READINGS IN EPISTEMOLOGY

Readings in Epistemology

Jack S. Crumley II
University of San Diego

Mayfield Publishing Company
Mountain View, California
London • Toronto

Library of Congress Cataloging-in-Publication Data

Readings in epistemology / [compiled by] Jack S. Crumley II.
    p. cm.
   Includes bibliographical references.
   ISBN 0-7674-0009-7
   1. Knowledge, Theory of. I. Crumley, Jack S.
   BD161 .R3415 1998
   121—dc21

                                           98-50660
                                             CIP

Manufactured in the United States of America

10 9 8 7 6 5 4 3 2 1

Mayfield Publishing Company
1280 Villa Street
Mountain View, California 94041

Sponsoring editor, Kenneth King; production, Publication Services; manuscript editor, Katherine Coyle; art director, Jeanne M. Schreiber; text and cover designer, Linda M. Robertson; manufacturing manager, Randy Hurst. The text was set in 9.5/12 Plantin Light by Publication Services and printed on 45# Highland Plus by Malloy Lithographing, Inc.

Text credits continue at the back of the book on pages 641-643, which constitute an extension of the copyright page.

 This book is printed on acid-free, recycled paper.

For Mom and Dad,
Karen and Thatcher,
and, of course, little Sammi

Preface

This anthology is designed primarily as a first course in epistemology for upper-division undergraduate students, although it can also be a useful resource for graduate students who are pursuing more detailed studies. One aim of the anthology is to provide convenient access to classical and historically significant sources and sources that have shaped and advanced contemporary epistemological debate.

The intent of this book is to provide comprehensive coverage of the areas that would be covered typically in epistemology courses and to provide a sufficient range of selections within the major sections of the book so that instructors can emphasize those areas of particular interest to them. Included are sections on the beginnings of epistemology, the analysis of knowledge, skepticism, foundationalism, coherentism, internalism and externalism, naturalized epistemology, *a priori* knowledge, and perception. Also included is a section on conceptions of justification, which provides a range of essays that focus on the nature of justification, including alternative conceptions of justification. I have included this section because it seems that recent epistemology often has focused on theoretical questions about the nature of justification, just as it has focused historically on the nature of knowledge. The particular selections themselves vary in difficulty from those that should be readily accessible to undergraduates to those that are more challenging. Again, the aim of providing this variation is to allow instructors to tailor their courses to their individual needs.

Each section begins with an accessible introductory essay to the main issues for the topic of that section and a synopsis of the selections that follow. The introductory essays aim to provide students with the conceptual and terminological background necessary for reading and understanding the essays. A list of readings for further study follows the last reading in each section. When confronted with scholarly articles, students sometimes have difficulty identifying the major ideas of the article; therefore, reading questions conclude each section. These questions are designed to help students focus on the central issues and arguments of the essays.

The selections include essays that represent alternative viewpoints to contemporary analytic epistemology. Where appropriate, these selections are integrated in the sections rather than set off in separate sections by themselves. This is intended to serve two purposes. First, it allows students to see that these alternative viewpoints are concerned with many of the same issues that motivate the mainstream analytic debate. Second, it provides students with a different vantage point from which to consider the assumptions and tendencies of contemporary analytic epistemology.

The central aim of this anthology is thus twofold: to provide instructors with a text that can be adapted to their individual needs and interests and to provide students with an anthology that eases them into the current epistemological debate.

Very special thanks are due to Leeanna Cummings, the department secretary, without whose assistance and advice this project would never have been completed. I also wish to thank the following reviewers for their thoughtful comments on the manuscript: Bruce A. Aune, University of Massachusetts at Amherst; Raymond Angelo Belliotti, State University of New York–Fredonia; Eric H. Gampel, California State University, Chico; Paul Haanstand, University of Utah; Sally Haslanger, Massachusetts Institute of Technology; Marc Lange, University of Washington, Seattle; Paul C. L. Tang, California State University, Long Beach; Adam Vinueza, University of Colorado; and Jeffrey P. Whitman, Susquehanna University.

Contents

READINGS IN EPISTEMOLOGY

PART I

Theory of Knowledge

1

Epistemology and the Nature of Knowledge

Epistemology is a *normative* discipline. It attempts to identify and defend the norms by which we measure or evaluate our beliefs. Epistemology—the word derives from the Greek word for knowledge, *episteme*—thus has the normative task of answering the question, What ought we to believe? It will be convenient to think of our beliefs as representations of the world around us, as indicating our view of what is going on in the world. We acquire our beliefs by many different processes. Some we acquire as the result of an argument, based on other beliefs we have. For example, on the basis of your beliefs that a quiz is usually given on Friday and that today is Friday, you come to believe that there will be a quiz today. Some beliefs we acquire simply as a result of the kind of beings we are, namely sensing beings. We hold some beliefs because of the testimony of other people—for example, parents, friends, teachers, or newspaper reporters. Still others we acquire as a result of more suspect processes, such as wishful thinking or self-deception. As representations of the world around us, our beliefs are either accurate or inaccurate.[1] Those that are accurate are true beliefs; those that are not are false beliefs. The truth or falsity of beliefs is one aspect of the way in which we normally evaluate beliefs; we discount the false belief and prefer the true. In seeking to identify norms for evaluating our myriad beliefs, the epistemologist seeks to identify those beliefs that are epistemically praiseworthy and those that are not, those that satisfy the norms and those that do not. Of course, it will not do for an epistemologist simply to assert that this or that is the set of norms or standards. The epistemologist must also attempt to defend the chosen standard or explain why the defense of it is the best.

Identification and defense of norms for the evaluation of our beliefs are evidenced in three principal issues that animate epistemology: the nature of knowledge, skepticism, and the regulation of our beliefs. Although they are intimately interrelated, initially it will be convenient to consider them somewhat separately.

It is a matter of common sense to acknowledge that not all of our beliefs are instances of knowledge. Some beliefs, even if true, we would be disinclined to consider knowledge. If, on your driving test, you guess that "c" is the correct answer to a certain question, and it turns out to be right, you would not think you *knew* that the answer was "c." Philosophers aim to identify the standards that our beliefs must satisfy if they are indeed instances of knowledge. Identifying these standards is sometimes described as analyzing the concept of knowledge, as spelling out the conditions under which some belief is a genuine case of knowledge. This analytic enterprise of specifying the conditions under which some belief is an instance of knowledge is a historically central task of epistemology. Beginning with Plato in the fourth century B.C.E., philosophers have attempted to identify the standards for distinguishing between beliefs that are instances of knowledge, and those that are not.

There is a close connection between *knowing* and the truth of a belief. Indeed, epistemologists standardly assume that knowing entails the truth of the belief. If Sara knows that there is a glass on the table, then it is true that there is a glass on the table. You might be wondering what standard we are to use for truth. When is a belief true? Interestingly, the task of analyzing the concept of knowledge is taken to be independent of the correct account of truth. That is, regardless of the correct standard of truth, knowledge implies truth. Nonetheless, we might take a moment to sketch some standard theories of truth.

There are three historically important theories of truth: *correspondence, coherence,* and *pragmatist.* There are different variations of each of these theories, but certain elements are common to the variations. Correspondence theories consider that a sentence or proposition is true if it matches or corresponds to certain features of the world.[2] The sentence, "There is a glass on the table," is true just in the case that there is indeed a glass on the table; the sentence matches, or corresponds, to the facts or the state of affairs. Similarly, if the content of Sara's belief is given by the sentence or proposition that there is a glass on the table, then Sara's belief is true just in the case that it corresponds to a state of affairs. Correspondence theories of truth are often associated with a doctrine known as *realism,* the view that the world has certain features, certain kinds of objects and properties, independently of what we believe about it. Versions of correspondence theory remain popular today.

Coherence theories see truth in a different light. Instead of thinking of individual sentences as true or false, coherence views hold that a sentence is true if it fits with, or coheres with, a family or set of sentences. Consider a very simple example, the sentence "It is raining outside." This sentence coheres, or fits, with other sentences, such as "The street is wet" and "People are carrying umbrellas." The truth of the first sentence derives from its fit with other sentences such as the latter two. The basic unit of truth, for the coherentist, is a set of sentences or propositions.

The pragmatic view of truth holds that a belief is true if it works or if it has certain kinds of consequences; the belief is cognitively useful. Sam's belief that there is a glass of tea on the table is true if that belief allows Sam to navigate his environment in a way that has certain desirable or advantageous consequences. If, as a consequence of this belief, Sam's thirst is quenched, then Sam's belief is true. We can see why this is thought of as the pragmatic view of truth: it is the cognitive and practical utility of beliefs that determines their truth.

These are sketches of the three theories of truth.[3] But we should not forget the essential point that analyses of the concept of knowledge are typically intended to be independent of any particular theory of truth. The standard view is that, whichever theory turns out to be correct, if one knows, then one has a true belief.

Knowledge, however, is more than just true belief. As Plato pointed out, a juror might have a true belief that a defendant is innocent, but this alone does not mean that the juror knows that the defendant is innocent. It was Plato's suggestion that what must be added to true belief is an account of the truth of that belief. Much of contemporary epistemology interprets the notion of account as *justification.* The concept of knowledge entails not only true belief but *justified* true belief. Just as there are different theories of truth, so there are different theories of justification. The nature of justified belief, or the nature of justification, turns out to be a much disputed and important issue in contemporary epistemology. We will return to the matter of justification below.

Consideration of the conditions of knowledge also leads epistemologists to examine the sources of knowledge. Our beliefs are generated in various ways, as noted above, and epistemologists attempt to identify which of these ways can yield knowledge. Two of the more historically important sources of knowledge are perception and reason. Perception, or the operations of our five senses, is for some the original source of all our knowledge. The empiricist view of knowledge, typified by David Hume, holds that all our knowledge about the world originates in perception or experience. Rationalism, on the other hand, as typified by Plato, holds that reason can be a source of knowledge. Prior to or independent of experience, reason provides us with beliefs that satisfy the conditions of knowledge. This type of knowledge is known as *a priori* knowledge, in contrast to *a posteriori* knowlege, which originates in the senses.

The analytic task of specifying the conditions for knowledge is closely connected to a second central issue in epistemology. Modern epistemology—epistemology since the seventeenth-century philosopher Rene Descartes—is often taken to be motivated by the project of responding to skepticism. Skepticism is the claim that we do not have the knowledge we think we have. The skeptic claims that once we identify the appropriate standard of knowledge, we will see that our beliefs fail to measure up. Now, the more sophisticated skeptic will not claim that he or she *knows* that we do not know. Rather, he or she will claim that if we reflect on the various areas in which we think we have knowledge, we will see that our beliefs do not satisfy the standards that we ourselves accept. We can now see the connection between the issue of skepticism and the task of analyzing the concept of knowledge. It is also at this point that the importance of the nature of justification becomes evident.

The skeptic can be viewed as claiming that we never have sufficient justification for thinking that our beliefs are true. Notice that the skeptic need not deny that our beliefs are true, but need only show that our reasons, our justification, are inadequate. It seems that an answer to the skeptic requires identification of the sort of justification necessary for knowledge and then a demonstration that at least some of our beliefs satisfy this standard. Different accounts of the kind of justification necessary for knowledge have been offered. One view, deriving from Descartes, is that a belief is an instance of knowledge only if it is certain, or there is no room for error. Another view holds that a belief is adequately justified only if there is more reason to believe it is true than to believe some skeptical alternative.

Some philosophers hold that a commitment to realism, the mind-independence of the world, opens the possibility of skepticism. If the world is what it is independently of what we believe, then our beliefs might fail to measure up. Since our beliefs do not determine the way the world is, our beliefs might not accurately represent the world. The mind-independence of the world opens the possibility that our beliefs could be wrong. The correct answers on Sara's driving test, for example, do not depend on what she thinks. Her beliefs might fail to measure up for just this reason. Indeed her beliefs might systematically fail to measure up. It is this possibility of systematic failure that skepticism envisages.

Implicit in the foregoing remarks about skepticism and the adequacy of our reasons is the third issue of concern in epistemology, the regulation of belief. Epistemology is a normative discipline. As a normative discipline, epistemology does not just describe the beliefs that we have or explain how we came to have them, but also attempts to answer the question, What should we believe? The regulation of belief is the identification (and of course the defense) of the principles that tell us what beliefs we ought to have. A natural answer to the question of what we should believe is to suggest that the beliefs we ought to have are justified beliefs. Descartes, for example, suggested that we ought to suspend belief

on those occasions when our beliefs are not appropriately justified. The task of regulating beliefs is thus intimately tied to the notion of justification.

A perhaps commonsense view of justification is that it means having reasons for a belief. But this view might not be sufficient. Sam might believe that he will pass his driving test because he believes his horoscope, which said that today is a good day for travel. Yet we might not be inclined to count Sam's belief as justified; he has reasons, but he does not have the right sort of reasons. We are inclined to think that good reasons, or the right sort of reasons, are those that support the *truth* of the belief. But we might think that the horoscope does not provide sufficient reason for thinking that the belief is *true*. We then have two aspects of justification: reasons and truth.

First, consider the notion of *having reasons* for thinking some belief is true. Because a person's reasons are often other beliefs, we might wonder whether there are any reasons for thinking that these other beliefs are themselves justified. It is not too difficult to see that this process of offering reasons, and then offering reasons for the reasons, might go on for a very long time. The two most important responses to this regress are *foundationalism* and *coherentism*. Foundationalists typically claim the existence of basic beliefs that are the ultimate sources of justification for our other beliefs. In the foundationalist view, a belief is justified only if it is basic or supported by one or more basic beliefs. Here we have a rough-and-ready formula for what we ought to believe: hold those beliefs that are either basic or in some way supported by basic beliefs.

Coherence theories of justification (one can be a coherentist about justification without accepting a coherentist theory of truth) reject the claim that there are basic beliefs. Instead, coherentists hold that a belief is justified only if it fits with, or coheres with, the holder's other beliefs. The person's beliefs stand or fall together. Again, we have a formula for what we ought to believe: hold those beliefs that are a part of a coherent set of beliefs.

This description of foundationalism and coherentism relies on an important assumption, namely, that justification, and hence the regulation of belief, turns on what reasons the person has. For many, this assumption is a central feature of modern epistemology. Justification requires that the person have reasons for believing, and that after thinking about it, the person could provide these reasons. As we have noted, not just any reasons will do. Nonetheless, justified beliefs are backed by reasons, in particular the person's reasons. This view of justification is a form of *internalism*.

Recent epistemological theories have called this assumption into question. Instead of focusing on the reasons for belief, some theorists have begun to focus on whether a belief is likely to be true. Such theorists claim that a belief is justified merely if that belief is likely to be true. Consequently, the focus shifts away from the perspective of the person holding the belief to that of a third person. According to such views, what matters for justification is how our beliefs are acquired. When Sam comes to believe that there is a glass of tea on the table, his belief is justified if it was acquired in an appropriate way. Which ways are appropriate? Those that tend to lead to true beliefs. Therefore, because Sam acquired his belief by seeing the glass, and because beliefs acquired by vision are likely to be true, Sam's belief is justified. This view of justification is a type of *externalism*.

To some it appears that moving from internalism to externalism sacrifices the thought that epistemology can provide individuals with a guide for regulating our beliefs. If we are to regulate our beliefs, we must be able to control them in some way. A traditional, internalist view holds that we can control our beliefs by focusing on the kind of reasons we have for those beliefs. But externalism deemphasizes this aspect of justification and instead focuses on the processes by which our beliefs are acquired. Externalism, according to some, attempts to answer the question, Is this the right process to use? instead of the agent-guiding question, "Do *I* have good reason to use this process?" Externalism thus substitutes a third-person perspective for a first-person perspective. Along with the foundationalism/coherentism distinction, the internalism/externalism distinction is one of the fundamental dividing lines in contemporary epistemology.

Epistemology is often considered to be a branch of philosophy, having its own subject matter, which, as we have seen, includes the analysis of knowledge, responding to the skeptic and identifying principles for the regulation of belief. More generally, normative epistemic properties, such as justification, are the unique subject matter of epistemology. *Naturalized epistemology,* a particular kind of externalism, questions whether epistemology is a distinct discipline. The naturalized epistemologist, for example, W. V. Quine, suggests that the best guide to the understanding of knowledge and justification is science. Epistemology is thus but a branch of science; it is one science among many. Of course, someone who doubts whether externalist theories are the right sort of epistemological theory will also doubt whether naturalized epistemology is the right approach to epistemology. Part of this dissatisfaction with naturalized epistemology stems from the view that epistemology is an inherently normative discipline, whereas the scientific task is typically descriptive and explanatory.

It is the normative theme that weaves together the various strands in the preceding, admittedly cursory, discussion. Disputes arise, of course, about how the normative element is to be understood and applied. Skeptics doubt that we satisfy the requisite epistemic norms; internalists think that the externalists have forsaken certain norms intrinsic to epistemology. Despite such disagreements, however, that normative character persists. Some very recent accounts, for example, attempt to identify the influence of social, historical, and cultural factors on the norms that interest epistemologists. But whether one adopts a traditional, internalist perspective, a naturalized perspective, or a more historical and cultural perspective, the intrinsically normative nature of epistemology remains virtually unquestioned.

The first serious epistemological discussions were those of Plato. Plato lived in Athens from about 429 to 347 B.C.E. When he was about thirty years old, his philosophical mentor, Socrates, was executed by the Athenian government. Plato's works are dialogues, conversations in which the interlocutors discuss various philosophical issues. The principal character in most of the dialogues is Socrates, who has, for some, the annoying habit of wanting to ask just one more question. But the character Socrates' aim is to arrive at the best answer that he can, given the particular circumstances of the conversation. Plato's work exercised a tremendous influence on the course of subsequent philosophy. Indeed, one twentieth-century philosopher claimed that the history of philosophy is but a footnote to

Plato. Plato's influence extends beyond philosophy, his dialogues being read by those interested in political science and literature, for example.

The excerpts that follow are from *Meno*, the *Republic*, and *Theaetetus*. In excerpts from *Meno*, Socrates suggests to Meno that coming to know is a process of recollection and that knowledge differs from true belief, and therefore is more valued, because it contains an account, or justification. The second selection is from Books VI and VII of the *Republic*. Socrates' interlocutors are Adeimantus and Glaucon. The character Socrates presents two of the most storied images in philosophy, the Divided Line and the Allegory of the Cave. Both images suggest that the proper objects of knowledge are grasped by the mind. In the selection from *Theaetetus*, Socrates considers and rejects Theaetetus' suggestion that perception is knowledge.

NOTES

1. The characterization of beliefs as representations implies that they are mental states—states of mind—with particular contents or information. Not everyone has accepted this characterization. Some, for example, have argued that we should view beliefs as dispositions to act in certain ways or in certain circumstances. More recently, some have argued that beliefs, at least as common sense views them, do not exist. This general issue is an important topic in the philosophy of mind and cannot be settled here. Describing beliefs as representations aims at capturing the idea that our beliefs are true or false and that they are about the world around us.

2. *Propositions* are held to be what *sentences* say or express. The English sentence "Snow is white" and the German sentence "Schnee ist weiss" are two different sentences. But both sentences have the same sense; they both express the same thing, namely the proposition that snow is white.

3. A more recent theory of truth is the redundancy theory. In this view, truth is not some special property or feature, such as correspondence or coherence, of sentences. To say that a sentence is true is just a redundant way of asserting the sentence. The sentence "'The glass is on the table' is true" tells us nothing more than the sentence "The glass is on the table." This type of theory is sometimes known as a deflationary view in that it rejects the idea that truth is some type of special property.

PLATO

from Meno

MENO. Yes, Socrates, but how do you mean that we do not learn, but that what we call learning is recollection? Can you teach me that this is so?

SOCRATES. As I said just now, Meno, you are a rascal. You now ask me if I can teach you, when I say there is no teaching but recollection, in order to show me up at once as contradicting myself.

MENO. No, by Zeus, Socrates, that was not my intention when I spoke, but just a habit. If you can somehow show me that things are as you say, please do so.

SOCRATES. It is not easy, but I am nevertheless willing to do my best for your sake. Call one of these many attendants of yours, whichever you like, that I may prove it to you in his case.

MENO. Certainly. You there, come forward.

SOCRATES. Is he a Greek? Does he speak Greek?

MENO. Very much so. He was born in my household.

SOCRATES. Pay attention then whether you think he is recollecting or learning from me.

MENO. I will pay attention.

SOCRATES. Tell me now, boy, you know that a square figure is like this? — I do.

SOCRATES. A square then is a figure in which all these four sides are equal? — Yes indeed.

SOCRATES. And it also has these lines through the middle equal? — Yes.

SOCRATES. And such a figure could be larger or smaller? — Certainly.

SOCRATES. If then this side were two feet, and this other side two feet, how many feet would the whole be? Consider it this way: if it were two feet this way, and only one foot that way, the figure would be once two feet? — Yes.

SOCRATES. But if it is two feet also that way, it would surely be twice two feet? — Yes.

SOCRATES. How many feet is twice two feet? Work it out and tell me. — Four, Socrates.

SOCRATES. Now let us have another figure twice the size of this one, with the four sides equal like this one. — Yes.

SOCRATES. How many feet will that be? — Eight.

SOCRATES. Come now, try to tell me how long each side of this will be. The side of this is two feet. What about each side of the one which is its double? — Obviously, Socrates, it will be twice the length.

SOCRATES. You see, Meno, that I am not teaching the boy anything, but all I do is question him. And now he thinks he knows the length of the line on which an eight-foot figure is based. Do you agree? — I do.

SOCRATES. And does he know? — Certainly not.

SOCRATES. He thinks it is a line twice the length? — Yes.

SOCRATES. Watch him now recollecting things in order, as one must recollect. Tell me, boy, do you say that a figure double the size is based on a line double the length? Now I mean such a figure as this, not long on one side and short on the other, but equal in every direction like this one, and double the size, that is, eight feet. See whether you still believe that it will be based on a line double the length. — I do.

SOCRATES. Now the line becomes double its length if we add another of the same length here? — Yes indeed.

SOCRATES. And the eight-foot square will be based on it, if there are four lines of that length? — Yes.

SOCRATES. Well, let us draw from it four equal lines, and surely that is what you say is the eight-foot square? — Certainly.

SOCRATES. And within this figure are four squares, each of which is equal to the four-foot square? —Yes.

SOCRATES. How big is it then? Is it not four times as big? — Of course.

SOCRATES. Is this square then, which is four times as big, its double? — No, by Zeus.

SOCRATES. How many times bigger is it? — Four times.

SOCRATES. Then, my boy, the figure based on a line twice the length is not double but four times as big? —You are right.

SOCRATES. And four times four is sixteen, is it not? —Yes.

SOCRATES. On how long a line then should the eight-foot square be based? Is it not based on this double line? — Yes. Now this four-foot square is based on a line half the length? —Yes.

SOCRATES. Very well. Is the eight-foot square not double this one and half that one? —Yes.

SOCRATES. Will it not be based on a line longer than this one and shorter than that one? Is that not so? — I think so.

SOCRATES. Good, you answer what you think. And tell me, was this one not two-feet long, and that one four feet? —Yes.

SOCRATES. The line on which the eight-foot square is based must then be longer than this one of two feet, and shorter than that one of four feet?— It must be.

SOCRATES. Try to tell me then how long a line you say it is. —Three feet.

SOCRATES. Then if it is three feet, let us add the half of this one, and it will be three feet? For these are two feet, and the other is one. And here, similarly, these are two feet and that one is one foot, and so the figure you mention comes to be? —Yes.

SOCRATES. Now if it is three feet this way and three feet that way, will the whole figure be three times three feet? — So it seems.

SOCRATES. How much is three times three feet? — Nine feet.

SOCRATES. And the double square was to be how many feet? — Eight.

SOCRATES. So the eight-foot figure cannot be based on the three-foot line? —Clearly not.

SOCRATES. But on how long a line? Try to tell us exactly, and if you do not want to work it out, show me from what line. — By Zeus, Socrates, I do not know.

SOCRATES. You realize, Meno, what point he has reached in his recollection. At first he did not know what the basic line of the eight-foot square was; even now he does not yet know, but then he thought he knew, and answered confidently as if he did know, and he did not think himself at a loss, but now he does think himself at a loss, and as he does not know, neither does he think he knows. —That is true.

SOCRATES. So he is now in a better position with regard to the matter he does not know?

MENO. I agree with that too.

SOCRATES. Have we done him any harm by making him perplexed and numb as the torpedo fish does? — I do not think so.

SOCRATES. Indeed, we have probably achieved something relevant to finding out how matters stand, for now, as he does not know, he would be glad to find out, whereas before he thought he could easily make many fine speeches to large audiences about the square of double size and said that it must have a base twice as long. — So it seems.

SOCRATES. Do you think that before he would have tried to find out that which he thought he knew though he did not, before he fell into perplexity and realized he did not know and longed to know? — I do not think so, Socrates.

SOCRATES. Has he then benefitted from being numbed? — I think.

SOCRATES. Look then how he will come out of his perplexity while searching along with me. I shall do nothing more than ask questions and not teach him. Watch whether you find me teaching and explaining things to him instead of asking for his opinion.

SOCRATES. You tell me, is this not a four-foot figure? You understand? — I do.

SOCRATES. We add to it this figure which is equal to it? —Yes.

SOCRATES. And we add this third figure equal to each of them? —Yes.

SOCRATES. Could we then fill in the space in the corner? — Certainly.

SOCRATES. So we have these four equal figures? — Yes.

SOCRATES. Well then, how many times is the whole figure larger than this one? — Four times.

SOCRATES. But we should have had one that was twice as large, or do you not remember? — I certainly do.

SOCRATES. Does not this line from one corner to the other cut each of these figures in two? — Yes.

SOCRATES. So these are four equal lines which enclose this figure? — They are.

SOCRATES. Consider now: how large is the figure? — I do not understand.

SOCRATES. Each of these lines cuts off half of each of the four figures inside it, does it not? — Yes.

SOCRATES. How many of this size are there in this figure? — Four.

SOCRATES. How many in this? — Two.

SOCRATES. What is the relation of four to two? — Double.

SOCRATES. How many feet in this? — Eight.

SOCRATES. Based on what line? — This one.

SOCRATES. That is, on the line that stretches from corner to corner of the four-foot figure? — Yes. — Clever men call this the diagonal, so that if diagonal is its name, you say that the double figure would be that based on the diagonal? — Most certainly, Socrates.

SOCRATES. What do you think, Meno? Has he, in his answers, expressed any opinion that was not his own?

MENO. No, they were all his own.

SOCRATES. And yet, as we said a short time ago, he did not know? — That is true.

SOCRATES. So these opinions were in him, were they not? — Yes.

SOCRATES. So the man who does not know has within himself true opinions about the things that he does not know? — So it appears.

SOCRATES. These opinions have now just been stirred up like a dream, but if he were

This is methodical

repeatedly asked these same questions in various ways, you know that in the end his knowledge about these things would be as accurate as anyone's. — It is likely.

SOCRATES. And he will know it without having been taught but only questioned, and find the knowledge within himself? — Yes.

SOCRATES. And is not finding knowledge within oneself recollection? — Certainly.

SOCRATES. Must he not either have at some time acquired the knowledge he now possesses, or else have always possessed it? — Yes.

SOCRATES. If he always had it, he would always have known. If he acquired it, he cannot have done so in his present life. Or has someone taught him geometry? For he will perform in the same way about all geometry, and all other knowledge. Has someone taught him everything? You should know, especially as he has been born and brought up in your house.

MENO. But I know that no one has taught him.

SOCRATES. Yet he has these opinions, or doesn't he?

MENO. That seems indisputable, Socrates.

SOCRATES. If he has not acquired them in his present life, is it not clear that he had them and had learned them at some other time? — It seems so.

SOCRATES. Then that was the time when he was not a human being? — Yes.

SOCRATES. If then, during the time he exists and is not a human being he will have true opinions which, when stirred by questioning, become knowledge, will not his soul have learned during all time? For it is clear that during all time he exists, either as a man or not. — So it seems.

SOCRATES. Then if the truth about reality is always in our soul, the soul would be immortal so that you should always confidently try to seek out and recollect what you do not know at present — that is, what do you not recollect?

MENO. Somehow, Socrates, I think that what you say is right.

SOCRATES. I think so too, Meno. I do not insist that my argument is right in all other respects,

This person seems to say that the slave boy even have knowledge of it

but I would contend at all costs both in the word and deed as far as I could that we will be better men, braver and less idle, if we believe that one must search for the things one does not know, rather than if we believe that it is not possible to find out what we do not know and that we must not look for it.

MENO. In this too I think you are right, Socrates. . . .

SOCRATES. I mean this: we were right to agree that good men must be beneficent, and that this could not be otherwise. Is that not so? — Yes.

SOCRATES. And that they will be beneficent if they give us correct guidance in our affairs. To this too we were right to agree? — Yes.

SOCRATES. But that one cannot guide correctly if one does not have knowledge; to this our agreement is likely to be incorrect. — How do you mean?

SOCRATES. I will tell you. A man who knew the way to Larissa, or anywhere else you like, and went there and guided others would surely lead them well and correctly? — Certainly.

SOCRATES. What if someone had had a correct opinion as to which was the way but had not gone there nor indeed had knowledge of it, would he not also lead correctly? — Certainly.

SOCRATES. And as long as he has the right opinion about that of which the other has knowledge, he will not be a worse guide than the one who knows, as he has a true opinion, though not knowledge. —In no way worse.

SOCRATES. So true opinion is in no way a worse guide to correct action than knowledge. It is this that we omitted in our investigation of the nature of virtue, when we said that only knowledge can lead to correct action, for true opinion can do so also. — So it seems.

SOCRATES. So correct opinion is no less useful than knowledge?

MENO. Yes, to this extent, Socrates. But the man who has knowledge will always succeed, whereas he who has true opinion will only succeed at times.

SOCRATES. How do you mean? Will he who has the right opinion not always succeed, as long as his opinion is right?

MENO. That appears to be so of necessity, and it makes me wonder, Socrates, this is being the case, why knowledge is prized far more highly than right opinion, and why they are different.

SOCRATES. Do you know why you wonder, or shall I tell you? — By all means tell me.

SOCRATES. It is because you have paid no attention to the statues of Daedalus, but perhaps there are none in Thessaly.

SOCRATES. What do you have in mind when you say this?

SOCRATES. That they too run away and escape if one does not tie them down but remain in place if tied down. — So what?

SOCRATES. To acquire an untied work of Daedalus is not worth much, like acquiring a runaway slave, for it does not remain, but it is worth much if tied down, for his works are very beautiful. What am I thinking of when I say this? True opinions. For true opinions, as long as they remain, are a fine thing and all they do is good, but they are not willing to remain long, and they escape from a man's mind, so that they are not worth much until one ties them down by (giving) an account of the reason why. And that, Meno my friend, is recollection, as we previously agreed. After they are tied down, in the first place they become knowledge, and then they remain in place. That is why knowledge is prized higher than correct opinion, and knowledge differs from correct opinion in being tied town.

MENO. Yes, by Zeus, Socrates, it seems to be something like that.

SOCRATES. Indeed, I too speak as one who does not have knowledge but is guessing. However, I certainly do not think I am guessing that right opinion is a different thing than knowledge. If I claim to know anything else—and I would make that claim about few things—I would put this down as one of the things I know.— Rightly so, Socrates.

SOCRATES. Well then, is it not correct that when true opinion guides the course of every action, it does no worse than knowledge?—I think you are right in this too.

SOCRATES. Correct opinion is then neither inferior to knowledge nor less useful in directing actions, nor is the man who has it less so than he who has knowledge. — That is so.

PLATO

from Republic

BOOK VI

And the one class of things we say can be seen but not thought, while the ideas can be thought but not seen.

By all means.

With which of the parts of ourselves, with which of our faculties, then, do we see visible things?

With sight, he said.

And do we not, I said, hear audibles with hearing, and perceive all sensibles with the other senses?

Surely.

Have you ever observed, said I, how much the greatest expenditure the creator of the senses has lavished on the faculty of seeing and being seen?

Why, no, I have not, be said.

Well, look at it thus. Do hearing and voice stand in need of an other medium so that the one may hear and the other be heard, in the absence of which third element the one will not hear and the other not be heard?

They need nothing, he said.

Neither, I fancy, said I, do many others, not to say that none require anything of the sort. Or do you know of any?

Not I, he said.

But do you not observe that vision and the visible do have this further need?

How?

Though vision may be in the eyes and its possessor may try to use it, and though color be present, yet without the presence of a third thing specifically and naturally adapted to this purpose, you are aware that vision will see nothing and the colors will remain invisible.

What is this thing of which you speak? he said.

The thing, I said, that you call light.

You say truly, he replied.

The bond, then, that yokes together visibility and the faculty of sight is more precious by no slight

form than that which unites the other pairs, if light is not without honor.

It surely is far from being so, he said.

Which one can you name of the divinities in heaven as the author and cause of this, whose light makes our vision see best and visible things to be seen?

Why, the one that you too and other people mean, he said, for your question evidently refers to the sun.

Is not this, then, the relation of vision to that divinity?

What?

Neither vision itself nor its vehicle, which we call the eye, is identical with the sun.

Why, no.

But it is, I think, the most sunlike of all the instruments of sense.

By far the most.

And does it not receive the power which it possesses as an influx, as it were, dispensed from the sun?

Certainly.

Is it not also true that the sun is not vision, yet as being the cause thereof is beheld by vision itself?

That is so, he said.

This, then, you must understand that I meant by the offspring of the good which the good begot to stand in a proportion with itself. As the good is in the intelligible region to reason and the objects of reason, so is this in the visible world to vision and the objects of vision.

How is that? he said. Explain further.

You are aware, I said, that when the eyes are no longer turned upon objects upon whose colors the light of day falls but that of the dim luminaries of night, their edge is blunted and they appear almost blind, as if pure vision did not dwell in them.

Yes, indeed, he said.

But when, I take it, they are directed upon objects illumined by the sun, they see clearly, and vision appears to reside in these same eyes.

Certainly.

Apply this comparison to the soul also in this way. When it is firmly fixed on the domain where truth and reality shine resplendent apprehends and knows them and appears to possess reason, but when it inclines to that region which is mingled with darkness, the world of becoming and passing away, it opines only and its edge is blunted, and it shifts its opinions hither and thither, and again seems as if it lacked reason.

Yes, it does.

This reality, then, that gives their truth to the objects of knowledge and the power of knowing to the knower, you must say is the idea of good, and you must conceive it as being the cause of knowledge, and of truth in so far as known. Yet fair as they both are, knowledge and truth, in supposing it to be something fairer still than these you will think rightly of it. But as for knowledge and truth, even as in our illustration it is right to deem light and vision sunlike, but never to think that they are the sun, so here it is right to consider these two their counterparts, as being like the good or boniform, but to think that either of them is the good is not right. Still higher honor belongs to the possession and habit of the good.

An inconceivable beauty you speak of, he said, if it is the source of knowledge and truth, and yet itself surpasses them in beauty. For you surely cannot mean that it is pleasure.

Hush, said I, but examine the similitude of it still further in this way.

How?

The sun, I presume you will say, not only furnishes to visibles the power of visibility but it also provides for their generation and growth and nurture though it is not itself generation.

Of course not.

In like manner, then, you are to say that the objects of knowledge not only receive from the presence of the good their being known, but their very existence and essence is derived to them from it, though the good itself is not essence but still transcends essence in dignity and surpassing power.

And Glaucon very ludicrously said, Heaven save us, hyperbole can no further go.

The fault is yours, I said, for compelling me to utter my thoughts about it.

And don't desist, he said, but at least expound the similitude of the sun, if there is anything that you are omitting.

Why, certainly, I said, I am omitting a great deal.

Well, don't omit the least bit, he said.

I fancy, I said, that I shall have to pass over much, but nevertheless so far as it is at present practicable I shall not willingly leave anything out.

Do not, he said.

Conceive then, said I, as we were saying, that there are these two identities, and that one of them is sovereign over the intelligible order and region and the other over the world of the eyeball, not to say the sky, but let that pass. You surely apprehend the two types, the visible and the intelligible.

I do.

Represent them then, as it were, by a line divided into two unequal sections and cut each section again in the same ratio-the section, that is, of the visible and that of the intelligible order-and then as an expression of the ratio of their comparative clearness and obscurity you will have, as one of the sections of the visible world, images. By images I mean, first, shadows, and then reflections in water and on surfaces of dense, smooth, and bright texture, and everything of that kind, if you apprehend.

I do.

As the second section assume that of which this is a likeness or an image, that is, the animals about us and all plants and the whole class of objects made by man.

I so assume it, he said.

Would you be willing to say, said I, that the division in respect of reality and truth or the opposite is expressed by the proportion-as is the opinable to the knowable so is the likeness to that of which it is a likeness?

I certainly would.

Consider then again the way in which we are to make the division of the intelligible section.

In what way?

By the distinction that there is one section of it which the soul is compelled to investigate by treating as images the things imitated in the former division, and by means of assumptions from which it proceeds not up to a first principle but down to a conclusion, while there is another section in which it advances from its assumption to a beginning or principle that transcends assumption, and in which it makes no use of the images employed by the other section, relying on ideas only and progressing systematically through ideas.

I don't fully understand what you mean by this, he said.

Well, I will try again, said I, for you will better understand after this preamble. For I think you are aware that students of geometry and reckoning and such subjects first postulate the odd and the even and the various figures and three kinds of angles and other things akin to these in each branch of science, regard them as known, and, treating them as absolute assumptions, do not deign to render any further account of them to themselves or others, taking it for granted that they are obvious to everybody. They take their start from these, and pursuing the inquiry from this point on consistently, conclude with that for the investigation of which they set out.

Certainly, he said, I know that.

And do you not also know that they further make use of the visible forms and talk about them, though they are not thinking of them but of those things of which they are a likeness, pursuing their inquiry for the sake of the square as such and the diagonal as such, and not for the sake of the image of it which they draw? And so in all cases. The very things which they mold and draw, which have shadows and images of themselves in water, these things they treat in their turn as only images, but what they really seek is to get sight of those realities which can be seen only by the mind.

True, he said.

This then is the class that I described as intelligible, it is true, but with the reservation first that the soul is compelled to employ assumptions in the investigation of it, not proceeding to a first principle because of its inability to extricate itself from and rise above its assumptions, and second, that it uses as images or likenesses the very objects that are themselves copied and adumbrated by the class below them, and that in comparison with these latter are esteemed as clear and held in honor.

I understand, said he, that you are speaking of what falls under geometry and the kindred arts.

Understand then, said I, that by the other section of the intelligible I mean that which the reason itself lays hold of by the power of dialectic, treating its assumptions not as absolute beginnings but literally as hypotheses, underpinnings, footings, and springboards so to speak, to enable it to rise to that which requires no assumption and is the starting point of all, and after attaining to that again taking hold of the first dependencies from it, so to proceed downward to the conclusion, making no use whatever of any object of sense but only of pure ideas moving on through ideas to ideas and ending with ideas.

I understand, he said, not fully, for it is no slight task that you appear to have in mind, but I do understand that you mean to distinguish the aspect of reality and the intelligible, which is contemplated by the power of dialectic, as something truer and more exact than the object of the so-called arts and sciences whose assumptions are arbitrary starting points. And though it is true that those who contemplate d them are compelled to use their understanding and not their senses, yet because they do not go back to the beginning in the study of them but start from assumptions you do not think they possess true intelligence about them although the things themselves are intelligibles when apprehended in conjunction with a first principle. And I think you call the mental habit of geometers and their like mind or understanding and not reason because you regard understanding as something intermediate between opinion and reason.

Your interpretation is quite sufficient, I said. And now, answering to these four sections, assume these four affections occurring in the soul-intellection or reason for the highest, understanding for the second, belief for the third, and for the last, picture thinking or conjecture-and arrange them in a proportion, considering that they participate in clearness and precision in the same degree as their objects partake of truth and reality.

I understand, he said. I concur and arrange them as you bid.

BOOK VII

Next, said I, compare our nature in respect of education and its lack to such an experience as this. Picture men dwelling in a sort of subterranean cavern with a long entrance open to the light on its entire width. Conceive them as having their legs and necks fettered from childhood, so that they remain in the same spot, able to look forward only, and prevented by the fetters from turning their heads. Picture further the light from a fire burning higher up and at a distance be hind them, and between the fire and the prisoners and above them a road along which a low wall has been built, as the exhibitors of pup pet shows have partitions before the men themselves, above which they show the puppets.

All that I see, he said.

See also, then, men carrying past the wall implements of all kinds that rise above the wall, and human images and shapes of animals as well, wrought in stone and wood and every material, some of these bearers presumably speaking and others silent.

A strange image you speak of, he said, and strange prisoners.

Like to us, I said. For, to begin with, tell me do you think that these men would have seen anything of themselves or of one another except the shadows cast from the fire on the wall of the cave that fronted them?

How could they, he said, if they were compelled to hold their heads unmoved through life?

And again, would not the same be true of the objects carried past them?

Surely.

If then they were able to talk to one another, do you not think that they would suppose that in naming the things that they saw they were naming the passing objects?

Necessarily.

And if their prison had an echo from the wall opposite them, when one of the passers-by uttered a sound, do you think that they would suppose anything else than the passing shadow to be the speaker?

By Zeus, I do not, said he.

Then in every way such prisoners would deem reality to be nothing else than the shadows of the artificial objects.

Quite inevitably, he said.

Consider, then, what would be the manner of the release and healing from these bonds and this folly if in the course of nature something of this sort should happen to them. When one was freed from his fetters and compelled to stand up suddenly and turn his head around and walk and to lift up his eyes to the light, and in doing all this felt pain and, because of the dazzle and glitter of the light, was unable to discern the objects whose shadows he formerly saw, what do you suppose would be his answer if someone told him that what he had seen before was all a cheat and an illusion, but that now, being nearer to reality and turned toward more real things, he saw more truly? And if also one should point out to him each of the passing objects and constrain him by questions to say what it is, do you not think that he would be at a loss and that he would regard what he formerly saw as more real than the things now pointed out to him?

Far more real, he said.

And if he were compelled to look at the light itself, would not that pain his eyes, and would he not turn away and flee to those things which he is able to discern and regard them as in very deed more clear and exact than the objects pointed out?

It is so, he said.

And if, said I, someone should drag him thence by force up the ascent which is rough and steep, and not let him go before he had drawn him out into the light of the sun, do you not think that he would find it painful to be so haled along, and would chafe at it, and when he came out into the light, that his eyes would be filled with its beams so that he would not be able to see even one of the things that we call real?

Why, no, not immediately, he said.

Then there would be need of habituation, I take it, to enable him to see the things higher up. And at first he would most easily discern the shadows and, after that, the likenesses or reflections in water of men and other things, and later, the things themselves, and from these he would go on to contemplate the appearances in the heavens and the moon, than by day the sun and the sun's light.

Of course.

And so, finally, I suppose, he would be able to look upon the sun itself and see its true nature, not by reflections in water or phantasms of it in an alien setting, but in and by itself in its own place

Necessarily, he said.

And at this point he would infer and conclude that this it is that provides the seasons and the courses of the year and presides over all things in the visible region, and is in some sort the cause of all these things that they had seen.

Obviously, he said, that would be the next step.

Well then, if he recalled to mind his first habitation and what passed for wisdom there, and his fellow bondsmen, do you not think that he would count himself happy in the change and pity them?

He would indeed.

And if there had been honors and commendations among them which they bestowed on one another and prizes for the man who is quickest to make out the shadows as they pass and best able to remember their customary precedences, sequences, and coexistences, and so most successful in guessing at what was to come, do you think he would be very keen about such rewards, and that he would envy and emulate those who were honored by these prisoners and lorded it among them, or that he would feel with Homer and greatly prefer while living on earth to be serf of another, a landless man, and endure anything rather than opine with them and live that life?

Yes, he said, I think that he would choose to endure anything rather than such a life.

And consider this also, said I. If such a one should go down again and take his old place would he not get his eyes full of darkness, thus suddenly coming out of the sunlight?

He would indeed.

Now if he should be required to contend with these perpetual prisoners in 'evaluating' these shadows while his vision was still dim and before his eyes were accustomed to the dark-and this time required for habituation would not be very short-would he not provoke laughter, and would it not be said of him that he had returned from his journey aloft with his eyes ruined and that it was not worth while even to attempt the ascent? And if it were possible to lay hands on and to kill the man who tried to release them and lead them up, would they not kill him?

They certainly would, he said.

This image then, dear Glaucon, we must apply as a whole to all that has been said, likening the region revealed through sight to the habitation of the prison, and the light of the fire in it to the power of the sun. And if you assume that the ascent and the contemplation of the things above is the soul's ascension to the intelligible region, you will not miss my surmise, since that is what you desire to hear. But Gods knows whether it is true. But, at any rate, my dream as it appears to me is that in the region of the known the last thing to be seen and hardly seen is the idea of good, and that when seen it must needs point us to the conclusion that this is indeed the

cause for all things of all that is right and beautiful, giving birth in the visible world to light, and the author of light and itself in the intelligible world being the authentic source of truth and reason, and that anyone who is to act wisely in private or public must have caught sight of this.

I concur, he said, so far as I am able.

Come then, I said, and join me in this further thought, and do not be surprised that those who have attained to this height are not willing to occupy themselves with the affairs of men, but their souls ever feel the upward urge and the yearning for that sojourn above. For this, I take it, is likely if in this point too the likeness of our image holds.

Yes, it is likely.

And again, do you think it at all strange, said I, if a man returning from divine contemplations to the petty miseries of men cuts a sorry figure and appears most ridiculous, if, while still blinking through the gloom, and before he has become sufficiently accustomed to the environing darkness, he is compelled in courtrooms or elsewhere to contend about the shadows of justice or the images that cast the shadows and to wrangle in debate about the notions of these things in the minds of those who have never seen justice itself?

It would be by no means strange, he said.

But a sensible man, I said, would remember that there are two distinct disturbances of the eyes arising from two causes, according as the shift is from light to darkness or from darkness to light, and, believing that the same thing happens to the soul too, whenever he saw a soul perturbed and unable to discern something, he would not laugh unthinkingly, but would observe whether coming from a brighter life its vision was obscured by the unfamiliar darkness, or whether the passage from the deeper dark of ignorance into a more luminous world and the greater brightness had dazzled its vision. And so he would deem the one happy in its experience and way of life and pity the other, and if it pleased him to laugh at it, his laughter would be less laughable than that at the expense of the soul that had come down from the light above.

That is a very fair statement, he said. Then, if this is true, our view of these matters must be this, that education is not in reality what some people proclaim it to be in their professions. What they aver is that they can put true knowledge into a soul that does not possess it, as if they were inserting vision into blind eyes.

They do indeed, he said.

But our present argument indicates, said I, that the true analogy for this indwelling power in the soul and the instrument whereby each of us apprehends is that of an eye that could not be converted to the light from the darkness except by turning the whole body. Even so this organ of knowledge must be turned around from the world of be coming together with the entire soul, like the scene-shifting periactus in the theater, until the soul is able to endure the contemplation of essence and the brightest region of being. And this, we say, is the good, do we not?

Yes.

Of this very thing, then, I said, there might be an art, an art of the speediest and most effective shifting or conversion of the soul, not an art of producing vision in it, but on the assumption that it possesses vision but does not rightly direct it and does not look where it should, an art of bringing this about.

Yes, that seems likely, he said.

Then the other so-called virtues of the soul do seem akin to those of the body. For it is true that where they do not pre-exist, they are afterward created by habit and practice. But the excellence of thought, it seems, is certainly of a more divine quality, a thing that never loses its potency, but, according to the direction of its conversion, becomes useful and beneficent, or, again, useless and harmful. Have you never observed in those who are popularly spoken of as bad, but smart men how keen is the vision of the little soul, how quick it is to discern the things that interest it, a proof that it is not a poor vision which it has, but one forcibly enlisted in the service of evil, so that the sharper its sight the more mischief it accomplishes?

I certainly have, he said.

Observe then, said I, that this part of such a soul, if it had been hammered from childhood, and had thus been struck free of the leaden weights, to speak, of our birth and becoming, which attaching themselves to it by food and similar pleasures and gluttonies turn downward the vision of the soul-if, I say, freed from these, it had suffered a conversion toward the things that are real and true, that same faculty of the same men would have been most keen in its vision of the higher things, just as it is for the things toward which it is now turned.

PLATO

from Theaetetus

SOCRATES. Consider, then, Theaetetus, this further point about what has been said. Now you answered that perception is knowledge, did you not?

THEAETETUS. Yes.

SOCRATES. If then, anyone should ask you, "By what does a man see white and black colours and by what does he hear high and low tones?" you would, I fancy, say, "By his eyes and ears."

THEAETETUS. Yes, I should.

SOCRATES. The easy use of words and phrases and the avoidance of strict precision is in general a sign of good breeding; indeed, the opposite is hardly worthy of a gentleman, but sometimes it is necessary, as now it is necessary to object to your answer, in so far as it is incorrect. Just consider; which answer is more correct, that our eyes are that by which we see or that through which we see, and our ears that by which or that through which we hear?

THEAETETUS. I think, Socrates, we perceive through, rather than by them, in each case.

SOCRATES. Yes, for it would be strange indeed, my boy, if there are many senses ensconced within us, as if we were so many wooden horses of Troy, and they do not all unite in one power, whether we should call it soul or something else, by which we perceive through these as instruments the objects of perception.

THEAETETUS. I think what you suggest is more likely than the other way.

SOCRATES. Now the reason why I am so precise about the matter is this: I want to know whether there is some one and the same power within ourselves by which we perceive black and white through the eyes, and again other qualities through the other organs, and whether you will be able, if asked, to refer all such activities to the body. But perhaps it is better that you make the statement in answer to a question than that I should take all the trouble for you. So tell me: do you not think that all the organs through which you perceive hot and hard and light and sweet are parts of the body? Or are they parts of something else?

THEAETETUS. Of nothing else.

SOCRATES. And will you also be ready to agree that it is impossible to perceive through one sense what you perceive through another; for instance, to perceive through sight what you perceive through hearing, or through hearing what you perceive through sight?

THEAETETUS. Of course I shall.

SOCRATES. Then if you have any thought about both of these together, you would not have perception about both together either through one organ or through the other.

THEAETETUS. No.

SOCRATES. Now in regard to sound and colour, you have, in the first place, this thought about both of them, that they both exist?

THEAETETUS. Certainly.

SOCRATES. And that each is different from the other and the same as itself?

THEAETETUS. Of course.

SOCRATES. And that both together are two and each separately is one?

THEAETETUS. Yes, that also.

SOCRATES. And are you able also to observe whether they are like or unlike each other?

THEAETETUS. May be.

SOCRATES. Now through what organ do you think all this about them? For it is impossible to grasp that which is common to them both either through hearing or through sight. Here is further evidence for the point I am trying to make: if it were possible to investigate the question whether the two, sound and colour, are bitter or not, you know that you will be able to tell by what faculty you will investigate it, and that is clearly neither hearing nor sight, but something else.

THEAETETUS. Of course it is,—the faculty exerted through the tongue.

SOCRATES. Very good. But through what organ is the faculty exerted which makes known to you that which is common to all things, as well as to these of which we are speaking—that which you call being and not-being, and the other attributes of things, about which we were asking just now? What organs will you assign for all these, through which that part of us which perceives gains perception of each and all of them?

THEAETETUS. You mean being and not-being, and likeness and unlikeness, and identity and difference, and also unity and plurality as applied to them. And you are evidently asking also through what bodily organs we perceive by our soul the odd and the even and everything else that is in the same category.

SOCRATES. Bravo, Theaetetus! you follow me exactly; that is just what I mean by my question.

THEAETETUS. By Zeus, Socrates, I cannot answer, except that I think there is no special organ at all for these notions, as there are for those others; but it appears to me that the soul views by itself directly what all things have in common.

SOCRATES. Why, you are beautiful, Theaetetus, and not, as Theodorus said, ugly; for he who speaks beautifully is beautiful and good. But besides being beautiful, you have done me a favour by relieving me from a long discussion, if you think that the soul views some things by itself directly and others through the bodily faculties; for that was my own opinion, and I wanted you to agree.

THEAETETUS. Well, I do think so.

SOCRATES. To which class, then, do you assign being; for this, more than anything else, belongs to all things?

THEAETETUS. I assign them to the class of notions which the soul grasps by itself directly.

SOCRATES. And also likeness and unlikeness and identity and difference?

THEAETETUS. Yes.

SOCRATES. And how about beautiful and ugly, and good and bad?

THEAETETUS. I think that these also are among the things the essence of which the soul most certainly views in their relations to one another, reflecting within itself upon the past and present in relation to the future.

SOCRATES. Stop there. Does it not perceive the hardness of the hard through touch, and likewise the softness of the soft?

THEAETETUS. Yes.

SOCRATES. But their essential nature and the fact that they exist, and their opposition to one another, and, in turn, the essential nature of this opposition, the soul itself tries to determine for us by reverting to them and comparing them with one another.

THEAETETUS. Certainly.

SOCRATES. Is it not true, then, that all sensations which reach the soul through the body, can be perceived by human beings, and also by animals, from the moment of birth; whereas reflections about these, with reference to their being and usefulness, are acquired, if at all, with difficulty and slowly, through many troubles, in other words, through education?

THEAETETUS. Assuredly.

SOCRATES. Is it, then, possible for one to attain "truth" who cannot even get as far as "being"?

THEAETETUS. No.

SOCRATES. And will a man ever have knowledge of anything the truth of which he fails to attain?

THEAETETUS. How can he, Socrates?

SOCRATES. Then knowledge is not in the sensations, but in the process of reasoning about them; for it is possible, apparently, to apprehend being and truth by reasoning, but not by sensation.

THEAETETUS. So it seems.

SOCRATES. Then will you call the two by the same name, when there are so great differences between them?

THEAETETUS. No, that would certainly not be right.

SOCRATES. What name will you give, then, to the one which includes seeing, hearing, smelling, being cold, and being hot?

THEAETETUS. Perceiving. What other name can I give it?

SOCRATES. Collectively you call it, then, perception?

THEAETETUS. Of course.

SOCRATES. By which, we say, we are quite unable to apprehend truth, since we cannot apprehend being, either.

THEAETETUS. No; certainly not.

SOCRATES. Nor knowledge either, then.

THEAETETUS. No.

SOCRATES. Then, Theaetetus, perception and knowledge could never be the same.

FOR FURTHER READING

Audi, Robert. *Belief, Justification, and Knowledge.* Belmont, Calif.: Wadsworth, 1988.

Ayer, A.J. *The Problem of Knowledge.* London: Penguin, 1956.

Chisholm, Roderick. *Theory of Knowledge.* 3rd ed. Englewood Cliffs, N.J.: Prentice Hall, 1988.

Harding, Sandra, and Merrill Hintikka, eds. *Discovering Reality: Feminist Perspectives on Epistemology, Methodology, and the Philosophy of Science.* Dordrecht, Netherlands: D. Reidel, 1983.

Lehrer, Keith. *Theory of Knowledge.* Boulder, Colo.: Westview Press, 1990.

Plato. *The Collected Dialogues of Plato.* Edited by Edith Hamilton and Huntington Cairns. New York: Pantheon Books, 1963.

Pojman, Louis. *What Can We Know? An Introduction to the Theory of Knowledge.* Belmont, Calif.: Wadsworth, 1995.

Taylor, A.E. *Plato, the Man and His Work.* London: Methuen, 1926.

White, Nicholas. *Plato on Knowledge and Reality.* Indianapolis: Hackett Publishing, 1976.

STUDY QUESTIONS

1. In *Meno,* Socrates asks the slave boy a series of questions about a geometric example. What general point is Socrates trying to make? Summarize why Socrates thinks the exchange with the slave boy shows that knowledge is but recollection.

2. In the last part of the selection from *Meno* Socrates says that correct opinion—what we would call true belief—and knowledge are alike in a particular way. What is this way? How are true opinions like the untied statues of Daedalus? Can you give an example of a true opinion that "flies away"? How, according to Socrates, does knowledge differ from correct opinion?

3. In the *Republic,* Socrates compares the "idea of good" to the sun. What is Socrates' aim here?

4. What are the four parts of the Divided Line? Which faculties or capacities correspond to which parts of the Divided Line? What do you think is the principal difference between the top and the bottom halves of the Line?

5. In the allegory of the Cave (Book VII of the *Republic*), Socrates again presents the same four stages of opinion and knowledge. At what level do most people live, in Socrates' view? Why would the person who breaks free of the cave not be thought of highly? What is your opinion of Socrates' allegory? Do you think

education is a kind of "turning around," as Socrates suggests near the end of the selection? Why or why not?

6. In *Theaetetus,* Socrates identifies certain qualities or properties that are known by the soul directly. Which are these? Can you give an example of properties known through the senses? Why do you think Socrates identifies these two types of properties? What is it that perception is unable to do that prevents it from yielding knowledge? Do you agree with Socrates? Why or why not?

2

Skepticism

We are accustomed to distinguishing between beliefs that we have doubts about and beliefs about which we are more confident. You might believe, for example, that it was Kepler who first proposed that the orbit of the planets is elliptical, but you might harbor some doubt, since you are aware that you occasionally confuse the exploits of Kepler with those of Copernicus. You would therefore not claim to *know* that Kepler first asserted that planets travel an elliptical path through the heavens. You have no such doubt, however, about many other things. You would unhesitatingly claim to know that you are looking at a book, that you remember what you had for breakfast, or that hydrogen atoms have but one electron. You might even be willing to claim that although you do not currently know whether Kepler or Copernicus deserves the credit, you certainly know how to find out. You can ask a knowledgeable friend or teacher; you can look it up in a book; or, feeling technologically inclined, you can look for it on the Internet. You are confident, not only that you know a great many things, but also that you have tried and trusted methods for increasing your knowledge.

Skepticism is the claim that we do not have the knowledge we think we have. When we examine our claims to knowledge more closely, we find that there is sufficient doubt that we know. Nor, according to the skeptic, can we appeal to our tried and trusted methods for help. Our normal methods may be familiar and trusted, but these methods—the means by which we acquire our beliefs—leave too much room for doubt.

More interesting forms of skepticism deny that we ever have knowledge of the world around us, that is, empirical knowledge. We use certain favored methods, such as perception or the methods of science, to acquire our beliefs about the world, and we think that these methods are adequate to provide us with knowledge. However, the skeptic claims that

they are in fact inadequate. There is too much doubt about the beliefs produced by such methods, and hence the beliefs do not count as knowledge. In putting forward skeptical hypotheses, the skeptic is not putting forward a new definition of knowledge or justification. Rather, the skeptic is claiming that the beliefs we acquire and the methods we use to acquire them do not measure up to our own standards of knowledge or justification.

Perception, the operations of our five senses, is perhaps the simplest and most trusted method for acquiring knowledge about the world. You look over at the table, see the glass of orange juice, and consequently reach for the glass. What could be more simple, more certain, or more obviously a case of knowledge? Nonetheless, the skeptic claims that when we look more closely at perception, we see that it provides us with less evidence than we originally thought. Perception provides us only with certain sensations or perceptual experiences. These sensations, according to the skeptic, are internal; they are mental states or properties. And the connection of these internal sensations to external objects and properties is tenuous. More to the point, we might have these very same sensations, the very same evidence, even if there were, for example, no glass of orange juice nearby. It is *possible* that we are the victim of hallucination or diabolically designed illusion. Our evidence does not adequately establish the truth of our belief; consequently we cannot be said to know that there is a glass of orange juice nearby.

There is an important pattern in this example. The skeptic doubts whether some method for acquiring knowledge is effective. The skeptic claims that the evidence we have for our beliefs does not adequately establish the truth of our beliefs as opposed to some competing claim. The skeptical scenario that we might be victims of hallucination or illusion is such a rival claim. If the rival claim is true, our normal beliefs are false. Our evidence, according to the skeptic, is insufficient to enable us to choose between our preferred interpretation of our experience—the familiar world and its properties—and the rival claim. Hence, we cannot be said to know.

The skeptic is not finished yet. The skeptic places constraints on what will count as an acceptable response to the skeptical challenge. In particular, if a certain method of belief acquisition is at issue, then we cannot use the suspect method to provide further evidence. If the method itself is in question, we cannot use that method to "verify" itself. A lawyer does not establish the credibility of a witness by asking the witness. Rather, the lawyer presents independent facts that corroborate the witness's testimony. Similarly, the skeptic wants independent evidence for the trustworthiness of the challenged method.

This last point illustrates the generality of the philosophical skeptic's question. The skeptic wants to know whether we have a certain kind of knowledge, such as perceptual knowledge. The skeptic wants us to explain why we think we have perceptual knowledge. But our explanation cannot appeal to the method in question or any evidence that depends on that method. Thus, if we are attempting to answer skeptical doubts about perception, it will not do to cite the scientific facts about vision, because scientific theories about vision ultimately depend on simple perceptual beliefs. Such "facts," the skeptic claims, are themselves dependent on beliefs acquired by means of perception. The skeptic, then, issues the challenge of showing that a certain method, in general, leads to knowledge.

What is an adequate response to skepticism? Some consider that an adequate response to the skeptic must show that we are certain of our beliefs, that there is no possibility of doubt or of the falsity of our beliefs. Still others hold that it is necessary only to show that we have more evidence or reason for our suspect beliefs than we do for the skeptic's rival claims. Another strategy sometimes employed in responses to skepticism is to show that the skeptical challenge entails assumptions or claims that are themselves dubious. The advocate of our claims to knowledge then asserts that the skeptic has not provided us with the evidence necessary for adopting such dubious assumptions. Consequently, we are not reasonably compelled to accept the skeptic's conclusions.

Skepticism comes in different guises. In addition to skepticism about perception, there are also, for example, skeptical challenges about induction and the reliability of memory. The selections in this section are divided into two parts, corresponding to two types of skeptical problem: the problem of our knowledge of the external world and the problem of our ability to extend our knowledge by means of induction. The first problem, the problem of the external world, is to explain how we know that the world is the way we think it is. We have certain experiences and sensations, and we have associated beliefs about what they tell us. But why should we think that our beliefs correspond to the world? What evidence do we have for this correspondence?

The skeptic wants us to make explicit the standards we use to discriminate among our various intuitions about what counts as good evidence and what does not. But the skeptic is not content with our merely making the standards explicit. More importantly, the skeptic wants us to explain why we count certain intuitions—such as our intuitions about the connections between sensations and objects—as legitimate, and others—such as the reading of tea leaves—as illegitimate.

It is worth noting that standards we count as legitimate can sometimes conflict with one another. Simple perception tells us that apples are red, the sun sets, and sugar is sweet. But science might be viewed as telling us a different story: there are no red or sweet electrons, and the sun does not really set so much as the earth rotates. Rene Descartes was not a skeptic, but he wanted to know how we might make sense of the knowledge that science seems to give us, a knowledge that appears to conflict with the deliverances of the senses. Descartes offers two of the most famous skeptical arguments. He claims that a particular belief is not an instance of knowledge unless it is indubitable, and he then argues that two kinds of belief do not satisfy this condition. In the Dream Argument, Descartes argues that perception alone cannot give us knowledge. In the Evil Demon Argument, he argues that some very general truths about the nature of the world are also open to doubt. In both arguments, Descartes' strategy is similar: he argues that the same evidence we cite in support of our beliefs would equally well support the Dream or Demon scenario.

The skeptical problem did not begin with Descartes. Near the beginning of the third century, the Greek skeptic Sextus Empiricus proposed *Pyrrhonian skepticism,* a skepticism designed to induce suspension of belief. He thought that the suspension of belief was the path to tranquility. The chief means for bringing about such suspension of belief are the *modes,* which are types of arguments that highlight the conflicts between our various perceptions. Since we have no independent means for choosing between the conflicting perceptions, our only reasonable option is to suspend belief

Some versions of the skeptical problem, such as that of Descartes, insist that knowledge requires beliefs that cannot be mistaken. A. J. Ayer considers whether there are such beliefs and concludes that there are none. He also provides a general outline for understanding the nature of the skeptical argument. He suggests that the skeptic insists that our claims to knowledge are supported only by the evidence we have at our disposal. The skeptic then insists that if we really know, the evidence must either deductively or inductively support our claims to knowledge. But our evidence does neither, according to the skeptic. Hence we do not know. This selection concludes with Ayer's description of four approaches to the skeptical problem.

The two essays by G.E. Moore and Norman Malcolm attempt to disprove the skeptical argument by arguing that some beliefs are instances of knowledge that at least some of our beliefs about the world are absolutely certain. Consequently, skepticism must be wrong. Malcolm begins by distinguishing two senses of "know," a strong and a weak sense. According to Malcolm, although we admit that our claims to knowledge are sometimes mistaken, there are occasions when we would not be willing to count anything as evidence against certain types of belief, and on those occasions we have knowledge in the strong sense.

Barry Stroud argues that the philosophical skeptic's question is completely general and that a satisfactory answer to the question must take account of this generality. In the first part of the selection, Stroud explains the sense in which philosophical

skepticism is completely general. He then argues that certain types of responses, what he calls "externalist" responses, do not adequately address this generality. For that reason, Stroud claims that externalist rejoinders to skepticism are unacceptable.

In the second part of Part II, we confront the issue of skepticism about induction. David Hume, an eighteenth-century philosopher, is credited with first having succinctly articulated this problem, and the selection here presents his argument. Hume's concern is whether we have adequate reason for thinking that a certain pattern of inference can provide us with knowledge or reasonable belief about what might occur in the future. Suppose that whenever we have experienced things of kind A, we have subsequently always experienced things of kind B. We typically infer that if we now experience an A, we can *reasonably* expect to experience a B. Hume argues that this pattern of inference depends on a principle, the Uniformity Principle, for which we can provide no adequate reason. Because our inductive inferences are reasonable only if we can give adequate reason for the Uniformity Principle, and because we cannot provide adequate reason for the Uniformity Principle, Hume claims that we do not have adequate reason for the conclusions of our inductive arguments. This general line of thought is further pursued in Bertrand Russell's "On Induction," written in the first decade of the twentieth century. Russell argues that not only the claims of science but even our simplest expectations of what will happen in the world around us depend on the inductive principle. Yet, in Russell's view, we cannot justify the inductive principle by any appeal to experience. In "Russell's Doubts about Induction," Paul Edwards protests that skepticism about induction unfairly changes the standard of what might count as confirming evidence or the reasonability of our inductive inferences.

Brian Skyrms, in an excerpt from *Choice and Chance,* examines the pragmatic justification of induction. The pragmatic justification claims that if any type of inference will lead to reasonable beliefs about our future experience, induction will. Skyrms concludes that despite the failure of the pragmatic approach to resolve the problem of induction, it does advance our understanding of the problem and opens an avenue for resolution. P. F. Strawson's selection elaborates what is sometimes called the "no problem" view of induction. Strawson argues that relying on inductive inferences is what it means to be rational. Interestingly, Strawson agrees with Hume that there is no *proof* that induction is trustworthy. But Strawson disagrees with Hume that we should either expect or try to give such proof.

In the final selection, Nelson Goodman argues that our inductive arguments in fact support competing conclusions. If we adopt one set of beliefs about the properties of objects, we will arrive at one sort of conclusion, but if we adopt another set of beliefs, we will arrive at a competing conclusion. The problem, the new riddle, is to find a means for deciding which set of properties we should adopt.

SEXTUS EMPIRICUS

from Outlines of Pyrrhonism

BOOK I

i. The Most Fundamental Difference among Philosophies

When people are investigating any subject, the likely result is either a discovery, or a denial of discovery and a confession of inapprehensibility, or else a continuation of the investigation. This, no doubt, is why in the case of philosophical investigations, too, some have said that they have discovered the truth, some have asserted that it cannot be apprehended, and others are still investigating.

Those who are called Dogmatists in the proper sense of the word think that they have discovered the truth—for example, the schools of Aristotle and Epicurus and the Stoics, and some others. The schools of Clitomachus and Carneades, and other Academics, have asserted that things can not be apprehended. And the Skeptics are still investigating. Hence the most fundamental kinds of philosophy are reasonably thought to be three: the Dogmatic, the Academic, and the Skeptical. The former two it will be appropriate for others to describe: in the present work we shall discuss in outline the Skeptical persuasion. By way of preface let us say that on none of the matters to be discussed do we affirm that things certainly are just as we say they are: rather, we report descriptively on each item according to how it appears to us at the time.

ii. The Accounts Constitutive of Skepticism

The Skeptical philosophy contains both a general and a specific account. In the general account we set out the distinctive character of Skepticism, saying what the concept of it is, what are its principles and what its arguments, what is its standard and what its aim, what are the modes of suspension of judgement, how we understand skeptical assertions, and what distinguishes Skepticism from neighboring phi-

losophies. The specific account is the one in which we argue against each of the parts of what they call philosophy.

Let us first deal with the general account, beginning our sketch with the names given to the Skeptical persuasion.

iii. The Nomenclature of Skepticism

The Skeptical persuasion, then, is also called Investigative, from its activity in investigating and inquiring; Suspensive, from the feeling that comes about in the inquirer after the investigation; Aporetic, either (as some say) from the fact that it puzzles over and investigates everything, or else from its being at a loss whether to assent or deny; and Pyrrhonian, from the fact that Pyrrho appears to us to have attached himself to Skepticism more systematically and conspicuously than anyone before him.

iv. What Is Skepticism?

Skepticism is an ability to set out oppositions among things which appear and are thought of in any way at all, an ability by which, because of the equipollence in the opposed objects and accounts, we come first to suspension of judgement and afterwards to tranquillity.

We call it an ability not in any fancy sense, but simply in the sense of 'to be able to'. Things which appear we take in the present context to be objects of perception, which is why we contrast them with objects of thought. 'In any way at all' can be taken either with 'an ability' (to show that we are to understand the word 'ability' in its straightforward sense, as we said), or else with 'to set out oppositions among the things which appear and are thought of' we say 'in any way at all' because we set up oppositions in a variety of ways—opposing what appears to what appears, what is thought of to what is thought of, and crosswise, so as to include all the oppositions. Or else we take the phrase with 'the things which appear and are thought of', to show that we are not to investigate how what appears or how what is thought of is thought of, but are simply to take them for granted.

By 'opposed accounts' we do not necessarily have in mind affirmation and negation, but take the phrase simply in the sense of 'conflicting accounts'. By 'equipollence' we mean equality with regard to being convincing or unconvincing: none of the conflicting accounts takes precedence over any other as being more convincing. Suspension of judgement is a standstill of the intellect, owing to which we neither reject nor posit anything. Tranquillity is freedom from disturbance or calmness of soul. We shall suggest in the chapter on the aim of skepticism how tranquillity accompanies suspension of judgement.

v. The Skeptic

The Pyrrhonian philosopher has been implicitly defined in our account of the concept of the Skeptical persuasion: a Pyrrhonian is someone who possesses this ability.

vi. The Principles of Skepticism

The causal principle of skepticism we say is the hope of becoming tranquil. Men of talent, troubled by the anomaly in things and puzzled as to which of them they should rather assent to, came to investigate what in things is true and what false, thinking that by deciding these issues they would become tranquil.

The chief constitutive principle of skepticism is the claim that to every account an equal account is opposed; for it is from this, we think, that we come to hold no beliefs.

vii. Do Skeptics Hold Beliefs?

When we say that Skeptics do not hold beliefs, we do not take 'belief' in the sense in which some say, quite generally, that belief is acquiescing in something; for Skeptics assent to the feelings forced upon them by appearances—for example, they would not say, when heated or chilled, 'I think I am not heated (or: chilled)'. Rather, we say that they do not hold beliefs in the sense in which some say that belief is assent to some unclear object of investigation in the sciences; for Pyrrhonists do not assent to anything unclear.

Not even in uttering the Skeptical phrases about unclear matters—for example, 'In no way more', or 'I determine nothing', or one of the other phrases which we shall later discuss—do they hold beliefs. For if you hold beliefs, then you posit as real the things you are said to hold beliefs about; but Skeptics posit these phrases not as necessarily being real. For they suppose that, just as the phrase 'Everything is false' says that it too, along with everything else, is false (and similarly for 'Nothing is true'), so also 'In no way more' says that it too, along with everything else, is no more so than not so, and hence it cancels itself along with everything else. And we say the same of the other Skeptical phrases. Thus, if people who hold beliefs posit as real the things they hold beliefs about, while Skeptics utter their own phrases in such a way that they are implicitly cancelled by themselves, then they cannot be said to hold beliefs in uttering them.

But the main point is this: in uttering these phrases they say what is apparent to themselves and report their own feelings without holding opinions, affirming nothing about external objects.

xi. The Standard of Skepticism

That we attend to what is apparent is clear from what we say about the standard of the Skeptical persuasion. 'Standard' has two senses: there are standards adopted to provide conviction about the reality or unreality of something (we shall talk about these standards when we turn to attack them); and there are standards of action, attending to which in everyday life we perform some actions and not others—and it is these standards which are our present subject.

We say, then, that the standard of the Skeptical persuasion is what is apparent, implicitly meaning by this the appearances; for they depend on passive and unwilled feelings and are not objects of investigation. (Hence no one, presumably, will raise a controversy over whether an existing thing appears this way or that; rather, they investigate whether it is such as it appears.)

Thus, attending to what is apparent, we live in accordance with everyday observances, without holding opinions—for we are not able to be utterly inactive. These everyday observances seem to be fourfold, and to consist in guidance by nature, necessitation by feelings, handing down of laws and customs, and teaching of kinds of expertise. By nature's guidance we are naturally capable of perceiving and thinking. By the necessitation of feelings, hunger conducts us to food and thirst to drink. By the handing down of customs and laws, we accept, from an everyday point of view, that piety is good and impiety bad. By teaching of kinds of expertise we are not inactive in those which we accept.

And we say all this without holding any opinions.

xii. What Is the Aim of Skepticism?

It will be apposite to consider next the aim of the Skeptical persuasion. Now an aim is that for the sake of which everything is done or considered, while it is not itself done or considered for the sake of anything else. Or: an aim is the final object of desire. Up to now we say the aim of the Skeptic is tranquillity in matters of opinions and moderation of feeling in matters forced upon us. For Skeptics began to do philosophy in order to decide among appearances and to apprehend which are true and which false, so as to become tranquil; but they came upon equipollent dispute, and being unable to decide this they suspended judgment. And when they suspended judgement, tranquillity in matters of opinion followed fortuitously.

For those who hold the opinion that things are good or bad by nature are perpetually troubled. When they lack what they believe to be good, they take themselves to be persecuted by natural evils and they pursue what (so they think) is good. And when they have acquired these things, they experience more troubles; for they are elated beyond reason and measure, and in fear of change they do anything so as not to lose what they believe to be good. But those who make no determination about what is good and bad by nature neither avoid nor pursue anything with intensity; and hence they are tranquil.

A story told of the painter Apelles applies to the Skeptics. They say that he was painting a horse and wanted to represent in his picture the lather on the horse's mouth; but he was so unsuccessful that he gave up, took the sponge on which he had been wiping off the colours from his brush, and flung it at the picture. And when it hit the picture, it produced a representation of the horse's lather. Now the Skeptics were hoping to acquire tranquillity by deciding the anomalies in what appears and is thought of; and being unable to do this they suspended judgement. But when they suspended judgement, tranquillity followed as it were fortuitously, as a shadow follows a body.

We do not, however, take Skeptics to be undisturbed in every way—we say that they are disturbed by things which are forced upon them; for we agree that at times they shiver and are thirsty and have other feelings of this kind. But in these cases ordinary people are afflicted by two sets of circumstances: by the feelings themselves, and no less by believing that these circumstances are bad by nature. Skeptics, who shed the additional opinion that each of these things is bad in its nature, come off more moderately even in these cases.

This, then, is why we say that the aim of Skeptics is tranquillity in matters of opinion and moderation of feeling in matters forced upon us. (Some eminent Skeptics have added as a further aim suspension of judgement in investigations.)

xiii. The General Modes of Suspension of Judgement

Since we have been saying that tranquillity follows suspension of judgement about everything, it will be apposite here to say how suspension of judgement comes about for us.

It comes about—to put it rather generally—through the opposition of things. We oppose what appears to what appears, or what is thought of to what is thought of; or crosswise. For example, we oppose what appears to what appears when we say: 'The same tower appears round from a distance and square from nearby'. We oppose what is thought of to what is thought of when, against those who seek to establish that there is Providence from the orderliness of the heavenly bodies, we oppose the view that often the good do badly while the bad do well and conclude from this that there is no Providence. We oppose what is thought of to what appears, as Anaxagoras did when to the view that snow is white, he opposed the thought that snow is frozen water and water is black and snow is therefore black.

In another sense we sometimes oppose present things to present things (as in the above examples) and sometimes present to past or future things. For example, when someone propounds to us an argument we cannot refute, we say to him: 'Before the founder of the school to which you adhere was born, the argument of the School, which is no doubt sound, was not yet apparent, although it was really there in nature. In the same way, it is possible that the argument opposing the one you have just propounded is really there in nature but is not yet apparent to us; so we should not yet assent to what is now thought to be a powerful argument' . . . .

xiv. The Ten Modes

. . . Nonetheless, so as to arrive at suspension of judgement even when resting the argument on a single person, such as the Sage they dream up, we bring out the mode which is third in order. This, we said, is the one deriving from the differences among the senses.

Now, that the senses disagree with one another is clear. For instance, paintings seem to sight to have recesses and projections, but not to touch. Honey appears pleasant to the tongue (for some people) but unpleasant to the eyes; it is impossible, therefore, to say whether it is purely pleasant or unpleasant. Similarly with perfume: it gratifies the sense of smell but displeases the sense of taste. Again, since spurge-juice is painful to the eyes but painless to the rest of the body, we will not be able to say whether, so far as its own nature goes, it is purely painless to bodies or painful. Rainwater is beneficial to the eyes, but is rough on the windpipe and lungs—so too is olive oil, though it comforts the skin. The sea-ray, when applied to the extremities, paralyses them, but can be put on the rest of the body harmlessly. Hence we will not be able to say what each of these things is like in its nature, although it is possible to say what they appear to be like on any given occasion.

More cases than these can be given; but so as not to waste time, given the purpose of our essay, we should say this. Each of the objects of perception which appears to us seems to impress us in a variety of ways—for example, an apple is smooth, fragrant, sweet, and yellow. It is unclear, then, whether in reality it has these qualities alone, or has only one quality but appears different depending on the different constitution of the sense-organs, or actually has more qualities than those which are apparent, some of them not making an impression on us.

That it has only one quality can be argued from what we said before about the nourishment dispersed in our bodies and the water dispersed in trees and the breath in flutes and pipes and similar instruments; for the apple can be undifferentiated but observed as different depending on the differences among the sense-organs by which it is grasped.

That the apple may have more qualities than those apparent to us we deduce as follows. Let us conceive of someone who from birth has touch, smell and taste, but who hears and sees nothing. He will suppose that there is absolutely nothing visible or audible, and that there exist only those three kinds of quality which he is able to grasp. So it is possible that we too, having only the five senses, grasp from among the qualities of the apple only those we are capable of grasping, although other qualities can exist, impressing other sense-organs in which we have no share, so that we do not grasp the objects perceptible by them.

But nature, someone will say, has made the senses commensurate with their objects. What nature?—given that there is so much undecidable dispute among the Dogmatists about the reality of what is according to nature. For if someone decides this question (namely, whether there is such a thing as nature), then if he is a layman he will not be convincing according to them, while if he is a philosopher he will be part of the dispute and under judgement himself rather than a judge.

So if it is possible that only those qualities exist in the apple which we think we grasp, and that there are more than them, and again that there are not even those which make an impression on us, then it will be unclear to us what the apple is like.

The same argument applies to the other objects of perception too. But if the senses do not apprehend external objects, the intellect is not able to apprehend them either (since its guides fail it), so by means of this argument too we shall be thought to conclude to suspension of judgement about external existing objects.

In order to end up with suspension of judgement even if we rest the argument on any single sense or actually leave the senses aside, we also adopt the fourth mode of suspension. This is the mode which gets its name from circumstances, where by 'circumstances' we mean conditions. It is observed, we say, in natural or unnatural states, in waking or sleeping, depending on age, on moving or being at rest, on hating or loving, on being in need or sated, on being drunk or sober, on anterior conditions, on being confident or fearful, on being in distress or in a state of enjoyment.

For example, objects produce dissimilar impressions on us depending on our being in a natural or an unnatural state, since people who are delirious or divinely possessed believe that they hear spirits, while we do not; and similarly they often say that they grasp an exhalation of storax or frankincense or the like, and many other things, while we do not perceive them. The same water seems to be boiling when poured on to inflamed places, but to us to be lukewarm. The same cloak appears orange to people with a blood-suffusion in the eye, but not to me; and the same honey appears sweet to me, but bitter to people with jaundice.

If anyone says that it is the mixing of certain humours which produces inappropriate appearances from existing objects in people who are in an unnatural state, we should say that, since healthy people too have mixed humours, it is possible that these humours make the external existing objects appear different to the healthy, while they are by nature the way they appear to those who are said to be in an unnatural state. For to grant one lot of humours but not the other the power of changing external objects has an air of fiction. Again, just as healthy people are in a state natural for the healthy but unnatural for the sick, so the sick are in a state unnatural for the healthy but natural for the sick, so that they too are in a state which is, relatively speaking, natural, and they too should be found convincing.

Different appearances come about depending on sleeping or waking. When we are awake we view things differently from the way we do when we are asleep, and when asleep differently from the way we do when awake; so the existence or non-existence of the objects becomes not absolute but relative—relative to being asleep or awake. It is likely, then, that when asleep we will see things which are unreal in waking life, not unreal once and for all. For they exist in sleep, just as the contents of waking life exist even though they do not exist in sleep.

Appearances differ depending on age. The same air seems cold to old men but mild to the young, the same colour appears faint to the elderly but intense to the young, and similarly the same sound seems to the former dim but to the latter clearly audible. Those who differ in age are also affected dissimilarly depending on their choices and avoidances. Children, for example, are serious about balls and hoops, while the young choose other things, and old men yet others. From this it is concluded that different appearances come about from the same existing objects depending on differences in age too.

Objects appear dissimilar depending on moving or being at rest. Things which we see as still when we are stationary seem to us to move when we sail past them. Depending on loving and hating: some people have an excessive revulsion against pork, while others consume it with great pleasure. Menander said:

> How foul he appears even in his looks since he has become like this! What an animal! Doing no wrong actually makes us beautiful.

And many men who have ugly girl-friends think them most attractive. Depending on being hungry or sated: the same food seems most pleasant to people who are hungry but unpleasant to the sated. Depending on being drunk or sober: things which we think shameful when sober do not appear shameful to us when we are drunk. Depending on anterior conditions: the same wine appears sour to people who have just eaten dates or figs, but it seems to be sweet to people who have consumed nuts or chickpeas. And the bathhouse vestibule warms people entering from outside but chills people leaving if they spend any time there. Depending on being afraid or confident: the same object seems fearful and dreadful to the coward but not so at all to someone bolder. Depending on being in distress or in a state of enjoyment: the same objects are annoying to people in distress and pleasant to people who are enjoying themselves.

Since, therefore, there are so many anomalies depending on conditions, and since at different times people come to be in different conditions, it is no doubt easy to say what each existing object appears to be like to each person, but not to say what it is like, since the anomalies are in fact undecidable.

For anyone who decides them is either in some of these conditions or in absolutely no condition at all. But to say that he is in no condition whatsoever (i.e.

neither healthy nor sick, neither moving nor at rest, of no particular age, and free from the other conditions) is perfectly incongruous. But if he is in some condition as he judges the appearances, he will be a part of the dispute. And again, he will not be an unbiased judge of external existing objects because he will have been contaminated by the conditions he is in. So a waking person cannot compare the appearances of sleepers with those of people who are awake, or a healthy person those of the sick with those of the healthy; for we assent to what is present and affects us in the present rather than to what is not present.

And there is another reason why the anomalies among the appearances are undecidable. Anyone who prefers one appearance to another and one circumstance to another does so either without making a judgement and without proof or making a judgement and offering a proof. But he can do so neither without these (for he will be unconvincing) nor yet with them. For if he judges the appearances he will certainly judge them by means of a standard. Now he will say of this standard either that it is true or that it is false. If false, he will be unconvincing. But if he says that it is true, then he will say that the standard is true either without proof or with proof. If without proof he will be unconvincing. But if with proof, he will certainly need the proof to be true— otherwise he will be unconvincing. Then when he says that the proof which he adopts to make the standard convincing is true, will he do so after judging it or without judging it? If he has not judged it he will be unconvincing. But if he has judged it, then clearly he will say that he has judged it by means of a standard—but we shall demand a proof of that standard, and then a standard for that proof. For a proof always requires a standard in order to be confirmed, and a standard always requires a proof in order to be shown to be true. A proof cannot be sound if there is no standard there already, nor can a standard be true if a proof has not already been made convincing. In this way standards and proofs fall into the reciprocal mode, by which both of them are found to be unconvincing: each waits to be made convincing by each other, and so each is as unconvincing as the other.

If, then, one cannot prefer one appearance to another either without a proof and a standard or with them, the different appearances which come about depending on different conditions will be undecidable. Hence so far as this mode too goes suspension of judgement about external existing objects is introduced.

The fifth argument is the one depending on positions and intervals and places—for depending on each of these the same objects appear different.

For example, the same colonnade appears foreshortened when seen from one end, but completely symmetrical when seen from the middle. The same boat appears from a distance small and stationary, but from close at hand large and in motion. The same tower appears from a distance round, but from close at hand square. These depend on intervals.

Depending on places: lamplight appears dim in sunlight but bright in the dark. The same oar appears bent in the water but straight when out of it. Eggs appear soft in the bird but hard in the air. Lyngurion appears liquid inside the lynx but hard in the air. Coral appears soft in the sea but hard in the air. And sound appears different when produced in a pipe, in a flute, or simply in the air.

Depending on positions: the same picture when laid down appears flat, but when put at a certain angle seems to have recesses and projections. Doves' necks appear different in colour depending on the different ways they turn them.

Since, then, all apparent things are observed in some place and some interval and in some position, and each of these produces a great deal of variation in appearances, as we have suggested, we shall be forced to arrive at suspension of judgement by these modes too.

For anyone wishing to give preference to some of these appearances over others will be attempting the impossible. If he makes his assertion simply and without proof he will not be convincing. But if he wants to use a proof, then if he says that the proof is false, he will turn himself about; and if he says that the proof is true, he will be required to give a proof of its being true, and another proof of that (since it too has to be true), and so *ad infinitum*. But it is impossible to establish infinitely many proofs. And so he will not be able to prefer one appearance to another with a proof either.

But if no one can decide among these appearances either without proof or with proof, the conclusion is suspension of judgement: we are no doubt able to say what each thing appears to be like in this position or from that interval or in this place, but we are not able, for the reasons we have given, to assert what it is like in its nature.

Sixth is the mode depending on admixtures. According to it we conclude that, since no existing object makes an impression on us by itself but rather together with something, it is perhaps possible to say what the mixture is like which results from the external object and the factor with which it is observed, but we cannot say purely what the external existing object is like.

That no external object makes an impression by itself but in every case together with something, and that it is observed as differing in a way dependent on this is, I think, clear. For instance, the colour of our skin is seen as different in warm air and in cold, and we cannot say what our colour is like in its nature but only what it is like as observed together with each of these. The same sound appears different together with clear air or with muggy air. Aromatic herbs are more pungent in the bathhouse and in the sun than in chilly air. And a body surrounded by water is light, surrounded by air heavy. . . .

The eighth mode is the one deriving from relativity, by which we conclude that, since everything is relative, we shall suspend judgement as to what things are independently and in their nature. It should be recognized that here, as elsewhere, we use 'is' loosely, in the sense of 'appears', implicitly saying 'Everything appears relative'.

But this has two senses: first, relative to the subject judging (for the external existing object which is judged appears relative to the subject judging), and second, relative to the things observed together with it (as right is relative to left). We have in fact already deduced that everything is relative, i.e. with respect to the subject judging (since each thing appears relative to a given animal and a given human and a given sense and a given circumstance), and with respect to the things observed together with it (since each thing appears relative to a given animal and a given composition and quantity and position).

We can also conclude in particular that everything is relative, in the following way. Do relatives differ or not from things which are in virtue of a difference? If they do not differ, then the latter are relatives too. But if they do differ, then, since everything which differs is relative (it is spoken of relative to what it differs from), things in virtue of a difference will be relative. Again, according to the Dogmatists, some existing things are highest genera, others lowest species, and others both genera and species. But all of these are relative. Everything, therefore, is relative. Further, some existing things are clear, others unclear, as they themselves say, and what is apparent is a signifier while what is unclear is signified by something apparent (for according to them 'the apparent is the way to see the unclear'). But signifier and signified are relative. Everything, therefore, is relative. Further, some existing things are similar, others dissimilar, and some are equal, others unequal. But these are relative. Everything, therefore, is relative.

And anyone who says that not everything is relative confirms that everything is relative. For by opposing us he shows that the very relativity of everything is relative to us and not universal.

So, since we have established in this way that everything is relative, it is clear that we shall not be able to say what each existing object is like in its own nature and purely, but only what it appears to be like relative to something. It allows that we must suspend judgment about the nature of objects. . . .

BOOK II

iv. Is There a Standard of Truth?

Of those who have discussed standards, some have asserted that there is one (e.g. the Stoics and certain others), some that there is not (among them, Xeniades of Corinth and Xenophanes of Colophon who says: 'but belief is found over all'); and we suspend judgement as to whether there is one or not.

Now they will say either that this dispute is decidable or that it is undecidable. If undecidable, they will immediately grant that one must suspend judgement; if decidable, let them say by what it will be judged when we neither possess an agreed standard nor even know if there is one but are investigating the matter.

Again, in order for the dispute that has arisen about standards to be decided, we must possess an agreed standard through which we can judge it; and in order for us to possess an agreed standard, the dispute about standards must already have been decided. Thus the argument falls into the reciprocal mode and the discovery of a standard is blocked—for we do not allow them to assume a standard by hypothesis, and if they want to judge the standard by a standard we throw them into an infinite regress.

Again, since a proof needs a standard which has been proved and a standard needs a proof which has been judged, they are thrown into the reciprocal mode.

Now, although we think that these considerations are actually enough to show the rashness of the Dogmatists in their account of standards, nevertheless, so that we may be able to bring some variety into our refutation of them, it is not absurd to persevere with the topic. Not that we propose to contest each of their opinions about standards one by one—for the dispute is vast, and in that way we too would necessarily fall into giving an unmethodical account. But since the standard we are investigating is thought to be threefold—that by which, that through which, and that in virtue of which—we shall tackle each of these in turn and establish its inapprehensibility; for in this way our account will be at once methodical and complete.

Let us begin with the standard by which; for along with it the others too seem in a way to reach an impasse.

xv. Induction

It is easy, I think, to reject the method of induction. For since by way of it they want to make universals convincing on the basis of particulars, they will do this by surveying either all the particulars or some of them. But if some, the induction will be infirm, it being possible that some of the particulars omitted in the induction should be contrary to the universal; and if all, they will labour at an impossible task, since the particulars are infinite and indeterminate. Thus in either case it results, I think, that induction totters.

RENÉ DESCARTES

from Meditations on the First Philosophy

MEDITATION I

Of the things which may be brought within the sphere of the doubtful.

It is now some years since I detected how many were the false beliefs that I had from my earliest youth admitted as true, and how doubtful was everything I had since constructed on this basis; and from that time I was convinced that I must once for all seriously undertake to rid myself of all the opinions which I had formerly accepted, and commence to build anew from the foundation, if I wanted to establish any firm and permanent structure in the sciences. But as this enterprise appeared to be a very great one, I waited until I had attained an age so mature that I could not hope that at any later date I should be better fitted to execute my design. This reason caused me to delay so long that I should feel that I was doing wrong were I to occupy in deliberation the time that yet remains to me for action. To-day, then, since very opportunely for the plan I have in view I have delivered my mind from every care (and am happily agitated by no passions) and since I have procured for myself an assured leisure in a peaceable retirement, I shall at last seriously and freely address myself to the general upheaval of all my former opinions.

Now for this object it is not necessary that I should show that all of these are false—I shall perhaps never arrive at this end. But inasmuch as reason already persuades me that I ought no less carefully to withhold my assent from matters which are not entirely certain and indubitable than from those which appear to me manifestly to be false, if I am able to find in each one some reason to doubt, this will suffice to justify my rejecting the whole. And for that end it will not be requisite that I should examine each in particular, which would be an endless undertaking; for owing to the fact that the destruction of the foundations of necessity brings with it the downfall of the rest of the edifice, I shall

only in the first place attack those principles upon which all my former opinions rested.

All that up to the present time I have accepted as most true and certain I have learned either from the senses or through the senses; but it is sometimes proved to me that these senses are deceptive, and it is wiser not to trust entirely to any thing by which we have once been deceived.

But it may be that although the senses sometimes deceive us concerning things which are hardly perceptible, or very far away, there are yet many others to be met with as to which we cannot reasonably have any doubt, although we recognise them by their means. For example, there is the fact that I am here, seated by the fire, attired in a dressing gown, having this paper in my hands and other similar matters. And how could I deny that these hands and this body are mine, were it not perhaps that I compare myself to certain persons, devoid of sense, whose cerebella are so troubled and clouded by the violent vapours of black bile, that they constantly assure us that they think they are kings when they are really quite poor, or that they are clothed in purple when they are really without covering, or who imagine that they have an earthenware head or are nothing but pumpkins or are made of glass. But they are mad, and I should not be any the less insane were I to follow examples so extravagant.

At the same time I must remember that I am a man, and that consequently I am in the habit of sleeping, and in my dreams representing to myself the same things or sometimes even less probable things, than do those who are insane in their waking moments. How often has it happened to me that in the night I dreamt that I found myself in this particular place, that I was dressed and seated near the fire, whilst in reality I was lying undressed in bed! At this moment it does indeed seem to me that it is with eyes awake that I am looking at this paper; that this head which I move is not asleep, that it is deliberately and of set purpose that I extend my hand and perceive it; what happens in sleep does not appear so clear nor so distinct as does all this. But in thinking over this I remind myself that on many occasions I have in sleep been deceived by similar illusions, and in dwelling carefully on this reflection I see so manifestly that there are no certain indications by which we may clearly distinguish wakefulness from sleep that I am lost in astonishment. And my astonishment is such that it is almost capable of persuading me that I now dream.

Now let us assume that we are asleep and that all these particulars, e.g. that we open our eyes, shake our head, extend our hands, and so on, are but false delusions; and let us reflect that possibly neither our hands nor our whole body are such as they appear to us to be. At the same time we must at least confess that the things which are represented to us in sleep are like painted representations which can only have been formed as the counterparts of something real and true, and that in this way those general things at least, i.e. eyes, a head, hands, and a whole body, are not imaginary things, but things really existent. For, as a matter of fact, painters, even when they study with the greatest skill to represent sirens and satyrs by forms the most strange and extraordinary, cannot give them natures which are entirely new, but merely make a certain medley of the members of different animals; or if their imagination is extravagant enough to invent something so novel that nothing similar has ever before been seen, and that then their work represents a thing purely fictitious and absolutely false, it is certain all the same that the colours of which this is composed are necessarily real. And for the same reason, although these general things, to wit, a body, eyes, a head, hands, and such like, may be imaginary, we are bound at the same time to confess that there are at least some other objects yet more simple and more universal, which are real and true; and of these just in the same way as with certain real colours, all these images of things which dwell in our thoughts, whether true and real or false and fantastic, are formed.

To such a class of things pertains corporeal nature in general, and its extension, the figure of extended things, their quantity or magnitude and number, as also the place in which they are, the time which measures their duration, and so on.

That is possibly why our reasoning is not unjust when we conclude from this that Physics, Astronomy, Medicine and all other sciences which have as their end the consideration of composite things, are very dubious and uncertain; but that Arithmetic, Geometry and other sciences of that kind which only treat of things that are very simple and very general, without taking great trouble to ascertain whether they are actually existent or not, contain some measure of certainty and an element of the indubitable. For whether I am awake or asleep, two and three together always form five, and the square can never have more than four sides, and it does not seem possible that truths so clear and apparent can be suspected of any falsity or uncertainty.

Nevertheless I have long had fixed in my mind the belief that an all-powerful God existed by whom I have been created such as I am. But how do I know that He has not brought it to pass that there is no earth, no heaven, no extended body, no magnitude, no place, and that nevertheless I possess the perceptions of all these things and that they seem to me to exist just exactly as I now see them? And, besides, as I sometimes imagine that others deceive themselves in the things which they think they know best, how do I know that I am not deceived every time that I add two and three, or count the sides of a square, or judge of things yet simpler, if anything simpler can be imagined? But possibly God has not desired that I should be thus deceived, for He is said to be supremely good. If, however, it is contrary to His goodness to have made me such that I constantly deceive myself, it would also appear to be contrary to His goodness to permit me to be sometimes deceived, and nevertheless I cannot doubt that he does permit this.

There may indeed be those who would prefer to deny the existence of a God so powerful, rather than believe that all other things are uncertain. But let us not oppose them for the present, and grant that all that is here said of a God is a fable; nevertheless in whatever way they suppose that I have arrived at the state of being that I have reached—whether they attribute it to fate or to accident, or make out that it is by a continual succession of antecedents, or by some other method—since to err and deceive oneself is a defect, it is clear that the greater will be the probability of my being so imperfect as to deceive myself ever, as is the Author to whom they assign my origin the less powerful. To these reasons I have certainly nothing to reply, but at the end I feel constrained to confess that there is nothing in all that I formerly believed to be true, of which I cannot in some measure doubt, and that not merely through want of thought or through levity, but for reasons which are very powerful and maturely considered; so that henceforth I ought not the less carefully to refrain from giving credence to these opinions than to that which is manifestly false, if I desire to arrive at any certainty in the sciences.

But it is not sufficient to have made these remarks, we must also be careful to keep them in mind. For these ancient and commonly held opinions still revert frequently to my mind, long and familiar custom having given them the right to occupy my mind against my inclination and rendered them almost masters of my belief; nor will I ever lose the habit of deferring to them or of placing my confidence in them, so long as I consider them as they really are, i.e. opinions in some measure doubtful, as I have just shown, and at the same time highly probable, so that there is much more reason to believe in than to deny them. That is why I consider that I shall not be acting amiss, if, taking of set purpose a contrary belief, I allow myself to be deceived, and for a certain time pretend that all these opinions are entirely false and imaginary, until at last, having thus balanced my former prejudices with my latter (so that they cannot divert my opinions more to one side than to the other), my judgment will no longer be dominated by bad usage or turned away from the right knowledge of the truth. For I am assured that there can be nei-

ther peril nor error in this course, and that I cannot at present yield too much to distrust, since I am not considering the question of action, but only of knowledge.

I shall then suppose, not that God who is supremely good and the fountain of truth, but some evil genius not less powerful than deceitful, has employed his whole energies in deceiving me; I shall consider that the heavens, the earth, colours, figures, sound, and all other external things are nought but the illusions and dreams of which this genius has availed himself in order to lay traps for my credulity; I shall consider myself as having no hands, no eyes, no flesh, no blood, nor any senses, yet falsely believing myself to possess all these things; I shall remain obstinately attached to this idea, and if by this means it is not in my power to arrive at the knowledge of any truth, I may at least do what is in my power (i.e. suspend my judgment), and with firm purpose avoid giving credence to any false thing, or being imposed upon by this arch deceiver, however powerful and deceptive he may be. But this task is a laborious one, and insensibly a certain lassitude leads me into the course of my ordinary life. And just as a captive who in sleep enjoys an imaginary liberty, when he begins to suspect that his liberty is but a dream, fears to awaken, and conspires with these agreeable illusions that the deception may be prolonged, so insensibly of my own accord I fall back into my former opinions, and I dread awakening from this slumber, lest the laborious wakefulness which would follow the tranquillity of this repose should have to be spent not in daylight, but in the excessive darkness of the difficulties which have just been discussed.

A. J. AYER

from Scepticism and Certainty

THE QUEST FOR CERTAINTY

The quest for certainty has played a considerable part in the history of philosophy: it has been assumed that without a basis of certainty all our claims to knowledge must be suspect. Unless some things are certain, it is held, nothing can be even probable. Unfortunately it has not been made clear exactly what is being sought. Sometimes the word 'certain' is used as a synonym for 'necessary' or for '*a priori*'. It is said, for example, that no empirical statements are certain, and what is meant by this is that they are not necessary in the way that *a priori* statements are, that they can all be denied without self-contradiction. Accordingly, some philosophers take *a priori* statements as their ideal. They wish, like Leibniz, to put all true statements on a level with those of formal logic or pure mathematics; or, like the existentialists, they attach a tragic significance to the fact that this cannot be done. But it is perverse to see tragedy in what could not conceivably be otherwise; and the fact that all empirical statements are contingent, that even when true they can be denied without self-contradiction, is itself a matter of necessity. If empirical statements had the formal validity which makes the truths of logic unassailable they could not do the work that we expect of them; they would not be descriptive of anything that happens. In demanding for empirical statements the safeguard of logical necessity, these philosophers have failed to see that they would thereby rob them of their factual content.

Neither is this the only way in which their ideal of *a priori* statements fails them. Such statements are, indeed, unassailable, in the sense that, if they are true, there are no circumstances in which they could have been false. One may conceive of a world in which they had no useful application, but their being useless would not render them invalid: even if the physical processes of addition or subtraction could

for some reason not be carried out, the laws of arithmetic would still hold good. But from the fact that *a priori* statements, if they are true, are unassailable in this sense, it does not follow that they are immune from doubt. For, as we have already remarked, it is possible to make mistakes in mathematics or in logic. It is possible to believe an *a priori* statement to be true when it is not. And we have seen that it is vain to look for an infallible state of intuition, which would provide a logical guarantee that no mistake was being made. Here too, it may be objected that the only reason that we have for concluding that any given *a priori* statement is false is that it contradicts some other which is true. That we can discover our errors shows that we have the power to correct them. The fact that we sometimes find ourselves to be mistaken in accepting an *a priori* statement, so far from lending favour to the suggestion that all those that we accept are false, is incompatible with it. But this still leaves it open for us to be at fault in any particular case. There is no special set of *a priori* statements of which it can be said that just these are beyond the reach of doubt. In very many instances the doubt would not, indeed, be serious. If the validity of some logical principle is put in question, one may be able to find a way of proving or disproving it. If it be suggested that the proof itself is suspect, one may obtain reassurance by going over it again. When one has gone over it again and satisfied oneself that there is nothing wrong with it, then to insist that it may still not be valid, that the conclusion may not really have been proved, is merely to pay lip-service to human fallibility. The doubt is maintained indefinitely, because nothing is going to count as its being resolved. And just for this reason it is not serious. But to say that it is not serious is not logically to exclude it. There can be doubt so long as there is the possibility of error. And there must be the possibility of error with respect to any statement, whether empirical or *a priori*, which is such that from the fact that someone takes it to be so it does not follow logically that it is so. We have established this point in our discussion of knowledge, and we have seen that it is not vitiated by the fact that in the case of *a priori* statements there may be no other ground for accepting them than that one sees them to be true.

Philosophers have looked to *a priori* statements for security because they have assumed that inasmuch as these statements may themselves be certain, in the sense of being necessary, they can be certainly known. As we have seen, it may even be maintained that only what is certainly true can be certainly known. But this, it must again be remarked, is a confusion. *A priori* statements can, indeed, be known, not because they are necessary but because they are true and because we may be entitled to feel no doubt about their truth. And the reason why we are entitled to feel no doubt about their truth may be that we can prove them, or even just that we can see them to be valid; in either case there is an appeal to intuition, since we have at some point to claim to be able to see the validity of a proof. If the validity of every proof had to be proved in its turn, we should fall into an infinite regress. But to allow that there are times when we may justifiably claim the right to be sure of the truth of an *a priori* statement is not to allow that our intuitions are infallible. One is conceded the right to be sure when one is judged to have taken every reasonable step towards making sure: but this is still logically consistent with one's being in error. The discovery of the error refutes the claim to knowledge; but it does not prove that the claim was not, in the circumstances, legitimately made. The claim to know an *a priori* statement is satisfied only if the statement is true; but it is legitimate if it has the appropriate backing, which may, in certain cases, consist in nothing more than the statement's appearing to be self-evident. Even so, it may fail: but if such claims were legitimate only when there was no logical possibility of error, they could not properly be made at all.

Thus, if the quest for certainty is simply a quest for knowledge; if saying that a statement is known for certain amounts to no more than saying that it is known, it may find its object in *a priori* statements, though not indeed in them uniquely. If, on the other hand, it is a search for conditions which exclude not merely the fact, but even the possibility, of error,

then knowledge of *a priori* statements does not satisfy it. In neither case is the fact that these *a priori* statements may themselves be certain, in the sense of being necessary, relevant to the issue. Or rather, as we have seen, it is relevant only if we arbitrarily decide to make it so.

ARE ANY STATEMENTS IMMUNE FROM DOUBT?

If our aim is never to succumb to falsehood, it would be prudent for us to abstain from using language altogether. Our behaviour might still be hesitant or misguided but it is only with the use of language that truth and error, certainty and uncertainty, come fully upon the scene. It is only such things as statements or propositions, or beliefs or opinions, which are expressible in language, that are capable of being true or false, certain or doubtful. Our experiences themselves are neither certain nor uncertain; they simply occur. It is when we attempt to report them, to record or forecast them, to devise theories to explain them, that we admit the possibility of falling into error, or for that matter of achieving truth. For the two go together: security is sterile. It is recorded of the Greek philosopher Cratylus that, having resolved never to make a statement of whose truth he could not be certain, he was in the end reduced simply to wagging his finger. An echo of his point of view is to be found in the disposition of some modern philosophers to regard the expression of purely demonstrative statements like 'this here now' as the ideal limit to which all narrative uses of language should approach. It is a matter in either case of gesticulating towards the facts without describing them. But it is just their failure to describe that makes these gestures defective as a form of language. Philosophers have been attracted by the idea of a purely demonstrative use of words because they have wanted to make the best of both worlds. They have sought as it were to merge their language with the facts it was supposed to picture; to treat its signs as symbols, and yet bestow upon them the solidity which belongs to the facts themselves, the facts being simply there without any question of doubt or error arising. But these aims are incompatible. Purely demonstrative expressions are in their way secure; but only because the information which they give is vanishingly small. They point to something that is going on, but they do not tell us what it is.

Some philosophers, however, have thought that they could go further than this. They have thought it possible to find a class of statements which would be both genuinely informative and at the same time logically immune from doubt. The statements usually chosen for this role contain a demonstrative component, but they are not wholly demonstrative; they contain also a descriptive component which is supposed to characterize some present state of the speaker, or some present content of his experience. The sort of example that we are offered is 'I feel a headache' or 'this looks to me to be red' or 'this is louder than that', where 'this' and 'that' refer to sounds that I am actually hearing or, more ambitiously, 'it seems to me that this is a table' or 'I seem to remember that such and such an event occurred'. Such statements may be false as well as true: nor is their truth a condition of their being made. I may, for example, be lying when I say that I feel a headache. But while I may be lying and so deceive others, I cannot, so it is maintained, myself be in any doubt or in anyway mistaken about the fact. I cannot be unsure whether I feel a headache, nor can I think that I feel a headache when I do not. And the same applies to the other examples. In all cases, so it is alleged, if one misdescribes the nature of one's present experience, one must be doing so deliberately. One must be saying something which one knows for certain to be false.

Since the only way in which any statement of fact can be discovered either to be true or false is by someone's having some experience, these statements which are supposed, as it were, to photograph the details of our experiences seem to occupy a privileged position: for it would appear that it is their truth or falsehood that provides the test for the validity all the others. For this reason they have sometimes been described as basic statements, or basic propositions. Or rather, it has been assumed that there must be some statements the recognition of whose truth or falsehood supplies the natural terminus to any process of empirical verification; and statements which are descriptive of the present contents of experiences are selected as the most worthy candidates. The reason why they are so distinguished is that it is thought that they alone are

directly and conclusively verifiable; of all statements which have a descriptive content they alone are not subject to any further tests. If they were subject to further tests the process of verification would not terminate with them. But where else, then, could it terminate? So these experiential statements, as we may call them, are taken as basic because they are held to be 'incorrigible'.

To say that these statements are incorrigible is not, however, to say that one's assessment of their truth or falsehood can ever be revised. Or if it does imply this, it is an error. Suppose that, feeling a headache, I write down in my diary the sentence 'I feel a headache'. To-morrow when I read this entry I may seem to remember that I did not make it seriously; and so I may decide that the statement which it expressed was false. In the circumstances envisaged this decision would be wrong; but this does not mean that I am not free to make it, or to revise it in its turn. But, it may be said, the statement which you subsequently reject is not the same as the one you originally accepted. The statement which is expressed by the sentence 'I feel a headache now' is different from the statement which is expressed by the sentence 'I felt a headache then' even though the pronoun refers to the same person in each case and 'now' and 'then' refer to the same moment. Now there is indeed a sense in which these sentences do have different meanings; the correct translation of one of them into a different language would not be a correct translation of the other. Granted that their reference is the same, the difference in their form shows that they are uttered at different times. But I think it would be wrong to conclude that they expressed different statements; for the state of affairs which makes what is expressed by either of them true is one and the same. Moreover, it seems strange to say that when I verify a prediction about the course of my experience, the statement which I actually verify is different from the statement which embodies the prediction, since one is expressed by a sentence in the present and the other by a sentence in the future tense. Yet this would follow from the assumption that if two sentences differ in this way the statements which they express cannot be the same. I think, therefore, that this assumption is to be rejected, and consequently that experiential statements are not incorrigible in the sense that once they have been discovered to be true they cannot subsequently be denied. Clearly, if we have discovered them to be true, we shall be in error if we subsequently deny them: all that I am now maintaining is that it is an error which it is within our power to make.

But in what sense then is it at all plausible to claim that these statements are incorrigible? Only, I think, in the sense that one's grounds for accepting them may be perfect. It is, therefore, misleading to talk of a class of incorrigible, or indubitable, statements as though 'being incorrigible' or 'being indubitable' were properties which belonged to statements in themselves. The suggestion is rather that there is a class of statements which in certain conditions only cannot be doubted; statements which are known incorrigibly when they are made by the right person in the right circumstances and at the right time. Thus, in my view at least, the sentences 'he has a headache', when used by someone else to refer to me, 'I shall have a headache', used by me in the past with reference to this moment, and 'I have a headache' all express the same statement; but the third of these sentences alone is used in such conditions as make it reasonable for me to claim that the statement is incorrigibly known. What is 'incorrigible' in this case is the strength of the basis on which I put the statement forward: not in the sense that the existence of such a basis cannot be denied or doubted by other persons, or by myself at other times, but that given its existence—and it is fundamental to the argument that I *am* given it—then, independently of all other evidence, the truth of the statement is perfectly assured. It is in this sense only that the statement may be regarded as not being subject to any further tests a claim which may seem more modest when it is remarked that even if I am given a conclusive basis for accepting the truth of what I say in such conditions, the gift is immediately withdrawn. The conditions change; the experience is past; and I am left free to doubt or deny that I ever had it, and so again to put in question the truth of the statement which for a moment I 'incorrigibly' knew.

The ground then, for maintaining that, while one is having an experience, one can know with absolute certainty the truth of a statement which does no more than describe the character of the experience in question is that there is no room here for any-

thing short of knowledge: there is nothing for one to be uncertain or mistaken about. The vast majority of the statements which we ordinarily make assert more than is strictly contained in the experiences on which they are based: they would indeed be of little interest if they did not. For example, I am now seated in a vineyard; and I can fairly claim to know that there are clusters of grapes a few feet away from me. But in making even such a simple statement as 'that is a bunch of grapes', a statement so obvious that in ordinary conversation, as opposed, say, to an English lesson, it would never be made, I am in a manner going beyond my evidence. I can see the grapes: but it is requisite also that in the appropriate conditions I should be able to touch them. They are not real grapes if they are not tangible; and from the fact that I am having just these visual experiences, it would seem that nothing logically follows about what I can or cannot touch. Neither is it enough that I can see and touch the grapes: other people must be able to perceive them too. If I had reason to believe that no one else could, in the appropriate conditions, see or touch them, I should be justified in concluding that I was undergoing a hallucination. Thus, while my basis for making this assertion may be very strong, so strong indeed as to warrant a claim to knowledge, it is not conclusive; my experience, according to this argument, could still be what it is even though the grapes which I think that I am perceiving really do not exist. But suppose now that I make an even less ambitious statement: suppose that I assert merely that I am seeing what now looks to me to be a bunch of grapes, without the implication that there is anything really there at all; so that my statement would remain true even if I were dreaming or suffering a complete hallucination. How in that case could I possibly be wrong? What other people may experience, or what I myself may experience at other times, does not affect the issue. My statement is concerned only with what appears to me at this moment, and to me alone: whether others have the same impression is irrelevant. I may indeed be using words eccentrically. It may be that it is not correct in English to describe what I seem to be seeing as a bunch of grapes. But this, so it is argued, does not matter. Even if my use of words be unconventional, what I mean to express by them must be true.

ARE MISTAKES ABOUT ONE'S OWN IMMEDIATE EXPERIENCE ONLY VERBAL?

For those who have the use of language, there is an intimate connection between identifying an object and knowing what to call it. Indeed on many occasions one's recognizing whatever it may be is simply a matter of one's coming out with the appropriate word. Of course the word must be meant to designate the object in question, but there are not, or need not be, two separate processes, one of fixing the object and the other of labelling it. The intention is normally to be found in the way in which the label is put on. There is, however, a sense in which one can recognize an object without knowing how to describe it. One may be able to place the object as being of the same sort as such and such another, or as having appeared before on such and such occasions, although one forgets what it is called or even thinks that it is called something which it is not. To a certain extent this placing of the object is already a fashion of describing it: we are not now concerned with the cases where recognition, conceived in terms of adaptive behaviour, is independent of the use of any symbols at all: but our finding a description of this sort is consistent with our ignoring or infringing some relevant linguistic rule. And this can happen also when the rule is of one's own making, or at least constituted by one's own practice. When the usage which they infringe is private, such lapses can only be exceptional; for unless one's practice were generally consistent, there would be no rule to break: but it is to be envisaged that they should now and then occur.

If this is so, one can be mistaken, after all, in the characterization of one's present experience. One can at least misdescribe it in the sense that one applies the wrong word to it; wrong because it is not the word which by the rules of one's language is correlated with an 'object' of the sort in question. But the reply to this may be that one would then be making only a verbal mistake. One would be misusing words, but not falling into any error of fact. Those who maintain that statements which describe some feature of one's present experience are incorrigible need not deny that the sentences which express them may be incorrectly formulated. What they are trying to exclude is the possibility of one's being factually mistaken.

But what is supposed to be the difference in this context between a verbal and a factual mistake? The first thing to remark is that we are dealing with words which, though general in their application, are also ostensive: that is, they are meant to stand for features of what is directly given in experience. And with respect to words of this kind, it is plausible to argue that knowing what they mean is simply a matter of being disposed to use them on the right occasions, when these are presented. It then appears to follow that to be in doubt as to the nature of something which is given, to wonder, for example, what colour this looks to me to be, is to be in doubt about the meaning of a word. And, correspondingly, to misdescribe what is given is to misuse a word. If I am not sure whether this looks crimson, what I am doubting is whether 'crimson' is the right word to describe this colour: if I resolve this doubt wrongly I have used the word 'crimson' when I should not or failed to use it when I should. This example is made easier to accept because the word 'crimson' has a conventional use. It is harder to see how I can use a word improperly when it is I alone who set the standard of propriety: my mistake would then have to consist in the fact that I had made an involuntary departure from some consistent practice which I had previously followed. In any event, it is argued, my mistake is not factual. If I were to predict that something, not yet presented to me, was going to look crimson, I might very well be making a factual mistake. My use of the word 'crimson' may be quite correct. It properly expresses my expectation: only the expectation is not in fact fulfilled. But in such a case I venture beyond the description of my present experience: I issue a draft upon the facts which they may refuse to honour. But for them to frustrate me I must put myself in their power. And this it is alleged I fail to do when I am merely recording what is directly given to me. My mistakes then can only be verbal. Thus we see that the reason why it is held to be impossible to make a factual error in describing a feature of one's present experience is that there is nothing in these circumstances which is allowed to count as one's being factually mistaken.

Against this, some philosophers would argue that it is impossible to describe anything, even a momentary private experience, without venturing beyond it. If I say that what I seem to see is crimson, I am saying that it bears the appropriate resemblance in colour to certain other objects. If it does not so resemble them I have classified it wrongly, and in doing so I have made a factual mistake. But the answer to this is that merely from the statement that a given thing looks crimson, it cannot be deduced that anything else is coloured or even that anything else exists. The fact, if it be a fact, that the colour of the thing in question does not resemble that of other things which are properly described as crimson does indeed prove that in calling it crimson I am making a mistake; I am breaking a rule which would not exist unless there were, or at any rate could be, other things to which the word applied. But in saying that this is crimson, I am not explicitly referring to these other things. In using a word according to a rule, whether rightly or wrongly, I am not talking about the rule. I operate it but I do not say how it operates. From the fact that I have to refer to other things in order to show that my description of something is correct, it does not follow that my description itself refers to them. We may admit that to describe is to classify; but this does not entail that in describing something one is bound to go beyond it, in the sense that one actually asserts that it is related to something else.

Let us allow, then, that there can be statements which refer only to the contents of one's present experiences. Then, if it is made a necessary condition for being factually mistaken that one should make some claim upon the facts which goes beyond the content of one's present experience, it will follow that even when these statements misdescribe what they refer to the error is not factual: and then there appears no choice but to say that it is verbal. The question is whether this ruling is to be accepted.

The assumption which lies behind it is that to understand the meaning of an ostensive word one must be able to pick out the instances to which it applies. If I pick out the wrong instances, or fail to pick out the right ones, I show that I have not learned how to use the word. If I hesitate whether to apply it to a given case, I show that I am so far uncertain of its meaning. Now there is clearly some truth in this assumption. We should certainly not say that someone knew the meaning of an ostensive word if he had no idea how to apply it; more than that, we require that his use of it should, in general, be both confident

and right. But this is not to say that in every single case in which he hesitates over the application of the word, he must be in doubt about its meaning. Let us consider an example. Suppose that two lines of approximately the same length are drawn so that they both come within my field of vision and I am then asked to say whether either of them looks to me to be the longer, and if so which. I think I might very well be uncertain how to answer. But it seems very strange to say that what, in such a case, I should be uncertain about would be the meaning of the English expression 'looks longer than'. It is not at all like the case where I know which looks to me the longer, but having to reply in French, and speaking French badly, I hesitate whether to say 'plus longue' or 'plus large'. In this case I am uncertain only about the proper use of words, but in the other surely I am not. I know quite well how the words 'looks longer than' are used in English. It is just that at in the present instance I am not sure whether, as a matter of fact, either of the lines does look to me to be longer than the other.

But if I can be in doubt about this matter of fact, I can presumably also come to the wrong decision. I can judge that this line looks to me to be longer than that one, when in fact it does not. This would indeed be a curious position to be in. Many would say that it was an impossible position, on the ground that there is no way of distinguishing between the way things look to someone and the way he judges that they look. After all he is the final authority on the way things look to him, and what criterion is there for deciding how things look to him except the way that he assesses them? But in allowing that he may be uncertain how a thing looks to him, we have already admitted this distinction. We have drawn a line between the facts and his assessment, or description, of them. Even so, it may be objected, there is no sense in talking of there being a mistake unless it is at least possible that the mistake should be discovered. And how could it ever be discovered that one had made a mistake in one's account of some momentary, private experience? Clearly no direct test is possible. The experience is past: it cannot be produced for reinspection. But there may still be indirect evidence which would carry weight. To return to our example, if I look at the lines again, it may seem quite clear to me that A looks longer than B, whereas I had previously been inclined to think that B looked longer than A, or that they looked the same length. This does not prove that I was wrong before: it may be that they look to me differently now from the way they did then. But I might have indirect, say physiological, evidence that their appearance, that is the appearance that they offer to me, has not changed. Or I may have reason to believe that in the relevant conditions things look the same to certain other people as they do to me: and then the fact that the report given by these other people disagrees with mine may have some tendency to show that I am making a mistake. In any event it is common ground that one can misdescribe one's experience. The question is only whether such misdescription is always to be taken as an instance of a verbal mistake. My contention is that there are cases in which it is more plausible to say that the mistake is factual.

If I am right. there is then no class of descriptive statements which·are incorrigible. However strong the experiential basis on which a descriptive statement is put forward, the possibility of its falsehood is not excluded. Statements which do no more than describe the content of a momentary, private experience achieve the greatest security because they run the smallest risk. But they do run some risk, however small, and because of this they too can come to grief. Complete security is attained only by statements like 'I exist' which function as gesticulations. But the price which they pay for it is the sacrifice of descriptive content.

We are left still with the argument that some statements must be incorrigible, if any are ever to be verified. If the statements which have been taken as basic are fallible like all the rest, where does the process of verification terminate? The answer is that it terminates in someone having some experience, and in his accepting the truth of some statement which describes it, or, more commonly, the truth of some more far-reaching statement which the occurrence of the experience supports. There is nothing fallible about the experience itself. What may be wrong is only one's identification of it. If an experience has been misidentified, one will be misled into thinking that some statement has been verified when it has not. But this does not mean that we never verify anything. There is no reason to doubt that the vast majority of our experiences are taken by us to be what they are; in which case they do verify the

statements which are construed as describing them. What we do not, and cannot, have is a logical guarantee that our acceptance of a statement is not mistaken. It is chiefly the belief that we need such a guarantee that has led philosophers to hold that some at least of the statements which refer to what is immediately given to us in experience must be incorrigible. But, as I have already remarked, even if there could be such incorrigible statements, the guarantee which they provided would not be worth very much. In any given case it would operate only for a single person and only for the fleeting moment at which he was having the experience in question. It would not, therefore, be of any help to us in making lasting additions to our stock of knowledge.

In allowing that the descriptions which people give of their experiences may be factually mistaken, we are dissociating having an experience from knowing that one has it. To know that one is having whatever experience it may be, one must not only have it but also be able to identify it correctly, and there is no necessary transition from one to the other; not to speak of the cases when we do not identify our experiences at all, we may identify them wrongly. Once again, this does not mean that we never know, or never really know, what experiences we are having. On the contrary it is exceptional for us not to know. All that is required is that we should be able to give an account of our experiences which is both confident and correct; and these conditions are very frequently fulfilled. It is no rebuttal of our claim to knowledge that, in this as in other domains, it may sometimes happen that we think we know when we do not.

The upshot of our argument is that the philosopher's ideal of certainty has no application. Except in the cases where the truth of a statement is a condition of its being made, it can never in any circumstances be logically impossible that one should take a statement to be true when it is false; and this holds good whatever the statement may be, whether, for example, it is itself necessary or contingent. It would, however, be a mistake to express this conclusion by saying, lugubriously or in triumph, that nothing is really certain. There are a great many statements the truth of which we rightly do not doubt; and it is perfectly correct to say that they are certain. We should not be bullied by the sceptic into renouncing an expression for which we have a legitimate use. Not that the sceptic's argument is fallacious; as usual his logic is impeccable. But his victory is empty. He robs us of certainty only by so defining it as to make it certain that it cannot be obtained.

THE PATTERN OF SCEPTICAL ARGUMENTS

There is, however, a special class of cases in which the problems created by the sceptic's logic are not so easily set aside. They are those in which the attack is directed, not against factual inference as such, but against some particular forms of it in which we appear to end with statements of a different category from those with which we began. Thus doubt is thrown on the validity of our belief in the existence of physical objects, or scientific entities, or the minds of others, or the past, by an argument which seeks to show that it depends in each case upon an illegitimate inference. What is respectively put in question is our right to make the transition from sense experiences to physical objects, from the world of common sense to the entities of science, from the overt behaviour of other people to their inner thoughts and feelings, from present to past. These are distinct problems, but the pattern of the sceptic's argument is the same in every case.

The first step is to insist that we depend entirely on the premises for our knowledge of the conclusion. Thus, it is maintained that we have no access to physical objects otherwise than through the contents of our sense-experiences, which themselves are not physical: we infer the existence of scientific entities, such as atoms and electrons, only from their alleged effects: another person's mind is revealed to us only through the state of his body or by the things he says and does: the past is known only from records or through our memories, the contents of which themselves belong to the present. Relatively to our knowledge of the evidence, our knowledge of the conclusion must in every case be indirect: and logically this could not be otherwise.

The second step in the argument is to show that the relation between premises and conclusion is not deductive. There can be no description of our sense-experiences, however long and detailed, from which it follows that a physical object exists. Statements

about scientific entities are not formally deductible from any set of statements about their effects, nor do statements about a person's inner thoughts and feelings logically follow from statements about their outward manifestations. However strong the present evidence for the existence of certain past events may be, it is not demonstrative. There would be no formal contradiction in admitting the existence of our memory-experiences, or of any other of the sources of our knowledge of the past, and yet denying that the corresponding past events had ever taken place.

But then, the argument proceeds, these inferences are not inductive either. Assuming inductive inference to be legitimate at all, it carries us, to use a phrase of Hume's, from instances of which we have experience to those of which we have none. But here it is essential that these instances of which we in fact have no experience should be such as we are capable of experiencing. Let it be granted, in spite of the problem of induction, that on the basis of what we do experience we are sometimes entitled to infer the existence of observed events: our reliance on argument will then be a substitute for the direct observations which, for some practical reason, we are unable to make. The position is quite different when the things whose existence we are claiming to infer not merely are not given to us in experience but never could be. For what foundation could there be in such a case for our inductive arguments and how could their success be tested? Some philosophers even consider it to be nonsensical to assert the existence of an object which could not, at least in principle, be observed; and clearly no amount of inductive evidence can warrant a meaningless conclusion. But even if one does not go so far as to call such conclusions meaningless, it must be admitted, according to this argument, that they can have no inductive backing. Experimental reasoning can carry us forward at a given level; on the basis of certain sense experiences it allows us to predict the occurrence of other sense-experiences; from observations of the way a person is behaving it allows us to infer that his future behaviour will take such and such a course. What it does not permit us is to jump from one level to another; to pass from premises concerning the contents of our sense-experiences to conclusions about physical objects, from premises concerning other people's overt behaviour to conclusions about their minds.

The last step is to argue that since these inferences cannot be justified either deductively or inductively, they cannot be justified at all. We are not entitled even to make the elementary move of inferring from our present experiences to the existence of past events, or, admitting the whole range of our experiences, to arrive at the existence of physical objects: and assuming that we had sufficient warrant for believing in the existence of the physical objects which make up the world of common sense, we still should not be entitled to make the transition from these to the entities of science, or from any physical phenomena to the existence of other minds. It would indeed be hard to find even a philosopher who was willing to accept these consequences. It is scarcely to be imagined that anyone should seriously maintain that we had no right whatsoever to be sure, or even moderately confident, of anything concerning physical objects, or the minds of others, or the past. But even if he shrinks from carrying his argument to what appears to be its logical conclusion, the sceptic may still insist that it presents a question for us to answer. No doubt we do know what he says we cannot know; we are at least called upon to explain how it is possible that we should.

The problem which is presented in all these cases is that of establishing our right to make what appears to be a special sort of advance beyond our data. The level of what, for the purposes of the problem, we take to be data varies; but in every instance they are supposed to fall short, in an uncompromising fashion, of the conclusion to which we look to them to lead us. For those who wish to vindicate our claim to knowledge, the difficulty is to find a way of bridging or abolishing this gap.

Concern with the theory of knowledge is very much a matter of taking this difficulty seriously. The different ways of trying to meet it mark out different schools of philosophy, or different methods of attacking philosophical questions. Apart from the purely sceptical position, which sets the problem, there are four main lines of approach. It is interesting that each of them consists in denying a different step in the sceptic's argument.

First, Naïve Realism. The naïve realist denies the first step of all. He will not allow that our knowledge of the various things which the sceptic wishes to put beyond our reach is necessarily indirect. His position is that the physical objects which we commonly perceive are, in a sense to be explained, directly 'given' to us, that it is not inconceivable that such things as atoms and electrons should also be directly perceived, that at least in certain favourable instances one can inspect the minds of others, that memory makes us directly acquainted with the past. The general attitude displayed is that of intuitionism. It is in the same spirit that philosophers maintain that they intuit moral values, or try to justify induction by claiming the power of apprehending necessary connections between events. But of course it is possible to take up the naïve realist's position on any one of these questions, without being committed to it on the others.

Secondly, Reductionism. The reductionist allows the first step in the sceptic's argument, but denies the second. Although his philosophical temper is diametrically opposed to that of the naïve realist, or indeed to intuitionism in any form, they have this much in common. Both of them try to close the gap which the sceptic relies on keeping open. But whereas the naïve realist does so by bringing the evidence up to the conclusion, the reductionist's policy is to bring the conclusion down to the level of the evidence. His view, which we shall presently examine, is that physical objects are logically constructed out of the contents of our sense-experiences, just as the entities of science are nothing over and above their so-called effects. In the same way, he holds that statements which appear to be about the minds of others are equivalent to statements about their physical manifestations, and that statements which appear to be about the past are equivalent to statements about what are ordinarily regarded as records of the past, that is to statements about the present and future. Thus the conclusion, being brought down to the level of the evidence, is presented in every case as being deducible from it. It is again to be noted that one may take a reductionist view of any one of these questions without being bound to apply it to the others.

Thirdly, we have what may be called the Scientific Approach. This is the position of those who admit the first two steps in the sceptic's argument but deny the third. Unlike their predecessors, they accept the existence of the gap between evidence and conclusion, but they hold that it can be bridged by a legitimate process of inductive reasoning. Thus they will maintain that physical objects, though not directly observable in the way the naïve realists suppose, can be known to us indirectly as the causes of our sensations, just as the existence of scientific entities can be inferred from their effects, without our having to identify the two. On this view, the deliverances of memory, and other records, make the existence of the past an overwhelmingly probable hypothesis. Knowing that we ourselves have inner thoughts and feelings, we can attribute them to others by analogy.

Finally, there is the method of Descriptive Analysis. Here one does not contest the premises of the sceptic's argument, but only its conclusion. No attempt is made either to close or to bridge the gap: we are simply to take it in our stride. It is admitted that the inferences which are put in question are not deductive and also that they are not inductive, in the generally accepted sense. But this, it is held, does not condemn them. They are what they are, and none the worse for that. Moreover, they can be analysed. We can, for example, show in what conditions we feel confident in attributing certain experiences to others: we can evaluate different types of record: we can distinguish the cases in which our memories or perceptions are taken to be reliable from those in which they are not. In short, we can give an account of the procedures that we actually follow. But no justification of these procedures is necessary or possible. One may be called upon to justify a particular conclusion, and then one can appeal to the appropriate evidence. But no more in these cases than in the case of the more general problem of induction, can there be a proof that what we take to be good evidence really is so. And if there cannot be a proof, it is not sensible to demand one. The sceptic's problems are insoluble because they are fictitious.

G. E. MOORE

A Defence of Common Sense

In what follows I have merely tried to state, one by one, some of the most important points in which my philosophical position differs from positions which have been taken up by *some* other philosophers. It may be that the points which I have had room to mention are not really the most important, and possibly some of them may be points as to which no philosopher has ever really differed from me. But, to the best of my belief, each is a point as to which many have really differed; although (in most cases, at all events) each is also a point as to which many have agreed with me.

I. The first point is a point which embraces a great many other points. And it is one which I cannot state as clearly as I wish to state it, except at some length. The method I am going to use for stating it is this. I am going to begin by enunciating, under the heading(1), a whole long list of propositions, which may seem, at first sight, such obvious truisms as not to be worth stating: they are, in fact, a set of propositions, every one of which (in my own opinion) I *know*, with certainty, to be true. I shall, next, under the heading (2), state a single proposition which makes an assertion about a whole set of *classes* of propositions—each class being defined, as the class consisting of all propositions which resemble *one* of the propositions in (1) in a certain respect. (2), therefore, is a proposition which could not be stated, until the list of propositions in (1), or some similar list, had already been given. (2) is itself a proposition which may seem such an obvious truism as not to be worth stating: and it is also a proposition which (in my own opinion) I *know*, with certainty, to be true. But, nevertheless, it is, to the best of my belief, a proposition with regard to which many philosophers have, for different reasons, differed from me; even if they have not directly denied (2) itself, they have held views incompatible with it. My first point, then, may be said to be that (2),

together with all its implications, some of which I shall expressly mention, is true.

(1)I begin, then, with my list of truisms, every one of which (in my own opinion) I *know*, with certainty, to be true. The propositions to be included in this list are the following:

There exists at present a living human body, which is *my* body. This body was born at a certain time in the past, and has existed continuously ever since, though not without undergoing changes; it was, for instance, much smaller when it was born, and for some time afterwards, than it is now. Ever since it was born, it has been either in contact with or not far from the surface of the earth; and, at every moment since it was born, there have also existed many other things, having shape and size in three dimensions (in the same familiar sense in which it has), from which it has been *at various distances* (in the familiar sense in which it is now at a distance both from that mantelpiece and from that bookcase, and at a greater distance from the bookcase than it is from the mantelpiece); also there have (very often, at all events) existed some other things of this kind with which it was in contact (in the familiar sense in which it is now *in contact* with the pen I am holding in my right hand and with some of the clothes I am wearing). Among the things which have, in this sense, formed part of its environment (i.e. have been either in contact with it, or at *some* distance from it, however *great*) there have, at every moment since its birth, been large numbers of other living human bodies, each of which has, like it, (*a*) at some time been born, (*b*)continued to exist from some time after birth, (*c*) been, at every moment of its life after birth, either in contact with or not far from the surface of the earth; and many of these bodies have already died and ceased to exist. But the earth had existed also for many years before my body was born; and for many of these years, also, large numbers of human bodies had, at every moment, been alive upon it; and many of these bodies had died and ceased to exist before it was born. Finally (to come to a different class of propositions), I am a human being, and I have, at different times since my body was born, had many different experiences, of each of many different kinds: e.g. I have often perceived both my own body and other things which formed part of its environment, including other human bodies; I have not only perceived things of this kind, but have also observed facts about them, such as, for instance, the fact which I am now observing, that that mantel piece is at present nearer to my body than that bookcase; I have been aware of other facts, which I was not at the time observing, such as, for instance, the fact, of which I am now aware, that my body existed yesterday and was then also for sometime nearer to that mantelpiece than to that bookcase; I have had expectations with regard to the future, and many beliefs of other kinds, both true and false; I have thought of imaginary things and persons and incidents, in the reality of which I did not believe; I have had dreams; and I have had feelings of many different kinds. And, just as my body has been the body of a human being, namely myself, who has, during his lifetime, had many experiences of each of these (and other) different kinds; so, in the case of very many of the other human bodies which have lived upon the earth, each has been the body of a different human being, who has, during the lifetime of that body, had many different experiences of each of these (and other) different kinds.

(2) I now come to the single truism which, as will be seen, could not be stated except by reference to the whole list of truisms, just given in (1). This truism also (in my own opinion) I *know*, with certainty, to be true; and it is as follows:

In the case of *very many* (I do not say *all*) of the human beings belonging to the class (which includes myself) defined in the following way, i.e. as human beings who have had human bodies, that were born and lived for some time upon the earth, and who have, during the lifetime of those bodies, had many different experiences of each of the kinds mentioned in (1), it is true that each has frequently, during the life of his body, known, with regard to *him*self or *his* body, and with regard to some time earlier than any of the times at which I wrote down

the propositions in (1), a proposition *corresponding* to each of the propositions in (1), in the sense that it asserts with regard to *him*self or *his* body and the earlier time in question (namely, in each case, the time at which he knew it), just what the corresponding proposition in (1) asserts with regard to *me* or *my* body and the time at which I wrote that proposition down.

In other words what (2) asserts is only (what seems an obvious enough truism) that each of *us* (meaning by 'us', very many human beings of the class defined) has frequently *known*, with regard to *him*self or *his* body and the time at which he knew it, everything which, in writing down my list of propositions in (1), I was claiming to know about *my*self or *my* body and the time at which I wrote that proposition down, i.e. just as *I* knew (when I wrote it down) 'There exists at present a living human body which is my body', so each of us has frequently known with regard to himself and some other time the different but corresponding proposition, which *he* could *then* have properly expressed by, 'There exists *at present* a human body which is *my* body'; just as *I* know 'Many human bodies other than mine have before now lived on the earth', so each of us has frequently known the different but corresponding proposition 'Many human bodies other than *mine* have before *now* lived on the earth'; just as *I* know 'Many human beings other than myself have before now perceived, and dreamed, and felt', so each of *us* has frequently known the different but corresponding proposition 'Many human beings other than *myself* have before *now* perceived, and dreamed, and felt'; and so on, in the case of *each* of the propositions enumerated in (1).

I hope there is no difficulty in understanding, so far, what this proposition (2) asserts. I have tried to make clear by examples what I mean by 'propositions *corresponding* to each of the propositions in (1)'. And what (2) asserts is merely that each of us has frequently known to be true a proposition *corresponding* (in that sense) to each of the propositions in (1)—a *different* corresponding proposition, of course, at each of the times—at which he knew such a proposition to be true.

But there remain two points, which, in view of the way in which some philosophers have used the English language, ought, I think, to be expressly mentioned, if I am to make quite clear exactly how much I am asserting in asserting (2).

The first point is this. Some philosophers seem to have thought it legitimate to use the word 'true' in such a sense that a proposition which is partially false may nevertheless also be true; and some of these, therefore, would perhaps *say* that propositions like those enumerated in (1) are, in their view, true, when all the time they believe that every such proposition is partially false. I wish, therefore, to make it quite plain that I am not using 'true' in any such sense. I am using it in such a sense (and I think this is the ordinary usage) that if a proposition is partially false, it follows that it is *not* true, though, of course, it may be *partially* true. I am maintaining, in short, that all the propositions in (1), and also many propositions corresponding to each of these, are *wholly* true; I am asserting this in asserting (2). And hence any philosopher, who does in fact believe, with regard to any or all of these classes of propositions, that every proposition of the class in question is partially false, is, in fact, disagreeing with me and holding a view incompatible with (2), even though he may think himself justified in *saying* that he believes some propositions belonging to all of these classes to be 'true'.

And the second point is this. Some philosophers seem to have thought it legitimate to use such expressions as, e.g. 'The earth has existed for many years past', as if they expressed something which they really believed, when in fact they believe that every proposition, which such an expression would *ordinarily* be understood to express, is, at least partially, false; and all they really believe is that there is some *other* set of propositions, related in a certain way to those which such expressions do actually express, which, unlike these, really are true. That is to say, they use the expression 'The earth has existed for many years past' to express, not what it would ordinarily be understood to express, but the proposition that some proposition, related to this in a certain way, is true; when all the time they believe that the proposition, which this expression would ordinarily be understood to express, is, at least partially, false. I wish, therefore, to make it quite plain that I was not using the expressions I used in (1) in any such subtle sense. I meant by each of them precisely what every reader, in reading them, will have

understood me to mean. And any philosopher, therefore, who holds that any of these expressions, if understood in this popular manner, expresses a proposition which embodies some popular error, is disagreeing with me and holding a view incompatible with (2), even though he may hold that there is some *other*, true, proposition which the expression in question might be legitimately used to express.

In what I have just said, I have assumed that there is some meaning which is *the* ordinary or popular meaning of such expressions as 'The earth has existed for many years past'. And this, I am afraid, is an assumption which some philosophers are capable of disputing. They seem to think that the question 'Do you believe that the earth has existed for many years past?' is not a plain question, such as should be met either by a plain 'Yes' or 'No', or by a plain 'I can't make up my mind', but is the sort of question which can be properly met by: 'It all depends on what you mean by "the earth" and "exists" and "years": if you mean so and so, and so and so, and so and so, then I do; but if you mean so and so, and so and so, and so and so, or so and so, and so and so, and so and so, or so and so, and so and so, and so and so, then I don't, or at least I think it is extremely doubtful.' It seems to me that such a view is as profoundly mistaken as any view can be. Such an expression as 'The earth has existed for many years past' is the very type of an unambiguous expression, the meaning of which we all understand. Anyone who takes a contrary view must, I suppose, be confusing the question whether we understand its meaning (which we all certainly do) with the entirely different question whether we *know what it means*, in the sense that we are able to *give a correct analysis* of its meaning. The question what is the correct analysis of *the* proposition meant *on any occasion* (for, of course, as I insisted in defining (2), a different proposition is meant at every different time at which the expression is used) by 'The earth has existed for many years past' is, it seems to me, a profoundly difficult question, and one to which, as I shall presently urge, no one knows the answer. But to hold that we do not know what, in certain respects, is the analysis of what we understand by such an expression, is an entirely different thing from holding that we do not understand the expression. It is obvious that we cannot even raise the question how what we do understand by it is to be analysed, unless we do understand it. So soon, therefore, as we know that a person who uses such an expression is using it in its ordinary sense, we understand his meaning. So that in explaining that I was using the expressions used in (1) in their ordinary sense (those of them which have an ordinary sense, which is not the case with quite all of them), I have done all that is required to make my meaning clear.

But now, assuming that the expressions which I have used to express (2) are understood, I think, as I have said, that many philosophers have really held views incompatible with (2). And the philosophers who have done so may, I think, be divided into two main groups. A. What (2) asserts is, with regard to a whole set of *classes* of propositions, that we have, each of us, frequently *known* to be true propositions belonging to *each* of these classes. And one way of holding a view incompatible with this proposition is, of course, to hold, with regard to one or more of the classes in question, that *no* propositions of that class *are* true—that all of them are, at least partially, false; since if, in the case of any one of these classes, *no* propositions of that class *are* true, it is obvious that nobody can have *known* any propositions of that class to be true, and therefore that *we* cannot have known to be true propositions belonging to *each* of these classes. And my first group of philosophers consists of philosophers who have held views incompatible with (2) for this reason. They have held, with regard to one or more of the classes in question, simply that no propositions of that class *are* true. Some of them have held this with regard to *all* the classes in question; some only with regard to *some* of them. But, of course, whichever of these two views they have held, they have been holding a view inconsistent with (2). B. Some philosophers, on the other hand, have not ventured to assert, with regard to *any* of the classes in (2), that no propositions of that class *are* true, but what they have asserted is that, in the case of some of these classes, no human being has ever *known*, with certainty, that any propositions of the class in question are true. That is to say, they differ profoundly from philosophers of group A, in that they hold that propositions of *all* these classes *may* be true; but nevertheless they hold a view incompatible with (2) since they hold, with regard to some of these classes, that none of us has ever *known* a proposition of the class in question to be true.

A. I said that some philosophers, belonging to this group, have held that no propositions belonging to *any* of the classes in (2) are wholly true, while others have only held this with regard to *some* of the classes in (2). And I think the chief division of this kind has been the following. Some of the propositions in (1) (and, therefore, of course, all propositions belonging to the corresponding classes in (2)) are propositions which cannot be true, unless some *material things* have existed and have stood *in spatial relations* to one another: that is to say, they are propositions which, *in a certain sense*, imply *the reality of material things*, and *the reality of Space*. E.g. the proposition that my body has existed for many years past, and has, at every moment during that time been either in contact with or not far from the earth is a proposition which implies both *the reality of material things* (provided you use 'material things' in such a sense that to deny the reality of material things implies that no proposition which asserts that human bodies have existed, or that the earth has existed, is wholly true) and also *the reality of Space* (provided, again, that you use 'Space' in such a sense that to deny the reality of Space implies that no proposition which asserts that anything has ever been in contact with or at a distance from another, in the familiar senses pointed out in (1), is wholly true). But others among the propositions in (1) (and, therefore, propositions belonging to the corresponding classes in (2)), do not (at least obviously) imply either the reality of material things or the reality of Space: e.g. the propositions that I have often had dreams, and have had many different feelings at different times. It is true that propositions of this second class do imply one thing which is also implied by all propositions of the first, namely that *(in a certain sense) Time is real*, and imply also one thing not implied by propositions of the first class, namely that *(in a certain sense) at least one Self is real*. But I think there are some philosophers, who, while denying that (in the senses in question) either material things or Space are real, have been willing to admit that Selves and Time are real, in the sense required. Other philosophers, on the other hand, have used the expression 'Time is not real', to express some view that they held; and some, at least, of these have, I think, meant by this expression something which is incompatible with the truth of *any* of the propositions in (1)—they have meant, namely, that *every* proposition of the sort that is expressed by the use of 'now' or 'at present', e.g. 'I am now both seeing and hearing' or 'There exists at present a living human body', or by the use of a *past* tense, e.g. 'I *have* had many experiences in the past', or 'The earth *has* existed for many years', are, at least partially, false.

All the four expressions I have just introduced, namely, 'Material things are not real', 'Space is not real', 'Time is not real', 'The Self is not real', are, I think, unlike the expressions I used in (1), really ambiguous. And it may be that, in the case of each of them, some philosopher has used the expression in question to express some view he held which was not incompatible with (2). With such philosophers, if there are any, I am not, of course, at present concerned. But it seems to me that the most natural and proper usage of each of these expressions is a usage in which it *does* express a view incompatible with (2); and, in the case of each of them, some philosophers have, I think, really used the expression in question to express such a view. All such philosophers have, therefore, been holding a view incompatible with (2).

All such views, whether incompatible with *all* of the propositions in (1), or only with *some* of them, seem to me to be quite certainly false; and I think the following points are specially deserving of notice with regard to them:

(*a*) If *any* of the classes of propositions in (2) is such that no proposition of that class is true, then no philosopher has ever existed, and therefore none can ever have held with regard to any such class, that no proposition belonging to it is true. In other words, the proposition that some propositions belonging to each of these classes are true is a proposition which has the peculiarity, that, if any philosopher has ever denied it, it follows from the fact that he has denied it, that he must have been wrong in denying it. For when I speak of 'philosophers' I mean, of course (as we all do), exclusively philosophers who have been human beings, with human bodies that have lived upon the earth, and who have at different times had many different experiences. If, therefore, there have been any philosophers, there have been human beings of this class; and if there have been human beings of this class, all the rest of what is asserted in (1) is certainly true too. Any view, therefore, incom-

patible with the proposition that many propositions corresponding to each of the propositions in (1) are true, can only be true, on the hypothesis that no philosopher has ever held any such view. It follows, therefore, that, in considering whether this proposition is true, I cannot consistently regard the fact that many philosophers, whom I respect, have, to the best of my belief, held views incompatible with it, as having any weight at all against it. Since, if I know that they have held such views, I am, *ipso facto*, knowing that they were mistaken; and, if I have no reason to believe that the proposition in question is true, I have still less reason to believe that they have held views incompatible with it; since I am more certain that they have existed and held *some* views, i.e. that the proposition in question is true, than that they have held any views incompatible with it.

(*b*) It is, of course, the case that all philosophers who have held such views have repeatedly, even in their philosophical works, expressed other views inconsistent with them: i.e. no philosopher has ever been able to hold such views consistently. One way in which they have betrayed this inconsistency, is by alluding to the existence of other philosophers. Another way is by alluding to the existence of the human race, and in particular by using 'we' in the sense in which I have already constantly used it, in which any philosopher who asserts that 'we' do so and so, e.g. that '*we* sometimes believe propositions that are not true', is asserting not only that he himself has done the thing in question, but that *very many other human beings, who have had bodies and lived upon the earth,* have done the same. The fact is, of course, that all philosophers have belonged to the class of human beings which exists only if (2) be true: that is to say, to the class of human beings who have frequently *known* propositions corresponding to each of the propositions in (1). In holding views incompatible with the proposition that propositions of all these classes are true, they have, therefore, been holding views inconsistent with propositions which they themselves *knew* to be true; and it was therefore, only to be expected that they should sometimes betray their knowledge of such propositions. The strange thing is that philosophers should have been able to hold sincerely, as part of their philosophical creed, propositions inconsistent with what they themselves *knew* to be true; and yet, so far as I can make out, this has really frequently happened. My position, therefore, on this first point, differs from that of philosophers belonging to this group A, not in that I hold anything which they don't hold, but only in that I don't hold as part of my philosophical creed, things which they do hold as part of theirs—that is to say, propositions consistent with some which they and I both hold in common. But this difference seems to me to be an important one.

(*c*) Some of these philosophers have brought forward, in favour of their position, arguments designed to show, in the case of some or all of the propositions in (1), that no propositions of that type can possibly be wholly true, because every such proposition entails both of two incompatible propositions. And I admit, of course, that if any of the propositions in (1) did entail both of two incompatible propositions it could not be true. But it seems to me I have an absolutely conclusive argument to show that none of them does entail both of two incompatible propositions. Namely this: All of the propositions in (1) are true; no true proposition entails both of two incompatible propositions; therefore, none of the propositions in (1) entails both of two incompatible propositions.

(*d*) Although, as I have urged, no philosopher who has held with regard to any of these types of proposition that no propositions of that type are true, has failed to hold also other views inconsistent with his view in this respect, yet I do not think that the view, with regard to any or all of these types, that no proposition belonging to them is true, is *in itself* a self-contradictory view, i.e. entails both of two incompatible propositions. On the contrary, it seems to me quite clear that it *might* have been the case that Time was not real, material things not real, Space not real, selves not real. And in favour of my view that none of these things, which might have been the case, *is* in fact the case, I have, I think, no better argument than simply this—namely, that all the propositions in (1) are, in fact, true.

B. This view, which is usually considered a much more modest view than A, has, I think, the defect that, unlike A, it really is self-contradictory, i.e. entails both of two mutually incompatible propositions.

Most philosophers who have held this view, have held, I think, that though each of us knows propositions corresponding to *some* of the propositions in (1), namely to those which merely assert that *I* myself have had in the past experiences of certain kinds at many different times, yet none of us knows *for certain* any propositions either of the type (*a*) which assert the existence of *material things* or of the type (*b*) which assert the existence of *other* selves, beside myself, and that *they* also have had experiences. They admit that we do in fact *believe* propositions of both these types, and that they *may* be true: some would even say that we know them to be highly probable; but they deny that we ever know them, *for certain*, to be true. Some of them have spoken of such beliefs as 'beliefs of Common Sense', expressing thereby their conviction that beliefs of this kind are very commonly entertained by mankind: but they are convinced that these things are, in all cases, only *believed*, not known for certain; and some have expressed this by saying that they are matters of Faith, not of Knowledge.

Now the remarkable thing which those who take this view have not, I think, in general duly appreciated, is that, in each case, the philosopher who takes it is making an assertion about 'us'—that is to say, not merely about himself, but about *many other human beings as well*. When he says 'No human being has ever *known* of the existence of other human beings', he is saying: 'There have been many other human beings beside myself, and none of them (including myself) has ever known of the existence of other human beings.' If he says: 'These beliefs are beliefs of Common Sense, but they are not matters of *knowledge*', he is saying: 'There have been many other human beings, beside myself, who have shared these beliefs, but neither I nor any of the rest has ever known them to be true.' In other words, he asserts with confidence that these beliefs *are* beliefs of Common Sense, and seems often to fail to notice that, *if* they are, they must be true; since the proposition that they are beliefs of Common Sense is one which logically entails propositions both of type (*a*) and of type (*b*); it logically entails the proposition that many human beings, beside the philosopher himself, have had human bodies, which lived upon the earth, and have had various experiences, including beliefs of this kind. This is why this position, as contrasted with positions of group A, seems to me to be self-contradictory. Its difference from A consists in the fact that it is making a proposition about *human knowledge* in general, and therefore is actually asserting the existence of many human beings, whereas philosophers of group A in stating their position are not doing this: they are only contradicting *other* things which they hold. It is true that a philosopher who says "'There have existed many human beings beside myself, and none of us has ever known of the existence of any human beings beside himself', is only contradicting himself if what he holds is 'There have *certainly* existed many human beings beside myself' or, in other words, '*I* know that there have existed other human beings beside myself'. But this, it seems to me, is what such philosophers have in fact been generally doing. They seem to me constantly to betray the fact that they regard the proposition that those beliefs *are* beliefs of Common Sense, or the proposition that they themselves are not the only members of the human race, as not merely true, but *certainly* true; and *certainly* true it cannot be, unless one member, at least, of the human race, namely themselves, has *known* the very things which that member is declaring that no human being has ever known.

Nevertheless, my position that I *know*, with certainty, to be true all of the propositions in (1), is certainly not a position, the denial of which entails both of two incompatible propositions. If I do *know* all these propositions to be true, then, I think, it is quite certain that other human beings also have known corresponding propositions: that is to say (2) also *is* true, and *I* know it to be true. But do I really *know* all the propositions in (1) to be true? Isn't it possible that I merely believe them? Or know them to be highly probable? In answer to this question, I think I have nothing better to say than that it seems to me that I *do* know them, with certainty. It is, indeed, obvious that, in the case of most of them, I do not know them *directly*: that is to say, I only know them because, in the past, I have known to be true *other* propositions which were evidence for them. If, for instance, I do know that the earth had existed for many years before I was born, I certainly only know this because I have known other things in the past which were evidence for it. And I certainly do not know exactly what the evidence was. Yet all this seems to me to be no good reason for doubting that I do know it. We are all, I think, in this strange posi-

tion that we do *know* many things, with regard to which we *know* further that we must have had evidence for them, and yet we do not know *how* we know them, i.e. we do not know what the evidence was. If there is any 'we', and if we know that there is, this must be so: for that there is a 'we' is one of the things in question. And that I do know that there is a 'we', that is to say, that many other human beings, with human bodies, have lived upon the earth, it seems to me that I do know, for certain.

If this first point in my philosophical position, namely my belief in (2), is to be given any name, which has actually been used by philosophers in classifying the positions of other philosophers, it would have, I think, to be expressed by saying that I am one of those philosophers who have held that the 'Common Sense view of the world' is, in certain fundamental features, *wholly* true. But it must be remembered that, according to me, *all* philosophers, without exception, have agreed with me in holding this: and that the real difference, which is commonly expressed in this way, is only a difference between those philosophers, who have *also* held views inconsistent with these features in 'the Common Sense view of the world', and those who have not.

The features in question (namely, propositions of any of the classes defined in defining (2)) are all of them features, which have this peculiar property—namely, that *if we know that they are features in the 'Common Sense view of the world', it follows that they are true*: it is self-contradictory to maintain that *we* know them to be features in the Common Sense view, and that yet they are not true; since to say that *we* know this, is to say that they are true. And many of them also have the further peculiar property that, *if they are features in the Common Sense view of the world (whether 'we' know this or not), it follows that they are true*, since to say that there is a 'Common Sense view of the world', is to say that they are true. The phrases 'Common Sense view of the world' or 'Common Sense beliefs' (as used by philosophers) are, of course, extraordinarily vague; and, for all I know, there may be many propositions which may be properly called features in 'the Common Sense view of the world' or 'Common Sense beliefs', which are not true, and which deserve to be mentioned with the contempt with which some philosophers speak of 'Common Sense beliefs'. But to speak with contempt of those 'Common Sense beliefs' which I have mentioned is quite certainly the height of absurdity. And there are, of course, enormous numbers of other features in 'the Common Sense view of the world' which, if these are true, are quite certainly true too: e.g. that there have lived upon the surface of the earth not only human beings, but also many different species of plants and animals, etc. etc.

II. What seems to me the next in importance of the points in which my philosophical position differs from positions held by *some* other philosophers, is one which I will express in the following way. I hold, namely, that there is no good reason to suppose either (A) that *every* physical fact is *logically* dependent upon some mental fact or (B) that *every* physical fact is *causally* dependent upon some mental fact. In saying this, I am not, of course, saying that there *are* any physical facts which are wholly independent (i.e. both logically and causally) of mental facts: I do, in fact, believe that there are; but that is not what I am asserting. I am only asserting that there is *no good reason* to suppose the contrary; by which I mean, of course, that none of the human beings, who have had human bodies that lived upon the earth, have, during the lifetime of their bodies, had any good reason to suppose the contrary. Many philosophers have, I think, not only believed either that *every* physical fact is *logically* dependent upon some mental fact ('physical fact' and 'mental fact' being understood in the sense in which I am using these terms) or that *every* physical fact is *causally* dependent upon some mental fact, or both, but also that they themselves had good reason for these beliefs. In this respect, therefore, I differ from them.

In the case of the term 'physical fact', I can only explain how I am using it by giving examples. I mean by 'physical facts', facts *like* the following: 'That mantelpiece is at present nearer to this body than that bookcase is', 'The earth has existed for many years past', 'The moon has at every moment for many years past been nearer to the earth than to the sun', 'That mantelpiece is of a light colour'. But, when I say 'facts *like* these', I mean, of course, facts like them *in a certain respect*; and what this respect is I cannot define. The term 'physical fact' is, however, in common use; and I think that I am using it in its ordinary sense. Moreover, there is no need for a def-inition to make my point clear; since among the examples I have given there are some with regard to which I hold that there is no reason to suppose *them* (i.e. these particular physical facts) either logically or causally dependent upon any mental fact.

'Mental fact', on the other hand, is a much more unusual expression, and I am using it in a specially limited sense, which, though I think it is a natural one, does need to be explained. There may be many other senses in which the term can be properly used, but I am only concerned with this one; and hence it is essential that I should explain what it is.

There may, possibly, I hold, be 'mental facts' of three different kinds. It is only with regard to the first kind that I am sure that there are facts of that kind; but if there were any facts of either of the other two kinds, they would be 'mental facts' in my limited sense, and therefore I must explain what is meant by the hypothesis that there are facts of those two kinds.

(*a*) My first kind is this. I am conscious now; and also I am seeing something now. These two facts are both of them mental facts of my first kind; and my first kind consists exclusively of facts which resemble one or other of the two *in a certain respect*.

(α) The fact that I am conscious now is obviously, in a certain sense, a fact, with regard to a particular individual and a particular time, to the effect that that individual is conscious at that time. And every fact which resembles this one in that respect is to be included in my first kind of mental fact. Thus the fact that I was also conscious at many different times yesterday is not itself a fact of this kind: but it entails that there *are* (or, as we should commonly say, because the times in question are past times, 'were') many other facts of this kind, namely each of the facts, which, at each of the times in question, I could have properly expressed by 'I am conscious *now*'. *Any* fact which is, in this sense, a fact with regard to an individual and a time (whether the individual be myself or another, and whether the time be past or present), to the effect that that individual *is* conscious at that time, is to be included in my first kind of mental fact: and I call such facts, facts of class (α).

(β) The second example I gave, namely the fact that I am seeing something now, is obviously related to the fact that I am conscious now in a peculiar manner. It not only *entails* the fact that I am conscious now (for from the fact that I am seeing something it *follows* that I am conscious: I *could* not have been seeing anything, unless I had been conscious, though I might quite well have been conscious without seeing anything) but it also is a fact, with regard to a *specific way* (or mode) of being conscious, to the effect that I am conscious in that way: in the same sense in which the proposition (with regard to any particular thing) 'This is red' both entails the proposition (with regard to the same thing) 'This is coloured', and is also a proposition, with regard to a *specific way* of being coloured, to the effect that that thing is coloured in that way. And any fact which is related in this peculiar manner to any fact of class (α), is also to be included in my first kind of mental fact, and is to be called a fact of class (β). Thus the fact that I am hearing now is, like the fact that I am seeing now, a fact of class (β); and so is any fact, with regard to myself and a past time, which could at that time have been properly expressed by 'I am dreaming now', 'I am imagining now', 'I am at present aware of the fact that . . . ', etc. etc. In short, any fact, which is a fact with regard to a particular individual (myself or another), a particular time (past or present), and *any particular kind of experience*, to the effect that that individual is having at that time an experience of that particular kind, is a fact of class (β): and only such facts are facts of class (β).

My first kind of mental facts consists exclusively of facts of classes (α) and (β), and consists of *all* facts of either of these kinds.

(*b*) That there are many facts of classes (α) and (β) seems to me perfectly certain. But many philosophers seem to me to have held a certain view with regard to the *analysis* of facts of class (α), which is such that, if it were true, there would be facts of another kind, which I should wish also to call 'mental facts'. I don't feel at all sure that this analysis is true; but it seems to me that it *may* be true; and since we can understand what is meant by the supposition that it is true, we can also understand what is meant by the supposition that there are 'mental facts' of this second kind.

Many philosophers have, I think, held the following view as to the analysis of what each of us knows, when he knows (at any time) 'I am conscious now'. They have held, namely, that there is a certain intrinsic property (with which we are all of us familiar and which might be called that of 'being an experience') which is such that, at any time at which any man knows 'I am conscious now', he is knowing, with regard to that property and himself and the time in question, 'There is occurring now an event which has this property (i.e. "is an experience") and which is an experience of *mine*', and such that this fact is what he expresses by 'I am conscious now'. And if this view is true, there must be many facts of each of three kinds, each of which I should wish to call 'mental facts'; viz. (1) facts with regard to some event, which has this supposed intrinsic property, and to some time, to the effect that that event is occurring at that time, (2) facts with regard to this supposed intrinsic property and some time, to the effect that *some* event which has that property is occurring at that time, and (3) facts with regard to some property, which is a *specific way* of having the supposed intrinsic property (in the sense above explained in which 'being red' is a specific way of 'being coloured') and some time, to the effect that some event which has that specific property is occurring at that time. Of course, there not only are not, but *cannot* be, facts of any of these kinds, unless there is an intrinsic property related to what each of us (on any occasion) expresses by 'I am conscious now', in the manner defined above; and I feel very doubtful whether there is any such property; in other words, although I know for certain both that I have had many experiences, and that I have had experiences of many different kinds, I feel very doubtful whether to say the first is the same thing as to say that there have been many events, each of which was an experience and an experience of mine, and whether to say the second is the same thing as to say that there have been many events, each of which was an experience of mine, and each of which also had a different property, which was a specific way of being an experience. The proposition that I have had experiences does not necessarily entail the proposition that there have been any events which were experiences; and I cannot satisfy myself that I am acquainted with any events of the supposed kind. But yet it seems to me possible that the proposed analysis of 'I am conscious now' is correct: that I am really acquainted with events of the supposed kind, though I cannot see that I am. And *if* I am, then I should wish to call the three kinds of facts defined above 'mental facts'. Of course, if there are 'experiences' in the sense defined, it would be possible (as many have held) that there *can* be no experiences which are not *some individual's* experiences; and in that case any fact of any of these three kinds would be logically dependent on, though not necessarily identical with, some fact of class (α) or class (β). But it seems to me also a possibility that, if there are 'experiences', there might be experiences which did not belong to any individual; and, in that case, there would be 'mental facts' which were neither identical with nor logically dependent on any fact of class (α) or class (β).

(*c*) Finally some philosophers have, so far as I can make out, held that there are or may be facts which are facts with regard to some individual, to the effect that he is conscious, or is conscious in some specific way, but which differ from facts of classes (α) and (β), in the important respect that they are not facts *with regard to any time*: they have conceived the possibility that there may be one or more individuals, who are *timelessly* conscious, and timelessly conscious in specific modes. And others, again, have, I think, conceived the hypothesis that the intrinsic property defined in (*b*) may be one which does not belong only to *events*, but may also belong to one or more wholes, which do *not* occur at any time: in other words, that there may be one or more *timeless* experiences, which might or might not be the experiences of some individual. It seems to me very doubtful whether any of these hypotheses are even possibly true; but I cannot see for certain that they are not possible: and, if they are possible, then I should wish to give the name 'mental fact' to any fact (if there were any) of any of the five following kinds, viz. (1) to any fact which is the fact, with regard to any individual, that he is *timelessly* conscious, (2) to any fact which is the fact, with regard to any individual, that he is *timelessly* conscious in any specific way, (3) to any fact which is the fact with regard to a *timeless* experience that it exists, (4) to any fact which is the fact with regard to the supposed intrinsic property 'being an experience', that something timelessly exists which has that property, and (5) to any fact which is the fact, with regard to any property, which is a specific mode of this supposed intrinsic property, that something timelessly exists which has that property.

I have, then, defined three different kinds of facts, each of which is such that, if there *were* any facts of that kind (as there certainly *are*, in the case of the first kind), the facts in question *would be* 'mental facts' in my sense; and to complete the definition of the limited sense in which I am using 'mental facts', I have only to add that I wish also to apply the name to one *fourth* class of facts: namely to any fact, which is the fact, with regard to any of these three kinds of facts, or any kinds included in them, *that there are facts of the kind in question*; i.e. not only will each individual fact of class (α) be, in my sense, a 'mental fact', but also the general fact 'that there are facts of class (α)', will itself be a 'mental fact'; and similarly in all other cases: e.g. not only will the fact that I am now perceiving (which is a fact of class(β)) be a 'mental fact', but also the general fact that *there are* facts, with regard to individuals and times, to the effect that the individual in question is perceiving at the time in question, will be a 'mental fact'.

A. Understanding 'physical fact' and 'mental fact' in the senses just explained, I hold, then, that there is no good reason to suppose that *every* physical fact is *logically* dependent upon some mental fact. And I use the phrase, with regard to two facts, F_1 and F_2, 'F_1 is *logically dependent* on F_2', wherever and only where F_1 *entails* F_2, either in the sense in which the proposition 'I am seeing now' *entails* the proposition 'I am conscious now', or the proposition (with regard to any particular thing) 'This is red' entails the proposition (with regard to the same thing) 'This is coloured', or else in the more strictly logical sense in which (for instance) the conjunctive proposition 'All men are mortal, and Mr. Baldwin is a man' entails the proposition 'Mr. Baldwin is mortal'. To say, then, of two facts, F_1 and F_2, that F_1 is *not* logically dependent upon F_2, is only to say that F_1 *might* have been a fact, even if there had been no such fact as F_2; or that the conjunctive proposition 'F_1 is a fact, but there is no such fact as F_2' is a proposition which is not self-contradictory, i.e. does not entail both of two mutually incompatible propositions.

I hold, then, that, in the case of *some* physical facts, there is no good reason to suppose that there is some mental fact, such that the physical fact in question could not have been a fact unless the mental fact in question had also been one. And my position is perfectly definite, since I hold that this is the case with all the four physical facts, which I have given as examples of physical facts. For example, there is no good reason to suppose that there is any mental fact whatever, such that the fact that that mantelpiece is at present nearer to my body than that bookcase could not have been a fact, unless the mental fact in question had also been a fact; and, similarly, in all the other three cases.

In holding this I am certainly differing from some philosophers. I am, for instance, differing from Berkeley, who held that that mantelpiece, that bookcase, and my body are, all of them, either 'ideas' or 'constituted by ideas', and that no 'idea' can possibly exist without being perceived. He held, that is, that this physical fact is logically dependent upon a mental fact of my fourth class: namely a fact which is the fact that there is at least one fact, which is a fact with regard to an individual and the present time, to the effect that that individual is now perceiving something. He does not say that this physical fact is logically dependent upon any fact which is a fact of any of my first three classes, e.g. on any fact which is the fact, with regard to a particular individual and the present time, that *that* individual is now perceiving something: what he does say is that the physical fact couldn't have been a fact, unless it had been a fact that there was *some* mental fact of this sort. And it seems to me that many philosophers, who would perhaps disagree either with Berkeley's assumption that my body is an 'idea' or 'constituted by ideas', or with his assumption that 'ideas' cannot exist without being perceived, or with both, nevertheless would agree with him in thinking that this physical fact is logically dependent upon *some* 'mental fact': e.g. they might say that it could not have been a fact, unless there had been, at some time or other, or, were timelessly, *some* 'experience'. Many, indeed, so far as I can make out, have held that *every* fact is logically dependent on every other fact. And, of course, they have held in the case of their opinions, as Berkeley did in the case of his, that they had good reasons for them.

B. I also hold that there is no good reason to suppose that *every* physical fact is *causally* dependent upon some mental fact. By saying that F_1 is *causally* dependent on F_2, I mean only that F_1 *wouldn't* have been a fact unless F_2 had been; *not* (which is what 'logically dependent' asserts) that F_1 *couldn't conceivably* have been a fact, unless F_2 had been. And I can illustrate my meaning by reference to the example which I have just given. The fact that that mantelpiece is at present nearer to my body than that bookcase, is (as I have just explained) so far as I can see, not *logically* dependent upon any mental fact; it *might* have been a fact, even if there had been no mental facts. But it certainly is *causally* dependent on many mental facts: my body *would* not have been here unless I had been conscious in various ways in the past; and the mantelpiece and the bookcase certainly *would* not have existed, unless other men had been conscious too.

But with regard to two of the facts, which I gave as instances of physical facts, namely the fact that the earth has existed for many years past, and the fact that the moon has for many years past been nearer to the earth than to the sun, I hold that there is no good reason to suppose that these are *causally* dependent upon any mental fact. So far as I can see, there is no reason to suppose that there is any mental fact of which it could be truly said: unless this fact had been a fact, the earth would not have existed for many years past. And in holding this, again, I think I differ from some philosophers. I differ, for instance, from those who have held that all material things were created by God, and that they had good reasons for supposing this.

III. I have just explained that I differ from those philosophers who have held that there is good reason to suppose that all material things were created by God. And it is, I think, an important point in my position, which should be mentioned, that I differ also from all philosophers who have held that there is good reason to suppose that there is a God at all, whether or not they have held it likely that he created all material things.

And similarly, whereas some philosophers have held that there is good reason to suppose that we, human beings, shall continue to exist and to be conscious after the death of our bodies, I hold that there is no good reason to suppose this.

IV. I now come to a point of a very different order.

As I have explained under I., I am not at all sceptical as to the *truth* of such propositions as 'The earth has existed for many years past', 'Many human bodies have each lived for many years upon it', i.e. propositions which assert the existence of material things: on the contrary, I hold that we all know, with certainty, many such propositions to be true. But I am very sceptical as to what, in certain respects, the correct *analysis* of such propositions is. And this is a matter as to which I think I differ from many philosophers. Many seem to hold that there is no doubt at all as to their *analysis*, nor, therefore, as to the analysis of the proposition 'Material things have existed', in certain respects in which I hold that the analysis of the propositions in question is extremely doubtful; and some of them, as we have seen, while holding that there is no doubt as to their *analysis*, seem to have doubted whether any such propositions are *true*. I, on the other hand, while holding that there is no doubt whatever that many such propositions are wholly true, hold also that no philosopher, hitherto, has succeeded in suggesting an analysis of them, as regards certain important points, which comes anywhere near to being certainly true.

It seems to me quite evident that the question how propositions of the type I have just given are to be analysed, depends on the question how propositions of another and simpler type are to be analysed. I know, at present, that I am perceiving a human hand, a pen, a sheet of paper, etc.; and it seems to me that I cannot know how the proposition 'Material things exist' is to be analysed, until I know how, in certain respects, these simpler propositions are to be analysed. But even these are not simple enough. It seems to me quite evident that my knowledge that I am now perceiving a human hand is a deduction from a pair of propositions simpler still—propositions which I can only express in the form 'I am perceiving *this*' and '*This* is a human hand'. It is the analysis of propositions of the latter kind which seems to me to present such great difficulties, while nevertheless the whole question as to the *nature* of material things obviously depends upon their analysis. It seems to me a surprising thing that so few philosophers, while saying a great deal as to what material things *are* and as to what it is to perceive them, have attempted to give a clear account as to what precisely they suppose themselves to *know* (or

to *judge*, in case they have held that we don't *know* any such propositions to be true, or even that no such propositions *are* true) when they know or judge such things as 'This is a hand,' 'That is the sun', 'This is a dog', etc. etc. etc.

Two things only seem to me to be quite certain about the analysis of such propositions (and even with regard to these I am afraid some philosophers would differ from me) namely that whenever I know, or judge, such a proposition to be true, (1) there is always some *sense-datum* about which the proposition in question is a proposition—some sense-datum which is *a* subject (and, in a certain sense, the principal or ultimate subject) of the proposition in question, and (2) that, nevertheless, *what* I am knowing or judging to be true about this sense-datum is not (in general) that it is *itself* a hand, or a dog, or the sun, etc. etc., as the case may be.

Some philosophers have I think doubted whether there are any such things as other philosophers have meant by 'sense-data' or 'sensa'. And I think it is quite possible that some philosophers (including myself, in the past) have used these terms in senses such that it is really doubtful whether there are any such things. But there is no doubt at all that there are sense-data, in the sense in which I am now using that term. I am at present seeing a great number of them, and feeling others. And in order to point out to the reader what sort of things I mean by sense-data, I need only ask him to look at his own right hand. If he does this he will be able to pick out something (and, unless he is seeing double, *only* one thing) with regard to which he will see that it is, at first sight, a natural view to take that that thing is identical, not, indeed, with his whole right hand, but with that part of its surface which he is actually seeing, but will also (on a little reflection) be able to see that it is doubtful whether it can be identical with the part of the surface of his hand in question. Things *of the sort* (in a certain respect) of which this thing is, which he sees in looking at his hand, and with regard to which he can understand how some philosophers should have supposed it to *be* the part of the surface of his hand which he is seeing, while others have supposed that it can't be, are what I mean by 'sense-data'. I therefore define the term in such a way that it is an open question whether the sense-datum which I now see in looking at my hand

and which is a sense-datum of my hand is or is not identical with that part of its surface which I am now actually seeing.

That what I know, with regard to this sense-datum, when I know 'This is a human hand', is not that it is *itself* a human hand, seems to me certain because I know that my hand has many parts (e.g. its other side, and the bones inside it), which are quite certainly *not* parts of this sense-datum.

I think it certain, therefore, that the analysis of the proposition 'This is a human hand' is, roughly at least, of the form 'There is a thing, and only one thing, of which it is true both that it is a human hand and that *this surface* is a part of its surface'. In other words, to put my view in terms of the phrase 'theory of representative perception', I hold it to be quite certain that I do not *directly* perceive *my hand*; and that when I am said (as I may be correctly said) to 'perceive' it, that I 'perceive' it means that I perceive (in a different and more fundamental sense) something which is (in a suitable sense) *representative* of it, namely, a certain part of its surface.

This is all that I hold to be *certain* about the analysis of the proposition 'This is a human hand'. We have seen that it includes in its analysis a proposition of the form 'This is part of the surface of a human hand' (where 'This', of course, has a different meaning from that which it has in the original proposition which has now been analysed). But this proposition also is undoubtedly a proposition about the sense-datum, which I am seeing, which is a sense-datum *of* my hand. And hence the further question arises: *What*, when I know '*This* is *part of the surface of* a human hand', am I knowing about the sense-datum in question? Am I, in this case really knowing about the sense-datum in question that it *itself* is part of the surface of a human hand? Or, just as we found in the case of 'This is a human hand', that what I was knowing about the sense-datum was certainly not that it *itself* was a human hand, so, is it perhaps the case, with this new proposition, that even here I am not knowing, with regard to the sense-datum, that it *itself* part of the surface of a hand? And, if so, what is it that I am knowing about the sense-datum itself?

This is the question to which, as it seems to me, no philosopher has hitherto suggested an answer which comes anywhere near to being *certainly* true.

There seem to me to be three, and only three, alternative types of answer possible; and to any answer yet suggested, of any of these types, there seem to me to be very grave objections.

(1) Of the first type, there is but one answer: namely, that in this case what I am knowing really is that the sense-datum *itself* is part of the surface of a human hand. In other words that, though I don't perceive *my hand* directly, I do *directly* perceive part of its surface; that the sense-datum itself *is* this part of its surface and not merely something which (in a sense yet to be determined) 'represents' this part of its surface; and that hence the sense in which I 'perceive' this part of the surface of my hand, is not in its turn a sense which needs to be defined by reference to yet a third more ultimate sense of 'perceive', which is the only one in which perception is direct, namely that in which I perceive the sense-datum.

If this view is true (as I think it may just possibly be), it seems to me certain that we must abandon a view which has been held to be certainly true by most philosophers, namely the view that our sense-data always really have the qualities which they sensibly appear to us to have. For I know that if another man were looking through a microscope at the same surface which I am seeing with the naked eye, the sense-datum which he saw would sensibly appear to him to have qualities very different from and incompatible with those which my sense-datum sensibly appears to me to have: and yet, if my sense-datum is identical with the surface we are both of us seeing, his must be identical with it also. My sense-datum can, therefore, be identical with this surface only on condition that it is identical with his sense-datum; and, since his sense-datum sensibly appears to him to have qualities incompatible with those which mine sensibly appears to me to have, his sense-datum can be identical with mine only on condition that the sense-datum in question either has not got the qualities which it sensibly appears to me to have, or has not got those which it sensibly appears to him to have.

I do not, however, think that this is a fatal objection to this first type of view. A far more serious objection seems to me to be that, when we see a thing double (have what is called 'a double image' of it), we certainly have *two* sense-data each *of* which is of the surface seen, and which cannot therefore both be identical with it; and that yet it seems as if, if any sense-datum is ever identical with the surface *of* which it is a sense-datum, each of these so-called 'images' must be so. It looks, therefore, as if every sense-datum is, after all, only 'representative' of the surface, *of* which it is a sense-datum.

(2) But, if so, what relation has it to the surface in question?

This second type of view is one which holds that when I know 'This is part of the surface of a human hand', what I am knowing with regard to the sense-datum which is *of* that surface, is, *not* that it is *itself* part of the surface of a human hand, but something of the following kind. There is, it says *some* relation, R, such that what I am knowing with regard to the sense-datum is either 'There is one thing and only one thing, of which it is true both that it is a part of the surface of a human hand, and that it has R to this sense-datum', or else 'There are a set of things, of which it is true both that that set, taken collectively, *are* part of the surface of a human hand, and also that each member of the set has R to this sense-datum, and that nothing which is not a member of the set has R to it'.

Obviously, in the case of this second type, many different views are possible, differing according to the view they take as to what the relation R is. But there is only one of them, which seems to me to have any plausibility; namely that which holds that R is an ultimate and unanalysable relation, which might be expressed by saying that 'xRy' means the same as 'y is an appearance or manifestation of x'. I.e. the analysis which this answer would give of 'This is part of the surface of a human hand' would be 'There is one and only one thing of which it is true both that it is part of the surface of a human hand, and that this sense-datum is an appearance or manifestation of it'.

To this view also there seem to me to be very grave objections, chiefly drawn from a consideration of the questions how we can possibly *know* with regard to any of our sense-data that there is one thing and one thing only which has to them such a supposed ultimate relation; and how, if we do, we can possibly *know* anything further about such things, e.g. of what size or shape they are.

(3) The third type of answer, which seems to me to be the only possible alternative if (1) and (2) are rejected, is the type of answer which J. S. Mill seems to have been implying to be the true one when he said that material things are 'permanent possibilities of sensation'. He seems to have thought that when I know such a fact as 'This is part of the surface of a human hand', what I am knowing with regard to the sense-datum which is the principal subject of that fact, is not that it is itself part of the surface of a human hand, nor yet, with regard to any relation, that *the* thing which has to it that relation is part of the surface of a human hand, but a whole set of hypothetical facts each of which is a fact of the form 'If *these* conditions had been fulfilled, I should have been perceiving a sense-datum intrinsically related to *this* sense-datum in *this* way', 'If *these* (other) conditions had been fulfilled, I should have been perceiving a sense-datum intrinsically related to *this* sense-datum in *this* (other) way', etc. etc.

With regard to this third type of view as to the analysis of propositions of the kind we are considering, it seems to me, again, just *possible* that it is a true one; but to hold (as Mill himself and others seem to have held) that it is *certainly*, or nearly certainly, true, seems to me as great a mistake, as to hold with regard either to (1) or to (2), that they are *certainly*, or nearly certainly, true. There seem to me to be very grave objections to it; in particular the three, (*a*) that though, in general, when I know such a fact as 'This is a hand', I certainly do know some hypothetical facts of the form 'If *these* conditions had been fulfilled, I should have been perceiving a sense-datum of *this* kind, which would have been a sense-datum of the same surface of which *this* is a sense-datum', it seems doubtful whether any conditions with regard to which I know this are not themselves conditions of the form 'If this and that *material thing* had been in those positions and conditions . . . ', (b) that it seems again very doubtful whether there is any intrinsic relation, such that my knowledge that (under *these* conditions) I should have been perceiving a sense-datum of *this* kind, which would have been a sense-datum of the same surface of which *this* is a sense-datum, is equivalent to a knowledge, with regard to that relation, that I should, under those conditions, have been perceiving a sense-datum related by it to *this* sense-datum, and (*c*) that, if it were true, the sense in which a material surface is 'round' or 'square', would necessarily be utterly different from that in which our sense-data sensibly appear to us to be 'round' or square.

V. Just as I hold that the proposition 'There are and have been material things' is quite certainly true, but that the question how this proposition is to be analysed is one to which no answer that has been hitherto given is anywhere near certainly true; so I hold that the proposition 'There are and have been many Selves' is quite certainly true, but that here again all the analyses of this proposition that have been suggested by philosophers are highly doubtful.

That I am now perceiving many different sense-data, and that I have at many times in the past perceived many different sense-data, I know for certain—that is to say, I know that there are mental facts of class (β), connected in a way which it is proper to express by saying that they are all of them facts about *me*; but how this kind of connection is to be analysed, I do not know for certain, nor do I think that any other philosopher knows with any approach to certainty. Just as in the case of the proposition 'This is part of the surface of a human hand', there are several extremely different views as to its analysis, each of which seems to me *possible*, but none nearly certain, so also in the case of the proposition 'This, that and that sense-datum are all at present being perceived by *me*', and still more so in the case of the proposition '*I* am now perceiving this sense-datum, and *I* have in the past perceived sense-data of these other kinds'. Of the *truth* of these propositions there seems to me to be no doubt, but as to what is the correct analysis of them there seems to me to be the gravest doubt—the true analysis may, for instance, *possibly* be quite as paradoxical as is the third view given above under IV as to the analysis of 'This is part of the surface of a human hand'; but whether it *is* as paradoxical as this seems to me to be quite as doubtful as in that case. Many philosophers, on the other hand, seem to me to have assumed that there is little or no doubt as to the correct analysis of such propositions; and many of these, just reversing my position, have also held that the propositions themselves are not true.

Two Types of Knowledge

"We must recognize that when we know something we either do, or by reflecting, can know that our condition is one of knowing that thing, while when we believe something, we either do or can know that our condition is one of believing and not of knowing: so that we cannot mistake belief for knowledge or vice versa."[1]

This remark is worthy of investigation. Can I discover *in myself* whether I know something or merely believe it?

Let us begin by studying the ordinary usage of "know" and "believe." Suppose, for example, that several of us intend to go for a walk and that you propose that we walk in Cascadilla Gorge. I protest that I should like to walk beside a flowing stream and that at this season the gorge is probably dry. Consider the following cases:

(1) You say "I believe that it won't be dry although I have no particular reason for thinking so." If we went to the gorge and found a flowing stream we should not say that you *knew* that there would be water but that you thought so and were right.

(2) You say "I believe that it won't be dry because it rained only three days ago and usually water flows in the gorge for at least that long after a rain." If we found water we should be inclined to say that you knew that there would be water. It would be quite natural for you to say "I knew that it wouldn't be dry"; and we should tolerate your remark. This case differs from the previous one in that here you had a *reason*.

(3) You say "I know that it won't be dry" and give the same reason as in (2). If we found water we should have very little hesitation in saying that you knew. Not only had you a reason, but you *said* "I know" instead of "I believe." It may seem to us that the latter should not make a difference—but it does.

(4) You say "I know that it won't be dry" and give a stronger reason, e.g., "I saw a lot of water flowing in the gorge when I passed it this morning." If we went and found water there would be no hesitation

at all in saying that you knew. If, for example, we later met someone who said "Weren't you surprised to see water in the gorge this afternoon?" you would reply "No, I *knew* that there would be water; I had been there earlier in the day." We should have no objection to this statement.

(5) Everything happens as in (4), except that upon going to the gorge we find it to be dry. We should not say that you knew, but that you *believed* that there would be water. And this is true even though you declared that you knew, and even though your evidence was the same as it was in case (4) in which you did know.

I wish to make some comments on the usage of "know, "knew," "believe," and "believed," as illustrated in the preceding cases:

(*a*) Whether we should say that you knew, depends in part on whether you had grounds for your assertion and on the strength of those grounds. There would certainly be less hesitation to say that you knew in case (4) than in case (3), and this can be due only to the difference in the strength of the grounds.

(*b*) Whether we should say that you knew, depends in part on how *confident* you were. In case (2), if you had said "It rained only three days ago and usually water flows in the gorge for at least that long after a rain; but, of course, I don't feel absolutely sure that there will be water," then we should *not* have said that you knew that there would be water. If you lack confidence that *p* is true, then others do not say that you know that *p* is true, even though *they* know that *p* is true. Being confident is a necessary condition for knowing.

(*c*) Prichard says that if we reflect we cannot mistake belief for knowledge. In case (4) you knew that there would be water, and in case (5) you merely believed it. Was there any way that you could have discovered by reflection, in case (5), that you did not know? It would have been useless to have reconsidered your grounds for saying that there would be water, because in case (4), where you *did* know, your grounds were identical. They could be at fault in (5) only if they were at fault in (4), and they were not at fault in (4). Cases (4) and (5) differ in only one respect—namely, that in one case you did subsequently find water and in the other you did not. Prichard says that we can determine by reflection whether we know something or merely believe it. But where, in these cases, is the material that reflection would strike upon? There is none.

There is only one way that Prichard could defend his position. He would have to say that in case (4) you did *not* know that there would be water. And it is obvious that he would have said this. But this is false. It is an enormously common usage of language to say, in commenting upon just such an incident as (4), "He knew that the gorge wouldn't be dry because he had seen water flowing there that morning." It is a usage that all of us are familiar with. We so employ "know" and "knew" every day of our lives. We do not think of our usage as being loose or incorrect—and it is not. As philosophers we may be surprised to observe that it *can* be that the knowledge that *p* is true should differ from the belief that *p* is true *only* in the respect that in one case *p* is true and in the other false. But that is the fact.

There is an argument that one is inclined to use as a proof that you did not know that there would be water. The argument is the following: It could have turned out that you found no water; if it had so turned out you would have been mistaken in saying that you would find water; therefore you could have been mistaken; but if you could have been mistaken then you did not know.

Now it certainly *could* have turned out that the gorge was quite dry when you went there, even though you saw lots of water flowing through it only a few hours before. This does not show, however, that you did not know that there would be water. What it shows is that *although you knew you could have been mistaken.*[2] This would seem to be a contradictory result; but it is not. It seems so because our minds are fixed upon another usage of "know" and "knew"; one in which "It could have turned out that I was mistaken," implies "I did not know."

When is "know" used in this sense? I believe that Prichard uses it in this sense when he says that when

we go through the proof of the proposition that the angles of a triangle are equal to two right angles we *know* that the proposition is true (p. 89). He says that if we put to ourselves the question: Is our condition one of knowing this, or is it only one of being convinced of it? then "We can only answer 'Whatever may be our state on other occasions, here we are knowing this.' And this statement is an expression of our *knowing* that we are knowing; for we do not *believe* that we are knowing this, we know that we are" (p. 89). He goes on to say that if someone were to object that we might be making a mistake "because for all we know we can later on discover some fact which is incompatible with a triangle's having angles that are equal to two right angles, we can answer that we *know* that there can be no such fact, for in knowing that a triangle must have such angles we also know that nothing can exist which is incompatible with this fact" (p. 90)

It is easy to imagine a non-philosophical context in which it would have been natural for Prichard to have said "I know that the angles of a triangle are equal to two right angles." Suppose that a young man just beginning the study of geometry was in doubt as to whether that proposition is true, and had even constructed an ingenious argument that appeared to prove it false. Suppose that Prichard was unable to find any error in the argument. He might have said to the young man: "There must be an error in it. I know that the angles of a triangle are equal to two right angles."

When Prichard says that "nothing can exist which is incompatible with" the truth of that proposition, is he prophesying that no one will ever have the ingenuity to construct a flawless-looking argument against it? I believe not. When Prichard says that "we" *know* (and implies that *he* knows) that the proposition is true and *know* that nothing can exist that is incompatible with its being true, he is not making any *prediction* as to what the future will bring in the way of arguments or measurements. On the contrary, he is asserting that *nothing* that the future might bring could ever count as evidence against the proposition. He is implying that he would not *call* anything "evidence" against it. He is using "know" in what I shall call its "strong" sense. "Know" is used in this sense when a person's statement "I know that *p* is true" implies that the person who makes the statement would look upon nothing whatever as evidence that p is false.

It must not be assumed that whenever "know" is used in connection with mathematical propositions it is used in the strong sense. A great many people have *heard* of various theorems of geometry, e.g., the Pythagorean. These theorems are a part of "common knowledge." If a schoolboy doing his geometry assignment felt a doubt about the Pythagorean theorem, and said to an adult "Are you *sure* that it is true? "the latter might reply "Yes, I know that it is." He might make this reply even though he could not give proof of it and even though he had never gone through a proof of it. If subsequently he was presented with a "demonstration" that the theorem is false, or if various persons reputed to have a knowledge of geometry soberly assured him that it is false, he might be filled with doubt or even be convinced that he was mistaken. When he said "Yes, I know that it is true," he did not pledge himself to hold to the theorem through thick and thin. He did not absolutely exclude the possibility that something could prove it to be false. I shall say that he used "know" in the "weak" sense.

Consider another example from mathematics of the difference between the strong and weak senses of "know." I have just now rapidly calculated that 92 times 16 is 1472. If I had done this in the commerce of daily life where a practical problem was at stake, and if someone had asked "Are you sure that $92 \times 16 = 1472$?" I might have answered "I *know* that it is; I have just now calculated it." But also I might have answered "I know that it is; but I will calculate it again to *make sure*." And here my language points to a distinction. I say that I *know* that $92 \times 16 = 1472$. Yet I am willing to *confirm* it—that is, there is something that I should *call* "making sure"; and, likewise, there is something that I should *call* "finding out that it is false." If I were to do this calculation again and obtain the result that $92 \times 16 = 1372$, and if I were to carefully check this latter calculation without finding any error, I should be disposed to say that I was previously mistaken when I declared that $92 \times 16 = 1472$. Thus when I say that I know that $92 \times 16 = 1472$, I allow for the possibility of a *refutation;* and so I am using "know" in its weak sense.

Now consider propositions like $2 + 2 = 4$ and $7 + 5 = 12$. It is hard to think of circumstances in which

it would be natural for me to say that I know that $2 + 2 = 4$, because no one ever questions it. Let us try to suppose, however, that someone whose intelligence I respect argues that certain developments in arithmetic have shown that $2 + 2$ does not equal 4. He writes out a proof of this in which I can find no flaw. Suppose that his demeanor showed me that he was in earnest. Suppose that several persons of normal intelligence became persuaded that his proof was correct and that $2 + 2$ does not equal 4. What would be my reaction? I should say "I can't see what is wrong with your proof; but it *is* wrong, because I *know* that $2 + 2 = 4$." Here I should be using "know" in its strong sense. I should not admit that any argument or any future development in mathematics could show that it is false that $2 + 2 = 4$.

The propositions $2 + 2 = 4$ and $92 \times 16 = 1472$ do not have the same status. There *can* be a demonstration that $2 + 2 = 4$. But a demonstration would be for me (and for any average person) only a curious exercise, a sort of *game*. We have no serious interest in proving that proposition.[3] It does not *need* a proof. It stands without one, and would not fall if a proof went against it. The case is different with the proposition that $92 \times 16 = 1472$. We take an interest in the demonstration (calculation) because the proposition *depends* upon its demonstration. A calculation may lead me to reject it as false. But $2 + 2 = 4$ does *not* depend on its demonstration. It does not depend on anything! And in the calculation that proves that $92 \times 16 = 1472$, there are steps that do not depend on any calculation (e.g., $2 \times 6 = 12$; $5 + 2 = 7$; $5 + 9 = 14$).

There is a correspondence between this dualism in the logical status of mathematical propositions and the two senses of "know." When I use "know" in the weak sense I am prepared to let an investigation (demonstration, calculation) determine whether the something that I claim to know is true or false. When I use "know" in the strong sense I am not prepared to look upon anything as an *investigation;* I do not concede that anything whatsoever could prove me mistaken; I do not regard the matter as open to any *question;* I do not admit that my proposition could turn out to be false, that any future investigation *could* refute it or cast doubt on it.[4]

We have been considering the strong sense of "know" in its application to mathematical propositions. Does it have application anywhere in the realm of *empirical* propositions—for example, to propositions that assert or imply that certain physical things exist? Descartes said that we have a "moral assurance" of the truth of some of the latter propositions but that we lack a "metaphysical certainty."[5] Locke said that the perception of the existence of physical things is not "so certain as our intuitive knowledge, or the deductions of our reason" although "it is an assurance that deserves the name of knowledge."[6] Some philosophers have held that when we make judgments of perception such as that there are peonies in the garden, cows in the field, or dishes in the cupboard, we are "taking for granted" that the peonies, cows, and dishes exist, but not knowing it in the "strict" sense. Others have held that all empirical propositions, including judgments of perception, are merely hypotheses.[7] The thought behind this exaggerated mode of expression is that any empirical proposition whatever *could* be refuted by future experience—that is, it *could* turn out to be false. Are these philosophers right?

Consider the following propositions:

(i) The sun is about ninety million miles from the earth.

(ii) There is a heart in my body.

(iii) Here is an ink-bottle.

In various circumstances I should be willing to assert of each of these propositions that I know it to be true. Yet they differ strikingly. This I see when, with each, I try to imagine the possibility that it is false.

(i) If in ordinary conversation someone said to me "The sun is about twenty million miles from the earth, isn't it?" I should reply "No, it is about ninety million miles from us." If he said "I think that you are confusing the sun with Polaris," I should reply "I *know* that ninety million miles is roughly the sun's distance from the earth." I might invite him to verify the figure in an encyclopedia. A third person who overheard our conversation could quite correctly report that I knew the distance to the sun, whereas the other man did not. But this knowledge of mine is little better than hearsay. I have seen that figure mentioned in a few books. I know nothing about the observations and calculations that led astronomers

to accept it. If tomorrow a group of eminent astronomers announced that a great error had been made and that the correct figure is twenty million miles, I should not insist that they were wrong. It would surprise me that such an enormous mistake could have been made. But I should no longer be willing to say that I *know* that ninety million is the correct figure. Although I should *now* claim that I know the distance to be about ninety million miles, it is easy for me to envisage the possibility that some future investigation will prove this to be false.

(ii) Suppose that after a routine medical examination the excited doctor reports to me that the X-ray photographs show that I have no heart. I should tell him to get a new machine. I should be inclined to say that the fact that I have a heart is one of the few things that I can count on as absolutely certain. I can feel it beat. I know it's there. Furthermore, how could my blood circulate if I didn't have one? Suppose that later on I suffer a chest injury and undergo a surgical operation. Afterwards the astonished surgeons solemnly declare that they searched my chest cavity and found no heart, and that they made incisions and looked about in other likely places but found it not. They are convinced that I am without a heart. They are unable to understand how circulation can occur or what accounts for the thumping in my chest. But they are in agreement and obviously sincere, and they have clear photographs of my interior spaces. What would be my attitude? Would it be to insist that they were all mistaken? I think not. I believe that I should eventually accept their testimony and the evidence of the photographs. I should consider to be false what I now regard as an absolute certainty.

(iii) Suppose that as I write this paper someone in the next room were to call out to me "I can't find an ink-bottle; is there one in the house?" I should reply "Here is an ink-bottle." If he said in a doubtful tone "Are you sure? I looked there before," I should reply "Yes, I know there is; come and get it."

Now could it turn out to be false that there is an ink-bottle directly in front of me on this desk? Many philosophers have thought so. They would say that many things could happen of such a nature that if they did happen it would be proved that I am deceived. I agree that many extraordinary things could happen, in the sense that there is no logical absurdity in the supposition. It could happen that when I next reach for this ink-bottle my hand should seem to pass *through* it and I should not feel the contact of any object. It could happen that in the next moment the ink-bottle will suddenly vanish from sight; or that I should find myself under a tree in the garden with no ink-bottle about; or that one or more persons should enter this room and declare with apparent sincerity that they see no ink-bottle on this desk; or that a photograph taken now of the top of the desk should clearly show all of the objects on it except the ink-bottle. Having admitted that these things *could happen*,[8] am I compelled to admit that if they did happen then it would be proved that there is no ink-bottle here *now*? Not at all! I could say that when my hand seemed to pass through the ink-bottle I should *then* be suffering from hallucination; that if the ink-bottle suddenly vanished it would have miraculously ceased to exist; that the other persons were conspiring to drive me mad, or were themselves victims of remarkable concurrent hallucinations; that the camera possessed some strange flaw or that there was trickery in developing the negative. I admit that in the next moment I could find myself under a tree or in the bathtub. But this is not to admit that it could be revealed in the next moment that I am now dreaming. For what I admit is that I might be instantaneously transported to the garden, but not that in the next moment I might *wake up* in the garden. There is nothing that could happen to me in the next moment that I should call "waking up"; and therefore nothing that could happen to me in the next moment would be accepted by me now as proof that I now dream.

Not only do I not *have* to admit that those extraordinary occurrences would be evidence that there is no ink-bottle here; the fact is that I *do not* admit it. There is nothing whatever that could happen in the next moment or the next year that would by me be called *evidence* that there is not an ink- bottle here now. No future experience or investigation could prove to me that I am mistaken. Therefore, if I were to say "I know that there is an ink-bottle here," I should be using "know" in the strong sense.

It will appear to some that I have adopted an *unreasonable* attitude toward that statement. There is, however, nothing unreasonable about it. It seems so because one thinks that the statement that here is an ink-bottle *must* have the same status as the statements that the sun is ninety million miles away and that I have a heart and that there will be water in the gorge this afternoon. But this is a *prejudice*.

In saying that I should regard nothing as evidence that there is no ink-bottle here now, I am not *predicting* what I should do if various astonishing things happened. If other members of my family entered this room and, while looking at the top of this desk, declared with apparent sincerity that they see no ink-bottle, I might fall into a swoon or become mad. I *might* even come to believe that there is not and has not been an ink-bottle here. I cannot foretell with certainty how I should react. But if it is *not* a prediction, what is the meaning of my assertion that I should regard nothing as evidence that there is no ink-bottle here?

That assertion describes my *present* attitude toward the statement that here is an ink-bottle. It does not prophesy what my attitude *would* be if various things happened. My present attitude toward that statement is radically different from my present attitude toward those other statements (e.g., that I have a heart).[9] I do *now* admit that certain future occurrences would disprove the latter. Whereas no imaginable future occurrence would be considered by me *now* as proving that there is not an ink-bottle here.

These remarks are not meant to be autobiographical. They are meant to throw light on the common concepts of evidence, proof, and disproof. Every one of us upon innumerable occasions of daily life takes this same attitude toward various statements about physical things, e.g., that here is a torn page, that this dish is broken, that the thermometer reads 70, that no rug is on the floor. Furthermore, the concepts of proof, disproof, doubt, and conjecture *require* us to take this attitude. In order for it to be possible that any statements about physical things should *turn out to be false* it is necessary that some statements about physical things *cannot* turn out to be false.

This will be made clear if we ask ourselves the question, When do we *say* that something turned out to be false? When do we use those words? Someone asks you for a dollar. You say "There is one in this drawer." You open the drawer and look, but it is perfectly empty. Your statement turned out to be false. This can be said because you *discovered* an empty drawer. It could not be said if it were only probable that the drawer is empty or were still open to question. Would it make sense to say "I had better make sure that it is empty; perhaps there is a dollar in it after all?" Sometimes; but not always. Not if the drawer lies open before your eyes. That remark is the prelude to a search. What search can there be when the emptiness of the drawer confronts you? In certain circumstances there is nothing that you would call "making sure" that the drawer is empty; and likewise nothing that you would call "its turning out to be false" that the drawer is empty. You *made* sure that the drawer is empty. One statement about physical things *turned out to be false* only because you *made sure* of another statement about physical things. The two concepts cannot exist apart. Therefore, it is impossible that *every* statement about physical things *could* turn out to be false.

In a certain important respect some a priori statements and some empirical statements possess the same logical character. The statements that $5 \times 5 = 25$ and that here is an ink-bottle, both lie beyod the reach of doubt. On both, my judgment and reasoning *rests*. If you could somehow undermine my confidence in either, you would not teach me *caution*. You would fill my mind with chaos! I could not even make *conjectures* if you took away those fixed points of certainty; just as a man cannot *try* to climb whose body has no support. A conjecture implies an understanding of what certainty would be. If it is not a certainty that $5 \times 5 = 25$ and that here is an ink-bottle, then I do not understand what it is. You cannot make me doubt either of these statements or treat them as hypotheses. You cannot persuade me that future experience could refute them. With both of them it is perfectly unintelligible to me to speak of a "possibility" that they are false. This is to say that I know both of them to be true, in the strong sense of "know." And I am inclined to think that the strong sense of "know" is what various philosophers have had in mind when they have spoken of "perfect," "metaphysical," or "strict certainty."[10]

It will be thought that I have confused a statement about my "sensations," or my "sense-data," or about the way something *looks* or *appears* to me, with a statement about physical things. It will be thought that the things that I have said about the statement "Here is an ink-bottle" could be true only

if that statement is interpreted to mean something like "There appears to me to be an ink-bottle here," i.e., interpreted so as not to assert or imply that any physical thing exists. I wish to make it clear that my statement "Here is an ink-bottle" is *not* to be interpreted in that way. It would be utterly fantastic for me in my present circumstances to say "There appears to me to be an ink-bottle here."

If someone were to call me on the telephone and say that he urgently needed an ink-bottle I should invite him to come here and get this one. If he said that it was extremely urgent that he should obtain one immediately and that he could not afford to waste time going to a place where there might not be one, I should tell him that it is an absolute certainty that there is one here, that nothing could be more certain, that it is something I absolutely guarantee. But if my statement "There is an ink-bottle here" were a statement about my "sensations" or "sense-data," or if it meant that there *appears* to me to be an ink-bottle here or that something here *looks* to me like an ink-bottle, and if that is all that I meant by it—then I should react quite differently to his urgent request. I should say that there is probably an ink-bottle here but that I could not *guarantee* it, and that if he needs one very desperately and at once then he had better look elsewhere. In short, I wish to make it clear that my statement "Here is an ink-bottle" is strictly about physical things and not about "sensations," "sense-data," or "appearances."[11]

Let us go back to Prichard's remark that we can determine by reflection whether we know something or merely believe it. Prichard would think that "knowledge in the weak sense" is mere belief and not knowledge. This is wrong. But if we let ourselves speak this way, we can then see some justification for Prichard's remark. For then he would be asserting, among other things, that we can determine by reflection whether we know something in the strong sense or in the weak sense. This is not literally true; however, there is this truth in it—that reflection can make us realize that we are *using* "I know it" in the strong (or weak) sense in a particular ease. Prichard says that reflection can show us that "our condition is one of knowing" a certain thing, or instead that "our condition is one of believing and not of knowing" that thing. I do not understand what could be meant here by "our condition." The way I should put it is that reflection on *what we should think* if certain things were to happen may make us realize that we should (or should not) call those things "proof" or "evidence" that what we claim to know is not so. I have tried to show that the distinction between strong and weak knowledge does not run parallel to the distinction between a priori and empirical knowledge but cuts across it, i.e., these two kinds of knowledge may be distinguished *within* a priori knowledge and *within* empirical knowledge.

Reflection can make me realize that I am using "know" in the strong sense; but can reflection show me that I *know* something in the strong sense (or in the weak)? It is not easy to state the logical facts here. On the one hand, if I make an assertion of the form "I know that *p*" it does not follow that *p*, whether or not I am using "know" in the strong sense. If I have said to someone outside my room "Of course, I know that Freddie is in here," and I am speaking in the strong sense, it does not *follow* that Freddie is where I claim he is. This logical fact would not be altered even if I *realized* that I was using "know" in the strong sense. My reflection on what I should say if . . . cannot show me that I *know* something. From the fact that I should not call anything "evidence" that Freddie is not here, it does not follow that he *is* here; therefore, it does not follow that I *know* he is here.

On the other hand, in an actual case of my using "know" in the strong sense, I cannot envisage a possibility that what I say to be true should turn out to be not true. If I were speaking of *another person's* assertion about something, I *could* think both that he is using "know" in the strong sense and that nonetheless what he claims he knows to be so might turn out to be not so. But *in my own case* I cannot have this conjunction of thoughts, and this is a logical and not a psychological fact. When *I* say that I know something to be so, using "know" in the strong sense, it is unintelligible to *me* (although perhaps not to others) to suppose that at anything could prove that it is not so and, therefore, that I do not know it.[12]

NOTES

1. H. A. Prichard, *Knowledge and Perception* (Oxford: The Clarendon Press, 1950), p. 88.
2. Some readers seem to have thought that I was denying here that "I knew that *p*" entails "that *p*." That was not my intention, and my words do not have that implication. If I had said "although you knew you were mistaken," I should have denied the above entailment and, also, I should have misused "knew." The difference between the strong and weak senses of "know" (and "knew") is not that this entailment holds for the strong but not for the weak sense. It holds for both. If it is false that p, then one does not (and did not) know that p.
3. Some logicians and philosophers have taken an interest in proving that $2 + 2 = 4$ (e.g., Leibniz, New Essays on the Understanding, Bk. IV, ch. 7, sec. 10; Frege, The Foundations of Arithmetic, sec. 6). They have wished to show that it can be deduced from certain premises, and to determine what premises and rules of inference are required in the deduction. Their interest has not been in the outcome of the deduction.
4. Compare these remarks about the strong sense of "know" with some of Locke's statements about "intuitive knowledge": ". . . in this the mind is at no pains of proving or examining. . . ." "This part of knowledge . . . leaves no room for hesitation, doubt, or examination. . . .

   "It is on this intuition that depends all the certainty and evidence of all our knowledge; which certainly every one finds to be so great, that he cannot imagine, and therefore not require a greater. . . ." Locke, Essay, Bk. IV, ch. 2, Sec. 1.
5. Descartes, Discourse on the Method, Part IV.
6. Locke, Essay, Book IV, ch. 11, sec. 3.
7. E.g., ". . . no proposition, other than a tautology, can possibly be anything more than a probable hypothesis." A. J. Ayer, Language, Truth and Logic, second ed. (New York: Dover Publications, Inc., 1951), p. 38.
8. My viewpoint is somewhat different here from what it is in "The Verification Argument." There I am concerned with bringing out the different ways in which such a remark as "these things *could* happen" can be taken. I wish to show, furthermore, that from none of the senses in which the remark is *true* does it follow that it is *not certain* that the things in question will *not* happen. Finally, I hold there, that it is perfectly certain that they will not happen. Here, I am not disagreeing with any of those points, but I am adding the further point that my admission that, in some sense, the things *could happen,* does not require me to admit that *if* they were to happen, that would be evidence that there is no ink-bottle here now.
9. The word "attitude" is not very satisfactory, but I cannot think of another noun that would do the

trick. By "my attitude" I mean, here, *what I should say and think* if various things were to happen. By "my *present* attitude" I mean what I should say and think now, when I imagine those things as happening, in contrast with what I should say and think at some future time if those things actually did happen at that time. It is this distinction that shows that my description of "my present attitude" is not a *prophecy.*

10. Descartes, for example, apparently took as his criterion for something's being "entirely certain" that he could not *imagine* in it the least ground of doubt: ". . . je pensai qu'il fallait . . . que je retasse comme absolument faux tout ce en quoi je pourrais imaginer le moindre doute, afin de voir s'il ne me resterait point après cela quelque chose en ma créance qui fut entièrement indubitable" (*Discourse,* Part IV). And Locke (as previously noted) said of "intuitive knowledge" that one *cannot imagine* a greater certainty, and that it "leaves no room for hesitation, doubt, or examination" (*Essay,* Bk. IV, ch. 2., sec. 1).

11. The remainder of the essay is newly written. The original conclusion was wrongly stated. The reader is referred to the following exchange between Richard Taylor and myself, in respect to the original paper: Taylor, "A Note on Knowledge and Belief," *Analysis,* XIII, June 1953; Malcolm, "On Knowledge and Belief," *Analysis,* XIV, March 1954; Taylor, "Rejoinder to Mr. Malcolm," *Analysis,* XIV, March 1954.

12. This is the best summary I can give of what is wrong and right in Prichard's claim that one can determine by reflection whether one knows something or merely believes it. A good part of the ideas in this essay were provoked by conversations with Wittgenstein. A brief and rough account of those talks is to be found in my *Ludwig Wittgenstein: A Memoir* (New York: Oxford University Press, 1958), pp. 87–92. Jaakko Hintikka provides an acute treatment of the topic of "knowing that one knows," with special reference to Prichard's claim. See his *Knowledge and Belief* (Ithaca: Cornell University Press, 1962), ch. 5.

Understanding Human Knowledge in General

The philosophical study of human knowledge seeks to understand what human knowledge is and how it comes to be. A long tradition of reflection on these questions suggests that we can never get the kind of satisfaction we seek. Either we reach the skeptical conclusion that we do not know the things we thought we knew, or we cannot see how the state we find ourselves in is a state of knowledge.

Most philosophers today still deny, or at the very least resist, the force of such reflections. In their efforts to construct a positive theory of knowledge they operate on the not-unreasonable assumption that since human perception, belief, and knowledge are natural phenomena like any other, there is no more reason to think they cannot be understood and explained than there is to think that digestion or photosynthesis cannot be understood and explained. Even if there is still much to be learned about human cognition, it can hardly be denied that we already know a great deal, at least in general, about how it works. Many see it now as just a matter of filling in the details, either from physiology or from something called "cognitive science." We might find that we understand much less than we think we do, but even so it would seem absurd simply to deny that there is such a thing as human knowledge at all, or that we can ever understand how it comes to be. Those traditional skeptical considerations, whatever they were, therefore tend to be ignored. They will be refuted in any case by a successful theory that explains how we do in fact know the things we do.

It would be as absurd to cast doubt on the prospects of scientific investigation of human knowledge and perception as it would be to declare limits to our understanding of human digestion. But I think that what we seek in epistemology—in the philosophical study of human knowledge—is not just anything we can find about how we know things. We try to understand human knowledge in general, and to do so in a certain special way. If the philosophical investigation of knowledge is something distinctive, or sets itself certain special or unique goals, one might question whether those goals can really be reached without thereby casting any doubt on investigations of human knowledge which lack those distinctive philosophical features. That is what I shall try to do. I want to raise and examine the possibility that, however much we came to learn about this or that aspect of human knowledge, thought, and perception, there might still be nothing that could satisfy us as a philosophical understanding of how human knowledge is possible.

When I say nothing could satisfy us I do not mean that it is a very difficult task and that we will never finish the job. It *is* very difficult, and we *will* never finish the job, but I assume that is true of most of our efforts to understand anything. Rather, the threat I see is that once we really understand what we aspire to in the philosophical study of knowledge, and we do not deviate from the aspiration to understand it in that way, we will be forever unable to get the kind of understanding that would satisfy us.

That is one reason I think skepticism is so important in epistemology. It is the view that we do not, or perhaps cannot, know anything, and it is important because it seems to be the inevitable consequence of trying to understand human knowledge in a certain way. Almost nobody thinks for a moment that skepticism could be correct. But that does not mean it is not important. If skepticism really is the inevitable outcome of trying to understand human knowledge in a certain way, and we think it simply could not be correct, that should make us look much more critically at that way of trying to understand human knowledge in the first place. But that is not what typically happens in philosophy. The goal itself is scarcely questioned, and for good reason. We feel human knowledge ought to be intelligible in that way.

The epistemological project feels like the pursuit of a perfectly comprehensible intellectual goal. We know that skepticism is no good; it is an answer, but it is not satisfactory. But being constitutionally unable to arrive at an answer to a perfectly comprehensible question is not satisfactory either. We therefore continue to acquiesce in the traditional problem and do not acknowledge that there is no satisfactory solution. We proceed as if it must be possible to find an answer, so we deny the force, and even the interest, of skepticism.

What we seek in the philosophical theory of knowledge is an account that is completely general in several respects. We want to understand how any knowledge at all is possible—how anything we currently accept amounts to knowledge. Or, less ambitiously, we want to understand with complete generality how we come to know anything at all in a certain specified domain.

For example, in the traditional question of our knowledge of the material bodies around us we want to understand how we know anything at all about any such bodies. In the philosophical problem of other minds we want to understand how any person ever comes to know anything at all about what is going on in the mind of any other person, or even knows that there are any other minds at all. In the case of induction we want to understand how anyone can ever have any reason at all to believe anything beyond what he himself has so far observed to be true. I take it to be the job of a positive philosophical theory of knowledge to answer these and similarly general questions.

One kind of generality I have in mind is revealed by what we would all regard as no answer at all to the philosophical problem. The question of other minds is how anyone can know what someone else thinks or feels. But it would be ludicrous to reply that someone can know what another person thinks or feels by asking a good friend of that person's. That would be no answer at all, but not because it is not true. I *can* sometimes find out what someone else thinks by asking his best friend. But that would not contribute to the solution to the philosophical problem of other minds. We are not simply looking for a list of all the ways of knowing. If we were, that way of knowing would go on the list. But in fact we seek a more inclusive description of all our ways of knowing that would explain our knowledge in general.

What is wrong with that particular way of knowing the mind of another is not that it is only one way among others. The trouble is that it explains how we know some particular fact in the area we are interested in by appeal to knowledge of some other fact in that same domain. I know what Smith thinks by knowing that Jones told me what Smith thinks. But knowing that Jones told me something is itself a bit of knowledge about the mind of another. So that kind of answer could not serve as, nor could it be generalized into, a satisfactory answer to the question how we know anything at all about any other minds. Not because it does not mention a legitimate way of knowing something about the mind of another. It does. Coming to know what Smith thinks by asking Jones is a perfectly acceptable way of knowing, and it is a different way of getting that knowledge from having Smith tell me himself, or from reading Smith's mail. There is nothing wrong with it in itself as an explanation. It is only for the general philosophical task that it is felt to be inadequate.

The same holds for everyday knowledge of the objects around us. One way I can know that my neighbor is at home is by seeing her car in front of her house, where she parks it when and only when she is at home. That is a perfectly good explanation of how I know that fact about one of the things around me. It is a different way of knowing where my neighbor is from seeing her through the window or hearing her characteristic fumblings on the piano. But it could not satisfy us as an explanation of how I know anything at all about any objects around me. It explains how I know something about one object around me—my neighbor—by knowing something about another object around me—her car. It could not answer the philosophical question as to how I know anything about any objects around me at all.

The kind of generality at stake in these problems takes its characteristic philosophical form when we come to see, on reflection, that the information available to us for knowing things in a particular domain is systematically less than we might originally have thought. Perhaps the most familiar instance of this is the *First Meditation* of Descartes, in which he asks about knowledge of the material world by means of the senses. It apparently turns out on reflection that the senses give us less than we might have thought; there is no strictly sensory information the possession of which necessarily amounts to knowledge of the material world. We could perceive exactly what we perceive now even if there were no material world at all. The problem then is to see how we ever come to get knowledge of the material world on that sensory basis.

In the case of other minds we find on reflection that the only evidence we can ever have or even imagine for the mental states of other people is their bodily behavior, including the sounds coming out of their mouths, or even the tears coming out of their eyes. But there is no strictly physical or behavioral information the possession of which necessarily amounts to knowledge of another person's mind or feelings. With induction the general distinction is perhaps even more obvious. The only reason we could ever have for believing anything about what we are not observing at the moment is something we have observed in the past or are observing right now. The problem then is how any knowledge of strictly past or even present fact amounts to knowledge of, or reasonable belief in, some unobserved or future fact.

These apparently simple, problem-generating moves come right at the beginning of epistemology. They are usually taken as so obvious and undeniable that the real problems of epistemology are thought to arise only after they have been made. In this paper I simply assume familiarity with them and with how easily they work. They are the very moves I think we eventually must examine more carefully if we are ever going to understand the real source of the dissatisfaction we are so easily driven to in philosophy. But for now I am concerned with the structure of the plight such reflections appear to leave us in.

If we start by considering a certain domain of facts or truths and ask how anyone could come to know anything at all in that domain, it will seem that any other knowledge that might be relevant could not be allowed to amount to already knowing something in the domain in question. Knowledge of anything at all in that domain is what we want to explain, and if we simply assume from the outset that the person has already got some of that knowledge we will not be explaining all of it. Any knowledge we do grant to the person will be of use to him only if he can somehow get from that knowledge to

some knowledge in the domain in question. Some inference or transition would therefore appear to be needed—for example, some way of going from what he is aware of in perception to knowledge of the facts he claims to know. But any such inference will be a good one, and will lead the person to knowledge, only if it is based on something the person also knows or has some reason to believe. He cannot just be making a guess that he has got good evidence. He has to know or at least have reason to believe something that will help get him from his evidential base to some knowledge in the domain in question. That "something" that he needs to know cannot simply be part of his evidential base, since it has to get him beyond that base. But it cannot go so far beyond that base as to imply something already in the domain in question either, since the knowledge of anything at all in that domain is just what we are trying to explain. So it would seem that on either possibility we cannot explain with the proper generality how the kind of knowledge we want to understand is possible. If the person does know what he needs to know, he has already got some knowledge in the domain in question, and if he does not, he will not be able to get there from his evidential base alone.

This apparent dilemma is a familiar quandary in traditional epistemology. I think it arises from our completely general explanatory goal. We want to explain a certain kind of knowledge, and we feel we must explain it on the basis of another, prior kind of knowledge that does not imply or presuppose any of the knowledge we are trying to explain. Without that, we will not be explaining the knowledge in question in the proper, fully general way. This felt need is what so easily brings into the epistemological project some notion or other of what is usually called "epistemic priority"—one kind of knowledge being prior to another. I believe it has fatal consequences for our understanding of our knowledge. It is often said that traditional epistemology is generated by nothing more than a misguided "quest for certainty," or a fruitless search for absolutely secure "foundations" for knowledge, and that once we abandon such a will-o'-the-wisp we will no longer be threatened by skepticism, or even much interested in it. But that diagnosis seems wrong to me—in fact, completely upside down. what some philosophers see as a poorly motivated demand for "foundations" of knowledge looks to me to be the natural consequence of seeking a certain intellectual goal, a certain kind of understanding of human knowledge in general.

In the philosophical problem of other minds, for example, we pick out observable physical movements or "behavior" and ask how on that basis alone, which is the only basis we have, we can ever know anything about the mind behind the "behavior." Those observable facts of "behavior" are held to be "epistemically prior" to any facts about the mind in the sense that it is possible to know all such facts about others' "behavior" without knowing anything about their minds. We insist on that condition for a properly general explanation of our knowledge of other minds. But in doing so we need not suppose that our beliefs about that "behavior" are themselves indubitable or incorrigible "foundations" of anything. Levels of relative epistemic priority are all we need to rely on in pressing the epistemological question in that way.

In the case of our knowledge of the material objects around us we single out epistemically prior "sensations" or "sense data" or "experiences" or whatever it might be, and then ask how on that basis alone, which is the only basis we have, we can know anything of the objects around us. We take it that knowledge of objects comes to us somehow by means of the senses, but if we thought of sensory knowledge as itself knowledge of material objects around us we would not get an appropriately general explanation of how any knowledge of any objects at all is possible by means of the senses. We would be explaining knowledge of some material objects only on the basis of knowledge of some others. "Data," "the given," "experiences," and so on, which traditional epistemologists have always trafficked in, therefore look to me much more like inevitable products of the epistemological enterprise than elusive "foundations," the unmotivated quest for which somehow throws us into epistemology in the first place.

But once we accept the idea of one kind of knowledge being prior to another as an essential ingredient in the kind of philosophical understanding we seek, it immediately becomes difficult even to imagine, let alone to find, anything that could satisfy us. How *could* we possibly know anything about the minds of

other people on the basis only of truths about their "behavior" if those truths do not imply anything about any minds? If we really are restricted in perception to "experiences" or "sense data" or "stimulations" which give us information that is prior to any knowledge of objects, how *could* we ever know anything about what goes on beyond such prior "data"? It would seem to be possible only if we somehow knew of some connection between what we are restricted to in observation and what is true in the wider domain we are interested in. But then knowing even that there was such a connection would be knowing something about that wider domain after all, not just about what we are restricted to in observation. And then we would be left with no satisfactorily general explanation of our knowledge.

In short, it seems that if we really were in the position the traditional account in terms of epistemic priority describes us as being in, skepticism would be correct. We could not know the things we think we know. But if, in order to resist that conclusion, we no longer see ourselves in that traditional way, we will not have a satisfactorily general explanation of all our knowledge in a certain domain.

Theorists of knowledge who accept the traditional picture of our position in the world obviously do not acknowledge what I see as its skeptical or otherwise unsatisfactory consequences. Some philosophers see their task as that of exhibiting the general structure of our knowledge by making explicit what they think are the "assumptions" or "postulates" or "epistemic principles" that are needed to take us from our "data" or evidence in a particular area to some richer domain of knowledge we want to explain. The fact that certain "postulates" or "principles" can be shown to be precisely what is needed for the knowledge in question is somehow taken to count in their favour. Without those "principles," it is argued, we wouldn't know what we think we know.

However illuminating such "rational reconstructions" of our knowledge might be, they cannot really satisfy us if we want to understand how we actually do know the things we think we know. If it had been shown that there is a certain "postulate" or "principle" which we have to have some reason to accept if we are to know anything about, say, the world around us, we would not thereby have come to understand how we do know anything about the world around us. We would have identified something we need, but its indispensability would not show that we do in fact have good reason to accept it. We would be left with the further question whether we know that that "principle" is true, and if so how. And all the rest of the knowledge we wanted to explain would then be hanging in the balance, since it would have been shown to depend on that "principle." Trying to answer the question of its justification would lead right back into the old dilemma. If the "principle" involved says or implies something richer than anything to be found in the prior evidential base—as it seems it must if it is going to be of any help—there will be nothing in that base alone that could give us reason to accept it. But if we assume from the outset that we do know or have some reason to accept that "principle," we will be assuming that we already know something that goes beyond our prior evidential base, and that knowledge itself will not have been explained. We would therefore have no completely general explanation of how we get beyond that base to any knowledge of the kind in question.

The threat of a regress in the support for any such "principles" leads naturally to the idea of two distinct sources or types of knowledge. If the "principles" or presuppositions of knowledge could be known independently, not on the basis of the prior evidence, but in some other way, it might seem that the regress could be avoided. This might be said to be what Kant learned from Hume: if all our knowledge is derived from experience, we can never know anything. But Kant did not infer from that conditional proposition the categorical skeptical conclusion he thought Hume drew from it. For Kant the point was that if we do have knowledge from experience we must also have some knowledge that is independent of experience. Only in that way is experiential knowledge possible. We must know some things *a priori* if we know anything at all.

As a way of explaining how we know the things we do, this merely postpones or expands the problem. It avoids the skeptical regress in sensory knowledge of the world by insisting that the basic "principles" or presuppositions needed for such empirical knowledge do not themselves depend on empirical, sensory support. But that says only that those "principles" are *not* known by experience; it does not explain how they are known. Merely being presupposed by our empirical knowledge confers no independent support. It has to be explained how we know anything at all *a priori,* and how in particular we know those very things we need for empirical knowledge. And then the old dilemma presents itself again. If our *a priori* knowledge of those "principles" is derived from something prior to them which serves as their evidential base, it must be shown how the further "principles" needed to take us from that base to the "principles" in question could themselves be supported. If we assume from the outset that we do know some "principles" *a priori*, not all of our *a priori* knowledge in general will have been explained. It would seem that *a priori* knowledge in general could be explained only in terms of something that is not itself *a priori* knowledge. But empirical knowledge cannot explain *a priori* knowledge—and it would be no help here even if it could—so either we must simply accept the unexplained fact that we know things *a priori* or we must try to explain it without appealing to any other knowledge at all.

I do not want to go further into the question of *a priori* knowledge. Not because it is not difficult and important in its own right, but because many theorists of knowledge would now argue that it is irrelevant to the epistemological project of explaining our knowledge of the world around us. They find they can put their finger precisely on the place where the traditional philosophical enterprise turns inevitably towards skepticism. And they hold that that step is wrong, and that without it there is no obstacle to finding a satisfactory account of our epistemic position that avoids any commitment to skepticism. This claim for a new "enlightened" theory of knowledge that does not take that allegedly skeptical step is what I want to question.

I have already sketched the hopeless plight I think the old conception leaves us in. The trouble in that conception is now thought to enter at just the point at which the regress I have described apparently gets started. To get from his "evidence" to any of the knowledge in question the person was said to need some "principle" or assumption that would take him from that "evidence" to that conclusion. But he would also need some reason for accepting that "principle"—he would have to know something else that supports it. And then he would need some reason for accepting that "something else," and it could not be found either in his evidential base or in the "principles" he originally needed to take him beyond that base. It must be found in something else in turn—another "something else"—and so on *ad infinitum*. What is wrong in this, it is now thought, is not the idea that the person cannot find such reasons, or that he can only find them somehow mysteriously *a priori*. What is wrong is the requirement that he himself has to find such reasons, that he has to be able to support his "principles," at all. The new "enlightened" approach to knowledge insists that there is a clear sense in which he does not.

The objection can be put another way. What is wrong with the traditional epistemological project that leads so easily to skepticism, it is said, is that the whole thing assumes that anyone who knows something must know that he knows it. He must himself know that his reasons are good ones, or that his prior "evidence" is adequate to yield knowledge of the kind in question. And then, by that same assumption, he must know that he knows that, and so on. But that assumption, it is argued, is not correct. It is obviously possible for someone to know something without knowing that he knows it. The theory of knowledge asks simply whether and how people know things. If that can be explained, that is enough. The fact that people sometimes do not know that they know things should not make us deny that they really do know those things—especially if we have a satisfactory theory that explains that knowledge.

Now it certainly seems right to allow that someone can know something even when we recognize that he does not know that he knows it. Think of the simplest ordinary examples. Someone is asked if he knows who won the battle of Hastings, and when it took place, and he tentatively replies "William the Conqueror, 1066." He knew the answer. He had learned it in school, perhaps, and had never forgotten it, but at the time he was asked he did not know whether he had really retained that information. He was not sure about the state of his knowledge, but as for the winner and the date of the battle of Hastings, he knew that all along. He knew more than he thought he did. So whether somebody knows something is one thing; whether he knows that he knows

it is something else. That seems to be a fact about our everyday assessments of people's knowledge.

The question is not whether that is a fact, but what significance it has for the prospects of the philosophical theory of knowledge. Obviously it turns on what a satisfactory philosophical account is supposed to do. The goal as I have presented it so far is to take ourselves and our ways of knowing on the one hand, and a certain domain of truths that we want to know about on the other, and to understand how we know any of those truths at all on the basis of prior knowledge that does not amount to already knowing something in the domain we are interested in. The question was what support we could find for the bridge that would be needed to get us from that prior basis to the knowledge in question. The present suggestion amounts in effect to saying that no independent or *a priori* support is needed on the part of the knower. All that is needed is that a certain proposition should be true; the person doesn't have to know that it is true in order to know the thing in question. If he has the appropriate prior knowledge or experience, and there is in fact a truth linking his having that knowledge or experience with his knowing something in the domain in question, then he does in fact know something in that domain, even if he is not aware of the favorable epistemic position he is in.

The truth in question will typically be one expressing the definition of knowledge, or of having reason to believe something. The search for such definitions is what many philosophers regard as the special job of the philosophical theory of knowledge. If knowing something could be defined solely in terms of knowledge or experience in some unproblematic, prior domain, then that definition could be fulfilled even if you didn't know that you knew anything in that domain. You yourself would not have to find a "bridge" from your evidential basis to the knowledge in question. As long as there actually was a "bridge" under your feet, whether you knew of it or not, there would be no threat of a skeptical regress.

In one form, this anti-skeptical strategy has been applied to the problem of induction. Hume had argued that if a long positive correlation observed to hold between two sorts of things in the past is going to give you some reason now to expect a thing of the second sort, given an observed instance of the first, you will also have to have some reason to think that what you have observed in the past gives you some reason to believe something about the future. P.F. Strawson replied that you need no such thing. Having observed a long positive correlation between two sorts of things under widely varied circumstances in the past is just what it is—what it means—to have reason to expect a thing of the second sort, given that a thing of the first sort has just appeared. If that is a necessary truth about reasonable belief it will guarantee that you do in fact have a reasonable belief in the future as long as you have had the requisite experience of the past and present. You do not have to find some additional reason for thinking that what you have observed in the past gives you good reason to believe something about the future.

This has come to be called an "externalist" account of knowledge or reasonable belief. It would explain knowledge in terms of conditions that are available from an "external," third-person point of view, independent of what the knower's own attitude towards the fulfillment of those conditions might be. It is not all smooth sailing. To give us what we need, it has to come up with an account of knowledge or reasonable belief that is actually correct—that distinguishes knowledge from lack of knowledge in the right way. I think the account just given of inductive reasons does not meet that test. As it stands, it does not state a necessary truth about reasons to believe. To come closer to being right, it would have to define the difference between a "law–like" generalization and a merely "accidental" correlation which does not give reason to believe it will continue. That task is by no means trivial, and it faces a "new riddle of induction" all over again. But if we do draw a distinction between having good reasons and not having them it would seem that there must be some account that captures what we do. It is just a matter of finding what it is.

The same goes for definitions of knowledge. One type of view says that knowing that p is equivalent to something like having acquired and retained a true belief that p as a result of the operation of a properly functioning, reliable belief-forming mechanism. That general scheme still leaves many things unexplained or undefined, and it is no trivial task to get it to come out right. But I am not concerned here with the details of "externalist" definitions of knowledge. My reservations about the philosophical

theory of knowledge are not just that it is difficult. I have doubts about the satisfactoriness of what you would have even if you had an "externalist" account of knowledge which as far as you could tell matched up completely with those cases in which we think other people know things and those in which we think they do not.

Here we come up against another, and perhaps the most important, dimension of generality I think we seek in the theory of knowledge. We want an account that explains how human knowledge in general is possible, or how anyone can know anything at all in a certain specified domain. The difficulty arises now from the fact that we as human theorists are ourselves part of the subject-matter that we theorists of human knowledge want to understand in a certain way. If we merely study another group and draw conclusions only about them, no such difficulty presents itself. But then our conclusions will not be completely general. They will be known to apply only to those others, and we will be no closer to understanding how our own knowledge is possible. We want to be able to apply what we find out about knowledge to ourselves, and so to explain how our own knowledge is possible.

I have already suggested why I think we cannot get a satisfactory explanation along traditional Cartesian lines. The promise of the new "externalist" strategy is that it would avoid the regress that seems inevitable in that project. A person who knows something does not himself have to know that what he has got in his prior evidential base amounts to knowledge in the domain in question. As long as he in fact satisfies the conditions of knowing something in the domain we are interested in, there is nothing more he has to do in order to know things in that domain. No regress gets started.

The question now is: can we find such a theory satisfactory when we apply it to ourselves? To illustrate what I find difficult here I return to Descartes, as we so often must do in this subject. Not to his skeptical argument in the *First Meditation*, but to the answer he gives to it throughout the rest of the *Meditations*. He eventually comes to think that he does know many of the things that seemed to be thrown into doubt by his earlier reflections on dreaming and the evil demon. He does so by proving that God exists and is not a deceiver and that everything in us, including our capacity to perceive and think, comes from God. So whatever we clearly and distinctly perceive to be true is true. God would not have it any other way. By knowing what I know about God I can know that He is not a deceiver and therefore that I do know the things I think I know when I clearly and distinctly perceive them. If I am careful, and keep God and his goodness in mind, I can know many things, and the threat of skepticism is overcome.

Many objections have been made to this answer to Descartes's question about his knowledge. One is the "externalist" complaint that Descartes's whole challenge rests on the assumption that you don't know something unless you know that you know it. Not only do my clear and distinct perceptions need some guarantee, but on Descartes's view I have to know what that guarantee is. That is why he thinks the atheist ·or the person who denies God in his heart cannot really know those things that we who accept Descartes's proof of God's existence and goodness can know. But according to "externalism" that requirement is wrong; you don't have to know that you know in order to know something.

Another and perhaps the most famous objection is that Descartes's proof of the guarantee of his knowledge is no good because it is circular. The knowledge he needs in order to reach the conclusion of God's existence and goodness is available to him only if God's existence and goodness have already been proved. What he calls his clear and distinct perception of God's existence will be knowledge of God's existence only if whatever he clearly and distinctly perceives is true. But that is guaranteed only by God, so he can't know that it is guaranteed unless he already knows that God exists.

Taking these two objections together, we can see that if the first is correct, the second is no objection at all. If Descartes is assuming that knowing requires knowing that you know, and if that assumption is wrong, then the charge of circularity has no force against his view. If "externalism" were correct, Descartes's inability to prove that God exists and guarantees the truth of our clear and distinct perceptions would be no obstacle to his knowing the truth of whatever he clearly and distinctly perceives. He would not have to know that he knows those things. As long as God did in fact exist and did in

fact make sure that his clear and distinct perceptions were true, Descartes would have the knowledge he started out thinking he had, even if God's existence and nature remained eternally unknown to him. The soundness of his proof would not matter. All that would matter for the everyday knowledge Descartes is trying to account for is the truth of its conclusion—God's existence and goodness. If that conclusion is in fact true, his inability to know that it is true would be no argument against his account.

To develop this thought further we can try to imagine what an "enlightened" or "externalist," but still otherwise Cartesian, theory might look like. It would insist that the knowing subject does not have to know the truth of the theory that explains his knowledge in order to have the knowledge that the theory is trying to account for. Otherwise, the theory would retain the full Cartesian story of God and his goodness and his guarantee of the truth of our clear and distinct perceptions. What would be wrong with accepting such an "enlightened" theory? If we are willing to accept the kind of theory that says that knowing that p is having acquired the true belief that p by some reliable belief-forming mechanism, why would we not be equally or even more willing to accept a theory that says that knowing that p is having acquired the true belief that p by clearly and distinctly perceiving it—a method of belief formation that is reliable because God guarantees that whatever is clearly and distinctly perceived is true? It is actually more specific than a completely general form of "externalism" or "reliabilism." It explains *why* the belief-forming mechanism is reliable. What, then, would be wrong with accepting it?

I think most of us simply don't believe it. We think that God does not in fact exist and is not the guarantor of the reliability of our belief-forming mechanisms. So we think that what this theory says about human knowledge is not true. Now that is certainly a defect in a theory, but is it the only thing standing in the way of our accepting it and finding it satisfactory? It seems to me it is not, and perhaps by examining its other defects, beyond its actual truth-value, we can identify a source of dissatisfaction with other "externalist" theories as well.

We have to admit that if the imagined "externalist" Cartesian theory were true, we would know many of the things we think we know. So skepticism would not be correct. But in the philosophical investigation of knowledge we want more than the falsity of skepticism and more than the mere possession of the knowledge we ordinarily think we've got. We want to understand how we know the things we know, how skepticism turns out not to be true. And even if this "enlightened" Cartesian story were in fact true, if we didn't know that it was, or if we didn't have some reason to believe that it was, we would be no further along towards understanding our knowledge than we would be if the theory were false. So we need some reason to accept a theory of knowledge if we are going to rely on that theory to understand how our knowledge is possible. That is what I think no form of "externalism" can give a satisfactory account of.

Suppose someone had said to Descartes, as they in effect did, "Look, you have no reason to accept any of this story about God and his guarantee of the truth of your clear and distinct perceptions. Of course, if what you say were true you would have the knowledge you think you have, but your whole proof of it is circular. You could justify your explanation of knowledge only if you already knew that what you clearly and distinctly perceive is true." Could an "enlightened" "externalist" Descartes reply: "That's right. I suppose I have to admit that I can give no good reason to accept my explanation. But that doesn't really bother me any more, now that I am an "externalist." Circularity in my proofs is no objection to my theory if "externalism" is correct. I still do believe my theory, after all, and as long as that theory is in fact true—whether I can give any reason to accept it or not—skepticism will be false and I will in fact know the things that I clearly and carefully claim to know.

I take it that that response is inadequate. The "externalist" Descartes I have imagined would not have a satisfactory understanding of his knowledge. It is crucial to what I want to say about "externalism" that we recognize some inadequacy in his position. It is admittedly not easy to specify exactly what the deficiency or the unsatisfactoriness of accepting that position amounts to. I think this much can be said: if the imagined Descartes responded only in that way he would be at best in the position of saying, "If the story that I accept is true, I do know the things I think I know. But I admit that if it is false, and a certain other story is true instead, then I do

not." If "externalism" is correct, what he would be saying here is true. His theory, if true, would explain his knowledge. The difficulty is that until he finds some reason to believe his theory rather than some other, he cannot be said to have explained how he knows the things he knows. That is not because he is assuming that a person cannot know something unless he knows that he knows it. He has explicitly abandoned that assumption. He admits that people know things whether they know the truth of his theory or not. The same of course holds for him. And he knows that implication. That is precisely what he is saying: if his theory is true he will know the things he thinks he knows. But he is, in addition, a theorist of knowledge. He wants to understand how he knows the things he thinks he knows. And he cannot satisfy himself on that score unless he can see himself as having some reason to accept the theory that he (and all the rest of us) can recognize would explain his knowledge if it were true. That is not because knowing implies knowing that you know. It is because having an explanation of something in the sense of understanding it is a matter of having good reason to accept something that would be an explanation if it were true.

The question now is whether an "externalist" scientific epistemologist who rejects Descartes's explanation and offers one of his own is in any better position when he comes to apply his theory to his own knowledge than the imagined "externalist" Descartes is in. He begins by asking about all knowledge in a specified domain. A philosophically satisfactory explanation of such knowledge must not explain some of the knowledge in the domain in question by appeal to knowledge of something else already in the domain. But the scientific student of human knowledge must know or have some reason to believe his theory of knowledge if he is going to understand how knowledge is possible. His theory about our belief-forming mechanisms and their reliability is a theory about the interactions between us and the world around us. It is arrived at by studying human beings, finding out how they get the beliefs they do, and investigating the sources of the reliability of those belief-forming mechanisms. Descartes claimed knowledge of God and his goodness, and of the relation between those supernatural facts and our earth-bound belief-forming mechanisms. A more naturalistic epistemologist's gaze does not reach so high. He claims knowledge of nothing more than the familiar natural world in which he thinks everything happens. But he will have an explanation of human knowledge, and so will understand how people know the things they do, only if he knows or has some reason to believe that his scientific story of the goings-on in that world is true.

If his goal was, among other things, to explain our scientific knowledge of the world around us, he will have an explanation of such knowledge only if he can see himself as possessing some knowledge in that domain. In studying other people, that presents no difficulty. It is precisely by knowing what he does about the world that he explains how others know what they do about the world. But if he had started out asking how anyone knows anything at all about the world, he would be no further along towards understanding how any of it is possible if he had not understood how he himself knows what he has to know about the world in order to have any explanation at all. He must understand himself as knowing or having reason to believe that his theory is true.

It might seem that he fulfills that requirement because his theory of knowledge is meant to identify precisely those conditions under which knowledge or good reason to believe something is present. If that theory is correct, and he himself fulfills those conditions in his own scientific investigations of human knowledge, he will in fact know that his theory of knowledge is true, or at least he will have good reason to believe it. He studies others and finds that they often satisfy the conditions his theory says are sufficient for knowing things about the world, and he believes that theory, and he believes that he too satisfies those same conditions in his investigations of those other people. He concludes that he does know how human beings know what they do, and he concludes that he therefore understands how he in particular knows the things he knows about the world. He is one of the human beings that his theory is true of. So the non-Cartesian, scientific "externalist" claims to be in a better position than the imagined "externalist" Descartes because he claims to know by a reliable study of the natural world that his explanation of human knowledge is correct and Descartes's is wrong. In accepting his own explanation he claims

to fulfill the conditions his theory asserts to be sufficient for knowing things.

I think this theorist would still be in no better position than the position the imagined "externalist" Descartes is in. If this theory is true, he will in fact know that his explanation is correct. In that sense he could be said to possess an explanation of how human beings know the things they know. In that same sense the imagined "externalist" Descartes would possess an explanation of his knowledge. He accepts something which, if true, would explain his knowledge. But none of this would be any help or consolation to them as epistemologists. The position of the imagined "externalist" Descartes is deficient for the theory of knowledge because he needs some reason to believe that the theory he has devised is true in order to be said to understand how people know the things they think they know. The scientific externalist" claims he does have reason to believe his explanation of knowledge and so to be in a better position than the imagined "externalist" Descartes. But the way in which he fulfills that condition, even if he does, is only in an "externalist" way, and therefore in the same way that the imagined Descartes fulfills the conditions of knowledge, if he does. *If* the scientific "externalist's" theory is correct about the conditions under which knowledge or reasonable belief is present, and if he does fulfill those conditions in coming to believe his own explanation of knowledge, then he is in fact right in thinking that he has good reason to think that his explanation is correct. But that is to be in the same position with respect to whether he has good reason to think his explanation is correct as the imagined "externalist" Descartes was in at the first level with respect to whether he knows the things he thinks he knows.

It was admitted that if that imagined Descartes's theory were true he would know the things he thinks he knows, but he could not be said to see or to understand himself as possessing such knowledge because he had no reason to think that his theory was true. The scientific "externalist" claims to have good reason to believe that his theory is true. It must be granted that if, in arriving at his theory, he did fulfill the conditions his theory says are sufficient for knowing things about the world, then if that theory is correct, he does in fact know that it is. But still, I want to say, he himself has no reason to think that he does have good reason to think that his theory is correct. He is at best in the position of someone who has good reason to believe his theory if that theory is in fact true, but has no such reason to believe it if some other theory is true instead. He can see what he *would* have good reason to believe if the theory he believes were true, but he cannot see or understand himself as knowing or having good reason to believe what his theory says.

I am aware that describing what I see as the deficiency in this way is not really satisfactory or conclusive. It encourages the "externalist" to re-apply his theory of knowing or having good reason to believe at the next level up, and to claim that he can indeed understand himself to have good reason to believe his theory because he has good reason to believe that he does have good reason to believe his theory. That further belief about his reasons is arrived at in turn by fulfilling what his theory says are the conditions for reasonably believing something. But then he is still in the same position two levels up that we found the imagined "externalist" Descartes to be in at the first level. If the imagined Descartes's claim to self-understanding was inadequate there, any similar claim will be equally inadequate at any higher level of knowing that one knows or having reason to believe that one has reason to believe. That is why our reaction to the original response of the imagined "externalist" Descartes is crucial. Recognition of its inadequacy is essential to recognizing the inadequacy of "externalism" that I have in mind. It is difficult to say precisely what is inadequate about that kind of response, especially in terms that would be acceptable to an "externalist." Perhaps it is best to say that the theorist has to see himself as having good reason to believe his theory in some sense of "having good reason" that cannot be fully captured by an "externalist" account.

So even if it is true that you can know something without knowing that you know it, the philosophical theorist of knowledge cannot simply insist on the point and expect to find acceptance of an "externalist" account of knowledge fully satisfactory. If he could, he would be in the position of someone who says: "I don't know whether I understand human knowledge or not. If what I believe about it is true and my beliefs about it are produced in what my theory says is the right way, I do know how human

knowledge comes to be, so in that sense I do understand. But if my beliefs are not true, or not arrived at in that way, I do not. I wonder which it is. I wonder whether I understand human knowledge or not." That is not a satisfactory position to arrive at in one's study of human knowledge—or of anything else.

It might be said that there can be such a thing as unwitting understanding, or understanding you don't know you've got, just as there can be unwitting knowledge, or knowledge you don't know you've got. Such "unwitting understanding," if there is such a thing, is the most that the "externalist" philosophical theorist about human knowledge could be said to have of his own knowledge. But even if there is such a thing, it is not something it makes sense to aspire to, or something to remain content with having reached, if you happen to have reached it. We want witting, not unwitting, understanding. That requires knowing or having some reason to accept the scientific story you believe about how people know the things they know. And in the case of knowledge of the world around us, that would involve already knowing or having some reason to believe something in the domain in question. Not all the knowledge in that domain would thereby be explained.

I do not mean that there is something wrong with our explaining how people know certain things about the world by assuming that they or we know certain other things about it. We do it all the time. It is only within the general epistemological enterprise that that otherwise familiar procedure cannot give us what we want. And when I say that "externalism" cannot give us what we want I do not mean that it possesses some internal defect which prevents it from being true. The difficulty I am pointing to is an unsatisfactoriness involved in *accepting* an "externalist" theory and claiming to understand human knowledge in general in that way. And even that is too broad. It is not that there is any difficulty in understanding other people's knowledge in those terms. It is only with self-understanding that the unsatisfactoriness or loss of complete generality makes itself felt. "Externalism," if it got the conditions of knowledge right, would work fine for other people's knowledge. As a third-person, observational study of human beings and other animals, it would avoid the obstacles to human understanding apparently involved in the first-person Cartesian project. But the question is whether we can take up such an "external" observer's position with respect to ourselves and our knowledge and still gain a satisfactorily general explanation of how we know the things we know. That is where I think the inevitable dissatisfaction comes in.

The demand for completely general understanding of knowledge in a certain domain requires that we see ourselves at the outset as not knowing anything in that domain and then coming to have such knowledge on the basis of some independent and in that sense prior knowledge or experience. And that leads us to seek a standpoint from which we can view ourselves without taking for granted any of that knowledge that we want to understand. But if we could manage to detach ourselves in that way from acceptance of any truths in the domain we are interested in, it seems that the only thing we could discover from that point of view is that we can never know anything in that domain. We could find no way to explain how that prior knowledge alone could yield any richer knowledge lying beyond it. That is the plight the traditional view captures. That is the truth in skepticism. If we think of our knowledge as arranged in completely general levels of epistemic priority in that way, we find that we cannot know what we think we know. Skepticism is the only answer.

But then that seems absurd. We realize that people do know many things in the domains we are interested in. We can even explain how they know such things, whether they know that they do or not. That is what the third-person point of view captures. That is the truth in "externalism." But when we try to explain how we know those things we find we can understand it only by assuming that we have got some knowledge in the domain in question. And that is not philosophically satisfying. We have lost the prospect of explaining and therefore understanding all of our knowledge with complete generality.

For these and other reasons I think we need to go back and look more carefully into the very sources of the epistemological quest. We need to see how the almost effortlessly natural ways of thinking embodied in that traditional enterprise nevertheless distort or misrepresent our position, if they do. But we should not think that if and when we come to see how the epistemological enterprise is not fully valid, or perhaps not even fully coherent, we will then possess a satisfactory explanation of how human knowledge in general is possible. We will have seen, at best, that we cannot have any such thing. And that too, I believe, will leave us dissatisfied.

DAVID HUME

Sceptical Doubts Concerning the Operations of the Understanding

PART I

All the objects of human reason or enquiry may naturally be divided into two kinds, to wit, *Relations of Ideas,* and *Matters of Fact.* Of the first kind are the sciences of Geometry, Algebra, and Arithmetic; and in short, every affirmation which is either intuitively or demonstratively certain. *That the square of the hypotenuse is equal to the square of the two sides,* is a proposition which expresses a relation between these figures. *That three times five is equal to the half of thirty,* expresses a relation between these numbers. Propositions of this kind are discoverable by the mere operation of thought, without dependence on what is anywhere existent in the universe. Though there never were a circle or triangle in nature, the truths demonstrated by Euclid would for ever retain their certainty and evidence.

Matters of fact, which are the second objects of human reason, are not ascertained in the same manner; nor is our evidence of their truth, however great, of a like nature with the foregoing. The contrary of every matter of fact is still possible; because it can never imply a contradiction, and is conceived by the mind with the same facility and distinctness, as if ever so conformable to reality. *That the sun will not rise to-morrow* is no less intelligible a proposition, and implies no more contradiction, than the affirmation, *that it will rise.* We should in vain, therefore, attempt to demonstrate its falsehood. Were it demonstratively false, it would imply a contradiction, and could never be distinctly conceived by the mind.

It may, therefore, be a subject worthy of curiosity, to enquire what is the nature of that evidence which assures us of any real existence and matter of fact, beyond the present testimony of our senses, or the records of our memory. This part of philosophy, it is observable, has been little cultivated, either by the ancients or moderns; and therefore our doubts and errors, in the prosecution of so important an enquiry, may be the more excusable; while we march through such difficult paths without any guide or direction. They may even prove useful, by exciting curiosity, and destroying that implicit faith and security, which is the bane of all reasoning and free enquiry. The discovery of defects in the common philosophy, if any such there be, will not, I presume, be a discouragement, but rather an incitement, as is usual, to attempt something more full and satisfactory than has yet been proposed to the public.

All reasonings concerning matter of fact seem to be founded on the relation of *Cause and Effect.* By means of that relation alone we can go beyond the evidence of our memory and senses. If you were to ask a man, why he believes any matter of fact, which is absent; for instance, that his friend is in the country, or in France; he would give you a reason; and this reason would be some other fact; as a letter received from him, or the knowledge of his former resolutions and promises. A man finding a watch or any other machine in a desert island, would conclude that there had once been men in that island. All our reasonings concerning fact are of the same nature. And here it is constantly supposed that there is a connexion between the present fact and that which is inferred from it. Were there nothing to bind them together, the inference would be entirely precarious. The hearing of an articulate voice and rational discourse in the dark assures us of the presence of some person: Why? because these are the effects of the human make and fabric, and closely connected with it. If we anatomize all the other reasonings of this nature, we shall find that they are founded on the relation of cause and effect, and that this relation is either near or remote, direct or collateral. Heat and light are collateral effects of fire, and the one effect may justly be inferred from the other.

If we would satisfy ourselves, therefore, concerning the nature of that evidence, which assures us of matters of fact, we must enquire how we arrive at the knowledge of cause and effect.

I shall venture to affirm, as a general proposition, which admits of no exception, that the knowledge of this relation is not, in any instance, attained by reasonings *a priori*; but arises entirely from experience, when we find that any particular objects are constantly conjoined with each other. Let an object be presented to a man of ever so strong natural reason and abilities; if that object be entirely new to him, he will not be able, by the most accurate examination of its sensible qualities, to discover any of its causes or effects. Adam, though his rational faculties be supposed, at the very first, entirely perfect, could not have inferred from the fluidity and transparency of water that it would suffocate him, or from the light and warmth of fire that it would consume him. No object ever discovers, by the qualities which appear to the senses, either the causes which produced it, or the effects which will arise from it; nor can our reason, unassisted by experience, ever draw any inference concerning real existence and matter of fact.

This proposition, *that causes and effects are discoverable, not by reason but by experience*, will readily be admitted with regard to such objects, as we remember to have once been altogether unknown to us; since we must be conscious of the utter inability, which we then lay under, of foretelling what would arise from them. Present two smooth pieces of marble to a man who has no tincture of natural philosophy; he will never discover that they will adhere together in such a manner as to require great force to separate them in a direct line, while they make so small a resistance to a lateral pressure. Such events, as bear little analogy to the common course of nature, are also readily confessed to be known only by experience; nor does any man imagine that the explosion of gunpowder, or the attraction of a loadstone, could ever be discovered by arguments *a priori*. In like manner, when an effect is supposed to depend upon an intricate machinery or secret structure of parts, we make no difficulty in attributing all our knowledge of it to experience. Who will assert that he can give the ultimate reason, why milk or bread is proper nourishment for a man, not for a lion or a tiger?

But the same truth may not appear, at first sight, to have the same evidence with regard to events, which have become familiar to us from our first appearance in the world, which bear a close analogy to the whole course of nature, and which are supposed to depend on the simple qualities of objects, without any secret structure of parts. We are apt to imagine that we could discover these effects by the mere operation of our reason, without experience. We fancy, that were we brought on a sudden into this world, we could at first have inferred that one Billiard-ball would communicate motion to another upon impulse; and that we needed not to have waited for the event, in order to pronounce with certainty concerning it. Such is the influence of custom, that, where it is strongest, it not only covers our natural ignorance, but even conceals itself, and seems not to take place, merely because it is found in the highest degree.

But to convince us that all the laws of nature, and all the operations of bodies without exception, are known only by experience, the following reflections may, perhaps, suffice. Were any object presented to us, and were we required to pronounce concerning the effect, which will result from it, without consulting past observation; after what manner, I beseech you, must the mind proceed in this operation? It must invent or imagine some event, which it ascribes to the object as its effect; and it is plain that this invention must be entirely arbitrary. The mind can never possibly find the effect in the supposed cause, by the most accurate scrutiny and examination. For the effect is totally different from the cause, and consequently can never be discovered in it. Motion in the second Billiard-ball is a quite distinct event from motion in the first; nor is there anything in the one to suggest the smallest hint of the other. A stone or piece of metal raised into the air, and left without any support, immediately falls: but to consider the matter *a priori*, is there anything we discover in this situation which can beget the idea of a downward, rather than an upward, or any other motion, in the stone or metal?

And as the first imagination or invention of a particular effect, in all natural operations, is arbitrary, where we consult not experience; so must we also esteem the supposed tie or connexion between the cause and effect, which binds them together, and renders it impossible that any other effect could result from the operation of that cause. When I see, for instance, a Billiard-ball moving in a straight line towards another; even suppose motion in the second ball should by accident be suggested to me, as the result of their contact or impulse; may I not conceive, that a hundred different events might as well follow from that cause? May not both these balls remain at absolute rest? May not the first ball return in a straight line, or leap off from the second in any line or direction? All these suppositions are consistent and conceivable. Why then should we give the preference to one, which is no more consistent or conceivable than the rest? All our reasonings *a priori* will never be able to show us any foundation for this preference.

In a word, then, every effect is a distinct event from its cause. It could not, therefore, be discovered in the cause, and the first invention or conception of it, *a priori*, must be entirely arbitrary. And even after it is suggested, the conjunction of it with the cause must appear equally arbitrary; since there are always many other effects, which, to reason, must seem fully as consistent and natural. In vain, therefore, should we pretend to determine any single event, or infer any cause or effect, without the assistance of observation and experience.

Hence we may discover the reason why no philosopher, who is rational and modest, has ever pretended to assign the ultimate cause of any natural operation, or to show distinctly the action of that power, which produces any single effect in the universe. It is confessed, that the utmost effort of human reason is to reduce the principles, productive of natural phenomena, to a greater simplicity, and to resolve the many particular effects into a few general causes, by means of reasonings from analogy, experience, and observation. But as to the causes of these general causes, we should in vain attempt their discovery; nor shall we ever be able to satisfy ourselves, by any particular explication of them. These ultimate springs and principles are totally shut up from human curiosity and enquiry. Elasticity, gravity, cohesion of parts, communication of motion by impulse; these are probably the ultimate causes and principles which we shall ever discover in nature; and we may esteem ourselves sufficiently happy, if, by accurate enquiry and reasoning, we can trace up the particular phenomena to, or near to, these general principles. The most perfect philosophy of the natural kind only staves off our ignorance a little longer: as perhaps the most perfect philosophy of the moral or metaphysical kind serves only to discover larger portions of it. Thus the observation of human blindness and weakness is the result of all philosophy, and meets us at every turn, in spite of our endeavours to elude or avoid it.

Nor is geometry, when taken into the assistance of natural philosophy, ever able to remedy this defect, or lead us into the knowledge of ultimate causes, by all that accuracy of reasoning for which it is so justly celebrated. Every part of mixed mathematics proceeds upon the supposition that certain laws are established by nature in her operations; and abstract reasonings are employed, either to assist experience in the discovery of these laws, or to determine their influence in particular instances, where it depends upon any precise degree of distance and quantity. Thus, it is a law of motion, discovered by experience, that the moment or force of any body in motion is in the compound ratio or proportion of its solid contents and its velocity; and consequently, that a small force may remove the greatest obstacle or raise the greatest weight, if, by any contrivance or machinery, we can increase the velocity of that force, so as to make it an overmatch for its antagonist. Geometry assists us in the application of this law, by giving us the just dimensions of all the parts and figures which can enter into any species of machine; but still the discovery of the law itself is owing merely to experience, and all the abstract reasonings in the world could never lead us one step towards the knowledge of it. When we reason *a priori*, and consider merely any object or cause, as it appears to the mind, independent of all observation, it never could suggest to us the notion of any distinct object, such as its effect; much less, show us the inseparable and inviolable connexion between them. A man must be very sagacious who could discover by reasoning that crystal is the effect of heat, and ice of cold, without being previously acquainted with the operation of these qualities.

PART II

But we have not yet attained any tolerable satisfaction with regard to the question first proposed. Each solution still gives rise to a new question as difficult as the foregoing, and leads us on to farther enquiries. When it is asked, *What is the nature of all our reasonings concerning matter of fact?* the proper answer seems to be, that they are founded on the relation of cause and effect. When again it is asked, *What is the foundation of all our reasonings and conclusions concerning that relation?* it may be replied in one word, Experience. But if we still carry on our sifting humour, and ask, *What is the foundation of all conclusions from experience?* this implies a new question, which may be of more difficult solution and explication. Philosophers, that give themselves airs of superior wisdom and sufficiency, have a hard task when they encounter persons of inquisitive dispositions, who push them from every corner to which they retreat, and who are sure at last to bring them to some dangerous dilemma. The best expedient to prevent this confusion, is to be modest in our pretensions; and even to discover the difficulty our selves before it is objected to us. By this means, we may make a kind of merit of our very ignorance.

I shall content myself, in this section, with an easy task, and shall pretend only to give a negative answer to the question here proposed. I say then, that, even after we have experience of the operations of cause and effect, our conclusions from that experience are not founded on reasoning, or any process of the understanding. This answer we must endeavour both to explain and to defend.

It must certainly be allowed, that nature has kept us at a great distance from all her secrets, and has afforded us only the knowledge of a few superficial qualities of objects; while she conceals from us those powers and principles on which the influence of these objects entirely depends. Our senses inform us of the colour, weight, and consistence of bread; but neither sense nor reason can ever inform us of those qualities which fit it for the nourishment and support of a human body. Sight or feeling conveys an idea of the actual motion of bodies; but as to that wonderful force or power, which would carry on a moving body for ever in a continued change of place, and which bodies never lose but by communicating it to others; of this we cannot form the most distant conception. But notwithstanding this ignorance of natural powers and principles, we always presume, when we see like sensible qualities, that they have like secret powers, and expect that effects, similar to those which we have experienced, will follow from them. If a body of like colour and consistence with that bread, which we have formerly eat, be presented to us, we make no scruple of repeating the experiment, and foresee, with certainty, like nourishment and support. Now this is a process of the mind or thought, of which I would willingly know the foundation. It is allowed on all hands that there is no known connexion between the sensible qualities and the secret powers; and consequently, that the mind is not led to form such a conclusion concerning their constant and regular conjunction, by anything which it knows of their nature. As to past *Experience*, it can be allowed to give *direct* and *certain* information of those precise objects only, and that precise period of time, which fell under its cognizance: but why this experience should be extended to future times, and to other objects, which for aught we know, may be only in appearance similar; this is the main question on which would insist. The bread, which I formerly eat, nourished me; that is, a body of such sensible qualities was, at that time, endued with such secret powers: but does it follow, that other bread must also nourish me at another time, and that like sensible qualities must always be attended with like secret powers? The consequence seems nowise necessary. At least, it must be acknowledged that there is here a consequence drawn by the mind; that there is a certain step taken; a process of thought, and an inference, which wants to be explained. These two propositions are far from being the same, *I have found that such an object has always been attended with such an effect,* and *I foresee, that other objects, which are, in appearance, similar, will be attended with similar effects.* I shall allow, if you please, that the one proposition may justly be inferred from the other: I know, in fact, that it always is inferred. But if you insist that the inference is made by a chain of reasoning, I desire you to produce that reasoning. The connexion between these propositions is not intuitive. There is required a medium, which may enable the mind to draw such an inference, if indeed it be drawn by reasoning and argument. What that medium is, I must confess, passes my comprehension; and it is incumbent on those to produce it, who assert that it really exists, and is the origin of all our conclusions concerning matter of fact.

This negative argument must certainly, in process of time, become altogether convincing, if many penetrating and able philosophers shall turn their enquiries this way and no one be ever able to discover any connecting proposition or intermediate step, which supports the understanding in this conclusion. But as the question is yet new, every reader may not trust so far to his own penetration, as to conclude, because an argument escapes his enquiry, that therefore it does not really exist. For this reason it may be requisite to venture upon a more difficult task; and enumerating all the branches of human knowledge, endeavour to show that none of them can afford such an argument.

All reasonings may be divided into two kinds, namely, demonstrative reasoning, or that concerning relations of ideas, and moral reasoning, or that concerning matter of fact and existence. That there are no demonstrative arguments in the case seems evident; since it implies no contradiction that the course of nature may change, and that an object, seemingly like those which we have experienced, may be attended with different or contrary effects. May I not clearly and distinctly conceive that a body, falling from the clouds, and which, in all other respects, resembles snow, has yet the taste of salt or feeling of fire? Is there any more intelligible proposition than to affirm, that all the trees will flourish in December and January, and decay in May and June? Now whatever is intelligible, and can be distinctly conceived, implies no contradiction, and can never be proved false by any demonstrative argument or abstract reasoning *a priori*.

If we be, therefore, engaged by arguments to put trust in past experience, and make it the standard of our future judgement, these arguments must be probable only, or such as regard matter of fact and real existence, according to the division above mentioned. But that there is no argument of this kind, must appear, if our explication of that species of reasoning be admitted as solid and satisfactory. We have said that all arguments concerning existence are founded on the relation of cause and effect; that our knowledge of that relation is derived entirely from experience; and that all our experimental conclusions proceed upon the supposition that the future will be conformable to the past. To endeav-our, therefore, the proof of this last supposition by probable arguments, or arguments regarding existence, must be evidently going in a circle, and taking that for granted, which is the very point in question.

In reality, all arguments from experience are founded on the similarity which we discover among natural objects, and by which we are induced to expect effects similar to those which we have found to follow from such objects. And though none but a fool or madman will ever pretend to dispute the authority of experience, or to reject that great guide of human life, it may surely be allowed a philosopher to have so much curiosity at least as to examine the principle of human nature, which gives this mighty authority to experience, and makes us draw advantage from that similarity which nature has placed among different objects. From causes which appear *similar* we expect similar effects. This is the sum of all our experimental conclusions. Now it seems evident that, if this conclusion were formed by reason, it would be as perfect at first, and upon one instance, as after ever so long a course of experience. But the case is far otherwise. Nothing so like as eggs; yet no one, on account of this appearing similarity, expects the same taste and relish in all of them. It is only after a long course of uniform experiments in any kind, that we attain a firm reliance and security with regard to a particular event. Now where is that process of reasoning which, from one instance, draws a conclusion, so different from that which it infers from a hundred instances that are nowise different from that single one? This question I propose as much for the sake of information, as with an intention of raising difficulties. I cannot find, I cannot imagine any such reasoning. But I keep my mind still open to instruction, if any one will vouchsafe to bestow it on me.

Should it be said that, from a number of uniform experiments, we *infer* a connexion between the sensible qualities and the secret powers; this, I must confess, seems the same difficulty, couched in different terms. The question still recurs, on what process of argument this *inference* is founded? Where is the medium, the interposing ideas, which join propositions so very wide of each other? It is confessed that the colour, consistence, and other sensible qualities of bread appear not, of themselves, to have any connexion with the secret powers of nourishment and support. For otherwise we could infer these secret powers from the first appearance of these sensible qualities, without the aid of experience; contrary to the sentiment of all philosophers, and contrary to plain matter of fact. Here, then, is our natural state of ignorance with regard to the powers and influence of all objects. How is this remedied by experience? It only shows us a number of uniform effects, resulting from certain objects, and teaches us that those particular objects, at that particular time, were endowed with such powers and forces. When a new object, endowed with similar sensible qualities, is produced, we expect similar powers and forces, and look for a like effect. From a body of like colour and consistence with bread we expect like nourishment and support. But this surely is a step or progress of the mind, which wants to be explained. When a man says, *I have found, in all past instances, such sensible qualities conjoined with such secret powers:* And when he says, *Similar sensible qualities will always be conjoined with similar secret powers,* he is not guilty of a tautology, nor are these propositions in any respect the same. You say that the one proposition is an inference from the other. But you must confess that the inference is not intuitive; neither is it demonstrative: Of what nature is it, then? To say it is experimental, is begging the question. For all inferences from experience suppose, as their foundation, that the future will resemble the past, and that similar powers will be conjoined with similar sensible qualities. If there be any suspicion that the course of nature may change, and that the past may be no rule for the future, all experience becomes useless, and can give rise to no inference or conclusion. It is impossible, therefore, that any arguments from experience can prove this resemblance of the past to the future; since all these arguments are founded on the supposition of that resemblance. Let the course of things be allowed hitherto ever so regular; that alone, without some new argument or inference, proves not that, for the future, it will continue so. In vain do you pretend to have learned the nature of bodies from your past experience. Their secret nature, and consequently all their effects and influence, may change, without any change in their sensible qualities. This happens sometimes, and with regard to some objects: Why may it not happen always, and with regard to all objects? What logic, what process of argument secures you against this supposition? My practice, you say, refutes my doubts. But you mistake the purport of my question. As an agent, I am quite satisfied in the point; but as a philosopher, who has some share of curiosity, I will not say scepticism, I want to learn the foundation of this inference. No reading, no enquiry has yet been able to remove my difficulty, or give me satisfaction in a matter of such importance. Can I do better than propose the difficulty to the public, even though, perhaps, I have small hopes of obtaining a solution? We shall at least, by this means, be sensible of our ignorance, if we do not augment our knowledge.

I must confess that a man is guilty of unpardonable arrogance who concludes, because an argument has escaped his own investigation, that therefore it does not really exist. I must also confess that, though all the learned, for several ages, should have employed themselves in fruitless search upon any subject, it may still, perhaps, be rash to conclude positively that the subject must, therefore, pass all human comprehension. Even though we examine all the sources of our knowledge, and conclude them unfit for such a subject, there may still remain a suspicion, that the enumeration is not complete, or the examination not accurate. But with regard to the present subject, there are some considerations which seem to remove all this accusation of arrogance or suspicion of mistake.

It is certain that the most ignorant and stupid peasants—nay infants, nay even brute beasts—improve by experience, and learn the qualities of natural objects, by observing the effects which result from them. When a child has felt the sensation of pain from touching the flame of a candle, he will be careful not to put his hand near any candle; but will expect a similar effect from a cause which is similar in its sensible qualities and appearance. If you assert, therefore, that the understanding of the child is led into this conclusion by any process of argument or ratiocination, I may justly require you to produce that argument; nor have you any pretence to refuse so equitable a demand. You cannot say that the argument is abstruse, and may possibly escape your enquiry; since you confess that it is obvious to the capacity of a mere infant. If you hesitate, therefore, a moment, or if, after reflection, you produce any intricate or profound argument, you, in a manner, give up the question, and confess that it is not reasoning which engages us to suppose the past resembling the future, and to expect similar effects from causes which are, to appearance, similar. This is the proposition which I intended to enforce in the present section. If I be right, I pretend not to have made any mighty discovery. And if I be wrong, I must acknowledge myself to be indeed a very backward scholar; since I cannot now discover an argument which, it seems, was perfectly familiar to me long before I was out of my cradle.

BERTRAND RUSSELL

On Induction

In almost all our previous discussions we have been concerned in the attempt to get clear as to our data in the way of knowledge of existence. What things are there in the universe whose existence is known to us owing to our being acquainted with them? So far, our answer has been that we are acquainted with our sense-data, and, probably, with ourselves. These we know to exist. And past sense-data which are remembered are known to have existed in the past. This knowledge supplies our data.

But if we are to be able to draw inferences from these data—if we are to know of the existence of matter, of other people, of the past before our individual memory begins, or of the future, we must know general principles of some kind by means of which such inferences can be drawn. It must be known to us that the existence of some one sort of thing, A, is a sign of the existence of some other sort of thing, B, either at the same time as A or at some earlier or later time, as, for example, thunder is a sign of the earlier existence of lightning. If this were not known to us, we could never extend our knowledge beyond the sphere of our private experience; and this sphere, as we have seen, is exceedingly limited. The question we have now to consider is whether such an extension is possible, and if so, how it is effected.

Let us take as an illustration a matter about which none of us, in fact, feel the slightest doubt. We are all convinced that the sun will rise tomorrow. Why? Is this belief a mere blind outcome of past experience, or can it be justified as a reasonable belief? It is not easy to find a test by which to judge whether a belief of this kind is reasonable or not, but we can at least ascertain what sort of general beliefs would suffice, if true, to justify the judgement that the sun will rise tomorrow, and the many other similar judgements upon which our actions are based.

It is obvious that if we are asked why we believe that the sun will rise tomorrow, we shall naturally answer, 'Because it always has risen every day'. We have a firm belief that it will rise in the future, because it has risen in the past. If we are challenged as to why we believe that it will continue to rise as heretofore, we may appeal to the laws of motion: the earth, we shall say, is a freely rotating body, and such bodies do not cease to rotate unless something interferes from outside, and there is nothing outside to interfere with the earth between now and tomorrow. Of course it might be doubted whether we are quite certain that there is nothing outside to interfere, but this is not the interesting doubt. The interesting doubt is as to whether the laws of motion will remain in operation until tomorrow. If this doubt is raised, we find ourselves in the same position as when the doubt about the sunrise was first raised.

The *only* reason for believing that the laws of motion will remain in operation is that they have operated hitherto, so far as our knowledge of the past enables us to judge. It is true that we have a greater body of evidence from the past in favour of the laws of motion than we have in favour of the sunrise, because the sunrise is merely a particular case of fulfillment of the laws of motion, and there are countless other particular cases. But the real question is: Do *any* number of cases of a law being fulfilled in the past afford evidence that it will be fulfilled in the future? If not, it becomes plain that we have no ground whatever for expecting the sun to rise tomorrow, or for expecting the bread we shall eat at our next meal not to poison us, or for any of the other scarcely conscious expectations that control our daily lives. It is to be observed that all such expectations are only *probable;* thus we have not to seek for a proof that they *must* be fulfilled, but only for some reason in favour of the view that they are *likely* to be fulfilled.

Now in dealing with this question we must, to begin with, make an important distinction, without which we should soon become involved in hopeless confusions. Experience has shown us that, hitherto, the frequent repetition of some uniform succession or coexistence has been a *cause* of our expecting the same succession or coexistence on the next occasion. Food that has a certain appearance generally has a certain taste, and it is a severe shock to our expectations when the familiar appearance is found to be associated with an unusual taste. Things which we see become associated, by habit, with certain tactile sensations which we expect if we touch them; one of the horrors of a ghost (in many ghost-stories) is that it fails to give us any sensations of touch. Uneducated people who go abroad for the first time are so surprised as to be incredulous when they find their native language not understood.

And this kind of association is not confined to men; in animals also it is very strong. A horse which has been often driven along a certain road resists the attempt to drive him in a different direction. Domestic animals expect food when they see the person who usually feeds them. We know that all these rather crude expectations of uniformity are liable to be misleading. The man who has fed the chicken every day throughout its life at last wrings its neck instead, showing that more refined views as to the uniformity of nature would have been useful to the chicken.

But in spite of the misleadingness of such expectations, they nevertheless exist. The mere fact that something has happened a certain number of times causes animals and men to expect that it will happen again. Thus our instincts certainly cause us to believe that the sun will rise tomorrow, but we may be in no better a position than the chicken which unexpectedly has its neck wrung. We have therefore to distinguish the fact that past uniformities *cause* expectations as to the future, from the question whether there is any reasonable ground for giving weight to such expectations after the question of their validity has been raised.

The problem we have to discuss is whether there is any reason for believing in what is called 'the uniformity of nature'. The belief in the uniformity of nature is the belief that everything that has happened or will happen is an instance of some general law to which there are *no* exceptions. The crude expectations which we have been considering are all subject to exceptions, and therefore liable to disappoint those who entertain them. But science habitually assumes, at least as a working hypothesis, that

general rules which have exceptions can be replaced by general rules which have no exceptions. 'Unsupported bodies in air fall' is a general rule to which balloons and aeroplanes are exceptions. But the laws of motion and the law of gravitation, which account for the fact that most bodies fall, also account for the fact that balloons and aeroplanes can rise; thus the laws of motion and the law of gravitation are not subject to these exceptions.

The belief that the sun will rise tomorrow might be falsified if the earth came suddenly into contact with a large body which destroyed its rotation; but the laws of motion and the law of gravitation would not be infringed by such an event. The business of science is to find uniformities, such as the laws of motion and the law of gravitation, to which, so far as our experience extends, there are no exceptions. In this search science has been remarkably successful, and it may be conceded that such uniformities have held hitherto. This brings us back to the question: Have we any reason, assuming that they have always held in the past, to suppose that they will hold in the future?

It has been argued that we have reason to know that the future will resemble the past, because what was the future has constantly become the past, and has always been found to resemble the past, so that we really have experience of the future, namely of times which were formerly future, which we may call past futures. But such an argument really begs the very question at issue. We have experience of past futures, but not of future futures, and the question is: Will future futures resemble past futures? This question is not to be answered by an argument which starts from past futures alone. We have therefore still to seek for some principle which shall enable us to know that the future will follow the same laws as the past.

The reference to the future in this question is not essential. The same question arises when we apply the laws that work in our experience to past things of which we have no experience—as, for example, in geology, or in theories as to the origin of the Solar System. The question we really have to ask is: 'When two things have been found to be often associated, and no instance is known of the one occurring without the other, does the occurrence of one of the two, in a fresh instance, give any good ground for expecting the other?' On our answer to this question must depend the validity of the whole of our expectations as to the future, the whole of the results obtained by induction, and in fact practically all the beliefs upon which our daily life is based.

It must be conceded, to begin with, that the fact that two things have been found often together and never apart does not, by itself, suffice to *prove* demonstratively that they will be found together in the next case we examine. The most we can hope is that the oftener things are found together, the more probable it becomes that they will be found together another time, and that, if they have been found together often enough, the probability will amount *almost* to certainty. It can never quite reach certainty, because we know that in spite of frequent repetitions there sometimes is a failure at the last, as in the case of the chicken whose neck is wrung. Thus probability is all we ought to seek.

It might be urged, as against the view we are advocating, that we know all natural phenomena to be subject to the reign of law, and that sometimes, on the basis of observation, we can see that only one law can possibly fit the facts of the case. Now to this view there are two answers. The first is that, even if *some* law which has no exceptions applies to our case, we can never, in practice, be sure that we have discovered that law and not one to which there are exceptions. The second is that the reign of law would seem to be itself only probable, and that our belief that it will hold in the future, or in unexamined cases in the past, is itself based upon the very principle we are examining.

The principle we are examining may be called the *principle of induction*, and its two parts may be stated as follows:

(*a*) When a thing of a certain sort A has been found to be associated with a thing of a certain other sort B, and has never been found dissociated from a thing of the sort B, the greater the number of cases in which A and B have been associated, the greater is the probability that they will be associated in a fresh case in which one of them is known to be present;

(*b*) Under the same circumstances, a sufficient number of cases of association will make the probability of a fresh association nearly a certainty, and will make it approach certainty without limit.

As just stated, the principle applies only to the verification of our expectation in a single fresh instance. But we want also to know that there is a probability in favour of the general law that things of the sort A are *always* associated with things of the sort B, provided a sufficient number of cases of association are known, and no cases of failure of association are known. The probability of the general law is obviously less than the probability of the particular case, since if the general law is true, the particular case must also be true, whereas the particular case may be true without the general law being true. Nevertheless the probability of the general law is increased by repetitions, just as the probability of the particular case, as. We may therefore repeat the two parts of our principle as regards the general law, thus:

(*a*) The greater the number of cases in which a thing of the sort A has been found associated with a thing of the sort B, the more probable it is (if no cases of failure of association are known) that A is always associated with B;

(*b*) Under the same circumstances, a sufficient number of cases of the association of A with B will make it nearly certain that A is always associated with B, and will make this general law approach certainty without limit.

It should be noted that probability is always relative to certain data. In our case, the data are merely the known cases of coexistence of A and B. There may be other data, which *might* be taken into account, which would gravely alter the probability. For example, a man who had seen a great many white swans might argue, by our principle, that on the data it was *probable* that all swans were white, and this might be a perfectly sound argument. The argument is not disproved by the fact that some swans are black, because a thing may very well happen in spite of the fact that some data render it improbable. In the case of the swans, a man might know that colour is a very variable characteristic in many species of animals, and that, therefore, an induction as to colour is peculiarly liable to error. But this knowledge would be a fresh datum, by no means proving that the probability relatively to our previous data had been wrongly estimated. The fact, therefore, that things often fail to fulfill our expectations is no evidence that our expectations will not *probably* be fulfilled in a given case or a given class of cases. Thus our inductive principle is at any rate not capable of being *disproved* by an appeal to experience.

The inductive principle, however, is equally incapable of being *proved* by an appeal to experience. Experience might conceivably confirm the inductive principle as regards the cases that have been already examined; but as regards unexamined cases, it is the inductive principle alone that can justify any inference from what has been examined to what has not been examined. All arguments which, on the basis of experience, argue as to the future or the unexperienced parts of the past or present, assume the inductive principle; hence we can never use experience to prove the inductive principle without begging the question. Thus we must either accept the inductive principle on the ground of its intrinsic evidence, or forgo all justification of our expectations about the future. If the principle is unsound, we have no reason to expect the sun to rise tomorrow, to expect bread to be more nourishing than a stone, or to expect that if we throw ourselves off the roof we shall fall. When we see what looks like our best friend approaching us, we shall have no reason to suppose that his body is not inhabited by the mind of our worst enemy or of some total stranger. All our conduct is based upon associations which have worked in the past, and which we therefore regard as likely to work in the future; and this likelihood is dependent for its validity upon the inductive principle.

The general principles of science, such as the belief in the reign of law, and the belief that every event must have a cause, are as completely dependent upon the inductive principle as are the beliefs of daily life. All such general principles are believed because mankind have found innumerable instances of their truth and no instances of their falsehood. But this affords no evidence for their truth in the future, unless the inductive principle is assumed.

Thus all knowledge which, on a basis of experience tells us something about what is not experienced, is based upon a belief which experience can neither confirm nor confute, yet which, at least in its more concrete applications, appears to be as firmly rooted in us as many of the facts of experience. The existence and justification of such beliefs—for the inductive principle, as we shall see, is not the only example—raises some of the most difficult and most debated problems of philosophy. We will, in the next chapter, consider briefly what may be said to account for such knowledge, and what is its scope and its degree of certainty.

PAUL EDWARDS

Russell's Doubts about Induction

I

A. In the celebrated chapter on induction in his *Problems of Philosophy,* Bertrand Russell asks the question: 'Have we any reason, assuming that they [laws like the law of gravitation] have always held in the past, to suppose that these laws will hold in the future?' Earlier in the same chapter he raises the more specific question: 'Do *any* number of cases of a law being fulfilled in the past afford evidence that it will be fulfilled in the future?' We may reformulate these questions in a way which lends itself more easily to critical discussion as follows:

(1) Assuming that we possess n positive instances of a phenomenon, observed in extensively varied circumstances, and that we have not observed a single negative instance (where n is a large number), have we any reason to suppose that the $n + 1$st instance will also be positive?

(2) Is there any number n of observed positive instances of a phenomenon which affords evidence that the $n + 1$st instance will also be positive?

It is clear that Russell uses 'reason' synonymously with 'good reason' and 'evidence' with 'sufficient evidence'. I shall follow the same procedure throughout this article.

Russell asserts that unless we appeal to a non-empirical principle which he calls the 'principle of induction', both of his questions must be answered in the negative. 'Those who emphasized the scope of induction,' he writes, 'wished to maintain that all logic is empirical, and therefore could not be expected to realize that induction itself, their own darling, required a logical principle which obviously could not be proved inductively, and must therefore be *a priori* if it could be known at all.' 'We must either accept the inductive principle on the ground of its

intrinsic evidence or forgo all justification of our expectations about the future.'

In conjunction with the inductive principle, on the other hand, question (1) at least, he contends, can be answered in the affirmative. 'Whether inferences from past to future are valid depends wholly, if our discussion has been sound, upon the inductive principle: if it is true, such inferences are valid.' Unfortunately Russell does not make it clear whether in his opinion the same is true about question (2).

As against Russell, I shall try to show in this article that question (1) can be answered in the affirmative without in any way appealing to a non-empirical principle. I shall also attempt to show that, without in any way invoking a non-empirical principle, numbers of observed positive instances do frequently afford us evidence that unobserved instances of the same phenomenon are also positive. At the outset, I shall concentrate on question (1) since this is the more general question. Once we have answered question (1) it will require little further effort to answer question (2).

I want to emphasize here that, to keep this paper within manageable bounds, I shall refrain from discussing, at any rate explicitly, the questions 'Are any inductive conclusions probable?' and 'Are any inductive conclusions certain?' I hope to fill in this gap on another occasion.

It will be well to conduct our discussion in terms of a concrete example. Supposing a man jumps from a window on the fiftieth floor of the Empire State Building. Is there any reason to suppose that his body will move in the direction of the street rather than say in the direction of the sky or in a flat plane? There can be no doubt that any ordinary person and any philosophically unsophisticated scientist would answer this question in the affirmative without in any way appealing to a non-empirical principle. He would say that there is an excellent reason to suppose that the man's body will move towards the street. This excellent reason, he would say, consists in the fact that whenever in the past a human being jumped out of a window of the Empire State Building his body moved in a downward direction; that whenever any human being anywhere jumped out of a house he moved in the direction of the ground; that, more generally, whenever a human body jumped or was thrown off an elevated locality in the neighbourhood of the earth, it moved downwards and not either upwards or at an angle of 180°; that the only objects which have been observed to be capable of moving upwards by themselves possess certain special characteristics which human beings lack; and finally in all the other observed confirmations of the theory of gravitation.

B. The philosophers who reject commonsense answers like the one just described, have relied mainly on three arguments. Russell himself explicitly employs two of them and some of his remarks make it clear that he also approves of the third. These three arguments are as follows: (*a*) Defenders of commonsense point to the fact that many inferences to unobserved events were subsequently, by means of direct observation, found to have resulted in true conclusions. However, any such appeal to observed results of inductive inferences is irrelevant. For the question at stake is: Have we ever a reason, assuming that all the large number of observed instances of a phenomenon are positive, to suppose that an instance which is still unobserved is also positive? The question is not: Have we ever a reason for supposing that instances which have by now been observed but were at one time unobserved are positive? In Russell's own words: 'We have experience of past futures, but not of future futures, and the question is: Will future futures resemble past futures? This question is not to be answered by an argument which starts from past futures alone.'

(*b*) Cases are known where at a certain time a large number of positive instances and not a single negative instance had been observed and where the next instance nevertheless turned out to be negative. 'We know that in spite of frequent repetitions there sometimes is a failure at the last.' The man, for instance, 'who has fed the chicken every day throughout its life at last wrings its neck instead'. Even in the case of the human being who is jumping out of the Empire State Building, 'we may be in

no better position than the chicken which unexpectedly has its neck wrung'.

(*c*) The number of positive and negative necessary conditions for the occurrence of any event is infinite or at any rate too large to be directly observed by a human being or indeed by all human beings put together. None of us, for example, has explored every corner of the universe to make sure that there nowhere exists a malicious but powerful individual who controls the movements of the sun by means of wires which are too fine to be detected by any of our microscopes. None of us can be sure that there is no such Controller who, in order to play a joke with the human race, will prevent the sun from rising tomorrow. Equally, none of us can be sure that there is nowhere a powerful individual who can, if he wishes, regulate the movement of human bodies by means of ropes which are too thin to be detected by any of our present instruments. None of us therefore can be sure that when a man jumps out of the Empire State Building he will not be drawn skyward by the Controller of Motion. Hence we have no reason to suppose that the man's body will move in the direction of the street and not in the direction of the sky.

In connection with the last of these three arguments attention ought to be drawn to a distinction which Russell makes between what he calls the 'interesting' and the 'uninteresting' doubt about induction. The uninteresting doubt is doubt about the occurrence of a given event on the ground that not all the conditions which are known to be necessary are in fact known to be present. What Russell calls the interesting doubt is the doubt whether an event will take place although all the conditions known to be necessary are known to obtain. Russell's 'interesting doubt', if I am not mistaken, is identical with Donald Williams's 'tragic problem of induction'.

II

As I indicated above, it is my object in this article to defend the commonsense answers to both of Russell's questions. I propose to show, in other words, that, without in any way calling upon a non-empirical principle for assistance, we often have a reason for supposing that a generalization will be confirmed in the future as it has been confirmed in the past. I also propose to show that numbers 'of cases of a law being fulfilled in the past' do often afford evidence that it will be fulfilled in the future.

However, what I have to say in support of these answers is so exceedingly simple that I am afraid it will not impress the philosophers who are looking for elaborate and complicated theories to answer these questions. But I think I can make my case appear plausible even in the eyes of some of these philosophers if I describe at some length the general method of resolving philosophical puzzles which I shall apply to the problem of induction.

Let us consider a simple statement like 'there are several thousand physicians in New York'. We may call this a statement of commonsense, meaning thereby no more than that anybody above a certain very moderate level of instruction and intelligence would confidently give his assent to it.

The word 'physician', as ordinarily used, is not entirely free from ambiguity. At times it simply means 'person who possesses a medical degree from a recognized academic institution'. At other times, though less often, it means the same as 'person who possesses what is by ordinary standards a considerable skill in curing diseases'. On yet other occasions when people say about somebody that he is a physician they mean both that he has a medical degree and that he possesses a skill in curing diseases which considerably exceeds that of the average layman.

Let us suppose that in the commonsense statement 'there are several thousand physicians in New York' the word 'physician' is used exclusively in the last-mentioned sense. This assumption will simplify our discussion, but it is not at all essential to any of the points I am about to make. It is essential, however, to realize that when somebody asserts in ordinary life that there are several thousand physicians in New York, he is using the word 'physician' in one or other of the ordinary senses just listed. By 'physician' he does not mean for example 'person who can speedily repair bicycles' or 'person who can cure any conceivable illness in less than two minutes'.

Now, supposing somebody were to say 'Really, there are no physicians at all in New York', in the belief that he was contradicting and refuting commonsense. Supposing that on investigation it turns out that by 'physician' he does not mean 'person who has a medical degree and who has considerably more skill in curing disease than the average layman'. It turns out that by 'physician' he means 'person who has a medical degree and who can cure any conceivable illness in less than two minutes'.

What would be an adequate reply to such an 'enemy of commonsense'? Clearly it would be along the following lines: 'What you say is true. There are no physicians in New York—in *your* sense of the word. There are no persons in New York who can cure any conceivable disease in less than two minutes. But this in no way contradicts the commonsense view expressed by "there are several thousand physicians in New York". For the latter asserts no more than that there are several thousand people in New York who have a medical degree and who possess a skill in curing disease which considerably exceeds that of the average layman. You are guilty of *ignoratio elenchi* since the proposition you refute is different from the proposition you set out to refute.'

Our discussion from here on will be greatly simplified by introducing a few technical terms. Let us, firstly, call '*ignoratio elenchi* by *redefinition*" any instance of *ignoratio elenchi* in which (i) the same sentence expresses both the proposition which ought to be proved and the proposition which is confused with it and where (ii) in the latter employment of the sentence one or more of its parts are used in a sense which is different from their ordinary sense or senses. Secondly, let us refer to any redefinition of a word which includes all that the ordinary definition of the word includes but which includes something else as well as a '*high* redefinition'; and to the sense which is defined by a high redefinition we shall refer as a high sense of the word. Thus 'person who has a medical degree and who is capable of curing any conceivable disease in less than two minutes' is a high redefinition of 'physician' and anybody using the word in that fashion is using it in a high sense. Thirdly, we shall refer to a redefinition of a word which includes something but not all of what the ordinary definition includes and which includes nothing else as a '*low* redefinition'; and the sense which is defined by a low redefinition we shall call a low sense of the word. 'Person capable of giving first aid' or 'person who knows means of alleviating pain' would be low redefinitions of 'physician'. Finally, it will be convenient to call a statement in which a word is used in a high or in a low sense a *redefinitional statement*. If the word is used in a high sense we shall speak of a highdefinitional statement; if it is used in a low sense we shall speak of a lowdefinitional statement.

A short while ago, I pointed out that the man who says 'there are no physicians in New York', meaning that there are no people in New York who have a medical degree and who can cure any conceivable illness in less than two minutes, is not really contradicting the commonsense view that there are physicians in New York. I pointed out that he would be guilty of what in our technical language is called an *ignoratio elenchi* by redefinition. Now, it seems to me that the relation between the assertion of various philosophers that past experience never constitutes a reason for prediction or generalization except perhaps in conjunction with a non-empirical principle and the commonsense view that past experience does often by itself constitute a reason for inferences to unobserved events has some striking resemblances to the relation between the redefinitional statement about physicians in New York and the commonsense view which this redefinitional statement fails to refute. And more generally, it strongly seems to me that almost all the bizarre pronouncements of philosophers—their 'paradoxes', their 'silly' theories—are in certain respects strikingly like the statement that there are no physicians in New York, made by one who means to assert that there are no people in New York who have medical degrees and who are capable of curing any conceivable disease in less than two minutes.

In making the last statement I do not mean to deny that there are also important differences between philosophical paradoxes and the highdefinitional statement about physicians. There are three differences in particular which have to be mentioned if my subsequent remarks are not seriously misleading. Firstly, many of the philosophical paradoxes are not without some point; they do often draw attention to likenesses and differences which ordinary usage obscures. Secondly, the redefinitions which are implicit in philosophical paradoxes do quite often, though by no means always, receive a certain backing from ordinary usage. Frequently, that is to say, there is a secondary sense or trend in ordinary usage which corresponds to the philosophical redefinition, the 'real' sense of the word. Thirdly, philosophical paradoxes are invariably ambiguous in a sense in which the highdefinitional statement about the physicians is not ambiguous.

Now, while fully admitting all these (and other) differences, I wish to insist on the great likenesses between philosophical paradoxes and the redefinitional statement about the physicians. And in this article I am mainly concerned with the likenesses, not with the differences. My main object of course is to point out the likenesses between the highdefinitional statement "there are no physicians in New York' and the statement that past experience never by itself affords a reason for making inferences to unobserved events. However, my points there will be clearer if I first make them in connection with another celebrated paradox.

Following Plato, Berkeley argued in favour of the view that heat and cold are not really 'in the object'. Ordinary people would unhesitatingly say that water of, e.g. 50° Centigrade is hot. Against this, Plato and Berkeley would point out that to a man who a moment before had held his hands in a jug of water with a temperature of 80° C. the water of 50° C. would appear cold. Similarly, to a race of individuals whose body-temperature was say 75° C., water of 50° would regularly appear cold. But the percepts of those to whom the water of 50° appears cold are just as genuine as the percepts of people to whom the water appears hot. Now, since it would be wrong to say that the water of 50° is really cold simply because of these genuine percepts of cold, it cannot any more rationally be said to be hot. The cold has 'just as good a right to be considered real' as the hot, and therefore, 'to avoid favouritism, we are compelled to deny that in itself' the water is either hot or cold.

It is not difficult to show that this argument is a case of *ignoratio elenchi* by redefinition. When an ordinary person says that water of 50° C. is hot all he means is that human beings, with their body-temperature being what it is, would in *all ordinary circumstances* have sense-impressions of heat on coming into contact with such water. In saying that water of 50° is hot, is *really* hot, an ordinary person in no way denies that under certain *special* conditions a human being would have genuine sense-impressions of cold. He also in no way denies that to a race of individuals whose body-temperature is 75° the water would genuinely appear cold. Pointing to these facts does therefore not refute the ordinary man. Berkeley is clearly guilty of a high redefinition of 'hot' or 'really hot'. To him something is hot only if, in addition to appearing hot to human beings in ordinary circumstances, it also appears hot to them under special circumstances and if it appears hot to beings with a body-temperature which is much greater than the actual body-temperature of human beings.

However, this is not quite accurate since, like most other philosophical paradoxes, the paradox about heat and cold has a double meaning. It would be inaccurate simply to say that Berkeley is guilty of *ignoratio elenchi* by redefinition. On the other hand, without in any way being inaccurate, it can be said that Berkeley and Plato have laid themselves open to the following dilemma: 'Either you mean by "hot" what is ordinarily meant by it—if you do, then what you say is plainly false; or else you are using "hot" in a high sense—if so what you say is true, but in that case you are guilty of *ignoratio elenchi* by redefinition. In either event you have failed to refute commonsense.' Very similar answers can also be made to Berkeley's and Russell's arguments concerning colours, shapes, and the other qualities which commonsense believes to exist independently of being perceived.

At the same time it must be admitted that Berkeley's arguments have a certain value. In ordinary speech we make a fairly rigid distinction between 'real' and 'unreal' data. Among the unreal data we lump together both the percepts which we have under special conditions (and percepts which do and would appear to beings differently constituted from ourselves) and what we experience, e.g., in dreams and hallucinations. 'Real' we call only those percepts which a normal observer has under certain standard conditions.

A classification of this sort obscures the many likenesses between the 'real' percepts and percepts appearing under special conditions, while also hiding the many differences between the latter and data which are experienced in dreams and hallucinations.

The situation becomes quite clear if we divide data into three and not merely into two groups, as follows:

the R-data: percepts appearing to a normal observer under standard conditions,

the A-data: percepts appearing to a normal observer under special conditions or to an abnormal observer in certain normal or special circumstances, and

the D-data: data appearing in dreams, hallucinations, etc.

It is unnecessary for our purposes to discuss exactly what are the likenesses between the R-data and the A-data. It is unnecessary, too, to discuss what exactly are the differences between the A-data and the D-data. It is sufficient to point out that while Berkeley is wrong in believing or suggesting that there are no differences between the R-data and the A-data, he is right in insisting that the differences between the R-data and the A-data are not nearly as great as ordinary speech suggests. In the case of colours, Berkeley's argument has the further merit of bringing out the fact that the expression 'X's real colour' has *two* perfectly proper senses. His argument helps one to realize that 'X's real colours' may mean 'the colour which X exhibits to a normal observer under certain standard conditions' *as well as* 'the colour which X exhibits to a normal observer under a finer instrument than the human eye, e.g. a microscope'.

III

A. Supposing a man, let us call him M, said to us, 'I have not yet found any physicians in New York.' Suppose we take him to Park Avenue and introduce him to Brown, a man who has a medical degree and who has cured many people suffering from diseases of the ear. Brown admits, however, that he has not been able to cure *all* the patients who ever consulted him. He also admits that many of his cures took a long time, some as long as eight years. On hearing this, M says, 'Brown certainly isn't a physician.'

Supposing we next take M to meet Black who has a medical degree and who can prove to M's and to our satisfaction that he has cured every patient who ever consulted him. Moreover, none of Black's cures took more than three years. However, on hearing that some of Black's cures took as long as two years and ten months, M says, 'Black certainly isn't a physician either.'

Finally we introduce M to White who has a medical degree and who has cured every one of his patients in less than six months. When M hears that some of White's cures took as long as five and a half months, he is adamant and exclaims,

'White—what a ridiculous error to call him a physician!'

At this stage, if not much sooner, all of us would impatiently ask M: What on earth do you mean by 'physician'? And we would plainly be justified in adding: Whatever you may mean by 'physician', in any sense in which we ever use the word, Black and Brown and White are physicians and very excellent ones at that.

Let us return now to Russell's doubt about the sun's rising tomorrow or about what would happen to a man who jumps out of the Empire State Building. Let us consider what Russell would say in reply to the following question: Supposing that the observed confirmatory instances for the theory of gravitation were a million or ten million times as extensive as they now are and that they were drawn from a very much wider field; would we then have a reason to suppose that the man will fall into the street and not move up into the sky? It is obvious that Russell and anybody taking his view would say 'No'. He would reply that though our *expectation* that the man's body will move in the direction of the street would be even stronger then than it is at present, we would still be without a *reason*.

Next, let us imagine ourselves to be putting the following question to Russell: Supposing the world were such that no accumulation of more than five hundred observed positive instances of a phenomenon has ever been found to be followed by a negative instance; supposing, for instance, that all the chickens who have ever been fed by the same man for 501 days in succession or more are still alive and that all the men too are still alive feeding the chickens every day—would the observed confirmations of the law of gravity in that case be a reason to suppose that the man jumping out of the Empire State Building will move in the direction of the street and not in the direction of the sky? I am not quite sure what Russell would say in reply to this question. Let us assume he would once again answer: 'No—Past experience would not even then ever be a *reason*.'

Thirdly and finally, we have to consider what Russell would say to the following question: Supposing we had explored every corner of the universe with instruments millions of times as fine and accurate as any we now possess and that we had yet failed to discover any Controller of the movements of human bodies—would we then in our predictions about the man jumping out of the Empire State Building be in a better position than the chicken is in predicting its meals? Would our past observations then be a reason for our prediction? Whatever Russell would in fact say to this, it is clear that his remarks concerning the 'interesting' doubt about induction require him to answer our question in the negative. He would have to say something like this: 'Our *expectation* that the man's body will move in a downward direction will be even stronger than it is now. However, without invoking a non-empirical principle, we shall not *really* be in a better position than the chicken. We should still fail to possess a *reason*.'

As in the case of the man who refused to say that Brown, Black, and White were doctors, our natural response to all this will be to turn to Russell and say: What do you mean by 'being in a better position'? What on earth do you mean by 'a reason'? And, furthermore, why should anybody be interested in a reason in your sense of the word?

Russell's remarks about the need for a general principle like his principle of induction to serve as major premiss in every inductive argument make it clear what he means by a reason: like the Rationalists and Hume (in most places), he means by 'reason' a *logically conclusive* reason and by 'evidence' *deductively conclusive* evidence. When 'reason' is used in this sense, it must be admitted that past observations can never by themselves be a reason for any prediction whatsoever. But 'reason' is not used in this sense when, in science or in ordinary life, people claim to have a reason for a prediction.

So far as I can see, there are three different trends in the ordinary usage of 'reason for an inductive conclusion' and according to none of them does the word mean 'logically conclusive reason'. Among the three trends one is much more prominent than the others. It may fitly be called the main sense of the word. According to this main sense, what we mean when we claim that we have a reason for a prediction is that the past observations of this phenomenon or of analogical phenomena are of a certain kind: they are exclusively or predominantly positive, the number of the positive observations is at least fairly large, and they come from extensively varied sets of circumstances. This is of course a very crude formulation. But for the purposes of this article it is, I think, sufficient.

Next, there is a number of trends according to which we mean very much less than this. Occasionally, for instance, we simply mean that it is *reasonable* to infer the inductive conclusion. And clearly it may be reasonable to infer an inductive conclusion for which we have no reason in the main sense. Thus let us suppose I know that Parker will meet Schroeder in a game in the near future and that it is imperative for me not to suspend my judgement but to come to a conclusion as to who will win. Supposing I know nothing about their present form and nothing also about the type of court on which the match is to be played. All I know is that Parker and Schroeder have in the previous two seasons met six times, Parker scoring four victories to Schroeder's two. In these circumstances it would be reasonable for me to predict that Parker will win and unreasonable to predict that Schroeder will win. Clearly however, in the main sense of the word I have no reason for either prediction.

Again there is a trend according to which any positive instance of a phenomenon is *a* reason for concluding that the next instance of the phenomenon will be positive. Thus in the circumstances described in the preceding paragraph, it would be quite proper to say we have *more reason* for supposing that Parker will win than for predicting Schroeder's victory. It would be quite proper also to say that we have *some reason* for supposing that Schroeder will win. It would be proper to say this even if Schroeder had won only one of the six matches. To all these and similar trends in the ordinary usage of 'reason for an inductive conclusion' I shall from now on refer as the second ordinary sense of the word.

There can be no doubt that, in both these ordinary senses of the word, we frequently have a reason for an inductive conclusion. In these senses we have an excellent reason for supposing that the man jumping out of the Empire State Building will move in the direction of the street, that the sun will rise tomorrow and that Stalin will die before the year 2000. The answer to question (1) is therefore a firm and clear 'Yes': in many domains we have a multitude of exclusively positive instances coming from extensively different circumstances.

The same is true if 'reason' is used in the third ordinary sense. However, I propose to reserve our discussion of that sense for Section V below. For the time being it will be convenient and, I think, not at all misleading to speak as if what I have called the main sense is the *only* ordinary sense of 'reason for an inductive conclusion'.

It should now be clear that, when Russell says that observed instances are never by themselves a reason for an inductive conclusion, he is guilty of an *ignoratio elenchi* by redefinition. His assertion that the premisses of an inductive argument never by themselves constitute a *logically conclusive* reason for an inductive conclusion in no way contradicts the commonsense assertion that they frequently constitute a reason *in the ordinary sense of the word*. Russell's definition of 'reason' is indeed in one respect not a redefinition since in certain contexts we do use 'reason' to mean 'deductively conclusive reason'. However, it is a redefinition in that we never in ordinary life use 'reason' in Russell's sense when we are talking about inductive arguments.

Moreover, if 'reason' means 'deductively conclusive reason', Russell's questions are no more genuinely questions than, e.g., the sentence 'Is a father a female parent?' For, since part of the definition of 'inductive inference' is inference from something observed to something unobserved, it is a *contradiction* to say that an inference is both inductive and at the same time in the same respect deductively conclusive. Russell's 'interesting' doubt, then, is no more sensible or interesting than the 'doubt' whether we shall ever see something invisible or find an object which is a father and also female or an object which is a man but not a human being.

In a similar fashion, Russell's remarks about the future future which we quoted in Section 1B constitute an *ignoratio elenchi* by redefinition. If the word 'future' is used in its ordinary sense in the statement 'the future will resemble the past and the present in certain respects', then we have plenty of evidence to support it. For in the ordinary sense of the word, 'future' simply means 'period which has to the past and the present the relation of happening after it'. In its ordinary sense, 'future' does *not* mean 'period which has to the past and the present the relation of happening after it *and* which can never itself be experienced *as a present*'. The period which is referred to by 'future' in its ordinary sense may very well one day be experienced as a present.

In the ordinary sense of the word 'future' there-fore, what Russell calls past futures *are* futures. They are futures in relation to certain other periods which preceded them. Now, the appeal to the fact that past futures resembled past pasts and past presents con-stitutes excellent inductive evidence for the conclu-sion that the future will resemble the past and the present. Stated fully, the argument is as follows: a period which has to the past and present the relation of happening after it will resemble the past and the present in certain respects because in the past peri-ods which stood in the same temporal relation to other periods were found to resemble those periods in these respects.

It should be emphasized that in the conclusion of this argument 'future' means 'future future', as that phrase would normally be understood. It refers to a period which by the time at which the statement is made has not yet been experienced, i.e. has not yet become a present or a past.

The appeal to the resemblance between past futures and past pasts and presents is not to the point only if in the sentence 'the future will resem-ble the past and the present' the word 'future' means 'period which has to the present the relation of occurring after it *and* which can never be experi-enced as a present'. In that case, of course, past futures are not really futures. For, when they were experienced they were experienced as presents. However, anybody who in ordinary life or in science says or implies that the future will resemble the past and the present does not use 'future' in this sense. He means to assert something about a future which may one day be experienced as a present.

B. If Russell had answered in the affirmative any of the three questions which we imagined ourselves to be addressing to him, his question (1) would be a genuine question in the sense that it could then not be disposed of by an examination of definitions alone. But even then Russell would have been guilty of *ignoratio elenchi* by high redefinition. For in order to have a reason, in the ordinary sense of the word, for inferring that the next instance of a certain phe-nomenon is positive it is not necessary to observe all the positive and negative necessary conditions for the occurrence of this instance. Nor is it necessary that the collection of positive observed instances should be larger or taken from more extensively dif-ferent circumstances than many we actually have. Nor, finally, is it necessary that breakdowns should never have occurred in *any* domain. All that is nec-essary in this connection is that there should have been no breakdowns in the same domain. Or if any did occur in the same domain they must have proved capable of correlation with certain special features which are known not to be present in the subject of the prediction.

Anybody who takes the trouble to observe the ordinary usage of the word 'reason' in connection with inductive arguments can easily check up on these claims.

It may be interesting to return for a moment to the case of the chicken which finally had its neck wrung. If we had explored every corner of the uni-verse with wonderfully fine instruments and failed to discover a Controller of human movements, then in any ordinary sense of 'being in a better position' we should undoubtedly be in a better position in the case of the man jumping out of the Empire State Building than the chicken in regard to its meals. If Russell even then denied that we are in a better position he is surely using the phrase 'being in a better position' in a strange sense. Or else he is asserting a very plain falsehood. For to say that pos-session of one set of observed facts, say P, puts one in a better position with regard to a certain induc-tive conclusion, say c, than possession of another set of observed facts, say Q, simply means that P is a reason for c while Q is not, or that P is a better rea-son than Q.

Moreover, even without having explored every corner of the universe, we *are* in a very much better position in the case of predicting the sun's rising or the movement of a man jumping from the Empire State Building than the chicken is regarding its meals. The truth is that Russell's analogy, although it is not wholly pointless, is very weak indeed. Its only merit consists in bringing out the fact that neither we nor the chicken have explored every corner of the universe. On the other hand, there are two important differences which Russell obscures when he says that even in the case of our most trusted sci-entific theories we may be in no better a position than the chicken. Firstly, the number of observed instances supporting our prediction in a case like the man's jumping from the Empire State Building is obviously much greater than the number of positive instances observed by the chicken. And secondly, although we cannot definitely say that there is nowhere a Controller of human motions, we certainly have no reason whatsoever to suppose that one exists. We have no reason whatsoever to suppose that a living individual, in any ordinary sense of 'control', controls the movements of human beings who jump out of a house. The chicken, on the other hand, if it knows anything, knows that it depends for its meals on another living object.

C. Let us now turn to question (2): Is there any number, n, of observed positive instances of a phenomenon which affords evidence that the $n + 1$st instance will also be positive? I have already mentioned the familiar fact that scientists as well as ordinary people of a certain level of intelligence do not rely for their inductive conclusions on the number of observed positive instances exclusively. However, it will be easier to discuss the question before us if we proceed on the assumption that according to commonsense the strength of past experience as evidence depends on the number of observed positive instances and on nothing else. All important points can be made more easily if we proceed on this assumption.

Now, in two senses the answer to question (2) must be admitted to be a clear 'No'. Firstly, even if there were in every domain or in some domains a number of observed positive instances which constitutes the dividing line between evidence and non-evidence or, as it is more commonly expressed, between sufficient and insufficient evidence, there is no reason whatsoever to suppose that the number would be the same for different domains. There is no reason to suppose that in the domain of animal learning, for example, the number is the same as in the domain of the movements of the heavenly bodies. But, secondly, there is no such number in *any* domain. For we are here clearly faced with a case of what is sometimes called 'continuous variation'. There is no more *a* number dividing sufficient from insufficient evidence than there is a number dividing bald people from those who are not bald or poor people from people who are not poor.

These facts, however, imply nothing against commonsense. For, from the fact that there is no rigid division between sufficient and insufficient evidence, it does not follow that there are no cases of sufficient evidence. From the fact that there is no number which constitutes the borderline between adequate collections of positive instances and those which are not adequate it does not follow that no number of positive instances is adequate. Although we cannot point to a number which divides bald people from people who are not bald, we can without any hesitation say that a man without a single hair on his head is bald while one with a million hairs on his head is not bald.

Furthermore, just as we can say about many people that they are bald and about many others that they are not bald although we have not counted the number of hairs on their heads and just as we can say that Rockefeller is rich although we cannot even approximately say what is the dollar-equivalent of his total possessions, so we can very often say *that* a number of observed instances constitutes sufficient evidence although we cannot say *what* this number is. The number of instances supporting the theory of gravitation which human beings have observed is for example more than sufficient evidence—in any ordinary sense of the word—for supposing that the man jumping out of the Empire State Building will move in a downward direction. But nobody knows what this number is. Human beings simply do not bother to keep records of all instances which confirm the law of gravity.

IV

A few words must now be said about the claim, made by Russell, Ewing, and others, that empiricism cannot provide a justification of induction since any inductive or empirical justification of induction would necessarily beg the question. If the principle of induction 'is not true', to use Russell's words, 'every attempt to arrive at general scientific laws from particular observations is fallacious, and Hume's scepticism is inescapable for an empiricist'. But 'the principle itself cannot, without circularity, be inferred from observed uniformities, since it is required to justify any such inference'.

In the light of our remarks about redefinitions it is easy to see that all claims of this nature are either mistaken or else cases of *ignoratio elenchi* by redefinition. Before showing this, it will be well to restate the principle of induction in a form which is less confusing than that which Russell uses. Let us try the following formulation:

> The greater the number of positive instances of a phenomenon which have been observed, assuming that no or none except easily explicable negative instances have been found, *and* the greater the number of kinds from which the positive instances are drawn, the less often does it happen that a new instance of the phenomenon turns out to be negative.

I admit that this statement is rather vague and I also admit that, unless one qualifies it so as to deprive it of all factual significance, one can find exceptions to it.

At the same time, it seems plain that the principle as here stated is very much closer to the truth than its contrary. Furthermore, whether or not it would be correct to regard the inductive principle as a *premiss* of all inductive arguments, it does seem to me part of the *reason* for every inductive conclusion. I mean by this that we would not apply 'reason' to a large number of positive and widely varied instances if the contrary of the inductive principle were true or nearer the truth than the inductive principle. Supposing, for example, it had been found in all domains that after 10,000 instances had been observed, all of them positive and gathered from very varied circumstances, chaos was found among the rest. After the 10,000th instance, in other words, predictions always became thoroughly unreliable. Supposing that in these circumstances we discover a new species of animal—let us call them grats. We want to find how long it takes the grats to solve a certain puzzle and find that all our first 10,000 subjects can solve it in less than an hour. Would we say, knowing what happened in all the many observed domains after the 10,000th instance, we had a reason for supposing that the 10,001st grat would also solve the puzzle in less than an hour? It seems clear that most of us would refuse to say this.

It is now apparent that my analysis in Section II of the main sense and also of the second ordinary sense of 'reason for an inductive conclusion' was incomplete. It will be sufficient here to indicate how my analysis requires to be supplemented in the case of the main sense. To say that *p* is a reason for an induc-

tive conclusion, in the main sense of 'reason', is to say firstly that part of *p* asserts what I earlier claimed the whole of *p* to assert *and* secondly that the rest of *p* asserts the inductive principle. Part of *p* asserts the inductive principle at least in the sense of asserting that it is much closer to the truth than its contrary.

Miss Ambrose, in her splendid article on induction, has tried to meet the charge of *petitio principii* by contending that the principle of induction is not a premiss of inductive arguments, but a principle of inference or substitution *according* to which 'inductive inferences are made'. But this seems to me an inadequate reply to the charge. For the enemies of commonsense might admit that what Miss Ambrose says is true of the principle as Russell is in the habit of formulating it. But they might then proceed to restate it in some such way as I have done, maintaining that in this sense it does form part of the reason for every inductive conclusion. At this stage they would undoubtedly renew their charge that the inductive argument cannot be supported by an inductive argument without begging the question.

And I want to show now that my admission that the inductive principle is part of the reason for every inductive conclusion implies nothing against commonsense or against empiricism. For this purpose it is necessary to distinguish two possible senses of any statement of the form 'All S are P'. Such a statement may either mean 'All *observed* S are P'; or it may mean 'All S *whatsoever* are P'. I propose to refer to statements of the first class as 'universal premisses' and to statements of the second class as 'universal conclusions'. Now, the charge of *petitio principii* could be sustained only if the inductive principle were meant as a universal *conclusion* when forming part of the evidence of inductive conclusions. But it is clear that when it forms part of the evidence of inductive conclusions, the inductive principle is or requires to be meant only as a universal *premiss*. We would refuse to regard a large collection of exclusively positive and widely varied instances of a phenomenon as a good reason for predicting that the next instance will also be positive if in all or most previous cases large collections of exclusively positive and widely varied instances turned out to be a thoroughly unreliable basis for prediction. However, given a large collection of exclusively positive and widely varied instances of a phenomenon, it would be sufficient for a correct application of 'reason' that in all or most *observed* cases large collections of exclusively positive and widely varied instances turned out to be a reliable basis for prediction. Any opinion to the contrary rests on the belief, exploded in the previous section, that according to ordinary usage 'reason for an inductive conclusion' means 'deductively conclusive reason for the inductive conclusion'.

V

I can well imagine that some people will not be moved by what I have said. Even if Russell himself were convinced, there are undoubtedly other philosophers who would take me to task for evading what they would declare to be the real issue. 'You may have shown,' it would be said, 'that in the ordinary sense of "reason" and "evidence" past observations do often constitute a good reason and sufficient evidence. But how do you know that what is a reason in the ordinary sense is *really* a *reason?* The fact that the sun has risen every day so far is admittedly a reason, in the ordinary sense, for supposing that it will again rise tomorrow. For to say this is simply to say that it has always risen in the past. But *can you predict* that the sun will again rise tomorrow simply because it has always risen in the past? The question, the interesting doubt about induction in this instance is not: Have we any reason in the ordinary sense for supposing that the sun will rise tomorrow? To this, we agree, the answer is "Yes". The real question is: Having a reason, in the ordinary sense, for believing that the sun will rise tomorrow, can we infer from this with any reliability that the sun will again rise tomorrow?'

Before I take up this objection I should like to fill in a gap in my analysis of the ordinary usage of the phrase 'reason for an inductive conclusion'. It will be remembered that in Section III I distinguished between three trends in the ordinary usage of this phrase. Firstly there is what I called the main sense of the word; secondly there is a set of trends which I grouped together as the second sense of the word; and finally there is a trend or sense to which I alluded but which I have so far not attempted to analyse. According to both senses I analysed, '*p* constitutes a reason for *c*' (where *c* stands for some inductive conclusion) asserts the existence of *observed*

events exclusively. Its truths need not at all be affected by the discovery that *c* is false.

Now, the third sense which I have not yet analysed is much less prominent than the main sense but, so far as I can see, much more prominent than the trends which I have grouped together as the second sense. When 'reason' is used in this third sense the observed facts referred to by 'reason' in the main sense are part of its referent, but they are not the whole of it. It is not indeed a necessary condition for the application of 'reason' (in this sense) to a set of propositions, say *p*, that the prediction based on *p* be *true*. But, where the prediction refers to a multitude of events, it is a necessary condition that it be considerably nearer the truth than its contrary. Where the prediction explicitly refers to a single event only, it is a necessary condition that a considerable majority of instantial predictions having the same relation to *p* be true. Thus, according to the third sense, we would have had a reason for believing that the man jumping out of the Empire State Building will move in a downward direction although subsequent observation shows him to move into the sky—provided that in most other cases, as yet unobserved at the time of making our prediction, human bodies did in similar circumstances move downwards. With our large collection of exclusively positive and widely varied past instances, we would have had a reason for believing that all men who will jump out of houses are going to move in a downward direction even if a few of them disappeared in the sky so long as *most* of them moved as we predicted. We would have had no reason in this third sense if in the case of a large proportion of subsequent jumps— approaching half the total number of new jumps— bodies failed to move in a downward direction.

It will be helpful to use different signs to distinguish between a reason in the main and a reason in the third sense. Let us use the sign 'reason *m*' to stand for reasons in the main sense and the sign 'reason *f*' to signify reasons in the third sense. Using this terminology, we may restate the objection outlined at the beginning of the present section as follows: 'You have shown that frequently people have reasons *m* for believing in inductive conclusions. However, the real question is whether, without appealing to a non-empirical principle, they ever have reasons *f*; and this you have not shown.' I could have stated this charge more easily by using the words 'probable' and 'certain'. But, as I explained earlier, an explicit discussion of the questions 'Are any inductive conclusions probable?' and 'Are any inductive conclusions certain?' is beyond my scope.

In reply to this charge, I wish to make two comments. The first of these is as follows: it simply is a fact that, given certain sets of observations, human beings can make true predictions. It simply is a fact that given reasons in the sense of reason m we very often also have reasons in the sense of reason f. This is a fact just as it is a fact that human beings can make genuine observations and just as it is a fact that certain objects have certain spatial relations to one another and that some events happen after other events. It is logically and also I think factually possible to have feelings of doubt and anxiety concerning the outcome of any prediction whatsoever. But it is also possible to have such doubts about the genuineness of observations at the present moment and about the reality of spatial and temporal relations. The possibility or the actual existence of such feelings no more implies that human beings cannot in certain circumstances make true predictions than it implies that they never make genuine observations or that there are no real relations in space and time.

Secondly, it seems to me that a person who has all the information which ordinary mortals have but who nevertheless asks, with an air of infinite puzzlement 'How can we now predict something which is not yet?' is tacitly confusing the statement 'c is true' with the statement 'c has been or is being directly verified'. 'c can now be correctly predicted' does indeed imply 'c is true', but it does not imply 'c has been directly verified'. To say that we have a reason f for c does imply that c is at least probable. It does not imply that c has already been directly tested. Now, if 'correctly predict' is used in any ordinary sense, then the question 'How can we now predict an event which is not yet?' produces no cramps and can easily be answered by referring to the truth of past predictions in certain circumstances. Questions like 'How can we now predict something which is not yet?' give rise to headaches only if 'c can now be

correctly predicted' is used in such a way as to imply 'c has been directly verified'. Sentences like this then produce cramps and headaches because they are not really questions at all. They are like rhetorical questions. The sentence 'How can we now predict something which is not yet?' is then another way of *asserting* the *necessary* proposition that in the high sense of 'predict' in which 'c can now be correctly predicted' implies 'c has been directly verified', it is impossible ever to predict a future event. But this of course does not at all contradict the commonsense view that in the ordinary sense of 'predict' we can frequently predict future events. This objection, too, is therefore an *ignoratio elenchi* by redefinition.

To be more precise: the sentence 'How can we now predict something which is not yet?' produces a cramp if one believes oneself to be asking the (easy) question which the sentence expresses with every word in it used in its ordinary sense when one is in fact *asserting* the necessary proposition that in a certain high sense of 'predict' we can never predict anything at all.

Following Moore, Mr. J. N. Findlay has forcibly drawn attention to the queerness of the philosopher's doubt when he utters sentences like 'But how can any one set of facts furnish a valid basis for an inference concerning another set of facts?', 'How do you know that one thing ever happens after another?' or 'How do you know that one thing is ever to the left of another?' Findlay suggests that we take a specific instance—e.g. what we would normally describe as a pencil lying to the left of a pen—point it out to the doubting philosopher, and say, 'This is how.' In the case of predictions we could take a piece of chalk and call out, 'I now predict that when I release this piece of chalk it will move in a downward direction.' We would then release it, and, as it falls in a downward direction, we would point to it and say, 'This is how we can know in advance.' Since the philosopher is just as familiar with these facts as we are and since he does not, in one important sense at least, query any of them, it is apparent that, without realizing it, he is using one or more of his words in a strange sense.

BRIAN SKYRMS

The Pragmatic Justification of Induction

Remember that the traditional problem of induction can be formulated as a dilemma: If the reasoning we use to rationally justify scientific inductive logic is to have any strength at all it must be either deductively valid or inductively strong. But if we try to justify scientific inductive logic by means of a deductively valid argument with premises that are known to be true, our conclusion will be too weak. And if we try to use an inductively strong argument, we are reduced to begging the question. Whereas the proponent of the *inductive* justification of scientific induction attempts to go over the second horn of the dilemma, the proponent of the *pragmatic* justification of induction attacks the first horn; he attempts to justify scientific inductive logic by means of a deductively valid argument.

The pragmatic justification of induction was proposed by Herbert Feigl and elaborated by Hans Reichenbach, both founders of the logical empiricist movement.[1] Reichenbach's pragmatic justification of induction is quite complicated, for it depends on what he believes are the details (at least the basic details) of scientific inductive logic. Thus no one can fully understand Reichenbach's arguments until he has studied Reichenbach's definition of probability and the method he prescribes for discovering probabilities. We shall return to these questions later; at this point we will discuss a simplified version of the pragmatic justification of induction. This version is correct as far as it goes. Only bear in mind that there is more to be learned.

Reichenbach wishes to justify scientific inductive logic by a deductively valid argument. Yet he agrees with Hume that no deductively valid argument with premises that are known to be true can give us the conclusion that scientific induction will give us true conclusions from true premises most of the time. He agrees with Hume that the conditions of Rational Justification, Suggestion I cannot be met. Since he fully intends to rationally justify scientific inductive logic, the only path open to him is to argue that the conditions of Rational Justification, Suggestion I need not be met in order to justify a system of inductive logic. He proceeds to advance his own suggestion as to what is required for rational justification and to attempt to justify scientific inductive logic in these terms.

If Hume's arguments are correct, there is no way of showing that scientific induction will give us true conclusions from true premises most of the time. But since Hume's arguments apply equally well to any system of inductive logic there is no way of showing that any competing system of inductive logic will give us true conclusions from true premises most of the time either. Thus scientific inductive logic has the same status as all other systems of inductive logic in this matter. No other system of inductive logic can be demonstrated to be superior to scientific inductive logic in the sense of showing that it gives true conclusions from true premises more often than scientific inductive logic.

Reichenbach claims that although it is impossible to show that any inductive method will be successful, it can be shown that scientific induction will be successful, if any method of induction will be successful. In other words, it is possible that no inductive logic will guide us to arguments that give us true conclusions from true premises most of the time, but if any method will then scientific inductive logic will also. If this can be shown, then it would seem fair to say that scientific induction has been rationally justified. After all, we must make some sort of judgments, conscious or unconscious, as to the inductive strength of arguments if we are to live at all. We must base our decisions on our expectations of the future, and we base our expectations of the future on our knowledge of the past and present. We are all gamblers, with the stakes being the success or failure of our plans of action. Life is an exploration of the unknown, and every human action presumes a wager with nature.

But if our decisions are a gamble and if no method is guaranteed to be successful, then it would seem rational to bet on that method which will be successful, if any method will. Suppose that you were force-ably taken into a locked room and told that whether or not you will be allowed to live depends on whether you win or lose a wager. The object of the wager is a box with red, blue, yellow, and orange lights on it. You know nothing about the construction of the box but are told that either all of the lights, some of them, or none of them will come on. You are to bet on one of the colors. If the colored light you choose comes on, you live; if not, you die. But before you make your choice you are also told that neither the blue, nor the yellow, nor the orange light can come on without the red light also coming on. If this is the only informa-tion you have, then you will surely bet on red. For although you have no guarantee that your bet on red will be successful (after all, all the lights might remain dark) you know that, if any bet will be successful, a bet on red will be successful. Reichenbach claims that scientific inductive logic is in the same privileged position vis-à-vis other systems of inductive logic as is the red light vis-à-vis the other lights.

This leads us to a new proposal as to what is required to rationally justify a system of inductive logic:

Rational Justification

Suggestion III: A system of inductive logic is rationally justified if we can show that the argu-ments that it adjudges inductively strong will give us true conclusions from true premises most of the time, if arguments adjudged induc-tively strong by any method will.

Reichenbach attempts to show that scientific inductive logic meets the conditions of Rational Justification, Suggestion III by a deductively valid argument. The argument goes roughly like this:

Either nature is uniform or it is not. If nature is uniform, scientific induction will be suc-cessful. If nature is not uniform, then no method will be successful.

If any method of induction will be successful, then scientific induction will be successful.

There is no question that this argument is deduc-tively valid, and the first and second premises are surely known to be true. But how do we know that the third premise is true? Couldn't there be some strange inductive method that would be successful even if nature were not uniform? How do we know that for any method to be successful nature must be uniform?

Reichenbach has a response ready for this chal-lenge. Suppose that in a completely chaotic universe, some method, call it method X, were successful. Then there is still at least one outstanding unifor-mity in nature: the uniformity of method X's suc-cess. And scientific induction would discover *that* uniformity. That is, if method X is successful on the whole, if it gives us true conclusions from true premises most of the time, then sooner or later the statement "Method X has been reliable in the past" will be true, and the following argument would be adjudged inductively strong by scientific inductive logic:

Method X has been reliable in the past.

Method X will be reliable in the future.

Thus if method X is successful, scientific induction will also be successful in that it will discover method X's reliability and, so to speak, license method X as a subsidiary method of prediction. This completes the proof that scientific induction will be successful if any method will.

The job may appear to be done, but in fact there is a great deal more to be said. In order to analyze just what has been proved and what has not, we shall use the idea of levels of inductive logic, which was developed in the last section. When we talk about a method, we are really talking about a system of inductive logic, while glossing over the fact that a system of inductive logic is composed of distinct levels of rules. Let us now pay attention to this fact. Since a system of inductive logic is composed of distinct levels of rules, in order to justify that system we would have to justify each level of its rules. Thus to justify scientific inductive logic we would have to justify level 1 rules of scientific inductive logic, level 2 rules of scientific inductive logic, level 3 rules of scientific inductive logic, etc. If each of these levels of rules is to be justified in accordance with the principle "It is rational to rely on a method that is successful if any method is successful," then the pragmatic justification of induction must establish the following:

1: Level 1 rules of scientific induction will be successful if level 1 rules of any system of inductive logic will be successful.

2: Level 2 rules of scientific induction will be successful if level 2 rules of any system of inductive logic will be successful.

$\vdots$ $\vdots$

k: Level k rules of scientific induction will be successful if level k rules of any system of inductive logic will be successful.

But if we look closely at the pragmatic justification of induction, we see that it does not establish this but rather something quite different.

Suppose that system X of inductive logic is successful on level 1. That is, the arguments that it adjudges to be inductively strong give us true conclusions from true premises most of the time. Then sooner or later an argument on level 2 which is adjudged inductively strong by scientific inductive logic, that is:

> Rules of level 1 of system X have been reliable in the past.
> _____
> Rules of level 1 of system X will be reliable in the future.

will come to have a premise that is known to be true. If the rules on level 1 of system X give true conclusions from true premises most of the time, then sooner or later it will be true that they have given us true conclusions from true premises most of the time *in the past*. And once we have this premise, scientific induction on level 2 leads us to the conclusion that they will be reliable in the future.

Thus what has been shown is that if any system of inductive logic has successful rules on level 1, then scientific induction provides a justifying argument for these rules on level 2. Indeed we can generalize this principle and say that if a system of inductive logic has successful rules on a given level, then scientific induction provides a justifying argument on the next highest level. More precisely, the pragmatist has demonstrated the following: If system X of inductive logic has rules on level k which pick out, as inductively strong arguments of level k,

those which give true conclusions from true premises most of the time, then there is an argument on level k + 1, which is adjudged inductively strong by the rules of level k + 1 of scientific inductive logic, which has as its conclusion the statement that the rules of system X on level k are reliable, and which has a premise that will sooner or later be known to be true.

Now this is quite different from showing that if any method works on any level then scientific induction will also work on *that* level, or even from showing that if any method works on level 1 then scientific induction will work on level 1. Instead what has been shown is that if any other method is generally successful on level 1 then scientific induction will have at least one notable success on level 2: it will eventually predict the continued success of that other method on level 1.

Although this is an interesting and important conclusion, it is not sufficient for the task at hand. Suppose we wish to choose a set of rules for level 1. In order to be in a position analogous to the wager about the box with the colored lights, we would have to know that scientific induction would be successful on level 1 if any method were successful on level 1. But we do not know this. For all we know, scientific induction might fail on level 1 and another method might be quite successful. If this were the case, scientific induction on level 2 would eventually tell us so, but this is quite a different matter.

In summary, the attempt at a pragmatic justification of induction has made us realize that a deductive justification of induction would be acceptable if it could establish that: if any system of inductive logic has successful rules on a given level, then scientific inductive logic will have successful rules on that level. But the arguments advanced in the pragmatic justification fail to establish this conclusion. Instead they show that if any system of inductive logic has successful rules on a given level, then scientific inductive logic will license a justifying argument for those rules on the next higher level.

Both the attempt at a pragmatic justification and the attempt at an inductive justification have failed to justify scientific induction. Nevertheless, both of them have brought forth useful facts about scientific induction, and we should try to utilize these facts. For instance, we might try to combine the pragmatic and inductive justifications of induction. That is, we might argue that the facts that were established in the pragmatic justification of induction provide a rationale for using scientific induction on higher levels to justify rules of induction on lower levels, and that the inductive justification of induction shows that, by this process, scientific induction is rationally justified on all levels. After all, the chief thorn in the side of the inductive justification of induction was the counterinductivist. And the pragmatic justification of induction shows one clear advantage of scientific induction over counterinduction. The counterinductivist cannot prove that if any method is successful on level 1, counterinduction on level 2 will eventually predict its continued success.

I am not advancing this view as *the* answer to the traditional problem of induction; it has several difficulties, one of which involves the word "eventually." What I am emphasizing is that there is still room for constructive thought on the problem, and that we can learn much from previous failures to solve it.

NOTE

1. However, the intellectual ancestry of the pragmatic justification can he traced back to Charles Saunders Peirce, the founder of American pragmatism and, in the opinion of many, the greatest philosopher that America has produced.

P. F. STRAWSON

from Hume, Wittgenstein and Induction

3. HUME: Reason and Nature

Is there any other way with skepticism which is not a variant on those I have referred to, i.e. is neither an attempt directly to refute it by rational argument drawing on commonsense or theological or quasi-scientific considerations nor an attempt indirectly to refute it by showing that it is in some way unintelligible or self-defeating? I think there is another way. There is nothing new about it, since it is at least as old as Hume; and the most powerful latter-day exponent of a closely related position is Wittgenstein. I shall call it the way of Naturalism; though this name is not to be understood in the sense of Quine's "naturalised epistemology."

In a famous sentence in Book II of the *Treatise* Hume limits the pretensions of reason to determine the ends of action. In a similar spirit, towards the end of Book I, he limits the pretensions of reason to determine the formation of beliefs concerning matters of fact and existence. He points out that all arguments in *support* of the skeptical position are totally inefficacious; and, by the same token, all arguments *against* it are totally idle. His point is really the very simple one that, whatever arguments may be produced on one side or the other of the question, we simply *cannot help* believing in the existence of body, and *cannot help* forming beliefs and expectations in general accordance with the basic canons of induction. He might have added, though he did not discuss this question, that the belief in the existence of other people (hence other minds) is equally inescapable. Hume regularly expresses his point by reference to Nature, which leaves us no option in these matters but "by absolute and uncontrollable necessity" determines us "to judge as well as to breathe and feel." Speaking of that total skepticism which, arguing from the fallibility of human judgment, would tend to undermine all belief and

opinion, he says: "Whoever has taken the pains to refute the cavils of this total scepticism has really disputed without an antagonist and endeavoured by arguments to establish a faculty which Nature has antecedently implanted in the mind and rendered unavoidable." He goes on to point out that what holds for total skepticism holds also for skepticism about the existence of body. Even the professed skeptic "*must assent* to the principle concerning the existence of body, though he cannot pretend by any arguments of philosophy to maintain its veracity"; for "nature has not left this to his choice, and has doubtless esteemed it an affair of too great importance to be entrusted to our uncertain reasonings and speculations." Hence " 'tis vain to ask Whether there be body or not? That is a point which we must take for granted in all our reasonings."

Here I interpolate some remarks which are not strictly to the present purpose but which are very much the purpose if one is considering the question of Hume himself. Hume contrasts the vain question, *Whether there be body or not?* with a question he says "we may well ask," viz. *What causes induce us to believe in the existence of body?*—thus seeming to anticipate Quine's program for a naturalized epistemology. But there follows, in Hume, what seems to be a striking inconsistency between principle and practice. For, having said that the existence of body is a point which we must take for granted in *all* our reasonings, he then conspicuously does *not* take it for granted in the reasonings which he addresses to the causal question. Indeed those reasonings famously point to a skeptical conclusion. So, as he himself is the first to acknowledge, there is an unresolved tension in Hume's position (a tension which may be found reminiscent in some ways of the tension between Kant's empirical realism and his transcendental idealism). One might speak of two Humes: Hume the skeptic and Hume the naturalist; where Hume's naturalism, as illustrated by the passages I quoted, appears as something like a refuge from his skepticism. An exponent of a more thoroughgoing naturalism could accept the question, *What causes induce us to believe in the existence of body?* as one we may well ask, as one that can be referred to empirical psychology, to the study of infantile development; but would do so in the justified expectation that answers to it would in fact take for granted the existence of body.

Hume, then, we may say, is ready to accept and to tolerate a distinction between two levels of thought: the level of philosophically critical thinking which can offer us no assurances against skepticism; and the level of everyday empirical thinking, at which the pretensions of critical thinking are completely overridden and suppressed by Nature, by inescapable natural commitment to belief: to belief in the existence of body and in inductively based expectations. (I hinted at a parallel with Kant; and a parallel there is, though it is only a loose one. There is a parallel in that Kant also recognizes two levels of thought: the empirical level at which we justifiably claim knowledge of an external world of causally related objects in space; and the critical level at which we recognize that this world is only appearance, appearance of an ultimate reality of which we can have no positive knowledge at all. The parallel, however, is only a loose one. Where Hume refers to an inescapable *natural disposition* to belief, Kant produces *argument* [transcendental argument] to show that what, at the empirical level, is rightly reckoned as empirical knowledge of an external world of law-governed objects is a necessary condition of self-awareness, of knowledge of our own inner states; and—a yet more striking difference—where, at the critical level, Hume leaves us with unrefuted skepticism, Kant offers us his own brand of idealism.)

Here I end my digression concerning the complex tensions in Hume's thought and the parallels with Kant; and return to a consideration of Hume as naturalist, leaving on one side Hume the skeptic. According to Hume the naturalist, skeptical doubts are not to be met by argument. They are simply to be neglected (except, perhaps, in so far as they supply a harmless amusement, a mild diversion to the intellect). They are to be neglected because they are *idle;* powerless against the force of nature, of our naturally implanted disposition to belief. This does not mean

that Reason has no part to play in relation to our beliefs concerning matters of fact and existence. It has a part to play, though a subordinate one: as Nature's lieutenant rather than Nature's commander. (Here we may recall and adapt that famous remark about Reason and the passions.) Our inescapable natural commitment is to a general frame of belief and to a general style (the inductive) of belief-formation. But *within* that frame and style, the requirement of Reason, that our beliefs should form a consistent and coherent system, may be given full play. Thus, for example, though Hume did not think that a rational justification of induction in general was either necessary or possible, he could quite consistently proceed to frame "rules for judging of cause and effect." Though it is Nature which commits us to inductive belief-formation in general, it is Reason which leads us to refine and elaborate our inductive canons and procedures and, in their light, to criticize, and sometimes to reject, what in detail we find ourselves naturally inclined to believe.

4. HUME AND WITTGENSTEIN

In introducing this way with skepticism, I associated the name of Wittgenstein with that of Hume. I have in mind primarily Wittgenstein's notes *On Certainty.* Like Hume, Wittgenstein distinguishes between those matters—those propositions—which are up for question and decision in the light of reason and experience and those which are not, which are, as he puts it, "exempt from doubt." Of course there are differences between Hume and Wittgenstein. We do not, for example, find in Wittgenstein any explicit repetition of Hume's quite explicit appeal to Nature. But, as we shall see, the resemblances, and even the echoes, are more striking than the differences. Above all, there is, in Wittgenstein's work, as in Hume's, the distinction between "what it is vain" to make a matter of inquiry, what "we must take for granted in all our reasonings," as Hume puts it, on the one hand, and what is genuinely matter for inquiry on the other.

Wittgenstein has a host of phrases to express this antithesis. Thus he speaks of a kind of conviction or belief as *"beyond being justified or unjustified; as it were, as something animal"* (359); and here we may find an echo of Hume's appeal to Nature and, even more, of Hume's remark that "belief is more properly an act of the sensitive than of the cogitative part of our nature." Again, Wittgenstein says that "certain propositions seem to *underlie* all questions and all thinking" (415); that "some propositions are *exempt from doubt*" (341); that "certain things are *in deed* [in der Tat, in practice] not doubted" (342); he speaks of "belief that is not founded" (253) but "in the entire system of our language-games *belongs to the foundations*" (411). Again, he speaks of "propositions which have *a peculiar logical role* in the system [of our empirical propositions]" (136); which belong to our *"frame of reference"* (83); which *"stand fast or solid"* (151); which constitute the "world-picture" which is "the *substratum* of all my enquiring and asserting" (162) or "the *scaffolding* of our thoughts" (211) or "the element in which arguments have their life" (105). This world-picture, he says, is not something he has because he has satisfied himself of its correctness. "No: it is the inherited background against which I distinguish between true and false" (94). He compares the propositions describing this world-picture to the rules of a game which "can be learned purely practically without learning any explicit rules" (95).

Though the general tendency of Wittgenstein's position is clear enough, it is not easy to extract a wholly clear consecutive statement of it from the mass of figures or metaphors which I have illustrated. Evidently his aim, at least in part, is to give a realistic account or description of how it actually is with our human systems or bodies of belief. Evidently, too, he distinguishes, as I have said, between those propositions, or actual or potential elements in our belief-systems, which we treat as subject to empirical confirmation or falsification, which we consciously incorporate in our belief-system (when we do) for this or that *reason* or on the basis of this or that *experience,* or which we actually treat as matter for inquiry or doubt—and, on the other hand, those elements of our belief-system which have a quite different character, alluded to by the figures of scaffolding, framework, background, substratum, etc. (The metaphors include that of foundations; but it is quite clear that Wittgenstein does not regard these propositions, or elements of the belief-system, as foundations in the traditional empiricist sense, i.e. as basic reasons, themselves resting on experience, for the rest of our beliefs. The metaphor of a scaffolding or framework, within which the activity of building or modifying the structure of our beliefs goes on, is a better one.)

Wittgenstein does not represent this distinction between two kinds of elements in our belief-systems as sharp, absolute, and unchangeable. On the contrary. And this is just as well in view of some of his examples of propositions of the second class, i.e. of propositions which are "exempt from doubt." (Writing in 1950–51, he gives as one example the proposition that no one has been very far [e.g. as far as the moon] from the surface of the earth.) It would have been helpful, though probably contrary to his inclinations, if he had drawn distinctions, or indicated a *principle* of distinction, *within* this class. An indication that there are such distinctions to be drawn comes at the end of an extended metaphor (96–99) in which he compares those propositions which are subject to empirical test to the waters moving in a river and those which are not so subject to the bed or banks of the river. The situation is not unchangeable in that there may sometimes be shifts of the bed or even of the bank. But, he concludes, "The bank of that river consists partly of hard rock, *subject to no alteration or only to an imperceptible one,* partly of sand which now in one place now in another gets washed away or deposited."

But how close, really, is Wittgenstein to Hume? There are points at which he may seem closer to Carnap. These are the points at which he seems disposed to express his sense of the difference between those propositions which are subject to empirical test and those which form the scaffolding, framework, foundations etc. of our thought (the hard rock of the river bank) by denying to the latter the status of propositions at all—comparing them, as we have seen, to rules "which can be learned purely practically." Thus he writes at one point: "No such proposition as 'There are physical objects' can be formulated" (36); and even that " 'There are physical objects' is nonsense" (35). But he is not very close to Carnap. Carnap speaks of a practical issue, a choice—a decision to adopt, or to persist in the use of, a certain framework. There is nothing of this in Wittgenstein. "It is not," he says, "as if we *chose* the game" (317). And elsewhere, though he is dissatisfied with the expression, we find: "I want to say: propositions of the form of empirical propositions, and not only propositions of logic, form the foundation of all operating with thoughts (with language)" (401). (There is here an evident allusion to the *Tractatus.*) Later, straightforwardly enough, we find: "certain propositions seem to underlie all questions and all thinking." The apparent shilly-shallying over "proposition" is perhaps palliated by the remarks at 319–20, where he speaks of a lack of sharpness in the boundary between rule and empirical proposition and adds that the concept 'proposition' is itself not a sharp one.

To sum up now the relations between Hume and Wittgenstein. Hume's position seems much the simpler. All that is explicitly mentioned by him as constituting the framework of all inquiry—what is to be "taken for granted in all our reasoning"—amounts to two things: acceptance of the existence of body and of the general reliability of inductive belief-formation. This is the groundwork; and its source is unambiguously identified. These unavoidable natural convictions, commitments, or prejudices are ineradicably implanted in our minds by Nature. Wittgenstein's position is, as we have seen, at least superficially more complicated. First, the propositions or crypto-propositions of the framework, though they may be taken to include the two Humean elements, are presumptively more various. Second, the framework is, up to a point at least, dynamically conceived: what was at one time part of the framework may change its status, may assume the character of a hypothesis to be questioned and perhaps falsified—some of what we would now regard as assumptions about supernatural agents or powers presumably come into this category—whereas other parts of the framework remain fixed and unalterable. Finally, and connectedly, Wittgenstein does not speak, as Hume does, of one exclusive source, viz. Nature, for these *préjugés.* Rather, he speaks of our learning, from childhood up, an activity, a practice, a social practice—of making judgements, of forming beliefs—to which the crypto-propositions have the special relation he seeks to illuminate by the figures of framework, scaffolding, substratum etc.; that is, they are not judgments we actually make or, in general, things we explicitly learn or are taught in the course of that practice, but rather reflect the general character of the practice itself, form a frame within which the

judgments we actually make hang together in a more or less coherent way.

In spite of the greater complication of Wittgenstein's position, we can, I think, at least as far as the general skeptical questions are concerned, discern a profound community between him and Hume. They have in common the view that our "beliefs" in the existence of body and, to speak roughly, in the general reliability of induction are not grounded beliefs and at the same time are not open to serious doubt. They are, one might say, outside our critical and rational competence in the sense that they define, or help to define, the area in which that competence is exercised. To attempt to confront the professional skeptical doubt with arguments in support of these beliefs, with rational justifications, is simply to show a total misunderstanding of the role they actually play in our belief-systems. The correct way with the professional skeptical doubt is not to attempt to rebut it with argument, but to point out that it is idle, unreal, a pretense; and then the rebutting arguments will appear as equally idle; the reasons produced in those arguments to justify induction or belief in the existence of body are not, and do not become, *our* reasons for these beliefs; there is no such thing as *the reasons for which we hold* these beliefs. We simply cannot help accepting them as defining the areas within which the questions come up of what beliefs we should rationally hold on such-and-such a matter. The point may be underlined by referring again to some attempts to rebut skepticism by argument.

Perhaps the best skepticism-rebutting argument in favor of the existence of body is the quasi-scientific argument I mentioned earlier: i.e., that the existence of a world of physical objects having more or less the properties which current science attributes to them provides the best available explanation of the phenomena of experience, just as accepted theories within physical science supply the best available explanations of the physical phenomena they deal with. But the implicit comparison with scientific theory simply proclaims its own weakness. We accept or believe the scientific theories (when we do) just because we believe they supply the best available explanations of the phenomena they deal with. That is our reason for accepting them. But no one accepts the existence of the physical world *because* it supplies the best available explanation etc. That is no one's reason for accepting it. Anyone who claimed it was his reason would be pretending. It is, as Hume declared, a point we are naturally bound to take for granted in all our reasonings and, in particular, in all those reasonings which underlie our acceptance of particular physical theories.

Similarly, the best argument against other-minds skepticism is, probably, that, given the non-uniqueness of one's physical constitution and the general uniformity of nature in the biological sphere as in others, it is in the highest degree improbable that one is unique among members of one's species in being the enjoyer of subjective states, and of the kind of subjective states one does enjoy in the kind of circumstances in which one enjoys them. But, again, this is no one's reason for believing in the existence of other minds, of other people, subjects of just such a range of sensations, emotions, and thoughts as he is aware of in himself. We simply react to others as to other *people*. They may puzzle us at times; but that is part of so reacting. Here again we have something which we have no option but to take for granted in all our reasoning.

5. "ONLY CONNECT": The Role of Transcendental Arguments

Suppose we accept this naturalist rejection both of skepticism and of skepticism-rebutting arguments as equally idle—as both involving a misunderstanding of the role in our lives, the place in our intellectual economy, of those propositions or crypto-propositions which the skeptic seeks to place in doubt and his opponent in argument seeks to establish. How, in this perspective, should we view arguments of the kind which Stroud calls "transcendental"? Evidently not as supplying the reasoned rebuttal which the skeptic perversely invites. Our naturalism is precisely the rejection of that invitation. So, even if we have a tenderness for transcendental arguments, we shall be happy to accept the criticism of Stroud and others that either such arguments rely on an unacceptably simple verificationism or the most they can establish is a certain sort of interdependence of conceptual capacities and beliefs: e.g., as I put it earlier, that in order for the intelligible formulation of skeptical doubts to be pos-

sible or, more generally, in or order for self-conscious thought and experience to be possible, we must take it, or *believe*, that we have knowledge of external physical objects or other minds. The fact that such a demonstration of dependence would not refute the skeptic does not worry our naturalist, who repudiates any such aim. But our naturalist might well take satisfaction in the demonstration of these connections—if they can indeed be demonstrated—for their own sake. For repudiation of the project of wholesale validation of types of knowledge-claim does not leave the naturalist without philosophical employment. E. M. Forster's motto—"only connect"—is as valid for the naturalist at the philosophical level as it is for Forster's characters (and us) at the moral and personal level. That is to say, having given up the unreal project of wholesale validation, the naturalist philosopher will embrace the real project of investigating the connections between the major structural elements of our conceptual scheme. If connections as tight as those which transcendental arguments, construed as above, claim to offer are really available, so much the better.

Of course, it is often disputed, both in detail and in general, that arguments of this kind do or can achieve even as much as the most that Stroud allowed them. Typically, a transcendental argument, as now construed, claims that one type of exercise of conceptual capacity is a necessary condition of another (e.g. that taking some experiences to consist in awareness of objects in physical space is a necessary condition of the self-ascription of subjective states as ordered in time or that being equipped to identify some states of mind in others is a necessary condition of being able to ascribe any states of mind to ourselves). I am not now concerned with the question of the validity of such arguments but with the general character of the criticisms to which they are typically subject. Typically, the criticism is that what is claimed to be a necessary condition has not been shown to be so and could not be shown to be so without eliminating all possible (or candidate) alternatives, a task which is not attempted. The transcendental arguer is always exposed to the charge that even if *he* cannot conceive of alternative ways in which conditions of the possibility of a certain kind of experience or exercise of conceptual capacity might be fulfilled, this inability may simply be due to lack of imagination on his part—a lack which makes him prone to mistake sufficient for necessary conditions.

It is not my present purpose to inquire how successfully arguments of the kind in question (on the present relatively modest construal of their aims) survive these criticisms; to inquire, that is, whether some or any of them are strictly valid. I am inclined to think that at least some are (e.g. self-ascription implies the capacity for other-ascription), though I must admit that few, if any, have commanded universal assent among the critics. But whether or not they are strictly valid, these arguments, or weakened versions of them, will continue to be of interest to our naturalist philosopher. For even if they do not succeed in establishing such tight or rigid connections as they initially promise, they do at least indicate or bring out conceptual connections, even if only of a looser kind; and, as I have already suggested, to establish the connections between the major structural features or elements of our conceptual scheme—to exhibit it, not as a rigidly deductive system, but as a coherent whole whose parts are mutually supportive and mutually dependent, interlocking in an intelligible way—to do this may well seem to our naturalist the proper, or at least the major, task of analytical philosophy. As indeed it does to me. (Whence the phrase, "descriptive [as opposed to validatory or revisionary] metaphysics.")

6. THREE QUOTATIONS

Vis-à-vis traditional skepticism, then, I am proposing that we adopt, at least provisionally (and everything in philosophy is provisional), the naturalist position. Or, perhaps, since we have yoked Wittgenstein to Hume in characterizing and illustrating the position, we should qualify the name and, since where Hume speaks only of Nature, Wittgenstein speaks of the language-games we learn from childhood up, i.e. in a social context, should call it, not simply 'naturalism', but 'social naturalism'. Whatever the name, I can perhaps illustrate the break that adoption of it constitutes with other attitudes with the help of two quotations: the first from the greatest of modern philosophers, the second from a philosopher whose title to respect is less con-

siderable, but who nevertheless seems to me to be on the right side of this point.

In the Preface to the second edition of *The Critique of Pure Reason* (B xi) Kant says: "it remains a scandal to philosophy and to human reason in general that the existence of things outside us . . . must be accepted merely on *faith* and that if anyone thinks good to doubt their existence, we are unable to counter his doubts by any satisfactory proof."

In *Being and Time* (I. 6) Heidegger ripostes: "The 'scandal of philosophy' is not that this proof has yet to be given, but that *such proofs are expected and attempted again and again.*"

To complete this short series of quotations, here is one, from Wittgenstein again, that neatly sums things up from the naturalist, or social naturalist, point of view: "It is so difficult to find the *beginning*. Or better: it is difficult to begin at the beginning. And not to try to go further back." (471)

To try to meet the skeptic's challenge, in whatever way, by whatever style of argument, is to try to go further back. If one is to begin at the beginning, one must refuse the challenge as our naturalist refuses it.

7. HISTORICISM: And the Past

But now, as Wittgenstein's first thought—as opposed to what he calls the better thought—in that quotation suggests, the question arises: Where exactly is the beginning? In other words, what are those structural features of our conceptual scheme, the framework features, which must be regarded as equally beyond question and beyond validation, but which offer themselves rather, for the kind of philosophical treatment which I have suggested and which might be called "connective analysis"? Hume, in Book I of the *Treatise,* concentrates, as we saw, on two such features: the habit of induction and the belief in the existence of body, of the physical world. Wittgenstein seems to offer, or suggest, a more miscellaneous collection, though he mitigates the miscellaneousness by the dynamic element in his picture, the provision for change: some things which at some time, or in some context or relation, may have the status of framework features, beyond question or test, may at another time, or in an other context or relation, become open to question or even be rejected; others are fixed and unalterable. Part, though not the whole, of the explanation of what may seem cloudy or unsatisfactory in Wittgenstein's treatment in *On Certainty* is that he is fighting on more than one front. He is not concerned only with the common framework of human belief-systems at large. He is also concerned to indicate what a realistic picture of individual belief-systems is like; and in such a picture room must be found for, as it were, local and idiosyncratic propositions (like "My name is Ludwig Wittgenstein") as elements in someone's belief-system which are, for him, neither grounded nor up for the question. But, obviously, no such proposition as that forms part of the common framework of human belief-systems at large.

But now it might be suggested that—even setting aside the point about individual belief-systems—Wittgenstein's admission of a dynamic element in the *collective* belief-system puts the whole approach in question. Earlier on, the unfortunate example, of the conviction that no one has been as far from the surface of the earth as the moon, was mentioned. One can think of more far-reaching beliefs. Surely the geocentric view of the universe—or at least of what we now call the solar system—at one time formed part of the framework of human thinking at large. Or, again, some form of creation-myth. Or some form of animism. If our "frame of reference," to use Wittgenstein's phrase, can undergo such radical revolutions as the Copernican (the real, not the Kantian, Copernican revolution), why should we assume that anything in it is "fixed and unalterable"? And if we drop that assumption, must we not be content to cast our metaphysics for a more modest— a historical or historicist—role; somewhat in the spirit of Collingwood, who declared that metaphysics was indeed an essentially historical study, the attempt to elicit what he called the "absolute presuppositions" of the science of the day? Metaphysical truth would thus be relativized to historical periods. Derelativization could be achieved only by explicitly assigning a system of presuppositions to its historical place. ("At such-and-such a period it *was* absolutely presupposed that . . ." or "As of now, it *is* absolutely presupposed that . . .")

In fact, there is no reason why metaphysics should tamely submit to historicist pressure of this kind. The human world-picture is of course subject to change.

But it remains a *human world-picture:* a picture of a world of physical objects (bodies) in space and time including human observers capable of action and of acquiring and imparting knowledge (and error) both of themselves and each other and of whatever else is to be found in nature. So much of a constant conception, of what, in Wittgenstein's phrase, is "Not subject to alteration or only to an imperceptible one," is given along with the very idea of historical alteration in the human world-view.

It is all of a piece with Wittgenstein's extreme aversion, in his later work, from any systematic treatment of issues, that he never attempted to specify which aspects of our world-picture, our frame of reference, are "not subject to alteration or only to an imperceptible one"; to which aspects our human or natural commitment is so profound that they stand fast, and may be counted on to stand fast, through all revolutions of scientific thought or social development. So far only those aspects have been specifically mentioned, or dwelt on to any extent, which have a relevance to—or show the irrelevance of—certain traditional skeptical problems: concerning the existence of body, knowledge of other minds and the practice of induction. I shall not attempt now to compile a list, or to engage in the connective metaphysical task of exhibiting the relations and interdependencies of the elements of the general structure. But, before I pass on to a different, though related, set of questions, I want to mention now one further aspect of our thought which seems to have a similarly inescapable character; and I choose it because of its relevance to some current discussions.

It is to be remembered that the point has been, not to offer a rational justification of the belief in external objects and other minds or of the practice of induction, but to represent skeptical arguments and rational counter-arguments as equally idle—not senseless, but idle—since what we have here are original, natural, inescapable commitments which we neither choose nor could give up. The further such commitment which I now suggest we should acknowledge is the commitment to belief in the reality and determinateness of the past. This is worth mentioning at the moment, not because it is a topic of traditional skeptical challenge, but because it is currently a topic of challenge from a certain kind of limited or moderate anti-realism, based on a particular, quasi-verificationist theory of meaning. Of course, it *could* be a topic of skeptical challenge, a challenge, e.g., taking a form which Russell once toyed with: i.e. "We have no guarantee, no certain knowledge, that the world didn't come into existence just five minutes ago; all our current experience, including our apparent memories, could be just as it is consistently with this being the case." But the current challenge is different. Roughly speaking (some of the challengers would probably say this is a good deal too rough), it allows, with respect to questions about the past, that there is a determinate fact of the matter in those cases to which our memories or conclusively confirming or falsifying evidence extend (or it is known could be brought to extend), but no determinate fact of the matter in any other cases. Only those questions about the past which we can answer (or bring ourselves into a position to answer) *have* answers, true or false. (One casualty of this view, evidently, is standard logic—which is deprived of the law of excluded middle.) Much subtlety of argument can be devoted to advancing this view and to opposing it. But my present concern is not to meet it with argument, but to suggest, again, that arguments on both sides are idle, since belief in the reality and determinateness of the past is as much part of that general framework of beliefs to which we are inescapably committed as is belief in the existence of physical objects and the practice of inductive belief formation. Indeed, it would be hard to separate the conception of objects which we have and our acceptance of inductively formed beliefs from that conception of the past. All form part of our mutually supportive natural metaphysics. We are equally happy to acknowledge, with the poet, that full many a flower is born to blush unseen and, with the naturalist metaphysician, that full many a historical fact is destined to remain unverified and unverifiable by subsequent generations.

NELSON GOODMAN

The New Riddle of Induction

1. THE OLD PROBLEM OF INDUCTION

At the close of the preceding lecture, I said that today I should examine how matters stand with respect to the problem of induction. In a word, I think they stand ill. But the real difficulties that confront us today are not the traditional ones. What is commonly thought of as the Problem of Induction has been solved, or dissolved; and we face new problems that are not as yet very widely understood. To approach them, I shall have to run as quickly as possible over some very familiar ground.

The problem of the validity of judgments about future or unknown cases arises, as Hume pointed out, because such judgments are neither reports of experience nor logical consequences of it. Predictions, of course, pertain to what has not yet been observed. And they cannot be logically inferred from what has been observed; for what *has* happened imposes no logical restrictions on what *will* happen. Although Hume's dictum that there are no necessary connections of matters of fact has been challenged at times, it has withstood all attacks. Indeed, I should be inclined not merely to agree that there are no necessary connections of matters of fact, but to ask whether there are any necessary connections at all—but that is another story.

Hume's answer to the question how predictions are related to past experience is refreshingly noncosmic. When an event of one kind frequently follows upon an event of another kind in experience, a habit is formed that leads the mind, when confronted with a new event of the first kind, to pass to the idea of an event of the second kind. The idea of necessary connection arises from the felt impulse of the mind in making this transition.

Now if we strip this account of all extraneous features, the central point is that to the question "Why one prediction rather than another?", Hume answers that the elect prediction is one that accords with a past regularity, because this regularity has established a habit. Thus among alternative statements about a future moment, one statement is distinguished by its consonance with habit and thus with regularities observed in the past. Prediction according to any other alternative is errant.

How satisfactory is this answer? The heaviest criticism has taken the righteous position that Hume's account at best pertains only to the source of predictions, not their legitimacy; that he sets forth the circumstances under which we make given predictions—and in this sense explains why we make them—but leaves untouched the question of our license for making them. To trace origins, runs the old complaint, is not to establish validity: the real question is not why a prediction is in fact made but how it can be justified. Since this seems to point to the awkward conclusion that the greatest of modern philosophers completely missed the point of his own problem, the idea has developed that he did not really take his solution very seriously, but regarded the main problem as unsolved and perhaps as insoluble. Thus we come to speak of 'Hume's problem' as though he propounded it as a question without answer.

All this seems to me quite wrong. I think Hume grasped the central question and considered his answer to be passably effective. And I think his answer is reasonable and relevant, even if it is not entirely satisfactory. I shall explain presently. At the moment, I merely want to record a protest against the prevalent notion that the problem of justifying induction, when it is so sharply dissociated from the problem of describing how induction takes place, can fairly be called Hume's problem.

I suppose that the problem of justifying induction has called forth as much fruitless discussion as has any half-way respectable problem of modern philosophy. The typical writer begins by insisting that some way of justifying predictions must be found; proceeds to argue that for this purpose we need some resounding universal law of the Uniformity of Nature, and then inquires how this universal principle itself can be justified. At this point, if he is tired, he concludes that the principle must be accepted as an indispensable assumption; or if he is energetic and ingenious, he goes on to devise some subtle justification for it. Such an invention, however, seldom satisfies anyone else; and the easier course of accepting an unsubstantiated and even dubious assumption much more sweeping than any actual predictions we make seems an odd and expensive way of justifying them.

2. DISSOLUTION OF THE OLD PROBLEM

Understandably, then, more critical thinkers have suspected that there might be something awry with the problem we are trying to solve. Come to think of it, what precisely would constitute the justification we seek? If the problem is to explain how we know that certain predictions will turn out to be correct, the sufficient answer is that we don't know any such thing. If the problem is to *find* some way of distinguishing antecedently between true and false predictions, we are asking for prevision rather than for philosophical explanation. Nor does it help matters much to say that we are merely trying to show that or why certain predictions arc *probable*. Oftcn it is said that whilc wc cannot tell in advance whether a prediction concerning a given throw of a die is true, we can decide whether the prediction is a probable one. But if this means determining how the prediction is related to actual frequency distributions of future throws of the die, surely there is no way of knowing or proving this in advance. On the other hand, if the judgment that the prediction is probable has nothing to do with subsequent occurrences, then the question remains in what sense a probable prediction is any better justified than an improbable one.

Now obviously the genuine problem cannot be one of attaining unattainable knowledge or of accounting for knowledge that we do not in fact have. A better understanding of our problem can be gained by looking for a moment at what is involved in justifying non-inductive inferences. How do we justify a *de*duction? Plainly, by showing that it conforms to the general rules of deductive inference. An argument that so conforms is justified or valid, even if its conclusion happens to be false. An argument that violates a rule is fallacious even if its conclusion happens to be true. To justify a deductive conclusion therefore requires no knowledge of the facts it pertains to. Moreover, when a deductive argument has been shown to conform to the rules of logical inference, we usually consider it justified without going on to ask what justifies the rules. Analogously, the basic task in justifying an inductive inference is to show that it conforms to the general rules of *in*duction. Once we have recognized this, we have gone a long way towards clarifying our problem.

Yet, of course, the rules themselves must eventually be justified. The validity of a deduction depends not upon conformity to any purely arbitrary rules we may contrive, but upon conformity to valid rules. When we speak of *the* rules of inference we mean the valid rules—or better, *some* valid rules, since there may be alternative sets of equally valid rules. But how is the validity of rules to be determined? Here again we encounter philosophers who insist that these rules follow from some self-evident axiom, and others who try to show that the rules are grounded in the very nature of the human mind. I think the answer lies much nearer the surface. Principles of deductive inference are justified by their conformity with accepted deductive practice. Their validity depends upon accordance with the particular deductive inferences we actually make and sanction. If a rule yields inacceptable inferences, we drop it as invalid. Justification of general rules thus derives from judgments rejecting or accepting particular deductive inferences.

This looks flagrantly circular. I have said that deductive inferences are justified by their conformity to valid general rules, and that general rules are justified by their conformity to valid inferences. But this circle is a virtuous one. The point is that rules and particular inferences alike are justified by being brought into agreement with each other. *A rule is amended if it yields an inference we are unwilling to accept; an inference is rejected if it violates a rule we are unwilling to amend.* The process of justification is the delicate one of making mutual adjustments between rules and accepted inferences; and in the agreement achieved lies the only justification needed for either.

All this applies equally well to induction. An inductive inference, too, is justified by conformity to general rules, and a general rule by conformity to accepted inductive inferences. Predictions are justified if they conform to valid canons of induction; and the canons are valid if they accurately codify accepted inductive practice.

A result of such analysis is that we can stop plaguing ourselves with certain spurious questions about induction. We no longer demand an explanation for guarantees that we do not have, or seek keys to knowledge that we can not obtain. It dawns upon us that the traditional smug insistence upon a hard-and-fast line between justifying induction and describing ordinary inductive practice distorts the problem. And we owe belated apologies to Hume. For in dealing with the question how normally accepted inductive judgments are made, he was in fact dealing with the question of inductive validity. The validity of a prediction consisted for him in its arising from habit, and thus in its exemplifying some past regularity. His answer was incomplete and perhaps not entirely correct; but it was not beside the point. The problem of induction is not a problem of demonstration but a problem of defining the difference between valid and invalid predictions.

This clears the air but leaves a lot to be done. As principles of *de*ductive inference, we have the familiar and highly developed laws of logic; but there are available no such precisely stated and well-recognized principles of inductive inference. Mill's canons hardly rank with Aristotle's rules of the syllogism, let alone with *Principia Mathematica*. Elaborate and valuable treatises on probability usually leave certain fundamental questions untouched. Only in very recent years has there been any explicit and systematic work upon what I call the constructive task of confirmation theory.

3. THE CONSTRUCTIVE TASK OF CONFIRMATION THEORY

The task of formulating rules that define the difference between valid and invalid inductive inferences is much like the task of defining any term with an established usage. If we set out to define the term "tree", we try to compose out of already understood words an expression that will apply to the familiar objects that standard usage calls trees, and that will not apply to objects that standard usage refuses to call trees. A proposal that plainly violates either condition is rejected; while a definition that meets these tests may be adopted and used to decide cases that are not already settled by actual usage. Thus the interplay we observed between rules of induction and particular inductive inferences is simply an instance of this characteristic dual adjustment between definition and usage, whereby the usage informs the definition, which in turn guides extension of the usage.

Of course this adjustment is a more complex matter than I have indicated. Sometimes, in the interest of convenience or theoretical utility, we deliberately permit a definition to run counter to clear mandates of common usage. We accept a definition of "fish" that excludes whales. Similarly we may decide to deny the term "valid induction" to some inductive inferences that are commonly considered valid, or apply the term to others not usually so considered. A definition may modify as well as extend ordinary usage.

Some pioneer work on the problem of defining confirmation or valid induction has been done by Professor Hempel. Let me remind you briefly of a few of his results. Just as deductive logic is concerned primarily with a relation between statements—namely the consequence relation—that is independent of their truth or falsity, so inductive logic as Hempel conceives it is concerned primarily with a comparable relation of confirmation between statements. Thus the problem is to define the relation that obtains between any statement S_1 and another S_2 if and only if S_1 may properly be said to confirm S_2 in any degree.

With the question so stated, the first step seems obvious. Does not induction proceed in just the opposite direction from deduction? Surely some of the evidence-statements that inductively support a general hypothesis are consequences of it. Since the consequence relation is already well defined by deductive logic, will we not be on firm ground in saying that confirmation embraces the converse relation? The laws of deduction in reverse will then be among the laws of induction.

Let's see where this leads us. We naturally assume further that whatever confirms a given statement confirms also whatever follows from that statement.

But if we combine this assumption with our proposed principle, we get the embarrassing result that every statement confirms every other. Surprising as it may be that such innocent beginnings lead to such an intolerable conclusion, the proof is very easy. Start with any statement S_1. It is a consequence of, and so by our present criterion confirms, the conjunction of S_1 and any statement whatsoever—call it S_2 But the confirmed conjunction, $S_1 \cdot S_2$, of course has S_2 as a consequence. Thus every statement confirms all statements.

The fault lies in careless formulation of our first proposal. While some statements that confirm a general hypothesis are consequences of it, not all its consequences confirm it. This may not be immediately evident; for indeed we do in some sense furnish support for a statement when we establish one of its consequences. We settle one of the questions at about it. Consider the heterogeneous conjunction:

> 8497 is a prime number and the other side of the moon is flat and Elizabeth the First was crowned on a Tuesday.

To show that any one of the three component statements is true is to support the conjunction by reducing the net undetermined claim. But support of this kind is not confirmation; for establishment of one component endows the whole statement with no credibility that is transmitted to other component statements. Confirmation of a hypothesis occurs only when an instance imparts to the hypothesis some credibility that is conveyed to other instances. Appraisal of hypotheses, indeed, is incidental to prediction, to the judgment of new cases on the basis of old ones.

Our formula thus needs tightening. This is readily accomplished, as Hempel points out, if we observe that a hypothesis is genuinely confirmed only by a statement that is an instance of it in the special sense of entailing not the hypothesis itself but its relativization or restriction to the class of entities mentioned by that statement. The relativization of a general hypothesis to a class results from restricting the range of its universal and existential quantifiers to the members of that class. Less technically, what the hypothesis says of all things the evidence statement says of one thing (or of one pair or other n-ad of things). This obviously covers the confirmation of the conductivity

of all copper by the conductivity of a given piece; and it excludes confirmation of our heterogeneous conjunction by any of its components. And, when taken together with the principle that what confirms a statement confirms all its consequences, this criterion does not yield the untoward conclusion that every statement confirms every other.

New difficulties promptly appear from other directions, however. One is the infamous paradox of the ravens. The statement that a given object, say this piece of paper, is neither black nor a raven confirms the hypothesis that all non-black things are non-ravens. But this hypothesis is logically equivalent to the hypothesis that all ravens are black. Hence we arrive at the unexpected conclusion that the statement that a given object is neither black nor a raven confirms the hypothesis that all ravens are black. The prospect of being able to investigate ornithological theories without going out in the rain is so attractive that we know there must be a catch in it. The trouble this time, however, lies not in faulty definition, but in tacit and illicit reference to evidence not stated in our example. Taken by itself, the statement that the given object is neither black nor a raven confirms the hypothesis that everything that is not a raven is not black as well as the hypothesis that everything that is not black is not a raven. We tend to ignore the former hypothesis because we know it to be false from abundant other evidence—from all the familiar things that are not ravens but are black. But we are required to assume that no such evidence is available. Under this circumstance, even a much stronger hypothesis is also obviously confirmed: that nothing is either black or a raven. In the light of this confirmation of the hypothesis that there are no ravens, it is no longer surprising that under the artificial restrictions of the example, the hypothesis that all ravens are black is also confirmed. And the prospects for indoor ornithology vanish when we notice that under these same conditions, the contrary hypothesis that no ravens are black is equally well confirmed.

On the other hand, our definition does err in not forcing us to take into account all the *stated* evidence. The unhappy results are readily illustrated. If two compatible evidence statements confirm two hypotheses, then naturally the conjunction of the evidence statements should confirm the conjunction of the hypotheses. Suppose our evidence consists of the statements E_1 saying that a given thing b is black, and E_2 saying that a second thing c is not black. By our present definition, E_1 confirms the hypothesis that everything is black, and E_2 the hypothesis that everything is non-black. The conjunction of these perfectly compatible evidence statements will then confirm the self-contradictory hypothesis that everything is both black and non-black. Simple as this anomaly is, it requires drastic modification of our definition. What given evidence confirms is not what we arrive at by generalizing from separate items of it, but—roughly speaking—what we arrive at by generalizing from the total stated evidence. The central idea for an improved definition is that, within certain limitations, what is asserted to be true for the narrow universe of the evidence statements is confirmed for the whole universe of discourse. Thus if our evidence is E_1 and E_2, neither the hypothesis that all things are black nor the hypothesis that all things are non-black is confirmed; for neither is true for the evidence-universe consisting of b and c. Of course, much more careful formulation is needed, since some statements that are true of the evidence-universe—such as that there is only one black thing—are obviously not confirmed for the whole universe. These matters are taken care of by the studied formal definition that Hempel develops on this basis; but we cannot and need not go into further detail here.

No one supposes that the task of confirmation theory has been completed. But the few steps I have reviewed—chosen partly for their bearing on what is to follow—show how things move along once the problem of definition displaces the problem of justification. Important and long unnoticed questions are brought to light and answered; and we are encouraged to expect that the many remaining questions will in time yield to similar treatment.

But our satisfaction is shortlived. New and serious trouble begins to appear.

4. THE NEW RIDDLE OF INDUCTION

Confirmation of a hypothesis by an instance depends rather heavily upon features of the hypothesis other than its syntactical form. That a given piece of copper conducts electricity increases the credibility of statements asserting that other pieces of copper conduct electricity, and thus confirms the hypothesis that all copper conducts electricity. But the fact that a given man now in this room is a third son does not increase the credibility of statements asserting that other men now in this room are third sons, and so does not confirm the hypothesis that all men now in this room are third sons. Yet in both cases our hypothesis is a generalization of the evidence statement. The difference is that in the former case the hypothesis is a *lawlike* statement; while in the latter case, the hypothesis is a merely contingent or accidental generality. Only a statement that is *lawlike*—regardless of its truth or falsity or its scientific importance—is capable of receiving confirmation from an instance of it; accidental statements are not. Plainly, then, we must look for a way of distinguishing lawlike from accidental statements.

So long as what seems to be needed is merely a way of excluding a few odd and unwanted cases that are inadvertently admitted by our definition of confirmation, the problem may not seem very hard or very pressing. We fully expect that minor defects will be found in our definition and that the necessary refinements will have to be worked out patiently one after another. But some further examples will show that our present difficulty is of a much graver kind.

Suppose that all emeralds examined before a certain time t are green. At time t, then, our observations support the hypothesis that all emeralds are green; and this is in accord with our definition of confirmation. Our evidence statements assert that emerald a is green, that emerald b is green, and so on; and each confirms the general hypothesis that all emeralds are green. So far, so good.

Now let me introduce another predicate less familiar than "green". It is the predicate "grue" and it applies to all things examined before t just in case they are green but to other things just in case they are blue. Then at time t we have, for each evidence statement asserting that a given emerald is green, a parallel evidence statement asserting that that emerald is grue. And the statements that emerald a is grue, that emerald b is grue, and so on, will each confirm the general hypothesis that all emeralds are grue. Thus according to our definition, the prediction that all emeralds subsequently examined will be green and the prediction that all will be grue are alike confirmed by evidence statements describing the same observations. But if an emerald subsequently examined is grue, it is blue and hence not green. Thus although we are well aware which of the two incompatible predictions is genuinely confirmed, they are equally well confirmed according to our present definition. Moreover, it is clear that if we simply choose an appropriate predicate, then on the basis of these same observations we shall have equal confirmation, by our definition, for any prediction whatever about other emeralds—or indeed about anything else. As in our earlier example, only the predictions subsumed under lawlike hypotheses are genuinely confirmed; but we have no criterion as yet for determining lawlikeness. And now we see that without some such criterion, our definition not merely includes a few unwanted cases, but is so completely ineffectual that it virtually excludes nothing. We are left once again with the intolerable result that anything confirms anything. This difficulty cannot be set aside as an annoying detail to be taken care of in due course. It has to be met before our definition will work at all.

Nevertheless, the difficulty is often slighted because on the surface there seem to be easy ways of dealing with it. Sometimes, for example, the problem is thought to be much like the paradox of the ravens. We are here again, it is pointed out, making tacit and illegitimate use of information outside the stated evidence: the information, for example, that different samples of one material are usually alike in conductivity, and the information that different men in a lecture audience are usually not alike in the number of their older brothers. But while it is true that such information is being smuggled in, this does not by itself settle the matter as it settles the matter of the ravens. There the point was that when the smuggled information is forthrightly declared, its effect upon the confirmation of the hypothesis in question is immediately and properly registered by the definition we are using. On the other hand, if to our initial evidence we add statements concerning the conductivity of pieces of other materials or concerning the number of older brothers of members of other lecture audiences, this will not in the least affect the confirmation, according to our definition, of the hypothesis concerning copper or of that concerning this lecture audience. Since our definition is insensitive to the bearing upon hypotheses of evidence so related to them even when the evidence is fully declared, the difficulty about accidental hypotheses cannot be explained away on the ground that such evidence is being surreptitiously taken into account.

A more promising suggestion is to explain the matter in terms of the effect of this other evidence not directly upon the hypothesis in question but *indirectly* through other hypotheses that *are* confirmed, according to our definition, by such evidence. Our information about other materials does by our definition confirm such hypotheses as that all pieces of iron conduct electricity, that no pieces of rubber do, and so on; and these hypotheses, the explanation runs, impart to the hypothesis that all pieces of copper conduct electricity (and also to the hypothesis that none do) the character of lawlikeness—that is, amenability to confirmation by direct positive instances when found. On the other hand, our information about other lecture audiences *disconfirms* many hypotheses to the effect that all the men in one audience are third sons, or that none are; and this strips any character of lawlikeness from the hypothesis that all (or the hypothesis that none) of the men in *this* audience are third sons. But clearly if this course is to be followed, the circumstances under which hypotheses are thus related to one another will have to be precisely articulated.

The problem, then, is to define the relevant way in which such hypotheses must be alike. Evidence for the hypothesis that all iron conducts electricity enhances the lawlikeness of the hypothesis that all zirconium conducts electricity, but does not similarly affect the hypothesis that all the objects on my desk conduct electricity. Wherein lies the difference? The first two hypotheses fall under the broader hypothesis—call it "*H*"—that every class of things of the same material is uniform in conductivity; the first and third fall only under some such hypothesis as—call it "*K*"—that every class of things that are either all of the same material or all on a desk is uniform in conductivity. Clearly the important difference here is that evidence for a statement affirming that one of the classes covered by *H* has the property in question increases the credibility of any statement affirming that another such class has this property; while nothing of the sort holds true with respect to *K*. But this is only to say that *H* is lawlike and *K* is not. We are faced anew with the very problem we are trying to solve: the problem of distinguishing between lawlike and accidental hypotheses.

The most popular way of attacking the problem takes its cue from the fact that accidental hypotheses seem typically to involve some spatial or temporal restriction, or reference to some particular individual. They seem to concern the people in some particular room, or the objects on some particular person's desk; while lawlike hypotheses characteristically concern all ravens or all pieces of copper whatsoever. Complete generality is thus very often supposed to be a sufficient condition of lawlikeness; but to define this complete generality is by no means easy. Merely to require that the hypothesis contain no term naming, describing, or indicating a particular thing or location will obviously not be enough. The troublesome hypothesis that all emeralds are grue contains no such term; and where such a term does occur, as in hypotheses about men in *this room,* it can be suppressed in favor of some predicate (short or long, new or old) that contains no such term but applies only to exactly the same things. One might think, then, of excluding not only hypotheses that actually contain terms for specific individuals but also all hypotheses that are equivalent to others that do contain such terms. But, as we have just seen, to exclude only hypotheses of which *all* equivalents contain such terms is to exclude nothing. On the other hand, to exclude all hypotheses that have *some* equivalent containing such a term is to exclude everything; for even the hypothesis

All grass is green

has as an equivalent

All grass in London or elsewhere is green.

The next step, therefore, has been to consider ruling out predicates of certain kinds. A syntactically universal hypothesis is lawlike, the proposal runs, if its predicates are 'purely qualitative' or 'non-positional'. This will obviously accomplish nothing if a purely qualitative predicate is then conceived either as one that is equivalent to some expression free of terms for specific individuals, or as one that is equivalent to no expression that contains such a term; for this only raises again the difficulties just pointed out. The claim appears to be rather that at least in the case of a simple enough predicate we can readily determine by direct inspection of its meaning whether or not it is purely qualitative. But even aside from obscurities in the notion of 'the meaning' of a predicate, this claim seems to me wrong. I simply do not know how to tell whether a predicate is qualitative or positional, except perhaps by completely begging the question at issue and asking whether the predicate is 'well-behaved'—that is, whether simple syntactically universal hypotheses applying it are lawlike.

This statement will not go unprotested. "Consider", it will be argued, "the predicates 'blue' and 'green' and the predicate 'grue' introduced earlier, and also the predicate 'bleen' that applies to emeralds examined before time *t* just in case they are blue and to other emeralds just in case they are green. Surely it is clear", the argument runs, "that the first two are purely qualitative and the second two are not; for the meaning of each of the latter two plainly involves reference to a specific temporal position." To this reply that indeed I do recognize the first two as well-behaved predicates admissible in lawlike hypotheses, and the second two as ill-behaved predicates. But the argument that the former but not the latter are purely qualitative seems to me quite unsound. True enough, if we start with "blue" and "green", then "grue" and "bleen" will be explained in terms of "blue" and "green" and a temporal term. But equally truly, if we start with "grue" and "bleen", then "blue" and "green" will be explained in terms of "grue" and "bleen" and a temporal term; "green", for example, applies to emeralds examined before time *t* just in case they are grue, and to other emeralds just in case they are bleen. Thus qualitativeness is an entirely relative matter and does not by itself establish any dichotomy of predicates. This relativity seems to be completely overlooked by those who contend that the qualitative character of a predicate is a criterion for its good behavior.

Of course, one may ask why we need worry about such unfamiliar predicates as "grue" or about accidental hypotheses in general, since we are unlikely to use them in making predictions. If our definition works for such hypotheses as are normally employed, isn't that all we need? In a sense, yes; but only in the sense that we need no definition, no theory of induction, and no philosophy of knowledge at all. We get along well enough without them in daily life and in scientific research. But if we seek a theory at all, we cannot excuse gross anomalies resulting from a proposed theory by pleading that we can avoid them in practice. The odd cases we have been considering are clinically pure cases that, though seldom encountered in practice, nevertheless display to best advantage the symptoms of a widespread and destructive malady.

We have so far neither any answer nor any promising clue to an answer to the question what distinguishes lawlike or confirmable hypotheses from accidental or nonconfirmable ones; and what may at first have seemed a minor technical difficulty has taken on the stature of a major obstacle to the development of a satisfactory theory of confirmation. It is this problem that I call the new riddle of induction.

5. THE PERVASIVE PROBLEM OF PROJECTION

At the beginning of this lecture, I expressed the opinion that the problem of induction is still unsolved, but that the difficulties that face us today are not the old ones; and I have tried to outline the changes that have taken place. The problem of justifying induction has been displaced by the problem of defining confirmation, and our work upon this has left us with the residual problem of distinguishing between confirmable and non-confirmable hypotheses. One might say roughly that the first question was "Why does a positive instance of a hypothesis give any grounds for predicting further instances?"; that the newer question was "What is a positive instance of a hypothesis?"; and that the crucial remaining question is "What hypotheses are confirmed by their positive instances?"

The vast amount of effort expended on the problem of induction in modern times has thus altered our afflictions but hardly relieved them. The original difficulty about induction arose from the recognition that anything may follow upon anything. Then, in attempting to define confirmation in terms of the converse of the consequence relation, we found ourselves with the distressingly similar difficulty that our definition would make any statement confirm any other. And now, after modifying our definition drastically, we still get the old devastating result that any

statement will confirm any statement. Until we find a way of exercising some control over the hypotheses to be admitted, our definition makes no distinction whatsoever between valid and invalid inductive inferences.

The real inadequacy of Hume's account lay not in his descriptive approach but in the imprecision of his description. Regularities in experience, according to him, give rise to habits of expectation; and thus it is predictions conforming to past regularities that are normal or valid. But Hume overlooks the fact that some regularities do and some do not establish such habits; that predictions based on some regularities are valid while predictions based on other regularities are not. Every word you have heard me say has occurred prior to the final sentence of this lecture; but that does not, I hope, create any expectation that every word you will hear me say will be prior to that sentence. Again, consider our case of emeralds. All those examined before time t are green; and this leads us to expect, and confirms the prediction, that the next one will be green. But also, all those examined are grue; and this does not lead us to expect, and does not confirm the prediction, that the next one will be grue. Regularity in greenness confirms the prediction of further cases; regularity in grueness does not. To say that valid predictions are those based on past regularities, without being able to say *which* regularities, is thus quite pointless. Regularities are where you find them, and you can find them anywhere. As we have seen, Hume's failure to recognize and deal with this problem has been shared even by his most recent successors.

As a result, what we have in current confirmation theory is a definition that is adequate for certain cases that so far can be described only as those for which it is adequate. The theory works where it works. A hypothesis is confirmed by statements related to it in the prescribed way provided it is so confirmed. This is a good deal like having a theory that tells us that the area of a plane figure is one half the base times the altitude, without telling us for what figures this holds. We must somehow find a way of distinguishing lawlike hypotheses, to which our definition of confirmation applies, from accidental hypotheses, to which it does not.

Today I have been speaking solely of the problem of induction, but what has been said applies equally to the more general problem of projection. As pointed out earlier, the problem of prediction from past to future cases is but a narrower version of the problem of projecting from any set of cases to others. We saw that a whole cluster of troublesome problems concerning dispositions and possibility can be reduced to this problem of projection. That is why the new riddle of induction, which is more broadly the problem of distinguishing between projectible and non-projectible hypotheses, is as important as it is exasperating.

Our failures teach us, I think, that lawlike or projectible hypotheses cannot be distinguished on any merely syntactical grounds or even on the ground that these hypotheses are somehow purely general in meaning. Our only hope lies in re-examining the problem once more and looking for some new approach. This will be my course in the final lecture.

FOR FURTHER READING

Audi, Robert. *Belief, Justification, and Knowledge.* Belmont, Calif.: Wadsworth, 1988.

Ayer, A. J. *The Problem of Knowledge.* London: Penguin Books, 1956.

BonJour, Laurence. *The Structure of Empirical Knowledge.* Cambridge: Harvard University Press, 1985.

Chisholm, Roderick. *Theory of Knowledge.* 3rd ed. Englewood Cliffs, N.J.: Prentice Hall, 1988.

Curley, E. M. *Descartes against the Skeptics.* Cambridge: Harvard University Press, 1978.

Dancy, Jonathan, and Ernest Sosa, eds. *A Companion to Epistemology.* Oxford: Basil Blackwell, 1992.

Davidson, Donald. "A Coherence Theory of Truth and Knowledge." In *Truth and Interpretation,* edited by E. LePore, 307–19.

Descartes, Rene. *Meditations.* Reprinted in *The Philosophical Works of Descartes,* vol. I, translated by Elizabeth Haldane and G. R. T. Ross. Cambridge: Cambridge University Press, 1968, 131–99.

Frankfurt, Harry G. *Demons, Dreamers, and Madmen.* Indianapolis: Bobbs Merrill, 1970.

Fumerton, Richard. *Metaepistemology and Skepticism.* Lanham, Md.: Rowman & Littlefield, 1995.

Hamlyn, D. W. *The Theory of Knowledge.* London: Macmillan Press, 1970.

Harman, Gilbert. *Thought.* Princeton: Princeton University Press, 1973.

Hookway, Christopher. *Skepticism.* London: Routledge and Kegan Paul, 1990.

Hume, David. *A Treatise of Human Nature.* Edited by L. A. Selby-Bigge. 2d ed. Revised by P. H. Nidditch. Oxford: Clarendon Press, 1978.

Hume, David. *An Enquiry Concerning Human Understanding.* Edited by L.A. Selby-Bigge. 3rd ed. Revised by P.H. Nidditch. Oxford: Clarendon Press, 1975.

Jackson, Frank. "Knowledge of the External World." In *The Handbook of Western Philosophy,* edited by G. H. R. Parkinson, 140–58.

Klein, Peter. *Certainty: A Refutation of Skepticism.* Minneapolis: University of Minnesota Press, 1981.

Kant, Immanuel. *Critique of Pure Reason.* Translated by Norman Kemp Smith. New York: St. Martin's Press, 1965.

Lehrer, Keith. *Theory of Knowledge.* Boulder, Colo.: Westview Press, 1990.

LePore, Ernest, ed. *Truth and Interpretation: Perspectives on the Philosophy of Donald Davidson.* Oxford: Basil Blackwell, 1985.

Luper-Foy, Steven, ed. *The Possibility of Knowledge.* Totowa, N.J.: Rowman & Littlefield, 1987.

Meyers, Robert G. *The Likelihood of Knowledge.* Dordrecht, Netherlands: Kluwer Academic Publishers, 1988.

Moore, G. E. *Philosophical Papers.* London: George Allen & Unwin, 1959.

Parkinson, G. H. R., ed. *The Handbook of Western Philosophy.* New York: Macmillan, 1988.

Popkin, Richard H. *The History of Skepticism from Erasmus to Spinoza.* Berkeley and Los Angeles: University of California Press, 1979.

Russell, Bertrand. *The Problems of Philosophy.* 1912. Reprint, London: Oxford University Press, 1959.

Schmitt, Frederick. *Knowledge and Belief.* London: Routledge, 1990.

Sextus, Empiricus. *Outlines of Skepticism.* Translated by Julia Annas and Jonathan Barnes. Cambridge: Cambridge University Press, 1994.

Strawson, P. F. *Introduction to Logical Theory.* London: Methuen, 1952.

Strawson, P. F. *Skepticism and Naturalism: Some Varieties.* New York: Columbia University Press, 1983.

Stroud, Barry. *Hume.* London: Routledge and Kegan Paul, 1977.

Stroud, Barry. *The Philosophical Significance of Skepticism.* Oxford: Clarendon Press, 1984.

Swinburne, Richard, ed. *The Justification of Induction.* Oxford: Oxford University Press, 1974.

Williams, Michael. *Unnatural Doubts.* Oxford: Blackwell, 1991.

Wilson, Margaret D. *Descartes.* London: Routledge and Kegan Paul, 1978.

Wright, J. P. *The Skeptical Realism of David Hume.* Minneapolis: University of Minnesota Press, 1983.

STUDY QUESTIONS

1. What does Sextus mean by "scepticism"? What is the aim of the sceptical attitude?

2. Sextus claims that we cannot trust our senses to tell us what qualities objects have. Explain three of the arguments Sextus gives in support of this claim. What is your opinion of these arguments? Suppose someone says that science tells us what qualities an object has; how might Sextus respond?

3. According to Descartes, what are the conditions under which a person knows? What kind of perceptual beliefs is the Dream Argument directed against? Explain why Descartes thinks this argument shows that perception does not yield knowledge. Do you agree with Descartes? Why or why not?

4. What kind of beliefs is the Evil Demon Argument directed against? Descartes thinks we cannot help believing, for example, that a triangle has three sides. Why, then, does he argue that we do not know that a triangle has three sides? For the Demon Argument to work, does not Descartes have to prove, or at least make plausible, that an evil demon actually exists? Explain.

5. What do you think Ayer means by "incorrigible beliefs"? Give an example of a putatively incorrigible belief. In this context, what is the difference between a factual mistake and a verbal mistake? Does Ayer think that it is possible that we could be factually mistaken about beliefs about our sensations or what we are thinking? Explain.

6. Explain Ayer's account of the skeptical challenge. What are the four different approaches to meeting this challenge? Which of these do you think is best? Why?

7. At the outset, Moore distinguishes two types of proposition; explain this distinction. Subsequently, Moore distinguishes two types of philosophers, those who claim that a certain kind of proposition is not true and those who claim that we do not know that a certain kind of proposition is true. Explain this distinction.

8. What is the "Common Sense view of the world"? According to Moore, if we know that a proposition is part of the Common Sense view of the world, what else do we know? Do you think Moore provides an adequate response to skepticism? Explain.

9. Explain the two senses of knowledge that Malcolm identifies, and give an example of each. Do you think that Malcolm provides an adequate response to the skeptic? Explain.

10. Explain what Stroud means by "externalist" responses to skepticism. Why does he think that such responses are inadequate responses to skepticism?

11. According to Hume, what is the only way by which we can come to know about matters of fact? How do we learn about causes and effects? Why does Hume think that reason is unable to teach us about cause and effects?

12. For Hume, what is the foundation of all our conclusions from experience? Why does Hume think that this foundation cannot be "justified" by reason? (First explain, as clearly as you can, what is the "foundation." Then identify the three ways of justifying this foundation and explain why Hume rejects each of them.)

13. Russell claims that the fact that past regularities cause expectations about the future does not mean that such past regularities make our expectations rational. What do you think he means by this? What is the principle of induction? Explain Russell's attitude towards this principle.

14. Edwards thinks that philosophers who reject the commonsense view of experience are committing a certain kind of fallacy. What is this fallacy, and why does Edwards think those who reject the commonsense view are guilty of it? What sense of "reason" does Edwards think justifies our ordinary inductive predictions? With whom do you agree, Russell or Edwards? Why?

15. Explain as succinctly as you can the pragmatic justification of induction. Why does Skyrms think that it does not solve the problem of induction?

16. What, according to Strawson, does it mean to say that an inductive inference is rational? According to Strawson, where does Hume go wrong? Do you agree with Hume or Strawson? Explain.

17. Goodman thinks we can see how to resolve the "old problem of induction" by looking at deductive inferences. Explain his strategy. What problem has replaced the problem of justifying induction? Explain as simply as you can "the new riddle of induction."

3

The Analysis of Knowledge

We often distinguish between such things as guessing correctly, believing truly, and knowing. In drawing such distinctions, we suggest that there is a difference between someone who knows and someone who merely guesses correctly. Epistemologists typically conceive part of their task as identifying conditions of such differences. Suppose, for example, Sara knows that the keys are on the desk and she is not merely guessing that the keys are there. We can ask what explains the difference between knowing and guessing correctly. What conditions are satisfied by Sara such that it is true that she knows? Of course, we can ask a much more general question. What conditions are satisfied whenever it is true that a person knows? Answering this question provides an analysis of the concept of knowledge. Less formally, when we provide an analysis of a concept, we are describing what that concept means.

Epistemologists attempt to explain the concept of knowledge by identifying the conditions that are necessary and sufficient for having knowledge or knowing. Generally, they are concerned with *propositional knowledge*, or "knowing that." For example, Sara knows that Caesar crossed the Rubicon or Sam knows that the bank will be closed tomorrow. The propositions "Caesar crossed the Rubicon" and "The banks will be closed tomorrow" are the content of Sara's and Sam's respective knowledge. In attempting to explain what it means for Sara or Sam, or anyone for that matter, to know, epistemologists try to identify each of the minimum requirements, or necessary conditions, for knowledge. A person cannot have knowledge unless each of these minimum or necessary conditions is met. Simply satisfying one necessary condition for knowledge does not imply that a person knows. Being 35 years of age is a necessary condition for being president of the United States, but it is certainly not enough. Receiving a majority of the Electoral College vote and being appropriately sworn in are a sufficient conditions—are enough—for being president. Epis-temologists identify the various necessary conditions that add up to, or are sufficient for, knowledge.

It might seem that there is such a large range of instances of propositional knowledge that there is no way to identify the necessary and sufficient conditions. For a time, however, there was widespread agreement on a *traditional* or *standard analysis of knowledge*. Let S stand for any Sam or Sara that we choose, and let p stand for any proposition. Epistemologists thought that the necessary and sufficient conditions for knowledge could be formulated as follows:

S knows that p if and only if:

1. p is true;

2. S believes that p; and

3. S is justified in believing that p.

We know that there is a difference between guessing correctly and knowing. The standard analysis of knowledge, however, asserts that there is a further difference between having a true belief and knowing. In order to know, a person must have a *justified* belief; there must be some reason for thinking that the belief is true.

In 1963 Edmund Gettier presented two counter-examples to show that conditions 1 through 3 may be necessary for knowledge, but they are not sufficient. A person could satisfy those three conditions and still fail to have knowledge. One of Gettier's counterexamples involves a man who believes on the basis of good evidence that he will get a certain job. He has ten coins in his pocket and infers that the man who will get the job has ten coins in his pocket. However, a coworker, who coincidentally has ten coins in his pocket, gets the job. The man has a justified true belief, but Gettier holds that this is not an instance of knowledge.

Keith Lehrer provides another Gettier-type example. Lehrer asks us to imagine a case in which Smith believes that someone in the office owns a Ford. Smith has seen a coworker, Nogot, driving a Ford, and friends tell Smith that Nogot owns a Ford. Smith consequently believes Nogot owns a Ford. On the basis of this belief Smith infers that someone in the office owns a Ford. Unbeknownst to Smith, however, Nogot does not own a Ford, but Havit does. Smith does have a justified belief because he has evidence for his belief that someone in the office owns a Ford. Further, Smith has a true belief; someone does own a Ford—Havit. However, it seems that Smith's reasons for his belief, his justification, are not the reasons that explain why his belief is true. Smith has a justified true belief but he does not have knowledge.

These examples illustrate a general failure of the traditional analysis. The traditional analysis does not place any restrictions on how the truth and justification conditions, 1 and 3 above, are satisfied. More precisely, the truth and justification conditions can be satisfied independently of one another. The reasons why the belief is justified might have nothing to do with why the belief is true.

It is fair to say that Gettier's brief paper was the catalyst for a turbulent period in epistemology. Epistemologists attempted to find ways to amend or revise the traditional analysis. The strength of the revisions was tested by their ability to deal with various Gettier-type counterexamples. Among the influential approaches that emerged were the causal theories and indefeasibility theories, which are the focus of the next three selections. We can get something of the flavor of the general approach by briefly considering another view, the no-false-premise view.

No-false-premise theorists argue that what goes wrong in Gettier cases involving inferential beliefs is that the belief depends on a false premise.[1] According to this view, a person has knowledge if and only if he or she has a justified true belief and that belief does not depend on any false premise or reason. A standard objection to this view is that a person might reason in such a way that the belief does not depend on any false premise, but the person would still know. To illustrate this objection, consider a modification of the Ford case, which is sometimes referred to as the case of the clever reasoner. Smith has the same evidence that Nogot owns a Ford—seeing Nogot drive a Ford, having co-workers tell him that Nogot drives a Ford. Smith's evidence thus consists of true propositions. Smith, however, does not explicitly base his conclusion that someone owns a Ford on the false premise

that Nogot owns a Ford. Smith simply infers from his other evidence that someone owns a Ford; he "skips over" the false premise and simply draws the conclusion that someone owns a Ford. This would be a case of justified true belief that is not knowledge, yet there is no false premise involved. Thus, it is claimed, the no-false-premise view fails to explain why such cases are not instances of knowledge. The no-false-premise view is too weak since it cannot "screen out" cases such as this.

No-false-premise theorists have attempted to respond to this sort of objection by distinguishing between essential and nonessential premises. They claim that a person knows only if the justifed true belief does not depend on any false essential premises. In the case of the clever reasoner, for example, the no-false-premise theorist argues that "Nogot owns a Ford" is an essential premise for Smith, despite the fact that Smith never explicitly considers or thinks about this premise. Clearly, the viability of the no-false-premise view depends on the plausibility of the notion of essential, but not explicitly considered, false premises.

This sketch of the no-false-premise view indicates something of the character of the Gettier-inspired debate. An epistemologist diagnoses the flaw that engenders Gettier counterexamples and presents an analysis of knowledge to remedy the flaw. This amended analysis is subsequently revised to meet still further counterexamples. In the end, a post-Gettier analysis is judged satisfactory to the extent that it can accommodate a wide range of counterexamples.

In "A Causal Theory of Knowing," Alvin Goldman claims that, in order to count as knowledge, a person's belief must be caused in an appropriate way. Goldman claims that beliefs acquired, by means of perception, for example, are caused in an appropriate way. If a perceptual belief is true and is caused in an appropriate way, then that belief is an instance of knowledge. Inferential beliefs—beliefs based on other beliefs—are instances of knowledge if the inference chain correctly reconstructs or mirrors the actual events. It is worth noting that Goldman recognizes that the causal analysis is a departure from more traditional conceptions of knowledge which in some way depend on the person's reasons for a belief. In effect, the justification condition is supplanted by a causal condition.

The selections by Keith Lehrer and John Pollock (*Knowledge, Truth and Evidence* and *The Gettier Problem*) are representative of a widely held view, indefeasibility theory. Indefeasibility analyses of knowledge suggest that Gettier cases arise because of a defect in the person's justification. According to these accounts, the person has a justified true belief but is unaware of other facts or true propositions. These other true propositions are *defeaters*. Were these other true propositions to become known to the person, the original justification would be lost or undermined. The person fails to have knowledge because the original justification cannot withstand learning about the defeaters. Indefeasibility theories propose that we amend our understanding of the kind of justification necessary for knowledge. Lehrer suggests that in genuine cases of knowledge a person could learn of a defeater, but would still be justified. Pollock develops a notion of objective justification, the kind of justification necessary for knowledge. The intuitive idea is that a person with knowledge has a true belief and has made all the right epistemic moves. In such a case, Pollock claims, a person will have the kind of justification necessary for knowledge only if acquiring more true beliefs would not "adversely affect" the person's original reasons.

This point is worth pursuing in a bit more detail, because the general idea is typical of indefeasibility theories. Suppose Sara has a justified true belief. That her belief is justified means that she has certain reasons for that belief; call these reasons her "original reasons." The indefeasibility theorists now suggest that Sara knows only if the following is true. Sara continue's acquiring true beliefs, even to the point that she aquires all the true beliefs a person might have. Despite all these additional true beliefs, nothing would have changed or need to be changed about her original reasons. Her original reasons would not be "adversely affected" by Sara's acquisition of further true beliefs. In such a case, Sara would be said to know. Thus, the indefeasibility theorist attempts to exploit the intuition that if a person knows, then learning more will not affect that knowledge.

The last selection, *The Fate of Knowledge in Social Science*, by Helen Longino, is somewhat different in orientation. Longino does not diagnose the Gettier problem and issue a prescription for its remedy. She is concerned, rather, with the understanding of the concept of knowledge. She sees knowledge as not just an individual endeavor but also a function of the epistemic norms of a community. She argues that we can identify an analysis of knowledge that is sensitive to the social nature of knowledge, and that knowledge should reflect the norms of a community and be responsive to the critical give-and-take characteristic of such social cognitive endeavors. She also argues that we should expand our conception of knowledge to include not only propositional knowledge but knowledge of *models* as well. She claims that models represent what we know when we understand the complex relationships and patterns that exist among various objects.

The myriad responses to Gettier problems are often technical and intensely analytic. They can seem preoccupied with fine discriminations in which the immediate significance is difficult to discern. As Pollock notes, the main idea is easier to grasp than to define. Epistemologists attempt to understand the nature of concepts important for our cognitive endeavors. We should not lose sight of "big picture" themes that emerge in the analysis of the concept of knowledge. For example, it has been suggested that in our ordinary cognitive transactions with the world, we run into hidden complications or unexpected surprises. Usually these complications or surprises do not affect the epistemic status of our beliefs. Sometimes, however, the unpredictable antics of the world can have significant epistemic effects. One of the themes suggested by the various analyses is that the person who knows has beliefs that better enable that person to cope with occasional surprises. The person who knows is cognitively better situated to make the right epistemic moves. Awareness of the features of cognitively preferable situations will enable us to discriminate genuine instances of knowledge from mere pretenders.

NOTE

1. Two accounts of the no-false-premise view can be found in Gilbert Harman, *Thought* (Princeton, NJ: Princeton University Press, 1973) and Robert Meyers, *The Likelihood of Knowledge* (Dordrecht, Netherlands: Kluwer Academic Publishers, 1988). The account that follows is drawn from Meyers, pp. 96–104.

EDMUND L. GETTIER

Is Justified True Belief Knowledge?

Various attempts have been made in recent years to state necessary and sufficient conditions for someone's knowing a given proposition. The attempts have often been such that they can be stated in a form similar to the following:[1]

(a) S knows that P   *IFF*
  (i) P is true,
  (ii) S believes that P, and
  (iii) S is justified in believing that P.

For example, Chisholm has held that the following gives the necessary and sufficient conditions for knowledge:[2]

(b) S knows that P   *IFF*
  (i) S accepts P,
  (ii) S has adequate evidence for P, and
  (iii) P is true.

Ayer has stated the necessary and sufficient conditions for knowledge as follows:[3]

(c) S knows that P   *IFF*
  (i) P is true,
  (ii) S is sure that P is true, and
  (iii) S has the right to be sure that P is true.

I shall argue that (a) is false in that the conditions stated therein do not constitute a *sufficient* condition for the truth of the proposition that S knows that P. The same argument will show that (b) and (c) fail if 'has adequate evidence for' or 'has the right to be sure that' is substituted for 'is justified in believing that' throughout.

I shall begin by noting two points. First, in that sense of 'justified' in which S's being justified in believing P is a necessary condition of S's knowing that P, it is possible for a person to be justified in believing a proposition that is in fact false. Secondly, for any proposition P, if S is justified in believing P, and P entails Q, and S deduces Q from P and accepts Q as a result of this deduction, then S is justified in believing Q. Keeping these two points in mind, I shall now present two cases in which the conditions stated in (a) are true for some proposition, though it is at the same time false that the person in question knows that proposition.

CASE I

Suppose that Smith and Jones have applied for a certain job. And suppose that Smith has strong evidence for the following conjunctive proposition:

(d) Jones is the man who will get the job, and Jones has ten coins in his pocket.

Smith's evidence for (d) might be that the president of the company assured him that Jones would in the end be selected, and that he, Smith, had counted the coins in Jones's pocket ten minutes ago. Proposition (d) entails:

(e) The man who will get the job has ten coins in his pocket.

Let us suppose that Smith sees the entailment from (d) to (e), and accepts (e) on the grounds of (d), for which he has strong evidence. In this case, Smith is clearly justified in believing that (e) is true.

But imagine, further, that unknown to Smith, he himself, not Jones, will get the job. And, also, unknown to Smith, he himself has ten coins in his pocket. Proposition (e) is then true, though proposition (d), from which Smith inferred (e), is false. In our example, then, all of the following are true: (*i*) (e) is true, (*ii*) Smith believes that (e) is true, and (*iii*) Smith is justified in believing that (e) is true. But it is equally clear that Smith does not *know* that (e) is true; for (e) is true in virtue of the number of coins in Smith's pocket, while Smith does not know how many coins are in Smith's pocket, and bases his belief in (e) on a count of the coins in Jones's pocket, whom he falsely believes to be the man who will get the job.

CASE II

Let us suppose that Smith has strong evidence for the following proposition:

(f) Jones owns a Ford.

Smith's evidence might be that Jones has at all times in the past within Smith's memory owned a car, and always a Ford, and that Jones has just offered Smith a ride while driving a Ford. Let us imagine, now, that Smith has another friend, Brown, of whose whereabouts he is totally ignorant. Smith selects three place names quite at random and constructs the following three propositions:

(g) Either Jones owns a Ford, or Brown is in Boston.

(h) Either Jones owns a Ford, or Brown is in Barcelona.

(i) Either Jones owns a Ford, or Brown is in Brest-Litovsk.

Each of these propositions is entailed by (f). Imagine that Smith realizes the entailment of each of these propositions he has constructed by (f), and proceeds to accept (g), (h), and(i) on the basis of (f). Smith has correctly inferred (g), (h),and (i) from a proposition for which he has strong evidence. Smith is therefore completely justified in believing each of these three propositions. Smith, of course, has no idea where Brown is.

But imagine now that two further conditions hold. First, Jones does *not* own a Ford, but is at present driving a rented car. And secondly, by the sheerest coincidence, and entirely unknown to Smith, the place mentioned in proposition (h) happens really to be the place where Brown is. If these two conditions hold, then Smith does *not* know that (h) is true, even though (*i*) (h) *is* true, (*ii*) Smith does believe that (h) is true, and (*iii*) Smith is justified in believing that (h) is true.

These two examples show that definition (a) does not state a *sufficient* condition for someone's knowing a given proposition. The same cases, with appropriate changes, will suffice to show that neither definition (b) nor definition (c) do so either.

NOTES

1. Plato seems to be considering some such definition at *Theaetetus* 201, and perhaps accepting one at *Meno* 98.
2. Roderick M. Chisholm, *Perceiving: a Philosophical Study,* Cornell University Press (Ithaca, New York, 1957), p. 16.
3. A. J. Ayer. *The Problem of Knowledge,* Macmillan (London, 1956), p. 34.

ALVIN I. GOLDMAN

A Causal Theory of Knowing

Since Edmund L. Gettier pointed out a certain important inadequacy of the traditional analysis of "*S* knows that *p*," several attempts have been made to correct that analysis.[1] In this paper I shall offer still another analysis (or sketch of an analysis) of "*S* knows that *p*," one which will avert Gettier's problem. My concern will be with knowledge of empirical propositions only. Although certain elements in my theory would be relevant to the analysis of knowledge of nonempirical truths, my theory is not intended to apply to knowledge of nonempirical truths.

Consider an abbreviated version of Gettier's second counterexample to the traditional analysis. Smith believes

(*q*) Jones owns a Ford

and has very strong evidence for it. Smith's evidence might be that Jones has owned a Ford for many years and that Jones has just offered Smith a ride while driving a Ford. Smith has another friend, Brown, of whose whereabouts he is totally ignorant. Choosing a town quite at random, however, Smith constructs the proposition

(*p*) Either Jones owns a Ford or Brown is in Barcelona.

Seeing that *q* entails *p*, Smith infers that *p* is true. Since he has adequate evidence for *q*, he also has adequate evidence for *p*. But now suppose that Jones does *not* own a Ford (he was driving a rented car when he offered Smith a ride), but, quite by coincidence, Brown happens to be in Barcelona. This means that *p* is true, that Smith believes *p*, and that Smith has adequate evidence for *p*. But Smith does not know *p*.

A variety of hypotheses might be made to account for Smith's not knowing *p*. Michael Clark, for example, points to the fact that *q* is false, and suggests this as the reason why Smith cannot be said to know *p*. Generalizing from this case, Clark[2] argues that, for *S* to know a proposition, each of *S*'s grounds for it must

be *true*, as well as his grounds for his grounds, etc. I shall make another hypothesis to account for the fact that Smith cannot be said to know *p*, and I shall generalize this into a new analysis of "*S* knows that *p*."

Notice that what *makes p* true is the fact that Brown is in Barcelona, but that this fact has nothing to do with Smith's believing *p*. That is, there is no *causal* connection between the fact that Brown is in Barcelona and Smith's believing *p*. If Smith had come to believe *p* by reading a letter from Brown postmarked in Barcelona, then we might say that Smith knew *p*. Alternatively, if Jones did own a Ford, and his owning the Ford was manifested by his offer of a ride to Smith, and this in turn resulted in Smith's believing *p*, then we would say that Smith knew *p*. Thus, one thing that seems to be missing in this example is a causal connection between the fact that makes *p* true [or simply: the fact that *p*] and Smith's belief of *p*. The requirement of such a *causal connection* is what I wish to add to the traditional analysis.

To see that this requirement is satisfied in all cases of (empirical) knowledge, we must examine a variety of such causal connections. Clearly, only a sketch of the important kinds of cases is possible here.

Perhaps the simplest case of a causal chain connecting some fact *p* with someone's belief of *p* is that of *perception*. I wish to espouse a version of the causal theory of perception, in essence that defended by H.P. Grice.[3] Suppose that *S* sees that there is a vase in front of him. How is this to be analyzed? I shall not attempt a complete analysis of this, but a necessary condition of *S*'s seeing that there is a vase in front of him is that there be a certain kind of causal connection between the presence of the vase and *S*'s believing that a vase is present. I shall not attempt to describe this causal process in detail. Indeed, to a large extent, a description of this process must be regarded as a problem for the special sciences, not for philosophy. But a certain causal process—viz., that which standardly takes place when we say that so-and-so *sees* such-and-such—must occur. That our ordinary concept of sight (i.e., knowledge acquired by sight) includes a causal requirement is shown by the fact that if the relevant causal process is absent we would withhold the assertion that so-and-so *saw* such-and-such. Suppose that, although a vase is directly in front of S, a laser photograph[4] is interposed between it and S, thereby blocking it from S's view. The photograph, however, is one of a vase (a different vase), and when it is illuminated by light waves from a laser, it looks to S exactly like a real vase. When the photograph is illuminated, S forms the belief that there is a vase in front of him. Here we would deny that S *sees* that there is a vase in front of him, for his view of the real vase is completely blocked, so that it has no causal role in the formation of his belief. Of course, S might *know* that there was a vase in front of him even if the photograph is blocking his view. Someone else, in a position to see the vase, might tell S that there is a vase in front of him. Here the presence of the vase might be a causal ancestor of S's belief, but the causal process would not be a (purely) *perceptual* one. S could not be said to *see* that there is a vase in front of him. For this to be true, there must be a causal process, but one of a very special sort, connecting the presence of the vase with S's belief.

I shall here assume that perceptual knowledge of facts is noninferential. This is merely a simplifying procedure, and not essential to my account. Certainly a percipient does not *infer* facts about physical objects from the state of his brain or from the stimulation of his sense organs. He need not know about these goings-on at all. But some epistemologists maintain that we directly perceive only sense data and that we infer physical-object facts from them. This view could be accommodated within my analysis. I could say that physical-object facts cause sense data, that people directly perceive sense data, and that they infer the physical object facts from the sense data. This kind of process would be fully accredited by my analysis, which will allow for knowledge based on inference. But for purposes of exposition it will be convenient to regard perceptual knowledge of external facts as independent of any inference.

Here the question arises about the *scope* of perceptual knowledge. By perception I can know noninferentially that there is a vase in front of me. But can I know noninferentially that the painting I am viewing is a Picasso? It is unnecessary to settle such issues here. Whether the knowledge of such facts is to be classed as inferential or noninferential, my analysis can account for it. So the scope of noninferential knowledge may be left indeterminate.

I turn next to memory, i.e., knowledge that is based, in part, on memory. Remembering, like perceiving, must be regarded as a causal process. S remembers p at time t only if S's believing p at an earlier time is a cause of his believing p at t. Of course, not every causal connection between an earlier belief and a later one is a case of remembering. As in the case of perception, however, I shall not try to describe this process in detail. This is a job mainly for the scientist. Instead, the kind of causal process in question is to be identified simply by example, by "pointing" to paradigm cases of remembering. Whenever causal processes are of that kind—whatever that kind is, precisely—they are cases of remembering.[5]

A causal connection between earlier belief (or knowledge) of p and later belief (knowledge) of p is certainly a necessary ingredient in memory.[6] To remember a fact is not simply to believe it at t_0 and also to believe it at t_1. Nor does someone's knowing a fact at t_0 and his knowing it at t_1 entail that he remembers it at t_1. He may have perceived the fact at t_0, forgotten it, and then relearned it at t_1 by someone's telling it to him. Nor does the inclusion of a memory "impression"—a feeling of remembering—ensure that one really remembers. Suppose S perceives p at t_0, but forgets it at t_1. At t_2 he begins to believe p again because someone tells him p, but at t_2 he has no memory impression of p. At t_3 we artificially stimulate in S a memory impression of p. It does not follow that S remembers p at t_3. The description of the case suggests that his believing p at t_0 has no causal effect whatever on his believing p at t_3; and if we accepted this fact, we would deny that he remembers p at t_3.

Knowledge can be acquired by a combination of perception and memory. At t_0, the fact p causes S to believe p, by perception. S's believing p at t_0 results, via memory, in S's believing p at t_1. Thus, the fact p is a cause of S's believing p at t_1, and S can be said to know p at t_1. But not all knowledge results from perception and memory alone. In particular, much knowledge is based on *inference*.

As I shall use the term 'inference,' to say that S knows p by inference" does not entail that S went through an explicit, conscious process of reasoning. It is not necessary that he have "talked to himself," saying something like "Since such-and-such is true, p must also be true." My belief that there is a fire in the neighborhood is based on, or inferred from, my belief that I hear a fire engine. But I have not gone through a process of explicit reasoning, saying "There's a fire engine; therefore there must be a fire." Perhaps the word 'inference' is ordinarily used only where explicit reasoning occurs; if so, my use of the term will be somewhat broader than its ordinary use.

Suppose S perceives that there is solidified lava in various parts of the countryside. On the basis of this belief, plus various "background" beliefs about the production of lava, S concludes that a nearby mountain erupted many centuries ago. Let us assume that this is a highly warranted inductive inference, one which gives S adequate evidence for believing that the mountain did erupt many centuries ago. Assuming this proposition is true, does S know it? This depends on the nature of the causal process that induced his belief. If there is a continuous causal chain of the sort he envisages connecting the fact that the mountain erupted with his belief of this fact, then S knows it. If there is no such causal chain, however, S does not know that proposition.

Suppose that the mountain erupts, leaving lava around the countryside. The lava remains there until S perceives it and infers that the mountain erupted. Then S does know that the mountain erupted. But now suppose that, after the mountain has erupted, a man somehow removes all the lava. A century later, a different man (not knowing of the real volcano) decides to make it look as if there had been a volcano, and therefore puts lava in appropriate places. Still later, S comes across this lava and concludes that the mountain erupted centuries ago. In this case, S cannot be said to know the proposition. This is because the fact that the mountain did erupt is not a cause of S's believing that it erupted. A necessary condition of S's knowing p is that his believing p be connected with p by a causal chain.

FIGURE 1

In the first case, where S knows p, the causal connection may be diagrammed as in Figure 1. (p) is the fact that the mountain erupted at such-and-such a time. (q) is the fact that lava is (now) present around the countryside. 'B' stands for a belief, the expression in parentheses indicating the proposition believed, and the subscript designating the believer. (r) is a "background" proposition, describing the ways in which lava is produced and how it solidifies. Solid arrows in the diagram represent causal connections; dotted arrows represent inferences. Notice that, in Figure 1, there is not only an arrow connecting (q) with S's belief of (q), but also an arrow connecting (p) with (q). In the suggested variant of the lava case, the latter arrow would be missing, showing that there is no continuous causal chain connecting (p) with S's belief of (p). Therefore, in that variant case, S could not be said to know (p).

I have said that p is causally connected to S's belief of p, in the case diagrammed in Figure 1. This raises the question, however, of whether the inferential part of the chain is itself a causal chain. In other words, is S's belief of q a cause of his believing p? This is a question to which I shall not try to give a definitive answer here. I am inclined to say that inference *is* a causal process, that is, that when someone *bases* his belief of one proposition on his belief of a set of other propositions, then his belief of the latter propositions can be considered a cause of his belief of the former proposition. But I do not wish to rest my thesis on this claim. All I do claim is that, if a chain of inferences is "added" to a causal chain, then the entire chain is causal. In terms of our diagram, a chain consisting of solid arrows plus dotted arrows is to be considered a causal chain, though I shall not take a position on the question of whether the dotted arrows represent causal connections. Thus, in Figure 1, p is a cause of S's belief of p, whether or not we regard S's belief of q a cause of his belief of p.[7]

Consider next a case of knowledge based on "testimony." This too can be analyzed causally. p causes

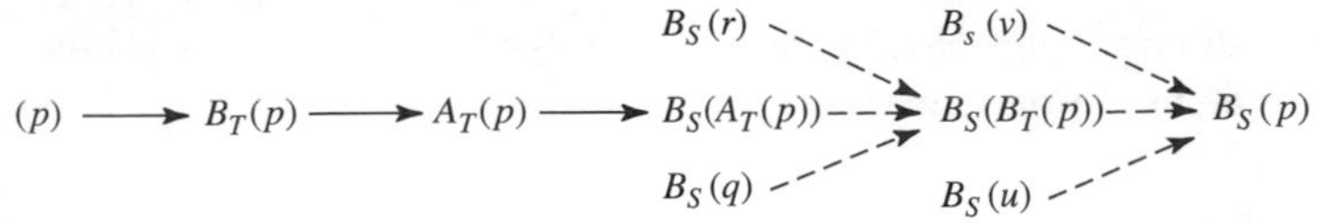

$$(p) \longrightarrow B_T(p) \longrightarrow A_T(p) \longrightarrow B_S(A_T(p)) \dashrightarrow B_S(B_T(p)) \dashrightarrow B_S(p)$$

with background propositions $B_S(r)$, $B_S(q)$, $B_s(v)$, $B_S(u)$ connected by dashed arrows.

FIGURE 2

a person T to believe p, by perception. T's belief of p gives rise to (causes) his asserting p. T's asserting p causes S, by auditory perception, to believe that T is asserting p. S infers that T believes p, and from this, in turn, he infers that p is a fact. There is a continuous causal chain from p to S's believing p, and thus, assuming that each of S's inferences is warranted, S can be said to know p.

This causal chain is represented in Figure 2. 'A' refers to an act of asserting a proposition, the expression in parentheses indicating the proposition asserted and the subscript designating the agent. (q), (r), (u), and (v) are background propositions. (q) and (r), for example, pertain to T's sincerity; they help S conclude, from the fact that T asserted p, that T really believes p.

In this case, as in the lava case, S knows p because he has correctly reconstructed the causal chain leading from p to the evidence for p that S perceives, in this case, T's asserting (p). This correct reconstruction is shown in the diagram by S's inference "mirroring" the rest of the causal chain. Such a correct reconstruction is a necessary condition of knowledge based on inference. To see this, consider the following example. A newspaper reporter observes p and reports it to his newspaper. When printed, however, the story contains a typographical error so that it asserts not-p. When reading the paper, however, S fails to see the word 'not', and takes the paper to have asserted p. Trusting the newspaper, he infers that p is true. Here we have a continuous causal chain leading from p to S's believing p; yet S does not know p. S thinks that p resulted in a report to the newspaper about p and that this report resulted in its printing the statement p. Thus, his reconstruction of the causal chain is mistaken. But, if he is to know p, his reconstruction must contain no mistakes. Though he need not reconstruct *every* detail of the causal chain, he must reconstruct all the important links.[8] An additional requirement for knowledge based on inference is that the knower's inferences be war-

ranted. That is, the propositions on which he bases his belief of p must genuinely confirm p very highly, whether deductively or inductively. Reconstructing a causal chain merely by lucky guesses does not yield knowledge.

With the help of our diagrams, we can contrast the traditional analysis of knowing with Clark's analysis (*op. cit.*) and contrast each of these with my own analysis. The traditional analysis makes reference to just three features of the diagrams. First, it requires that p be true; i.e., that (p) appear in the diagram. Secondly, it requires that S believe p; i.e., that S's belief of p appear in the diagram. Thirdly, it requires that S's inferences, if any, be warranted; i.e., that the sets of beliefs that are at the tail of a dotted arrow must jointly highly confirm the belief at the head of these arrows. Clark proposes a further requirement for knowledge. He requires that *each* of the beliefs in S's chain of inference be *true*. In other words, whereas the traditional analysis requires a fact to correspond to S's belief of p, Clark requires that a fact correspond to *each* of S's beliefs on which he based his belief of p. Thus, corresponding to each belief on the right side of the diagram there must be a fact on the left side. (My diagrams omit facts corresponding to the "background" beliefs.)

As Clark's analysis stands, it seems to omit an element of the diagrams that my analysis requires, viz., the arrows indicating causal connections. Now Clark might reformulate his analysis so as to make implicit reference to these causal connections. If he required that the knower's beliefs include *causal beliefs* (of the relevant sort), then his requirement that these beliefs be true would amount to the requirement that there *be* causal chains of the sort I require. This interpretation of Clark's analysis would make it almost equivalent to mine, and would enable him to avoid some objections that have been raised against him. But he has not explicitly formulated his analysis this way, and it therefore remains deficient in this respect.

Before turning to the problems facing Clark's analysis, more must be said about my own analysis. So far, my examples may have suggested that, if S knows p, the fact that p is a cause of his belief of p. This would clearly be wrong, however. Let us grant that I can know facts about the future. Then, if we required that the known facts cause the knower's belief, we would have to countenance "backward" causation. My analysis, however, does not face this dilemma. The analysis requires that there be a causal *connection* between p and S's belief, not necessarily that p be a *cause* of S's belief. p and S's belief of p can also be causally connected in a way that yields knowledge if both p and S's belief of p have a *common* cause. This can be illustrated as follows.

T intends to go downtown on Monday. On Sunday, T tells S of his intention. Hearing T say he will go downtown, S infers that T really does intend to go downtown. And from this S concludes that T *will* go downtown on Monday. Now suppose that T fulfills his intention by going downtown on Monday. Can S be said to know that he would go downtown? If we ever can be said to have knowledge of the future, this is a reasonable candidate for it. So let us say S did know that proposition. How can my analysis account for S's knowledge? T's going downtown on Monday clearly cannot be a cause of S's believing, on Sunday, that he would go downtown. But there is a fact that is the *common* cause of T's going downtown and of S's belief that he would go downtown, viz., T's intending (on Sunday) to go downtown. This intention resulted in his going downtown and also resulted in S's believing that he would go downtown. This causal connection between S's belief and the fact believed allows us to say that S *knew* that T would go downtown.

The example is diagrammed in Figure 3. (p) = T's going downtown on Monday. (q) = T's intending (on Sunday) to go downtown on Monday. (r) = T's telling S (on Sunday) that he will go downtown on Monday. (u) and (v) are relevant background propositions pertaining to T's honesty, resoluteness, etc. The diagram reveals that q is a cause both of p and of S's belief of p. Cases of this kind I shall call *Pattern 2* cases of knowledge. Figures 1 and 2 exemplify *Pattern 1* cases of knowledge.

Notice that the causal connection between q and p is an essential part of S's knowing p. Suppose, for example, that T's intending (on Sunday) to go downtown does not result in, or cause, T's going downtown on Monday. Suppose that T, after telling S that he would go downtown, changes his mind. Nevertheless, on Monday he is kidnapped and forced, at the point of a gun, to go downtown. Here both q and p actually occur, but they are not causally related. The diagram in Figure 3 would have to be amended by deleting the arrow connecting (q) with (p). But if the rest of the facts of the original case remain the same, S could not be said to know p. It would be false to say that S knew, on Sunday, that T would go downtown on Monday.

Pattern 2 cases of knowledge are not restricted to knowledge of the future. I know that smoke was coming out of my chimney last night. I know this because I remember perceiving a fire in my fireplace last night, and I infer that the fire caused smoke to rise out of the chimney. This case exemplifies Pattern 2. The smoke's rising out of the chimney is not a causal factor of my belief. But the fact that there was a fire in the fireplace was a cause both of my belief that smoke was coming out of the chimney and of the fact that smoke was coming out of the chimney. If we supplement this case slightly, we can make my knowledge exemplify *both* Pattern 1 and Pattern 2. Suppose that a friend tells me today that he perceived smoke coming out of my chimney last night and I base my continued belief of this fact on his testimony. Then the fact was a cause of my current belief of it, as well as an *effect* of another fact that caused my belief. In general, numerous and diverse kinds of causal connections can obtain between a given fact and a given person's belief of that fact.

Let us now examine some objections to Clark's analysis and see how the analysis presented here fares against them. John Turk Saunders and Narayan Champawat[9] have raised the following counterexample to Clark's analysis:

> Suppose that Smith believes
>   (p) Jones owns a Ford
> because his friend Brown whom he knows to be generally reliable and honest yesterday told Smith that Jones had always owned a Ford. Brown's information was correct, but today Jones sells his Ford and replaces it with a Volkswagen. An hour later Jones is pleased to

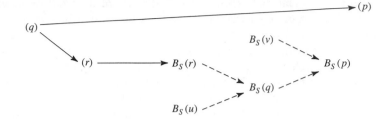

FIGURE 3

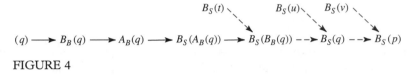

FIGURE 4

find that he is the proud owner of two cars: he has been lucky enough to win a Ford in a raffle. Smith's belief in p is not only justified and true, but is fully grounded, e.g., we suppose that each link in the . . . chain of Smith's grounds is true (p. 8).

Clearly Smith does not know p; yet he seems to satisfy Clark's analysis of knowing.

Smith's lack of knowledge can be accounted for in terms of my analysis. Smith does not know p because his believing p is not causally related to p, Jones's owning a Ford *now*. This can be seen by examining Figure 4. In the diagram, (p) = Jones's owning a Ford now; (q) = Jones's having always owned a Ford (until yesterday); (r) = Jones's winning a Ford in a raffle today. (t), (u), and (v) are background propositions. (v), for example, deals with the likelihood of someone's continuing to own the same car today that he owned yesterday. The subscript 'B' designates Brown, and the subscript 'S' designates Smith. Notice the absence of an arrow connecting (p) with (q). The absence of this arrow represents the absence of a causal relation between (q) and (p). Jones's owning a Ford in the past (until yesterday) is not a cause of his owning one now. Had he continued owning the same Ford today that he owned yesterday, there would be a causal connection between q and p and, therefore, a causal connection between p and Smith's believing p. This

causal connection would exemplify Pattern 2. But, as it happened, it is purely a coincidence that Jones owns a Ford today as well as yesterday. Thus, Smith's belief of p is not connected with p by Pattern 2, nor is there any Pattern 1 connection between them. Hence, Smith does not know p.

If we supplement Clark's analysis as suggested above, it can be saved from this counterexample. Though Saunders and Champawat fail to mention this explicitly, presumably it is one of Smith's beliefs that Jones's owning a Ford yesterday would *result* in Jones's owning a Ford now. This was undoubtedly one of his grounds for believing that Jones owns a Ford now. (A complete diagram of S's beliefs relevant to p would include this belief.) Since this belief is false, however, Clark's analysis would yield the correct consequence that Smith does not know p. Unfortunately, Clark himself seems not to have noticed this point, since Saunders and Champawat's putative counterexample has been allowed to stand.

Another sort of counterexample to Clark's analysis has been given by Saunders and Champawat and also by Keith Lehrer. This is a counterexample from which his analysis cannot escape. I shall give Lehrer's example (*op. cit.*) of this sort of difficulty. Suppose Smith bases his belief of

(p) Someone in his office owns a Ford

on his belief of four propositions

(*q*) Jones owns a Ford.

(*r*) Jones works in his office.

(*s*) Brown owns a Ford.

(*t*) Brown works in his office.

In fact, Smith knows *q*, *r*, and *t*, but he does not know *s* because *s* is false. Since *s* is false, not *all* of Smith's grounds for *p* are true, and, therefore, on Clark's analysis, Smith does not know *p*. Yet clearly Smith does know *p*. Thus, Clark's analysis is *too strong*.

Having seen the importance of a causal chain for knowing, it is fairly obvious how to amend Clark's requirements without making them too weak. We need not require, as Clark does, that *all* of S's grounds be true. What is required is that enough of them be true to ensure the existence of at least *one* causal connection between *p* and S's belief of *p*. In Lehrer's example, Smith thinks that there are two ways in which he knows *p*: via his knowledge of the conjunction of *q* and *r*, and via his knowledge of the conjunction of *s* and *t*. He does not know *p* via the conjunction of *s* and *t*, since *s* is false. But there is a causal connection, via *q* and *r*, between *p* and Smith's belief of *p*. And this connection is enough.

Another sort of case in which one of S's grounds for *p* may be false without preventing him from knowing *p* is where the false proposition is a dispensable background assumption. Suppose S bases his belief of *p* on 17 background assumptions, but only 16 of these are true. If these 16 are strong enough to confirm *p*, then the 17th is dispensable. S can be said to know *p* though one of his grounds is false.

Our discussion of Lehrer's example calls attention to the necessity of a further clarification of the notion of a "causal chain." I said earlier that causal chains with admixtures of inferences are causal chains. Now I wish to add that causal chains with admixtures of logical connections are causal chains. Unless we allow this interpretation, it is hard to see how facts like "Someone in the office owns a Ford" or "All men are mortal" could be *causally* connected with beliefs thereof.

The following principle will be useful: *If x is logically related to y and if y is a cause of z, then x is a cause of z.* Thus, suppose that *q* causes S's belief of *q* and that *r* causes S's belief of *r*. Next suppose that S

infers *q* & *r* from his belief of *q* and of *r*. Then the facts *q* and *r* are causes of S's believing *q* & *r*. But the fact *q* & *r* is logically related to the fact *q* and to the fact *r*. Therefore, using the principle enunciated above, the fact *q* & *r* is a cause of S's believing *q* & *r*.

In Lehrer's case another logical connection is involved: a connection between an existential fact and an instance thereof. Lehrer's case is diagrammed in Figure 5. In addition to the usual conventions, logical relationships are represented by double solid lines. As the diagram shows, the fact *p*—someone in Smith's office owning a Ford—is logically related to the fact *q* & *r*—Jones's owning a Ford and Jones's working in Smith's office. The fact *q* & *r* is, in turn, logically related to the fact *q* and to the fact *r*. *q* causes S's belief of *q* and, by inference, his belief of *q* & *r* and of *p*. Similarly, *r* is a cause of S's belief of *p*. Hence, by the above principle, *p* is a cause of S's belief of *p*. Since Smith's inferences are warranted, even setting aside his belief of *s* & *t*, he knows *p*.

In a similar way, universal facts may be causes of beliefs thereof. The fact that all men are mortal is logically related to its instances: John's being mortal, George's being mortal, Oscar's being mortal, etc. Now suppose that S perceives George, John, Oscar, etc., to be mortal (by seeing them die). He infers from these facts that all men are mortal, an inference which, I assume, is warranted. Since each of the facts, John is mortal, George is mortal, Oscar is mortal, etc., is a cause of S's believing that fact, each is also a cause of S's believing that all men are mortal. Moreover, since the universal fact that all men are mortal is logically related to each of these particular facts, this universal fact is a cause of S's belief of it. Hence, S can be said to know that all men are mortal. In analogous fashions, S can know various other logically compound propositions.

We can now formulate the analysis of knowing as follows:

S knows that p if and only if:
The fact p is causally connected in an "appropriate" way with S's believing p.

"Appropriate," knowledge-producing causal processes include the following:

(1) perception

(2) memory

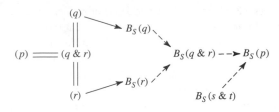

FIGURE 5

(3) a causal chain, exemplifying either Pattern 1 or 2, which is correctly reconstructed by inferences, each of which is warranted. (Background propositions warrant an inference only if they are true.)10

(4) combinations of (1), (2), and (3)

We have seen that this analysis is *stronger* than the traditional analysis in certain respects: the causal requirement and the correct-reconstruction requirement are absent from the older analysis. These additional requirements enable my analysis to circumvent Gettier's counterexamples to the traditional one. But my analysis is *weaker* than the traditional analysis in another respect. In at least one popular interpretation of the traditional analysis, a knower must be able to justify or give evidence for any proposition he knows. For S to know p at t, S must be able, at t, to *state* his justification for believing p, or his grounds for p. My analysis makes no such requirement, and the absence of this requirement enables me to account for cases of knowledge that would wrongly be excluded by the traditional analysis.

I know now, for example, that Abraham Lincoln was born in 1809.[11] I originally came to know this fact, let us suppose, by reading an encyclopedia article. I believed that this encyclopedia was trustworthy and that its saying Lincoln was born in 1809 must have resulted from the fact that Lincoln was indeed born in 1809. Thus, my original knowledge of this fact was founded on a warranted inference. But now I no longer remember this inference. I remember that Lincoln was born in 1809, but not that this is stated in a certain encyclopedia. I no longer have any pertinent beliefs that highly confirm the proposition that Lincoln was born in 1809. Nevertheless, I know this proposition now. My original knowledge of it was preserved until now by the causal process of memory.

Defenders of the traditional analysis would doubtlessly deny that I really do know Lincoln's birth year. This denial, however, stems from a desire to protect their analysis. It seems clear that many things we know were originally learned in a way that we no longer remember. The range of our knowledge would be drastically reduced if these items were denied the status of knowledge.

Other species of knowledge without explicit evidence could also be admitted by my analysis. Notice that I have not closed the list of "appropriate" causal processes. Leaving the list open is desirable, because there may be some presently controversial causal processes that we may later deem "appropriate" and, therefore, knowledge-producing. Many people now doubt the legitimacy of claims to extrasensory perception. But if conclusive evidence were to establish the existence of causal processes connecting physical facts with certain persons' beliefs without the help of standard perceptual processes, we might decide to call such beliefs items of knowledge. This would be another species of knowledge in which the knower might be unable to justify or defend his belief. My analysis allows for the possibility of such knowledge, though it doesn't commit one to it.

Special comments are in order about knowledge of our own mental states. This is a very difficult and controversial topic, so I hesitate to discuss it, but something must be said about it. Probably there are some mental states that are clearly distinct from the subject's beliefs that he is in such a state. If so, then there is presumably a causal process connecting the existence of such states with the subject's belief thereof. We may add this kind of process to the list of "appropriate" causal processes. The more difficult cases are those in which the state is hardly distinguishable from the subject's believing that he is in that state. My being in pain and my believing that I am in pain are hardly distinct states of affairs. If there is no distinction here between the believing and the believed, how can there be a causal connection between them? For the purposes of the present analysis, we may regard identity as a "limiting" or "degenerate" case of a causal connection, just as zero may be regarded as a "limiting" or "degenerate" case of a number. It is not surprising that knowledge of one's own mental state should turn out to be a limiting or degenerate case of knowledge. Philosophers have long recognized its peculiar status. While some philosophers have regarded it as a paradigm case of knowledge, others have claimed that we have no "knowledge" of our mental states at all. A theory of knowledge that makes knowledge of one's own mental states rather different from garden-variety species of knowledge is, in so far forth, acceptable and even welcome.

In conclusion, let me answer some possible objections to my analysis. It might be doubted whether a causal analysis adequately provides the meaning of the word 'knows' or of the sentence (-schema) "S knows p." But I am not interested in giving the *meaning* of "S knows p"; only its *truth conditions*. I claim to have given one correct set of truth conditions for "S knows p." Truth conditions of a sentence do not always provide its meaning. Consider, for example, the following truth-conditions statement: "The sentence 'Team T wins the baseball game' is true if and only if team T has more runs at the end of the game than the opposing team." This statement fails to provide the meaning of the sentence 'Team T wins the baseball game'; for it fails to indicate an essential part of the meaning of that sentence, viz., that to win a game is to achieve the presumed goal of playing it. Someone might fully understand the truth conditions given above and yet fail to understand the meaning of the sentence because he has no understanding of the notion of "winning" in general.

Truth conditions should not be confused with verification conditions. My analysis of "S knows p" does not purport to give procedures for *finding out* whether a person (including oneself) knows a given proposition. No doubt, we sometimes do know that people know certain propositions, for we sometimes know that their beliefs are causally connected (in appropriate ways) with the facts believed. On the other hand, it may often be difficult or even impossible to find out whether this condition holds for a given proposition and a given person. For example, it may be difficult for me to find out whether I really do remember a certain fact that I seem to remember. The difficulties that exist for *finding out* whether someone knows a given proposition do not constitute difficulties for my analysis, however.

In the same vein it should be noted that I have made no attempt to answer skeptical problems. My analysis gives no answer to the skeptic who asks that I start from the content of my own experience and then prove that I know there is a material world, a past, etc. I do not take this to be one of the jobs of giving truth conditions for "S knows that p."

The analysis presented here flies in the face of a well-established tradition in epistemology, the view that epistemological questions are questions of logic or justification, not causal or genetic questions. This traditional view, however, must not go unquestioned. Indeed, I think my analysis shows that the question of whether someone knows a certain proposition is, in part, a causal question, although, of course, the question of what the correct analysis is of "S knows that p" is not a causal question.

NOTES

1. "Is Justified True Belief Knowledge?" Analysis, XXIII.6, ns 96 (June 1963): 121–123. New analyses have been proposed by Michael Clark, "Knowledge and Grounds: A Comment on Mr. Gettier's Paper," Analysis, XXIV.2, ns 98 (December 1963): 46–48; Ernest Sosa, "The Analysis of 'Knowledge That P,'" Analysis, XXV. 1, ns 103 (October 1964): 1–3; and Keith Lehrer, "Knowledge, Truth, and Evidence," Analysis, XXV.5, ns 105 (April 1965): 168–175. An outline of a causal theory of knowing appears in Robert Binkley, "A Theory of Practical Reason," The Philosophical Review, LXXIV.4, ns 412 (October 1965): 423–448 (cf. pp. 432–435).

2. Op. cit. Criticisms of Clark's analysis will be discussed below.

3. "The Causal Theory of Perception," Proceedings of the Aristotelian Society, Supp. Vol. XXXV (1961).

4. If a laser photograph (hologram) is illuminated by light waves, especially waves from a laser, the effect of the hologram on the viewer is exactly as if the object were being seen. It preserves three-dimensionality completely, and even gives appropriate parallax effects as the viewer moves relative to it. Cf. E. N. Leith and J. Upatnieks, "Photography by Laser," Scientific American, CCXII, 6 (June 1965): 24.

5. For further defense of this kind of procedure, with attention to perception, cf. Grice, op. cit. A detailed

causal analysis of remembering is presented by C. B. Martin and Max Deutscher, "Remembering," *The Philosophical Review,* LXXV.2, ns 414 (April 1966): 161—196.

6. Causal connections can hold between states of affairs, such as believings, as well as between events. If a given event or state, in conjunction with other events or states, "leads to" or "results in" another event state (or the same state obtaining at a later time), it will be called a "cause" of the latter. I shall also speak of "facts" being causes.

7. A fact can be a cause of a belief even if it does not *initiate* the belief. Suppose I believe that there is a lake in a certain locale, this belief having started in a manner quite unconnected with the existence of the lake. Continuing to have the belief, I go to the locale and perceive the lake. At this juncture, the existence of the lake becomes a cause of my believing that there is a lake there. This is analogous to a table top that is supported by four legs. When a fifth leg is inserted flush beneath the table top, it too becomes a cause of the table top's not falling. It has a causal role in the support of the table top even though, before it was inserted, the table top was adequately supported.

8. Clearly we cannot require someone to reconstruct every detail, since this would involve knowledge of minute physical phenomena, for example, of which ordinary people are unaware. On the other hand, it is difficult to give criteria to identify which details, in general, are "important." This will vary substantially from case to case.

9. "Mr. Clark's Definition of 'Knowledge'," *Analysis,* XXV.1, ns 103 (October 1964): 8–9.

10. Perhaps background propositions that help warrant *S*'s inference must be *known* by *S*, as well as true. This requirement could be added without making our analysis of "*S* knows that *p*" circular. For these propositions would not include *p*. In other words, the analysis of knowledge could be regarded as recursive.

11. This kind of case is drawn from an unpublished manuscript of Gilbert Harman.

KEITH LEHRER

Knowledge, Truth and Evidence

If a man is not completely justified in believing something, then he does not know it. On the other hand, if what he believes is true and he is completely justified in believing it, then it would seem that he knows it. This suggests that we may analyze the statement

   S knows h

as the conjunction of

   (i) h is true,

   (ii) S believes h, and

   (iii) S is completely justified in believing h.

Professor Gettier has recently shown this analysis to be defective. To meet the kind of counterexample he has formulated, it is necessary to add some fourth condition to the proposed analysis.

The primary concern of my paper will be to solve the problem that Professor Gettier has raised. However, before turning to that problem, I wish to make a few remarks concerning the third condition to avoid misunderstanding. Firstly, a person may be completely justified in believing something which is in fact false. We shall consider examples of this shortly.

Secondly, though there may be some cases in which a person is completely justified in believing something in the absence of any evidence to justify his belief, the analysis offered here is intended to apply only to those cases in which a person must have evidence to be completely justified in believing what he does. There are a number of ways in which a person who has evidence for what he believes may nevertheless fail to be completely justified in believing what he does. A person may, for example, fail to be completely justified simply because the evidence that he has is not adequate to completely justify his belief.

Moreover, if a person has evidence adequate to completely justify his belief, he may still fail to be completely justified in believing what he does

because his belief is not *based on* that evidence. What I mean by saying that a person's belief is not based on certain evidence is that he would not appeal to that evidence to justify his belief. For example, a detective who rejects the truthful testimony of a reliable eye-witness to a crime, but accepts the lying testimony of an ignorant meddler, when both tell him that Brentano committed the crime, would fail to be completely justified in believing this. For his belief is not based on the adequate evidence supplied by the truthful eye-witness but is instead based on the inadequate evidence supplied by an ignorant man.

Again, even if a person has evidence adequate to completely justify his belief and his belief is based on that evidence, he may still fail to be completely justified in believing what he does. For he may be unable to provide any plausible line of reasoning to show how one could reach the conclusion he believes from the evidence that he has. For example, a detective who has a complicated mass of evidence that is conclusive evidence for the conclusion that Little Nelson is the leader of the gang might reach that conclusion from his evidence by what is nothing more than a lucky guess. Imagine that the only line of reasoning he can supply to show how he reached his conclusion is entirely fallacious or that he can supply none. In that case the detective would not be completely justified in believing what he does.

Finally, a man may be completely justified in believing something but fail to believe it because he does not appreciate the strength of his evidence. In this case, the man lacks knowledge because of a lack of belief rather than of justification for belief.

With these qualifications having been noted, let us now turn to the problem of amending the proposed analysis of knowledge to meet the counterexample Professor Gettier has presented against it.

Gettier argues that if a person is completely justified in believing P and he deduces H from P, and believes H on the basis of P, then he is completely justified in believing H. Given this principle we can construct a counterexample to the proposed analysis. Imagine the following: I see two men enter my office whom I know to be Mr. Nogot and Mr. Havit. I have just seen Mr. Nogot depart from a Ford, and he tells me that he has just purchased the car. Indeed, he shows me a certificate that states that he owns the Ford. Moreover, Mr. Nogot is a friend of mine whom I know to be honest and reliable. On the basis of this evidence, I would be completely justified in believing

P1: Mr. Nogot, who is in my office, owns a Ford.

I might deduce from this that

H: Someone in my office owns a Ford.

I would then be completely justified in believing H. However, imagine that, contrary to my evidence, Mr. Nogot has deceived me and that he does not own a Ford. Moreover, imagine that Mr. Havit, the only other man I see in my room, does own a Ford, though I have no evidence that he (or I) owns a Ford. In this case, which I shall hereafter refer to as *case one,* though H is true, and I am completely justified in my belief that it is true, I do not know that it is true. For, the reason that H is true is that Mr. Havit owns a Ford, and I have no evidence that this is so.

We have said that a person is completely justified in believing a statement only if he has adequate evidence to completely justify his belief and his belief is based on that evidence. It might seem that since

P1: Mr. Nogot, who is in my office, owns a Ford

is false, it is also false that I have evidence adequate to completely justify my belief that

H: Someone in my office owns a Ford.

But this is incorrect. Leaving P1 aside, I have adequate evidence for H that consists entirely of *true* statements. The evidence is that which I have for P1, namely, that I see Mr. Nogot in my office, have just seen him get out of a Ford, etc. All these things are true and provide evidence adequate to completely justify my believing H. Moreover, my belief that H is true is based on that evidence, though it is also based on P1.

Nevertheless, it might seem reasonable to add to the proposed analysis of knowledge a fourth condition to the effect that if a person knows something, then his belief is not based on any false statements. Thus in addition to the previous three conditions, we would add the condition

(iv) It is not the case that S believes h on the basis of any false statement.

But this condition is much too strong. Imagine that case one is modified so that in addition to the evidence that I have for believing that Mr. Nogot owns a Ford, I have equally strong evidence for believing that Mr. Havit owns a Ford. Moreover, imagine that my belief that someone in my office owns a Ford is based both on the false statement

P1: Mr. Nogot, who is in my office, owns a Ford

and on the true statement

P2: Mr. Havit, who is in my office, owns a Ford.

In this case, which I shall refer to as *case two,* it would be correct to say that I know

H: Someone in my office owns a Ford.

But condition (iv) is not satisfied, and therefore must be rejected.

I know H in case two, because in addition to the evidence that I have for the false statement P1 which entails (but is not entailed by) H, I also have evidence for the true statement P2 which entails H, and this additional evidence is adequate to completely justify my believing H. This suggests that the following condition might be more satisfactory than the one we have just considered:

(iv a) If S is completely justified in believing any false statement p which entails (but is not entailed by)h, then S has evidence adequate to completely justify his believing h in addition to the evidence he has for p.

This condition is not satisfied in case one. In that case I do not have evidence adequate to completely justify my believing

H: Someone in my office owns a Ford

in addition to the evidence I have for the false statement

P1: Mr. Nogot, who is in my office, owns a Ford

which entails H. Thus, condition (iv a) will yield the correct result that I do not know H in case one. So far so good, but now let us consider case two.

In case two, I know

H: Someone in my office owns a Ford

because I have adequate evidence for the true statement

P2: Mr. Havit, who is in my office, owns a Ford.

However, in this case I also have adequate evidence for the false statement

P3: Mr. Nogot and Mr. Havit, who are in my office, own Fords

and, consequently, I would be completely justified in believing P3. But P3 entails H, and, unfortunately, I have no evidence for H in addition to the evidence that I have for P3. The only evidence that I have for H is precisely the evidence that I have for the false statement P3 which entails H. Thus, condition (iv a) would yield the incorrect result that I do not know H in case two, and, consequently, this condition must also be rejected.

To avoid this difficulty, we could formulate a condition to the effect that if a person is completely justified in believing a false statement which entails a true one, then some part of his evidence must be adequate to completely justify his believing the true statement but not adequate to completely justify his believing the false statement. In case two, the evidence that I have for

P2: Mr. Havit, who is in my office, owns a Ford

is adequate to completely justify my believing the true statement

H: Someone in my office owns a Ford

but not adequate to completely justify my believing the false statements

P1: Mr. Nogot, who is in my office, owns a Ford

or

P3: Mr. Nogot and Mr. Havit, who are in my office, own Fords.

The fourth condition would read as follows:

(iv b) If S is completely justified in believing any false statement p which entails (but is not entailed by) h, then S has some evidence adequate to completely justify his believing h but not adequate to completely justify his believing p.

This condition will not be satisfied in case one, because in that case I do not have any evidence that would be adequate to completely justify my believing

H: Someone in my office owns a Ford

that would not completely justify my believing

P1: Mr. Nogot, who is in my office, owns a Ford.

This is a desired result, because I do not know H in that case. But this condition must also be rejected.

The reason is that there are statements which a person might be completely justified in believing in the absence of any evidence to support them. I shall defend the claim that there are such statements presently, but let us assume for the moment that R is such a statement. Moreover, assume that R is false. Now, imagine the following. I have adequate evidence to completely justify my believing

P2: Mr. Havit, who is in my office, owns a Ford

but do not have any evidence for P1, and again P2 is true. In this case, which I shall refer to as *case three*, we may suppose that the evidence I have for P2 is irrelevant to R and that I am completely justified in believing the conjunction of P2 and R. However, this conjunction is a false statement, because R is false, and it entails

H: Someone in my office owns a Ford.

Thus I have no evidence adequate to completely justify my believing H that is not also adequate to completely justify my believing the false statement which is the conjunction of P2 and R and which entails H. So, condition (iv b) would not be satisfied in this case, even though I know that H is true.

The proof that there are statements which a person is completely justified in believing in the absence of any evidence to support them is this. Assume that evidence e is adequate to completely justify my believing h. In that case, the statement that e materially implies h is one that I am completely justified in believing in the absence of any evidence to support it or its denial.

To solve the problem it is essential to notice what would result were I to suppose in the cases we have considered that those statements are false which are in fact false and which entail H. For example, if I were to suppose in case one that

P1: Mr. Nogot, who is in my office, owns a Ford

is false, I would not in that case be justified in appealing to the evidence that I have for P1 to justify my believing H. Consequently, I would not be completely justified in believing H in case one if I were to suppose that P1 is false.

On the other hand, if I were to suppose in case two that P1 is false, we would not obtain the same result. For in that case I have adequate evidence for P2 as well as P1, and, consequently, I would still be justified in believing H on the basis of the evidence I have for P2. Moreover, even if I were to suppose that the conjunction of P1 and P2 is false in case two, I would still be completely justified in believing H. For I could reason as follows. To suppose that the conjunction of P1 and P2 is false, I need only suppose that one of the conjuncts is false. If P1 is false, then I would be completely justified in believing H on the basis of the evidence that I have for P2. If P2 is false, then I would be completely justified in believing H on the basis of the evidence that I have for P1. Therefore, even if I were to suppose that the conjunction is false, since I am not thereby committed to supposing that both conjuncts are false, I would still be completely justified in believing H.

Similarly, in case three I would be completely justified in believing H even if I were to suppose the conjunction of P2 and R is false. For I could reason that to suppose the conjunction is false does not commit me to supposing that both conjuncts are false, and, consequently, I may suppose that R is false and P2 is true. I would then be completely justified in believing H on the basis of the evidence I have for P2.

We now have the following results. In case one I would not be completely justified in believing H if I were to suppose that P1 is false, but in case two I would be completely justified in believing H even if I were to suppose that P1 is false or if I were to suppose that the conjunction of P1 and P2 is false, and in case three I would be completely justified in believing H even if I were to suppose that the conjunction of R and P2 is false. Since I know H to be true in case two and three but not in case one, I propose the following as a fourth condition in the analysis of knowledge:

(iv c) If S is completely justified in believing any false statement p which entails (but is not entailed by) h, then S would be completely justified in believing h even if S were to suppose that p is false.

This condition, as we have seen, is satisfied in case two and three but not in case one. Consequently, by adding it to our analysis of knowledge, we gain the result that our analysis is satisfied in just those cases in which we have knowledge and not otherwise.

In connection with these remarks, it is important to notice certain facts about the role of supposition in justification. In the first place, a man need not believe what he supposes to be true. I may suppose that something is true (perhaps to comply with the wishes of another) and examine the consequence of such a supposition without believing what I suppose. I may suppose that P1 is false and examine the consequences of that supposition without believing what I suppose. Secondly, a man need not count as evidence all that he supposes. I may suppose that the conjunction of P1 and P2 is false without counting that as evidence that I have. For my supposition might be entirely unjustified. Thirdly, suppositions which are neither believed nor counted as evidence may still have the role of preventing a person from appealing to certain evidence that he has to justify his beliefs. Thus, were I to suppose in case one that P1 is false, I would not believe this nor would I count it as evidence that I have, but that supposition would prevent me from appealing to the evidence I have for P1 to justify my believing H.

With these qualifications, I propose the conjunction of conditions (i), (ii), (iii) and (iv c) as an analysis of knowledge.

JOHN POLLOCK

The Gettier Problem

1. INTRODUCTION

It is rare in philosophy to find a consensus on any substantive issue, but for some time there was almost complete consensus on what is called 'the justified true belief analysis of knowing'. According to that analysis:

S knows P if and only if:
(1)   P is true;
(2)   S believes P; and
(3)   S is justified in believing P.

In the period immediately preceding the publication of Gettier's landmark article "Is justified true belief knowledge?", this analysis was affirmed by virtually every writer in epistemology. Then Gettier published his article and single-handedly changed the course of epistemology. He did this by presenting two clear and undeniable counterexamples to the justified true belief analysis. Recounting the example given in chapter one, consider Smith who believes falsely but with good reason that Jones owns a Ford. Smith has no idea where Brown is, but he arbitrarily picks Barcelona and infers from the putative fact that Jones owns a Ford that either Jones owns a Ford or Brown is in Barcelona. It happens by chance that Brown is in Barcelona, so this disjunction is true. Furthermore, as Smith has good reason to believe that Jones owns a Ford, he is justified in believing this disjunction. But as his evidence does not pertain to the true disjunct of the disjunction, we would not regard Smith as knowing that either Jones owns a Ford or Brown is in Barcelona.

Gettier's paper was followed by a spate of articles attempting to meet his counterexamples by adding a fourth condition to the analysis of knowing. The first attempts to solve the Gettier problem turned on the observation that in Gettier's examples, the epistemic agent arrives at his justified true belief by reasoning from a false belief. That suggested the addition of a fourth condition something like the following:

S's grounds for believing P do not include any false beliefs.

It soon emerged, however, that further counterexamples could be constructed in which knowledge is lacking despite the believer's not inferring his belief from any false belief. Alvin Goldman [1976] constructed the following example. Suppose you are driving through the countryside and see what you take to be a barn. You see it in good light and from not too great a distance, it looks the way barns look, and so on. Furthermore, it is a barn. You then have justified true belief that it is a barn. But in an attempt to appear more opulent than they are, the people around here have taken to constructing very realistic barn facades that cannot readily be distinguished from the real thing when viewed from the highway. There are many more barn facades around than real barns. Under these circumstances we would not agree that you know that what you see is a barn, even though you have justified true belief. Furthermore, your belief that you see a barn is not inferred in any way from a belief about the absence of barn facades. Most likely the possibility of barn facades is something that will not even have occurred to you, much less have played a role in your reasoning.

We can construct an even simpler perceptual example. Suppose S sees a ball that looks red to him, and on that basis he correctly judges that it is red. But unbeknownst to S, the ball is illuminated by red lights and would look red to him even if it were not red. Then S does not know that the ball is red despite his having justified true belief to that effect. Furthermore, his reason for believing that the ball is red does not involve his believing that the ball is not illuminated by red lights. Illumination by red lights is related to his reasoning only as a defeater, not as a step in his reasoning. These examples, of other related examples indicate that justified true belief can fail to be knowledge because of the truth values of propositions that do not play a direct role in the reasoning underlying the belief. This observation led to a number of "defeasibility" analyses of knowing. The simplest defeasibility analysis would consist of adding a fourth condition requiring that there be no true defeaters. This might be accomplished as follows:

> There is no true proposition Q such that if Q were added to S's beliefs then he would no longer be justified in believing P.

But Keith Lehrer and Thomas Paxson [1969] presented the following counterexample to this simple proposal:

> Suppose I see a man walking to the library and remove a book from the library by concealing it beneath his coat. Since I am sure the man is Tom Grabit, whom I have often seen before when he attended my classes, I report that I know that Tom Grabit has removed the book. However, suppose further that Mrs. Grabit, the mother of Tom, has averred that on the day in question, Tom was not in the library, indeed, was thousands of miles away, and that Tom's identical twin brother, John Grabit, was in the library. Imagine, moreover, that I am entirely ignorant of the fact that Mrs. Grabit has said these things. The statement that she has said these things would defeat any justifications I have for believing that Tom Grabit removed the book, according to our present definition of defeasibility.
>
> The preceding might seem acceptable until we finish the story by adding that Mrs. Grabit is a compulsive and pathological liar, that John Grabit is a fiction of her demented mind, and that Tom Grabit took the book as I believed. Once this is added, it should be apparent that I did know that Tom Grabit removed the book. (p. 228)

A natural proposal for handling the Grabit example is that in addition to there being a true defeater there is a true defeater defeater, and that restores knowledge. For example, in the Grabit case it is true that Mrs. Grabit reported that Tom was not in the library but his twin brother John was there (a defeater), but it is also true that Mrs. Grabit is a compulsive and pathological liar and John Grabit is a fiction of her demented mind (a defeater defeater). It is difficult, however, to construct a precise principle that handles these correctly by appealing to true defeaters and true defeater defeaters. It will not do to amend the above as follows:

> If there is a true proposition Q such that if Q were added to S's beliefs then he would no longer be justified in believing P, then there is also a true proposition R such that if Q and R were both added to S's beliefs then he would be justified in believing P.

The simplest difficulty for this proposal is that adding R may add new reasons for believing P rather than restoring the old reasons. It is not trivial to see how to formulate a fourth condition incorporating defeater defeaters. I think that such a fourth condition will ultimately provide the solution to the Gettier problem, but no proposal of this sort has been worked out in the literature. I will pursue this further in the next section.

2. OBJECTIVE EPISTEMIC JUSTIFICATION

The Gettier problem has spawned a large number of proposals for the analysis of knowledge. As the literature on the problem has developed, the proposals have become increasingly complex in the attempt to meet more and more complicated counterexamples to simpler analyses. The result is that even if some very complex analysis should turn out to be immune from counterexample, it would seem *ad hoc*. We would be left wondering why we employ any such complicated concept. I will suggest that our concept of knowledge is actually a reasonably simple one. The complexities required by increasingly complicated Gettier-type examples are not complexities in the concept of knowledge, but instead reflect complexities in the structure of our epistemic norms.

In the discussion of externalism I commented on the distinction between subjective and objective senses of 'should believe' and how that pertains to epistemology. The subjective sense of 'should believe' concerns what we should believe given what we actually do believe (possibly incorrectly). The objective sense of 'should believe' concerns what we should believe given what is in fact true. But what we should believe given what is true is just the truths, so the objective sense of 'should believe' gets identified with truth. The subjective sense, on the other hand, is ordinary epistemic justification. What I now want to suggest, however, is that there is an intermediate sense of 'should believe', that might also be regarded as objective but does not reduce to truth.

It is useful to compare epistemic judgments with moral judgments. Focusing on the latter, let us suppose that a person S subjectively should do **A.** This will be so *for particular reasons.* There may be relevant facts of which the person is not apprised that bear upon these reasons. It might be the case that even in the face of all the relevant facts, S should still do **A.** That can happen in either of two ways: (1) among the relevant facts may be new reasons for doing **A** of which S has no knowledge; or (2) the relevant facts may, on sum, leave the original reasons intact. What I have been calling 'the objective sense of "should" appeals to both kinds of considerations, but there is also an important kind of moral evaluation that appeals only to considerations of the second kind. This is the notion of the original reasons surviving intact, and it provides us with another variety of objective moral evaluation. We appraise a person and his act simultaneously by saying that he has a moral obligation to perform the act (he subjectively should do it) and his moral obligation derives from what are in fact good reasons (reasons withstanding the test of truth). It seems to me that we are often in the position of making such appraisals, although moral language provides us with no simple way of expressing them. The purely objective sense of 'should' pertains more to acts than to agents, and hence does not express moral obligation. Therefore, it should not be confusing if I express appraisals of this third variety artificially by saying that S has an *objective obligation* to do **A** when he has an obligation to do **A** and the obligation derives from what are in fact good reasons (in the face of all the relevant facts).

How might objective obligations be analyzed? It might at first be supposed that S has an objective obligation to do **A** if and only if (1) S subjectively

should do **A,** and (2) there is no set of truths X such that if these truths were added to S's beliefs (and their negations removed in those cases in which S disbelieves them) then it would be true that S subjectively should do **A** *for the same reason.* This will not quite do, however. It takes account of the fact that moral reasons are defeasible, but it does not take account of the fact that the defeaters are also defeasible. For example, S might spy a drowning man and be in a position to save him with no risk to himself. Then he subjectively should do so. But suppose that, unbeknownst to S, the man is a terrorist who fell in the lake while he was on his way to blow up a bus station and kill many innocent people. Presumably, if S knew that then he would no longer have a subjective obligation to save the man, and so it follows by the proposed analysis that S does not have an objective obligation to save the man. But suppose it is also the case that what caused the man to fall in the lake was that he underwent a sudden religious conversion that persuaded him to give up his evil ways and devote the rest of his life to good deeds. If S knew this, then he would again have a subjective obligation to save the man for the same reasons as his original reasons, and so he has an objective obligation to save the man. There is, however, no way to accommodate this on the proposed analysis. On that basis, if a set of truths defeats an obligation, there is no way to get it undefeated again by appealing to a broader class of truths.

What the analysis of objective should require is that if S were apprised of "enough" truths (all the relevant ones) then he would still be subjectively obligated to do **A.** This can be cashed out as requiring that there is a set of truths such that if S were apprised of them then he would be subjectively obligated in the same way as he originally was, and those are all the relevant truths in the sense that if he were to become apprised of any further truths that would not make any difference. Precisely:

S has an objective obligation to do **A** if and only if:
(1)   S subjectively should do **A;** and
(2)   there is a set **X** of truths such that, given any more inclusive set **Y** of truths, necessarily, if the truths in **Y** were added to S's beliefs (and their negations removed in those cases in which

which S disbelieves them) then it would still be true *for the same reason* that subjectively should do **A**.

Now let's return to epistemology. An important difference between moral judgments and epistemic judgments is that basic moral judgments concern obligation whereas basic epistemic judgments concern permissibility. This reflects an important difference in the way moral and epistemic norms function. In morality, reasons are reasons for obligations. Anything is permissible that is not proscribed. In epistemology, on the other hand, epistemic justification concerns what beliefs you are permitted to hold (not 'obliged to hold'), and reasons are required for permissibility. Thus the analogy between epistemology and morality is not exact. The analogue of objective moral obligation is "objective epistemic permissibility", or as I will say more simply, *objective epistemic justification*. I propose to ignore our earlier concept of objective epistemic justification because it simply reduces to truth. Our new concept of objective epistemic justification can be defined as follows, on analogy to our notion of objective moral obligation:

S is objectively justified in believing P if and only if:
(1)   S is (subjectively) justified in believing P); and
(2)   there is a set **X** of truths such that, given any more inclusive set **Y** of truths, necessarily, if the truths in **Y** were added to S's beliefs (and their negations removed in those cases in which S disbelieves them) and S believed P *for the same reason* then he would still be (subjectively) justified in believing P.

Despite the complexity of its definition, the concept of objective epistemic justification is a simple and intuitive one. As is so often the case with technical concepts, the concept is easier to grasp than it is to define. It can be roughly glossed as the concept of getting the right answer while doing everything right. I am construing 'S is justified in believing P' in such a way that it entails that S does believe P, so objective justification entails justified belief. It also entails truth, because if P were false and we added ~P to **Y** then S would no longer be justified in

believing P. Thus, objective epistemic justification entails justified true belief.

My claim is now that objective epistemic justification is very close to being the same thing as knowledge. We will find in section three that a qualification is required to turn objective justification into knowledge, but in the meantime it can be argued that the Gettier problem can be resolved by taking objective epistemic justification to be a necessary condition for knowledge. This enables us to avoid the familiar Gettier-type examples that create difficulties for other analyses of knowledge. Consider one of Gettier's original examples. Jones believes, correctly, that Brown owns a Ford. He believes this on the grounds that he has frequently seen Brown drive a particular Ford, he has ridden in it, he has seen Brown's auto registration which lists him as owning that Ford, and so forth. But unknown to Jones, Brown sold that Ford yesterday and bought a new one. Under the circumstances, we would not agree that Jones now knows that Brown owns a Ford, despite the fact that he has justified true belief to that effect. This is explained by noting that Jones is not objectively justified in believing that Brown owns a Ford. This is because there is a truth—namely, that Brown does not own the Ford Jones thinks he owns—such that if Jones became apprised of it then his original reasons would no longer justify him in believing that Jones owns a Ford, and becoming apprised of further truths would not restore those original reasons.

To take a more complicated case, consider Goldman's barn example. Suppose you are driving through the countryside and see what you take to be a barn. You see it in good light and from not too great a distance, and it looks like a barn. Furthermore, it is a barn. You then have justified true belief that it is a barn. But the countryside here is littered with very realistic barn facades that cannot readily be distinguished from the real thing when viewed from the highway. There are many more barn facades than real barns. Under these circumstances we would not agree that you know that what you see is a barn, even though you have justified true belief. This can be explained by noting that if you were aware of the preponderance of barn facades in the vicinity then you would not be justified in believing you see a barn, and your original justification could not be restored by learning other truths (such as that it is really a barn). Consequently, your belief that you see a barn is not objectively justified.

Finally, consider the Grabit example. Here we want to say that I really do know that Tom Grabit stole the book, despite the fact that Mrs. Grabit alleged that Tom was thousands of miles away and his twin brother John was in the library. That she said this is a true defeater, but there is also a true defeater defeater, viz., that Mrs. Grabit is a compulsive and pathological liar and John Grabit is a fiction of her demented mind. If we include *both* (if these truths in the set **X** then I remain justified *for my original reason* in believing that Tom stole the book, so in this case my belief is objectively justified despite the existence of a true defeater.

To a certain extent, I think that the claim that knowledge requires objective epistemic justification provides a solution to the Gettier problem. But it might be disqualified as a solution to the Gettier problem on the grounds that the definition of objective justification is vague in one crucial respect. It talks about being justified, *for the same reason*, in believing P. I think that that notion makes pre-theoretic good sense, but to spell out what it involves requires us to construct a complete epistemological theory. That, I think, is why the Gettier problem has proven so intractable. The complexities in the analysis of knowing all have to do with filling out this clause. The important thing to realize, however, is that these complexities have nothing special to do with knowledge per se. What they pertain to is the structure of epistemic justification and the way in which beliefs come to be justified on the basis of other beliefs and nondoxastic states. Thus even if it is deemed that we have not yet solved the Gettier problem, we have at least put the blame where it belongs—not on knowledge but on the structure of epistemic justification and the complexity of our epistemic norms.

Let us turn then to the task of filling in some of the details concerning epistemic justification. In chapter two, I proposed an analysis of epistemic justification in terms of ultimately undefeated arguments. That analysis proceeded within the context of a subsequently rejected foundationalist theory, but basically the same analysis can be resurrected within direct realism. For this purpose we must take

arguments to proceed from internal states (both doxastic and nondoxastic states) to doxastic states, the links between steps being provided by reasons. Within direct realism, reasons are internal states. They are generally doxastic states, but not invariably. At the very least, perceptual and memory states can also be reasons.

Our epistemic norms permit us to begin reasoning from certain internal states without those states being supported by further reasoning. Such states can be called *basic states*. Paramount among these are perceptual and memory states. Arguments must always begin with basic states and proceed from them to nonbasic doxastic states. What we might call *linear arguments* proceed from basic states to their ultimate conclusions through a sequence of steps each consisting of a belief for which the earlier steps provide reasons. It seems likely, however, that we must allow arguments to have more complicated structures than those permitted in linear arguments. Specifically, we must allow "subsidiary arguments" to occur within the main argument. A subsidiary argument can begin with premises that are merely assumed for the sake of the argument rather than because they have already been justified. For instance, in the forms of conditional proof familiar from elementary logic, in establishing a conditional $(P \supset Q)$, we may begin by taking P as a premise (even though it has not been previously established), deriving Q from it, and then "discharging" the assumption of the antecedent to obtain the conditional $(P \supset Q)$. It seems that something similar occurs in epistemological arguments. We can accommodate this by taking *an argument conditional on a set* **X** *of propositions* to be an argument beginning not just from basic states but also from doxastic states that consist of believing the members of **X**. Then an argument that justifies a conclusion for a person may have embedded in it subsidiary arguments that are conditional on propositions the person does not believe. For present purposes we need not pursue all the details of the permissible structures of epistemiological arguments, but the general idea of conditional arguments will be useful below.

An argument *supports* a belief if and only if that belief occurs as a step in the argument that does not occur within any subsidiary argument. A person *instantiates* an argument if and only if he is in the basic states from which the argument begins and he believes the conclusion of the argument on the basis of that argument. Typically, in reasoning to a conclusion one will proceed first to some intermediate conclusions from which the final conclusion is obtained. The notion of holding a belief on the basis of the argument is to be understood as requiring that one also believes the intermediate conclusions on the basis of the initial parts of the argument.

Epistemic justification consists of holding a belief on the basis of an ultimately undefeated argument, that is, instantiating an ultimately undefeated argument supporting the belief. To repeat the definition of an ultimately undefeated argument, every argument proceeding from basic states that S is actually in will be *undefeated at level 0* for S. Of course, arguments undefeated at level 0 can embed subsidiary arguments that are conditional on propositions S does not believe. Some arguments will support defeaters for other arguments, so we define an argument to be undefeated at level 1 if and only if it is not defeated by any other arguments undefeated at level 0. Among the arguments defeated at level 0 may be some that supported defeaters for others, so if we take arguments undefeated at level 2 to be arguments undefeated at level 0 that are not defeated by any arguments undefeated at level 1, there may be arguments undefeated at level 2 that were arguments defeated at level 1. In general, we define an argument to be *undefeated at level n + 1* if and only if it is undefeated at level 0 and is not defeated by any arguments undefeated at level n. An argument is *ultimately undefeated* if and only if there is some point beyond which it remains permanently undefeated; that is, for some N, the argument remains undefeated at level n for every n > N.

This gives us a picture of the structure of epistemic justification. Many details remain to be filled in, but we can use this picture without further elaboration to clarify the concept of objective epistemic justification. Roughly, a belief is objectively justified if and only if it is held on the basis of some ultimately undefeated argument **A,** and either **A** is not defeated by any argument conditional on true propositions not believed by S, or if it is then there are further true propositions such that the initial defeating arguments will be defeated by arguments conditional on the enlarged set of true propositions.

This can be made precise by defining an *argument conditional on* **Y** to be any argument proceeding from basic states S is actually in together with doxastic states consisting of believing members of **Y.** We then say that an argument instantiated by S (not an argument conditional on **Y**) is *undefeated at level n + 1 relative to* **Y** if and only if it is undefeated by any argument undefeated at level n relative to **Y.** An argument is *ultimately undefeated relative to* **Y** if and only if there is an N such that it is undefeated at level n relative to **Y** for every n > N. Then the concept of objective epistemic justification can be made more precise as follows:

> S is objectively justified in believing P if and only if S instantiates some argument **A** supporting P which is ultimately undefeated relative to the set of all truths.

I will take this to be my official definition of objective epistemic justification. I claim, then, that the Gettier-style counterexamples to the traditional definition of knowledge can all be met by taking knowledge to require objective epistemic justification. This makes precise the way in which knowledge requires justification that is either undefeated by true defeaters, or if defeated by true defeaters then those defeaters are defeated by true defeater defeaters, and so on.

A common view has been that the reliability of one's cognitive processes is required for knowledge, and thus reliabilism has a place in the analysis of knowledge quite apart from whether it has a place in the analysis of epistemic justification. The observation that knowledge requires objective epistemic justification explains the appeal of the idea that knowledge requires reliability. Nondefeasible reasons logically entail their conclusions, so they are always perfectly reliable, but defeasible reasons can be more or less reliable under various circumstances. Discovering that the present circumstances are of a type in which a defeasible reason is unreliable consitiutes a defeater for the use of that reason. Objective justification requieres that if a belief is held on the basis of a defeasible reason then there are no true defeaters (or if there are then there are true defeater defeaters, and so on). Thus knowledge automatically requires that one's reasons be reliable under the present circumstances. Reliabilisim has a place in knowledge even if it has none in justification. It is worth emphasizing, however, that considerations of reliability are not central to the concept of knowledge. Rather than having to be imposed on the analysis in an *ad hoc* way, they emerge naturally from the observation that knowledge requires objective epistemic justification.

3. SOCIAL ASPECTS OF KNOWLEDGE

It is tempting to simply identify knowledge with objective epistemic justification. As I have pointed out, objective justification includes justified true belief, and it is immune from Gettier-style counterexamples. It captures the idea underlying defeasibility analyses. The basis idea is that *believed* defeaters can prevent justification, and defeaters that are true but not believed can prevent knowledge while leaving justification intact. However, there are also some examples that differ in important ways from the Gettier-style examples we have discussed so far, and they are not so easily handled in terms of there being true defeaters. These examples seem to have to with social aspects of knowing. The philosopher most prominently associated with these examples is Gilbert Harman. One of Harman's examples is as follows:

Suppose that Tom enters a room in which many people are talking excitedly although he cannot understand what they are saying. He sees a copy of the morning paper on a table. The headlines and main story reveal that a famous civil-rights leader has been assassinated. On reading the story he comes to believe it; it is true. . . .

Suppose that the assassination has been denied, even by eyewitnesses, the point of the denial being to avoid a racial explosion. The assassinated leader is reported in good health; the bullets are said, falsely, to have missed him and hit someone else. The denials occurred too late to prevent the original and true story from appearing in the paper that Tom has seen; but everyone else in the room has heard about the denials. None of them know what to believe. They all have information that Tom lacks. Would we judge Tom to be the only one who

knows that the assassination has actually occurred? . . . I do not think so. ([1968], p.172)

This example cannot be handled in the same way as the Grabit example. As in the Grabit example there is a true defeater, viz., that the news media have reported that the assassination did not occur. But just as in the Grabit example, there is also a true defeater defeater, viz., that the retraction of the original story was motivated by an attempt to avoid race riots and did not necessarily reflect the actual facts. The appeal to true defeaters and true defeater defeaters should lead us to treat this example just like the Grabit example, but that gives the wrong answer. The Grabit example is one in which the believer has knowledge, whereas the newspaper example is one in which the believer lacks knowledge.

Harman gives a second kind of example in a recent article:

In case one, Mary comes to know that Norman is in Italy when she calls his office and is told he is spending the summer in Rome. In case two, Norman seeks to give Mary the impression that he is in San Francisco by writing her a letter saying so, a letter he mails to San Francisco where a friend then mails it on to Mary. This letter is in the pile of unopened mail on Mary's desk before her when she calls Norman's office and is told he is spending the summer in Rome. In this case (case two), Mary does not come to know that Norman is in Italy.

It is unimportant in this case that Mary could obtain the misleading evidence. If the evidence is unobtainable, because Norman forgot to mail the letter after he wrote it, or because the letter was delivered to the wrong building where it will remain unopened, then it does not keep Mary from knowing that Norman is in Italy. ([1981], p. 164)

Again, there is a true defeater, viz., that the letter reports Norman to be in San Francisco. But there is also a true defeater defeater, viz., that the letter was written with the intention to deceive. So Mary's belief is objectively justified. Nevertheless, we want to deny that Mary knows that Norman is in Italy.

Harman ([1981], p. 164) summarizes these examples by writing, "There seem to be two ways in which such misleading evidence can undermine a person's knowledge. The evidence can either be evidence that it would be possible for the person to obtain himself or herself or evidence possessed by others in a relevant social group to which the person in question belongs." We might distinguish between these two examples by saying that in the first example there is a true defeater that is "common knowledge" in Tom's social group, whereas in the second example there is a true defeater that is "readily available" to Mary. I will loosely style these "common knowledge" and "ready availability" defeaters.

It is worth noting that a common knowledge defeater can be defeated by a defeater defeater that is also common knowledge. For example, if it were common knowledge that the news media was disclaiming the assassination, but also common knowledge that the disclaimer was fraudulent, then Tom would retain his knowledge that the assassination occurred even if he were unaware of both the disclaimer and its fraudulence. The same thing is true of ready availability defeaters. If Norman had a change of heart after sending the false letter and sent another letter explaining the trick he played on Mary, and both letters lay unopened on Mary's desk when she called Norman's office, her telephone call would give her knowledge that Norman is in Italy.

What is more surprising is that common knowledge and ready availability defeaters and defeater defeaters can be combined to result in knowledge. For instance, if Norman's trick letter lays unopened on Mary's desk when she makes the call, she will nevertheless acquire knowledge that Norman is in Italy if Norman is an important diplomat and, unbeknownst to her, the news media have been announcing all day that Norman is in Rome but has been trying to fool people about his location by sending out trick letters. This shows that despite the apparent differences between common knowledge and ready availability defeaters, there must be some kind of connection between them.

My suggestion is that these both reflect a more general social aspect of knowledge. We are "socially expected" to be aware of various things. We are expected to know what is announced on television, and we are expected to know what is in our mail. If we fail to know all these things and that makes a difference to whether we are justified in believing some true proposition P, then our objectively justified belief in P does not constitute knowledge. Let us say that a proposition is *socially sensitive for S* if and only if it is of a sort S is expected to believe when true. My claim is that Harman's examples are best handled by taking them to involve cases in which there are true socially sensitive defeaters. This might be doubted on the grounds that not all readily available truths are socially sensitive. For instance, supposed that instead of having his trick letter mailed from San Francisco, Norman had a friend secrete it under Mary's doormat. We are not socially expected to check regularly under our doormats, but nevertheless this is something we can readily do and so information secreted under our doormats counts as readily available. It does not, however, defeat knowledge. If the trick letter were secreted under Mary's doormat, we would regard her as knowing that Norman is in Italy. Suppose, on the other hand, that we lived in a society in which it is common to leave messages under doormats and everyone is expected to check his doormat whenever he comes home. In that case, if the trick letter were under Mary's doormat but she failed to check there before calling Norman's office, we would not regard that call as providing her with knowledge. These examples seem to indicate that it is social sensitivity and not mere ready availability that enables a truth to defeat a knowledge claim.

My suggestion is that we can capture the social aspect of knowledge by requiring a knower to hold his belief on the basis of an argument ultimately undefeated relative not just to the set of all truths, but also to the set of all socially sensitive truths. My proposal is:

> S knows P if and only if S instantiates some argument **A** supporting P which is (1) ultimately undefeated relative to the set of all truths, and (2) ultimately undefeated relative to the set all truths socially sensitive for S.

This proposal avoids both the Gettier problem and the social problems discussed by Harman. At this stage in history it would be rash to be very confident of any analysis of knowledge, but I put this forth tentatively as an analysis that seems to handle all of the known problems.

REFERENCES

Goldman, Alvin. "Discrimination and Perceptual Knowledge." *Journal of Philosophy* 73 (1976), 771–91.

Harman, G. "Knowledge, Inference and Explanation." *American Philosophical Quarterly* 5 (1968), 164–73.

Harman, G. "Reasoning and Evidence One Does Not Possess." In Peter French, et al., eds. *Midwest Studies in Philosophy,* vol. 5. Minneapolis: University of Minnesota Press, 1981, 163–82.

Lehrer, Keith, and Thomas D. Paxon Jr. "Knowledge: Undefeated Justified True Belief." *Journal of Philosophy* 66 (1969), 225–37.

HELEN E. LONGINO

The Fate of Knowledge in Social Theories of Science

INTRODUCTION

My project has been to develop an analysis of scientific inquiry that both acknowledges the social dimensions of inquiry and keeps room for the normative and prescriptive concerns that have been the traditional preoccupation of philosophers.[1] Is such a project really feasible? Many sociologists and philosophers answer in the negative.

Philip Kitcher (1991 and this volume), for example, claims that in spite of my intention to provide a new account of objectivity and a way of thinking about inquiry that integrates its social and cognitive dimensions (see Longino 1990), the account I do provide cannot rise above a relativism that is incapable of distinguishing between evolutionary theory and creationism (or your disreputable program of choice). He does this by extracting from my account a definition of knowledge that exhibits this weakness. That definition will be the subject of my remarks later in the chapter.

Sociologists and anthropologists of science, on the other hand, have taken themselves to offer a significant challenge to the philosopher. Through a number of different case studies, they have argued that scientific knowledge is not developed by the application of procedures ratified by epistemological norms of the sort recognized by philosophers. Instead scientists negotiate, borrow, barter, and steal—use any means necessary—to get their interpretations accepted, their aim being to survive or win in the game of science. Science is socially constructed. This motto has become both a rallying cry and a banal comment. It turns out, however, that it does not mean the same thing to all. And the difference makes a difference.

Philosophers have engaged most with the "strong program" in the sociology of science associated with the University of Edinburgh and represented in the work of Barry Barnes and David Bloor (Barnes 1977; Bloor 1976 [2nd edn, 1991]; Barnes and Bloor 1982). This program has attracted the attention of a number of philosophers—for example, a sympathetic if critical reading by Mary Hesse (1980), and much less temperate responses from Larry Laudan (1984), among others. According to the strong program, both good and bad, successful and unsuccessful science must be explained in the same way. One can't explain good science by appealing to rationality and bad science by appealing to distorting social factors. In both kinds of case, what does the explanatory work is interests: ideological/political interests; professional interests; individual career interests. Science is socially constructed in the sense that the congruence of a hypothesis or theory with the social interests of the members of a scientific community determines its acceptance by that community (rather than a congruence of theory/hypothesis with the world).

The strong program theorists present two sorts of theoretical argument. Appeals to Wittgenstein's later philosophy or to Mary Hesse's Quinean account of concept formation undergird an argument to the social nature of classification systems. The relativism is supported by arguments challenging the notion of privileged descriptive categories or of a common basic level of sense experience, and by arguments concerning the impossibility of a noncircular justification of principles of inference. There is no general argument to the effect that all scientific judgments have a social content. Instead, the various case studies are intended to exhibit a congruence between the scientific positions and the social values of participants in scientific debates. The combination of theoretical arguments with the case studies then has this form: cognitive, or rational, factors cannot explain why S thought as she or he did (because they fail in any case), therefore the appeal of T for S was precisely the congruence of T with S's social values. Beliefs and attitudes about society or one's proper place in it determine scientific content or what scientific content is accepted. But the fact that the boundaries of classificatory categories are conventional and determined by a linguistic community does not show that the boundaries are adopted because of their semantic relation with social values. And what the arguments against basic experiential categories or "rational" justifications of inductive reasoning really support are anti-foundationalism, not relativism. So while the case studies are intriguing, they do not demonstrate that in every instance of scientific judgment the protagonists had no reason but interests for the scientific choices they made.

In many ways more compelling are the empirical laboratory studies done by Karin Knorr-Cetina, Bruno Latour, and others. Although they have different social-theoretical frameworks within which they present their studies they show that science is social in a different sense than it is social for the strong program theorists: the procedures of science are social in the sense of involving social interactions. Moreover, the "slice of life" documentation of those interactions shows (in the laboratory cases studied) that the procedures by which scientists certify results and validate hypotheses involve a hodge-podge of "internal" and "external" considerations. These theorists then conclude from this that it is not possible to distinguish between the purely cognitive and the social—or interest-laden—bases of hypotheses. The normative concerns of philosophers are, hence, idle: the wheels of prescription may spin in philosophy, but they fail to engage the gears in actual epistemic communities.

Latour (1987), for example, enunciates as a rule of method that if we want to understand scientists and engineers we must follow them as they enroll allies and establish networks, and not appeal to anything like "mind" or cognition until all the routes of social explanation have been exhausted. He clearly thinks that, when all such explanations *have* been exhausted, there will be nothing left in need of explanation. The allies that can be enrolled include not just other members of the scientist's community, but the elements of nature whose behavior the scientist is trying to explain, predict, use, or reproduce in the laboratory. Latour's language rather playfully suggests that natural "actants" can find it in their

interest or not in their interest to cooperate with the investigator. But it's not clear that an unpacking of "enrolling allies" would not reintroduce the cognitive elements Latour wishes to banish.[2]

Karin Knorr-Cetina, in an essay (1983) outlining the elements of her constructivist approach to science, claims that the features of scientific practice that it reveals "defeat the hope of the philosopher of science to find the set of criteria that govern scientific selections." In this essay she construes "the epistemological question" as the question, "How is that which we come to call knowledge constituted and accepted?"—a question to which she gives answers invoking the social processes and interactions in the laboratory and between the laboratory and its worldly environment. What I find striking about this "defeat" of the philosopher is that the game is won before it is even engaged, by the way the questions are cast. With respect to her epistemological question, one might respond that no, the epistemological question is not how that which we come to call knowledge is constituted and accepted, but what we think we're saying when we claim knowledge or make a knowledge attribution. What distinguishes knowledge from other doxastic states, such as opinion or belief? With respect to the defeat of the philosopher, we might respond that the hope of the philosopher of science is not to find the criteria that do govern scientific selections, but to find the criteria that ought to govern them.

This brief review suggests that both the sociologist and any philosopher at least as traditional as Kitcher agree that the fate of knowledge as it is treated in social theories of science is to collapse into what is believed or what is accepted. If philosophers are interested in analyzing the concept of knowledge and in figuring out what norms our use of such a concept commits us to, why should we remain interested in the sociological approach? There are at least two reasons. Firstly, whether or not we are naturalists, philosophers have rightly or wrongly taken the sciences to be the best model we have of knowledge production. Studies of how it actually works should surely be of interest to us even if they challenge our preconceptions. While Knorr-Cetina's investigations reveal social interaction at the heart of the scientific enterprise, her results do not defeat or displace the philosopher so much as raise new questions or change the field upon which philosophical concerns are engaged. Secondly, feminists have been interested in this work because it provides a model for thinking about how masculinist interests could get incorporated into so-called good science as well as in methodologically disreputable science. Feminists have offered analyses of the content of specific research programs in the sciences that demonstrate their congruence with (and, in cases, support of) masculinist ideology and their satisfaction of methodological norms. It is puzzling how this could happen on most philosophically orthodox accounts of scientific practice. Any general account that throws the standing of methodological norms into question has thus seemed a more attractive alternative. But what the empirical work demands is an account of knowledge that incorporates the social dimensions of science into the epistemology of inquiry, rather than one that shows that (much) practice departs from traditional epistemological conventions. The latter demonstration permits the riposte that good science does not express the biases decried by feminist critics, while the former enables demonstrations of masculinism in the most prized of research programs (cf. Longino 1992).

Both the feminists and the sociologists can be understood as rejecting what we might call an "unconditioned subject," that is, a knower guided only by content- and value-neutral methodological rules (cf. Longino 1993). Individual knowers are instead conditioned by various aspects of their social location—from their dependence on government agencies and industry for funding, to their location in an intellectual lineage, to their position in the race, gender, and class grid of their society. The problem with recognizing the social locatedness and, hence, conditioned character of individual epistemic subjects is that it seems to force us into choosing between relativism and demonstrating the epistemic superiority of one among the various social locations. I wish to reject this choice, which I see as arising from a continued commitment to individualism in epistemology. The question towards which the rest of this essay is addressed is whether any recognizable concept of knowledge can be recovered from a more thoroughly social account of inquiry.

WHEREIN IS KNOWLEDGE SOCIAL?

Elsewhere (Longino 1990), I argued that an individualist bias in philosophy stood in the way of solutions to problems—such as underdetermination—confronting the possibility of scientific knowledge. Some may see the solution afforded by a social account of knowledge as worse than the problem. I would argue, in contrast, that scientific knowledge is produced by cognitive processes that are fundamentally social and that an adequate normative theory of knowledge must be a normative theory of social knowledge—a theory whose norms apply to social practices and processes of cognition.

Although in that earlier work, I appealed to present features of scientific practice, the main argument was an epistemological one: only if we understand scientific inquiry as fundamentally social, and scientific knowledge as the outcome of discursive interactions, is it possible to claim that scientific inquiry is objective. Here I would like to concentrate on a different sort of argument, namely, conceptual arguments to the effect that observation and justificatory reasoning—central elements of scientific knowledge construction—are themselves social.

1. Observation. Ethnomethodologists and sociologists practicing discourse analysis have argued that establishing what the (observational) data are is a social matter. Ascertaining what the results of an experiment are, what is a real result and what an artifact of the experimental situation, what are new data (constituting a genuine anomaly) and what an experiment gone wrong, is accomplished by "negotiation," or critical discussions among group members.

Michael Lynch has used ethnomethodological analysis to uncover the conversational work that anchors the interpretation of data. In a piece on digital imaging in astronomy Lynch and Samuel Edgerton (1988) describe the intersubjective and socially interactive process of interpreting and clarifying the salient features of galactic images. Karin Knorr-Cetina has made similar sorts of observations, although without the trappings of ethnomethodology. In a paper with Klaus Amann (1990), she reports on a study of a molecular biology laboratory using gel electrophoresis techniques to identify the molecular constituents of a sample of

DNA. The two sociologists identify various discursive interactions that propel a group of investigators to progressively more definite accounts of what is actually exhibited on a given film. The final representations, the ones used in publication, are constructed by synthesizing a number of films—introducing a second level of integrative sociality.

Of course, what happens in one or two laboratories is not evidence that scientific observation is intrinsically social, rather than contingently so on the occasions reported. But more conceptual considerations do support thinking of scientific observation as dialogical in nature. Observational data consist in observation reports that are ordered and organized. This ordering rests on a consensus as to the centrality of certain categories (the speed of a reaction vs. the color of its product), the boundaries of concepts and classes (just what counts as an acid), the ontological and organizational commitments of a model or theory, and so on. Observation is not simple sense perception (whatever that might be), but an organized sensory encounter that registers what is perceived. I leave open whether this registering is linguistic (see below); it does involve classification and categorization that notes similarity and dissimilarity with other items of interest.

Furthermore, not just any observation will do. To have value as data, observations must have a stability that allows their transfer from one laboratory to another. If we are going to treat observational data as data, we need assurances that an apparent or purported regularity really is one. The requirement of the repeatability of experiments is a requirement for the intersubjective accessibility of data serving as evidence because it is a requirement that anyone similarly placed with similar equipment would see (perceive) the same thing. Nature has been enrolled as an ally when the experimenter has found a way to stabilize her or his results across different perspectives.[3] Even when an experiment is not actually repeated (which is the case for the majority of experiments), the presupposition of its results being used as evidential data is that anyone similarly placed would observe the same thing.

Harry Collins (1983, 1991) has argued that only in cases of controversial science (e.g., cold fusion, parapsychology, molecular memory) does anyone go to the trouble of actually trying to produce the same results with the same methods. We might say that only in such cases does anyone attempt actually to determine the publicity or intersubjective accessibility of experimental results. Collins is trying to expose the repeatability requirement as window dressing not supported by actual practices. On the view urged here, the invocation of the repeatability criterion in controversial cases demonstrates that the presupposition in the "normal" case of the unchecked taking of a set of observations or measurements as data is that they are and will remain stably accessible across changes in context or point of view. In the case of doubt as to its satisfaction, the presupposition is tested by bringing different perceivers to the situation (identical or a replica) and ascertaining intersubjective invariance. From this point of view, then, the studies of Lynch and Knorr-Cetina are not at all surprising. If intersubjective invariance is an important feature of observational data, then of course experimenters will consult with one another to establish or impose definiteness on initially "flexible" data. Indeed, since one of the professional aims of researchers is to get their data and interpretations taken up by others, the very kind of sociality to which Knorr-Cetina and Latour draw our attention guarantees that researchers will aim for intersubjective invariance of observation. Otherwise, their work will perish.

The point here is not that an individual scientist could not engage in experimentation or make observations on her own. Indeed, the sensory capacities of individuals are crucial. The claim of sociality is the claim that the status of the scientist's activity as *observation* depends on her relations with others—in particular, her openness to their correction of her reports. This is what enables the transformation of "it seems to me that *p*" into "*p*." There is no way other than the interaction of multiple perspectives to ascertain the observational status of individual perceptions.[4]

2. Reasoning. The second main cognitive element in the production of scientific knowledge is reasoning, which traces lines of evidentiary support between data and theories and hypotheses. Individual brains or minds, of course engage in calculation. But reasoning (at least scientific reasoning) is not mere calculation; it is bringing the appropriate considerations to bear on judgments.

Justificatory reasoning is part of a practice of challenge and response: challenge to a claim is met by the offering of reasons to believe it, which reasons can then be challenged on grounds both of truth and of relevance, provoking additional reasoning. Reasoning, thus, gets its point in a social context—a context of interaction among individuals, rather than of interaction between an individual and the object of her or his cogitations. What counts as an appropriate consideration, as a reason, is determined and stabilized through discursive interactions.

In the empirical sciences, observational and experimental data function as the appropriate sorts of considerations. But even when described and categorized, their precise relevance to particular hypotheses and theories is not self-evident.[5] Both ascertaining the evidential relevance of data to a hypothesis and accepting a hypothesis on the basis of evidence require a reliance on substantive and methodological background assumptions. Just as not any old observations will do, so not just any old assumptions will do. In general, every assumption upon which it is permissible to rely is a function of consensus among the scientific community, is learned as part of one's apprenticeship as a scientist, and is largely invisible to practitioners within the community. Although invisible, or transparent, to members of the community, all such assumptions are articulable and hence, in principle, public. This in-principle publicity makes them available to critical examination as a consequence of which they may be abandoned, modified, or reinforced. Just as not all experiments are repeated, not all assumptions are in fact so scrutinized; but the presumption in inference is that they would survive, if scrutinized.

This critical examination is a social activity, requiring the participation of multiple points of view to ensure that the hypotheses accepted by a community do not represent someone's idiosyncratic interpretation of observational or experimental data. The inferences that build scientific knowledge, then, are not the inferences made by individual researchers, but inferences that proceed through discursive interactions. Of course, the invisibility—within a community—of many of its background assumptions as assumptions means that a closed community will not be able to exhibit those assumptions for critical scrutiny. These sorts of worries also affect the discussion of observation: the degree of intersubjective invariance of a set of observations will be limited by the degree of perspectival variation. These are the worries that generate the normative aspects of this view to be discussed in the following sections.

Knowing

The results of both reasoning and observation are socially processed before incorporation into the body of ideas ratified for circulation and use. What deserves the honorific "knowledge," on this view, is an outcome of the critical dialogue about observation, reasoning, and material practices among individuals and groups holding different points of view. It is constructed not by individuals, but by an interactive dialogic community. The conceivability of such a figure as Robinson Crusoe is frequently invoked as a counterexample to the above claims. Isn't it possible for some particular isolated individual to engage in inquiry that would qualify as scientific, to produce systematic knowledge of her surroundings that would count as science? Cannot she engage in that critical scrutiny on her own? Several points need to be made in rejoinder. First of all, in imagining Crusoe's critical scrutiny of her reasoning and observation, we simply import the community into Crusoe's head. Secondly, Crusoe's conversation with herself is parasitic on her past and potential interaction with others. She must rely on meanings and practices developed in the social setting from which she has been set adrift; and she must regard the results of her cognitive activity as tentative, awaiting ratification by the community of which she is still, in intention, a part. We can regard her activities as science only if they stand in this relation to the activities of others. Individuals are not replaced by a transcendent social entity, on the view being advocated. Rather, without individuals there would be no knowledge: it is through their sensory system that the natural world enters cognition; it is their proposals that are subject to critical scrutiny by other individuals, their imaginations which generate novelty. The activities of knowledge construction, however, are the activities of individuals in interaction, of individuals in certain relations (of criticism and response) with others.

A knowledge-constructive community extends beyond the laboratory in several important ways. As

Knorr-Cetina (1981) reminds us, researchers are sensitive to the opportunities (for further support, interest) that can be engaged by taking certain research directions rather than others. And whether anyone pays attention will depend on how researchers can link their work up with that pursued elsewhere. The critical exchanges occur not only within the laboratory or research unit, but between it and other researchers as well as members of the larger community who have an interest in the outcomes. The dialogue will then involve aspects which are not classically cognitive—enrolling, in Latour's words, various sorts of allies who can provide an audience or increase the prospects of future development and/or funding. But it also involves elements that are epistemic in nature: is the pattern on film A sufficiently like the pattern on film B? Is this result an expression of the material under investigation or an artifact of the instrumental set-up? It is not purity, but responsiveness to epistemic considerations that is important. As David Hull (1988) says of the systematists he chronicled, knowledge may be a by-product of the activities that obtain the primary results (e.g. credit) desired by scientists; but, because of the rules by which the game is played, it is still a product. It is not purity, but responsiveness to epistemic considerations that is important in determining epistemological status.

While intersubjective interaction is a necessary feature of scientific cognition, not just any form of interaction will do. If the point of intersubjective interaction is to transform the subjective into the objective, then those interactions must not simply preserve and distribute one subjectivity over all others, but must constitute genuine and mutual checks.[6] This end can be served by specifying features of the design and constitution of a community that facilitate transformative criticism and enable a consensus to qualify as knowledge. Four such features or conditions can be identified.

1. There must be publicly recognized forums for the criticism of evidence, of methods, and of assumptions and reasoning.

2. There must be uptake of criticism. The community must not merely tolerate dissent; its beliefs and theories must change over time in response to the critical discourse taking place within it.

3. There must be publicly recognized standards by reference to which theories, hypotheses, and observational practices are evaluated and by appeal to which criticism is made relevant to the goals of the inquiring community. With the possible exception of empirical adequacy, there needn't be and probably isn't a set of standards common to all communities. The general family of standards from which those locally adopted are drawn includes such cognitive virtues as accuracy, coherence, and breadth of scope, and such social virtues as fulfilling technical or material needs or facilitating certain kinds of interactions between a society and its material environment or among the society's members. The point of requiring public standards is that, by explicitly or implicitly professing adherence to those standards, individuals and communities adopt criteria of adequacy by which they may be evaluated. The satisfaction of goals of inquiry is not ascertained privately, but by evaluation with respect to shared values and standards. This evaluation may be performed by anyone, not just by members of the community sharing all standards. Furthermore, standards are not a static set, but may themselves be criticized and transformed in reference to other standards, goals, or values held temporarily constant. Indeed, as in the case of observation and the assumptions underlying justificatory reasoning, the presupposition of reliance on such standards is that they have survived similar critical scrutiny.

4. Finally, communities must be characterized by equality of intellectual authority. What consensus exists must be the result not of the exercise of political or economic power, or of the exclusion of dissenting perspectives, but a result of critical dialogue in which all relevant perspectives are represented. This criterion is meant to impose duties of inclusion; it does not require that each individual, no matter what her or his past record or state of training, should be granted equal authority on every matter.

Education is required to prepare members of a society to make useful contributions, and researchers with a lot of experience or a record of "getting things right" may be more deserving of attention than others.[7] Exclusive attention to those who have earned the greatest cognitive authority, however, can lead to the neglect of new or "different" voices that ought to be heard. The more important function of measurements of degree of cognitive authority, then, is identifying—so as to be able to disregard—those who consistently get things wrong. The public standards mentioned in condition 3 have two objects. One is to impose obligations on acknowledged members of a knowledge-productive community to attend, restricting them to criticism that is relevant to their cognitive and practical aims. The other is to limit the sorts of criticisms to which a community must attend, restricting them to those which affect the satisfaction of its goals. The point of condition 4 is that such criticism may originate from an indeterminate number of points of view, none of which may be arbitrarily excluded from the community's interactions without cognitive impairment.

These features are features of an idealized epistemic community. In practice, then, they are criteria of knowledge-productive capacity that take the critical interactions of communities and their institutions as their domain of application. As such they constitute norms applying to the social practices and processes of cognition, norms whose satisfaction assures that theories and hypotheses accepted in the community will not incorporate the idiosyncratic biases (heuristic or social) of an individual or subgroup. We might call them "conditions of effective criticism." A community satisfying these conditions—that is, a community with means of disseminating and responding to criticism, whose members hold themselves answerable individually and collectively to a set of standards and reach consensus as a result of discursive interactions including all relevant perspectives and uninhibited by political or economic power—will qualify as a knowledge-productive community. Since the norms represent ideals that can be partially satisfied, this qualification is a matter of degree.

What's Known

Elsewhere (Longino 1993), I have proposed that this account of knowledge is most compatible with the treatment of scientific theories as models. There I appealed to the model treatment as an escape from what looks like a fatal dilemma. The account requires diversity in the community to generate critical discourse. But if diversity is seriously pursued, the consensus required for the application of theories to problems will be elusive; and if consensus is pursued, then critical oppositional positions will at some point have to be silenced, or at least ignored. Do we then aim for consensus or dissensus?

This dilemma seems forced upon us if we are still in the grip of an ideal of absolute and unitary truth—a final truth—whose attainment is the goal of scientific inquiry. Linked with this ideal is a residual individualism. The account of theories as models is intended to address the first source of the dilemma. Let me address the residual individualism first. "The community" is a misleading sobriquet. In a context of thinking about scientific knowledge we may be tempted to suppose that it refers to some entity—for example, the global scientific community, the scientific community whose aim is discovery of the truth about the world. Subcommunities may then be thought of as microcosmic replicas of the global community, each adding its mite to the stack. This is a bad picture. To think or see in these terms is still to see the knowledge-productive features of a knower as internal to the knower, or as a matter of the relation between knower and known, rather than a matter of the relatedness of the knower to other knowers. It is to fail to take into account the situated character of communities, their location in history and their constitution by their histories and their orientations to specific goals. It is to see pluralism as a means to its own overcoming in a final consensus.

The alternative is to see communities as themselves fluid entities overlapping both in values and standards and in membership. No community is ever complete in the sense of containing all possible perspectives within itself. Scientific knowledge is not a product of the final consensus, but consists in whatever theoretical apprehensions of the natural world are stable enough to permit elaboration and application for some period of time. Temporary and provisional unity around some goals and standards within a community permits the elaboration of ideas and hypotheses sufficiently for their application to problems. Whether their success can be called "knowledge" depends on the inclusion in their dialogue of all those perspectives having a bearing on the subject matter. It is on this matter of inclusiveness that attributions of knowledge are most clearly a matter of gradation. The notion of all relevant perspectives involves a diachronicity impossible to achieve, including as it must an as yet unrealized future. What perspectives must be included in community dialogue? Those that are live options for anyone both sharing some of the community's goals and with whom the community could reasonably be supposed to be in contact. This is of course dependent on the technologies of travel and communication available to a community.

If there is no "perfect" community but only successions of multiply related communities pursuing inquiry to satisfy local goals, then the ideal of an absolute and unitary truth—a final truth—is an empty notion. It decontextualizes what is meaningful only within the context of its constitution. The notion of models is introduced in part to provide an object or medium of knowledge suited to the provisionality, partiality, and pluralism inherent in this conception of epistemic communities. What counts as a model for this purpose is a pretty heterogeneous assemblage: sets of equations, specifications of structure, visual representations, mental maps, diagrams, three-dimensional objects like the wire and plastic models of the DNA molecule, or four-dimensional models that incorporate change or motion. The model approach to theories is intended as an alternative to the view that theories are sets of propositions. On this latter view, the adequacy of a theory is a matter of the truth by correspondence of the propositions constituting the theory. A model, by contrast, is neither true nor false; but its structure, or the structure of a subset of its elements, may be identical to a structure in the world. This isomorphism permits the mapping of the relations and structures and processes of the model onto some portion of the world. Elements of any portion of the world stand in many relations to many other elements. A model selects among those relations, presenting the results of that selection as a coherent, interrelated set. Many models can be isomorphic to some portion of the world as long as elements in the models stand in the same relations to each other as some set of elements in that portion of the world do to each other. The choice of a model, therefore, is not just a function of its isomorphism (or the iso-

morphism of a subset of its elements) with a portion of the world, but also a function of the relations it picks out being ones in which the users of the model are interested. It must represent the world in a way that facilitates the interactions its users seek to have with the modelled domain.

There is another reason to think of theories as models. Often research programs are guided not by an explicit theory, but by a sense of how things in the domain under study are related. This sense remains unarticulated in the generality in which it is held, and is expressed only in specific accounts of particular instances. I have called such a sense an explanatory model (Longino 1990), for it functions as a model of how explanations of particular phenomena in a domain are to be structured. In behavioral endocrinology, for example, behavioral patterns of various sorts are attributed to hormonal exposures at critical periods of organismic development. There is no explicit general theory, only a number of studies linking different behaviors to different hormone levels. Each of these, however, acquires significance on account of its similarity to the others. It is as though researchers are working with a general picture of a class of systems behaving in similar fashion, without ever articulating a general theory that then requires support. Such a theory, as a picture, is nevertheless a crucial element in the research, determining the way researchers look at and think about the systems under study, the questions they ask, and the experiments they design.

Models, whether tacit or elaborately articulated, guide our interactions with and interventions in the world. To see the products of scientific inquiry as models is to understand scientific knowledge not as reified in a set of propositions detachable from knowers, but as an ability to understand the structural features of a model and to understand and act in the world as it manifests that structure. Treating theories as models, then, also enables the expression of one of the ways in which scientific inquiry shapes and in a sense produces the world in which we live. Inquiry gives certain features, relationships, and processes significance by incorporating them into a coherent (if still partial) framework. A model works to the extent that it is possible to interact with the modelled domain as though it were constituted of just those elements. As Ian Hacking suggests in his discussions of laboratory sciences, one of the keys to the success of those sciences is the ability of researchers to create in the laboratory a world in which only those elements and processes postulated in a model are interacting (Hacking 1988). It is a small step to the supposition that what is recreated in the laboratory is what's real about the natural domain under study.

WHAT'S KNOWLEDGE

This is all very well, you might say, but what has happened to knowledge in the course of this analysis? Like the sociologist, haven't I simply retained the term but jettisoned the concept? This is essentially the question asked by Philip Kitcher in the comments mentioned earlier. He does this by extracting an analysis along the lines of a traditional analysis of "*S* knows that *p*"—including an attitudinal clause, a success clause, and a procedural clause—from earlier versions of ideas of the sort developed in the preceding section. He uses his critique of this analysis to argue that the account from which it is drawn is incapable of expressing what we intend to convey by knowledge claims or attributions. I disagree with this verdict—in part because I think the analysis extracted doesn't quite capture the ideas, and in part because I disagree with Kitcher's assessment of what he does include. Let me first discuss Kitcher's extraction, and then present an alternative version.

Kitcher proposes the following as a reconstruction of the account of knowledge.

> KNOWLEDGE I. *S* knows that *p* if and only if
> (i) *S* believes that *p*;
> (ii) *p* is effective in directing *S*'s actions towards the attainment of goals that are validated by the society to which *S* belongs; and
> (iii) *S*'s belief is produced by a process that the society in question would validate (providing it meets criteria of proper cognitive design).

He worries that both the second and the third clause would permit us (counterintuitively) to say that creationists know that the world was created between four and seven thousand years ago. He pre-

sents the analysis as an analysis of propositional knowledge because he views proponents of models as committed to some propositions—for example, that a model is isomorphic with, or similar to, the modelled domain—and thus sees no reason to abandon the analysis of scientific knowledge as propositional knowledge or truth as the appropriate dimension of evaluation. I shall take up these issues in turn, drawing on the remarks of the previous sections.

Creationism. Kitcher's point in bringing up creationism is to demonstrate that, despite my aspirations to offer an analysis robust enough to support the normative judgments we make about knowledge (e.g., she knows, he doesn't), the analysis actually offered fails. So, for creationism substitute any egregiously wrong-headed set of claims about the natural world. Kitcher claims that both the second and third clauses of his extraction allow the creationist to know that the world was created between four and five thousand years ago. The second clause requires that *p* be effective in directing *S*'s actions towards the attainment of goals that are validated by the society to which *S* belongs. Something like this is consistent with the sociologists' accounts.

Now, for all my suspicion of truth, I think Kitcher is right to question its replacement by this pragmatic criterion. How does it allow egregiously wrong-headed beliefs to be knowledge? Kitcher does not elaborate, but it is worth doing so to see just why an exclusively pragmatic criterion of success will not do. Since it is not clear how a proposition by itself could be effective, let us suppose that what is meant is that acceptance of or belief that *p* is effective. What goals might be served by belief or acceptance that the world was created four to seven thousand years ago? Perhaps awe of the almighty, which is surely a goal validated by the creationist's society. But awe of the almighty is itself an intermediate goal, instrumental in achievement of the final goal, which is presumably salvation, or eternal life with god. How the second clause permits flawed beliefs depends on how it is read. If to be effective in directing someone's actions towards the attainment of a given goal requires that the goal be realizable, then the creationist knows only if eternal life with god is a genuine possibility (and god chooses to reward such belief with eternal life). If attainability is not required, then the creationist may know as long as acceptance of p effectively directs S's actions towards that goal, even if it is not realizable. What's counterintuitive about this clause is that, in general, beliefs which have no real-world correlates would be admitted as instances of knowledge (provided the other clauses were met). Even if god had created the world billions of years ago, she might reward the hapless creationist with salvation just for believing against so many odds, thus making S's belief effective in the ways required. Part of what is counterintuitive is that it is the fact of S's acceptance that is effective, rather than any relation between the content of what is accepted and elements, structures, and processes represented by that content. The earlier discussion of models invoked satisfaction of goals as an important element in assessing the adequacy of representations, but only as a supplement to model isomorphism. The kind of example just developed shows that efficacy in goal satisfaction is not a sufficient success condition in itself. Furthermore, in the case of a proposition, success need only consist in its content's being the case. Goal satisfaction is not required. Thus, I reject Kitcher's reconstruction of the success clause.

Kitcher also faults the third clause for permitting creationist knowledge. That is the clause requiring that S's belief that p be produced by a process that the society in question would validate (subject, of course, to that society's meeting criteria of proper cognitive design). How does this clause ratify wrong-headed beliefs? A society will validate processes of inquiry that result in its or its members' having beliefs which satisfy clause (ii). But the parenthetical addition of proper cognitive design is important here. Let us suppose that proper cognitive design means satisfying the four conditions of effective criticism discussed above. That means that there must be critical exchanges in which the full variety of perspectives are represented and that they are treated as equally capable of generating significuit challenges to theories. For the creationist belief to be ratified by this clause, all participants to the dialogue would have to share an overriding commitment to the goal of salvation or to the intermediate goal of fostering awe of the almighty. But this is to limit the included perspectives by content, not by past performance.

Kitcher thinks the creationist claims cannot be criticized without the adoption of methodological norms that are not forced on individuals (or groups) simply by virtue of their commitment to a practice of open criticism and discussion. But this is not at all obvious. A practice of genuinely open criticism and discussion requires an openness to all perspectives: no claim or belief can be held immune to criticism. Creationism must withstand critical scrutiny and challenge to count as knowledge. Moreover, the supposition that additional methodological norms would be required presupposes an insulation of cognitive goals from practical and social goals—an insulation that we have no good reason to assume. A commitment to salvation that ratified procedures of inquiry warranting creationist beliefs about the origin of the universe would be in conflict with other goals of an inquiring community, and could be shown to be in such conflict if the community were indeed open. So, while I think Kitcher's version of the procedural clause is reasonably close to what I've been arguing for, his rejection of it is based on a lack of appreciation for its strength.

Propositions versus Models. If an account of propositional knowledge is to be given within the social approach, all that really requires modification is the third condition. The following is a better reconstruction than Kitcher's.

KNOWLEDGE II. If $S_1 \ldots S_n$ are members of an epistemic community C, then $S_1 \ldots S_n$ know that p if and only if
(i) $S_1 \ldots S_n$ believe that p;
(ii) p; and
(iii) $S_1 \ldots S_n$'s believing that p is the result of warranting practices adopted by C in circumstances characterized by
a. public forums for critical interaction,
b. uptake of criticism,
c. public standards, and
d. equality of intellectual authority among diverse perspectives.

Kitcher attributes an account of propositional knowledge to me for two reasons. Firstly, propositions are standard objects of knowledge in philosophical analysis, and their conditions of success and failure are clear: truth and falsity. Of this point, more in a moment. Secondly, he states that in spite of my talk of models, I'm still committed to a treatment of propositional knowledge. There are two ways to understand this latter claim. One is as the assertion that models are all well and good, but we still have propositional knowledge. To which I say, yes, I can know that the cat is on the roof, and I can know that the dial is at .5 on the meter, but a great deal of what we call "scientific knowledge" is just not like that kind of knowledge. That is, much of what we call "scientific knowledge" has as its object not singular propositions about mid-sized objects, but patterns and relationships among entities beyond our powers of sensory detection and between such entities and the objects and relationships we do detect. We have a choice, then, between limiting the possible objects of knowledge to those within our powers of detection and attempting to find an analysis that permits us to speak of knowledge in those cases in which direct determination of truth and falsity is not possible. Treating models as media of knowledge is one way of developing a more expansive conception of knowledge.[8]

A second interpretation of the claim that in spite of my talk of models I'm still committed to a treatment of knowledge as propositional knowledge is that, even in a model treatment of theories, whatever knowledge is involved is propositional knowledge, namely, knowledge that the model is similar to the real-world system of which it is a model. There are three problems with this view. Firstly, it unnecessarily restricts knowledge to the contemplative and fails to give expression to the ways in which scientific knowledge involves active engagement with its objects. Secondly, knowledge of similarity may not be what is asserted in claims to knowledge. We can know that a model is empirically adequate—that is, that a subset of its elements is isomorphic with a subset of the elements of the modelled domain—without knowing or needing to know the full extent or respect of similarity of the model to the modelled domain. Thirdly, given the elasticity of "similar," it is not clear what one knows when one knows that a model is similar to a real-world system. So it is not clear that propositional knowledge of this sort is any better or clearer than possible alternatives.

The more general point about propositions and models is that both are means of representation used in the sciences. Absent a principled argument to the effect that one rather than the other medium of representation can count as knowledge, any analysis of scientific knowledge in the sciences ought to be able to accommodate both forms. Talking about models as media of knowledge enables us to include as cases of knowledge those representations of portions of the natural world that are nonpropositional, that are nevertheless empirically adequate, and that provide us with a framework within which to carry out inquiry and successfully to pursue practical projects. The point of extending an analysis of knowledge to include such representations is to show how the distinction between knowledge and opinion can be preserved under such extension. What follows, then, is a proposal that draws on the earlier discussion. While it is modelled on the traditional form of analyses of knowledge, both the object of analysis and the analyzing conditions depart from it somewhat in content.

KNOWLEDGE III. If $S_1 \ldots S_n$ are members of an epistemic community, W is some real-world system or portion of real-world system, and M is a model (of that system), then $S_1 \ldots S_n$ know W as M if and only if

(i) $S_1 \ldots S_n$ represent W as M, and act with respect to W as if it were M;

(ii) a subset of elements of M is sufficiently isomorphic to a subset of elements of W to enable $S_1 \ldots S_n$ to satisfy their goals with respect to W; and

(iii) $S_1 \ldots S_n$'s representing W as M is the result of warranting practices adopted by C in circumstances characterized by

a. public forums for critical interaction,

b. uptake of criticism,

c. public standards, and

d. equality of intellectual authority among diverse perspectives.

The knowledge defined here is similar to knowledge by acquaintance. It differs from traditional accounts of acquaintance (e.g., Russell's) in that it is mediated rather than direct. This mediation makes possible both partiality and pluralism, since it leaves open that W may also be known as M', i.e. that M does not exhaust the features (processes/interactions/elements) of W. M and M' may equally be ways of knowing W. To illustrate with a mundane example: my students know me as a teacher; while my mother knows me as a daughter. Different features of my personality, capacities, and so on are highlighted in these representations of me which determine how these different knowers will act with regard to me. Their different representations also elicit different behaviors from me. Thus I confirm those representations in the contexts in which they are activated. Or think of a collection of objects of different materials and two models: one containing the two-place transitive relation (larger than) and names for the objects; the other containing the two-place transitive relation (heavier than) and names for the objects. These models will order the elements in the domain differently, but each can be an adequate representation of the domain for certain purposes.[9] The analyzing conditions are intended to preserve the pluralism and partiality inherent in this expression of the analysandum.

The attitudinal condition has two components: representation and action. Both are required as a replacement for belief. "Representation" conveys the intentionality of belief, while "action" conveys its commitment. The medium of representation, however, is not (or not necessarily) a proposition, but may be a set of equations, a diagram, a mental map, a structure made of linguistic or physical elements. The point of the representation is the kinds of actions it makes possible for $S_1 \ldots S_n$ in W, whether they be designing a new superconducting material, orienting the Hubble space telescope, or preparing a bacterial plasmid for production of some biological substance. This aspect of the condition expresses the active and productive character of scientific knowledge.

The success condition requires partial isomorphism of the model, rather than truth of constituent propositions. The requirement of isomorphism is a very weak requirement, especially when the isomorphism is only partial. It is satisfied as long as some elements of M stand to one another in relations structurally identical to those in which some elements of W stand to one another. It is not necessary that all the structural relations of a set of elements be represented in order that a given model or portion of a model be isomorphic with that set. Not every possible model will be (partially) isomorphic with its intended domain, but many models will be.[10]

Given that isomorphilism is so easily obtainable, it is not a sufficient condition of success. The success condition requires a degree of isomorphism sufficient to enable $S_1 \ldots S_n$ to act in W in such a way as to satisfy their goals. Clearly, isomorphism of the observational elements of M with the experienced elements of M is necessary to meet this condition, which leaves open whether any more isomorphism is required or even to be had.

This success condition also allows for changes in the sorts of experiences we may wish for or can have. Technological changes make possible finer experiential discriminations, and what counts as a satisfactory level of isomorphism at one time in the context of one set of needs and capacities may not count as such in the context of a different set. Hence, more extensive or different isomorphism may be required at a different time. While this condition has some of the flexibility of the more purely pragmatic version, its externalism enables escape from the problems attendant upon that version because it requires a relation with the modelled domain that holds independently of the fact that $S_1 \ldots S_n$ so represent it. Their goals are satisfied by acting in W in the ways made possible by representing W as M, not as a reward for faith.

The procedural condition is essentially the same in both proffered analyses and in this version is explicitly supplemented with the criteria of knowledge-productive capacity. When these are explicit, it's less plausible to think that the warranting procedures would permit egregiously wrong-headed views to count as knowledge. And if they did, I think we would be required to reconsider our judgment of egregious wrong-headedness. That is, if a community C's representation of W as M continues to be warranted by the procedures of C that have been modified in response to free and open criticism referencing some goals of C, then it is not clear that there are any further grounds (beyond simple disagreement) for criticism. The worry so often expressed is Kitcher's worry: won't this analysis license creationism? The correct response to such a worry is two-fold. Firstly, if the creationists meet the conditions, they are not the creationists we love to hate. Secondly, it is satisfaction of condition 3 that gives even Western scientific communities whatever claim they have to our doxastic allegiance. For the only non-question-begging response to challenge must be this: "We are open to criticism; we do change in response to it; and while we may not have included all possible perspectives in the discursive interactions that underwrite our methodological procedures, we've included as many as we have encountered (or more than others have)." It doesn't follow, however, that the standards and warranting procedures could not change further in response to new sorts of criticisms.(Indeed, if feminist, environmentalist, and other critics of the sciences are successful, the standards and the knowledge they legitimate will change.) The point is that there is nothing further—that appeal to standards or methodological norms beyond those ratified by the discursive interactions of an inquiring community is an appeal to transcendent principles that inevitably turn out to be local.

CONCLUSION

In this essay, I've argued that the sociologists are wrong to dismiss the concerns of philosophers, but that philosophers are equally wrong to ignore the empirical studies of sociologists. Philosophical analysis converges with sociological observation in concluding that the processes of knowledge construction in the sciences are importantly social. This does not mean that norms are idle, but that they must be articulated for social rather than individual processes, and that the norms that bind individuals are those that come out of the public standards of a community. I've discussed a set of conditions for effective discursive interaction and shown that the distinction between knowledge and opinion that underlies our use of those terms, and hence the normative content of "knowledge," can be expressed within the terms of a social theory of scientific knowledge.

The view has elements of both construction and constraint. We select representations partly on the basis of their efficacy in satisfying our needs. But that very efficacy is a function of those representations' relations with their intended domains, and hence our selection is constrained by the need for some isomorphism with those domains. Furthermore, to count as knowledge, those representations must be the outcome of discursive interactions in circumstances that meet the identifiable

conditions for effective community criticism. Not every representation counts as knowledge. The idea of social construction often evokes visions of science displaced by social interests and social content. But on the view of social knowledge developed here, such displacement would occur only in contexts of flawed discursive interaction. While the account of inquiry shows how social values can permeate scientific inquiry, the sociality that constrains is procedural. Norms of practice emerge as communities engage in specific practices with specific goals. Norms of inquiry are generated and validated by communities of inquirers with specific cognitive needs. Philosophers can reflect on the congruence (or incongruence) of practices, norms, and goals, and participate in the discursive interactions that constitute knowledge construction in our communities. We can reflect on the conditions for effective discursive interactions. All we are proscribed from doing is articulating context-independent rules (as distinct from conditions) of inquiry that must hold for all communities. The epistemology that results may lack the grandeur of traditional theories of knowledge that legislated for all, but what it lacks in grandeur it will gain in robustness.

NOTES

1. I wish to thank Richard Grandy and Jeffry Ramsey for discussing earlier drafts of this essay with me, Fred Schmitt for his extensive and provocative comments, and all those who responded to spoken versions of this essay.
2. For an argument to this effect, see Brown (1989).
3. The condition of reproducibility, which involves stability across different apparatus as well as across different observers (see Cartwright 1991), signifies an even stronger alliance than repeatability.
4. This is the epistemological dimension of what Joseph Rouse (1987) and Jerome Ravetz (1970) discuss as standardization—a practical aim whose satisfaction enables the transfer of results from laboratory to laboratory and to the world outside the laboratory.
5. None of this is to deny that theoretical considerations play a role in the selection, reporting, and description of observational and experimental results. For a good account of the role of theory in observation, see Hesse (1980).

6. Goldman's (1987b) rejection of consensus reflects a similar concern. He's rightly worried that mere consensus doesn't rule out error, but his commitment to epistemological individualism prevents him from exploring conditions under which consensus might function as a criterion of justifiability.

7. This is the argument in Kitcher (1992).

8. Another way is to adopt a pluralistic definition of truth that allows more latitude in the sorts of propositions whose truth we deem ourselves able to ascertain. (See Hacking 1992).

9. Thanks to John Martin for this example.

10. Nor does invocation of isomorphism presuppose a preexistent determinate structure of the world that models must somehow match to be adequate. The isomorphism requirement is compatible with the view that determinacy is determinability in some system of representation.

REFERENCES

Barnes, B. *Scientific Knowledge and Social Theory.* London: Routledge, 1974.

Barnes, B., and D. Bloor "Relativism, Rationalism and the sociology of knowledge.: In M. Hollis and S. Lukes, eds. *Rationality and Relativism.* Cambridge, MA: MIT Press, 1982.

Bloor, D. *Knowledge and Social Imagery.* London: Routledge, 1976, 2d ed, Chicago: University of Chicago Press, 1991.

Brown, H. *Rationality.* London: Routledge, 1989.

Cartwright, N. "Replicability, Reproducibility, and Robustness: Comments on Harry Collins.: *History of Political Economy* 23 (1991), 143–55.

Collins, H. *"An Empirical Relativisit Program in the Sociology of Science."* In Knorr-Cetina and Mulkay, 1983.

Collins H. *"The Meaning of Replication and the Science of Economics."* History of Political Economy, 23 (1991).

Hesse, M. *Revolutions and Reconstructions in the Philosophy of Science.* Bloomington: Indiana University Press, 1980.

Kitcher, P. "Socializing Knowledge." *Journal of Philosophy* 88 (1991), 670–76.

Kitcher, P. *The Advancement of Science.* Oxford: Oxford University Press, 1993.

Knorr-Cetina, K. "The Ethnographic Study of Scientific Work." In Knorr-Cetina and Mulkay, 1983.

Knorr-Cetina, K. *The Manufacture of Knowledge.* Oxford: Pergamon Press, 1981.

Knorr-Cetina, K. and M. Mulkay, eds. *Science Observed: Perspective on Social Studies of Science.* London: Sage, 1983.

Latour, B. *Science in Action.* Cambridge: Harvard University Press, 1987.

Longino, H. "Essential Tensions." In E. McMullin, 1991b.

Longino, H. "Science, Power, Knowledge: Description and Prescription in Feminist Philosophy of Science." In Alcoff and Potter, 1993.

Longino, H. *Science as Social Knowledge.* Princeton: Princeton University Press, 1990.

Ravetz, J. *Science and Its Social Problems.* New York: Oxford, 1970.

FOR FURTHER READING

Armstrong, D.M. *Belief, Truth and Knowledge.* London: Cambridge University Press, 1973.

Austin, David F., ed. *Philosophical Analysis: A Defense by Example.* Dordrecht, Netherlands: Kluwer Academic Publishers, 1988.

Ayer, A. *The Problem of Knowledge.* Harmondsworth, U.K.: Penguin Books, 1956.

Chisholm, Roderick. *The Foundations of Knowing.* Minneapolis: University of Minnesota Press, 1982.

Chisholm, Roderick. *Theory of Knowledge.* 3rd ed. Englewood Cliffs, N.J.: Prentice Hall, 1988.

Conee, Earl. "Why Solve the Gettier Problem." In *Empirical Knowledge,* edited by Paul Moser, pp. 261-5.

Feldman, Richard. "An Alleged Defect in Gettier Counterexamples." In *Emirical Knowledge,* edited by Paul Moser, pp. 241-3.

French, Peter, et al., eds. *Midwest Studies in Philosophy,* vol. V. Minneapolis: University of Minnesota, 1980.

Goldman, Alvin. "A Causal Theory of Knowing." In *Knowing: Essays on the Analysis of Knowledge,* edited by Michael D. Roth and Leon Galis. New York: Random House, 1970.

Harman, Gilbert. *Thought.* Princeton: Princeton University Press, 1973.

Harrison, Jonothan. "Does Knowing Imply Believing?" In *Knowing: Essays on the Analysis of Knowledge,* edited by Michael D. Roth and Leon Galis, New York: Random House, 1970.

Johnson, Oliver. "The Standard Definition." In *Midwest Studies in Philosophies,* edited by Peter French, et al. Minneapolis: University of Minnesota, 1980.

Kaplan, Mark. "It's Not What You Know That Counts." *Journal of Philosophy*, 82 (1985), 350-63.

Lehrer, Keith. "Knowledge, Truth and Evidence." In *Knowing: Essays on the Analysis of Knowledge,* edited by Michael D. Roth and Leon Galis. New York: Random House, 1970.

Lehrer, Keith. *Knowledge.* Oxford: Oxford University Press, 1974.

Lehrer, Keith. *Theory of Knowledge.* Boulder, Colo.: Westview Press, 1990.

Luper-Foy, Steven, ed. *The Possibility of Knowledge.* Totowa, NJ: Rowman & Littlefield, 1987.

Meyers, Robert G. *The Likelihood of Knowledge.* Dordrecht, Netherlands: Kluwer Academic Publishers, 1988.

Pappas, George, and Marshall Swain, eds. *Essays on Knowledge and Justification.* Ithica, N.Y.: Cornell University Press, 1978.

Pollock, John. *Contemporary Theories of Knowledge.* Totowa, NJ: Rowan & Littlefield, 1986.

Radford, Colin. "Knowledge by Examples." In *Knowing: Essays on the Analysis of Knowledge,* edited by Michael D. Roth and Leon Galis, New York: Random House, 1970.

Roth, Michael D., and Leon Galis, eds. *Knowing; Essays on the Analysis of Knowledge* New York: Random House, 1970.

Schmitt, Fredrick, ed. *Socializing Epistemology: The Social Dimensions of Knowledge.* Lanham, MD: Rowman & Littlefield, 1994.

Shope, Robert K. *The Analysis of Knowing: A Decade of Research.* Princeton, N.J.: Princeton University Press, 1983.

Swain, Marshall. *Reasons and Knowledge.* Ithaca, N.Y.: Cornell University Press, 1981.

Swain, Marshall. "Epistemic Defeasibility." In *Essays on Knowledge and Justification,* edited by George Pappas and Marshall Swain. Ithaca, N.Y.: Cornell University Press, 1978.

STUDY QUESTIONS

1. Gettier argues that the justified true belief analysis is not sufficient for knowledge. Explain what he means by this. Choose one of the cases Gettier offers and explain why this shows that the justified true belief analysis is not sufficient.

2. Goldman suggests that what is missing from the traditional analysis is the requirement of a causal connection. Using one of the cases cited, explain what he means by this. Why does Goldman think that ordinary cases of perception yield knowledge?

3. Goldman claims that we can give a causal analysis for instances of inferential knowledge based on other beliefs that a person has. Using the cases of the lava and the faulty newspaper report, explain what condition must be satisfied, according to Goldman, in order to have inferential knowledge.

4. According to Goldman, what is the difference betwen giving the truth conditions of a sentence and giving its verification conditions?

5. According to Lehrer, can a person have evidence for a belief, yet not be completely justified? Explain. Can a person have evidence adequate to completely justify a belief, but not be completely justified in believing? Explain.

6. Why does Lehrer reject as a further condition for knowledge the fact that a person does not hold the belief on the basis of any false statement? In case two, as Lehrer calls it, S is completely justified in believing a false statement. Why does Lehrer think that S still has knowledge in this case?

7. Why does Pollock think the simplest version of the indefeasibility analysis must be rejected? In your own words, explain what Pollock means by "objective epistemic justification." Why does Pollock think a person in the Grabit case does have objective epistemic jusification?

8. What does Pollock mean by an ultimately undefeated argument? What must be added to objective epistemic justification to turn it into knowledge?

9. As Longino describes it, what is the sociological approach to knowledge? What is wrong with this approach? Why should the epistemologists nonetheless be concerned about the sociological approach? Why does Longino think that elements of the scientific enterprise, specifically observation and justificatory reasoning, are social in nature?

10. Why does Longino think that the analysis of knowledge should include models as the objects of knowledge? The traditional analysis of knowledge requires the justification of a belief. Explain how Longino's final account of knowledge, "Knowledge III," incorporates the notion of justification. Explain how her view differs from a more traditional understanding of justification.

PART II

Theory of Justification

4

Conceptions of the Nature of Justification

Although the concept of justification is basic for epistemology, there are many different conceptions of the *nature* of justification. As with other fundamental epistemic concepts, justification is an intrinsically normative concept. Epistemologists may, however propose dramatically different frameworks for elaborating the core normative features of justification.

How we understand the concept of justification depends in part on our understanding of epistemic goals and the methods appropriate to attaining those goals. Consider, for example, the typical analysis that a belief is justified only if there are good reasons for thinking it is true. This sort of view is reflected in Laurence BonJour's selection, "The Concept of Epistemic Justification," in which he holds that there is a conceptual connection between truth and justification. The epistemic goal explicit in this type of analysis is to acquire true beliefs. Some, however, resist the idea that we should follow along the traditional path, taking truth to be our epistemic goal. This is not the only point of contention in elaborating the concept of justification.

It is obvious that we require some understanding of the notion of "good reasons" for believing. It is possible to interpret "good reasons" in either a first- or third-person perspective, and the resulting theories of justification will differ markedly. If a first-person perspective is adopted, then a theory may emphasize the reasons that support a belief. On the other hand, if a third-person perspective is adopted, a theory may emphasize the causal, psychological processes that bring about the belief. But even the third-person perspective can be interpreted individualistically or socially. A theory of justification might focus on facts about the individual person, or it may focus on various social factors and mechanisms that lead to people forming beliefs. Still another complicating factor in a theory of justification is determining the method

we are to use to analyze the concept of justification. This sort of issue can lead to challenging the theoretical foundations and core assumptions of epistemology.

A prominent conception of the nature of justification is the *deontological* conception. In this view, specific epistemic obligations or epistemic duties are required in order to justify a belief. Acquiring true beliefs or believing only on sufficient evidence are examples of epistemic obligations sometimes proposed. Descartes, for example, could be interpreted as holding a deontological conception. Our epistemic obligation may be to hold only those beliefs that are certain or infallible. Similarly, one might understand Hume as arguing that our epistemic obligation is to believe only on the basis of sufficient evidence.

It is thought by some that the deontological conception of justification inaccurately describes the way in which we acquire our beliefs. Having an obligation implies the ability to satisfy that obligation, or, more simply, "ought implies can." If we try to apply the "ought implies can" principle to epistemological matters, the deontological view appears to face an awkward dilemma. Either belief is voluntary, which seems counterintuitive—do you think you voluntarily believe you are looking at a book?—or the deontological view is mistaken as an account of justification. This line of thought is pursued by William Alston in "Conceptions of Epistemic Justification."

One response to this problem is to hold that we can have obligations that we may be unable to satisfy. This is the approach taken by Richard Feldman in "Epistemic Obligations." Feldman argues that the best account of our epistemic obligation is to believe on the basis of evidence.

It might seem that the claim to believe only on the basis of evidence is a generally salutary injunction.

William James challenges this view in his 1896 essay "The Will to Believe." James argues that most of the propositions that affect the way we live and the decisions we make are not the sort of propositions for which the evidence speaks unambiguously. He does not seem to be thinking of the type of propositions that frequently occupy epistemologists. Moreover, James argues that we can scarcely suspend belief about these propositions; to suspend belief in the proposition that God exists is a commitment. James thus attempts to defend the idea that it is not only truth and evidence for truth that matters; in some cases, the practical difference a belief makes matters more.

The essays by Richard Rorty and Richard Foley similarly challenge some of the deeper assumptions of traditional epistemology, especially the assumptions of what is occasionally called "analytic epistemology." In "Pragmatism, Relativism, and Irrationalism," Rorty develops some Jamesean themes. For Rorty, the importance of a philosopher like James is his resistance to a "theory of knowledge." Concepts such as justification and knowledge are not the sort of concepts that can be analyzed. Practice (how we act and live), not theory, is the principal concern of the pragmatist. Rorty holds that once one adopts the type of pragmatist perspective he describes, apparently pejorative aspects of relativism and irrationalism lose much of their bite. One aspect of Rorty's defense of pragmatism is his attempt to understand the epistemological project in a larger historical and social context.

Richard Foley, in his "What Am I to Believe?" departs from a traditional conception of rationality or justification. This traditional conception has two elements, as we have already noticed. There is a first-person aspect, which Foley calls "egocentric," and a truth-directed third-person perspective. Unfortunately, Foley argues, neither of these perspectives gives us an adequate answer to the question "What should we believe?" In its current incarnation, epistemology is not in a position to give us the sort of intellectual advice we desire. Epistemology also, according to Foley, inevitably depends on our beliefs and assumptions. This is not troubling to Foley, since he thinks that we must abandon the presumption that we are in need of intellectual advice, as that is understood in the classical and contemporary epistemological tradition. Foley thinks that by the time we turn to epistemological theory our intellectual standards are already shaped and alternative standards are rarely real options for us.

The essays in this chapter reflect but a part of the diversity that can be found in current epistemological theory. Epistemology is not confined to the dualisms—rationalism and empiricism, foundationalism and coherentism—that so often seem to dominate the discipline. In subsequent chapters we will explore some of the more orthodox developments, as well as the newer, controversial orthodoxies in the conception of the nature of justification. We will also have the opportunity to see some different developments of the epistemological enterprise.

LAURENCE BONJOUR

The Concept of Epistemic Justification

The concept of epistemic justification is clearly the central concept in the whole theory of knowledge, and this book is largely devoted to exploring in detail certain of its facets and ramifications. But my immediate task is more modest and more basic: to consider how epistemic justification differs from other species of justification and to explore in a very preliminary way some of the problems raised by the concept thus arrived at.

The reason that the first issue requires discussion is that the concept of justification is plainly a generic one—roughly that of a reason or warrant of some kind meeting some appropriate standard. There are many specific varieties of justification actually in use and in principle as many as anyone cares to construct. Thus one may justify an action by appeal to moral standards; a business decision by appeal to business standards; an interpretation of a religious text by appeal to theological standards; and so on. What is involved in each of these examples is plainly some species of justification, but the particular standards of justification which are relevant in each case are obviously very different. Moreover, the choice of standards, in the more interesting cases at least, is not at all arbitrary. Rather there is an underlying rationale involved in each sort of case by reference to which the choice of standards is made and relative to which those standards might themselves be appropriately justified or rationalized. The immediate problem is thus to distinguish epistemic justification, the species of justification appropriate or relevant to knowledge, from other actual and possible species of justification.

Now it might be thought that the solution to this problem is obvious and straightforward: epistemic justification is that species of justification which is appropriate to *beliefs* or *judgments,* rather than to actions, decisions, and so on. But this initially plausible suggestion is only partly correct. It seems correct that only beliefs, or cognitive states resembling

beliefs, are even candidates for epistemic justification. It may even be the case, though this would be very hard to show, that epistemic justification is the species of justification which is somehow most appropriate to beliefs. But there are other species of justification which also can apply to beliefs, so that mere applicability to beliefs cannot be the sole distinguishing characteristic of epistemic justification.

A pair of examples may help to illustrate this point. First, suppose that I have a dear friend who has stood by me and supported me through many trials and crises, often at considerable cost to himself. Now this friend stands accused of a horrible crime, everyone else believes him to be guilty, and there is substantial evidence for this conclusion. Suppose too that I have no independent evidence concerning the matter and also that my friend knows me well enough that an insincere claim to believe in his innocence will surely be detected. If in these difficult circumstances I can bring myself to believe in his innocence, it is surely plausible to say that there is a sense in which I am justified in so believing; indeed such a belief might well be regarded as obligatory. But the justification in question is plainly not epistemic justification, but rather a kind of *moral* justification: even if my friend is in fact innocent, I obviously do not *know* on this basis that he is innocent, no matter how compelling a reason *of this sort* I may have for my belief.

A different sort of justification for believing, still nonepistemic in character, is illustrated by Pascal's famous wager and by an analogous example offered by William James. Pascal argues, roughly, that it is rational to believe that God exists because, on the one hand, if God exists, belief will be enormously rewarded and failure to believe horribly punished; and, on the other hand, if God does not exist, the consequences of either believing or not believing will be very minor by comparison. James imagines a situation in which I must leap over a chasm to escape from some danger: it is uncertain whether I can jump that far, but I know that I will make a better effort and thus have a better chance of success if I believe that I can. In such a situation, he argues, I am justified in believing that I can make the leap, even though I have no real evidence that this is so. The point here is that even if these arguments are otherwise acceptable (notoriously there are difficulties at least with Pascal's), the *kind* of justification which they provide for the beliefs in question is not the right kind to satisfy the requirement for knowledge—no matter how strong it is in its own way and no matter whether the beliefs in question happen in fact to be true. It is what might be called prudential or pragmatic justification, not epistemic justification.

What then is the differentia which distinguishes epistemic justification, the species of justification appropriate to knowledge, from these other species of justification? The answer is to be found, I submit, by reflecting on the implicit rationale of the concept of knowledge itself. What after all is the point of such a concept, and what role is epistemic justification supposed to play in it? Why should we, as cognitive beings, *care* whether our beliefs are epistemically justified? Why is such justification something to be sought and valued?

Once the question is posed in this way, the following answer seems obviously correct, at least in first approximation. What makes us cognitive beings at all is our capacity for belief, and the goal of our distinctively cognitive endeavors is *truth:* we want our beliefs to correctly and accurately depict the world. If truth were somehow immediately and unproblematically accessible (as it is, on some accounts, for God) so that one could in all cases opt simply to believe the truth, then the concept of justification would be of little significance and would play no independent role in cognition. But this epistemically ideal situation is quite obviously not the one in which we find ourselves. We have no such immediate and unproblematic access to truth, and it is for this reason that justification comes into the picture. The basic role of justification is that of a *means* to truth, a more directly attainable mediating link between our subjective starting point and our objective goal. We cannot, in most cases at least, bring it about directly that our beliefs are true, but

we can presumably bring it about directly (though perhaps only in the long run) that they are epistemically justified. And, *if our standards of epistemic justification are appropriately chosen,* bringing it about that our beliefs are epistemically justified will also tend to bring it about, in the perhaps even longer run and with the usual slippage and uncertainty which our finitude mandates, that they are true. If epistemic justification were not conducive to truth in this way, if finding epistemically justified beliefs did not substantially increase the likelihood of finding true ones, then epistemic justification would be irrelevant to our main cognitive goal and of dubious worth. It is only if we have some reason for thinking that epistemic justification constitutes a path to truth that we as cognitive beings have any motive for preferring epistemically justified beliefs to epistemically unjustified ones. Epistemic justification is therefore in the final analysis only an instrumental value, not an intrinsic one.

The distinguishing characteristic of epistemic justification is thus its essential or internal relation to the cognitive goal of truth. It follows that one's cognitive endeavors are epistemically justified only if and to the extent that they are aimed at this goal, which means very roughly that one accepts all and only those beliefs which one has good reason to think are true. To accept a belief in the absence of such a reason, however appealing or even mandatory such acceptance might be from some other standpoint, is to neglect the pursuit of truth; such acceptance is, one might say, *epistemically irresponsible.* My contention here is that the idea of avoiding such irresponsibility, of being epistemically responsible in one's believings, is the core of the notion of epistemic justification.

It is this essential relation to truth which distinguishes epistemic justification from other species of justification aimed at different goals. Of course, at times the degree of epistemic justification may fall short of that required for knowledge and thus fail to make it likely to any very high degree that the belief in question is true. But any degree of epistemic justification, however small, must increase to a commensurate degree the chances that the belief in question is true (assuming that these are not already maximal), for otherwise it cannot qualify as epistemic justification at all.

WILLIAM ALSTON

Concepts of Epistemic Justification

I

Justification, or at least 'justification', bulks large in recent epistemology. The view that knowledge consists of true justified belief (+ . . .) has been prominent in this century, and the justification of belief has attracted considerable attention in its own right. But it is usually not at all clear just what an epistemologist means by 'justified', just what concept the term is used to express. An enormous amount of energy has gone into the attempt to specify conditions under which beliefs of one or another sort are justified; but relatively little has been done to explain *what it is* for a belief to be justified, what that is for which conditions are being sought. The most common procedure has been to proceed on the basis of a number of (supposedly) obvious cases of justified belief, without pausing to determine what property it is of which these cases are instances. Now even if there were some single determinate concept that all these theorists have implicitly in mind, this procedure would be less than wholly satisfactory. For in the absence of an explicit account of the concept being applied, we lack the most fundamental basis for deciding between supposed intuitions and for evaluating proposed conditions of justification. And in any event, as philosophers we do not seek merely to speak the truth, but also to gain an explicit, reflective understanding of the matters with which we deal. We want to know not only when our beliefs are justified, but also what it is to enjoy that status. True, not every fundamental concept can be explicated, but we shall find that much can be done with this one.

And since, as we shall see in this paper, there are several distinct concepts that are plausibly termed "concepts of epistemic justification", the need for analysis is even greater. By simply using 'justified' in an unexamined, intuitive fashion, the epistemologist is covering up differences that make important differences to the shape of a theory of justification. We cannot fully understand the stresses and strains in thought about justification until we uncover the most crucial differences between concepts of epistemic justification.

Not all contemporary theorists of justification fall under these strictures. Some have undertaken to given an account of the concept of justification they are using. But none of them provide a map of this entire conceptual territory.

In this essay I am going to elaborate and interrelate several distinct concepts of epistemic justification, bringing out some crucial issues involved in choosing between them. I shall give reasons for disqualifying some of the contenders, and I shall explain my choice of a winner. Finally I shall vouchsafe a glimpse of the enterprise for which this essay is a propaedeutic, that of showing how the differences between these concepts make a difference in what it takes for the justification of belief, and other fundamental issues in epistemology.

Before launching this enterprise, we must clear out of the way a confusion between one's *being* justified in believing that *p*, and one's *justifying* one's belief that *p*, where the latter involves one's *doing* something to show that *p*, or to show that one's belief was justified, or to exhibit one's justification. The first side of this distinction is a state or condition one is in, not anything one does or any upshot thereof. I might *be* justified in believing that there is milk on the table because I see it there, even though I have done nothing to show that there is milk on the table or to show that I am justified in believing there to be. It is amazing how often these matters are confused in the literature. We will be concentrating on the "be justified" side of this distinction, since that is of more fundamental epistemological interest. If epistemic justification were restricted to those cases in which the subject carries out a "justification", it would *obviously* not be a necessary condition of knowledge or even of being in a strong position to acquire knowledge. Most cases of perceptual knowledge, for example, involve no such activity.

II

Let's begin our exploration of this stretch of conceptual territory by listing a few basic features of the concept that would seem to be common ground.

(1) It applies to beliefs, or alternatively to a cognitive subject's having a belief. I shall speak indifferently of S's belief that p being justified and of S's being justified in believing that p. This is the common philosophical concept of belief, in which S's believing that p entails neither that S knows that p nor that S does not know that p. It is not restricted to conscious or occurrent beliefs.

(2) It is an evaluative concept, in a broad sense in which this is contrasted with 'factual'. To say that S is justified in believing that p is to imply that there is something all right, satisfactory, in accord with the way things should be, about the fact that S believes that p. It is to accord S's believing a positive evaluative status.

(3) It has to do with a specifically *epistemic* dimension of evaluation. Beliefs can be evaluated in different ways. One may be more or less prudent, fortunate, or faithful in holding certain belief. Epistemic justification is different from all that. Epistemic evaluation is undertaken from what we might call the "epistemic point of view". That point of view is defined by the aim at maximizing truth and minimizing falsity in a large body of beliefs. The qualification "in a large body of beliefs" is needed because otherwise one could best achieve the aim by restricting one's beliefs to those that are obviously true. That is a rough formulation. How large a body of beliefs should we aim at? Is any body of beliefs of a given size, with the same truth-falsity ratio, equally desirable, or is it more important, epistemically, to form beliefs on some matters than others? And what relative weights should be assigned to the two aims at maximizing truth and minimizing falsity? We can't go into all that here; in any event, however these issues are settled, it remains true that our central cognitive aim is to amass a large body of beliefs with a favorable truth-falsity ratio. For a belief to be epistemically justified is for it, somehow, to be awarded high marks relative to that aim.

(4) It is a matter of degree. One can be more or less justified in believing that p. If, e.g., what justifies one is some evidence one has, one will be more or less justified depending on the amount and strength of the evidence. In this paper, however, I shall, for the sake of simplicity, treat justification as absolute. You may, if you like, think of this as the degree of justification required for some standard of acceptability.

III

Since any concept of epistemic justification is a concept of some condition that is desirable or commendable from the standpoint of the aim at maximizing truth or minimizing falsity, in distinguishing different concepts of justification we will be distinguishing different ways in which conditions can be desirable from this standpoint. As I see it, the major divide in this terrain has to do with whether believing and refraining from believing are subject to obligation, duty, and the like. If they are, we can think of the favorable evaluative status of a certain belief as consisting in the fact that in holding that belief one has fulfilled one's obligations, or refrained from violating one's obligations, to achieve the fundamental aim in question. If they are not so subject, the favorable status will have to be though of in some other way.

I shall first explore concepts of the first sort, which I shall term 'deontological', since they have to do with how one stands, in believing that p, vis-à-vis duties or obligations. Most epistemologists who have attempted to explicate justification have set out a concept of this sort. It is natural to set out a deontological concept on the model of the justification of behavior. Something I *did* was justified just in case it was *not in violation* of any relevant duties, obligations, rules, or regulations, and hence was not something for which I could rightfully be blamed. To say that my expenditures on the trip were justified is not to say that I was obliged to make those expenditures (e.g., for taxis), but only that it was all right for me to do so, that in doing so I was not in violation of any relevant rules or regulations. And to say that I was justified in making that decision on my own, without consulting the executive committee, is not to say that I was required to do it on my own (though that *may* also be true); it is only to say that the departmental by-laws permit the chairman to use his own discretion in matters of this kind. Similarly, to say that a belief was deontologically justified is not to say that the subject was obligated to believe this, but only that he was permitted to do so, that believing this did not involve any violation of relevant obligations. To say that I am justified in believing that salt is composed of sodium and chlorine, since I have been assured of this by an expert, is not to say that I am obligated to believe this, though this might also be true. It is to say that I am permitted to believe it, that believing it would not be a violation of any relevant obligation, for example, the obligation to refrain from believing that *p* in the absence of adequate reasons for doing so. As Carl Ginet puts it, "One is *justified* in being confident that *p* if and only if it is not the case that one ought not to be confident that *p*; one could not be justly reproached for being confident that *p*."

Since we are concerned specifically with the *epistemic* justification of belief, the concept in which we are interested is not that of *not violating obligations of any sort in believing,* but rather the more specific concept of *not violating "epistemic", "cognitive", or "intellectual" obligations in believing.* Where are such obligations to be found? If we follow out our earlier specification of "epistemic point of view", we will think of our basic epistemic obligation as that of doing what we can to achieve the aim at maximizing truth and minimizing falsity within a large body of beliefs. There will then be numerous more specific obligations that owe their status to the fact that fulfilling them will tend to the achievement of that central aim. Such obligations might include *to refrain from believing that p in the absence of sufficient evidence and to accept whatever one sees to be clearly implied by something one already believes (or, perhaps, is already justified in believing).* Of course other positions might be taken on this point. One might suppose that there are a number of ultimate, irreducible intellectual duties that cannot be derived from any basic goal of our cognitive life. Or alternative versions of the central aim might be proposed. Here we shall think in terms of the basic aim we have specified, with more specific obligations derived from that.

Against this background we can set out our first concept of epistemic justification as follows, using 'd' for 'deontological':

(I)   S is J_d in believing that *p iff* in believing that *p* S is not violating any epistemic obligations.

There are important distinctions between what we may call "modes" of obligation, justification, and other normative statuses. These distinctions are by no means confined to the epistemic realm. Let's introduce them in connection with moral norms for behavior. Begin with a statement of obligation in "objective" terms, a statement of the objective state of affairs I might be said to be obliged to bring about. For example, it is my obligation as a host to make *my guest, G, feel welcome.* Call that state of affairs 'A'. We may think of this as an *objective* conception of my obligation as a host. I have fulfilled that obligation *iff* G feels welcome. But suppose I did what I sincerely believed would bring about A? In that case surely no one could blame me for dereliction of duty. That suggests a more *subjective* conception of my obligation as *doing what I believed was likely to bring about A.* But perhaps I should not be let off as easily as that. "You should have realized that what you did was not calculated to make G feel welcome." This retort suggests a somewhat more stringent formulation of my obligation than the very permissive subjective conception just specified. It suggests that I can't fulfill my obligation by doing just anything I happen to believe will bring about A. I am not off the hook unless *I did what the facts available to me indicate will have a good chance of leading to A.* This is still a subjective conception in that what it takes to fulfill my obligation is specified from my point of view; but it takes my point of view to range over not all my beliefs, but only my justified beliefs. This we might call a *cognitive* conception of my obligation. Finally, suppose that I did what I had adequate reason to suppose would produce A, and I did produce A, but I didn't do it for that reason. I was just amusing myself, and I would have done what I did even if I had known it would not make G feel welcome. In that case I might be faulted for moral irresponsibility, however well I rate in the other modes. This suggests that we may call a motivational conception of my obligation as *doing what I believed (or was justified in believing) would bring about A, in order to bring about A.*

We may sum up these distinctions as follows:

(II) S has fulfilled his *objective* obligation *iff* S has brought about A.

(III) S has fulfilled his *subjective* obligation *iff* S has done what he believed to be most likely to bring about A.

(IV) S has fulfilled his *cognitive* obligation *iff* S did what he was justified in believing to be most likely to bring about A.

(V) S has fulfilled his *motivational* obligation *iff* S has done what he did because he supposed it would be most likely to bring about A.

We can make analogous distinctions with respect to the justification of behavior or belief, construed as the absence of any violation of obligations. Let's indicate how this works out for the justification of belief.

(VI) S is *objectively* justified in believing that *p iff* S is not violating any objective obligation is believing that *p*.

(VII) S is *subjectively* justified in believing that *p iff* S is not violating any subjective obligation in believing that *p*.

(VIII) S is *cognitively* justified in believing that *p iff* S is not violating any cognitive obligation in believing that *p*.

(IX) S is *motivationally* justified in believing that *p iff* S is not violating any motivational obligation in believing that *p*.

If we assume that only one intellectual obligation is relevant to the belief in question, viz., the obligation to believe that *p* only if one has adequate evidence for *p*, we can be a bit more concrete about this.

(X) S is objectively justified in believing that *p iff* S has adequate evidence for *p*.

(XI) S is subjectively justified in believing that *p iff* S believes that he *p*ossesses adequate evidence for *p*.

(XII) S is cognitively justified in believing that *p iff* S is justified in believing that he possesses adequate evidence for *p*.

(XIII) S is motivationally justified in believing that *p iff* S believes that *p* on the basis of adequate evidence, or, alternatively, on the basis of what he believed, or was justified in believing, was adequate evidence.

I believe that we can safely neglect (XI). To explain why, I will need to make explicit what it is to have adequate evidence for *p*. First, a proposition, *q*, is adequate evidence for *p* provided they are related in such a way that if *q* is true then *p* is at least probably true. But I *have* that evidence only if I believe that *q*. Furthermore I don't "have" it in such a way as to thereby render my belief that *p* justified unless I know or am justified in believing that *q*. An unjustified belief that *q* wouldn't do it. If I believe that Begin has told the cabinet that he will resign, but only because I credited an unsubstantiated rumor, then even if Begin's having told the cabinet that he would resign is an adequate indication that he will resign, I will not thereby be justified in believing that he will resign.

Now I might very well *believe* that I have adequate evidence for *q* even though one or more of these conditions is not satisfied. I might mistakenly believe that my evidence is adequate support, and I might mistakenly suppose that I am justified in accepting it. But, as we have just seen, if I am not justified in accepting the evidence for *p*, then my believing it cannot render me justified in believing that *p*, however adequate that evidence. I would also hold, though this is perhaps more controversial, that if the evidence is not in fact adequate, my having that evidence cannot justify me in believing that *p*. Thus, since my believing that I have adequate evidence is compatible with these nonjustifying states of affairs, we cannot take subjective justification, as defined in (XI), to constitute epistemic justification.

That leaves us with three contenders. Here I will confine myself to pointing out that there is strong tendency for J_d to be used in a cognitive rather than a purely objective form. J_d is, most centrally, a concept of freedom from blameworthiness, a concept of being "in the clear" so far as one's intellectual obligations are concerned. But even if I don't have adequate evidence for *p*, I could hardly be blamed for believing that *p* (even assuming, as we are in this discussion, that there is something wrong with believing in the absence of adequate evidence), provided I am justified in supposing that I have adequate evidence. So long as that condition holds, I have done the right thing, or refrained from doing the wrong thing, so far as I am able to tell; and what more could be required of me? But his means that it is (XII), rather than (X), that brings out what it takes for freedom from blame, and so brings out what it takes for being J_d.

What about the motivational form? We can have J_d in any of the first three forms with or without the motivational form. I can have adequate evidence for p and believe that p, whether or not my belief is based on that evidence; and so for the other two. But the motivational mode is parasitic on the other modes, in that the precise form taken by the motivational mode depends on the status of the (supposed) evidence on which the belief is based. This "unsaturated" character of the motivational mode is reflected in the threefold alternative that appears in our formulation of (XIII). If S bases his belief that p on actually possessed adequate evidence, then (XIII) combines with (X). If the evidence on which it is based is only believed to be adequate evidence, or only justifiably believed to be adequate evidence, then (XIII) combines with (XI) and (XIII). Of course, it may be based on actually possessed adequate evidence, which is justifiably believed to be such, in which case S is justified in all four modes. Thus the remaining question concerning J_d is whether a "motivational rider" should be put on (XII). Is it enough for J_d that S be justified in believing that he has adequate evidence for p, or should it also be required that S's belief that p be based on that evidence? We will address this question in Section v in the form it assumes for a quite different concept of justification.

IV

We have explained *being $\mathcal{J}_d$ in believing that p* as *not violating any intellectual obligations in believing that p*. And, in parallel fashion, being J_d in refraining from believing that p would consist in not having violated any intellectual obligations in so doing. But if it is possible for me to violate an obligation in refraining

from believing that p, it must be that I can be obliged, under certain conditions, to believe that p. And, by the same token, if I can violate obligations in believing that p, then I can be obliged to refrain from believing that p. And this is the way we have been thinking of it. Our example of an intellectual obligation has been the obligation to refrain from believing that p in the absence of adequate evidence. On the other side, we might think of a person as being obliged to believe that p if confronted with conclusive evidence that p (where that includes the absence of sufficient overriding evidence to the contrary).

Now it certainly looks as if I can be obliged to believe or to refrain from believing, only if this is in my direct voluntary control; only if I can, here and now, believe that p or no just by willing (deciding, choosing . . .). And that is the way many epistemologists seem to construe the matter. At least, many formulations are most naturally interpreted in this way. Think back, for example, on Chisholm's formulation of our intellectual obligation. Chisholm envisages a person thinking of a certain proposition as a candidate for belief, and then effectively choosing belief or abstention on the basis of those considerations. Let's call the version of J_d that presupposes direct voluntary control over belief (and thus thinks of an obligation to believe as an obligation to bring about belief here and now), 'J_{dv}' ('v' for 'voluntary').

I find this assumption of direct voluntary control over belief quite unrealistic. There are strong reasons for doubting that belief is usually, or perhaps ever, under direct voluntary control. First, think of the beliefs I acquire about myself and the world about me through experience—through perception, self-consciousness, testimony, and simple reasoning based on these data. When I see a car coming down the street, I am not capable of believing or disbelieving, this at will. In such familiar situations the belief-acquisition mechanism is isolated from the direct influence of the will and under the control of more purely cognitive factors.

Partisans of a voluntary control thesis will counter by calling attention to cases in which things don't appear to be so cut and dried: cases of radical underdetermination by evidence, as when a general has to dispose his forces in the absence of sufficient information about the position of enemy forces; or cases of the acceptance of a religious or philosophical position where there seem to be a number of equally viable alternatives. In such cases it can appear that one makes a decision as to what to believe and what not to believe. My view on these matters is that insofar as something is chosen voluntarily, it is something other than a belief or abstention from belief. The general chooses to proceed on the working assumption that the enemy forces are disposed in such-and-such a way. The religious convert to whom it is not clear that the beliefs are correct has chosen to live a certain kind of life, or to selectively subject himself to certain influences. And so on. But even if I am mistaken about these kinds of cases, it is clear that for the vast majority of beliefs nothing like direct voluntary control is involved. And so J_{dv} could not possibly be a generally applicable concept of epistemic justification.

If I am right in rejecting the view that belief is, in general or ever, under direct voluntary control, are we foreclosed from construing epistemic justification as freedom from blameworthiness? Not necessarily. We aren't even prevented from construing epistemic justification as the absence of obligation-violations. We *will* have to avoid thinking of the relevant obligations as obligations to believe or refrain from believing, on the model of obligations to answer a question or to open a door, or to do anything else over which we have immediate voluntary control. If we are to continue to think of intellectual obligations as having to do with believing, it will have to be more on the model of the way in which obligations bear on various other conditions over which one lacks direct voluntary control but which one can influence by voluntary actions, such conditions as being overweight, being irritable, being in poor health, or having friends. I can't institute, nullify, or alter any of those conditions here and now just by deciding to do so. But I can do things at will that will influence those conditions, and in that way they may be to some extent under my indirect control. One might speak of my being obliged to be in good health or to have a good disposition, meaning that I am obliged to do what I can (or as much as could reasonably be expected of me) to institute and preserve those states of affairs. Since, however, I think it less misleading to say exactly what I mean, I will not speak of our being obliged to weigh a certain amount or to have a good disposition, or to

believe a proposition; I will rather speak of our having obligations to do what we can, or as much as can reasonably be expected of us, to influence those conditions.

The things we can do to affect our believings can be divided into (1) activities that bring influences to bear, or withhold influences from, a particular situation, and (2) activities that affect our belief-forming habits. (1) includes such activities as checking to see whether I have considered all the relevant evidence, getting a second opinion, searching my memory for analogous cases, and looking into the question of whether there is anything markedly abnormal about my current perceptual situation. (2) includes training myself to be more critical of gossip, talking myself into being either more or less subservient to authority, and practicing greater sensitivity to the condition of other people. Moreover it is plausible to think of these belief-influencing activities as being subject to intellectual obligations. We might, for instance, think of ourselves as being under an obligation to do what we can (or what could reasonably be expected of us) to make our belief-forming processes as reliable as possible.

All this suggests that we might frame a deontological conception of justification according to which one is epistemically justified in believing that *p iff* one's believing that *p* is not the result of one's failure to fulfill one's intellectual obligations vis-à-vis one's belief-forming and maintaining activities. It would, again, be like the way in which one is or isn't to blame for other conditions that are not under direct voluntary control but that one can influence by one's voluntary activities. I am to blame for being overweight (being irritable, being in poor health, being without friends) only if that condition is in some way due to my own past failures to do what I should to limit my intake or to exercise or whatever. If I would still be overweight even if I had done everything I could and should have done about it, then I can hardly be blamed for it. Similarly, we may say that I am subject to reproach for believing that *p*, provided that I am to blame for being in that doxastic condition, in the sense that there are things I could and should have done, such that if I had done them I would not now be believing that *p*. If that is the case, I am unjustified in that belief. And if it is *not* the case, if there are no unfulfilled obligations the fulfilling of which would have inhibited that belief formation, then I am justified in the belief.

Thus we have arrived at a deontological concept of epistemic justification that does not require belief to be under direct voluntary control. We may label this concept 'J_{di}' ('i' for 'involuntary'). It may be more formally defined as follows:

(XIV) S is J_{di} in believing that *p* at *t iff* there are not intellectual obligations that (1) have to do with the kind of belief-forming or sustaining habit the activation of which resulted in S's believing that *p* at *t*, or with the particular process of belief formation or sustenance that was involved in S's believing that *p* at *t*, and (2) which are such that:

(A) S had those obligations prior to *t*.

(B) S did not fulfill those obligations.

(C) If S had fulfilled those obligations, S would not have believed that *p* at *t*.

As it stands, this account will brand too many beliefs as unjustified, just because it is too undiscriminating in the counterfactual condition, C. There are ways in which the nonfulfillment of intellectual obligations can contribute to a belief acquisition without rendering the belief unjustified. Suppose that I fail to carry out my obligation to spend a certain period in training myself to observe things more carefully. I use the time thus freed up to take a walk around the neighborhood. In the course of this stroll I see two dogs fighting thereby acquiring the belief that they are fighting. There was a relevant intellectual obligation I didn't fulfill, which is such that if I had fulfilled it I wouldn't have acquired that belief. But if that is a perfectly normal perceptual belief, it is surely not thereby rendered unjustified.

Here the dereliction of duty contributed to belief formation simply by facilitating access to the data. That's not the kind of contribution we had in mind. The sorts of cases we were thinking of were those most directly suggested by the two sorts of intellectual obligations we distinguished: (a) cases in which

the belief was acquired by the activation of a habit that we would not have possessed had we fulfilled our intellectual obligations; (b) cases in which we acquire, or retain, the belief only because we are sheltered from adverse considerations in a way we wouldn't be if we had done what we should have done. Thus we can avoid counterexamples like the above by reformulating C as follows:

(C) If S had fulfilled those obligations, then S's belief-forming habits would have changed, or S's access to relevant adverse considerations would have changed, in such a way that S would not have believed that *p* at *t*.

But even with this refinement J_{di} does not give us what we expect of epistemic justification. The most serious defect is that it does not hook up in the right way with an adequate truth-conducive ground. I may have done what could reasonably be expected of me in the management and cultivation of my doxastic life and still hold a belief on outrageously inadequate grounds. There are several possible sources of such a discrepancy. First, there is what we might call "cultural isolation". If I have grown up in an isolated community in which everyone unhesitatingly accepts the traditions of the tribe as authoritative, then if I have never encountered anything that seems to cast doubt on the traditions and have never thought to question them, I can hardly be blamed for taking them as authoritative. There is nothing I could reasonably be expected to do what would alter that belief-forming tendency. And there is nothing I could be expected to do that would render me more exposed to counterevidence. (We can suppose that the traditions all have to do with events distant in time and/or space, matters on which I could not be expected to gather evidence on my own.) I am J_{di} in believing these things. And yet the fact that it is the tradition of the tribe that *p* may be a very poor reason for believing that *p*.

Then there is deficiency in cognitive powers. Rather than looking at the more extreme forms of this, let's consider a college student who just doesn't have what it takes to follow abstract philosophical reasoning, or exposition for that matter. Having read Book IV of Locke's *Essay*, he believes that it is Locke's view that everything is a matter of opinion, that one person's opinion is just as good as another's, and that what is true for me may not be true for you. And it's not just that he didn't work hard enough on this particular point, or on the general abilities involved. There is nothing that he could and should have done such that he done so, he would have gotten this straight. He is simply incapable of appreciating the distinction between "One's knowledge is restricted to one's own ideas" and "Everything is a matter of opinion". No doubt teachers of philosophy tend to assume too quickly that this description applies to some of their students, but surely there can be such cases, cases in which either no amount of time and effort would enable the student to get straight on the matter, or it would be unreasonable to expect the person to expend that amount of time or effort. And yet we would hardly wish to say that the student is justified in believing what he does about Locke.

Other possible sources of a discrepancy between J_{di} and epistemic justification are poor training that the person lacks the time or resources to overcome, and an incorrigible doxastic incontinence. ("When he talks like that, I just can't help believing what he says.") What this spread of cases brings out is that J_{di} is not sufficient for epistemic justification; we may have done the best we can, or at least the best that could reasonably be expected of us, and still be in a very poor epistemic position in believing that p; we could, blamelessly, be believing p for outrageously bad reasons. Even though J_{di} is the closest we can come to a deontological concept of epistemic justification if belief is not under direct voluntary control, it still does not give us what we are looking for.

V

Thus neither version of J_d is satisfactory. Perhaps it was misguided all along to think of epistemic justification as freedom from blameworthiness. Is there any alternative, given the nonnegotiable point that we are looking for a concept of epistemic evaluation? Of course there is. By no means all evaluation, even all evaluation of activities, states, and aspects of human beings, involves the circle of terms that includes 'obligation', 'permission', 'right', 'wrong', and 'blame'. We can evaluate a person's abilities, personal appearance, temperament, or state of

health as more or less desirable, favorable, or worthwhile, without taking these to be within the person's direct voluntary control and so subject to obligation in a direct fashion (as with J_{dv}), and without making the evaluation depend on whether the person has done what she should to influence these states (as with J_{di}). Obligation and blame need not come into it all. This is most obvious when we are dealing with matters that are not even under indirect voluntary control, like one's basic capacities or bodily build. Here when we use positively evaluative terms like 'gifted' or 'superb', we are clearly not saying that the person has done all she could to foster or encourage the condition in question. But even where the condition is at least partly under indirect voluntary control, as with personal appearance or state of health, we need not be thinking in those terms when we take someone to present a pleasing appearance or to be in splendid health. Moreover, we can carry out these evaluations from a certain point of view. We can judge that someone has a fine bodily constitution from an athletic or from an aesthetic point of view, or that someone's manner is a good one from a professional or from a social point of view.

In like fashion one can evaluate S's believing that p as a good, favorable, desirable, or appropriate thing without thinking of it as fulfilling or not violating an obligation, and without making this evaluation depend on whether the person has done what she could to carry out belief-influencing activities. As in the other cases, it could simply be a matter of the possession of certain good-making characteristics. Furthermore, believing can be evaluated from various points of view, including the epistemic, which, as we have noted, is defined by the aim at maximizing truth and minimizing falsity. it may be a good thing that S believes that p for his peace of mind, or from the standpoint of loyalty to the cause, or as an encouragement to the redoubling of his efforts. But none of this would render it a good thing for S to believe that p from the epistemic point of view. To believe that p because it gives peace of mind or because it stimulates effort may not be conducive to the attainment of truth and the avoidance of error.

All of this suggests that we can frame a concept of epistemic justification that is "evaluative", in a narrow sense of that term in which it contrasts with 'deontological', with the assessment of conduct in terms of obligation, blame, right, and wrong. Let's specify an "evaluative" sense of epistemic justification as follows:

(XV) S is J_e in believing that p *iff* S's believing that p, as S does, is a good thing from the epistemic point of view.

This is a way of being commendable from the epistemic point of view that is, or can be, quite different from the subject's not being to blame for any violation of intellectual obligations. The qualification "as S does" is inserted to make it explicit that in order for S to be J_e in believing that p, it need not be the case that any believing of p by S would be a good thing epistemically, much less any believing of p by anyone. It is rather that there are aspects of *this* believing of p by S that make it a good thing epistemically. There could conceivably be person-proposition pairs such that any belief in that proposition by that person would be a good thing epistemically, but this would be a limiting case and not typical of our epistemic condition.

Is there anything further to be said about this concept? Of course we should avoid building anything very substantive into the constitution of the concept. After all, it is possible for epistemologists to differ radically as to the conditions under which one or another sort of belief is justified. When this happens, they are at least sometimes using the same concept of justification; otherwise they wouldn't be disagreeing over what is required for justification, though they could still disagree over which concept of justification is most fundamental or most useful. Both our versions of J_d are quite neutral in this way. Both leave it completely open as to what intellectual obligations we have, and hence as to what obligations must not be violated if one is to be justified. But while maintaining due regard for the importance of neutrality. I believe that we can go beyond (XV) in fleshing out the concept.

We can get a start on this by considering the following question. If goodness from an epistemic point of view is what we are interested in, why shouldn't we identify justification with truth, at least extensionally? What could be better from that point of view than truth? If the name of the game is the maximization of truth and the minimization of falsity in our beliefs, then plain unvarnished truth is hard to beat. This consideration, however, has not moved epistemologists to identify justification with truth, or even to take truth as a necessary and sufficient condition for justification. The logical independence of truth and justification is a staple of the epistemological literature. But why should this be? It is obvious that a belief might be J_d without being true and vice versa, but what reason is there for taking J_e to be independent of truth?

I think the answer to this has to be in terms of the "internalist" character of justification. When we ask whether S is justified in believing that p, we are, as we have repeatedly been insisting, asking a question from the standpoint of an aim at truth; but we are not asking whether things are in fact as S believes. We are getting at something more "internal" to S's perspective on the world". This internalist feature of justification made itself felt in our discussion of J_d when we pointed out that to be J_{dv} is to fail to violate any relevant intellectual obligations, *so far as one can tell*; it is to be J_{dv} in what we call the "cognitive" mode. With respect to J_e the analogous point is that although this is goodness vis-à-vis the aim at truth, it consists not in the beliefs fitting the way the facts actually are, but something more like the belief's being true "so far as the subject can tell from what is available to the subject". In asking whether S is J_e in believing that p, we are asking whether the truth of p is strongly indicated by what S has to go on; whether, given what S had to go on, it is at least quite likely that p is true. We want to know whether S had *adequate grounds* for believing that p, where *adequate* grounds are those sufficiently indicative of the truth of p.

If we are to make the notion of *adequate grounds* for central J_e, we must say more about it. A belief has a certain ground, G, when it is "based on" G. What is it for a belief, B, to be *based on* G? That is a difficult question. So far as I know, there is no fully satisfactory general account in the literature, nor am I able to supply one. But we are not wholly at a loss. We do have a variety of paradigm cases; the difficulty concerns just how to generalize from them and just where to draw the line. When one infers p and q and *thereby* comes to accept p, this is a clear case of basing one belief on another. Again, when I come to believe that this is a tree because this visually appears to me to be the case, that is another paradigm; here my belief that that is a tree is based on my visual experience, or, if you prefer, on certain aspects of that experience. The main difficulties arise with respect to cases in which no conscious inference takes place but in which we are still inclined to say that one belief is based on another. Consider, for instance, my forming the belief that you are angry on seeing you look and act in a certain way. I perform no conscious inference from a proposition about your demeanor and behavior to a proposition about your emotional state. Nevertheless, it seems plausible to hold that I did learn about your demeanor and behavior through seeing it, and that the beliefs I thereby formed played a crucial role in my coming to believe that you are angry. More specifically, it seems that the former beliefs gave rise to the latter belief; that if I hadn't acquired the former, I would not have acquired the latter; and, finally, that if I am asked why I suppose that you are angry, I would cite the behavior and demeanor as my reason (perhaps only as "the way he looked and acted"). How can we get this kind of case together with the conscious-inference cases into a general account? We might claim that they are all cases of inference, some of them being unconscious. But there are problems as to when we are justified in imputing unconscious inferences. We might take it that what lets in our problem cases is the subject's disposition to cite the one belief(s) as his reason for the other belief; and then make our general condition a disjunction of conscious inference from q and a tendency to cite q as the reason. But then what about subjects (small children and lower animals) that are too unsophisticated to be able to answer questions as to what their reasons are? Can't their beliefs be based on something when no conscious inference is performed? Moreover, this disjunctive criterion will not include cases in which belief is based on an experience, rather than on other beliefs. A third suggestion concerns causality. In all the cases mentioned thus far it is plausible to suppose that the belief that q was among the causes of the belief that p. This suggests that we might try to cut the Gordian knot by boldly identifying "based on" with "caused by". But this runs into the usual difficulties of simple causal theories.

Many items enter into the causation of a belief, for example, various neurophysiological happenings, that clearly don't qualify as even part of what the belief is based on. To make a causal account work, we would have to beef it up into "caused by q in a certain way". And what way is that? Some way that is paradigmatically exemplified by our paradigms? But how to state this way in such a fashion that it applies equally to the nonparadigmatic cases?

In the face of these perplexities our only recourse is to keep a firm hold on our paradigms and work with a less than ideally determinate concept of a relationship that holds in cases that are "sufficiently like" the paradigms. That will be sufficient to do the job over most of the territory.

Let's return to "grounds". What a belief is based on we may term the ground of the belief. A ground, in a more dispositional sense of the term, is the sort of item on which a belief can be based. We have already cited beliefs and experiences as possible grounds, and these would seem to exhaust the possibilities. Indeed, some epistemologists would find this too generous already, maintaining that beliefs can be based only on other beliefs. They would treat perceptual cases by holding that the belief that a tree is over there is based on the *belief that* there visually appears to me to be a tree over there, rather than, as we are suggesting, on the visual appearance itself. I can't accept that, largely because I doubt that all perceptual believers have such beliefs about their visual experience, but I can't pause to argue the point. Suffice it to say that since my opponents' position is, to be as generous as possible, controversial, we do not want to build a position on this issue into the *concept* of epistemic justification. We want to leave open at least the *conceptual* possibility of *direct* or *immediate* justification by experience (and perhaps in other ways also), as well as *indirect* or *mediate* justification by relation to other beliefs (inferentially in the most explicit cases). Finally, to say that a subject *has adequate* grounds for her belief that p is to say that she has other justified beliefs, or experiences, on which the belief could be based and which are strongly indicative of the truth of the belief. The reason for the restriction to *justified* beliefs is that a gound shouldn't be termed adequate unless it can confer justification on the belief it grounds. But we noted earlier that if I infer my belief that p, even by impeccable logic, from an *unjustified* belief that *q*, the former belief is not thereby justified.

To return to the main thread of the discussion, we are thinking of S's being J_e in believing that *p* as involving S's having adequate grounds for that belief. That is, we are thinking of the possession of those adequate grounds as constituting the goodness of the belief from the epistemic point of view. The next thing to note is that the various "modes" of J_d apply here as well.

Let's begin by noting an objective-subjective distinction. To be sure, in thinking of J_e as *having truth-indicative grounds within one's "perspective on the world"*, we are already thinking of it as more subjective than flat-out truth. But within that perspectival conception we can set the requirements as more objective or more subjective. There is more than one respect in which the possession of adequate grounds could be "subjectivized". First, there is the distinction between the existence of the ground and its adequacy. S is *objectively* J_e in believing that *p* if S (a) does in fact have grounds that are (b) in fact adequate grounds for that belief. A (more or less) *subjective* version would replace (a) or (b) or both with the requirement that the subject believe this to be the case. Of the two partially subjective versions, it may well be doubted that the one in which only (a) is subjectivized is possible. For if I believe mistakenly that I have grounds for the belief, can there be any matter of fact as to whether those nonexistent grounds are adequate? Perhaps. If my belief is specific enough as to what grounds I am supposing myself to possess, it could be objectively true or false that such grounds would be adequate. But in any event, lacking time to go into all possible variations, I shall confine attention to the subjectivization of (b). So our first two modes will be:

(XVI) Objective—S does have adequate grounds for believing that p.

(XVII) Subjective—S has grounds for believing that p and he believes them to be adequate.

And here too we have a "justified belief", or "cognitive" variant on the subjective version.

(XVIII) Cognitive—S has grounds for believing that p and he is justified in believing them to be adequate.

We can dismiss (XVII) by the same arguments we brought against the subjective version of J_d. The mere fact that I believe, however unjustifiably or irresponsibly, that my grounds for believing that *p* are adequate could scarcely render me justified in believing that *p*. If I believe them to be adequate just because I have an egotistical penchant to overestimate my powers, that could hardly make it rational for me to believe that *p*. But here we will not find the same reason to favor (XVII) over (XVI). With J_d the cognitive version won out because of what it takes for blameworthiness. But whether one is J_e in believing that *p* has nothing to do with whether he is subject to blame. It depends rather on whether his believing that *p* is *good thing* from the epistemic point of view. And however justifiably S believes that his grounds are adequate, if they are not, then his believing that *p* on those grounds is not a good move in the truth-seeking game. Even if he isn't to blame for making that move, it is a bad move nonetheless. Thus J_e is properly construed in the objective mode.

We are also confronted with the question of whether J_e should be construed "motivationally". Since we have already opted for an objective reading, the motivational version will take the following form:

(XIX) Motivational—S's belief that p is based on adequate grounds.

So our question is whether it is enough for justification that S *have* adequate grounds for his belief, whether used or not, or whether it is also required that the belief be based on those grounds. We cannot settle this question on the grounds that were available for J_{dv}, since with J_e we are not thinking of the subject as being obliged to take relevant consideration into account in *choosing* whether to believe that *p*.

There is something to be said on both sides of this issue. In support of the first, source-irrelevant position (XVI without XIX), it can be pointed out that S's *having a justification* for believing that *p* is independent of whether S does believe that p; I can have adequate grounds for believing that *p*, and so *have* a justification, even thought I do not in fact believe in *p*. Hence it can hardly be a requirement for having a justification for *p* that my nonexistent belief have a certain kind of basis. Likewise my having adequate grounds for believing that *p* is sufficient for this being *a rational thing for me to believe.*

But, says the opponent, suppose that S does believe that p. If simply having adequate grounds were sufficient for this belief to be justified, then, provided S does have the grounds, her belief that p would be justified however frivolous the source. But surely a belief that stems from wishful thinking would not be justified, however strong one's (unutilized) grounds for it.

Now the first thing to say about this controversy is that both antagonists win, at least to the extent that each of them is putting forward a viable concept, and one that is actually used in epistemic assessment. There certainly is the concept of *having* adequate grounds for the belief that p, whether or not one does believe that p, and there equally certainly is the concept of one's belief being based on adequate grounds. Both concepts represent favorable epistemic statuses. *Ceteris paribus*, one is better off believing something for which one has adequate grounds than believing something for which one doesn't. And the same can be said for the contrast between having a belief that is based on adequate grounds and having one that isn't. Hence I will recognize that these are both concepts of epistemic justification, and I will resist the pressure to decide which is *the* concept.

Nevertheless, we can seek to determine which concept is more fundamental to epistemology. On this issue it seems clear that the motivational concept is the richer one and thereby embodies a more complete account of a belief's being a good thing from the epistemic point of view. Surely there is something epistemically undesirable about a belief that is generated in an intellectually disreputable way, however adequate the unutilized grounds possessed by the subject. If, possessing excellent reasons for supposing that you are trying to discredit me professionally, I nevertheless believe this, not for those reasons but out of paranoia, in such a way that even if I didn't have those reasons I would have believed this just as firmly, it was undesirable from the point of view of the aim at truth for me to form that belief as I did. So if we are seeking the most inclusive concept of what makes a belief a good thing epistemically, we will want to include a consideration of what the belief is based on. Hence I will take (XIX) as the favored formulation of what makes a belief a good thing from the epistemic point of view.

I may add that (XVI) can be seen as derivative from (XIX). To simply *have* adequate grounds is to be in such a position that *if* I make use of that position as a basis for believing that p, I will thereby be justified in that belief. Thus (XVI) gives us a concept of a potential for (XIX); it is a concept of having resources that are sufficient for believing justifiably, leaving open the question of whether those resources are used.

The next point to be noted is that (XIX) guarantees only prima facie justification. As often noted, it is quite possible for my belief that p to have been formed on the basis of evidence that in itself adequately supports p, even though the totality of the evidence at my disposal does not. Thus the evidence on which I came to believe that the butler committed the murder might strongly support that hypothesis, but when arriving at the belief I was ignoring other things I know or justifiably believe that tend to exculpate the butler; the total evidence at my disposal is not sufficient support for my belief. In that case we will not want to count my belief as justified all things considered, even though the grounds *on the basis of which* it was formed were themselves adequate. Their adequacy is, so to say *overridden* by the larger perspectival context in which they are set. Thus (XIX) gives us prima facie justification, what will be justification provided it is not canceled by further relevant factors. Unqualified justification requires an additional condition to the effect that S does not also have reasons that suffice to override the justification provided by the grounds on which the belief is based. Building that into (XIX), we get:

(XX) Motivational—S's belief that p is based on adequate grounds, and S lacks overriding reasons to the contrary.

Even though (XX) requires us to bring in the unused portions of the perspective, we cannot simplify the condition by ignoring the distinction between what provides the basis and what doesn't, and make the crucial condition something like "The totality of S's perspective provides adequate support". For then we would run up against the considerations that led us to prefer (XIX) to (XVI).

We have distinguished two aspects of our evaluative concept of justification, the strictly evaluative portion—goodness from the epistemic point of view—and the very general statement of the relevant good making characteristic, *based on adequate grounds in the absence of overriding reasons to the contrary*. In taking the concept to include this second component we are opting for the view that this concept, though unmistakably evaluative rather than "purely factual" in character, is not so purely evaluative as to leave completely open the basis on which this evaluative status supervenes. I do not see how to justify this judgment by reference to any more fundamental considerations. It is just that in reflecting on epistemic justification, thought of in evaluative (as contrasted with deontological) terms, it seems clear to me that the range of possible bases for epistemic goodness is not left completely open by the concept, that it is part of what we mean in terming a belief justified, that the belief was based on adequate grounds (or, at least, that the subject had adequate grounds for it). Though this means that J_e is not maximally neutral on the question of what it takes for justification, it is still quite close to that. It still leaves open whether there is immediate justification and if so on the basis of what, how strong a ground is needed for justification, what dimensions of strength there are for various kinds of grounds, and so on.

Let's codify our evaluative concept of justification as follows:

(XXI) S is J_{eg} in believing that *p iff* S's believing that *p*, as S did, was good thing from the epistemic point of view, in that S's belief that *p* was based on adequate grounds and S lacked sufficient overriding reasons to the contrary.

In the subscript, 'g' stands for 'grounds'.

My supposition that all justification of belief involves adequate grounds may be contested. This does seem incontrovertible for the beliefs based on other beliefs and for perceptual beliefs based on experience. But what about beliefs in self-evident propositions where the self-evidence is what justifies me in the belief? On considering the proposition that two quantities equal to the same quantity are equal to each other, this seems obviously true to me; and I shall suppose, though this is hardly uncontroversial, that in those circumstances I am justified in believing it. But where are the adequate

grounds on which my belief is based? It is not that there are grounds here about whose adequacy we might well have doubts; it is rather that there seems to be nothing identifiable as grounds. There is nothing here that is distinguishable from my belief and the proposition believed, in the way evidence or reasons are distinct from that for which they are evidence or reasons, or in the way my sensory experience is distinct from the beliefs about the physical world that are based on it. Here I simply consider the proposition and straightaway accept it. A similar problem can be raised for normal beliefs about one's own conscious states. What is the ground for a typical belief that one feels sleepy? If one replies "One's consciousness of one's feeling of sleepiness", then it may be insisted, with some show of plausibility, that where one is consciously feeling sleepy, there is no difference between one's feeling sleepy and one's being conscious that one is feeling sleepy.

This is a very large issue that I will not have time to consider properly. Suffice it to say that one may treat these as limiting cases in which the ground, though real enough, is minimally distinguishable either from the belief it is grounding or from the fact that makes the belief true. In the first-person belief about one's own conscious state the ground coincides with the fact that makes the belief true. Since the fact believed is itself an experience of the subject, there need be nothing "between" the subject and the fact that serves as an indication of the latter's presence. The fact "reveals itself" directly. Self-evident propositions require separate treatment. Here I think that we can take the *way* the proposition appears to one, variously described as "obviously true", "self-evident", and "clear and distinct", as the ground on which the belief is based. I accept the proposition because it *seems* to me so obviously true. This is less distinct from the belief than an inferential or sensory experiential ground, since it has to do with how I am aware of the proposition. Nevertheless, there is at least a minimal distinctness. I can form an intelligible conception of someone's failing to believe that *p*, where *p* seems obviously true. Perhaps this person has been rendered unduly skeptical by overexposure to the logical paradoxes.

VI

Let's go back to the idea that the "based on adequate grounds" part of J_{eg} is there because of the "internalist" character of justification. Contrasts between internalism and externalism have been popular in epistemology lately, but the contrast is not always drawn in the same way. There are two popular ways, both of which are distinct from what I have in mind. First there is the idea that justification is internal in that it depends on what support is available for the belief from 'within the subject's perspective", in the sense of what the subject knows or justifiably believes about the world. This kind of internalism restricts justification to mediate or discursive justification, justification by reasons. Another version takes "the subject's perspective" to include whatever is "directly accessible" to the subject, accessible just on the basis of reflection; internalism on this version restricts justifiers to what is directly accessible to the subject. This, unlike the first version, does not limit us to mediate justification, since experience can be taken to be at least as directly accessible as beliefs and knowledge.

In contrast to both these ways of drawing the distinction, what I take to be internal about justification is that whether a belief is justified depends on what it is based on (grounds); and grounds must be other psychological state(s) of the same subject. I am not absolutely certain that grounds are confined to beliefs and experiences, even if experiences are not confined to sensations and feelings but also include, e.g., the way a proposition seems obvious to one, and religious and aesthetic experiences; but these are the prime candidates, and any other examples must belong to some kind of which these are the paradigms. So in taking it to be conceptually true that one is justified in believing that p iff one's belief that p is based on an adequate ground, I take justification to be "internal" in that it depends on the way in which the belief stems from the believer's psychological states, which are "internal" to the subject in an obvious sense. What would be an externalist contrast with this kind of internalism? We shall see one such contrast in a moment, in discussing the relation of J_{eg} to reliabilism. Moreover, it contrasts with the idea that one can be justified in a certain belief just because of the status of the proposition believed (necessary, infallible). My sort of internalism is different from the first one mentioned above, in that experiences as well as beliefs can figure as grounds. And it is different from the second if, as I believe, what a belief is based on may not be directly accessible. This will be the case if, as seems plausible, much belief formation goes on below the conscious level. It would seem, for example, that as we move about the environment, we are constantly forming short-term perceptual beliefs without any conscious monitoring of this activity.

The most prominent exponents of an explicitly nondeontological conception of epistemic justification have been reliabilists, who have either identified justification with reliability, or have taken reliability to be an adequate criterion of justification. The reliability that is in question here is the reliability of belief formation and sustenance. To say that a belief was formed in a reliable way is, roughly, to say that it was formed in a way that can be depended on generally to form true rather than false beliefs, at least from inputs like the present one, and at least in the sorts of circumstances in which we normally find ourselves. Thus if my visual system, when functioning as it is at present in yielding my belief that there is a tree in front of me, generally yields true beliefs about objects that are fairly close to me and directly in front of me, then my present belief that there is a tree in front of me was formed in a reliable manner.

Now it may be supposed that J_{eg}, as we have explained it, is just reliability of belief formation with an evaluative frosting. For where a belief is based on adequate grounds, that belief has been formed in a reliable fashion. In fact, it is plausible to take reliability as a *criterion* for adequacy of grounds. If my grounds for believing that p are not such that it is generally true that beliefs like that formed on grounds like that are true, they cannot be termed 'adequate'. Why do we think that wanting State to win the game is not an adequate reason for supposing that it has won, whereas the fact that a victory has been reported by several newspapers is an adequate reason? Surely it has something to do with the fact that beliefs like that when formed on the first sort of grounds are not *generally* true, while they are *generally* true when formed on grounds of the second sort. Considerations like this may lead us to suppose that J_{eg}, in effect, identifies justification with reliability.

Nevertheless the internalist character of justification prevents it from being identified with reliability, and even blocks an extensional equivalence. Unlike justification, reliability of belief formation is not limited to cases in which a belief is based on adequate grounds within the subject's psychological states. A reliable mode of belief formation *may* work through the subject's own knowledge and experience. Indeed, it is plausible to suppose that all of the reliable modes of belief formation available to human beings are of this sort. But it is quite conceivable that there should be others. I might be so constituted that beliefs about the weather tomorrow which apparently just "pop into my mind" out of nowhere are in fact reliably produced by a mechanism of which we know nothing, and which does not involve the belief being based on anything. Here we would have reliably formed beliefs that are not based on adequate grounds from within my perspective, and so are not J_{eg}.

Moreover, even within the sphere of beliefs based on grounds, reliability and justification do not necessarily go together. The possibility of divergence here stems from another feature of justification embodied in our account, the way in which unqualified justification requires not only an adequate ground but also the absence of sufficient overriding reasons. This opens up the possibility of a case in which belief is formed on the basis of grounds in a way that is in fact highly reliable, even though the subject has strong reasons for supposing the way to be unreliable. These reasons will (or may) override the prima facie justification provided by the grounds on which the belief was based. And so S will not be justified in the belief, even though it was reliably generated.

Consider, in this connection, a case presented by Alvin Goldman.

Suppose that Jones is told on fully reliable authority that a certain class of his memory beliefs are almost all mistaken. His parents fabricate a wholly false story that Jones suffered from amnesia when he was seven but later developed *pseudo*-memories of that period. Though Jones listens to what his parents say

and has excellent reason to trust them, he persists in believing the ostensible memories from his seven-year-old past.

Suppose that Jones, upon recalling his fifth birthday party, believes that he was given an electric train for this fifth birthday because, as it seems to him, he remembers being given it. By hypothesis, his memory mechanism is highly reliable, and so his belief about his fifth birthday was reliably formed. But this belief is not adequately supported by the *totality* of what he justifiably believes. His justifiable belief that he has no real memory of his first seven years overrides the support from his ostensible memory. Thus, Jones is not J_{eg} in his memory belief, because the "lack of overriding reasons to the contrary" requirement is not satisfied. But reliability is subject to no such constraint. Just as reliable mechanisms are not restricted to those that work through the subject's perspective, so it is not a requirement on he reliability of belief formation that the belief be adequately supported by the totality of subject's perspective. However, many and however strong the reasons Jones has for distrusting his memory, the fact remains that his memory beliefs are still reliably formed. Here is another way in which the class of beliefs that are J_{eg} and the class of reliably formed beliefs can fail to coincide.

I would suggest that, of our candidates, J_{eg} most fully embodies what we are looking for under the heading of "epistemic justification". (1) Like its deontological competitors it is an evaluative concept, in a broad sense, a concept of a favorable status from an epistemic point of view. (2) Unlike J_{dv}, it does not presuppose that belief is under direct voluntary control. (3) Unlike J_{di}, it implies that the believer is in a strong epistemic position in believing that p, that is to say, that there is something about the way in which he believes that p that renders it at least likely that the belief is true. Thus it renders it intelligible that justification is something we should prize from an epistemic point of view. (4) Unlike the concept of a reliable mode of belief formation it represents this "truth-conductivity" as a matter of the belief's being based on an adequate ground within the subject's own cognitive states. Thus it recognizes the "internalist" character of justification; it recognizes that in asking whether a belief is justified we are interested in the prospects for the truth of the belief, given what the subject "has to go on". (5) Thus the concept provides broad guidelines for the specification of conditions of justification, but within those guidelines there is ample room for disagreement over the precise conditions for one or another type of belief. The concept does not leave us totally at a loss as to what to look for. But in adopting J_{eg} we are not building answers to substantive epistemological questions into the concept. As the only candidate to exhibit all these desiderata, J_{eg} is clearly the winner.

VII

It may be useful to bring together the lessons we have learned from this conceptual exploration.

(1) Justifying, an activity of showing or establishing something, is much less central for epistemology than is "being justified", as a state or condition.

(2) It is central to epistemic justification that *what justifies* is restricted to the subject's "perspective", to the subject's knowledge, justified belief, or experience.

(3) Deontological concepts of justification are either saddled with an indefensible assumption of the voluntariness of belief (J_{dv}) or allow for cases in which one believes that p without having any adequate ground for the belief (J_{di}).

(4) The notion of one's belief being based on adequate grounds incorporates more of what we are looking for in a concept of epistemic justification than the weaker notion of having adequate grounds for belief.

(5) Justification is closely related to reliability, but because of the perspectival character noted in (2), they do not completely coincide; much less can they be identified.

(6) The notion of believing that p in a way that is good from an epistemic point of view in that the belief is based on adequate grounds (J_{eg}) satisfies the chief desiderata for a concept of epistemic justification.

VIII

The ultimate payoff of this conceptual exploration is the increased sophistication it gives us in dealing with substantive epistemological issues. Putting our scheme to work is a very large enterprise, spanning a large part of epistemology. In conclusion I will give one illustration of the ways in which our distinctions can be of help in the trenches. For this purpose I will restrict myself to the broad contrast between J_{dv} and J_{eg}.

First, consider what we might term "higher level requirements" for S's being justified in believing that p. I include under that heading all requirements that S know or justifiably believe something *about* the epistemic status of p, or about the strength of S's grounds for p. This would include requirement that S be justified in believing that:

(1) R is an adequate reason for p (where R is alleged to justify S's belief that p).

(2) Experience e is an adequate indication that p (where e is alleged to justifiy S's belief that p).

On J_{eg} there is no temptation to impose such requirements. If R *is* an adequate reason (e is an adequate indication), then if one believes that p on that basis, one is *thereby* in a strong position, epistemically; and the further knowledge, or justified belief, that the reason is adequate (the experience is an adequate indication), though no doubt quite important and valuable for other purposes, will do nothing to improve the truth-conduciveness of one's believing that p. But on J_{dv} we get a different story. If it's a question of being blameless in believing that p, it can be persuasively argued that this requires not only forming the belief on what is in fact an adequate ground, but doing so in the light of the realization that the ground is an adequate one. If I decide to believe that p without knowing whether the ground is adequate, am I not subject to blame for proceeding irresponsibly in my doxastic behavior, whatever the actual strength of the ground? If the higher level requirements are plausible only if we are using J_{dv}, then the dubiousness of that concept will extend to those requirements.

In the above paragraph we are considering whether S's being justified in believing that his ground is adequate is a *necessary* condition of justification. We can also consider whether it is sufficient. Provided that S is justified in believing that his belief that p is based on an adequate ground, G, does it make any difference, for his being justified in believing that p, whether the ground *is* adequate? Our two contenders will line up here as they did on the previous issue. For J_{eg} the mere fact that S is justified in supposing that G is adequate will cut no ice. What J_{eg} requires is that S *actually be* in an epistemically favorable position; and although S's being justified in supposing G to be adequate is certainly good evidence for that, it doesn't *constitute* being in such a position. Hence J_{eg} requires that the ground of the belief actually be an adequate one. As for J_{dv}, where it is a question of whether S is blameworthy in believing that p, what is decisive is how S's epistemic position appears within S's perspective on the world. If, so far as S could tell, G is an adequate ground, then S is blameless, that is, J_{dv}, in believing that p on G. Nothing else could be required for justification in that sense. If S has chosen his doxastic state by applying the appropriate principles in the light of all his relevant knowledge and justified belief, then he is totally in the clear. Again the superior viability of J_{eg}, as over against J_{dv}, should tip the scales in favor of the more objective requirements of adequacy.

RICHARD FELDMAN

Epistemic Obligations

I

Suppose an unfortunate student, Jones, is about to take an oral exam with an unusually difficult teacher. In fact, the failure rate on oral exams with this teacher is grim indeed: only 10% of the students who take the exam pass it. One slightly encouraging fact is that people who are optimistic about their chances for passing the exam tend to do a little better: 20% of them pass it. Apparently, the teacher's evaluations are improved by sincere manifestations of confidence. Let us also suppose that Jones, the student, has no particularly good information about his own abilities on the material to be covered on the tests. Assume next that Jones is a relatively normal person and that he has a strong desire to pass the test. Assume finally that Jones is aware of all of this and is considering the proposition that he will pass the exam.

We may ask what, given this information, Jones ought to believe. Should he believe that he will pass the oral exam? When Jones considers the proposition that he will pass the exam, he must take exactly one of three attitudes toward it: he must either believe it, disbelieve it, or suspend judgment with respect to it. One of these attitudes will be the one that he ought to have.

One may find oneself with conflicting intuitions about what Jones should do. On the one hand, it surely is in Jones's interest to believe that he'll pass; one could hardly blame him for doing whatever he could to improve his chances. Since he wants to pass and knows that the best way to increase his chances is to believe that he'll pass, he should believe that he'll pass. At the very least, this way of thinking about the case makes it seem clear that it is permissible for him to believe that he'll pass. In other words, it is not the case that he ought to believe that he won't pass.

On the other hand, his evidence makes passing look unlikely, and this inclines us to say that believing that he'll pass "flies in the face of the facts." After he finds out that he's failed and we're dealing with his disappointment, we might say that he should have realized that he wouldn't pass. That is, given his information, he should not have believed that he would pass. So, it seems that there is some basis for saying that he shouldn't believe that he'll pass, as well as some basis for saying that he should believe that he'll pass.

The apparent conflict between these inclinations can be resolved easily. The inclination to say that Jones ought to believe that he'll pass concerns a *practical* or *prudential* sense of obligation. Sometimes it makes sense to treat beliefs like other actions and to evaluate their practical or prudential merit. Jones's optimistic belief scores well in this evaluation, and this accounts for our judgment that it is a belief he ought to have. The contrary intuition concerns *epistemic* obligation. The peculiarly epistemic judgment concerns not these practical merits but rather the propriety of a disinterested believer in Jones's situation having that belief. Since Jones's optimistic belief does not come out so well on these grounds, it is epistemically improper. Epistemic obligation, then, concerns obligations to believe to which the practical benefits of beliefs are not relevant. They are obligations that arise from a purely impartial and disinterested perspective.

Epistemic obligation also differs from *moral* obligation. There maybe cases in which having a belief is morally significant. If there are such cases, then it may be that the moral factors lead one to a different belief than the epistemic factors. Thus, for example, one might have a moral duty to trust one's friends and family, thereby making it morally obligatory that one believe their claims. At the same time, one's purely epistemic obligation may well lead the other way. In allowing for this possibility, I may be disagreeing with the well-known claim of William K. Clifford (1886), who said that "It is wrong, always, everywhere, and for every one, to believe anything upon insufficient evidence." (p. 346). If 'wrong' here expresses moral wrongness, as the context suggests it does, then Clifford is claiming that one never is morally permitted to believe what is not supported by one's evidence. And, given what I will argue later, this is equivalent to saying that one is never morally permitted to believe what one is not epistemically permitted to believe. Equivalently, if one epistemically ought to believe something, then, on Clifford's view, one also morally ought to believe it. That, as I said, seems wrong to me, since the moral consequences of an epistemically obligatory belief might be very bad. Thus, I think epistemic and moral obligation are distinct.

This discussion of the ethics of belief, of the moral status of beliefs, suggests an obvious and important issue. It is generally held that something can be obligatory only if it is a free action, only if it is something over which the agent has control. But it is doubtful that beliefs are, for the most part, free, voluntary, or controllable actions. Hence, it seems that there can't be any epistemic obligations to have beliefs. I respond to this claim in the next section. In subsequent sections I will develop an account of what our epistemic obligations are.

II

The objection to there being any epistemic obligations concerns doxastic voluntarism, the view that having a belief is something a person does voluntarily and can control. Alvin Plantinga (1986) has recently defended a version of this objection, arguing that if accepting a "proposition is not up to me, then accepting . . . .[that] . . . . proposition cannot be a way in which I can fulfill my obligation to the truth, or, indeed *any* obligation."(p 12). Plantinga thinks that it is as absurd to hold that one has epistemic obligations if doxastic voluntarism is false as it is to hold that one has obligations regarding which way to fall—up or down—after one has gone off a cliff.

Plantinga's point can be formulated as a simple argument, which I will call 'The Voluntarism Argument':

1. Doxastic voluntarism is false.

2. If doxastic voluntarism is false, then no one has epistemic obligations.

3. Therefore, no one has epistemic obligations.

The Voluntarism Argument has considerable plausibility. There is a long tradition that makes only voluntary or controllable actions the subject of obligations, so (2) seems true. And it does seem that we can't control our beliefs. In the ordinary course of events, one finds oneself with some beliefs and rather little one can do about them. If revelations about your favorite politician cause you to believe that he is dishonest, then you might wish that you didn't have this belief. Although you may be able to put the matter out of mind, you can't, at will, change your belief about the topic. Similarly, all the perceptual beliefs that you have seem just to come over you. When I go outside on a typical winter day in Rochester, the belief that it is cold and gray outside just comes over me. In general, there is rather little we can do about our beliefs. They seem not to be matters under our control. So, (1) seems to be correct as well.

Despite the apparent truth of (1) and (2), philosophers have denied each premise. Although some philosophers, perhaps Descartes, have thought that beliefs are voluntarily adopted and maintained, few have rejected (1) on this basis. A more plausible reason for rejecting (1) has been advanced by John Heil (1983). His idea is that although we can't "directly" control our beliefs (in some sense of 'direct'), we can indirectly control them. There are things we can do to alter the ways in which we form beliefs and the kind of information which we receive. I can, for example, study logic and probability theory with the aim of reducing the number of mistaken inferences I draw. I might read the publications of some political or religious groups with the aim of eventually coming to accept the general set of beliefs they support. These and any number of other voluntary actions will affect my beliefs, and I may perform the actions for that very purpose. Hence, I do have some sort of indirect control over my beliefs. And this indirect control over beliefs makes some sort of doxastic voluntarism true, so (1) is false.

Heil is surely right about there being some sense in which we can indirectly control our beliefs. Perhaps, this shows that not every version of doxastic involuntarism is true. However, defenders of The Voluntarism Argument are likely to contend that (1) and (2) are true when 'doxastic voluntarism' is taken to refer the view that people have the relevant sort of "direct" control over their beliefs. They would argue that indirect control of the sort Heil discusses is not sufficient for there to be epistemic obligations. At most, they would grant that Heil has shown that there can be obligations to perform the sort of belief inducing actions Heil mentions. He has not shown that there can be epistemic obligations to believe or disbelieve anything. I'm inclined to agree with Heil's critics here, although the meanings of 'direct' and 'indirect' are sufficiently obscure to make these issues extremely difficult to sort out.

In any case, we are willing to say of people that they should or should not believe things even in cases in which they do not have the ability to undertake courses of action that might affect their beliefs in the relevant way. So, our intuitive judgments do not limit epistemic obligations to cases in which we have the sort of indirect control Heil describes. Thus, an equally damaging version of The Voluntarism Argument, restricted to cases of this sort, can be constructed.

Examples of the sorts of cases I have in mind are ones in which seemingly unchangeable psychological factors determine one's beliefs. For example, I just can't help believing that I see some tables and chairs now. Moreover, it is unlikely that I could embark upon any course of action, even the study of skepticism, which would lead me to believe otherwise in similar situations. Despite my inability to avoid this belief, this is exactly what I should believe in my current situation. Similarly, as a result of some psychological factors one may be unable to do anything about some of one's beliefs about oneself or one's family. For example, some people never believe that they are successful or talented, no matter what their accomplishments. Such people often should have better opinions of themselves, but there may be nothing they can do to change their negative attitude. Thus, there seem to be epistemic obligations even in cases in which we don't have the limited sort of control Heil describes. But the modified Voluntarism Argument has the conclusion that we don't have epistemic obligations in these cases. Thus defenders of epistemic obligations need a response to that argument that goes beyond Heil's. They need a way to reconcile the apparent truth of doxastic involuntarism with their inclination to ascribe epistemic obligations even in these cases.

Another way to respond to the Voluntarism Argument is to deny (2), the claim that if voluntarism is false, then there are no epistemic obligations. One might reject (2) on the basis of the idea that epistemic obligations pertain not to doxastic states but rather to actions that lead to doxastic states. Thus, my epistemic obligations may be to gather lots of evidence, to listen carefully to evidence, to listen carefully to critics, and the like. While I grant that there may be obligations to perform actions such as these, I think that this response simply evades the point at issue here. My concern is with obligations to believe and the question is whether there can be any such obligations if doxastic voluntarism is false. The existence of these other obligations, whether they are called 'epistemic obligations' or not, is thus beside the point.

A more promising variant on this objection to (2) has been proposed by Keith Lehrer (1981). Lehrer suggests that the notion of belief should be replaced in some epistemological analyses with that of acceptance. The difference between the two "concerns the element of optionality. Sometimes a person cannot decide what to believe at a moment, but he can decide what to accept. . . . Believing is not an action. Accepting is." (p. 79–80). Since accepting is an action over which one has control, one can have obligations to accept or not accept certain propositions. Accounts of these obligations could be constructed that are perfectly analogous to the accounts of obligations to believe that will be considered later. This sort of view preserves the traditional connection between obligation and voluntariness, is consistent with the apparent fact that beliefs are not voluntarily formed or retained, yet makes sense of something like epistemic obligation. I will argue shortly that it is possible to have obligations with respect to involuntary behavior, but those who reject that conclusion may translate all subsequent discussion of obligations regarding beliefs into talk of obligations to accept propositions.

I think that the best response to The Voluntarism Argument is to deny (2) on the grounds that there can be obligations concerning involuntary behavior. It may be true that with respect to *some* sorts of obligation, one has obligations of those sorts only if one has control over the relevant actions, only if one can act (and can avoid acting) in the obligatory way. This seems most clearly true with respect to moral obligation. Perhaps there are also notions of prudential obligation and "all things considered" obligation that obtain only when the person has control over the obligatory behavior. It is never the case that one is obligated, in these senses, to do things one can't avoid doing (or must do).

However, it is equally clear that there are obligations and requirements that obtain in the absence of our ability to fulfill them. Here are some examples. In the beginning of a semester teachers typically tell their students what they are obligated to do as students in the class. We might say that students have an academic obligation to do that work. We also say, more naturally, that they are required to do the work. It often happens that later in the semester students report that they are unable to complete the work. Teachers respond to such claims in any number of ways, but I doubt that any say, "Well, if you can't do it, it follows that you are not required to do it." We are more apt to tell them what we do to students who don't complete their requirements.

To make the case more concrete, and like some Plantinga (1986) considers in his defense of The Voluntarism Argument, suppose a student comes to me and says that he cannot write a term paper because he has a brain lesion that makes him fall asleep whenever he thinks about the paper topic. In this case, it may be best for me to change his requirements or to advise him to switch to another course in which he can fulfill his requirements. His inability plainly does not make it the case that he does not have these academic obligations or course requirements. (His inability makes him not morally required to do the work.) Thus, the student's course requirements include doing work he is unable to do. Similarly, course requirements may include doing something that a student can't refrain from doing. If, somehow, a brain lesion or a malicious demon makes a student unable to avoid doing logic problems identical to those assigned by the logic teacher, it does not follow that he was not required to do those problems. These kinds of obligations or requirements do not imply freedom or control.

Similar considerations apply to some other obligations. When I took out a mortgage on my house I incurred a legal obligation to pay the bank each month a certain sum of money. The amount is roughly equal to my entire monthly salary. If my salary goes down, or I lose my job and I can't pay, I'm sure that officials in the bank's foreclosure department would properly be unimpressed by the argument: "I can't pay you the money you say I owe you; therefore, I have no financial obligation to pay you that money." I still am legally (or financially) obligated to pay, even though I can't do it. On the other hand, if I arrange things so that the money is automatically taken out of my bank account and it is impossible for me to change that, I may be unable to avoid paying the mortgage. I retain my obligation to pay.

I conclude from these examples that there can be non-moral and non-prudential obligations that one can't fulfill and ones that one can't avoid fulfilling. Thus, I think that it is plausible to hold that there can be epistemic obligations that one can't fulfill and ones that one can't avoid fulfilling. Sometimes, one can't believe what one ought to believe and sometimes one can't help believing what one ought to believe. There can be epistemic obligations even if doxastic voluntarism is false.

Some examples, mentioned above, seem to me to give this view support. Normally, while observing the world one forms a lot of perceptual beliefs that are in the relevant sense unavoidable. Yet, many of those beliefs are ones that one should have. For example, when one is looking at a table in clear light one should believe that one sees a table, rather than defy or suspend judgment about the proposition. Fortunately, then, in these cases most of us can't help doing what we epistemically ought to do. But people who are driven to beliefs by hopes, fears, or other emotions may be unable to believe what they epistemically ought to believe.

I can think of two objections to my claim that epistemic obligations don't require doxastic voluntarism. The first grants that some sorts of obligations don't carry implications of freedom and control, but adds that some do and that epistemic obligations are of the latter sort. I've admitted that moral and prudential obligations may obtain only where there is control, but claimed that legal and financial obligations can obtain in the absence of freedom and control. My suggestion is that epistemic obligations are of the latter sort and the response is that they are of the former sort.

I believe that this objection is mistaken. Two remarks are in order. First, I think that the examples support my side. That is, it is natural to say things like "He should (or shouldn't) believe that" even in cases in which there is no freedom or control. The examples already described indicate that. Second, as I hope to show later in this paper, a plausible account of epistemic obligations can be developed which makes it clear that epistemic obligations don't have much to do with freedom and control. Of course, the force of this point turns on the merits of the account to be developed later.

I turn now to the second response to my claim that (2) is false. Recall that my defense relies on the claim that there are some obligations, such as academic and legal ones, that do not require voluntarism. The response is that academic and legal obligations are not, strictly speaking, cases of simple obligation at all. They are, rather, cases of conditional obligation. What's true of the student might be put this way: given that he wants to pass this course, he ought to write the paper. What's true of me is: given that I want to keep my house, I ought to pay my mortgage. Couple these accounts of the obligations present in these cases with the denial of a rule of detachment for obligation statements and one then has the basis for denying that I have presented any cases of obligations that cannot be fulfilled. That is, from these conditional obligations and the facts that the student does want to pass the course and I do want to keep my house, it does not follow that the student ought to do the work or that I ought to pay the mortgage. Hence, we do not yet have cases of unfulfillable unconditional obligations.

If financial and academic obligations are best understood as conditional obligations, and one can have conditional obligations that one cannot fulfill (or cannot avoid fulfilling), then, I think, epistemic obligations can also be understood as conditional obligations that one might be unable to fulfill. If epistemic obligations are best interpreted as conditional obligations, then perhaps they are conditional upon the desire to be epistemically excellent: to say that you epistemically ought to believe p is to say that given that you want to achieve epistemic excellence, you ought to believe p.

I don't particularly want to defend this analysis. However, I will concede to anyone who insists that the examples I have given of unfulfillable obligations are really only examples of unfulfillable conditional obligations. My claim about epistemic obligations could then be recast as the claim that epistemic obligations are also conditional obligations and they may also be unfulfillable. And if this is the case, then my main claim is this section remains unrefuted: ordinary talk about epistemic obligations, talk about what one ought to believe, carries no implications about doxastic voluntarism. We can, then, look into the nature of epistemic obligations without worrying further about whether doxastic voluntarism is true.

III

I turn next to discussion of the most widely accepted account of what our epistemic obligations are. This view traces back at least to William James (1911). James says,

> There are two ways of looking at our duty in the matter of opinion,—ways entirely different, and yet ways about whose difference the theory of knowledge seems hitherto to have shown little concern. We *must know the truth*: and *we must avoid error*,—these are our first and great commandments as would-be knowers; but they are not two ways of stating an identical commandment, they are two separable laws. . . . By choosing between them we may end by coloring differently our whole intellectual life. . . . For my part, I can believe that worse things than being duped may happen to a man. (pp. 17–19.)

James states his view in terms of two related "commandments" or imperatives: know the truth and avoid error. In telling us to avoid error, James is telling us that we should not believe falsehoods. And his directive that we know the truth implies that we should believe truths. So, James's idea seems to be that we should believe truths and should not believe falsehoods. His claim that these are two separable and independent commandments can be easily demonstrated. We can succeed in believing lots of truths by believing everything. If one does this (assuming that one can believe both a proposition and its negation), then one will surely have managed to believe all the truths, or at least all the truths among the propositions one considers. But that hardly achieves any sort of epistemic excellence. On the other hand, by believing very little we surely manage to avoid error. But this excessive conservativism does not achieve epistemic excellence either. It is by attaining a suitable mix of the two goals that we will achieve epistemic excellence. That, according to the Jamesian view, is what we ought to do.

An account of epistemic obligation along Jamesian lines has become a philosophical commonplace. In setting out his own account of epistemic requirements, Roderick Chisholm (1977) cites the passage from James just quoted as his source. Keith Lehrer (1981) uses a notion of reasonableness as the fundamental notion in his account of knowledge, and he says the following about his concept: "When we use the notion of reasonableness in our definition, we mean reasonable for the purpose of pursuing truth. The pursuit of truth involves an interest in obtaining a story free of error, or as much so as we can, and obtaining the whole story, or as much as we can. These combined interests may pull in opposite directions, but they both bear the stamp of legitimacy in the quest for truth." (p. 87). Roderick Firth (1978) discusses, but does not ultimately defend, an analysis of epistemic warrant in terms of "a duty to believe propositions if and only if they are true." (p.224.) The Jamesian flavor in these passages is obvious.

Other writers describe a view very much like James's as 'standard' or 'familiar'. Paul Moser (1985) writes, "A familiar characterization of epistemic obligation states that it is the (*prima facie*) obligation one has, *qua* truth-seeker, to maximize true belief and to minimize, if not to avoid, false belief." (p. 214). Peter Markie (1986) describes the end (or goal) of believing all and only what is true about the matter under investigation as "the standard epistemic imperative". (p. 37). Richard Foley (1987) says that ". . . a distinctly epistemic goal. . . [is]. . . what epistemologists often have said it to be, now to believe those propositions that are true and now not to believe those propositions that are false." Each of the three writers just mentioned eventually defends an account of epistemic obligation along Jamesian lines and describes such accounts as familiar or standard.

While James's view may seem straightforward enough, there actually is some difficulty in figuring out exactly what his claims amount to. James speaks of "commandments", Chisholm speaks of "requirements", Moser speaks of "obligations", Markie and Foley both speak of "ends" and Markie frames the idea in terms of an imperative. While all of these ideas may be fairly similar, there are differences worthy of our attention, and it is not entirely obvious just how the Jamesian line can be put into plausible account of epistemic obligations.

As a first attempt at a Jamesian view about epistemic obligation, we might try the following:

(1) S is epistemically obligated to believe p if p is true and S is epistemically obligated to disbelieve p if p is false.

(1) is subject to several obvious and decisive objections.

First of all, it is clear that sometimes one epistemically ought to suspend judgement about some propositions. However, (1) implies that everyone should believe every truth and disbelieve every falsehood, thereby leaving no room for suspension of judgment. Suppose a coin I know to be fair has been tossed, I have not seen how it landed, and do not have any other information about how it landed. Surely, I ought to suspend judgment about the proposition that it came up heads. But (1) says that I ought to believe it came up heads if it did come up heads and disbelieve that if it didn't. That's clearly wrong. I ought to suspend judgment in this and many other cases in which I have no good information about the truth value of the proposition in question.

It is equally clear that sometimes people should believe propositions that are in fact false. Suppose that some proposition, p, is false but all the evidence anyone has indicated that p is true, and some person carefully collects and weighs all the evidence, and then believes p on the basis of that evidence. Then surely that person is believing what he epistemically ought to believe. It may be that the evidence is in some sense misleading, but if the person has no way to know that, then the mere falsity of his belief does not demonstrate that he failed to do what he epistemically should have done. To say, for example, that ancient school children should have believed that the Earth was (roughly) round, since it is roughly round, is to miss the point of epistemic obligation altogether. By believing that the Earth is flat such children were believing exactly what they should have believed, given the situation they were in.

But if (1) is false, and so seriously off the mark, what could James have had in mind in asserting it? And what have others had in mind in endorsing his view? I believe that we can arrive at an answer to these questions by considering an analogy. Investors are often urged to "buy low and sell high". That is, they should buy stocks that are at a low point and will go up and they should sell stocks that are at a high point and will go down. Thus, we might say

(2) S ought to buy stock x if the price of x will go up and S ought to sell x if the price of x will go down.

While (2) may seem to express some truth, there is at least one straightforward interpretation under which it is plainly false. Suppose that, as a matter of fact, some stock is about to go up, but all available indications are that it is about to go down. Perhaps it has just been discovered that the company's sole product is defective, e.g., house paint that is water-soluble after it dries. There seems to be a clear sense in which, assuming one knows this, one ought not buy the stock. (Ignore the possibility that one might do well by being a "contrarian".) If all the information one has suggests that a stock will go down, then it is a bad idea to buy it. In some sense of 'ought', one ought not buy such stocks. One ought to follow the best indicators of future price that one has. So, (2), at least with 'ought' understood this way, is false.

There is, however, some truth in the vicinity of (2). It is:

(3) One's goals as an investor are to buy stocks that will go up and to sell stocks that will go down.

(3) specifies some *goals* of investing. Although (3) may seem trivial, it is not. You might explain to children who know nothing about the stock market that these are the goals of investing. One could, in fact, disagree about whether (3) is entirely accurate or complete. Some would claim that one's goals are, or should be, different, or at least broader. Profits may not be the only goal. Perhaps investing in companies that meet some political or social values one has is important as well. So (3) is a plausible and non-trivial claim about investment objectives.

More specific investment advice can be seen as advice about how best to satisfy the goal specified in (3). So, when one is told that one ought to buy stocks in companies in expanding rather than declining industries, one is being told about a means to an end. Our obligations, perhaps, are to do what is best (in some sense) to accomplish some end. There is much that remains to be said about all of this. There are, in particular, questions about what exactly counts as the "best" means for achieving these investment ends. But I will ignore these issues for now and return to the epistemic case, which I think is quite similar.

I think that James's remarks are best seen as comments about epistemic ends, not about epistemic obligations. This makes James's view most similar to the one expressed by Foley in the passage quoted above. He has told us what we are to strive for as epistemic agents. He has told us nothing about what means we ought to follow in order to achieve those ends. Thus, I think that a truth about epistemic ends can be formulated as follows:

(4) One's goals as a rational believer are to believe things that are true and to avoid believing things that are false.

Again, this may seem trivial, but it isn't. (4) calls our attention to what the proper epistemic ends are. According to this view, it is not to believe things that are edifying or expansive. It is not to believe what makes us feel good. It is not to have opinions that differ from those of our parents. It is to get at the truth. Telling this to children, or to college freshmen, could be useful and enlightening. But (4) leaves open entirely what the proper means to this end are. The passage from James simply has nothing to say about how we ought to go about achieving this end.

Thus, I think that what's true and Jamesian is (4). But (4) isn't a statement about epistemic obligations. One simple statement about obligations somehow connected to (4) is (1). But (1) is false. We have, then, no adequate account of epistemic obligations.

IV

Chisholm (1977) has defended an account of epistemic obligations that is clearly derived from James's account, but which seems to avoid the objections to (1) raised in the previous section. Chisholm writes,

> We may assume that every person is subject to a purely intellectual requirement—that of trying his best to bring it about that, for every proposition h that he considers, he accepts h if and only if h is true. (p. 14).

This statement may be formulated as the following account of epistemic obligation:

> (5) For any proposition p and person S, if S considers p then S is epistemically obligated to try his best to bring it about that S believes p if and only if p is true.

This could, of course, be broken up into two principles, one saying that a person is obligated to try to believe p if p is true and the other saying that the person is obligated to try to avoid believing p if p is false. Thus Chisholm's view connects with James's in an obvious way. James has said, in principle (4), that the two epistemic ends are to believe truths and to avoid believing falsehoods. Chisholm has said that our epistemic obligation is to try our best to achieve these ends with respect to the propositions we consider.

One obstacle to determining exactly what implications (5) has is the fact that (5) gives no directive about the relative weights given to the obligation to try to believe truths and the obligation to try to avoid believing falsehoods. One might be cautious, and weigh the obligation to try to avoid error more heavily. On the other hand, one might advocate a more adventurous attitude, and emphasize the obligation to try for the truth more strongly. James himself seems to support the latter view, in his remark that he "can believe that worse things than being duped may happen to a man." (1911, p. 19). I think that this is a suggestion to the effect that it is better to be bold, and form beliefs in an effort to get at the truth, than it is to be cautious and avoid belief in an effort to avoid error. I will not pursue this issue, however, because I think that there are more fundamental questions to be raised about (5), and I want to turn to them instead.

I will consider two objections to Chisholm's view. The first objection is that it construes our epistemic obligations far too narrowly, mentioning only obliga-tions to try for the truth and to try to avoid error, omitting many other important epistemic goals. Plantinga (1986) raises this sort of objection in his discussion of Chisholm. He writes, "Obviously, something must be said about *other* epistemic values: the importance of considering *important* propositions, of having beliefs on certain topics, of avoiding unnecessary clutter and trivial dilettantism, etc." (p. 6). Thus, Plantinga thinks Chisholm construes our epistemic obligations too narrowly, considering only our obligation to the truth and ignoring our obligation to be what we might call "good epistemic agents".

I do not wish to deny that there is plausibility in the view that we ought, in some sense, to be good epistemic agents. However, I think that being a good epistemic agent in this sense is irrelevant to the central notion of epistemic obligation, and irrelevant to the sort of obligation with which Chisholm is concerned. Thus I deny that Chisholm has given too narrow an account of our epistemic obligations. I grant, however, that there may be another sort of obligation, distinct from the one with which he is concerned, to which Plantinga is calling attention. Thus, I think that Plantinga's objections to (5) fail.

To see what Chisholm has in mind, it is useful to focus on these questions: given that I am in the situation that I am in, and given that I am considering proposition p, what should I do—believe it, disbelieve it, or suspend judgment about it? Which of these three options is epistemically best? In thinking about these questions, one is to consider only these three options and only the end of getting at the truth about p. The particularly epistemic aspect of this is supposed to exclude from consideration other factors, such as which attitude would feel good or be comforting or be morally valuable. Also irrelevant to this judgment are the long-term epistemic consequences of adopting the belief. It is the truth about p now that matters. Thus, if believing something now would somehow lead me to believe lots of truths later, that long-term epistemic benefit is also irrelevant to this judgment. Foley, in the passage quoted previously, brings out the relevant point by emphasizing the key question related to epistemic obligation is "what should I believe *now*?"

In thinking about this question, being a good epistemic agent in the broader ways that Plantinga mentions is just irrelevant. Whether I have been, am, or will be a good agent—whether I consider important propositions, etc.—has no bearing on what attitude I epistemically ought to take toward p now. A person can fulfill the narrower obligations without being a good epistemic agent in the broader sense. He might have the attitude he ought to have toward each proposition he considers even though he spends most of his time considering a sequence of "unimportant" propositions of the form "n + 1 > n" and even if he seeks his intellectual stimulation by going bowling. All that he must do in order to fulfill his narrower epistemic obligations is to have the appropriate attitude toward the propositions he does consider.

Other things that have broader epistemic relevance are also irrelevant to this core notion of epistemic obligation. Consider the suggestion that one ought to seek and consider all relevant evidence. That may be a good idea, but when my question is what I should believe *now*, seeking more evidence just isn't one of my options. Suppose I haven't thought very carefully about some proposition, but the little evidence I have seen suggests that the proposition is true. I ask, "Should I believe that proposition now?" If you tell me that I should seek more evidence, than my original question remains unanswered. Perhaps I should seek more evidence or think about the matter further, but until I have a chance to do that, what should I believe? What should I believe *now*? It is this latter question, I think, that is the central epistemic question, and these issues about epistemic agency are quite clearly irrelevant to it.

It is clear, I think, that there are at least two different questions associated with epistemic obligation. One is the question about what to believe, or what attitude to take toward a particular proposition. This is the question I have been trying to focus on in the preceding paragraphs. There is also a legitimate set of questions about what actions ought to be pursued in an effort to obtain evidence, what issues ought to be the focus of attention and the like. My main point here is that these latter questions are distinct from and independent of the former one. The reason for this, again, is that even if it is true that I should seek more evidence or perform some other action in connection with some proposition,

there always remains the question of what attitude I should take toward that proposition now, before (or while) I perform that action.

Sometimes it seems true that a person should seek more evidence concerning some proposition. It is important to realize that this does not imply that the person should suspend judgment about the proposition until that additional evidence is in. Whether I should seek additional evidence typically depends upon how important it is that I get a well-founded belief about the topic in question. An example, described by Heil (1986) makes the point well. Suppose that you are in charge of an agency responsible for testing drugs and deciding whether they are to be sold to the public. You might have considerable evidence indicating that a particular drug is safe, sufficient evidence to make it reasonable for you to believe that it is safe. Of your three doxastic options, believing that it is safe is the one you ought to have. At the same time, it may also be true that because of the importance of being right, and the potential risks of allowing an unsafe drug on the market, you ought to seek further evidence about its safety.

This example shows the independence of questions about what actions regarding evidence gathering ought to be performed from questions about what ought to be believed. Since it is this latter sort of obligation with which Chisholm is concerned, the example helps us to see the error in Plantinga's contention that Chisholm has construed epistemic obligations too narrowly

The example just considered, as well some others to be described below, suggest that the sorts of considerations Plantinga mentions are really relevant to some sort of practical obligations, not to any purely epistemic concerns. Whether the drug tester should seek more evidence seems to be a clear case of a decision problem in which the expected value of the possible actions is to be weighted. If the potential side effects of the drug are severe, more testing may be appropriate. If the drug offers a cure for a serious illness not yet treatable, perhaps foregoing additional testing would be prudent. There seems to be no purely epistemic considerations that decide this matter.

Other cases also suggest that epistemic considerations do not determine what evidence gathering activities are appropriate. To someone who tells me that I should seek additional evidence about some proposition, I might appropriately respond that there are better things for me to do with my time. Maybe it would be better for me to play with my daughter or take my dog for a walk. But these considerations are practical, not epistemological. There's never any purely epistemological considerations that decide these practical questions. Whether I should be a better epistemic agent is always a practical question. The narrower question about what I should believe now, the question I want to focus on, is the central epistemological question.

Thus, I conclude that this first objection to (5) is mistaken. In thinking that these broader sorts of vaguely epistemological obligations that we may have are relevant to the central notion of epistemic obligation, Plantinga has conflated the epistemic aspects of a broader notion of practical obligation with the central notion of epistemic obligation.

A second objection to Chisholm's view, is, I think, more successful. Chisholm says very little about what counts as "trying one's best", but on at least one plausible interpretation, his view is clearly unsatisfactory. Other, more satisfactory interpretations, are possible, but then the view is in serious need of additional detail.

On Chisholm's view, one's goal is to believe all and only the truths one considers, and one's obligation is to try one's best to achieve that goal. But what counts as trying one's best? Suppose p is a truth I consider. In one straightforward sense of 'try my best to believe truths,' if p is true, then I've tried my best with respect to p if I bring it about that I do believe p. And if p is false, then I've tried my best to avoid error if I've tried in a way that brings it about that I don't believe p. More generally, on one reading of 'try my best to believe truths and avoid falsehood', I've fulfilled my obligation to do this if I've tried in the way that in fact makes me believe all and only truths. What could possibly be a better way to try to achieve a goal than to do what in fact makes one achieve that goal? There's at least one reading of 'try my best' that makes the answer "Nothing". In this sense, one has tried one's best when one has tried in the way that has the best results.

But this reading of 'try my best' saddles (5) with implausible implications that Chisholm surely did not intend. On this reading, when I've done whatever I can to bring it about that I believe truths, then I've done my best. Thus, if there is any way I can try that will make me believe p, and p is true, then I am obligated to try in that way. This is the case even if what I must do is make myself believe what my evidence clearly suggests to be false. Plainly, this is not what Chisholm intended. He surely agrees that there are times when doing one's epistemic best, doing what one epistemically should, will lead to avoidable false beliefs.

I suspect that what Chisholm has in mind is that some general ways or methods to try to believe the truth are better than others and that we epistemically ought to follow the best method. Thus, we might pose the following:

(6) For any proposition p and person S and time t, if S considers p at t, then S is epistemically obligated to believe p at t if and only if, if S were to follow the best available method for trying to believe truths and avoid believing falsehoods at t, then S would believe p at t.

The methods in (6) are limited to methods to be followed at the moment. They are not to include longer term strategies such as looking for lots of evidence. But if this sort of account is to work, some possibly successful ways must be eliminated from the running. For example, one might concoct a way to try for the truth by listing all the truths a person considers and describing the way to try for the truth as trying to believe all the propositions on that list at the appropriate times. Perhaps trying in this way would in fact lead him to believe all the truths. Or, perhaps there is some other way in which the person could try that would have this result. This would saddle (6) with the same absurd consequences as (5). It would have the plainly mistaken result that one is epistemically obligated to believe each of the truths one considers, or at least those one can believe, regardless of the evidence one has and the situation one is in. As we have seen, that is plainly mistaken. The problem, in short, is that there are unnatural and gerrymandered "methods" for trying to believe truths that one could follow. Some of these cooked up methods can be very successful. But their mere success does not make them the ones one ought to follow.

In the next section I will discuss a different account of epistemic obligations. It is possible that the account to be discussed differs from (6) only in that it makes explicit what would have been said in a generous interpretation of (6). It may also be that it is what Chisholm had in mind originally. That is, it may be that the account to be suggested simply specifies what Chisholm was thinking of when he said that one should try one's best to believe truths and avoid believing falsehoods. It has the advantage, however, of avoiding the problems found in formulations (5) and (6).

V

In objecting to (6) I assumed that the best method for trying to believe truths and disbelieve falsehoods is the one that is in fact most effective. There is another way to try to believe truths and perhaps Chisholm would regard this as the best way to do so. In any case, I believe that this other way to try for the truth leads to a more satisfactory account of epistemic obligations.

This other method to try to believe truths and avoid believing falsehoods is to believe what is supported or justified by one's evidence and to avoid believing what is not supported by one's evidence. One who follows this method does not believe things because it feels good to believe them or because of some long-term benefits that result from doing so. One who follows this method just believes at any time exactly what the evidence he then has supports. Thus, I propose:

(7) For any person S and proposition p and time t, S epistemically ought to believe p at t if and only if p is supported by the evidence S has at t.

Since psychological or other factors may force or preclude one from believing what is supported by one's evidence, (7) does not imply that one always can believe, or can avoid believing, what one should believe. It is therefore an account of epistemic obligation that does not require the truth of doxastic voluntarism. Moreover, (7) obviously avoids the successful objections to the other accounts of epistemic obligation previously considered.

In his most recent published discussion of this topic, Chisholm (1986) proposes something along the lines of (7). He writes: "I have previously written, incautiously, that one's primary intellectual duties are to acquire truth and to avoid error. What I should have said is that one's primary intellectual duties are to believe *reasonably* and to avoid believing *unreasonably*." (pp. 90–91). Since what it is reasonable for a person to believe at any time is what is supported by the person's evidence, what Chisholm says here turns out to be quite similar to (7). To accept (7) as an account of epistemic obligations is not to reject a Jamesian view entirely. (4), the claim that one's epistemic goal is to get at the truth, is consistent with (7) and I believe that it is also true. But one's epistemic duties or obligations concern the way to get to this goal and the epistemically dutiful way to get there is to believe in accordance with one's evidence. That's what one is epistemically obligated to do.

REFERENCES

Chisholm, R.: 1977, *Theory of Knowledge, 2nd edition*, Prentice Hall, Englewood Cliffs, NJ.

Chisholm, R.: 1986, 'The Place of Epistemic Justification', *Philosophical Topics* 14, pp. 85–92.

Clifford, W.L.: 1866, *Lectures and Essays, 2nd Edition*, Macmillan, London.

Feldman, R. and Conee, E.: 1985, 'Evidentialism', *Philosophical Studies* 48, pp. 15–34.

Firth, R.: 1978, 'Are Epistemic Concepts Reducible to Ethical Concepts?' in A.I. Goldman and J. Kim, (eds.) *Values and Morals*, D. Reidel, Dordrecht, pp. 215–225.

Foley, R.: 1987, *The Theory of Epistemic Rationality*, Harvard University Press, Cambridge.

Heil, J.: 1983, 'Doxastic Agency', *Philosophical Studies* 43, pp. 355–364. Heil, J.: 1986, 'Believing Reasonably', presented at The University of Rochester, October, 1986.

James, W.: 1911, *The Will To Believe and Other Essays in Popular Philosophy*, David McKay, New York, 1911.

Lehrer, K.: 1981, 'A Self Profile', in Bogdan, R. (ed) *Keith Lehrer*, D. Reidel, Dordrecht, pp. 3–104.

Markie, P.: 1986, *Descartes's Gambit*, Cornell University Press, Ithaca.

Moser, P.: 1985, *Empirical Justification*, D. Reidel, Dordrecht.

Plantinga, A: 1986, 'Chisholmian Internalism', presented at Brown University, November, 1986.

WILLIAM JAMES

The Will to Believe

In the recently published Life by Leslie Stephen of his brother, Fitz-James, there is an account of a school to which the latter went when he was a boy. The teacher, a certain Mr. Guest, used to converse with his pupils in this wise: "Gurney, what is the difference between justification and sanctification?—Stephen, prove the omnipotence of God!" etc. In the midst of our Harvard freethinking and indifference we are prone to imagine that here at your good old orthodox College conversation continues to be somewhat upon this order; and to show you that we at Harvard have not lost all interest in these vital subjects, I have brought with me to-night something like a sermon on justification by faith to read to you,—I mean an essay in justification *of* faith, a defence of our right to adopt a believing attitude in religious matters, in spite of the fact that our merely logical intellect may not have been coerced. 'The Will to Believe,' accordingly, is the title of my paper.

I have long defended to my own students the lawfulness of voluntarily adopted faith; but as soon as they have got well imbued with the logical spirit, they have as a rule refused to admit my contention to be lawful philosophically, even though in point of fact they were personally all the time chock-full of some faith or other themselves. I am all the while, however, so profoundly convinced that my own position is correct, that your invitation has seemed to me a good occasion to make my statements more clear. Perhaps your minds will be more open than those with which I have hitherto had to deal. I will be as little technical as I can, though I must begin by setting up some technical distinctions that will help us in the end.

I

Let us give the name of *hypothesis* to anything that may be proposed to our belief; and just as the electricians speak of live and dead wires, let us speak of any hypothesis as either *live* or *dead*. A live hypothesis is one which appeals as a real possibility to him to whom it is proposed. If I ask you to believe in the Mahdi, the notion makes no electric connection with your nature,—it refuses to scintillate with any credibility at all. As an hypothesis it is completely dead. To an Arab, however (even if he be not one of the Mahdi's followers), the hypothesis is among the mind's possibilities: it is alive. This shows that deadness and liveness in an hypothesis are not intrinsic properties, but relations to the individual thinker. They are measured by his willingness to act. The maximum of liveness in an hypothesis means willingness to act irrevocably. Practically, that means belief; but there is some believing tendency wherever there is willingness to act at all.

Next, let us call the decision between two hypotheses an *option*. Options may be of several kinds. They may be—1, *living* or *dead*; 2, *forced* or *avoidable*; 3, *momentous* or *trivial*; and for our purposes we may call an option a *genuine* option when it is of the forced, living, and momentous kind.

1. A living option is one in which both hypotheses are live ones. If I say to you: "Be a theosophist or be a Mohammedan," it is probably a dead option, because for you neither hypothesis is likely to be alive. But if I say: "Be an agnostic or be a Christian," it is otherwise: trained as you are, each hypothesis makes some appeal, however small, to your belief.

2. Next, if I say to you: "Choose between going out with your umbrella or without it," I do not offer you a genuine option, for it is not forced. You can easily avoid it by not going out at all. Similarly, if I say, "Either love me or hate me," "Either call my theory true or call it false," your option is avoidable. You may remain indifferent to me, neither loving nor hating, and you may decline to offer any judgment as to my theory.

But if I say, "Either accept this truth or go without it," I put on you a forced option, for there is no standing place outside of the alternative. Every dilemma based on a complete logical disjunction, with no possibility of not choosing, is an option of this forced kind.

3. Finally, if I were Dr. Nansen and proposed to you to join my North Pole expedition, your option would be momentous; for this would probably be your only similar opportunity, and your choice now would either exclude you from the North Pole sort of immortality altogether or put at least the chance of it into your hands. He who refuses to embrace a unique opportunity loses the prize as surely as if he tried and failed. *Per contra,* the option is trivial when the opportunity is not unique, when the stake is insignificant, or when the decision is reversible if it later prove unwise. Such trivial options abound in the scientific life. A chemist finds an hypothesis live enough to spend a year in its verification: he believes in it to that extent. But if his experiments prove inconclusive either way, he is quit for his loss of time, no vital harm being done.

It will facilitate our discussion if we keep all these distinctions well in mind.

II

The next matter to consider is the actual psychology of human opinion. When we look at certain facts, it seems as if our passional and volitional nature lay at the root of all our convictions. When we look at others, it seems as if they could do nothing when the intellect had once said its say. Let us take the latter facts up first.

Does it not seem preposterous on the very face of it to talk of our opinions being modifiable at will? Can our will either help or hinder our intellect in its perceptions of truth? Can we, by just willing it, believe that Abraham Lincoln's existence is a myth, and that the portraits of him in McClure's Magazine are all of some one else? Can we, by any effort of our will, or by any strength of wish that it were true, believe ourselves well and about when we are roaring with rheumatism in bed, or feel certain that the sum of the two one-dollar bills in our pocket must be a hundred dollars? We can say any of these things, but we are absolutely impotent to believe them; and of just such things is the whole fabric of the truths that we do believe in made up,—matters of fact, immediate or remote, as Hume said, and relations between ideas, which are either there or not there for us if we see them so, and which if not there cannot be put there by any action of our own.

In Pascal's Thoughts there is a celebrated passage known in literature as Pascal's wager. In it he tries to force us into Christianity by reasoning as if our concern with truth resembled our concern with the stakes in a game of chance. Translated freely his words are these: You must either believe or not believe that God is—which will you do? Your human reason cannot say. A game is going on between you and the nature of things which at the day of judgment will bring out either heads or tails. Weigh what your gains and your losses would be if you should stake all you have on heads, or God's existence: if you win in such case, you gain eternal beatitude; if you lose, you lose nothing at all. If there were an infinity of chances, and only one for God in this wager, still you ought to stake your all on God; for though you surely risk a finite loss by this procedure, any finite loss is reasonable, even a certain one is reasonable, if there is but the possibility of infinite gain. Go, then, and take holy water, and have masses said; belief will come and stupefy your scruples,— *Cela vous fera croire et vous abêtira.* Why should you not? At bottom, what have you to lose?

You probably feel that when religious faith expresses itself thus, in the language of the gaming-table, it is put to its last trumps. Surely Pascal's own personal belief in masses and holy water had far other springs; and this celebrated page of his is but an argument for others, a last desperate snatch at a weapon against the hardness of the unbelieving heart. We feel that a faith in masses and holy water adopted willfully after such a mechanical calculation would lack the inner soul of faith's reality; and if we were ourselves in the place of the Deity, we should probably take particular pleasure in cutting off believers of this pattern from their infinite reward. It is evident that unless there be some pre-existing tendency to believe in masses and holy water, the option offered to the will by Pascal is not a living option. Certainly no Turk ever took to masses and holy water on its account; and even to us Protestants these means of salvation seem such foregone impossibilities that Pascal's logic, invoked for them specifically, leaves us unmoved. As well might the Mahdi write to us, saying, "I am the Expected One whom God has created in his effulgence. You shall be infinitely happy if you confess me; otherwise you shall be cut off from the light of the sun. Weigh, then, your infinite gain if I am genuine against your finite sacrifice if I am not!" His logic would be that of Pascal; but he would vainly use it on us, for the hypothesis he offers us is dead. No tendency to act on it exists in us to any degree.

The talk of believing by our volition seems, then, from one point of view, simply silly. From another point of view it is worse than silly, it is vile. When one turns to the magnificent edifice of the physical sciences, and sees how it was reared; what thousands of disinterested moral lives of men lie buried in its mere foundations; what patience and postponement, what choking down of preference, what submission to the icy laws of outer fact are wrought into its very stones and mortar; how absolutely impersonal it stands in its vast augustness,—then how besotted and contemptible seems every little sentimentalist who comes blowing his voluntary smoke-wreaths, and pretending to decide things from out of his private dream! Can we wonder if those bred in the rugged and manly school of science should feel like spewing such subjectivism out of their mouths? The whole system of loyalties which grow up in the schools of science go dead against its toleration; so that it is only natural that those who have caught the scientific fever should pass over to the opposite extreme, and write sometimes as if the incorruptibly truthful intellect ought positively to prefer bitterness and unacceptableness to the heart in its cup.

It fortifies my soul to know

That, though I perish, Truth is so—

sings Clough, while Huxley exclaims: "My only consolation lies in the reflection that, however bad our posterity may become, so far as they hold by the plain rule of not pretending to believe what they have no reason to believe, because it may be to their advantage so to pretend [the word 'pretend' is surely here redundant], they will not have reached the lowest depth of immorality." And that delicious *enfant terrible* Clifford writes: "Belief is desecrated when given to unproved and unquestioned statements for the solace and private pleasure of the believer. . . . Whoso would deserve well of his fellows in this matter will guard the purity of his belief with a very fanaticism of jealous care, lest at any time it should rest on an unworthy object, and catch a stain which can never be wiped away. . . . If [a] belief has been accepted on insufficient evidence [even though the belief be true, as Clifford on the same page explains] the pleasure is a stolen one. . . . It is sinful because it is stolen in defiance of our duty to mankind. That duty is to guard ourselves from such beliefs as from a pestilence which may shortly master our own body and then spread to the rest of the town. . . . It is wrong always, everywhere, and for every one, to believe anything upon insufficient evidence."

III

All this strikes one as healthy, even when expressed, as by Clifford, with somewhat too much of robustious pathos in the voice. Free-will and simple wishing do seem, in the matter of our credences, to be only fifth wheels to the coach. Yet if any one should thereupon assume that intellectual insight is what remains after wish and will and sentimental preference have taken wing, or that pure reason is what then settles our opinions, he would fly quite as directly in the teeth of the facts.

It is only our already dead hypotheses that our willing nature is unable to bring to life again. But what has made them dead for us is for the most part a previous action of our willing nature of an antagonistic kind. When I say 'willing nature,' I do not mean only such deliberate volitions as may have set up habits of belief that we cannot now escape from,—I mean all such factors of belief as fear and hope, prejudice and passion, imitation and partisanship, the circumpressure of our caste and set. As a matter of fact we find ourselves believing, we hardly know how or why. Mr. Balfour gives the name of 'authority' to all those influences, born of the intellectual climate, that make hypotheses possible or impossible for us, alive or dead. Here in this room,

we all of us believe in molecules and the conservation of energy, in democracy and necessary
progress, in Protestant Christianity and the duty of
fighting for 'the doctrine of the immortal Monroe,'
all for no reasons worthy of the name. We see into
these matters with no more inner clearness, and
probably with much less, than any disbeliever in
them might possess. His unconventionality would
probably have some grounds to show for its conclusions; but for us, no insight, but the *prestige* of the
opinions, is what makes the spark shoot from them
and light up our sleeping magazines of faith. Our
reason is quite satisfied, in nine hundred and ninety-
nine cases out of every thousand of us, if it can find
a few arguments that will do to recite in case our
credulity is crtiticized by some one else. Our faith is
faith in some one else's faith, and in the greatest
matters this is most the case. Our belief in truth
itself, for instance, that there is a truth, and that our
minds and it are made for each other,—what is it
but a passionate affirmation of desire, in which our
social system backs us up? We want to have a truth;
we want to believe that our experiments and studies
and discussions must put us in a continually better
and better position towards it; and on this line we
agree to fight out our thinking lives. But if a pyrrhonistic skeptic asks us *how we know* all this, can
our logic find a reply? No! certainly it cannot. It is
just one volition against another,—we willing to go
in for life upon a trust or assumption which he, for
his part, does not care to make.

As a rule we disbelieve all facts and theories for
which we have no use. Clifford's cosmic emotions
find no use for Christian feelings. Huxley belabors
the bishops because there is no use for sacerdotal-
ism in his scheme of life. Newman, on the contrary,
goes over to Romanism, and finds all sorts of reasons good for staying there, because a priestly system is for him an organic need and delight. Why do
so few 'scientists' even look at the evidence for
telepathy, so called? Because they think, as a leading
biologist, now dead, once said to me, that even if
such a thing were true, scientists ought to band
together to keep it suppressed and concealed. It
would undo the uniformity of Nature and all sorts
of other things without which scientists cannot carry
on their pursuits. But if this very man had been
shown something which as a scientist he might *do*

with telepathy, he might not only have examined the
evidence, but even have found it good enough. This
very law which the logicians would impose upon
us—if I may give the name of logicians to those who
would rule out our willing nature here—is based on
nothing but their own natural wish to exclude all elements for which they, in their professional quality of
logicians, can find no use.

Evidently, then, our non-intellectual nature does
influence our convictions. There are passional tendencies and volitions which run before and others
which come after belief, and it is only the latter that
are too late for the fair; and they are not too late
when the previous passional work has been already
in their own direction. Pascal's argument, instead of
being powerless, then seems a regular clincher, and
is the last stroke needed to make our faith in masses
and holy water complete. The state of things is evidently far from simple; and pure insight and logic,
whatever they might do ideally, are not the only
things that really do produce our creeds.

IV

Our next duty, having recognized this mixed-up
state of affairs, is to ask whether it be simply reprehensible and pathological, or whether, on the contrary, we must treat it as a normal element in making
up our minds. The thesis I defend is, briefly stated,
this: *Our passional nature not only lawfully may, but
must, decide an option between propositions, whenever it
is a genuine option that cannot by its nature be decided
on intellectual grounds; for to say, under such circumstances, "Do not decide, but leave the question open," is
itself a passional decision,—just like deciding yes or
no,—and is attended with the same risk of losing the
truth.* The thesis thus abstractly expressed will, I
trust, soon become quite clear. But I must first
indulge in a bit more of preliminary work.

V

It will be observed that for the purposes of this discussion we are on 'dogmatic' ground,—ground, I
mean, which leaves systematic philosophical skepticism altogether out of account. The postulate that

there is truth, and that it is the destiny of our minds to attain it, we are deliberately resolving to make, though the skeptic will not make it. We part company with him, therefore, absolutely, at this point. But the faith that truth exists, and that our minds can find it, may be held in two ways. We may talk of the *empiricist* way and of the *absolutist* way of believing in truth. The absolutists in this matter say that we not only can attain to knowing truth, but we can *know when* we have attained to knowing it; while the empiricists think that although we may attain it, we cannot infallibly know when. To *know* is one thing, and to know for certain *that* we know is another. One may hold to the first being possible without the second; hence the empiricists and the absolutists, although neither of them is a skeptic in the usual philosophic sense of the term, show very different degrees of dogmatism in their lives.

If we look at the history of opinions, we see that the empiricist tendency has largely prevailed in science, while in philosophy the absolutist tendency has had everything its own way. The characteristic sort of happiness, indeed, which philosophies yield has mainly consisted in the conviction felt by each successive school or system that by it bottom-certitude had been attained. "Other philosophies are collections of opinions, mostly false; *my* philosophy gives standing-ground forever,"—who does not recognize in this the key-note of every system worthy of the name? A system, to be a system at all, must come as a *closed* system, reversible in this or that detail, perchance, but in its essential features never!

Scholastic orthodoxy, to which one must always go when one wishes to find perfectly clear statement, has beautifully elaborated this absolutist conviction in a doctrine which it calls that of 'objective evidence.' If, for example, I am unable to doubt that I now exist before you, that two is less than three, or that if all men are mortal then I am mortal too, it is because these things illumine my intellect irresistibly. The final ground of this objective evidence possessed by certain propositions is the *adaequatio intellectus nostri cum re.* The certitude it brings involves an *aptitudinem ad extorquendum certum assensum* on the part of the truth envisaged, and on the side of the subject a *quietem in cognitione,* when once the object is mentally received, that leaves no possibility of doubt behind; and in the whole trans-

action nothing operates but the *entitas ipsa* of the object and the *entitas ipsa* of the mind. We slouchy modern thinkers dislike to talk in Latin,—indeed, we dislike to talk in set terms at all; but at bottom our own state of mind is very much like this whenever we uncritically abandon ourselves: You believe in objective evidence, and I do. Of some things we feel that we are certain: we know, and we know that we do know. There is something that gives a click inside of us, a bell that strikes twelve, when the hands of our mental clock have swept the dial and meet over the meridian hour. The greatest empiricists among us are only empiricists on reflection: when left to their instincts, they dogmatize like infallible popes. When the Cliffords tell us how sinful it is to be Christians on such 'insufficient evidence,' insufficiency is really the last thing they have in mind. For them the evidence is absolutely sufficient, only it makes the other way. They believe so completely in an anti-Christian order of the universe that there is no living option: Christianity is a dead hypothesis from the start.

VI

But now, since we are all such absolutists by instinct, what in our quality of students of philosophy ought we to do about the fact? Shall we espouse and endorse it? Or shall we treat it as a weakness of our nature from which we must free ourselves, if we can?

I sincerely believe that the latter course is the only one we can follow as reflective men. Objective evidence and certitude are doubtless very fine ideals to play with, but where on this moonlit and dream-visited planet are they found? I am, therefore, myself a complete empiricist so far as my theory of human knowledge goes. I live, to be sure, by the practical faith that we must go on experiencing and thinking over our experience, for only thus can our opinions grow more true; but to hold any one of them—I absolutely do not care which—as if it never could be reinterpretable or corrigible, I believe to be a tremendously mistaken attitude, and I think that the whole history of philosophy will bear me out. There is but one indefectibly certain truth, and that is the truth that pyrrhonistic skepticism itself leaves standing,—the truth that the present phenomenon of consciousness exists. That, however, is the bare starting-point of knowledge, the mere admission of a stuff to be philosophized about. The various philosophies are but so many attempts at expressing what this stuff really is. And if we repair to our libraries what disagreement do we discover! Where is a certainly true answer found? Apart from abstract propositions of comparison (such as two and two are the same as four) propositions which tell us nothing by themselves about concrete reality, we find no proposition ever regarded by any one as evidently certain that has not either been called a false-hood, or at least had its truth sincerely questioned by some one else. The transcending of the axioms of geometry, not in play but in earnest, by certain of our contemporaries (as Zöllner and Charles H. Hinton), and the rejection of the whole Aristotelian logic by the Hegelians, are striking instances in point.

No concrete test of what is really true has ever been agreed upon. Some make the criterion external to the moment of perception, putting it either in revelation, the *consensus gentium,* the instincts of the heart, or the systematized experience of the race. Others make the perceptive moment its own test,—Descartes, for instance, with his clear and distinct ideas guaranteed by the veracity of God; Reid with his 'common-sense,' and Kant with his forms of synthetic judgment *a priori.* The inconceivability of the opposite; the capacity to be verified by sense; the possession of complete organic unity or self-relation, realized when a thing is its own other,—are standards which, in turn, have been used. The much lauded objective evidence is never triumphantly there; it is a mere aspiration or *Grenzbegriff,* marking the infinitely remote ideal of our thinking life. To claim that certain truths now possess it, is simply to say that when you think them true and they *are* true, then their evidence is objective, otherwise it is not. But practically one's conviction that the evidence one goes by is of the real objective brand, is only one more subjective opinion added to the lot. For what a contradictory array of opinions have objective evidence and absolute certitude been claimed! The world is rational through and through,—its existence is an ultimate brute fact; there is a personal God,—a personal God is inconceivable; there is an extra-mental physical world immediately known,—the mind can only know its own ideas; a moral imperative exists,—obligation is only the resultant of desires; a permanent spiritual principle is in everyone,—there are only shifting states of mind; there is an endless chain of causes,—there is an absolute first cause; an eternal necessity,—a freedom; a purpose,—no purpose; a primal One,—a primal Many; a universal continuity,—an essential discontinuity in things; an infinity,—no infinity. There is this,—there is that; there is indeed nothing which some one has not thought absolutely true, while his neighbor deemed it absolutely false; and not an absolutist among them seems ever to have considered that the trouble may all the time be essential, and that the intellect, even with truth directly in its grasp, may have no infallible signal for knowing whether it be truth or no. When, indeed, one remembers that the most striking practical application to life of the doctrine of objective certitude has been the conscientious labors of the Holy Office of the Inquisition, one feels less tempted than ever to lend the doctrine a respectful ear.

But please observe, now, that when as empiricists we give up the doctrine of objective certitude, we do not thereby give up the quest or hope of truth itself. We still pin our faith on its existence, and still believe that we gain an ever better position towards it by systematically continuing to roll up experiences and think. Our great difference from the scholastic lies in the way we face. The strength of his system lies in the principles, the origin, the *terminus a quo* of his thought; for us the strength is in the outcome, the upshot, the *terminus ad quem.* Not where it come from but what it leads to is to decide. It matters not to an empiricist from what quarter an hypothesis may come to him: he may have acquired it by fair means or by foul; passion may have whispered or accident suggested it; but if the total drift of thinking continues to confirm it, that is what he means by its being true.

VII

One more point, small but important, and our preliminaries are done. There are two ways of looking at our duty in the matter of opinion,—ways entirely different, and yet ways about whose difference the theory of knowledge seems hitherto to have shown very little concern. *We must know the truth;* and *we must avoid error,*—these are our first and great commandments as would-be knowers; but they are not two ways of stating an identical commandment, they are two separable laws. Although it may indeed happen that when we believe the truth *A,* we escape as an incidental consequence from believing the falsehood *B,* it hardly ever happens that by merely disbelieving *B* we necessarily believe *A.* We may in escaping *B* fall into believing other falsehoods, *C* or *D,* just as bad as *B;* or we may escape *B* by not believing anything at all, not even *A.*

Believe truth! Shun error!—these, we see, are two materially different laws; and by choosing between them we may end by coloring differently our whole intellectual life. We may regard the chase for truth as paramount, and the avoidance of error as secondary; or we may, on the other hand, treat the avoidance of error as more imperative, and let truth take its chance. Clifford, in the instructive passage which I have quoted, exhorts us to the latter course. Believe nothing, he tells us, keep your mind in suspense forever, rather than by closing it on insufficient evidence incur the awful risk of believing lies. You, on the other hand, may think that the risk of being in error is a very small matter when compared with the blessings of real knowledge, and be ready to be duped many times in your investigation rather than postpone indefinitely the chance of guessing true. I myself find it impossible to go with Clifford. We must remember that these feelings of our duty about either truth or error are in any case only expressions of our passional life. Biologically considered, our minds are as ready to grind out falsehood as veracity, and he who says, "Better go without belief forever than believe a lie!" merely shows his own preponderant private horror of becoming a dupe. He maybe critical of many of his desires and fears, but this fear he slavishly obeys. He cannot imagine any one questioning its binding force. For my own part, I have also a horror of being duped; but I can believe that worse things than being duped may happen to a man in this world: so Clifford's exhortation has to my ears a thoroughly fantastic sound. It is like a general informing his soldiers that it is better to keep out of battle forever than to risk a single wound. Not so are victories either over enemies or over nature gained. Our errors are surely not such awfully solemn things. In a world where we are so certain to incur them in spite of all our caution, a certain lightness of heart seems healthier than this excessive nervousness on their behalf. At any rate, it seems the fittest thing for the empiricist philosopher.

VIII

And now, after all this introduction, let us go straight at our question. I have said, and now repeat it, that not only as a matter of fact do we find our passional nature influencing us in our opinions, but that there are some options between opinions in which this influence must be regarded both as an inevitable and as a lawful determinant of our choice.

I fear here that some of you my hearers will begin to scent danger, and lend an inhospitable ear. Two first steps of passion you have indeed had to admit as necessary,—we must think so as to avoid dupery, and we must think so as to gain truth; but the surest path to those ideal consummations, you will probably consider, is from now onwards to take no further passional step.

Well, of course, I agree as far as the facts will allow. Wherever the option between losing truth and gaining it is not momentous, we can throw the chance of *gaining truth* away, and at any rate save ourselves from any chance of *believing falsehood,* by not making up our minds at all till objective evidence has come. In scientific questions, this is almost always the case; and even in human affairs in general, the need of acting is seldom so urgent that a false belief to act on is better than no belief at all. Law courts, indeed, have to decide on the best evidence attainable for the moment, because a judge's duty is to make law as well as to ascertain it, and (as a learned judge once said to me) few cases are worth spending much time over: the great thing is to have them decided on *any* acceptable principle, and got out of the way. But in our dealings with objective nature we obviously are recorders, not makers, of the truth: and decisions for the mere sake of deciding promptly and getting on to the next business would be wholly out of place. Throughout the breadth of physical nature facts are what they are quite independently of us, and seldom is there any such hurry about them that the risks of being duped by believing a premature theory need be faced. The questions here are always trivial options, the hypotheses are hardly living (at any rate not living for us spectators), the choice between believing truth or falsehood is seldom forced. The attitude of skeptical balance is therefore the absolutely wise one if we would escape mistakes. What difference, indeed, does it make to most of us whether we have or have not a theory of the Röntgen rays, whether we believe or not in mind-stuff, or have a conviction about the causality of conscious states? It makes no difference. Such options are not forced on us. On every account it is better not to make them, but still keep weighing reasons *pro et contra* with an indifferent hand.

I speak, of course, here of the purely judging mind. For purposes of discovery such indifference is to be less highly recommended, and science would be far less advanced than she is if the passionate desires of individuals to get their own faiths confirmed had been kept out of the game. See for example the sagacity which Spencer and Weismann now display. On the other hand, if you want an absolute duffer in an investigation, you must, after all, take the man who has no interest whatever in its results: he is the warranted incapable, the positive fool. The most useful investigator, because the most sensitive observer, is always he whose eager interest in one side of the question is balanced by an equally keen nervousness lest he become deceived. Science has organized this nervousness into a regular *technique,* her so-called method of verification; and she has fallen so deeply in love with the method that one may even say she has ceased to care for truth by itself at all. It is only truth as technically verified that interests her. The truth of truths might come in merely affirmative form, and she would decline to touch it. Such truth as that, she might repeat with Clifford, would be stolen in defiance of her duty to mankind. Human passions, however, are stronger than technical rules. "Le coeur a ses raisons," as Pascal says, "que la raison ne connaît pas;" and however indifferent to all but the bare rules of the game the umpire, the abstract intellect, may be, the concrete players who furnish him the materials to judge of are usually, each one of them, in love with some pet 'live hypothesis' of his own. Let us agree, however, that wherever there is no forced option, the dispassionately judicial intellect with no pet hypothesis, saving us, as it does, from dupery at any rate, ought to be our ideal.

The question next arises: Are there not somewhere forced options in our speculative questions, and can we (as men who may be interested at least as much in positively gaining truth as in merely escaping dupery) always wait with impunity till the coercive evidence shall have arrived? It seems *a priori* improbable that the truth should be so nicely adjusted to our needs and powers as that. In the great boarding-house of nature, the cakes and the butter and the syrup seldom come out so even and leave the plates so clean. Indeed, we should view them with scientific suspicion if they did.

IX

Moral questions immediately present themselves as questions whose solution cannot wait for sensible proof. A moral question is a question not of what sensibly exists, but of what is good, or would be good if it did exist. Science can tell us what exists; but to compare the *worths,* both of what exists and of what does not exist, we must consult not science, but what Pascal calls our heart. Science herself consults her heart when she lays it down that the infinite ascertainment of fact and correction of false belief are the supreme goods for man. Challenge the statement, and science can only repeat it oracularly, or else prove it by showing that such ascertainment and correction bring man all sorts of other goods which man's heart in turn declares. The question of having moral beliefs at all or not having them is decided by our will. Are our moral preferences true or false, or are they only odd biological phenomena, making things good or bad for *us,* but in themselves indifferent? How can your pure intellect decide? If your heart does not *want* a world of moral reality, your head will assuredly never make you believe in one. Mephistophelian skepticism, indeed, will satisfy the head's play-instincts much better than any rigorous idealism can. Some men (even at the student age) are so naturally cool-hearted that the moralistic hypothesis never has for them any pungent life, and in their supercilious presence the hot young moralist always feels strangely ill at ease. The appearance of knowingness is on their side, of *naïveté* and gullibility on his. Yet, in the inarticulate heart of him, he clings to it that he is not a dupe, and that there is a realm in which (as Emerson says) all their wit and intellectual superiority is no better than the cunning of a fox. Moral skepticism can no more be refuted or proved by logic than intellectual skepticism can. When we stick to it that there *is* truth (be it of either kind), we do so with our whole nature, and resolve to stand or fall by the results. The skeptic with his whole nature adopts the doubting attitude; but which of us is the wiser, Omniscience only knows.

Turn now from these wide questions of good to a certain class of questions of fact, questions concerning personal relations, states of mind between one man and another. *Do you like me or not?*—for example. Whether you do or not depends, in countless instances, on whether I meet you half-way, am willing to assume that you must like me, and show you trust and expectation. The previous faith on my part in your liking's existence is in such cases what makes your liking come. But if I stand aloof, and refuse to budge an inch until I have objective evidence, until you shall have done something apt, as the absolutists say, *ad extorquendum assensum meum,* ten to one your liking never comes. How many women's hearts are vanquished by the mere sanguine insistence of some man that they *must* love him! he will not consent to the hypothesis that they cannot. The desire for a certain kind of truth here brings about that special truth's existence, and so it is in innumerable cases of other sorts. Who gains promotions, boons, appointments, but the man in whose life they are seen to play the part of live hypotheses, who discounts them, sacrifices other things for their sake before they have come, and takes risks for them in advance? His faith acts on the powers above him as a claim, and creates its own verification.

A social organism of any sort whatever, large or small, is what it is because each member proceeds to his own duty with a trust that the other members will simultaneously do theirs. Wherever a desired result is achieved by the cooperation of many independent persons, its existence as a fact is a pure consequence of the precursive faith in one another

of those immediately concerned. A government, an army, a commercial system, a ship, a college, an athletic team, all exist on this condition, without which not only is nothing achieved, but nothing is even attempted. A whole train of passengers (individually brave enough) will be looted by a few highwaymen, simply because the latter can count on one another, while each passenger fears that if he makes a movement of resistance, he will be shot before any one else backs him up. If we believed that the whole carfull would rise at once with us, we should each severally rise, and train-robbing would never even be attempted. There are, then, cases where a fact cannot come at all unless a preliminary faith exists in its coming. *And where faith in a fact can help create the fact,* that would be an insane logic which should say that faith running ahead of scientific evidence is the 'lowest kind of immorality' into which a thinking being can fall. Yet such is the logic by which our scientific absolutists pretend to regulate our lives!

X

In truths dependent on our personal action, then, faith based on desire is certainly a lawful and possibly an indispensable thing.

But now, it will be said, these are all childish human cases, and have nothing to do with great cosmical matters, like the question of religious faith. Let us then pass on to that. Religions differ so much in their accidents that in discussing the religious question we must make it very generic and broad. What then do we now mean by the religious hypothesis? Science says things are; morality says some things are better than other things; and religion says essentially two things.

First, she says that the best things are the more eternal things, the overlapping things, the things in the universe that throw the last stone, so to speak, and say the final word. "Perfection is eternal,"—this phrase of Charles Secrétan seems a good way of putting this first affirmation of religion, an affirmation which obviously cannot yet be verified scientifically at all.

The second affirmation of religion is that we are better off even now if we believe her first affirmation to be true.

Now, let us consider what the logical elements of this situation are *in case the religious hypothesis in both its branches be really true.* (Of course, we must admit that possibility at the outset. If we are to discuss the question at all, it must involve a living option. If for any of you religion be a hypothesis that cannot, by any living possibility be true, then you need go no farther. I speak the 'saving remnant' alone.) So proceeding, we see, first that religion offers itself as a *momentous* option. We are supposed to gain, even now, by our belief, and to lose by our non-belief, a certain vital good. Secondly, religion is a *forced* option, so far as that good goes. We cannot escape the issue by remaining skeptical and waiting for more light, because, although we do avoid error in that way *if religion be untrue,* we lose the good, *if it be true,* just as certainly as if we positively chose to disbelieve. It is as if a man should hesitate indefinitely to ask a certain woman to marry him because he was not perfectly sure that she would prove an angel after he brought her home. Would he not cut himself off from that particular angel-possibility as decisively as if he went and married some one else? Skepticism, then, is not avoidance of option; it is option of a certain particular kind of risk. *Better risk loss of truth than chance of error,*—that is your faith-vetoer's exact position. He is actively playing his stake as much as the believer is; he is backing the field against the religious hypothesis, just as the believer is backing the religious hypothesis against the field. To preach skepticism to us as a duty until 'sufficient evidence' for religion be found, is tantamount therefore to telling us, when in presence of the religious hypothesis, that to yield to our fear of its being error is wiser and better than to yield to our hope that it may be true. It is not intellect against all passions, then; it is only intellect with one passion laying down its law. And by what, forsooth, is the supreme wisdom of this passion warranted? Dupery for dupery, what proof is there that dupery through hope is so much worse than dupery through fear? I, for one, can see no proof; and I simply refuse obedience to the scientist's command to imitate his kind of option, in a case where my own stake is important enough to give me the right to choose my own form of risk. If religion be true and the evidence for it be still insufficient, I do not wish, by putting your extinguisher upon my nature (which feels to me as if it

had after all some business in this matter), to forfeit my sole chance in life of getting upon the winning side,—that chance depending, of course, on my willingness to run the risk of acting as if my passional need of taking the world religiously might be prophetic and right.

All this is on the supposition that it really may be prophetic and right, and that, even to us who are discussing the matter, religion is a live hypothesis which may be true. Now, to most of us religion comes in a still further way that makes a veto on our active faith even more illogical. The more perfect and more eternal aspect of the universe is represented in our religions as having personal form. The universe is no longer a mere *It* to us, but a *Thou,* if we are religious; and any relation that may be possible from person to person might be possible here. For instance, although in one sense we are passive portions of the universe, in another we show a curious autonomy, as if we were small active centres on our own account. We feel, too, as if the appeal of religion to us were made to our own active good-will, as if evidence might be forever withheld from us unless we met the hypothesis half-way. To take a trivial illustration: just as a man who in a company of gentlemen made no advances, asked a warrant for every concession, and believed no one's word without proof, would cut himself off by such churlishness from all the social rewards that a more trusting spirit would earn, so here, one who should shut himself up in snarling logicality and try to make the gods extort his recognition willy-nilly, or not get it at all, might cut himself off forever from his only opportunity of making the gods' acquaintance. This feeling, forced on us we know not whence, that by obstinately believing that there are gods (although not to do so would be so easy both for our logic and our life) we are doing the universe the deepest service we can, seems part of the living essence of the religious hypothesis. If the hypothesis *were* true in all its parts, including this one, then pure intellectualism, with its veto on our making willing advances, would be an absurdity; and some participation of our sympathetic nature would be logically required. I, therefore, for one, cannot see my way to accepting the agnostic rules for truth-seeking, or willfully agree to keep my willing nature out of the game. I cannot do so for this plain reason, that *a rule of thinking which would absolutely prevent me from acknowledging certain kinds of truth if those kinds of truth were really there, would be an irrational rule.* That for me is the long and short of the formal logic of the situation, no matter what the kinds of truth might materially be.

I confess I do not see how this logic can be escaped. But sad experience makes me fear that some of you may still shrink from radically saying with me, *in abstracto,* that we have the right to believe at our own risk any hypothesis that is live enough to tempt our will. I suspect, however, that if this is so, it is because you have got away from the abstract logical point of view altogether, and are thinking (perhaps without realizing it) of some particular religious hypothesis which for you is dead. The freedom to 'believe what we will' you apply to the case of some patent superstition; and the faith you think of is the faith defined by the schoolboy when he said, "Faith is when you believe something that you know ain't true." I can only repeat that this is misapprehension. *In concreto,* the freedom to believe can only cover living options which the intellect of the individual cannot by itself resolve; and living options never seem absurdities to him who has them to consider. When I look at the religious question as it really puts itself to concrete men, and when I think of all the possibilities which both practically and theoretically it involves, then this command that we shall put a stopper on our heart, instincts, and courage, and *wait*—acting of course mean-while more or less as if religion were *not* true—till dooms-day, or till such time as our intellect and senses working together may have raked in evidence enough,—this command, I say, seems to me the queerest idol ever manufactured in the philosophic cave. Were we scholastic absolutists, there might be more excuse. If we had an infallible intellect with its objective certitudes, we might feel ourselves disloyal to such a perfect organ of knowledge in not trusting to it exclusively, in not waiting for its releasing word. But if we are empiricists, if we believe that no bell in us tolls to let us know for certain when truth is in our grasp, then it seems a piece of idle fantasticality to preach so solemnly our duty of waiting for the bell. Indeed we *may* wait if we will,—I hope you do not think that I am denying that,—but if we do so, we do so at our peril as much as if we believed. In

either case we *act,* taking our life in our hands. No one of us ought to issue vetoes to the other, nor should we bandy words of abuse. We ought, on the contrary, delicately and profoundly to respect one another's mental freedom: then only shall we bring about the intellectual republic; then only shall we have that spirit of inner tolerance without which all our outer tolerance is soulless, and which is empiricism's glory; then only shall we live and let live, in speculative as well as in practical things.

I began by a reference to Fitz James Stephen; let me end by a quotation from him. "What do you think of yourself? What do you think of the world? . . . These are questions with which all must deal as it seems good to them. They are riddles of the Sphinx, and in some way or other we must deal with them. . . . In all important transactions of life we have to take a leap in the dark. . . . If we decide to leave the riddles unanswered, that is a choice; if we waver in our answer, that, too, is a choice: but whatever choice we make, we make it at our peril. If a man chooses to turn his back altogether on God and the future, no one can prevent him; no one can show beyond reasonable doubt that he is mistaken. If a man thinks otherwise and acts as he thinks, I do not see that any one can prove that *he* is mistaken. Each must act as he thinks best; and if he is wrong, so much the worse for him. We stand on a mountain pass in the midst of whirling snow and blinding mist, through which we get glimpses now and then of paths which may be deceptive. If we stand still we shall be frozen to death. If we take the wrong road we shall be dashed to pieces. We do not certainly know whether there is any right one. What must we do? 'Be strong and of a good courage.' Act for the best, hope for the best, and take what comes. . . . If death ends all, we cannot meet death better."

NOTES

1. Since belief is measured by action, he who forbids us to believe religion to be true, necessarily also forbids us to act as we should if we did believe it to be true. The whole defence of religous faith hinges upon action. If the section required or inspired by the religious hypothesis is in no way different from that dictated by the naturalistic hypothesis, then

religious faith is a pure superfluity, better pruned away, and controversy about its legitimacy is a piece of idle trifling, unworthy of serious minds. I myself believe, of course, that the religious hypothesis gives to the world an expression which specifically deter-mines our reactions, and makes them in a large part unlike what they might be on a purely naturalistic scheme of belief.

2. Liberty, Equality, Fraternity, p. 353, 2d edition. London, 1874.

RICHARD RORTY

Pragmatism, Relativism, and Irrationalism

PART 1. PRAGMATISM

"Pragmatism" is a vague, ambiguous, and over-worked word. Nevertheless, it names the chief glory of our country's intellectual tradition. No other American writers have offered so radical a suggestion for making our future different from our past, as have James and Dewey. At present, however, these two writers are neglected. Many philosophers think that everything important in pragmatism has been preserved and adapted to the needs of analytic philosophy. More specifically, they view pragmatism as having suggested various holistic corrections of the atomistic doctrines of the early logical empiricists. This way of looking at pragmatism is not wrong, as far as it goes. But it ignores what is most important in James and Dewey. Logical empiricism was one variety of standard, academic, neo-Kantian, epistemologically-centered philosophy. The great pragmatists should not be taken as suggesting an holistic variation of this variant, but rather as breaking with the Kantian epistemological tradition altogether. As long as we see James or Dewey as having "theories of truth" or "theories of knowledge" or "theories of morality" we shall get them wrong. We shall ignore their criticisms of the assumption that there ought to *be* theories about such matters. We shall not see how radical their thought was—how deep was their criticism of the attempt, common to Kant, Husserl, Russell, and C. I. Lewis, to make philosophy into a foundational discipline.

One symptom of this incorrect focus is a tendency to overpraise Peirce. Peirce is praised partly because he developed various logical notions and various technical problems (such as the counterfactual conditional) which were taken up by the logical empiricists. But the main reason for Peirce's undeserved apotheosis is that his talk about a general theory of signs looks like an early discovery of the importance of language. For all his genius, however, Peirce never made up his mind what he wanted a general theory of signs *for*, nor what it might look like, nor what its relation to either logic or epistemology was supposed to be. His contribution to pragmatism was merely to have given it a name, and to have stimulated James. Peirce himself remained the most Kantian of thinkers—the most convinced that philosophy gave us an all-embracing ahistorical context in which every other species of discourse could be assigned its proper place and rank. It was just this Kantian assumption that there was such a context, and that epistemology or semantics could discover it, against which James and Dewey reacted. We need to focus on this reaction if we are to recapture a proper sense of their importance.

This reaction is found in other philosophers who are currently more fashionable than James or Dewey—for example, Nietzsche and Heidegger. Unlike Nietzsche and Heidegger, however, the pragmatists did not make the mistake of turning against the community which takes the natural scientist as its moral hero—the community of secular intellectuals which came to self-consciousness in the Enlightenment. James and Dewey rejected neither the Enlightenment's choice of the scientist as moral example, nor the technological civilization which science had created. They wrote, as Nietzsche and Heidegger did not, in a spirit of social hope. They asked us to liberate our new civilization by giving up the notion of "grounding" our culture, our moral lives, our politics, our religious beliefs, upon "philosophical bases." They asked us to give up the neurotic Cartesian quest for certainty which had been one result of Galileo's frightening new cosmology, the quest for "enduring spiritual values" which had been one reaction to Darwin, and the aspiration of academic philosophy to form a tribunal of pure reason which had been the neo-Kantian response to Hegelian historicism. They asked us to think of the Kantian project of grounding thought or culture in a permanent ahistorical matrix as *reactionary*. They viewed Kant's idealization of Newton, and Spencer's of Darwin, as just as silly as Plato's idealization of Pythagoras, and Aquinas' of Aristotle.

Emphasizing this message of social hope and liberation, however, makes James and Dewey sound like prophets rather than thinkers. This would be misleading. They had things to say about truth, knowledge, and morality, even though they did not have *theories* of them, in the sense of sets of answers to the textbook problems. In what follows, I shall offer three brief sloganistic characterizations of what I take to be their central doctrine.

My first characterization of pragmatism is that it is simply antiessentialism applied to notions like "truth," "knowledge," "language," "morality," and similar objects of philosophical theorizing. Let me illustrate this by James's definition of "the true" as "what is good in the way of belief." This has struck his critics as not to the point, as unphilosophical, as like the suggestion that the essence of aspirin is that it is good for headaches. James's point, however, was that there *is* nothing deeper to be said: truth is not the sort of thing which *has* an essence. More specifically, his point was that it is no use being told that truth is "correspondence to reality." Given a language and a view of what the world is like, one can, to be sure, pair off bits of the language with bits of what one takes the world to be in such a way that the sentences one believes true have internal structures isomorphic to relations between things in the world. When we rap out routine undeliberated reports like "This is water," "That's red," "That's ugly," "That's immoral," our short categorical sentences can easily be thought of as pictures, or as symbols which fit together to make a map. Such reports do indeed pair little bits of language with little bits of the world. Once one gets to negative universal hypotheticals, and the like, such pairing will become messy and *ad hoc,* but perhaps it can be done. James's point was that carrying out this exercise will not enlighten us about why truths are good to believe, or offer any clues as to why or whether our present view of the world is, roughly, the one we should hold. Yet nobody would have asked for a "theory" of truth if they had not wanted answers to these latter questions. Those who want truth to have an essence want knowledge, or rationality, or inquiry, or the relation

between thought and its object, to have an essence. Further, they want to be able to use their knowledge of such essences to criticize views they take to be false, and to point the direction of progress toward the discovery of more truths. James thinks these hopes are vain. There are no essences anywhere in the area. There is no wholesale, epistemological way to direct, or criticize, or underwrite, the course of inquiry.

Rather, the pragmatists tell us, it is the vocabulary of practise rather than of theory, of action rather than contemplation, in which one can say something useful about truth. Nobody engages in epistemology or semantics because he wants to know how "This is red" pictures the world. Rather, we want to know in what sense Pasteur's views of disease picture the world accurately and Paracelsus' inaccurately, or what exactly it is that Marx pictured more accurately than Machiavelli. But just here the vocabulary of "picturing" fails us. When we turn from individual sentences to vocabularies and theories, critical terminology naturally shifts from metaphors of isomorphism, symbolism, and mapping to talk of utility, convenience, and likelihood of getting what we want. To say that the parts of properly analyzed true sentences are arranged in a way isomorphic to the parts of the world paired with them sounds plausible if one thinks of a sentence like "Jupiter has moons." It sounds slightly less plausible for "The earth goes round the sun," less still for "There is no such thing as natural motion," and not plausible at all for "The universe is infinite." When we want to praise or blame assertions of the latter sort of sentence, we show how the decision to assert them fits into a whole complex of decisions about what terminology to use, what books to read, what projects to engage in, what life to live. In this respect they resemble such sentences as "Love is the only law" and "History is the story of class struggle." The whole vocabulary of isomorphism, picturing, and mapping is out of place here, as indeed is the notion of being true *of objects*. If we ask what objects these sentences claim to be true of, we get only unhelpful repetitions of the subject terms— "the universe," "the law," "history." Or, even less helpfully, we get talk about "the facts," or "the way the world is." The natural approach to such sentences, Dewey tells us, is not "Do they get it right?", but more like "What would it be like to believe that? What would happen if I did? What would I be committing myself to?" The vocabulary of contemplation, looking, *theoria,* deserts us just when we deal with theory rather than observation, with programming rather than input. When the contemplative mind, isolated from the stimuli of the moment, takes large views, its activity is more like deciding what to *do* than deciding that a representation is accurate. James's dictum about truth says that the vocabulary of practice is unelimiinable, that no distinction of kind separates the sciences from the crafts, from moral reflection, or from art.

So a second characterization of pragmatism might go like this: there is no epistemological difference between truth about what ought to be and truth about what is, nor any metaphysical difference between facts and values, nor any methodological difference between morality and science. Even non-pragmatists think Plato was wrong to think of moral philosophy as discovering the essence of goodness, and Mill and Kant wrong in trying to reduce moral choice to rule. But every reason for saying that they were wrong is a reason for thinking the epistemological tradition wrong in looking for the essence of science, and in trying to reduce rationality to rule. For the pragmatists, the pattern of all inquiry–scientific as well as moral—is deliberation concerning the relative attractions of various concrete alternatives. The idea that in science or philosophy we can substitute "method" for deliberation between alternative results of speculation is just wishful thinking. It is like the idea that the morally wise man resolves his dilemmas by consulting his memory of the Idea of the Good, or by looking up the relevant article of the moral law. It is the myth that rationality consists in being constrained by rule. According to this Platonic myth, the life of reason is not the life of Socratic conversation but an illuminated state of consciousness in which one never needs to ask if one has exhausted the possible descriptions of, or explanations for, the situation. One simply arrives at true beliefs by obeying mechanical procedures.

Traditional, Platonic, epistemologically-centered philosophy is the search for such procedures. It is the search for a way in which one can avoid the need for conversation and deliberation and simply tick off the way things are. The idea is to acquire beliefs about interesting and important matters in a way as—much like visual perception as possible—by confronting an object and responding to it as programmed. This urge to substitute *theoria* for *phronesis* is what lies behind the attempt to say that "There is no such thing as natural motion" pictures objects in the same way as does "The cat is on the mat." It also lies behind the hope that some arrangement of objects may be found which is pictured by the sentence "Love is better than hate," and the frustration which ensues when it is realized that there may be no such objects. The great fallacy of the tradition, the pragmatists tell us, is to think that the metaphors of vision, correspondence, mapping, picturing, and representation which apply to small, routine assertions will apply to large and debatable ones. This basic error begets the notion that where there are no objects to correspond to we have no hope of rationality, but only taste, passion, and will. When the pragmatist attacks the notion of truth as accuracy of representation he is thus attacking the traditional distinctions between reason and desire, reason and appetite, reason and will. For none of these distinctions make sense unless reason is thought of on the model of vision, unless we persist in what Dewey called "the spectator theory of knowledge."

The pragmatist tells us that once we get rid of this model we see that the Platonic idea of the life of reason is impossible. A life spent representing objects accurately would be spent recording the results of calculations, reasoning through sorites, calling off the observable properties of things, construing cases according to unambiguous criteria, getting things right. Within what Kuhn calls "normal science," or any similar social context, one can, indeed, live such a life. But conformity to *social* norms is not good enough for the Platonist. He wants to be constrained not merely by the disciplines of the day, but by the ahistorical and nonhuman nature of reality itself. This impulse takes two forms—the original Platonic strategy of postulating novel *objects* for treasured propositions to correspond to, and the Kantian strategy of finding *principles* which are definatory of the essence of knowledge, or representation, or morality, or rationality. But this difference is unimportant compared to the common urge to escape the vocabulary and practices of one's own time and find something ahistorical and necessary to cling to. It is the urge to answer questions like "Why believe what I take to be true?" "Why do what I take to be right?" by appealing to something *more* than the ordinary, retail, detailed, concrete reasons which have brought one to one's present view. This urge is common to nineteenth-century idealists and contemporary scientific realists, to Russell and to Husserl; it is definatory of the Western philosophical tradition, and of the culture for which that tradition speaks. James and Dewey stand with Nietzsche and Heidegger in asking us to abandon that tradition, and that culture.

Let me sum up by offering a third and final characterization of pragmatism: it is the doctrine that there are no constraints on inquiry save conversational ones—no wholesale constraints derived from the nature of the objects, or of the mind, or of language, but only those retail constraints provided by the remarks of our fellow-inquirers. The way in which the properly-programmed speaker cannot help believing that the patch before him is red has *no* analogy for the more interesting and controversial beliefs which provoke epistemological reflection. The pragmatist tells us that it is useless to hope that objects will constrain us to believe the truth about them, if only they are approached with an unclouded mental eye, or a rigorous method, or a perspicuous language. He wants us to give up the notion that God, or evolution, or some other underwriter of our present world-picture, has programmed us as machines for accurate verbal picturing, and that philosophy brings self-knowledge by letting us read our own program. The only sense in which we are constrained to truth is that, as Peirce suggested, we can make no sense of the notion that the view which can survive all objections might be false. But objections—conversational constraints—cannot be anticipated. There is no method for knowing *when* one has reached the truth, or when one is closer to it than before.

I prefer this third way of characterizing pragmatism because it seems to me to focus on a fundamental choice which confronts the reflective mind: that between accepting the contingent character of starting-points, and attempting to evade this contingency. To accept the contingency of starting-points is to accept our inheritance from, and our conversation with, our fellow-humans as our only source of guidance. To attempt to evade this contingency is to hope to become a properly-programmed machine. This was the hope which Plato thought might be fulfilled at the top of the divided line, when we passed beyond hypotheses. Christians have hoped it might be attained by becoming attuned to the voice of God in the heart, and Cartesians that it might be fulfilled by emptying the mind and seeking the indubitable. Since Kant, philosophers have hoped that it might be fulfilled by finding the a priori structure of any possible inquiry, or language, or form of social life. If we give up this hope, we shall lose what Nietzsche called "metaphysical comfort," but we may gain a renewed sense of community. Our identification with our community—our society, our political tradition, our intellectual heritage—is heightened when we see this community as *ours* rather than *nature's*, *shaped* rather than *found*, one among many which men have made. In the end, the pragmatists tell us, what matters is our loyalty to other human beings clinging together against the dark, not our hope of getting things right. James, in arguing against realists and idealists that "the trail of the human serpent is over all," was reminding us that our glory is in our participation in fallible and transitory human projects, not in our obedience to permanent nonhuman constraints.

PART II. RELATIVISM

"Relativism" is the view that every belief on a certain topic, or perhaps about *any* topic, is as good as every other. No one holds this view. Except for the occasional cooperative freshman, one cannot find anybody who says that two incompatible opinions on an important topic are equally good. The philosophers who get *called* "relativists" are those who say that the grounds for choosing between such opinions are less algorithmic than had been thought. Thus one may be attacked as a relativist for holding that familiarity of terminology is a criterion of theory-choice in physical science, or that coherence with the institutions of the surviving parliamentary democracies is a criterion in social philosophy. When such criteria are invoked, critics say that the resulting philosophical position assumes an unjustified primacy for "our conceptual framework," or our purposes, or our institutions. The position in question is criticized for not having done what philosophers are employed to do: explain why our framework, or culture, or interests, or language, or whatever, is at last on the right track—in touch with physical reality, or the moral law, or the real numbers, or some other sort of object patiently waiting about to be copied. So the real issue is not between people who think one view as good as another and people who do not. It is between those who think our culture, or purpose, or intuitions cannot be supported except conversationally, and people who still hope for other sorts of support.

If there *were* any relativists, they would, of course, be easy to refute. One would merely use some variant of the self-referential arguments Socrates used against Protagoras. But such neat little dialectical strategies only work against lightly-sketched fictional characters. The relativist who says that we can break ties among serious and incompatible candidates for belief only by "nonrational" or "noncognitive" considerations is just one of the Platonist or Kantian philosopher's imaginary playmates, inhabiting the same realm of fantasy as the solipsist, the skeptic, and the moral nihilist. Disillusioned, or whimsical, Platonists and Kantians occasionally play at being one or another of these characters. But when they do they are never offering relativism or skepticism or nihilism as a serious suggestion about how we might do things differently. These positions are adopted to make *philosophical* points—that is, moves in a game played with fictitious opponents, rather than fellow-participants in a common project.

The association of pragmatism with relativism is a result of a confusion between the pragmatist's attitude toward *philosophical* theories with his attitude towards *real* theories. James and Dewey are, to be sure, metaphilosophical relativists, in a certain limited sense. Namely: they think there is no way to choose, and no point in choosing, between incompatible philosophical theories of the typical Platonic or Kantian type. Such theories are attempts to ground some element of our practices on something external to these practices. Pragmatists think that any such philosophical grounding is, apart from elegance of execution, pretty much as good or as bad as the practice it purports to ground. They regard the project of grounding as a wheel that plays no part in the mechanism. In this, I think, they are quite right. No sooner does one discover the categories of the pure understanding for a Newtonian age than somebody draws up another list that would do nicely for an Aristotelian or an Einsteinian one. No sooner does one draw up a categorical imperative for Christians than somebody draws up one which works for cannibals. No sooner does one develop an evolutionary epistemology which explains why our science is so good than somebody writes a science-fiction story about bug-eyed and monstrous evolutionary epistemologists praising bug-eyed and monstrous scientists for the survival value of their monstrous theories. The reason this game is so easy to play is that none of these philosophical theories have to do much hard work. The real work has been done by the scientists who developed the explanatory theories by patience and genius, or the societies which developed the moralities and institutions in struggle and pain. All the Platonic or Kantian philosopher does is to take the finished first-level product, jack it up a few levels of abstraction, invent a metaphysical or epistemological or semantical vocabulary into which to translate it, and announce that he has *grounded* it.

"Relativism" only seems to refer to a disturbing view, worthy of being refuted, if it concerns real theories, not just philosophical theories. Nobody really cares if there are incompatible alternative formulations of a categorical imperative, or incompatible sets of categories of the pure understanding. We do care about alternative, concrete, detailed cosmologies, or alternative concrete, detailed proposals for political change. When such an alternative is proposed, we debate it, not in terms of categories or principles but in terms of the various concrete advantages and disadvantages it has. The reason relativism is talked about so much among Platonic and Kantian philosophers is that they think being relativistic about philosophical theories—attempts to "ground" first-level theories—leads to being relativistic about the first-level theories themselves. If anyone really believed that the worth of a theory depends upon the worth of its philosophical grounding, then indeed they would be dubious about physics, or democracy, until relativism in respect to philosophical theories had been overcome. Fortunately, almost nobody believes anything of the sort.

What people do believe is that it would be good to hook up our views about democracy, mathematics, physics, God, and everything else, into a coherent story about how everything hangs together. Getting such a synoptic view often does require us to change radically our views on particular subjects. But this holistic process of readjustment is just muddling through on a large scale. It has nothing to do with the Platonic-Kantian notion of grounding. That notion involves finding constraints, demonstrating necessities, finding immutable principles to which to subordinate oneself. When it turns out that suggested constraints, necessities, and principles are as plentiful as blackberries, nothing changes except the attitude of the rest of culture towards the philosophers. Since the time of Kant, it has become more and more apparent to nonphilosophers that a really professional philosopher can supply a philosophical foundation for just about anything. This is one reason why philosophers have, in the course of our century, become increasingly isolated from the rest of culture. Our proposals to guarantee this and clarify that have come to strike our fellow-intellectuals as merely comic.

PART III. IRRATIONALISM

My discussion of relativism may seem to have ducked the real issues. Perhaps nobody is a relativist. Perhaps "relativism" is *not* the right name for what so many philosophers find so offensive in pragmatism. But surely there *is* an important issue around somewhere. There is indeed an issue, but it is not easily stated, nor easily made amenable to argument. I shall try to bring it into focus by developing it in two different contexts, one microcosmic and the other macrocosmic. The microcosmic issue concerns philosophy in one of its most parochial senses—namely, the activities of the American Philosophical Association. Our Association has traditionally been agitated by the question of whether we should be free-wheeling and edifying, or argumentative and professional. For my purposes, this boils down to an issue about whether we can be pragmatists and still be professionals. The macrocosmic issue concerns philosophy in the widest sense—the attempt to make everything hang together. This is

the issue between Socrates on the one hand and the tyrants on the other—the issue between lovers of conversation and lovers of self-deceptive rhetoric. For my purposes, it is the issue about whether we can be pragmatists without betraying Socrates, without falling into irrationalism.

I discuss the unimportant microcosmic issue about professionalism first because it is sometimes confused with the important issue about irrationalism, and because it helps focus that latter issue. The question of whether philosophy professors should edify agitated our Association in its early decades. James thought they should, and was dubious about the growing professionalization of the discipline. Arthur Lovejoy, the great opponent of pragmatism, saw professionalization as an unmixed blessing. Echoing what was being said simultaneously by Russell in England and by Husserl in Germany, Lovejoy urged the sixteenth annual meeting of the APA to aim at making philosophy into a science. He wanted the APA to organize its program into well-structured controversies on sharply defined problems, so that at the end of each convention it would be agreed who had won. Lovejoy insisted that philosophy could either be edifying and visionary *or* could produce "objective, verifiable, and clearly communicable truths," but not both. James would have agreed. He too thought that one could *not* be both a pragmatist and a professional. James, however, saw professionalization as a failure of nerve rather than as a triumph of rationality. He thought that the activity of making things hang together was *not* likely to produce "objective, verifiable, and clearly communicable truths," and that this did not greatly matter.

Lovejoy, of course, won this battle. If one shares his conviction that philosophers should be as much like scientists as possible, then one will be pleased at the outcome. If one does not, one will contemplate the APA in its seventy-sixth year mindful of Goethe's maxim that one should be careful what one wishes for when one is young, for one will get it when one is old. Which attitude one takes will depend upon whether one sees the problems we discuss today as permanent problems for human thought, continuous with those discussed by Plato, Kant, and Lovejoy—or as modern attempts to breathe life into dead issues. On the Lovejoyan account, the gap between philosophers and the rest of high culture is of the same sort as the gap between physicists and laymen. The gap is not created by the artificiality of the problems being discussed, but by the development of technical and precise ways of dealing with real problems. If one shares the pragmatists' anti-essentialism, however, one will tend to see the problems about which philosophers are now offering "objective, verifiable, and clearly communicable" solutions as historical relics, left over from the Enlightenment's misguided search for the hidden essences of knowledge and morality. This is the point of view adopted by many of our fellow-intellectuals, who see us philosophy professors as caught in a time-warp, trying to live the Enlightenment over again.

I have reminded you of the parochial issue about professionalization not in order to persuade you to one side or the other, but rather to exhibit the source of the anti-pragmatist's passion. This is his conviction that conversation necessarily aims at agreement and at rational consensus, that we converse in order to make further conversation unnecessary. The anti-pragmatist believes that conversation only makes sense if something like the Platonic theory of Recollection is right—if we all have natural starting-points of thought somewhere within us, and will recognize the vocabulary in which they are best formulated once we hear it. For only if something like that is true will conversation have a natural goal. The Enlightenment hoped to find such a vocabulary—nature's own vocabulary, so to speak. Lovejoy—who described himself as an "unredeemed *Aufklärer*"—wanted to continue the project. Only if we had agreement on such a vocabulary, indeed, could conversation be reduced to argumentation—to the search for "objective, verifiable, and clearly communicable" solutions to problems. So the anti-pragmatist sees the pragmatist's scorn for professionalism as scorn for consensus, for the Christian and democratic idea that every human has the seeds of truth within. The pragmatist's attitude seems to him elitist and dilettantish, reminiscent of Alcibiades rather than of Socrates.

Issues about relativism and about professionalization are awkward attempts to formulate this opposition. The real and passionate opposition is over the question of whether loyalty to our fellow-humans presupposes that there is something perma-

nent and unhistorical which explains *why* we should continue to converse in the manner of Socrates, something which guarantees convergence to agreement. Because the anti-pragmatist believes that without such an essence and such a guarantee the Socratic life makes no sense, he sees the pragmatist as a cynic. Thus the microcosmic issue about how philosophy professors should converse leads us quickly to the macrocosmic issue: whether one can be a pragmatist without being an irrationalist, without abandoning one's loyalty to Socrates.

Questions about irrationalism have become acute in our century because the sullen resentment which sins against Socrates, which withdraws from conversation and community, has recently become articulate. Our European intellectual tradition is now abused as "merely conceptual" or "merely ontic" or as "committed to abstractions." Irrationalists propose such rubbishy pseudo-epistemological notions as "intuition" or an "inarticulate sense" of tradition or "thinking with the blood" or "expressing the will of the oppressed classes." Our tyrants and bandits are more hateful than those of earlier times because, invoking such self-deceptive rhetoric, they pose as intellectuals. Our tyrants write philosophy in the morning and torture in the afternoon; our bandits alternately read Hölderlin and bomb people into bloody scraps. So our culture clings, more than ever, to the hope of the Enlightenment, the hope that drove Kant to make philosophy formal and rigorous and professional. We hope that by formulating the *right* conceptions of reason, of science, of thought, of knowledge, of morality, the conceptions which express their *essence*, we shall have a shield against irrationalist resentment and hatred. Pragmatists tell us that this hope is vain. On their view, the Socratic virtues—willingness to talk, to listen to other people, to weigh the consequences of our actions upon other people—are *simply* moral virtues. They cannot be inculcated nor fortified by theoretical research into essence. Irrationalists who tell us to think with our blood cannot be rebutted by better accounts of the nature of thought, or knowledge, or logic. The pragmatists tell us that the conversation which it is our moral duty to continue is *merely* our project, the European intellectual's form of life. It has no metaphysical nor epistemological guarantee of sucess. Further (and this is the crucial point) *we do not know what "success" would mean except simply "continuance."* We are not conversing because we have a goal, but because Socratic conversation is an activity which is its *own* end. The anti-pragmatist who insists that agreement is its goal is like the basketball player who thinks that the reason for playing the game is to make baskets. He mistakes an essential moment in the course of an activity for the end of the activity. Worse yet, he is like a basketball fan who argues that all men by nature desire to play basketball, or that the nature of things is such that balls can go through hoops.

For the traditional, Platonic or Kantian philosopher, on the other hand, the possibility of *grounding* the European form of life—of showing it to be more than European, more than a contingent human project—seems the central task of philosophy. He wants to show that sinning against Socrates is sinning against our nature, not just against our community. So he sees the pragmatist as an irrationalist. The charge that pragmatism is "relativistic" is simply his first unthinking expression of disgust at a teaching which seems cynical about our deepest hopes. If the traditional philosopher gets beyond such epithets, however, he raises a question which the pragmatist must face up to: the *practical* question of whether the notion of "conversation" *can* substitute for that of "reason." "Reason," as the term is used in the Platonic and Kantian traditions, is interlocked with the notions of truth as correspondence, of knowledge as discovery of essence, of morality as obedience to principle, all the notions which the pragmatist tries to deconstruct. For better or worse, the Platonic and Kantian vocabularies are the ones in which Europe has described and praised the Socratic virtues. It is not clear that we know how to describe these virtues without those vocabularies. So the deep suspicion which the pragmatist inspires is that, like Alcibiades, he is essentially frivolous—that he is commending uncontroversial common goods while refusing to participate in the only activity which can preserve those goods. He seems to be sacrificing our common European project to the delights of purely negative criticism.

The issue about irrationalism can be sharpened by noting that when the pragmatist says "All that can be done to explicate 'truth', 'knowledge', 'morality', 'virtue' is to refer us back to the concrete details

of the culture in which these terms grew up and developed," the defender of the Enlightenment takes him to be saying "Truth and virtue are simply what a community agrees that they are." When the pragmatist says "We have to take truth and virtue as whatever emerges from the conversation of Europe," the traditional philosopher wants to know what is so special about Europe. Isn't the pragmatist saying, like the irrationalist, that *we* are in a privileged situation simply by being *us*? Further, isn't there something terribly dangerous about the notion that truth can only be characterized as "the outcome of doing more of what we are doing now" ? What if the "we" is the Orwellian state? When tyrants employ Lenin's blood-curdling sense of "objective" to describe their lies as "objectively true," what is to prevent them from citing Peirce in Lenin's defense?

The pragmatist's first line of defense against this criticism has been created by Habermas, who says that such a definition of truth works only for the outcome of *undistorted* conversation, and that the Orwellian state is the paradigm of distortion. But this is *only* a first line, for we need to know more about what counts as "undistorted." Here Habermas goes transcendental and offers principles. The pragmatist, however, must remain ethnocentric and offer examples. He can only say: "undistorted" means employing *our* criteria of relevance, where *we* are the people who have read and pondered Plato, Newton, Kant, Marx, Darwin, Freud, Dewey, etc. Milton's "free and open encounter," in which truth is bound to prevail, must itself be described in terms of examples rather than principles—it is to be more like the Athenian market-place than the council-chamber of the Great King, more like the twentieth century than the twelfth, more like the Prussian Academy in 1925 than in 1935. The pragmatist must avoid saying, with Peirce, that truth is *fated* to win. He must even avoid saying that truth *will* win. He can only say, with Hegel, that truth and justice lie in the direction marked by the successive stages of European thought. This is not because he knows some "necessary truths" and cites these examples as a result of this knowledge. It is simply that the pragmatist knows no better way to explain his convictions than to remind his interlocutor of the position they both are in, the contingent starting points they both share, the floating, ungrounded conversations of which they are both members. This means that the pragmatist cannot answer the question "What is so special about Europe?" save by saying "Do you have anything non-European to suggest which meets *our* European purposes better?" He cannot answer the question 'What is so good about the Socratic virtues, about Miltonic free encounters, about undistorted communication?" save by saying "What else would better fulfill the purposes *we* share with Socrates, Milton, and Habermas?"

To decide whether this obviously circular response is enough is to decide whether Hegel or Plato had the proper picture of the progress of thought. Pragmatists follow Hegel in saying that "philosophy is its time grasped in thought." Anti-pragmatists follow Plato in striving for an escape from conversation to something atemporal which lies in the background of all possible conversations. I do not think one can decide between Hegel and Plato save by meditating on the past efforts of the philosophical tradition to escape from time and history. One can see these efforts as worthwhile, getting better, worth continuing. Or one can see them as doomed and perverse. I do not know what would count as a noncircular metaphysical or epistemological or semantical argument for seeing them in either way. So I think that the decision has to be made simply by reading the history of philosophy and drawing a moral.

Nothing that I have said, therefore, is an argument in favor of pragmatism. At best, I have merely answered various superficial criticisms which have been made of it. Nor have I dealt with the central issue about irrationalism. I have not answered the deep criticism of pragmatism which I mentioned a few minutes ago: the criticism that the Socratic virtues cannot, as a practical matter, be defended save by Platonic means, that without some sort of metaphysical comfort nobody will be able *not* to sin against Socrates. William James himself was not sure whether this criticism could be answered. Exercising his own right to believe, James wrote: "If this life be not a real fight in which something is eternally gained for the universe by success, it is no better than a game of private theatricals from which we may withdraw at will." "It *feels*," he said, "like a fight."

For us, footnotes to Plato that we are, it *does* feel that way. But if James's own pragmatism were taken seriously, if pragmatism became central to our culture and our self-image, then it would no longer feel that way. We do not know how it would feel. We do not even know whether, given such a change in tone, the conversation of Europe might not falter and die away. We just do not know. James and Dewey offered us no guarantees. They simply pointed to the situation we stand in, now that both the Age of Faith and the Enlightenment seem beyond recovery. They grasped our time in thought. We did not change the course of the conversation in the way they suggested we might. Perhaps we are still unable to do so; perhaps we never shall be able to. But we can nevertheless honor James and Dewey for having offered what very few philosophers have succeeded in giving us: a hint of how our lives might be changed.

RICHARD FOLEY

What Am I to Believe?

The central issue of Descartes's *Meditations* is an intensely personal one. Descartes asks a simple question of himself, one that each of us can also ask of ourselves, "What am I to believe?" One way of construing this question—indeed, the way Descartes himself construed it—is as a methodological one. The immediate aim is not so much to generate a specific list of propositions for me to believe. Rather, I want to formulate for myself some general advice about how to proceed intellectually.

If this is what I want, I am not likely to be content with telling myself that I am to use reliable methods of inquiry. Nor will I be content with telling myself to believe only that which is likely to be true given my evidence. It is not as if such advice is mistaken. It is just unhelpful. I knew all along that it is better for me to use reliable methods rather than unreliable ones, and I also knew that it is better for me to believe that which is likely to be true rather than that which is not. Besides, I cannot simply read off from the world what methods are reliable ones, nor can I read off when something is likely to be true given my evidence. These are just the sorts of things about which I want advice.

An appeal to the prevailing intellectual standards will not provide what I am looking for either. I will not be satisfied with a recommendation that tells me to conduct my inquiries in accordance with the standards of my community, or alternatively in accordance with the standards of those recognized in my community as experts. I will want to know whether these standards are desirable ones. The dominant standards in a community are not always to be trusted and those of the recognized experts are not either.

My question is a more fundamental one and also a more egocentric one. It is not that I think that the task of working out intellectual guidelines is one that is best conducted by myself in solitude. If I do think this, I am being foolish. A task of this sort is better

done in full public view, with results being shared. This increases the chances of correction and decreases the chances of self-deception. In the end, however, I must make up my own mind. I must make up my own mind about what is true and who is reliable and what is worth respecting in my intellectual tradition. It is this that prompts the question, what am I to believe? The question is one of how I am to go about making up my own mind.

Here is one way of answering this question: I am to make up my mind by marshalling my intellectual resources in a way that conforms to my own deepest epistemic standards. If I conduct my inquiries in such a way that I would not be critical of the resulting beliefs even if I were to be deeply reflective, then these beliefs are rational for me in an important sense, an egocentric sense. There are various ways of trying to spell out exactly what this amounts to, but for purposes here the details can be left open. The basic idea is that if I am to be egocentrically rational, I must not have internal reasons for retraction, ones whose force I myself would acknowledge were I to be sufficiently reflective.

An answer of this sort has the right egocentric flavor, but as advice it is not very satisfying. It seems misdirected. When I am trying to formulate some intellectual advice for myself, or more generally when I am deliberating about what to believe and how to proceed intellectually, my concern is not with my own standards. The point of my deliberations is not to find out what I think or would think on deep reflection about the reliability of various methods. My concern is with what methods are in fact reliable; it is with the objective realities, not my subjective perceptions.

Be this as it may, the recommendation that I conform to my own standards is an appropriate answer to the egocentric question, "What am I to believe?" More precisely, it is an appropriate answer if the question is interpreted as one about what I am to believe insofar as my ends are epistemic. Even more precisely, it is an appropriate philosophical answer to this question, the one that should be given if the question is pushed to its limit. The reflection prompted by the egocentric question initially has an outward focus. The object of my concern is the world. I wonder whether this or that is true. If pushed hard enough, however, the reflection ultimately curls back upon me. I become concerned with my place in the world, especially my place as an inquirer. I want to know what methods of inquiry are suitable for me insofar as I am trying to determine whether this or that is true. Should I trust the evidence of my senses? Should I use scientific methods? Should I rely on sacred texts? Should I have confidence in my intuitions?

These questions can lead to still others. They can make me wonder about the criteria that I am presupposing in evaluating various methods. Meta-issues thus begin to occupy me. My primary concern is no longer with whether it would be more reliable for me to use this method rather than that one. Nor is it with what each would have me believe. Rather, it is with my criteria for evaluating these various methods and in turn with the criteria for these criteria, and so on. This is the point at which the egocentric question can be appropriately answered by talking about me. What am I to believe? Ultimately, I am to believe that which is licensed by my own deepest epistemic standards. An answer of this sort is the appropriate one for epistemologists. It is the appropriate answer for those whose reflections on the egocentric question take them to this level.

Insofar as nonepistemologists raise the question of what they are to believe, they are principally interested in a different kind of answer. They want an answer that gives them marks of truth and reliability. Epistemologists also want such marks, but once their deliberations reach the metalevel that is characteristic of epistemology, they are forced to admit that regardless of how they marshal their intellectual resources, there are no non-question-begging guarantees that the way that they are marshalling them is reliable. Vulnerability to error cannot be avoided. It is built into us and our methods. However, vulnerability to self-condemnation is not, and it is essentially this that egocentric rational-

ity demands. It demands that we have beliefs that we as truth-seekers would not condemn ourselves for having even if we were to be deeply reflective. This is the post-Cartesian answer to the Cartesian question.

It is also an answer that is bound to be disappointing to anyone who thinks that an essential part of the epistemologist's job is to provide intellectual guidance. Much of the attractiveness of the Cartesian method of doubt is that it purports to do just this. It purports to provide us with a way of proceeding intellectually, and a concrete one at that. The proposed method tends to strike the contemporary reader as overly demanding, but it would nonetheless seem to be to Descartes's credit, indeed part of his greatness, that he at least attempted to provide such guidance. Contemporary epistemology is apt to seem barren by comparison. Concrete intellectual advice has all but disappeared from it. Of course, no one expects epistemologists to provide advice about local intellectual concerns. The specialist is better placed to give us that—the physicist, the mathematician, the meteorologist, whoever the relevant expert happens to be. What we might like from epistemologists, however, is useful advice about the most basic matters of intellectual inquiry, but it is just this that contemporary epistemology fails to provide.

This is to be regretted only if epistemologists are in a privileged position to give such advice, but they are not. They may be in a privileged position to say something about the general conditions of rational belief. Likewise, they may be able to say interesting things about the conditions of knowledge and other related notions. The mistake is to assume that these conditions should provide us with useful guidelines for the most basic matters of intellectual inquiry. They cannot. The conditions will either be misdirected or not fundamental enough or both.

Consider the proposal that at least in one sense, being rational is essentially a matter of using methods that are reliable. Perhaps this is so, but if a proposal of this sort is meant to provide me with intellectual guidance, I must be able to distinguish reliable from unreliable methods. However, this is precisely one of the matters about which I will want advice. It is also a matter about which epistemologists are not in a privileged position to give advice, except indirectly. They may have useful and even surprising things to say about what reliability is, but once these things are said, it will be up to the rest of us to apply what they say. We will have to determine what methods and procedures are in fact reliable. So, no condition of this sort will be able to provide me with fundamental intellectual advice. On the contrary, if such conditions are to help guide inquiry, I must already be able to make the kind of determinations that they themselves imply are fundamental for me to make if I am to be rational. I reliably must be able to pick out which methods are reliable.

The same is true of other proposals. One proposal, for instance, is that I am rational only if I conform to the standards of the acknowledged experts. If I am to use this to guide inquiry, I once again must be able to make determinations of just the sort that are said to be fundamental to my being rational. How am I to determine what the relevant expert standards are? Presumably by conducting an inquiry that itself conforms to the standards of the experts. But which standards are these, I want to know.

Suppose that the proposal is more inwardly looking. In particular, consider the proposal that it is rational in an important sense, an egocentric sense, for me to believe only that which I would not be motivated to retract even on deep reflection. If what I want is advice, this proposal is a non-starter. It is misdirected. Besides, I do not have the time to be deeply reflective about everything that I believe. So, even here I would be confronted with the problem of knowing how to apply the recommendation. How am I to determine whether my practices and my resulting beliefs conform with my own deep epistemic standards, the ones that I would approve of on reflection? Presumably by conforming to those very standards. But what I want to know, and what is often by no means obvious, is how I am to do this, short of being deeply reflective about all of these practices and beliefs?

The only way to avoid problems of this sort is to make the conditions of rationality ones to which we have immediate and unproblematic access. But this has a familiar and unpromising ring to it. Recall Bertrand Russell's epistemology, for example. He claimed that we are directly acquainted with certain truths and that these truths make various other propositions probable for us. If this kind of episte-mology is to provide us with fundamental intellectual advice, we must be capable of determining immediately and unproblematically when we are directly acquainted with something and when we are not. Likewise, we must be capable of determining immediately and unproblematically what propositions are made probable by the truths with which we are directly acquainted. Otherwise we will want advice about how to make these kinds of determinations. Russell's epistemology leaves room for the possibility that we do have these capabilities. Being directly acquainted with something is itself the sort of phenomenon with which we can be directly acquainted. Similarly, according to Russell's epistemology, we can be directly acquainted with the truth that one thing makes another thing probable.

An epistemology of direct acquaintance or something closely resembling it is our only alternative if we expect the conditions of rationality to give us useful advice about those matters that the conditions themselves imply are fundamental to our being rational. It is also the kind of epistemology that few are willing to take seriously anymore. But if not, we must give up the idea that epistemology is in the business of giving fundamental intellectual advice. For that matter, we must give up the whole idea that there is such advice to be had. There can be no general recipe for the conduct of our intellectual lives, if for no other reason than that questions can always arise about how to follow the recipe, questions to which the recipe itself can give no useful answer.

By contrast, consider the kind of advice that logic professors sometimes give their students. They sometimes tell them to try to solve difficult proofs from "both ends," working alternatively down from the premises and up from the desired conclusion. This is advice that is often useful for students, but it is also advice that has no pretenses of being about the most fundamental issues of inquiry. It is not even about the most fundamental matters of logical inference. This is no accident. It is useful precisely because it is embedded in a prior intellectual enterprise, one in which certain skills and abilities are taken for granted.

This is an obvious enough point once it is made explicit, but it is nonetheless a point that is easy enough to overlook. It is overlooked, for instance, by those internalists who argue against externalist conditions of rational belief on the grounds that they are unhelpful insofar as we are interested in advice about how to go about improving our belief systems. As a complaint against externalism, this will not do, but not because externalist conditions of rational belief provide us with useful advice. They do not. It is not especially useful to be told that we are to have beliefs that are products of reliable cognitive processes, for example. The problem, rather, is that internalist conditions of rational belief do not provide us with genuinely useful advice either.

Of course, internalists have often thought otherwise. One of Descartes's conceits, for example, was that the method of doubt provides advice to inquirers that is at once both useful and fundamental. By this I do not mean that Descartes intended his method to be used by everyone, even the fishmonger and the butcher. He did not. He intended it to be used only by philosopher-scientists, and he intended that even they use it only for a special purpose. It was not to be used in their everyday lives. It was to be used only for the purpose of conducting secure theoretical inquiry. However, the method was intended to provide advice at the most fundamental level about how to conduct such inquiry.

But, in fact, it fails to do this. It faces the same difficulties as other attempts to give intellectual advice that is both fundamental and useful. Either it presupposes that philosopher-scientists can make determinations of a sort that the recommendation itself says is fundamental or it is misdirected advice or perhaps both. Which of these difficulties Descartes's advice is subject to depends on how we understand it.

Suppose the advice is for philosopher-scientists to believe just those propositions whose truth they cannot doubt when they bring them clearly to mind. Then the advice faces both difficulties. First, it is not fundamental enough. It need not be immediately obvious to philosopher-scientists just what is indubitable for them in this sense and what is not. They thus can have questions about that which the advice says is fundamental to their being rational, and these will be questions that the advice cannot help them answer. Second, the advice is misdirected. It is advice that looks inward rather than outward. Insofar as the goal of philosopher-scientists is to conduct theoretical inquiry in an absolutely secure

manner, their interest is to find propositions that cannot be false rather than ones that cannot be doubted. Of course, Descartes thought that there was a linkage between the two. He thought that what cannot be subjectively doubted cannot be objectively false, but there is no reason to think that he was right about this.

Suppose, then, that we interpret Descartes as offering more objective advice. He is telling philosopher-scientists to believe just those propositions that are clear and distinct for them, and he is stipulating from the very beginning that only truths can be genuinely clear and distinct. Then this exacerbates the first difficulty. If philosopher-scientists try to take the advice to heart, the question of whether something really is clear and distinct in this sense becomes one of the fundamental issues about which they will want advice.

So, contrary to his hopes, Descartes did not succeed in providing advice that is both useful and fundamental. More precisely, he did not succeed in providing advice about the conduct of inquiry as opposed to its goals. For despite the above difficulties, we can still view Descartes as making a recommendation about what our intellectual goal should be. He is advising us to make certainty our goal, at least for theoretical purposes. We should try to believe as much as possible without encountering the risk of error. Of course, even this is advice that few of us would be willing to take seriously. The goal is far too demanding. Almost all of us are willing to put up with some risks of error in our theoretical pursuits.

But the important point here is that even if I did have this as my intellectual goal, Descartes has no good, substantive advice for me about how to achieve it. The advice he gives is either misdirected or not fundamental enough. If the advice is to believe what is clear and distinct, where by definition only truths are clear and distinct, it is not fundamental enough. If the advice is to believe what I cannot doubt, it is misdirected. At best, it is a piece of meta-advice. Indeed, when stripped of its spurious guarantees of truth, the advice amounts only to this: insofar as my goal is to believe as much as possible without risk, then from my perspective the way to go about trying to achieve this goal is to believe just that which strikes me as being risk-free and then hope for the best.

This is a sensible enough recommendation but also an altogether safe one. After all, someone can give me this kind of advice even if she has no convictions one way or the other about whether or not I am constituted in such a way that what I find impossible to doubt is in fact true. It is not much different from telling me to do what I think is best about the problem I have confided to her, even when she has no idea whether what I think best really is best.

Of course, if she were presumptuous enough, she could go on to advise me about what I myself deep-down really think is the best way to deal with the problem. Indeed, this would be the counterpart of Descartes's strategy. He first recommends that I believe just those propositions that I cannot doubt, and he then tries to tell me, albeit with a notorious lack of success, which propositions these are. On the other hand, if she is not in this way presumptuous, if she simply tells me to do what I think is best and then leave matters at that, this is not so much genuine advice as a substitute for it. She is not trying to tell me what is best for me. She leaves this to me to figure out for myself.

The recommendation that I have beliefs that I as a truth-seeker would not condemn myself for having, even if I were to be deeply reflective, has a similar status. This recommendation is internalistic in character, since it emphasizes matters of perspective. But insofar as it is conceived as a piece of advice, it is at best meta-advice. If it were interpreted as an attempt to provide me with something more than this—if it were interpreted, for example, as an attempt to provide me with serious, substantive intellectual guidance—it would be clearly inadequate. So, this cannot be the charitable way to interpret it. It must instead be conceived as a different kind of recommendation.

What kind of recommendation? It is a recommendation about the conditions of rational belief-more exactly, the conditions for a certain kind of rational belief, egocentrically rational belief. The goal is to provide a notion of rational belief that is both enlightening and recognizable: enlightening in that it helps us think more clearly about related notions—truth, knowledge, skepticism, dogmatism, and intellectual disagreement, to name a few; and recognizable in that it helps us to understand the

ascriptions of rationality that we want to make, both the ones we are inclined to make in our everyday lives and also the ones we are inclined to make when doing epistemology.

This conception takes epistemology, even internalist epistemology, out of the business of giving intellectual advice. The primary epistemological project is to offer an account of the conditions of rational belief, and there is no reason why this project must generate useful advice. Indeed, epistemology is not even the part of philosophy that is most closely tied to the giving of intellectual advice. Studies in logic and probability are more likely to generate useful advice than is epistemology proper. But even here, expectations should not be too high. Nothing extensive in the way of advice will come out of these studies either.

In part, this is so because logic and probability theory do not tell how to react when we discover logical inconsistency and probabilistic incoherence. There will be any number of ways for us to restore consistency or coherency. Similarly, when inconsistency or incoherency threatens, there will be any number of ways for us to avoid them. In neither case does logic or probability theory have anything to tell us about which of these many ways is preferable.

So, there will not be much in the way of concrete positive advice that can come out of either logic or probability theory. In addition, there are limits even to the usefulness of the negative advice they are able to generate. Part of this is because of a familiar problem. Insofar as the advice is always to avoid inconsistency and incoherency, this is often difficult advice to follow. To do so, we need to be able to determine whether or not a set of opinions is inconsistent or incoherent, but the original advice cannot help with this. For help with this problem, we will need new advice—in effect, advice about how to apply the original advice.

Moreover, there is an even more basic limitation on this advice. It is not always good advice. It is not always and everywhere desirable to avoid inconsistency and incoherency. Doing so might make my overall situation worse. It might even make it intellectually worse. If I recognize that my opinions are inconsistent or incoherent, I know that they cannot possibly all be accurate. So, I know that my opinions are less than ideal. But from this it does not immediately follow that it is irrational for me to have these opinions. What is rational for me in such situations depends upon what realistic alternatives I have. In betting situations, it is often rational to adopt a strategy that I know in advance is less than ideal, one in which I am sure to lose at least some of my bets. Moreover, this can be rational even when there are available to me other strategies that hold out at least some possibility of a flawless outcome. These other strategies may be unduly daring or unduly cautious. The same is true of beliefs. Sometimes it is rational for me to have beliefs that I know cannot possibly all be accurate. Indeed, this is the real lesson of the lottery, the preface, and other such paradoxes.

None of this is to say that logic and probability theory do not have a special role to play in intellectual guidance. They obviously do. Logical inconsistency and probabilistic incoherence indicate that my opinions are less than ideal. They thus put me on guard about these opinions. What they do not tell me is how to react to this situation. From the fact that my opinions are less than ideal, it does not automatically follow that I must on pains of irrationality change any of these opinions. And even in those cases where I do have to change something, nothing in logic or probability theory tells me which opinions to change. They give me no concrete advice about this.

Of course, things are different when it is issues of logic and probability theory that are themselves being debated. Similarly, they are different when other specifically philosophical issues are being debated. The relevant philosophical experts will then be in a special position to give me substantive advice. But when it is not philosophical matters that are at issue, advice will have to come from other sources. Fortunately, there is no shortage of such sources. Most are relatively specific in nature. I am confronted with an intellectual problem. So, I go to an expert on the topic in question or consult a reference work or perhaps simply ask a knowledgeable friend.

There are also sources that hold out the hope of more general advice, and it is no accident that among the richest of these are ones in which philosophers have become more and more interested—cognitive science and the history of science. Of course, there are other philosophical motives for interest in these fields. Nevertheless, there is a story to be told here, one whose rough outlines are that as it became increasingly obvious that epistemology could not be expected to give fundamental intellectual advice, philosophers became increasingly interested in empirical disciplines that had human intellectual inquiry as part of their subject matter.

It is not as if these disciplines can be expected to provide the kind of fundamental advice that epistemology fails to provide. If this were their aim, they would encounter all the familiar problems. There would be problems of how to apply the advice, for example. But with these disciplines, unlike epistemology, there is not even a pretense of their being able to provide fundamental advice. This is so not just because we can have questions about the way inquiry is conducted within these disciplines themselves, although this is true enough. It is also because the kind of information that these disciplines are in a position to provide will itself call for interpretation. The fact that scientists have historically used procedures of a certain kind or the fact that we are disposed to make inferences of a certain kind are themselves facts that need to be evaluated before they can provide us with intellectual advice. We will especially want to know whether these procedures and inferences are reliable ones. But to answer this question, we will need to appeal to something more than the history of science and cognitive science.

On the other hand, if what we seek is not advice about the most fundamental matters of inquiry but rather some useful rules of thumb, these disciplines can be of help. At their best, they are able to provide a rich supply of data from which, with persistence and with the help of still other disciplines, we may be able to tease out some useful advice.

Sometimes it may not even take much teasing, especially for negative advice. Recent cognitive science is filled with studies that purport to show recurrent patterns of error in the way that we make inferences. The errors arise, for example, from an insensitivity to sample size or an under-utilization of known prior probabilities in making predictions or an inclination in certain kinds of situations to assign a higher probability to a conjunction than one of its conjuncts. These are data from which we can fashion intellectual advice for ourselves—advice that alerts us about our tendency to make these kinds of errors.

Extracting intellectual advice from the history of science is seldom so straightforward a matter, but it, too, can provide us with useful data. It does so in part because historical examples are less easily manipulable than purely hypothetical ones. This is not to say that dreamed-up examples cannot instruct. They obviously can, and indeed they are often more convenient, since they are more neat than real life examples. They can be designed to our purposes, with extraneous features deleted. But, of course, this is just the danger as well. It is sometimes all too easy to tailor them to suit our purposes. Actual cases in all of their detail are not so malleable.

Suppose, then, that I have looked at the history of science and at the findings of cognitive science and at various other studies that provide data, about human inquiry. So, I now have all this data. How am I to go about using the data to generate some rules of thumb for the conduct of inquiry? Sometimes it will be obvious, since sometimes the data will reveal that I have a tendency to make what I myself readily concede to be errors. But matters will not always be so obvious, and besides, I want positive as well negative advice. Is there any general advice to be had about this, the process of using the available data to generate intellectual advice?

Those who have been influenced by contemporary moral theory might advise me to employ something akin to the method of wide reflective equilibrium. The rough idea would be that I am to begin with my initial intuitions about what constitute sound methods of inquiry. Then I am to test these intuitions against all the data and all the cases that strike me as relevant—data from cognitive science about characteristic patterns of inference, cases from the history of science, imaginary cases, and anything else that I take to be relevant. Finally, I am to use my best judgment to resolve any conflicts among these intuitions, data, and cases. Sometimes I will judge that my original intuitions are sound. Other times the data or the cases will convince me to alter the original intuitions, and still other times I will be disposed to alter both by a process of give-and-take.

The problem with this recommendation is the familiar one. It is not so much mistaken as unhelpful. At best, it is meta-advice. Indeed, it is essentially the same meta-advice that is implicit in the notion of egocentric rationality. It tells me essentially this: take into account all the data that I think to be relevant and then reflect on the data, solving conflicts in the way that I judge best. On the other hand, it does not tell me what kinds of data are relevant, nor does it tell me what is the best way to resolve conflicts among the data. It leaves me to muck about on these questions as best I can.

And muck I must, for this is part of the human intellectual predicament. It is not that there is no useful intellectual advice to be had. There obviously is. It is just that philosophy is not in a particularly privileged position to provide it. The kind of intellectual advice that philosophy has been sometimes thought to be in a privileged position to give—viz., general advice about the most fundamental issues of intellectual inquiry—is precisely the kind of advice that cannot be usefully given. Attempts to provide this kind of advice are inevitably misdirected or not sufficiently fundamental.

On the other hand, philosophy in general and epistemology in particular has no special claim on more modest kinds of advice—e.g., specific advice on local intellectual concerns or general rules of thumb about the conduct of inquiry. The relevant expert is better positioned for the former, while the latter is best produced by reflection upon all of the available data. We can potentially use anything to fashion intellectual rules of thumb, from the findings of cognitive science to studies in the history of science to mnemonic devices and other intellectual tricks, even relatively trivial ones, such as carrying nines, for example.

This is a project to which philosophers can make important and diverse contributions. They can help us to appreciate that there are various ends at which inquiry might be aimed, for example. Some of these ends are epistemic in nature, in that they are concerned with the accuracy and comprehensiveness of our belief systems. Others are more pragmatic. Moreover, there are distinctions to be made even among those ends that are epistemic. Some are synchronic (roughly, getting things as right as we can for the moment), while others are diachronic (roughly, getting things right eventually). Such distinctions can be important when we are trying to provide ourselves with intellectual advice, since certain kinds of recommendations—for example, the recommendation that we prefer the simplest of otherwise equal hypotheses—will seem plausible relative to some of these aims and not so plausible relative to others.

There is much else of relevance that philosophers can tell us. They can tell us what it is to have an explanation of something, or what it is to have a merely verbal disagreement as opposed to a substantive one. They can distinguish different sorts of arguments for us, emphasizing that different criteria are appropriate for evaluating these arguments. More generally, they can act as intellectual gadflies, examining and criticizing the developments in other intellectual disciplines. And of course, they can also try to describe the conditions under which inquiry is conducted rationally, only these conditions will not be of a sort that provides us with much useful intellectual guidance.

There are those who will insist that this will not do. They will insist that one of our most important intellectual projects is that of generating sound intellectual advice and that we need guidance about how to conduct this project. There are better and worse ways of doing so, and it is epistemology's special role to instruct us about this. Nothing else is positioned to do so. Science, for example, cannot do so, since what we need is advice that is prior to inquiry rather than the result of inquiry. It is only epistemology that can provide us with this kind of fundamental guidance.

This is a view that sees epistemology as the arbiter of intellectual procedures. The presupposition is that epistemology can be prior to other inquiries and that as such it is capable of providing us with a non-question-begging rationale for using one set of intellectual procedures rather than another. Just the reverse is true. Epistemology begins at a late stage of inquiry. It builds on preexisting inquiry and without that inquiry it would be subjectless. One consequence of this is that there is no alternative to using antecedent opinion and methods in thinking about our intellectual procedures. There is no way of doing epistemology *ex nihilo*, and hence it is no more capable of giving us non-question-begging advice about basic issues of intellectual procedure than is anything else.

There is deeper presupposition that also must be abandoned, the presupposition that it is important for us to have such advice. Descartes and the Enlightenment figures who followed him—Locke, for example—thought that this was important,

since they thought that the alternative was intellectual anarchy, and perhaps as a result religious and political anarchy as well. Their assumptions seemed to be that there are countless ways of proceeding intellectually, that we are pretty much free to choose among them as we please, and that there must be a non-question-begging rationale for preferring one of these ways over the others if intellectual chaos is to be avoided. Descartes and Locke saw it as their task, the task of the epistemologist, to provide such a rationale.

If this were an accurate description of our intellectual situation, they might have been right. But in fact, this is not our situation. It is not as if we are each given a menu of basic intellectual procedures and that our task is either to find a non-question-begging way of choosing among these procedures or to face intellectual anarchy. Our problem tends to be the opposite one. By the time we reach the point at which it occurs to us that there might be fundamentally different kinds of intellectual procedures, we are largely shaped intellectually. We come to this point equipped not only with a battery of assumptions about the world but also a battery of intellectual skills and habits. All of our intellectual inquiries are grounded in these resources, and the bulk of our intellectual lives must be conducted using them in largely automatic fashion. We have no choice about this. Fundamental rules for the direction of the mind would do us little good even if we had them. We would not have the time or resources to make proper use of them. Insofar as our goal is intellectual improvement, the emphasis is better placed on the development of skills and habits that we think will help make us more reliable inquirers.

The project of building up such skills and habits lacks the drama of the Cartesian project. It is inevitably a piecemeal project. To engage in it, we must draw upon an enormous number of background assumptions, skills, and habits, ones that for the time being we are content to use rather than reform. Questions can still arise about this background. We may realize that had we been born with significantly different cognitive equipment or into a significantly different environment, these assumptions, skills, and habits might have been considerably different. These possibilities are mainly of theoretical interest, however. They are of interest for epistemology. They can be used to discuss skeptical worries, for instance. On the other hand, they normally will not be of much interest insofar as our purpose is epistemic improvement. After all, most of these fundamentally different ways of proceeding will not be real options for us. It is not as if we are radically free to reconstitute ourselves intellectually in any way that we see fit and that we need some guidance about whether to do so or how to do so.

Of course, we are not entirely without options. We cannot alter our fundamental intellectual procedures by a simple act of will, but by making incremental changes over a long enough period of time, we perhaps could train ourselves to use procedures that are very different from those that we currently employ. Perhaps there are even ways of bringing about the changes more immediately. Drugs might do the trick, for instance. There are those who have recommended peyote or LSD as a way to truth. But even here, insofar as our worry is intellectual chaos, the search need not be for a non-question-begging way of deciding which procedures, our present ones or the drug-induced ones, are the more reliable. It is enough to point out that from our present undrugged perspective, most of us have no reason to think that the drugged perspective is the more reliable one. Quite the contrary, from our current perspective it seems far less reliable. Thus, insofar as our ends are epistemic, we have no motivation to drug ourselves.

Descartes and Locke notwithstanding, our primary intellectual threat is not that of chaos, and our primary intellectual need is not for advice about the most fundamental matters of intellectual outlook. We cannot help but be largely guided by our intellectual inheritance on these matters. The primary threat is rather that of intellectual conformity, and our primary need is for intellectual autonomy. Little in life is more difficult than resisting domination by one's intellectual environment. It is all too easy for us to be intellectual lemmings. We do not have the ability to cast off wholesale the effects of our environment and adopt a radically new intellectual outlook, so this cannot be the basis of our intellectual autonomy. It is instead based upon our ability to use our existing opinions arid existing methods to examine our opinions and methods. It resides in our ability to make ourselves into an object of study, to evaluate and monitor ourselves, and moreover to do so not so much in terms of the prevailing standards but rather in terms of our own standards. This ability creates a space for intellectual autonomy.

But it is only a space. Self-monitoring in terms of our own personal standards does not altogether eliminate the threat of intellectual domination. As Foucault emphasized recently and as Marx had argued earlier, the most effective kind of control is that which is internalized. We accept as our own the very norms by which we are controlled. Be this as it may, our only alternative is to monitor ourselves for this as well, to try as best we can to make ourselves aware of this possibility and thus prevent it. Of course, there is no guarantee that we will be successful. If the domination is thorough enough, leaving no trace of its influence, then no amount of self-monitoring will do much good.

But in this respect, the possibility of complete and utter domination is not much different from the possibility of complete and utter deception. Just as a powerful enough demon could use our own experiences to deceive us thoroughly without our being aware of it, so too a powerful enough dominating force could use our own standards to control us thoroughly without our being aware of it. But neither of these gives us a rationale to be dismissive of our intellectual projects. The possibility of radical error does not mean that knowledge is altogether impossible for us, and the possibility of radical domination does not mean that intellectual autonomy is altogether impossible for us.

Our intellectual standards cannot help but show the effects of our intellectual environment, but they need not be swallowed up by it. My standards can and presumably sometimes do differ from the standards of the people who surround me. When they do, intellectual autonomy as well as egocentric rationality requires that I conform to my standards rather than the prevailing ones.

FOR FURTHER READING

Alston, William. *Epistemic Justification*. Ithaca, N.Y.: Cornell University Press, 1989.

Audi, Robert. *Belief, Justification, and Knowledge*. Belmont, Calif.: Wadsworth, 1988.

Audi, Robert. *The Structure of Justification.* New York: Cambridge University Press, 1993.

BonJour, Laurence. *The Structure of Empirical Knowledge.* Cambridge, Mass.: Harvard University Press, 1985.

Chisholm, Roderick. *Theory of Knowledge,* 3rd ed. Englewood Cliffs, N.J.: Prentice Hall, 1988.

Cohen, Stewart. "Justification and Truth." *Philosophical Studies* 46 (1984), 279–295.

Conee, Earl. "The Basic Nature of Epistemic Justification." *Monist* 71 (1988), 389–404.

Dancy, Jonathan, and Ernest Sosa, eds. *A Companion to Epistemology.* Oxford: Basil Blackwell, 1992.

Feldman, Richard, and Earl Conee. "Evidentialism." In *Philosophical Studies* 48 (1985), 15–34.

Foley, Richard. *Working without a Net.* Oxford: Oxford University Press, 1993.

French, Peter, et al., eds. *Midwest Studies in Philosophy,* Vol. V. Minneapolis: University of Minnesota, 1980.

Fumerton, Richard. *Metaepistemology and Skepticism.* Lanham, Md.: Rowman & Littlefield, 1995.

Goldman, Alvin. *Epistemology and Cognition.* Cambridge, Mass.: Harvard University Press, 1986.

Lehrer, Keith. *Theory of Knowledge.* Boulder, Colo.: Westview Press, 1990.

Moser, Paul. *Empirical Knowledge,* 2nd ed. Lanham, Md.: Rowman & Littlefield, 1996.

Pollock, John. *Contemporary Theories of Knowledge.* Totowa, N.J.: Rowman & Littlefield, 1986.

Rorty, Richard. *Consequences of Pragmatism.* Minneapolis: University of Minnesota Press, 1982.

Schmitt, Frederick. *Knowledge and Belief.* London: Routledge, 1990.

Stich, Stephen. *The Fragmentation of Reason.* Cambridge, Mass.: MIT Press, 1990.

Tomberlin, James, ed. *Philosophical Perspectives, 2, Epistemology.* Atascadero, Calif.: Ridgeview Press, 1988.

Wagner, Richard, and Steven Warner, eds. *Naturalism: A Critical Appraisal.* Notre Dame: University of Notre Dame Press, 1993.

STUDY QUESTIONS

1. According to BonJour, how does epistemic justification differ from other kinds of justification? Explain BonJour's reasoning for this. What does BonJour mean by "epistemic responsibility?" How is this notion related to that of justification?

2. Alston distinguishes between *being* justified in believing and *justifying* one's belief. What is this distinction?

3. Describe the features that are characteristic of deontological conceptions of justification. What does Alston mean by the claim that many of our beliefs are involuntary? Why is this a problem for the deontological conception of justification? Does Alston think that the deontological conception is aided by the claim that we have indirect control over our beliefs? Why or why not?

4. Alston describes three ways of drawing the internalist/externalist distinction. Briefly explain each. Which does Alston prefer? Explain what Alston means by "adequate grounds," and explain why this concept is important. Do you think that Alston's preferred conception of epistemic justification is adequate? Explain.

5. Feldman considers the "Voluntarism Argument" at some length. What is this argument? Explain Feldman's assessment of attempts to reject the first premise of this argument. Why does Feldman think the second premise should be rejected? What is your opinion of Feldman's defense of the claim that we have epistemic obligations?

6. Why does Feldman reject the Jamesian view of epistemic obligation? Why does he reject Chisholm's view of epistemic obligation? Why does Feldman think that this view avoids the problems encountered by doxastic voluntarism? In what ways does Feldman think his account of epistemic obligation incorporates the appropriate elements of both James' and Chisholm's view?

7. James distinguishes between different kinds of options; what are these? Does James think we can control our beliefs? Explain. Why does James think that "believe the truth and avoid error" is not one rule, but two?

8. James rejects the idea that we should hold only those beliefs for which we have "evidence." Why does he think this? Do you agree or disagree with James? Why?

9. Explain the three characterizations of pragmatism given by Rorty. Why does Rorty think epistemology is wrong to look for "essences"? In Rorty's view, what are the only real constraints on inquiry? What do you think he has in mind here? How does Rorty attempt to rebut the claim that pragmatism is committed to irrationalism?

10. Foley suggests that contemporary epistemology attempts to provide theories of rational or justified belief. Why does he think internalist theories are unable to provide us with intellectual advice or guidance? When Foley claims that some intellectual advice is not "fundamental enough," what does he mean by this?

11. Explain what Foley thinks is the Descartes-Locke view of our intellectual threat and our intellectual need. Why does he reject this view?

5

Foundationalism

On occasion we are requested to provide reasons or evidence for our beliefs. If someone asks you why you believe it will rain this weekend, you might cite, for example, the forecast in the newspaper or a weather report on the local news. Having reasons or evidence for our beliefs leads to greater confidence in them; it leads us to think of our beliefs as more trustworthy, and less likely to be arbitrary or the result of wishful thinking. Our commonsense notions of trustworthiness or confidence are in part what epistemologists mean by justified beliefs. The justification of beliefs requires evidence or reasons for them.

The justificatory status of our beliefs is only as good as the reasons for them. If a builder uses inferior materials to build a house, such as cracked timber or concrete that is not strong enough, then our confidence in the stability of the house diminishes. The house is only as secure as the elements that hold it up. Similarly, our beliefs are only as secure as the elements that support them. Thus, when someone tries to explain her confidence in a particular belief, we might not share that confidence if we think the support is rather insecure. Our beliefs are trustworthy only if they are supported by reasons or evidence that are themselves trustworthy. Of course, it is not difficult to imagine that we might then wonder why the supporting reasons are trustworthy. Suppose that Sara tells Sam she believes it will rain this weekend. If she tells Sam she believes that rain is inevitable because the AccuWeather service says it will rain, Sam might question her confidence in the service's forecasts. The trustworthiness of the belief about the weekend weather depends on the trustworthiness of the reason. It is not difficult to imagine that we can continue to ask about the trustworthiness, or the justificatory status, of the supporting reasons. For each supporting reason, it is possible to ask what supports that reason.

The preceding paragraph describes an informal version of the *Regress Argument*. The Regress Argument suggests that a belief is justified only if there is some support for the belief. In turn, the Regress Argument suggests, we can ask what supports the support. We might think that our beliefs are legitimately justified only if we can find some resolution to the Regress Argument.

Inferential beliefs depend on other beliefs for their justification. The justification for inferential beliefs lies in the supporting beliefs, which themselves must be justified. Again, it is here that the Regress Argument takes hold. There are four possible responses to the argument.

1. The regress terminates in beliefs that are themselves unjustified.

2. The regress does not terminate; it simply continues.

3. The regress leads us to see that the source of justification is the network of beliefs.

4. The regress terminates in beliefs that are justified, but do not depend on other beliefs for their justification.

The first two options are unacceptable, and it is not difficult to see why. We can think of the Regress Argument as asking about the initial source of justification. If our inferential beliefs derive their justification from other beliefs, what is the source of this property of justification? Seen in this way, the first option says that justification magically appears. Justification can begin with beliefs that are themselves wholly arbitrary and untrustworthy. This is a little like saying that if you use cheap, inferior materials to get the house built, you don't have to worry about the house collapsing. As long as one has other beliefs that serve as reasons for a belief, that belief is justified.

This implies that any beliefs, no matter how untrustworthy, could serve to justify other beliefs. This is not the epistemic security we have in mind when we ask what the reasons are for a belief.

The second option is not much better. Suppose you are interested in buying a certain house, but before you sign anything, you want an outside opinion about whether the house is well constructed. I offer, for a modest fee, to investigate whether the house is indeed well constructed and stable. Several months later you call me asking why you have not received my report. I tell you that, if you had read the small print, you would have noticed that my investigation is an ongoing, never-ending process. Surely this is not the way to determine the trustworthiness of a building. Nor is it the best way to determine the trustworthiness of our beliefs.

A more interesting possibility emerges with the third option. The third option is characteristic of a family of views known as coherentism. Central to coherentism is the claim that justification arises not from individual beliefs, but from a network or group of beliefs that are connected in various ways. According to coherentism, there are no individual sources of justification; instead justification arises from the fabric of our beliefs. Critics of coherentism (as we will see) allege that this network character of justification cannot be right. Why should the mere fact that an individual belief belongs to a group of beliefs make the individual belief more trustworthy? The group itself would need to be trustworthy, but how can this trustworthiness of the group come about if the elements of the group are not themselves trustworthy? Thus, it is claimed that coherentism cannot explain the source of the justification of our beliefs.

If coherentism is rejected, foundationalism is the only remaining response to the Regress Argument. *Foundationalism* is a view about the best solution to the Regress Argument. Foundationalist theories hold that the ultimate justification of our beliefs derives from beliefs that are themselves justified, but do not depend on other beliefs for their justification. Since other possible responses to the argument are inadequate, it is thought that foundationalism provides the only plausible solution. Of course, we need to be told more about the nature of such beliefs and their relation to the beliefs they support.

Foundationalism divides justified beliefs into two categories. *Basic beliefs* are the ultimate source of justification. Such beliefs are the source of justification for nonbasic beliefs and are directly justified, since their justification does not derive from other beliefs. It is natural to ask what kinds of belief could serve as basic beliefs: What types of belief are directly justified? The answer to this question depends on whether one thinks we are looking for fallible or infallible justification of our beliefs.

Classic or infallible foundationalism claims that basic beliefs must be infallibly justified. A belief is justified only if there is no possibility of mistake in having that belief. *Modest* or fallible foundationalism, on the other hand, holds that basic beliefs are fallibly justified. The justification of such beliefs may be overridden by new information or new reasons. Whether one requires fallible or infallible justification determines the type of beliefs that counts as basic.

Suppose Sam sees a glass on the table and, as a result, comes to believe that there is a glass in front of him. Moments later Sam might realize that he was only seeing a reflection or that he had mistaken some other object for a glass. These sorts of perceptual mistakes, although perhaps rare, are nonetheless real possibilities. Such mistakes suggest that perceptual beliefs are not infallibly justified; they are at best fallibly justified.

Still Sam might have a belief that is infallibly justified. When his error is pointed out, Sam could well respond that it *seemed* to him that there was a glass on the table. His perceptual experiences or his sensations were just what they would have been had their been a glass on the table. It seemed—to Sam—as if there was a glass; about this he could not be mistaken. Here is a kind of belief that has been held to be infallible—beliefs *about* one's sensations or experiences. Since there is no possibility of mistake, Sam's belief is justified. And, since his belief about his sensations does not depend on other beliefs, it is directly justified. Sam doesn't have to consult his other beliefs to determine the nature of his sensations. Hence, Sam's belief that it seems that there is a glass on the table is a basic belief. More generally, beliefs about sensations seem a promising candidate for directly and infallibly justified beliefs. Whether we actually have such infallible beliefs is a subject of some controversy. The prospects for infallible foundationalism are considered in the selection by Keith Lehrer, "Infallible Foundations." Lehrer rejects infallible foundationalism because introspective beliefs—beliefs about what we think—and beliefs about our sensations are not infallible.

Although Descartes is taken as a paradigmatic example of a classic foundationalist, today many foundationalists are modest or fallible foundationalists. With this view, it is possible to see perceptual beliefs as a kind of basic belief. Again, consider Sam's perceptual belief that there is a glass in front of him. As we noted, the belief is clearly fallible; is there any reason to think that it is justified, despite not depending on other beliefs for its justification?

One line of thought is the following. Sam has the perceptual belief that he does because he has sensations of a green, cylindrical object. Sam's having the sensations make it likely that his belief is true, even though they don't guarantee that his belief is true. Sam's belief is justified, but it does not depend on other beliefs for its justification, since sensations are not beliefs. Sam's belief is then a basic belief. Perceptual beliefs are a type of basic belief according to some modest foundationalists.

The difference between basic and nonbasic beliefs also distinguishes infallible from fallible foundationalism. The typical characterization of infallible foundationalism is that basic beliefs must deductively support nonbasic beliefs. Fallible foundationalism holds that basic beliefs may provide inductive support for nonbasic beliefs.

Perhaps by now the central objection to foundationalism is apparent to you. Are there any basic beliefs? More precisely, are there any beliefs that are justified but do not depend on other beliefs for their justification? Critics have tried to show that any belief must inevitably rely on other beliefs for its justification. Infallible foundationalists have the burden of showing that there are infallibly justified beliefs.

Descartes is no doubt the most celebrated infallible foundationalist. In his first *Meditation,* Descartes set about to discover the "firm and lasting foundations" of his beliefs, beliefs which were not liable to

error. In the current selection, meditations II and III, Descartes argues that he is able to find such a belief: "I am, I exist, is necessarily true each time that I pronounce it, or that I mentally conceive it." It is this belief that is the foundational departure point for Descartes' ensuing investigations. Moreover, Descartes claims to isolate a criterion—clarity and distinctness—that enables him to extend his knowledge beyond the foundational belief that he identifies.

William Alston, in "Two Types of Foundationalism," argues that foundationalism need not be committed to the claim that a person must be able to show that their basic beliefs are justified. This objection to foundationalism, sometimes called the "levels argument," attempts to show that there are no basic beliefs, since any basic belief depends on still another belief to show that it is justified. Alston argues that there is reason to accept this iterative notion of foundationalism.

Robert Audi, in "The Foundationalism-Coherentism Controversy," examines the major points of contention between modest foundationalism and coherentism. There are, according to Audi, features of coherentism that the modest foundationalist can accept. However, coherentism cannot explain the original source of the justification of our beliefs. Thus, modest foundationalism is preferable to coherentism.

In the concluding selection, from *The Man of Reason,* Genevieve Lloyd examines the way in which a certain conception of reason has developed. Lloyd argues that in principle the individualism implicit in Descartes' method made knowledge accessible to everyone. However, women were unable to participate fully in the pursuit of knowledge, since that pursuit occurred in the public and collective context of scientific inquiry and women were excluded from that public arena.

As is apparent in these selections, the distinctive claim of foundationalism is also its fundamental challenge. Explaining and defending the claim that there are beliefs that do not depend on other beliefs for their justification—basic beliefs—is the most important task for the foundationalist.

RENÉ DESCARTES

from Meditations on the First Philosophy

MEDITATION II

Of the Nature of the Human Mind; and
that it is more easily known than the Body.

The Meditation of yesterday filled my mind with so many doubts that it is no longer in my power to forget them. And yet I do not see in what manner I can resolve them; and, just as if I had all of a sudden fallen into very deep water, I am so disconcerted that I can neither make certain of setting my feet on the bottom, nor can I swim and so support myself on the surface. I shall nevertheless make an effort and follow anew the same path as that on which I yesterday entered, i.e. I shall proceed by setting aside all that in which the least doubt could be supposed to exist, just as if I had discovered that it was absolutely false; and I shall ever follow in this road until I have met with something which is certain, or at least, if I can do nothing else, until I have learned for certain that there is nothing in the world that is certain. Archimedes, in order that he might draw the terrestrial globe out of its place, and transport it elsewhere, demanded only that one point should be fixed and immoveable; in the same way I shall have the right to conceive high hopes if I am happy enough to discover one thing only which is certain and indubitable.

I suppose, then, that all the things that I see are false; I persuade myself that nothing has ever existed of all that my fallacious memory represents to me. I consider that I possess no senses; I imagine that body, figure, extension, movement and place are but the fictions of my mind. What, then, can be esteemed as true? Perhaps nothing as all, unless that there is nothing in the world that is certain.

But how can I know there is not something different from those things that I have just considered, of which one cannot have the slightest doubt? Is there not some God, or some other being by whatever name we call it, who puts these reflections into my mind? That is not necessary, for is it not possible that I am capable of producing them myself? I myself, am I not at least something? But I have already denied that I had senses and body. Yet I hesitate, for what follows from that? Am I so dependent on body and senses that I cannot exist without these? But I was persuaded that there was nothing in all the world, that there was no heaven, no earth, that there were no minds, nor any bodies: was I not then likewise persuaded that I did not exist? Not at all; of a surety I myself did exist since I persuaded myself of something [or merely because I thought of something]. But there is some deceiver or other, very powerful and very cunning, who ever employs his ingenuity in deceiving me. Then without doubt I exist also if he deceives me, and let him deceive me as much as he will, he can never cause me to be nothing so long as I think that I am something. So that after having reflected well and carefully examined all things, we must come to the definite conclusion that this proposition: I am, I exist, is necessarily true each time that I pronounce it, or that I mentally conceive it.

But I do not yet know clearly enough what I am, I who am certain that I am; and hence I must be careful to see that I do not imprudently take some other object in place of myself, and thus that I do not go astray in respect of this knowledge that I hold to be the most certain and most evident of all that I have formerly learned. That is why I shall now consider anew what I believed myself to be before I embarked upon these last reflections; and of my former opinions I shall withdraw all that might even in a small degree be invalidated by the reasons which I have just brought forward, in order that there may be nothing at all left beyond what is absolutely certain and indubitable.

What then did I formerly believe myself to be? Undoubtedly I believed myself to be a man. But what is a man? Shall I say a reasonable animal? Certainly not; for then I should have to inquire what an animal is, and what is reasonable; and thus from a single question I should insensibly fall into an infinitude of others more difficult; and I should not wish to waste the little time and leisure remaining to me in trying to unravel subtleties like these. But I shall rather stop here to consider the thoughts which of themselves spring up in my mind, and which were not inspired by anything beyond my own nature alone when I applied myself to the consideration of my being. In the first place, then, I considered myself as having a face, hands, arms, and all that system of members composed on bones and flesh as seen in a corpse which I designated by the name of body. In addition to this I considered that I was nourished, that I walked, that I felt, and that I thought, and I referred all these actions to the soul: but I did not stop to consider what the soul was, or if I did stop, I imagined that it was something extremely rare and subtle like a wind, a flame, or an ether, which was spread throughout my grosser parts. As to body I had no manner of doubt about its nature, but thought I had a very clear knowledge of it; and if I had desired to explain it according to the notions that I had then formed of it, I should have described it thus: By the body I understand all that which can be defined by a certain figure: something which can be confined in a certain place, and which can fill a given space in such a way that every other body will be excluded from it; which can be perceived either by touch, or by sight, or by hearing, or by taste, or by smell: which can be moved in many ways not, in truth, by itself, but by something which is foreign to it, by which it is touched [and from which it receives impressions]: for to have the power of self-movement, as also of feeling or of thinking, I did not consider to appertain to the nature of body: on the contrary, I was rather astonished to find that faculties similar to them existed in some bodies.

But what am I, now that I suppose that there is a certain genius which is extremely powerful, and, if I may say so, malicious, who employs all his powers in deceiving me? Can I affirm that I possess the least of all those things which I have just said pertain to the nature of body? I pause to consider, I revolve all these things in my mind, and I find none of which I can say that it pertains to me. It would be tedious to stop to enumerate them. Let us pass to the attributes of soul and see if there is any one which is in me? What of nutrition or walking [the first mentioned]? But if it is so that I have no body it is also true that I can neither walk nor take nourishment. Another attribute is sensation. But one cannot feel without body, and besides I have thought I perceived many things during sleep that I recognised in my waking moments as not having been experienced at all. What of thinking? I find here that thought is an attribute that belongs to me; it alone cannot be separated from me. I am, I exist, that is certain. But how often? Just when I think; for it might possibly be the case if I ceased entirely to think, that I should likewise cease altogether to exist. I do not now admit anything which is not necessarily true: to speak accurately I am not more than a thing which thinks, that is to say a mind or a soul, or an understanding, or a reason, which are terms whose significance was formerly unknown to me. I am, however, a real thing and really exist; but what thing? I have answered: a thing which thinks.

And what more? I shall exercise my imagination [in order to see if I am not something more]. I am not a collection of members which we call the human body: I am not a subtle air distributed through these members, I am not a wind, a fire, a vapour, a breath, nor anything at all which I can imagine or conceive; because I have assumed that all these were nothing. Without changing that supposition I find that I only leave myself certain of the fact that I am somewhat. But perhaps it is true that these same things which I supposed were non-existent because they are unknown to me, are really not different from the self which I know. I am not sure about this, I shall not dispute about it now; I can only give judgment on things that are known to me. I know that I exist, and I inquire what I am, I whom I know to exist. But it is very certain that the knowledge of my existence taken in its precise significance does not depend on things whose existence is not yet known to me; consequently it does not depend on those which I can feign in imagination. And indeed the very term *feign* in imagination proves to me my error, for I really do this if I image myself a something, since to imagine is nothing else than to contemplate the figure or image of a corporeal thing. But I already know for certain that I am, and that it may be that all these images, and speaking generally, all things that relate to the nature of body are nothing but dreams [and chimeras]. For this reason I see clearly that I have as little reason to say, 'I shall stimulate my imagination in order to know more distinctly what I am,' than if I were to say, 'I am now awake, and I perceive somewhat that is real and true: but because I do not yet perceive it distinctly enough, I shall go to sleep of express purpose, so that my dreams may represent the perception with greatest truth and evidence.' And, thus, I know for certain that nothing of all that I can understand by means of my imagination belongs to this knowledge which I have of myself, and that it is necessary to recall the mind from this mode of thought with the utmost diligence in order that it may be able to know its own nature with perfect distinctness.

But what then am I? A thing which thinks. What is a thing which thinks? It is a thing which doubts, understands, [conceives], affirms, denies, wills, refuses, which also imagines and feels.

Certainly it is no small matter if all these things pertain to my nature. But why should they not so pertain? Am I not that being who now doubts nearly everything, who nevertheless understands certain things, who affirms that one only is true, who denies all the others, who desires to know more, is averse from being deceived, who imagines many things, sometimes indeed despite his will, and who perceives many likewise, as by the intervention of the bodily organs? Is there nothing in all this which is as true as it is certain that I exist, even though I should always sleep and though he who has given me being employed all his ingenuity in deceiving me? Is there likewise any one of these attributes which can be distinguished from my thought, or which might be said to be separated from myself? For it is so evident of itself that it is I who doubts, who understands, and who desires, that there is no reason here to add anything to explain it. And I have certainly the power of imagining likewise; for although it may happen (as I formerly supposed) that none of the things which I imagine are true, nevertheless this power of imagining does not cease to be really in use, and it forms part of my thought. Finally, I am the same who feels, that is to say, who perceives certain things, as by the organs of sense, since in truth I see light, I hear noise, I feel heat. But it will be said that these phenomena are false and that I am dreaming. Let it be so; still it is at least quite certain that it seems to me that I see light, that I hear noise and that I feel heat. That cannot be false; properly speaking it is what is in me called feeling; and used in this precise sense that is no other thing than thinking.

From this time I begin to know what I am with a little more clearness and distinction than before; but nevertheless it still seems to me, and I cannot prevent myself from thinking, that corporeal things, whose images are framed by thought, which are tested by the senses, are much more distinctly known than that obscure part of me which does not come under the imagination. Although really it is very strange to say that I know and understand more distinctly these things whose existence seems to me dubious, which are unknown to me, and which do not belong to me, than others of the truth of which I am convinced, which are known to me and which pertain to my real nature, in a word, than myself. But I see clearly how the case stands: my mind loves to wander, and cannot yet suffer itself to be retained within the just limits of truth. Very good, let us once more give it the freest rein, so that, when afterwards we seize the proper occasion for pulling up, it may the more easily be regulated and controlled.

Let us begin by considering the commonest matters, those which we believe to be the most distinctly comprehended, to wit, the bodies which we touch and see; not indeed bodies in general, for these general ideas are usually a little more confused, but let us consider one body in particular. Let us take, for example, this piece of wax: it has been taken quite freshly from the hive, and it has not yet lost the sweetness of the honey which it contains; it still retains somewhat of the odour of the flowers from which it has been culled; its colour, its figure, its size are apparent; it is hard, cold, easily handled, and if you strike it with the finger, it will emit a sound. Finally all the things which are requisite to cause us distinctly to recognise a body, are met with in it. But notice that while I speak and approach the fire what remained of the taste is exhaled, the smell evaporates, the colour alters, the figure is destroyed, the size increases, it becomes liquid, it heats, scarcely can one handle it, and when one strikes it, no sound is emitted. Does the same wax remain after this change? We must confess that it remains; none would judge otherwise. What then did I know so distinctly in this piece of wax? It could certainly be nothing of all that the senses brought to my notice, since all these things which fall under taste, smell, sight, touch, and hearing, are found to be changed, and yet the same wax remains.

Perhaps it was what I now think, viz. that this wax was not that sweetness of honey, nor that agreeable scent of flowers, nor that particular whiteness, nor that figure, nor that sound, but simply a body which a little while before appeared to me as perceptible under these forms, and which is now perceptible under others. But what, precisely, is it that I imagine when I form such conceptions? Let us attentively consider this, and, abstracting from all that does not belong to the wax, let us see what remains. Certainly nothing remains excepting a certain extended thing which is flexible and movable. But what is the meaning of flexible and movable? Is it not that I imagine that this piece of wax being round is capable of becoming square and of passing from a square to a triangular figure? No, certainly it is not that, since I imagine it admits of an infinitude of similar changes, and I nevertheless do not know how to compass the infinitude by my imagination, and consequently this conception which I have of the wax is not brought about by the faculty of imagination. What now is this extension? Is it not also unknown? For it becomes greater when the wax is melted, greater when it is boiled, and greater still when the heat increases; and I should not conceive [clearly] according to truth what wax is, if I did not think that even this piece that we are considering is capable of receiving more variations in extension than I have ever imagined. We must then grant that I could not even understand through the imagination what this piece of wax is, and that it is my mind alone which perceives it. I say this piece of wax in particular, for as to wax in general it is yet clearer. But what is this piece of wax which cannot be understood excepting by the [understanding or] mind? It is certainly the same that I see, touch, imagine, and finally it is the same which I have always believed it to be from the beginning. But what must particularly be observed is that

its perception is neither an act of vision, nor of touch, nor of imagination, and has never been such although it may have appeared formerly to be so, but only an intuition of the mind, which may be imperfect and confused as it was formerly, or clear and distinct as it is at present, according as my attention is more or less directed to the elements which are found in it, and of which it is composed.

Yet in the meantime I am greatly astonished when I consider [the great feebleness of mind] and its proneness to fall [insensibly] into error; for although without giving expression to my thoughts I consider all this in my own mind, words often impede me and I am almost deceived by the terms of ordinary language. For we say that we see the same wax, if it is present, and not that we simply judge that it is the same from its having the same colour and figure. From this I should conclude that I knew the wax by means of vision and not simply by the intuition of the mind; unless by chance I remember that, when looking from a window and saying I see men who pass in the street, I really do not see them, but infer that what I see is men, just as I say that I see wax. And yet what do I see from the window but hats and coats which may cover automatic machines? Yet I judge these to be men. And similarly solely by the faculty of judgment which rests in my mind, I comprehend that which I believed I saw with my eyes.

A man who makes it his aim to raise his knowledge above the common should be ashamed to derive the occasion for doubting from the forms of speech invented by the vulgar; I prefer to pass on and consider whether I had a more evident and perfect conception of what the wax was when I first perceived it, and when I believed I knew it by means of the external senses or at least by the common sense as it is called, that is to say by the imaginative faculty, or whether my present conception is clearer now that I have most carefully examined what it is, and in what way it can be known. It would certainly be absurd to doubt as to this. For what was there in this first perception which was distinct? What was there which might not as well have been perceived by any of the animals? But when I distinguish the wax from its external forms, and when, just as if I had taken from it its vestments, I consider it quite naked, it is certain that although some error may still be found in my judgment, I can nevertheless not perceive it thus without a human mind.

But finally what shall I say of this mind, that is, of myself, for up to this point I do not admit in myself anything but mind? What then, I who seem to perceive this piece of wax so distinctly, do I not know myself, not only with much more truth and certainty, but also with much more distinctness and clearness? For if I judge that the wax is or exists from the fact that I see it, it certainly follows much more clearly that I am or that I exist myself from the fact that I see it. For it may be that what I see is not really wax, it may also be that I do not possess eyes with which to see anything; but it cannot be that when I see, or (for I no longer take account of the distinction) when I think I see, that I myself who think am nought. So if I judge that the wax exists from the fact that I touch it, the same thing will follow, to wit, that I am; and if I judge that my imagination, or some other cause, whatever it is, persuades me that the wax exists, I shall still conclude the same. And what I have here remarked of wax may be applied to all other things which are external to me [and which are met with outside of me]. And further, if the [notion or] perception of wax has seemed to me clearer and more distinct, not only after the sight or the touch, but also after many other causes have rendered it quite manifest to me, with how much more [evidence] and distinctness must it be said that I now know myself, since all the reasons which contribute to the knowledge of wax, or any other body whatever, are yet better proofs of the nature of my mind! And there are so many other things in the mind itself which may contribute to the elucidation of its nature, that those which depend on body such as these just mentioned, hardly merit being taken into account.

But finally here I am, having insensibly reverted to the point I desired, for, since it is now manifest to me that even bodies are not properly speaking known by the senses or by the faculty of imagination, but by the understanding only, and since they are not known from the fact that they are seen or touched, but only because they are understood, I see clearly that there is nothing which is easier for me to know than my mind. But because it is difficult to rid oneself so promptly of an opinion to which one was accustomed for so long, it will be well that I should halt a little at this point, so that by the length of my

meditation I may more deeply imprint on my memory this new knowledge.

MEDITATION III

Of God: That He Exists

I shall now close my eyes, I shall stop my ears, I shall call away all my senses, I shall efface even from my thoughts all the images of corporeal things, or at least (for that is hardly possible) I shall esteem them as vain and false; and thus holding converse only with myself and considering my own nature, I shall try little by little to reach a better knowledge of and a more familiar acquaintanceship with myself. I am a thing that thinks, that is to say, that doubts, affirms, denies, that knows a few things, that is ignorant of many [that loves, that hates], that wills, that desires, that also imagines and perceives; for as I remarked before, although the things which I perceive and imagine are perhaps nothing at all apart from me and in themselves, I am nevertheless assured that these modes of thought that I call perceptions and imaginations, inasmuch only as they are modes of thought, certainly reside [and are met with] in me.

And in the little that I have just said, I think I have summed up all that I really know, or at least all that hitherto I was aware that I knew. In order to try to extend my knowledge further, I shall now look around more carefully and see whether I cannot still discover in myself some other things which I have not hitherto perceived. I am certain that I am a thing which thinks; but do I not then likewise know what is requisite to render me certain of a truth? Certainly in this first knowledge there is nothing that assures me of its truth, excepting the clear and distinct perception of that which I state, which would not indeed suffice to assure me that what I say is true, if it could ever happen that a thing which I conceived so clearly and distinctly could be false; and accordingly it seems to me that already I can establish as a general rule that all things which I perceive very clearly and very distinctly are true.

At the same time I have before received and admitted many things to be very certain and manifest, which yet I afterwards recognised as being dubious. What then were these things? They were the earth, sky, stars and all other objects which I apprehended by means of the senses. But what did I clearly [and distinctly] perceive in them? Nothing more than that the ideas or thoughts of these things were presented to my mind. And not even now do I deny that these ideas are met with in me. But there was yet another thing which I affirmed, and which, owing to the habit which I had formed of believing it, I thought I perceived very clearly, although in truth I did not perceive it at all, to wit, that there were objects outside of me from which these ideas proceeded, and to which they were entirely similar. And it was in this that I erred, or, if perchance my judgment was correct, this was not due to any knowledge arising from my perception.

But when I took anything very simple and easy in the sphere of arithmetic or geometry into consideration, e.g. that two and three together made five, and other things of the sort, were not these present to my mind so clearly as to enable me to affirm that they were true? Certainly if I judged that since such matters could be doubted, this would not have been so for any other reason than that it came into my mind that perhaps a God might have endowed me with such a nature that I may have been deceived even concerning things which seemed to me most manifest. But every time that this preconceived opinion of the sovereign power of a God presents itself to my thought, I am constrained to confess that it is easy to Him, if He wishes it, to cause me to err, even in matters in which I believe myself to have the best evidence. And, on the other hand, always when I direct my attention to things which I believe myself to perceive very clearly, I am so persuaded of their truth that I let myself break out into words such as these: Let who will deceive me, He can never cause me to be nothing while I think that I am, or some day cause it to be true to say that I have never been, it being true now to say that I am, or that two and three make more or less than five, or any such thing in which I see a manifest contradiction. And, certainly, since I have no reason to believe that there is a God who is a deceiver, and as I have not yet satisfied myself that there is a God at all, the reason for doubt which depends on this opinion alone is very slight, and so to speak metaphysical. But in order to be able altogether to remove it, I must inquire whether there is a God as soon as the occasion presents itself; and if I find that there is a God, I must

also inquire whether He may be a deceiver; for without a knowledge of these two truths I do not see that I can ever be certain of anything.

And in order that I may have an opportunity of inquiring into this in an orderly way [without interrupting the order of meditation which I have proposed to myself, and which is little by little to pass from the notions which I find first of all in my mind to those which I shall later on discover in it] it is requisite that I should here divide my thoughts into certain kinds, and that I should consider in which of these kinds there is, properly speaking, truth or error to be found. Of my thoughts some are, so to speak, images of the things, and to these alone is the title 'idea' properly applied; examples are my thought of a man or of a chimera, of heaven, of an angel, or [even] of God. But other thoughts possess other forms as well. For example in willing, fearing, approving, denying, though I always perceive something as the subject of the action of my mind, yet by this action I always add something else to the idea which I have of that thing; and of the thoughts of this kind some are called volitions or affections, and others judgments.

Now as to what concerns ideas, if we consider them only in themselves and do not relate them to anything else beyond themselves, they cannot properly speaking be false; for whether I imagine a goat or a chimera, it is not less true that I imagine the one than the other. We must not fear likewise that falsity can enter into will and into affections, for although I may desire evil things, or even things that never existed, it is not the less true that I desire them. Thus there remains no more than the judgments which we make, in which I must take the greatest care not to deceive myself. But the principal error and the commonest which we may meet with in them, consists in my judging that the ideas which are in me are similar or conformable to the things which are outside me; for without doubt if I considered the ideas only as certain modes of my thoughts, without trying to relate them to anything beyond, they could scarcely give me material for error.

But among these ideas, some appear to me to be innate, some adventitious, and others to be formed [or invented] by myself; for, as I have the power of understanding what is called a thing, or a truth, or a thought, it appears to me that I hold this power from no other source than my own nature. But if I now hear some sound, if I see the sun, or feel heat, I have hitherto judged that these sensations proceeded from certain things that exist outside of me; and finally it appears to me that sirens, hippogryphs, and the like, are formed out of my own mind. But again I may possibly persuade myself that all these ideas are of the nature of those which I term adventitious, or else that they are all innate, or all fictitious: for I have not yet clearly discovered their true origin.

And my principal task in this place is to consider, in respect to those ideas which appear to me to proceed from certain objects that are outside me, what are the reasons which cause me to think them similar to these objects. It seems indeed in the first place that I am taught this lesson by nature; and, secondly, I experience in myself that these ideas do not depend on my will nor therefore on myself—for they often present themselves to my mind in spite of my will. Just now, for instance, whether I will or whether I do not will, I feel heat, and thus I persuade myself that this feeling, or at least this idea of heat, is produced in me by something which is different from me, i.e. by the heat of the fire near which I sit. And nothing seems to me more obvious than to judge that this object imprints its likeness rather than anything else upon me.

Now I must discover whether these proofs are sufficiently strong and convincing. When I say that I am so instructed by nature, I merely mean a certain spontaneous inclination which impels me to believe in this connection, and not a natural light which makes me recognise that it is true. But these two things are very different; for I cannot doubt that which the natural light causes me to believe to be true, as, for example, it has shown me that I am from the fact that I doubt, or other facts of the same kind. And I possess no other faculty whereby to distinguish truth from falsehood, which can teach me that what this light shows me to be true is not really true, and no other faculty that is equally trustworthy. But as far as [apparently] natural impulses are concerned, I have frequently remarked, when I had to make active choice between virtue and vice, that they often enough led me to the part that was worse; and this is why I do not see any reason for following them in what regards truth and error.

And as to the other reason, which is that these ideas must proceed from objects outside me, since they do not depend on my will, I do not find it any the more convincing. For just as these impulses of which I have spoken are found in me, notwithstanding that they do not always concur with my will, so perhaps there is in me some faculty fitted to produce these ideas without the assistance of any external things, even though it is not yet known by me; just as, apparently, they have hitherto always been found in me during sleep without the aid of any external objects.

And finally, though they did proceed from objects different from myself, it is not a necessary consequence that they should resemble these. On the contrary, I have noticed that in many cases there was a great difference between the object and its idea. I find, for example, two completely diverse ideas of the sun in my mind; the one derives its origin from the senses, and should be placed in the category of adventitious ideas; according to this idea the sun seems to be extremely small; but the other is derived from astronomical reasonings, i.e. is elicited from certain notions that are innate in me, or else it is formed by me in some other manner; in accordance with it the sun appears to be several times greater than the earth. These two ideas cannot, indeed, both resemble the same sun, and reason makes me believe that the one which seems to have originated directly from the sun itself, is the one which is most dissimilar to it.

All this causes me to believe that until the present time it has not been by a judgment that was certain [or premeditated], but only by a sort of blind impulse that I believed that things existed outside of, and different from me, which, by the organs of my senses, or by some other method whatever it might be, conveyed these ideas or images to me [and imprinted on me their similitudes].

But there is yet another method of inquiring whether any of the objects of which I have ideas within me exist outside of me. If ideas are only taken as certain modes of thought, I recognise amongst them no difference or inequality, and all appear to proceed from me in the same manner; but when we consider them as images, one representing one thing and the other another, it is clear that they are very different one from the other. There is no doubt that those which represent to me substances are something more, and contain so to speak more objective reality within them [that is to say, by representation participate in a higher degree of being or perfection] than those that simply represent modes or accidents; and that idea again by which I understand a supreme God, eternal, infinite, [immutable], omniscient, omnipotent, and Creator of all things which are outside of Himself, has certainly more objective reality in itself than those ideas by which finite substances are represented.

Now it is manifest by the natural light that there must at least be as much reality in the efficient and total cause as in its effect. For, pray, whence can the effect derive its reality, if not from its cause? And in what way can this cause communicate this reality to it, unless it possessed it in itself? And from this it follows, not only that something cannot proceed from nothing, but likewise that what is more perfect—that is to say, which has more reality within itself—cannot proceed from the less perfect. And this is not only evidently true of those effects which possess actual or formal reality, but also of the ideas in which we consider merely what is termed objective reality. To take an example, the stone which has not yet existed not only cannot now commence to be unless it has been produced by something which possesses within itself, either formally or eminently, all that enters into the composition of the stone [i.e. it must possess the same things or other more excellent things than those which exist in the stone] and heat can only be produced in a subject in which it did not previously exist by a cause that is of an order [degree or kind] at least as perfect as heat, and so in all other cases. But further, the idea of heat, or of a stone, cannot exist in me unless it has been placed within me by some cause which possesses within it at least as much reality as that which I conceive to exist in the heat or the stone. For although this cause does not transmit anything of its actual or formal reality to my idea, we must not for that reason imagine that it is necessarily a less real cause; we must remember that [since every idea is a work of the mind] its nature is such that it demands of itself no other formal reality than that which it borrows from my thought, of which it is only a mode [i.e. a manner or way of thinking]. But in order that an idea should contain some one certain objective reality rather than another, it must without doubt derive it from some cause in which there is at least as much

formal reality as this idea contains of objective reality. For if we imagine that something is found in an idea which is not found in the cause, it must then have been derived from nought; but however imperfect may be this mode of being by which a thing is objectively [or by representation] in the understanding by its idea, we cannot certainly say that this mode of being is nothing, nor, consequently, that the idea derives its origin from nothing.

Nor must I imagine that, since the reality that I consider in these ideas is only objective, it is not essential that this reality should be formally in the causes of my ideas, but that it is sufficient that it should be found objectively. For just as this mode of objective existence pertains to ideas by their proper nature, so does the mode of formal existence pertain to the causes of those ideas (this is at least true of the first and principal) by the nature peculiar to them. And although it may be the case that one idea gives birth to another idea, that cannot continue to be so indefinitely; for in the end we must reach an idea whose cause shall be so to speak an archetype, in which the whole reality [or perfection] which is so to speak objectively [or by representation] in these ideas is contained formally [and really]. Thus the light of nature causes me to know clearly that the ideas in me are like [pictures or] images which can, in truth, easily fall short of the perfection of the objects from which they have been derived, but which can never contain anything greater or more perfect.

And the longer and the more carefully that I investigate these matters, the more clearly and distinctly do I recognise their truth. But what am I to conclude from it all in the end? It is this, that if the objective reality of any one of my ideas is of such a nature as clearly to make me recognise that it is not in me either formally or eminently, and that consequently I cannot myself be the cause of it, it follows of necessity that I am not alone in the world, but that there is another being which exists, or which is the cause of this idea. On the other hand, had no such idea existed in me, I should have had no sufficient argument to convince me of the existence of any being beyond myself; for I have made very careful investigation everywhere and up to the present time have been able to find no other ground.

But of my ideas, beyond that which represents me to myself, as to which there can here be no difficulty, there is another which represents a God, and there are others representing corporeal and inanimate things, others angels, others animals, and others again which represent to me men similar to myself.

As regards the ideas which represent to me other men or animals, or angels, I can however easily conceive that they might be formed by an admixture of the other ideas which I have of myself, of corporeal things, and of God, even although there were apart from me neither men nor animals, nor angels, in all the world.

And in regard to the ideas of corporeal objects, I do not recognise in them anything so great or so excellent that they might not have possibly proceeded from myself; for if I consider them more closely, and examine them individually, as I yesterday examined the idea of wax, I find that there is very little in them which I perceive clearly and distinctly. Magnitude or extension in length, breadth, or depth, I do so perceive; also figure which results from a termination of this extension, the situation which bodies of different figure preserve in relation to one another, and movement or change of situation; to which we may also add substance, duration and number. As to other things such as light, colours, sounds, scents, tastes, heat, cold and the other tactile qualities, they are thought by me with so much obscurity and confusion that I do not even know if they are true or false, i.e. whether the ideas which I form of these qualities are actually the ideas of real objects or not [or whether they only represent chimeras which cannot exist in fact]. For although I have before remarked that it is only in judgments that falsity, properly speaking, or formal falsity, can be met with, a certain material falsity may nevertheless be found in ideas, i.e. when these ideas represent what is nothing as though it were something. For example, the ideas which I have of cold and heat are so far from clear and distinct that by their means I cannot tell whether cold is merely a privation of heat, or heat a privation of cold, or whether both are real qualities, or are not such. And inasmuch as [since ideas resemble images] there cannot be any ideas which do not appear to represent some things, if it is correct to say that cold is merely a privation of heat, the idea which represents it to me as something real and positive will not be improperly termed false, and the same holds good of other similar ideas.

To these it is certainly not necessary that I should attribute any author other than myself. For if they are false, i.e. if they represent things which do not exist, the light of nature shows me that they issue from nought, that is to say, that they are only in me in so far as something is lacking to the perfection of my nature. But if they are true, nevertheless because they exhibit so little reality to me that I cannot even clearly distinguish the thing represented from non-being, I do not see any reason why they should not be produced by myself.

As to the clear and distinct idea which I have of corporeal things, some of them seem as though I might have derived them from the idea which I possess of myself, as those which I have of substance, duration, number, and such like. For [even] when I think that a stone is a substance, or at least a thing capable of existing of itself, and that I am a substance also, although I conceive that I am a thing that thinks and not one that is extended, and that the stone on the other hand is an extended thing which does not think, and that thus there is a notable difference between the two conceptions—they seem, nevertheless, to agree in this, that both represent substances. In the same way, when I perceive that I now exist and further recollect that I have in former times existed, and when I remember that I have various thoughts of which I can recognise the number, I acquire ideas of duration and number which I can afterwards transfer to any object that I please. But as to all the other qualities of which the ideas of corporeal things are composed, to wit, extension, figure, situation and motion, it is true that they are not formally in me, since I am only a thing that thinks; but because they are merely certain modes of substance [and so to speak the vestments under which corporeal substance appears to us] and because I myself am also a substance, it would seem that they might be contained in me eminently.

Hence there remains only the idea of God, concerning which we must consider whether it is something which cannot have proceeded from me myself. By the name God I understand a substance that is infinite [eternal, immutable], independent, all-knowing, all-powerful, and by which I myself and everything else, if anything else does exist, have been created. Now all these characteristics are such that the more diligently I attend to them, the less do they appear capable of proceeding from me alone; hence, from what has been already said, we must conclude that God necessarily exists.

For although the idea of substance is within me owing to the fact that I am substance, nevertheless I should not have the idea of an infinite substance—since I am finite—if it had not proceeded from some substance which was veritably infinite.

Nor should I imagine that I do not perceive the infinite by a true idea, but only by the negation of the finite, just as I perceive repose and darkness by the negation of movement and of light; for, on the contrary, I see that there is manifestly more reality in infinite substance than in finite, and therefore that in some way I have in me the notion of the infinite earlier than the finite—to wit, the notion of God before that of myself. For how would it be possible that I should know that I doubt and desire, that is to say, that something is lacking to me, and that I am not quite perfect, unless I had within me some idea of a Being more perfect than myself, in comparison with which I should recognise the deficiencies of my nature?

And we cannot say that this idea of God is perhaps materially false and that consequently I can derive it from nought [i.e. that possibly it exists in me because I am imperfect], as I have just said is the case with ideas of heat, cold and other such things; for, on the contrary, as this idea is very clear and distinct and contains within it more objective reality than any other, there can be none which is of itself more true, nor any in which there can be less suspicion of falsehood. The idea, I say, of this Being who is absolutely perfect and infinite, is entirely true; for although, perhaps, we can imagine that such a Being does not exist, we cannot nevertheless imagine that His idea represents nothing real to me, as I have said of the idea of cold. This idea is also very clear and distinct; since all that I conceive clearly and distinctly of the real and the true, and of what conveys some perfection, is in its entirety contained in this idea. And this does not cease to be true although I do not comprehend the infinite, or though in God there is an infinitude of things which I cannot comprehend, nor possibly even reach in any way by thought; for it is of the nature of the infinite that my nature, which is finite and limited, should not comprehend it; and it is sufficient that I should understand this, and that I should judge that all things which I clearly perceive and in which I know that there is some perfection, and possibly likewise an infinitude of properties of which I am ignorant, are in God formally or eminently, so that the idea which I have of Him may become the most true, most clear, and most distinct of all the ideas that are in my mind.

WILLIAM ALSTON

Two Types of Foundationalism

Foundationalism is often stated as the doctrine that knowledge constitutes a structure the foundations of which support all the rest but themselves need no support. To make this less metaphorical we need to specify the mode of support involved. In contemporary discussions of foundationalism knowledge is thought of in terms of true justified belief (with or without further conditions); thus the mode of support involved is justification, and what gets supported a belief. The sense in which a foundation needs no support is that it is not justified by its relation to other justified beliefs; in that sense it does not "rest on" other beliefs. Thus we may formulate foundationalism as follows:

(I) Our justified beliefs form a structure, in that some beliefs (the foundations) are justified by something other than their relation to other justified beliefs; beliefs that *are* justified by their relation to other beliefs all depend for their justification on the foundations.

Notice that nothing is said about *knowledge* in this formulation. Since the structure alleged by foundationalism is a structure of the justification of belief, the doctrine can be stated in terms of that component of knowledge alone. Indeed, one who thinks that knowledge has nothing to do with justified belief is still faced with the question of whether foundationalism is a correct view about the structure of epistemic justification.

Two emendations will render this formulation more perspicuous. First, a useful bit of terminology. Where what justifies a belief includes the believer's having certain other justified beliefs, so related to the first belief as to embody reasons or grounds for it, we may speak of *indirectly (mediately) justified belief*. And, where what justifies a belief does not include any such constituent, we may speak of *directly (immediately) justified belief*. Correspondingly, a case of knowl-

edge in which the justification requirement is satisfied by indirect (mediate) justification will be called *indirect (mediate) knowledge*; and a case in which the justification requirement is satisfied by direct (immediate) justification will be called *direct (immediate) knowledge*.

Second, we should make more explicit how mediate justification is thought to rest on immediately justified belief. The idea is that, although the other beliefs involved in the mediate justification of a given belief may themselves be mediately justified, if we continue determining at each stage how the supporting beliefs are justified, we will arrive, sooner, or later, at directly justified beliefs. This will not, in general, be a single line of descent; typically the belief with which we start will rest on several beliefs, each of which in turn will rest on several beliefs. So the general picture is that of multiple branching from the original belief.

With this background we may reformulate foundationalism as follows (turning the "foundation" metaphor on its head):

(II) Every mediately justified belief stands at the origin of a (more or less) multiply branching tree structure at the tip of each branch of which is an immediately justified belief.

(II) can be read as purely hypothetical (*if there are any mediately justified beliefs, then...*) or with existential import (There are mediately justified beliefs, and...). Foundationalists typically make the latter claim, and I shall understand the doctrine to carry existential import.

(II) can usefully be divided into two claims:

(A) There are directly justified beliefs.

(B) A given person has a stock of directly justified beliefs sufficient to generate chains of justification that terminate in whatever indirectly justified beliefs he has.

In other words, (A) there are foundations, and (B) they suffice to hold up the building.

In this essay we shall restrict our attention to (A). More specifically, we shall be concerned with a certain issue over what it takes for a belief to serve as a foundation.

I. THE SECOND LEVEL ARGUMENT

Let's approach this issue by confronting foundationalism with a certain criticism, a recent version of which can be found in Bruce Aune.[1]

> The line of reasoning behind the empiricist's assumption is, again, that while intra-language rules may validly take us from premise to conclusion, they cannot themselves establish empirical truth. If the premises you start with are false, you will have no guarantee that the conclusions you reach are not false either. Hence, to attain knowledge of the actual world, you must ultimately have premises whose truth is acceptable independently of any inference and whose status is accordingly indubitable. Only by having such premises can you gain a starting point that would make inference worthwhile. For convenience, these indispensable basic premises may be called "intrinsically acceptable." The possibility of empirical knowledge may then be said to depend on the availability of intrinsically acceptable premises.
>
> If this line of thought is sound, it follows that utter scepticism can be ruled out only if one can locate basic empirical premises that are intrinsically acceptable. Although philosophers who attack scepticism in accordance with this approach generally think they are defending common sense, it is crucial to observe that they cannot actually be doing so. The reason for this is that, from the point of view of common experience, there is no plausibility at all in the idea that intrinsically acceptable premises, as so defined, ever exist. Philosophers defending such premises fail to see this because they always ignore the complexity of the situation in which an empirical claim is evaluated.
>
> I have already given arguments to show that introspective claims are not, in themselves, intrinsically infallible, they may be regarded as virtually certain if produced by a reliable (sane, clear-headed) observer, but their truth is not a consequence of the mere fact that they are confidently made. To establish a similar conclusion regarding the observation claims of everyday life only the sketchiest arguments are needed. Obviously the mere fact that such a claim is made does not assure us of its truth. If we know that the observer is reliable, made his observation in good light, was reasonably close to the object, and so on, then we may immediately regard it as acceptable. But its acceptability is not intrinsic to the claim itself. . . . I would venture to say that any spontaneous claim, observational or introspective, carries almost no presumption of truth, when considered entirely by itself. If we accept such a claim as true, it is only because of our confidence that a complex body of background assumptions—concerning observers, standing conditions, the kind of object in question—and, often, a complex mass of further observations all point to the conclusion that it is true.
>
> Given these prosaic considerations, it is not necessary to cite experimental evidence illustrating the delusions easily brought about by, for example, hypnosis to see that no spontaneous claim is acceptable wholly on its own merits. On the contrary, common experience is entirely adequate to show that clear-headed men never accept a claim merely because it is made, without regard to the peculiarities of the agent and of the conditions under which it is produced. For such men, the acceptability of every claim is always determined by inference. If we are prepared to take these standards of acceptability seriously, we must accordingly admit that the traditional search for intrinsically acceptable empirical premises is completely misguided. (pp. 41–43)

Now the target of Aune's critique differs in several important respects from the foundationalism defined above. First and most obviously, Aune supposes that any "intrinsically acceptable premises" will be infallible and indubitable, and some of his arguments are directed specifically against these features. Second, there is an ambiguity in the term 'intrinsically acceptable'. Aune introduces it to mean "whose truth is acceptable independently of any inference"; this looks roughly equivalent to our 'directly justified'. However, in arguing against the supposition that the "observation claims of everyday life" are intrinsically acceptable, he says that "the mere fact that such a claim is made does not assure us of its truth", thereby implying that to be intrinsically acceptable a claim would have to be justified just by virtue of being made. Now it is clear that a belief (claim) of which this is true is directly justified, but the converse does not hold. A perceptual belief will also be directly justified, as that term was explained above, if what justifies it is the fact that the perceiver "is reliable, made his observation in good light, was reasonably close to the object, and so on", *provided it is not also required that he be justified in believing that these conditions are satisfied.* Thus this argument of Aune's has no tendency to show that perceptual beliefs cannot be directly justified, but only that they cannot enjoy that special sort of direct justification which we may term "self-justification".

Some of Aune's arguments, however, would seem to be directed against any immediate justification, and a consideration of these will reveal a third and more subtle discrepancy between Aune's target(s) and my version of foundationalism. Near the end of the passage Aune says:

> If we accept such a claim [observational or introspective] as true, it is only because of our confidence that a complex of background assumptions . . . all point to the conclusion that it is true.

And again:

> For such men [clear-headed men], the acceptability of every claim is always determined by inference.

It certainly looks as if Aune is arguing that whenever a claim (belief) is justified, it is justified by inference (by relation to other justified beliefs); and that would be the denial of 'There are directly justified beliefs'. But look more closely. Aune is discussing not what would justify the issuer of an introspective or observational claim in his belief, but rather what it would take to justify "us" in accepting his claim; he is arguing from a third-person perspective. Now it does seem clear that I cannot be immediately justified in accepting *your* introspective or observational claim as true. If I am so justified, it is because I am justified in supposing that you issued a claim of that sort, that you are in a normal condition and know the language, and (if it is an observational claim) that conditions were favorable for your accurately perceiving that sort of thing. But that is only because I, in contrast to you, am justified in believing that p (where what you claimed is that p, and where I have no independent access to p) only if I am justified in supposing that you are justified in believing that p. My access to p is through your access. It is just because *my* justification in believing that p presupposes my being justified in believing that you are justified, that my justification has to be indirect. That is why I have to look into such matters as conditions of observation and your normality. Thus what Aune is really pointing to is the necessity for "inferential" backing for any higher level belief to the effect that someone is justified in believing that p. (I shall call such higher level beliefs *epistemic beliefs*). His argument, if it shows anything, shows that no epistemic belief can be immediately justified. But it does nothing to show that the original observer's or introspector's belief that p was not immediately justified. Hence his argument is quite compatible with the view that an introspective belief is self-justified and with the view that an observational belief is justified just by being formed in favorable circumstances.

As a basis for further discussion I should like to present my own version of an argument against the possibility of immediate justification for epistemic beliefs—what I shall call the *second level argument*:

(A1) Where S's belief that p is mediately justified, any justification for the belief that S is *justified in believing that p* is obviously mediate. For one could not be justified in this latter belief unless it were based on a justified belief that S is justified in accepting the grounds on which his belief that p is based. But even where S is immediately justified in believing that p, the higher level belief will still be mediately justified, if at all. For in taking a belief to be justified, we are evaluating it in a certain way. And, like any evaluative property, epistemic justification is a supervenient property, the application of which is based on more fundamental properties. A belief is justified because it possesses what Roderick Firth has called "warrant-increasing properties". Hence in order for me to be justified in believing that S's belief that p is justified, I must be justified in certain other beliefs, viz., that S's *belief that p* possesses a certain property, Q, and that Q renders its possessor justified. (Another way of formulating this last belief is: a belief that there is a valid epistemic principle to the effect that any belief that is Q is justified.) Hence in no case can an epistemic belief that S is justified in believing that p, itself be immediately justified.

Before proceeding I shall make two comments on this argument and its conclusion.

(1) It may appear that the conclusion of the argument is incompatible with the thesis that one cannot be justified in believing that p without also being justified in believing that one is justified in believing that p. For if being immediately justified in believing that p necessarily carried with it being justified in believing that I am justified in believing that p, it would seem that this latter justification would be equally immediate. I would not shirk from such an incompatibility, since I feel confident in rejecting that thesis. It is not clear, however, that there is any such incompatibility. It all depends on how we construe the necessity. If, for example, it is that my being justified in believing that p necessarily puts me into possession of the *grounds* I need for being justified in the higher level belief, then that is quite compatible with our conclusion that the latter can only be mediately justified.

(2) The conclusion should not be taken to imply that one must perform any conscious inference to be justified in an epistemic belief, or even that one must be explicitly aware that the lower level belief has an appropriate warrant-increasing property.

Here, as in other areas, one's grounds can be possessed more or less implicitly. Otherwise we would have precious little mediate knowledge.

I have already suggested that the second level argument is not really directed against (II). To be vulnerable to this argument, a foundationalist thesis would have to require of foundations not only that *they* be immediately justified, but also that the believer be immediately justified in believing that they are immediately justified. A position that does require this we may call *iterative foundationalism*, and we may distinguish it from the earlier form (*simple foundationalism*) as follows (so far as concerns the status of the foundations):

> Simple Foundationalism: For any epistemic subject, S, there are p's such that S is immediately justified in believing that p.

> Iterative Foundationalism: For any epistemic subject, S, there are p's such that S is immediately justified in believing that p and S is immediately justified in believing that he is immediately justified in believing that p.

It would not take much historical research to show that both positions have been taken. What I want to investigate here is which of them there is most reason to take. Since the classic support for foundationalism has been the regress argument, I shall concentrate on determining which form emerges from that line of reasoning.

II. THE REGRESS ARGUMENT

The regress argument seeks to show that the only alternatives to admitting epistemic foundations are circularity of justification or an equally unpalatable infinite regress of justification. It may be formulated as follows:

(A2) Suppose we are trying to determine whether S is mediately justified in believing that p. To be so justified he has to be justified in believing certain other propositions, $q, r, \ldots$ that are suitably related to p (so as to constitute adequate grounds for p). Let's say we have identified a set of such propositions each of which S believes. Then he is justified in believing that p only if he is justified in believing each of those propositions. And, for each of these propositions $q, r,$ . . . that he is not immediately justified in believing, he is justified in believing it only if he is justified in believing some other propositions that are suitably related to it. And for each of these latter propositions . . .

Thus in attempting to give a definitive answer to the original question we are led to construct a more or less extensive tree structure, in which the original belief and every other putatively mediately justified belief form nodes from which one or more branches issue, in such a way that every branch is a part of some branch that issues from the original belief. Now the question is: what form must be assumed by the structure in order that S be mediately justified in believing that p? There are the following conceivable forms for a given branch:

(a) It terminates in an immediately justified belief.

(b) It terminates in an unjustified belief.

(c) The belief that p occurs at some point (past the origin), so that the branch forms a loop.

(d) The branch continues infinitely.

Of course some branches might assume one form and others another.

The argument is that the original belief will be mediately justified only if every branch assumes form (a). Positively, it is argued that on this condition the originally mentioned necessary condition for the original belief's being mediately justified is satisfied, and, negatively, it is argued that if any branch assumes any of the other forms, it is not.

(1) Where every branch has form (a), this necessary condition is satisfied for every belief in the structure. Since each branch terminates in an immediately justified belief that is justified without necessity for further justified beliefs, the regress is ended along each branch. Hence justification is transferred along each branch right back to the original belief.

(2) For any branch that exhibits form (b), no element, even the origin, is justified, at least by this structure. Since the terminus is not justified, the prior element, which is justified only if the terminus is, is not justified. And, since it is not justified, its predecessor, which is justified only if it is, is not justified either. And so on, right back to the origin, which therefore itself fails to be justified.

(3) Where we have a branch that forms a closed loop, again nothing on that branch, even the origin, is justified, so far as its justification depends on this tree structure. For what the branch "says" is that the belief that p is justified only if the belief that r is justified, and that belief is justified only if . . . , and the belief that z is justified only if the belief that p is justified. So what this chain of necessary conditions tells us is that the belief that p is justified only if the belief that p is justified. True enough, but that still leaves it completely open whether the belief that p is justified.

(4) If there is a branch with no terminus, that means that no matter how far we extend the branch, the last element is still a belief that is mediately justified if at all. Thus, as far as this structure goes, wherever we stop adding elements, we have still not shown that the relevant necessary condition for the mediate justification of the original belief is satisfied. Thus the structure does not exhibit the original belief as mediately justified.

Hence the original belief is mediately justified only if every branch in the tree structure terminates in an immediately justified belief. Hence every mediately justified belief stands at the origin of a tree structure at the tip of each branch of which is an immediately justified belief.

Now this version of the argument, analogues of which occur frequently in the literature, supports only simple foundationalism. It has no tendency to show that there is immediately justified epistemic belief. So long as S is directly justified in believing some t for each branch of the tree, that will be quite enough to stop the regress; all that is needed is that he *be* justified in believing t without thereby incurring the need to be justified in believing some further proposition. But perhaps there are other versions that yield the stronger conclusion. Indeed, in surveying the literature one will discover versions that differ from (A2) in one or both of the following respects:

1. Their starting points (the conditions of which they seek to establish) are cases of being justified in believing that one knows (is justified in believing) that p, rather than, more generally, cases of being justified in believing that p.

2. They are concerned to establish what is necessary for showing that p, rather than what is necessary for being justified in believing that p.

Let's consider whether regress arguments with one or the other of these features will yield iterative foundationalism.

First let's consider an argument that differs from (A2) only in the first respect. In his essay "Theory of Knowledge" in a volume devoted to the history of twentieth-century American philosophy, R. M. Chisholm launches a regress argument as follows:

To the question "What justification do I have for thinking that I know that a is true?" one may reply: "I know that b is true, and if I know that b is true then I also know that a is true". And to the question "What justification do I have for thinking I know that b is true?" one may reply: "I know that c is true, and if I know that c is

true then I also know that b is true". Are we thus led, sooner or later, to something, n, of which one may say "What justifies me in thinking I know that n is true is simply the fact that n is true"? (p. 263)

Chisholm then supports an affirmative answer to this last question by excluding other alternatives in a manner similar to that of (A2).

Now the crucial question is: why does Chisholm conclude not just that mediate justification of claims to know requires *some* immediately justified beliefs, but that it requires immediately justified *epistemic* beliefs? Of course, having granted the general position that any mediately justified belief rests on some immediately justified belief(s), one might naturally suppose that mediately justified *epistemic* beliefs will rest on immediately justified *epistemic* beliefs. But we should not assume that all cases of mediate knowledge rest on foundations that are similar in content. On the contrary, every version of foundationalism holds that from a certain set of basic beliefs one erects a superstructure that is vastly different from these foundations. From knowledge of sense data one derives knowledge of public physical objects, from knowledge of present occurrences one derives knowledge of the past and future, and so on. So why suppose that *if* mediate epistemic beliefs rest on foundations, those foundations will be epistemic beliefs? We would need some special reason for this. And neither Chisholm nor, to my knowledge, anyone else has given any such reason. All rely on essentially the same argument as (A2), which at most yields the weaker conclusion. They seem to have just assumed uncritically that the foundations on which epistemic beliefs rest are themselves epistemic.

Thus, altering the regress argument in the first way does not provide grounds for iterative foundationalism. Let's turn to the second modification. In order to maximize our chances, let's combine it with the first and consider what it would take to *show*, for some p, that I am justified in believing that p. It is easy to see how one might be led into this. One who accepted the previous argument might still feel dissatisfied with simple foundationalism. "You have shown," he might say, "that it is *possible* to be justified in believing that p without having any immediately justified epistemic belief. But are we *in fact* justified in believing any p? To answer that question you will have to *show*, for some p, that you are justified in believing it. And the question is, what is required for that? Is it possible to do that without immediately justified epistemic belief?"

Now if we are to show, via a regress argument, that immediately justified epistemic belief is necessary for showing that I am justified in believing any p, it must be because some requirement for showing sets up a regress that can be stopped only if we have such beliefs. What could that requirement be? Let's see what is required for showing that p. Clearly, to show that p I must adduce some other (possibly compound) proposition, q. What restrictions must be put on a q and my relations thereto?

(1) It is true that q.

(2) q constitutes adequate grounds for p.

These requirements give rise to no regress, or at least none that is vicious. Even if no proposition can be true without some other proposition's being true, there is nothing repugnant about the notion of an infinity of true propositions. Hence we may pass on.

(3) I am justified in believing that q.

This requirement clearly does give rise to a regress, viz., that already brought out in (A2). We have seen that immediately justified epistemic belief is not required to end that regress; so again we may pass on.

(4) I am justified in believing that I am justified in believing that q.

I am not prepared to admit this requirement, my reasons being closely connected with the point that one may be justified in believing that q without even believing that one is so justified, much less being justified in believing that one is so justified. However, it is not necessary to discuss that issue here. Even if (4) is required, it will simply set up a regress of the sort exemplified by Chisholm's argument, an argument we have seen to have no stronger conclusion than simple foundationalism.

(5) I am able to show that q.

This looks more promising. Clearly this requirement gives rise to a regress that is different from that of (A2). If I can show that p by citing q only if I am able to show that q, and if, in turn, I am able to show that q by citing r only if I am able to show that r, it is clear that we will be able to avoid our familiar alternatives of circularity and infinite regress only if at some point I arrive at a proposition that I can show to be correct without appealing to some other proposition. In deciding whether this argument provides support for iterative foundationalism, we must consider first whether requirement (5) is justified and, second, whether immediately justified epistemic belief would stop the regress so generated.

The requirement looks plausible. For, if I cannot show that q, then it looks as if I won't be able to settle whether or not it is the case that q, and in that case how can I claim to have settled the question about p? But this plausibility is specious, stemming from one of the protean forms assumed by that confusion of levels typified by the confusion of knowing that p with knowing that one knows that p. It's quite true that an inability to show that q will prevent me from showing *that I have shown that p*; for to do the latter I have to show that the grounds I have cited for p are correct. But why suppose that it also prevents me from showing that p? Can't I prove a theorem in logic without being able to prove that I have proved it? The former requires only an ability to wield the machinery of first order logic, which one may possess without the mastery of metalogic required for the second. Similarly, it would seem that I can show that p, by adducing true adequate grounds I am justified in accepting, without being able to *show* that those grounds are true.

But even if requirement (5) were justified and the show-regress were launched, immediately justified epistemic beliefs would be powerless to stop it. Let's say that I originally set out to show that I am justified in believing that a, and in the regress of showings thus generated I eventually cite as a ground *that I am immediately justified in believing that z* (call this higher level proposition "Z"), where I am in fact immediately justified in believing that Z. How will this latter fact enable me to *show* that Z? As a result of being immediately justified in believing that Z, I may have no doubt about the matter; I may feel no need to show *myself* that Z. But of course that doesn't imply that *I have shown* that Z. However immediate my justification for accepting Z, I haven't *shown* that Z unless I adduce grounds for it that meet the appropriate conditions. And once I do that, we are off to the races again. The regress has not been stopped. In the nature of the case it cannot be stopped. In this it differs from the original regress of *being* justified. *Showing* by its very nature requires the exhibition of grounds. Furthermore, grounds must be different from the proposition to be shown. (This latter follows from the "pragmatic" aspect of the concept of showing. To show that p is to present grounds that one can justifiably accept without already accepting p. Otherwise showing would lack the point that goes toward making it what it is.) Hence, there are no conceivable conditions under which I could show that p without citing other propositions that, by requirement (5), I must be able to show. If we accept requirement (5), if an infinite structure of abilities to show is ruled out, and if circularity is unacceptable, it follows that it is impossible ever to show anything. (That would seem to be an additional reason for rejecting [5].) Since immediately justified epistemic belief would do nothing to stop the regress, this kind of regress argument can provide no support for iterative foundationalism.

III. FUNCTIONS OF FOUNDATIONALISM

Thus, although simple foundationalism is strongly supported by (A2), we have failed to find any argument that supports iterative foundationalism. And the second level argument strikes at the latter but not the former. Hence it would seem that foundationalism has a chance of working only in its simple form. This being the case, it is of some interest to determine the extent to which simple foundationalism satisfies the demands and aspirations that foundationalism is designed to satisfy, other than stopping the regress of justification. I shall consider two such demands.

Answering Skepticism

Skepticism assumes various forms, many of which no sort of foundationalism could sensibly be expected to answer. For example, the extreme skeptic who refuses to accept anything until it has been shown to be true and who will not allow his opponent any premises to use for this purpose obviously cannot be answered, whatever one's position. Talking

with him is a losing game. Again there are more limited skepticisms in which one sort of knowledge is questioned (e.g., knowledge of the conscious states of other persons) but others are left unquestioned (e.g., knowledge of the physical environment). Here the answering will be done, if at all, by finding some way of deriving knowledge of the questioned sort from knowledge of the unquestioned sort. The role of a general theory of knowledge will be limited to laying down criteria for success in the derivation, and differences over what is required for foundations would seem to make no difference to such criteria.

The kind of "answer to skepticism" that one might suppose to be affected by our difference is that in which the skeptic doubts that we have any knowledge, a successful answer being a demonstration there is some. One may think that the possession of immediate epistemic knowledge will put us in a better position to do that job. Whether it does, and if so how, depends on what it takes to show that one knows something. The discussion of showing in Section II yielded the following conditions for S's showing that p:

(1) It is true that p.
(2) S cites in support of p a certain proposition q such that:
    (A) It is true that q.
    (B) q is an adequate ground for p.
    (C) S is justified in believing q.

We rejected the further conditions that S be able to show that q. However, since we are here concerned with showing something to a skeptic, it may be that some further requirement should be imposed. After all, we could hardly expect a skeptic to abandon his doubt just on the *chance* that his interlocuter is correct in the grounds he gives. The skeptic will want to be given some reason for supposing those grounds to be correct, and this does not seem unreasonable. But we can't go back to the unqualified requirement that every ground adduced be established or even establishable without automatically making showing impossible. Fortunately there is an intermediate requirement that might satisfy a reasonable skeptic while not rendering all showing impossible. Let's require that S be able to show that r, for any r among his grounds concerning which his audience has any real doubt. This differs from the unqualified requirement in leaving open the possibility that there will be grounds concerning which no reasonable person who has reflected on the matter will have any doubt; and if there be such, it may still be possible for S to succeed in showing that p. Thus we may add to our list of conditions:

> (D) If there is real doubt about q, S is able to show that q.

Now when p is 'S knows that a', the question is whether one or more of these conditions is satisfiable only if S has immediately justified epistemic beliefs. Let's consider the conditions in turn. As for (1), S can in fact know that a without having any directly justified epistemic belief, even if it should be the case that one can't know that a without knowing that one knows that a. For, as we saw in Section II, there is no reason to doubt that all justified beliefs *that one knows or is justified in believing something* are themselves *mediately* justified. As for (2A) and (2B), there should be no temptation to suppose that they depend on iterative foundationalism. As for whether the grounds are true, that is clearly quite independent of my epistemic situation vis-à-vis those grounds, and hence quite independent of whether I have any immediately justified epistemic beliefs, here or elsewhere. Even if one or more of the grounds should themselves be claims to knowledge, the question of what is required for their truth can be handled in the same way as requirement (1). And adequacy, being a matter of relations between propositions, cannot depend on what sort of justification S has for one or another belief. As for (2C), the discussion in Sections I and II failed to turn up any reasons for supposing that immediately justified epistemic belief is required for my being justified in believing anything. That leaves (2D). But this has already been covered. To satisfy (2D) I have to be able to *show* that (some of) my grounds are true. But that will not require conditions that are different in kind from those already discussed. Hence we may conclude that iterative foundationalism is not a presupposition of our showing that we do have knowledge. Of course it remains an open question whether we are in fact capable of showing that we know something. But if we are incapable, it is not because of the lack of immediately justified epistemic belief.

Self-consciously Reconstructing Knowledge from the Foundations

Suppose that we are assailed by general doubts as to whether we really know anything. In order to lay such doubts to rest we seek as many items as possible of which we can be absolutely certain, each on its own apart from any support from anything else we might know, since at that initial stage we are not supposing, with respect to any particular item, that it counts as knowledge. Having identified a number of such isolated certainties, we proceed to seek ways in which further knowledge can be established on that basis, thus validating as much knowledge as possible. Here is an enterprise that really does require iterative foundationalism. If the enterprise is to succeed, then we must, with respect to at least the initial certainties, be immediately justified not only in believing the proposition in question to be true but also in believing that we are immediately justified in believing it to be true. For otherwise, how could we identify the proposition in question as one of the foundations? We can't be mediately justified in supposing ourselves to know it immediately, for at that stage we have nothing else to go on to provide a basis for that higher level belief.

Obviously, my description of this enterprise is modeled on Descartes' procedure in the *Discourse* and *Meditations*. Nevertheless, there are differences, more marked in the *Meditations*, but present in both. For one thing Descartes was not working with a true-justified-belief conception of knowledge, and so what he says has to be "translated" into contemporary "justification" talk. More crucially, Descartes does not rest content with an immediate recognition of isolated certainties. He requires a discursive proof of their status, thus giving rise to the notorious Cartesian circle. We might think of the program I have sketched as the Cartesian program, translated into "justification" talk, and without the requirement that the status of the foundations be established by an appeal to the omnipotence and goodness of God.

If iterative foundationalism is both without strong support and subject to crushing objections, it looks as if we will have to do without a self-conscious reconstruction of knowledge. How grievous a loss is this? Why should anyone want to carry out such a reconstruction? Well, if knowledge does have a foundational structure, it seems intolerable that we should be unable to spell this out. And it may seem that such a spelling out would have to take the present form. But that would be an illusion. If there are foundations, one can certainly identify them and determine how other sorts of knowledge are based on them without first taking on the highly artificial stance assumed by Descartes. One can approach this problem, as one approaches any other, making use of whatever relevant knowledge or justified belief one already possesses. In that case immediate epistemic knowledge is by no means required, just as we have seen it is not required to show that one is justified in holding certain beliefs. If iterative foundationalism is false, we can still have as much epistemic knowledge as you like, but only after we have acquired quite a lot of first level knowledge. And why should that not satisfy any epistemic aspirations that are fitting for the human condition?

IV. ENVOI

As we have seen, the main reason for adopting foundationalism is the seeming impossibility of a belief's being mediately justified without resting ultimately on immediately justified belief. And the main reason for rejecting it (at least the main antecedent reason, apart from the difficulties of working it out) is that reason one version of which we found in the quotation from Aune. That is, it appears that the foundationalist is committed to adopting beliefs in the absence of any reasons for regarding them as acceptable. And this would appear to be the sheerest dogmatism. It is the aversion to dogmatism, to the apparent arbitrariness of putative foundations, that leads many philosophers to embrace some form of coherence or contextualist theory, in which no belief is deemed acceptable unless backed by sound reasons.

The main burden of this paper is that with simple foundationalism one can have the best of both arguments; one can stop the regress of justification without falling into dogmatism. We have already seen that Aune's form of the dogmatism argument does not touch simple foundationalism. For that form of the argument attacks only the ungrounded

acceptance of claims *to knowledge or justification*; and simple foundationalism is not committed to the immediate justification of any such higher level claims. But one may seek to apply the same argument to lower level beliefs. Even simple foundationalism, the critic may say, must allow that some beliefs may be accepted in the absence of any reasons for supposing them to be true. And this is still arbitrary dogmatism. But the simple foundationalist has an answer. His position does not require anyone to accept any belief without having a reason for doing so. Where a person *is* immediately justified in believing that *p*, he may find adequate reasons for the higher level belief that he is immediately justified in believing that *p*. And if he has adequate reasons for accepting this epistemic proposition, it surely is not arbitrary of him to accept the proposition that *p*. What better reason could he have for accepting it?

Lest the reader dismiss this answer as a contemptible piece of sleight-of-hand, let me be more explicit about what is involved. Though the simple foundationalist requires *some* immediately justified beliefs in order to terminate the regress of justification, his position permits him to recognize that all epistemic beliefs require mediate justification. Therefore, for any belief that one is immediately justified in believing, one *may* find adequate reasons for accepting the proposition that one is so justified. The curse (of dogmatism) is taken off immediate justification at the lower level, just by virtue of the fact that propositions at the higher level are acceptable only on the basis of reasons. A foundational belief, *b*, is immediately justified just because some valid epistemic principle lays down conditions for its being justified which do not include the believer's having certain other justified beliefs. But the believer will be justified in believing *that* he is immediately justified in holding *b* only if he has *reasons* for regarding that principle as valid and for regarding *b* as falling under that principle. And if he does have such reasons, he certainly cannot be accused of arbitrariness or dogmatism in accepting *b*. The absence of reasons for *b* is "compensated" for by the reasons for the correlated higher level belief. Or, better, the sense in which one can have reasons for accepting an immediately justified belief is necessarily different from that in which one can have reasons for accepting a mediately justified belief. Reasons in the former case are necessarily "meta" in character; they have to do with reasons for regarding the belief as justified. Whereas in the latter case, though one *may* move up a level and find reasons for the higher level belief that the original belief is mediately justified, it is also required that one have adequate reasons for the lower level belief itself.

We should guard against two possible misunderstandings of the above argument. First, neither simple foundationalism nor any other epistemology can guarantee that one will, or can, find adequate reasons for a given epistemic proposition, or for any other proposition. The point rather is that there is nothing in the position that rules out the possibility that, for any immediately justified belief that one has, one can find adequate reasons for the proposition that one is so justified. Second, we should not take the critic to be denying the obvious point that people are often well advised, in the press of everyday life, to adopt beliefs for which they do not have adequate reasons. We should interpret him as requiring only that an *ideal* epistemic subject will adopt beliefs only for good and sufficient reason. Hence he insists that our epistemology must make room for this possibility. And, as just pointed out, simple foundationalism does so.

The dogmatism argument may be urged with respect to *showing* that *p*, as well as with respect to accepting the proposition that *p*. That is, the critic may argue that foundationalism is committed to the view that "foundations cannot be argued for". Suppose that in trying to show that *p* I adduce some grounds, and, the grounds being challenged, I try to show that they are true, and . . . in this regress I finally arrive at some foundation *f*. Here, according to the critic, the foundationalist must hold that the most I can (properly) do is simply *assert f*, several times if necessary, and with increasing volume. And again this is dogmatism. But again simple foundationalism is committed to no such thing. It leaves something for the arguer to do even here, viz., try to establish the higher level proposition that he is immediately justified in believing that *f*. And, if he succeeds in doing this, what more could we ask? Unless someone demands that he go on to establish the grounds appealed to in that argument—to which again the simple foundationalist has no objection in principle. Of course, as we saw earlier, the demand that one establish every ground in a demonstration is a self defeating demand. But the point is that the simple foundationalist need not, any more than the coherence theorist, mark out certain points at which the regress of showing *must* come to an end. He allows the possibility of one's giving reasons for an assertion whenever it is appropriate to do so, even if that assertion is of a foundation.

NOTE

1. *Knowledge, Mind and Nature* (New York: Random House, 1967).

KEITH LEHRER

Infallible Foundations

THE FOUNDATION AS A GUARANTEE OF TRUTH

We are adopting an entirely different approach that cuts across traditional lines. Rationalists and empiricists often share a common conception which leads to a foundation theory. They conceive of justification as being a guarantee of truth. Empiricists think that experience can guarantee the truth of basic beliefs and rationalists think that reason is the guarantee of truth. Basic beliefs are basic because they cannot be false; their truth is guaranteed. With this initial guarantee of truth in basic beliefs, the next problem is how to extend this guarantee to other beliefs.

Our earlier analysis of knowledge offers a simple explanation of why this doctrine should be held. Since one condition of knowledge is truth, it follows that no belief constitutes knowledge unless it is true. Thus, if our justification fails to guarantee the truth of what we accept, then it may leave us with a false belief. In that case, we lack knowledge, so justification sufficient to ensure us knowledge must, some foundation theorists have argued, guarantee the truth of what we accept.

Another motive for the doctrine of infallible foundationalism is a consequence of our account of acceptance. If the goal of acceptance is to accept something just in case it is true, then acceptance, which guarantees its own truth, provides us with a prophylactic against accepting something false. Thus, though a fallible foundation theorist may deny that we need a guarantee for the truth of basic beliefs, a central thesis of the traditional foundation theory was that basic beliefs are immune from error and refutation. If basic beliefs were erroneous and refutable, then all that was justified by basic beliefs, all that was built upon them in the edifice of justification, might be undone by error. The very founda-tion of all justification might prove unsound. If there is nothing to ensure that such basic beliefs are true, then, *ipso facto*, there is nothing to ensure the truth of those beliefs they justify. All justification might rest on a false foundation. . . .

INCORRIGIBLE FOUNDATIONS

A foundation theory alleging that basic beliefs guarantee their truth faces two problems. The first is to show that there are some basic beliefs which can guarantee their own truth. The second is to show how basic beliefs can guarantee the truth of other beliefs. Let us consider the first problem. Philosophers have maintained that some beliefs guarantee their own truth and are thus self-justified because they are *incorrigible*. We shall now examine the tenability of this thesis. What is meant by saying that a belief is incorrigible?

Let us begin with the intuitive notion that an incorrigible belief is one such that the person who has it cannot be mistaken in believing what she does. We are immediately faced with the tricky little word 'can', a semantic chameleon. What are we to understand it to mean? We may wisely begin with a technical notion and then, should that prove insufficiently subtle, turn to some modification. Let us begin with the notion of *logical possibility*.

It is logically impossible that someone has a female brother or that some number is larger than itself. Logical impossibility is a familiar notion, though it is clear that some modal notion, possibility, for example, must be taken as primitive. So, if we assume the notion of a possible world, for example, then we can say that something is logically impossible if and only if it does not obtain in any possible world. We sometimes speak of the logical impossibility of certain sentences. For example, we might say that the sentence, 'John has a female brother,' is logically impossible. However, when we say such things we are speaking elliptically. It is what is *stated* by the sentence that is logically impossible. What the sentence 'John has a female brother' states is that John has a female brother, and that is logically impossible. This explains why the sentence is not true in any possible world and, therefore, is contradictory or analytically false. We thus come full tilt to the controversial notion of *analyticity*.

It is notoriously difficult to provide any satisfactory definition or criterion of analyticity or related notions. Some philosophers thus disregard the notion of analyticity as a philosophical relic of semantic battles lost long ago. This conclusion is premature. Some logical notion, whether that of contradictoriness, possibility, or impossibility, may be taken as basic and undefined. Once we concede that logical possibility or some other logical notion must be taken as basic and undefined, we must also admit there are going to be cases in which it is difficult to ascertain whether something is logically possible. This is partly because the distinction between logic and other areas of inquiry is not clearly drawn. Nevertheless, there are many cases in which the application of the concept will be sufficiently precise for useful employment. . . .

Amended Definition of Incorrigibility

The solution to this problem is a simple amendment of the definition of incorrigibility, one which will, moreover, insure that incorrigible beliefs achieve the goal of acceptance. We said that the objective of acceptance is to accept that p if and only if it is true that p. The definition of incorrigibility given above logically insures that whenever a person's acceptance of p is incorrigible, then, if a person accepts that p, it is true that p, but this is only one objective of acceptance. The other is to accept that p if it is true that p. To insure logically that incorrigible beliefs attain the objectives of acceptance, we should define incorrigibility as follows:

The belief that p is incorrigible for S if and only if (i) it is logically necessary that if S believes that p, then it is true that p and (ii) it is logically necessary that if it is true that p, then S believes that p.

Incorrigible beliefs so defined fulfill the objectives of acceptance as a matter of logical necessity. The first condition might be called the *infallibility* condition because it requires that one cannot fail to attain truth in what one believes, and the second condition might be called the *irresistibility* condition because it requires that one cannot resist believing what is true. Beliefs that fulfill the infallibility condition will be said to be *infallible* beliefs, while those that fulfill the irresistibility condition will be said to be *irresistible* beliefs.

This definition of incorrigibility is equivalent to saying that a belief that p is incorrigible for S just in case (i) it is logically impossible that S believe that p and that it be false that p and (ii) it is logically impossible that it be true that p and that S not believe that p. The first condition, the infallibility condition, is the one that proved insufficient in consideration of necessary truths, but the addition of the second, the irresistibility condition, mends the difficulty. Though it is logically impossible that a person should believe a mathematical truth (for example, that 25 times 26 equals 650) and be in error, it is perfectly possible that a person should fail to believe such a truth. In this case the irresistibility condition is not satisfied, the belief is not irresistible. Thus, the truth that 25 times 26 equals 650 is not an incorrigible belief for a person when it is logically possible that the person not believe this because it is not an irresistible belief.

Many beliefs that a person has about herself are alleged to be incorrigible in this sense. The favorites are beliefs about conscious mental states of the moment, such as a sharp pain, the idea being that a person cannot be mistaken about what is consciously occurring in her mind at the moment it is occurring. Rather than beginning with a discussion of a belief about some mental or psychological state, though, let us go back to Descartes and consider the bare belief of a person that she exists, whatever else might be true about her.

Consider, for example, my belief that I exist. My belief that I exist cannot possibly be false, and it is plausible to affirm that I cannot possibly fail to believe it. Consider my belief that I believe something. It is logically impossible that I believe that I believe something and do not believe something. The belief is clearly infallible. Moreover, it is plausible to maintain that I cannot fail to believe that I believe something when, in fact, I do believe something and, thus, that the belief is irresistible as well. Thus, the belief that I exist and the belief that I believe something are infallible beliefs which are plausible candidates for the role of incorrigible beliefs as so defined.

Infallible Beliefs About Thoughts

The foregoing example concerning beliefs about believing something must be distinguished from a closely related one. Once it is conceded that the belief that one believes something is infallible, it might be inferred that if a person believed that he believes that so and so, then his belief that he believes that so and so is also infallible. This is doubtful, however. I cannot both believe something and be in error in believing that I believe something, but I can believe that I believe some specific thing, that my belief has some specific content, and be in error. The sort of belief that concerns us is acceptance in the interests of obtaining truth and avoiding error, and, as we noted in the last chapter, such belief is a functional state implying a readiness to infer and act in specified ways. The inferences and actions of a person may reveal that he does not accept what he sincerely says and even believes he accepts. If a man says he believes a woman is capable of performing a job as well as the man she has replaced and yet immediately infers, without investigation, that everything that goes wrong in the office is her fault, he does not really believe she is as capable as the man she replaced. His chauvinism shows that he does not accept what he says, even if he believes he does. One could offer similar arguments to show that it is logically possible for a person to be mistaken about what she hopes, fears, and wishes.

Are any mental occurrences the objects of infallible beliefs? The best candidates are thoughts and sensations. Let us consider thoughts first. We sometimes say of a person that he thinks that so and so when we are using the term 'think' to mean something very much like belief. That is not the sense of the term we shall consider now. Instead, consider the participial use of the term 'thinking' which describes an occurrent episode, for example, thinking that

Mary is a colonel. Here we use the term to refer to the thoughts that are now occurring to us or our ongoing mental processes. Can a person be mistaken in his beliefs about such occurrences?

Suppose I am thinking that Bacon is the author of *Hamlet*. Suppose, secondly, that I believe that Bacon is identical with Shakespeare, that is, that the man known to us as the author, Shakespeare, is none other than Bacon. However, though I believe this identity to hold, let us also imagine that this belief is not before my mind, I am not thinking of this identity at the time at which I am thinking that Bacon is the author of *Hamlet*. Now, suppose I am asked what I was thinking. I might conclude that I was thinking that Shakespeare was the author of *Hamlet* because, believing that Bacon is Shakespeare, I also believe that thinking that Bacon is such and such is the same thing as thinking that Shakespeare is such and such. Am I correct?

The answer is no. Suppose my thinking, in this instance, consists of my talking to myself, of mulling things over in silent soliloquy, though we admit that not all thinking consists of such silent soliloquy. Nevertheless, there are some cases in which thinking consists of talking to oneself, and by focusing on such cases we shall be able to reveal the way in which a person can be mistaken about what he is thinking. Suppose that when I was thinking that Bacon is the author of *Hamlet*, my thinking consisted of saying to myself: 'Bacon is the author of *Hamlet*.' Now, it is perfectly clear that to say, 'Bacon is the author of *Hamlet*' is one thing, and to say, 'Shakespeare is the author of *Hamlet*,' another. Thus, thinking that Bacon is the author of *Hamlet* is not necessarily the same thing as thinking that Shakespeare is the author of *Hamlet*. We may, therefore, imagine that I was not thinking the latter when I was thinking the former. Thus, when I reported that I was thinking that Shakespeare is the author of *Hamlet*, and believed what I said, I was quite mistaken. Hence, believing that one is thinking such and such does not logically imply that one is thinking that.

There are several objections to this line of thought which must be met. The first is that even though my thinking that Bacon is the author of *Hamlet* might, in some way, consist of my saying, 'Bacon is the author of *Hamlet*' to myself, it still does not follow that I was not thinking that Shakespeare is the author of *Hamlet* when saying to myself 'Bacon is the author of *Hamlet*'. Maybe I was thinking that Shakespeare is the author of *Hamlet*, but my so thinking did not consist of my saying 'Shakespeare is the author of *Hamlet*' to myself.

The reply to this objection is that there is no reason to say I was thinking Shakespeare was the author of *Hamlet* when I was saying something quite different to myself. My reason for saying that I was thinking Shakespeare is the author of *Hamlet* is a faulty inference. From the premise that Bacon is Shakespeare I inferred that thinking Bacon is such and such is the same thing as thinking Shakespeare is such and such. The inference is as faulty as the inference from that premise to the conclusion that saying Bacon is such and such is the same thing as saying Shakespeare is such and such. This inference is incorrect, even if the two men are identical, because I did not say that they were identical. Hence, when I said Bacon was such and such, I did not say that Shakespeare was such and such.

The argument just enunciated may be obscured by the consideration that if Bacon and Shakespeare are the same, then what I said of the one man is true if and only if what I said of the other is true. However, we can avoid this issue by assuming my belief that Bacon is Shakespeare to be false. Indeed, most scholars of Elizabethan literature do assume this. In that case, when I am saying that Shakespeare is the author of *Hamlet*, what I am saying is true, while, when I am saying that Bacon is the author of *Hamlet*, what I am saying is false. Hence, saying the one thing cannot be identical with saying the other. The same holds for thinking. If, when I am thinking that Shakespeare is the author of *Hamlet*, what I am thinking is true, while, when I am thinking that Bacon is the author of *Hamlet*, what I am thinking is false—then my thinking the first cannot be identical with my thinking the second. Hence, if I believe that I am thinking Shakespeare is the author of *Hamlet* because I believe I am thinking Bacon is the author of *Hamlet*, as was the case in the example cited, the former belief may be mistaken, even though the latter is correct.

Moreover, I can falsely believe that I am thinking Shakespeare is the author of *Hamlet* at the very same time I am actually thinking that Bacon is the author of *Hamlet*. To see that this is so, notice first of all that I can believe that I am thinking that Bacon is the author of *Hamlet* at the very time at which I am thinking that. My believing that I am thinking can coexist with the thinking and yet be quite distinct from the thinking. When a person talks to herself, she need not believe what she says. If my belief that I am thinking that Bacon is the author of *Hamlet* can exist at the same time as my thinking that, then obviously my false belief that I am thinking Shakespeare is the author of *Hamlet* can exist at the same time as my thinking Bacon is the author of *Hamlet*.

From the preceding argument we may conclude that a person can make all sorts of mistakes about what is presently going on in her mind. The preceding argument may be adopted to show that when a person believes that she is surmising that *p*, doubting that *p*, or pondering that *p*, she may be mistaken in her belief. It would be the most unforgivable pedantry to rerun the preceding argument for each of these states. Moreover, any mental state that has a specific content, the content that *p*, as an object is a state about which one can be mistaken. This should be clear from the preceding argument. Thus, we have subverted the pretentious claim of introspection to be the source of infallible belief concerning the content of even our present thoughts.

Fallible Beliefs About Sensations

Are beliefs about sensations infallible? Following a philosophical tradition, we may refer to the objects of sensory experiences as sensations whether the experience is tactile, visual, auditory, and so forth. Armstrong has argued that reports about the sensations one is having are reports that can be mistaken even though no verbal slip or other verbal confusion is involved. It will be useful for our purposes to reformulate his thesis and arguments in terms of belief. The change is not fundamental. Armstrong argues that we might at some time have exceedingly good evidence both that a person was not lying or making a verbal error, and that she did not have the sensation she said she had. To this end, imagine that we have reached a level of neurological understanding beyond the present and have established that a person experiences a certain sensation when and only when in a certain brainstate, call it state 143. Let us imagine that the sensation is a visual one, for example, that sort of visual experience that a normal person has when confronted with red objects in daylight. We may call this a sensation of red.

Moreover, suppose we can give a person a drug which will make him truthful in answering questions. Now imagine we give a person such a drug, he reports a sensation of red, and we are able to observe that he is not in brain state 143. On the basis of the evidence that he is drugged, we conclude that he believes what he says. On the basis of the neurological evidence that he is not in brain state 143, we conclude that he is not having a sensation of red. This story, Armstrong would have us concede, is at least logically possible. If it is logically possible and involves no contradiction in conception, then it is logically possible that the person in question believes that he has a sensation of red when he does not have it.

The basic assumption of the example is that we could have evidence which shows a person believes he is having a sensation he is not having. If it is conceded that such evidence would render it highly probable that the person is not having the sensation without thereby rendering it at least as probable that he does not believe he is having the sensation, then the argument succeeds. We know it is a theorem of probability that if evidence renders a hypothesis highly probable, then it renders any logical consequence of that hypothesis at least as probable. Let us abbreviate the hypothesis that the person is not having the sensation by 'NS' and the hypothesis that he does not believe he has the sensation by 'NB', and the evidence Armstrong mentions by 'E'. Now suppose the evidence E renders NS highly probable but does not render NB probable. This would show that believing one has a sensation does not logically imply having the sensation, because NS does not logically imply NB.

Nevertheless, the argument is defective. We all agree that an experimenter might have evidence which would convince her that it is highly probable that the man in the example believes that he has a sensation but does not. It would seem to her that evidence E renders NS highly probable, but fails to render NB equally probable. There are, however, two divergent explanations of our experimenter's attitude. One is that the evidence only seems not to render NB highly probable. If a person does not recognize that one hypothesis logically implies a second, then evidence that favors the first hypothesis might not seem to favor the second, even though in fact it does.

Let us consider an example in which evidence renders one hypothesis highly probable, but does not seem to render highly probable a logical consequence of it. Imagine that I see a red die on my desk, and let us suppose my sensory evidence renders it highly probable that there is a red die there. This evidence then also renders it highly probable that there is a cube on my desk, since a die is by definition a cube. Now, suppose that I do not know that it logically follows from the fact that something is a cube that it has twelve edges. In that case, though I maintain that my evidence renders it highly probable that there is a cube on my desk, I might deny that the evidence renders it highly probable that there is a twelve-edged object on my desk. Even so, the latter would be an error. The evidence that renders it highly probable that there is a cube on my desk must render it at least as probable that there is a solid object having twelve edges on my desk, for the former logically implies the latter.

The application of these considerations to the issue at hand is to illustrate two different ways of explaining the reaction of our fictitious experimenter. One is to assume what the experimenter does. The other is to assume that the experimenter simply failed to notice that believing one has a sensation logically implies that one has it. On the latter assumption she has failed to notice that her evidence renders it highly improbable that the subject believes he has a sensation. This second explanation is consistent with the infallibility of beliefs about sensations. These two ways of explaining why the experimenter thinks what she does are on exactly equal footing. We need some other argument to shake the dialectical ground beneath them.

Sensations and Incorrigibility: A Counterexample

Another argument is readily available. A person might believe that one sensation is the same as another when this belief is erroneous and, consequently, that he is having one sensation when he is having quite a different one. Let us consider an example of confusing two sensations, those of hurting and itching. Imagine that a not very enlightened man goes to his doctor and is inclined to believe what the doctor says even when her medical deliverance is somewhat preposterous. The doctor tells the man that it is not surprising that his sensation is sometimes one of pain and sometimes one of itching because itches are really pains. All itches, she says, are pains, though some are very mild. Such is the authority of the doctor, and such the credulity of the man, that her word is taken as creed. From that moment on, he never doubts that itches are pains, and, though they feel different, he firmly believes that he is in pain, even if only very slightly so, whenever he has the slightest itch. When he itches, therefore, he erroneously believes that he is in pain, even if only very slightly so. Thus, his beliefs that he is in pain are often erroneous and are by no means infallible.

It should be apparent that the man in question might have been misled by his esteemed medical sage into believing that any sensation was another when in fact it was not. He might, without understanding how such things could possibly be true, believe that they are. Hence, beliefs about sensations, like beliefs about thoughts, are fallible and corrigible. In general, very little of what we believe about our own mental and psychological states is incorrigible. Error can, as a matter of logic, insert itself stealthily between belief and what is believed in this matter as in others.

Other Alleged Counterexamples

Other counterexamples to the thesis that beliefs about sensations are incorrigible concern people who are in a more or less aberrant state. Consider a man who believes he is about to undergo some painful experience, for example, that he is about to be touched by some very hot object, though in fact the object is cold to the touch. Because he expects to feel a burning sensation, he could believe that he is feeling such a sensation during the first moment or two that the cold object is touching his flesh. This belief would then be false. The difficulty with such a counterexample is that it is problematic whether expecting to feel a burning sensation produces false beliefs or a burning sensation.

Another kind of counterexample concerns those who are mentally aberrant and undergoing hallucinations. For example, suppose that a very paranoid man complains that he is suffering excruciating pain because little green Martians are cutting into his flesh. If he then goes on to tell us that the reason he shows no sign of being in pain (he does not grimace, wince, and so forth) is that he does not want to let the Martians know they are succeeding in making him suffer, we might begin to think he believes he is in pain when he is not. The man might in fact not be undergoing any pain whatsoever, even though he does genuinely believe that he is suffering. He might later, when the aberrance has vanished, report that this is what had happened. Some philosophers might doubt that the usual concepts of belief and sensation apply in such peculiar cases as this, and others would have other doubts. Such examples may be genuine counterexamples, however.

FALLIBILITY AND INFERENCE: Summary of the Argument

The arguments concerning the fallibility of beliefs concerning thought and sensation may be summarized as follows. Whatever one can believe as a result of introspection, one can instead believe as a result of inference, and the inference can be based on false premises. If a woman believes she is in pain as a result of feeling pain, then, of course, she will be correct in believing that she is in pain. If, however, a man believes that he is in pain because some scientific or religious authority figure tells him that he is in pain, then what he believes may well be false. In such a case, the person has accepted a premise, namely, that what the scientific or religious authority figure says is true which, together with the premise that the authority says the person is in pain, leads the person to infer and, therefore, to believe that he or she is in pain and to believe this falsely when the authority is untruthful.

Inference from the testimony of an authority is only one example of how false beliefs about one's mental states may result from inference. It may seem strange to imagine people coming to believe they have some thought or sensation as a result of inference from testimony, but this is the strangeness of the human mind, not of logic. People may believe things in ways that are quite unreasonable and mentally deranged. As a result of these mad beliefs, they may come to believe things about anything, about their very own thoughts and sensations, which they would otherwise never believe.

ROBERT AUDI

The Foundationalism–Coherentism Controversy: Hardened Stereotypes and Overlapping Theories

Foundationalism and coherentism each contain significant epistemological truths. Both positions are, moreover, intellectually influential even outside epistemology. But most philosophers defending either position have been mainly concerned to argue for their view and to demolish the other, which they have often interpreted through just one leading proponent. It is not surprising, then, that philosophers in each tradition often feel misunderstood by those in the other. The lack of clarity—and unwarranted stereotyping—about both foundationalism and coherentism go beyond what one would expect from terminological and philosophical diversity: there are genuine obscurities and misconceptions. Because both positions, and especially foundationalism, are responses to the epistemic regress problem, I want to start with that. Once it is seen that this perennial conundrum can take two quite different forms, both foundationalism and coherentism can be better understood.

I. TWO CONCEPTIONS OF THE EPISTEMIC REGRESS PROBLEM

It is widely agreed that the epistemic regress argument gives crucial support to foundationalism. Even coherentists, who reject the argument, grant that the regress problem which generates it is important in motivating their views. There are at least two major contexts—often not distinguished—in which the regress problem arises. Central to one is pursuit of the question of how one knows or is justified in believing some particular thing, most typically a proposition about the external world, e.g. that one saw a bear in the woods. This context is often colored by conceiving such questions as skeptical chal-

lenges, and this is the conception of them most important for our purposes. The challenges are often spearheaded by "How do you know?" Central to the other main context in which the regress problem arises are questions about what *grounds* knowledge or justification, or a belief taken to be justified or to constitute knowledge, where there is no skeptical purpose, or at least no philosophically skeptical one. Other terms may be used in framing these questions. People interested in such grounds may, for instance, want to know the source, basis, reasons, evidence, or rationale for a belief. We must consider the regress problem raised in both ways. I begin with the former.

Suppose I am asked how I know that *p*, say that there are books in my study. The skeptic, for instance, issues the question as a challenge. I might reply by citing a ground of the belief in question, say *q*: I have a clear recollection of books in my study. The skeptic then challenges the apparent presupposition that I know the ground to hold; after all, if I do have a ground, it seems natural to think that I should be able (at least on reflection) not just to produce it, but also to justify it: how else can I be entitled to take it as a ground? Thus, if "How do you know?" is motivated by a skeptical interest in knowledge, the question of how I know is likely to be reiterated, at least if my ground, *q*, is not self-evident; for unless *q* is self-evident, and in that sense a self-certifying basis for *p*, the questioner—particularly if skeptical—will accept my citing *q* as answering "How do you know that *p*?", only on the assumption that I *also* know that *q*. How far can this questioning reasonably go?

For epistemologists, the problem posed by "How do you know?" and "What justifies you?" is to answer such questions without making one or another apparently inevitable move that ultimately undermines the possibility of knowledge or even of justification. Initially, there seem to be three unpleasant options. The first is to rotate regressively in a vicious circle, say from p to q as a ground for p, then to r as a ground for q, and then back to p as a ground for r. The second option is to fall into a vicious regress: from p to q as a ground for p, then to r as a ground for q, then to s as a ground for r, and so on to infinity. The third option is to stop at a purported ground, say s, that does not constitute knowledge or even justified belief; but the trouble with this is that if one neither knows nor justifiedly believes s, it is at best difficult to see how citing s can answer the question of how one knows that p. The fourth option is to stop with something that is known or justifiedly believed, say r, but *not* known on the basis of any further knowledge or justified belief. Here the problem as many see it is that r, not being believed on any further ground, serves as just an arbitrary way of stopping the regress and is only capriciously taken to be known or justifiedly believed. Thus, *citing r as a final answer to the chain of queries seems dogmatic. I want to call this difficulty—how to answer, dialectically, questions about how one knows, or about what justifies one—the *dialectical form of the regress problem*.

Imagine, by contrast, that we consider either the entire body of a person's apparent knowledge, as Aristotle seems to have done, or a representative item of apparent knowledge, say my belief that there are books in my study, and ask on what this apparent knowledge is grounded (or based) and whether, if it is grounded on some further belief, *all* our knowledge or justified belief could be so grounded. We are now asking a structural question about knowledge, not requesting a verbal response in defense of a claim to it. No dialectic need even be imagined; we are considering a person's overall knowledge, or some presumably representative item of it, and asking how that body of knowledge is structured or how that item of knowledge is grounded. Again we get a regress problem: how to specify one's grounds without vicious circularity or regress or, on the other hand, stopping with a belief that does not constitute knowledge (or is not justified) or seems only capriciously regarded as knowledge. Call this search for appropriate grounds of knowledge the *structural form of the regress problem*.

To see how the two forms of the regress problem differ, we can think of them as arising from different ways of asking "How do you know?" It can be asked with *skeptical force*, as a challenge to people who either claim to know something or (more commonly) presuppose that some belief they confidently hold represents knowledge. Here the question is roughly equivalent to "Show me that you know." It can also be asked with *informational force*, as where someone simply wants to know by what route, such as observation or testimony, one came to know something. Here the question is roughly equivalent to "How is it that you know?" The skeptical form of the question does *not* presuppose that the person in question really has any knowledge, and, asked in this noncommittal way, the question tends to generate the dialectical form of the regress. The informational form of the question typically *does* presuppose that the person knows the proposition in question. It is easy to assume that it does not matter in which way we formulate the problem. But it does matter, for at least four reasons.

Knowing versus Showing That One Knows

First, the dialectical form of the regress problem invites us to think that an adequate answer to "How do you know?" *shows* that we know. This is so particularly in the context of a concern to reply to skepticism. For the skeptic is not interested in the information most commonly sought when people ask how someone knows, say information about the origin of the belief, e.g. in first-hand observation as opposed to testimony. It is, however, far from clear that an adequate answer to the how-question must be an adequate answer to the show-question. If I tell you how I know there were injuries in the accident by citing the testimony of a credible witness who saw it, you may be satisfied; but I have not shown that I know (as I might by taking you to the scene), and the skeptic who, with the force of a challenge, asks how I know will not be satisfied. I have answered the informational form of the question, but not the skeptical form.

First-Order versus Second-Order Knowledge

Second, when the regress problem is dialectically formulated, any full non-skeptical answer to "How do you know that p?" will tend to imply an epistemic self-ascription, say "I know that q"; thus, my answer is admissible only if I both have the concept of knowledge—since I would otherwise not understand what I am attributing to myself—and am at least dialectically warranted in asserting that I do know that q. If you ask, informationally, how I know that there were injuries, I simply say (for instance) that I heard it from Janet, who saw them. But if you ask, skeptically, how I know it, I will realize that you will not accept evidence I merely *have*, but only evidence I *know;* and I will thus tend to say something to the effect that I *know* that Janet saw the injuries. Since this in effect claims knowledge of knowledge, it succeeds only if I meet the second-order standard for having knowledge that I know she saw this. If, however, the regress problem is structurally formulated, it is sufficient for its solution that there *be* propositions which, whether or not I believe them *prior* to being questioned, are both warranted for me (reasonable for me *to* believe) and together justify the proposition originally in question. For this to be true of me, I need only meet a first-order standard, e.g. by remembering the accident, and thereby be justified in believing that there were injuries.

Having, Giving, and Showing a Solution

Third, and largely implicit in the first two points, the two formulations of the regress problem differ as to what must hold in order for there to *be,* and for S to *give,* an adequate answer to "How do you know?" or "What justifies you?" On the structural formulation, if there *are* warranted propositions of the kind just described, as where I am warranted in believing that there were injuries, the problem (as applied to p, the proposition in question) *has* a solution; and if I *cite* them in answering "How do you know that p?" I *give* a solution to the problem. The problem has a solution because of the mere existence of propositions warranted for me; and the solution is given, and the problem thus actually solved, by my simply affirming those propositions in answering "How do you know?" By contrast, when the problem is dialectically formulated, it is taken to have a solution only if there not only *are* such propositions, but I can show by *argument* that there are; and to give a solution I must not merely cite these propositions

but also show that they are justified and that they in turn justify p. Thus, I cannot adequately say how I know there are books in my study by citing my recollection of them unless I can show by argument that it is both warranted and justifies concluding that there are indeed books there. Raising the structural form of the problem presupposes only that if I know that p, I have grounds of this knowledge that are expressible in propositions warranted for me; it does not presuppose that I can formulate the grounds or show that they imply knowledge. The structural form thus encourages us to conceive solutions as *propositional,* in the sense that they depend on the evidential propositions warranted for me; the dialectical form encourages conceiving solutions, as *argumental,* because they depend on what *arguments* about the evidence are accessible to me. I must be able to enter the dialectic with good arguments for p, not simply to be warranted in believing evidence propositions that justify p.

The Process of Justification versus the Property of Justification

Fourth, a dialectical formulation, at least as applied to justification (and so, often, to knowledge as at least commonly embodying justification), tends to focus our attention on the *process* of justification, i.e., of justifying a proposition, though the initial question concerns whether the relevant belief has the *property* of justification, i.e., of being justified. The skeptical forms of the questions "How do you know?" and "What justifies you?" tend to start a process of argument; "Show me that you know" demands a response, and what is expected is a process of justifying the belief that p. The informational form of those questions tends to direct one to cite a ground, such as clear recollection, and the knowledge or (property of) justification in question may be simply taken to be based on this ground. "By what route (or on what basis) do you know?" need not start a process (though it may). It implies that providing a good ground—one in virtue of which the belief that p has the property of being justified—will fully answer the question. Granted, the epistemologist pursuing the regress problem in either form must use second-order formulations (though in different ways); still, the criteria for knowledge and justified belief tend to differ depending on which approach is dominant in determining those criteria.

If I am correct in thinking that the dialectical and structural formulations of the regress problem are significantly different, which of them is preferable in appraising the foundationalism-coherentism controversy? One consideration is neutrality; we should try to avoid bias toward any particular epistemological theory. The dialectical formulation, however, favors coherentism, or at least non-foundationalism. Let me explain.

Foundationalists typically posit beliefs that are grounded in experience or reason and are direct—and so not grounded through other, mediating beliefs—in two senses. First, they are *psychologically direct:* non-inferential (in the most common sense of that term), and thus not held on the basis of (hence through) some further belief. Second, they are *epistemically direct:* they do not depend (inferentially) for their status as knowledge, or for any justification they have, on other beliefs, justification, or knowledge. The first kind of direct belief has no psychological intermediary of the relevant kind, such as belief. The second kind has no evidential intermediary, such as knowledge of a premise for the belief in question. Roughly, epistemically direct beliefs are not inferentially *based on* other beliefs or knowledge, and this point holds whether or not there is any actual *process* of inference. Now imagine that, in dealing with the dialectical form of the regress problem, say in answering the question of how I know I have reading material for tonight, I cite, as an appropriate ground, my knowing that there are books in my study. In choosing this as an example of knowledge, I express a belief that I do in fact know that there are books in the study. But am I warranted in this *second-order* belief, as I appear to be warranted simply in believing that there *are* books in the study (the former belief is construed as second-order on the assumption that knowing entails believing, and the belief that one knows is thus in some sense a belief about another belief)? Clearly it is far less plausible to claim that my second-order belief that I *know* there are books in my study is epistemically direct than to claim this status for my *perceptual* belief that there *are* books in it; for the latter seems non-inferentially based on my seeing them, whereas the former seems inferential, e.g. based on beliefs

about epistemic status. Thus, foundationalists are less likely to seem able to answer the dialectical formulation of the problem, since doing that requires positing direct second-order knowledge (or at least direct, second-order justified belief).

In short, the dialectical form of the problem seems to require foundationalists to posit foundations of a higher order, and a greater degree of complexity, than they are generally prepared to posit. The same point emerges if we note that "How do you know?" can be repeated, and in some fashion answered, indefinitely. Indeed, because this question (or a similar one) is central to the dialectical formulation, that formulation tends to be inimical to foundationalism, which posits at least one kind of natural place to stop the regress: a place at which, even if a skeptical challenge *can* be adequately answered, having an answer to it is not necessary for having knowledge or justified belief.

It might seem, on the other hand, that the structural formulation, which stresses our actual cognitive makeup, is inimical toward coherentism, or at least non-foundationalism. For given our knowledge of cognitive psychology it is difficult to see how a normal person might *have* anything approaching an infinite chain of beliefs constituting knowings; hence, an infinite chain of answers to "How do you know?" seems out of the question. But this only cuts against an infinite regress approach in epistemology, not against any finitistic coherentism, which seems the only kind ever plausibly defended. Indeed, even assuming—as coherentists may grant—that much of our knowledge in fact arises, non-inferentially, from experiential states like seeing, the structural formulation of the problem allows *both* that, as foundationalists typically claim, there is non-inferential knowledge, and that, as coherentists typically claim, non-inferential beliefs are dialectically defensible indefinitely and (when true) capable of constituting knowledge only by virtue of coherence. The structural formulation may not demand that such defenses be available indefinitely; but it also does not preclude this nor even limit the mode of defense to circular reasoning.

I believe, then, that the structural formulation is not significantly biased against coherentism. Nor is it biased in favor of internalism over externalism about justification, where internalism is roughly the view that what justifies a belief, such as a visual impression, is internal in the sense that one can become (in some way) aware of it through reflection or introspection (internal processes), and externalism denies that what justifies a belief is always accessible to one in this sense. The dialectical formulation, by contrast, tends to favor internalism, since it invites us to see the regress problem as solved in terms of what propositions warranted for one are *also* accessible to one in answering "How do you know that *p*?" If the structural formulation is biased against internalism or coherentism, I am not aware of good reasons to think so, and I will work with it here.

II. THE EPISTEMIC REGRESS ARGUMENT

If we formulate the regress problem structurally, then a natural way to state the famous epistemic regress argument is along these lines. First, suppose I have knowledge, even if only of something so simple as there being a patter outside my window. Could all my knowledge be inferential? Imagine that this is possible by virtue of an infinite epistemic regress—roughly, an infinite series of knowings, each based (inferentially) on the next. Just assume that a belief constituting inferential knowledge is based on knowledge of some other proposition, or at least on a further belief of another proposition; the further knowledge or belief might be based on knowledge of, or belief about, something still further, and so on. Call this sequence an *epistemic chain*; it is simply a chain of beliefs, with at least the first constituting knowledge, and each belief linked to the previous one by being based on it. A standard view is that there are just four kinds: an epistemic chain might be infinite or circular, hence in either case unending and in that sense regressive, third, it might terminate with a belief that is not knowledge; and fourth, it might terminate with a belief constituting direct knowledge. The epistemic regress problem is above all to assess these chains as possible sources (or at least carriers) of knowledge or justification.

The foundationalist response to the regress problem is to offer a regress argument favoring the fourth possibility as the only genuine one. The argument can be best formulated along these lines:

1. If one has any knowledge, it occurs in an epistemic chain (possibly including the special case of a single link, such as a perceptual or a priori belief, which constitutes knowledge by virtue of being anchored directly in experience or reason);

2. the only possible kinds of epistemic chains are the four mutually exclusive kinds just sketched;

3. knowledge can occur only in the last kind of chain; hence,

4. if one has any knowledge, one has some direct knowledge.

Some preliminary clarification is in order before we appraise this argument.

First, the conclusion, being conditional, does not presuppose that there *is* any knowledge. This preserves the argument's neutrality with respect to skepticism, as is appropriate since the issue concerns *conceptual* requirements for the possession of knowledge. The argument would have existential import, and so would not be purely conceptual, if it presupposed that there *is* knowledge and hence that at least one knower exists. Second, I take (1) to imply that inferential knowledge depends on at least one epistemic chain for its status *as* knowledge. I thus take the argument to imply the further conclusion that any inferential knowledge one has exhibits (inferential) *epistemic dependence* on some appropriate inferential connection, via some epistemic chain, to some non-inferential knowledge one has. Thus, the argument would show not only that if there is inferential knowledge, there *is* non-inferential knowledge, but also that if there is inferential knowledge, that very knowledge is *traceable* to some non-inferential knowledge as its foundation.

The second point suggests a third. If two epistemic chains should *intersect,* as where a belief that *p* is both foundationally grounded in experience and part of a circular chain, then if the belief is knowledge, that knowledge *occurs in* only the former chain, though the knowledge qua *belief* belongs to both chains. Knowledge, then, does not occur in a chain merely because the belief constituting it does. Fourth, the argument concerns the structure, not the content, of a body of knowledge and of its constituent epistemic chains. The argument may thus be used regardless of what purported items of knowledge one applies it to in any particular person. The argument does not presuppose that in order to have knowledge, there are specific things one must believe, or that a body of knowledge must have some particular content.

A similar argument applies to justification. We simply speak of *justificatory chains* and proceed in a parallel way, substituting justification for knowledge. The conclusion would be that if there are any justified beliefs, there are some non-inferentially justified beliefs, and that if one has any inferentially justified belief, it exhibits (inferential) *justificatory dependence* on an epistemic chain appropriately linking it to some non-inferentially justified belief one has, that is, to a foundational belief. In discussing foundationalism, I shall often focus on justification.

Full-scale assessment of the regress argument is impossible here. I shall simply comment on some important aspects of it to provide a better understanding of foundationalism and of some major objections to it.

Appeal to infinite epistemic chains has seldom seemed to philosophers to be promising. Let me suggest one reason to doubt that human beings are even capable of having infinite sets of beliefs. Consider the claim that we can have an infinite set of arithmetical beliefs, say that 2 is twice 1, that 4 is twice 2, etc. Surely for a finite mind there will be some point or other at which the relevant proposition cannot be grasped. The required formulation (or entertaining of the proposition) would, on the way "toward" infinity, become too lengthy to permit understanding it. Thus, even if we could read or entertain it part by part, when we got to the end we would be unable to remember enough of the first part to grasp and thereby believe what the formulation expresses. Granted, we could believe that the formulation just read expresses *a* truth; but this is not sufficient for believing *the truth* that it expresses. That truth is a specific mathematical statement; believing, of a formulation we cannot even get before our minds, or remember, in toto, that it expresses *some* mathematical truth is not sufficient for believing, or even grasping, the true statement in question. Since we cannot understand the formulation as a whole, we cannot grasp that truth; and

what we cannot grasp, we cannot believe. I doubt that any other lines of argument show that we can have infinite sets of beliefs; nor, if we can, is it clear how infinite epistemic chains could account for any of our knowledge. I thus propose to consider only the other kinds of chain.

The possibility of a circular epistemic chain as a basis of knowledge has been taken much more seriously. The standard objection has been that such circularity is vicious, because one would ultimately have to know something on the basis of itself—say p on the basis of q, q on the basis of r, and r on the basis of p. A standard reply has been that if the circle is wide enough and its content sufficiently rich and coherent, the circularity is innocuous. I bypass this difficult matter, since I believe that coherentism as most plausibly formulated does not depend on circular chains.

The third alternative, namely that an epistemic chain terminates in a belief which is not knowledge, has been at best rarely affirmed; and there is little plausibility in the hypothesis that knowledge can originate through a belief of a proposition S does not know. If there are exceptions, it is where, although I do not know that p, I am justified, to *some* extent, in believing that p, as in making a reasonable estimate that there are at least thirty books on a certain shelf. Here is a different case. Suppose it vaguely seems to me that I hear strains of music. If, on the basis of the resulting, somewhat justified belief that there is music playing, I believe that my daughter has come home, and she has, do I know this? The answer is not clear. But this apparent indeterminacy would not help anyone who claims that knowledge can arise from belief which does not constitute knowledge. For it is equally unclear, and for the same sort of reason, whether my belief that there is music playing is *sufficiently* reasonable—say, in terms of how good my perceptual grounds are—to give me knowledge that music is playing. The stronger our tendency to say that I know she is home, the stronger our inclination to say that I do after all know that there are strains of music in the air. Notice something else. In the only cases where the third kind of chain seems likely to ground knowledge (or justification), there is a degree—apparently a substantial degree—of justification. If there can be an epistemic chain which ends with belief that is not knowledge only because it ends, in this way, with justification, then we are apparently in the general vicinity of knowledge. We seem to be at most a few degrees of justification away. Knowledge is not emerging from nothing, as it were—the picture originally evoked by the third kind of epistemic chain—but from something characteristically much like it: justified true belief. There would thus be a foundation after all: not bedrock, but perhaps ground that is nonetheless firm enough to yield a foundation we can build upon.

The fourth possibility is that epistemic chains which originate with knowledge end in non-inferential knowledge: knowledge not inferentially based on further knowledge (or further justified belief). That knowledge, in turn, is apparently grounded in experience, say in my auditory impression of music or in my intuitive sense that if A is one mile from B, then B is one mile from A. This non-inferential grounding of my knowledge can explain how that knowledge is (epistemically) direct. It arises, non-inferentially—and so without any intermediary premise that must be known along the way—from (I shall assume) one of the four classical kinds of foundational material, namely, perception, memory, introspection, and reason.

Such direct grounding in experience also seems to explain why a belief so grounded may be expected to be *true;* for experience seems to connect the beliefs it grounds to the reality they are apparently about, in such a way that what is believed concerning that reality tends to be the case. For empirical beliefs at least, this point seems to explain best why we have those beliefs. Let me illustrate all this. Normally, when I know that there is music playing, it is just because I hear it, and not on the basis of some further belief of mine; hence, the chain grounding my knowledge that my daughter has come home is anchored in my auditory perception, which in turn reflects the musical reality represented by my knowledge that there is music playing. This reality explains both my perception and, by explaining that, indirectly explains my believing the proposition I know on the basis of this perception—that my daughter is home.

The non-inferentially grounded epistemic chains in question may differ in many ways. They differ *compositionally,* in the sorts of beliefs constituting them, and *causally,* in the kind of causal relation holding between one belief and its successor. This relation, for instance, may or may not involve the predecessor belief's being necessary or sufficient for its successor: perhaps, on grounds other than the music, I would have believed my daughter was home; and perhaps not, depending on how many indications of her presence are accessible to me. Such chains also differ *structurally,* in the kind of *epistemic transmission* they exhibit; it may be deductive, as where I infer a theorem from an axiom by rigorous rules of deductive inference, or inductive, as where I infer from the good performance of a knife that others of that kind will also cut well; or the transmission of knowledge or justification may combine deductive and inductive elements. Epistemic chains also differ *foundationally,* in their ultimate grounds, the anchors of the chains; the grounds may, as illustrated, be perceptual or rational, and they may vary in justificational strength.

Different proponents of the fourth possibility have held various views about the character of the *foundational knowledge,* i.e., the beliefs constituting the knowledge that makes up the final link and anchors the chain in experience or reason. Some, including Descartes, have thought that the appropriate beliefs must be infallible, or at least indefeasibly justified. But in fact all that the fourth possibility requires is *non-inferential knowledge,* knowledge not (inferentially) based on other knowledge (or other justified belief). Non-inferential knowledge need not be of self-evident propositions, nor constituted by indefeasibly justified belief, the kind whose justification cannot be defeated. The case of introspective beliefs, which are paradigms of those that are non-inferentially justified, supports this view, and we shall see other reasons to hold it.

III. FALLIBILIST FOUNDATIONALISM

The foundationalism with which the regress argument concludes is quite generic and leaves much to be determined, such as how *well* justified foundational beliefs must be if they are to justify a superstructure belief based on them. In assessing the foundationalist-coherentist controversy, then, we need a more detailed formulation. The task of this section is to develop one. I start with a concrete example.

As I sit reading on a quiet summer evening, I sometimes hear a distinctive patter outside my open window. I immediately believe that it is raining. It may then occur to me that if I do not bring in the lawn chairs, the cushions will be soaked. But this I do not believe immediately, even if the thought strikes me in an instant; I believe it on the basis of my prior belief that it is raining. The first belief is perceptual, being grounded directly in what I hear. The second is inferential, being grounded not in what I perceive but in what I believe. My belief that it is raining expresses a premise for my belief that the cushions will be soaked. There are many beliefs of both kinds. Perception is a major source of beliefs; and, from beliefs we have through perception, many others arise inferentially. The latter, inferential beliefs are then based on the former, perceptual beliefs. When I see a headlight beam cross my window and immediately believe, perceptually, that a car's light is moving out there, I may, on the basis of that belief, come to believe, inferentially, that someone has entered my driveway. From this proposition in turn I might infer that my doorbell is about to ring; and from that I might infer still further propositions. Assuming that knowledge implies belief, the same point holds for knowledge: much of it is perceptually grounded, and much of it is inferential. There is no definite limit on how many inferences one may draw in such a chain, and people differ in how many they tend to draw. Could it be, however, that despite the apparent obviousness of these points, there really *is* no non-inferential knowledge or belief, even in perceptual cases? If inference can take us forward indefinitely beyond perceptual beliefs, why may it not take us backward indefinitely from them? To see how this might be thought to occur, we must consider more systematically how beliefs arise, what justifies them, and when they are sufficiently well grounded to constitute knowledge.

Imagine that when the rain began I had not trusted my ears. I might then have believed just the weaker proposition that there was a pattering sound and only on that basis, and after considering the situation, come to believe that it was raining. We need not stop here, however. For suppose I do not trust my sense of hearing. I might then believe merely that it *seems* to me that there is a patter, and only on that basis believe that there is such a sound. But surely this cannot go much further, and in fact there is no need to go even this far. Still, what theoretical reason is there to stop? It is not as if we had to articulate all our beliefs. Little of what we believe is at any one time before our minds being inwardly voiced. Indeed, perhaps we can have infinitely many beliefs, as some think we do. But, as I have already suggested, it is simply not clear that a person's cognitive system can sustain an infinite set of beliefs, and much the same can be said regarding a circular cognitive chain.

Even if there could be infinite or circular belief chains, foundationalists hold that they cannot be sources of knowledge or justification. The underlying idea is in part this. If knowledge or justified belief arises through inference, it requires belief of at least one premise; and that belief could produce knowledge or justified belief of a proposition inferred from the premise only if the premise belief is itself an instance of knowledge or is at least justified. But if the premise belief is justified, it must be so by virtue of *something*—otherwise it would be self-justified, and hence one kind of foundational belief after all. If, however, experience cannot do the justificatory work, then the belief must derive its justification from yet another set of premises, and the problem arises all over again: what justifies that set? In the light of such points, the foundationalist concludes that if any of our beliefs are justified or constitute knowledge, then some of our beliefs are justified, or constitute knowledge, simply because they arise (in a certain way) from experience or reflection (including intuition as a special case of reflection). Indeed, if we construe experience broadly enough to include logical reflection and rational intuition, then experience may be described as the one overall source. In either case, there appear to be at least four basic sources of knowledge and justified belief: perception; consciousness, which grounds, e.g., my knowledge that I am thinking about the structure of justification; reflection, which is, for instance, the basis of my justified belief that if A is older than B and B is older than C, then A is older than C; and memory: I can be justified in believing that, say, I left a light on simply by virtue of the sense of recalling my having done so.

Particularly in the perceptual cases, some foundationalists tend to see experience as a mirror of nature. This seems to some foundationalists a good, if limited, metaphor because it suggests at least two important points: first, that some experiences are *produced* by external states of the world, somewhat as light produces mirror images; and second, that (normally) the experiences in some way *match* their causes, for instance in the color and shape one senses in one's visual field. If one wants to focus on individual perceptual beliefs, one might think of a thermometer model; it suggests both the causal connections just sketched, but also, perhaps even more than the mirror metaphor, *reliable* responses to the external world. From this causal-responsiveness perspective, it is at best unnatural to regard perceptual beliefs as inferential. They are not formed by inference from anything else believed but directly reflect the objects and events that cause them.

The most plausible kind of foundationalism will be fallibilist (moderate) in at least the following respects—and I shall concentrate on foundationalism about justification, though much that is said will also hold for foundationalism about knowledge. First, as a purely philosophical thesis about the *structure* of justification, foundationalism should be neutral with respect to skepticism and should not entail that there *are* justified beliefs. Second, if it is fallibilistic, it must allow that a justified belief, even a foundational one, be false. To require here justification of a kind that entails truth is to require that justified foundational beliefs be infallible. Third, superstructure beliefs may be only inductively, hence fallibly, justified by foundational ones and thus (unless they are necessary truths) can be false even when the latter are true. Just as one's warranted beliefs may be fallible, one's inferences may be, also, leading from truth to falsity. If the proposition is sufficiently supported by evidence one justifiedly believes, one may justifiedly hold it on the basis of that evidence, even if one could turn out to be in error. Fourth, a fallibilist foundationalism must allow for *discovering* error or lack of justification, in foundational as well as in superstructure beliefs. Foundational beliefs may be discovered to conflict either with other such beliefs or with sufficiently well-supported superstructure beliefs.

These four points are quite appropriate to the inspiration of the theory as expressed in the regress argument: it requires epistemic unmoved movers, but not unmovable movers. Solid ground is enough, even if bedrock is better. There are also different kinds of bedrock, and not all of them have the invulnerability apparently belonging to beliefs of luminously self-evident truths of logic. Even foundationalism as applied to knowledge can be fallibilistic; for granting that false propositions cannot be known, foundationalism about knowledge does not entail that one's *grounds* for knowledge (at any level) are indefeasible. Perceptual grounds, e.g., may be overridden; and one can fail (or cease) to know a proposition not because it is (or is discovered to be) false, but because one ceases to be justified in believing it.

I take *fallibilist foundationalism*, as applied to justification, to be the inductivist thesis that

I. For any S and any t, (1) the structure of S's body of justified beliefs is, at t, foundational in the sense that any inferential (hence nonfoundational) justified beliefs S has depend for their justification on one or more noninferential (thus in a sense foundational) justified beliefs of S's; (2) the justification of S's foundational beliefs is at least typically defeasible; (3) the inferential transmission of justification need not be deductive; and (4) nonfoundationally justified beliefs need not derive *all* of their justification from foundational ones, but only enough so that they would remain justified if (other things remaining equal) any other justification they have (say, from coherence) were eliminated.

This is fallibilist in at least three ways. Foundational beliefs may turn out to be unjustified or false or both; superstructure beliefs may be only inductively, hence fallibly, justified by foundational ones and hence can be false even when the latter are true; and possibility of *discovering* error or lack of justification, even in foundational beliefs, is left open: they may be found to conflict either with other such beliefs or with sufficiently well-supported superstructure beliefs. Even foundationalism as applied to knowledge can forswear infallibility. For although false beliefs cannot be knowledge, what is known can be both contingent—and so might have been false—*and* based on defeasible grounds—and so might cease to be known. We can lose knowledge when our grounds for it are defeated by counterevidence. Even introspective grounds are overridable (as argued in Chapter 5); hence, even self-knowledge is defeasible.

Since I am particularly concerned to clarify foundationalism in contrast to coherentism, I want to focus on the roles fallibilist foundationalism allows for coherence (conceived in any plausible way) in relation to justification. There are at least two important roles coherence may apparently play.

The first role fallibilist foundationalism allows for coherence—or at least for incoherence—is negative. Incoherence may defeat justification or knowledge, even the justification of a directly justified, hence foundational, belief (or one constituting knowledge), as where my justification for believing I am hallucinating books prevents me from knowing, or remaining justified in believing, certain propositions incoherent with it, say that the books in my study are before me. If this is not ultimately a role for coherence itself—which is the opposite and not merely the absence of incoherence—it *is* a role crucial for explaining points stressed by coherentism. Coherentists have not taken account of the point that incoherence is not merely the absence of coherence and cannot be explicated simply through analyzing coherence, nor accounted for as an epistemic standard only by a coherentist theory (a point to which I shall return); but they have rightly noted, for instance, such things as the defeasibility of the justification of a memorial belief owing to its incoherence with perceptual beliefs, as where one takes oneself to remember an oak tree in a certain spot, yet, standing near the very spot, can find no trace of one. Because fallibilist foundationalism does not require indefeasible justification on the part of the relevant memory belief, there is no anomaly in its defeat by perceptual evidence.

Second, fallibilist foundationalism can employ an *independence principle*, one of a family of principles commonly emphasized by coherentists, though foundationalists need not attribute its truth to coherence. This principle says that the larger the number of independent mutually coherent factors

one believes to support the truth of a proposition, the better one's justification for believing it (other things being equal). The principle can explain, e.g., why my justification for believing, from what I hear, that my daughter has come home increases as I acquire new beliefs supporting that conclusion, say that there is a smell of popcorn. For I now have a confirmatory belief which comes through a different sense (smell) and does not depend for its justification on my other evidence beliefs.

Similar principles consistent with foundationalism can accommodate other cases in which coherence apparently enhances justification, for instance where a proposition's explaining, and thereby cohering with, something one justifiably believes, tends to confer some justification on that proposition. Suppose I check three suitcases at the ticket counter. Imagine that as I await them at the baggage terminal I glimpse two on the conveyor at a distance and tentatively believe that they are mine. The propositions that (a) the first is mine, (b) the second is, and (c) these two are side by side—which I am fully justified in believing because I can clearly see how close they are to each other—would be explained by the hypothesis that my three suitcases are now coming off together; and that hypothesis, in turn, derives some justification from its explaining what I already believe. When I believe the further proposition, independent of (a)–(c), that my third suitcase is coming just behind the second, the level of my justification for the hypothesis rises.

Fallibilist foundationalism thus allows for coherence to play a significant though restricted role in explicating justification, and it provides a major place for incoherence in this task. But there remains a strong contrast between the two accounts of justification, as we shall soon see.

IV. HOLISTIC COHERENTISM

The notion of coherence is frequently appealed to in epistemological and other contexts, but it is infrequently explicated. Despite the efforts that have been made to clarify coherence, explaining what it is remains difficult. It is not mere consistency, though *in*consistency is the clearest case of incoherence. Whatever coherence is, it is a cognitively *internal* relation, in the sense that it is a matter of how one's beliefs (or other cognitive items) are related *to one another*, not to anything outside one's system of beliefs, such as one's perceptual experience. Coherence is sometimes connected with explanation; it is widely believed that propositions which stand in an explanatory relation cohere with one another and that this coherence counts toward that of a person's beliefs of the propositions in question. If the wilting of the leaves is explained by billowing smoke from a chemical fire, then presumably the proposition expressing the first event coheres with the proposition expressing the second (even if the coherence is not obvious and is relative to the context). Probability is also relevant: if the probability of one proposition you believe is raised by that of a second you believe, this at least counts toward the coherence of the first of the beliefs with the second. The relevant notions of explanation and probability are themselves philosophically problematic, but our intuitive grasp of them can still help us understand coherence.

In the light of these points, let us try to formulate a plausible version of coherentism as applied to justification. The central coherentist idea concerning justification is that a belief is justified by its coherence with other beliefs one holds. The unit of coherence may be as large as one's entire set of beliefs, though some may be more significant in producing the coherence than others, say because of differing degrees of their closeness in subject matter to the belief in question. This conception of coherentism would be accepted by a proponent of the circular view, but the thesis I want to explore differs from that view in not being *linear:* it does not take justification for believing that *p*, or knowledge that *p*, to emerge from an inferential line running from premises for *p* to that proposition as a conclusion from them, and from other premises to the first set of premises, and so on until we return to the original proposition as a premise. On the circular view, no matter how wide the circle or how rich its constituent beliefs, there is a line from any one belief in a circular epistemic chain to any other. In practice I may never trace the entire line, as by inferring one thing I know from a second, the second from a third, and so on until I reinfer the first. Still, on this view there is such a line for every belief constituting knowledge.

Coherentism need not, however, be linear, and I believe that the most plausible versions are instead holistic. A moderate version of *holistic coherentism* might be expressed as follows:

> II. For any *S* and any *t*, if *S* has any justified beliefs at *t*, then, at *t*, (1) they are each justified by virtue of their coherence with one or more others of *S*'s beliefs; and (2) they would remain justified even if (other things remaining equal) any justification they derive from sources other than coherence were eliminated.

The holism required is minimal, since the unit of coherence may be as small as one pair of beliefs—though it may also be as large as the entire system of *S*'s beliefs (including the belief whose justification is in question, since we may take such partial "self-coherence" as a limiting case). But the formulation also applies to the more typical cases of holistic coherentism; in these cases a justified belief coheres with a substantial number of other beliefs, but not necessarily with all of one's beliefs. Some beliefs, like those expressing basic principles of one's thinking, can be justified only by coherence with a large and diverse group of related beliefs. Coherentist theories differ concerning the sense (if any) in which the set of beliefs whose coherence determines the justification of some belief belonging to it must be a "system."

To illustrate holistic coherentism, consider a question that evokes a justification. Ken wonders how, from my closed study, I know (or why I believe) that my daughter is home. I say that there is music playing in the house. He next wants to know how I can recognize my daughter's music from behind my closed doors. I reply that what I hear is the wrong sort of thing to come from any nearby house. He then asks how I know that it is not from a passing car. I say that the volume is too steady. He now wonders whether I can distinguish, with my door closed, my daughter's vocal music from the singing of a neighbor in her yard. I reply that I hear an accompaniment. In giving each justification I apparently go only one step along the inferential line: initially, for instance, just to my belief that there is music playing in the house. For my belief that my daughter is home *is* based on this belief about the music. After that, I do not even mention anything that this belief, in turn, is based on; rather, I defend my beliefs as appropriate, in terms of an entire pattern of interrelated beliefs I hold. And I may appeal to many different parts of the pattern. For coherentism, then, beliefs representing knowledge do not lie at one end of a grounded chain; they fit a coherent pattern and are justified through their fitting it in an appropriate way.

Consider a variant of the case. Suppose I had seemed to hear music of neither the kind my daughter plays nor the kind the neighbors play nor the sort I expect from passing cars. The proposition that this is what I hear does not cohere well with my belief that the music is played by my daughter. Suddenly I recall that she was bringing a friend, and I remember that her friend likes such music. I might now be justified in believing that my daughter is home. When I finally hear her voice, I know that she is. The crucial thing here is how, initially, a kind of *incoherence* prevents justification of my belief that she is home, and how, as relevant pieces of the pattern develop, I become justified in believing, and (presumably) come to know, that she is. Arriving at a justified belief, on this view, is more like answering a question by looking up diverse information that suggests the answer than like deducing a theorem from axioms.

Examples like this show how a holistic coherentism can respond to the regress argument *without* embracing the possibility of an epistemic circle (though its proponents need not reject that either). It may deny that there are only the four kinds of possible epistemic chains I have specified. There is apparently another possibility, not generally noted: that the chain terminates with belief which is *psychologically direct* but *epistemically indirect* or, if we are talking of coherentism about justification, *justificationally indirect*. Hence, the last link is, as belief, direct, since it is non-inferential; yet, as knowledge, it is *indirect*, not in the usual sense that it is inferential but rather in the broad sense that the belief constitutes knowledge only by virtue of receiving support from other knowledge or belief. Thus, my belief that there is music playing is psychologically direct because it is simply grounded, causally, in my hearing and is not (inferentially) based on any other belief; yet my *knowledge* that there is music is not epistemically direct. It is epistemically, but not inferentially, based on the coherence of my belief that

there is music with my other beliefs, presumably including many that constitute knowledge themselves. It is thus knowledge *through*, though not by inference from, other knowledge—or at least through justified beliefs; hence it is epistemically indirect and this non-foundational.

There is another way to see how this attack on the regress argument is constructed. The coherentist grants that the belief element *in* my knowledge is non-inferentially grounded in perception and is in that sense direct; but the claim is that the belief constitutes knowledge only by virtue of coherence with my other beliefs. The strategy, then—call it the *wedge strategy*—is to sever the connection foundationalism usually posits between the psychological and the epistemic. In the common cases, foundationalists tend to hold, the basis of one's *knowledge* that *p*, say a perceptual experience, is also the basis of one's belief that *p*; similarly, for justified belief, the basis of its justification is usually also that of the belief itself. For the coherentist using the wedge strategy, the epistemic ground of a belief need not be a psychological ground. Knowledge and justification are a matter of how well the system of beliefs hangs together, not of how well grounded the beliefs are—and they may indeed hang: one could have a body of justified beliefs, at least some of them constituting knowledge, even if *none* of them is justified by a belief or experience in which it is psychologically grounded.

In a sense, of course, coherentism does posit a *kind* of foundation for justification and knowledge: namely, coherence. But so long as coherentists deny that justification and knowledge can be *non-inferentially* grounded in experience or reason, this point alone simply shows that they take justification and knowledge to be based on something (to be supervenient properties, as some would put it). Justification and knowledge are still grounded in the coherence of elements which themselves admit of justification and derive their justification (or status as knowledge) from coherence with other such items rather than from grounding in elements like sensory impressions (say of music), which, though not themselves justified or unjustified, confer justification on beliefs they ground.

Apparently, then, the circularity objection to coherentism can be met by construing the thesis holistically and countenancing psychologically direct beliefs. One could insist that if a non-inferential, thus psychologically direct, belief constitutes knowledge, it *must* be direct knowledge. But the coherentist would reply that in that case there will be two kinds of direct knowledge: the kind the foundationalist posits, which derives from grounding in a basic experiential or rational source, and the kind the coherentist posits, which derives from coherence with other beliefs and not from being based on those sources. This is surely a plausible response.

Is the holistic coherentist trying to have it both ways? Not necessarily. Holistic coherentism can grant that a variant of the regress argument holds for belief, since the only kind of inferential belief chain that it is psychologically realistic to attribute to us is the kind terminating in direct (non-inferential) belief. But even on the assumption that knowledge is constituted by (certain kinds of) beliefs, it does not follow that direct belief which constitutes knowledge is also direct *knowledge*. Epistemic dependence, on this view, does not imply inferential or psychological dependence; hence, a noninferential belief can depend for its status as knowledge on other beliefs. Thus, the coherentist may grant a kind of *psychological foundationalism*—which says (in part) that if we have any beliefs at all, we have some direct (non-inferential) ones—yet deny epistemological foundationalism, which requires that there be knowledge which is epistemically (and normally also psychologically) direct, if there is any knowledge at all. Holistic coherentism may grant experience and reason the status of psychological foundations of our belief systems, but it denies that they are the basic sources of justification or knowledge.

V. FOUNDATIONALISM, COHERENTISM, AND DEFEASIBILITY

Drawing on our results above, this section considers how fallibilist foundationalism and holistic coherentism differ and, related to that, how the controversy is sometimes obscured by failure to take account of the differences.

There is one kind of case that seems both to favor foundationalism and to show something

about justification that coherentism in any form misses. It might seem that coherence theories of justification are decisively refuted by the possibility of *S*'s having, if just momentarily, only a single belief which is nonetheless justified, say that there is music playing. For this belief would be justified without cohering with any others *S* has. But could one have just a single belief? Could I, for instance, believe that there is music playing yet not believe, say, that there are (or could be) musical instruments, melodies, and chords? It is not clear that I could; and foundationalism does not assume this possibility, though the theory may easily be wrongly criticized for implying it. Foundationalism is in fact consistent with *one* kind of coherentism—*conceptual coherentism*. This is a coherence theory of the acquisition of concepts which says that a person acquires concepts, say of musical pieces, only in relation to one another and must acquire an entire family of related concepts in order to acquire any concept.

It remains questionable, however, whether my justification for believing that there is music playing ultimately *derives* from the coherence of the belief with others, i.e., whether coherence is even partly the basis of my justification in holding this belief. Let us first note an important point. Suppose the belief turns out to be *in*coherent with a second, such as my belief that I am standing before the phonograph playing the music yet see no movement of its turntable; now the belief may *cease* to be justified, since if I really hear the phonograph, I should see its turntable moving. But this shows only that the belief's justification is *defeasible*—liable to being either overridden (roughly, outweighed) or undermined—should sufficiently serious incoherence arise. It does not show that the justification derives from coherence. In this case the justification of my belief grounded in hearing may be overridden. My better-justified beliefs, including the belief that a phonograph with a motionless turntable cannot play, may make it more reasonable for me to believe that there is *not* music playing in the house.

The example raises another question regarding the possibility that coherence is the source of my justification, as opposed to incoherence's constraining it. Could incoherence override the justification of my belief if I were not *independently* justified in believing that a proposition incoherent with certain other ones is, or probably is, false, e.g. in believing that if I do not see the turntable moving, then I do not hear music from the phonograph? For if I lacked such independent justification, should I not suspend judgment on, or even reject, the other propositions and retain my original belief? And aren't the relevant other beliefs or propositions—those that can override or defeat my justification—precisely the kind for which, directly or inferentially, we have some degree of justification through the experiential and rational sources, such as visual perception of a stockstill turntable? Note that the example shows that these beliefs or propositions need not be a priori; thus it is not open to coherentists to claim that only the a priori is an exception to the thesis that justification is determined by coherence.

A similar question arises regarding the crucial principles themselves. Could incoherence play the defeating role it does if we did not have a kind of foundational justification for principles to the effect that certain kinds of evidences or beliefs override certain other kinds? More generally, can we *use,* or even benefit from, considerations of coherence in acquiring justification, or in correcting mistaken presuppositions of justification, if we do not bring to the various coherent or incoherent patterns principles not derived from those very patterns? If, without such principles to serve as justified standards that guide belief formation and belief revision, we can become justified by coherence, then coherence would seem to be playing the kind of generative role that foundational sources are held to play in producing justification. One could become justified in believing that p by virtue of coherence even if one had no justified principles by which one could, for instance, inferentially connect the justified belief that p with others that cohere with it.

There is a second case, in which one's justification is simply undermined: one ceases to be justified in believing the proposition in question, though one does not become justified in believing it false. Suppose I seem to see a black cat, yet there no longer appears to be one there if I move five feet to my left. This experience could justify my believing, and lead me to believe, that I might be hallucinating. This belief in turn is to a degree incoherent with, and undermines the justification of, my visual belief that the cat is there, though it does not by itself jus-

tify my believing that there is *not* a cat there. Again, however, I am apparently justified, independently of coherence, in believing a proposition relevant to my overall justification for an apparently foundational perceptual belief: namely, the proposition that my seeing the cat there is incoherent with my merely hallucinating it there. The same seems to hold for the proposition that my seeing the cat there coheres with my feeling fur if I extend my hand to the feline focal point of my visual field. Considerations like these suggest that coherence has the role it does in justification only because *some* beliefs are justified independently of it.

Both examples illustrate an important distinction that is often missed. It is between defeasibility and epistemic dependence or, alternatively, between *negative epistemic dependence,* which is a form of defeasibility, and *positive epistemic dependence,* the kind beliefs bear to the source(s) from which they *derive* any justification they have or, if they represent knowledge, their status as knowledge. The defeasibility of a belief's justification by incoherence does not imply that, as coherentists hold, its justification positively depends on coherence. If my garden is my source of food, I (positively) depend on it. The fact that people could poison the soil does not make their non-malevolence part of my food *source* or imply a (positive) dependence on them, such as I have on the sunshine. Moreover, it is the sunshine that (with rainfall and other conditions) explains both my having the food and the amount I have. The non-malevolence is necessary for, but does not explain, this; it alone, under the relevant conditions of potential for growth, does not even tend to produce food.

So it is with perceptual experience as a source of justification. Foundationalists need not deny that a belief's justification negatively depends on something else, for as we have seen they need not claim that justification must be indefeasible. It may arise, unaided by coherence, from a source like perception; yet it remains defeasible from various quarters—including conflicting perceptions. Negative dependence, however, does not imply positive dependence. The former is determined by the absence of something—defeaters; the latter is determined by the presence of something—justifiers. Justification can be defeasible by incoherence and thus overridden or undermined should incoherence arise, without owing its existence to coherence. Fallibilist foundationalism is not, then, a blend of coherentism, and it remains open just what positive role, if any, it must assign to coherence in explicating justification.

There is a further point that fallibilist foundationalism should stress, and in appraising the point we learn more about both coherentism and justification. If I set out to *show* that my belief is justified— as the dialectical formulation of the regress problem invites one to think stopping the regress of justification requires—I do have to cite propositions that cohere with the one to be shown to be justified for me, say that there is music in my house. In some cases, these are not even propositions one already believes. Often, in defending the original belief, one forms new beliefs, such as the belief one acquires, in moving one's head, that one can vividly see the changes in perspective that go with seeing a black cat. More important, these beliefs are highly appropriate to the *process* of self-consciously justifying one's belief; and the result of that process is twofold: forming the second-order belief that the original belief is justified and showing that the latter is justified. Thus, coherence is important in showing that a belief is justified. In *that* limited sense coherence is a pervasive element in justification: it is pervasive in the process of *justifying,* especially when that is construed as showing that one has justification.

Why, however, should the second-order beliefs appropriate to *showing* that a belief is justified be necessary for its *being* justified? They need not be. Indeed, why should one's simply having a justified belief imply even that one could be justified in holding the second-order beliefs appropriate to showing that it is justified? It would seem that just as a little child can be of good character even if unable to defend its character against attack, one can have a justified belief even if, in response to someone who doubts this, one could not show that one does. Supposing I have the sophistication to form a second-order belief that my belief that there is a cat before me is justified, the latter belief can be justified so long as the former is *true;* and it can be *true* that my belief about the cat is justified even if I am not justified in holding it or am unable to show that it is true. Justifying a second-order belief is a sophisti-

cated process. The process is particularly sophisticated if the second-order belief concerns a special property like the justification of the original belief. Simply being justified in a belief about, say, the sounds around one is a much simpler matter. But confusion is easy here, particularly if the governing context is an imagined dialectic with a skeptic. Take, for instance, the question of how a simple perceptual belief "is justified." The very phrase is ambiguous. The question could be "By what process, say of reasoning, has the belief been (or might it be) justified?" or, on the other hand, "In virtue of what is the belief justified?" These are very different questions. The first invites us to conceive justification as a process of which the belief is a beneficiary, the second to conceive it as a property that a belief has, whether in virtue of its content, its genesis, or others of its characteristics or relations. Both aspects of the notion are important, but unfortunately much of our talk about justification makes it easy to run them together. A justified belief could be one that *has* justification or one that *has been* justified; and a request for someone's justification could be a request for a list of justifying factors or for a recounting of the process by which the person justified the belief.

Once we forswear the mistakes just pointed out, what argument is left to show the (positive) dependence of perceptual justification on coherence? I doubt that any plausible one remains, though given how hard it is to discern what coherence is, we cannot be confident that no plausible argument is forthcoming. Granted, one could point to the oddity of saying things like, "I am justified in believing that there is music playing, but I cannot justify this belief." Why is this odd if not because, when I have a justified belief, I can give a justification for it by appeal to beliefs that cohere with it? But consider this. Typically, in asserting something, say that there were lawsuits arising from an accident, I imply that, in some way or other, I *can* justify what I say, especially if the belief I express is, like this one, not plausibly thought to be grounded in a basic source such as perception. In the quoted sentence I deny that I can justify what I claim. The foundationalist must explain why that is odd, given that I can be justified in believing propositions even when I cannot show that I am (and may not even believe I am). The main point needed to explain this is that it is apparently my *asserting* that my belief is justified, rather than its being so, that gives the appearance that I must be able to give a justification of the belief. Compare "*She* is justified in believing that there is music playing, but (being an intuitive and unphilosophical kind of person) she cannot justify that proposition." This has no disturbing oddity, because the person said to have justification is not the one claiming it. Since she might be shocked to be asked to justify the proposition and might not know how to justify it, this statement might be true of her. We must not stop here, however. There are at least two further points.

First, there is quite a difference between *showing* that one is justified and simply *giving* a justification. I can give my justification for believing that there is music simply by indicating that I hear it. But this does not show that I am justified, at least in the sense of 'show' usual in epistemology. That task requires not just exhibiting what justifies one but also indicating conditions for being justified *and* showing that one meets them. It is one thing to cite a justifier, such as a clear perception; it is quite another to show that it meets a sufficiently high standard to *be* a justifier of the belief it grounds. Certainly skeptics—and probably most coherentists as well—have in mind something more like the latter process when they ask for a justification. Similarly—and this is the second point—where a regress of justification is, for fallibilist foundationalism, stopped by giving a (genuine) justification for the proposition in question, and the regress problem can be considered soluble because such stopping is possible, the skeptic will not countenance any stopping place, and certainly not any solution, that is not dialectically defended by argument showing that one is justified.

To be sure, it may be that at least typically when we do have a justified belief we can give a justification for it. When I justifiedly believe that there is music playing, I surely can give a justification: that I hear it. But I need not *believe* that I hear it *before* the question of justification arises. That question leads me to focus on my circumstances, in which I first had a belief solely about the music. I also had a *disposition,* based on my auditory experience, to form the belief that I *hear* the music, and this is largely why, in the course of justifying that belief, I then *form* the further belief that I do hear it. But a dispo-

sition to believe something does not imply an actual belief of it, not even a dispositional one, as opposed to one manifesting itself in consciousness. If I am talking loudly and excitedly in a restaurant, I may be disposed to believe this—so much so that if I merely think of the proposition that I am talking loudly, I will form the belief that I am and lower my voice. But this disposition does not imply that I *already* believe that proposition—if I did, I would not be talking loudly in the first place. In the musical case, I tend to form the belief that I hear the music if, as I hear it, the question of whether I hear it arises; yet I need not have subliminally believed this already. The justification I offer, then, is not by appeal to coherence with other beliefs I already had—such as that I saw the turntable moving—but by reference to what has traditionally been considered a basic source of both justification and knowledge: perception. It is thus precisely the kind of justification that foundationalists are likely to consider appropriate for a non-inferential belief. Indeed, one consideration favoring foundationalism about both justification and knowledge, at least as an account of our everyday epistemic practices, including much scientific practice, is that typically we cease to offer justification or to defend a knowledge claim precisely when we reach a basic source.

VI. COHERENCE, FOUNDATIONS, AND JUSTIFICATION

There is far more to say in clarifying both foundationalism and coherentism. But if what I have said so far is correct, then we can at least understand their basic thrusts. We can also see how coherentism may respond to the regress argument—in part by distinguishing psychological from epistemic directness. And we can see how foundationalism may reply to the charge that, once made moderate enough to be plausible, it depends on coherence criteria rather than on grounding in experience and reason. The response is in part to distinguish negative from positive epistemic dependence and to argue that foundationalism does not make justification depend positively on coherence, but only negatively on (avoiding) incoherence.

One may still wonder, however, whether fallibilist foundationalism concedes enough to coherentism. Granted that it need not restrict the role of coherence any more than is required by the regress argument, it still denies that coherence is (independently) necessary for justification. As most plausibly developed, fallibilist foundationalism also denies that coherence is a *basic* (nonderivative) source of justification—or at least that if it is, it can produce *enough* justification to render a belief unqualifiedly justified or (given truth and certain other conditions) to make it knowledge. A single drop of even the purest water will not quench a thirst. The moderate holistic coherentism formulated above is parallel in this: while it may grant foundationalism its typical psychological picture of how belief systems are structured, it denies that foundational justification is (independently) necessary for justification and that it is a basic source of justification, except possibly of degrees of justification too slight for knowledge or unqualifiedly justified belief.

The issue here is the difference in the two conceptions of justification. Broadly, foundationalists tend to hold that justification belongs to a belief, whether inferentially or directly, by virtue of its grounding in experience or reason; coherentists tend to hold that justification belongs to a belief by virtue of its coherence with one or more other beliefs. This is apparently a difference concerning basic sources. To be sure, my formulation may make coherentism sound foundationalistic, because justification is grounded not in an inferential relation to premises but in coherence itself, which sounds parallel to experience or reason. But note three contrasts with foundationalism: (1) the source of coherence is *cognitive,* because the coherence is an internal property of the belief system, whereas foundationalism makes no such restriction; (2) coherence is an inferential or at least epistemic generator, in the sense that it arises, with or without one's having inferential beliefs, from relations among beliefs or their propositional objects, e.g. from entailment, inductive support, or explanation of one belief or proposition by another, whereas experiential sources and (for pure coherentists) even rational sources are a non-inferential generator of belief (these sources can produce and thereby explain belief, but they do not, according to coherentism, justify it); and (3) S has *inferential access* to the coherence-making relations: S can wield them in inferentially justifying the belief that p, whereas foundationalism does not require such access to its basic sources. Still, I want to pursue just how deep the difference between foundationalism and coherentism is; for once foundationalism is moderately expressed and grants the truth of conceptual coherentism, and once coherentism is (plausibly) construed as consistent with psychological foundationalism, it may appear that the views differ far less than the prevailing stereotypes would have us think.

It should help if we first contrast fallibilist foundationalism with *strong foundationalism* and compare their relation to coherentism. If we use Descartes' version as a model, strong foundationalism is deductivist, takes foundational beliefs as indefeasibly justified, and allows coherence at most a limited generative role. To meet these conditions, it may reduce the basic sources of justification to reason and some form of introspection. Moreover, being committed to the indefeasibility of foundational justification, it would not grant that incoherence can defeat such justification. It would also concede to coherentists, and hence to any independence principle they countenance, at most a minimal positive role, say by insisting that if a belief is supported by two or more independent cohering sources, its justification is increased at most "additively," that is, only by combining the justification transmitted separately from each relevant basic source.

By contrast, what fallibilist foundationalism denies regarding coherence is only that it is a basic (hence sufficient) source of justification. Thus, coherence by itself does not ground justification, and hence the independence principle does not apply to sources that have *no* justification; at most, the principle allows coherence to raise the level of justification originally drawn from other sources to a level higher than it would reach if those sources did not mutually cohere. Similarly, if inference is a basic source of coherence (as some coherentists seem to believe), it is not a basic source of justification. It may enhance justification, as where one strengthens one's justification for believing someone's testimony by inferring the same point from someone else's. But inference *alone* does not generate justification. Suppose I believe several propositions without a shred of evidence and merely through wishful thinking. I might infer any number of others; yet even if by good luck I arrive at a highly coherent set of beliefs, I do not automatically gain justification for believing any of them. If I am floating in mid-ocean, strengthening my boat with added nails and planks may make it hang together more tightly and thereby make me feel secure; but if nothing indicates my location, there is no reason to expect this work to get me any closer to shore. Coherence may, to be sure, enable me to draw a beautiful map; but if there are no experiences I may rely on to connect it with reality, I may follow it forever to no avail. Even to be justified in *believing* that it will correspond with reality, I must have some experiential source to work from.

A natural coherentist reply is that when we consider examples of justified belief, not only do we always find some coherence, we also apparently find the right sort to account for the justification. This reply is especially plausible if—as I suggest is reasonable—coherentism as usually formulated is modified to include, in the coherence base, *dispositions to believe.* Consider my belief that music is playing. It coheres both with my beliefs about what records are in the house, what music my daughter prefers, my auditory capacities, etc., *and* with many of my dispositions to believe, say to form the belief that no one else in the house would play that music. Since such dispositions can themselves be well grounded, say in perception, or poorly grounded, e.g. in prejudice, they admit of justification and, when they produce beliefs, can lead to reasonable inferences. These dispositions are thus appropriate for the coherence base, and including them among generators of coherence is particularly useful in freeing coherentism from implausibly positing all the beliefs needed for the justificational capacities it tends to take to underlie justified belief. We need not "store" beliefs of all the propositions needed for our own system of justified belief; the disposition to believe them is enough. Given this broad conception of coherence, it is surely plausible to take coherence as at least necessary for justified belief. And it might be argued that its justification is based on coherence, not on grounding in experience.

Let us grant both that the musical case does exhibit a high degree of coherence among my beliefs

and dispositions to believe and even that the coherence is necessary for the justification of my belief. It does not follow that the justification is based on the coherence. Coherence could still be at best a *consequential necessary condition* for justification, one that holds as a result of the justification itself or what that is based on, as opposed to a *constitutive necessary condition,* one that either expresses part of what it *is* for a belief to be justified or constitutes a basic source of it. The relation of coherence to the properties producing it might be analogous to that of heat to friction: a necessary product of it, but not part of what constitutes it.

If coherence is a constitutive necessary condition for justification, and especially if it is a basic source of it, we might expect to find cases in which the experiential and rational sources are absent, yet there is sufficient coherence for justified belief. But this is precisely what we do not easily find, if we ever find it. If I discover a set of my beliefs that intuitively cohere very well yet receive no support from what I believe (or at least am disposed to believe) on the basis of experience or reason, I am not inclined to attribute justification to any of them. To be sure, if the unit of coherence is large enough to include my actual beliefs, then because I have so many that *are* grounded in experience or reason (indeed, few that are not), I will almost certainly not in fact have any beliefs that, intuitively, seem justified yet are not coherent with some of my beliefs so grounded. This complicates assessment of the role of coherence in justification. But we can certainly imagine beings (or ourselves) artificially endowed with coherent sets of beliefs *not* grounded in experience or reason; and when we do, it appears that coherence does not automatically confer justification.

One might conclude, then, that it is more nearly true that coherence is based on justification (or whatever confers justification) than that the latter is based on the former. Further, the data we have so far considered can be explained on the hypothesis that both coherence among beliefs and their justification rest on the beliefs' being grounded (in an appropriate way) in the basic sources. For particularly if a coherence theory of the acquisition of concepts is true, one perhaps cannot have a belief justified by a basic source without having beliefs—or at least dispositions to believe—related in an intimate (and intuitively coherence-generating) way to that belief. One certainly cannot have a justified belief unless incoherence defeats its justification. Given these two points, it is to be expected that on a fallibilist foundationalism, justification will normally imply coherence, both in the positive sense involving mutual support and in the weak sense of the absence of potential incoherence. There is some reason to think, then, that coherence is not a basic source of justification and is at most a consequentially necessary condition for it.

There is at least one more possibility to be considered, however: that *given* justification from foundational sources, coherence can generate more justification than *S* would have from those sources alone. If so, we might call coherence a *conditionally basic* source, in that, where there is already some justification from other sources, it can produce new justification. This bears on interpreting the independence principle. It is widely agreed that our justification increases markedly when we take into account independent sources of evidence, as where I confirm that there is music playing by moving closer to enhance my auditory impression and by visually confirming that a phonograph is playing. Perhaps what explains the dramatic increase in my overall justification here is not just "additivity" of foundational justification but also coherence as a further source of justification.

There is plausibility in this reasoning, but it is not cogent. For one thing, there really are no such additive quantities of justification. Perhaps we simply combine degrees of justification, so far as we can, on analogy with combinations of independent probabilities. Thus, the probability of at least one heads on two fair coin tosses is not $1/2 + 1/2$ (the two independent probabilities), which would give the event a probability of 1 and make it a certainty; the probability is $3/4$, i.e., 1 minus the probability of two tails, which is $1/4$. Insofar as degrees of justification are quantifiable, they combine similarly. Moreover, the relevant probability rules do not seem to depend on coherence; they seem to be justifiable by *a priori* reasoning in the way beliefs grounded in reason are commonly thought to be justifiable, and they appear to be among the principles one must *presuppose* if one is to give an account of how coherence contributes to justification. The

(limited) analogy between probability and justification, then, does not favor coherentism and may well favor foundationalism.

There remains a contrast between, say, having six independent credible witnesses tell me that *p* on separate occasions which I do not connect with one another, and having them do so on a single occasion when I can note the coherence of their stories. In the first case, while my isolated beliefs cohere, I have no belief that they do, nor even a sense of their collective weight. This is not, to be sure, a case of six increments of isolated foundational justification versus a case of six cohering items of evidence. Both cases exhibit coherence; but in the second there is an additional belief (or justified disposition to believe): *that* six independent witnesses agree. Foundationalists as well as coherentists can plausibly explain how this additional belief increases the justification one has in the first case. It would be premature, then, to take cases like this to show that coherence is even a conditionally basic source of justification. It may only reflect other sources of justification, rather than contribute any.

VII. EPISTEMOLOGICAL DOGMATISM AND THE SOURCES OF JUSTIFICATION

Of the problems that remain for understanding the foundationalism-coherentism controversy, the one most readily clarified by the results of this chapter, is the dogmatism objection. This might be expressed as follows. If one can have knowledge or justified belief without being able to show that one does, and even without a premise from which to derive it; then the way is open to claim just about anything one likes, defending it by cavalierly noting that one can be justified without being able to show that one is. Given the conception of the foundationalism-coherentism controversy developed here, we can perhaps throw some new light on how the charge of dogmatism is relevant to each position.

The notion of dogmatism is not easy to characterize, and there have apparently been few detailed discussions of it in recent epistemological literature. My focus will be dogmatism as an epistemological attitude or stance, not as a trait of personality. I am mainly interested in what it is to hold a belief dogmatically. This is probably the basic notion in any case: a general dogmatic attitude, like the personality trait of dogmatism, is surely in some way a matter of having or tending to have dogmatically held beliefs.

It will be useful to start with some contrasts. Dogmatism in relation to a belief is not equivalent to stubbornness in holding it; for even if a dogmatically held belief cannot be easily given up, one could be stubborn in holding a belief simply from attachment to it, and without the required disposition to defend it or regard it as better grounded than alternatives. For similar reasons, psychological certainty in holding a belief does not entail dogmatism. Indeed, even if one is both psychologically certain of a simple logical truth *and* disposed to reject denials of it with confidence and to suspect even well-developed arguments against it as sophistical, one does not qualify as dogmatic. The content of one's view is important: even moderate insistence on a reasonably disputed matter may bespeak dogmatism; stubborn adherence to the self–evident need not. An attitude that would be dogmatic in holding one belief may not be so in holding another.

Dogmatic people are often closed-minded, and dogmatically held beliefs are often closed-mindedly maintained; but a belief held closed-mindedly need not be held dogmatically: it may be maintained with a guilty realization that emotionally one simply cannot stand to listen to challenges of it, and with an awareness that it might be mistaken. Moreover, although people who hold beliefs dogmatically are often intellectually pugnacious in defending them, or even in trying to win converts, such pugnacity is not sufficient for dogmatism. Intellectual pugnacity is consistent with a keen awareness that one might be mistaken, and it may be accompanied by open-minded argumentation for one's view. Nor need a dogmatically held belief generate such pugnacity; I might be indisposed to argue, whether from confidence that I know or from temperament, and my dogmatism might surface only when I am challenged.

One thing all of these possible conceptions of dogmatism have in common is lack of a second-order component. But that component may well be necessary for a dogmatic attitude, at least of the full-blooded kind. Typically, a dogmatically held belief is maintained with a conviction (often unjustified) to the effect that one is right, e.g. that one knows, is amply justified, is properly certain, or can just see the truth of the proposition in question. Such a second-order belief is not, however, sufficient for a dogmatic attitude. This is shown by certain cases of believing simple logical truths. These can be held both with such a second-order belief and in the stubborn way typical of a dogmatic attitude yet not bespeak a dogmatic attitude. It might be held that in this case they would at least be held *dogmatically;* but if the imagined tenacity is toward, say, the principle that if a = b, and b = c, then a = c, one could not properly call the attitude dogmatic, and we might better speak of maintaining the belief steadfastly rather than dogmatically.

It might be argued, however, that even if the only examples of dogmatism so far illustrated are the second-order ones, there are still two kinds of dogmatism: first– and second-order. It may be enough, for instance, that one be *disposed* to have a certain belief, usually an unwarrantedly positive one, about the status of one's belief that *p*. Imagine that Tom thinks that Mozart is a far greater composer than Haydn, asserts it without giving any argument, and sloughs off arguments to the contrary. If he does not believe, but is disposed to believe on considering the matter, that his belief is, say, obviously correct, then he may qualify as dogmatically holding it. Here, then, there is no actual second-order attitude, but only a disposition to form one upon considering the status of one's belief. I want to grant that this kind of first-order pattern may qualify as dogmatism; but the account of it remains a second-order one, and it still seems that the other first-order cases we have considered, such as mere stubbornness in believing, are not cases of dogmatism. They may exhibit believing dogmatically, but that does not entail dogmatism as an epistemic attitude or trait of character, any more than doing something lovingly entails a loving attitude, or being a loving person. It appears, then, that at least the clear cases of dogmatically holding beliefs imply either second-order attitudes or certain dispositions to form them.

There may be no simple, illuminating way to characterize dogmatism with respect to a belief that *p*; but if there is, the following elements should be reflected at least as typical conditions and should provide the materials needed in appraising the foundationalism-coherentism controversy: (1) confidence that p, and significantly greater confidence than one's evidence or grounds warrant; (2) unjustified resistance to taking plausible objections seriously when they are intelligibly posed to one; (3) a willingness, or at least a tendency, to assert the proposition flat-out even in the presence of presumptive reasons to question it, including simply the conflicting views of one or more persons whom S sees or should see to be competent concerning the subject matter; and (4) a (second-order) belief, or disposition to believe, that one's belief is clearly true (or certainly true). Note, however, that (i) excessive confidence can come from mere foolhardiness and can be quite unstable; (ii) resistance to plausible objections may be due to intellectual laziness; (iii) a tendency to assert something flat-out can derive from mere bluntness; and (iv) a belief that one is right might arise not from dogmatism but merely from conceit, intellectual mistake (such as a facile anti-skepticism), or sheer error. Notice also that the notion of dogmatism is not just psychological, but also epistemic.

Of the four elements highly characteristic of dogmatism, the last may have the best claim to be an unqualifiedly necessary condition, and perhaps one or more of the others is necessary. The four are probably jointly sufficient; but this is not self-evident, and I certainly doubt that we can find any simple condition that is nontrivially sufficient, such as believing that one knows, or is justified in believing, that p (which one does believe), while also believing one has no reasons for believing that p. This condition is not sufficient because it could stem from a certain view of knowledge and reasons, say a view on which one never has reasons (as opposed to a basis) for believing simple, self-evident propositions. The condition also seems insufficient because it could be satisfied by a person who lacks the first three of the typical conditions just specified.

Let us work with the full-blooded conception of a dogmatically held belief summarized by conditions (1)–(4). What, then, may we say about the standard charge that foundationalism is dogmatic, in a sense implying that it invites proponents to hold certain beliefs dogmatically? This charge has been leveled on a number of occasions, and some plausible replies have been made. Given the earlier sections of this chapter, it should be plain that the charge is more likely to seem cogent if foundationalism is conceived as answering the dialectical regress problem, as it has apparently been taken to do by, e.g., Chisholm. For in this case a (doxastic) stopping place in the regress generated by 'How do you know that p?' will coincide with the assertion of a second-order belief, such as that I know that q, e.g. that there is a window before me; and since knowledge claims are commonly justifiable by evidence, flatly stopping the regress in this way will seem dogmatic. Even if such a claim is justified by one's citing a non-doxastic state of affairs, such as a visual experience of a window, one is still asserting the existence of this state of affairs and hence apparently expressing knowledge: making what seems a tacit claim *to* it, though not actually claiming to *have* it.

We can formulate various second-order foundationalisms, for instance one which says that if S knows anything, then there is something that S directly knows S knows. But a foundationalist need not hold such a view, nor would one who does be committed to maintaining that many kinds of belief constitute such knowable foundations, i.e., are knowledge one can know one has, or that every epistemic chain terminates in them. In any event, moderate foundationalists will be disinclined to hold a second-order foundationalism, even if they think that we do in fact have some second-order knowledge. For one thing, if foundational beliefs are only defeasibly justified, it is likely to be quite difficult to know that they are justified, because this requires warrant for attributing certain grounds to the belief and may also require justification for believing that certain defeaters are absent. This is not to deny that there are kinds of knowledge which one may, without having evidence for this, warrantedly and non-dogmatically say one has, for instance where the first-order knowledge is of a simple self-evident proposition. My point is that foundationalism as such, at least in moderate versions, need not make such second-order knowledge (or justification) a condition for the existence of knowledge (or justification) in general.

If we raise the regress problem in the structural form, there is much less temptation to consider foundationalism dogmatic. For there is no presumption that, with respect to anything I know, I non-inferentially know that I know it (and similarly for justification). Granted, on the assumption that by and large I am entitled, without offering evidence, to assert what I directly know, it may seem that even moderate foundationalism justifies me in holding—and expressing—beliefs dogmatically. But this is a mistake. There is considerable difference between what I know or justifiably believe and what I may warrantedly assert without evidence. It is, e.g., apparently consistent with knowing that p, say that there is music playing, that I have some reason to doubt that p; I might certainly have reason to think others doubt it and that they should not be spoken to as if their objections could not matter. Thus, I might know, through my own good hearing, that p, yet be unwarranted in saying that I know it, and warranted, with only moderate confidence, even in saying simply that it is true. Here 'It is true' would *express*, but not *claim*, my knowledge; 'I know it' explicitly claims knowledge and normally implies that I have justification for beliefs about my objective grounds, not just about my own cognitive and perceptual state.

Nothing said here implies that one *cannot* be justified in believing what one holds dogmatically. That one's attitude *in* holding that p is not justified does not imply that one's holding that p is itself not justified. It might be possible, for all I have said, that in certain cases one might even be justified, overall, in taking a dogmatic attitude toward certain propositions. This will depend on, among other things, the plausibility of the proposition in question and the level of justification one has for believing that one is right. But typically, dogmatic attitudes are not justified, and moderate foundationalism, far from implying otherwise, can readily explain this.

Furthermore, once the defeasibility of foundational beliefs is appreciated, then even if one does think that one may assert the propositions in question without offering evidence, one will not take the attitudes or other stances required for holding a belief dogmatically. As the example of my belief about the music illustrates, most of the time one is likely to be open to counterargument and may indeed tend to be no more confident than one's grounds warrant. To be sure, fallibilism alone, even when grounded in a proper appreciation of defeasibility, does not preclude dogmatism regarding many of one's beliefs. But it helps toward this end, and it is natural for moderate foundationalists to hold a fallibilistic outlook on their beliefs, especially their empirical beliefs, and to bear it in mind in framing an overall conception of human experience.

If foundationalism has been uncritically thought to encourage dogmatism, coherentism has often been taken to foster intellectual openness. But this second stereotypic conception may be no better warranted than the first. Much depends, of course, on the kind of coherentism and on the temperament of its proponent. Let us consider these points in turn.

What makes coherentism seem to foster tolerance is precisely what leads us to wonder how it can account for knowledge (at least without a coherence theory of truth). For as coherentists widely grant, there are indefinitely many coherent systems of beliefs people might in principle have; hence, to suppose that mine embodies knowledge and thus truth, or even justification and thus a presumption of truth, while yours does not, is prima facie unwarranted. But the moment the view is developed to yield a plausible account of knowledge of the world (an external notion), say by requiring a role for observation beliefs and other cognitively spontaneous beliefs, as some coherentists do, or by requiring beliefs accepted on the basis of a desire to believe truth and avoid error, as others do, it becomes easy to think—and one can be warranted in thinking—that one's beliefs are more likely to constitute knowledge, or to be justified, than someone else's, especially if the other person(s) holds views incompatible with one's own. Indeed, while coherentism makes it easy to see how counterargument can be launched from a wide range of opposing viewpoints, it also provides less in the way of foundational appeals by which debates may be settled—and pretensions quashed. Is one likely to be less dogmatic where one thinks one can always encounter reasoned opposition from someone with a different coherent belief system, right or wrong, than where one believes one can be decisively shown to be mistaken by appeal to foundational sources of knowledge and justification? The answer is not clear; in any given case it will depend on a number of variables, including the temperament of the subject and the propositions in question. And could not my confidence that, using one or another coherent resource, I can always continue to argue for my view generate overconfidence just as much as my thinking that I (defeasibly) know something through experience or reason? Indeed, if coherence is as vague a notion as it seems, it seems quite possible both to exaggerate the extent of its support for one's own beliefs and underestimate the degree of coherence supporting an opposing belief. It turns out that coherentism can also produce dogmatism, even if its proponents have tended to be less inclined toward it than some foundationalists.

If there has been such a lesser inclination, it may be due to temperament, including perhaps a greater sympathy with skepticism, as much as to theoretical commitments. In any case, whether one dogmatically holds certain of one's beliefs surely does depend significantly on whether one is dogmatic in temperament or in certain segments of one's outlook. It may be that the tendency to seek justification in large patterns runs stronger in coherentists than in foundationalists, and that the latter tend more than the former to seek it instead in chains of argument or of inference. If so, this could explain a systematic difference in the degree of dogmatism found in the two traditions. But these tendencies are only contingently connected with the respective theories. Foundationalism can account for the justificatory importance of large patterns, and coherentists commonly conceive argument and inference as prime sources of coherence. One can also wax dogmatic in insisting that a pattern is decisive in justification, as one can dogmatically assert that a single perceptual belief is incontrovertibly veridical.

One source of the charge of dogmatism, at least as advanced by philosophers, is of course the sense that skepticism is being flatly denied. Moreover, the skeptic in us tends to think that any confident assertion of a non-self-evident, non-introspective proposition is dogmatic. On this score, foundationalism is again likely to seem dogmatic if it is conceived as an answer to the dialectical regress formulation. For it may then seem to beg the question against skepticism. But again, foundationalism is not committed to the existence of any knowledge or justified belief; and even a foundationalist who maintains that there

is some need not hold that we directly know that there is. Granted, foundationalists are more likely to say, at some point or other, that skepticism is just wrong than are coherentists, who (theoretically) can always trace new justificatory paths through the fabric of their beliefs. But if this is true, it has limited force: perhaps in some such cases foundationalists would be warranted in a way that precludes being dogmatic, and perhaps coherentists are in effect repeating themselves in a way consistent with dogmatic reassertion of the point at issue.

It turns out, then, that fallibilist foundationalism is not damaged by the dogmatism objection and coherentism is not immune to it. Far from being dogmatic, fallibilist foundationalism implies that even where one has a justified belief one cannot show to be justified, one may (and at least normally can) *give* a justification for it. As to coherentism, it, too, may be a refuge for dogmatists, at least those clever enough to find a coherent pattern by which to rationalize the beliefs they dogmatically hold.

CONCLUSION

The foundationalism-coherentism controversy cannot be settled in a single essay. But we can now appreciate some often neglected dimensions of the issue. One dimension is the formulation of the regress problem itself; another is the distinction between defeasibility and epistemic dependence; still another is that between consequential and constitutive necessary conditions; and yet another is between an unqualifiedly and a conditionally basic source. Even if coherence is neither a constitutive necessary condition for justification nor even a conditionally basic source of it, there is still reason to consider it important for justification. It may even be a *mark* of justification, a common effect of the same causes as it were, or a virtue with the same foundations. Coherence is certainly significant as suggesting a negative constraint on justification; for incoherence is a paradigm of what defeats justification.

I have argued at length for the importance of the regress problem. It matters considerably whether we conceive the problem dialectically or structurally, at least insofar as we cast foundationalism and coherentism in terms of their capacity to solve it. Indeed, while both coherentism and foundationalism can be made plausible on either conception, coherentism is perhaps best understood as a response to the problem *in* some dialectical formulation, and foundationalism is perhaps best understood as a response to it in some structural form. Taking account of both formulations of the regress problem, I have suggested plausible versions of both foundationalism and coherentism. Neither has been established, though fallibilist foundationalism has emerged as the more plausible of the two. In clarifying them, I have stressed a number of distinctions: between the process and the property of justification, between dispositional beliefs and dispositions to believe, between epistemically and psychologically foundational beliefs, between defeasibility and epistemic dependence, between constitutive and consequential necessary conditions for justification, and between unqualified and conditionally basic sources of it. Against this background, we can see how fallibilist foundationalism avoids some of the objections commonly thought to refute foundationalism, including its alleged failure to account for the defeasibility of most and perhaps all of our justification, and for the role of coherence in justification. Indeed, fallibilist foundationalism can even account for coherence as a mark of justification; the chief tension between the two theories concerns not whether coherence is necessary for justification, but whether it is a basic source of it.

It is appropriate in closing to summarize some of the very general considerations supporting a fallibilist foundationalism, since that is a position which some have apparently neglected—or supposed to be a contradiction in terms—and others have not distinguished from coherentism. First, the theory provides a plausible and reasonably straightforward solution to the regress problem. It selects what seems the best option among the four and does not interpret that option in a way that makes knowledge or justification either impossible, as the skeptic would have it, or too easy to achieve, as they would be if they required no grounds at all or only grounds obtainable without the effort of observing, thinking, or otherwise taking account of experience. Second, in working from the experiential and rational sources it takes as epistemically basic, fallibilist

foundationalism (in its most plausible versions) accords with reflective common sense: the sorts of beliefs it takes as non-inferentially justified, or as constituting non-inferential knowledge, are pretty much those that, on reflection, we think people are justified in holding, or in supposing to be knowledge, without any more than the evidence of the senses or of intuition. Third, fallibilist foundationalism is psychologically plausible, in two major ways: the account it suggests of the experiential and inferential genesis of many of our beliefs apparently fits what is known about their origins and development; and, far from positing infinite or circular belief chains, whose psychology is at least puzzling, it allows a fairly simple account of the structure of cognition. Beliefs arise both from experience and from inference; some serve to unify others, especially those based on them; and their relative strengths, their changes, and their mutual interactions are all explicable within the moderate foundationalist assumptions suggested. Fourth, the theory serves to integrate our epistemology with our psychology and even biology, particularly in the crucial case of perceptual beliefs. What causally explains why we hold them—sensory experience—is also what justifies them.

From an evolutionary point of view, moreover, many of the kinds of beliefs that the theory (in its most plausible versions) takes to be non-inferentially justified—introspective and memorial beliefs as well as perceptual ones—are plainly essential to survival. We may need a map, and not merely a mirror, of the world to navigate it; but if experience does not generally mirror reality, we are in no position to move to the abstract level on which we can draw a good map. If a mirror without a map is insufficiently discriminating, a map without a mirror is insufficiently reliable. Experience that does not produce beliefs cannot guide us; beliefs not grounded in experience cannot be expected to be true.

Finally, contrary to the dogmatism charge, the theory helps to explain cognitive pluralism. Given that different people have different experiences, and that anyone's experiences change over time, people should be expected to differ from one another in their non-inferentially justified beliefs and, in their own case, across time; and given that logic does not dictate what is to be inferred from one's premises, people should be expected to differ considerably in their inferential beliefs as well. Logic does, to be sure, tell us what *may* be inferred; but it neither forces inferences nor, when we draw them, selects which among the permissible ones we will make. Particularly in the case of inductive inference, say where we infer a hypothesis as the best explanation of some puzzling event, our imagination comes into play; and even if we were to build from the same foundations as our neighbors, we would often produce quite different superstructures.

A properly qualified foundationalism, then, has much to recommend it and exhibits many of the virtues that have been commonly thought to be characteristic only of coherentist theories. Fallibilist foundationalism can account for the main connections between coherence and justification, and it can provide principles of justification to explain how justification that can be plausibly attributed to coherence can also be traced—by sufficiently complex and sometimes inductive paths—to basic sources in experience and reason.

GENEVIEVE LLOYD

from The Man of Reason: "Male" and "Female" in Western Philosophy

INTRODUCTION

The claim that Reason is 'male', in the context of current philosophical debate, must inevitably conjure up the idea that what is true or reasonable for men might be not at all so for women. Contemporary philosophical concern about our ideals of rationality is, not surprisingly, largely preoccupied with issues of relativism—with the possibility that truth might be relative to particular cultures, or to periods of time. Relativism is a major challenge to Reason's traditional claims to universality—to its capacity to yield ultimately true representations of one real world. In the context of such concern with beliefs and truth, to allege that Reason, despite its pretensions to be gender-free, might after all be thoroughly 'male', may well seem preposterous. To suggest that the celebrated objectivity and universality of our canons of rational belief might not in fact transcend even sexual difference seems to go beyond even the more outrageous versions of cultural relativism. It seems highly implausible to claim that what is true or reasonable varies according to what sex we are. But the implausibility of such 'sexual relativism' can mask other, no less important, respects in which Reason is indeed 'male'.

There is more at stake in assessing our ideals of Reason than questions of the relativity of truth. Reason has figured in western culture not only in the assessment of beliefs, but also in the assessment of character. It is incorporated not just into our criteria of truth, but also into our understanding of what it is to be a person at all, of the requirements that must be met to be a good person, and of the proper relations between our status as knowers and the rest of our lives. Past philosophical reflection on what is distinctive about human life, and on what should be the priorities of a well-lived life, has issued in character ideals centered on the idea of Reason; and the supposed universality and neutrality of these ideals can be seriously questioned. It is with the maleness of these character ideals—the maleness of the Man of Reason—that this book is primarily concerned.

The maleness of the Man of Reason, I will try to show, is no superficial linguistic bias. It lies deep in our philosophical tradition. This is not to say that women have their own truth, or that there are distinctively female criteria for reasonable belief. It is, however, to make a claim which is no less a scandal to the pretensions of Reason. Gender, after all, is one of the things from which truly rational thought is supposed to prescind. Reason is taken to express the real nature of the mind, in which, as Augustine put it, there is no sex. The aspiration to a Reason common to all, transcending the contingent historical circumstances which differentiate minds from one another, lies at the very heart of our philosophical heritage. The conviction that minds, in so far as they are rational, are fundamentally alike underlies many of our moral and political ideals. And the aspiration has inspired, too, our ideals of objective knowledge. The claim, repudiated by relativism, that Reason delivers to us a single objective truth has often been substantiated by appeal to Reason's supposed transcendence of all that differentiates minds from one another.

Our trust in a Reason that knows no sex has, I will argue, been largely self-deceiving. To bring to the surface the implicit maleness of our ideals of Reason is not necessarily to adopt a 'sexual relativism' about rational belief and truth; but it does have important implications for our contemporary understanding of gender difference. It means, for example, that there are not only practical reasons, but also conceptual ones, for the conflicts many women experience between Reason and femininity. The obstacles to female cultivation of Reason spring to a large extent from the fact that our ideals of Reason have historically incorporated an exclusion of the feminine, and that femininity itself has been partly constituted through such processes of exclusion. The historical treatment I will offer of the maleness of Reason bears, too, on the problems of adequately assessing the ideal, current in some contemporary feminist thought, of a distinctively female thought-style. A full treatment of the complexities of these issues lies beyond the scope of this book. What emerges about the historical maleness of Reason, however, does help to illuminate some of the perplexity these questions induce in men and women alike.

REASON AS ATTAINMENT

Introduction

In *The Philosophy of Right,* Hegel contrasted the 'happy ideas, taste and elegance' characteristic of female consciousness with male attainments which demand a 'universal faculty'. 'Women are educated—who knows how?—as it were by breathing in ideas, by living rather than by acquiring knowledge. The status of manhood, on the other hand, is attained only by the stress of thought and much technical exertion.' These kinds of connection between maleness and achievement are not confined to Hegel. In western thought, maleness has been seen as itself an achievement, attained by breaking away from the more 'natural' condition of women. Attitudes to Reason and its bearing on the rest of life have played a major part in this; a development that occurred in the seventeenth century has been particularly crucial.

In the illustrations, in the last chapter, of Reason's superiority over other aspects of human nature, it was seen as a distinctive human trait, with ramifications in all areas of life—the practical, no less than the contemplative—even if, as with Augustine, this was regarded as an inferior diversion of Reason. In the seventeenth century, Reason came to be seen not just as a distinguishing feature of human nature, but as an achievement—a skill to be learned, a distinctively methodical way of thinking,

sharply differentiated from other kinds of thought—and its relationships with other aspects of human nature were also transformed. The most thorough going and influential version of Reason as methodical thought was the famous method of Descartes. Something happened here which proved crucial for the development of stereotypes of maleness and femaleness, and it happened in some ways despite Descartes's explicit intentions.

Descartes's Method

In its Greek origins, the basic meaning of 'method' was a road or path to be followed; and the metaphor of a path whose goal is understanding recurs throughout the entire philosophical tradition which grew from Greek thought. The method which proceeds without analysis, says Socrates in Plato's *Phaedrus,* is 'like groping of a blind man'. The follower of true method is preserved from such blind wandering by understanding the reason for which things are done in a certain order. Descartes used the same metaphors. In expounding his 'rules for the direction of the mind', he attacked those truth-seekers who 'conduct their minds along unexplored routes, having no reason to hope for success, but merely being willing to risk the experiment of finding whether the truth they seek lies there'. It is, he says, as if a man seeking treasure were to 'continuously roam the streets, seeking to find something that a passer-by might have chanced to drop'. But, although his description of the goal remained much the same, Descartes completely transformed the relationship between Reason and method which had been central in the intellectual tradition since the time of Socrates.

The original Socratic ideal of method, illustrated by the definition of love, is expounded in the concluding sections of the *Phaedrus.* Right method, says Socrates, involves processes of generalization, the 'survey of scattered particulars, leading to their comprehension in one idea'; and processes of division into species, 'according to the natural formation, where the joint is, not breaking any part as a bad carver might'. These processes are aids to speaking and thinking; they belong in the art of rhetoric. But they are also supposed to be guides to truth, helping those who practice them to discern a 'one and many' in Nature. Most of the ingredients for later developments in the idea of method can be found in these brief *Phaedrus* passages: the idea of an orderly procedure; of an analysis to be conducted in relation to an end to be achieved; the connections between method and teaching; the importance of understanding the nature of the soul, in which persuasion is supposed to be induced. The ability to impart the Socratic art of rhetoric involves grasping its nature and relating its parts to the end which is supposed to be achieved in the soul. However, Socrates' general description of the art of rhetoric passed into the tradition as a general rubric which could be extended to any art: the teacher must have an understanding of what the art deals with and be able to analyse and evaluate its parts in relation to the achievement of its end.

Aristotle developed the idea of a systematic treatment of the art of arguing and debating into a concern with a rational way—a reasoned procedure—for arriving at sound conclusions. But the relation of reason to the 'way' or 'method' was similar to the original Socratic version. Reason—whether applied to the art of persuasion, to other arts, or more narrowly to the investigations which are supposed to yield truth—was incorporated into method. Method was a reasoned way of pursuing an activity; and it was the grasp of this internal reason which was supposed to enable the activity to be taught..

In Descartes's system, in contrast, method became not so much a reasoned way of proceeding—a path to be followed rationally—as a way of reasoning: a precisely ordered mode of abstract thinking. And the right order of thought was to be determined not by the variable subject-matter and ends of the activities at issue, but by the natural operations of the mind itself. Descartes's actual definitions of method are on the surface not very different from earlier ideas of method. By a method, he says in his *Rules for the Direction of the Mind,* he means 'certain and simple rules such that, if a man observe them accurately, he shall never assume what is false as true, and will never spend his mental efforts to no purpose, but will always gradually increase his knowledge and so arrive at a true understanding of all that does not surpass his powers'. To see what is really distinctive and important about Descartes's method we must see it in the context of the meta-physical doctrine for which he is most notorious—the radical separateness of mind and body—and also in the context of his immediate predecessors in the development of ideas of method.

Descartes's method, he insisted, is unitary and yields truth regardless of subject-matter. He criticized his Aristotelian scholastic predecessors for holding that the certainty of mathematics was unattainable in other sciences and that the method of each science should vary with differences in the material it investigated. A single and identical method, he thought, could be applied to all the various sciences, for the sciences taken together were nothing else but the very unity of human reason itself. This vision of the unity of the sciences as reflecting that of Reason arose directly from Descartes's radical separation of mind and body. Where body is involved, the formation of one habit inhibits that of others. The hand that adapts itself to agricultural operations is thereby less likely to be adept at harp playing. But the sciences consist entirely in the cognitive exercise of the mind. The traditional conception of a multiplicity of methods for different subject-areas thus rests on a faulty assimilation of mind to body. The sciences do not share in the inevitable multiplicity of the bodily arts. Knowing one truth does not have the restricting effect that is the consequence of mastering a bodily art; in fact it aids us in finding out other truths. So the sciences, taken all together, are identical with human wisdom, which always remains one and the same, however applied to different subjects.

All this is strongly opposed to what Descartes saw as the arbitrariness of the prevailing scholastic curriculum divisions. This concern was not new. Descartes's humanist predecessors had also been dissatisfied with the arbitrary methods of presentation of the traditional disciplines which, they thought, created needless difficulties for students. In the sixteenth century, Peter Ramus had devised 'one simple method' to bring order into the subjects taught in universities. Ramus's method proceeded from universal and general principles down to the more specific and singular, an order which he supposed to reflect the different degrees of clarity among the parts of a discipline. The clearer was to precede the more obscure, following the order and progression from universal to singular. Aristotle had distinguished what is prior in nature and what is prior to us. Ramus's ideal was a right order and progression of thought, which would reflect the priority in nature of the universal over the particular. But there was no real justification for his conviction that what was prior in being should also be clearer to students.

For Descartes, the idea of a right order of thought was grounded in an understanding of the nature of the mind. The correspondence between the basic structures of human thought and the order of the world, he argued, is divinely guaranteed. To find and to follow the mind's most basic operations was for him not just a prerequisite for ease in learning. His organization of subject-matter in accordance with what is more apparent to an attentive mind was not just a pedagogical device. Clarity and distinctness were the marks of truth. His method was directed to uncovering those basic ideas whose truth was assured by the fact that a veracious God created both the mind and the material world. Method was not confined to pedagogy; it was linked with criteria of truth.

As a development in the politics of learning, the significance of this approach to method cannot be overestimated. Earlier Renaissance reforms of educational procedures often found themselves in conflict with those who saw following the 'natural' processes of the mind as less important than following approved methods of strict demonstration and proof, however difficult these may have been to impart to students. Descartes's method undercut this conflict. Its aim went beyond the transmission of an already established art or the successful pursuit of a course of study; it aimed at valid knowledge. It should not be seen, he insisted, as a means of persuasion, belonging in the art of rhetoric; it belonged, rather, with the discovery of new truth. But such discovery was assured precisely through following the natural processes of thought. At the same time, Descartes's grounding of this unified method in the unity of Reason itself, accessible through introspection, enabled him to separate method entirely from the realm of public pedagogy and disputation.

The implications for Reason of thus severing the links between method and public procedures of discourse, debate and successful argument were far reaching. The right ordering of ideas was no longer associated with the best arrangement of the school curricula, but with private abstract thought, which can be pursued quite independently of public educational structures and procedures. Persuasion was internalized as what is clear and apparent to an attentive mind—the mark of truth itself. Reasoning in accordance with this new method does not demand conformity with the subtle forms of argument accepted as valid in the public disputations of the schools. The emphasis is entirely on unaided Reason. Descartes presented the method as simply a systematization of the innate faculty of Reason or 'good sense'—the power of 'forming good judgment and of distinguishing the true from false'. And this natural light of Reason is supposedly equal in all.

Descartes saw his method as opening the way to a new egalitarianism in knowledge. In a letter written shortly after the publication of the *Discourse on Method,* he commented that his thoughts on method seemed to him appropriate to put in a book where he wished that 'even women' might understand something. From our perspective, this tone may sound patronizing, but the remark is to be understood against the background of associations between earlier Renaissance versions of method and pedagogical procedures. By and large, it was only boys who were given systematic formal education outside the home. The exclusion of women from method was a direct consequence of their exclusion from the schools in which it was pursued. Descartes's egalitarian intentions come out also in his insistence on writing the *Discourse of Method* in the vernacular, rather than in Latin, the learned language of the schools. The work, he stressed, should appeal to those who avail themselves only of their natural reason in its purity. The point was political as well as practical. The use of Latin was in many ways the distinguishing mark of the learned. Women, being educated mostly at home rather than in schools, had no direct access to the learned, Latin-speaking world. The teaching of Latin to boys thus marked the boundaries between the private world of the family, in which the vernacular was used, and the external world of learning, to which males had access. The accessibility of the new method even to women was thus a powerful symbol of the transformation which it marked in the relationship between method and autonomous, individual reasoning.

In place of the subtleties of scholastic disputation, which can only, he thought, obscure the mind's clarity, Descartes offered a few supposedly simple procedures, the rationale of which was to remove all obstacles to the natural operations of the mind. The general rubric of the method was to break down the more complex operations of the mind into their simplest forms and then recombine them in an orderly series. The complex and obscure is reduced to simple, self-evident 'intuitions', which the mind scrutinizes with 'steadfast, mental gaze', then combines in orderly chains of deductions. Anyone who follows this method can feel assured that 'no avenue to the truth is closed to him from which everyone else is not also excluded, and that his ignorance is due neither to a deficiency in his capacity nor to his method of procedure'.

Descartes's method, with its new emphasis on the privacy of the mind's natural operations, promised to make knowledge accessible to all, even to women. Such was his intent. The lasting influence of his method, however, was something quite different, though no less a product of his radical separation of mind and body. In the context of associations already existing between gender and Reason, his version of the mind-body relationship produced stark polarizations of previously existing contrasts. This came about not through any intellectual move made within his system, but as a by-product of his transformation of the relations between Reason and its opposites. Descartes strongly repudiated his medieval predecessors' idea of divided soul, which had Reason—identified with the authentic character of a human being—struggling with lesser parts of the soul. For him, the soul was not to be divided into higher (intellectual) and lower (sensitive) parts; it was an indivisible unity, identified with pure intellect. He replaced the medieval philosophers' divisions between higher and lower parts of the soul with the dichotomy between mind and body. In this limited respect, Descartes's system echoed the thought of the early Plato. In place of the older divisions within the soul he introduced a division between the soul—now identified again with the mind—and body; the non-rational was no longer part of the soul, but pertained entirely to body.

There is within us but one soul, and this soul has not in itself any diversity of parts; the same

part that is subject to sense impressions is rational, and all the soul's appetites are acts of will. The error which has been committed in making it play the part of various personages, usually in opposition one to another, only proceeds from the fact that we have not properly distinguished its functions from those of the body, to which alone we must attribute everything which can be observed in us that is opposed to our reason.

The drama of dominance between human traits persisted in Descartes's philosophy, but it was played out as a struggle between the soul itself—equated with pure intellect—and body. He saw the encroachments of non-intellectual passion, sense or imagination as coming not from lower parts or aspects of the soul, but from altogether outside the soul—as intrusions from body. Descartes's method is founded on this alignment between the bodily and the non-rational. It involves forming the habit of distinguishing intellectual from corporeal matters. And this search for the purely intellectual—the clear and distinct—made possible polarizations of previously existing contrasts, which had previously been drawn within the boundaries of the soul. Those aspects of human nature which Reason must dominate had not previously been so sharply delineated from the intellectual. The distinction between Reason and its opposites could now coincide with Descartes's very sharp distinction—than which, as he says, none can be sharper—between mind and body.

Descartes's alignment between the Reason-non-Reason and mind-body distinctions brought with it the notion of a distinctive kind of rational thought as a highly restricted activity. Augustine had presented the mind's dealings with practical matters as a diversion of a unitary Reason from its superior function of contemplation. This diversion was at risk of entanglement with sense, but it was not thereby different in kind from the Reason employed in contemplative thought. Descartes separated thought of the kind that yields certainty much more sharply from the practical concerns of life. It was for him a highly rarefied exercise of intellect, a complete transcending of the sensuous—a highly arduous activity which cannot be expected to occupy more than a very small part of a normal life. In the *Discourse on Method,* he stressed the contrasts between the demands of enquiry into truth and the attitudes appropriate to the practical activities of life. The foundations of the enquiry into truth demand that the mind rigorously enact the metaphysical truth of its separateness from body. This securing of the foundations of knowledge is a separate activity from the much more relaxed pursuits of everyday life, where mind must accept its intermingling with body. Descartes's separation of mind and body yielded a vision of a unitary pure thought, ranging like the common light of the sun over a variety of objects. Its unitariness, however, served also to separate it from the rest of life.

Pure thought of this rarefied kind secures the foundations of science. However, most of scientific activity itself involves exercise of the imagination rather than of pure intellect, scientific investigation, although it demands sustained effort and training, occupies an intermediate position between pure intellect and the confusion of sense. The rest of life is rightly given over to the sway of the senses, to that muddled zone of confused perception where mind and body intermingle. In his correspondence with Princess Elizabeth, Descartes again stressed that arduous clear and distinct thought, of the kind that secures the foundations of science, can and should occupy only a small part of a well-spent life. If we can take seriously his autobiographical remarks to her—as he insists she should—it is something to which he himself devoted only a few hours a year. It is though pure intellect, transcending the intrusion of body, that we grasp the separateness of mind and body on which true science is founded. The greater part of the life of a Cartesian self is lived in the zone of confused, sensuous awareness. However, it is sustained there by the metaphysical truth, which pure thought can grasp, of the absolute separateness of mind and body; and by the possibility of a complete science grounded in this truth. Underlying the confusion of the senses, there is a crystalline realm of order, where sharply articulated structures of thought perfectly match the structure of intelligible reality. These clear, matching structures of mind and matter underlie the confused realm of the sensuous produced by the intermingling of both. Individual minds can rest assured that there is an underlying right order of thought, which provides a secure underpinning for lives lived predominantly in the realm of the sensuous; the confusions of sense and imagination hold no ultimate threat.

Arduous as the grasp of the metaphysical basis of Descartes's method may be, the method itself was supposed to be accessible to all. And within the terms of the system there is, in all this no differentiation between male and female minds. Both must be seen as equally intellectual substances, endowed with good sense or Reason. The difference in intellectual achievement between men and women, no less than that between different men, must arise not from some being more rational than others, but 'solely from the fact that our thoughts pass through diverse channels and the same objects are not considered by all'. But removing method from the restraints of public pedagogy did not, in practice, make knowledge any more accessible to women. Descartes's method may be essentially private and accessible to all. But for him, no less than Bacon, the new science was, none the less, a collective endeavor. It is by 'joining together the lives and labours of many', he says in the concluding section of the *Discourse on Method*, that science will progress. It is through a corporate exercise, however non-corporeal may be its ultimate metaphysical foundation, that the new science will advance, rendering humanity the promised goal of becoming 'masters and possessors of nature'. Descartes thought his account of the mind opened the way to a newly egalitarian pursuit of knowledge. But the channels through which those basically equal resources of Reason had to flow remained more convoluted, even for noble women, than for men. Elizabeth poignantly expressed the situation in one of her letters to Descartes:

> the life I am constrained to lead does not allow me enough free time to acquire a habit of meditation in accordance with your rules. Sometimes the interest of my household, which I must not neglect, sometimes conversations and civilities I cannot eschew, so thoroughly deject this weak mind with annoyances or boredom that it remains, for a long time afterward, useless for anything else.

The realities of the lives of women, despite their supposed equality in Reason, precluded them, too, from any significant involvement in the collective endeavours of science, the developing forms of which quickly outstripped the private procedures of Descartes's method.

It is not just impinging social realities, however, which militate against sexual equality in this new version of Reason's relations with science. There are aspects of Descartes's thought which—however unintentionally—provided a basis for a sexual division of mental labour whose influence is still very much with us. Descartes's emphasis on the equality of Reason had less influence than his formative contribution to the ideal of a distinctive kind of Reason—a highly abstract mode of thought, separable, in principle, from the emotional complexities and practical demands of ordinary life. This was not the only kind of thought which Descartes recognized as rational. In the Sixth Meditation he acknowledged that the inferior senses, once they have been set aside from the search for truth—where they can only mislead and distort—are reliable guides to our well-being. To trust them is not irrational. He does not maintain that we are rational only when exercising arduous pure thought, engaged in intellectual contemplation and assembling chains of deduction. Indeed, he thinks it is not rational to spend an excessive amount of time in such purely intellectual activity. None the less, through his philosophy, Reason took on special associations with the realm of pure thought, which provides the foundations of sciences, and with the deductive ratiocination which was of the essence of his method. And the sharpness of his separation of the ultimate requirements of truth-seeking from the practical affairs of everyday life reinforced already existing distinctions between male and female roles, opening the way to the idea of distinctive male and female consciousness.

We owe to Descartes an influential and pervasive theory of mind, which provides support for a powerful version of the sexual division of mental labour. Women have been assigned responsibility for that realm of the sensuous which the Cartesian Man of Reason must transcend, if he is to have true knowledge of things. He must move on to the exercise of disciplined imagination, in most of scientific activity; and to the rigours of pure intellect, if he would grasp the ultimate foundations of science. Woman's task is to preserve the sphere of the intermingling of mind and body, to which the Man of Reason will repair for solace, warmth, and relaxation. If he is to exercise the exalted form of Reason, he must leave soft emotions and sensuousness behind; woman will keep them intact for him. The way was thus opened for women to be associated with not just a lesser presence of Reason, but a different kind of intellectual character, construed as complementary to 'male' Reason. This crucial development springs from the accentuation of women's exclusion from Reason, now conceived—in its highest form—as an attainment.

FOR FURTHER READING

Alston, William. *Epistemic Justification*. Ithaca, N.Y.: Cornell University Press, 1989.

Armstrong, D. M. *Belief, Truth and Knowledge*. London: Cambridge University Press, 1973.

Audi, Robert. *Belief, Justification, and Knowledge*. Belmont, Calif.: Wadsworth, 1988.

Audi, Robert. *The Structure of Justification*. New York: Cambridge University Press, 1993.

BonJour, Laurence. *The Structure of Empirical Knowledge*. Cambridge, Mass.: Harvard University Press, 1985.

Chisholm, Roderick. *The Foundations of Knowing*. Minneapolis: University of Minnesota Press, 1982.

Chisholm, Roderick. *Theory of Knowledge*, 3rd ed. Englewood Cliffs, N. J.: Prentice Hall, 1988.

Dancy, Jonathan, and Ernest Sosa, eds. *A Companion to Epistemology*. Oxford: Basil Blackwell, 1992.

Descartes, Rene. *Meditations*. Reprinted in *The Philosophical Works of Descartes*, Vol I, translated by Elizabeth Haldane and G. R. T. Ross. Cambridge, U.K.: Cambridge University Press, 1968.

Fales, Evan. *A Defense of the Given*. Lanham, Md.: Rowman & Littlefield, 1996.

Fumerton, Richard. *Metaepistemology and Skepticism*. Lanham, Md.: Rowman & Littlefield, 1995.

Goldman, Alan. *Empirical Knowledge*. Berkeley: University of California Press, 1988.

Haack, Susan. *Evidence and Inquiry: Towards Reconstruction in Epistemology*. Oxford: Basil Blackwell, 1993.

Lehrer, Keith. *Knowledge*. Oxford: Oxford University Press, 1974.

Lehrer, Keith. *Theory of Knowledge*. Boulder, Colo.: Westview Press, 1990.

Lewis, Clarence I. *Mind and the World Order*. New York: Charles Scribner's Sons, 1929.

Lloyd, Genevieve. *The Man of Reason: "Male" and "Female" in Western Philosophy*. Minneapolis: University of Minnesota Press, 1984.

Moser, Paul. *Empirical Knowledge,* 2d ed. Lanham, Md.: Rowman & Littlefield, 1996.

Pollock, John. *Contemporary Theories of Knowledge.* Totowa, N. J.: Rowman & Littlefield, 1986.

Sosa, Ernest. *Knowledge in Perspective.* Cambridge, U.K.: Cambridge University Press, 1991.

Williams, Michael. *Unnatural Doubts.* Oxford: Blackwell, 1991.

STUDY QUESTIONS

1. What proposition does Descartes think he knows for certain? Why does he think he knows this proposition? Do you agree with Descartes that this proposition is infallible—that is, it cannot be mistaken? Explain. What kind of thing does Descartes think he is? How does he arrive at this conclusion?

2. What "rule" does Descartes think he can use to determine whether he knows other propositions? How does Descartes think he acquired the idea of God, of an infinitely perfect being? Why does he think such a being exists?

3. Alston identifies two types of foundationalism, iterative and simple. Explain the distinction between showing that one is justified and being justified. Explain how this distinction is related to iterative and simple foundationalism.

4. Why does Alston reject the "second level" argument? In this connection, explain what Alston means by "epistemic beliefs." Does he think that foundationalism must accept the idea that we have immediately justified epistemic beliefs? Explain.

5. Does Lehrer think we have *any* infallible beliefs? Explain. Lehrer uses the Bacon/Shakespeare example to show that a person can be mistaken about what he or she is thinking. Explain how Lehrer arrives at this conclusion.

6. Why does Lehrer reject Armstrong's argument that beliefs (or thoughts) about one's sensations are fallible? Why does Lehrer think our beliefs about sensations are fallible?

7. Explain Audi's distinction between the dialectical and structural forms of the regress argument. Explain how this distinction is important for the contrast between knowing and showing that one knows and for the contrast between the process and the property of justification.

8. What is the distinction between linear and holistic coherentism? Explain the central features of holistic coherentism. Audi grants that the justification of a belief may negatively depend on other beliefs. Why does he reject positive epistemic dependence as a condition of justification? Why does Audi think that fallible foundationalism is preferable to holistic coherntism?

9. Why, according to Lloyd, is Descartes' separation of mind and body important for our understanding of reason? Why does Descartes' method make knowledge accessible to women? Why, then, were women precluded from participating equally in scientific inquiry? How did Descartes' view contribute to the already existing distinction between male and female, according to Lloyd?

6

Coherence Theory

Coherence theory rejects foundationalism's central claim that there are epistemically prior, or basic, beliefs. Coherentism also rejects the thought that the source of justification is found in basic beliefs. The positive thesis of coherentism is that justification arises from the interconnection between beliefs. The basic unit of epistemic appraisal is a set or group of beliefs.

The history of coherence theory is somewhat checkered. Unlike foundationalism, it is difficult to find a moment in epistemology when coherence stepped firmly onto the stage. Coherentists, however, have not been absent from the epistemological drama, and have appeared at various points in the twentieth century.

In the early twentieth century both F. H. Bradley and Brand Blanshard defended coherence theory, but their commitment to coherentist justification was motivated by their commitment to a coherence theory of truth. In this view, a proposition is true if it is a member of a coherent set of propositions. Various criteria have been suggested for a coherent set, but two that seem prominent are logical consistency and explanatory connections. Logically consistent sets of propositions are sets in which the propositions can be true at the same time. In addition to Blanshard, contemporary epistemologists such as Wilfried Sellars have also countenanced the thought that a set is coherent if every proposition in the set either explains or is explained by some other proposition.

The standard criticism of the coherence theory of truth is that it is too liberal. Two conflicting propositions might both count as true since they belong to different, yet incompatible, coherent sets. (Think, for example, of two different religions.) The response of coherentists like Bradley and Blanshard is neatly summarized by Jonathan Dancy:

What these coherentists are saying is that the [coherentist] enterprise is to start from the data of experience and to construct a set of beliefs around those data which will order the data in the most systematic (coherent) way. To do this we may need to reject *some* of the data, but we cannot reject them all because our very aim is to make sense of what we have as data. So the set of beliefs which we do construct *must* be empirically grounded, and this grounding in the data of experience guarantees that there will be only one set which constitutes 'the most systematic ordering'.

This appeal to the need for an empirical grounding manages to exclude all the more fanciful putatively coherent sets of propositions from our reckoning.[1]

Critics of coherentism sometimes worry that the coherentist view permits even propositions belonging to imaginative, yet coherent sets to count as true or justified. This shows a misunderstanding of the nature and point of the coherentist enterprise. Coherentists aim to make sense of our experience, and consequently must take into account the evidence afforded us by our senses. Incorporating sensory evidence thus limits the contending sets of propositions, and the coherentist might rightly remark that good empiricists ought not to try to say in advance which of the contenders is the right set. Contemporary coherentists, such as Keith Lehrer and Laurence BonJour, also hold that systems of belief are constrained by what we learn from our senses. It should be noted, however, that Lehrer and BonJour are not interested in defending a coherence theory of truth, but a coherence theory of justification.

Coherentist views took a more epistemological turn with W.V. Quine's "Two Dogmas of Empiricism" (see Section 9). Near the end of this essay, Quine argues that we cannot hope to take our beliefs one by one and confirm or disconfirm them according to the evidence of our senses. Instead, Quine argues that it is the *system* of beliefs that confronts the "tribunal of experience."[2] We can reject the information we obtain from a particular experience as long as we are willing to revise other beliefs we have. Quine refers to this view as holism because of its relation to another of Quine's views, the holistic theory of meaning. In this view, the meaning of a term is determined by the set of sentences in which it occurs, not by the unique sensory experiences associated with it. Nonetheless, Quine's view has an obvious affinity with coherentism. Indeed, Donald Davidson, who has made significant contributions to philosophy of language, philosophy of mind, and epistemology, acknowledges the influence of Quine, and has on various occasions defended a coherence theory of knowledge and justification. Davidson argues that only beliefs can justify other beliefs; experience or sensation is the wrong type of thing to play a justificatory role, because experiences are of a different cognitive type than beliefs.

Very recent accounts of coherentist justification tend to construe coherence in one of two ways—a global property of a system of beliefs or a relational property among beliefs. When considered globally, coherence is a property of a system of beliefs. In Laurence BonJour's view, for example, a particular belief is justified because it is a member of a coherent system. But this is a derivative sense of justification. According to BonJour, one must establish that a set of beliefs is coherent and then show that the coherence leads to likely truth. He calls this the "metajustificatory argument," which is presented in the second part of the selection by BonJour. Hence, the system as a whole is justified, and the particular belief is justified by virtue of its membership in the system of beliefs.

Coherence is also understood as a relational property. Keith Lehrer claims that a proposition is justified if it fits or coheres with a person's other beliefs. Lehrer interprets the coherence relation along the following lines. A belief coheres with other beliefs if it is more reasonable to accept that belief than any of its competitors. The competitors of a belief are propositions that either deny or cast doubt on that belief. It is more reasonable to accept a belief if doing so is more likely, given what else the agent believes, to lead to the person having true beliefs and avoiding false beliefs. As a very simple example,

suppose that Sam is considering the proposition that a quiz will be given the day before vacation. The most obvious competitor of this proposition is that no quiz will be given. Suppose that Sam also believes that a quiz is scheduled to be given and that the teacher does not like changing the schedule. Now, suppose that Sam reflects on the proposition and its competitor with the goal of accepting what is likely to be true. Given what else he believes regarding the schedule and the teacher's aversion to it, then the proposition that a quiz is forthcoming is more reasonable than its competitor. Hence, the proposition coheres with Sam's other beliefs, and Sam is justified in accepting it. Coherence, for Lehrer, is a relation between a belief and other beliefs the agent has. Lehrer elaborates these ideas in the essay "Knowledge Reconsidered."

The *Isolation Objection* maintains that coherence accounts cut justification off from the world. The justification of belief implies the likely truth of belief. Likely truth, however is not simply a function of relations between beliefs; it depends on the world. But coherentist justification is a function of the relations between beliefs. So, coherentist justification does not necessarily imply that beliefs are likely to be true, and thus cuts justification off from the world. Some critics have pursued a similar line, insisting that the coherentist cannot explain how our beliefs acquire their initial credibility.

The first selection is from Laurence BonJour's *The Structure of Empirical Knowledge*. BonJour explains the features that increase the coherence of a system of beliefs. In the latter part of the selection, he argues that a coherent system of beliefs is likely to be true. The "metajustificatory argument," as BonJour calls it, depends in part on the *Observation Requirement*. BonJour holds that a coherent system of beliefs must accord a prima facie reliability to perceptual beliefs.

In "Circularity and Coherence," Robert Meyers discusses some of the traditional objections to coherentist accounts of justification and presses the argument that coherentists cannot explain the source of justification, or the source of the initial epistemic credibility of our beliefs.

The last selection is from Linda Alcoff's *Real Knowing: New Versions of the Coherence Theory*. She argues that epistemology must take account of social practices and real-life contexts and must look beyond the narrow borders of traditional analytic or continental philosophy to developments in social theory and postmodernist views. She claims that coherentism is especially suited to do so since, among other features, it takes account of the "actual mechanisms most often used to judge new contenders for belief. . . ." Central to the position she develops is a view about the nature of truth, which she elaborates in "Coherentism in Context."

NOTES

1. Jonathan Dancy, *Introduction to Contemporary Epistemology* (Oxford: Blackwell, 1985), p. 114.
2. This is sometimes called the "Quine-Duhem Thesis."

LAURENCE BONJOUR

from The Structure of Empirical Knowledge

5.3 The Concept of Coherence

What, then, is coherence? Intuitively, coherence is a matter of how well a body of beliefs "hangs together": how well its component beliefs fit together, agree or dovetail with each other, so as to produce an organized, tightly structured system of beliefs, rather than either a helter-skelter collection or a set of conflicting subsystems. It is reasonably clear that this "hanging together" depends on the various sorts of inferential, evidential, and explanatory relations which obtain among the various members of a system of beliefs, and especially on the more holistic and systematic of these. Thus various detailed investigations by philosophers and logicians of such topics as explanation, confirmation, probability, and so on, may be reasonably taken to provide some of the ingredients for a general account of coherence. But the main work of giving such an account, and in particular one which will provide some relatively clear basis for *comparative* assessments of coherence, has scarcely been begun, despite the long history of the concept.

My response to this problem, for the moment at least, is a deliberate—though, I think, justified—evasion. It consists in pointing out that the task of giving an adequate explication of the concept of coherence is not uniquely or even primarily the job of coherence theories. This is so because coherence—or something resembling it so closely as to be subject to the same sort of problem—is, and seemingly must be, a basic ingredient of virtually all rival epistemological theories as well. We have already seen that weak foundationalism essentially involves an appeal to coherence. And it seems clear that even moderate and strong foundationalisms cannot avoid an appeal to something like coherence in giving an account of knowledge of the past, theoretical knowledge, and other types of knowledge which (on any view) go be-

yond direct experience. Thus it is not surprising that virtually all of the leading proponents of comprehensive foundationalist views, whether weak, moderate, or strong, employ the notion of coherence in their total epistemological accounts—though sometimes under other names, such as "congruence" (Lewis) or "concurrence" (Chisholm). Even "contextualist" views, which attempt to repudiate the whole issue of global justification, make a similar appeal. The conclusion strongly suggested is that something like coherence is indispensable to any nonskeptical epistemological position which is even *prima facie* adequate. And if this is so, the absence of an adequate explication of coherence does not count against coherence theories any more than against their rivals.

The foregoing response is dialectically cogent in defending coherence theories against other, nonskeptical epistemologies, but it must be admitted that it is of little use vis-à-vis the skeptic, who may well argue that what it shows is that all nonskeptical epistemologies are fundamentally flawed by virtue of their dependence on this inadequately explicated concept. But although this challenge must be taken seriously, it is far from obvious that it is even close to being decisive. A better account of coherence is beyond any doubt something devoutly to be sought; but it is, I think, quite plausible to say, as Ewing does, that what proponents of coherence "are doing is to describe an ideal that has never yet been completely clarified but is none the less immanent in all our thinking," and to hold on this basis that our intuitive grasp of this notion, though surely not ideally satisfactory, will suffice so long as the only alternative is skepticism—which itself carries, after all, a significant burden of implausibility.

In any case, however, there is little point in talking at length about coherence without a somewhat clearer idea of what is involved. Thus I will attempt to provide in this section a reasonable outline of the concept of coherence, while recognizing that it falls far short of what would be ideal. The main points are: first, coherence is not to be equated with mere consistency; second, coherence, as already suggested, has to do with the mutual inferability of the beliefs in the system; third, relations of explanation are one central ingredient in coherence, though not the only one; and, fourth, coherence may be enhanced through conceptual change.

First. A serious and perennial mistake in discussing coherence, usually committed by critics but occasionally also by would-be proponents of coherence theories, is to assume that coherence means nothing more than logical consistency, the absence of explicit contradiction. It is true that consistency is one requirement for coherence, that inconsistency is obviously a very serious sort of incoherence. But it is abundantly clear, as many coherentists have pointed out, that a system of beliefs might be perfectly consistent and yet have no appreciable degree of coherence.

There are at least two ways in which this might be so. The more obvious is what might be called *probabilistic inconsistency*. Suppose that my system of beliefs contains both the belief that P and also the belief that it is extremely improbable that P. Clearly such a system of beliefs may perfectly well be logically consistent. But it is equally clear from an intuitive standpoint that a system which contains two such beliefs is significantly less coherent than it would be without them and thus that probabilistic consistency is a second factor determining coherence.

Probabilistic consistency differs from straightforward logical consistency in two important respects. First, it is extremely doubtful that probabilistic inconsistency can be entirely avoided. Improbable things do, after all, sometimes happen, and sometimes one can avoid admitting them only by creating an even greater probabilistic inconsistency at an- other point. Second, probabilistic consistency, unlike logical consistency, is plainly a matter of degree, depending on (a) just how many such conflicts the system contains and (b) the degree of improbability involved in each case. Thus we have two initial conditions for coherence, which we may formulate as follows:

(1) A system of beliefs is coherent only if it is logically consistent.

(2) A system of beliefs is coherent in proportion to its degree of probabilistic consistency.

But these two requirements are still not enough. Imagine a set of beliefs, each member of which has simply no bearing at all on the subject matter of any of the others, so that they make no effective contact with each other. This lack of contact will of course assure that the set is both logically and probabilistically consistent by ruling out any possibility of conflict; but it will also assure that the members of the set fail to hang together in any very significant way. Thus consider the following two sets of propositions, A and B. A contains "this chair is brown," "electrons are negatively charged," and "today is Thursday." B contains "all ravens are black," "this bird is a raven," and "this bird is black." Clearly both sets of propositions are free of contradiction and are also probabilistically consistent. But in the case of A, this consistency results from the fact that its component propositions are almost entirely irrelevant to each other; though not in conflict, they also fail to be positively related in any significant way. And for this reason, set A possesses only a very low degree of coherence. In the case of set B, in contrast, consistency results from the fact that the component propositions, rather than being irrelevant to each other, fit together and reinforce each other in a significant way; from an epistemic standpoint, any two of them would lend a degree of positive support to the third (though only very weak support in two out of the three cases). Thus set B, though obviously much too small to have a really significant degree of coherence, is much more coherent than set A. As the classical proponents of coherence have always insisted, coherence must involve some sort of positive connection among the beliefs in question, not merely the absence of conflict.

Second. But what sort of positive connection is required and how strong must it be? The obvious answer to the first question is that the connections in question are *inference relations:* namely, any sort of relation of content which would allow one belief or set of beliefs, if justified, to serve as the premise(s) of a cogent epistemic-justificatory argument for a further belief. The basic requirement for such an inference relation, as suggested in the earlier discussion of epistemic justification, is that it be to some degree truth-preserving; any sort of relation which meets this requirement will serve as an appropriate positive connection between beliefs, and no other sort of connection seems relevant here.

This much would be accepted by most, if not all, proponents of coherence theories. The main thing that divides them is the issue of how close and pervasive such inferential connections are required to be. One pole with regard to this issue is represented by the classical absolute idealists. Blanshard's formulation is typical:

> Fully coherent knowledge would be knowledge in which every judgment entailed, and was entailed by, the rest of the system.

(In interpreting this formulation it is important to remember that Blanshard, like many others in this tradition, believes in synthetic entailments and indeed holds the admittedly dubious view that causal connections are one species of entailment.) The main problem with this view is that it is quite impossible even to imagine a system of beliefs which would satisfy such a requirement; as Blanshard himself admits, even such a system as Euclidean geometry, often appealed to as a paradigm of coherence, falls far short. Thus it is plausible to weaken the requirement for coherence at least to the degree advocated by Ewing, who requires only that each proposition in a coherent system be entailed by the rest taken together, not that the reciprocal relation hold. (We will see shortly that weakening the requirement in this way creates a problem which forces Ewing to add a further, related requirement.)

At the opposite extreme is Lewis's account of "congruence," a concept which plays a crucial role in his account of memory knowledge:

> A set of statements . . . will be said to be congruent if and only if they are so related that the antecedent probability of any one of them will be increased if the remainder of the set can be assumed as given premises.

This is obviously an extremely weak requirement. A system of beliefs which satisfied it at only the most minimal level would possess a vastly lower degree of systematic interconnection than that envisaged by the idealists, in two significantly different respects. First, reducing the requirement from entailment to merely some increase in probability obviously allows a weakening of the inferential connections which constitute coherence. But this is no objection to Lewis's account, so long as it is understood that coherence is a matter of degree, and that a lower degree of inferential interconnection carries with it only a lower degree of coherence. Second, however, Lewis's account, and indeed Ewing's as well, by making the inferential connection between the individual belief in question and the rest of the system one-way rather than reciprocal, creates the possibility that a system of beliefs could count as coherent to as high a degree as one likes by being composed of two or more subsystems of beliefs, each internally connected by strong inference relations but none having any significant connection with the others. From an intuitive standpoint, however, it is clear that such a system, though coherent to some degree, would fall very far short of ideal coherence. Ideal coherence requires also that the entire system of beliefs form a unified structure, that there be laws and principles which underlie the various subsystems of beliefs and provide a significant degree of inferential connection between them. We are obviously very close here to the ideal of a "unified science," in which the laws and terms of various disparate disciplines are reduced to those of some single master discipline, perhaps physics; while such a specific result is not essential for coherence, it would represent one way in which a high degree of coherence could be achieved, and something in this general direction seems to be required.

Ewing attempts to meet this difficulty by adding as a separate requirement for coherence the condition that no set of beliefs smaller than the whole system be logically independent of the rest of the system, and a similar requirement could be added to Lewis's account as well. It would be better, however, to make this further aspect of coherence also a matter of degree, since there are obviously many intermediate cases between a completely unified system and a system with completely isolated subsystems. Putting all of this together results in the following two additional conditions for coherence:

(3) The coherence of a system of beliefs is increased by the presence of inferential connections between its component beliefs and increased in proportion to the number and strength of such connections.

(4) The coherence of a system of beliefs is diminished to the extent to which it is divided into subsystems of beliefs which are relatively unconnected to each other by inferential connections.

It should be noted that condition (3), in addition to summarizing the preceding discussion, includes one important idea which did not emerge explicitly there: each individual belief can be involved in many different inferential relations, and the degree to which this is so is also a determinant of coherence.

Third. The foregoing account, though it seems to me to be on the right track, is obviously still extremely sketchy. One way to reduce this sketchiness somewhat is to consider the major role which the idea of *explanation* plays in the overall concept of coherence. As I have already suggested by mentioning the ideal of unified science, the coherence of a system of beliefs is enhanced by the presence of explanatory relations among its members.

Indeed, if we accept something like the familiar Hempelian account of explanation, this claim is to some extent a corollary of what has already been said. According to that account, particular facts are explained by appeal to other facts and general laws from which a statement of the explanandum fact may be deductively or probabilistically inferred; and lower-level laws and theories are explained in an analogous fashion by showing them to be deducible from more general laws and theories. Thus the presence of relations of explanation within a system of beliefs enhances the inferential interconnectedness of the system simply because explanatory relations *are* one species of inference relations.

Explanatory connections are not just additional inferential connections among the beliefs of a system, however; they are inferential connections of a particularly pervasive kind. This is so because the basic goal of scientific explanation is to exhibit events of widely differing kinds as manifestations of a relatively small number of basic explanatory principles. As Hempel remarks: "What scientific explanation, especially theoretical explanation, aims at is . . . an objective kind of insight that is achieved by a systematic unification, by exhibiting the phenomena as manifestations of common underlying structures and processes that conform to specific, testable, basic principles." What Hempel calls "systematic unification" is extremely close to the concept of coherence.

One helpful way to elaborate this point is to focus on the concept of *anomaly*. For my purposes, an anomaly is a fact or event, especially one involving some sort of recurring pattern, which is claimed to obtain by one or more of the beliefs in the system of beliefs, but which is incapable of being explained (or would have been incapable of being predicted) by appeal to the other beliefs in the system. (Obviously such a status is a matter of degree.) The presence of such anomalies detracts from the coherence of the system to an extent which cannot be accounted for merely by appeal to the fact that the belief in an anomalous fact or event has fewer inferential connections to the rest of the system than would be the case if an explanation were available. In the context of a coherentist position, such beliefs will have to be inferentially connected to the rest of the system in other, nonexplanatory ways if there is to be any justification for accepting them (see the discussion of observation in Chapter 6), and such connections may be very extensive. The distinctive significance of anomalies lies rather in the fact that they undermine the claim of the allegedly basic explanatory principles to be genuinely basic, and thus threaten the overall coherence of the system in a much more serious way. For this reason, it seems advisable to add one more condition to our list of conditions for coherence:

(5) The coherence of a system of beliefs is decreased in proportion to the presence of unexplained anomalies in the believed content of the system.

Having insisted on the close connection between coherence and explanation, we must nonetheless resist the idea that explanatory connections are all there is to coherence. Certain proponents of coherentist views, notably Sellars and Harman, have used phrases like "explanatory coherence" in speaking of coherence, seeming to suggest (though I doubt whether any of those using it really intend such a suggestion) that coherence depends *entirely* on explanatory connections. One could of course adopt a conception of coherence which is restricted in this way, but there is no reason at all—from an epistemological standpoint—to do so. The epistemologically significant concept of coherence is bound up with the idea of *justification,* and thus any sort of inference relation which could yield some degree of justification also enhances coherence, whether or not such a relation has any explanatory force.

A simple example (borrowed from Lehrer who in turn borrowed it from Bromberger) may help to illustrate this point. Suppose that I am standing three feet from a pole which is four feet high. Next to my foot is a mouse, and on top of the pole is perched an owl. From these conditions I may obviously infer, using the Pythagorean theorem, that the mouse is five feet from the owl. This inference is surely adequate to justify my believing that the mouse is five feet from the owl, assuming that I am justified in believing these other propositions. And intuitively speaking, this inferential connection means that the belief that the mouse is five feet from the owl coheres with the rest of my beliefs to quite a significant extent. But none of this has any apparent connection with explanation. In particular, as Lehrer points out, this inference does not in any way help to *explain* why the mouse is so close to the owl. Thus it is a mistake to tie coherence too closely to the idea of explanation. Of course, it is still true that the coherence of the system in question would be enhanced by adding an explanation for the presence of the mouse in such close proximity to the owl: given the usual behavior of mice around owls, the presence of the mouse at that distance is an explanatory and predictive anomaly. The point is simply that coherence is also enhanced by inferential connections of a nonexplanatory sort.

Fourth. The final point is really just a corollary of the one just made. To the extent that coherence is closely bound up with explanation and systematic unification, achieving a high degree of coherence may well involve significant conceptual change. This point is most clear in the area of theoretical science, though it has much broader application. A typical situation of theoretical explanation involves one or more anomalies at the "observational" level: apparently well-established facts formulated in the available system of concepts for which no adequate explanation seems to be available in those terms. By devising a new system of theoretical concepts the theoretician makes an explanation available and thus enhances the coherence of the system. In this way the progress of theoretical science may be plausibly viewed as a result of the search for greater coherence.

The foregoing account of coherence is a long way from being as definitive as desirable. I submit, however, that it does indeed identify a concept which, in Ewing's phrase, is "immanent in all our thinking," including all our most advanced scientific

thinking; and also that the concept thus identified, though vague and sketchy in many ways, is nonetheless clear enough to make it reasonable to use it, albeit with caution, in dealing with the sorts of epistemological issues under discussion here. In particular, it seems clear that the concept is not so vague as to be at all easy to satisfy.

8.3 THE METAJUSTIFICATORY ARGUMENT

In the present section, I will offer a sketch, at a highly intuitive level, of a metajustificatory argument for the sort of coherentist position that is suggested by Chapters 5, 6, and 7. It will be useful to begin by reflecting a bit on what such an argument would have to accomplish. What is needed, in first approximation, is an argument to show that a system of empirical beliefs that is justified according to the standards of a coherence theory of this sort is thereby also likely to correspond to reality. There are several preliminary points to be noted about such an argument.

To begin with, it is important to distinguish between the result of applying a set of standards for epistemic justification at a particular time and the result of applying those standards consistently over the relatively long run, that is, relative to the present account of justification, between a system of beliefs which is coherent at a moment and a system which remains coherent over the long run. Although it would obviously be very useful if it were somehow possible to argue that even the short-run results of applying a certain account of justification were likely to be true, so strong a result does not seem to be necessary, and there is moreover no moderately plausible general account of empirical justification for which it has ever been achieved. It would be quite enough, I submit, if it could be shown that adhering to coherentist standards over the long run is likely eventually to yield beliefs which correspond to reality, and it is this more modest result at which the argument to be offered here is aimed. Establishing even this result would presumably make it epistemically reasonable to adopt and apply such a standard of justification even in the short run (assuming that there is no alternative standard which offers a more immediate prospect of success).

But even this is more than we can hope to show, at least without a significant further qualification. It is vital to realize that adhering to a coherentist standard of the sort in question over the long run might produce either of two very different sorts of results: (a) the system of beliefs, though coherent at particular moments, might involve constant and relatively wholesale changes over time, so as not to even approach any *stable* conception of the world; or (b) the system of beliefs might gradually *converge* on some definite view of the world and thereafter remain relatively stable, reflecting only those changes (such as the passage of time and the changes associated with it) which are allowed or even required by the general picture of the world thus presented. (Intermediate cases are obviously possible, but these do not require explicit consideration.) The point is that it is only in the latter sort of case—the case in which the belief system converges on and eventually presents a relatively stable long-run picture of the world, thus achieving coherence over time as well as at particular times—that the coherence of the system provides any strong reason for thinking that the component beliefs are thereby likely to be true. Just why this is so will emerge more clearly later. As just noted, such stability over time is one aspect of the idea of dynamic coherence invoked earlier, but it is sufficiently crucial to the metajustificatory argument to deserve explicit mention from here on in. (It would be reasonable to regard a reasonable degree of stability as a necessary condition for even speaking of a single ongoing system of beliefs; but it seems more perspicuous to list it explicitly as a distinct requirement.)

It must also be emphasized that it is the Observation Requirement formulated in section 7.1 which guarantees that the system of beliefs will receive ongoing observational *input,* and it is the preservation of coherence in the face of such input which, as we will see, provides the basic reason for thinking that a system of beliefs is likely to be true. Thus the continued satisfaction of the Observation Requirement is an essential presupposition of the argument in question, and the proposed metajustificatory thesis will have to specify that the coherent system in question meets this condition.

Finally, coherence is obviously, on any reasonable view, a matter of degree (as is stability). Hence the conclusion of the envisaged argument should be that the likelihood that a system of beliefs corresponds to reality varies in proportion to its degree of coherence (and stability), other things being equal.

Thus, summing up this preliminary discussion, what is needed is a defense of something like the following thesis, which I will refer to as MJ.

> A system of beliefs which (a) remains coherent (and stable) over the long run and (b) continues to satisfy the Observation Requirement is likely, to a degree which is proportional to the degree of coherence (and stability) and the longness of the run, to correspond closely to independent reality.

This is obviously very approximate, but it will suffice well enough for present purposes.

How might thesis MJ be defended? The intuitive idea behind the argument to be explored here is that the kind of situation described in the thesis requires an *explanation* of some sort. The coherence-cum-stability of a system of beliefs is complicated and fragile, easily disrupted or destroyed, and thus it is inherently unlikely that a system of beliefs which is constantly receiving the sort of input that is assured by the Observation Requirement would remain coherent from moment to moment without constant revisions which would destroy its stability. Some explanation is therefore needed for why it continues to do so, and the obvious one is that the beliefs of the system match the independent reality which they purport to describe closely enough to minimize the potential for disruptive input.

A somewhat more detailed formulation of this argument would involve the following two main premises:

> P_1. If a system of beliefs remains coherent (and stable) over the long run while continuing to satisfy the Observation Requirement, then it is highly likely that there is some explanation (other than mere chance) for this fact, with the degree of likelihood being proportional to the degree of coherence (and stability) and the longness of the run.
>
> P_2. The best explanation, the likeliest to be true, for a system of beliefs remaining coherent (and stable) over the long run while continuing to sat-

isfy the Observation Requirement is that (a) the cognitively spontaneous beliefs which are claimed, within the system, to be reliable are systematically caused by the sorts of situations which are depicted by their content, and (b) the entire system of beliefs corresponds, within a reasonable degree of approximation, to the independent reality which it purports to describe; and the preferability of this explanation increases in proportion to the degree of coherence (and stability) and the longness of the run.

I have tried to make these premises as perspicuous as possible, rather than worrying about whether they formally entail MJ. The general intent should be clear enough: if it is highly likely that there is an explanation for the system's long-run coherence and if the explanation in terms of truth is the likeliest to be true of the alternative explanations available, then that explanation will be likely to be true to some significant degree. Whether it will be likelier to be true than not or likely enough to satisfy the requirements for knowledge will depend on just how likely it is that there is some explanation and on just how much more likely the truth explanation is in relation to the other alternatives; and, according to P_1 and P_2, these matters will in turn depend on the degree of coherence (and stability) and the longness of the run. All of these things would have to be discussed in detail in a really complete version of the argument. But it would be a major step in the right direction if a reasonably convincing *prima facie* case could be made for P_1 and P_2.

Of these two premises, P_1 is by far the less problematic. Indeed, it seems to me quite plausible at an intuitive level to claim that P_1 is self-evidently true. The rationale here is simple and obvious: if there were no further factor (of a sort which could provide an explanation) operative in the production of the system of beliefs in question, if the cognitively spontaneous beliefs which satisfy the Observation Requirement were genuinely produced by chance or at random, then it is very likely that the coherence of the system would be continually disrupted and that it could be restored, if at all, only by making enough changes in the content of the system to disrupt its stability or else by rejecting enough of the observational beliefs to violate the Observation

Requirement. Thus if this sort of disruption fails to occur, even in the long run, it becomes highly likely that some further factor is present which would provide an explanation for this fact, and this likelihood increases the longer this situation continues—which is precisely what P_1 claims.

Premise P_2, on the other hand, is vastly more problematic and will obviously require much more extended discussion. What needs to be shown is that the explanatory hypothesis in question, which I will refer to as the *correspondence hypothesis,* is more likely to be true relative to the conditions indicated than is any alternative explanation. The underlying claim is that a system of beliefs for which the correspondence hypothesis was false would be unlikely to remain coherent (and continue to satisfy the Observation Requirement) unless it were revised in the direction of greater correspondence with reality—thereby destroying the stability of the original system and gradually leading to a new and stable system of beliefs for which the correspondence hypothesis is true. But is there any reason to think that such a claim is correct? This issue can only be dealt with by considering in some detail the alternative explanations of coherence-cum-stability that do not invoke the correspondence hypothesis.

The primary alternatives fall into two main groups, requiring significantly different treatment. In the first place there are alternative explanations that envision a world of approximately the same general sort as the one in which we presently believe, consisting of objects and processes occurring in space and time, and in which our putative observational beliefs are systematically caused in some way by features of that world, but in which the resulting system of beliefs nevertheless presents a picture of the world in question which is in some important way inaccurate, incomplete, or distorted; I will call such alternatives *normal hypotheses.* And, in the second place, there are alternatives which employ one or more of the distinctively skeptical possibilities which are prominent in the philosophical literature, such as Cartesian demons or brains in vats; I will refer to these as *skeptical hypotheses.* Normal hypotheses will be considered in the balance of the present section, while skeptical hypotheses will be reserved for separate treatment in the next. . . .

8.4 SKEPTICAL HYPOTHESES

I turn from normal hypotheses to the distinctively skeptical hypotheses that have been the special concern of philosophers, especially since the time of Descartes. Perhaps my cognitively spontaneous beliefs and hence the picture of the world which I base upon them, rather than being caused by a relatively ordinary world of objects and processes in space and time, are caused in some radically different way. Perhaps, as Descartes envisaged, they are caused by an all-powerful evil demon or spirit who employs all his power to deceive me into believing that there is an ordinary world of the sort that I think there is, even though nothing of the kind actually exists. Perhaps I am merely a subject in the laboratory of a malevolent psychologist who feeds me delusory experiences via electrode stimulation: I might be firmly fastened to his laboratory table, or I might even be merely a brain floating in a vat of nutrients. Perhaps I am mad, and my observational beliefs are systematically generated by my own unconscious mind, giving me once again a coherent picture of a totally unreal world. And there are obviously many further possibilities as well.

Such skeptical hypotheses pose a problem which any nonskeptical epistemology must respond to in some way; it will not do to simply close one's eyes to the problem by "refusing to entertain the skeptical question." But they are in no way a distinctive problem for coherence theories; nor, so far as I can see, is there any very compelling reason to think that the problem thus posed will be more difficult for a coherence theory to deal with. Thus a consideration of this brand of skepticism is not essential to a defense of a coherentist position against rival nonskeptical epistemologies. But since such skeptical hypotheses do constitute alternatives to the explanation for the long-run coherence-cum-stability of my system of beliefs that is offered by the correspondence hypothesis, I must, if I am to be fully justified (for the reason suggested in the previous section) in accepting that hypothesis, have good reasons for thinking that these skeptical alternatives are significantly less likely to be true than it is.

The epistemological literature contains a wide variety of responses to skeptical hypotheses of this kind, but most of these are quite unsatisfactory when viewed from our present perspective. Some attempt to argue, on broadly verificationist grounds, that the skeptical views in question are either meaningless or else somehow not genuinely distinct from nonskeptical views; I can see no merit in such positions and will not discuss them further. But even among those views which do not resort to verificationism, most do not even attempt to show that such hypotheses are *less likely to be true* than are the nonskeptical views with which they compete. Many such views attempt instead to rule out skepticism on broadly methodological or pragmatic grounds—for example, because it unduly restricts or limits future inquiry—where such grounds are usually conceded (if the issue is raised at all) to have nothing to do with likelihood of truth. But although views of this sort do perhaps provide a kind of justification or rationale for preferring the nonskeptical view to the skeptical one, this justification is plainly not *epistemic* justification, as that notion was explained above, and hence provides no reason for regarding the nonskeptical beliefs in question as knowledge. In effect, positions which rely on responses to skepticism of this sort are themselves merely sophisticated versions of skepticism; they offer a non-epistemic reason for preferring our ordinary beliefs to the skeptical alternatives, while admitting all the while that the skeptical alternative is no less likely to be true.

Perhaps the most familiar response to these skeptical possibilities is the claim that they should be rejected because they are less *simple* than alternatives like the correspondence hypothesis. As will emerge, such a view seems to me to be very roughly on the right track, but it initially faces two serious problems. First, it is not at all obvious, in part due to the serious obscurity of the notion of simplicity itself, that the correspondence hypothesis *is* simpler than such skeptical hypotheses. Second, and even more serious, such views typically make no attempt at all to argue that the simpler hypothesis should be preferred, not on some other basis (such as the methodological or pragmatic ones just mentioned), but rather because it is in virtue of its simplicity more likely to be true. Nor, once this issue is explicitly raised, is it at all clear that such an argument is available: why, after all, should it be supposed that reality is more likely to be simple than complex? And without such an argument, the appeal to simplicity, like the general methodological appeals discussed earlier, becomes quite irrelevant to the main epistemological issue because whatever justification it might confer would not count as *epistemic* justification.

Thus attempts of this sort to evade or "dissolve" the problem posed by such skeptical hypotheses are epistemologically unhelpful, and the apparent upshot is that an adequate response will have to confront the issue directly by arguing on some basis that such hypotheses are significantly less likely to be true, given the fact of a long-run coherent (and stable) system of beliefs, than is the correspondence hypothesis.

What would such an argument have to look like? It is a fact of probability theory, which I assume may be relied on here, that the relative probability of two hypotheses on the same evidence is a function of the following two factors: first, the probability of that evidence relative to each hypothesis; and second, the antecedent or prior probability of each hypothesis. Since it is clear (see below for elaboration) that an appropriately chosen skeptical hypothesis can make the first of these factors at least as great as it is for the correspondence hypothesis, an argument in favor of the greater probability or likelihood of the correspondence hypothesis must be based on the second factor: that is, it must argue that such skeptical hypotheses are antecedently less likely to be true than is the correspondence hypotheses. And since any appeal to empirical considerations would obviously beg the question in the present context, the antecedent probability or likelihood in question will have to be entirely *a priori* in character. But even philosophers who are not skeptical of appeals to the *a priori* in general are likely to have qualms about the notion of *a priori* probability.

I believe, however, that a case can perhaps be made for the needed result, though there is room here for only a preliminary and highly intuitive adumbration. The basic suggestion, to be elaborated in the balance of this section, is that it is the very versatility of skeptical hypotheses of the variety in question, their ability to explain any sort of experience equally well, which renders them not merely methodologically less satisfactory as explanations but less likely to be true, given the fact of a coherent (and stable) system of beliefs.

It will be useful to begin by considering a parallel case that is somewhat analogous to our main concern, one which will also add some degree of respectability to the idea of *a priori* probabilities: the hypothesis that the coherence-cum-stability of the system of beliefs is due purely to chance. I argued earlier that this hypothesis is extremely unlikely, though not quite impossible, relative to the fact of a coherent (and stable) system of beliefs, since it is extremely likely that observational beliefs produced by chance would eventually upset the coherence of the system. But if this is so, consider the following modified version of the chance hypothesis:

> My cognitively spontaneous observational beliefs are produced purely by chance; and chance, quite fortuitously, produces in fact only observational beliefs which will fit into my coherent system of beliefs and not disturb its stability.

(Call observational beliefs of the sort just specified *coherence-conducive observations*.) Relative to *this* version of the chance hypothesis, the *elaborated chance hypothesis* as it may be called, it is obviously extremely likely that the system of beliefs will remain coherent (and stable), since it is specified as a part of the hypothesis itself that only coherence-conducive observations will occur; this elaborated chance hypothesis thus explains the continued coherence (and stability) of the system at least in the minimal sense of providing a premise from which the thesis that the system will have these features follows with high probability or likelihood. But it also seems clear on an intuitive level that this hypothesis is nonetheless not at all likely to be true relative to the evidence provided by the existence of a coherent (and stable) system of beliefs, indeed no more likely than is the simple chance hypothesis.

But we must attempt to understand why this is so. It would probably be possible to find methodological reasons for rejecting this hypothesis as an explanation, but as already suggested the relevance of such considerations to likelihood of truth is obscure. The only apparent alternative is to claim that such a hypothesis is extremely unlikely to be true on a purely *a priori* basis, unlikely enough that it remains extremely unlikely to be true even when its capacity to make the evidence in question highly probable is taken into account. If general doubts about *a priori* knowledge are set aside (for discussion, see Appendix A), such a claim seems to me quite plausible. Indeed, the reason why the antecedent, *a priori* likelihood or probability of the elaborated chance hypothesis is extremely low is fundamentally the same as that given above for the relative unlikelihood of the simple chance hypothesis vis-à-vis the fact of a coherent (and stable) system of beliefs: the internal tension or probabilistic incompatibility between (a) the claim that the observational beliefs are produced purely by chance, and (b) the claim that they continue even in the long run to satisfy the complicated and demanding pattern required in order to be coherence-conducive. If these two claims are considered separately, the latter is unlikely relative to the former, and hence also the former relative to evidence constituted by the latter; whereas if they are combined into one hypothesis, this same incompatibility, now internal to the hypothesis itself, makes that hypothesis unlikely to be true on a purely *a priori* or intrinsic basis. This case suggests a sense of the contract between simplicity and complexity which is relevant to likelihood of truth: a hypothesis is complex rather than simple in this sense to the extent that it contains elements within it, some of which are unlikely to be true relative to others, thus making the hypothesis as a whole unlikely on a purely *a priori* basis to be true; it is simple to the extent that this is not the case. Such an account is admittedly crude, but will nonetheless suffice for present purposes.

Turning now to skeptical hypotheses proper, it will be helpful to focus on one particular version of skepticism. I will choose for this purpose the familiar Cartesian evil demon hypothesis and will assume, somewhat rashly perhaps, that what is said about this version of skepticism can be extended without major modifications to other versions.

In considering the evil demon hypothesis, however, it is important to distinguish between two crucially different forms which it may take, forms which closely parallel the two forms of the chance hypothesis just considered. The first form postulates merely that there is an all-powerful evil demon who causes my experience, that is, my cognitively spontaneous beliefs, without saying anything more about the demon's motives and purposes or about what sorts of beliefs he is inclined to produce; whereas the second form postulates in addition, as a part of the explanatory hypothesis itself, that the demon has certain specific desires, purposes, and so on, in virtue of

which he will single-mindedly continue to produce in me, even in the long run, coherence-conducive observations. Hypotheses of the first kind are *simple demon hypotheses,* while hypotheses of the second kind are *elaborated demon hypotheses.* These two sorts of hy-potheses require significantly different, though related, treatment.

A simple demon hypothesis, though it does provide an explanation of sorts for the long-run existence of a coherent (and stable) system of beliefs, fails to provide a very good explanation for the existence of such a system and hence is not very likely, relative to such an explanandum, to be true. The basic point here is quite parallel to that made earlier about the simple chance hypothesis. Just as it is quite unlikely, though admittedly possible, that the cognitively spontaneous beliefs produced by chance would continue to be coherence-conducive, so also is it just as unlikely, though again still possible, that those produced by an otherwise unspecified evil demon would continue to do so. Like pure chance, such an unspecified demon is capable of producing, and equally likely to produce, virtually any configuration of beliefs, and the simple demon hypothesis provides no reason at all for expecting him to confine himself to those which will fit coherently into my cognitive system. The upshot is that the continued coherence-cum-stability of my system of beliefs is excellent, though not totally conclusive, evidence *against* simple demon hypotheses, simply because it is a result which would be extremely unlikely to occur if such hypotheses were true.

This is scarcely a startling result, for it is obvious that it is elaborated demon hypotheses which provide the major skeptical challenge, even though the distinction between these and simple demon hypotheses is not usually made explicit. And against an appropriate elaborated demon hypothesis, the foregoing argument is entirely ineffective: in contrast to simple demon hypothesis, an elaborated demon hypothesis of the right sort will make it extremely likely or even certain that my cognitively spontaneous beliefs will be coherence-conducive and hence extremely likely that my system of beliefs will remain coherent (and stable) in the long run. Such a hypothesis can stipulate both that the demon's single overriding purpose is to provide me with such observations and also that it has sufficient power and knowledge to accomplish this end. Indeed, it seems clear that the system's remaining coherent (and stable) is, if anything, *more* likely in relation to such a hypothesis than it is in relation to the correspondence hypothesis. Thus if the claim that the correspondence hypothesis is the explanation for the coherence (and stability) of the system of beliefs which is most likely to be true is to be maintained, some other objection to such elaborated demon hypotheses will have to be found. And, as already suggested, there seems to be only one real possibility at this point: just as the claim was made above that the elaborated chance hypothesis is antecedently extremely unlikely to be true, that its *a priori* probability or likelihood is extremely low, so also must an analogous claim be made about elaborated demon hypotheses.

The argument for this claim will closely parallel that offered above for the elaborated chance hypothesis. Just as the relation of tension or probabilistic incompatibility that holds between the simple chance hypothesis and the fact of the long-run coherence (and stability) of my system of beliefs is internalized by the elaborated chance hypothesis, so also the analogous relation of incompatibility which was just argued to exist between simple demon hypotheses and the existence of such a system is internalized by elaborated demon hypotheses, with the result that an elaborated demon hypothesis of the sort just indicated is very unlikely, on purely *a priori* grounds, to be true. The unlikelihood that a demon would have just such desires and purposes (and that these would not change) seems no less great than the unlikelihood that an unspecified demon would produce just such observations. Just as an unspecified demon is equally capable of producing all possible configurations of observations, so that it is very unlikely that he will produce the very special sort of configuration required to be coherence-conducive, so also a demon is capable of having *any* set of desires and purposes, thus making the quite special set of desires and purposes which would lead him to produce a coherence-conducive set of observations equally unlikely. For this reason, the elaborated demon hypothesis is, like the elaborated chance hypothesis, extremely unlikely to be true.

But this result, even if plausible on its own, is obviously not enough to show that the elaborated de-

mon hypothesis is significantly *less* likely to be true relative to the evidence provided by a coherent (and stable) system of beliefs than is the rival correspondence hypothesis. That hypothesis, after all, involves a considerable internal complexity of its own, and some reason accordingly needs to be given for thinking that this complexity does not render it for basically parallel reasons just as unlikely, or even more unlikely, to be true than are the demon hypotheses.

The principle point at which the correspondence hypothesis seems to be vulnerable to an argument which would parallel the one already offered against the elaborated chance and elaborated demon hypotheses is in its assertion that the cognitively spontaneous beliefs which are claimed within the system to be reliable are systematically caused by the kinds of external situations which they assert to obtain. It does not seem especially more or less likely *a priori* that there should be a world of the sort in question and that it should cause beliefs in some way or other than that there should be a demon which causes beliefs, leaving the two sorts of hypotheses roughly on a par in this respect. But if this is so, then it can be argued that the correspondence hypothesis is just as unlikely to be true on a purely *a priori* basis as are demon hypotheses. It is unlikely, relative to all the possible ways in which beliefs could be caused by the world, that they would be caused in the specific way required by the correspondence hypothesis.

The clearest way to elaborate this point is to distinguish, in a way which parallels the distinction between simple and elaborated demon hypotheses, two versions of the claim that cognitively spontaneous beliefs are caused by an ordinary world of objects in space and time: (1) a simple version which claims simply that they are thus caused, without specifying anything about what specific sort of cause produces what specific sort of belief; and (2) an elaborated version which claims, in the way required by the correspondence hypothesis, that the cause of such cognitively spontaneous beliefs, or rather of those specific kinds of cognitively spontaneous beliefs which are judged to be reliable from within the system, is normally the sort of external situation that the belief asserts to obtain. The claim is then that relative to the simple hypothesis (1), the existence of a coherent (and stable) system of beliefs is extremely unlikely, because that hypothesis fails to make it at all likely that the causation of such observation beliefs will take place in any way which will lead to long-run coherence (and stability); hence, relative to the fact of a long-run coherent (and stable) system of beliefs, hypothesis (1) is extremely unlikely to be true. And if this is right, then hypothesis (2) will itself be extremely unlikely to be true for the same sort of reason that was offered against elaborated demon hypotheses and the elaborated chance hypothesis: it embodies within itself two elements, one of which is extremely unlikely to be true relative to the other, and hence has an extremely low *a priori* probability or likelihood. The apparent result is that there is no reason for thinking that the correspondence hypothesis, which essentially involves this unlikely causal claim, is any more likely to be true than some appropriate elaborated demon hypothesis, so that our attempt at a metajustification of the envisaged coherentist account of empirical justification fails at this crucial point.

Part of the claim advanced in this argument seems undeniably correct. Because of the many different ways in which cognitively spontaneous beliefs could be caused by a world of the sort in question, it is highly unlikely on a purely *a priori* basis that they would be caused in the quite specific way demanded by the correspondence hypothesis, and thus also *a priori* unlikely that the correspondence hypothesis is true. From the standpoint of a coherence theory, this amounts to saying that it is *a priori* quite unlikely that there should exist cognitive beings like us who succeed in having knowledge of an independent world. The central issue is whether this unlikelihood is approximately as great as the corresponding unlikelihood for simple demon hypotheses, or whether, on the contrary, reasons might perhaps be found for thinking that it is significantly smaller, thus resulting in a significantly greater degree of relative likelihood for the correspondence hypothesis. I believe that such reasons can be found, though I can offer only a brief sketch of them here.

The crucial point here is that although the elaborated causal hypothesis (2) is admittedly extremely unlikely relative to the general claim that the beliefs in question are caused by a normal world, there are two correlative reasons why it is less so than the foregoing argument might suggest. In the first place, it is not the case (as it was for the simple demon hypothesis) that the simple causal hypothesis (1) makes all or virtually all possible patterns of beliefs and of belief causation equally likely to occur. While the whole point of a skeptical hypothesis like that of the evil demon is to be completely and equally compatible with any resulting pattern of experience, and thus neither refutable nor disconfirmable by any such pattern, this is not true of the hypothesis that beliefs are caused by a spatio-temporal world of a more or less ordinary sort. Such a world, unlike a demon, is not merely a neutral producer of beliefs. On the contrary, having as it does a definite and orderly character of its own, such a world would be expected *a priori* to cause beliefs in ways which reflected that character to some degree, not in a completely random fashion. Thus hypotheses which involve such patterns of causation, of which the elaborated causal hypothesis (2) is one, become substantially more likely to be true.

Second, and more important, there is avaliable a complicated albeit schematic account in terms of biological evolution and to some extent also cultural and conceptual evolution which explains how cognitive beings whose spontaneous beliefs are connected with the world in the right way could come to exist—an explanation which, speaking very intuitively, arises from within the general picture provided by hypothesis (2) and by the correspondence hypothesis, rather than being arbitrarily imposed from the outside. My suggestion is that the availability of such an account—as a coherent conceptual possibility, not as an established empirical fact—reduces the internal tension between the elements of hypothesis (2) and hence decreases the unlikelihood of that hypothesis, and that of the correspondence hypothesis which embodies it, enough to give it a very significant edge over the demon hypotheses considered above, for which no such internal account appears to be readily available.

This is not to deny that some sort of account could be supplied for the demon as well, perhaps by a clever fantasist: an account, based upon some stipulated demonology, of why the demon comes to have the right set of desires and purposes. The point is rather that such an account would be essentially external to those aspects of the demon which serve to generate our belief and hence unlikely, in relation to those aspects, to be true. There is and can be nothing about the demon considered merely as a producer of beliefs which makes such an account any more likely to be true than any other. Thus the internal probablisitic tension which pertains to an elaborated demon hypothesis would not be in any way lessened by the providing of such an account. If the situation were analogous with regard to the correspondence hypothesis, if that hypothesis amounted simply to stipulating that some of the beliefs caused by the world just happen to satisfy casual hypothesis (2), or stipulating some purely external account (for example, by appeal to a diety of some sort) of how such a world comes to satisfy hypothesis (2), then the situation would indeed be parallel. But this, I have argued, is not the case.

For both of these reasons, I suggest, the degree of *a priori* unlikelihood which pertains to the correspondence hypothesis, though admittedly large, is substantially less than that which pertains to elaborated demon hypotheses, making the correspondence hypothesis substantially more likely to be true as an explanation of the long-run coherence (and stability) of my system of beliefs. And this result,

taken together with the argument of the previous section, makes it reasonable to accept thesis MJ.

Even at this schematic and admittedly problematic stage, this sketch of how a metajustification might be given for a coherentist account of the justification of empirical beliefs seems to me sufficient, when combined with the argument of the previous section, to seriously undermine the third of the standard objections to coherence theories: the claim that such an account of justification can be shown to be truth-conducive only by adopting an untenable coherence theory of the nature of truth itself. Thus the standard objections to coherentist accounts of empirical justification prove to be much less compelling than is usually thought. And, though much more obviously remains to be done, this result, combined with the severe objections faced by the various versions of foundationalism, is enough, I submit, to establish a coherence theory of the sort offered here as the leading candidate for a correct theory of empirical knowledge.

KEITH LEHRER

Knowledge Reconsidered

I have been grateful to the philosophical world for the attention *Knowledge* received in the periodical literature. After fourteen years, I should be surprised and disappointed if I still believed exactly what I wrote then. My recent reflections and writings on the theory of knowledge developed out of the many important and useful criticisms of my earlier effort and seem to me to be consistent with the theory of *Knowledge*. I have, however, changed my mind in various respects. This chapter represents the state of my art.

The earlier work sought to define justification in terms of probability relative to a background system. I no longer think that is tenable. Justification may be defined in terms of reasonableness which contains probability as a factor, a critically important factor, but there are other factors that are not reducible to probability. The subjective account of complete justification in *Knowledge* was supplemented with an account of justification not being defeated by the correction of errors in the justifying background system. I, like Pollock, still defend the notion that undefeated justification is the basis of knowledge, but I would offer a more objective account of complete justification. The requirement in *Knowledge* that justification be undefeated incorporated a condition similar to what Goldman has called *reliabilism*. An objective probability of truth greater than competitors relative to the background system was required for undefeated justification. My sort of probabilism was systematic rather than historical, however. I do not think it is a necessary condition of knowledge or justification that a belief have some specified causal history.

Coherence remains for me the central notion in epistemology, though I insist with Cohen that there must be some connection between the justification of a belief and the truth of the belief. In this, I differ from pure internalists. The dispute between externalism and internalism is not so clear cut as the defenders of each position think, however. Enlightened

internalists, those maintaining the justification of a belief can be completely determined by reflection, Chisholm for example, are left with the need to deal with the Gettier problem. In so doing, they naturally require that justification not be connected with falsity, and this requirement imposes an external condition. The purest internalists who bar external conditions from entering into an account of justification find externalism creeping in through Gettier's back door. Enlightened externalists, Goldman, for example, find it necessary to require that a person not believe anything which would undermine beliefs arising from external processes, thus introducing reference to background beliefs, that is, to internal conditions. As a rough and ready aid to the classification of theories, I have no objection to the distinction between externalism and internalism, but the dispute over the matter is more useful for igniting dialectic passion than for reaching the truth in the matter. Knowledge arises when there is the appropriate sort of match between all of what a person believes and external reality. The object of epistemology is to find the right mix of internal factors and external relationships to explicate what is required.

I shall, instead of attempting to refine distinctions between one kind of theory and another for the purpose of proceeding to bash the category of my adversary, help myself to what insights I find in the work of others and see whether this strategy might yield better results. I shall, accordingly, combine aspects of theories advocated by foundation theorists, causal theorists, faculty theorists, and what have you, to articulate the sort of coherence theory I wish to defend. If the resulting theory seems to be more of some other sort of theory than a coherence theory, I would not protest against another label. A critic of another theory of mine, a theory of consensus, once dubbed it a monster theory. Since the theory I shall present contains what may seem an unnatural combination of ingredients, I propose to call it the *monster* theory. I hope to convince you the monster is an admirable one, deserving of friendly treatment, though requiring some discipline to render it domestically acceptable.

THE MONSTER THEORY

The theory has two components. One is definitional or formal. This constitutes an analysis or explication of knowledge. It leaves open substantive issues. The formal analysis of knowledge I shall offer is compatible with a wide variety of epistemologies, among them some foundation theories for example. I think it advisable to distinguish this part of the theory from those parts that should be more controversial, though there is no dearth of philosophers inclined to controvert what follows next. I shall present the key definitions and explain them.

> DK. S knows that p at t if and only if (i) p, (ii) S accepts that p at t, (iii) S is justified in accepting that p at t, and (iv) there is nothing that defeats the justification that S for accepting p at t.

This definition is intended to be a definition schema of the open sentence to the left of the "if and only if" rather than one implicitly quantified over some domain of entities for the variable p. That is a nicety, but I wish to leave open the question of whether knowing is a relation between a subject and a class of entities, propositions for example. The definition is traditional and is correct as far as it goes. It is insufficiently articulate to meet objections or to provide the sort of illumination philosophers demand of theories, or at least of the theories of others, however. One can reasonably request explication of the key terms, "justified" and "undefeated" for example, but this in no way implies the definition is incorrect or otherwise unsatisfactory.

A word of comment about the nature of analysis may be useful before proceeding to define the so far undefined notions. Analysis rests on an equivalence relation. I do not claim an analysis is an equivalence holding for all conceivable cases. Some examples, though conceivable, are not really consistent. Reid made the point long ago that conceivability is not an adequate test of logical possibility. I do not claim the

analysis holds even for all logically possible cases. The definition should be thought of more like a definition of "force" in physics. It is a nomological equivalence. Thus, I would rule out as irrelevant any test case that was inconsistent with the laws of nature even if it was logically possible. For the most part, discussion proceeds in terms of such cases and so I do not think this restriction is really novel. Another respect in which the intended definition is like the definition of "force" in physics is that, once the primitive terms are themselves defined, the defined notion should be more precise than the ordinary notion. As a result, some borderline cases of knowledge as the term is ordinarily applied may be excluded as not being cases of knowledge in the more precise defined sense. Such borderline cases like logical possibilities that are nomologically impossible may be of interest, but they do not constitute test cases for the definition, that is, they cannot serve as counterexamples.

Finally, I make no assumption that the notions used to define "know" are ordinary notions. They are technical. As will become clear, some of them are my creations, or so I believe. A colleague remarked he could find no reason to believe the ordinary conception of knowledge, assuming there to be such a thing, must be such that there would be other ordinary conceptions constituting necessary and sufficient conditions. That may be true, but it is irrelevant, I think, to a philosophical and historically adequate conception of analysis. Philosophers have not for the most part tried to define ordinary terms or concepts in terms of other ordinary terms or concepts, though they sometimes have said and more often thought they were doing so. They have created new terms and conceptions to use to analyze some target term or concept. I think this is obvious from the history of science and philosophy. A more controversial claim is that we create new terms and concepts that cannot be defined in terms of the old ones. That I also hold, but this is not the place to argue for it.

With those remarks on behalf of DK, let me explain my intentions in attempting to analyze the conditions employed in DK. It is not my attempt to finally arrive at some ultimate conceptual primitives used to define all the rest. I shall, in fact, begin by taking a locution as primitive, but I do not wish to he taken as an advocate of a compositional theory of concept formation. According to such a theory, all concepts that we understand are understood by us because they reduce by definition to some primitive concepts we initially understand. I doubt the compositional theory of concept formation is true. There is an intelligible notion of a term or concept being primitive relative to some system we develop. What is primitive relative to one system, however, may be defined in another system containing the same total set of terms or concepts as the first. I shall take some terms as primitive relative to the system I develop, but I do not claim what I take as primitive is metaphysically or psychologically primitive. Anything taken as primitive in one system may be defined in another system or in an expansion of the original. Nothing is ultimately undefinable.

What we can achieve in philosophy is the articulation of principles, among them definitions or equivalence principles, compatible with the laws of nature, including the laws of human nature. If, therefore, my analysis yields the result that subhuman, superhuman, diminished human, or nonhuman beings do not know anything, that is consistent with my purposes. I am concerned with human knowledge. There are, I am sure, states very like human knowledge which other beings possess, but that is not my concern here.

ACCEPTANCE

I shall take the term "accept" as primitive, but my use of it requires some explanation. Reflection on various cases of knowledge have convinced me that, though there is some common positive propositional attitude toward the content known, that is, that p, there is no ordinary use of any term exactly coinciding with the required propositional attitude. I use the expression 'propositional attitude' for the sake of tradition to describe such mental attitudes as believing, thinking, and accepting such and such without committing myself to the doctrine that these attitudes are relations to a proposition. I use the term "content" in the theory-neutral sense to refer to what the person believes, thinks, or accepts. It is a special use of the term "accepts" I employ. When I say a person accepts that p at t, I mean the person accepts that p for the specific purpose of obtaining truth and avoiding error with re-

spect to p. The point of these qualifications is that a person may accept something for a variety of purposes, to increase felicity by accepting what one would like to be true, or to please someone else who is keen on having one accept what they say, but these purposes are not the ones germane to knowledge. The purposes of obtaining truth and avoiding error are the relevant ones. Even accepting p for these general purposes is not sufficient, however, in that one might think accepting p is useful for the purpose of accepting other things that are true and avoiding accepting other things that are false, while having no idea whether p is true. Such acceptance for these general purposes is not what is required for knowledge either. What is required is a certain kind of acceptance of p specifically aimed at being correct about p and avoiding being mistaken about p.

My reasons for preferring acceptance to belief as a condition of knowledge are partly theoretical and partly linguistic. The term "accept" in one of its uses seems to me to be a relative term in which there is some implicit reference to some purpose or aim, while the term "believe" does not have this feature. Of course, belief like acceptance may arise from a variety of causes, some being related to the truth of the content, such as vision, and others being unrelated, such as wishful thinking, as Goldman has insisted. But believing something, however caused, is not a relative conception in the way accepting something is. To accept something is to accept something for a purpose, to please another, to make one happy, to concede something for the sake of argument, or, finally, to obtain truth. What one accepts for one purpose, moreover, one may reject for another. This aspect of acceptance or "acceptance" is a useful feature of the notion or term in the analysis. The required propositional attitude in the analysis of knowledge is one having truth seeking as its purpose. In *Knowledge,* where I used the notion of belief, it was necessary to select a subclass of beliefs, those the person would retain if solely interested in obtaining truth and avoiding error, which introduced a counterfactual element unnecessarily. The notion of acceptance allows us to build in the purpose of truth seeking without introducing any counterfactual element.

There is another more theoretical and psychological reason for preferring acceptance to belief. Belief sometimes arises in an individual against his or her better judgment. It also sometimes fails to arise when one's better judgment tells one it should. The point is not that acceptance is voluntary, though some kinds of acceptance are voluntary in some instances, but that belief and rational judgment may sometimes conflict. When, on the basis of the evidence one rationally affirms p, one accepts that p whether or not this produces belief. Such acceptance plays a determinate role in inference and further acceptance without necessarily yielding belief. A student of a certain sort, one lacking confidence, may always feel he will fail each examination before taking it, though, being, in fact, a brilliant and a thorough scholar, he knows he will pass the typical midterm graded by a generous instructor. His feeling he will fail deters us from saying he believes he will pass, though, on the basis of evidence about his abilities, preparation, past successes, and dispositions of the instructor, he, when seeking to accept what is true, accepts he will pass. He knows he will pass. The problem is that the rational intellect, or, in more modern terms, the central system, does not always determine belief. We may know something is the case before we believe it; indeed, our knowing it to be the case may result in our coming to believe it. In short, there may be conflict between a lower-level unreflective system and a higher-level reflective one. Acceptance without belief may result when there is an absence of belief corresponding to what one accepts in the interests of obtaining truth and avoiding error.

The foregoing remarks should not be taken as implying that acceptance of the required sort must always be reflective. In receiving information, we have need of a system that is virtually automatic in responding to sensory evidence. So belief carries over into acceptance unless there is conflict with background information. When there is conflict, belief and acceptance may diverge. Thus a person accepts that p exactly when the person either believes that p without conflict with background information or reflectively judges that p on the basis of background information. When there is no conflict between belief and background information, there is a kind of routine positive evaluation by something like a central cognitive system, but that is psychological speculation only and no part of my account of acceptance.

Perhaps the simplest account of acceptance may be put as follows. When a person considers and judges that p, the person comes into a mental state that has a certain sort of functional role in thought and inference. A person may come to be in a similar mental state having a similar functional role in thought and inference without the state having arisen from such consideration and judgment. A mental state having the appropriate sort of functional role with respect to the content that p is what I have referred to as accepting that p. It is not essential to such a mental state having such a functional role that a person have considered and judged that p, though it may arise in that way. Of course, if the state of accepting that p does not arise from consideration and judgment, the person will not think or infer that he or she did consider and judge that p, but he or she may otherwise use the content that p in the same manner as one who did so judge. Thus, accepting that p is a mental state assigning a similar functional role to the content that p in truth seeking inference and thought as a mental state arising from considering and judging that p. Accepting that p is a sort of positive attitude toward a content, that p, resulting in employment of the content, that p, as background information in thought and inference.

The notion of acceptance gives rise to the notion of an acceptance system, a system articulating what a person accepts, which replaces the notion of a corrected doxastic system in *Knowledge as* the justification-generating system. The acceptance system is defined as follows:

D1. A system X is an acceptance system of S if and only if X contains just statements of the form—S accepts that p—attributing to S just those things that S accepts with the objective of obtaining truth and avoiding error with respect to the specific thing accepted.

JUSTIFICATION

Justification arises, as I have argued and continue to aver, from coherence with a background system. This proposal is expressed in the following schema:

D2. S is justified in accepting that p at t on the basis of system X of S at t if and only if p coheres with the system X of S at t.

I shall first give a formal rather than a material account of justification by defining justification in terms of a comparative notion of reasonableness. The account is formal in the sense that epistemologists advocating diverse theories of justification could, consistent with their substantive differences, accept the definition in question. A foundation theorist could claim that what makes one thing more reasonable than another is some relation to a foundation whose reasonableness is not derived from anything else. A reliabilist could maintain that what makes one thing more reasonable than another is that the first is the result of a more reliable process, and so forth. Thus, the sort of definition I shall offer, if not theory neutral, is compatible with most current theories of justification.

I shall eventually offer some account of the notion of reasonableness. Here, however, I shall, following Chisholm, take as primitive the notion of one thing being more reasonable for a person than another. I shall sometimes apply this notion in a relativized extended manner and speak of it being more reasonable for a person to accept p than q on one assumption than on another on the basis of some system X at some time t. For the sake of formal elegance, the latter relativized expression might be taken as primitive and the notions that are not relativized to any assumptions or systems could be defined in terms of the relativized expression by treating the assumptions as vacuous and the system as empty.

It has been my contention that a person is justified in accepting something just in case either any skeptical hypothesis a skeptic might raise to shed doubt on what the person accepts is less reasonable for the person to accept than what is called in question, or it is no less reasonable for the person to accept the skeptical hypothesis conjoined with some consideration neutralizing the skeptical impact than to accept the skeptical hypothesis alone. In *Knowledge,* I assumed such skeptical hypotheses must be less probable than what they call into question, but the requirement now seems to me too restrictive. My claim that I see my hand before me is more probable and more reasonable than the skeptical hypothesis that my senses are deceiving me. My claim is, however, no more probable or reasonable than the skeptical observation that our senses sometimes deceive us. This observation, which sheds doubt on my claim that I see my hand before me, is, however, neutralized by the observation that my senses are not now deceiving me.

Treating skeptical hypotheses as competitors we may, therefore, define notions of a competitor, of beating a competitor, and of neutralizing a competitor as follows.

D3. S is justified in accepting p at t on the basis of system X of S at t if and only if all competitors of p are beaten or neutralized for S on X at t.

D4. c competes with p for S on X at t if and only if it is more reasonable for S to accept that p on the assumption that c is false than on the assumption that c is true on the basis of X at t.

D5. p beats c for S on X at t if and only if c competes with p for S on X at t, and it is more reasonable for S to accept p than to accept c on X at t.

D6. n neutralizes c as a competitor of p for S on X at t if and only if c competes with p for S on X at t, the conjunction of c and n does not compete with p for S on X at t, and it is reasonable for S to accept the conjunction of c and n as to accept c alone on X at t.

This formal definition of justification does not presuppose a coherence theory of justification and is, as I have noted, consistent with competing theories of knowledge and justification.

A comment on my use of the skeptic and her hypotheses is essential. I am not supposing that a person who is justified in accepting something has considered any skeptical hypotheses. I have never before considered the hypothesis that there is a submicroscopic beetle, the brain beetle, that lives in all our brains and, when actively moving about among the cerebral passageways during procreation, disturbs the connections in the occipital lobes producing visual hallucination. Bt it is and was, even prior to my imagining the existence of the brain beetle, more reasonable for me to believe I see my hand than that such a hypothesis is true. I would explain the greater reasonableness of the one belief than the other in terms of background beliefs about hands and beetles, but the fact of the greater reasonableness of one than the other is, I contend, more obvious than any philosophical explanation of the fact. I do not suggest a skeptic would be moved by this claim or that it is an adequate reply to a philosophical skeptic. My use of the skeptic and her skeptical machinations is merely a heuristic device to focus attention on competitors of a given claim.

These definitions may also be consistent with an approach that might seem quite at odds with them, namely, the proposal of Dretske that skeptical alternatives are irrelevant to whether one knows. It would be possible to interpret him as maintaining that, even though the skeptical hypotheses compete with other claims and cannot be beaten or neutralized, they are nevertheless irrelevant to whether a person knows. Of course, Dretske has denied justification is a condition of knowledge, but I think it would be implausible to interpret him as claiming irrelevant alternatives are unbeaten and unneutralized competitors. On the contrary, it seems more reasonable to interpret his claims as implying the irrelevant skeptical alternatives are not really competitors, though they might seem to be. I would find that claim philosophically odd, but it seems to me in the spirit of Dretske's position to claim skeptical alternatives do not count, epistemically speaking. I, on the contrary, think skeptical alternatives do count, that is, are competitors, because the usual perceptual claims seem to me to be less reasonable on the assumption that the skeptical hypotheses are true than on the assumption that they are false. Another possible interpretation of the relevant alternatives approach within the present framework is to admit the skeptical alternatives are competitors but to contend they are beaten as a consequence of their irrelevance. The definitions are, I propose, logically consistent with the relevant alternatives approach.

It is now, however, time to turn to the more substantiative issue of what makes a person justified in accepting something. My answer is that what makes a person justified in accepting something is coherence with a background system, but I contend there is more than one sort of system and, consequently, more than one sort of justification required for knowledge. It would be possible to define one sort of justification, undefeated justification, that logically implies all the others, but it is more illuminating intuitively to break down this notion of justification into components. The first sort of justification is relative to the acceptance system of a person specified above. We may define it as follows:

> D7. S is personally justified in accepting that p at t if and only if S is justified in accepting that p on the basis of the acceptance system of S at t.

Notice this definition does not employ the notion of coherence. Coherence enters into the determination of justification by determining whether one thing is more or less reasonable to accept than another. Thus,

> D2. S is justified in accepting that p at t on the basis of the system X of S at t if and only if p coheres with the system X of S at t

is a substantiative claim about justification. The substantiative issues in epistemology depend on what makes something justified and, hence, on my view of the matter, on what makes something cohere with some system.

What makes something cohere in the relevant sense with the acceptance system of a person to yield personal justification? The objectives of justification are to obtain truth and avoid error with respect to the thing accepted. So coherence in the relevant sense depends on what the acceptance system tells us about our chances of obtaining those objectives. Hence, in *Knowledge* I argued coherence was a matter of probability, subjective or personal probability. Probability still strikes as a determinant, but the story is more complicated for familiar reasons. Explanatory power, which Sellars and Harman consider a central determinant, may be reflected, I have argued, in high prior probability assignments. There is nothing to preclude us from assigning a higher prior probability to explanatory hypotheses. At some point, however, explanatory power requires explanatory comprehensiveness, and, given the conjunction principles concerning probability, a reduction in probability. In seeking to obtain truth and avoid error, we are interested in obtaining the whole truth, as well as in obtaining nothing but the truth, and the acceptance of the whole truth would involve greater risk of error than accepting only a part. Something must make the risk reasonable, and what makes it reasonable cannot be probability. For the probability diminishes as truth becomes more comprehensive. To take the example above, it is just as reasonable for me to accept the conjunction that our senses sometimes deceive us *and* that my eyes do not deceive me when I now see my hand as to accept simply that our senses sometimes deceive us, but the conjunction is not as probable. What makes the conjunction as reasonable is the fuller description and removal of the false innuendo that my eyes might be deceiving me.

One principal determinant of what makes it more reasonable to accept one thing than another on the basis of my acceptance system is what I accept about the conditions under which some source, method, or state is trustworthy in the quest for truth and the avoidance of error. I accept that the testimony of others is, under various circumstances, a trustworthy guide to truth, just as I accept that my eyes are, under various circumstances, a trustworthy guide. In some instances, it is some state of myself, a distinct memory of something, of my telephone number for example, I accept as a trustworthy guide to truth. What I accept about the trustworthiness of states of acceptance themselves provides a doxastic connection between acceptance and truth. I accept that certain states of acceptance are trustworthy guides to truth, and, since justification aims at truth, those states of acceptance are justified for me on the basis of my acceptance system. In this way, to use a metaphor from Glymour, my acceptance system bootstraps what I accept to justified acceptance.

The preceding remarks indicate the truth in reliabilism and other causal, nomological, and counterfactual theories of knowledge. The truth is a doxastic truth. It is the result of doxastic ascent. We not only accept things about the external world, we also accept things about the connection between ourselves, about what we judge and believe, and the external world. I do not, of course, suggest the doxastic connection is the result of deliberation, though few escape the burden of reflecting on when their internal states are trustworthy, and those few suffer a disability. As I noted above, however, we accept things we have never thought about, and everyone trusts their senses and draws inferences on the assumption that they are to be trusted. For that reason, I maintain people accept things about the trustworthiness of their mental states, acceptance included, because their thoughts and inferences exhibit a state functionally similar to one arising from conscious consideration of the matter.

THE TRILEMMA

The foregoing remarks raise a problem the solution of which provides the solution to a traditional epistemological problem. The new problem and the old are closely connected. The new problem is that if justified acceptance that p requires, as I allege, accepting the acceptance of p as a trustworthy guide to truth, the question naturally arises as to whether this higher-order acceptance must itself be justified. If so, this would require further doxastic ascent, acceptance that the higher-order acceptance was trustworthy, and a regress threatens. Before turning to the solution to the problem, we will find it useful to notice a similarity between this problem and a traditional trilemma. The trilemma was formulated by Sextus Empiricus by contending justification must either proceed in a circle, lead to a regress, or be ended by some mere assumption. The third alternative has been described by a modern author as an artificial breaking off of inquiry.

The traditional problem might be formulated as follows. The sort of justification required for knowledge must be justification for accepting that p for the purpose of obtaining truth and avoiding error with respect to the claim that p. To have this sort of justification one must at least accept that accepting p is a trustworthy means to the purpose in question. But merely accepting this is insufficient. One must be justified in accepting it. Such justification would lead either to a circle, to a regress, or to the mere assumption that something is justified. Foundation theories have traditionally embraced the third alternative. They affirm something is immediately, directly, or intrinsically self-justified and have been favored by many for that reason. Externalist and reliabilist solutions have either denied justification is necessary for knowledge or affirmed that some beliefs are justified because of the causal, nomological, counterfactual, or statistical relationship to truth. Denying knowledge requires justification does not, of course, solve the trilemma with respect to justification, and the other solution is like the solution of the foundationalist.

There is a correct insight in these solutions, but, in my opinion, there is something philosophically unsatisfying in them. The dissatisfaction with the foundationalist is that it abrogates the connection between justification and truth. Justification has as its purpose the attainment of truth and the avoidance of error, and, as a result, the mere postulation or assumption that something is justified, even if it is, leaves one with an unanswered question. What reason have we for thinking such intrinsic justification serves the purpose of attaining truth and avoiding error? The reliabilist and his externalist cohorts supply an answer to the question, namely, that there is some specified connection between justification and truth, for example, that the belief-forming process instantiates some truth productive rule or method. Their solution leaves us with a residual dissatisfaction. If their account is correct, then, though we can see the justified beliefs of another serve the purpose of attaining truth and avoiding error, the person having the belief might have no idea his or her beliefs serve the purpose in question. To see the point, suppose a person is justified in some belief solely on reliabilist grounds but has no idea of these grounds at all. Imagine she asks herself the following question: "What reason have I for thinking this belief is justified for the purpose of attaining truth or avoiding error?" Her answer must be, "None whatever." Hence the dissatisfaction with this solution to the trilemma. Both solutions have something to offer, but what they omit is the doxastic connection supplying a person with a reason, whether appealed to or not, for thinking accepting what one does serves the interests of truth. On the other hand, the attempt to supply such a reason in every case appears to lead to a circle or a regress the avoidance of which is an attraction of the views considered.

There is a solution to the trilemma which, at the same time, solves the problem of doxastic ascent. The first step in the solution is to recall once again that a person may accept something she has not considered. Such acceptance is a mental state having a functional role in thought and inference similar to a mental state arising from conscious consideration and judgment except for those thoughts and inferences pertaining to the process of consideration and judgment. This step allows me to contend people accept they are trustworthy evaluators of truth and error, though they have not consciously considered the matter in these terms. When I say people accept they are trustworthy evaluators of truth and error, I mean this plays a role in their thought and inference. A per-

son who sees her black hair thinks of herself as black haired, draws inferences in accord with this, for example, that her hair is darker than blond and that she should check *black* next to hair color on her military identification papers. All this shows she accepts that she can tell the color of her hair when she sees it, that is, that she can determine the truth of the matter. When, however, I say a person accepts that she is a trustworthy evaluator of truth, I do not mean to suggest she accepts that she can tell whether every claim is true or false. What I mean by saying a person is a trustworthy evaluator of truth and error is that when she accepts something as true for the purpose of accepting what is true and avoiding accepting what is false, her accepting what she does is a trustworthy guide to truth in the matter. It is to say she has the capacity to accept what is true and avoid accepting what is false. To say someone has such a capacity is not to say she is an infallible guide to truth. A person may be trustworthy, though fallible, in the quest for truth as in other matters. A trustworthy bookkeeper may be paid richly for her trustworthiness, though her work is not entirely free from error.

With these preliminary remarks before us, let us consider how to solve the problems in question. It is clear that the claim

T. I am a trustworthy evaluator of truth

has a special potency for suppyling me with a reason for regarding acceptance as serving the purpose of attaining truth and avoiding error. For, whatever I accept for this pupose, principle T supplies me with a reason for thinking what I accept is true, to wit, that my accepting something is a trustworthy guide to truth. A person could reason, though he need not, that I accept that p in the interests of attaining truth and avoiding error, and, since I am a trustworthy evaluator of truth, my accepting p indicates that p is true. So every regress is ended and every cicrcle avoided by appeal to T, except, of course, when T itself comes into question.

What are we to say with respect to T itself? Am I intrinsically justified in accepting T? Does the attempt to justify T take us to an ever higher level of doxastic ascent generating a regress? Or does the attempt to justify T lead us in a short circle in which T provides us with a reason for accepting itself? There is a sense in which the answer to all of these questions is positive. Let us begin with the last. Thomas Reid articulated a similar principle, though he put the matter in a negative form, affirming our faculties are not fallacious. He went on to say that as evidence resembles light in many respects, so it resembles light in that as light reveals the illuminated object it also reveals itself. The obvious point is that just as principle T has the capacity to provide a reason for accepting the other things we do, so it provides us with a reason for accepting itself. The argument is short and neat. If I accept p, whatever p might be, in the quest for truth, principle T provides me with a reason for thinking my acceptance is a guide to truth, for that is what T tells me. But then, let principle T be what I accept. If I accept T in the interests of obtaining truth and avoiding error, principle T provides me with a reason for thinking my acceptance of T is a guide to truth, for principle T is perfectly general in application.

It is easy to explain how a person becomes justified in accepting T when the person, in fact, accepts that T. The following is a true principle:

TR If S accepts that T at t, then it is more reasonable for S to accept that T than to accept the denial of T on the basis of the acceptance system of S at t.

TR appears to me, unless the acceptance system of S is quite peculiar, to imply

If S accepts T at t, then all competitors of T are either beaten or neutralized on the basis of the acceptance system of S at t,

which in turn implies

If S accepts that T at t, then S is personally justified in accepting that T at t.

I do not think that it is necessarily true that it is more reasonable for a person to accept what he or she does than to accept its denial. If, for example, a person were to accept the denial of T, then the person might accept many other things even though it was no more reasonable for the person to accept those things than their denials. Indeed, any acceptance system not containing the acceptance of T, or something having similar consequences, seems likely to be a system in which it is no more reasonable for a person to accept what he or she does than to accept the denial. In the absence of any views about whether one's accepting something is a guide to truth, the mere fact that one accepts it is no reason for one to suppose it to be true. So, T has the following peculiarity. For a person to be justified in accepting anything, the person must accept T or something having similar consequences, and if the person does accept T, then the person is justified in accepting T as well as other things, though not necessarily all other things, the person accepts. Thus, principle T is surely a bootstrapping principle, pulling itself up by its own bootstraps, but it is also a make-or-break principle for the justification of other things as well.

Given the correctness of TR and what it implies, one might be inclined to argue, as did Reid, that TR is a first principle, the foundation or the root of justification and knowledge. Acceptance of T has many of the features of a basic belief in foundational epistemology, and I have no objection to the suggestion that either T or TR is a first principle. I would, however, note that principle T may be confirmed and established through experience. Someone accepting that principle would as the result of experience learn to modify and qualify what they subsequently accept about the world, but that principle would be supported rather than undermined by such experience. So T is not beyond confirmation, though, to be sure, such confirmation presupposes acceptance of it. More important, however, principle TR has an important feature other proposed foundational principles lack. The content of T provides an explanation of why one is justified in accepting TR. Principle T tells me my accepting something is a guide to truth. The purpose of justification is to obtain truth and avoid error in what I accept. Therefore, the content of principle T explains why I am justified in accepting it, namely, that my accepting it is a means to fulfilling the purpose of justification.

Other principles proposed as first principles, ones affirming that when a person accepts something about his present mental states or distinctly perceived objects, the person is justified in accepting what he accepts, leave us without any explanation of why someone interested in truth should be justified in accepting those things. It may be implicitly assumed that a person will accept that what one accepts about one's present mental states or objects one distinctly perceives are very unlikely to be in error, that is, are a trustworthy guide to truth, and is justified in so doing. If that is explicitly assumed, however, the alleged first principle concerning present mental states and distinct perceptions can be justified by appeal to a more general principle telling us when what we accept is a trustworthy guide to truth. Principle TR is not simply postulated or merely assumed to be a first principle. On the contrary, the content of principle T combined with the objectives of justification provides a reason for considering acceptance of it to be justified. Other proposed first principles, on the other hand, are simply postulated or merely assumed. Thus, we have avoided the alternatives of the trilemma by arguing that accepting T can personally justify a person in accepting T for the purpose of obtaining truth and avoiding error.

A detractor might, of course, object that what we have done is to use principle T to justify itself and, therefore, have fallen into the smallest possible circle of justification rather than having avoided it. Similarly, such a detractor might object that, to be strictly accurate, we are not appealing to principle T to justify itself but to a higher-order principle referring to truths of a lower level to which T belongs, and, therefore, we are falling into an infinite regress proceeding from each level to the next higher level in order to justify versions of T indexed to the various levels in the truth hierarchy. This detractor is not one with which I should care to dispute but one which I would seek to mollify. I suggest there is nothing vicious in the regress or the circle mentioned, and I have no objection to principle TR being represented as a circular or regressive principle of justification. Rather, I contend there is no logical defect involved. The regress does not commit us to carrying out an infinite series of acts. On the contrary, it simply shows us that an infinite series of T principles at various levels are each such that, when accepted, one is justified in accepting them. The circle shows the peculiar but significant way in which the content of T explains why one who accepts it is personally justified in doing so.

If the circular element seems pernicious, this might result from skeptical reflection on TR. A skeptic might retort to the claim that someone accepting T is justified in accepting it that the person has assumed that T is true in order to justify accepting T. Assuming the very thing one must justify is, the skeptic might continue, to argue in a pernicious circle. My reply is that appeal to principle TR is dialectically unsatisfactory as a premise for replying to a skeptic challenging the acceptance of T, but that does not show that TR is false or that a person lacks a reason for regarding his or her acceptance of T as justified when he or she accepts T. The reason is not the sort of reason for replying to a skeptical challenge. It is, nevertheless, a reason that explains the truth of TR. To understand the point, suppose a skeptic were simply to deny the truth of T when I assert it. I have no reply to his denial that would not gratuitously beg the question. If T is false, then I am not a trustworthy evaluator of truth, and it would be pointless for me to attempt to show the truth lies on my side. On the other hand, if I proceed to offer argument, I have assumed I am a trustworthy evaluator of truth and gratuitously begged the question. In this dispute, a wise person would do as Reid said he would, hold his hand over his mouth in silence. Yet, accepting T as I do, I am justified in so doing, whether I say so or remain silent.

UNDEFEATED JUSTIFICATION

A skeptic might remain undaunted by the foregoing considerations and argue that if T is, in fact, false, then, though a person accepting T as true may be personally justified in accepting T and the common sense claims supported by T on the basis of what the person accepts, the person is not objectively justified in accepting T or the other claims supported thereby. For, she might continue, the only reason the person has to justify accepting T is T itself, or something depending on T, and T is false. If the justification a person has for what she accepts depends essentially on some reason or premise that is false, then the justification is defeated by the error on which it rests. Suppose the evil demon hypothesis of Descartes or the brain-in-vat hypothesis of Putnam is true, she might suggest, then T would be false, we would lack one sort of justification we require for knowledge, and we would be ignorant.

I agree with such a skeptic. There is some ambiguity in the notion of justification, however, that can lead to perplexity. Cohen noted a person in an evil demon universe is justified in accepting what he does because the person accepts what he or she does in an epistemically impeccable manner. When such a person accepts that he sees his hand before him, he has exactly the same reasons for thinking what he accepts is true as any person in the actual world. He cannot be faulted in any way and is, therefore, justified in what he accepts. I agree that the person is, in one sense, justified in what he accepts, but I agree with the skeptic who says that if T is false, then the justification the person has for accepting what he does is defeated by an error on which it rests. I would put this by saying the person is personally justified, perhaps epistemically virtuous as well, but the justification is defeated. The point is of critical importance in epistemology. Gettier noted the importance originally, arguing that justified true belief was not sufficient for knowledge, but the implications extend far beyond the problem he originally raised to the truth contained in externalism, reliabilism, and probabilism. Undefeated objective justification that does not rest on any error depends on the truth of T, that is, on our actually being trustworthy evaluators of truth.

The view I am defending might be described as doxastic reliabilism, a doxastic cousin of historical reliabilism of Goldman. Goldman has proposed that whether a belief is justified in the requisite sense depends on whether or not it is the result of a reliable belief-forming process, where the notion of resulting from a process is broadly construed to cover both origination and sustenance of a belief. I have argued that acceptance rather than belief is the key notion and that the sort of origination and sustenance Goldman, Swain, and others appeal to are not necessary to justification. I agree with him that reliability or probability is central. But it is the state of accepting something that must be a reliable or trustworthy guide to truth rather than the process that originates or sustains acceptance. I can imagine a person accepting something out of prejudice who acquires information giving him knowledge that his prejudice was true. So the acceptance leading to knowledge need not originate from the information that yields knowledge. It need not be causally or counterfactually sustained by it either. In the normal case, someone would, of course, be causally influenced by information received. In the odd and perhaps not very important case, however, a person might, if the originating prejudice lost its influence, be mentally shattered by the experience or, less catastrophically, might fall under the influence of some other prejudice which sustains his belief. The role of

information in acceptance is to render acceptance a trustworthy guide to truth. Any causal influence of the information upon acceptance is coincidental to justification or knowledge in all cases except those in which the content of what is accepted is itself causal. It is the state of acceptance itself rather than the process from which it results that must be a trustworthy guide to truth in order to yield objective or undefeated justification.

The notion of undefeated justification is, intuitively put, justification based on an acceptance system that is, in a special sense, beyond criticism. The sense in which the justification based on the acceptance system must be beyond criticism is simply that no consistent elimination of acceptance when the content of what one accepts is false, or consistent replacement of acceptance in such cases by acceptance of the denial of the false content, would destroy the justification. This might be explained by the heuristic of a justification game. The question is whether my justification for accepting p is undefeated. Imagine my acceptance system A is as follows:

L accepts that p_1

L accepts that p_2

A = L accepts that p_3

L accepts that p_n

Now imagine the following game with an omniscient critic. She is allowed to eliminate any member from A when p_i is false, or replace it with

L accepts that not-p_i,

or leave it unchanged. Let us call these *allowed* changes. She may make as many allowed changes as she wishes with one constraint. If she eliminates a member of A because p_i is false and p_i logically entails p_k and p_k is also false, then acceptance of p_k by L must also be eliminated if originally included in A. Similarly, if she replaces a member of A with the acceptance of the denial of p_i because p_i is false and p_i logically entails p_k and p_k is false, then she must replace acceptance of p_k with acceptance of the denial of p_k if originally included in A. Such elimination or replacement of things falsely accepted is in this way *deductively closed* in the acceptance system of S. The intuitive justification for such a constraint of deductive closure is that if p_i logically entails p_k and p_k is false, then accepting p_i is an error because accepting p_k is an error. Therefore, correcting errors of acceptance requires that if the error of accepting p_i is corrected, then the error of accepting p_k which guarantees that accepting p_i is an error must also be corrected. Let us call the result of such changes system M. Suppose I am personally justified in accepting that p at t. If the critic can form a system M with the result that I am not justified in accepting p on the basis of M at t, then the critic wins the game, and my justification is defeated. If, on the other hand, my acceptance is such that no such system M has the result that I am not justified in accepting p on the basis of M at t, then I win, and my justification is undefeated.

There is obviously a set of systems, M, resulting from different allowed changes the critic might make in the acceptance system given her omniscience of truth and error. Let us call the set of such systems the ultrasystem of S at t. We may then define undefeated justification as follows:

D8. S is justified in accepting that p at t in a way that is undefeated if and only if S is justified in accepting p at t on the basis of every system that is a member of the ultrasystem of S at t.

Similarly, we may define what it means to say that a system M defeats a personal justification of S for accepting that p at t as follows:

D9. M defeats the personal justification of S for accepting p at t if and only if S is personally justified in accepting p at t, but S is not justified in accepting p at t on system M at t where M is member of the ultrasystem of S at t.

The notion of something being a member of an ultrasystem explained above may be defined as follows:

D10. A system M is a member of the ultrasystem of S at t if and only if either M is the acceptance system of S at t or results from eliminating one or more statements of the form—S accepts that q—when q is false, replacing one or more statements of the form—S accepts that q—with a statement of the form—S accepts that not-q—when q is false, or any combination of such eliminations and replacements in the acceptance system of S at t with

the constraint that if q logically entails r which is false and also accepted, then—S accepts that r—must be also be eliminated or replaced in the same way as—S accepts that q—was.

In *Knowledge*, I defined undefeated justification in terms of just one member of the ultrasystem in which all cases of error in the acceptance system were replaced with acceptance of the denial of the false system. Carter pointed out, correctly I think, that such replacement might inadvertently manufacture some new justification for accepting p other than the justification resulting from the acceptance system and that S, having no conception of such a justification, is not entitled to the epistemic benefits of such manufacture. He then proposed another system be used to define undefeated justification, one in which all cases of error were simply eliminated. For some time that seemed to me correct, but it then occurred to me that just as replacement might inadvertently manufacture justification to which S was not entitled, so elimination might unblock some justification to which S was equally unentitled. The solution to the problem proposed above, based on a suggestion by Kuys, is that for justification to be undefeated it must survive under any elimination or replacement of error in the acceptance system generating the justification.

It does seem to me, however, that an important notion of justification results from Carter's proposal. If we adopt the technical term *verific system* to describe the system resulting from elimination of all error, the verific system may be defined as follows:

D11. A system V is a verific system of S at t if and only if V is a subsystem of the acceptance system of S at t resulting from eliminating all statements of the form—S accepts that p—when p is false. (V is a member of the ultrasystem of S.)

Similarly, a technical notion of justification, verific justification, may be defined in terms of such a system as follows:

D12. S is verifically justified in accepting that p at t if and only if S is justified in accepting that p on the basis of the verific system of S at t.

We are in a position to define a kind of justification, *complete* justification, which, though entailed by undefeated justification, is a more natural and intuitive notion of justification. When a person is justified on the basis of what she accepts and would remain so even if she eliminated all errors in what she accepts, I think it is appropriate to say she is *completely* justified. We may, therefore, define complete justification as follows:

D13. S is completely justified in accepting that p at t if and only if S is personally justified in accepting p at t and S is verifically justified in accepting p at t.

If the personal justification a person has for accepting p is undefeated, then the person is completely justified as well. Thus, complete justification, if added to the definition of knowledge, would not be an independent condition. It does, however, capture an important notion of justification. There were a number of philosophers, Pailthorp and Thalberg among them, who were inclined to deny one is completely justified in accepting a conclusion one has deduced from a false premise one was justified in accepting, contrary to Gettier's contention. I do not think this observation provides a solution to the Gettier problem, but I do think there is a sense in which it is correct to say that a person who has deduced a conclusion from a false premise is not really completely justified in accepting the conclusion on the basis of the deduction even if, as luck would have it, the person would have been completely justified had the premise been true. In short, then, there is a sense in which the person is justified, personally justified, in accepting what the person does in the Gettier examples, though there are other senses in which the person is not justified. The person is not completely justified, for example. The word "completely" is here used grammatically as an intensifier, and, consequently, people will differ in their intuitions regarding whether a person deducing a true conclusion from a false but justified premise is completely justified depending on how important he or she considers the falsity of the premise to be. The notion of complete justification does, however, capture the sense in which we feel that a person proceeding from false premises has not completely justified his or her conclusion.

With these definitions and observations before us, let us return to principle T, to wit, that I am a trustworthy evaluator of truth. If T is true, the justification a person has for accepting T based on accepting T would, in normal circumstance, be undefeated. Thus, what is crucial to knowledge is the following principle:

TRU. If T is true, and S accepts that T at t as a result, then it is more reasonable for S to accept that T than to accept the denial of T on the basis of the ultrasystem of S at t.

Again, unless the acceptance system of S is peculiar, one would expect all competitors of T to be beaten or neutralized on the basis of the verific system and the ultrasystem of S, and, therefore, expect the following principles to be true:

If T is true, and S accepts that T at t as a result, then S is completely justified in accepting that T at t.
If T is true, and S accepts that T at t as a result, then S is justified in accepting that T in a way that is undefeated at t.

Thus, the acceptance of T, if T is true, may be expected to yield knowledge of the truth of T. We may not be able to refute the skeptic who denies the truth of T or who advances some skeptical hypotheses implying the falsity of T. If, however, we are correct in thinking the skeptic is in error and in accepting the truth of T, then, skeptical machinations not withstanding, we know that T is true and know many other things as a result of this knowledge. We may not have the satisfaction of being able to dialectically refute the skeptic without begging the question, but we may, nevertheless, know that the skeptical hypotheses are false. This knowledge does not result from the irrelevance of the skeptical alternatives as some allege but from our being personally justified in accepting that we are not dreaming, hallucinating, deceived by an evil demon, brains in vats, and, assuming we are right in this, from our justification being complete and undefeated.

KNOWLEDGE REDUCED

The foregoing complicated set of definitions reduces to a simple formula for the definition of knowledge. Knowledge is undefeated justified acceptance. That is a formal feature of the theory. The substantive part is a coherence theory of justification in which personal justification results from a special relationship between the things one accepts, a wholly internal matter. One is personally justified in accepting something because the things one accepts inform one that such acceptance is a trustworthy guide to truth. The attainment of truth and avoidance of error are the objectives of justification. To obtain knowledge, however, such subjective justification does not suffice. An external connection is required. There must be a match between what one accepts as a trustworthy guide to truth and what really is a trustworthy guide to truth sufficient to sustain justification as error is corrected by elimination or replacement. Given the importance I attach to the trustworthiness of acceptance in yielding undefeated justification and knowledge, the substantive part of my theory might be called doxastic reliabilism, but, given that the acceptance of our trustwor-thiness yields, in the normal case, justification of its own acceptance, the theory might as well be called foundational coherentism. To obtain knowledge we need the right mix of internal coherence, reliability, and self-justification. The monster theory may appear dialectically promiscuous, but fidelity to a single approach strikes me as epistemic puritanism. The simple theory, though ever seductive, is usually the mistress of error. The queen of truth is a more complicated woman but of better philosophical parts.

NOTE

Research on this paper was supported by a grant from the National Science Foundation and a fellowship from the John Simon Guggenheim Memorial Foundation. I am indebted to John Pollock, Alvin Goldman, Peter Klein, Scott Sturgeon, and Marian David for comments on early drafts.

Circularity and Coherence

The main objection to the coherence theory is that it is circular. In the past, it was commonplace to dismiss the theory on this ground without worrying about the details. Following Sellars (1963), recent exponents of the theory such as Lehrer (1974, 1986) have argued that the objection can be met. I will argue that circularity actually covers two distinct problems. One is that perceptual beliefs and the covering belief that we are reliable perceivers must be justified *before* the other, leading to a regress that can only be broken by moving in a circle. I think Sellars has a plausible reply to this. The other version of the objection is more troublesome and, I think, ultimately fatal. It is that the theory takes all warrant to be relative to other beliefs and so cannot accept new epistemic input into the system. Let us consider them in turn.

I. As we saw, the theory holds that first-level knowledge (i.e., knowledge of appearances or, if the defender accepts direct realism, knowledge of nearby physical objects) presupposes knowledge of reliability. The obvious way to show that a mechanism is reliable is to show that past successes outweigh failures; that is, that more true beliefs result from the mechanism than false. From this, we can posit an underlying mechanism to explain the regularity. Having a true belief on this occasion, then, cannot be an accident. This commits the theory to holding that the lower level depends on a higher one for its credibility since perceptual beliefs have no warrant, according to the theory, unless the more general statement does. The problem is that such generalizations are empirical and can be justified only by appeal to perceptual beliefs. This leads to a chain of justification in which the perceptual depends on the more general which in turn depends on the perceptual.

This is not immediately a circle. The perceptual judgments that justify reliability need not be the same ones we are validating by justifying reliability. My belief that this is red might be credible only because I can show that I am a reliable indicator of colors, but my judgment about my reliability might be based on the testimony of others (ultimately my parents or teachers perhaps) and not rest on any color judgments. Nevertheless it is difficult to see how we could avoid a circle. Since perception can only be justified if appropriate generalizations about reliability are justified and these must themselves be based on perception, it seems inevitable that we will be forced to hold at some point that the two levels justify each other. It is also difficult to understand how we could have inductive support for the generalization without having acquired justified perceptual beliefs over a period of time before the generalization becomes justified. Yet, according to the theory, none of these particular beliefs are justified until enough have been acquired to justify the generalization that we are reliable. The coherentist holds, in other words, that the perceptual judgments must be justified *before* the generalization even though this must be justified *before* the perceptual mechanisms can yield any justified beliefs. The result is a regress.

Sellars discusses this objection in part VIII of 'Empiricism and the Philosophy of Mind' (1963, p. 164). He argues that Jones could know that he is reliable because he can now cite prior occasions on which his spontaneous utterances were confirmed even though those utterances were not justified on those occasions. The theory "requires only that it is correct to say that Jones *now* knows, thus remembers, that these particular facts *did* obtain. It does not require that it be correct to say that at the time these facts did obtain he *then knew* them to obtain." There is thus no regress (1963, p. 169).

The point is that we can recall evidence of reliability even though our perceptual judgments at the earlier time were not warranted until we can defend our reliability. At t_1, I might respond to stimuli correctly and at t_2 become aware that I am a reliable perceiver because I responded correctly at t_1. The perceptual judgments at t_1 are not justified, according to Sellars, because I am not able to defend my reliability; after t_2, however, they are because I remember the earlier occasions and can show that I am reliable. Sellars can thus argue that there is no circle or regress; level-1 and level-2 beliefs become justified together at t_2.

Sellars assumes that the circularity objection is a problem about the temporal sequence of justification. As he sees it, the objection is that perceptual judgments must be justified *before* the generalization if empiricism is true whereas the coherence theory is committed to holding that the generalization that supports reliability must be justified *before* the perceptual judgments. His solution is that the two levels can become justified at the same time, breaking the chain.

This assumes that propositions can become justified in groups rather than one at a time. I think this is an important insight on Sellars' part. The problem is to make sense out of this holistic justification. How can cognitive acts occur in quantum steps, in "batteries," as he says (1963, p. 148), rather than one at a time? For the moment, I will concentrate on this aspect of his answer and assume that there are no special problems about the mutual dependence of the levels.

We might distinguish two forms of coherence theory depending on how extensive the justificatory units are taken to be. A broader theory will hold that nothing is justified unless everything is, or, in other words, that the entire body of empirical knowledge is of a piece, no part of which can stand on its own. Such a theory is reminiscent of the 19th century theories that "truth" at any stage in science is partial until we reach the completed system. A narrower theory would hold that beliefs become justified in groups smaller than the sum total of knowledge. The broader theory is the epistemic analogue to Wittgenstein's extreme claim that "understanding a sentence means understanding a language" (1958, p. 5). I don't think there is any reason to attribute the broader theory to Sellars, however. Perceptual claims fall into groups relating to the senses involved and kinds of properties perceived, e.g., color, shape. One might be a good perceiver of shapes and yet be color blind and tone deaf. Sellars could hold that the claims that have to be justified together need not extend to all the senses or all sensed qualities.

This still does not explain the essential claim of holism, namely, that justification occurs in quantum leaps rather than incrementally. It might be said that the problem is not with the size of the unit, but with the claim that justification occurs in jumps at all. So far as I can see, Sellars does not explain this process; and, as we will see, he also has a problem with the circularity of justification considered nontemporally. The obscurity of holism, however, is not peculiar to Sellars' theory or to coherence theories of justification, but, I think, is a problem for empiricism in general.

Consider the empiricist account of color sensation. Most have held that we can acquire the concept of red simply by having a sensation of red. We then go on to justify the proposition that something appears (say) red; from this, along with other beliefs, we can justify beliefs about apples and cars. There are two ways in which this theory is plausible only if several mental acts occur at once.

First, color sensations require experience of contrasting colors. If we experienced only one color, we probably would not have any color sensations at all. A person with limited experience of shades of red also has a more rudimentary understanding of red than a person who has had wide experience. This suggests that a color concept cannot be acquired by a single sensation, or even by many sensations of the same color. We need a range of different sensations. If this is right, the empiricist is committed to holding that color concepts occur in batteries rather than one at a time regardless of his views on coherence versus foundations.

Holism is also implied by the traditional account of concept acquisition. Foundationalists usually hold that we get a concept by (a) having repeated sensations over time, (b) recognizing the similarities, then (c) finally acquiring the concept. When this happens, we become aware of the appearance and, so, acquire the premises we need to justify other propositions; e.g., we come to believe that something looks red. The process from (a) to (c) is thought to be temporal in that the sensations occur first and the concepts later. This turns out to be incoherent, however. A sensation is an awareness of a certain sort of appearance. It is thus a cognitive state and can occur only if one already has the concept. In other words, to have a sensation of red in this sense, one must have the concept of red; step (a) is impossible unless we have the concept of red even though we are supposed to have sensations before concepts. (See Meyers, 1981, for a fuller statement of the problem).

The only way to salvage the theory—and, I think, what was intended all along—is to hold that sensations in step (a) are not cognitive, but are physical stimulations of the sense organs. These do not result in awareness until the similarities have been recognized and one has the concept. On this interpretation, the theory holds that the sensation (in the cognitive sense, i.e., the awareness of the color), having the concept and coming to know that something looks red *all occur at once*. If this is the only defensible version of the traditional theory, the foundationalist is just as committed to quantum jumps as the coherence theory and so cannot rest his case solely on the obscurity of holism.

2. The more basic problem is the coherence theory's claim that all justification is immanent. We might admit that background beliefs play a role in evaluating propositions. But we cannot hold that we can increase the credibility of one proposition simply by believing another. I do not increase the credibility of believing that the mayor is Republican by also believing that 90 per cent of the voters are Republican. First, the beliefs have to be arrived at independently. If I believe that 90 per cent of the voters are Republican *because* I believe that the mayor is, the first belief cannot increase the credibility of the belief about the mayor. How can the warrant of p be increased by believing q if one of the factors influencing my believing q is my believing p? Second, supporting propositions must have independent warrant as well. Suppose we come to believe q by flipping a coin. Belief in q is causally independent of p in this case, but it does not raise the credibility of p unless there also is some ground for q or q has some initial credibility of its own. As we shall see, this second problem is crucial.

Stated generally, the objection is that, if coherence is the sole criterion, all warrant is relative to other beliefs and there is no reason to think one set is preferable to any other no matter how bizarre or fabulous. Lewis (1952, p. 173) put the problem as follows:

If no probability statement is categorically assertable, without probability qualification,

then I think the whole system of such could provide no better assurance of anything in it than that which attaches to a well-written novel. I see no hope for such a coherence theory which repudiates data of experience which are simply given—or no hope unless a postulate be added to the effect that *some* synthetic statements are probable a priori; the postulate, for example, that every perceptual belief has *some* probability just on account of being a perceptual belief.

Several points should be noted about this. Lewis recognizes that the given is not the only option to coherence; we might postulate initial probability. He also suggests that we must have certainty although he concedes that intrinsic probability might do. (See Cornman, 1977, for a discussion and rejection of Lewis' requirement of certainty.) But the main point is that coherence will not warrant any beliefs if it is the only source of warrant, i.e., if no propositions are "categorically assertable."

The coherentist might reply that coherence has to be applied globally to all our beliefs and not just selectively to some. This would rule out subsets of beliefs that are coherent in themselves (as a novel might be) but incoherent with the rest of our beliefs. The theory does not have to accept every piece of internally coherent fiction as actual history; if it fails to cohere with our other beliefs, we are warranted in treating it as fiction. But this is not the most serious challenge. Lewis is also arguing that warrant cannot rest solely on immanent relations among beliefs, *no matter how extensive the set.* The entire set of our beliefs might be like a well-written novel, if there is no independent source of warrant. Coherence with this set then does not make it knowledge.

This is a familiar objection, but its force is often underestimated. Bonjour (1976, p. 289) takes the objection to be that coherence is not sufficient to pick out one unique system of beliefs since there are always equally plausible alternatives. His answer to this takes just half a paragraph (pp. 302–303). He argues that since the coherence theory can allow for input through observation, we cannot construct alternatives at will; new beliefs will always be entering the system and "there is no reason to think that one objective world will go on providing coherent input to incompatible systems in the long run." (The answer is repeated in his later treatment (1985, p. 144).)

This takes the objection to be that coherence leaves our theory of the world underdetermined, even in the long run. As Bonjour notes, however, all theories are subject to the same objection, including foundations theories. This is not the central problem, however. Spontaneous beliefs might add to our stock of beliefs; they might also force rejection of old beliefs where there are inconsistencies. But none of this shows that we ought to worry about inconsistencies between these beliefs and our old beliefs, if the only warranting condition is coherence. If coherence is the only ground of credibility for a belief, only those that cohere with other beliefs will have any warrant. If a new belief challenges old beliefs, we have no reason to worry about it unless it has independent warrant and this is just what it lacks, according to the coherence theory. And if a new belief coheres with old beliefs, we have no reason to cheer since neither it nor the other beliefs have independent warrant; it is all warrant relative to other beliefs, none of which we have any reason to accept on their own merits. Lewis' objection is that at best the coherence theory gives relative warrant just as we find in a novel where everything fits but nothing has warrant in itself. The statements in the novel form a circle: each is credible *given the others* but none has any claim to acceptance in itself.

Lehrer (1986, p. 21) takes a different strategy. Bonjour (1976, pp. 291 ff.) thinks each belief must be justified by appeal to an argument; in the case of perception, one must be able to give the covering argument about one's reliability. Lehrer holds that some beliefs are justified without argument even though they are justified only because of coherence with other beliefs. His aim is to avoid the charge of circularity while still taking coherence to be the only justifying condition. Roughly, his view is that a proposition has credibility only if it coheres with one's "acceptance system," i.e., the set of propositions one accepts (see 1986, pp. 8–9, for details). Like Bonjour, Lehrer does not have to hold that each observational belief is coherent with this system; it is enough that the reliability of the process that generates such a belief cohere with it. But Lehrer does not require that this dependence be spelled out in an argument in order for observation to provide warrant. If the knower has beliefs about his reliability and these stand in suitable relations with others, they are justified and new beliefs generated by them have warrant as well, even though he can't put all this together as an argument.

This still does not avoid the circularity, however. Lehrer holds that p has credibility only if the beliefs in the acceptance system have credibility. The credibility of p is still relative to the credibility of the other beliefs. The question is: what is the source of credibility for these propositions? Again the answer has to be coherent with other beliefs in the acceptance system. Clearly the warrant is all relative to other beliefs, which in turn have no independent warrant of their own. As a result, there is no fresh warrant, i.e., no epistemic input. New beliefs are occurring spontaneously all the time, but this is just a psychological fact. A novelist has new "beliefs" about his characters as he writes, but they do not make the work more historical even if they cohere perfectly with what went before. The fact that we do not have to provide the argument to show that a source is reliable, then, does not save the theory from the charge of circularity, that is, from the charge that relations among beliefs must be supplemented with some other source of warrant.

I think Lehrer would argue that at best this shows that the coherence theory is circular—which is hardly surprising—but that there is no reason to think that the circle is vicious. In a similar fashion, Sellars admits that the theory is circular since perceptual beliefs and its presuppositions must be justified together in spite of their dependency. (This, I think, is what is meant by "nonlinear" justification, a term stressed by Bonjour (1985, pp. 90–93).) Sellars obviously thinks this strategy defuses circularity while acknowledging it. Is this an acceptable reply?

The issue is whether the mutual dependence of beliefs is viciously circular. I think a good case can be made for thinking it is. The most plausible account of vicious circularity is that the argument "p therefore q" is viciously circular if and only if you could not know that the premise p is true (or be warranted in accepting it) without knowing that the conclusion q is also, even though p is intended as the ground for q. This puts the notion in terms of arguments, but it need not be considered to be a claim about inference or the acquisition of beliefs in time. The point is that p cannot provide a ground for q if it cannot be known or warranted independently of q, no matter how strong the coherence relation between them. (A non-vicious circle is an argument in which the premiss depends on the conclusion but is known independently. If the premiss and conclusion are equivalent, the argument may be said to be circular but not viciously so, since the premiss might be known independently of the conclusion even though the conclusion implies the premiss.)

An example of a vicious circle is this. Suppose someone believes (1) that the resurrection of Jesus proves the Bible to be reliable; his ground for this is (2) that 500 witnesses saw Jesus after his death, and his ground for this is (3) that the Bible says that 500 people saw him. This justification is obviously circular, but it is also viciously so. The grounds for accepting the Bible's reliability are certain claims that are acceptable only by assuming its reliability. The only ground offered for thinking that 500 witnesses saw Jesus is that the Bible says so; this then cannot be used to show its reliability as a source of knowledge. (Compare Moore's example, 1966, p. 44.)

If we apply this notion to the coherence theory, the circle does seem to be vicious. Since the reliability of perceptual mechanisms is an empirical question and hence rests on perception, it seems impossible for one to know (or have warrant) for perceptual reliability without perceptual judgments having warrant even though such judgments are (according to the coherence theory) credible only on condition that we know that we are reliable. The fact that one can come to believe the propositions all at once does not show that their epistemic dependence is acceptable any more than the fact that one can come to believe the different propositions in the Bible case at the same time shows that it isn't viciously circular to base the Bible's reliability on claims that assume its reliability. We might claim that this circle is "virtuous" or christen it a holistic justification or say that it is "nonlinear," but none of this is convincing without an account of how such justification differs from the Bible case. Without such an account, these terms amount to nothing more than a refusal to admit the viciousness of the circle by calling it something else—a common

enough fault where viciousness is concerned but hardly an adequate defense.

However the coherentist replies, one response is clearly inadmissible. He cannot argue that justification rests solely on some large number of our beliefs being true regardless of whether we can show this non-circularly or not. This would make knowledge depend on relations between our beliefs and facts external to them even though he claims that all justification is internal and immanent. (Lehrer's notion of "verific justification," i.e., coherence with the acceptance system after it has been purged of error, suggests this response (1986, p. 8).) I will argue in the next chapter that this externalist reply is an acceptable answer to most skeptical arguments. However, the coherentist cannot appeal to it without giving up his theory. He holds that the fact of reliability is not enough to make a perceptual mechanism a source of warrant; we also need a covering argument or at least a covering belief, if we accept Lehrer's version. If he is forced to defend coherence on the ground that enough of the test set is true even though we have no independent covering argument for this, why do we need such an argument in the case of perception? In fact, the coherence theory cuts itself off from an externalist defense by insisting that all justification is internal and immanent.

REFERENCES

BonJour, L. "The Coherence Theory of Empirical Knowledge." *Philosophical Studies*, 30 (1976), 281–312.

BonJour, L. *The Structure of Empirical Knowledge*. Cambridge, MA: Harvard University Press, 1985.

Cornman, J. "On Acceptability Without Certainty." *Journal of Philosophy* 74 (1977), 29–47.

Lehrer, K. "The Coherence Theory of Knowledge." *Philosophical Topics* 14 (1986), 5–25.

Lehrer, K. *Knowledge*. Oxford: Oxford University Press, 1974.

Lewis, C. I. "The Given Element in Experience." *Philosophicl Review*. 61 (1952), pp. 168–175.

Meyers, Robert. "Sellar's Rejection of Foundations." *Philosophical Studies*. 39 (1981), 61–78.

Sellars, Wilfrid. *Science, Perception and Reality*. London: Humanities Press, 1963.

Wittgenstein, Ludwig. *The Blue and Brown Books*. New York: Harper and Row, 1958.

from Real Knowing: New Versions of Coherence Theory

WHY COHERENCE? WHY EPISTEMOLOGY?

Epistemology has too often operated as a private conversation presuming to sit in judgment on the whole expanse of human knowledge yet separating itself from actually existing knowers. Epistemologists pare down the complex variety of real knowing practices to a few supposedly paradigmatic cases ("Jones owns a Ford") whose simplicity is purported to allow a close examination of epistemic justification. As a result, philosophers continue to struggle over finely tuned analyses of simple inferences, observational beliefs, and memory while other fields have moved light years ahead in developing more complex and realistic accounts of socially and historically situated belief-formation. In an era that has seen knowledge increasingly produced through international networks in virtual space-time, too many epistemologists seem content to spend their lives analyzing the belief "The cat is on the mat." Sometimes it seems as if the information age has passed philosophy by.

This book arises out of a concern that epistemologists must begin to reflect on and address recent developments in the analysis of how knowledge and meaning are actually produced, how science truly proceeds, and how certain bodies of theory get to count as knowledge. No longer can we envision an individual knower grappling with nature's secrets, or a text as having a single, decisive interpretation. No longer can we assume that power and desire are eliminable elements for either justification or belief-formation. Nor can we romanticize science or the university as politically neutral meritocracies unsullied by racist and sexist hierarchies of class, nor plausibly maintain that such facts have no significant bearing on the theoretical products of these institutions.

Of course, I am romanticizing "our" agreement on these issues. On the basis of the statements I have just made, many analytic philosophers will close this book right now. Even Richard Rorty, the enfant terrible of the American Philosophical Association, tends to dismiss much of current continental philosophy, which invokes concepts such as "power" and "desire," as faddish, anarchist nonsense. In a similarly dismissive move, many continental philosophers seem to believe that epistemology and perhaps philosophy itself have outlived their paradigms and must face the revolutionary firing squad. Michel Foucault himself, despite his concern with knowledge, evidently believed that epistemology was obsolescent. I have little sympathy for either of these dismissals. As I shall argue in the following pages, there is an ongoing need for theorizing knowledge in a fashion that is epistemic and not just sociological, that is, which understands that the line of demarcation between truth and falsehood is not in every case completely determined by and reducible to ideology, mob rule, or unconscious desires. The dawning recognition that such elements as desire and power are *always* involved in the determination of validity conditions for knowledge does not entail the claim that they are *all* that is involved. At the same time, there is a pressing need to produce epistemologies that will acknowledge the ubiquity of these elements in all processes of knowing. The task of epistemologists is therefore not outdated; it just has become more difficult.

Why Epistemology?

This book is located within what is, I hope, an emerging paradigm shift in epistemology that might broadly call itself "social epistemology" (although the work that currently uses that name is still too narrow, in my estimation).[1] This new paradigm is identifiable by its project to address both of the following concerns: the need for a normative theory of knowledge that can offer an epistemic account of how evaluative distinctions between competing claims should (and can) be made, and the need for an account of knowledge that is self-conscious about the interconnections between knowledge, power, and desire. Such a project would try to answer the following questions: Given a richer and more politically attuned analysis of the production of knowledge, how should we *epistemically* characterize a validity claim? Which criteria should be given priority in demarcating better and worse theoretical claims? How, given our new (forced) self-consciousness, are we to conceptualize the precise nature of the relationship between politics and knowledge?

These questions suggest and, I will argue, require a dialogue between analytic and continental philosophy. Analytically trained epistemologists have made significant contributions to our understanding of knowledge, justification, and belief, but they have generally been unwilling to explore the implications that follow from recent work in the sociology of knowledge, feminist epistemologies, continental theories of meaning and interpretation, and the whole press of forces which are demanding that we begin to take a close look at the politics of knowledge. Epistemologists should not continue to act like ostriches in the face of these new developments and pretend that they are either wholly and completely false or entirely irrelevant to contemporary epistemological theory. The corresponding mistake, made by many continental philosophers and those influenced by them, is to pretend that we need only expose the faulty presumptions of reference and the fictional binaries in traditional accounts of knowledge. But this critical focus conveniently overlooks the continental philosophers' own claims to epistemic authority, claims that need not rest on referential ontologies to be authoritative. By refusing to offer new validity conditions for justified belief, these theorists only protect their own implicit epistemological commitments from scrutiny. Part of the task of this book is to reveal these commitments, in the work of Hans-Georg Gadamer and Foucault, so as to assess and learn from them.

I shall argue that no account of knowledge, *pace* the wishes of many analytic and continental philosophers (surprisingly in agreement on this point), can be separated ultimately from an account of truth and ontology. Any claim to validity, authorization, or legitimation implies a position on how the world is to be conceptualized and understood in its relation to the sphere of the social and the knowledge under dispute. Claims to know are claims *about something,* and the way in which this "aboutness" is understood, as well as the way the "something" is conceptualized, needs to be explored. Traditional realist notions of reference and representation do not exhaust all the possibilities. I believe that Jacques Derrida no less than Roderick Chisholm has a metaphysics implicit in his discourse on *différance* and the (inevitable) deferral of meaning. (This statement sounds counterintuitive because we have come to define truth monolithically as correspondence, as I will discuss shortly.) In analytic terms, my claim is simply that justification requires truth-conduciveness, and that truth is nonreducible to language; in other words, the validity conditions for any serious speech act will involve a presupposed commitment to specific metaphysical views. Analytic philosophy cannot skirt the question of the ontology of truth or hide its ontological commitments behind its semantics, as I shall try to show: Alfred Tarski's equivalency schema ("P" is true iff p) does not say everything there is to say about truth, and the correspondence theory can no longer be taken as self-evident. Similarly, continental philosophy cannot repudiate dominant notions of truth without implying an alternative conception of reality as well as an alternative criterion of validity. The point is not so much to shift the research agenda of continental philosophy to epistemological reconstruction as it is to suggest that such reconstruction has already implicitly begun in writings that offer metacritiques of philosophy. But the question of truth must be brought out into the open.

It will be obvious by now that my usage of terms such as epistemology, metaphysics, and ontology swims upstream from current philosophical fashions. In these pages *metaphysics* will not refer only to the working out of first principles; *epistemology* will not refer to a foundationalist, antiskeptical project; nor will *ontology* refer to the carving up of essential categories. These traditional definitions represent specific problematics or research programs, not the whole or defining criteria of the enterprises. I want to promote a usage of these terms which will be more general and therefore more inclusive, and so in these pages *epistemology* will refer to the theorizing of knowledge, and *metaphysics* and *ontology* will refer to the theorizing of reality, full stop.

Besides, what is most original about contemporary postmodernist (for want of a better word) theory is not that epistemology and metaphysics have finally been abandoned, although it is true that how knowledge and reality are conceptualized and understood has been radically transformed. Postmodernism is still engaged in the work of conceptualizing knowledge and reality in some way recognizably continuous with the philosophical work that has gone before. Its originality lies, rather, in its large-scale attack on the borders and boundaries between philosophy and other enterprises of theoretical thinking. The autonomy and integrity of epistemology, for example—considered to be unique and separable from sociology, political theory, and psychology, among other disciplines—can no longer hold firm. The new theory understands that questions about the justification of belief require cross-disciplinary exploration, and that such forays cannot be restricted to the biological sciences or to artificial intelligence studies, as analytic philosophers seem to think. I realize many philosophers hold that sociology and related disciplines may tell us how beliefs *actually* attain justification, but that epistemology alone pursues the question how they *should* attain justification. But this border between the normative and the sociological is perhaps the most important border that needs to be crossed, as this study will try to show. Let those of us working in the United States never forget that border control has no intrinsic value.

Why Coherence?

It is precisely the breakup of the old borders between disciplines, and of the dichotomies and dualisms marking those borders, that brings us to coherence epistemologies. If Rorty is correct (which he is, occasionally), Donald Davidson's conversion to coherentism was motivated by the project to think past a subject/object dualism or mediation which posits the two as separable poles with language in between.[2] Rorty also associates this coherentist project with Harold Bloom's claim that the meaning of a poem can be found only in its relations to other poems, a view that (in its numerous and varied incarnations) has become de rigueur among contem-

porary literary critics. A further movement toward coherence can be found among the historicist philosophers of science, including Imre Lakatos, Larry Laudan, and even Karl Popper, for whom both the meaning and the validation of scientific theories is to be found ultimately in their relationships to other theories.[3]

Throughout these disparate fields of inquiry, coherentism signifies the view that would seek to explain meaning, knowledge, and even truth by reference to the interrelationships between assorted epistemically salient elements. A typical formulation of coherentism goes as follows: "A belief is justified to the extent to which the belief-set of which it is a member is coherent."[4] What it means for a set of beliefs to be coherent is more variously defined. Some minimalist formulations of coherence require only simple consistency, while other, stronger versions require mutual entailment. The problem with the latter requirement is that it renders most actual belief sets incoherent and therefore unjustified, whereas the problem with the former is that it would force us into the position of accepting a huge number of questionable or even fictional systems as justified beliefs if only they have internal consistency. A middle position which avoids these problems requires that the elements in a belief set be mutually explanatory. This involves symmetrical relations of support rather than the relations of logical dependence implied in the concept of mutual entailment. Explanatory support can be offered by inference, correlation, analogy, or even similarity.

If a coherence theory of truth is adopted along with a coherence theory of justification, then it is held that "a proposition is true iff it is a member of a coherent set."[5] This more robust form of coherentism is the one I shall be principally interested in, since it alone offers the possibility for reconceptualizing the ontology of truth. Ontologically, robust coherentism has the neo-Hegelian aspiration to locate knowledge in such a way that the binary between nature and human construction is transcended. Knowledge has most often been defined as a kind of affinity between two essentially dissimilar entities: a linguistic item and a bit of nature or a phenomenological experience, a mental entity and a corporeal one, a systematized set of propositions and a Ding an sich. Truth has been located at the intersection, as a bridge spanning the chasm between two "worlds" or as piercing an obstructive "veil."

Coherentist epistemology, at least in its more robust manifestations and certainly as I shall treat it here, is an attempt to reconfigure and transform—not merely rearrange—the basic building blocks of truth: knowledge, reality, social practice. If this project is a viable one, it holds out the promise of avoiding the problems of both foundationalist philosophies and epistemologically nihilist ones.

Foundationalist epistemologies that identify knowledge in terms of its relationship to a mind-independent reality have become increasingly difficult to maintain. One of the principal reasons for this is the changing conception of the sciences since the nineteenth century. Science, and particularly natural science, has served as the paradigm of justified belief in the West since Bacon (although the cause of its valued status arguably has had more to do with the role science could play in the societies of burgeoning commodity capitalism and colonialism than with Bacon's formulation of the scientific method—on this view, his contribution was to provide an ideological articulation for the latest form of epistemological authoritarianism). Nonetheless, scientific beliefs had seemed to instantiate a level of objectivity elusive for other fields of inquiry. Bacon's formulation ensured this identification between science and objectivity by claiming that it is nature herself (this is Bacon's gendering, not mine) that determines which theories will be confirmed, which knowledge claims accepted and which rejected, rather than the desire of some experimental scientist or the consensus of judgment among communities of scientists.

But as science has become more and more removed from commonsense beliefs and observable experience, or, to use W. V. O. Quine's terminology, as the recognized disparity between our meager input and our torrential output has expanded, this assumption of the determining role of nature has become increasingly implausible. The past hundred years have witnessed a growing amount of evidence against and suspicion about this belief. Since Popper, it has become widely accepted, for example, that it is impossible actually to *confirm* theoretical claims in science. This is not to say that there is no reason to continue to accept science's claims, but to suggest that we must reconsider what their accept-

ability *means*. There is no available method by which we can isolate singular scientific claims for epistemic evaluation. Nor have we been able to rid science of its reliance on and use of irreducible metaphysical assumptions. The project of finding a justification for our dependence on induction has failed, at least thus far. We have not been able to explicate methodically the rules for induction or the most reliable processes for the discovery of hypotheses. For the most widely used and confirmed theory of the twentieth century—quantum mechanics—we have failed to translate its implications into a coherent ontology. And ironically, despite obvious advances in technological production, many philosophers concur that we have no way to prove that, at least in traditional realist terms, the knowledge we have about nature has actually progressed.

For many of us, the implication to be drawn from these failures, and from the growing sense that we cannot completely erase the effects of the knower on the known, is that we need to redefine and rethink what claims "to know," in science as well as elsewhere, actually mean. Analytic philosophers are overly fond of using such examples as whether "it is raining" to support correspondence theories of truth, but relatively few truth claims (and certainly none of the interesting and complicated ones) permit such easy characterizations. When any of the sciences are used in place of immediate sensory experience as the paradigm of knowledge, it quickly becomes apparent that our assumptions about truth as correspondence to the intrinsic features of a mind-independent reality and our notion of reason as a transhistorical and rule-governed methodology are dubitable and inadequate, if not laughably simplistic.

Quine and Chisholm represent two of the most important responses to this predicament that analytic epistemologists have developed. Quine has opted for a radically redefined empiricism in which coherence is the primary criterion for truth, since it is the coherence requirement that defines what can count as evidentiary support. For Quine this criterion operates outside of history, culture, or political influence. Chisholm has attempted to create a new foundation, this time not based on Descartes's skimpy enthymeme or Kant's synthetic a priori truths or Moritz Schlick's thin, unstatable observation reports but on self-presenting, incorrigible phenomenological states.

The problem here is how to move from such subjective, internal states to the torrential output of claimed knowledge. A third major response has been to reduce epistemology to semantics and deny the necessity for an ontology of truth at all (paradoxically, both Tarski and Rorty would fit here). Interestingly, all three responses involve a kind of avoidance of the problem of truth that highlights justification as the central concern of epistemology and relegates the issue of truth and its ontology to a minor if not nonparticipatory status.

I find it fascinating that, though they arise out of a significantly different historical problematic, continental treatments of knowledge have largely turned away from the ontology of truth as well. The reasons given for this turn include the new skepticism toward a naive scientific realism discussed above, but are also based on the ultimately undecidable status of meaning. If meaning is based not on identity (as it would be if it were determined by reference, for example) but rather on difference, then meaning can have no intrinsic content that remains stable outside the constantly shifting terms within multiple contexts which determine it. Unlike sameness or identity, which could offer a determinate meaning, difference always involves an open relation ("difference from x," where x is an undefined variable) and therefore it is never fixed or finally decided. In Derrida's early writings he claimed that truth talk in the West has denied this instability of meaning and has pursued identity through a metaphysics of presence, a transcendentalized ontology which would stabilize meaning. But this pursuit, according to Derrida, is grounded in a philosophical error with violent political effects. Claims to truth are inevitably grounded on elements which would undermine the claims if they were made perspicuous, and thus they inherently require exclusion and. avoidance. It is the business of deconstruction to reveal this unpleasant underside of truth-claims, the constitutive exclusions by which truth-claims maintain their illusion of full presence or identity. While Derrida has never contested either the value of truth or its existence, his belief in the infinite deferral of meaning contests truth's claim to stability and thus (so Derrida thinks) to any ontological status. The only recourse is to be anti-ontological. "Discourse, therefore, if it is originally violent, can only *do itself violence,* can only negate itself in order to affirm itself, make war upon the war which institutes it without ever *being able* to reappropriate this negativity, to the extent that it is discourse. . . . This secondary war, as the avowal of violence, is the least possible violence."[6] Derrida realizes that this anti-ontological project can never be fully carried out, but he has consistently held that the inherent violence of presence cannot be reduced by an affirmation of another presence. Thus, truth must exist without ontology.

The poststructuralist turn away from ontology has also been motivated by an acknowledgment of the constitutive influence of what is called the "other" of reason: most notably, desire and power. As already indicated, deconstruction is motivated not just by the paradoxical nature of validity claims, with their erroneous understanding of how meaning operates, but by the political absolutism that is produced by a metaphysics of presence. Truth talk serves to close down discussion and debate by claiming a relationship to a realm that is constant and fixed and therefore beyond challenge or debate. For Jean-Francois Lyotard, claims to truth, which by definition would presume to structure the field of possible moves within a language game, are "terrorist." If truth exists, it exists in the realm of the ineffable; within language, there is only heteroglossia. Therefore, "consensus has become an outmoded and suspect value."[7] According to Lyotard, we should not strive for consensus or for coherence or for any stable system, but for an open system like science, in which the only constant value is the ability to generate new and different rules.[8] Thus, many poststructuralists conclude that the problems with foundationalism point not so much toward the need for a radical rethinking of knowledge or a reconstruction of epistemology as toward a repudiation of the possibility and desirability of offering any determinate account of knowledge, or any normative epistemology at all. What I am calling epistemological nihilism is this rejection of normativity, which is based on a cynicism about the possibility of improving on the *epistemic* status of what passes for knowledge.

The dilemma between rearticulated foundationalisms and epistemologies of pure negativity is not only unsatisfactory: the thought of it can make one queasy. On the one side we have epistemologies which continue to be rooted in ahistorical pretensions, and on the other we have an apparently unresolvable nihilism. Both orientations divert us from the work at hand: reconstructing epistemology and reconceptualizing the ontology of truth with a newly awakened recognition of the complexities involved.

My working hypothesis in this book will be that, beyond or alongside the theoretical tendencies just described, there is a discernible move toward coherentism on both sides of the analytic/continental divide in philosophy. This move is motivated by a desire for a newly reconstructed epistemology, by which I mean not merely developing a new, specific theory of knowledge but reorienting epistemology's understanding of its own program of inquiry, including its goals, methods, and disciplinary location. Through an exploration of the work of Davidson, Gadamer, Foucault, and Hilary Putnam I will develop the main contours of this reconstruction and attempt to demonstrate that it can help resolve some of the impasses that are now inhibiting discussions of coherence. I will not try to develop an account of coherentist epistemology that synthesizes all the works discussed. That would be too ambitious, and the disparity between such thinkers as Davidson and Foucault is too great to produce a single epistemology, or a coherent one! Nor is my aim in this study to put forward a new and better, fully developed theory of knowledge. Rather, I intend to explore developments and themes in the new coherentist accounts of knowledge that can address long-standing objections to coherence and thus shift the debate over coherentism to new ground. I will also try to show how, through these newly articulated coherentisms, epistemology can survive the emerging self-consciousness of its own political, historical, and social embeddedness.

But why coherence in particular? A coherentist account of knowledge has the potential to clear important hurdles that previous epistemologies—primarily foundationalist ones—are inherently incapable of overcoming. There are at least three such hurdles that will be discussed throughout this book.

First, coherentism can provide a more realistic and feasible account of the way in which beliefs are justified than accounts that would require an uninterpreted, pretheoretical, self-presenting experiential state or mode of cognition. Coherentism traditionally holds that beliefs are justified by other beliefs, which means that a correspondence relation between beliefs and an extradiscursive, transparent reality is not required for knowledge. The experience and empirical evidence that play a determining role in the confirmation of many beliefs can be acknowledged as themselves the product (at least in part) of interpretation and theoretical commitments. This follows because on a coherentist view experience and evidence are recognized as beliefs, not self-presenting phenomenological states whose meaning is transparent. Coherentism also takes account of the actual mechanisms most often used to judge new contenders for belief: their plausibility in light of the beliefs one already holds and the tendency we all have to conserve beliefs. Coherentism thus posits a picture of belief-formation that does not require the knower to be able to suspend all of her or his beliefs, and that does not present a pristine mind confronting a transparent reality, what John Dewey called the "spectator theory of knowledge" and Theodor Adorno named "peephole metaphysics." In contrast to such metaphysics, coherentism starts with a knower who always already has a great many beliefs, and thus is always already "in the world." Coherentism further recognizes that these prior beliefs interpret and inform every experience the knower has. This makes it easier for coherentism to shift from an individualist account of knowing to a collectivist account—a shift long overdue in Western epistemologies—because coherentism posits the knower as always already committed to a variety of beliefs based on the testimony of others. And this suggests that for coherentism the interpersonal and cooperative nature of belief-justification will more readily be included as part of the central issues for an epistemology to address, rather than being thought of as side issues or even irrelevant considerations. (Of course, it is true that Anglo-American coherentisms have by and large failed to address this issue. But I am arguing here for the *potential* of coherentist epistemologies, a potential that is developed by the theorists I shall be discussing).

A second advantage is that coherentism can provide a way to show how and why apparently disparate elements are and even should be involved in theory-choice and belief-justification. Political considerations, moral commitments, even metaphysical beliefs, have not been considered germane to the justification of beliefs that claim referentiality or truth, and desire and power—the "other" of reason—are regarded as even less relevant. To admit the ineliminable influence of such elements would seem to spell the demise of any hope for knowledge. But this is only because traditionally dominant accounts of justification have presented, as Peirce said long ago, a linear, single-line, inferential model of knowledge in which politics, values, and desire could only be seen as obstacles at worst, irrelevant at best.[9] Coherentist models, in which the process of justification involves not a single linear chain of inference but a complicated, heterogeneous web of belief, make it much easier to see how different kinds of elements can be involved not only in justification but in justification-conferring. On a linear model, the claim that authoritarianism is involved in the justification of master-molecule theories will seem highly implausible; the two ideas may appear metaphorically similar but it will be difficult to show how a biological theory could reasonably follow from a political premise which operates in a different plane of discourse. On a coherentist model, however, the metaphorical similarity between political authoritarianism and mastermolecule theories can be seen to offer mutual support, and thus the relevance of various political assumptions to theory-choice in the sciences can be more easily explained, and explained in a way that does not attribute intentional bias to most scientists (or, for that matter, philosophers). Where coherence is taken to be the principal criterion for knowledge, and where the entire web is involved in the process (though different parts of the web are involved to different degrees), it becomes much easier to account for the inclusion of politics in science, ethics in epistemology, and desire in philosophy.[10]

The third advantage that coherentist accounts can claim accrues only to what I have called more robust accounts, when coherence is taken to involve in some manner the definition of truth rather than (as Laurence Bonjour argues, for example) simply the means by which one can achieve truth in the sense of correspondence. Less prejudicially, I will refer to the latter as coherentist accounts of justification, whereas when a coherentist account theorizes both justification and truth via coherence I will refer to it as a coherentist epistemology. I will argue that an advantage of the latter is that it can offer what might be called an immanent account of knowledge.

Coherence epistemology is frequently cited as the principal contender against and ultimate contrast with a foundationalist view.[11] I believe that this opposition is based primarily on the fact that coherentism offers an immanent account of knowledge against foundationalism's transcendental account. For coherentism, knowledge is ultimately a product of phenomena that are immanent to human belief systems and practices, social organizations, and lived reality, whereas for foundationalism, if a belief is to count as knowledge it must ultimately be able to establish some link to transcendent phenomenon or to something that is entirely extrinsic to human existence (that is, the way the world would be if we had never existed). Whereas foundationalism ties justification to an external realm beyond beliefs and belief sets and understands truth as a relationship of a certain sort with this external realm, coherentism holds to an understanding of knowledge as immanent. Justification is an immanent feature of beliefs in that it refers to their interrelationships, and if truth is defined as what coheres, truth is also emergent from immanent relationships rather than from relationships with an external or transcendental realm.

This immanent account is advantageous principally because it does not require us to first posit and then find access to a realm defined as beyond all human interpretation and knowledge. Nor does it necessitate establishing a God's-eye view so that we can step outside of language, all belief systems, and interpretive modes to check on the correspondence between human claims and an extrahuman reality. This is not because coherentism posits a Berkeleyan idealism in which reality is conceived to be causally determined by "mind" or simply to consist in mental properties, but because, at least as I shall tell the story, coherentism starts from a Hegelian phenomenological ontology that sets up no absolute separation between human beings and the world but sees us as always already in the world, engaged in practical activities, encumbered with myriad beliefs and commitments, and constitutively linked in various complex ways to that about which we are seeking to know. This is a more metaphysically adequate descriptive starting point from which to think about knowledge, and it has the added bonus of making the problem of skepticism vanish from the frame. It also allows us, as I shall argue in later chapters, to account for the historical and social embeddedness of all truth-claims without lapsing into epistemological nihilism.

For all these reasons, which shall be developed in more detail in the pages that follow, coherentism has at least the potential to provide a more realistic account of the way in which we make our epistemic commitments. Like Marx, I will hold that no absolute separation should exist between the way in which we actually justify our beliefs and the way in which we *should* justify them: all prescriptive proposals must be grounded firmly in current, actual practices since these alone can circumscribe the possible. This is not to say that the realm of the actual will dictate the epistemic good, but that there is a normative relevance to having realistic accounts of the production of knowledge.

The above three points serve to justify this excursion into coherentist epistemology by arguing that coherence can overcome some of the current impasses in the theorizing of knowledge. But what about the theoretical impasses within coherence accounts themselves? There are certainly many of these. Coherentism has been charged with irreducible vagueness, with justifying coherent fictions, with being unable to privilege experience or empirical sources of evidence, with placing overly stringent requirements on justification, and with entailing an absolute relativism between coherent systems. These traditional objections have recently been given adequate answers by Ralph C. S. Walker, Bonjour, Davidson, Jonathan Dancy, and others, and thus should not continue to debilitate the development of coherentist accounts.[12] There are still more objections, however, which have not been answered adequately as yet, and thus continue to deserve serious attention. I will use the authors discussed herein to suggest new refutations to these objections. Both the objections and the answers to them that I shall develop are briefly outlined below.

(1) The criterion of coherence itself as the test of knowledge would seem to have no necessary connection to truth; the fact that a claim coheres to a body of beliefs does not establish it as true or likely to be true unless that body of beliefs can be shown to be true. The puzzle then becomes, if one wants what is sometimes called a pure coherence theory, how to establish that a body of beliefs is true on the basis of coherence alone, since it is certainly the case that a body of beliefs may attain a high level of coherence without being truthful. This has been perhaps the most serious objection to coherence accounts of

knowledge since their inception, and no fully adequate answer has been developed that does not simply define knowledge as coherence or base its claim on making an appeal to noncoherentist elements. I will argue that the new versions of coherentism discussed here, and most importantly the work of Gadamer, suggest a new answer to this old objection, principally through devising a new ontology of truth or an account of the relationship between true beliefs and reality. This new ontology is not merely an ad hoc, opportunist maneuver tacked on in order to establish the truth-conduciveness of coherence as a criterion of knowledge, but a different ontology with independent arguments in its favor.

(2) The second objection I will address does not originate among analytic philosophers. In fact, what I am calling an objection here does not even address itself to coherence epistemology, and yet it presents in my view one of the most serious obstacles coherentism must face. Joseph Rouse has recently offered a critique of accounts that present science as a "field of practices rather than a network of statements."[13] He suggests that the work of Thomas Kuhn, among others, constitutes a significant trend in philosophy of science away from "representationalist, theory-dominant" accounts in favor of ones that highlight science's practical and experimental everyday character. To distill science into the set of truth-claims in statement form collected in journal articles and textbooks, or to equate its documentary aspects with the entirety of "science," is phenomenologically incorrect and has led to many egregious mistakes in the epistemologies of science, since such distillations present distorted images of the actual processes by which theories are chosen.

I would make a broader claim about knowledge as a whole, similar to Rouse's claim about philosophies of science. To distill the amalgam of knowing practices into a string of propositions to which I can give or from which I may withhold mental assent, is a mistake begun by Descartes and mystifyingly persistent in contemporary epistemology. Aristotle knew that propositional knowledge was not the only kind of knowledge, as did Gilbert Ryle, Wittgenstein, and the American pragmatists. I suggest that feminist epistemologies and recent continental accounts of knowledge are also more open to the idea that knowledge is, as Rouse describes science, a field of practices only some of which can be translated into propositional form and represented in a logical schema.

Coherentist accounts of knowledge have repeated this erroneous focus on propositions. Coherence accounts, remember, tie everything to beliefs: webs of belief, systems of statements, networks of propositions.[14] Coherence describes justification as a process whereby a grouping of beliefs is brought to bear on a contending belief. Thus it is clear that coherence epistemologies are very much predisposed to view knowledge as consisting entirely in statements and sets of statements.

Foucault's work can be usefully applied to this problem, since he suggests a form of coherentism that does not focus mostly or exclusively on statements but includes a larger constellation of elements. Foucault, continuing the tradition of Aristotle, Ryle, Wittgenstein, and the pragmatists, conceives of knowledge not only as beliefs but also as networks of practices and forms of life. For Foucault, the coherence necessary for knowledge must link a wide range of disparate elements—modes of perception, experimental methods, skills, experiential interiority, and institutions—all interwoven with power effects and various pleasures. Foucault's understanding of knowledge thus makes it possible to avoid the statement-dominant problem and suggests an expanded conception of coherence whose many advantages I will strive to retrieve from their obscurity.

(3) A final objection I will take seriously is one that will be found not in analytic circles but among poststructuralists. This objection would hold that coherence itself is a misguided goal, because it is doomed to failure and based on totalitarian impulses. This would surely be Lyotard's and Gilles Deleuze's claim, if they were to address themselves directly to coherence epistemologies. The attribution of coherence requires similarity, sameness, and thus the denial or de-emphasis of difference. Such denials of difference are well known to have played an important role in many forms of oppression, in their attempts to force non-identicals together by erasing specificities and in their assumption that likeness has a higher value than its converse. For these reasons, the preferred aim among poststructuralists is never coherence or even consistency but heteroglossia, heterotropy, paradox, fragmentation, and paralogy. The desire for coherence is seen as a desire for control and domination, an obsession with identity, which thus produces an epistemology well-suited not only for Western imperialism but for the anal-retentive.

Fragmentation and contradiction are indeed inevitable, and the achieved balance of coherence is partial and momentary, both fallible and unstable. The view that difference is a priori problematic is both pernicious and un-necessary. But coherence does not require identity or the elimination of difference, only a way to eliminate debilitating contradictions. The pursuit of coherence and the criterion of coherence as the test of epistemic adequacy remains defensible. As Richard Bernstein and Nancy Fraser have pointed out, the problem with poststructuralism is its one-sided valorization of negativity and rupture and its inability to produce the reconstructive analyses called for by its own critiques.[15] The productive contributions of negativity and difference and the inevitability of rupture and instability do not entail that coherent systems of thought and practices cannot be developed, though they should scale down our expectations of how much can be realistically achieved, and for how long.

Furthermore, the desire for coherence can come from a variety of sources, not all of which are pernicious or pathological; it is ironically a universalist error for poststructuralists to hold that coherentist aspirations are always grounded in something politically retrograde. Consider the desire to appease one's conflicting moral commitments as far as possible, which Martha Nussbaum discusses in rich concreteness within an argument that overall seeks to establish the very impossibility of perfect coherence.[16] Or consider the desire for coherence that Simone de Beauvoir describes in her analysis of the forced contradictions between constructed femininities and the achievement of personhood.[17] While ruptures may be inevitable, the desire for coherence is inevitable as well and can often be productive. Fragmentation and conflict can be painful to live through, and while I too share the current sensibilities toward finding positive elements in irreconcilable differences rather than uselessly pining for a lost sense of oneness, it remains the case that harmony is at least some of the time an understandable as well as realistic goal.

The cautious attitude toward coherence that poststructuralism displays is also shared by some critical theorists who work in the tradition of the Frankfurt School. Adorno argued that for those of us interested in social criticism and social change within the context of "affirmative culture" (commodity capitalism), it is of paramount necessity to find and produce negation and contradiction. But the productive effects of determinate negation (a goal shared by all self-respecting neo-Hegelians) only work within a context where the contradiction produced by the negation pushes forward a new and higher synthesis, motivated precisely by the discomfort caused by conflict and the absence of coherence. Rupture thus produces social change *because* of the desire for coherence, and the subsequent determination of those who recognize the current contradictions to rebuild new, more coherent structures.

It is also important to note that coherence can be variously defined. It need not, and in fact usually is not, equated with strict sameness or logical entailment, but with compatibility and a consistency alongside—a kind of epistemic peaceful coexistence. The dangers of authoritarianism can be offset by such milder formulations and may in fact be overstated.

I have tried to establish in this Introduction why the project of epistemology must continue, and why coherentist accounts are worth pursuing. The question that remains is, why explore the work of Gadamer, Davidson, Foucault, and Putnam within this context? An answer can only unfold in the chapters that follow.

COHERENCE IN CONTEXT

Perhaps nobody yet has been truthful enough about what "truthfulness" is.

-Friedrich Nietzsche, *Beyond Good and Evil*

In English the words "realm" and "real" share a common root, and in premodern times the word "real" meant "regal" or "royal," that is, "pertaining to the king."[18] In Spanish the word *real* still means both "real" and "royal." Such an association implies a connection between what is real and what is in the royal jurisdiction, that is, what the king controls, owns, and has dominion over. In premodern mythic Europe, the royal realm comprised all that the king could see, all the lands and peoples visible from the elevated overlook of the king's castle. This overlay of epistemic structure onto a political dominion had an effect on the ontology of truth; it might even be said to have constituted an ontology of truth whereby the real was that which was visible to the king.

This notion of the real implies a corollary concept of truth that combines both perspectivism and authoritarianism, a concept that accords with the practical history of European epistemic conventions in which epistemic credibility correlated with rank and privilege, and justification was conferred only on the perspective of the authorities.[19] The identity of these authorities was the source of much dispute, and religious leaders contended with their secular competitors for the position of truth's arbiter. Whether it was the prerogative of the Inquisitor or of the king and his court, knowledge was a possession only for elites. If you were a peasant, serf, or tradesman, your judgment in such matters about the Christian character of your neighbor Mary Smyth would be deemed irrelevant when the ranking regional cleric came to the village and pronounced her a witch. If your daughter had been "seduced" by a member of the local gentry and you went to court to accuse the noble of unfair treatment, the magistrate only need hear the noble's denial of the charge to assess his judgment of the case in the noble's favor. Peasants, women, slaves, children, Jews and many other nonelites were "known" to be liars, epistemically unreliable and unable to distinguish justified beliefs from falsehoods. Women were too irrational, peasants too ignorant, children too immature, and Jews too cunning. Slaves, as Aristotle famously argued, were so naturally prone to deceit that they had to be tortured to tell the truth.

Historical progression between epochs never creates absolute breaks; there are no total displacements, only gradations of change.[20] Is it any wonder, then, that the Enlightenment epistemologies that came after Scholasticism, whether rationalist or empiricist, continued to carry this legacy of authoritarian perspectivism? The Enlightenment attributed epistemic justification only to those subjects who could demonstrate the proper epistemic attitude, characterized by the use of reason and the maintenance of an objective stance. Unsurprisingly, these subjects turned out to be the dominant male elite. As sociologist of science Steven Shapin puts it, "Gentility powerfully assisted credibility."[21] Who could attain the new stance of objectivity required by the scientific method? Certainly not women, children, the insane, or anyone driven by impassioned commitments, whether religious or political. Shapin has shown that, in seventeenth-century England, slaves, peasants, and any other workers beholden to others for their livelihood (a group which, notice, included *all* women) were assumed to flatter, cajole, and appear agreeable of necessity, and hence to develop only with difficulty the virtue of truthfulness. Shapin's recent foray into the genealogy of modern epistemology in his book, *The Social History of Truth*, demonstrates that lower-class people who were beholden to others for their livelihood were considered unreliable because they had to acquiesce in order to support themselves; the very rich and powerful were also considered unreliable because a strict adherence to the facts might compromise their ability to protect the interests of the court and to thwart their many enemies.

> It was very widely understood in sixteenth- and seventeenth-century English society that the possession of great power and responsibility might compromise integrity, and that places of power were places where truth could thrive only with the greatest difficulty. . . . By contrast, the middle position might be accounted the place where scope for free action was greatest. Here one might be content with one's portion and be free of the necessity to secure more; here one might have easy communication with those afraid of greater men; and here one might have no need of preferment and no fear of superiors.[22]

Thus it turned out that "simple independent gentlemen," who were of independent means and in a middle-class position between the powerful and the powerless, nearly alone among the population had qualifications sufficient to pursue the truth objectively. Scientists, in particular, became the newly authorized epistemic agents, and during these centuries (recognized) scientists were nearly always Gentile males who had income-generating property. Truth was what this elite said it was.[23]

Who could master reason? Only those with a temperament sufficient for objectivity (that is, detachment), which certainly excluded the same groups listed above (peasants, women, and so forth),

and only those with sufficient education in the new doctrines of science. Thus scientists and "men of reason" were accorded the highest epistemic authority through their exclusive ability to wield reason, on the assumption that independent gentlemen had no political, social, or economic vested interest that they might want to protect or that might cloud their perceptiveness to certain areas of lived reality. This epistemic structure proved even more impervious to contestation because the open perspectivism of the monarchists and the papacy was replaced by the cloaked perspectivism of Bacon and Boyle. The Enlightenment is sometimes presented as an era which validated every adult human being's rational capacities: this is an anachronistic misreading. The fact that universal suffrage was not achieved until the twentieth century was not an aberration; it is entirely consistent with the Enlightenment's elitist conception of epistemic abilities.

The lesson to be drawn from this is not that epistemology is reducible to a strategic discourse for the maintenance of elite power. Bacon and Boyle, as well as others such as Locke and Kant, produced a rich legacy of thought about knowledge, as did the Scholastics despite their beliefs in divine authority. Critical rereadings of Enlightenment epistemologies show that they were partly structured around the legitimation of domination, but this was not their only organizing principle or theoretical effect.[24] A more attentive and contextualized reading of Western epistemology's history shows that, contrary to the usual assumption, it has never really eschewed perspectivism, as long as the perspectives that were privileged were those of the dominant elites. Nietzsche knew this, but he had no motivation to extend epistemic authority beyond the heroic masculine few who could brave God's demise. Nietzsche's only goal in revealing the inherent perspectivism in philosophy was to criticize the cowardice of universalist systems that refused to acknowledge their own self-regarding motivations.[25] His work does help to show that the subjectivity of the knower is not a new preoccupation in philosophy. Nor has it been eliminated in the modernist epistemologies, despite claims to the contrary. The problem is not simply that epistemologists have recently tried to eliminate subjectivity but failed. Rather, a symptomatic reading of the sort I have been discussing here suggests that, although modernist epistemologists have attempted to eliminate subjectivity as an overt feature of their accounts of knowledge, they have allowed a very particular subjectivity to structure their epistemologies in a more covert manner, with predictably self-validating results. Thus, it is not that we must now come to see that perspectivism is the best epistemological account, but rather that a covert perspectivism has been accepted all along.

Foundationalist epistemologies with universalist aspirations have been imprinted and constrained by what is visible, not to the king, but to the (middle-class male) philosopher, a fact which no doubt can account for, among other things, the valorization of propositional over practical knowledge, and of mental work over manual. What has been generally visible to the philosopher are the types of direct sensory knowledge available to educated males, a rudimentary understanding of science, and the prevailing common sense (read: ideology) of the European dominant classes. The sensory knowledge typically available to women and to men of the lower classes was generally out of range, as was non-European knowledge and the social perspectives of the oppressed. As a result, among philosophers metaphysical conceptions of disembodiedness flourished, a sharp evaluative demarcation was made between science and "magic," and "civilization" was identified as coextensive with European liberal societies. It is no coincidence that foundationalist epistemologies have identified the foundations for all justified belief in some variation of this rather arbitrary collection: European science (the foundation for logical positivism), the sensory experience of philosophers (the foundation for empiricism), and the available "common sense" or intuitions proper to the philosophers' gender and station (the foundation for rationalism). Thus, foundationalism has been built on top of a very particular perspectivism, through which it gained its plausibility within the philosophical milieu.

To repeat, the task in epistemology today is not, by acknowledging this perspectivism, to deconstruct or self-destruct. As many philosophers since Hegel have understood, we must come to grips with the implications of the historical and social locatedness of knowledge. This will force us to acknowledge that the Western canonical tradition (which, of course, is not *simply* Western) includes elitist epistemologies that worked to privilege dominant European males and was therefore both Eurocentric and patriarchal. But this tradition is no monolith structured by a single coherent ideology which can be assessed as a totality; it consists of polychromatic, sometimes contradictory strands which vary not only in content but also in validity and effects. Thus, what is needed is to begin to root out the philosophical underpinnings of epistemological domination, and to develop accounts of knowing that can acknowledge its multiple and heterogeneous sites of production and forms of articulation—a project that will in some respects continue the self-critical tradition of the Enlightenment and make use of its tools.

Attempting to construct a new and more effective transcendental universal will not, however, work to root out authoritarian perspectivism, since this would only replicate the erasure of the historical and social location in which all knowing is grounded. It is not perspectivism per se that is the problem with modernist epistemologies: it is the authoritarianism of their perspective.

In fact, although Hegel inaugurated the project of developing an epistemology with explicit historical and social dimensions, his own contribution toward it retained the desire to establish the absoluteness of knowledge despite its historical limits.[26] For Hegel the ultimate truth was represented by the perfect identity of subject and object, a notion which effects not a mediation of difference but its elimination. A Nietzschean-cum-Foucauldian genealogy of this conception of absoluteness, a conception in which representation does not admit of degrees and there is a singular truth about the world, would no doubt reveal that it is rooted at least in part in the desire for mastery over an infinite totality. It begets an epistemology of imperialism, or, in Hegel's terms, a freedom of the few. An epistemic mastery over the total whole is fundamentally incompatible with a recognition of knowledge's intersubjective nature as well as its perspectival roots. Intersubjective relations, unlike relations between a subject and an object, cannot generate that sort of total mastery or total identity; rather, they point toward limitation, a back-and-forth movement, and, where possible, a harmony of difference rather than an erasure of it. Perspective cannot yield totalization. Hegel's epistemological perspectivism ingenuously maintained Europe's supremacy by claiming mastery over the totality—even while it acknowledged its incapacity to transcend its own location—through a historicist dialectic in which European knowledge sublated all other forms, acknowledging their existence but subsuming them within its own higher universal.[27] In this system, all knowledge is perspectival, but all perspectives are not equal, and thus Hegelian epistemology instantiates once again the authoritarian perspectivism characteristic of the Enlightenment. Therefore, although the Hegelian legacy helped to inaugurate within the West a process of historical self-reflection, this legacy is only partially trustworthy. We are still in the process of uncovering the ineliminable unconscious, irrational, and political elements at work in the production of accepted knowledges. Modernism inaugurated this self-reflexive moment, but its ability to transcend Eurocentrism was limited by its own historical context. Today, the illusion of Anglo-European supremacy is much more difficult to maintain.

Although I share a commitment to epistemology and metaphysics with most analytic philosophers, then, the principal justification I would give is different. Hilary Putnam, for example, says that it is just a fact that human beings will always want to discuss knowledge and reality, as if these are "natural" problems arising from human experience. In the same way, Jean-Paul Sartre thought at one time that individual alienation from others was a natural problem outside of history or the particularities of social structures. Hume perhaps started this tradition within epistemology, suggesting that skeptical doubts are the inevitable outcome of any sustained reflection on human knowledge. It may be that these claims are right, or at least partially so. It may be that critical self-reflection is a persistently recurring feature of human practice. While the specific direction or content of that reflection may change (like Michael Williams, I have skeptical doubts about the inevitability of epistemological skepticism), perhaps there will always be some such reflective activity. Today, however, we can appeal to more immediate, historically specific reasons to engage in philosophical work on knowledge and reality than timeless human dispositions. As I have argued, we particularly need to do this work today because of its social and

political importance. Currently our choices consist of an authoritarian perspectivism or an all-pervasive repudiation of knowledge, both of which are unsatisfactory. I would argue that this debate reaches beyond the confines of our universities and pervades many popular arenas of discourse and practice as well, where it is expressed in the common sense of our era. This dilemma obviously cannot be resolved or redirected simply by esoteric work in the academy, but the university is certainly one of the many sites in which dominant notions of knowledge are being remolded.

The project of contemporary epistemology, as I have described it, should be to reconceptualize epistemic justification and truth in a manner that is normative and epistemological and not merely sociological and political, though it must involve these dimensions of knowing as well. In the remainder of this final chapter I want to build on the works discussed previously to argue that a robust coherentist epistemology is particularly capable of offering such a reconceptualization. The virtue of a robust coherentist epistemology is that it can incorporate an acknowledgment of inherent perspectival constraints in its formulation of knowing without sacrificing the link between knowing and truth. This means that coherentism has explanatory value in its favor; it offers a way to make sense of the political legacy of modernist science and epistemology without completely reducing these to ideology or to a collection of extraepistemic forces. I realize that one cannot defend coherentism by arguing for its explanatory value without making a circular argument, because explanatory value in the end amounts to coherence. Circularity in this context is not vicious, however: I am not trying to show how coherentism defeats skepticism, but how it can usefully account for our knowing practices and optimally guide them.

I will also argue that we can disentangle coherentism from the authoritarian perspectivism of Eurocentric patriarchies. If the entire web of belief is brought to bear on the justification of new claims, and the meaning of truth is immanent to a lived reality rather than transcendental, then Michel Foucault's long list of discursive and nondiscursive elements—including subject-positions, institutional practices, systems of exclusion, epistemes, and so forth—can be recognized as operative in the production of knowledge. This approach comprises no transcendental foundation, but instead incorporates an inherent partiality to the understanding of epistemic justification. Justification must always be understood as indexed to a context made up of very particular elements which are incapable of conferring absolute justification in the special philosophical sense of an absolute founded on a transcendental.

Toward this possibility, what I am calling immanent epistemology is aligned with a similarly immanent formulation of realism, a realism without the transcendental evocations of a realm beyond human cognition or interference. An immanent realism would be one that eschewed the Cartesian bifurcations between "man" and world, culture and nature, mind and reality. Cartesian metaphysics posits these binary terms as ultimately independent and autonomous, ontologically distinguishable, and separated by an abyss. We must remember that such an ontology of binarisms is a social construct and does not conform to the phenomenological experience of living or to the conditions of scientific practice.[28] The concept of a thing-in-itself is, after all, just a concept. The fact that we cannot attain it does not automatically mean we lose out on a piece of reality, but just that a particular concept has been found not to fit reality. What is much more real than a conceptual thing-in-itself is the lived world we share, a world of complexity, ambiguity, and richness that exceeds simple dualism.

Dualistic ontologies of self/world are not consistent with our best theories about the self, which understand human subjectivity as the product, reflection, and conduit for natural and intersubjective elements. Binary ontologies emerged out of specific Western masculine identity issues and nascent capitalist formations; they also provided an explanation for experienced phenomena such as false belief, dreams, and hallucinations (all of which the ancients had difficulty accounting for).[29] Dualism offered a philosophical articulation for the rapidly changing worldview and the alienations associated with capitalist expansion. If Hegel was right to say that "philosophy is its time grasped in thought," bifurcated ontologies represent a philosophical articulation of the widespread and deeply felt alienation experienced in the modern West after its encounter with the "new" world.

My point here is that a coherentist ontology of truth need not be thought of as a consolation prize that we get when we give up the hope of achievmg "real" truth. In fact, coherentism has some advantages over transcendental conceptions of truth, and some of these advantages arguably involve an increased metaphysical accuracy of description. It remains the case, however, that dualism provided a powerful explanation for false belief. If reality is separated from the mind, the mind can represent that reality either accurately or inaccurately. Change in justified beliefs can be explained without involving ontological changes in reality. False belief and dreams need no counterpart or reference point in the world if the mind is essentially autonomous. The issue of how to characterize changed beliefs is one that arises not only within the context of philosophical reflection based on modernist as sumptions, but also within the context of everyday, real knowing. After having learned new, disturbing facts about my ex-husband, do I reassess the "reality" of our marriage entirely? Was my previous happiness simply the product of a false belief? Whom was I married to: the man as I know him to be now or the man I thought him to be then? Or, to use examples that involve fewer complicated personal identity issues, I used to believe that the United States was the home of the brave and the land of the free. I no longer hold this belief. I also used to believe that margarine is better for your health than butter, and that sugar intake is linked to hyperactivity. Recent studies have convinced me otherwise, though I wonder what the next studies will suggest. How would a coherentist account of truth characterize such changes? A nonbifurcated realism seems to require that changes in justified belief imply changes in reality itself. How would an immanent conception of truth account for false belief?

I want to think through these deliberately unconventional examples rather than the stock-in-trade examples regularly used in epistemology and philosophy of science, such as changed beliefs about the shape of the earth, phlogiston, ether; or the makeup of oxygen. After all, these latter examples are really relatively easy to explain. The claims in natural science involve complicated inferences and large-scale theories, far removed from immediate experiences including either direct observation or affect. Even beliefs about the shape of the earth involve inference for most of us, and within my phenomenologicalty accessible world (given that I am not an astronaut), the world is pretty flat (in fact, where I grew up in Florida we used to say that you could stand on top of a car and see the whole state).

When a claim is especially theory-laden—as in the assertion that electrons and quarks exist—it is intuitively obvious that there is no simple fact of the matter. To insist that electrons must either exist or not exist is to transport the practical rules for everyday discourse about observable items (for example, "Either there is a girl in your room or there is not!") beyond their application. Putnam's internal realism can account for scientific changes quite easily by indexing claims to conceptual paradigms or research programs that have their own set of categories and posited entities. Scientific ontologies are internal to models of reality.

But surely it would be unnecessarily purist to say that such claims within science cannot therefore claim truth. This would be to lapse back to a dualist assumption that electrons must be entirely a human projection if we cannot verify their existence in any simple or direct manner. If we think of the ontology of truth in more complicated ways than simplistic one-on-one correspondences, it is possible to account for the actual sorts of changes that routinely occur in scientific explanation, which rarely take the form of "p and then not-p" but more often seem to be something like "P-Q-R-S-T-U-V and then P-Q-R-#-S-T-U".

Because of the way in which variables hang together; rarely if ever capable of being pulled apart, changes in scientific belief are not well represented as simple negations. Thus, correspondence theorists need not feel compelled to say that belief A was false and now belief B is true, though with some nervous insecurity about belief B's likely longevity. Nor will it ever be necessary to claim, as some thought coherence theorists might, that belief A was true at time t_1 but belief B is now true at time t_2. We can account for changes more easily by offering partial, complex reports in which it may make the most sense to say that prior, discarded theories contained some truths. This is just to say, of course, that we can take advantage of the notion of scientific knowledge as a progressive accumulation to account for change in a way that does not entail simple negations. Such theories need not involve the claim that

science's accumulation of knowledge about reality represents an increase in the percentage of science that corresponds to a transcendental world. Rather; partial changes that involve accumulations can deliver improved practices, greater explanatory reach, and other advantages that refer to the goals set by the research program rather than to a transcendental concept of reality.

Let me return, then, to the examples I raised earlier; which represent realistic problems one might encounter in the process of living. When one radically changes beliefs about other people, states of affairs, or even one's own history and character; how should this be portrayed? Correspondence accounts would seem to have no trouble. They would simply say that my ex-husband was such as he was all along, that my belief that he was my true soul mate was based on lies and mistakes, and was not true. Either the United States is a free country or it is not. Either sugar and butter are obstacles to physical well-being or they are not.

Coherentism has a decided advantage here. If truth refers to a constellation of elements, then a change in belief occasioned by an increase or alteration in the relevant constellation is not a simple negation, but an *altered truth*. What was the character of my ex-husband and the nature of our marriage? I was happy for several years, we developed a strong level of emotional intimacy and mutual support, and subsequent revelations about him can never completely change that history. But my assessment of him and of our relationship lacked some important elements, and the coherence of that assessment did not survive an enlarged and altered reconstellation of knowledge. It is not simply that he changed, or that I changed, though of course we both did. It is that the truth about my lived reality and even our shared lived reality changed. Thus, the belief I had at time t_1 remains true despite the fact that now, at time t_2, a different belief referring to the same person is true.

The two beliefs are not simple contradictories. They do not refer to or involve precisely the same set of constellations. Nor are they equal, with no standard of assessment to distinguish between their relative validities. Ordinarily, unless there exist strong reasons to do otherwise, we privilege later beliefs which are based on fuller experience. We also ordinarily forgive earlier beliefs, however, recognizing their temporal situatedness. It is true that I might say, "How could I have been so blind?" in regard to my ex-husband or the political realities of the United States. Radical changes of belief (especially about such important matters) generally prompt some self-examination. I might ask what weakness in my cognitive capacities and character produced such apparent blindness, though instead of using those terms I would more likely ask, "Why was I such an idiot?" But unless self-examination leads me to decide that I willfully deceived myself, avoided clear indications, and created my own dream world of happiness, I am likely to accept the earlier belief as true in part. I will conclude that my husband had some positive qualities, that we had some genuine happiness together, but that there was more to the story than I knew at the time. By the same token, I will likely conclude that, in my own narrow corner of the United States, my earlier beliefs were also true in part. All was not unending oppression. Thus, because they are beliefs *about* different things (including myself), I can accept both earlier and later beliefs as true without creating metaphysical incoherence or accepting an outright contradiction or succumbing to a dysfunctional relativism. We do it all the time.

In regard to the delights of sugar and butter (I can only hope this example has not become outdated by the time this reaches print), part of what has changed over the years is health science's theoretical orientations, for example, toward holism and away from the assumption that diseases have single causes, and toward a fuller recognition of the significance of individual physical and lifestyle differences. Whether butter is dangerous to your health depends in part on the kind of life you lead and your genetic inheritance. It also depends on what ingredients are going into margarine this season. Of course, it is also true that new studies sometimes contradict old studies, even when the presuppositions remain stable. In this case, from a new constellation of elements a new truth emerges, arguably better than the first because it is based on a more extensive constellation. We might even want to say sometimes that a prior claim was simply false, though every changed conclusion need not elicit this explanation, and to make charges of false belief we need not have recourse to a transcendental ontology. In fact, given the complexity of life, of science, and of human belief, the reference to a transcendental ontology might create more conceptual problems than it can solve. One would think that most philosophers of

science would be prepared to acknowledge this after struggling for a century to maintain scientific realism in the face of scientific developments.

What I am trying to develop here is a concept of immanent realism. In the discussion that follows I shall largely elaborate this concept by contrasting it with Putnam's internal realism and the contextual realism put forward by Williams, and then I shall return to the set of issues I raised in the Introduction. I realize that I am not following the expected route, which would involve defending this notion of an immanent epistemology against the usual list of possible objections an epistemology must address, and thus that my case may well look underdeveloped and underargued. But I am not really interested in showing how it can defeat skepticism, explain the possibility of human knowledge, or set out a clear and limited set of criteria for justification. I am more concerned with the need to avoid a hyperrationalistic account of knowledge, to correct the statement-dominant tendency in epistemology, and to explain its politics. But I will begin with some more traditional concerns.

On Putnam's account of internal or pragmatic realism, there is no version-free description of the real, and given the fact that there are different versions, more than one (true) description of the real is possible. Putnam denies that this amounts to a subjective idealism or that truth is a matter of arbitrary or conventional construction, since once a language game or version has been chosen, truth can be determined objectively. The success of this denial, however, hinges on how a version is chosen. Putnam's answer to this question is basically pragmatics: versions of reality that become dominant have a utility which is related in some sense to human flourishing (which Putnam defines very broadly).

This theory of the real conflicts with a belief in the existence of intrinsic properties, since intrinsic properties are by definition version-independent and therefore independent of any theoretical language or description. Putnam implies that the search for intrinsic properties which will remain stable across versions is like the search for the Holy Grail, highly motivating, perhaps, but hopeless.

I have suggested that internal realism is quite useful in accounting for the changes in science's ontological attributions, but the concept of immanent realism which I find more broadly useful is distinct from internal realism in the following way. Internal realism refers principally to versions or models of reality while immanent realism refers to contexts. To say there are no properties that are version-independent is different from saying there are no properties that are context-independent. Version-dependence involves being incapable of description outside of a theoretical version of reality with its own ontological categories; thus Putnam's realism is internal, or on *this side* of the man/world Kantian schema. Context-dependence involves a relationship not just to theoretical description but to a more inclusive context, which is defined as including not only theory, version, and language game, but also historical, spatio-temporal, and social location. There are no properties of things that are context-independent, just as mass and extension change according to the nearest planet and the current velocity. The notion of property, no less than the demarcation of "things," involves a host of contextual elements, outside of which the notion will lose its meaning. Thus "context" has an ontological dimension that "version" does not, even though ontologies are dependent on versions. Moreover, contexts are not located only on "this side" of the man/world Kantian schema; they work more effectively than versions to break this schema down and overcome its binary separation. Contexts are not mind-made versions of the world, but portions or locations of the world, historically and socially specific.

The best term to capture this concept is "immanence," a word that suggests opposition to a transcendental conception of reality which is by definition beyond all human practice or intervention. Immanent does not imply internal; the latter term demands the existence of an external whereas immanence, although it is often contrasted with transcendence, requires no opposite. Internal and external are conceptualized in terms of physical space in a way that transcendental and immanent need not be. The word "internal" may also connote subjectivity, an association I want to avoid. The term "contextual" has a possible application here, but "context" by itself does not automatically suggest that more than traditional subjectivity is involved; contexts may be assumed to resemble Putnam's versions or a subjective perspective. Even if context is defined more broadly, I prefer the phrase "immanent realism" to "contextual realism" because of the former's conno-

tations within the historical canon of philosophy. Immanent, unlike either internal or contextual, connotes for philosophers the material world, the profane, the human realm, without a God or an absolute knowledge. Consider Aristotle, Hume, Kierkegaard, Marx and Nietzsche: an unlikely assortment, but each offering a philosophy securely tethered to the realm of immanence. Their grounding in and valorization of immanence does not entail an implicit commitment to the existence of a transcendent realm; certainly Kierkegaard maintained such a commitment, but it was not entailed by his conceptualization of immanence. I'll return to this issue when I discuss Williams's notion of contextual realism.

On this account of immanent realism, false beliefs and changes in beliefs are explained by changes in the constitutive elements of knowledge, such as an enlarged discursive formation to which one has access, or an altered perspective gained from an altered social location. These changes cannot be sequestered on either side of the subject/object distinction; they cannot be split in this way. False belief results from some inadequate constellation of epistemic ingredients. Without the subject/object binary, however, truth is not reducible to an epistemic term—this would once again involve trying to locate truth somewhere on that bifurcated neo-Kantian map. On an immanent realist view, the difference between a true claim and a false claim is not always or simply that one represents and the other does not; the difference is in the nature, quality, and comprehensiveness of the representation.

Immanent realism makes it possible to understand why context must always be introduced as a significant variable in determinations of truth, because for an immanent realist the aboutness of truth is not transcendental. (The term context is of course plastic enough to involve an entire ethos of political, social, historically situated human praxis, that is, thought and action in combination.) Is immanent realism necessarily different from traditional accounts of truth? Every concept of truth, after all, must allow for some indexical truths: truths indexed to specific speakers and locations (for example, "I am not pregnant"). But generally only one truth per index is allowed for, whereas immanent realism, like Putnam's version-dependent realism, must allow for plural truths even in one specific indexed location. Different versions applied to the same indexed location might produce different true claims: if, for example, "pregnancy" were defined more broadly, not as that condition which occurs between conception and birth but as a state involving the very capability of reproduction. Some fundamentalist arguments would seem to imply a notion of pregnancy not far from this, when they proscribe contraceptive devices that block conception and refer to such devices as methods of abortion.

Immanent realism will thus be broader than version-dependent (or internal) realism because it introduces more elements to which truth must be indexed, beyond mere versions or ontologically descriptive theories. It is not only versions that produce particular truths when applied in particular locations, but the larger context, which can include such elements as epistemes, subject-positions, and institutions of power/knowledge. Immanent realism has a further significant advantage over version-dependent realism in displacing the centrality of the knower or subject. In Putnam's internal realism, truth is dependent on theory, which is developed by subjects, and thus truth is dependent on constructions of the subject. This may account for why Putnam's view is often confused with forms of idealism: his view is human-centered. On an immanent realist view, truth is an emergent property of all the elements involved in the context, including but not limited to theory. Immanent realism can therefore acknowledge more readily the formative effects that language, discourse, and power/knowledges have on the production of truths, rather than privileging the knowing subject as the necessary center of the knowing process. Here, then, might lie the route to a nonauthoritarian epistemology, one that incorporates an ineliminable partiality and a context-based account of knowing which is, in effect, a more plausible description of real knowing.

. . .

Coherentism on Balance

I want to turn next to a reassessment of coherentism's promised advantages and the major hurdles it must overcome, issues I raised in the Introduction. I have already dealt at some length in this chapter with the advantage coherentism offers in its notion of an immanent account of realism. Part of this argument is that it provides a more realistic ontology of truth. This can also help with the long-standing difficulty epistemology has had in understanding the historical di-

mension of truth. A number of European philosophers since Hegel have expressed the belief that, as Max Horkheimer and Theodor Adorno put it, "the core of truth is historical."[30] To many Anglo-American philosophers this claim appears to entail that truth, or what we call truth, is in reality ideological, for ideology can be historical whereas our traditional conception of truth or scientific knowledge cannot be. The result is that European proponents of a historical concept of truth are continuously read in the United States as champions of subjectivism and/or irrationalism, or of the belief that the content of human knowledge has little to do with "real" truth.[31]

On a coherentist ontology of truth, however, the conclusion that historical truth must be irrational can be avoided, because on this account, truth can be historical without necessarily descending into ideology and unreason. If truth is *not* a representation of the intrinsic features of reality, if it is rather the product of an interaction between reality and human beings, then truth, and not merely justified belief, can be thought of as historical. We need not relinquish our intuition that truth is beyond our subjective control, but we must relinquish the idea that truth is something wholly other to us, intrinsic or inherent to a reality where our input has been erased or discarded. Truth is historically relative, on this view, without being irrational, subjectivist, or ideological.

I also asserted in the Introduction that coherentist epistemology is based on a more realistic description of actual knowing, principally because it posits a knower who is always already in the world, replete with a large variety of epistemic commitments. The problem with Descartes' thought experiment, in which he tried to imagine giving up all of his beliefs until he reached an indubitable bedrock, was that this very thought experiment was conducted, and could only have been conducted, by holding a number of important beliefs. Descartes had to hold onto beliefs about what counts as dubitability and indubitability, for example. Positioned as he was in time and place, he also continued to be affected by ideologies of many sorts. It is no miracle that at the end of his thought experiment, most of his former beliefs which he temporarily set aside turned out to retain their justifiability, so that he could readopt them in good conscience. The lesson to draw from this miracle is not that we are all helplessly bound by ideology, but that Descartes' proposed method will not work to ensure the epistemic adequacy of our beliefs because it is based on an inaccurate, illusionary account of human knowing.

Coherentism recognizes the unavoidable fact of our prior commitments, our situatedness in specific contexts, and our general tendency from within a set of cognitively relevant practices to conserve that which we think we already know. Gadamer and Davidson argue that neither knowledge nor the identification of error can be achieved in any other context. But Gadamer also shows that this situation need not create closed, self-justifying systems because the horizon of one's prior judgments is constantly evolving through interaction with new texts and new experiences. The worry that coherentism will work to justify arbitrary sets of coherent beliefs and make them immutable to external critique is as unrealistic as Descartes' thought experiment: coherentism within the context of lived reality is rarely applied in this way and when it is, it usually has disastrous results and few followers. Coherentism sets no a priori boundaries around what must cohere and what can be set aside as irrelevant, but in reality such a priori boundaries are unnecessary. The boundaries needed can only be determined locally, within the context of specific situations.

A third advantage I promised with coherentism was its ability to explain how and why apparently disparate elements can be shown to be cognitively linked without recourse to a strong version of false consciousness. That is, it is not simply the case that scientists have been ideologically determined to welcome master-molecule theories or linear accounts of genetic causes, but that theories even in the sciences are given credibility or lent support from beliefs and practices elsewhere that are coherent with their presuppositions, general orientation, or metaphysical commitments.[32]

Helen Longino has recently developed an account of science to show how background assumptions which contain metaphysical commitments as well as contextual values enter necessarily into the process of theory choice.[33] The influence of these assumptions and values cannot be restricted to the so-called context of discovery because they have an important impact on the formulation of hypotheses, the decision to regard certain hypotheses as plausible, the kinds of analogies and models that get seriously entertained, and the determination of the kind of evidence considered sufficient to justify theories. After all these factors are set in place, the process of theory-choice may indeed be seen to conform to a paradigm of objectivity since, as Longino and others have pointed out, once you determine the scale that will be used to assess temperature, the determination of the temperature is really an objective matter. The realm of objectivity in this traditional sense does not, however, extend very far. The models of justification that are considered plausible and thus are up for debate and consideration, the goals of the inquiry itself, its unexamined assumptions about the locus and contours of its research topic—all these elements are significantly influenced by what Longino calls contextual values, which are themselves a function in part of who the scientist is.

A relevant example can be given about traditional epistemology itself. Epistemology has most often assumed that knowing occurs between an individual and an object or world.[34] This typically Western assumption of individualism (which operates as both an ontological assumption and a value) dictates the kinds of problems and hurdles epistemologists set themselves to overcome. For example, how can *I* (by myself) justify my beliefs? How can the massive number of beliefs *I* hold be justified on the basis of my own narrow observational input? How, for naturalized epistemology, can *I* describe the complex brain states involved in various epistemic functions? Most knowledge, however, is produced through collective endeavor and is largely dependent on the knowledge produced by others. It is not achieved by individuals. If epistemology were to dispense with its individualist assumption and begin with a conception of knowing as collective, a different agenda of issues would suggest itself. For example, we would need a more complicated understanding of the epistemic interrelationships of a knowing community; we would want to understand the relation between modes of social organization and the types of beliefs that appear reasonable; and we would need to explore the influence of the political relationships between individuals on their epistemic relationships.

This analysis indicates that the formative assumptions and values of any group of epistemologists, whether privileged European-American males or a national minority, can have a significant impact on the epistemological theories the group produces. This view need not devolve into a dysfunctional, absolute relativism, especially if we begin to acknowledge such influences so that they can be identified for debate and discussion. To assume that the entanglement of political issues entails a radical relativism is to assume that political debate is doomed to irrationality. But political issues are no less susceptible to rational consideration and discussion than epistemological ones. A coherentist epistemology can accommodate and even prompt such discussions by recognizing the interdependence of our disparate commitments.

I mentioned earlier that coherentism faces a number of hurdles, best described as challenges that continental theory would pose if it were to address coherentism directly. The first of these—the concern that coherentism perpetuates a statement-dominant perception of knowledge—has been, I trust, adequately covered. As we have seen, the work of Foucault and Putnam presents cognition within a context of practice, a context that is constitutive both of knowledge and of the criteria of adequacy it must satisfy. On this view, the measure of coherence does not operate simply within a body of beliefs, but within a system of practices encompassing but not reduced to beliefs.

The second hypothetical objection I raised has not yet been addressed in much detail. This objection was concerned with the political danger of valorizing a coherence that requires similarity and sameness and de-emphasizes difference. For someone like Jean-Francois Lyotard, the pursuit of coherence would be inherently oppressive, because it values connection over disjunction and thus will always try to subvert fragmentation. On this view, the drive for coherence is a drive for control over the whole field of discourse, wherein the whole can be mapped out and arranged according to a single plan, theme, or motif. It thus conflicts with the freedom to break apart, to create new, dissonant formations, and to promote a difference that cannot be incorporated. The pursuit of coherence would be a kind of epistemological totalitarianism.

In his latest polemic against postmodernism, Christopher Norris takes up the related issue of association made between truth and violence.[35] Arguing against Foucault, Paul de Man, and Richard Rorty as well as Page DuBois, Norris considers the case made by postmodernists that philosophical truth is grounded in domination and the desire for mastery and control.

DuBois' recent book, *Torture and Truth,* is especially useful for a consideration of this issue because she makes the argument more explicit and develops a historical case study of the Greeks to support the association between "the appeal to a unitary Truth" and the attempt to maintain "differentials of wealth, power, and privilege."[36] Contrary to an authoritarian truth, she argues, "the idea of equality has its own dynamic, a pressure towards the consideration of all in view as entitled to the privileges of rule by the people."[37] But in its antidemocratic, Platonic origins, truth has been codified as "privileged epistemic access, as a matter of penetrating to secrets which can only be revealed through various kinds of expert hermeneutical technique, or procedures vouchsafed to those few knowing individuals who possess the requisite degree of authentic understanding."[38] The result is a doubled association between truth and violence: the metaphorical violence of claims which, by posing as absolutes authorized by a metaphysics of presence, necessarily exclude and erase others; and the material violence of torture used persistently in the West to extract truth from inferiors who, because they lacked the requisite rationality or reliability of credible witnesses, had to be tortured to produce truthful testimony.

Norris takes issue with the epistemological skepticism resulting from such arguments and promotes an open dialogic exchange á la Jurgen Habermas as an alternative route to truth which will eliminate or minimize oppression. "What is wrong with [the postmodernist argument] . . . is that it fails to take account of the crucial difference between truths imposed by arbitrary fiat, through presumptive access to *the Truth* as revealed by some authorized body of priests or commissars, and truth-claims advanced in the public sphere of open argumentative debate" (289). Norris admits that the Platonic dialogic model was never really open, but he contests the claim that this is an inherent problem with any model of dialogue. The kinship between torture and truth holds only for truth-claims that appeal to "presumptive sources of revealed or self-authenticating truth" (292).

Norris thus focuses the political critique of truth on the notion of revealed wisdom, where only an authority of some kind can discern it. But surely any concept of transcendental truth would have the effect of obviating the need for open discussion. An infallible, absolute, and stable truth inevitably closes down dialogue by providing the final word. A truth situated within collective lived experience in history, rather than outside of it, calls for collective, decentered procedures of inquiry. In this regard, Norris' dismissal of Foucault as simply a skeptic is unfortunate. Norris never seriously considers Foucault's notion of local truth, which could provide the beginnings of an alternative epistemology that would justify Norris's valorization of public debate. Local truth defies a priori, outside assessments made without consultation or dialogic exchange.

I agree with Norris that an epistemological skepticism inspired by postmodernism is to be rejected, but he portrays the debate here as too starkly characterized by mutually exclusive positions, even while he accuses postmodernists of taking this approach. For Norris, on the one side stand skepticism and relativism, on the other epistemology and truth. Only "logic, reason, and reflexive autocritique . . . can resist the kinds of dogmatic imposition which derive their authority from a mystified resort to notions of absolute, transcendent truth" (288). But how do logic, reason, and self-criticism gain epistemic value? Why does Norris think that they can completely eliminate relativism? The argument against postmodern skepticism cannot be successful without an account of truth and the truth-conduciveness of justificatory processes. To defend the ideal of open public dialogue Norris needs to offer epistemological and not simply political arguments.

Epistemologically, there is no way to get around the fact that claims of truth involve exclusion, control, and the repudiation of opponents. The sphere of truth cannot be made politically correct according to the latest formulations. Norris poses Habermas's dialogic model as a better alternative to postmodernism's relativist abdication of truth on the grounds that the dialogic model is epistemically better and politically just as good, that is, just as inclusive and nonoppressive. The better tack, I think, is to look at how oppression is being defined in these critiques of truth. For Lyotard, any ordering at all leads to exclusion and the inhibition of creativity. This claim assumes, however, a liberal individualist definition of freedom as the absence of restraint on individual action, and thus defines processes that involve exclusion and inhibition as necessarily unfree.

A more complex and realistic account of freedom would understand it as constituted within a social context which is necessarily ordered in a variety of ways. Freedom requires a context, just as resistance, in the postmodernist view, requires (and is the natural by-product of) power. The process of achieving truth must involve open dialogic exchange without *arbitrary* exclusions such as those based on sexism or racism, but it must also involve exclusions based on epistemic status. Truth is not therefore necessarily on the side of oppression in its self-privileging or its assumption of authority.

All authorities are not authoritarian. As Gadamer counsels, we must critique Enlightenment assumptions that the deference for tradition and authority is in every case unjustified and always sustains tyranny. Not only must we make distinctions between different sorts of traditions and authorities rather than characterizing them all monolithically, but we must also understand tradition and authority as open to the new, as within history and therefore never fixed, and as constituted in part by those who give deference and thus interpret and apply the tradition. If every authority is seen as authoritarian, the result is a tyranny of structurelessness in which strong personalities hold sway and dominant ideas are left unaccountable. The point in epistemology, as well as in politics, is not to subvert every authority but to make authorities accountable, to acknowledge their fallibility, and to incorporate an analysis of power within any critique of their knowledge claims.

The same can be said for an epistemology based on coherence. The drive for coherence provides structure and a criterion of adjudication. The attempt to harmonize difference will necessitate some exclusion and control, but let us remember that coherence is a limit concept, or a heuristic; there is no possibility that we will ever achieve a totalizing coherence that will remain stable and thus prove stultifying. Given that, the danger that the structuring of coherence imposes is perhaps not so dangerous. As Foucault well knew, it is uselessly utopian to pursue the complete elimination of all structures of power/knowledge. For both epistemic and political reasons, what is needed is a decentered form of structuring, which can destabilize authorities so that they cannot become authoritarian. Coherence epistemologies posit no self-justifying states, no indubitable bedrock, that would create a foundation beyond challenge. Where the ultimate criterion is coherence within a large constellation of elements in a temporally and spatially specific context, rather than a foundation purportedly linked to a truth outside of history, truth will always be temporary and unstable.

I do not believe this shift can be made without a new ontological paradigm. Thomas Kuhn was right to argue that an old paradigm will not fall, no matter how many anomalies it is unable to explain, until a new one has been developed to take its place. The transcendentalized conception of truth will retain its intuitive stranglehold on philosophical discourses until a new ontological imagery can be developed and made persuasive. Moreover, if we acknowledge that these ideas are not unconnected to social location and history, it is easy to diagnose transcendental versions of realism as the overdetermined product of cultural crisis, social alienation, the economic reification of nature, dominant Western masculine identity distortions, the unselfconscious translation of religion into science, and the list could go on. We are passing into a new era. Anglo-European economic hegemony will be displaced as capital is decentered. Economic exploitation of the earth will be modified as prior methods become infeasible. Social relations between men and women will take new forms, as will racial identifications and ethnic politics. Some of the crises of modernism will take new shapes. These will not necessarily be moves toward "progress" in some absolute or overall sense, but there will definitely be movement. Epistemology needs to catch up.

NOTES

1. See, e.g., Steve Fuller; *Social Epistemology* (Bloomington: Indiana University Press, 199 1) in which the "social turn" is described without mentioning or citing a single feminist theorist working in this area and without raising any issues in regard to gender or race. "Social" here evidently refers to the society of white men.

2. Richard Rorty, *Contingency, Irony, Solidarity* (Cambridge: Cambridge University Press, 1989), p. 10.

3. See Robert D'Amico, *Historicism and Knowledge,* chapter 2, for a compelling argument that Popper is a historicist (New York: Routledge, 1989).

4. Jonathan Dancy, *Introduction to Contemporary Epistemology* (Oxford: Basil Blackwell, 1985), p.116.

5. Ibid., p. 112.

6. Jacques Derrida, "Violence and Metaphysics: An Essay on the Thought of Emmanuel Levinas," trans. Alan Bass, in *Writing and Difference* (Chicago: University of Chicago Press, 1978), p. 130.

7. Jean-Francois Lyotard, *The Postmodern Condition,* trans. Geoff Bennington and Brian Massumi (Minneapolis: University of Minnesota Press, 1984), p. 66.

8. Ibid., p. 64.

9. Charles Sanders Peirce, *Collected Papers* (Cambridge: Harvard University Press), 5:265, quoted in Richard J. Bernstein, *The New Constellation* (Cambridge: MIT Press, 1992), p. 327.

10. Linda Alcoff, "Justifying Feminist Social Science," *Hypatia* 2 (Fall 1987): 107–27; Lynn Hankinson Nelson, *Who Knows: From Quine to a Feminist Empiricism* (Philadelphia: Temple University Press, 1990).

11. An intriguing exception to this is Michael Williams, who has recently argued that coherentism is a form of foundationalism. See his *Unnatural Doubts: Epistemological Realism and the Basis of Scepticism* (Cambridge, Mass.: Basil Blackwell, 1991). I discuss this analysis in Chapter 7.

12. Ralph C. S. Walker, *The Coherence Theory of Truth* (London: Routledge, 1989), pp. 1–40; Laurence Bonjour, *The Structure of Empirical Knowledge* (Cambridge: Harvard University Press, 1985), pp. 94–153; Donald Davidson, "A Coherence Theory of Truth and Knowledge" and "Empirical Content," in *Truth and Interpretation: Perspectives on the Philosophy of Donald Davidson,* ed. Ernest LePore (Oxford: Basil Blackwell, 1986), pp.307–32; and Dancy, *Introduction,* pp. 110–40.

13. Joseph Rouse, *Knowledge and Power: Toward a Political Philosophy of Science* (Ithaca: Cornell University Press, 1987), p. 26.

14. Walker is one of the few coherence theorists to discuss the problem of coherentism's exclusive focus on beliefs and propositions (*Coherence Theory,* pp. 84, 94).

15. See Bernstein, *New Constellation;* Nancy Fraser, *Unruly Practices* (Minneapolis: University of Minnesota Press, 1989).

16. Martha Nussbaum, *The Fragility of Goodness: Luck and Ethics in Greek Tragedy and Philosophy* (Cambridge: Cambridge University Press, 1986).

17. Simone de Beauvoir, *The Second Sex,* trans. H. M. Parshley (New York: Random House, 1952).

18. See Marilyn Frye, *The Politics of Reality: Essays in Feminist Theory* (Trumansburg, N.Y: Crossing Press, 1983), p. 155. This chapter was inspired by her illuminating discussion of the ways in which philosophy and language can conceal forcible exclusions and thus neatly erase oppression with a metaphysical flourish. See also *Webster's Unabridged Dictionary,* 2d ed.

19. See Steven Shapin, *A Social History of Truth: Civility and Science in Seventeenth Century England* (Chicago: University of Chicago Press, 1994), pp. 86–95.

20. Alasdair Macintyre, 'Epistemological Crises, Dramatic Narrative, and tile Philosophy of Science," in *Paradigms and Revolutions: Applications and Appraisals of Thomas Kuhn's Philosophy of Science,* ed. Gary Gutting (Notre Dame: University of Notre Dame Press, 1980), pp. 54–74

21. See Shapin, *Social History of Truth,* p. 124. For an excellent explanation of why cultural studies of science are relevant to epistemology, see Joseph Rouse, "What Are Cultural Studies of Scientific Knowledge?" *Configurations* 1 (1992): 1–22.

22. Shapin, *Social History of Truth,* pp. 100–101.

23. Ibid., esp. chap. 3.

24. There is a growing tradition in the philosophical canon of new readings that juxtapose rhetorical analysis and philosophy. See, for example, Michele LeDoeuff, *The Philosophical Imaginary,* trans. Colin Gordon (Stanford: Stanford University Press, 1989); Susan Bordo, *The Flight to Objectivity: Essays on Cartesianism and Culture* (Albany: SUNY Press, 1987); Andrea Nye, *Words of Power: A Feminist Reading of the History of Logic* (New York: Routledge, 1990); Genevieve Lloyd, *The Man of Reason:"Male" and "Female" in Western Philosophy* (Minneapolis: University of Minnesota Press, 1984); Robert C. Solomon, *The Bully Culture: Enlightenment, Romanticism, and the Transcendental Pretense* (Lanham, Md.: Rowman and Littlefield, 1993).

25. See, e.g., *Beyond Good and Evil,* trans. by Walter Kaufmann (New York: Random House, 1966), sec. 198.

26. See Michael S. Roth, *Knowing and History: Appropriations of Hegel in Twentieth-Century France* (Ithaca: Cornell University Press, 1988).

27. See Robert Young, *White Mythologies* (New York. Routledge, 1990), chap. 1.

28. See Rouse, *Knowledge and Power: Toward a Political Philosophy of Science* (Ithaca, New York: Cornell University Press, 1987), esp. chap. 2.

29. See Bordo, *Flight to Objectivity;* Merchant, *Death of Nature.*

30. Max Horkheimer and Theodor W. Adorno, *Dialectic of Enlightenment,* trans. John Cumming (New York: Continuum, 1944), p. 1.

31. One example of this is Hilary Putnam's reading of Foucault in *Reason, Truth, and History* (Cambridge: Cambridge University Press, 1981), p.167.

32. Helen Longino, *Science as Social Knowledge: Values and Objectivity in Scientific Inquiry* (Princeton: Princeton University Press, 1990), chap. 7

33. Longino, *Science as Social Knowledge,* chap. 5. Her analysis, although primarily directed at knowing within science, can be applied to epistemology as well.

34. This example is discussed in Lynn Hankinson Nelson, *Who Knows? From Quine to a Feminist Empiricism* (Philadelphia: Temple University Press, 1990), esp. chap. 6.

35. Christopher Norris, *The Truth about Postmodernism* (Oxford: Basil Blackwell, 1993).

36. Quoted in ibid., p. 265.

37. Ibid.

38. Ibid., p. 262.

FOR FURTHER READING

Alcoff, Linda. *Real Knowing: New Versions of Coherence Theory.* Ithaca, N.Y.: Cornell University Press, 1996.

Audi, Robert. *Belief, Justification, and Knowledge.* Belmont, Calif.: Wadsworth, 1988.

Audi, Robert. *The Structure of Justification.* New York: Cambridge University Press, 1993.

Bender, John, ed. *The Current State of Coherence Theory.* Dordrecht, Netherlands: Kluwer Academic Publishers, 1989.

BonJour, Laurence. *The Structure of Empirical Knowledge.* Cambridge: Harvard University Press, 1985.

Dancy, Jonathan, and Ernest Sosa, eds. *A Companion to Epistemology.* Oxford: Basil Blackwell, 1992.

Davidson, Donald. "A Coherence Theory of Truth and Knowledge." In *Truth and Interpretation: Perspectives on the Philosophy of Donald Davidson,* edited by Ernest LePore. Oxford: Basil Blackwell, 1985.

Davidson, Donald. "Empirical Content." In *Truth and Interpretation: Perspectives on the Philosophy of Donald Davidson,* edited by Ernest LePore. Oxford: Basil Blackwell, 1985.

Day, Timothy Joseph. "Circularity, Non-linear Justification, and Holistic Coherentism." In *The Current State of Coherence Theory,* edited by John Bender. Dordrecht, Netherlands: Kluwer Academic Publishers, 1989.

Fumerton, Richard. *Metaepistemology and Skepticism.* Lanham, Md. Rowman & Littlefield, 1995.

Haack, Susan. *Evidence and Inquiry: Towards Reconstruction in Epistemology.* Oxford: Basil Blackwell, 1993.

Harman, Gilbert. *Thought.* Princeton: Princeton University Press, 1973.

Lehrer, Keith. *Knowledge.* Oxford: Oxford University Press, 1974.

Lehrer, Keith. *Self-Trust: A Study of Reason, Knowledge, and Autonomy.* Oxford: Oxford University Press, 1997.

Lehrer, Keith. Theory of Knowledge. Boulder, Colo.: Westview Press, 1990.

LePore, Ernest, ed. *Truth and Interpretation: Perspectives on the Philosophy of Donald Davidson.* Oxford: Basil Blackwell, 1985.

Meyers, Robert G. *The Likelihood of Knowledge.* Dordrecht, Netherlands: Kluwer Academic Publishers, 1988.

Moser, Paul. *Empirical Knowledge,* 2d ed. Lanham, Md. Rowman & Littlefield, 1996.

Pollock, John. *Contemporary Theories of Knowledge.* Totowa, N.J.: Rowman & Littlefield, 1986.

Quine, W. V. O. *From a Logical Point of View,* 2d ed. New York: Harper, 1961.

Sosa, Ernest. *Knowledge in Perspective.* Cambridge, U.K.: Cambridge University Press, 1991.

Thagard, Paul. *Conceptual Revolutions.* Princeton, N.J.: Princeton University Press, 1992.

Van Cleve, James. "Epistemic Supervenience and the Circle of Belief." *Monist* 68 (1985), 90–104.

Williams, Michael. *Unnatural Doubts.* Oxford: Blackwell, 1991.

STUDY QUESTIONS

1. In BonJour's view, what are the criteria for the coherence of a system of beliefs? Explain the role of inference relations in BonJour's view.
2. What is the purpose of a metajustificatory argument, according to BonJour? The Observation Requirement—the requirement that a system of beliefs accord prima facie reliability to perceptual beliefs—plays an essential role in the metajustificatory argument. Explain the outlines of the metajustifacatory argument and the role of the Observation Requirement.
3. Explain the distinction between the simple and the elaborated demon hypotheses. Why does BonJour think that our commonsense view of why we have certain perceptions is more likely to be true than the elaborated demon hypothesis?
4. What does Lehrer mean by "acceptance?" How does acceptance differ from belief? In Lehrer's view, what is the connection between coherence and acceptance? Between coherence and reasonability?
5. Why does Lehrer think that foundationalism breaks the connection between justification and truth? Why does Lehrer think that a person is justified in accepting that he or she is a trustworthy evaluator of truth? Why does Lehrer think that we may know, even if we cannot show that the skeptic is mistaken?
6. What is the circularity objection to holism, according to Meyers? Does he think that this shows that foundationalism is superior to coherentism? Explain.
7. Meyers claims that the basic problem with coherence theory is its commitment to the notion that all justification is immanent. What does Meyers mean by this? Why does Meyers think that coherence theorists cannot explain the independent credibility of perceptual beliefs?
8. Why does Alcoff think that coherence theory, as opposed to foundationalism, provides the best account of justification and knowledge?
9. Alcoff claims that there has been a covert perspectivism in epistemology, despite epistemologists' claims to the contrary. Why does she think this? Can you explain how, according to Alcoff, a coherentist theory of truth allows us to explain or make sense of "real world" changes in belief? Why does Alcoff think that Descartes's method is mistaken? Why does she think that coherentism can avoid the problem faced by Descartes's method?

PART III

Recent Controversies

7

Internalism and Externalism

It is widely thought that one of the characteristic features of epistemology since Descartes is the commitment to *internalism*. Roderick Chisholm provides a succinct formulation of the view:

> We presuppose . . . that the things we know are justified for us in the following sense: *we* can know what it is, on any occasion, that constitutes our grounds, or reason, or evidence for thinking that we know.[1]

Chisholm claims that whenever we have a justified belief we are able to tell what constitutes the justifying basis of the belief. Understood in this way, internalism is the view that justification requires that we have access to the reasons for our beliefs.

It is not difficult to see why internalism is thought to be characteristic of traditional epistemology. Since Descartes, a traditional project for the epistemologist is to provide a response to the skeptic. The skeptic wants to know whether we have adequate reasons for our beliefs. Responding to the skeptic involves at least two aspects: providing the reasons for our beliefs and explaining why those reasons are indeed adequate. The first aspect seems to indicate that we know, or at least could come to know, the reasons for our beliefs.

Internalism can also be connected to a second traditional feature of epistemology. As noted in the Introduction, an aim of epistemology is the regulation of belief. Descartes suggests, for example, that we ought to suspend judgment in those cases where our beliefs are dubitable or susceptible to error. If our reasons for a belief are inadequate to rule out the possibility of mistake, we should not count that belief as epistemically praiseworthy. Of course, in order to assess the adequacy or inadequacy of our reasons, we must first identify those reasons.

Internalism thus emphasizes the reasons for our belief. Whether such beliefs are likely to be true is, in a qualified sense, of secondary importance. It is not unusual for internalists to insist that a person's belief can be justified even if there is no chance that the belief is true. In the internalist view, to do the right thing, the *epistemically* right thing, is to do the best that one can do. And doing the best one can do is a function of the kinds of reason available to the agent.

Externalism, a recent development in epistemology, departs from this standard assumption that sound epistemological theory requires a commitment to internalism.[2] Externalists claim that what matters for justification and consequently knowledge is whether our beliefs are likely to be true. A typical externalist view is that our beliefs are likely to be true if they are correctly acquired. For example, externalists claim that perception produces beliefs that are likely to be true, whereas wishful thinking does not. Thus, beliefs acquired as the result of perception are justified and beliefs acquired as the result of wishful thinking are not. Of course, a person's reasons can make a difference as to whether a belief is justified, but reasons are important only insofar as they play a role in an appropriate process of belief acquisition. Externalism is a normative view in that externalists identify standards or norms that our beliefs must satisfy if they are to count as knowledge or justified.

Reliabilism is one of the most widely held versions of externalism. A simple version of reliabilism holds that a belief is justified if it is the product of a reliable belief-forming process. Notice that in this view the agent's reasons or the agent's perspective is not the determining factor in justification.

Internalists argue that externalism is too dramatic a departure from traditional epistemology. Consider, for example, skepticism about induction. We are unable, according to the skeptic, to provide a justification for accepting the conclusions of inductive inferences. Imagine that inductive inferences generally result in true beliefs. Then, if reliabilism is the correct account of justification, beliefs based on induction are justified since they are acquired by a reliable process. A reliabilist will not face the same difficulty faced by the traditionalist because the long-standing problem of induction is no longer a problem.

Of course, the more traditional internalist claims that this approach ignores the real question. What we want to know, according to the internalist, is whether induction *is* a reliable process. The traditional problem of induction requires that we have some reason for thinking that induction is a reliable process. Externalists seemingly avoid this question by claiming that if induction is reliable, then inductive beliefs are justified. Of course, externalists are free to insist that some argument must be given by internalists for persisting in the traditional epistemological projects.

Two types of arguments seem to be at the center of the dispute between externalists and internalists. The first, as we have noted, concerns whether accessibility to one's reasons is necessary for justification. Externalists argue that there are cases of justified belief where the reasons seem inaccessible. Typically, two sorts of example are cited. Small children have justified beliefs, but do not seem to have reasons at their disposal. If three-year-old Sammy remembers seeing the blue ball in the bedroom, and runs to the bedroom to retrieve it, then it would seem that Sammy has a justified belief. But it is unlikely that Sammy could offer any reasons for his belief. It is unlikely that he could provide us with any sort of reason supporting the general veracity of memory beliefs. A second type of example is that of forgetting one's reasons. Suppose Sara constructs a truth table for DeMorgan's Theorem, thus assuring herself of its truth. Years later she forgets that she did so; indeed she remembers nothing of truth tables. She does remember, however, that neither Sam nor Sara goes to the store means the same as that both Sam and Sara do not go to the store. Again, it seems that she has a justified belief, according to externalists, but does not have access to her reasons for that belief.

One line of response sometimes adopted by internalists is to distinguish between possessing information and being justified or knowing. Small children may possess certain information, but not have epistemically praiseworthy beliefs. In response to cases such as Sara's, it is suggested that Sara has a second-order reason because she remembers that she once had a reason. If she does not have even this second-order reason, then convinced internalists might simply dig in their heels and claim that she does not have a justified belief.

A second central source of dispute between internalists and externalists is the voluntary character of belief. Certain versions of internalism imply that in cases where we do not have adequate reasons, we should refrain from having beliefs. Externalists maintain however, that we are obligated to refrain from having such beliefs only if we can control whether we have the beliefs. But many of our beliefs seem to be involuntary in nature; they are not obviously under our control. Perceptual beliefs are notorious examples of beliefs that are acquired involuntarily. As I look out my window and see the canyon just off my balcony, I cannot refrain from believing that there is a grove of trees near a small building. Indeed the involuntary character of perceptual beliefs is doubtless a salutary and beneficial thing. If I am about to step off the curb to cross the street, and involuntarily form the perceptual belief that a truck is careening down the avenue, then I am at least practically better off. To the extent that internalism is committed to *doxastic voluntarism*, the voluntary nature of our beliefs, it loses some of its motivation.

Internalists recognize that many of our beliefs are involuntary, but they dissent from the externalist claim that the involuntary character of beliefs undermines internalism. Some internalists suggest that we can exercise an indirect control over our beliefs by becoming more aware of the circumstances in which our beliefs might be trustworthy. Still others suggest that despite the involuntary character of our beliefs, we are not relieved of the epistemic obligation to believe on the basis of the best reasons we have. A third line of response is to suggest that the epistemic appraisal of belief is independent of the voluntary character of belief. Descartes, for example, recognizes that some of our beliefs are psychologically irresistible. That a triangle has three sides and that colored things have shape are beliefs we cannot refrain from having. We might, however, refuse to count such beliefs as epistemically praiseworthy.

These arguments suggest that internalist and externalist alike have targeted important but different aspects of justification. These aspects reveal a fundamental tension in our notion of justification, a tension that will not easily be relieved.

Alvin Goldman's "What Is Justified Belief?" is one of the foundational essays of reliabilism. Goldman outlines his aim as finding an account of justification that does not depend on any epistemic concepts. After rejecting various possibilities, he outlines what he calls "historical process reliabilism." Interestingly, Goldman explicitly rejects the idea that a person must believe that a belief forming process is reliable.

This concession is exploited in Laurence BonJour's essay "Externalist Theories of Empirical Knowledge." BonJour argues that reliabilism commits us to the seemingly odd consequence that instances of knowledge and justified belief can be irrational; from the agent's perspective, such beliefs might be based on no reasons at all. According to BonJour, this consequence shows that mere reliability is not sufficient for knowledge or justification.

In "Strong and Weak Justification," Goldman sketches a response to what has been called the new evil demon problem. Internalists ask us to imagine a demon world, a world in which we have exactly the same sort of perceptual experience we have in this world, and subsequently form the same perceptual beliefs. Since it is a demon world, none of our perceptual beliefs are true. It seems plausible to hold that our perceptual beliefs in the demon world would be justified, yet they are clearly not reliable. Hence, reliability does not seem necessary for justification. Goldman responds to this case by suggesting that we distinguish between strong and weak justification. Inhabitants of the demon world are weakly justified, since they are epistemically blameless for using an unreliable cognitive process. They have no reason to think that perception is unreliable, and they cannot be faulted for failing to have such reasons.

In his essay "the Internalism/Externalism Controversy," Richard Fumerton considers various ways of characterizing the dispute between internal-ists and externalists. His positive suggestion is that the externalists attempt to analyze epistemic concepts by appealing to nomological concepts, concepts that invoke a kind of causal necessity.

The last two essays, by Robert Audi and Ernest Sosa, attempt to carve out a middle ground between internalism and externalism. Audi explores the connection between justification and attempts to explain how a generally internalist notion of justification can accommodate reliabilist intuitions. Central to Audi's argument is the distinction between the process and the property of justification, or the teleological and the ontological views of justification. According to Audi, our justificatory practice is aimed at truth. Thus, in the process of justifying a belief, we typically cite those reasons or states that we take to reliably indicate truth.

Sosa outlines a view that he calls "virtue perspectivism." Justified beliefs arise as a result of certain cognitive faculties that are attuned to truth. They arise from those cognitive capacities that manifest intellectual virtue. Elsewhere, Sosa attempts to accommodate internalist and reliabilist scruples by distinguishing between apt and justified beliefs. Apt beliefs are those that are the result of intellectually virtuous cognitive capacities, while justified beliefs are apt beliefs, but we are aware of the source of such apt beliefs. In "Knowledge and Intellectual Virtue," Sosa claims that justification and knowledge arise from the operation of intellectual virtuous faculties. Sosa identifies two types of knowledge, *animal* and *reflective*. The former arises as a direct response of an intellectually virtuous faculty to the enviroment, while reflective knowledge arises when one understands the role or place of such a response.

NOTES

1. Roderick Chisolm *Theory of Knowledge,* 2d ed. (Englewood Cliffs, N.J.: Prentice Hall, 1977), 17.
2. Frederick F. Schmitt has recently argued that strains of externalism can be found in more traditional epistemologists. See *Knowledge and Belief.* (London: Routledge, 1990).

ALVIN I. GOLDMAN

What Is Justified Belief?

The aim of this paper is to sketch a theory of justified belief. What I have in mind is an explanatory theory, one that explains in a general way why certain beliefs are counted as justified and others as unjustified. Unlike some traditional approaches, I do not try to prescribe standards for justification that differ from, or improve upon, our ordinary standards. I merely try to explicate the ordinary standards, which are, I believe, quite different from those of many classical, e.g., 'Cartesian', accounts.

Many epistemologists have been interested in justification because of its presumed close relationship to knowledge. This relationship is intended to be preserved in the conception of justified belief presented here. In previous papers on knowledge,[1] I have denied that justification is necessary for knowing, but there I had in mind 'Cartesian' accounts of justification. On the account of justified belief suggested here, it *is* necessary for knowing, and closely related to it.

The term 'justified', I presume, is an evaluative term, a term of appraisal. Any correct definition or synonym of it would also feature evaluative terms. I assume that such definitions or synonyms might be given, but I am not interested in them. I want a set of *substantive* conditions that specify when a belief is justified. Compare the moral term 'right'. This might be defined in other ethical terms or phrases, a task appropriate to meta-ethics. The task of normative ethics, by contrast, is to state substantive conditions for the rightness of actions. Normative ethics tries to specify non-ethical conditions that determine when an action is right. A familiar example is act-utilitarianism, which says an action is right if and only if it produces, or would produce, at least as much net happiness as any alternative open to the agent. These necessary and sufficient conditions clearly involve no ethical notions. Analogously, I want a theory of justified belief to specify in non-epistemic terms when a belief is justified. This is not the only kind of theory of justifiedness one might seek, but it is one important kind of theory and the kind sought here.

In order to avoid epistemic terms in our theory, we must know which terms are epistemic. Obviously, an exhaustive list cannot be given, but here are some examples: 'justified', 'warranted', 'has (good) grounds', 'has reason (to believe)', 'knows that', 'sees that', 'apprehends that', 'is probable' (in an epistemic or inductive sense), 'shows that', 'establishes that', and 'ascertains that'. By contrast, here are some sample non-epistemic expressions: 'believes that', 'is true', 'causes', 'it is necessary that', 'implies', 'is deducible from', and 'is probable' (either in the frequency sense or the propensity sense). In general, (purely) doxastic, metaphysical, modal, semantic, or syntactic expressions are not epistemic.

There is another constraint I wish to place on a theory of justified belief, in addition to the constraint that it be couched in non-epistemic language. Since I seek an explanatory theory, i.e., one that clarifies the underlying source of justificational status, it is not enough for a theory to state 'correct' necessary and sufficient conditions. Its conditions must also be appropriately deep or revelatory. Suppose, for example, that the following sufficient condition of justified belief is offered: 'If S senses redly at t and S believes at t that he is sensing redly, then S's belief at t that he is sensing redly is justified.' This is not the kind of principle I seek; for, even if it is correct, it leaves unexplained *why* a person who senses redly and believes that he does, believes this justifiably. Not every state is such that if one is in it and believes one is in it, this belief is justified. What is distinctive about the state of sensing redly, or 'phenomenal' states in general? A theory of justified belief of the kind I seek must answer this question, and hence it must be couched at a suitably deep, general, or abstract level.

A few introductory words about my *explicandum* are appropriate at this juncture. It is often assumed that whenever a person has a justified belief, he knows that it is justified and knows what the justification is. It is further assumed that the person can state or explain what his justification is. On this view, a justification is an argument, defense, or set of reasons that can be given in support of a belief. Thus, one studies the nature of justified belief by considering what a person might *say* if asked to defend, or justify, his belief. I make none of these sorts of assumptions here. I leave it an open question whether, when a belief *is* justified, the believer *knows* it is justified. I also leave it an open question whether, when a belief is justified, the believer can *state* or *give* a justification for it. I do not even assume that when a belief is justified there is something 'possessed' by the believer which can be called a 'justification'. I do assume that a justified belief gets its status of being justified from some processes or properties that make it justified. In short, there must be some justification-conferring processes or properties. But this does not imply that there must be an argument, or reason, or anything else, 'possessed' at the time of belief by the believer.

I

A theory of justified belief will be a set of principles that specify truth-conditions for the schema "S's belief in p at time t is justified", i.e., conditions for the satisfaction of this schema in all possible cases. It will be convenient to formulate candidate theories in a recursive or inductive format, which would include (A) one or more base clauses, (B) a set of recursive clauses (possibly null), and (C) a closure clause. In such a format, it is permissible for the predicate 'is a justified belief' to appear in recursive clauses. But neither this predicate, nor any other epistemic predicate, may appear in (the antecedent of) any base clause.[2]

Before turning to my own theory, I want to survey some other possible approaches to justified belief. Identification of problems associated with other attempts will provide some motivation for the theory I shall offer. Obviously, I cannot examine all, or even very many, alternative attempts. But a few sample attempts will be instructive.

Let us concentrate on the attempt to formulate one or more adequate base clause principles.[3] Here is a classical candidate:

(1) If S believes p at t, and p is indubitable for S (at t), then S's belief in p at t is justified.

To evaluate this principle, we need to know what 'indubitable' means. It can be understood in at least two ways. First, 'p is indubitable for S' might mean: 'S has no *grounds* for doubting p'. Since 'ground' is an epistemic term, however, principle (1) would be inadmissible on this reading, for epistemic terms may not legitimately appear in the antecedent of a base-clause. A second interpretation would avoid this difficulty. One might interpret 'p is indubitable for S' psychologically, i.e., as meaning 'S is psychologically incapable of doubting p'. This would make principle (1) admissible, but would it be correct? Surely not. A religious fanatic may be psychologically incapable of doubting the tenets of his faith, but that doesn't make his belief in them justified. Similarly, during the Watergate affair, someone may have been so blinded by the aura of the Presidency that even after the most damaging evidence against Nixon had emerged he was still incapable of doubting Nixon's veracity. It doesn't follow that his belief in Nixon's veracity was justified.

A second candidate base-clause principle is this:

(2) If S believes p at t, and p is self-evident, then S's belief in p at t is justified.

To evaluate this principle, we again need an interpretation of its crucial term, in this case 'self-evident'. On one standard reading, 'evident' is a synonym for 'justified'. '*Self*-evident' would therefore mean something like 'directly justified', 'intuitively justified', or 'non-derivatively justified'. On this reading 'self-evident' is an epistemic phrase, and principle (2) would be disqualified as a base-clause principle.

However, there are other possible readings of 'p is self-evident' on which it isn't an epistemic phrase. One such reading is: 'It is impossible to understand p without believing it'.[4] According to this interpretation, trivial analytic and logical truths might turn out to be self-evident. Hence, any belief in such a truth would be a justified belief, according to (2).

What does 'it is *impossible* to understand *p* without believing it' mean? Does it mean '*humanly* impossible'? That reading would probably make (2) an unacceptable principle. There may well be propositions which humans have an innate and irrepressible disposition to believe, e.g., 'Some events have causes'. But it seems unlikely that people's inability to refrain from believing such a proposition makes every belief in it justified.

Should we then understand 'impossible' to mean 'impossible in principle', or 'logically impossible'? If that is the reading given, I suspect that (2) is a vacuous principle. I doubt that even trivial logical or analytic truths will satisfy this definition of 'self-evident'. Any proposition, we may assume, has two or more components that are somehow organized or juxtaposed. To understand the proposition one must 'grasp' the components and their juxtaposition. Now in the case of *complex* logical truths, there are (human) psychological operations that suffice to grasp the components and their juxtaposition but do not suffice to produce a belief that the proposition is true. But can't we at least *conceive* of an analogous set of psychological operations even for simple logical truths, operations which perhaps are not in the repertoire of human cognizers but which might be in the repertoire of some conceivable beings? That is, can't we conceive of psychological operations that would suffice to grasp the components and componential-juxtaposition of these simple propositions but do not suffice to produce *belief* in the propositions? I think we can conceive of such operations. Hence, for any proposition you choose, it will be possible for it to be understood without being believed.

Finally, even if we set these two objections aside, we must note that self-evidence can at best confer justificational status on relatively few beliefs, and the only plausible group are beliefs in necessary truths. Thus, other base-clause principles will be needed to explain the justificational status of beliefs in contingent propositions.

The notion of a base-clause principle is naturally associated with the idea of 'direct' justifiedness, and in the realm of contingent propositions first-person-current-mental-state propositions have often been assigned this role. In Chisholm's terminology, this conception is expressed by the notion of a '*self-presenting*' state or proposition. The sentence 'I am thinking', for example, expresses a self-presenting proposition. (At least I shall *call* this sort of content a 'proposition', though it only has a truth value given some assignment of a subject who utters or entertains the content and a time of entertaining.) When such a proposition is true for person S at time t, S is justified in believing it at t: in Chisholm's terminology, the proposition is 'evident' for S at t. This suggests the following base-clause principle.

(3) If p is a self-presenting proposition, and p is true for S at t, and S believes p at t, then S's belief in p at t is justified.

What, exactly, does 'self-presenting' mean? In the second edition of *Theory of Knowledge*, Chisholm offers this definition: "h is self-presenting for S at $t =$ $_{df}$. h is true at t; and necessarily, if h is true at t, then h is evident for S at t."[5] Unfortunately, since 'evident' is an epistemic term, 'self-presenting' also becomes an epistemic term on this definition, thereby disqualifying (3) as a legitimate base-clause. Some other definition of self-presentingness must be offered if (3) is to be a suitable base-clause principle.

Another definition of self-presentation readily comes to mind. 'Self-presentation' is an approximate synonym of 'self-intimation', and a proposition may be said to be self-intimating if and only if whenever it is true of a person that person believes it. More precisely, we may give the following definition.

(SP) Proposition p is self-presenting if and only if: necessarily, for any S and any t, if p is true for S at t, then S believes p at t.

On this definition, 'self-presenting' is clearly not an epistemic predicate, so (3) would be an admissible principle. Moreover, there is initial plausibility in the suggestion that it is *this* feature of first-person-current-mental-state proposition—viz., their truth guarantees their being believed—that makes beliefs in them justified.

Employing this definition of self-presentation, is principle (3) correct? This cannot be decided until we define self-presentation more precisely. Since the operator 'necessarily' can be read in different ways, there are different forms of self-presentation and correspondingly different versions of principle (3). Let us focus on two of these readings: a *'nomological'* reading and a *'logical'* reading. Consider first the nomological reading. On this definition a proposition is self-presenting just in case it is nomologically necessary that if p is true for S at t, then S believes p at t.[6]

Is the nomological version of principle (3)—call it '(3_N)'—correct? Not at all. We can imagine cases in which the antecedent of (3_N) is satisfied but we would not say that the belief is justified. Suppose, for example, that p is the proposition expressed by the sentence 'I am in brain-state B', where 'B' is shorthand for a certain highly specific neural state description. Further suppose it is a nomological truth that anyone in brain-state B will ipso facto *believe* he is in brain-state B. In other words, imagine that an occurrent belief with the content 'I am in brain-state B' is realized whenever one is in brain-state B.[7] According to (3_N), any such belief is justified. But that is clearly false. We can readily imagine circumstances in which a person goes into brain-state B and therefore has the belief in question, though this belief is by no means justified. For example, we can imagine that a brain-surgeon operating on S artificially induces brain-state B. This results, phenomenologically, in S's suddenly believing—out of the blue—that he is in brain-state B, without any relevant antecedent beliefs. We would hardly say, in such a case, that S's belief that he is in brain-state B is justified.

Let us turn next to the logical version of (3)—call it '(3_L)'—in which a proposition is defined as self-presenting just in case it is logically necessary that if p is true for S at t, then S believes p at t. This stronger version of principle (3) might seem more promising. In fact, however, it is no more successful than (3_N). Let p be the proposition 'I am awake' and assume that it is logically necessary that if this proposition is true for some person S and time t, then S believes p at t. This assumption is consistent with the further assumption that S frequently believes p when it is false, e.g., when he is dreaming. Under these circumstances, we would hardly accept the contention that S's belief in this proposition is always justified. But nor should we accept the contention that the belief is justified when it is *true*. The truth of the proposition logically guarantees that the

belief is *held*, but why should it guarantee that the belief is *justified?*

The foregoing criticism suggests that we have things backwards. The idea of self-presentation is that truth guarantees belief. This fails to confer justification because it is compatible with there being belief without truth. So what seems necessary—or at least sufficient—for justification is that belief should guarantee truth. Such a notion has usually gone under the label of *'infallibility'*, or *'incorrigibility'*. It may be defined as follows.

(INC) Proposition p is incorrigible if and only if: necessarily, for any S and any t, if S believes p at t, then p is true for S at t.

Using the notion of incorrigibility, we may propose principle (4).

(4) If p is an incorrigible proposition, and S believes p at t, then S's belief in p at t is justified.

As was true of self-presentation, there are different varieties of incorrigibility, corresponding to different interpretations of 'necessarily'. Accordingly, we have different versions of principle (4). Once again, let us concentrate on a nomological and a logical version, (4_N) and (4_L) respectively.

We can easily construct a counterexample to (4_N) along the lines of the belief-state/brain-state counterexample that refuted (3_N). Suppose it is nomologically necessary that if anyone believes he is in brain-state B then it is true that he is in brain-state B, for the only way this belief-state is realized is through brain-state B itself. It follows that 'I am in brain-state B' is a nomologically incorrigible proposition. Therefore, according to (4_N), whenever anyone believes this proposition at any time, that belief is justified. But we may again construct a brain-surgeon example in which someone comes to have such a belief but the belief isn't justified.

Apart from this counterexample, the general point is this. Why should the fact that S's believing p guarantees the truth of p imply that S's belief is justified? The nature of the guarantee might be wholly fortuitous, as the belief-state/brain-state example is intended to illustrate. To appreciate the point, consider the following related possibility. A person's mental structure might be such that whenever he believes that p will be true (of him) a split second later, then p is true (of him) a split second later. This is because, we may suppose, his believing it brings it about. But surely we would not be compelled in such a circumstance to say that a belief of this sort is justified. So why should the fact that S's believing p guarantees the truth of p *precisely at the time of belief* imply that the belief is justified? There is no intuitive plausibility in this supposition.

The notion of *logical* incorrigibility has a more honored place in the history of conceptions of justification. But even principle (4_L), I believe, suffers from defects similar to those of (4_N). The mere fact that belief in p logically guarantees its truth does not confer justificational status on such a belief.

The first difficulty with (4_L) arises from logical or mathematical truths. Any true proposition of logic or mathematics is logically necessary. Hence, any such proposition p is logically incorrigible, since it is logically necessary that, for any S and any t, if S believes p at t then p is true (for S at t). Now assume that Nelson believes a certain very complex mathematical truth at time t. Since such a proposition is logically incorrigible, (4_L) implies that Nelson's belief in this truth at t is justified. But we may easily suppose that this belief of Nelson is not at all the result of proper mathematical reasoning, or even the result of appeal to trustworthy authority. Perhaps Nelson believes this complex truth because of utterly confused reasoning, or because of hasty and ill-founded conjecture. Then his belief is not justified, contrary to what (4_L) implies.

The case of logical or mathematical truths is admittedly peculiar, since the truth of these propositions is assured independently of any beliefs. It might seem, therefore, that we can better capture the idea of 'belief logically guaranteeing truth' in cases where the propositions in question are *contingent*. With this in mind, we might restrict (4_L) to *contingent* incorrigible propositions. Even this amendment cannot save (4_L), however, since there are counter-examples to it involving purely contingent propositions.

Suppose that Humperdink has been studying logic—or, rather, pseudologic—from Elmer Fraud, whom Humperdink has no reason to trust as a logician. Fraud has enunciated the principle that any disjunctive proposition consisting of at least 40 distinct disjuncts is very probably true. Humperdink now encounters the proposition p, a contingent proposition with 40 disjuncts, the 7th disjunct being 'I exist'. Although Humperdink grasps the proposition fully, he doesn't notice that it is entailed by 'I exist'. Rather, he is struck by the fact that it falls under the disjunction rule Fraud has enunciated (a rule I assume Humperdink is not *justified* in believing). Bearing this rule in mind, Humperdink forms a belief in p. Now notice that p is logically incorrigible. It is logically necessary that if anyone believes p, then p is true (of him at that time). This simply follows from the fact that, first, a person's believing anything entails that he exists, and second, 'I exist' entails p. Since p is logically incorrigible, principle (4_L) implies that Humperdink's belief in p is justified. But surely, given our example, that conclusion is false. Humperdink's belief in p is not at all justified.

One thing that goes wrong in this example is that while Humperdink's belief in p logically implies its truth, Humperdink doesn't *recognize* that his believing it implies its truth. This might move a theorist to revise (4_L) by adding the requirement that S 'recognize' that p is logically incorrigible. But this, of course, won't do. The term 'recognize' is obviously an epistemic term, so the suggested revision of (4_L) would result in an inadmissible base-clause.

II

Let us try to diagnose what has gone wrong with these attempts to produce an acceptable base-clause principle. Notice that each of the foregoing attempts confers the status of 'justified' on a belief without restriction on *why* the belief is held, i.e., on what *causally initiates* the belief or *causally sustains* it. The logical versions of principles (3) and (4), for example, clearly place no restriction on causes of belief. The same is true of the nomological versions of (3) and (4), since nomological requirements can be satisfied by simultaneity or cross-sectional laws, as illustrated by our brain-state/belief-state examples. I suggest that the absence of causal requirements accounts for the failure of the foregoing principles. Many of our counterexamples are ones in which the belief is caused in some strange or unacceptable way, e.g., by the accidental movement of a brain-surgeon's hand, by reliance on an illicit, pseudo-logical principle, or by the blinding aura of the Presidency. In general, a strategy for defeating a noncausal principle of justifiedness is to find a case in which the principle's antecedent is satisfied but the belief is caused by some faulty belief-forming process. The faultiness of the belief-forming process will incline us, intuitively, to regard the belief as unjustified. Thus, correct principles of justified belief must be principles that make causal requirements, where 'cause' is construed broadly to include sustainers as well as initiators of belief (i.e., processes that determine, or help to overdetermine, a belief's continuing to be held.)[8]

The need for causal requirements is not restricted to base-clause principles. Recursive principles will also need a causal component. One might initially suppose that the following is a good recursive principle: 'If S justifiably believes q at t, and q entails p, and S believes p at t, then S's belief in p at t is justified'. But this principle is unacceptable. S's belief in p doesn't receive justificational status simply from the fact that p is entailed by q and S justifiably believes q. If what causes S to believe p at t is entirely different, S's belief in p may well not be justified. Nor can the situation be remedied by adding to the antecedent the condition that S justifiably believes that q entails p. Even if he believes this, and believes q as well, he might not put these beliefs together. He might believe p as a result of some other wholly extraneous considerations. So once again, conditions that fail to require appropriate causes of a belief don't guarantee justifiedness.

Granted that principles of justified belief must make reference to causes of belief, what kinds of causes confer justifiedness? We can gain insight into this problem by reviewing some faulty processes of belief-formation, i.e., processes whose belief-outputs would be classed as unjustified. Here are some examples: confused reasoning, wishful thinking, reliance on emotional attachment, mere hunch or guesswork, and hasty generalization. What do these faulty processes have in common? They share the feature of *unreliability:* they tend to produce *error* a large proportion of the time. By contrast, which species of belief-forming (or belief-sustaining) processes are intuitively justification-conferring? They include standard perceptual processes, remembering, good reasoning, and introspection. What these

processes seem to have in common is *reliability:* the beliefs they produce are generally true. My positive proposal, then, is this. The justificational status of a belief is a function of the reliability of the process or processes that cause it, where (as a first approximation) reliability consists in the tendency of a process to produce beliefs that are true rather than false.

To test this thesis further, notice that justifiedness is not a purely categorical concept, although I treat it here as categorical in the interest of simplicity. We can and do regard certain beliefs as more justified than others. Furthermore, our intuitions of comparative justifiedness go along with our beliefs about the comparative reliability of the belief-causing processes.

Consider perceptual beliefs. Suppose Jones believes he has just seen a mountain-goat. Our assessment of the belief's justifiedness is determined by whether he caught a brief glimpse of the creature at a great distance, or whether he had a good look at the thing only 30 yards away. His belief in the latter sort of case is (*ceteris paribus*) more justified than in the former sort of case. And, if his belief is true, we are more prepared to say he *knows* in the latter case than in the former. The difference between the two cases seems to be this. Visual beliefs formed from brief and hasty scanning, or where the perceptual object is a long distance off, tend to be wrong more often than visual beliefs formed from detailed and leisurely scanning, or where the object is in reasonable proximity. In short, the visual processes in the former category are less reliable than those in the latter category. A similar point holds for memory beliefs. A belief that results from a hazy and indistinct memory impression is counted as less justified than a belief that arises from a distinct memory impression, and our inclination to classify those beliefs as *'knowledge'* varies in the same way. Again, the reason is associated with the comparative reliability of the processes. Hazy and indistinct memory impressions are generally less reliable indicators of what actually happened; so beliefs formed from such impressions are less likely to be true than beliefs formed from distinct impressions. Further, consider beliefs based on inference from observed samples. A belief about a population that is based on random sampling, or on instances that exhibit great variety, is intuitively more justified than a belief based on biased sampling, or on instances from a narrow sector of the population. Again, the degree of justifiedness seems to be a function of reliability. Inferences based on random or varied samples will tend to produce less error or inaccuracy than inferences based on non-random or non-varied samples.

Returning to a categorical concept of justifiedness, we might ask just *how* reliable a belief-forming process must be in order that its resultant beliefs be justified. A precise answer to this question should not be expected. Our conception of justification is *vague* in this respect. It does seem clear, however, that *perfect* reliability isn't required. Belief-forming processes that *sometimes* produce error still confer justification. It follows that there can be justified beliefs that are false.

I have characterized justification-conferring processes as ones that have a 'tendency' to produce beliefs that are true rather than false. The term 'tendency' could refer either to *actual* long-run frequency, or to a 'propensity', i.e., outcomes that would occur in merely *possible* realizations of the process. Which of these is intended? Unfortunately, I think our ordinary conception of justifiedness is vague on this dimension too. For the most part, we simply assume that the 'observed' frequency of truth versus error would be approximately replicated in the actual long-run, and also in relevant counterfactual situations, i.e., ones that are highly 'realistic', or conform closely to the circumstances of the actual world. Since we ordinarily assume these frequencies to be roughly the same, we make no concerted effort to distinguish them. Since the purpose of my present theorizing is to capture our ordinary conception of justifiedness, and since our ordinary conception is vague on this matter, it is appropriate to leave the theory vague in the same respect.

We need to say more about the notion of a belief-forming 'process'. Let us mean by a 'process' a *functional operation* or procedure, i.e., something that generates a *mapping* from certain states—'inputs'—into other states— 'outputs'. The outputs in the present case are states of believing this or that proposition at a given moment. On this interpretation, a process is a *type* as opposed to a *token*. This is fully appropriate, since it is only types that have statistical properties such as producing truth 80% of the time; and it is precisely such statistical properties

that determine the reliability of a process. Of course, we also want to speak of a process as *causing* a belief, and it looks as if types are incapable of being causes. But when we say that a belief is caused by a given process, understood as a functional procedure, we may interpret this to mean that it is caused by the particular *inputs* to the process (and by the intervening events 'through which' the functional procedure carries the inputs into the output) on the occasion in question.

What are some examples of belief-forming 'processes' construed as functional operations? One example is reasoning processes, where the inputs include antecedent beliefs and entertained hypotheses. Another example is functional procedures whose inputs include desires, hopes, or emotional states of various sorts (together with antecedent beliefs). A third example is a memory process, which takes as input beliefs or experiences at an earlier time and generates as output beliefs at a later time. For example, a memory process might take as input a belief *at* t_1 that Lincoln was born in 1809 and generate as output a belief *at* t_n that Lincoln was born in 1809. A fourth example is perceptual processes. Here it isn't clear whether inputs should include states of the environment, such as the distance of the stimulus from the cognizer, or only events within or on the surface of the organism, e.g., receptor stimulations. I shall return to this point in a moment.

A critical problem concerning our analysis is the degree of generality of the process-types in question. Input-output relations can be specified very broadly or very narrowly, and the degree of generality will partly determine the degree of reliability. A process-type might be selected so narrowly that only one instance of it ever occurs, and hence the type is either completely reliable or completely unreliable. (This assumes that reliability is a function of *actual* frequency only.) If such narrow process-types were selected, beliefs that are intuitively unjustified might be said to result from perfectly reliable processes; and beliefs that are intuitively justified might be said to result from perfectly unreliable processes.

It is clear that our ordinary thought about process-types slices them broadly, but I cannot at present give a precise explication of our intuitive principles. One plausible suggestion, though, is that the relevant processes are *content-neutral*. It might be argued, for example, that the process of *inferring p whenever the Pope asserts p* could pose problems for our theory. If the Pope is infallible, this process will be perfectly reliable; yet we would not regard the belief-outputs of this process as justified. The content-neutral restriction would avert this difficulty. If relevant processes are required to admit as input beliefs (or other states) with *any* content, the aforementioned process will not count, for its input beliefs have a restricted propositional content, viz., '*the Pope* asserts *p*'.

In addition to the problem of 'generality' or 'abstractness' there is the previously mentioned problem of the '*extent*' of belief-forming processes. Clearly, the causal ancestry of beliefs often includes events outside the organism. Are such events to be included among the 'inputs' of belief-forming processes? Or should we restrict the extent of belief-forming processes to '*cognitive*' events, i.e., events within the organism's nervous system? I shall choose the latter course, though with some hesitation. My general grounds for this decision are roughly as follows. Justifiedness seems to be a function of how a cognizer deals with his environmental input, i.e., with the goodness or badness of the operations that register and transform the stimulation that reaches him. ('Deal with', of course, does not mean *purposeful* action; nor is it restricted to *conscious* activity.) A justified belief is, roughly speaking, one that results from cognitive operations that are, generally speaking, good or successful. But '*cognitive*' operations are most plausibly construed as operations of the cognitive faculties, i.e., 'information-processing' equipment *internal* to the organism.

With these points in mind, we may now advance the following base-clause principle for justified belief.

(5) If S's believing *p* at *t* results from a reliable cognitive belief-forming process (or set of processes), then S's belief in *p* at *t* is justified.

Since 'reliable belief-forming process' has been defined in terms of such notions as belief, truth, statistical frequency, and the like, it is not an epistemic term. Hence, (5) is an admissible base clause.

It might seem as if (5) promises to be not only a successful base clause, but the only principle needed whatever, apart from a closure clause. In other words, it might seem as if it is a necessary as well as

a sufficient condition of justifiedness that a belief be produced by reliable cognitive belief-forming processes. But this is not quite correct, given our provisional definition of 'reliability'.

Our provisional definition implies that a reasoning process is reliable only if it generally produces beliefs that are true, and similarly, that a memory process is reliable only if it generally yields beliefs that are true. But these requirements are too strong. A reasoning procedure cannot be expected to produce true belief if it is applied to false premises. And memory cannot be expected to yield a true belief if the original belief it attempts to retain is false. What we need for reasoning and memory, then, is a notion of '*conditional reliability*'. A process is conditionally reliable when a sufficient proportion of its output-beliefs are true *given that its input-beliefs are true*.

With this point in mind, let us distinguish *belief-dependent* and *belief-independent* cognitive processes. The former are processes *some* of whose inputs are belief-states.[9] The latter are processes *none* of whose inputs are belief-states. We may then replace principle (5) with the following two principles, the first a base-clause principle and the second a recursive-clause principle.

(6_A) If S's belief in *p* at *t* results ("immediately") from a belief-independent process that is (unconditionally) reliable, then S's belief in *p* at *t* is justified.

(6_B) If S's belief in *p* at *t* results ("immediately") from a belief-dependent process that is (at least) conditionally reliable, and if the beliefs (if any) on which this process operates in producing S's belief in *p* at *t* are themselves justified, then S's belief in *p* at *t* is justified.[10]

If we add to (6_A) and (6_B) the standard closure clause, we have a complete theory of justified belief. The theory says, in effect, that a belief is justified if and only if it is '*well-formed*', i.e., it has an ancestry of reliable and/or conditionally reliable cognitive operations. (Since a dated belief may be over-determined, it may have a number of distinct ancestral trees. These need not all be full of reliable or conditionally reliable processes. But at least one ancestral tree must have reliable or conditionally reliable processes throughout.)

The theory of justified belief proposed here, then, is an *Historical* or *Genetic* theory. It contrasts with the dominant approach to justified belief, an approach that generates what we may call (borrowing a phrase from Robert Nozick) *'Current Time-Slice'* theories. A Current Time-Slice theory makes the justificational status of a belief wholly a function of what is true of the cognizer *at the time* of belief. An Historical theory makes the justificational status of a belief depend on its prior history. Since my Historical theory emphasizes the reliability of the belief-generating processes. it may be called *'Historical Reliabilism'*.

The most obvious examples of Current Time-Slice theories are 'Cartesian' Foundationalist theories, which trace all justificational status (at least of contingent propositions) to current mental states. The usual varieties of Coherence theories, however, are equally Current Time-Slice views, since they too make the justificational status of a belief wholly a function of *current* states of affairs. For Coherence theories, however, these current states include all other beliefs of the cognizer, which would not be considered relevant by Cartesian Foundationalism. Have there been other Historical theories of justified belief? Among contemporary writers, Quine and Popper have Historical epistemologies, though the notion of 'justification' is not their avowed *explicandum*. Among historical writers, it might seem that Locke and Hume had Genetic theories of sorts. But I think that their Genetic theories were only theories of ideas, not of knowledge or justification. Plato's theory of recollection, however, is a good example of a Genetic theory of knowing.[11] And it might be argued that Hegel and Dewey had Genetic epistemologies (if Hegel can be said to have had a clear epistemology at all).

The theory articulated by (6_A) and (6_B) might be viewed as a kind of 'Foundationalism,' because of its recursive structure. I have no objection to this label, as long as one keeps in mind how different this 'diachronic' form of Foundationalism is from Cartesian, or other 'synchronic' varieties of, Foundationalism.

Current Time-Slice theories characteristically assume that the justificational status of a belief is something which the cognizer is able to know or determine at the time of belief. This is made explicit, for example, by Chisholm.[12] The Historical theory I endorse makes no such assumption. There are many facts about a cognizer to which he lacks 'privileged access', and I regard the justificational status of his beliefs as one of those things. This is not to say that a cognizer is necessarily ignorant, at any given moment, of the justificational status of his current beliefs. It is only to deny that he necessarily has, or can get, knowledge or true belief about this status. Just as a person can know without knowing that he knows, so he can have justified belief without knowing that it is justified (or believing justifiably that it is justified).

A characteristic case in which a belief is justified though the cognizer doesn't know that it's justified is where the original evidence for the belief has long since been forgotten. If the original evidence was compelling, the cognizer's original belief may have been justified; and this justificational status may have been preserved through memory. But since the cognizer no longer remembers how or why he came to believe, he may not know that the belief is justified. If asked now to justify his belief, he may be at a loss. Still, the belief *is* justified, though the cognizer can't demonstrate or establish this.

The Historical theory of justified belief I advocate is connected in spirit with the causal theory of knowing I have presented elsewhere.[13] I had this in mind when I remarked near the outset of the paper that my theory of justified belief makes justifiedness come out closely related to knowledge. Justified beliefs, like pieces of knowledge, have appropriate histories; but they may fail to be knowledge either because they are false or because they founder on some other requirement for knowing of the kind discussed in the post-Gettier knowledge-trade.

There is a variant of the Historical conception of justified belief that is worth mentioning in this context. It may be introduced as follows. Suppose S has a set B of beliefs at time t_0, and some of these beliefs are *un*justified. Between t_0 and t_1 he reasons from the entire set B to the conclusion p, which he then accepts at t_1. The reasoning procedure he uses is a very sound one, i.e., one that is conditionally reliable. There is a sense or respect in which we are tempted to say that S's belief in p at t_1 is 'justified'. At any rate, it is tempting to say that the *person* is justified in believing p at t. Relative to his antecedent cognitive state, he did as well as could be expected: the *transition* from his cognitive state at t_0 to his cognitive state at t_1 was entirely sound. Although we may acknowledge this brand of justifiedness—it might be called *'Terminal-Phase Reliabilism'*—it is not a kind of justifiedness so closely related to knowing. For a person to know proposition p, it is not enough that the *final phase* of the process that leads to his belief in p be sound. It is also necessary that some entire history of the process be sound (i.e., reliable or conditionally reliable).

Let us return now to the Historical theory. In the next section of the paper, I shall adduce reasons for strengthening it a bit. Before looking at these reasons, however, I wish to review two quite different objections to the theory.

First, a critic might argue that *some* justified beliefs do not derive their justificational status from their causal ancestry. In particular, it might be argued that beliefs about one's current phenomenal states and intuitive beliefs about elementary logical or conceptual relationships do not derive their justificational status in this way. I am not persuaded by either of these examples. Introspection, I believe, should be regarded as a form of retrospection. Thus, a justified belief that I am 'now' in pain gets its justificational status from a relevant, though brief, causal history.[14] The apprehension of logical or conceptual relationships is also a cognitive process that occupies time. The psychological process of 'seeing' or 'intuiting' a simple logical truth is very fast, and we cannot introspectively dissect it into constituent parts. Nonetheless, there are mental operations going on, just as there are mental operations that occur in *idiots savants,* who are unable to report the computational processes they in fact employ.

A second objection to Historical Reliabilism focuses on the reliability element rather than the causal or historical element. Since the theory is intended to cover all possible cases, it seems to imply that for any cognitive process C, if C is reliable in possible world W, then any belief in W that results from C is justified. But doesn't this permit easy counterexamples? Surely we can imagine a possible world in which wishful thinking is reliable. We can imagine a possible world where a benevolent demon so arranges things that beliefs formed by wishful thinking usually come true. This would make wish-

ful thinking a reliable process in that possible world, but surely we don't want to regard beliefs that result from wishful thinking as justified.

There are several possible ways to respond to this case and I am unsure which response is best, partly because my own intuitions (and those of other people I have consulted) are not entirely clear. One possibility is to say that in the possible world imagined, beliefs that result from wishful thinking *are* justified. In other words we reject the claim that wishful thinking could never, intuitively, confer justifiedness.[15]

However, for those who feel that wishful thinking couldn't confer justifiedness, even in the world imagined, there are two ways out. First, it may be suggested that the proper criterion of justifiedness is the propensity of a process to generate beliefs that are true *in a non-manipulated environment,* i.e., an environment in which there is no purposeful arrangement of the world either to accord or conflict with the beliefs that are formed. In other words, the suitability of a belief-forming process is only a function of its success in *'natural'* situations, not situations of the sort involving benevolent or malevolent demons, or any other such manipulative creatures. If we reformulate the theory to include this qualification, the counterexample in question will be averted.

Alternatively, we may reformulate our theory, or reinterpret it, as follows. Instead of construing the theory assaying that a belief in possible world W is justified if and only if it results from a cognitive process that is reliable in W, we may construe it as saying that a belief in possible world W is justified if and only if it results from a cognitive process that is reliable *in our world.* In short, our conception of justifiedness is derived as follows. We note certain cognitive processes in the actual world, and form beliefs about which of these are reliable. The ones we believe to be reliable are then regarded as justification-conferring processes. In reflecting on hypothetical beliefs, we deem them justified if and only if they result from processes already picked out as justification-conferring, or processes very similar to those. Since wishful thinking is not among these processes, a belief formed in a possible world W by wishful thinking would not be deemed justified, even if wishful thinking is reliable *in W.* I am not sure that this is a correct reconstruction of our intuitive conceptual scheme, but it would accommodate the benevolent demon case, at least if the proper thing to say in that case is that the wishful-thinking-caused beliefs are unjustified.

Even if we adopt this strategy, however, a problem still remains. Suppose that wishful thinking turns out to be reliable *in the actual world*![16] This might be because, unbeknownst to us at present, there is a benevolent demon who, lazy until now, will shortly start arranging things so that our wishes come true. The long-run performance of wishful thinking will be very good, and hence even the new construal of the theory will imply that beliefs resulting from wishful thinking (in *our* world) are justified. Yet this surely contravenes our intuitive judgment on the matter.

Perhaps the moral of the case is that the standard format of a 'conceptual analysis' has its shortcomings. Let me depart from that format and try to give a better rendering of our aims and the theory that tries to achieve that aim. What we really want is an *explanation* of why we count, or would count, certain beliefs as justified and others as unjustified. Such an explanation must refer to our *beliefs* about reliability, not to the actual *facts*. The reason we *count* beliefs as justified is that they are formed by what we *believe* to be reliable belief-forming processes. Our beliefs about which belief-forming processes are reliable may be erroneous, but that does not affect the adequacy of the explanation. Since we *believe* that wishful thinking is an unreliable belief-forming process, we regard beliefs formed by wishful thinking as unjustified. What matters, then, is what we *believe* about wishful thinking, not what is *true* (in the long run) about wishful thinking. I am not sure how to express this point in the standard format of conceptual analysis, but it identifies an important point in understanding our theory.

III

Let us return, however, to the standard format of conceptual analysis, and let us consider a new objection that will require some revisions in the theory advanced until now. According to our theory, a belief is justified in case it is caused by a process that is in fact reliable, or by one we generally believe to be reliable. But suppose that although one of S's be-

liefs satisfies this condition, S has no reason to believe that it does. Worse yet, suppose S has reason to believe that his belief is caused by an *un*reliable process (although *in fact* its causal ancestry is fully reliable). Wouldn't we deny in such circumstances that S's belief is justified? This seems to show that our analysis, as presently formulated, is mistaken.

Suppose that Jones is told on fully reliable authority that a certain class of his memory beliefs is almost all mistaken. His parents fabricate a wholly false story that Jones suffered from amnesia when he was seven but later developed *pseudo*-memories of that period. Though Jones listens to what his parents say and has excellent reason to trust them, he persists in believing the ostensible memories from his seven-year-old past. Are these memory beliefs justified? Intuitively, they are not justified. But since these beliefs result from genuine memory and original perceptions, which are adequately reliable processes, our theory says that these beliefs are justified.

Can the theory be revised to meet this difficulty? One natural suggestion is that the actual reliability of a belief's ancestry is not enough for justifiedness; in addition, the cognizer must be *justified in believing* that the ancestry of his belief is reliable. Thus one might think of replacing (6_A), for example, with (7). (For simplicity, I neglect some of the details of the earlier analysis.)

(7) If S's belief in p at t is caused by a reliable cognitive process, and S justifiably believes at t that his p-belief is so caused, then S's belief in p at t is justified.

It is evident, however, that (7) will not do as a base clause, for it contains the epistemic term 'justifiably' in its antecedent.

A slightly weaker revision, without this problematic feature, might next be suggested, viz.,

(8) If S's belief in p at t is caused by a reliable cognitive process, and S believes at t that his p-belief is so caused, then S's belief in p at t is justified.

But this won't do the job. Suppose that Jones believes that his memory beliefs are reliably caused despite all the (trustworthy) contrary testimony of his parents. Principle (8) would be satisfied, yet we wouldn't say that these beliefs are justified.

Next, we might try (9), which is stronger than (8) and, unlike (7), formally admissible as a base clause.

(9) If S's belief in p at t is caused by a reliable cognitive process, and S believes at t that his p-belief is so caused, and this meta-belief is caused by a reliable cognitive process, than S's belief in p at t is justified.

A first objection to (9) is that it wrongly precludes unreflective creatures—creatures like animals or young children, who have no beliefs about the genesis of their beliefs—from having justified beliefs. If one shares my view that justified belief is, at least roughly, *well-formed* belief, surely animals and young children can have justified beliefs.

A second problem with (9) concerns its underlying rationale. Since (9) is proposed as a substitute for (6_A), it is implied that the reliability of a belief's own cognitive ancestry does not make it justified. But, the suggestion seems to be, the reliability of a *meta-belief*'s ancestry confers justifiedness on the first-order belief. Why should that be so? Perhaps one is attracted by the idea of a 'trickle-down' effect: if an n + 1-level belief is justified, its justification trickles down to an n-level belief. But even if the trickle-down theory is correct, it doesn't help here. There is no assurance from the satisfaction of (9)'s antecedent that the meta-belief itself is *justified*.

To obtain a better revision of our theory, let us re-examine the Jones case. Jones has strong evidence against certain propositions concerning his past. He doesn't *use* this evidence, but if he *were* to use it properly, he would stop believing these propositions. Now the proper use of evidence would be an instance of a (conditionally) reliable process. So what we can say about Jones is that he *fails* to use a certain (conditionally) reliable process that he could and should have used. Admittedly, had he used this process, he would have 'worsened' his doxastic states: he would have replaced some true beliefs with suspension of judgment. Still, he couldn't have known this in the case in question. So, he failed to do something which, epistemically, he should have done. This diagnosis suggests a fundamental change in our theory. The justificational status of a belief is not only a function of the cognitive processes *actually* employed in producing it; it is also a function of processes that could and should be employed.

With these points in mind, we may tentatively propose the following revision of our theory, where we again focus on a base-clause principle but omit certain details in the interest of clarity.

(10) If S's belief in p at t results from a reliable cognitive process, and there is no reliable or conditionally reliable process available to S which, had it been used by S in addition to the process actually used, would have resulted in S's not believing p at t, then S's belief in p at t is justified.

There are several problems with this proposal. First, there is a technical problem. One cannot use an additional belief-forming (or doxastic-state-forming) process *as well as* the original process if the additional one would result in a different doxastic state. One wouldn't be using the original process at all. So we need a slightly different formulation of the relevant counter-factual. Since the basic idea is reasonably clear, however, I won't try to improve on the formulation here. A second problem concerns the notion of *'available'* belief-forming (or doxastic-state-forming) processes. What is it for a process to be 'available' to a cognizer? Were scientific procedures 'available' to people who lived in pre-scientific ages? Furthermore, it seems implausible to say that all 'available' processes ought to be used, at least if we include such processes as gathering *new* evidence. Surely a belief can sometimes be justified even if additional evidence-gathering would yield a different doxastic attitude. What I think we should have in mind here are such additional processes as calling previously acquired evidence to mind, assessing the implications of that evidence, etc. This is admittedly somewhat vague, but here again our ordinary notion of justifiedness is vague, so it is appropriate for our analysans to display the same sort of vagueness.

This completes the sketch of my account of justified belief. Before concluding, however, it is essential to point out that there is an important use of 'justified' which is not captured by this account but can be captured by a closely related one.

There is a use of 'justified' in which it is not implied or presupposed that there is a *belief* that is justified. For example, if S is trying to decide whether to believe p and asks our advice, we may tell him that he is 'justified' in believing it. We do not thereby imply that he *has* a justified *belief,* since we know he is still suspending judgement. What we mean, roughly, is that he *would* or *could* be justified if he were to believe *p.* The justificational status we ascribe here cannot be a function of the causes of *S*'s believing *p,* for there is no belief by *S* in *p.* Thus, the account of justifiedness we have given thus far cannot explicate *this* use of 'justified'. (It doesn't follow that this use of 'justified' has no connection with causal ancestries. Its proper use may depend on the causal ancestry of the cognizer's cognitive state, though not on the causal ancestry of his believing *p.*)

Let us distinguish two uses of 'justified': an *ex post* use and an *ex ante* use. The *ex post* use occurs when there exists a belief, and we say *of that belief* that it is (or isn't) justified. The *ex ante* use occurs when no such belief exists, or when we wish to ignore the question of whether such a belief exists. Here we say of the *person,* independent of his doxastic state vis-à-vis *p,* that *p* is (or isn't) suitable for him to believe.[17]

Since we have given an account of *ex post* justifiedness, it will suffice if we can analyze *ex ante* justifiedness in terms of it. Such an analysis, I believe, is ready at hand. *S* is *ex ante* justified in believing *p* at *t* just in case his total cognitive state at *t* is such that from that state he could come to believe *p* in such a way that this belief would be *ex post* justified. More precisely, he is *ex ante* justified in believing *p* at *t* just in case a reliable belief-forming operation is available to him such that the application of that operation to his total cognitive state at *t* would result, more or less immediately, in his believing *p* and this belief would be *ex post* justified. Stated formally, we have the following:

(11) Person *S* is *ex ante* justified in believing *p* at *t* if and only if there is a reliable belief-forming operation available to *S* which is such that if *S* applied that operation to his total cognitive state at *t,* *S* would believe *p* at *t*-plus-delta (for a suitably small delta) and that belief would be *ex post* justified.

For the analysans of (11) to be satisfied, the total cognitive state at *t* must have a suitable causal ancestry. Hence, (11) is implicitly an Historical account of *ex ante* justifiedness.

As indicated, the bulk of this paper was addressed to *ex post* justifiedness. This is the appropriate analysandum if one is interested in the connection between justifiedness and knowledge, since what is crucial to whether a person *knows* a proposition is whether he has an actual *belief* in the proposition that is justified. However, since many epistemologists are interested in *ex ante* justifiedness, it is proper for a general theory of justification to try to provide an account of that concept as well. Our theory does this quite naturally, for the account of *ex ante* justifiedness falls out directly from our account of *ex post* justifiedness.[18]

NOTES

1. Goldman 1967, 1975, 1976.
2. Notice that the choice of a recursive format does not prejudice the case for or against any particular theory. A recursive format is perfectly general. Specifically, an explicit set of necessary and sufficient conditions is just a special case of a recursive format, i.e. one in which there is no recursive clause.
3. Many of the attempts I shall consider are suggested by material in William Alston 1971.
4. Such a definition (though without the modal term) is given, for example, by W. V. Quine and J. S. Ullian 1970, p. 21. Statements are said to be self-evident just in case "to understand them is to believe them".
5. Chisholm 1977, p. 22.
6. I assume, of course, that 'nomologically necessary' is *de re* with respect to '*S*' and '*t*' in this construction. I shall not focus on problems that may arise in this regard, since my primary concerns are with different issues.
7. This assumption violates the thesis that Davidson calls 'The Anomalism of the Mental'. Cf. Davidson 1970. But it is unclear that this thesis is a necessary truth. Thus, it seems fair to assume its falsity in order to produce a counterexample. The example neither entails nor precludes the mental-physical identity theory.
8. Keith Lehrer's example of the gypsy lawyer is intended to show the inappropriateness of a causal requirement. (See Lehrer 1974, pp. 124–125.) But I find this example unconvincing. To the extent that I clearly imagine that the lawyer fixes his belief solely as a result of the cards, it seems intuitively

wrong to say that he *knows*—or has a *justified belief*—that his client is innocent.

9. This definition is not exactly what we need for the purposes at hand. As Ernest Sosa points out, introspection will turn out to be a belief-dependent process since sometimes the input into the process will be a belief (when the introspected content is a belief). Intuitively, however, introspection is not the sort of process which may be merely conditionally reliable. I do not know how to refine the definition so as to avoid this difficulty, but it is a small and isolated point.

10. It may be objected that principles (6_A) and (6_B) are jointly open to analogues of the lottery paradox. A series of processes composed of reliable but less-than-perfectly-reliable processes may be extremely unreliable. Yet applications of (6_A) and (6_B) would confer justifiedness on a belief that is caused by such a series. In reply to this objection, we might simply indicate that the theory is intended to capture our ordinary notion of justifiedness, and this ordinary notion has been formed without recognition of this kind of problem. The theory is not wrong *as* a theory of the ordinary (naive) conception of justifiedness. On the other hand, if we want a theory to do more than capture the ordinary conception of justifiedness, it might be possible to strengthen the principles to avoid lottery-paradox analogues.

11. I am indebted to Mark Pastin for this point.

12. Cf. Chisholm 1977, pp. 17, 114–116.

13. Cf. Goldman 1967. The reliability aspect of my theory also has its precursors in earlier papers of mine on knowing: Goldman 1975, 1976.

14. The view that introspection is retrospection was taken by Ryle, and before him (as Charles Hartshorne points out to me) by Hobbes, Whitehead, and possibly Husserl.

15. Of course, if people in world *W* learn *inductively* that wishful thinking is reliable, and regularly base their beliefs on this inductive inference, it is quite unproblematic and straightforward that their beliefs are justified. The only interesting case is where their beliefs are formed *purely* by wishful thinking, without using inductive inference. The suggestion contemplated in this paragraph of the text is that,

in the world imagined, even pure wishful thinking would confer justifiedness.

16. I am indebted here to Mark Kaplan.

17. The distinction between *ex post* and *ex ante* justifiedness is similar to Roderick Firth's distinction between *doxastic* and *propositional* warrant. See Firth 1978.

18. Research on this paper was begun while the author was a fellow of the John Simon Guggenheim Memorial Foundation and of the Center for Advanced Study in the Behavioral Sciences. I am grateful for their support. I have received helpful comments and criticism from Holly S. Goldman, Mark Kaplan, Fred Schmitt, Stephen P. Stich, and many others at several universities where earlier drafts of the paper were read.

REFERENCES

Alston, William P. 1971. "Varieties of Privileged Access." *American Philosophical Quarterly* 8, 223–241.

Chisholm, R.M. 1977. *Theory of Knowledge.* 2d ed. Englewood Cliffs, N.J.: Prentice Hall.

Davidson, D. 1970. "The Anomalism of the Mental." In Foster and Swanson 1970.

Foster L., and Swanson, J.W., eds. 1970. *Experience and Theory.* Amherst: University of Massachusetts Press.

Goldman, Alvin I. 1967. "A Causal Theory of Knowing." *Journal of Philosophy* 64, 357–372. Reprinted in Pappas and Swain 1978. [4, 5, 7]

Goldman, Alvin I. 1975. "Innate Knowledge." In Stich 1975.

Goldman, Alvin I. 1976. "Discrimination and Perceptual Knowledge." *Journal of Philosophy* 73, 771–791. Reprinted in Pappas and Swain 1978.

Lehrer, Keith. 1974. *Knowledge.* Oxford: Oxford University Press.

Pappas, George S., and Swain, Marshall, eds. 1978. *Essays on Knowledge and Justification.* Ithaca: Cornell University Press.

Quine, W.V.O., and Ullian, J.S. 1978. *The Web of Belief.* 2d ed. New York: Random House.

Stich, Stephen P. 1975. *Innate Ideas.* Berkeley: University of California Press.

LAURENCE BONJOUR

Externalist Theories of Empirical Knowledge

Of the many problems that would have to be solved by a satisfactory theory of empirical knowledge, perhaps the most central is a general structural problem which I shall call *the epistemic regress problem*: the problem of how to avoid an infinite and presumably vicious regress of justification in one's account of the justification of empirical beliefs. *Foundationalist* theories of empirical knowledge, as we shall see further below, attempt to avoid the regress by locating a class of empirical beliefs whose justification does not depend on that of other empirical beliefs. Externalist theories, the topic of the present paper, represent one species of foundationalism.

I

I begin with a brief look at the epistemic regress problem. The source of the problem is the requirement that beliefs that are to constitute knowledge must be *epistemically justified*. Such a requirement is of course an essential part of the "traditional" conception of knowledge as justified true belief, but it also figures in at least most of the revisions of that conception which have been inspired by the Gettier problem. Indeed, if this requirement is understood in a sufficiently generic way, as meaning roughly that the acceptance of the belief must be epistemically rational, that it must not be epistemically irresponsible, then it becomes hard to see how any adequate conception of knowledge can fail to include it.

How then are empirical beliefs epistemically justified? Certainly the most obvious way to show that such a belief is justified is by producing a justificatory argument in which the belief to be justified is shown to follow inferentially from some other (perhaps conjunctive) belief, which is thus offered as a reason for accepting it. Beliefs whose justification would, if made explicit, take this form may be said to be *inferentially justified*. (Of course, such a justificatory argument would usually be explicitly rehearsed only in the face of some specific problem or challenge. Notice also that an inferentially justified belief need not have been *arrived at* through inference, though it often will have been.)

The important point about inferential justification, however, is that if the justificandum belief is to be genuinely justified by the proffered argument, then the belief that provides the premise of the argument must itself be justified in some fashion. This premise belief might of course itself be inferentially justified, but this would only raise a new issue of justification with respect to the premise(s) of this new justificatory argument, and so on, so that empirical knowledge is threatened by an infinite and seemingly vicious regress of epistemic justification, with a thoroughgoing skepticism as the eventual outcome. So long as each new step of justification is inferential, it appears that justification can never be completed, indeed can never really even get started, and hence that there is no justification and no knowledge. Thus the epistemic regress problem.

What is the eventual outcome of this regress? There are a variety of possibilities, but the majority of philosophers who have considered the problem have believed that the only outcome that does not lead more or less directly to skepticism is *foundationalism*: the view that the regress terminates by reaching empirical beliefs (a) that are genuinely justified, but (b) whose justification is not inferentially dependent on that of any further empirical belief(s), so that no further issue of empirical justification is thereby raised. These non-inferentially justified beliefs, or *basic beliefs* as I shall call them, are claimed to provide the foundation upon which the edifice of empirical knowledge rests. And the central argument for foundationalism is simply that all other possible outcomes of the regress lead inexorably to skepticism.[1]

This argument has undeniable force. Nonetheless, the central concept of foundationalism, the concept of a basic belief, is itself by no means unproblematic. The fundamental question that must be answered by any acceptable version of foundationalism is: *how are basic beliefs possible*? How, that is, is it possible for there to be an empirical belief that is epistemically justified in a way completely independent of any believed premises that might provide reasons for accepting it? As Chisolm suggests, a basic belief seems to be in effect an epistemologically unmoved (or perhaps self-moved) mover. But such a status is surely no less paradoxical in epistemology than it is in theology.

This intuitive difficulty with the idea of a basic empirical belief may be elaborated by considering briefly the fundamental concept of epistemic justification. There are two points to be made. First, the idea of justification is generic, admitting in principle of many different species. Thus, for example, the acceptance of an empirical belief might be morally justified, or pragmatically justified, or justified in some still different sense. But a belief's being justified in one of these other senses will not satisfy the justification condition for knowledge. What knowledge requires is *epistemic* justification. And the distinguishing characteristic of this particular species of justification is, I submit, its internal relationship to the cognitive goal of *truth*. A cognitive act is epistemically justified, on this conception, only if and to the extent that is aimed at this goal-which means at a minimum that one accepts only beliefs that there is adequate reason to think are true.

Second, the concept of epistemic justification is fundamentally a normative concept. It has to do with what one has a duty or obligation to do, from an epistemic or intellectual standpoint. As Chisholm suggests, one's purely intellectual duty is to accept beliefs that are true, or likely to be true, and reject beliefs that are false, or likely to be false. To accept beliefs on some other basis is to violate one's epistemic duty—to be, one might say, *epistemically irresponsible*—even though such acceptance might be desirable or even mandatory from some other, nonepistemic standpoint.

Thus if basic beliefs are to provide a suitable foundation for empirical knowledge, if inference from them is to be the sole basis for the justification

of other empirical beliefs, then that feature, whatever it may be, in virtue of which an empirical belief qualifies as basic, must also constitute an adequate reason for thinking that the belief is true. And now if we assume, plausibly enough, that the person for whom a belief is basic must *himself* possess the justification for that belief if *his* acceptance of it is to be epistemically rational or responsible, and thus apparently that he must believe *with justification* both (a) that the belief has the feature in question and (b) that beliefs having that feature are likely to be true, then we get the result that this belief is not basic after all, since its justification depends on that of these other beliefs. If this result is correct, then foundationalism is untenable as a solution to the regress problem.[2]

What strategies are available to the foundationalist for avoiding this objection? One possibility would be to grant that the believer must be in possession of the reason for thinking that his basic belief is true but hold that the believer's cognitive grasp of that reason does not involve further *beliefs,* which would then require justification, but instead cognitive states of a different and more rudimentary kind: *intuitions* or *immediate apprehensions,* which are somehow capable of conferring justification upon beliefs without themselves requiring justification. Some such view as this seems implicit in most traditional versions of foundationalism.[3]

My concern in the present paper, however, is with an alternative foundationalist strategy, one of comparatively recent innovation. One way, perhaps somewhat tendentious, to put this alternative approach is to say that according to it, though there must in a sense be a reason why a basic belief is likely to be true, the person for whom such a belief is basic need not have any cognitive grasp of this reason. On this view, the epistemic justification or reasonableness of a basic belief depends on the obtaining of an appropriate relation, generally causal or nomological in character, between the believer and the world. This relation, which is differently characterized by different versions of the view, is such as to make it either nomologically certain or else highly probable that the belief is true. It would thus provide, *for anyone who knew about it,* an undeniably excellent reason for accepting such a belief. But according to proponents of the view under discussion, the person for whom the belief is basic need not (and in general will not) have any cognitive grasp of any kind of this reason or of the relation that is the basis for it in order for this basic belief to be justified; all these matters may be entirely *external* to the person's subjective conception of the situation. Thus the justification of a basic belief need not involve any further beliefs (or other cognitive states) so that no further regress of justification is generated. D. M. Armstrong calls this an "externalist" solution to the regress problem, and I shall adopt this label.

My purpose in this paper is to examine such externalist views. I am not concerned with problems of detail in formulating a view of this kind, though some of these will be mentioned in passing, but rather with the overall acceptability of an externalist solution to the regress problem and thus of an externalist version of foundationalism. I shall attempt to argue that externalism is not acceptable. But there is a methodological problem with respect to such an argument which must be faced at the outset, since it determines the basic approach of the paper.

When viewed from the general standpoint of the western epistemological tradition, externalism represents a very radical departure. It seems safe to say that until very recent times, no serious philosopher of knowledge would have dreamed of suggesting that a person's beliefs might be epistemically justified simply in virtue of facts or relations that were external to his subjective conception. Descartes, for example, would surely have been quite unimpressed by the suggestion that his problematic beliefs about the external world were justified if only they were in fact reliably related to the world—whether or not he had any reason for thinking this to be so. Clearly his conception, and that of generations of philosophers who followed, was that such a relation could play a justificatory role only if the believer possessed adequate reason for thinking that it obtained. Thus the suggestion embodied in externalism would have been regarded by most epistemologists as simply irrelevant to the main epistemological issue, so much so that the philosopher who suggested it would have been taken either to be hopelessly confused or to be simply changing the subject (as I note below, this may be what some externalists in fact intend to be doing). The problem, however, is that this very rad-

icalism has the effect of insulating the externalist from any very direct refutation: any attempt at such a refutation is almost certain to appeal to premises that a thoroughgoing externalist would not accept. My solution to this threatened impasse will be to proceed on an intuitive level as far as possible. By considering a series of examples, I shall attempt to exhibit as clearly as possible the fundamental intuition about epistemic rationality that externalism seems to violate. Although this intuition may not constitute a conclusive objection to the view, it is enough, I believe, to shift the burden of proof decisively to the externalist. In the final section of the paper, I shall consider briefly whether he can discharge this burden.

II

Our first task will be the formulation of a clear and relatively adequate version of externalism. The recent epistemological literature contains a reasonably large number of externalist and quasi-externalist views. Some of these, however, are not clearly relevant to our present concerns, either because they are aimed primarily at the Gettier problem, so that their implications for a foundationalist solution of the regress problem are not made clear, or because they *seem,* on the surface at least, to involve a repudiation of the very conception of epistemic justification or reasonableness as a requirement for knowledge. Views of the latter sort seem to me to be very difficult to take seriously; but if they are seriously intended, they would have the consequence that the regress problem, at least in the form discussed here, would simply not arise, so that there would be no need for any solution, foundationalist or otherwise. My immediate concern here is with versions of externalism that claim to *solve* the regress problem and thus that also claim that the acceptance of beliefs satisfying the externalist conditions is epistemically justified or rational or warranted. Only such an externalist position genuinely constitutes a version of foundationalism, and hence the more radical views, if any such are in fact seriously intended, may safely be left aside for the time being.

The most completely developed externalist view of the sort we are interested in is that of Armstrong, as presented in his book, *Belief, Truth and Knowledge*.[4] Armstrong is explicitly concerned with the regress problem, though he formulates it in terms of knowledge rather than justification. And it seems reasonably clear that he wants to say that beliefs satisfying his externalist criterion are epistemically justified or rational, though he is not as explicit as one might like on this point.[5] In what follows, I shall in any case assume such an interpretation of Armstrong and formulate his position accordingly.

Another version of externalism, which fairly closely resembles Armstrong's except for being limited to knowledge derived from visual perception, is offered by Dretske in *Seeing and Knowing*.[6] Goldman, in several papers, also suggests views of an externalist sort,[7] and the view that Alston calls "Simple Foundationalism" and claims to be the most defensible version of foundationalism seems to be essentially externalist in character.[8] The most extreme version of externalism would be one that held that the external condition required for justification is simply the *truth* of the belief in question. Such a view could not be held in general, of course, without obliterating the distinction between knowledge and mere true belief, thereby turning every lucky guess into knowledge. But it might be held with respect to some more limited class of beliefs. Such a view is mentioned by Alston as one possible account of privileged access,[9] and seems, surprisingly enough, to be advocated by Chisolm (though it is very hard to be sure that this is what Chisholm really means).[10]

Here I shall concentrate mainly on Armstrong's view. Like all externalists, Armstrong makes the acceptability of a basic belief depend on an external relation between the believer and his belief, on the one hand, and the world, on the other, specifically a law-like connection: "there must be a *law-like connection* between the state of affairs *Bap* [i.e., *a*'s believing that *p*] and the state of affairs which makes '*p*' true, such that, given *Bap*, it must be the case that *p*." [166] This is what Armstrong calls the "thermometer-model" of non-inferential knowledge: just as the readings of a reliable thermometer lawfully reflect the temperature, so one's basic beliefs lawfully reflect the states of affairs that make them true. A person whose beliefs satisfy this condition is in effect a reliable cognitive instrument; and it is, according to Armstrong, precisely in virtue of this reliability that these basic beliefs are justified.

Of course, not all thermometers are reliable, and even a reliable one may be accurate only under certain conditions. Similarly, it is not a requirement for the justification of a basic belief on Armstrong's view that all beliefs of that general kind or even all beliefs of that kind held by that particular believer be reliable. Thus the law linking the having of the belief with the state of affairs that makes it true will have to mention properties, including relational properties, of the believer beyond his merely having that belief. Incorporating this modification yields the following schematic formulation of the conditions under which a non-inferential belief is justified and therefore basic: a non-inferential belief is justified if and only if there is some property H of the believer, such that it is a law of nature that whenever a person satisfies H and has that belief, then the belief is true. [197][11] Here H may be as complicated as one likes and may include facts about the believer's mental processes, sensory apparatus, environment, and so on. But presumably, though Armstrong does not mention this point, H is not to include anything that would entail the truth of the belief; such a logical connection would not count as a law of nature.

Armstrong adds several qualifications to this account, aimed at warding off various objections, of which I shall mention only two. First, the nomological connection between the belief and the state of affairs that makes it true is to be restricted to "that of *completely reliable sign* to thing signified." [182] What this is intended to exclude is the case where the belief itself *causes* the state of affairs that makes it true. In such a case, it seems intuitively that the belief is not a case of knowledge even though it satisfies the condition of complete reliability formulated above. Second, the property H of the believer which is involved in the law of nature must not be "too specific"; there must be a "real possibility" of a recurrence of the situation described by the law. What Armstrong is worried about here is the possibility of a "veridical hallucination," i.e., a case in which a hallucinatory belief happens to be correct. In such a case, if the state of affairs that makes the belief true happens to be part of the cause of the hallucination and if the believer and his environment are described in enough detail, it might turn out to be nomologically necessary that such a state of affairs obtain, simply because all alternative possible causes for the hallucinatory belief have been ruled out by the specificity of the description. Again, such a case intuitively should not count as a case of knowledge, but it would satisfy Armstrong's criterion in the absence of this additional stipulation. (Obviously this requirement of non-specificity or repeatability is extremely vague and seems in fact to be no more than an *ad hoc* solution to this problem; but I shall not pursue this issue here.)

There are various problems of detail, similar to those just discussed, which could be raised about Armstrong's view, but these have little relevance to the main theme of the present paper. Here I am concerned with the more fundamental issue of whether Armstrong's view, or any other externalist view of this general sort, is acceptable as a solution to the regress problem and the basis for a foundationalist account of empirical knowledge. When considered from this perspective, Armstrong's view seems at the very least to be in need of considerable refinement in the face of fairly obvious counterexamples. Thus our first task will be to develop some of these counterexamples and suggest modifications in the view accordingly. This discussion will also lead. however, to a fundamental intuitive objection to all forms of externalism.

III

Although it is formulated in more general terms, the main concern of an externalist view like Armstrong's is obviously those non-inferential beliefs which arise from ordinary sources like sense-perception and introspection. For it is, of course, these beliefs which will on any plausible foundationalist view provide the actual foundations of empirical knowledge. Nevertheless, cases involving sense-perception and introspection are not very suitable for an intuitive assessment of externalism, since one central issue between externalism and other foundationalist and non-foundationalist views is precisely whether in such cases a further basis for justification beyond the externalist one is typically present. Thus it will be useful to begin by considering the application of externalism to other possible cases of non-inferential

knowledge, cases of a less familiar sort where it will be easier to stipulate in a way that will be effective on an intuitive level that only the externalist sort of justification is present. Specifically, in this section and the next, our focus will be on possible cases of clairvoyant knowledge. Clairvoyance, the alleged psychic power of perceiving or intuiting the existence and character of distant states of affairs without the aid of any sensory input, remains the subject of considerable scientific controversy. Although many would like to dismiss out of hand the very idea of such a cognitive power, there remains a certain amount of evidence in favor of its existence which it is difficult to entirely discount. But in any case, the actual existence of clairvoyance does not matter at all for present purposes, so long as it is conceded to represent a coherent possibility. For externalism, as a general philosophical account of the foundations of empirical knowledge, must of course apply to all possible modes of non-inferential empirical knowledge, and not just to those that in fact happen to be realized.

The intuitive difficulty with externalism that the following discussion is intended to delineate and develop is this: on the externalist view, a person may be ever so irrational and irresponsible in accepting a belief, when judged in light of his own subjective conception of the situation, and may still turn out to be epistemically justified, i.e., may still turn out to satisfy Armstrong's general criterion of reliability. This belief may in fact be reliable, even though the person has no reason for thinking that it is reliable— or even though he has good reason to think that it is not reliable. But such a person seems nonetheless to be thoroughly irresponsible from an epistemic standpoint in accepting such a belief, and hence not justified, contrary to externalism. The following cases may help bring out this problem more clearly.

Consider first the following case:

Case I. Samantha believes herself to have the power of clairvoyance, though she has no reasons for or against this belief. One day she comes to believe, for no apparent reason, that the President is in New York City. She maintains this belief, appealing to her alleged clairvoyant power, even though she is at the same time aware of a massive amount of apparently cogent evidence, consisting of news reports, press releases, allegedly live television pictures, etc., indicating that the President is at that time in Washington, D.C. Now the President is in fact in New York City, the evidence to the contrary being part of a massive official hoax mounted in the face of an assassination threat. Moreover, Samantha does in fact have completely reliable clairvoyant power, under the conditions that were then satisfied, and her belief about the President did result from the operation of that power.

In this case, it is clear that Armstrong's criterion of reliability is satisfied. There will be some complicated description of Samantha, including the conditions then operative, from which it will follow, by the law describing her clairvoyant power, that her belief is true.[12] But it seems intuitively clear nevertheless that this is not a case of justified belief or of knowledge: Samantha is being thoroughly irrational and irresponsible in disregarding cogent evidence that the President is not in New York City on the basis of a clairvoyant power which she has no reason at all to think that she possesses; and this irrationality is not somehow canceled by the fact that she happens to be right. Thus, I submit, Samantha's irrationality and irresponsibility prevent her belief from being epistemically justified.

This case and others like it suggest the need for a further condition to supplement Armstrong's original one: not only must it be true that there is a lawlike connection between a person's belief and the state of affairs that makes it true, such that given the belief, the state of affairs cannot fail to obtain, but it must also be true that the person in question does not possess cogent reasons for thinking that the belief in question is false. For, as this case seems to show, the possession of such reasons renders the acceptance of the belief irrational in a way that cannot be overridden by a purely externalist justification.

Nor is this the end of the difficulty for Armstrong. Suppose that the clairvoyant believer, instead of having evidence against the particular belief in question, has evidence against his possession of such a cognitive power, as in the following case:

Case II. Casper believes himself to have the power of clairvoyance, though he has no reasons for this belief. He maintains his belief despite the

fact that on the numerous occasions on which he has attempted to confirm one of his allegedly clairvoyant beliefs, it has always turned out apparently to be false. One day Casper comes to believe, for no apparent reason, that the President is in New York City, and he maintains this belief, appealing to his alleged clairvoyant power. Now in fact the President is in New York City; and Casper does, under the conditions that were then satisfied, have completely reliable clairvoyant power, from which this belief in fact resulted. The apparent falsity of his other clairvoyant beliefs was due in some cases to his being in the wrong conditions for the operation of his power and in other cases to deception and misinformation.

Is Casper justified in believing that the President is in New York City, so that he then knows that this is the case? According to Armstrong's account, even with the modification just suggested, we must apparently say that the belief is justified and hence a case of knowledge: the reliability condition is satisfied, and Casper possesses no reason for thinking that the President is not in New York City. But this result still seems mistaken. Casper is being quite irrational and irresponsible from an epistemic standpoint in disregarding evidence that his beliefs of this sort are not reliable and should not be trusted. And for this reason, the belief in question is not justified.

In the foregoing case, Casper possessed good reasons for thinking that he did not possess the sort of cognitive ability that he believed himself to possess. But the result would be the same, I believe, if someone instead possessed good reasons for thinking that *in general* there could be no such cognitive ability, as in the following case:

Case III. Maud believes herself to have the power of clairvoyance, though she has no reasons for this belief. She maintains her belief despite being inundated by her embarrassed friends and relatives with massive quantities of apparently cogent scientific evidence that no such power is possible. One day Maud comes to believe, for no apparent reason, that the President is in New York City, and she maintains this belief, despite the lack of any independent evidence, appealing to her alleged clairvoyant power. Now in fact

the President is in New York City, and Maud does, under the conditions then satisfied, have completely reliable clairvoyant power.
Moreover, her belief about tile President did result from the operation of that power.

Again, Armstrong's criterion of reliability seems to be satisfied. But it also seems to me that Maud, like Casper, is not justified in her belief about the President and does not have knowledge. Maud has excellent reasons for thinking that no cognitive power such as she believes herself to possess is possible, and it is irrational and irresponsible of her to maintain her belief in that power in the face of that evidence and to continue to accept and maintain beliefs on this dubious basis.

Cases like these two suggest the need for a further modification of Armstrong's account: in addition to the law-like connection between belief and truth and the absence of any reasons against the particular belief in question, it must also be the case that the believer in question has no cogent reasons, either relative to his own case or in general, for thinking that such a law-like connection does *not* exist, i.e., that beliefs of that kind are not reliable.

IV

So far the modifications suggested for Armstrong's criterion are consistent with the basic thrust of externalism as a response to the regress problem. What emerges is in fact a significantly more plausible externalist position. But these cases and the modifications made in response to them also suggest an important moral which leads to a basic intuitive objection to externalism: external or objective reliability is not enough to offset subjective irrationality. If the acceptance of a belief is seriously unreasonable or unwarranted from the believer's own standpoint, then the mere fact that unbeknownst to the believer its existence in those circumstances lawfully guarantees its truth will not suffice to render the belief epistemically justified and thereby an instance of knowledge. So far we have been concerned only with situations in which the believer's subjective irrationality took the form of ignoring positive grounds in his possession for questioning either that

specific belief or beliefs arrived at in that way. But now we must ask whether even in a case where these positive reasons for a charge of irrationality are not present, the acceptance of a belief where only an externalist justification is available cannot still be said to be subjectively irrational in a sense that rules out its being epistemically justified.

We may begin by considering one further case of clairvoyance, in which Armstrong's criterion with all the suggested modifications is satisfied:

Case IV. Norman, under certain conditions that usually obtain, is a completely reliable clairvoyant with respect to certain kinds of subject matter. He possesses no evidence or reasons of any kind for or against the general possibility of such a cognitive power, or for or against the thesis that he possesses it. One day Norman comes to believe that the President is in New York City, though he has no evidence either for or against this belief. In fact the belief is true and results from his clairvoyant power, under circumstances in which it is completely reliable.

Is Norman epistemically justified in believing that the President is in New York City, so that his belief is an instance of knowledge? According to the modified externalist position, we must apparently say that he is. But is this the right result? Are there not still sufficient grounds for a charge of subjective irrationality to prevent Norman's being epistemically justified?

One thing that might seem relevant to this issue, which I have deliberately omitted from the specification of the case, is whether Norman believes himself to have clairvoyant power, even though he has no justification for such a belief. Let us consider both possibilities. Suppose, first, that Norman does have such a belief and that it contributes to his acceptance of his original belief about the President's whereabouts in the sense that were Norman to become convinced that he did not have this power, he would also cease to accept the belief about the President.[13] But is it not obviously irrational, from an epistemic standpoint, for Norman to hold such a belief when he has no reasons at all for thinking that it is true or even for thinking that such a power is possible? This belief about his clairvoyance fails after all to possess even an externalist justification.

And if we say that the belief about his clairvoyance is epistemically irrational and unjustified, must we not say the same thing about the belief about the President which *ex hypothesi* depends upon it?[14]

A possible response to this challenge would be to add one further condition to our modified externalist position, *viz.*, that the believer not even *believe* that the law-like connection in question obtains, since such a belief will not in general be justified (or at least that his continued acceptance of the particular belief that is at issue not depend on his acceptance of such a general belief). In our present case, this would mean that Norman must not believe that he has the power of clairvoyance (or at least that his acceptance of the belief about the President's whereabouts not depend on his having such a general belief). But if this specification is added to the case, it now becomes more than a little puzzling to understand what Norman thinks is going on. From his standpoint, there is apparently no way in which he *could* know the President's whereabouts. Why then does he continue to maintain the belief that the President is in New York City? Why is not the mere fact that there is no way, as far as he knows or believes, for him to have obtained this information a sufficient reason for classifying this belief as an unfounded hunch and ceasing to accept it? And if Norman does not do this, is he not thereby being epistemically irrational and irresponsible?

For these reasons, I submit, Norman's acceptance of the belief about the President's whereabouts is epistemically irrational and irresponsible, and thereby unjustified, whether or not he believes himself to have clairvoyant power, so long as he has no justification for such a belief. Part of one's epistemic duty is to reflect critically upon one's beliefs, and such critical reflection precludes believing things to which one has, to one's knowledge, no reliable means of epistemic access.[15]

We are now face-to-face with the fundamental—and seemingly obvious—intuitive problem with externalism: *why* should the mere fact that such an external relation obtains mean that Norman's belief is epistemically justified, when the relation in question is entirely outside his ken? As remarked earlier, it is clear that one who knew that Armstrong's criterion was satisfied would be in a position to construct a simple and quite cogent justifying argument for

the belief in question: if Norman has property H (being a completely reliable clairvoyant under the existing conditions and arriving at the belief on that basis), then he holds the belief in question only if it is true; Norman does have property H and does hold the belief in question; therefore, the belief is true. But Norman himself is by stipulation not in a position to employ this argument, and it is unclear why the mere fact that it is, so to speak, potentially available in the situation should justify *his* acceptance of the belief. Precisely what generates the regress problem in the first place, after all, is the requirement that for a belief to be justified for a particular person, not only is it necessary that there be true premises somehow available in the situation which could in principle provide a basis for a justification, but also that the believer in question know or at least justifiably believe some such set of premises and thus be in a position to employ the corresponding argument. The externalist position seems to amount merely to waiving this general requirement in a certain class of cases, and the question is why this should be acceptable in these cases when it is not acceptable generally. (If it were acceptable generally, then it seems likely that *any* true belief would be justified, unless some severe requirement is imposed as to how immediately available such premises must be. But any such requirement seems utterly arbitrary, once the natural one of actual access by the believer is abandoned.) Thus externalism looks like a purely *ad hoc* solution to the epistemic regress problem.

One reason why externalism may seem initially plausible is that if the external relation in question genuinely obtains, then Norman will in fact not go wrong in accepting the belief, and it is, *in a sense*, not an accident that this is so. But how is this supposed to justify Norman's belief? From his subjective perspective, it *is* an accident that the belief is true. Of course, it would not be an accident from the standpoint of our hypothetical external observer who knows all the relevant facts and laws. Such an observer, having constructed the justifying argument sketched above, would be thereby in a position to justify *his own* acceptance of the belief. Thus Norman, as Armstrong's thermometer image suggests, could serve as a useful epistemic instrument for such an observer, a kind of cognitive thermometer; and it is to this fact, as we have seen, that Armstrong appeals in arguing that a belief like Norman's can be correctly said to be reasonable or justifiable. [183] But none of this is seems in fact to justify Norman's *own* acceptance of the belief, for Norman, unlike the hypothetical external observer, has no reason at all for thinking that the belief is true. And the suggestion here is that the rationality or justifiability of Norman's belief should be judged from Norman's own perspective, rather than from one that is unavailable to him.[16]

This basic objection to externalism seems to me to be intuitively compelling. But it is sufficiently close to being simply a statement of what the externalist wants to deny to make it helpful to buttress it a bit by appealing to some related intuitions.

First, we may consider an analogy with moral philosophy. The same conflict between perspectives which we have seen to arise in the process of epistemic assessment can also arise with regard to the moral assessment of a person's action: the agent's subjective conception of what he is doing may differ dramatically from that which would in principle be available to an external observer who had access to facts about the situation that are beyond the agent's ken. And now we can imagine an approximate moral analogue of externalism which would hold that the moral justifiability of an agent's action was, in certain cases at least, properly to be determined from the external perspective, entirely irrespective of the agent's own conception of the situation.

Consider first the moral analogue of Armstrong's original, unmodified version of externalism. If we assume, purely for the sake of simplicity, a utilitarian moral theory, such a view would say that an action might on occasion be morally justified simply in virtue of the fact that in the situation then obtaining, it would as a matter of objective fact lead to the best overall consequences—even if the agent planned and anticipated that it would lead to a very different, perhaps extremely undesirable, consequences. But such a view seems plainly mistaken. There is no doubt a point to the objective, external assessment: we can say correctly that it turns out to be objectively a good thing that the agent performed the action. But this is not at all inconsistent with saying that his action was morally unjustified and reprehensible, given his subjective conception of the likely consequences.

Thus our envisaged moral externalism must at least be modified in a way that parallels the modifications earlier suggested for epistemological externalism. Without attempting to make the analogy exact, it will suffice for our present purposes to add to the original requirement for moral justification, viz., that the action will in fact lead to the best overall consequences, the further condition that the agent not believe or intend that it lead to undesirable consequences. Since it is also, of course, not required by moral externalism that the agent believe that the action will lead to good consequences, the sort of case we are now considering is one in which an agent acts in a way that will in fact produce the best overall consequences, but has *no belief at all* about the likely consequences of his action. Although such an agent is no doubt preferable to one who acts in the belief that his action will lead to undesirable consequences, surely he is not morally justified in what he does. On the contrary, he is being highly irresponsible, from a moral standpoint, in performing the action in the absence of any evaluation of what will result from it. His moral duty, from our assumed utilitarian standpoint, is to do what will lead to the best consequences, but this duty is not satisfied by the fact that he produces this result willy-nilly, without any idea that he is doing so.[17] And similarly, the fact that a given sort of belief is objectively reliable, and thus that accepting it is in fact conducive to arriving at the truth, need not prevent our judging that the epistemic agent who accepts it without any inkling that this is the case violates his epistemic duty and is epistemically irresponsible and unjustified in doing so.

Second, we may appeal to the connection between knowledge and rational action. Suppose that Norman, in addition to the clairvoyant belief described earlier, also believes that the Attorney-General is in Chicago. This latter belief, however, is not a clairvoyant belief but is based upon ordinary empirical evidence in Norman's possession, evidence strong enough to give the belief some fairly high degree of reasonableness, but *not* strong enough to satisfy the requirement for knowledge.[18] Suppose further that Norman finds himself in a situation where he is forced to bet a very large amount, perhaps even his life or the life of someone else, on the whereabouts of either the President or the Attorney-General. Given his epistemic situation as described, which bet is it more reasonable for him to make? It seems relatively clear that it is more reasonable for him to bet the Attorney-General is in Chicago than to bet that the President is in New York City. But then we have the paradoxical result that from the externalist standpoint it is more rational to act on a merely reasonable belief than to act on one that is adequately justified to qualify as knowledge (and which in fact *is* knowledge). It is very hard to see how this could be so. If greater epistemic reasonableness does not carry with it greater reasonableness of action, then it becomes most difficult to see why it should be sought in the first place. (Of course, the externalist could simply bite the bullet and insist that it is in fact more reasonable for Norman to bet on the President's whereabouts than the Attorney-General's, but such a view seems very implausible.)

I have been attempting in this section to articulate the fundamental intuition about epistemic rationality, and rationality generally, that externalism seems to violate. This intuition the externalist would of course reject, and thus my discussion does not constitute a refutation of the externalist position on its own ground. Nevertheless it seems to me to have sufficient intuitive force at least to place the burden of proof squarely on the externalist. In the final section of the paper, I shall consider briefly some of the responses that seem to be available to him.

VI

One possible defense for the externalist in the face of the foregoing intuitive objection would be to narrow his position by restricting it to those commonsensical varieties of non-inferential knowledge which are his primary concern, viz., sense-perception and introspection, thereby rendering the cases set forth above strictly irrelevant. Such a move seems, however, utterly *ad hoc*. Admittedly it is more difficult to construct intuitively compelling counterexamples involving sense-perception and introspection, mainly because our intuitions that beliefs of those kinds are in fact warranted in *some* way or other are very strong. But this does nothing to establish that the externalist account of their warrant is the correct one. Thus unless the externalist can give some positive account of why the same conclusion that seems to hold for non-standard cases like clairvoyance does not also hold for sense-perception and introspec-

tion, this narrowing of his position seems to do him no good.

If the externalist cannot escape the force of the objection in this way, can he perhaps balance it with positive arguments in favor of his position? Many attempts to argue for externalism are in effect arguments by elimination and depend on the claim that alternative accounts of empirical knowledge are unacceptable, either because they cannot solve the regress problem or for some other reason. Most such arguments, depending as they do on a detailed consideration of the alternatives, are beyond the scope of the present paper. But one such argument depends only on very general features of the competing positions and thus can usefully be considered here.

The basic factual premise of this argument is that in very many cases that are commonsensically instances of justified belief and of knowledge, there seem to be no justifying factors explicitly present beyond those appealed to by the externalist. An ordinary person in such a case may have no idea at all of the character of his immediate experience, of the coherence of his system of beliefs, etc., and yet may still have knowledge. Alternative theories, so the argument goes, may describe correctly cases of knowledge involving a knower who is extremely reflective and sophisticated, but they are obviously too demanding and too grandiose when applied to these more ordinary cases. In these cases, *only* the externalist condition is satisfied, and this shows that no more than that is necessary for justification and for knowledge, though more might still be epistemically desirable.

Although the precise extent to which it holds could be disputed, in the main this factual premise must be simply conceded. Any non-externalist account of empirical knowledge that has any plausibility will impose standards for justification which very many beliefs that seem commonsensically to be cases of knowledge fail to meet in any full and explicit fashion. And thus on such a view, such beliefs will not *strictly speaking* be instances of adequate justification and of knowledge. But it does not follow that externalism must be correct. This would follow only with the addition of the premise that the judgments of common sense in this area are sacrosanct, that any departure from them is enough to demonstrate that a theory of knowledge is inadequate. But such a premise seems entirely too strong. There seems in fact to be no basis for more than a reasonably strong presumption in favor of the correctness of common sense, but one which is still quite defeasible. And what it would take to defeat this presumption depends in part on how great a departure from common sense is being advocated. Thus, although it would take very strong grounds to justify a very strong form of skepticism, not nearly so much would be required to make acceptable the view that what common sense regards as cases of justification and of knowledge are in fact only rough approximations to an epistemic ideal which *strictly speaking* they do not satisfy.

Of course, a really adequate reply to the externalist would have to spell out in some detail the precise way in which such beliefs really do approximately satisfy some acceptable alternative standard, a task which obviously cannot be attempted here. But even without such elaboration, it seems reasonable to conclude that this argument in favor of externalism fails to carry very much weight as it stands and would require serious buttressing in order to give it any chance of offsetting the intuitive objection to externalism: either the advocacy and defense of a quite strong presumption in favor of common sense, or a detailed showing that alternative theories cannot in fact grant to the cases favored by common sense even the status of approximations to justification and to knowledge.

The other pro-externalist argument I want to consider does not depend in any important way on consideration of alternative positions. This argument is hinted at by Armstrong [185–88], among others, but I know of no place where it is developed very explicitly. Its basic claim is that only an externalist theory can handle a certain version of the lottery paradox.

The lottery paradox is standardly formulated as a problem confronting accounts of inductive logic that contain a rule of acceptance or detachment, but we shall be concerned here with a somewhat modified version. This version arises when we ask how much or what degree of epistemic justification is required for a belief to qualify as knowledge, given that the other necessary conditions for knowledge are satisfied Given the intimate connection, discussed earlier, between epistemic justification and likelihood of truth, it seems initially reasonable to take likelihood or probability of truth as a measure of the degree of

epistemic justification, and thus to interpret the foregoing question as asking how likely or probable it must be, relative to the justification of one's belief, that the belief be true, in order for that belief to satisfy the justification requirement for knowledge. Most historical theories of knowledge tended to answer that knowledge requires *certainty* of truth, relative to one's justification. But more recent epistemological views have tended to reject this answer, for familiar reasons, and to hold instead that knowledge requires only a reasonably high likelihood of truth. And now, if this high likelihood of truth is interpreted in the obvious way as meaning that, relative to one's justification, the numerical probability that one's belief is true must equal or exceed some fixed value, the lottery paradox at once rears its head.

Suppose, for example, that we decide that a belief is adequately justified to satisfy the requirement for knowledge if the probability of its truth, relative to its justification, is 0.99 or greater. Imagine now that a lottery is to be held, about which we know the following facts: exactly 100 tickets have been sold, the drawing will indeed be held, it will be a fair drawing, and there will be only one winning ticket. Consider now each of the 100 propositions of the form:

Ticket number *n* will lose

where *n* is replaced by the number of one of the tickets. Since there are 100 tickets and only one winner, the probability of each such proposition is 0.99; and hence if we believe each of them, our individual beliefs will be adequately justified to satisfy it the requirement for knowledge. And then, given only the seemingly reasonable assumptions, first, that if one has adequate justification for believing each of a set of propositions, one also has adequate justification for believing the conjunction of the members of the set, and, second, that if one has adequate justification for believing a proposition, one also has adequate justification for believing any further proposition entailed by the first proposition, it follows that we are adequately justified in believing that no ticket will win, contradicting our other information.

Clearly this is a mistaken result, but how is it to be avoided? In the first place, it will plainly do no good to simply increase the level of numerical probability required for adequate justification. For no matter how high it is raised, short of certainty, it will obviously be possible to duplicate the paradoxical result by simply choosing a large enough lottery. Nor do the standard responses to the lottery paradox, whatever their merits may be in dealing with other versions of the paradox, seem to be of much help here. Most of them are ruled out simply by insisting that we do know that empirical propositions are true, not merely that they are probable, and that such knowledge is not in general relative to particular contexts of inquiry. This leaves only the possibility of avoiding the paradoxical result by rejecting the two assumptions stated in the preceding paragraph. But this would be extremely implausible—involving in effect a denial that one may always justifiably deduce conclusions from one's putative knowledge—and in any case would still leave the intuitively unacceptable result that one could on this basis come to know separately the 99 true propositions about various tickets losing (though not of course the false one). In fact, it seems intuitively clear that I do not *know* any of these propositions to be true: if I own one of the tickets, I do not know that it will lose, even if in fact it will, and would not know no matter how large the total number of tickets might be.

At this stage, it may seem that the only way to avoid the paradox is to return to the traditional idea that any degree of probability or likelihood of truth less than certainty is insufficient for knowledge, that only certainty, relative to one's justification, will suffice. The standard objection to such a view is that it seems to lead at once to the skeptical conclusion that we have little or no empirical knowledge. For it seems quite clear that there are no empirical beliefs, with the possible and extremely problematic exception of beliefs about one's own mental states, for which we have justification adequate to exclude all possibility of error. Such a solution seems as bad as the original problem.

It is at this point that externalism may seem to offer a way out. For an externalist position allows one to hold that the justification of an empirical belief must make it certain that the belief is true, while still escaping the clutches of skepticism. This is so precisely because the externalist justification need not be within the cognitive grasp of the believer or indeed of anyone. It need only be true that there is *some* description of the believer, however complex and practically unknowable it may be, which, together with some true law of nature, ensures the truth of the belief. Thus, e.g., my perceptual belief that there is a cup on my desk is not certain, on any view, relative to the evidence or justification that is in my possession; I might be hallucinating or there might be an evil demon who is deceiving me. But it seems reasonable to suppose that if the belief is indeed true, then there is *some* external description of me and my situation and some true law of nature, relative to which the truth of the belief is guaranteed, and if so it would satisfy the requirement for knowledge.

In some ways, this is a neat and appealing solution to the paradox. Nonetheless, it seems doubtful that it is ultimately satisfactory. In the first place, there is surely something intuitively fishy about solving the problem by appealing to an in-principle guarantee of truth which will almost certainly in practice be available to no one. A second problem, which cannot be elaborated here, is that insisting on this sort of solution seems likely to create insuperable difficulties for knowledge of general and theoretical propositions. But in any case, the externalist solution seems to yield intuitively incorrect results in certain kinds of cases. A look at one of these may also suggest the beginnings of a more satisfactory solution.

Consider then the following case:

Case V. Agatha, seated at her desk, believes herself to be perceiving a cup on the desk. She also knows, however, that she is one of a group of 100 people who have been selected for a philosophical experiment by a Cartesian evil demon. The conditions have been so arranged that all 100 will at this particular time seem to themselves to be perceiving a cup upon their respective desks, with no significant differences in the subjective character of their respective experiences. But in fact, though 99 of the people will be perceiving a cup in the normal way, the last one will be caused by the demon to have a complete hallucination (including perceptual conditions, etc.) of a non-existent cup. Agatha knows all this, but she does not have any further information as to whether she is the one who is hallucinating, though as it happens she is not.

Is Agatha epistemically justified in her belief that there is a cup on the desk and does she know this to be so? According to the externalist view, we must say that she is justified and does know. For there is, we may assume, an external description of Agatha and her situation relative to which it is nomologically certain that her belief is true. (Indeed, according to Armstrong's original, unmodified view, she would be justified and would know even if she also knew instead that 99 of the 100 persons were being deceived by the demon, so long as she was in fact the odd one who was perceiving normally.) But this result is, I submit, intuitively mistaken. If Agatha knows that she is perceiving a cup, then she also knows that she is not the one who is being deceived. But she does not know this, for reasons that parallel those operative in the lottery case.

Is there then no way out of the paradox? The foregoing case and others like it seem to me to suggest the following approach to at least the present version of the paradox, though I can offer only an exceedingly brief sketch here. Intuitively, what the lottery case and the case of Agatha have in common is the presence of a large number of relevantly similar, alternative possibilities, all individually very unlikely, but such that the person in question *knows* that at least one of them will in fact be realized. In such a case, since there is no relevant way of distinguishing among these possibilities, the person cannot believe with adequate justification and *a fortiori* cannot know that any particular possibility will not be realized, even though the probability that it will not be realized may be made as high as one likes by simply increasing the total number of possibilities. Such cases do show that high probability is not by itself enough to satisfy the justification condition for knowledge. They do not show, however, that certainty is required instead. For what rules out knowledge in such a case is not merely the fact that the probability of truth is less than certainty but also the fact that the person *knows* that at least one of these highly probable propositions is false. It is a necessary condition for justification and for knowledge that this not be so. But there are many cases in which a person's justification for a belief fails to make it certain that the belief is true, but in which the person also does not know that some possible situation in which the belief would be false is one of a set of relevantly similar, alternative possibilities, at least one of which will definitely be realized. And in

such a case, the lottery paradox provides no reason to think that the person does not know.[19]

An example may help to make this point clear. Consider again my apparent perception of the cup on my desk. I think that I do in fact know that there is a cup there. But the justification that is in my possession surely does not make it certain that my belief is true. Thus, for example, it seems to be possible, relative to my subjective justification, that I am being deceived by an evil demon, who is causing me to have a hallucinatory experience of the cup, together with accompanying conditions of perception. But it does not follow from this that I do not know that there is a cup on the desk, because it does not follow and I do not know that there is some class of relevantly similar cases in at least one of which a person is in fact deceived by such a demon. Although it is only probable and not certain that there is no demon, it is still possible for all I *know* that never in the history of the universe, past, present, or future, is there a case in which someone in a relevantly similar perceptual situation is actually deceived by such a demon. And, as far as I can see, the same thing is true of all the other ways in which it is possible that my belief might be mistaken. If this is so, then the lottery paradox provides no obstacle to my knowledge in this case.[20]

This response to the lottery paradox seems to me to be on the right track. It must be conceded, however, that it is in considerable need of further development and may turn out to have problems of its own. But that is a subject for another paper.[21]

There is one other sort of response, mentioned briefly above, which the externalist might make to the sorts of criticisms developed in this paper. I want to remark on it briefly, though a full-scale discussion is impossible here. In the end it may be possible to make intuitive sense of externalism only by construing the externalist as simply abandoning the traditional idea of epistemic justification or rationality and along with it anything resembling the traditional conception of knowledge. I have already mentioned that this may be precisely what the proponents of externalism intend to be doing, though most of them are anything but clear on this point.[22]

Against an externalist position that seriously adopts such a gambit, the criticisms developed in the present paper are of course entirely ineffective.

If the externalist does not want even to claim that beliefs satisfying his conditions are epistemically justified or reasonable, then it is obviously no objection that they seem in some cases to be quite unjustified and unreasonable. But, as already noted, such a view, though it may possess some other sort of appeal constitutes a solution to the epistemic regress problem or to any problem arising out of the traditional conception of knowledge only in the radical and relatively uninteresting sense that to reject that conception entirely is also, of course, to reject any problems arising out of it. Such "solutions" would seem to be available for any philosophical problem at all, but it is hard to see why they should be taken seriously.

NOTES

1. For a fuller discussion of the regress argument, including a discussion of other possible outcomes of the regress, see my paper "Can Empirical Knowledge have a Foundation?" *American Philosophical Quarterly* 15 (1978): 1–13. That paper also contains a brief anticipation of the present discussion of externalism.
2. It could, of course, still be claimed that the belief in question was *empirically* basic, so long as both the needed justifying premises were justifiable on an *a priori* basis. But this would mean that it was an *a priori* truth that a particular empirical belief was likely to be true. In the present paper, I shall simply assume, without further discussion, that this seemingly unlikely state of affairs does not in fact obtain.
3. For criticism of this view, see the paper cited in note 1.
4. D. M. Armstrong, *Belief, Truth and Knowledge* (London, Press, 1973). Bracketed references in the text will be to the pages of this book.
5. The clearest passages are at p. 183, where Armstrong says that a belief satisfying his externalist condition, though not "based on reasons," nevertheless "might be said to be reasonable (justifiable), because it is a sign, a completely reliable sign, that the situation believed to exist does in fact exist"; and at p. 189, where he suggests that the satisfaction of a slightly weaker condition, though it does not yield knowledge, may still yield rational belief. There is no reason to think that any species of rationality or reasonableness other than the epistemic is at issue in either of these passages. But though these passages seem to me to adequately support my interpretation of Armstrong, the strongest support may well derive simply from

the fact that he at no point *disavows* a claim of epistemic rationality. (See also the parenthetical remark in the middle of p.77.)
6. Fred I. Dretske, *Seeing and Knowing* (London, 1969), chap. III. Dretske also differs from Armstrong in requiring in effect that the would-be knower also believe that the externalist condition is satisfied, but not of course that this belief be justified.
7. Goldman does this most clearly in "Discrimination and Perceptual Knowledge," *Journal of Philosophy* 73 (1976): 771–91, and in "What is Justified Belief?" forthcoming. See also "A Causal Theory of Knowing," *Journal of Philosophy* 64 (1967): 355–72, though this last paper is more concerned with the Gettier problem than with a general account of the standards of epistemic justification.
8. William P. Alston, "Two Types of Foundationalism," *Journal of Philosophy* 73 (1976): 165–85; see especially p. 168.
9. Alston, "Varieties of Privileged Access," in Roderick Chisholm and Robert Swartz, *Empirical Knowledge* (Englewood Cliffs, N.J., 1973), pp. 396–99. Alston's term for this species of privileged access is "truth sufficiency."
10. See Chisholm, Theory of Knowledge, 2nd ed. (Englewood Cliffs, N.J., 1977), p. 22, where Chisholm offers the following definition of the concept of a state of affairs being self-presenting:

h is *self-presenting* for S at t = Df *h* occurs at *t*; and necessarily, if *h* occurs at *t* then *h* is evident [i.e., justified] for S at *t*.

Despite the overtones of the term "self-presentation," nothing in this passage seems to require that believer have any sort of immediate awareness of the state in question; all that is required is that it actually occur, i.e., that his belief be true. On the other hand, Chisholm also, in the section immediately preceding this definition, quotes with approval a passage from Leibniz which appeals to the idea of "direct awareness" and of the absence of mediation "between the understanding and its objects," thus suggesting the non-externalist variety of foundationalism (pp.20–21).
11. Armstrong actually formulates the criterion as a criterion of knowledge, rather than merely of justification the satisfaction of the belief condition is built into the criterion and this, with the satisfaction of the indicated justification condition, entails that the truth condition is satisfied.
12. This assumes that clairvoyant beliefs are caused in some distinctive way, so that an appropriately

complete description of Samantha will rule out the possibility that the belief is a mere hunch and will connect appropriately with the law governing her clairvoyance.

13. This further supposition does not prevent the belief about the President's whereabouts from being non-inferential, since it is not in any useful sense Norman's reason for accepting that specific belief.

14. This is the basic objection to Dretske's version of externalism, mentioned above. Dretske's condition requires that one have an analogously unjustified (though true) belief about the reliability of one's perceptual belief.

15. The only apparent answer here would be to claim that the reasonable presumption is in favor of one's having such reliable means of access, unless there is good reason to the contrary. But it is hard to see why such a presumption should he thought reasonable.

16. Mark Pastin, in a critical study of Armstrong, has suggested that ascriptions of knowledge depend on the epistemic situation of the ascriber rather than on that of the ascribee at this point, so that I am correct in ascribing knowledge to Norman so long as I know that his belief is reliable (and hence also that the other conditions of knowledge are satisfied), even if Norman does not. But I can see no very convincing rationale for this claim. See Pastin, "Knowledge and Reliability: A Study of D. M. Armstrong's Belief, Truth and Knowledge," *Metaphilosophy 9* (1978)150–62. Notice further that if the epistemic regress problem is in general to be dealt with along externalist lines, then my knowledge that Norman's belief is reliable would depend on the epistemic situation of a further external observer, who ascribes knowledge to me. And similarly for the knowledge of that observer, etc., ad infinitum. I do not know whether this regress of external observers is vicious, but it seems clearly to deprive the appeal to such an observer of .any value as a practical criterion.

17. Of course there are eases in which one must act, even though one has no adequate knowledge of the likely consequences; and one might attempt to defend epistemic externalism by arguing that in epistemic contexts the analogous situation always obtains. But there are several problems with such a response. First, to simply assume that this is always so seems to be question-begging, and the externalist can argue for this claim only by refuting all alternatives to his position. Second, notice that in ethical contexts this situation usually, perhaps always, obtains only when not acting will lead definitely to bad consequences, not just to the failure to obtain good ones; and there seems to be no parallel to this in the epistemic ease. Third, and most important, the justification for one's action in such a case would depend not on the external fact, if it is a fact, that the action leads to good consequences, but simply on the fact that one could do no better, given the unfortunate state of one's knowledge; thus this position would not be genuinely a version of moral externalism, and analogously for the epistemic case.

18. I am assuming here, following Chisholm, that knowledge requires a degree of justification stronger than that required to make a belief merely reasonable.

19. I do not, alas, have any real account to offer here of the notion of relevant similarity. Roughly, the idea is that two possibilities are relevantly similar if there is no known difference between them that has a bearing on the likelihood that they will be realized. But this will not quite do. For consider a lottery case in which there are two tickets bearing each even number and only one for each odd number. Intuitively, it seems to me, this difference does not prevent all the tickets, odd and even, from being relevantly similar, despite the fact that it is twice as likely that an even ticket will be drawn.

20. But if this account is correct, I may still fail to know in many other cases in which common sense would say fairly strongly that I do. E.g., do I know that my house has. not burned down since I left it this morning? Ordinarily we are inclined to say that we do know such things. But if it is true, as it might well be, that I also know that of the class of houses relevantly similar to mine, at least one will burn down at some point , then I do not, on the present account, know that my house has not burned down, however improbable such a catastrophe may be. (On the other hand, knowledge would not he ruled out by the present principle simply because I knew that certain specific similar houses, other than mine, have in the past burned down or even that they will in the future burn down. For I know, ex hypothesi. that my house is not one of those. The force of the principle depends on my knowing that at least one possibility which might for all I know be the one I am interested in will be realized, not just on descriptively similar possibilities being realized.)

21. This response to the lottery paradox derives in part from discussions with C. Anthony Anderson.

22. The clearest example of such a position is in Goldman's paper "Discrimination and Perceptual Knowledge," cited above, where he rejects what he calls "Cartesian-style justification" as a requirement for perceptual knowledge, in favor of an externalist account. He goes on to remark, however, that one could use the term "justification" in such a way that satisfaction of his externalist conditions "counts as justification," though a kind of justification "entirely different from the sort of justification demanded by Cartesianism" (p. 790). What is unclear is whether this is supposed to be a purely verbal possibility, which would then be of little interest, or whether it is supposed to connect with something like the concept of epistemic rationality explicated in section I. Thus it is uncertain whether Goldman means to repudiate the whole idea of epistemic rationality, or only some more limited view such as the doctrine of the given (reference to which provides his only explanation of what he means by "Cartesianism" in epistemology).

ALVIN I. GOLDMAN

Strong and Weak Justification

It is common in recent epistemology to distinguish different senses, or conceptions, of epistemic justification. The proposed oppositions include the objective/subjective, internalist/externalist, regulative/nonregulative, resource-relative/resource-independent, personal/verific, and deontological/evaluative conceptions of justification.[1] In some of these cases, writers regard both members of the contrasting pair as legitimate; in other cases only one member. In this paper I want to propose another contrasting pair of conceptions of justification, and hold that *both* are defensible and legitimate. The contrast will then be used to construct a modified version of reliabilism, one which handles certain problem cases more naturally than my previous versions of reliabilism.

I

I should begin by acknowledging the undesirability of multiplying senses of any term beyond necessity. Lacking good evidence for multivocality of a target analysandum, a unified analysis should be sought. But sometimes there is indeed good evidence for multivocality. Here is a case in point for the term 'justified'.

Consider a scientifically benighted culture, of ancient or medieval vintage. This culture employs certain highly unreliable methods for forming beliefs about the future and the unobserved. Their methods appeal to the doctrine of signatures, to astrology, and to oracles. Members of the culture have never thought of probability theory or statistics, never dreamt of anything that could be classed as 'experimental method'.[2] Now suppose that on a particular occasion a member of this culture forms a belief about the outcome of an impending battle by using one of the aforementioned methods, say, by consulting zodiacal signs in a culturally approved fashion.

Call this method M. Is this person's belief justified, or warranted?

One feels here a definite tension, a tug in opposite directions. There is a strong temptation to say, no, this belief is not justified or warranted. Yet from a different perspective one feels inclined to say, yes, the belief is justified.

The attraction of the negative answer is easily explained. It is natural to regard a belief as justified only if it is generated by proper, or adequate, methods. But method M certainly looks improper and inadequate. This point can be reinforced in the following way. Epistemologists have widely supposed—and I concur—that a necessary condition for having knowledge is having justified belief. But the belief under consideration has no chance to qualify as knowledge, assuming it is wholly based on zodiacal signs. Even if it happens to be true, even if there is nothing 'Gettierized' about the case, the believer cannot be credited with *knowing* (beforehand) the outcome of the battle. The natural explanation is that his belief fails to be justified.

Why, then, is some attraction felt toward a positive answer? This seems to stem from the cultural plight of our believer. He is situated in a certain spatio-historical environment. Everyone else in this environment uses and trusts method M. Moreover, our believer has good reasons to trust his cultural peers on many matters, and lacks decisive reasons for distrusting their confidence in astrology. While it is true that a scientifically trained person, set down in this same culture, could easily find ways to cast doubt on method M, our believer is not so trained, and has no opportunity to acquire such training. It is beyond his intellectual scope to find flaws in M. Thus, we can hardly *fault* him for using M, nor fault him therefore for believing what he does. The belief in question is epistemically *blameless*, and that seems to explain why we are tempted to call it *justified*.[3]

As this case illustrates, there are two distinct ideas or conceptions of epistemic justification. On one conception, a justified belief is (roughly) a *well-formed* belief, a belief formed (or sustained) by proper, suitable, or adequate methods, procedures, or processes. On another conception, a justified belief is a *faultless*, *blameless*, or *nonculpable* belief. As our example suggests, the first of these conceptions is stronger, or more stringent, than the second. It requires the belief to be formed by methods that are *actually* proper or adequate, whereas the second conception makes no such requirement. I therefore call the first conception the *strong* conception and the second the *weak*. Each of these seems to me a legitimate conception. Each captures some chunks of intuition involving the term 'justified' (in its epistemic applications).

Granting the distinction between strong and weak justification, my next task is to delineate more precisely the conditions attached to these respective conceptions. Before turning to this, however, let me mention another distinction relevant to the theory of justified belief.

In *Epistemology and Cognition* (hereinafter E & C) I propose a distinction between belief-forming *processes* and belief-forming *methods*.[4] 'Processes' are basic psychological processes, roughly, wired-in features of our native cognitive architecture. 'Methods' are learnable algorithms, heuristics, or procedures for forming beliefs, such as procedures that appeal to instrument readings, or statistical analyses. All beliefs are formed partly by processes. We cannot do anything in the cognitive realm without using basic psychological operations. Learned methods, by contrast, are not universally required, although the vast majority of an adult's beliefs are probably indebted to such methods. Now *fully* justified beliefs, I propose, must be formed by adequate processes *and* adequate methods, if methods are used at all. (At least this is so for strong justification.) But it is possible to form a belief by a combination of adequate process and inadequate method, or by a combination of inadequate process and adequate method. I therefore distinguish two levels of justifiedness: primary justifiedness, corresponding to the level of processes, and secondary justifiedness, corresponding to the level of methods. A complete account of justifiedness must present conditions for both of these levels.

The strong/weak distinction I have introduced enters at each level: the level of processes and the level of methods. So let me try to sketch conditions of strong and weak justification for each level separately. I begin with the level of methods.

II

Strong justification at the level of methods requires the use of *proper* or *adequate* methods. What makes a method proper or adequate? A natural and appealing answer is a reliabilist answer: a method is proper or adequate just in case it is reliable, i.e., leads to truth a sufficiently high percent of the time. This answer meshes perfectly with our intuitions about the scientifically benighted believer. His belief is not strongly justified precisely because the method of consulting zodiacal signs is not a reliable way of getting truths about the outcomes of battles.

What exactly is meant by calling a method or process 'reliable' needs further discussion. I shall address this issue in due course. Another sort of issue, however, needs comment. High reliability may not suffice for method-level justifiedness because even highly reliable methods may be *less* reliable than other available methods. Some people might argue for a *maximum* reliability condition, not merely a *satisficing* reliability condition. I am going to set this matter aside. There are enough other questions to be dealt with in this paper, and the proposed switch to maximum reliability would not seriously affect the other epistemological topics on which I shall focus.

However, I do not mean to imply that use of a highly reliable method is sufficient for method-level, or secondary, justifiedness. Two other conditions are necessary. First, it is necessary that the method have been *acquired* in a suitable fashion. If a person adopts a method out of the blue, and by chance it happens to be reliable, his use of that method does not confer secondary justifiedness. The method must be acquired by other methods, or ultimately processes, that are either reliable or meta-reliable.[5] A further necessary condition of secondary justifiedness is that the believer's cognitive state, at the time he uses the method, should not *undermine* the correctness, or adequacy, of the method. Very roughly, it should not be the case that the believer *thinks* that the method is unreliable, nor is he justified in regarding the method as unreliable. Of course, the latter condition should be spelled out in non-justificational terms, something I undertake (sketchily) in *E & C* but will not repeat here.[6]

Chisholm expresses the worry that the reliable-method condition is too *easy* to satisfy.[7] He considers the case of a man who comes to believe that there are nine planets by reading the tea-leaves. Now suppose that this reading took place on a Friday afternoon at 2:17, and suppose that nobody on any other occasion consults tea-leaves about the number of planets at 2:17 on a Friday afternoon. Then, says Chisholm, this man followed a method that always leads to truth, a method one could describe by saying, 'To find out anything about the number of planets, consult tea-leaves at 2:17 on a Friday afternoon.'

Notice, however, that *this* is not plausibly the method the man has *used*. For a method to be used, it must be represented in the cognizer's head (though not necessarily consciously). But presumably neither the day of the week nor the time of day was part of the recipe for belief formation that the man represented in his head. Although *we* can introduce those features into a description of his action, it doesn't follow that they were parts of the method *he used*.[8] But the method he *did* use—consulting the tea-leaves—is not reliable.

Admittedly, a cognizer *might* incorporate these temporal factors into a method, and such a method could be reliable (at least in the sense Chisholm specifies). But use of this reliable method would not suffice for secondary (method-level) justifiedness. As indicated, the believer must acquire the method in a suitable fashion. That condition is (apparently) not met in Chisholm's example. If a new example were constructed in which it *is* met, then I think the cognizer's belief *would*, intuitively, be justified.

The plausibility of the reliability approach can be bolstered by considering degrees of justifiedness. Although my main analysandum is the categorical notion of justified belief, a brief digression on the comparative notion may be instructive. Chisholm, of course, has rightly stressed the idea of multiple grades of epistemic status.[9] Can such a notion be captured within reliabilism? Quite naturally, I believe. Ceteris paribus, one belief is better justified than another belief just in case the methods (or processes) that generate (or sustain) the former are more reliable than those that generate the latter.

A simple example will illustrate this idea. Suppose one student does a long addition problem by adding columns from top to bottom, in the canonical fashion. This student arrives at a belief in the answer. A second student goes through the same procedure, yielding the same answer, but then 'checks her work' by doing it all over again. Or perhaps she does the problem the second time by proceeding bottomup, or by using a calculator. In any event, she uses a *compound* method, M_2, which contains the first method, M_1, as its first component. The compound method involves forming a belief only when both procedures yield the same answer. It is plausible to say that both students have justified beliefs, but that the second has a *more* justified, or *better* justified, belief than her classmate. Why? The natural answer is: method M_2 is more reliable than M_1. Indeed, the difference in degree of justifiedness seems to correspond precisely to the difference in reliability of the methods. If the compound method has only marginally greater reliability, then it yields, intuitively, only marginally greater justifiedness. If the compound method has substantially greater reliability, justifiedness is substantially increased. This supports the idea that reliability is the underlying ingredient in justifiedness.

III

Returning from this digression, but staying at the level of methods, I turn now from strong to weak justification. The weak notion of justification, it will be recalled, is that of blameless, or non-culpable, belief. We must be careful here, however. A well-formed belief, whose method is well-acquired and non-undermined, is also presumably blameless. So the strong notion of justifiedness entails blamelessness. But I want the notions of strong and weak justification to be *opposing* notions. This means that the weak notion of justification that interests me is not precisely that of blamelessness, but the narrower notion of *mere* blamelessness. That is, the weak notion is that of *ill-formed*-but-blameless belief.

With this point clarified, let me propose some conditions for weakly justified belief (at the level of methods). More precisely, I shall try to provide only some *sufficient* conditions for weak justifiedness, not necessary conditions. S's belief in p is weakly justified (at the secondary level) if (1) the method M by which the belief is produced is unreliable (i.e., not sufficiently reliable), but (2) S does not believe that M is unreliable, and (3) S neither possesses, nor has available to him/her, a reliable way of telling that M is unreliable. (By this I mean that S has neither reliable method nor reliable process which, if applied to his/her present cognitive state, would lead S to believe that M is unreliable.) It is plausible that a further condition should also be added, viz., (4) there is no process or method S *believes* to be reliable which, if used, would lead S to believe that M is unreliable.

The proposed conditions seem to capture our case of the scientifically benighted cognizer. That cognizer's belief in the outcome of the impending battle is in fact ill-formed, i.e., formed by an unreliable method. But he does not believe that his method is unreliable. Moreover, there is no reliable method (or process) in his possession, or available to him, that would lead him to believe that his astrology-based method is unreliable. Finally, there is no method or process he *believes* to be reliable that would lead him to this judgment.

Our judgment of the benighted cognizer does depend, admittedly, on exactly what he knows, or has been told, about the accuracy of past astrology-based predictions, especially battle predictions. If he is told that in *all* such cases the predictions were falsified, we would surely deny that his use of the astrology-based method is defensible. After all, he does possess a native process of *induction*, which can be applied to such data! But let the case be one in which he receives relatively few well-substantiated reports of battle outcomes. Some of these corroborate the prior predictions, as chance would dictate. Where outcomes reportedly go against the predictions, the community's astrology experts explain that the predictions had been based on misapplications of the method. The experts have techniques for 'protecting' their theory from easy falsification, and only sophisticated methodologies or astronomical theories would demonstrate the indefensibility

of such tactics; but these are not available. (Needless to say, if this particular example of a benighted cognizer does not fully suit the reader, other examples to make the same point might readily be constructed).

Clearly, the truth of the contention that no way of detecting the target method's unreliability is *possessed* or *available* to a cognizer depends on exactly how the terms 'possessed' and 'available' are understood. It might be argued, for instance, that sophisticated scientific methodology is always in fact 'available' to people, even when such a methodology is not in use by members of their culture. The proper response, I suggest, is that the notions of availability and possession are vague and variable. They are open to a number of interpretations, each reasonably plausible and pertinent in at least some contexts.

The vagueness or variability of 'possession' has been stressed in connection with *evidence* possession by Richard Feldman[10]; I also mention it a bit in *E & C*.[11] At one extreme, 'possessing', or 'having', a piece of evidence at a given time could mean consciously thinking of that evidence. At another extreme, it could mean having that evidence stored somewhere in memory, however difficult it may be to retrieve or access the item. An intermediate view would be that a piece of evidence is 'possessed' only if it is either in consciousness or *easily* accessible from memory.

Similar ambiguities arise for the term 'available'. But here there are not only different possible locations *in the head* but different locations and degrees of accessibility in the *social* world. Is a piece of evidence socially 'available' no matter how difficult or costly it would be to find it? There are no clear-cut answers here, neither in the case of *evidence* nor in the case of *methods*, which is what directly concerns me here. Different speakers (and listeners) use varying standards, depending on context and intention. So it is best to leave the notions of possession and availability in their natural, vague state, rather than try to provide artificial precision. It follows, of course, that the notion of weak justification inherits this vagueness. But there is plenty of evidence that epistemic concepts, including justification and knowledge, *have* this kind of vagueness.[12] However, under very natural and commonly used standards, no process or method is possessed or available to our benighted cognizer for telling that his astrology-based battle-predicting method is unreliable. Hence, his battle predictions based on that method are weakly justified. (This probably follows as well from one very moderate constraint I shall later impose on 'availability'.)

IV

Let me turn now to primary justifiedness: justifiedness at the level of processes. In this treatment I shall adopt the simple format for presenting reliabilism that I used in "What Is Justified Belief?"[13], rather than the preferable but more unwieldy format of process-permitting rule systems found in *E & C*. However, I shall later opt for the preferable rule-system format.

The proposed account of *strong* justification at the primary level closely parallels the account at the secondary level. A belief of person S is strongly justified at the primary level if and only if (1) it is produced (or sustained) by a sufficiently reliable cognitive process, and (2) that the producing process is reliable is not undermined by S's cognitive state.

The proposed conditions for *weak* justification at the primary level also parallel those at the secondary level. S's belief is weakly justified at the primary level if (1) the cognitive process that produces the belief is unreliable, but (2) S does not believe that the producing process is unreliable, and (3) S neither possesses, nor has available to him/her, a reliable way of telling that the process is unreliable. Finally, a further condition may be appropriate: (4) there is no process or method S *believes* to be reliable which, if used, would lead S to believe that the process is unreliable. Once again, interpretation of the terms 'possession' and 'available' is subject to variation. I shall not try to give a unique interpretation to these vague terms. As indicated earlier, though, I shall shortly impose one plausible constraint on availability.

V

I want to turn immediately now to an example of central interest, the case of a cognizer in a Cartesian demon world. Focus on the perceptual beliefs of such a cognizer. These beliefs are regularly or invariably false, but they are caused by the same internal processes that cause our perceptual beliefs. In the Cartesian demon world, however, those processes are unreliable. (I assume that either there is just a lone cognizer using those processes in that world or that the demon fools enough people to render those processes insufficiently reliable.) Then according to the proposed account of *strong* justifiedness, the cognizer's beliefs are not justified.

This sort of case is an ostensible problem for reliabilism, because there is a strong temptation to say that a cognizer in a demon world *does* have justified perceptual beliefs. The course of his experience, after all, may be indistinguishable from the course of your experience or mine, and we are presumably justified in holding our perceptual beliefs. So shouldn't his beliefs be justified as well?[14]

Under the present theory the treatment of the demon case is straightforward. The victim of the demon fails to have *strongly* justified beliefs, but he does have *weakly* justified beliefs. While his beliefs are not *well-formed*, they are *blameless* and *nonculpable*. His cognitive processes are not reliable (in his world), but (A) he does not believe that they are unreliable, (B) he has no reliable way of telling this, and (C) there is no method or process he *believes* to be reliable which would lead him to this conclusion. So on the weak conception of justifiedness, the resulting beliefs are justified.

Is it really true that the demon victim has no reliable way of telling that his perceptual processes are unreliable? What seems fairly clear is that none of his cognitive processes we normally deem reliable would lead him to the conclusion that his perceptual processes are unreliable. Surely if he uses his memories of past perceptual beliefs, memories of subsequent 'validations' of these by further perceptual checks, and then makes a standard inductive generalization, he will conclude that his perceptual processes *are* reliable. However, it might be contended that a reliable method is *available* to him that would yield the conclusion that his processes are unreliable. This is the 'single-output' method that would have him start with his antecedent corpus of beliefs and produce the conclusion, 'My perceptual processes are unreliable'. This single-output method is reliable since the one belief it produces is true!

I make two replies to this proposal. First, to call this a 'method' is surely to trivialize the notion of a method. I admit, though, that I have no convenient way of restricting methods that would rule this out. (*Perhaps* all single-output formulas should be excluded; but I am unsure of this.) However, even if we persist in calling this a 'method', there is little plausibility in saying that it is *available* to the demon victim. Availability should not be construed as mere in-principle constructibility and usability. It must at least be required that the cognizer could naturally be led to that method by some processes and/or methods he already employs, operating on his actual beliefs and experiences. But that is false in the present case. All his antecedent beliefs, processes, and methods run *against* the acceptance of this single-output 'method'. So there is no relevant sense in saying that this method is possessed by, or available to, this cognizer. Hence, his perceptual beliefs are indeed weakly justified.

VI

It is clear that this version of reliabilism accommodates the intuition that the demon victim has justified beliefs—at least on one conception of justification. What relation does this version bear to other versions of reliabilism? In *E & C* a reliabilist theory is proposed that handles the demon-world case rather differently. That theory is formulated in terms of right systems of process-permitting rules. A belief qualifies as justified (at the process level) just in case it is produced by processes that conform with some right rule system. (A non-undermining proviso is also included.) A rule system is right just in case it is reliable, i.e., compliance with that rule system would produce beliefs with a sufficiently high truth ratio.

These formulations do not resolve all questions of interpretation about the theory. Suppose we ask whether a belief B, in some possible world W, is justified. The answer depends on whether the processes that cause B in W are permitted by a right rule system. But is the rightness of a rule system a function of the system's reliability *in* W? Or is it fixed in some other way?

In *E & C*[15] I suggest that rightness of rule systems is rigid. A given rule system is either right in all

possible worlds or wrong in all possible worlds; it does not vary across worlds. Furthermore, rightness is not determined by the system's reliability in the *actual* world, for example, but rather by its reliability in what I call *normal worlds*. A very special sense of 'normal worlds' is delineated. A normal world is understood as a world consistent with our general *beliefs* about the actual world, beliefs about the sorts of objects, events, and changes that occur in the actual world. The upshot of this theory is that the appraisal of a demon victim's beliefs does not depend on whether his perceptual belief-forming processes are reliable in the demon world, but on whether they are reliable in normal worlds. Since they presumably *are* reliable in normal worlds, even this victim's beliefs qualify as justified according to the theory. Moreover, even if it should turn out that the actual world is a demon world, and our own beliefs are systematically illusory, these beliefs would (or could) still be justified. As long as the processes are reliable in normal worlds—which in this scenario does not include the actual world—these beliefs will be justified.

The normal-worlds version of reliabilism has the virtue of saving intuitions about justification in demon world cases. It also has other attractions. It seems to me natural to expect that reliability should be assessed in normal situations (or worlds) rather than all possible situations. When one says of a car that it is very reliable, one doesn't imply that it will start and run smoothly in *all* weather conditions; not at −50 degrees Fahrenheit, for example. One only implies that it will start in *normal* conditions.[16] However, this sense of 'normalcy' probably refers to *typical* situations. It doesn't imply anything like my *doxastic* sense of 'normalcy'. What might rationalize the doxastic sense? In writing *Epistemology and Cognition*, I had planned a chapter on concepts. One thesis I planned to defend is that our concepts are constructed against certain background assumptions, comprised of what we believe about what typically happens in the actual world. I expected this approach to concepts to underpin the doxastic-normalcy conception of reliability. Unfortunately, I did not manage to work out such an approach in detail.

In any case, there are a number of problems facing the account of justification that focuses on normal worlds (construed doxastically). First, *which* general beliefs about the actual world are relevant in fixing normal worlds? There seem to be too many choices. Second, whichever general beliefs are selected, it looks as if dramatically different worlds might conform to these beliefs. Does a rule system count as right only if it has a high truth ratio in *all* those worlds?[17] Third, when the theory says that normal worlds are fixed by the general beliefs *we* have about the actual world, what is the referent of 'we'?[18] Is it *everyone* in the actual world, i.e., the whole human race? Different members of the human race have dramatically divergent general beliefs. How are the pertinent general beliefs to be extracted?[19]

Finally, even if these problems could be resolved, it isn't clear that the normal-worlds approach gets things right. Consider a possible non-normal world W, significantly different from ours. In W people commonly form beliefs by a process that has a very high truth-ratio in W, but would not have a high truth-ratio in normal worlds. Couldn't the beliefs formed by the process in W qualify as justified?[20]

To be concrete, let the process be that of forming beliefs in accord with feelings of clairvoyance. Such a process presumably does not have a high truth ratio in the actual world; nor would it have a high truth ratio in normal worlds. But suppose W contains clairvoyance waves, analogous to sound or light waves. By means of clairvoyance waves people in W accurately detect features of their environment just as we detect features of our environment by light and sound. Surely, the clairvoyance belief-forming processes of people in world W *can* yield justified beliefs.

For all the foregoing reasons, it seems wise to abandon the normal-worlds version of reliabilism. Fortunately, this does not leave reliabilism incapable of meeting the demon-world problem. The present version of reliabilism accommodates the intuition that demon-world believers have justified beliefs by granting that they have *weakly* justified beliefs.

If the normal-worlds interpretation of rightness is abandoned, what should be put in its place (in the account of *strong* justification)? As the foregoing example suggests, it is probably unwise to rigidify rightness; better to let it vary from world to world. Perhaps the best interpretation is the most straightforward one: a rule system is right in W just in case it has a high truth-ratio in W.

There are reasons, however, why reliabilism cannot rest content with this interpretation. I shall mention them briefly although I cannot fully address the issues they raise. First, some rule system might be used rather sparsely in a given world, say the actual world. Its performance in that world might therefore be regarded as a poor indication of its true colors: either too favorable or too unfavorable. For this reason, it seems advisable to assess its rightness in W not simply by its performance in W, but by its performance in a set of worlds very close to W. In other words, we should be interested in the probability of a rule-system yielding truths in the propensity, or modal frequency, interpretation of probability.[21]

A similar conclusion is mandated by a related consideration. There are many different possible ways of complying with, or instantiating, a given rule system. Even if we take the outside environment as fixed, some rules might be used frequently in one scenario but infrequently in another. (Remember, the rules are *permission* rules; they do not say what processes *must* be used, or when.) These different scenarios, or compliance profiles, would presumably generate different truth ratios. The multiplicity of compliance profiles is noted in *E & C*,[22] where it is acknowledged that new refinements in the reliability theory are needed. Several plausible developments readily suggest themselves. First, one might require that *all* compliance profiles, even the lowest, should generate a specified, tolerably high, truth ratio. Alternatively, one might propose one or another weaker requirement, e.g., that the mean compliance profile, or the modal profile (in the statistical sense), should have a certain high truth ratio. Although I won't examine these ideas further, all are in the spirit of reliabilism.

Another technical problem is worth mentioning. *E & C* formulates reliabilism in terms of rule *systems* because many single processes would not have determinate truth ratios. Consider an inference process, or a memory process, for example. Whether it yields true or false beliefs depends on the truth values of the prior beliefs which it takes as inputs. Thus, only an entire system of processes, or a system of process-permitting rules, holds the prospect of having asociated truth ratios. However, a problem now arises. If you start with a given system, R, that has a very high truth ratio, adding a single unreliable rule might not reduce the truth ratio very much. So R*, obtained from R by adding such a rule, might still pass the reliability test. But if R* contains a poor rule, we don't want to count it as right. Let us call this the epistemic *free rider* problem.

I propose the following solution. It is not enough that a rule system itself have a sufficiently high truth ratio (in whatever fashion this gets spelled out or refined). It must also be required that none of its *subsets* should have an *in*sufficiently high truth ratio. Since the unit set of a member rule is a subset of the rule system, this requirement disbars rule systems with any individually unreliable rules.

VII

Let me leave these detailed points about the strong conception of justifiedness, and consider a worry about its general contours.[23] In particular, let me focus on the 'world-bound' character of reliabilism, as it emerges in the present formulation of strong justifiedness. Since the rightness of a rule system is now allowed to vary from world to world, even from one experientially indistinguisable world to another, it looks as if there is an element of *luck* in whether a belief is strongly justified or not. If we are in the world we *think* we are in, our perceptual beliefs are (in the main) strongly justified. If we are in a demon world, on the other hand, our perceptual beliefs are not strongly jusified. But these two worlds are experientially indistinguisable. So it seems to be a matter of luck whether or not our beliefs are strongly justified. But can invidious epistemic judgements properly rest on luck?

Note first that luck is a generally acknowledged component in other epistemic achievements, specifically *knowledge*. Justification does not logically imply truth, so even if one has a justified belief it is still a matter of luck whether one gets truth, and hence a matter of luck whether one attains knowledge. A similar moral follows from Gettier examples. People in experientially indistinguisable worlds might differ in their knowledge attainments because their true justified beliefs are Gettierized in one of the worlds but not the other. Since luck is a component in knowledge, why should it be shocking to find it in justifiedness?

The critic might retort that while it is conscionable to let luck figure in knowledge, it is unconscionable to let it figure in justification, which is an evaluative notion. But, I reply, should luck be excluded from evaluative contexts? Several writers have pointed out that it seems to enter into moral and legal evaluation.[24] Two equally reckless truck drivers, one who unluckily strikes a child and one who does not, may incur different amounts of disapproval and punishment. A similar point might be made in a slightly different vein about aesthetic evaluation. We can evaluate a painter's artistic feats even while admitting that these feats are partly due to luck: the luck of natural talent and the good fortune of excellent training.

But shouldn't there be *some* style of justificational evaluation that eliminates or minimizes luck? This seems plausible. It is precisely what is captured with the concept of weak justification. So the present theory also makes room for anti-luck cravings.

VIII

Does my duplex theory of justification amount to an acknowledgement that internalism is partly correct? Is it a partial abandonment of externalism? I find this hard to answer because the terms 'internalism' and 'externalism' do not have generally accepted definitions. Internalism might be the view that whether you are justified in believing a proposition is directly accessible to you from the internal perspective, or by immediate reflection. If this is how internalism is defined, though, it is not clear that the weak conception of justification is a brand of internalism. Whether you possess a way of telling, or have available a way of telling, that certain belief-forming processes are reliable or unreliable may not be something directly accessible to you by immediate reflection. I also doubt whether the weak conception of justification would fully appeal to internalists. Most internalists, I suspect, would like a more demanding conception of justification.

So I do not know whether the duplex theory of justification amounts to a marriage of externalism and internalism. I have no objection to this union, if that indeed is what it is. The important point is that it captures many intuitions about justified belief and does so in a broadly reliabilist framework.

NOTES

1. Objective and subjective senses are distinguished in Pollock (1979) and Goldman (1986), the latter using the terms 'real' and 'apparent' justification. Externalist and internalist conceptions are discussed by Armstrong (1973), Goldman (1980), BonJour (1980, 1985), and Alston (1986). The regulative and non-regulative options are discussed by Kornblith (1983), Goldman (1980, 1986), and Pollock (1986). Resource-relative and resource-independent conceptions are distinguished in Goldman (1986). Lehrer (1981) presents the personal and verific conceptions. Alston (1985) delineates deontological and evaluative conceptions (among many others).

2. Alston (1985) has a similar example of 'cultural isolation'.

3. Justifiedness as freedom from blameworthiness is one of the conceptions discussed by Alston (1985). A related conception of justifiedness as freedom from (epistemic) irresponsibility is presented by Kornblith (1983) and BonJour (1985).

4. See Goldman (1986), pp. 92–95.

5. A process or method is meta-reliable if, roughly, the methods (or processes) it tends to produce or preserve are mostly reliable. There are, however, a variety of alternative ways of spelling out the spirit of this idea. See Goldman (1986), pp. 27, 52–53, 115–116, 374–377.

6. See pp. 62-63, 111–112.

7. Chisholm (1982), p. 29.

8. Similarly, just because a perceptual belief is formed on a Friday, or in an environment with rose-tinted light, this does not mean that the cognizer has used *processes* of 'perceptual belief-formation on a Friday', or 'perceptual belief-formation in rose-tinted light'. In general, external circumstances such as date, time of day, physical objects in the environment, conditions of observation, etc. are not parts of a person's *cognitive processes*. The reason for this is not quite the same, however, as the reason in the case of methods. It isn't because these factors are not represented in the cognizer's head; processes in my sense are not the sorts of things that are represented explicitly in the head. Rather, they are *general operating characteristics* of the cognitive system. This is what restricts them to purely internal features or mechanisms. Many examples of process types given in the critical literature on reliabilism violate the exclusion of external factors, e.g., most cases discussed in Alvin Plantinga

(1986), pp. 10–11. Observance of this exclusion does not by itself, of course, solve the 'generality problem' confronting reliabilism. But exclusion of external conditions is essential to understanding the kind of referent that the term 'cognitive process' is intended to have.

9. See Chisholm (1966, 1977).

10. In Feldman (1986).

11. Goldman (1986), p. 204.

12. For a persuasive discussion of one dimension of contextual vagueness, see Cohen (1986); also Sosa (1974) and Dretske (1980).

13. Goldman (1979).

14. This point has been emphasized by a number of writers, including Pollock (1984), Cohen (1984), Lehrer and Cohen (1983), Ginet (1985), Foley (1985), and Luper-Foy (1985).

15. Page 107.

16. This example is due to Matthias Steup.

17. This point was raised by Alvin Plantinga, in correspondence.

18. This point was raised by Ernest Sosa in a lecture at the NEH Summer Institute on the Theory of Knowledge, Boulder, Colorado, 1986.

19. Sosa also raised other difficulties, in the lecture cited in note 18, but I won't try to review them all.

20. This general point, and the core of the example that follows, is due to Stewart Cohen, in correspondence.

21. See van Fraassen (1980), chap. 6.

22. Chapter 5, note 23, p. 395.

23. A different kind of objection should be addressed as well. I maintain that strong justification, involving generally reliable methods and processes, is necessary for knowledge. But Richard Foley (1985, p. 195) raises the following objection. It is possible for someone to know that a demon has been deceiving most people and himself as well, but no longer is deceiving him. He can then know by means of his perceptual processes, even though these processes are not generally reliable (nor usually reliable *for him*). I grant that a person in such a situation can have knowledge, but I deny that it would be obtained purely perceptually. Rather, it would be obtained by *inference* from the person's knowledge that the demon is *currently* allowing his visual processes to function properly (i.e., reliably). Foley does not specify how knowledge about the demon's new practice might be obtained, but it is compatible with the imagined example that this knowledge be obtained by reliable processes, as reliabilism requires. From such knowledge about the

demon's new practice, plus the fact that it now looks to the person as if, say, there is a javelina in the bush (a belief acquired by reliable introspection), the cognizer can reliably infer that there *is* a javelina in the bush. Thus, as Foley says, knowledge acquired with the help of perceptual processes is possible, even if these processes are not generally reliable; but this does not contravene reliabilism.

24. See Williams (1976) and Nagel (1979).

REFERENCES

Alston, William (1985). "Concepts of Epistemic Justification," *The Monist*, 68: 57–89.

Alston, William (1986). "Internalism and Externalism in Epistemology," *Philosophical Topics*, 14: 179–221.

Armstrong, D.M. (1973). *Belief, Truth and Knowledge* (Cambridge: Cambridge University Press).

BonJour, Laurence (1980). "Externalist Theories of Empirical Knowledge," in P. French, T. Uehling, and H. Wettstein, eds., *Midwest Studies in Philosophy* vol. 5, *Studies in Epistemology* (Minneapolis: University of Minnesota Press).

BonJour, Laurence (1985). *The Structure of Empirical Knowledge* (Cambridge, Mass.: Harvard University Press).

Chisholm, Roderick (1966). *Theory of Knowledge* (Englewood Cliffs, N.J.: Prentice-Hall, 1966).

Chisholm, Roderick (1977). *Theory of Knowledge*, 2nd ed. (Englewood Cliffs, N. J.: Prentice-Hall).

Chisholm, Roderick (1982). *The Foundations of Knowing* (Minneapolis: University of Minnesota Press).

Cohen, Stewart (1984). "Justification and Truth," *Philosophical Studies*, 46: 279–295.

Cohen, Stewart (1986). "Knowledge and Context", *Journal of Philosophy*, 83: 574–583.

Dretske, Fred (1980). "The Pragmatic Dimension of Knowledge", *Philosophical Studies*, 40: 363–378.

Feldman, Richard (1986). "Having Evidence," read at the NEH Summer Institute on the Theory of Knowledge, Boulder, Colorado.

Foley, Richard (1985). "What's Wrong with Reliabilism?" *The Monist*, 68: 188–202.

Ginet, Carl (1985). "*Contra* Reliabilism," *The Monist*, 68: 175–187.

Goldman, Alvin (1979). "What Is Justified Belief?", in George Pappas, ed., *Justification and Knowledge* (Dordrecht: D. Reidel).

Goldman, Alvin (1980). "The Internalist Conception of Justification," in P. French, T. Uehling, and H. Wettstein, eds., *Midwest Studies in Philosophy*, vol. 5, *Studies in Epistemology* (Minneapolis: University of Minnesota Press).

Goldman, Alvin (1986). *Epistemology and Cognition* (Cambridge, Mass.: Harvard University Press).

Kornblith, Hilary (1983). "Justified Belief and Epistemically Responsible Action," *Philosophical Review*, 92: 33–48.

Lehrer, Keith (1981). "A Self Profile," in Radu Bogdan, ed., *Keith Lehrer* (Dordrecht: D. Reidel).

Lehrer, Keith and Stewart Cohen (1983). "Justification, Truth, and Coherence," *Synthese*, 55:191–207.

Luper-Foy, Steven (1985). "The Reliabilist Theory of Rational Belief," *The Monist* 68: 203–225.

Nagel, Thomas (1979). "Moral Luck," in *Mortal Questions* (Cambridge: Cambridge University Press).

Plantinga, Alvin (1986). "Epistemic Justification," *Nous*, 20:1–18.

Pollock, John (1979). "A Plethora of Epistemological Theories," in George Pappas, ed., *Justification and Knowledge* (Dordrecht: D. Reidel).

Pollock, John (1984). "Reliability and Justified Belief," *Canadian Journal of Philosophy*, 14: 103–114.

Pollock, John (1986). *Contemporary Theories of Knowledge* (Totowa, N.J.: Rowman & Littlefield).

Sosa, Ernest (1974). "How Do You Know?" *American Philosophical Quarterly*, 11: 113–122.

Van Fraassen, Bas (1980). *The Scientific Image* (Oxford: Oxford University Press)

Williams, Bernard (1976). "Moral Luck," *Proceedings of the Aristotelian Society*, supplementary vol.1.

RICHARD FUMERTON

The Internalism/Externalism Controversy

Much of contemporary epistemology takes place in the shadow of the internalism/externalism debate. Its current place on the centre stage of epistemology seems appropriate given the dramatic revolution in our thought about historical and contemporary epistemological inquiry that would seem to be forced by certain paradigm externalist views. But although the controversy seems to strike deep at the heart of fundamental epistemological issues, I am not certain that it has been clearly defined. It seems to me that philosophers are choosing sides without a thorough understanding of what the respective views entail.

In this paper I want to explore a number of different ways of defining the technical distinction between internalist and externalist epistemologies. As is so often the case with technical philosophical distinctions, it is probably foolish to insist that there is only one "correct" way to define the distinction. I am interested in developing a way of understanding the controversy so that it leaves many philosophers already recognized as paradigm internalists and externalists in their respective categories, but this is not my main goal. Indeed, while my ultimate suggestion as to how to understand internalism will include as internalists many in the history of philosophy, it may be harder to find contemporary epistemologists who satisfy my internalist criteria. My primary concerns are to define the controversy in such a way that it a) involves a fundamentally important distinction, and b) articulates the source of the underlying dissatisfaction that internalists feel toward paradigm externalist analyses of epistemic concepts. At the very least, I want to articulate *this* internalist's view as to the critical mistake of externalism. As one who thinks that externalist analyses of epistemic concepts are somehow irrelevant to the traditional and appropriate philosophical interest in knowledge and justified belief, I am obviously inter-

ested in converting philosophers to my own brand of internalism, and the extreme version of foundationalism that it involves. My hope is that when philosophers realize the underlying source of their unhappiness with externalist epistemology, they will come home to a version of foundationalism that has been neglected too long. By way of achieving this last goal, I will also examine and object to one of the methodological assumptions underlying externalist epistemologies. But let us begin by trying to define the concepts of internalism and externalism.

INTERNALISM AND INTERNAL STATES

The term "internalism" might suggest the view that S's knowing that P or having a justified belief that P, consists in S being in some *internal* state. We might, then, understand the externalist as one who is committed to the view that two individuals could be in identical "internal" states of mind while one knows, or has evidence, or has a justified belief, while the other does not. This is surely tempting, but everything hinges on how we understand "same internal state" and "same state of mind". If we include among the properties that define a state of mind *relational* properties, then it would seem obvious that an *externalist* can, and would, embrace the thesis that if my state of mind is identical to yours then I'll know what you know, I'll be justified in believing what you are justified in believing. Goldman, Nozick, Armstrong, and Dretske, to consider just a few externalists, are all willing to pick out a complex relational property that my belief has in virtue of which it constitutes knowledge or justified belief.[1] The relational property will typically be a complex nomological property, such as the property of being caused by a process which satisfies a certain description, or being such that it would not have occurred had not certain other conditions obtained. One gets all sorts of variations on externalism depending on how the relevant nomological relations are characterized. If we are trying to define a view that these externalists reject, then, we cannot simply define internalism as maintaining that one knows or has a justified belief in virtue of being in a certain kind of state of mind when we let the relevant kind be determined in part by its relational properties.

Shall we then say that an internalist identifies knowledge and justified belief with internal states of mind, meaning by internal states of mind, *nonrelational* properties of a mind? The externalist, correspondingly, would maintain only that two individuals could exemplify the same nonrelational properties while one knows or has a justified belief and the other does not. We could, but then we are going to be hardpressed to find very many internalists. Certainly, on this understanding of externalism, everyone who holds that a justified true belief can constitute knowledge even when the justification is logically compatible with the belief being false is committed to an externalist account of knowledge.[2] A non-redundant truth condition in the traditional analysis of knowledge clearly introduces a condition that goes beyond the nonrelational properties of the knower. But even if we restrict our attention to the concept of justified belief, there seem to be precious few philosophers who would identify the having of a justified belief with the exemplification of some nonrelational property (properties).

One of the classic foundationalist approaches to understanding noninferential knowledge identifies at least one condition for such knowledge as *direct acquaintance* with facts. I'll have more to say about this view later, but for now I would merely observe that at least some externalists take such positions to be paradigms of the sort of internalist epistemologies they are rejecting.[3] But clearly when someone like Russell talked about being acquainted with a fact, he intended to be referring to a *relation* that a subject bears to a fact. Having a noninferentially justified belief, on such a view, would *not* be identical with exemplifying nonrelational properties, and a Russellean would *not* argue that if two people were in the same nonrelational states they would have the same justified beliefs. It is not even clear that the ex-

ternalists' favorite internalist, Descartes, would satisfy the above characterization of an internalist. If, for example, Descartes accepted a relational analysis of believing something to be the case, or having an idea of something, the states of mind that for him constitute knowledge and justified belief would not be nonrelational properties of a self. The only philosophers who could be internalists in the above sense are philosophers who embrace an adverbial theory of consciousness and identify some of the nonrelational properties, exemplification of which constitutes consciousness, with knowledge and justified belief. If one must believe all that in order to be an internalist, not very many philosophers, myself included, would want any part of the view.

Philosophers who have tried to ground knowledge and justified belief in acquaintance with facts have sometimes construed the facts with which one *can* be acquainted as themselves "modifications" of the mind. This might in turn suggest that one could usefully define the internalist as someone who is committed to the view that knowledge and justified belief must be identified either with nonrelational properties of the mind *or* with relational properties of the mind where the relata of the relations are the mind and its nonrelational properties. Such a definition would house more analyses of justified belief under the roof of internalism although any analysis of knowledge involving a nonredundant *truth* condition would still be externalist. But it is important to realize that such a definition of internalism would still leave philosophers who ground justified belief in acquaintance with nonmental facts (e.g., the neutral monist's sense data, the epistemological direct realist's surfaces of physical objects, the Platonist's forms and their relations, the realist's universals and their relations) in the externalist's camp. And I don't think the paradigm externalist wants their company. More importantly, it looks as though we are defining the internalism/externalism debate in a *peculiar* way by putting into opposite camps *fundamentally* similar views. It seems to me that if I am trying to ground the concept of justified belief in acquaintance with nonrelational properties of the mind, and you are trying to ground the concept of justified belief in acquaintance with nonmental sense data, our views are fundamentally alike. The internalism/externalism controversy will not be getting at a *significant* issue if one of these views gets described as a form of internalism while the other is described as a form of externalism.

INTERNALISM AND ITERATION

There is, of course, more than one natural way to understand the suggestion that conditions for knowledge or justification are internal to the cognizer, or are "in the mind" of the cognizer. When philosophers talked about sense data being "in the mind," for example, at least sometimes they seemed to be pointing to a feature of our *knowledge* of them.[4] Sense data are "in the mind" in the sense that one has a kind of privileged access to them. And this analogy suggests another way of trying to understand what is really at issue between the internalist and the externalist. At least some philosophers want to understand the internalist as someone who maintains that the necessary and sufficient conditions for satisfying epistemic concepts are conditions to which one has a privileged and direct access. "Access," of course, is itself an epistemic term. On this analysis of internalism, then, the internalist might be thought of as someone who is committed to the view that knowledge entails knowing (perhaps directly) that one knows; having a justified belief entails justifiably believing that one has a justified belief.

The above involves a very strong interpretation of having access to the conditions of knowledge and justified belief. A weaker conception of access could construe access as *potential* knowledge or justified belief. Thus a weaker version of internalism along these lines might insist that for a person to be justified in believing a proposition P that person must have "available" to him a method for discovering what the nature of that justification is. Let us consider both this strong and weak attempt to understand internalism as the view that having knowledge or justified belief entails having epistemic access to the conditions for knowledge and justified belief.

As someone who has always thought of himself as an internalist, one of my first concerns with the *strong* requirement of access is that it might saddle the internalist with a view that requires the *impossible* of knowledge and justified belief. As I shall make clear in my concluding remarks, I don't care if, on my analysis of epistemic terms, it turns out that dogs, computers, my Aunt Mary, or even the philosophically sophisticated, do not have *philosophically relevant* knowledge of, or justification for believing, what they think they know or are justified in believing. But I do not want to *define* knowledge and justified belief in such a way that having knowledge and justified belief involves a vicious regress. And the requirements that one must know that one knows P in order to know P; justifiably believe that one is justified in believing P in order to justifiably believe P, certainly seem to flirt with the prospect of a vicious regress.

In elaborating this point, one might, however, usefully distinguish inferential justification from noninferential justification. I *have* defended elsewhere (in [6], Chapter 2; and [7]) the very strong principle that if one is to be justified in *inferring* one proposition P from another E one must be 1) justified in believing E *and* 2) justified in believing that E makes epistemically probable P. Foundationalists have traditionally maintained that if one accepts such a principle, the only way to avoid an infinite number of infinite regresses is to recognize the existence of noninferentially justified beliefs (including, of course, noninferentially justified beliefs in propositions of the form 'E makes probable P'). My reservations with the strong requirement of access, then, have to do with the general thesis that *all* justification involves access to the conditions of justification. In his recent book [2], Bonjour seems to defend a version of internalism defined in terms of a requirement of strong access and he argues, quite plausibly, that foundationalists are going to have an exceedingly difficult time ending the regress of justification within the context of this strong internalism.[5] If a belief that P has some feature X in virtue of which it is supposed to be noninferentially justified, Bonjour's internalism requires us to justifiably believe that the feature X is present and that it makes probable the truth of P. The regress we were trying to end with noninferential justification is obviously about to begin again. If one accepts this incredibly strong version of internalism, it seems to me that one will not be able to escape Bonjour's argument. Indeed it is all too evident that Bonjour cannot escape his own argument as it might be applied to his coherentist alternative to foundationalism. To his credit, Bonjour recognizes that his internalism requires that in order to have empirical justification, one must have *access* to what one believes and the relevant relations of coherence. Since the only kind of epistemic access to empirical propositions he recognizes is through coherence, one will have to find beliefs which cohere with beliefs about what one believes. But the problem rearises with respect to getting access to those beliefs and again we encounter a vicious regress. Bonjour tries to save his view with his "doxastic presumption" (101–05) (you just take it for granted that your metabeliefs are by and large right), but it seems to me that if one reads the text closely, Bonjour as much as admits that his view entails the most radical of skepticisms with respect to empirical justification (105).

The only way one can satisfy the requirement of strong access for justification is to allow the possibility of a mind having an infinite number of increasingly complex intentional states. If, for example, I hold (as I do) that my belief that P is noninferentially justified when I am acquainted with the fact that P, the thought that P, and the relation of correspondence between the thought that P and the fact that P (call these conditions X) I am not, on the above view, an internalist unless I am willing to assert that in order for X to constitute my noninferential justification for believing P, I must be acquainted with the fact that X, the thought that X, and the relation of correspondence between the thought that X and the fact that X (call *these* Y). And I must also hold that I am acquainted with the fact that Y, and so on. Now I am not saying that this view is obviously impossible to hold. One can suppose that people have an infinite number of thoughts (perhaps dispositional) and one can think of the "layers" of acquaintance as being like perfectly transparent sheets laid one on top of another. But do we, as internalists, want to let ourselves be painted into a corner this tight where the only escape is a view that might not even be intelligible?

While it is not precisely the same problem of a formal vicious regress, the possible limitations of the mind when it comes to considering facts of ever expanding complexity might also make a proponent of the acquaintance theory of noninferential justification reluctant to accept even the *weaker* requirement of access. Speaking for myself, I am not sure I can even keep things straight when I try to form the

thought that my thought that my thought that my thought that P corresponds to my thinking that P corresponds to P. And this is still only a few levels away from the first order thought that P.

"Internalism" is, to be sure, a technical expression, but do we want to put a view like mine that refuses to accept either the strong or the weak requirement of access, but that defines noninferential justification in part by reference to the concept of direct acquaintance with facts, on the externalist side of the internalist/externalist controversy? My suspicion is that this is not how the issue is being understood. And to further reinforce the idea that we are not getting at the heart of the controversy by considering requirements of "access", we should reflect on how easily a mischievous externalist can "play along" with access requirements of internalism. For purposes of illustration let us take one of the paradigmatic externalist analyses of epistemic terms, the reliabilist analysis of justification offered by Goldman in [8].[6] In that article Goldman initially suggests the following recursive analysis of justification: A belief is justified if it results either from 1) a belief-independent process that is unconditionally reliable, or 2) a belief-dependent process that is conditionally reliable, where the "input" beliefs are themselves justified. Belief-independent processes do not have beliefs as their "input," and what makes them unconditionally reliable is that the "output" beliefs are usually true. Belief-dependent processes have as their "input" at least some beliefs, and what makes them conditionally reliable is that the "output" beliefs are usually true *when* the "input" beliefs are true. Qualifications having to do with the availability of alternative processes and the consequences of their hypothetical use are later suggested, but they need not concern us for the point I presently wish to discuss.

Now it is obviously a feature of Goldman's paradigmatic externalism that it does not require that a person whose belief is justified by being the result of some process have epistemic access to that process. My beliefs can be reliably produced even if I have no reason whatsoever for supposing that they are reliably produced. And this might seem to suggest that the important feature of externalism is its rejection of access requirements for justified belief. But suppose the externalist gets tired of hearing internalists complaining about allowing the possibility of having a justified belief with no justification for believing that it is justified.[7] It is useful to ask whether a reliabilist could remain within the spirit of reliabilism and at the same time allow that reliable processes yield justified beliefs only when one is justified in believing that the processes are reliable. Certainly, a reliabilist could accept our weak requirement of access—a reliabilist could allow that a reliable process $P1$ generates justified beliefs only if there is *available* a justification for believing that $P1$ is reliable. Interpreting this justification on the relabilist's model would presumably require there being available a process $P2$ which could generate the belief that $P1$ is reliable. Of course, given the requirement of weak access, $P2$ would itself generate justified beliefs only if there were available a reliable process $P3$ which could generate the belief that $P2$ is reliable, and so on. But it is not obvious that all of these reliable processes or methods need be different (a reliabilist, as far as I can see, can allow, for example, the inductive justification of induction, perceptual justification of the reliability of perception, and so on) and in any event since they need only be available (as opposed to actually used) it is not clear that the regress is vicious.

Could a reliabilist accept even a strong requirement of access? Could a reliabilist even allow that a process $P1$ generates justified beliefs only if the believer actually justifiably believes that the process is reliable? This is clearly more problematic for there would actually have to be some reliable process $P2$ generating the belief that $P1$ is reliable, and some reliable process $P3$ generating the belief that $P2$ is reliable and so on. The coherence of such a view rests on considerations concerning the potential complexity of the mind that we have already discussed in the context of wondering whether classical foundationalism can cope with strong access requirements. But suppose, for the sake of argument, that our hypothetical reliabilist convinces us that the mind has a kind of infinite complexity that renders harmless even this regress. The important question to ask is whether this hypothetical reliabilist paying his externalist lip service to our requirements of access would make the dissatisfied internalist happy. And I think that the answer is that he obviously would not. As long as the reliabilist/externalist keeps offering reliabilist/externalist accounts of knowing that

one knows or being justified in believing that one has a justified belief, the internalist isn't going to feel that anything has been accomplished by getting this reliabilist to accept the view that knowing entails knowing that one knows; having a justified belief entails being justified in believing that one has a justified belief. The obvious moral to draw is that the fundamental disagreement between internalists and externalists is not really a disagreement over such questions as whether inferential justification entails actual or potential justified belief in the legitimacy of the inference, or more generally whether justification entails actual or potential access to the fact that the conditions of justification are satisfied.

INTERNALISM AND NORMATIVITY

One of the more nebulous criteria for distinguishing internalist and externalist analyses involves the suggestion that externalists ignore the *normativity* of epistemic judgments. And, certainly, many of the objections levelled at reliabilism, for example, make the claim that unreliability to which one has no actual or potential access cannot decide questions about the rationality or irrationality of beliefs because charges of irrationality are relevant to evaluations of epistemic *praise* and *blame*. If my beliefs are produced by unreliable processes when there is no possible way for me to find that out, in what sense am I to be blamed for having the belief? The inhabitants of demon worlds are no more blameworthy for their demon induced false beliefs than are the inhabitants on non-demon worlds.[8]

Now in one sense I am perfectly prepared to admit, qua internalist, that when one characterizes a belief as irrational one is *criticizing* that belief, and since I think that externalist accounts are radically mistaken analyses of philosophically relevant epistemic concepts, I obviously think they have incorrectly analyzed the nature of this epistemic criticism. But being a kind of criticism is a very broad criterion for being normative. We criticize beliefs for being irrational, but we also criticize knives for being dull, cars for being too expensive, theories for being false. But does that make judgments about the dullness of knives, the cost of cars, and the falsehood of theories, normative judgments? Perhaps in a sense a judgment about the dullness of knives is *relevant* to a normative judgment about the goodness of that knife in that we usually consider dullness to be a property that makes the knife ineffective for achieving certain ends peculiar to the use of knives. But this is grist for the reliabilist's mill. We criticize the processes producing beliefs for being unreliable, the reliabilist might argue, because such processes typically fail to produce what we want from them—true beliefs.

Surely both internalists and externalists will agree that in some sense charges of irrationality can be construed as *criticisms*. But it is important to distinguish this virtual truism, a truism that isn't going to differentiate the two views, from so-called deontic analyses of epistemic terms, where a deontic analysis *defines* epistemic concepts using value terms. Deontic analyses of epistemic terms may well be incompatible with at least paradigm externalist views, but as an internalist I certainly don't want to be stuck with defending a deontic analysis of epistemic concepts. To *criticize* a person's *belief* is not to suggest that the person is morally reprehensible for having that belief. And this is so even if we successfully avoid the standard "conflicting duties" objections to deontic analyses that were raised against the view that Chisholm suggested in [3] (You've got the duty to believe you will get well—it might help—even though your evidence indicates you will probably die). Specifically, I would argue that a person's belief can be epistemically criticized even if we decide that the person is so far gone, is so irrational, that we do not think it even causally possible for him to figure out why his beliefs are irrational. Such a person is presumably not to be *blamed* for believing anything. He may be doing the very best he can with the potential he has, even though his best effort still results in the having of irrational beliefs. Put another way, we do not (should not) ethically criticize an irrational *person* for holding beliefs that we nevertheless *criticize* as irrational. Again, I do not think that the externalist has a plausible understanding of the conditions under which we philosophically criticize a belief as being irrational, but for the reasons I have tried to indicate, I do not think it is useful to try to understand the internalist/externalist debate as one over the normativity of epistemic judgments. In fact, I would argue that pure deontic analyses of epistemic terms involve a mistake very much like the mistake of externalism.

EXTERNALISM AND WHAT'S REALLY WRONG WITH IT

For someone whose primary interest is in defining the controversy, this section heading might seem unnecessarily contentious. But you will recall that my concern is to understand the internalist/externalist debate in such a way as to make clear what I take to be the source of the internalist's dissatisfaction with the view, and particularly this internalist's dissatisfaction with the view.

Old philosophical views have a way of resurfacing under new labels. And the roots of externalism go back further than the "naturalistic epistemology" encouraged by Quine. Rather, I think they lie with an old controversy concerning the correct analysis of epistemic probability. While the Russell of [15] clearly took epistemic probability to be a *sui generis* concept (see his discussion of the principle of induction) the Russell of [16] was bound and determined to reduce epistemic probability to a frequency conception of probability.[9] A crude attempt to define epistemic probability in terms of frequency might hold that one proposition E makes probable another proposition P when the pair is of a kind e/p such that usually when a proposition of the first kind is true, a proposition of the second kind is true. For our present purposes we can ignore the difficult questions involving the interpretation of the relevant frequencies, questions to which Russell devoted a great deal of attention. There is, it seems to me, an obvious connection between a frequency analysis of epistemic probability and the fundamental claims of such externalist epistemologies as reliabilism. Both are trying to understand fundamental epistemic concepts in terms of *nomological* concepts. The externalist/naturalist in epistemology (like his counterpart in ethics) is trying to define away the concepts fundamental to his discipline; he is trying to analyze fundamental epistemic concepts in terms of other non-epistemic concepts. Goldman's hard core reliabilism wants to explicate justified belief in terms of either a frequency or propensity (if that is any different) concept of probability. Nozick wants to define epistemic concepts in terms of nomological connections between facts and beliefs of the sort expressed by contingent subjunctive conditionals (in [14]). Armstrong appeals to this same concept of nomological necessity in trying to understand knowledge (in [1]). And if externalism involves a fundamental philosophical error, I would suggest that it is analogous to the alleged mistake of naturalism in ethics, or more accurately, the alleged mistake in ethics of trying to define the indefinable. I would urge you to consider the suggestion that it is a defining characteristic of an internalist epistemology that it takes fundamental epistemic concepts to be *sui generis*. No matter how much lip service our hypothetical reliabilist tries to pay to our insistence that justified belief entails being actually or potentially aware of the conditions of justification, he won't satisfy us as long as he continues to define the epistemic terms with which he pays us lip service in his naturalistic (nomological) way. It is the nomological analyses of epistemic concepts that leads us to keep moving up a level to ask the externalist how he knows that he knows, or knows that he knows that he knows. The externalist might be able to give correct answers within the framework of his view, but we, as internalists, will keep asking the questions until his answer invokes a concept of knowledge or justified belief not captured in terms of nomological connection. The real internalist/externalist controversy, I would suggest, concerns the extent to which sui generis epistemic concepts can be analyzed employing, or even be viewed as supervenient upon (where being supervenient upon involves a necessary connection stronger then causation), such nonepistemic nomological concepts as causation, universal and probabilistic law, and contingent subjunctive conditionals. Ironically, I never have been convinced that there is a naturalistic or definist fallacy in ethics. As an internalist, I am convinced that there is something analogous in epistemology and that it is at the heart of the internalism/externalism debate.

What are these sui generis epistemic concepts that defy reduction or analysis? This is obviously a question about which those who reject the externalists' views will themselves disagree. Perhaps the most famous contemporary philosopher associated with internalism today is Roderick Chisholm and despite periodic flirtations with deontic analyses of

epistemic terms, I think one must ultimately take seriously his insistence that we take as primitive the concept of one proposition being more reasonable to believe than another (in, for example, [4]). I would myself locate the fundamental sui generis epistemic concepts elsewhere.

In rejecting externalism, I have tried to be clear that I reject it only as an analysis of philosophically relevant epistemic concepts. Knowing, or having a justified belief, in the externalist's sense doesn't satisfy our philosophical curiosity, doesn't answer our philosophical questions, because qua philosophers trying to be rational, we want more than to be automata responding to stimuli with beliefs. I would argue that we want *facts*, including facts about which propositions make probable others, before our consciousness. This notion of a fact being before consciousness is, of course, itself an epistemic concept, and my suggestion is that one of the fundamental sui generis concepts that defy further analysis or reduction is the concept of direct acquaintance with a fact that in part[10] defines the concept of noninferential knowledge. And in the case of inferential knowledge, what one really wants as an internalist is direct acquaintance with the fact that one's evidence makes epistemically probable one's conclusion. Acquaintance with evidential connections would clearly be impossible if evidential connections are to be understood in terms of frequencies or other nomological connections, and that indicates that the other epistemic concept which resists further analysis is the old Keynesean notion of making probable as a sui generis relation between propositions, analogous to, but obviously different from, entailment.[11] I haven't the space to develop this view here—I have done so elsewhere.[12] My only concern is to sketch the *kind* of view, with its reliance on sui generis epistemic concepts, that I would take to be paradigmatically internalist.

A PRESUPPOSITION OF EXTERNALISM

I would like to conclude by briefly commenting on what I take to be a primary motivation of externalist analyses of epistemic concepts. I have said that there are a number of different views as to what the sui generis epistemic concepts might be, and the ease with which one can avoid skepticism depends very much on the details of the view one accepts. But certainly if one accepts the extreme version of foundationalism I recommend, complete with its insistence that one must have noninferential justification for believing propositions asserting evidential connections, the externalist is going to think that the task of avoiding skepticism is impossible. The typical externalist is convinced that one simply cannot be acquainted with facts. And even the internalist will undoubtedly admit that the kinds of facts with which we can be directly acquainted constitute a tiny fraction of what we think we know. When it comes to inferential knowledge, one must take seriously Humean complaints about the phenomenological inaccessibility of the relevant probability connection even if one ultimately rejects those complaints. If one cannot find in thought sui generis probability relations holding between propositions, one may well despair of resolving skeptical problems within the framework of radical foundationalism. On the problem of justifying belief in propositions describing the external world, for example, one might begin to suspect that Hume was right when he suggested with respect to what man ends up believing that

> Nature has not left this to his choice, and has doubtless esteem'd it an affair of too great importance to be trusted to our uncertain reasonings and speculations. ([11], p. 187).

Hume's hypothesis, I suspect, is accepted by externalists, but they do not want its truth to cheat us out of knowledge and justified belief. One of the most attractive features of most versions of externalism is that is makes it easy for us to know what we think we know. As long as nature (we now prefer to talk about evolution) has ensured that we respond to certain stimuli with correct representations of the world, we will know and have justified belief. Indeed, given externalist epistemologies, there is no difficulty in any creature or machine capable of representing reality achieving knowledge and justified belief.

It seems to me, however, that contemporary epistemology has too long let its philosophical analyses of epistemic terms be *driven* by the desire to avoid skepticism, by the desire to accommodate "commonsense intuitions" about what we know or are justified in believing. It is true that we describe ourselves as knowing a great many things. We also say that the dog knows that its master is home, the rat knows that it will get water when it hears the bell, and the salmon knows that it must get upstream to lay its eggs. But it seems clear to me that one need not take seriously our love of anthropomorphizing when analyzing the concepts of knowledge and justified belief that concern philosophers. If Wittgenstein and his followers did nothing else they surely have successfully argued that terms like "know" are used in a wide variety of ways in a wide variety of contexts. As philosophers, however, we can and should try to focus on the philosophically relevant use of epistemic terms. And the philosophically relevant epistemic concepts are those, satisfaction of which, resolves philosophical curiosity and doubt. I remain convinced that the kind of knowledge a philosopher wants, the kind of knowledge that will resolve philosophical doubt, involves the kind of direct confrontation with reality captured by the concept of direct acquaintance. While this is not the place to argue the issue, Hume *may* have been right—it may not be possible to justify in a philosophically satisfying way much of what we unreflectively believe. If this should be true, we may still satisfy, of course, the externalist's criteria for knowledge and justified belief, and these criteria may even mark a perfectly clear and useful distinction between beliefs and the kind of relations they bear to the world. Internalists will continue to feel, however, that the externalist has *redefined* fundamental epistemic questions so as to make them irrelevant to traditional philosophical concerns.

NOTES

1. Goldman in [8], [9], and [10]; Nozick in [14]; Armstrong in [1]; and Dretske in (among others) [5].
2. This point is made by Luper-Foy in [13].
3. See Nozick in [14], p. 281.
4. Not always. Sometimes "in the mind" meant logically dependent on the mind—the mind was thought of as a necessary condition for their existence.
5. The argument is presented on p. 32 but is discussed in a number of places throughout the book.

6. I realize that Goldman has presented a more so-phisticated view in his recent book [10]. But it is a view which strays rather far from his reliabilist in-tuitions. The idea that justification is a function of reliability in normal worlds where normal worlds are defined in terms of *beliefs* about this world is equivalent to abandoning the idea that justification involves beliefs which are (actually) reliably pro-duced. Indeed the view seems to me to come closer to a version of coherentism than reliabilism. In any event, I gather from a paper he read at a confer-ence in honor of Roderick Chisholm, [9], that he is now more inclined to go back to "hard core" relia-bilism for at least one fundamental concept of jus-tification.

7. It is interesting to note that in [9] and [10] Goldman comes very close to accepting something at least analogous. He allows that the use of a method can generate a strongly justified belief only if the method has been acquired in a suitable fash-ion, acquired by other methods, or ultimately pro-cesses, that are either reliable or meta-reliable. He does *not* impose the requirement on *all* processes, however, and in any event his requirement seems to concern the reliable generation of methods, not *beliefs* about methods.

8. In [10], Goldman himself seems to be more con-cerned with hooking up *one* sense of justification, what he calls weak justification, to considerations of blameworthiness and praiseworthiness. The aforementioned retreat from pure reliabilism in [9] was presumably aimed at achieving this same end.

9. See particularly [16], Part V, Chapters V and VI.

10. Notice that I have nowhere argued that an inter-nalist cannot make reference to concepts other than the *sui generis* epistemic concepts in analyses of epistemic terms.

11. See Keynes's discussion of this issue in [12], Chapter 1.

12. See particularly Chapter 2 of [6].

REFERENCES

1. D. M. Armstrong, *Belief, Truth, and Knowledge* (London: Routledge and Kegan Paul, 1968).
2. Laurence Bonjour, *The Structure of Empirical Knowledge* (Cambridge: Harvard University Press, 1985).
3. R. M. Chisholm, *Perceiving* (Ithaca: Cornell University Press, 1957).
4. R. M. Chisholm, *Theory of Knowledge,* 2nd Edition, (Englewood Cliffs, N.J.: Prentice-Hall, 1977).
5. Fred Dretske, *Seeing and Knowing* (London: Routledge and Kegan Paul, 1969).
6. Richard Fumerton, *Metaphysical and Epistemological Problems of Perception* (Lincoln and London: University of Nebraska Press, 1985).
7. Richard Fumerton, "Inferential Justification and Empiricism," *Journal of Philosophy,* 73 (1976), 557–69.
8. Alvin Goldman, "What Is Justified Belief," in Pappas, ed., *Justification and Knowledge* (Dordrecht: Reidel, 1979), 1–23.
9. Alvin Goldman, "Strong and Weak Justification," a paper read at Brown University, Fall, 1986, at a conference in honor of R. M. Chisholm.
10. Alvin Goldman, *Epistemology and Cognition* (Cambridge: Harvard University Press, 1986).
11. David Hume, *A Treatise of Human Nature,* ed by L. A. Selby-Bigge (London: Oxford University Press, 1888).
12. John M. Keynes, *Treatise on Probability* (London, Macmillan, 1921).
13. Steven Luper-Foy, "The Reliabilist Theory of Rational Belief," *The Monist,* April, 1985, 203–25.
14. Robert Nozick, *Philosophical Explanations* (Cambridge: Harvard University Press, 1981).
15. Bertrand Russell, *The Problems of Philosophy* (Oxford: Oxford University Press, 1959).
16. Bertrand Russell, *Human Knowledge: Its Scope and Limits* (New York: Simon and Schuster, 1948).

ROBERT AUDI

Justification, Truth, and Reliability

There are two quite different strands in the concept of justification, its normative character and its connection with truth. There is a tendency to take one of these as fundamental. That may explain why recent treatments of justification have often been dominated by one or the other of two contrasting views: epistemic deontologism,[1] which takes a belief to be justified provided the subject (S) meets his epistemic obligations relevant to that belief; and reliabilism, which conceives a belief's justification as determined by the reliability—roughly, the tendency to yield true beliefs—of the process(es) by which it is produced or sustained. This paper develops a third account of justification. The account has affinities to both views, but it aims at a better integration of the apparently disparate central strands in justification. My starting point is the relation between justification and truth.

I. JUSTIFICATION AND TRUTH

It is widely held that (epistemic) justification and truth are connected; but I believe that contemporary epistemologists have not adequately explicated this connection.[2] I want to clarify and account for it. At least two pitfalls must be avoided here. One mistake is excessive focus on the process of justification, particularly that of justifying beliefs in response to skepticism. This mistake is especially likely if one is preoccupied with the normative aspect of justification, which is very prominent in attempts to justify a belief by explicit appeal to a standard. The other mistake is excessive focus on the property of justification, justifiedness. That mistake is especially tempting for those preoccupied with the link between justification and truth, which may seem discernible simply by analyzing the notion of justified belief. We must not only avoid such mistakes, but

also account for the relation between the process and the property. This relation has been somewhat neglected, perhaps because many philosophers have concentrated on the process or the property, or conflated the one with the other. I shall discuss the relation in some detail.

Whatever the connection between justification—whether as process or property—and truth, justification does not entail truth. Granted, there may well be strong axiomatic justification: a kind possessed by beliefs which are based simply on understanding the proposition believed and cannot be unjustified, e.g. beliefs of simple self-evident propositions, say that if some dogs are mammals, some mammals are dogs. Strong axiomatic justification apparently *does* connect the *concepts* of justification and truth; for it is a kind of justification whose possession seems to entail truth. Descartes apparently thought that (suitably reflective) beliefs that one now exists are so justified; and he sought to build truth into the entire ediface of justified beliefs by showing that they are all either so justified or deductively based on beliefs that are. But if any empirical beliefs (beliefs of empirical propositions) possess strong axiomatic justification, it is only certain beliefs about oneself; and unless—as is doubtful—all other justified beliefs are deductively based on these, we must still ask how, for beliefs about the external world, justification is connected with truth.

If entailment does not constitute the general connection between justification and truth, what weaker tie might? Consider a case. Judy and Jack are taking a train on a fall evening. His view is obscured and he asks what color the foliage is. She might say, "Green," to which he might reply, "Can it still be green this far north?" A natural answer would be, "I can see it clearly, and it certainly looks green." It is significant that this answer *both* responds to a challenge of the truth of her statement and expresses a justification for her believing it. Imagine, moreover, that Jack perversely rejoins: "I know your seeing it clearly and its looking green to you justifies your belief, but is that relevant to its *truth*?" What are we to make of this? It is not a skeptical response, such as noting that she could be wrong. He admits that she has a justification and questions whether it is relevant to the truth of her justified belief. So understood, his rejoinder seems unintelligible. I believe that it appears unintelligible precisely because of the conceptual connection between (epistemic) justification and truth: it seems to be at least partly constitutive of justification that, in *some* way, it *counts toward truth*.

It is difficult to explicate the idea that justification counts toward truth. There are at least two interpretations, one stressing the property of justification, the other the process. The first is ontological, the second teleological. On the ontological view, when something (such as what Judy cites) justifies a belief, then, in a suitable range of relevantly similar possible worlds, notably worlds like ours where the same sort of thing is believed on the same sort of basis, this belief is true. One may perhaps equally well speak of relevantly similar circumstances; and there are other ways to express the basic idea.[3] On the teleological view, the conceptual connection between justification and truth is a matter of justification's "aiming" at truth, not in the consequentialist sense that what justifies produces or indicates true belief, but in the sense that the proper aim of giving a justification of a belief is to show (or argue for) its truth. The teleological view, then, ties justification to *seeking truth* and makes the *practice* of justification, above all the giving of justifications, fundamental in the connection between the concepts of justification and truth. The ontological view makes the *property* of justification, justifiedness, fundamental in this. It ties justification to *indicating truth*. Clearly, the two views can agree on what properties are suitable in giving a justification; and both hold that justification admits of degree and that if one belief is better justified than a second, then what justifies the first counts more toward truth than what justifies the second. But as we shall see, the differences between the views are more important than their similarities.

On the ontological view, correct generation principles for justification exhibit it as grounded in a state of affairs somehow connected with the truth of the belief in question. The state of affairs may be said to be truth-conducive; to count toward the truth of the belief; or to entail its prima facie truth (or a tendency toward truth). All these terms suggest fallibility: that at least normally a justified belief can be false because of some untoward circumstance.[4] Propositions may also be said to be justified, e.g. where someone asks whether there is any justification for a conjectured mathematical claim. We may speak of propositional justification here.[5] One other case should be mentioned: that of S's being justified relative to a proposition, as where S is justified *in* believing something obviously implied by propositions S believes. Here we may also speak of the relevant proposition, say p, being justified *for* S. This is person-relative propositional justification.[6] It does not entail S's actually believing that p; it occurs when there is something about S, whether an evidential belief or something phenomenal, e.g. having a visual impression of green, such that his believing it would be justified if he believed it on that basis. Such justification may also be said to derive from something about S, on the basis of which he could believe p, which *does* justify p. A full account of justification should clarify all three kinds.

One reason that reliabilism is attractive as an account of justification should now be evident. It explains the connection between justification and truth—at least if this connection is viewed ontologically. For if what justifies a belief is, say, production by a process that tends to yield true beliefs, then a justified belief has a (causal) basis that counts toward its truth. What justifies it will by its very nature be truth-conducive. By contrast, deontologism cannot readily account for an ontological connection between justification and truth. For—unless deontologists can find plausible principles of obligation whose satisfaction *entails* a reliable basis for beliefs—one could apparently meet one's intellectual obligations without one's bases for one's beliefs counting toward their truth. My problem, in part, is to explicate the relation between justification and truth in a way that avoids various difficulties of each of these theories, yet preserves some of their merits.

II. THE GENERATION OF JUSTIFICATION

A good way to explore the connection between justification and truth is to consider what sorts of epistemic principles might account for justification. First, however, some preliminary points. (1) I take justification to be a supervenient property. It supervenes on nonnormative properties like being in a sensory state, having a memory impression, and understanding a proposition. Let us also assume the following two points, typically accepted by reliabilists and deontologists alike. (2) Two beliefs cannot differ in justificatory status without differing in the sorts of non-normative properties cited: the relevant supervenience base properties. (3) As (2) suggests, the justifiedness of a belief is somehow determined by those properties. If all this is so, then the most plausible generation principles for direct (roughly, non-inferential) justification will exhibit it as grounded in non-normative properties.

My fourth preliminary point is that generation principles (like other epistemic principles) differ in many dimensions. They may be *momentary,* applying to justification at a single time, or *cross-temporal,* applying to justification over time or at multiple times. They may be *content-specific,* e.g. restricted to beliefs about perceptibles; or *content-neutral* say in applying to *any* proposition S seems to remember. A principle might be called *empirical* if it applies only to empirical beliefs, *a priori* if its scope is a priori beliefs, and *epistemically mixed* if it applies to both sorts. And a principle may of course be *absolute* or *prima facie.*

There is a further distinction, specially significant for competing conceptions of justification. A generation principle may or may not exhibit *subjective accessibility*: roughly, the factors it represents as conferring justification may or may not be available to S's direct awareness[7] through ordinary (even if searching) reflection. Thus, if Judy's belief that the foliage is green is justified by its looking green to her, then a principle accounting for this justification would be an accessibility principle if, by ordinary reflection, she can become (directly) aware of how the foliage looks to her. Can she? That depends on whether, by ordinary reflection, she can become

aware of (a) how *the foliage* looks to her, where this entails her having a perceptual relation to it; or only of (say) (b) *its looking to her as if the foliage is green,* where (b) is phenomenal: a matter of the content of her experience, say an impression of green foliage. Suppose that only (b) is available to her direct awareness. Then a different sort of generation principle is needed, one that represents a state like (b) as prima facie justifying her belief that the foliage is green.

It is evident that some potential justifiers are more readily accessible to awareness than others. Moreover, a generation principle can exhibit *mixed accessibility,* representing justification as arising from a combination of factors, some accessible and others, e.g. conditions of observation, not. If we assume that only the (mentally) internal is directly accessible, a theorist who holds that correct generation principles exhibit unmixed accessibility might be called a *pure internalist;* one who holds that they do not may be called an *externalist.*[8] Some views are more externalist than others; the degree of a view's externalism is proportional to the number and importance of the inaccessible justification generators it countenances relative to the number and importance of the accessible ones it countenances. It is doubtful that *pure* externalism, positing no subjectively accessible generators, has been seriously defended; pure internalism has been held and may indeed be entailed by certain kinds of coherentism.[9] Internalism and externalism are each associated with major epistemological drives. We should consider those drives before discussing particular epistemic principles.

I have spoken of the property and the process of justification. The two notions are systematically linked, and their relation is too little appreciated. A major connection is this: a belief is justified (has the property of justifiedness) if and only if it has one or more other, non-normative properties such that (i) in virtue of them it is justified, and (ii) *citing* them can, at least in principle, both show that it is justified and (conceptually) *constitute* justifying it. Call this *the process-property integration thesis.* Both epistemically and conceptually, it ties the properties on which justifiedness supervenes to the process of justifying the belief in question; and while it does not entail that S can readily cite them in justifying it, it does entail that the properties are so usable: that a property can confer justification only if citing it can constitute showing justification. One might think the property is more fundamental than the process; but we need not assume that, and my concern is with relations between the two that are independent of which, if either, is more fundamental to justification.

The process-property integration thesis, at least if it is (as it seems) conceptually true, helps to explain why it is natural to think of justification as generated by base properties S can adduce in response to a challenge. For if the thesis is a conceptual truth, then if we think of S's belief that p as justified, we should tend to think of it as having properties the citing of which *justifies* it; and, given how closely we associate the process and the property of justification, we should tend to think of these base properties as the sort S *can* cite, at least on reflection, in justifying it. Pure internalism entails that these points hold for all justified beliefs. Indeed, in part for this reason, the integration thesis helps to motivate at least a moderate internalism *independently* of deontologism: whether justification derives from meeting obligations or not, one cannot use only inaccessible justifiers in the process of (comprehendingly) justifying one's beliefs, and it is at best difficult to see how the integration thesis could be conceptually true if all of the properties conferring justification were inaccessible. If, however, one reflects on the relation between justification and truth, it is also natural to expect generation principles to cite factors in virtue of which the beliefs which the principles count as justified are likely to be true. And for beliefs about the external world, the best candidates for such factors, e.g. production of the belief by *veridical* perception, do not seem directly accessible to awareness.

There is, then, a tension we must resolve: if we conceive justification as something one can give upon reflection, we tend to think of generators of justification as subjectively accessible; if we conceive justification as truth-conducive, we tend to think of its generators more objectively, as factors that render the beliefs they justify likely to be true. Granted, the tension perhaps need not arise for introspective beliefs; perhaps they are necessarily both grounded in subjectively accessible mental states and reliably

produced. But with beliefs about the external world, the pure internalist is hard pressed to account for the apparently necessary connection between justification and truth, and the externalist is hard pressed to account for the apparently necessary availability of justifiers to the subject upon appropriate reflection.

If one conceives justification deontologically, this tension is reinforced. For if being justified consists in meeting epistemic obligations, then, by reflecting, one should be able to know one has met them. If, relative to my purview, my epistemic behavior is faultless, surely I have fulfilled my epistemic obligations. Granted, an epistemic deontologist, like an ethical one, *can* distinguish objective and subjective obligation and tie justification to the former. This may be an implausible move, but its possibility serves to bring out that it is the sense that justification must be available to S, and not a deontological view of justification as such, that generates the tension: it stems from basic properties of justification, not some special conception of it. One might posit two or more concepts of justification; but while I grant the plausibility of that view, I want to resolve the tension in a conceptually more economical way, and I assume there is a single, though complex, practice of justification, and an associated property of justifiedness, each discernible both in standard epistemic parlance and in the epistemological tradition since Plato.

III. SOME EPISTEMIC PRINCIPLES

Given the points made so far, we can explore some epistemic principles that may partly account for direct justification.[10] These will not be a *complete* set, one that accounts for all directly justified beliefs, nor can I take up indirect justification. Moreover, I discuss only momentary principles, and to minimize controversy the sample principles may not be the strongest warranted. Let us begin with *empirical grounding*—with principles concerning empirical beliefs—and explore introspective, perceptual, and memorial principles. A kind of *a priori grounding* will then be examined.

Take introspection first, and start with thinking, traditionally taken as a paradigmatic subject of directly justified beliefs. It is arguable that if S believes that S is thinking, this belief is justified. Granted, such beliefs may generate only strong prima facie justification, and hence may entail justification on balance only in the absence of certain overriders, e.g. S's having a well justified belief of an obvious contrary.[11] To simplify, let us use the prima facie formulation. If we do, we can presumably generalize to something like

P₁ For any occurrent mental state m, if S believes, noninferentially and attentively, that S is in m, then this belief is prima facie justified,

where an occurrent mental state is a mental process or phenomenal state, and attentively believing a proposition does not imply reflection, but only something like focusing carefully on it. Should P₁ stipulate that m's occurring is the *basis* of S's belief, since a brain manipulator could perhaps instill a false, groundless belief that one is, e.g., reasoning? I leave this open and assume that S's belief would still be prima facie justified.[12]

Now consider a perceptual principle. Take first something about visual experience: if S has a spontaneous visual experience in which it appears to him that there is an x which is F, and on this basis he believes this, then this belief is prima facie justified, where F is a visual property, such as a shape or color, 'x' ranges over physical objects of the sort that have such properties, and its appearing to him that there is an x which is F is a phenomenal state that does not entail his believing this, but only a disposition to believe it. I offer no characterization of visual properties, but make no controversial assumptions about them. It is more important to comment on the spontaneity requirement. Suppose Jack can induce visual experiences in himself at will. The induced visual experiences might well not yield prima facie justification; presumably, only spontaneous ones do. Spontaneous visual experiences are not, however, just those actually caused by a perceived object; and some nonveridical spontaneous experiences, such as an impression of water on the road ahead, can yield prima facie justification. If the suggested principle were not prima facie, the analysis of spontaneity would be a major concern; but since some of the slack can be taken up in setting out what overrides the prima facie justification, we can leave our for-

mulation as it is for purposes of discussion. (Indeed, it might be enough to require only that S take the experience to be spontaneous, or at least *not* be disposed to take it to be otherwise.)

If our visual principle is a reasonable model, a plausible counterpart for perceptual experience in general, substituting the notion of an impression that x is F for its appearing to S that there is an x which is F, would be

P₂ If S has a spontaneous perceptual experience in which S has the impression that x is F (an x-is-Fish impression), and on this basis attentively believes that x is F, then this belief is prima facie justified,

where F is a perceptual property, for instance a tactual one, x is some object (such as foliage) appropriate to the impression, and having a perceptual, e.g. visual, impression is a conscious, phenomenal state. P₂ is like P₁ in applying to *de dicto* beliefs; similar principles can be framed for *de re* cases. Since the relevant notion of spontaneity may be plausibly taken to be phenomenal, I construe P₂ as a subjective accessibility principle even on the strong assumption that this requires access to the spontaneity *as well as* the impression. If, however, the relevant notion is *genetic,* this must perhaps be left open, since it is not clear that one is ever directly aware of such genetic aspects of a perceptual experience.

The next case to be explored is that of memory beliefs. Consider

P₃ If S has a spontaneous, confident memorial impression that p (where p is internally consistent), then if S attentively believes p on this basis, this belief is prima facie justified.

A memory impression need not embody an image, but is a state of consciousness in which one has a sense of pastness regarding either the object(s) or event(s) which p is about or one's acquaintance with its subject matter; and the confidence of such an impression is not a matter of its actually producing belief, but of a tendency to produce confident belief that p. The sense of pastness is phenomenal, though often so unintrusive that it allows total concentration on what is remembered, as where, in writing a letter, one simply recalls and conveys remembered facts and events. This sense may be unanalyzable;

but we can say that while it does not entail believing p, nor even having a correct memory regarding p, it does entail being disposed to believe p. Lewis held a principle like P3, but perhaps more permissive.[13] It may be impossible to account for our intuitions about memorial beliefs without some such principle. We could try a *de re* principle: if the *truth* of p produces S's spontaneous, confident memorial impression that p, then if S believes it on the basis of that impression, this belief is prima facie justified. This is plausible, but to account for justified but false memorial beliefs we need a principle which, like P3, links memorial justification to suitable memory impressions.

In the kinds of empirical grounding of direct justification we have considered, then, there are recurring features. The relevant principles seem to apply only to prima facie justification; the generators need not be such that S has (or readily can have) *direct* awareness of what it is *about* them that justifies him; and, though we have not discussed them, there are versions applicable to both personal and propositional justification, as well as *de dicto* and *de re* versions. Let us now turn to a priori grounding.

Consider the logical truth that if no men are women, no women are men. Surely one believes such truths simply on the basis of understanding them (which I take to entail understanding the concepts figuring essentially in them). The same holds for such apparently necessary truths as that nothing is red and green all over at once. These could be believed on the basis of other propositions; but that is not normal, nor does one need such further beliefs for justifiably believing either kind of necessary truth. Using the notion of believing a proposition simply on the basis of understanding it, we may plausibly hold at least this restricted principle:

P4 If p is a necessary truth which, simply on the basis of understanding it, S attentively believes, then S's belief that p is prima facie justified.

It is appropriate to speak of a priori grounding in P4 because the justification is based on reason broadly conceived. Indeed, it may well be that *any* belief attentively held simply on the basis of understanding its content is prima facie justified. Neither that principle nor P4 entails that all necessary truths, even all "simple" ones, are knowable a priori. P4 does not even entail that where S's prima facie justification is not overridden, S knows that p. Nor is that true: think of mathematical theorems for which justified belief seems undeniable given a proof sketch, yet knowledge requires stronger reasons (or a completed proof).

As applied to most people, P4 will not account for their justification in believing any but quite simple necessary truths; but in principle one could believe a fairly complicated proposition simply on the basis of understanding it, and could be prima facie justified by so believing it, since the belief could be grounded in understanding its content and not on experience or any evidence for it one might have. However, unqualified justification is not entailed by the antecedent of P4 because, e.g., S may simultaneously have sufficiently good reason to disbelieve p. Many more generation principles could be considered, and a great deal must be said to explicate even P1–P4. But our brief discussion of them is sufficient to prepare us for the very general questions I now want to pursue concerning both their status and justification in general.

IV. THE STATUS OF THE EPISTEMIC PRINCIPLES

The prima facie qualification in P_1–P_4 deserves special comment. To understand them, we must also consider their epistemological status and their modality. I shall address these three topics in turn.

Regarding the prima facie qualification, at least four points are important. First, I am using 'prima facie justified' not in the *conditional sense* of 'justified provided certain conditions are met and otherwise not at all justified', but in a certain *defeasibility sense*, namely, 'having some degree of justification and justified on balance if the justification is not defeated'. Second, the prima facie justified belief that p may fail to be justified on balance because S has a (sufficiently) justified belief of an incompatible or disconfirming proposition. (It must also be sufficiently obvious to S, or at least to a hypothetical person who is a standard of rationality, that the relevant proposition counts against p; for S may have other relevant beliefs, e.g. one which warrants his thinking p and q compatible.) A third factor is S's simply being justified *in* believing an appropriately conflicting proposition, say *q*: even if *S* does not believe *q*, his being justified in believing it might override his justification for *p*; for he might be such that he "ought" to believe *q* and not to believe *p*. Fourth, consider circumstantial factors. Suppose that one's memory is very unreliable regarding a certain period in one's life. Or, suppose that when Judy forms the belief that the foliage is green, the sun is nearly down and her glance is hasty. Such factors might preclude the relevant memory and perceptual beliefs' having justification on balance: defeating though not overriding it.

There is an issue here. A pure internalist will argue that external circumstances are relevant only derivatively, through internal variables; e.g., that the justification of Judy's perceptual belief is defeated because she ought to *believe* her light insufficient to discern the color of the foliage. An externalist will argue that actual unreliability may directly undermine justification. We need not settle this: our question is the sorts of factors covered by the prima facie qualification. It should now be clear both why the qualification is appropriate and that we have a good enough idea of its scope so that its use does not trivialize the principles. Whether, a priori, we can specify *all* the factors that defeat prima facie justification, and thus formulate principles generating justification on balance, I leave open.

We come now to the epistemological status of the principles. Our broadest question is whether they are knowable a priori, i.e., roughly, through reflecting on them and the concepts figuring in them, and independently of experiential evidence (I do not assume that they cannot *also* be known experientially, say through testimony). If they are knowable a priori, they might be analytic or, more likely, conceptual synthetic truths: non-analytic, yet true by virtue of ("synthetic") relations of the relevant concepts. If they are empirical, they are presumably nomic. For one thing, they seem to support counterfactuals and to have explanatory power. Let us focus on P2.

An instance of P2 would be: If Jack has a spontaneous visual impression of green foliage before him, and on this basis attentively believes that the foliage before him is green, then this belief is prima facie justified. How might we know this? It will not do to say that the principle was arrived at by reflection on

justification and so is a priori; for one way a principle can be arrived at by reflection seems compatible with its being indirectly testable and nomic, rather than a priori.[14] Consider, on the other hand, what is relevant to assessing P2. Surely it is reflection, both on the principle itself and on the kind of hypothetical cases usually appealed to in assessing philosophical theses; and even if we do not sharply distinguish a priori from empirical propositions, it is plausible to distinguish among propositions in respect of their position in a spectrum from direct observational testability to highly indirect confirmability or disconfirmiability through experience, and to place at least some philosophical theses very far toward the latter end.

If we take such considerations seriously, we are likely to conclude that P2 is a priori, at least *if* we think philosophical theses in general are. But let us be careful. A reliabilist might reply that what occurs to us is this: if it seems to *S* that the foliage is green and he thereby believes it is, then probably *S*'s belief is produced by something in virtue of which it is true, here the green foliage; hence, we accept P2 because we accept the reliability of perceptual processes. If such thinking underlies acceptance of P2, then, since the reliability of the genesis of an empirical belief is not knowable a priori, epistemic principles based on reliability are not knowable a priori either. If we know P2, it is because we know empirically that a suitable proportion of (such) visually produced beliefs is true. Call this idea *subsumptivism:* the covering principle (a philosophical one) is that a reliably produced belief is justified, and the instantial premise is that spontaneously arising perceptual beliefs are reliably produced (since they tend to be true). P2, then, is true.

Leaving aside how, on this approach, we could know epistemic principles themselves without pulling ourselves up by our bootstraps (since we would apparently have to presuppose some to get the information about reliability needed in order to know the others),[15] does subsumptivism account for our acceptance of principles like P1–P4? Here are two relevant points. First, we simply cannot say what sorts of beliefs are directly justified except by referring to the kinds of generators and sustainers discussed in Section III—introspective, perceptual, memorial, and intuitive (or rational). Secondly, a challenge to principles expressing the justificatory force of these elements may properly be met, not only by pointing to a reliable connection, but, more importantly, by a response exhibiting the sense that a basic conceptual truth has been denied. If, e.g., someone said that the fact that S attentively believes he is imaging is no reason to regard his belief that he is imaging as justified, we are likely to wonder if he really means this, or understands the terms he uses. Notice that the issue is what counts toward justification, not what yields unqualified justification. This line of reasoning, then, is consistent with a skeptical denial that such beliefs are necessarily justified *on balance*.

To be sure, challenging certain deeply entrenched empirical propositions can elicit similar incredulity. But there is at least one difference: testability.[16] The epistemic principles we are discussing are not observationally testable. Even to begin to test one, we would apparently have to presuppose its soundness, or that of some principle of empirical grounding; and in any case it is not clear what observable outcomes would confirm or disconfirm it. Perhaps our experience could alter in a way that leads us to cease using the concept of justification which the principles in part constitute, but that is another matter. Accountability to experience in *this* sense is different from testability. We might also come to use 'justify' and its relatives in new senses. But we assess the principles by reflection, not by observing actual cognitive behavior, e.g. by seeing how often beliefs grounded in a certain way are true. Being such that we might have used, or might come to use, others, the principles might be said to be *historically contingent*, but they are *conceptually necessary*. The indicated distinction is not sharp, but it is real.

V. JUSTIFICATION AND THE PRESUMPTION OF RELIABILITY

If P_1–P_4 are a priori, we face a serious difficulty: when a justification is offered, why is questioning the reliability of the generators, such as perceptual experience, *necessarily* relevant? If it is not a conceptual truth that these factors reliably indicate truth, why should reliability matter in the important

way it does in assessing attempts to justify a belief? The answer, I think, is that because of the conceptual connection between justification and truth, an objection to the effect that what purportedly generates justification is not truth-conducive *is* relevant to a principle representing that generator as conceptually sufficient for justification. But if this is so, we face a serious problem, at least if the connection between justification and truth is ontological. The problem is to account for the relation between justification and reliability: if our epistemic generation principles are a priori and there is an a priori connection between justification and truth, then apparently some degree of reliability in the generating elements must be knowable a priori; yet their reliability seems a wholly empirical matter.

To see the issue more concretely, imagine a Cartesian demon who acts in such a way that our experience could be just as it is and yet at least the majority of our beliefs about the external world false. By P_1–P_4 we could have a great many justified beliefs. But would their justification count toward their truth in such a world? One would think not. But if P_1–P_4 are a priori, it is reasonable to consider them necessary, as I shall at least for the sake of argument (if some a priori propositions are contingent, these principles do not seem to be among them). Then, if one satisfies them, one must have justified beliefs. Apparently, however, justification is truth-conducive, and one's justified beliefs thus tend to be true. What, then, of the case where our justificatory experience is systematically misleading and at least the majority of our beliefs about the world false? Or, supposing that case is not possible, what of one in which, though we often have true beliefs about the world, we at least as often have false ones about it, and we have no way to tell the true from the false?

At least three historically important positions can be viewed as answering this problem. One is Cartesianism, which, on one interpretation, construes the connection between justification and truth as entailment and then secures the possibility of justified beliefs about the external world by proving God's existence from indubitable premises and appealing to the divine nature to provide a deductive path from beliefs justified by immediate experience to beliefs about the external world. The second view is phenomenalism, which, as often set out, is like Cartesianism in taking the connection between justification and truth as entailment, but instead secures that deductive path by constructing external objects out of experience. The third view is Kantian. It rejects the phenomenalist account of external objects, which it takes to be unknowable in themselves; but it may be interpreted as securing the connection between justification and truth for objects of experience by imposing a priori conditions on their nature which guarantee that (under appropriate conditions) they tend to be as they appear. I cannot accept these views; but the difficulty of the problem increases their appeal, and some of their claims are warranted. Perhaps Descartes was right in thinking that the only deductive path from justification to truth about the external world is theistic; phenomenalism may be correct in claiming that the only indefeasibly justified empirical beliefs are about mind-dependent objects; and Kant is apparently right in maintaining that experience provides no deductive justification for beliefs about external things in themselves. Can we understand the relation between justification and truth if we assume a realist rather than a phenomenalist or idealist conception of truth, the a priori and necessary status of correct epistemic principles, and the truth-conduciveness of justification? This problem is the concern of the next section.

VI. JUSTIFICATION AND THE EXTERNAL WORLD

Imagine that Jack is in a world rigged by a demon so that his perceptual experience is systematically misleading. Thus, if it seems to him that the foliage is green and he thereby believes it is, he is wrong; but he cannot acquire good reason to believe he is wrong because attempted confirmation will be manipulated. He will, e.g., tactually hallucinate foliage if he tries to touch it. Can his belief that the foliage is green still be prima facie justified? By P2, it can. What the demon does might preclude justification on balance, but it need not. To sharpen our problem, however, assume Jack's belief is justified on balance. Must we conclude that since, owing to the demon, its falsity is guaranteed, the sense in which it is jus-

tified is not the one we seek to capture? In answering, we should consider at least two defenses of the view that there is an ontological connection between justification and truth. One appeals to relevantly similar possible worlds, the other to the metaphysics of perceptual objects.

According to the first defense, Jack's manipulated but perceptually well grounded belief has truth-conducive properties because, in a suitable range of worlds similar to his, such perceptually grounded beliefs are true, since, for one thing, those worlds have no demon. To support the truth-conduciveness of the belief's grounds, one might note that it *would* be true if there were not a special reason for its falsity: demonic machinations. Demons cannot, then, utterly sever the connection between justification and truth, as if it were contingent. What they do is wrench Jack's justification from its usual ontological counterpart: veridicality. On this view, then, what P2 implies for all possible worlds is not that most of the relevant justified perceptual beliefs actually are true, but rather that they are all grounded in truth-conducive elements. Thus, there is enough of a connection between justification and truth to save a proponent of principles like P1–P4 from either endorsing an idealist conception of truth or granting that belief with no objective probability of truth can satisfy the principles.

This defense, however, is at best inconclusive. On what basis may we suppose that worlds relevantly similar to ours (or Jack's) have no demons (or other causes of systematic error)? Perhaps we do not *take* a world to be like ours if perceptually well grounded beliefs therein are usually false. But to call only worlds in which such beliefs are usually true relevantly similar seems to presuppose that most of our justified perceptual beliefs *are* true, and the defense may thus beg the question. Granted, given our concept of our world, it is plausible to say that our perceptually justified beliefs are true unless there is a special reason for their falsity; but if a demon *does* inhabit relevantly similar worlds, his machinations are no longer "special," or at least are too pervasive to permit our claiming that in relevantly similar worlds justified beliefs are usually true. Moreover, granting that certain of our justified empirical beliefs can be falsified only by a sufficiently *systematic* demon, this at most shows that if at least one sense yields true beliefs, the deceptiveness of the others might be discovered, not that all our justified beliefs rest on truth-conducive factors.

One might try to defend the ontological connection view about (empirical) justification and truth in a second way, one that might explain why principles like P_1–P_4 are natural for a realist. First, we shift direction: instead of looking from experience to external objects, we look from them toward experience. Next, we avoid not only separating the concept of truth from that of justification, but also separating that of reality from that of justification. We do not characterize reality independently of truth and then understand truth in terms of representing reality, or characterize truth independently of reality and then conceive reality as whatever truth represents. The two notions are inextricably connected; hence, if either is essentially related to justification, the other should be also. Perhaps, then, one way to think of reality, or at least of real things to which P_1-P_3 apply, is in terms of what *must* be true if such a priori principles of justification are truth-conducive.

Part of the suggested point is this: it is implicit in our concept of a real empirical object that it can impinge on our senses, that, under certain conditions, it tends to affect our senses, and that it is the sort of thing which best explains our spontaneous perceptual experiences. This is not idealism. It does not, e.g., imply that apart from perceivers there are no real objects. The point is rather that it is partly because of what reality is, and not only because of what justification is, that justified beliefs are truth-conducive. Call this view *epistemic realism*. Its central claim is that accessibility to the sorts of experiences that confer epistemic justification is implicit in the concepts of the kinds of things to which P_1–P_3 apply: tables and chairs, earth and water, colors and sounds, movements of trees, and flashes of light. Could a table be such that it (conceptually) could not be perceptually taken to be one? Could a flash of light be such that it could not be perceived or produce a memory impression? Certainly a table could be designed to cause us to hallucinate something else each time we approach it, and always to elude our touch. But tables are in principle perceptible, and by their very nature *tend* to be seen, touched, etc., when approached head-on by a normal observer in normal light. If these points are cor-

rect, then the sorts of things to which P_1–P_3 apply are intrinsically the kind about which the formation of justified beliefs is to be expected whenever normal perceivers are near them under appropriate conditions.

Here we must be careful, however. The view in question is that real objects are epistemically constituted: necessarily such that they *tend* to produce justified beliefs (and knowledge) about them. This does not entail that most of our perceptual beliefs *are* true. But the more modest view that justification is truth-conducive seems to be supported by epistemic realism. For, arguably the best explanation of, or at least a somewhat probable inference from, say, my perceptually taking there to be a table beneath my arms, is that there really is one there. If epistemic realism is correct, this is not simply an epistemic point about justifiable explanatory hypotheses: the concept of a table *is* in part the concept of something that has (and can explain) such effects as perceptual experiences of the sort underlying my belief; and apparently this applies to nothing else. Other real objects *can* produce the same experiences, but what else is conceptually fitted to this role? If an hallucinogenic machine plays the role, it presumably does so through something that inhibits or distorts its normal effects. It is intrinsically liable to be exposed as a fraud. These and other points implicit in epistemic realism suggest that the spontaneous perceptual belief that there is a table beneath my arms has a special status: if it is appropriately grounded in my experience, it is, to some degree, truth-conducive.

Unfortunately, the desired connection between justification and truth cannot be guaranteed by this line either. Granted, a table before one in normal light may be intrinsically fitted to produce a perceptual experience through which one truly believes that it *is* before one. But if we assume only that one has an experience *as of* a table, what entails a likelihood that there is one there? Perhaps what in *fact* best explains such experiences is that there is a table before one. But this is uncontroversial only so far as it rests on the epistemic point that such experience *justifies* one in believing this. We may not say, *a priori*, that there being a table there best explains such experiences, in a sense implying an objective likelihood that there is one, nor that nothing else (e.g., demonic machinations) is as well fitted to the role of causing such experiences. We cannot, in this way at least, move from the ontology of perceivable objects to the epistemology of perception. Reason may tell us that no competing explanations we are aware of, including skeptical explanations, are better; and this may help us answer skepticism; but that explanations presupposing the general veridicality of sense experience tend to be true is not knowable a priori.

If the considerations we have examined are the most plausible kind favoring an ontological connection between justification and truth, then apparently we cannot establish any such connection a priori. What epistemic realism does do, however, is help to unify P₁–P₄ (and similar principles). For it implies not only that objects are epistemically constituted, but that their essential properties, such as shape and texture, include those corresponding to the very modalities through which we know them: perception, for external objects; introspection, for mental phenomena (in our own case); and reason, for abstract objects. Moreover, we have seen no reason to deny that there is an a priori teleological relation between justification and truth. Reflection alone shows that the process of justifying a belief has, as its appropriate—even intrinsic—aim, showing or arguing for its truth (or at least probable truth). This is why it is conceptually improper to say such things as that one is trying to justify one's belief that *p* but is not at all concerned to show *p* to be true or probable. So far as we understand this, we take the kind of justification to be non-epistemic, e.g. moral justification for *retaining* (or causing oneself to hold) the belief. One could satisfy the *behavioral* conditions for giving a justification without being motivated to show that *p*, though this would not be (fully) *engaging* in our practice of justification: the practice whose character I have been illustrating, in which the concept of justification of belief is anchored. (If there are other concepts of justification, I believe they derive from this one.) That the intrinsic aim of the process is to show truth is not a psychological claim: it is a relevance requirement, and it largely determines what counts as an appropriate objection.

An equally important point is that the elements, such as perceptual states, that we cite in this process *can* be seen, a priori, to count toward that aim. This is not because, in engaging in the practice of justifi-

cation, we must take them to entail truth or probable truth, but because the kinds of principles in which the elements figure, principles like P₁–P₃, are constitutive of the practice. Engaging in the practice entails that one take such justifiers as perceptual experience normally to be in some way truth-conducive; it does not require taking them to be *necessarily* such. Their de facto reliability (and thereby truth-conduciveness) is necessarily a presupposition *of* the practice; their necessary reliability is not, nor is it presupposed *in* the practice. We cannot know that, in every possible world, conformity with the principles conduces to forming true beliefs; but we can know a priori in any possible world they generate (prima facie) justified beliefs. For the concept of justified belief is in part constituted by the very principles that license our appeal to these elements.

VII. RELIABILITY AND JUSTIFICATION

In the light of the framework developed above, we can clarify the relation between (empirical) justification and reliability. I begin with negative points. While reliability is apparently not built into P₁–P₃ as a priori principles, they can be seen a priori to provide grounds for holding beliefs. While they are not, as on an idealist view, partly constitutive of truth, they are partly constitutive of epistemically permissible attempts to show truth. Thus, justification does not necessarily imply truth or (objective) probability of truth; yet it is necessary that the process of justification "aim" at truth. Truth is a teleological aim of the practice to which that process belongs, though it need not be a motivational aim of those engaging in the practice. The sorts of generative factors figuring in P₁–P₄ are intrinsically suited to this process: given a proper appeal to them, one aims right, in the sense of 'properly', whether or not one hits the target. Perhaps a Cartesian demon could falsify our belief that there is a world out there; but he could not leave our experience unchanged and deprive us of any good reason to think there is.

For all the importance of the connection between justification and reliability, however, reliability does not constitute justification as understood here (or in normal contexts in which we justify beliefs).

Imagine a perfectly reliable process that generates true beliefs, but does so neither through the elements in P_1–P_4 nor by anything accessible to S, apart, say, from his making a scientific study of his beliefs to discover what explains their truth. Thus, Jan might simply find herself believing, of people she meets, that they were born on some particular day; and these beliefs might arise from an undiscovered process so connected with her and them as to guarantee her correctness. Surely such beliefs are not justified—at least before she learns of her success—though perhaps they can be knowledge.[17] Thus, their reliable production is not sufficient to justify them. (I bypass problems about how to specify precisely *what types* of belief-generating processes are reliable; it turns out that this is very difficult for reliabilism.[18])

It might be objected that one's *citing* the reliable production of Jan's beliefs *does* justify them. Suppose it does. That there *is* a justification for a belief does not entail that S justifiably *holds* it,[19] and indeed the justification here is of her "beliefs" only in the sense of their propositional objects (or perhaps belief-types). For the reliable production of her beliefs to justify them she must have access to it, which she can obtain only by using principles like P_1–P_3. The reason why her beliefs are not justified here is, then, not that she cannot *give* a justification for them. One may be unable (in practice, at least) to give a justification for one's quite justified belief that one is, say, imaging red. Yet this belief might be introspectively grounded and instantiate P_1; and while the elements in P_1–P_3 that generate empirical justification do surely tend to yield true beliefs, I am aware of no sound epistemic principles that exhibit mere reliable production of a belief, unconnected with either accessible factors or epistemic principles like P_1–P_4, as sufficient for its justification. (The examples of generation principles which reliabilists tend to use are similar to P_1–P_3; none has to my knowledge adopted principles grounding justification in any but very familiar processes.)

Recall the process-property integration thesis, which asserts a conceptual connection between the property of justification (justifiedness) and the process of justification, and implies that for every justified belief there is a possible process of justifying the belief by invoking certain properties of it. If this paper is correct, the integration, as applied to us, is not only between the justifiedness of our beliefs and *possible* justificatory processes, but between it and our *actual practice* of justification. It appears that the basic justificatory elements to which we have appealed are by their nature the sorts of things that S can cite, given a grasp of ordinary facts and ordinary epistemic principles, in offering a justification. This usability is crucial because the practice of justification is, if not more fundamental than the property, at least the place where that property is anchored.

This point does not presuppose, though it may support, a deontological view of justification. An underlying truth in that view is that unless justifiers were usable in giving justification, the process and the property of justification could not be integrated as they are: the property seems to be precisely the sort of thing the process, as normally practiced, can show a belief to have, and the process is judged largely by its success in showing the relevant belief to have an appropriate set of the properties (such as we have discussed) which confer justification. The process and the property of justification seem to be made for each other—or by each other. This integration can exist whether or not the property supervenes on fulfillment of duties.

VIII. JUSTIFICATION AND KNOWLEDGE

In the integration of process and property, justification differs from knowledge. There is no process of knowledge, as opposed to coming to know. And showing one knows is very different from showing one is justified: the former entails showing that one is in an *epistemically successful* state, and apparently does not entail that one's getting there meets, or is, even indirectly, guided by, any normative standards; the latter entails showing that one is in an *epistemically acceptable* state, which one cannot be in without meeting normative standards. One need not *do* anything in fulfillment of the appropriate standards, as on the paradigm deontological views, but one's cognitive state must meet them. Justification, we might say, is roughly a matter of a *right to believe*, and is anchored in a social practice; knowledge is roughly a matter of *being right* (in a suitable way), and is anchored to the world. If this contrast is sound, it helps to explain why generators of knowledge, unlike generators of justification, apparently need not be things one can de facto appeal to in showing that someone knows something.

The connection just stressed, between the property and the process of justification, is important both because, negatively, it helps us see that reliability does not constitute justification, and because, positively, it helps us see why reliability seems so prominent in generation principles like P1–P4. Since the property of justification is, teleologically speaking, truth-conducive, the sorts of factors we conceive as justifiers should also be factors we think of as tending to produce true beliefs. This is not because we have discovered the (contingent) reliability of these factors and subsumed them under the principle that reliable belief-generators confer justification; it is more nearly because, given the purposes of our justificatory practice, nothing could serve, in the basic way they do, as a justificatory element, unless we *conceived* it as (at least contingently) truth-conducive. If we are trying to show that a belief has a property which is truth-conducive, the base properties we cite will clearly be ones we take to conduce to truth. We may err about the reliability of a given factor; but as we come to believe that a type of factor does reliably indicate truth, we tend to count citing it as providing (at least indirect) justification. In this way, *justification appropriates reliability*, or, at least, sufficiently widely assumed reliability. Because of this appropriation, moreover, our concept of justification can evolve as certain of our beliefs about reliable cognitive generation become sufficiently deep.

An ethical analogy is useful here. Suppose that what constitutes the rightness of an act is its conforming to certain moral rules, such as principles that require keeping promises. If the teleological basis of our practice embodying these rules is largely to enhance human welfare, it is to be expected that rightness will supervene on (perhaps among other things) such properties of an act as its conformity with rules which, if followed, conduce to our welfare. Citing such properties will then provide reasons for the rightness of an act. Rightness might even be extensionally equivalent to some compli-

cated property of this sort. But it would not follow that rightness is analyzable in terms of such a property. On the other hand, because of the purposes of our moral practices, citing considerations of welfare to justify ascriptions of rightness will be so natural that denying their relevance may seem to deny conceptual connections. Similarly for justifiedness: it may be constituted by a belief's conformity with epistemic principles like P1–P4; and because our justificatory practice is based largely on a concern to grasp truths, it is to be expected that justification will supervene on properties of a belief (such as perceptual generation) in virtue of which we conceive of it as likely to be true. But it does not follow that justification is analyzable in terms of such properties as production by a truth-conducive (or reliable) process. Still, we will justify beliefs in terms of properties we believe are truth-conducive; and when a property is so conceived, denying its relevance to the justification of a belief that has it will seem conceptually deviant.

The contrasts I have drawn are easily misinterpreted. While I have argued that justification is not analyzable in terms of reliability, I grant that reliability may be the basis of a kind of *theory* of justification, as utilitarianism—the ethical analogue of reliabilism, I think—gives us a kind of theory of the right. It is not only that justifiedness could be extensionally equivalent to some sort of truth-conduciveness. There is a sense in which reliability can explain justification, or at least explain why we conceive as justificatory the factors we do so conceive. Recall first how the concept of justification is linked to a practice whose underlying concern is (partly) to lead us to believe truth and avoid error. The conceptual connection between justification and truth is tied, at least teleologically, to this concern; and perhaps evolutionary factors partly explain why we have the conception we do have of what confers justification, and why we are correct in taking the basic elements, such as sensory experience, as reliable. Could we have survived if the beliefs we take to be justified, and on which we regularly stake our lives, were not, with sufficient frequency, true? If all this is so, it is to be expected that we regard generators of belief as justificatory only if we also consider them reliable. On the other hand, just as happiness *can* be maximized by an act that is not right and a right act can fail to maximize happiness, a belief can be reliably produced—as in our divination case—without being justified, or be justified without being so produced. That beliefs we take to be so produced are characteristically beliefs we also consider justified does not show that reliable generation constitutes justification.

IX. SOME IMPLICATIONS OF THE ACCOUNT: Second-Order Beliefs and Epistemological Naturalism

Plainly, there *can* be directly justified beliefs if principles even close to P1–P4 are sound. But can we *show* that there are? Nothing said above precludes this. To be sure, in arguing that we have justified beliefs it may be impossible to satisfy skeptics. I do not claim that anything I say would impress skeptics. I simply want to suggest how far the position of this paper can take us in an anti-skeptical direction.

Suppose that one can know a priori that certain kinds of occurrent mental state beliefs are prima facie justified (P1). If so, and surely if one can, as may well be possible, also know this directly, then one may justifiably believe it. Now suppose one believes P1 *and* that one is now in the occurrent state of thinking about skepticism. Apparently one may thereby justifiably believe that one has a prima facie justified belief that one is thinking about skepticism. Thus, there is some reason to think that we may justifiably believe that we have justified beliefs.

Can this second-order belief be *shown* to be true? Would arguing from the premises that (a) such occurrent mental state beliefs are prima facie justified, and (b) one is now in the occurrent mental state of thinking about skepticism, to the conclusion that one justifiably believes that one is in that state, show that one justifiably believes this? Much depends on how showing is conceived. On a weak interpretation, if one is justified in believing one's (true) premises, and validly (and non-circularly) argues from them to a conclusion, one has shown it. But it might be claimed that unless one's premises are self-evident, one must be able to say something on their behalf. There may also be dialectical conditions for showing, e.g. that in asserting the premises one not "presuppose" anything denied by a plausible case against the conclusion. Skeptics tend to prefer stronger notions. This issue cannot be settled here, and I conclude that it may be only on a weak, though significant, notion of showing, that one can show that one has a justified belief. Those preferring a stronger notion might deny that showing, in *this* way, that there are justified second-order beliefs cuts against a skeptical denial that there are.

What about beliefs regarding the external world? If one may assume that a perceptual experience one is having is spontaneous, P2 could be used, in the way just sketched, to show that one justifiably believes, say, that the foliage is green. Perhaps, however, one may not assume, without inductive evidence, that a perceptual experience is spontaneous. I think there is a sense of 'spontaneous', strong enough to sustain second-order use of P2, for which one may believe this without inductive evidence; but until this matter is settled, principles like P2 do not allow our confidently concluding that we may justifiably believe that we have justified beliefs about the world.

We may conclude here, then, only that principles like P1–P3 provide *some* basis for our justifiably believing that we have justified beliefs about the world, and that they are, for at least one plausible notion of showing, a basis for rejecting skepticism concerning these beliefs. Suppose, on the other hand, that we do not conceive epistemic principles as a priori, but rather as, e.g., knowable only by virtue of knowing the actual reliability of belief generators. Could we justifiably believe that we have justified (empirical) beliefs? Let us assume so, since such second-order beliefs *could* be reliably produced. Could we show that we have justified empirical beliefs? In the weak sense just sketched, we could, provided we could justifiably and correctly believe the epistemic principle that reliably produced beliefs are justified, and that some belief of ours is so produced. Suppose we could fulfill this condition. Dialectically, at least, such a reliabilism still seems worse off than the normativism of this paper, in showing that we have justified beliefs. For one apparently could not argue for the crucial reliabilist epistemic principle—say, that spontaneous perceptual beliefs tend to be true—without presupposing it as one's basis for picking out justified beliefs as confirming instances of it. P2, by contrast, would be supported a priori and could be identified intuitively and apart from empirical knowledge of reliable processes. It may be, of course, that neither view enables us to show, in a strong sense, that any significant skeptical thesis is false; but the contrast is still important in understanding how, for non-skeptics, each kind of view accounts for second-order justification.

With respect to skepticism about knowledge the case is similar. Even if knowledge does not entail justification, showing that S has it requires using some epistemic principle and some proposition about S, say that a belief of S's is produced in a certain way. There is the added difficulty that the belief must be true, so that showing it constitutes knowledge entails showing, in *some* sense of 'show', that it is true. Let us pursue this.

Some philosophers, and certainly most skeptics, believe that premises show something only if they *entail* it. If this is true, prospects for showing that there is knowledge of the external world are dim. For it is doubtful that any plausible epistemic principles license *deduction* of propositions about the world from premises one is obviously justified in assuming, e.g. that one has an impression of green. But surely showing, as opposed to proving, does not require entailing grounds. Thus, if certain epistemic principles can be known a priori, perhaps they may be used to show that there is knowledge of the external world. That attempt may not succeed, but I do not see that it must fail. Let me elaborate briefly.

Nothing I have said presupposes that there is direct knowledge of epistemic principles. Such knowledge, or justified belief, can be a priori without being direct. But perhaps we are directly justified in believing (and even directly know) some epistemic principles, e.g. that if S is thinking about skepticism and on this basis noninferentially and attentively believes he is, then this belief is justified. Given P4, our believing this principle is at least prima facie justified, provided—what seems plausible—that the principle is a necessary truth which we attentively believe simply on the basis of understanding it. If one is justified, directly, in believing some epistemic principles, then the prospects for showing that one has justified (empirical) beliefs, or even (empirical) knowledge—say, that one is thinking about skepti-

cism—are improved. For one thing, if our justification for believing such principles is direct, their truth should be apparent, perhaps even close to self-evident, other than by the often controversial route through prior premises. Surely we are at least more likely to succeed in any strong kind of showing than on the assumption that epistemic principles are known empirically and indirectly.[20]

Much less needs to be said here about beliefs of necessary truths. Skeptics have been far less concerned with beliefs of prima facie necessary truths, and the case for skepticism regarding them is weaker. Surely there are necessary truths, such as very simple logical ones, which we are directly justified in believing. Moreover, let us assume that we can justifiably believe (directly) some of the relevant epistemic principles, e.g. P4. If, in addition, we are justified in believing some simple logical truths to *be* necessary and to be believed by us on the basis of understanding them, then we can justifiably hold (and perhaps know and even show the truth of) second-order beliefs to the effect that we are prima facie justified in our belief of some necessary truth, say that if no men are women, no women are men.

The suggested apriorist view of epistemic principles has been constructed to take account of not only the relation between justification and reliability, but also possible relations between our justificatory practice and evolutionary considerations. Is the view, then, naturalistic? Let us distinguish between a *substantively naturalistic* epistemology and a *conceptually naturalistic* one.[21] The former takes epistemological propositions, such as P1–P4, to be empirical and the latter simply uses no irreducibly normative concepts. Then, while the view is not substantively naturalistic, it could be conceptually naturalistic, depending on how normative concepts are to be understood. I have argued that justification is not analyzable in terms of reliability, but have not ruled out its being a natural property. This seems doubtful, however, and the position of this paper seems best regarded as a *teleological normativism*. It has affinities to intuitionism, but is not a deontologism and differs from, e.g., W. D. Ross's view at least in providing a way to unify the constitutive principles, in conceiving the relevant practice as having an underlying teleological aim, and, of course, in taking (epistemic) justification, unlike rightness, to apply to beliefs rather than actions. Moreover, just as reliabilism is not the only naturalistic epistemology, deontologism, while a kind of normativism, is not the only kind. For justification can be constituted by a priori, normative standards which justified beliefs must satisfy, even if such satisfaction is not a matter of one's fulfilling obligations.

CONCLUSION

My main subject is justification, and I want to reiterate that, as irrational divination suggests, knowledge should not be simply assumed to entail justification. Even if it does not, problems beset attempts to analyze it naturalistically.[22] Still, if it does not entail justification, perhaps the problems facing a naturalistic analysis of justification need not preclude such an analysis of knowledge. On some conceptions of naturalism, of course, a naturalistic view cannot countenance the synthetic a priori. But to insist on this is surely to assimilate naturalism as a metaphysical and conceptual view to empiricism. The historical association between naturalism and empiricism is strong, but they are independent.

Our direct concern has been what is often called epistemic justification. We may call it epistemic without assuming that knowledge entails justification, because, for one thing, whether this entailment holds or not, the relevant sort of justification counts towards a belief's being knowledge. However, the generic notion of justification is connected both with all the other propositional attitudes and with actions, and our results bear on that notion. One might think the concept occurring in those cases is radically different; but this view should be resisted if we can frame a good general account of justification. If we take off from the truth-conduciveness of the justifiers of belief, the likely bridge between epistemic and non-epistemic justification is a non-epistemic analogue of truth. Suppose we adopt a realist conception of value, of desirability, and of the justification of actions. We might then conceive non-epistemic justification, say of valuing good conversation, as supervening on the sorts of properties that count (at least teleologically) toward possession— objective instantiation—of these normative characteristics, e.g. toward the actual intrinsic goodness of

conversation.[23] There are, then, significant parallels to the epistemological case, both in the generation principles and in the justificatory practices.

Thus, if this paper is correct, its results can be incorporated into a wider theory of justification. Such a theory must not only lay out generation principles in more detail than has been possible here, but also formulate transmission principles. If, however, the account of direct justification explored here is a good starting point, we can readily extend it both to other cases of direct justification and to the transmission of justification. We should find generation principles whose modal and epistemic status is similar to those explored here; we should find analogues of truth, such as objective value; and we should find counterparts of reliability. What generates the direct justification of a valuation, e.g., should be the kind of property conducive to the relevant sort of thing's being objectively valuable.

I do not present the teleological normativist account of justification as clearly correct; but it may be a good foil for both reliabilism and deontologism, and one of its merits is its ready applicability to non-epistemic justification. The account also provides a basis for understanding both the nature of epistemic generation principles and their connection with truth. Epistemic justification is seen as inseparably tied to a justificatory practice whose proper aim is to foster true beliefs and avoid false ones. In part because the concept of justification is tied to this practice, it is subject to accessibility requirements. Inaccessible justifiers could hardly serve as the basis of our epistemic practice, which embodies readily applicable standards of criticism and judgment. These requirements, in turn, are reflected in the elements which the principles constitutive of the practice represent as conferring direct justification. Those elements apparently cannot be shown a priori to be truth-conducive, but we can show a priori that justification has a teleological connection with truth.

It is true that there may well be at least one sort of justification, the strong axiomatic kind, that does entail truth. This case illustrates the conceptual connection between the two notions, but it also offers a paradigm to which—unless we follow Descartes— we must not assimilate all justification. For justification in general does not entail truth; the ontological connection implicit in strong axiomatic justification belongs only to the a priori and perhaps a few kinds of empirical belief about the internal world. The justifiedness of beliefs in general may, however, be viewed as the actual—or more often—potential upshot of a process whose intrinsic *aim* is reaching truth: justifiedness need not arise from a process of justification, as only a small proportion of our justified beliefs do; but it must be attainable through that process. Precisely because of this aim, the elements we regard as justificatory, such as sensory and memorial experiences, are elements that we also normally take to be at least in fact reliable indicators of truth; and as our beliefs about reliability change, our conception of what justifies, and even of justification itself, can evolve. But our concept of justification does not appear analyzable in terms of reliability; it seems irreducibly normative and inextricably connected to a normative practice.[24]

NOTES

1. The analogy to deontology regarding moral justification is intended and will be pursued. For illuminating treatments of the contrast between normative and reliabilist conceptions of justification, see William P. Alston, e.g. "Concepts of Epistemic Justification," *The Monist* 68 (1985), and "Epistemic Circularity," *Philosophy and Phenomenological Research* 46 (1986).

2. Philosophers have said that the process of justification aims at truth, but this needs clarification (to which I try to contribute below). Among the recent works that treat the connection between justification and truth in a way relevant to this paper are John L. Pollock, *Knowledge and Justification* (Princeton, 1974), esp. chap. 1; Laurence BonJour, *The Structure of Empirical Knowledge* (Cambridge, Mass., 1985), esp. chap. 1; Ernest Sosa, "The Foundations of Foundationalism," *Noûs* 13 (1979); Roderick M. Chisholm, "A Version of Foundationalism," *Midwest Studies in Philosophy* 5 (1980); Keith Lehrer and Stewart Cohen, "Justification, Truth, and Coherence," *Synthese* 55 (1983); and the papers cited in note 1.

3. One might, e.g., speak of prima facie truth, where *S*'s belief that *p* is prima facie true provided it is either true or there is an appropriate single explanation both of why *p* seems true to *S* and why *p* is either false or in no way implied by what justifies *S*

e.g. a hallucination. This will not apply to all false belief; for it requires a restricted kind of explanation. But perhaps that kind cannot be fully specified, and perhaps there need not be such explanations for every justified false belief. I thus prefer the notion of truth-conduciveness.

4. A belief is indefeasibly justified if nothing could undermine its justification. Perhaps *S* could not unjustifiably believe a simple logical truth such as that if A = B, then B = A, even if *S* could believe it for bad reasons.

5. I have discussed such justification in Chapter 7.

6. Person-relative propositional justification is treated in Chapter 7. The notion is roughly equivalent to what Roderick Firth calls "propositional justification" in "Are Epistemic Concepts Reducible to Ethical Concepts?", in A. I. Goldman and J. Kim, eds., *Values and Morals* (Dordrecht, 1978). For criticism of Firth's paper and a case for construing epistemic principles differently than I do with respect to a causal element linking a belief to what justifies it, see Richard Foley, "Epistemic Luck and the Purely Epistemic," *American Philosophical Quarterly* 21 (1984).

7. Direct awareness is unmediated; e.g., *S* is not directly aware of how something appears to him if it is only *through* his being aware of something else that he is aware of it. But time and introspection may be needed to become directly aware of certain kinds of things.

8. My use of 'externalism' and 'internalism' is at least close to one of their most common uses. For relevant discussions see D. M. Armstrong, *Belief, Truth and Knowledge* (Cambridge, 1973), esp. chap. 11; Laurence BonJour, "Externalist Theories of Empirical Knowledge," *Midwest Studies in Philosophy* 5 (1980); and William P. Alston, "Internalism and Externalism in Epistemology," *Philosophical Topics* 14 (1986).

9. This is suggested by a statement of Keith Lehrer's coherentism, in *Knowledge* (Oxford, 1974): "There is nothing other than one's belief to which one can appeal in the justification of belief. There is no exit from the circle of one's beliefs" (p. 188). But apparently not all the crucial properties of one's beliefs are accessible. If not, the view is internalist not in the accessibility sense, but only in the weaker sense that it bases justification on mental factors.

10. I have discussed direct justification in Chapters 1 and 2, this volume. Given the results of those studies and the supporting works they cite, I assume there *are* directly justified beliefs. I also assume that

while there are different conceptions of justification, there is a univocal concept of it expressed in speaking, pretheoretically, of justified belief.

11. This idea is hard to make precise; clearly not just any incompatible proposition is such that one's believing it undermines one's justification for p. It might, e.g., take a sophisticated argument, which S cannot follow, to show the inconsistency. More important, the sources of undermining justification must also be explicable by our overall theory of justification.

12. There are counterparts of P1 for dispositional mental states, e.g. wanting; for person-relative propositional justification, e.g. for the proposition that S is thinking being justified *for him*; and for *de re* cases, such as one's justifiably believing, of one's desire, that it is intense. I cannot discuss such variants, even in perceptual cases.

13. C. I. Lewis, *An Analysis of Knowledge and Valuation* (LaSalle, 1946), chap. 11. He says, e.g., that "whatever is remembered, whether as explicit recollection or merely in the form of our sense of the past, is *prima facie* credible because so remembered."

14. This claim is defended (indirectly) in my paper "The Concept of Wanting," *Philosophical Studies* 21 (1973).

15. For assessments of the circularity problem described here, see Alston's "Epistemic Circularity" (cited in note 1); and James Van Cleve, "Foundationalism, Epistemic Principles, and the Cartesian Circle," *Philosophical Review* 88 (1979).

16. That even what seem to be analytic truths can be testable is argued in "The Concept of Wanting," cited in note 14; the principles under study here would not meet even the weak criterion of testability used there.

17. For a plausible account of knowledge that supports this see Frederick I. Dretske, *Knowledge and the Flow of Information* (Cambridge, Mass., 1981).

18. For plausible criticism of reliabilist accounts of justification, see John L. Pollock, "Reliability and Justified Belief," *Canadian Journal of Philosophy* 14 (1984); Richard Feldman, "Reliability and Justification," *The Monist* 68 (1985); Richard Foley, "What's Wrong with Reliabilism?," *The Monist* 68 (1985); and Paul K. Moser, *Empirical Justification* (Dordrecht, 1985), esp. chap. 4.

19. That there is no entailment here is argued in Chapter 7.

20. Considerations showing how difficult it would be, on the assumption that epistemic principles are empirical, to show that we have justified beliefs, are set out in Alston's "Epistemic Circularity," cited in note 1.

21. This distinction is introduced and developed in Chapter 3.

22. For an indication of some of these problems, see Chapter 6.

23. I have pursued this line of inquiry in some detail in Chapter 13.

24. This paper has benefited from comments by many people from discussions at Notre Dame, Syracuse, Texas Tech, Wayne State University, and an NEH Summer Seminar which I directed in 1987. For comments on a very early version I thank John Heil, Eric Russert Kraemer, George S. Pappas, and especially Albert Casullo. The incisive and extensive remarks of William P. Alston were of great help at several points. I have also benefited much from detailed critical comments, on two versions, by Jonathan Kvanvig, Paul Moser, and Bruce Russell. John Bender, Richard Foley, Andrew Naylor, Kevin Possin, and Thomas Vinci also made many helpful points, and the report of the Editor, Ernest Sosa, on the penultimate version led to many further improvements.

Knowledge and Intellectual Virtue

I

An intellectual virtue is a quality bound to help maximize one's surplus of truth over error; or so let us assume for now, though a more just conception may include as desiderata also generality, coherence, and explanatory power, unless the value of these is itself explained as derivative from the character of their contribution precisely to one's surplus of truth over error. This last is an issue I mention in order to lay it aside. Here we assume only a teleological conception of intellectual virtue, the relevant end being a proper relation to the truth, exact requirements of such propriety not here fully specified.

Whatever exactly the end may be, the virtue of a virtue derives not simply from leading us to it, perhaps accidentally, but from leading us to it reliably: e.g., "in a way *bound* to maximize one's surplus of truth over error." Rationalist intuition and deduction are thus prime candidates, since they would always lead us aright. But it is not so clearly virtuous to admit no other faculties, seeing the narrow limits beyond which intuition and deduction will never lead us. What other faculties might one admit?

II

There are faculties of two broad sorts: those that lead to beliefs from beliefs already formed, and those that lead to beliefs but not from beliefs. The first of these we call "transmission" faculties, the second "generation" faculties. Rationalist deduction is hence a transmission faculty and rationalist intuition a generation faculty. Supposing reason a single faculty with subfaculties of intuitive reason and inferential reason, reason itself is then both a transmission faculty and a generation faculty. The other most general faculties traditionally recognized are,

of course, perception, introspection, and memory. Shall we simply admit these, so as to break the narrow limits of reason in our search for truth?

Memory would seem a transmission faculty.[1] If I remember that the square of the hypotenuse is equal to the sum of the squares of the legs then my present belief to that effect derives in a certain way from my earlier belief to that same effect. If we think of memory thus it is then as little fallible as deductive reason. Given the truth of its input beliefs, there is no chance whatever for a false output, just as in deduction. Indeed memory then seems if anything more secure than deduction, since the object of the input belief is the very same as that of the output belief. We go from belief at time t in the Pythagorean Theorem to belief at a later time t′ in that very same proposition. There should hence be no rationalist compunction about such transmission memory as a further faculty beside intuitive and deductive reason.

Possession of an excellent transmissive memory is yet compatible with frequent error in one's ostensible memories. Someone might have an excellent ability to retain beliefs once acquired, and yet suffer from a terrible propensity to believe new things out of the blue which come as apparent memories, as beliefs from the past.

Turn next to intuitive reason, a faculty of grasping relatively simple necessary truths, an ability or power by which one cannot consider without accepting any necessary truth that is simple enough. Someone might then be gifted with such a faculty, while all the same suffering from a terrible propensity to believe things out of the blue as apparent truths of intuitive reason, as apparently truths that he grasps just because of their simple and obvious necessity, while in fact (a) other operative causes suffice on their own to bring about the beliefs in question, and (b) the intrinsic character of the propositions believed—their simple necessity—would *not* alone call forth his assent upon consideration.

If the possibility of a propensity to error in one's ostensible intuitions does not rule out intuitive reason, then the similar potential for error in one's ostensible memories cannot alone rule out transmissive memory, even for strict rationalism.

Whereas memory is like deductive reason in being a transmission faculty, perception is rather like intuitive reason in being a generation faculty. Both the external perception of the senses and the internal perception of introspection generate beliefs out of states that are not beliefs. [More strictly: "out of states that are not beliefs at the same or at higher levels in the hierarchy of beliefs B(P), B(B(P)), B(B(B(P))), etc." This in order to allow for the introspection of B(P) by B(B(P)).]

The perceptual faculty of sight, for example, generates beliefs about the colors and shapes of surfaces seen fully, within a certain range, and in adequate light. Such beliefs issue from visual impressions derived in turn from the seen objects. Here again we have the familiar possibility in a new form: now it is someone with excellent sight subject besides to frequent hallucinations. His ostensible visual perceptions are thus highly error-prone but that should not cancel the virtue of his faculty of sight so long as both erring intuition and erring memory retain their status. And similar reasoning applies to introspection as well.

If on the other hand perception as a faculty can ever conceivably lead us astray, then perhaps what makes a belief perceptual is its basis in experience as if P, leaving it open whether or not the belief derives from a perceptual process originating in a fact corresponding to the object of belief: namely, P. Such perception *can* of course lead us astray. It does so whenever a perceptual belief turns out to be in error. Such perception would then be *essentially* an experience-belief (input-output) device and it would seem a dubious virtue for any epistemic community so circumstanced that it nearly always would lead them astray.

That is a promising tack for external perception but dubious for other general faculties. Take for instance memory. Even if on occasion we accept P because of what seems phenomenologically a memory feeling or inclination to accept P, surely not every case of memory can be conceived thus. Here we run against the fact that nothing in the operation of memory need play experience's role as input for perception. One may simply find oneself believing that the square of the hypotenuse equals the sum of the squares of the legs with no separate memory feeling of any sort. Yet that might still be a perfectly acceptable case of remembering. And something similar holds good for reason, both intuitive and deductive.

III

What makes a faculty intellectually virtuous? *Its* performance or powers, surely? If so what is required in a faculty is that *it* not lead us astray in our quest for truth: that *it* outperform feasible competitors in its truth/error delivery differential. This even if one is often wrong, or nearly always wrong, in one's beliefs as to the outputs of that faculty. Someone may be gifted with comprehensive and accurate recall well above the average for his epistemic kind. What if in addition he is nearly always wrong when he both believes something and takes himself to believe it on the basis of memory—wrong both on the source of his belief, which in fact is not memory, and also wrong in the belief itself, which in fact is false? Would this invalidate the claim to knowledge of any deliverance of his excellent memory, even one about whose source he forms no further belief?

How to determine the truth/error delivery differential of a faculty will depend on whether it is generative or transmissive. For a generative faculty the relevant differential covers all deliverances of that faculty. But it can't be right to charge against a transmissive faculty errors that enter with its inputs, for which it bears no responsibility. The relevant differential for a transmissive faculty is accordingly the truth/error differential over outputs yielded by *true* inputs. Intuitive reason, deductive reason, and propositional memory all hence deliver a truth/error differential apparently undiminished by falsehood. But neither introspection nor perception may seem so favored.

Introspection may seem not so favored in general, if defined as acquisition or sustainment of belief about one's own mental state on the basis of one's own mental state. For one can look within and attribute n sides to a visual image that in fact has n + 1 sides. Dependent as it is on the favor of external conditions, outer perception is all the more prone to lead us astray. And it seems unavailing to plead that misleading perception is no true perception. Despite perfection *in the subject himself* outer perception can still go astray through unfavorable *external* conditions, a difference from inner perception whose consequences we need to explore.

Pure introspection, it may be argued, is not guessing or miscounting or any such error-prone process that may *build* on introspection but is not exhaustively introspection. Of course not just *any* belief about one's own mental state counts as pure introspection. Pure introspection requires a certain causal aetiology: it requires that one's belief about a mental state of one's own have its source in that very mental state. But not just in any way whatever may the mental state serve as source of one's belief: not when one miscounts the sides of one's image, for instance. Here it is not just *introspection* that plays a role, but also *counting* (a process with external application liable perhaps to lead us astray).

Pure introspection is a cognitive process that in normal conditions reflects the actual character of one's mental states and as such cannot normally cause error. Through greater attentiveness and circumspection one can normally improve the quality of one's introspection and thus enhance its accuracy. But except for rare special phenomena—excruciating pain, for example—it does seem plausible that abnormal conditions could always frustrate one's best attempts at accurate introspection. Such abnormality could derive from a variety of causes including hypnosis, brainwashing, and neural engineering.

Yet why call the source of a belief "introspection" when it derives wholly from the suggestion of a hypnotist? And if a belief is not after all a deliverance of introspection when a mere hypnotic suggestion, why call it pure introspection if it derives *even partly* from hypnosis and partly from a somewhat misdescribed internal phenomenon? If we follow this line, then pure introspection seems again no less infallible than rational intuition. In each case we have a faculty in the subject leading causally from given facts to the belief in them. The process can of course go wrong in various ways—haste, perhaps, or inattentiveness, or hypnosis—but when it goes wrong we are denied a *pure* exemplar of introspection or intuition, as the case may be.

If we do yield to such purism on reason both intuitive and deductive, on memory, and on introspection, with what right can we deny the same treatment to outer perception? When some abnormality dupes us through illusion or hallucination, we could absolve the faculty of perception by alleging that any such error cannot be charged to *pure* perception: "Pure perception requires normal conditions, internal *and* external, and hence precludes the presence of abnormalities responsible for such illusion or hallucination."

But it is hard to credit someone with good perception if he is frequently enough duped by illusion or hallucination: we need to reconsider purism in general.

IV

We are thus back to our question: If someone's ostensible intuitions, deductions, memories, introspections, and perceptions are mostly wrong, how can we credit him with intellectually virtuous faculties of reason, memory, and perception, when the virtue of such virtues would have to derive from their maximizing our differential of truth over error? There is, perhaps, a plausible response: "What makes something an *ostensible* x is that it *seems* an x, but a belief can *seem* a deliverance of reason, or of memory, or of perception, without really being such. Thus the fact that *ostensible* deliverances of X are nearly always wrong is quite compatible with *true* deliverances of X being nearly always right, and hence quite compatible with X's being an intellectually virtuous faculty." Yet it still seems absurd to credit someone with good perception if he is frequently duped by hallucination or illusion, even when such anomalies issue from a variety of sporadic causes. Most especially does that seem absurd if the responsible causes are intrinsic to the subject himself.

Someone prone to frequent illusions or hallucinations of mainly internal origin cannot be credited with good visual perception in an epistemically most relevant sense. This even if in normal external conditions he *does* reflect with unsurpassed accuracy the colors and shapes in his environment, by virtue of his excellent eyesight. Perhaps then such receptiveness is necessary for virtue but *not* sufficient.

Perhaps one needs to mirror such properties not just in the sense of showing their impact when they are appropriately placed and mediated in one's environment, but in the fuller sense that includes *also* a further requirement: that one show the characteristic trace of such impact *only* under the action of the correlated sensible properties, in normal conditions.

The key element of a specific perceptual faculty would then be some quality enabling the subject to reflect accurately the presence *or absence* of some correlated range of properties and relations. The presence of such properties would project characteristic images or traces in the subject, whose presence or absence could then guide his perceptual beliefs. Under this fuller conception of a virtuous perceptual faculty, then, to the extent one is prone to illusion or hallucination in certain conditions, to that extent is diminished whatever relevant faculty one might still retain: to that extent is it diminished in its ability to justify in such conditions.

Unfortunately, that analysis does not carry over easily to other traditional faculties. There is nothing that plays for them the role played by sensory images or "traces" for outer perception. Ostensible memories, it may be recalled, will not serve, since they amount not to pre-belief images (except for the very special cases in which personal memory does function via imagistic traces), but to the beliefs themselves believed retained in memory. And something similar holds good in each of the other cases: introspection, intuition, and deduction.

For faculties other than outer perception we are hence left with a question: is there nothing in them analogous to the hallucinations or illusions that make a subject's perception less virtuous than it might be? Must we say that such faculties are always error-free, since there is no way of understanding how their true operation could possibly lead to error? Our understanding of how belief can be *perceptual* though false depends on understanding perception as essentially an experience-belief mechanism fallible through the occasional failure of an experience to reflect what experience of that sort normally reflects. What can play the role of experience for any of the other faculties?

Is there any sort of belief-guiding pre-belief appearance in the operation of introspection, of memory, of intuition, or of deduction? In the absence of any such appearance, moreover, how can any belief be in error while yet an introspective, memory, intuitive or deductive belief?

Take memory. Shall we say that any belief about the past will count as a memory belief? Surely not: one can *infer* to new beliefs about the past, which do not then issue from memory. Shall we say that any belief is due to memory which is just there at a time with no inferential or experiential lineage? Surely not: a belief due to present subliminal suggestion is not a memory belief, nor is one implanted by advanced neural technology. How then can we conceive of a *memory* belief without involving its aetiology? There seems no way. But once we do involve such aetiology, how then do we understand the lineage required for legitimacy as memory while still allowing the possibility of error due to the misoperation of *memory* (and not to flaws in the original inputs)?

Suppose $B_t(P)$ can derive by memory from $B_{t'}(Q)$ where $t > t'$ and $P \neq Q$ (failing which it is hard to see how error could possibly arise from the operation of memory). This entails a hard question: How may P and Q be related for it to be possible that B(P) derive by memory from B(Q)? Can they differ to any width?

Everyone is of course familiar with the decay of information in memory. Thus one may ostensibly remember a friend's phone number as 245-6088 when really it is 245-9088. But here we must ask: Is the presence of the "6" due to the operation of *memory*? Or is it due to nothing more than guessing in the absence of true memory, or perhaps to an unfortunate disposition to switch the "6" and the "9"? "Well, it *feels* no different than any of the other six digits!" True, but can that be a good guide to when we do and when we do not have memory, if a hypnotist might have created that same feeling for all seven digits, *none* in that case being a deliverance of memory? The relevant feeling, so far as I can tell, might be just the feeling of confidence in the absence of reasons, and *that* hypnosis can provide. Therefore it cannot be such a feeling that *makes* a belief a memory belief, however well or ill it might serve as symptom or criterion. And we are thus left with our main questions: (a) What then *can* constitute the character of a belief of being a memory belief if not the causal aetiology of that belief? (b) If it *is* its causal aetiology that makes a belief of P a pure memory belief, what short of an earlier belief of P can serve as relevant cause? "Nothing" seems in each case a defensible answer. And until we are shown some flaw in this answer it will seem defensible to suppose memory infallible when pure.

Since the relevant considerations seem applicable not just to memory but equally to introspection, intuition, and deduction, each of these raises the same question of how it may be understood so as to allow error. The difficulties already encountered suggest a shift in the burden of proof: Why *not* conceive of such faculties as infallible?

V

There is one other subfaculty of reason beside intuitive reason and deductive reason, and that is of course ampliative reason, whether inductive or explanatory. This is just reason in its role as seeker of coherence and comprehensiveness, however, and granted the *possibility* that our most coherent and comprehensive account of a certain matter fails to accord with the brute facts, such ampliative reason must take a place next to external perception among fallible faculties. Just as with external perception, our most justified ampliative procedure may yet lead us into error. But there is nothing here to require revision of the view that intuition, deduction, introspection, and memory are all infallible.

Yet there is one remaining scruple. We made an exception by admitting the fallibility of perception for one main reason: because there can be perceptually justified yet false beliefs. And this fits with our notion that a belief's justification derives from the endowments and conduct that lie behind it. For the falsehood of a perceptually justified belief may go unreflected in the subject's perception because of external abnormalities that he could not possibly have grasped. In such circumstances his perceptual false belief shows no defect or misconduct in the subject, and may be perceptually justified. That is why we had to allow perception to be exceptional in being fallible. But is there not a similar reason to allow fallibility in each of the other faculties?

Take a student gifted with excellent memory who attributes *An Essay Concerning Human Understand-*

ing to David Hume. Given his excellent memory proven right on countless occasions, is he not justified in accepting what he ostensibly remembers? And don't we then have as much reason to admit the fallibility of memory as that of perception?

Take again a logician gifted with excellent deductive powers who goes through a relatively simple proof and somehow fails for once to detect an invalidating flaw. Might he not be justified still in believing the (false) conclusion on the basis of his inference from the (true) premises? And are we not thereby forced to admit the (transmissive) fallibility of deduction?

Or take, finally, someone of normal sophistication and acumen who believes in the existence of a class of all classes that are not self-members. Given his normal ability to understand simple necessary truths and to grasp their truth, might he not be justified through intuition in accepting that untruth about classes at least until shown an opposing demonstration? And are we not thereby forced to admit the fallibility of intuition?

To the contrary, in none of these cases is there really no plausible alternative to admitting the fallibility of the relevant faculty: memory, deduction, or intuition. For in each of them it is at least equally plausible to insist that the false belief derives *not* from the operation of true memory, or true deduction, or true intuition, but from various other interfering causes. Thus, to take just one example, at the point where the logician makes his mistake he is *not* following any relevant rule of deduction. How then can that part of his procedure be true deduction as opposed to, say, blundering through inattention?

But if in no such case does the belief really have its source in the corresponding faculty, whence can it derive its justification? In each case the justification can plausibly be attributed to coherence-seeking ampliative reason, as follows. In each case, the subject (a) is aware of his gift, of his relevant faculty F and its reliability, (b) finds himself with a belief B which he justifiably attributes to his faculty F, and (c) on the basis of (a) and (b) justifiably sustains his belief B. And that is all compatible with the falsity of B. Hence the way in which ostensible memory, deduction, and intuition can lead one into error is roundabout, and compatible after all with the infallibility of the corresponding faculties. In each case, the source of the false belief is not the corresponding faculty F (memory itself, or deduction, or intuition) but rather ampliative, coherence-seeking reason. It is such reason which when provided with the assumptions: (a) that the subject's faculty F is normally reliable (as proved time and time again already), and (b) that present belief B derives from F, a reasonable assumption in the circumstances; reaches on that twofold basis the conclusion (c) that belief B must be true, which sustains the subject in upholding B. In each case, however, B turns out to be false, and—we may now reasonably add—turns out *not* to be a deliverance of F after all.

Thus may we after all explain the apparent fallibility of introspection, intuition, deduction, and memory as illusory reflections of the true fallibility of ampliative, explanatory reason, which may take a belief B for a deliverance of a faculty F when B is neither true *nor* a deliverance of F. (And the objection that no subject S is so reflective as is required by our explanation would receive a twofold response: (a) emphasis on the implicit character of the assumptions attributed to S; and (b) appeal to the distinction between animal knowledge and reflective knowledge in Section IX below.)

VI

The question does remain whether intuitive reason (for example) would be of any use to epistemology if ostensible intuitions could always fail to be real and the true ones were indistinguishable from the false ones. But what is it here to distinguish a true one if not to know that it is a true one? And if that's all it is, then why can't the rationalist respond that we *can* tell a true intuition after all, since we can intuit-cum-introspect that an intuition of ours is such, *even if not all ostensible intuition-cum-introspection is real.*

But surely that response would not be plausible if ostensible intuitions almost never turned out to be real. Exactly why not, however, if in any case where ostensible intuition turned out to be real the output belief *would* come out of an infallible process (not simply a reliable process, note, but an infallibly reliable process)? Why should it make a difference how many other cases seem cases of such a process with-

out really being so or what ratio there is of real to false ostensible cases?

Besides, why should one's fallibility with regard to the source S of one's belief B and its justification impugn such justification if the justification derives from source S itself and not from one's knowledge of it. Requiring that one always know the source of one's justification, would seem to land us in a vicious regress.

Despite such doubts from the other side, however, it still seems absurd to allow that someone can know that p because his belief that p does derive from intuition even though his ostensible intuitions almost never turn out to be real.

VII

There is anyhow an alternative to explore before yielding to anything so implausible as human infallibility. According to our alternative, we first define a *faculty* of retentive memory, and only then define a retentive memory belief as a belief deriving causally from the exercise of that faculty. This provides an alternative answer to our question: "If it is its causal aetiology that makes a belief of P a pure memory belief, what short of an earlier belief of P can serve as relevant cause?" And this alternative answer leaves it open that retentive memory be fallible. Whether it is or is not fallible now depends on how we conceive of the faculty itself, on how we define it.

Consider first the notion of a faculty in general. The primary meaning attributed to "faculty" by my dictionary is: "ability, power." Faculties are therefore presumably in the general family of dispositions. Here are some simple examples of dispositional properties:

(a) Being an incline-roller: being a thing x such that were x placed at the top of an inclined plane in certain conditions (absence of obstacles, etc.), then x would roll down.

(b) Being a level-roller: being a thing x such that were x placed on a level plane surface and pushed in certain conditions, then x would roll.

(c) Being a round-snug-fitter: being a thing x such that were x placed with a certain orientation on a hole of a certain diameter, x would fit snugly.

Both a basketball and a bicycle tire would have dispositions or powers a, b, and c. And in each case of an ordinary object and an ordinary disposition something intrinsic to the object would ground its having the disposition in question: some intrinsic property or some set of intrinsic properties. Thus it's the roundness of a basketball that grounds its having each of the three dispositions or powers: a, b, and c. But it's rather the cylindrical intrinsic character of the tire that grounds its possession of each of a, b, and c. How now shall we think of faculties: as dispositions or as grounding intrinsic characters of dispositions? Faculties seem abilities to do certain sorts of things in certain sorts of circumstances rather than what *underlies* the possession of such abilities. Otherwise, since many different intrinsic characters or natures can underlie possession of the same ability (as happens with a ball and a tire *vis-à-vis* dispositions a, b, and c) we would have to speak of different faculties in the tire and the ball, which seems wrong. (It is of course somewhat forced to speak of faculties at all in something that is not an agent, but then similar examples could surely be contrived in which a human and an extraterrestrial would take the place of the basketball and the tire, respectively.)

If indeed cognitive faculties are viewed as abilities or powers, how more specifically is it done? Here is one possibility: To each faculty there corresponds a set of accomplishments of a distinctive sort. Indeed the faculty is *defined* as the ability to attain such accomplishments. Now of course an accomplishment attainable in given circumstances may be unattainable in other circumstances. Therefore, abilities correlate with accomplishments only relative to circumstances. There is for example our ability to tell (directly) the color and shape of a surface, so long as it is facing, "middle-sized," not too far, unscreened, and in enough light, and so long as one looks at it while sober, and so on. And similarly for other perceptual faculties. Compare also our ability to tell simple enough necessary truths, at least once having attained an age of reason and discernment; and our ability to retain simple enough beliefs in which we have sufficient interest. In each case our remarkably extensive species-wide accomplishments of a certain sort are explained by appeal to a corresponding ability, to a cognitive faculty; or at least we are thus provided the beginning of an explanation, an explanation sketch. But in none of these cases is there really any pretense to infallibility. All we're in a position to require is a good success ratio. Common sense is simply in no position to specify substantive circumstances in which the exercise of sight is bound to be infallible. (By substantive circumstances here is meant circumstances that are not vacuous or trivial in the way of "being such as to be right about the facing surface.") Of course that is not to say that there aren't underlying abilities which are in fact infallible: it's just to say that if there are such abilities common sense is at this point unable to formulate them. (Compare the fact that corresponding to common-sense generalizations about falling bodies and the like science did discover underlying principles with a good claim to being substantive and exceptionless.)

Any actuality involving an individual as essential constituent displays abilities or powers of that individual. The dance of a puppet displays not only abilities of the puppeteer but also powers of the puppet. The powers in the puppet that serve as partial source of its behavior are not however of the sort sufficient to make it an agent, much less a responsible agent. Similarly, someone hypnotized into believing something to his mind groundless would seem too much a puppet of external fate to count as knowing what he believes. His belief does of course display certain powers seated in him as well as certain abilities of the hypnotist. But the powers constituting susceptibility to hypnosis are hardly of the sort to give knowledge or epistemically justified belief. (At least that seems so if one is hypnotized unaware *in our world as it stands*. But it also seems plausible both (a) that we can embellish the example so that hypnosis does provide knowledge, at least in the way the reading of an encyclopedia may do so, and (b) that we can conceive of a world where even being hypnotized unawares does regularly enable people to know things by being hypnotized into believing them.)

What powers or abilities do then enable a subject to know or at least to acquire epistemic justification? They are presumably powers or abilities to distinguish the true from the false in a certain subject field, to attain truth and avoid error in that field.

One's power or ability must presumably make one such that, normally at least, in one's ordinary habitat, or at least in one's ordinary circumstances when making such judgments, one *would* believe what is true and *not* believe what is false, concerning matters in that field.

Just how fields are to be defined is determined by the lay of interesting, illuminating generalizations about human cognition, which psychology and cognitive science are supposed in time to uncover. In any case, fields must not be narrowed arbitrarily so as to secure artificially a sort of pseudoreliability. Human intellectual virtues are abilities to attain cognitive accomplishments in "natural" fields, which would stand out by their place in useful, illuminating generalizations about human cognition.

Faculty F is a *more refined subfaculty* of faculty F′ iff the field f(F) of F includes but is not included by the field f(F′) of F′. Thus the visual faculties of an expert bird-watcher would presumably include many more refined subfaculties of the faculties of color and shape perception that he shares with ordinary people. Moreover, the visual faculties of a bird-watcher with 20-20 vision would presumably include many more refined subfaculties of the faculties that he shares with those who fall well short of his visual acuity.

Faculty F is *more reliable* than faculty F′ iff the likelihood with which F would enable one to discriminate truth from falsehood in f(F) is higher than the likelihood with which F′ would enable one to make such discrimination in f(F′).

Thus may we explain why in certain conditions one is better justified in taking a surface (S) to be polygonal (P) than in taking it to be heptagonal (H): there may then be faculties F and F′ such that (a) F′ yields the belief that S is P; (b) F yields the belief that S is H; (c) F is a more refined subfaculty of F′; and (d) F′ is more reliable than F.

VIII

Infallible faculties are required by rationalism. But pure rationalism with its *perfectly* reliable certainty is a failed epistemology. A more realistic successor claims our attention today:

Reliabilism is the view that a belief is epistemically justified if and only if it is produced or sustained by a cognitive process that reliably yields truth and avoids error.

There are two main sorts of objection to such reliabilism and they pull in opposite directions. One questions the sufficiency of such reliability for justification. The other questions its necessity.

Consider first someone gifted with a sort of clairvoyance or special sense who considers the deliverances of his gift to be inexplicable superstition, and has excellent reason for his dim view. How plausible would it be to suppose him justified in his clairvoyant beliefs?[2]

From the opposite direction, consider the victim of a Cartesian Evil Demon. If his experience and reasoning are indistinguishable from those of the best justified among us, can we in fairness deny him the justification that we still claim for ourselves? Yet if we do grant him such justification, then *unreliable* processes do yield him much belief that is in fact justified (given our hypothesis).

A response to the first sort of objection modifies radical reliabilism by requiring for justification not only that the belief in question be caused by a reliable process, but also that there be no equally reliable process in the subject's repertoire whose use by him in combination with the process that he actually does use would not have yielded that same belief. Such alternative methods would of course include the recall and use through reasoning of relevant evidence previously unused though stored in memory, including evidence about the reliability of one's pertinent faculties.[3]

That revision will not deal with the problem from the other direction, however, the problem of the justified victim of the Evil Demon. And there is besides a further problem. For if a process is reliable but fallible, it can on occasion fail to operate properly. But that opens the possibility that a process can yield a belief B through *improper* operation where by lucky accident B turns out to be true anyhow. Take for example memory, and suppose it fallible. Suppose, in particular, that memory could take a belief that a friend's phone number is 245-9088 as input and yield as output later belief that it is 245-6088. Might not one's memory be such that on a given occasion it *would* in fact have that unfortunate result but for the effect of extremely rare and random inversion-preventing radiation? Would the (correct) output belief properly earn it status as epistemically justified? If so, since no reasoning via falsehood seems involved, would the belief also amount to knowledge? If these are good questions, parallel questions can obviously be raised about our various perceptual faculties.

What in brief is the problem? Apparently, though a belief is caused by a reliable but fallible cognitive process, that process may actually operate improperly and cause the true belief only through the intervention of some highly unusual factor whose presence is merely a lucky accident. Would the belief then fall short of sound epistemic justification, and not be a true instance of knowledge? What might be missing? Perhaps some closer connection between the belief and its truth? Perhaps these cannot be so independent as when they come together only by lucky accident, the way they do in our example of fallible memory.

Compare the Gettier case in which S acquires the belief that p in a highly reliable way and deduces from it that (p ∨ q), where this last belief turns out to be true but only because it's true that q, since in fact it is false that p. If S has no reason to think it true that q, and no reason to think that (p ∨ q) except his having inferred it deductively from his belief that p, then it seems clear his belief that (p ∨ q) turns out to be true only by luck (in some appropriate sense) and is not a case of knowledge.[4]

Finally, compare also the case where we are out driving and spot a barn by its barnlike look from our perspective on the highway; where unknown to us it is the one true barn left standing in that vicinity, in the midst of barn facades all presenting equally realistic barnlike looks, and many such facsimiles may be found for miles in either direction. If visual perception remains a reliable process, then by reliabilism our belief would seem justified; yet although it is true, it seems clearly no knowledge.[5]

These three examples pose a problem not so much for reliabilism as a theory of justification, as for the combination of such a theory of justification with a conception of knowledge as justified true belief.[6]

IX

Here is a short story. Superstitious S believes whatever he reads in the horoscope simply because one day in August it predicted no snow. Tricky T intends to offer S a lemon of a used car and plants the following in the horoscope under S's sign: "You will be offered a business proposition by T. The time is ripe for accepting business propositions." Does S know that T will offer him a deal? T planted the message and would have done so if he had been going to offer S a deal, and would not have done so if he had not been going to offer S a deal. So it is not *just* a lucky guess nor is it *just* a happy accident that S is right in thinking that a deal is forthcoming, given his daily use of the horoscope. In fact here S not only believes the truth that p; but also he would believe that p if it were true that p (in nearby possible worlds where it is true that p), and he would not believe that p if it were false that p (in nearby possible worlds where it is false that p). One thing seems clear: S does not know in such a case. What S lacks, I suggest, is *justification*. His reason for trusting the horoscope is not adequate—to put it kindly. What is such justification?

A being of epistemic kind K is prima facie justified in believing P if and only if his belief of P manifests what, relative to K beings, is an intellectual virtue, a faculty that enhances their differential of truth over error. But such prima facie justification may of course be overridden in special cases: e.g., through his learning that the conditions are not normal for the use of that faculty.[7]

It is of prudential importance to the subject himself to know how reliable and trustworthy his own judgments are in various categories. That is also moreover of prudential importance to his fellows and of social importance collectively to his epistemic kind. Testimony is of paramount importance to the *epistemic* weal and progress of any social, language-using species.

That is why we take an interest not only in the truth of beliefs but also in their justification. What interests us in justification is essentially the trustworthiness and reliability of the subject with regard to the field of his judgment, in situations normal for judgments in that field. That explains also why what does matter for justification is how the subject performs with regard to factors internal to him, and why it does not matter for justification if external factors are abnormal and unfavorable so that despite his impeccable performance S does not know. What we care about in justification are the epistemic endowments and conduct of the subject, his intellectual virtues.

From this standpoint we may distinguish between two general varieties of knowledge as follows:

One has *animal knowledge* about one's environment, one's past, and one's own experience if one's judgments and beliefs about these are direct responses to their impact—e.g., through perception or memory—with little or no benefit of reflection or understanding.

One has *reflective knowledge* if one's judgment or belief manifests not only such direct response to the fact known but also understanding of its place in a wider whole that includes one's belief and knowledge of it and how these come about.[8]

Since a direct response supplemented by such understanding would in general have a better chance of being right, reflective knowledge is better justified than corresponding animal knowledge.

Note that no human blessed with reason has merely animal knowledge of the sort attainable by beasts. For even when perceptual belief derives as directly as it ever does from sensory stimuli, it is still relevant that one has *not* perceived the signs of contrary testimony. A reason-endowed being automatically monitors his background information and his sensory input for contrary evidence and automatically opts for the most coherent hypothesis even when he responds most directly to sensory stimuli. For even when response to stimuli is most direct, *if* one were also to hear or see the signs of credible contrary testimony that would change one's response. The beliefs of a *rational* animal hence would seem never to issue from *unaided* introspection, memory, or perception. For reason is always at least a silent partner on the watch for other relevant data, a silent partner whose very *silence* is a contributing cause of the belief outcome.

Both animal and reflective knowledge require a true belief whose justification by its source in intellectual virtue is prima facie but not overridden.

Possible overriders of such justification would have to be wider intrinsic states of the subject diminishing significantly the probability that the belief in question be true. The probability that it be true since yielded by the intellectual virtue is then significantly greater than the probability that it be true given the wider intrinsic state.

Overriders come in two varieties: the opposing and the disabling. An overrider of prima facie justification for believing P is opposing iff it would provide prima facie justification for believing the opposite: not-P. Otherwise it is a disabling overrider.[9]

If one has visual experience as if there is a pink surface before one, the reception of good testimony that there is no pink surface in the room would provide an opposing overrider. But if the good testimony says only that there is a red light shining on the surface before one, that provides a disabling overrider. What is it in either of these cases that defeats one's prima facie justification when one accepts such testimony?

In our eyes anyone who still believes in a pink surface before him after accepting either testimony above would lack justification—this because we consider rational coherence the best overall guide. Even if the testimony is in each case false, given only adequate reason to accept it, one still loses one's justification to believe in the pink surface. Ironically that is so even for someone who does respond directly to the experience of pink with the corresponding belief and whose belief turns out true while the testimony is false. Here it would *seem* that the subject is at least as well off epistemically as his neighbor who also responds to pink experience while ignorant of the (misleading) testimony, and at least as well off as the nearby young child who could not have understood the testimony even had he heard it. But that is an illusion. Once having attained years of reason and discretion, and once in possession of the credible testimony, one errs not to give it due weight, which may betray a flawed epistemic character. This is important news to fellow members of one's epistemic kind, and even to one's own higher self, as is revealed in one's loss of "justification" for belief in the pink surface.

But not just *any* sort of incoherence would betray such a flaw. The author who sincerely takes responsibility in his preface for the "errors that surely remain" is not guilty of epistemic misconduct for continuing to accept individually the contents of his carefully wrought treatise, nor would he sin by accepting their conjunction could he somehow manage to conjoin them. The convinced skeptic with the reasoned conclusion that perceptual beliefs about one's environment are never justified does not lose all justification for his many such beliefs in the course of a normal day. Yet both the author and the skeptic are of course guilty of a sort of incoherence. But how can this be so? How can such incoherence differ relevantly from that of the victim of credible-hence-accepted but misleading testimony who arbitrarily retains what the testimony discredits?

According to our leading idea, the relevant difference must reside in a difference for one's prospects towards getting in the best relation to the truth. This is borne out by reflecting that anyone who lets skeptical arguments mislead him to the cynical extent of a massive withdrawal of doxastic commitment would save his coherence at enormous cost in truth. And the same goes for the honest and sincere author at work on his preface.

X

An intellectual virtue may be viewed as a subject-grounded ability to tell truth from error infallibly or at least reliably in a correlated field. To be epistemically justified in believing is to believe out of intellectual virtue. To know you need at least epistemic justification. But there are two prominently different sorts of knowledge: the animal and the reflective. Animal knowledge is yielded by reaction to the relevant field unaided by reflection on the place of one's belief and its object within one's wider view. Even for such knowledge it is not just the reliability of the cognitive process yielding the relevant belief that provides its justification. Nor is it enough to require further the absence of any equally reliable process in the subject's repertoire whose use by him combined with the process actually used would not have yielded that belief. For even that will not preclude a subject with excellent eyesight subject however to internal hallucinogenic interference 99% of the time, one deprived of any way to distinguish his cases of true vision from the hallucinations. Such a subject can hardly be granted even animal knowledge in his rare cases of true vision, surely, nor even warranted or jus-

tified belief. Though he has a reliable cognitive process of true vision, he yet does not have a relevant faculty in an epistemically most relevant sense: he does not have a faculty F correlated with a "natural" field f(F) such that F is constituted by the ability to discern truth from error with high reliability over f(F). Despite his occasionally operative true vision, our victim of frequent, stable, and long-standing hallucinogenic irregularities does not have the sort of ability constitutive of an epistemically relevant faculty.

Since justified belief seems anyhow insufficient for knowledge (see the objections early in Section VIII above), it is tempting to bypass justification and try some wholly fresh approach.[10] Yet justification proves stubbornly required for knowledge. The next chapter argues for a split of epistemic justification into two concepts: justification proper and epistemic aptness. Each of these is needed for a full understanding of our knowledge.[11]

SUMMARY

I. A teleological conception of intellectual virtue.

II. Transmission faculties and generation faculties. Examples of each. What makes a belief of a certain sort a belief of that sort: e.g., what makes a memory belief a memory belief, and what makes a perceptual belief a perceptual belief?

III. What makes a faculty intellectually virtuous? Purity of faculties: pure reason, pure memory, pure introspection, and pure perception.

IV. Ostensible intuition (etc.) versus real intuition (etc.). The epistemological relevance of this distinction. The role of sensory experience in determining ostensible perception. The absence of any correlate of such experience for intuition, deduction, memory, or introspection.

V. Ampliative reason: as clearly fallible as external perception. How the fallibility of ampliative reason may help explain the apparent fallibility of introspection, intuition, deduction, and memory.

VI. Why should the high likelihood of error in *ostensible* deliverances of source S impugn the justification of beliefs that flow from S if S itself is highly error-free or even infallible? Yet somehow it seems very implausible to count as justified a belief B with source S and held by person X even though for X ostensible deliverances of S are nearly always wrong.

VII. What yielded the (implausible) infallibility of retentive memory (in Section II) was our view of a retentive-memory belief of proposition P on the part of person X as a belief of P caused by an earlier belief of P on the part of X himself (roughly). The faculty of retentive memory was then conceived as the ability to retain beliefs thus. And similarly for intuition, deduction, and introspection. An alternative is examined here: to reverse the order of definition. Instead of defining the faculty of memory as what leads to memory beliefs, we first define the faculty of memory (in some other way) and then define memory beliefs as beliefs that flow from the faculty of memory. According to our alternative proposal, epistemically relevant faculties are abilities to distinguish reliably the true from the false in certain "natural" subject fields.

VIII. Infallible faculties comport with the perfect reliability required by rationalism. Contemporary reliabilism jibes better with our highly reliable but fallible faculties. Four examples are considered which pose as many problems for the combination of reliabilism as a theory of justification with a conception of knowledge as justified true belief.

IX. The chapter concludes with some general reflections on the nature of justification and two of its main varieties, which leads, in the following chapter, to a proposed split in our concept of epistemic justification.

NOTES

1. Actually this is true only of one sort of memory, "retention." For a notion of generative memory see Carl Ginet's *Knowledge, Perception, and Memory* (Dordrecht: D. Reidel, 1975), esp. ch. 7, sec. 2, pp. 148–53.

2. Cf. Laurence Bonjour, "Externalist Theories of Empirical Knowledge," *Midwest Studies in Philosophy* 5 (1980): 53–75. Cf. also William Alston,

"What's Wrong with Immediate Knowledge?" *Synthese* 55 (1983): 73–97.

3. Cf. Alvin Goldman, "What Is Justified Belief?" in George S. Pappas, ed., *Justification and Knowledge* (Dordrecht: D. Reidel, 1979).

4. Cf. Edmund Gettier, "Is Justified True Belief Knowledge?" *Analysis* 23 (1963): 121–3.

5. Cf. Alvin Goldman, "Discrimination and Perceptual Knowledge," *Journal of Philosophy* 73 (1976): 771–91.

6. For alternative reactions to our recent difficulties, see Robert Nozick, *Philosophical Explanations* (Cambridge, Mass.: Harvard University Press, 1981), ch. 3, esp. part I; and Peter Klein, "Real Knowledge," *Synthese* 55 (1983): 143–65.

7. That epistemic justification is prima facie and defeasible is argued already in Roderick M. Chisholm's *Theory of Knowledge* (Englewood Cliffs, N.J.: Prentice Hall, 1966), p. 46.

8. That the "wider whole" essentially involved in good reasoning is wider than might appear is argued by Gilbert Harman in "Reasoning and Evidence One Does Not Possess," *Midwest Studies in Philosophy* 5 (1980): 163–82.

9. Cf. John Pollock, *Knowledge and Justification* (Princeton, N.J.: Princeton University Press, 1974).

10. For example, Robert Nozick's in his *Philosophical Explanations, op. cit.* Compare Fred Dretske's *Knowledge and the Flow of Information* (Cambridge, Mass.: MIT Press/Bradford Books, 1981). For Dretske's *précis* of his book, discussion by several commentators, and replies by the author, see *The Behavioral and Brain Sciences* 6 (1983): 55–90.

11. An earlier version of this essay was part of the Special Session on Knowledge and Justification at the Twelfth World Congress of Philosophy (Montreal, August 1983).

FOR FURTHER READING

Almeder, Robert. *Blind Realism.* Lanham, Md.: Rowman & Littlefield, 1992.

Alston, William. *Epistemic Justification.* Ithica, N.Y.: Cornell University Press, 1989.

Audi, Robert. *Belief, Justification, and Knowledge.* Belmont, Calif.: Wadsworth, 1988.

Audi, Robert. *The Structure of Justification.* New York: Cambridge University Press, 1993.

BonJour, Laurence. *The Structure of Empirical Knowledge.* Cambridge: Harvard University Press, 1985.

Dancy, Jonathan, and Ernest Sosa, eds. *A Companion to Epistemology.* Oxford: Basil Blackwell, 1992.

Feldman, Richard. "Epistemic Obligation." In *Philosophical Perspectives, 2, Epistemology,* ed. James Tomberlin, 240-56.

Feldman, Richard. "Reliability and Justification." *Monist,* 68 (1985), 159–74.

Foley, Richard. "What's Wrong with Reliabilism?" *Monist* 68 (1985), 188–202.

Foley, Richard. *Working without a Net.* Oxford: Oxford University Press, 1993.

French, Peter et. al., eds. *Midwest Studies in Philosophy,* Vol. V. Minneapolis: University of Minnesota, 1980.

Fumerton, Richard. *Metaepistemology and Skepticism.* Lanham, Md.: Rowman & Littlefield, 1995.

Goldman, Alvin "What Is Justified Belief?" In *Naturalizing Epistemology,* ed. Hilary Kornblith, 91–113.

Goldman, Alvin. "Epistemic Folkways and Scientific Epistemology." In *Empirical Knowledge,* ed. Paul Moser, 423–46.

Goldman, Alvin. "Reliabilism." In *A Companion to Epistemology,* ed. Jonathan Dancy, pp. 433–36.

Goldman, Alvin. "Strong and Weak Justification." In *Philosophical Perspectives, 2,* ed. James Tomberlin (Ridgeview Press, 1988), 62.

Goldman, Alvin. *Epistemology and Cognition.* Cambridge: Harvard University Press, 1986.

Kim, Jaegwon. "Concepts of Supervenience." *Philosophical and Phenomenological Research,* 65 (1984), 257–70.

Kitcher, Philip. "The Naturalists Return." *Philosophical Review,* 101 (1992), 53–114.

Kornblith, Hilary, ed. *Naturalizing Epistemology.* Cambridge: MIT Press, 1987.

Lehrer, Keith. *Theory of Knowledge.* Boulder, Colo.: Westview Press, 1990.

Luper-Foy, Steven, ed. *The Possibility of Knowledge.* Totowa, N.J.: Rowman & Littlefield, 1987.

Luper-Foy, Steven. "The Reliabilist Theory of Rational Belief." *Monist* 68 (1985), 203–25.

Meyers, Robert G. *The Likelihood of Knowledge.* Dordrecht, Netherlands: Kluwer Academic, 1988.

Moser, Paul. *Empirical Knowledge,* 2d ed. Lanham, Md.: Rowman & Littlefield, 1996.

Pollock, John. *Contemporary Theories of Knowledge.* Totowa, N.J.: Rowman & Littlefield, 1986.

Schmitt, Fredrick. *Knowledge and Belief.* London: Routledge, 1990.

Sosa, Ernest. *Knowledge in Perspective.* Cambridge: Cambridge University Press, 1991.

Swain, Marshall. *Reasons and Knowledge.* Ithaca, N.Y.: Cornell University Press, 1981.

Tomberlin, James, ed. *Philosophical Perspectives, 2, Epistemology,* Atascadero, Calif.: Ridgeview Press, 1988.

STUDY QUESTIONS

1. Why does Goldman think that an analysis of justified belief should not rely on any epistemic terms? Explain how Goldman uses this restriction to discount other accounts of justified belief.

2. Goldman claims that previous attempts to explain justified belief failed to take into account what causally initiates or causally sustains a belief. Why does he think this is important? What kinds of causes are important for justified belief, according to Goldman? How does Goldman's historical theory differ from current time-slice theories?

3. Goldman suggests that his initial version of reliabilism, the hisorical process view, must be modified in light of an objection. What is this objection, and how does Goldman propose to modify his theory?

4. BonJour claims that there are two central features of epistemic justification—what are they? According to BonJour, what are the features of Armstrong's externalism?

5. What does BonJour think is the intuitive difficulty with externalism? BonJour considers three examples that lead him to modify externalism; what is this modification? Explain how BonJour uses the case of Norman, the clairvoyant, to illustrate the fundamental difficulty for externalism. Do you agree with BonJour? Why or why not?

6. In "Strong and Weak Justification," Goldman distinguishes two concepts of epistemic justification? What are they, and how do they differ? Which conception does Goldman identify with strong justification? What is the difference between processes and methods?

7. Explain, in your own words, the notions of strong and weak justification. How does Goldman use these notions to handle the case of a person in a Cartesian demon world? Does Goldman think that this solution is a concession to internalism? Explain.

8. Mental properties that involve reference to things outside the mind are said to be *relational properties* of mind; such properties involve a relation between the mind and something outside

of it. Explain why Fumerton thinks that we cannot use the relational/nonrelational distinction to explain the internalist/externalist distinction.

9. Explain the difference between strong and weak accessibility requirements for justification. Why does Fumerton think that accessibility is not the appropriate way to explain the internalist/externalist distinction? What is Fumerton's view of how we should understand this distinction? Given this view, why does Fumerton think that externalism is mistaken?

10. Audi's essay concerns the connection between justification and truth. He suggests that the ontological view of this connection emphasizes the property of justification, while the teleogical view emphasizes the process of justification. Explain what he has in mind here. Explain what Audi meant by the *process-property integration thesis*.

11. What is a generation principle? Does Audi think that his perceptual principle is compatible with an accessibility requirement? Explain. Why does Audi think such principles are knowable a priori? Why does Audi think that epistemic realism is relevant to the teleological connection between justification and truth?

12. Why does Audi reject reliabilism as an analysis of justification? Can you explain why Audi thinks the connection between the process and the property of justification helps explain why reliability is relevant to justification?

13. What is an intellectual virtue, according to Sosa? When is a faculty intellectually virtuous? Does Sosa think that a faculty must be infallible in order to be intellectually virtuous?

14. What is Sosa's account of (prima facie) justification? Explain Sosa's distinction between animal and reflective knowledge. Does Sosa think we have animal knowledge? Explain. How does the distinction between animal and reflective knowledge enable Sosa to deal with the objections to reliabilism?

Naturalized Epistemology

The relation between epistemology and the sciences has become a matter of controversy during recent decades. One aim of traditional epistemology is to provide a theoretical understanding of epistemic concepts, such as knowledge and justification. The task of the traditional epistemologist is to provide principled answers to questions such as "How are knowledge and justification possible?" and "What standards must a belief meet in order to count as justified or an instance of knowledge?" According to the traditional epistemologist, it would be a mistake to think that these questions might be answered by first looking to the sciences. If we want to know whether perceptual beliefs are justified or provide us with knowledge of the world around us, it would be a mistake to begin by consulting, say, a textbook on the neurophysiology of vision. Consulting a science book presumes *that* we know. The epistemologist is asking *whether* we know, and if we do, of what that knowledge consists. Assertions of scientific knowledge cannot be used in the epistemologist's investigations if the epistemologist wants to understand how such knowledge is possible in the first place. Not only does the appeal to science seem to jump the epistemological gun, science seems to provide the wrong sort of answers. Science describes and explains; it is not in the business of answering normative questions. Science claims to tell us what is the case. It does not tell us what we ought to believe. It does not, indeed cannot according to some, tell us whether we ought to believe the myriad scientific claims.

These brief remarks suggest that epistemology differs from science in at least two ways. First, the methods of epistemology differ from the methods of the sciences. Scientific method takes for granted precisely what the epistemologist wants to explain. When the scientist claims that there are certain *known* facts that confirm or undermine a given hypothesis, the epistemologist balks. Such known facts come at the conclusion of the epistemologist's in-

quiry, not at the beginning. This seems to suggest that the epistemologist's method is independent of and *prior to* the empirical methods of the scientist. In this sense, the epistemologist relies on *a priori* methods.

If the methods of scientist and epistemologist seem to differ, so also does the subject matter. Induction is not only the layperson's daily guide, it is the scientist's ever present companion. The epistemologist is less interested in the new hypotheses that induction yields, and more interested in our entitlement to use induction. Ought we to believe the results of our inductive inferences? Until we answer this question, the traditional epistemologist claims, we cannot appeal to the results of science. The subject matter of the sciences is the descriptive and explanatory, while the subject matter of epistemology is the normative.

As portrayed here, there is a gulf between epistemological questions and scientific questions. In order to build a bridge between the two, construction begins on the epistemological side; the task of the epistemologist shows how we get from the epistemological issues to the scientific. We are *entitled* to start on the scientific questions only after we have answered the epistemological questions. Epistemology thus retains its conceptual and methodological priority.

You may be thinking that there is something not quite right about this picture of the relationship between science and epistemology. Science, after all, appears to have been on a roll since the middle of the seventeenth century—saving lives, turning the mysterious into the obvious, making possible better bridges, buildings, telescopes, microscopes, and for the forgetful among us, wristwatches that do not need to be wound. Underlying these technological advances are the theoretical advances of science that have moved us from vapors and spirits to protons and electrons, quarks and quasars. Surely, you might be thinking, the success of science says something about the scientist's right to use the scientific method.

Philosophers, too, have recently questioned the accuracy of this picture of the relationship between epistemology and science. In its most dramatic version, naturalized epistemology is the view that neither the methods nor the subject matter of epistemology are distinct from the sciences. Epistemology is continuous with and an extension of the empirical sciences.

The motivation for naturalized epistemology begins, in part, with an observation not too distant from the commonsense worry noted above. Since Descartes, epistemology has endeavored to find the foundations for empirical knowledge. Epistemologists have yet to arrive at a consensus about the nature of such foundations. Consequently, it might be thought that the project of finding foundations is misconceived.

A more substantive motivation might be found in the following. As traditionally conceived, epistemology aims to identify the appropriate reasons for our beliefs. We are entitled to various beliefs only if we have the right sort of reasons. The point of such reasons is to show the *truth* of our beliefs. We want to know why our beliefs are true or likely to be true. But if it is truth we desire, then why not look to our best guide to the truth—science? Science is the closest thing we have to an ultimate arbiter of the truth. If we wonder whether the popcorn we buy at the movies is healthy to eat, we look to science. If we wonder what causes earthquakes, illness, or black holes in space, we turn to science. Science, in short, provides us with the best reasons for believing. So why, asks the naturalized epistemologist, would we not turn to science to answer our more epistemological questions? The best way to show that knowledge is possible is, after all, to show that it is actual. And science, for example cognitive psychology and cognitive neurobiology, can show us how we come to have the true beliefs that we do. Further, the naturalized epistemologist claims, science is the best judge of the truth precisely because of its method.

This is but an intuitive motivation of naturalized epistemology, but it is enough to frame the issues of this chapter. Naturalized epistemologists claim that the traditional epistemological project is misconceived. They claim that epistemological questions are in fact scientific questions, and they should be approached in the same way as other scientific questions. Thus, neither the subject matter nor the methods of epistemology are independent of the sciences. Skeptical questions arise within a general scientific framework—the assumption of physical objects and their properties—and we are then free to use science to respond to the skeptical challenge.

Traditional epistemologists object to the naturalist's reconfiguring of epistemology. A prominent feature of their objections is the essentially normative character of epistemology. The traditionalist emphasizes the importance of the question, What ought we to believe? while maintaining that the naturalized epistemologist is restricted to description and explanation. The traditionalist claims that the naturalized epistemologist is committed to giving a naturalistic explanation of normative properties and characteristics. Unless there is such a naturalistic explanation, naturalized epistemology will miss the point of the epistemological picture. Of course, the traditionalist doubts that there is any legitimate naturalistic explanation forthcoming.

A third position between the naturalized and traditional epistemologist is discernible. This position is naturalistic, but it attempts to retain the more central aspects of the traditional picture. This type of view holds that all properties are natural properties. There is always some naturalistic basis of any property, even the evaluative properties that interest epistemologists. The evaluative properties come about because of an arrangement or configuration of other natural properties. If Sara justifiably believes that there is a red pen on the desk, then there are certain natural properties, properties discernible by one or more of the sciences, that account for the justified character of her belief. In attempting to retain the evaluative character of epistemology, this intermediate position also allows that the *a priori* methods of the traditionalist have a role to play in our epistemological inquiries. For example, we might employ *a priori* methods in order to identify our epistemic goals. There is no doubt that this position is naturalistic. To the extent that it is, it will of course be subject to the traditionalist's criticisms. But this intermediate position does attempt to avoid the putatively obvious failings of a more radical naturalized epistemology.

The first three essays represent W. V. Quine's view of naturalized epistemology. In the first, "Epistemology Naturalized," Quine explains why he thinks that the traditional project of epistemology ought to be abandoned. Quine argues that traditional epistemology, conceived as a kind of classic foundationalism, is unable to identify any "first philosophy" that might give us the principles for belief evaluation. Instead we should recognize that epistemology is continuous with the natural sciences, and we should look to science for our understanding of the relation between theory and evidence. Indeed, in the second essay, "The Nature of Natural Knowledge," Quine argues that skeptical worries are scientific worries; they arise within the framework of scientific theorizing, and we are thus permitted to use the results of science to answer the skeptic. In the final, brief selection, "Norms and Aims," Quine identifies what he considers to be the normative character of naturalized epistemology.

In "What is Naturalized Epistemology," Jaegwon Kim argues that the principal defect of naturalized epistemology is that it forsakes the normative character of epistemology, a feature that is inherited from the intrinsic normative character of the concept of belief. In "On Naturalizing Epistemology," Robert Almeder surveys the various objections to naturalized epistemology and assesses the relative strength of these objections. Almeder concludes that the variety of arguments offered in support of Quinean naturalized epistemology do not support the view that traditional epistemology should be replaced.

The final essay, "Feminist Epistemology: An Interpretation and a Defense," by Elizabeth Anderson, is an attempt to locate feminist epistemology as a kind of naturalized epistemology. Anderson argues that a naturalized feminist epistemology is a branch of social epistemology, which recognizes rational inquiry as an essentially social endeavor. She also identifies four categories by which we might recognize the normative implications of feminist epistemology.

W. V. O. QUINE

Epistemology Naturalized

Epistemology is concerned with the foundations of science. Conceived thus broadly, epistemology includes the study of the foundations of mathematics as one of its departments. Specialists at the turn of the century thought that their efforts in this particular department were achieving notable success: mathematics seemed to reduce altogether to logic. In a more recent perspective this reduction is seen to be better describable as a reduction to logic and set theory. This correction is a disappointment epistemologically, since the firmness and obviousness that we associate with logic cannot be claimed for set theory. But still the success achieved in the foundations of mathematics remains exemplary by comparative standards, and we can illuminate the rest of epistemology somewhat by drawing parallels to this department.

Studies in the foundations of mathematics divide symmetrically into two sorts, conceptual and doctrinal. The conceptual studies are concerned with meaning, the doctrinal with truth. The conceptual studies are concerned with clarifying concepts by defining them, some in terms of others. The doctrinal studies are concerned with establishing laws by proving them, some on the basis of others. Ideally the obscurer concepts would be defined in terms of the clearer ones so as to maximize clarity, and the less obvious laws would be proved from the more obvious ones so as to maximize certainty. Ideally the definitions would generate all the concepts from clear and distinct ideas, and the proofs would generate all the theorems from self-evident truths.

The two ideals are linked. For, if you define all the concepts by use of some favored subset of them, you thereby show how to translate all theorems into these favored terms. The clearer these terms are, the likelier it is that the truths couched in them will be obviously true, or derivable from obvious truths. If in particular the concepts of mathematics were all reducible to the clear terms of logic, then all the truths of mathematics would go over into truths of logic; and surely the truths of logic are all obvious or at least potentially obvious. i.e.. derivable from obvious truths by individually obvious steps.

This particular outcome is in fact denied us, however, since mathematics reduces only to set theory and not to logic proper. Such reduction still enhances clarity, but only because of the interrelations that emerge and not because the end terms of the analysis are clearer than others. As for the end truths, the axioms of set theory, these have less obviousness and certainty to recommend them than do most of the mathematical theorems that we would derive from them. Moreover, we know from Gödel's work that no consistent axiom system can cover mathematics even when we renounce self-evidence. Reduction in the foundations of mathematics remains mathematically and philosophically fascinating, but it does not do what the epistemologist would like of it: it does not reveal the ground of mathematical knowledge, it does not show how mathematical certainty is possible.

Still there remains a helpful thought, regarding epistemology generally, in that duality of structure which was especially conspicuous in the foundations of mathematics. I refer to the bifurcation into a theory of concepts, or meaning, and a theory of doctrine, or truth; for this applies to the epistemology of natural knowledge no less than to the foundations of mathematics. The parallel is as follows. Just as mathematics is to be reduced to logic, or logic and set theory, so natural knowledge is to be based somehow on sense experience. This means explaining the notion of body in sensory terms; here is the conceptual side. And it means justifying our knowledge of truths of nature in sensory terms; here is the doctrinal side of the bifurcation.

Hume pondered the epistemology of natural knowledge on both sides of the bifurcation, the conceptual and the doctrinal. His handling of the conceptual side of the problem, the explanation of body in sensory terms, was bold and simple: he identified bodies outright with the sense impressions. If common sense distinguishes between the material apple and our sense impressions of it on the ground that the apple is one and enduring while the impressions are many and fleeting, then, Hume held, so much the worse for common sense; the notion of its being the same apple on one occasion and another is a vulgar confusion.

Nearly a century after Hume's *Treatise*, the same view of bodies was espoused by the early American philosopher Alexander Bryan Johnson. "The word iron names an associated sight and feel," Johnson wrote.

What then of the doctrinal side, the justification of our knowledge of truths about nature? Here, Hume despaired. By his identification of bodies with impressions he did succeed in construing some singular statements about bodies as indubitable truths, yes; as truths about impressions, directly known. But general statements, also singular statements about the future, gained no increment of certainty by being construed as about impressions.

On the doctrinal side, I do not see that we are farther along today than where Hume left us. The Humean predicament is the human predicament. But on the conceptual side there has been progress. There the crucial step forward was made already before Alexander Bryan Johnson's day, although Johnson did not emulate it. It was made by Bentham in his theory of fictions. Bentham's step was the recognition of contextual definition, or what he called paraphrasis. He recognized that to explain a term we do not need to specify an object for it to refer to, nor even specify a synonymous word or phrase; we need only show, by whatever means, how to translate all the whole sentences in which the term is to be used. Hume's and Johnson's desperate measure of identifying bodies with impressions ceased to be the only conceivable way of making sense of talk of bodies, even granted that impressions were the only reality. One could undertake to explain talk of bodies in terms of talk of impressions by translating one's whole sentences about bodies into whole sentences about impressions, without equating the bodies themselves to anything at all.

This idea of contextual definition, or recognition of the sentence as the primary vehicle of meaning,

was indispensable to the ensuing developments in the foundations of mathematics. It was explicit in Frege, and it attained its full flower in Russell's doctrine of singular descriptions as incomplete symbols.

Contextual definition was one of two resorts that could be expected to have a liberating effect upon the conceptual side of the epistemology of natural knowledge. The other is resort to the resources of set theory as auxiliary concepts. The epistemologist who is willing to eke out his austere ontology of sense impressions with these set-theoretic auxiliaries is suddenly rich: he has not just his impressions to play with, but sets of them, and sets of sets, and so on up. Constructions in the foundations of mathematics have shown that such set-theoretic aids are a powerful addition; after all, the entire glossary of concepts of classical mathematics is constructible from them. Thus equipped, our epistemologist may not need either to identify bodies with impressions or to settle for contextual definition; he may hope to find in some subtle construction of sets upon sets of sense impressions a category of objects enjoying just the formula properties that he wants for bodies.

The two resorts are very unequal in epistemological status. Contextual definition is unassailable. Sentences that have been given meaning as wholes are undeniably meaningful, and the use they make of their component terms is therefore meaningful, regardless of whether any translations are offered for those terms in isolation. Surely Hume and A. B. Johnson would have used contextual definition with pleasure if they had thought of it. Recourse to sets, on the other hand, is a drastic ontological move, a retreat from the austere ontology of impressions. There are philosophers who would rather settle for bodies outright than accept all these sets, which amount, after all, to the whole abstract ontology of mathematics.

This issue has not always been clear, however, owing to deceptive hints of continuity between elementary logic and set theory. This is why mathematics was once believed to reduce to logic, that is, to an innocent and unquestionable logic, and to inherit these qualities. And this is probably why Russell was content to resort to sets as well as to contextual definition when in *Our Knowledge of the External World* and elsewhere he addressed himself to the epistemology of natural knowledge, on its conceptual side.

To account for the external world as a logical construct of sense data—such, in Russell's terms, was the program. It was Carnap, in his *Der logische Aufbau der Welt* of 1928, who came nearest to executing it.

This was the conceptual side of epistemology; what of the doctrinal? There the Humean predicament remained unaltered. Carnap's constructions, if carried successfully to completion, would have enabled us to translate all sentences about the world into terms of sense data, or observation, plus logic and set theory. But the mere fact that a sentence is *couched* in terms of observation, logic, and set theory does not mean that it can be *proved* from observation sentences by logic and set theory. The most modest of generalizations about observable traits will cover more cases than its utterer can have had occasion actually to observe. The hopelessness of grounding natural science upon immediate experience in a firmly logical way was acknowledged. The Cartesian quest for certainty had been the remote motivation of epistemology, both on its conceptual and its doctrinal side; but that quest was seen as a lost cause. To endow the truths of nature with the full authority of immediate experience was as forlorn a hope as hoping to endow the truths of mathematics with the potential obviousness of elementary logic.

What then could have motivated Carnap's heroic efforts on the conceptual side of epistemology, when hope of certainty on the doctrinal side was abandoned? There were two good reasons still. One was that such constructions could be expected to elicit and clarify the sensory evidence for science, even if the inferential steps between sensory evidence and scientific doctrine must fall short of certainty. The other reason was that such constructions would deepen our understanding of our discourse about the world, even apart from questions of evidence; it would make all cognitive discourse as clear as observation terms and logic and, I must regretfully add, set theory.

It was sad for epistemologists, Hume and others, to have to acquiesce in the impossibility of strictly deriving the science of the external world from sensory evidence. Two cardinal tenets of empiricism remained unassailable, however, and so remain to this day. One is that whatever evidence there is for science is sensory evidence. The other, to which I shall recur, is that all inculcation of meanings of words must rest ultimately on sensory evidence. Hence the continuing attractiveness of the idea of a *logischer Aufbau* in which the sensory content of discourse would stand forth explicitly.

If Carnap had successfully carried such a construction through, how could he have told whether it was the right one? The question would have had no point. He was seeking what he called a *rational reconstruction*. Any construction of physicalistic discourse in terms of sense experience, logic, and set theory would have been seen as satisfactory if it made the physicalistic discourse come out right. If there is one way there are many, but any would be a great achievement.

But why all this creative reconstruction, all this make-believe? The stimulation of his sensory receptors is all the evidence anybody has had to go on, ultimately, in arriving at his picture of the world. Why not just see how this construction really proceeds? Why not settle for psychology? Such a surrender of the epistemological burden to psychology is a move that was disallowed in earlier times as circular reasoning. If the epistemologist's goal is validation of the grounds of empirical science, he defeats his purpose by using psychology or other empirical science in the validation. However, such scruples against circularity have little point once we have stopped dreaming of deducing science from observations. If we are out simply to understand the link between observation and science, we are well advised to use any available information, including that provided by the very science whose link with observation we are seeking to understand.

But there remains a different reason, unconnected with fears of circularity, for still favoring creative reconstruction. We should like to be able to *translate* science into logic and observation terms and set theory. This would be a great epistemological achievement, for it would show all the rest of the concepts of science to be theoretically superfluous. It would legitimize them—to whatever degree the concepts of set theory, logic, and observation are themselves legitimate—by showing that everything done with the one apparatus could in principle be done with the other. If psychology itself could deliver a truly translational reduction of this kind, we should welcome it; but certainly it cannot, for certainly we did not grow up learning definitions of physicalistic language in terms of a prior language of set theory, logic, and observation. Here, then, would be good reason for persisting in a rational reconstruction: we want to establish the essential innocence of physical concepts, by showing them to be theoretically dispensable.

The fact is, though, that the construction which Carnap outlined in *Der logische Aufbau Der Welt* does not give translational reduction either. It would not even if the outline were filled in. The crucial point comes where Carnap is explaining how to assign sense qualities to positions in physical space and time. These assignments are to be made in such a way as to fulfill, as well as possible, certain desiderata which he states, and with growth of experience the assignments are to be revised to suit. This plan, however illuminating, does not offer any key to *translating* the sentences of science into terms of observation, logic, and set theory.

We must despair of any such reduction. Carnap had despaired of it by 1936, when, in "Testability and meaning," he introduced so-called *reduction forms* of a type weaker than definition. Definitions had shown always how to translate sentences into equivalent sentences. Contextual definition of a term showed how to translate sentences containing the term into equivalent sentences lacking the term. Reduction forms of Carnap's liberalized kind, on the other hand, do not in general give equivalences; they give implications. They explain a new term, if only partially, by specifying some sentences which are implied by sentences containing the term, and other sentences which imply sentences containing the term.

It is tempting to suppose that the countenancing of reduction forms in this liberal sense is just one further step of liberalization comparable to the earlier one, taken by Bentham, of countenancing contextual definition. The former and sterner kind of rational reconstruction might have been represented as a fictitious history in which we imagined our ancestors introducing the terms of physicalistic discourse on a phenomenalistic and set-theoretic basis by a succession of contextual definitions. The new and more liberal kind of rational reconstruction is a fictitious history in which we imagine our ancestors introducing those terms by a succession rather of reduction forms of the weaker sort.

This, however, is a wrong comparison. The fact is rather that the former and sterner kind of rational reconstruction, where definition reigned, embodied no fictitious history at all. It was nothing more nor less than a set of directions—or would have been, if successful—for accomplishing everything in terms of phenomena and set theory that we now accomplish in terms of bodies. It would have been a true reduction by translation, a legitimation by elimination. *Definire est eliminare*. Rational reconstruction by Carnap's later and looser reduction forms does none of this.

To relax the demand for definition, and settle for a kind of reduction that does not eliminate, is to renounce the last remaining advantage that we supposed rational reconstruction to have over straight psychology; namely, the advantage of translational reduction. If all we hope for is a reconstruction that links science to experience in explicit ways short of translation, then it would seem more sensible to settle for psychology. Better to discover how science in fact developed and learned than to fabricate a fictitious structure to a similar effect.

The empiricist made one major concession when he despaired of deducing the truths of nature from sensory evidence. In despairing now even of translating those truths into terms of observation and logico-mathematical auxiliaries, he makes another major concession. For suppose we hold, with the old empiricist Peirce, that the very meaning of a statement consists in the difference its truth would make to possible experience. Might we not formulate, in a chapter-length sentence in observational language, all the difference that the truth of a given statement might make to experience, and might we not then take all this as the translation? Even if the difference that the truth of the statement would make to experience ramifies indefinitely, we might still hope to embrace it all in the logical implications of our chapter-length formulation, just as we can axiomatize an infinity of theorems. In giving up hope of such translation, then, the empiricist is conceding that the empirical meanings of typical statements about the external world are inaccessible and ineffable.

How is this inaccessibility to be explained? Simply on the ground that the experiential implications of a typical statement about bodies are too complex for finite axiomatization, however lengthy? No, I have a different explanation. It is that the typical statement about bodies has no fund of experiential implications it can call its own. A substantial mass of theory, taken together, will commonly have experiential implications; this is how we make verifiable predictions. We may not be able to explain why we arrive at theories which make successful predictions, but we do arrive at such theories.

Sometimes also an experience implied by a theory fails to come off; and then, ideally, we declare the theory false. But the failure falsifies only a block of theory as a whole, a conjunction of many statements. The failure shows that one or more of those statements is false, but it does not show which. The predicted experiences, true and false, are not implied by any one of the component statements of the theory rather than another. The component statements simply do not have empirical meanings, by Peirce's standard; but a sufficiently inclusive portion of theory does. If we can aspire to a sort of *logischer Aufbau der Welt* at all, it must be to one in which the texts slated for translation into observational and logico-mathematical terms are mostly broad theories taken as wholes, rather than just terms or short sentences. The translation of a theory would be a ponderous axiomatization of all the experiential difference that the truth of the theory would make. It would be a queer translation, for it would translate the whole but none of the parts. We might better speak in such a case not of translation but simply of observational evidence for theories; and we may, following Peirce, still fairly call this the empirical meaning of the theories.

These considerations raise a philosophical question even about ordinary unphilosophical translation, such as from English into Arunta or Chinese. For, if the English sentences of a theory have their meaning only together as a body, then we can justify their translation into Arunta only together as a body. There will be no justification for pairing off the component English sentences with component Arunta sentences, except as these correlations make the translation of the theory as a whole come out right. Any translations of the English sentences into Arunta sentences will be as correct as any other, so long as the net empirical implications of the theory as a whole are preserved in translation. But it is to be expected that many different ways of translating the component sentences, essentially different individu-

ally, would deliver the same empirical implications for the theory as a whole; deviations in the translation of one component sentence could be compensated for in the translation of another component sentence. Insofar, there can be no ground for saying which of two glaringly unlike translations of individual sentences is right.

For an uncritical mentalist, no such indeterminacy threatens. Every term and every sentence is a label attached to an idea, simple or complex, which is stored in the mind. When on the other hand we take a verification theory of meaning seriously, the indeterminacy would appear to be inescapable. The Vienna Circle espoused a verification theory of meaning but did not take it seriously enough. If we recognize with Peirce that the meaning of a sentence turns purely on what would count as evidence for its truth, and if we recognize with Duhem that theoretical sentences have their evidence not as single sentences but only as larger blocks of theory, then the indeterminacy of translation of theoretical sentences is the natural conclusion. And most sentences, apart from observation sentences, are theoretical. This conclusion, conversely, once it is embraced, seals the fate of any general notion of propositional meaning or, for that matter, state of affairs.

Should the unwelcomeness of the conclusion persuade us to abandon the verification theory of meaning? Certainly not. The sort of meaning that is basic to translation, and to the learning of one's own language, is necessarily empirical meaning and nothing more. A child learns his first words and sentences by hearing and using them in the presence of appropriate stimuli. These must be external stimuli, for they must act both on the child and on the speaker from whom he is learning. Language is socially inculcated and controlled; the inculcation and control turn strictly on the keying of sentences to shared stimulation. Internal factors may vary *ad libitum* without prejudice to communication as long as the keying of language to external stimuli is undisturbed. Surely one has no choice but to be an empiricist so far as one's theory of linguistic meaning is concerned.

What I have said of infant learning applies equally to the linguist's learning of a new language in the field. If the linguist does not lean on related languages for which there are previously accepted translation practices, then obviously he has no data but the concomitances of native utterance and observable stimulus situation. No wonder there is indeterminacy of translation—for of course only a small fraction of our utterances report concurrent external stimulation. Granted, the linguist will end up with unequivocal translations of everything; but only by making many arbitrary choices—arbitrary even though unconscious—along the way. Arbitrary? By this I mean that different choices could still have made everything come out right that is susceptible in principle to any kind of check.

Let me link up, in a different order, some of the points I have made. The crucial consideration behind my argument for the indeterminacy of translation was that a statement about the world does not always or usually have a separable fund of empirical consequences that it can call its own. That consideration served also to account for the impossibility of an epistemological reduction of the sort where every sentence is equated to a sentence in observational and logico-mathematical terms. And the impossibility of that sort of epistemological reduction dissipated the last advantage that rational reconstruction seemed to have over psychology.

Philosophers have rightly despaired of translating everything into observational and logico-mathematical terms. They have despaired of this even when they have not recognized, as the reason for this irreducibility, that the statements largely do not have their private bundles of empirical consequences. And some philosophers have seen in this irreducibility the bankruptcy of epistemology. Carnap and the other logical positivists of the Vienna Circle had already pressed the term "metaphysics" into pejorative use, as connoting meaninglessness; and the term "epistemology" was next. Wittgenstein and his followers, mainly at Oxford, found a residual philosophical vocation in therapy: in curing philosophers of the delusion that there were epistemological problems.

But I think that at this point it may be more useful to say rather that epistemology still goes on. though in a new setting and a clarified status. Epistemology, or something like it, simply falls into place as a chapter of psychology and hence of natural science. It studies a natural phenomenon, viz., a physical human subject. This human subject is accorded a certain experimentally controlled input—certain patterns of irradiation in assorted frequencies, for instance—and in the full-

ness of time the subject delivers as output a description of the three-dimensional external world and its history. The relation between the meager input and the torrential output is a relation that we are prompted to study for somewhat the same reasons that always prompted epistemology; namely, in order to see how evidence relates to theory, and in what ways one's theory of nature transcends any available evidence.

Such a study could still include, even, something like the old rational reconstruction, to whatever degree such reconstruction is practicable; for imaginative constructions can afford hints of actual psychological processes, in much the way that mechanical simulations can. But a conspicuous difference between old epistemology and the epistemological enterprise in this new psychological setting is that we can now make free use of empirical psychology.

The old epistemology aspired to contain, in a sense, natural science; it would construct it somehow from sense data. Epistemology in its new setting, conversely, is contained in natural science, as a chapter of psychology. But the old containment remains valid too, in its way. We are studying how the human subject of our study posits bodies and projects his physics from his data, and we appreciate that our position in the world is just like his. Our very epistemological enterprise, therefore, and the psychology wherein it is a component chapter, and the whole of natural science wherein psychology is a component book—all this is our own construction or projection from stimulations like those we were meting out to our epistemological subject. There is thus reciprocal containment, though containment in different senses: epistemology in natural science and natural science in epistemology.

This interplay is reminiscent again of the old threat of circularity, but it is all right now that we have stopped dreaming of deducing science from sense data. We are after an understanding of science as an institution or process in the world, and we do not intend that understanding to be any better than the science which is its object. This attitude is indeed one that Neurath was already urging in Vienna Circle days, with his parable of the mariner who has to rebuild his boat while staying afloat in it.

One effect of seeing epistemology in a psychological setting is that it resolves a stubborn old enigma of epistemological priority. Our retinas are irradiated in two dimensions, yet we see things as three-dimensional without conscious inference. Which is to count as observation—the unconscious two-dimensional reception or the conscious three-dimensional apprehension. In the old epistemological context the conscious form had priority, for we were out to justify our knowledge of the external world by rational reconstruction, and that demands awareness. Awareness ceased to be demanded when we gave up trying to justify our knowledge of the external world by rational reconstruction. What to count as observation now can be settled in terms of the stimulation of sensory receptors, let consciousness fall where it may.

The Gestalt psychologists' challenge to sensory atomism, which seemed so relevant to epistemology forty years ago, is likewise deactivated. Regardless of whether sensory atoms or Gestalten are what favor the forefront of our consciousness, it is simply the stimulations of our sensory receptors that are best looked upon as the input to our cognitive mechanism. Old paradoxes about unconscious data and inference, old problems about chains of inference that would have to be completed too quickly—these no longer matter.

In the old anti-psychologistic days the question of epistemological priority was moot. What is epistemologically prior to what? Are Gestalten prior to sensory atoms because they are noticed, or should we favor sensory atoms on some more subtle ground? Now that we are permitted to appeal to physical stimulation, the problem dissolves; A is epistemologically prior to B if A is causally nearer than B to the sensory receptors. Or, what is in some ways better, just talk explicitly in terms of causal proximity to sensory receptors and drop the talk of epistemological priority.

Around 1932 there was debate in the Vienna Circle over what to count as observation sentences, or *Protokollsatze*. One position was that they had the form of reports of sense impressions. Another was that they were statements of an elementary sort about the external world, e.g., "A red cube is standing on the table." Another, Neurath's, was that they had the form of reports of relations between percipients and external things: "Otto now sees a red cube on the table." The worst of it was that there seemed to be no objective way of settling the matter: no way of making real sense of the question.

Let us now try to view the matter unreservedly in the context of the external world. Vaguely speaking, what we want of observation sentences is that they be the ones in closest causal proximity to the sensory receptors. But how is such proximity to be gauged? The idea may be rephrased this way: observation sentences are sentences which, as we learn language, are most strongly conditioned to concurrent sensory stimulation rather than to stored collateral information. Thus let us imagine a sentence queried for our verdict as to whether it is true or false; queried for our assent or dissent. Then the sentence is an observation sentence if our verdict depends only on the sensory stimulation present at the time.

But a verdict cannot depend on present stimulation to the exclusion of stored information. The very fact of our having learned the language evinces much storing of information, and of information without which we should be in no position to give verdicts on sentences however observational. Evidently then we must relax our definition of observation sentence to read thus: a sentence is an observation sentence if all verdicts on it depend on present sensory stimulation and on no stored information beyond what goes into understanding the sentence.

This formulation raises another problem: how are we to distinguish between information that goes into understanding a sentence and information that goes beyond? This is the problem of distinguishing between analytic truth, which issues from the mere meanings of words, and synthetic truth, which depends on more than meanings. Now I have long maintained that this distinction is illusory. There is one step toward such a distinction, however, which does make sense: a sentence that is true by mere meanings of words should be expected, at least if it is simple, to be subscribed to by all fluent speakers in the community. Perhaps the controversial notion of analyticity can be dispensed with, in our definition of observation sentence, in favor of this straightforward attribute of community-wide acceptance.

This attribute is of course no explication of analyticity. The community would agree that there have been black dogs, yet none who talk of analyticity would call this analytic. My rejection of the analyticity notion just means drawing no line between what goes into the mere understanding the sentences of a language and what else the community sees eye-to-eye on. I doubt that an objective distinction can be made between meaning and such collateral information as is community-wide.

Turning back then to our task of defining observation sentences, we get this: an observation sentence is one on which all speakers of the language give the same verdict when given the same concurrent stimulation. To put the point negatively, an observation sentence is one that is not sensitive to differences in past experience within the speech community.

This formulation accords perfectly with the traditional role of the observation sentence as the court of appeal of scientific theories. For by our definition the observation sentences are the sentences on which all members of the community will agree under uniform stimulation. And what is the criterion of membership in the same community? Simply general fluency of dialogue. This criterion admits of degrees, and indeed we may usefully take the community more narrowly for some studies than for others. What count as observation sentences for a community of specialists would not always so count for a larger community.

There is generally no subjectivity in the phrasing of observation sentences, as we are now conceiving them; they will usually be about bodies. Since the distinguishing trait of an observation sentence is intersubjective agreement under agreeing stimulation, a corporeal subject matter is likelier than not.

The old tendency to associate observation sentences with a subjective sensory subject matter is rather an irony when we reflect that observation sentences are also meant to be the intersubjective tribunal of scientific hypotheses. The old tendency was due to the drive to base science on something firmer and prior in the subject's experience; but we dropped that project.

The dislodging of epistemology from its old status of first philosophy loosed a wave, we saw, of epistemological nihilism. This mood is reflected somewhat in the tendency of Polányi, Kuhn, and the late Russell Hanson to belittle the role of evidence and to accentuate cultural relativism. Hanson ventured even to discredit the idea of observation, arguing that so-called observations vary from observer to observer with the amount of knowledge that the observers bring with them. The veteran physicist looks at some apparatus and sees an x-ray tube. The neo-

phyte, looking at the same place, observes rather "a glass metal instrument replete with wires, reflectors, screws, lamps, and pushbuttons." One man's observation is another man's closed book or flight of fancy. The notion of observation as the impartial and objective source of evidence for science is bankrupt. Now my answer to the x-ray example was already hinted a little while back: what counts as an observation sentence varies with the width of community considered. But we can also always get an absolute standard by taking in all speakers of the language, or most. It is ironical that philosophers, finding the old epistemology untenable as a whole, should react by repudiating a part which has only now moved into clear focus.

Clarification of the notion of observation sentence is a good thing, for the notion is fundamental in two connections. These two correspond to the duality that I remarked upon early in this lecture: the duality between concept and doctrine, between knowing what a sentence means and knowing whether it is true. The observation sentence is basic to both enterprises. Its relation to doctrine, to our knowledge of what is true, is very much the traditional one: observation sentences are the repository of evidence for scientific hypotheses. Its relation to meaning is fundamental too, since observation sentences are the ones we are in a position to learn to understand first, both as children and as field linguists. For observation sentences are precisely the ones that we can correlate with observable circumstances of the occasion of utterance or assent, independently of variations in the past histories of individual informants. They afford the only entry to a language.

The observation sentence is the cornerstone of semantics. For it is, as we jut saw, fundamental to the learning of meaning. Also, it is where meaning is firmest. Sentences higher up in theories have no empirical consequences they can call their own; they confront the tribunal of sensory evidence only in more or less inclusive aggregates. The observation sentence, situated at the sensory periphery of the body scientific, is the minimal verifiable aggregate; it has an empirical content all its own and wears it on its sleeve.

The predicament of the indeterminacy of translation has little bearing on observation sentences. The equating of an observation sentence of our language to an observation sentence of another language is mostly a matter of empirical generalization; it is a matter of identity between the range of stimulations that would prompt assent to the one sentence and the range of stimulations that would prompt assent to the other.

It is no shock to the preconceptions of old Vienna to say that epistemology now becomes semantics. For epistemology remains centered as always on evidence, and meaning remains centered as always on verification; and evidence is verification. What is likelier to shock preconceptions is that meaning, once we get beyond observation sentences, ceases in general to have any clear applicability to single sentences; also that epistemology merges with psychology as well as with linguistics.

This rubbing out of boundaries could contribute to progress, it seems to me, in philosophically interesting inquiries of a scientific nature. One possible area is perceptual norms. Consider, to begin with, the linguistic phenomenon of phonemes. We form the habit, in hearing the myriad variations of spoken sounds, of treating each as an approximation to one or another of a limited number of norms—around thirty altogether—constituting so to speak a spoken alphabet. All speech in our language can be treated in practice as sequences of just those thirty elements, thus rectifying small deviations. Now outside the realm of language also there is probably only a rather limited alphabet of perceptual norms altogether toward which we tend unconsciously to rectify all perceptions. These, if experimentally identified, could be taken as epistemological building blocks, the working elements of experience. They might prove in part to be culturally variable, as phonemes are, and in part universal.

Again there is the area that the psychologist Donald T. Campbell calls evolutionary epistemology. In this area there is work by Hüseyin Yilmaz, who shows how some structural traits of color perception could have been predicted from survival value. And a more emphatically epistemological topic that evolution helps to clarify is induction, now that we are allowing epistemology the resources of natural science."

W. V. O. QUINE

The Nature of Natural Knowledge[1]

Doubt has oft been said to be the mother of philosophy. This has a true ring for those of us who look upon philosophy primarily as the theory of knowledge. For the theory of knowledge has its origin in doubt, in scepticism. Doubt is what prompts us to try to develop a theory of knowledge. Furthermore, doubt is also the first step to take in developing a theory of knowledge, if we adopt the line of Descartes.

But this is only half of a curious interplay between doubt and knowledge. Doubt prompts the theory of knowledge, yes; but knowledge, also, was what prompted the doubt. Scepticism is an offshoot of science. The basis for scepticism is the awareness of illusion, the discovery that we must not always believe our eyes. Scepticism battens on mirages, on seemingly bent sticks in water, on rainbows, after-images, double images, dreams. But in what sense are these illusions? In the sense that they seem to be material objects which they in fact are not. Illusions are illusions only relative to a prior acceptance of genuine bodies with which to contrast them. In a world of immediate sense data with no bodies posited and no questions asked, a distinction between reality and illusion would have no place. The positing of bodies is already rudimentary physical science; and it is only after that stage that the sceptic's invidious distinctions can make sense. Bodies have to be posited before there can be a motive, however tenuous, for acquiescing in a non-committal world of the immediate given.

Rudimentary physical science, that is, common sense about bodies, is thus needed as a springboard for scepticism. It contributes the needed notion of a distinction between reality and illusion, and that is not all. It also discerns regularities of bodily behaviour which are indispensable to that distinction. The sceptic's example of the seemingly bent stick owes its force to our knowledge that sticks do not bend by immersion; and his examples of mirages, after-images, dreams, and the rest are similarly parasitic upon positive science, however primitive.

I am not accusing the sceptic of begging the question. He is quite within his rights in assuming science in order to refute science; this, if carried out, would be a straightforward argument by *reductio ad absurdum*. I am only making the point that sceptical doubts are scientific doubts.

Epistemologists have coped with their sceptical doubts by trying to reconstruct our knowledge of the external world from sensations. A characteristic effort was Berkeley's theory of vision, in which he sought our clues for a third dimension, depth, in our two-dimensional visual field. The very posing of this epistemological problem depends in a striking way upon acceptations of physical science. The goal of the construction, namely the depth dimension, is of course deliberately taken from the science of the external world; but what particularly wants noticing is that also the accepted basis of the construction, the two-dimensional visual field, was itself dictated by the science of the external world as well. The light that informs us of the external world impinges on the two-dimensional surface of the eye, and it was Berkeley's awareness of this that set his problem.

Epistemology is best looked upon, then, as an enterprise within natural science. Cartesian doubt is not the way to begin. Retaining our present beliefs about nature, we can still ask how we can have arrived at them. Science tells us that our only source of information about the external world is through the impact of light rays and molecules upon our sensory surfaces. Stimulated in these ways, we somehow evolve an elaborate and useful science. How do we do this, and why does the resulting science work so well? These are genuine questions, and no feigning of doubt is needed to appreciate them. They are scientific questions about a species of primates, and they are open to investigation in natural science, the very science whose acquisition is being investigated.

The utility of science, from a practical point of view, lies in fulfilled expectation: true prediction.

This is true not only of sophisticated science, but of its primitive progenitor as well; and it may be good strategy on our part to think first of the most primitive case. This case is simple induction. It is the expectation, when some past event recurs, that the sequel of that past event will recur too. People are prone to this, and so are other animals.

It may be felt that I am unduly intellectualizing the dumb animals in attributing expectation and induction to them. Still the net resultant behaviour of dumb animals is much on a par with our own, at the level of simple induction. In a dog's experience, a clatter of pans in the kitchen has been followed by something to eat. So now, hearing the clatter again, he goes to the kitchen in expectation of dinner. His going to the kitchen is our evidence of his expectation, if we care to speak of expectation. Or we can skip this intervening variable, as Skinner calls it, and speak merely of reinforced response, conditioned reflex, habit formation.

When we talk easily of repetition of events, repetition of stimuli, we cover over a certain significant factor. It is the *similarity* factor. It can be brought into the open by speaking of events rather as unique, dated, unrepeated particulars, and then speaking of similarities between them. Each of the noisy episodes of the pans is a distinct event, however similar, and so is each of the ensuing dinners. What we can say of the dog in those terms is that he hears something similar to the old clatter and proceeds to expect something similar to the old dinner. Or, if we want to eliminate the intervening variable, we can still say this: when the dog hears something similar to the old clatter and, going to the kitchen, gets something similar to the old dinner, he is reinforced in his disposition to go to the kitchen after each further event similar to the old clatter.

What is significant about this similarity factor is its subjectivity. Is similarity the mere sharing of many attributes? But any two things share countless attributes—or anyway any two objects share membership in countless classes. The similarity that matters, in the clatter of the pans, is similarity for the dog. Again I seem to appeal to the dog's mental life, but again I can eliminate this intervening variable. We can analyse similarity, for the dog, in terms of his dispositions to behaviour: his patterns of habit formation. His habit of going to the kitchen after a

clatter of pans is itself our basis for saying that the clatter events are similar for the dog, and that the dinner events are similar for the dog. It is by experimental reinforcement and extinction along these lines that we can assess similarities for the dog, determining whether event a is more similar to b than to c for him. Meanwhile his mental life is as may be.

Now our question 'Why is science so successful?' makes some rudimentary sense already at this level, as applied to the dog. For the dog's habit formation, his primitive induction, involved extrapolation along similarity lines: episodes similar to the old clattering episode engendered expectation of episodes similar to the old dinner episode. And now the crux of the problem is the subjectivity of similarity. Why should nature, however lawful, match up at all with the dog's subjective similarity ratings? Here, at its most primitive, is the question 'Why is science so successful?'

We are taking this as a scientific question, remember, open to investigation by natural science itself. Why should the dog's implicit similarity ratings tend to fit world trends, in such a way as to favour the dog's implicit expectations? An answer is offered by Darwin's theory of natural selection. Individuals whose similarity groupings conduce largely to true expectations have a good chance of finding food and avoiding predators, and so a good chance of living to reproduce their kind.

What I have said of the dog holds equally of us, at least in our pursuit of the rudimentary science of common sense. We predict in the light of observed uniformities, and these are uniformities by our subjective similarity standards. These standards are innate ones, overlaid and modified by experience; and natural selection has endowed us, like the dog, with a head start in the way of helpful, innate similarity standards.

I am not appealing to Darwinian biology to justify induction. This would be circular, since biological knowledge depends on induction. Rather I am granting the efficacy of induction, and then observing that Darwinian biology, if true, helps explain why induction is as efficacious as it is.

We must notice, still, a further limitation. Natural selection may be expected only to have encouraged similarity standards conducive to rough and ready anticipations of experience in a state of nature. Such standards are not necessarily conducive to deep science. Colour is a case in point. Colour dominates our scene; similarity in colour is similarity at its most conspicuous. Yet, as J. J. C. Smart points out, colour plays little role in natural science. Things can be alike in colour even though one of them is reflecting green light of uniform wave length while the other is reflecting mixed waves of yellow and blue. Properties that are most germane to sophisticated science are camouflaged by colour more than revealed by it. Over-sensitivity to colour may have been all to the good when we were bent on quickly distinguishing predator from prey or good plants from bad. But true science cuts through all this and sorts things out differently, leaving colour largely irrelevant.

Colour is not the only such case. Taxonomy is rich in examples to show that visual resemblance is a poor index of kinship. Natural selection has even abetted the deception; thus some owls have grown to resemble cats, for their own good, and others resemble monkeys. Natural selection works both to improve a creature's similarity standards and to help him abuse his enemies' similarity standards.

For all their fallibility, our innate similarity standards are indispensable to science as an entering wedge. They continue to be indispensable, moreover, even as science advances. For the advance of science depends on continued observation, continued checking of predictions. And there, at the observational level, the unsophisticated similarity standards of common sense remain in force.

An individual's innate similarity standards undergo some revision, of course, even at the common-sense level, indeed even at the sub-human level, through learning. An animal may learn to tell a cat from an owl. The ability to learn is itself a product of natural selection, with evident survival value. An animal's innate similarity standards are a rudimentary instrument for prediction, and then learning is a progressive refinement of that instrument, making for more dependable prediction. In man, and most conspicuously in recent centuries, this refinement has consisted in the development of a vast and bewildering growth of conceptual or linguistic apparatus, the whole of natural science. Biologically, still, it is like the animal's learning about cats and owls; it is a learned improvement over simple induction by innate similarity standards. It makes for more and better prediction.

Science revises our similarity standards, we saw; thus we discount colour, for some purposes, and we liken whales to cows rather than to fish. But this is not the sole or principal way in which science fosters prediction. Mere improvement of similarity standards would increase our success at simple induction, but this is the least of it. Science departs from simple induction. Science is a ponderous linguistic structure, fabricated of theoretical terms linked by fabricated hypotheses, and keyed to observable events here and there. Indirectly, via this labyrinthine superstructure, the scientist predicts future observations on the basis of past ones; and he may revise the superstructure when the predictions fail. It is no longer simple induction. It is the hypothetico-deductive method. But, like the animal's simple induction over innate similarities, it is still a biological device for anticipating experience. It owes its elements still to natural selection—notably, the similarity standards that continue to operate at the observational level. The biological survival value of the resulting scientific structure, however, is as may be. Traits that were developed by natural selection have been known to prove lethal, through over-development or remote effects or changing environment. In any event, and for whatever good it may do us, the hypothetico-deductive method is delivering knowledge hand over fist. It is facilitating prediction.

I said that science is a linguistic structure that is keyed to observation at some points. Some sentences are keyed directly to observation: the observation sentences. Let us examine this connection. First I must explain what I mean by an observation sentence. One distinctive trait of such a sentence is that its truth value varies with the circumstances prevailing at the time of the utterance. It is a sentence like 'This is red' or 'It is raining', which is true on one occasion and false on another; unlike 'Sugar is sweet', whose truth value endures regardless of occasion of utterance. In a word, observation sentences are occasion sentences, not standing sentences.

But their being occasion sentences is not the only distinctive trait of observation sentences. Not only must the truth value of an observation sentence depend on the circumstances of its utterance; it must depend on intersubjectively observable circumstances. Certainly the fisherman's sentence 'I just felt a nibble' is true or false depending on the circumstances of its utterance; but the relevant circumstances are privy to the speaker rather than being out in the open for all present witnesses to share. The sentence 'I just felt a nibble' is an occasion sentence but not an observation sentence, in my sense of the term.

An observation sentence, then, is an occasion sentence whose occasion is intersubjectively observable. But this is still not enough. After all, the sentence 'There goes John's old tutor' meets these requirements; it is an occasion sentence, and all present witnesses can see the old tutor plodding by. But the sentence fails of a third requirement: the witnesses must in general be able to appreciate that the observation which they are sharing is one that verifies the sentence. They must have been in a position, equally with the speaker, to have assented to the sentence on their own in the circumstances. They are in that position in the case of 'This is red' and 'It is raining' and 'There goes an old man', but not in the case of 'There goes John's old tutor.'

Such, then, is an observation sentence: it is an occasion sentence whose occasion is not only intersubjectively observable but is generally adequate, moreover, to elicit assent to the sentence from any present witness conversant with the language. It is not a report of private sense data; typically, rather, it contains references to physical objects.

These sentences, I say, are keyed directly to observation. But how *keyed*, now—what is the nature of the connection? It is a case of conditioned response. It is not quite the simplest kind; we do not say 'red' or 'This is red' whenever we see something red. But we do assent if asked. Mastery of the term 'red' is acquisition of the habit of assenting when the term is queried in the presence of red, and only in the presence of red.

At the primitive level, an observation sentence is apt to take the form of a single word, thus 'ball', or 'red'. What makes it easy to learn is the intersubjective observability of the relevant circumstances at the time of utterance. The parent can verify that the child is seeing red at the time, and so can reward the child's assent to the query. Also the child can verify that the parent is seeing red when the parent assents to such a query.

In this habit formation the child is in effect determining, by induction, the range of situations in which the adult will assent to the query 'red', or approve the child's utterance of 'red'. He is extrapolating along similarity lines; this red episode is similar to that red episode by his lights. His success depends, therefore, on substantial agreement between his similarity standards and those of the adult. Happily the agreement holds; and no wonder, since our similarity standards are a matter partly of natural selection and partly of subsequent experience in a shared environment. If substantial agreement in similarity standards were not there, this first step in language acquisition would be blocked.

We have been seeing that observation sentences are the starting-points in the learning of language. Also, they are the starting-points and the check points of scientific theory. They serve both purposes for one and the same reason: the intersubjective observability of the relevant circumstances at the time of utterance. It is this, intersubjective observability at the time, that enables the child to learn when to assent to the observation sentence. And it is this also, intersubjective observability at the time, that qualifies observation sentences as check points for scientific theory. Observation sentences state the evidence, to which all witnesses must accede.

I had characterized science as a linguistic structure that is keyed to observation at some points. Now we have seen how it is keyed to observation: some of the sentences, the observation sentences, are conditioned to observable events in combination with a routine of query and assent. There is the beginning, here, of a partnership between the theory of language learning and the theory of scientific evidence. It is clear, when you think about it, that this partnership must continue. For when a child learns his language from his elders, what has he to go on? He can learn observation sentences by consideration of their observable circumstances, as we saw. But how can he learn the rest of the language, including the theoretical sentences of science? Somehow he learns to carry his observation terms over into theoretical contexts, variously embedded. Somehow he learns to connect his observation sentences with standing sentences, sentences whose truth values do not depend on the occasion of utterance. It is only by such moves, however ill understood, that anyone masters the non-observational part of his mother tongue. He can learn the observational part in firm and well-understood ways, and then he must build out somehow, imitating what he hears and linking it tenuously and conjecturally to what he knows, until by dint of trial and social correction he achieves fluent dialogue with his community. This discourse depends, for whatever empirical content it has, on its devious and tenuous connections with the observation sentences; and those are the same connections, nearly enough, through which one has achieved one's fluent part in that discourse. The channels by which, having learned observation sentences, we acquire theoretical language, are the very channels by which observation lends evidence to scientific theory. It all stands to reason; for language is man-made and the locutions of scientific theory have no meaning but what they acquired by our learning to use them.

We see, then, a strategy for investigating the relation of evidential support, between observation and scientific theory. We can adopt a genetic approach, studying how theoretical language is learned. For the evidential relation is virtually enacted, it would seem, in the learning. This genetic strategy is attractive because the learning of language goes on in the world and is open to scientific study. It is a strategy for the scientific study of scientific method and evidence. We have here a good reason to regard the theory of language as vital to the theory of knowledge.

When we try to understand the relation between scientific theory and the observation sentences, we are brought up short by the break between occasion sentences and standing sentences; for observation sentences are of the one kind while theoretical sentences are of the other. The scientific system cannot digest occasion sentences; their substance must first be converted into standing sentences. The observation sentence 'Rain' or 'It is raining' will not do; we must put the information into a standing sentence: 'Rain at Heathrow 1600 G.M.T. 23 February 1974.' This report is ready for filing in the archives of science. It still reports an observation, but it is a standing report rather than an occasion sentence. How do we get from the passing observation of rain to the standing report?

This can be explained by a cluster of observations and observation sentences, having to do with other matters besides the rain. Thus take the term 'Heathrow'. Proper names of persons, buildings, and localities are best treated as observation terms,

on a par with 'red' and 'rain'. All such terms can be learned by ostension, repeated sufficiently to suggest the intended scope and limits of application. 'Here is Heathrow,' then, is an observation sentence on a par with 'It is raining'; and their conjunction, 'Raining at Heathrow,' is an observation sentence as well. It is an occasion sentence still, of course, and not a standing report of observation. But now the two further needed ingredients, hour and date, can be added as pointer readings: 'The clock reads 1600' and 'The calendar reads 23 February 1974' are further observation sentences. Taking the conjunction of all four, we still have an observation sentence: 'Rain at Heathrow with clock at 1600 and calendar at 23 February 1974.' But it is an observation sentence with this curious trait: it gives lasting information, dependent no longer on the vicissitudes of tense or of indicator words like 'here' and 'now'. It is suitable for filing.

True, the clock and calendar may have been wrong. As an observation sentence our report must be viewed as stating the temporal readings and not the temporal facts. The question of the temporal facts belongs to scientific theory, somewhat above the observational level. Theoretical repercussions of this and other observations could eventually even prompt a modest scientific hypothesis to the effect that the clock or the calendar had been wrong.

I think this example serves pretty well as a paradigm case, to show how we can get from the occasion sentences of observation to the standing reports of observation that are needed for scientific theory. But this connection is by no means the only connection between observation sentences and standing sentences. Thus consider the universal categorical, 'A dog is an animal.' This is a standing sentence but it is not, like the example of rain at Heathrow, a standing report of observation. Let us resume our genetic strategy: how might a child have mastered such a universal categorical?

I shall venture one hypothesis, hoping that it may be improved upon. The child has learned to assent to the observation term 'a dog' when it is queried in the conspicuous presence of dogs, and he has learned to assent to 'an animal' likewise when it is queried in the conspicuous presence of dogs (though not only dogs). Because of his close association of the word 'dog' with dogs, the mere sound of the word 'dog' disposes him to respond to the subsequent query 'an animal' as he would have done if a dog had been there; so he assents when he hears 'a dog' followed by the query, 'an animal?'. Being rewarded for so doing, he ever after assents to the query 'A dog is an animal?' In the same way he learns a few other examples of the universal categorical. Next he rises to a mastery of the universal categorical construction 'An S is a P' in general: he learns to apply it to new cases on his own. This important step of abstraction can perhaps be explained in parallel fashion to the early learning of observation sentences, namely, by simple induction along similarity lines; but the similarity now is a language-dependent similarity.

Much the same account can be offered for the learning of the seemingly simpler construction, mere predication: 'Fido is a dog,' 'Sugar is sweet.'

The child has now made creditable progress from observation sentences towards theoretical language, by mastering predication and the universal categorical construction. Another important step will be mastery of the relative clause; and I think I can give a convincing hypothesis of how this comes about. What is conspicuous about the relative clause is its role in predication. Thus take a relative clause, 'something that chases its tail', and predicate it of Dinah: 'Dinah is something that chases its tail.' This is equivalent to the simple sentence 'Dinah chases its tail' (or 'her tail'). When we predicate the relative clause, the effect is the same as substituting the subject of the predication for the pronoun of the relative clause. Now my suggestion regarding the learning of the relative clause is that the child learns this substitution transformation. He discovers that the adult is prepared to assent to a predication of a relative clause in just the circumstances where he is prepared to assent to the simpler sentence obtained by the substitution.

This explains how the child could learn relative clauses in one standard position: predicative position. He learns how to eliminate them, in that position, by the substitution transformation—and how to introduce them into that position by the converse transformation, superstitution. But then, having learned this much, he is struck by an analogy between relative clauses and ordinary simple predicates or general terms; for these also appear in predicative position. So, pursuing the analogy, he presses relative clauses into other positions where general terms have been appearing—notably into the universal categorical construction. Or, if the child does not press this analogy on his own, he is at any rate well prepared to grasp adult usage and follow it in the light of the analogy. In this way the relative clause gets into the universal categorical construction, from which it cannot be eliminated by the substitution transformation. It is there to stay.

We can easily imagine how the child might learn the truth functions—negation, conjunction, alternation. Take conjunction: the child notices, by degrees, that the adult affirms 'p and q' in only those circumstances where he is disposed, if queried, to assent to 'p' and also to 'q'.

We have now seen, in outline and crude conjecture, how one might start at the observational edge of language and work one's way into the discursive interior where scientific theory can begin to be expressed. Predication is at hand, and the universal categorical, the relative clause, and the truth functions. Once this stage is reached, it is easy to see that the whole strength of logical quantification is available. I shall not pause over the details of this, except to remark that the pronouns of relative clauses take on the role of the bound variable of quantification. By further conjectures in the same spirit, some of them more convincing and some less, we can outline the learner's further progress, to where he is bandying abstract terms and quantifying over properties, numbers, functions, and hypothetical physical particles and forces. This progress is not a continuous derivation, which, followed backward, would enable us to reduce scientific theory to sheer observation. It is a progress rather by short leaps of analogy. One such was the pressing of relative clauses into universal categoricals, where they cease to be eliminable. There are further such psychological speculations that I could report, but time does not allow.

Such speculations would gain, certainly, from experimental investigation of the child's actual learning of language. Experimental findings already available in the literature could perhaps be used to sustain or correct these conjectures at points, and further empirical investigations could be devised. But a speculative approach of the present sort seems required to begin with, in order to isolate just the factual questions that bear on our purposes. For our objective here is still philosophical—a better understanding of the relations between evidence and scientific theory. Moreover, the way to this objective requires consideration of linguistics and logic along with psychology. This is why the speculative phase has to precede, for the most part, the formulation of relevant questions to be posed to the experimental psychologist.

In any event the present speculations, however inaccurate, are presumably true to the general nature of language acquisition. And already they help us to understand how the logical links are forged that connect theoretical sentences with the reports of observation. We learn the grammatical construction 'p and q' by learning, among other things, to assent to the compound only in circumstances where we are disposed to assent to each component. Thus it is that the logical law of inference which leads from 'p and q' to 'p' is built into our habits by the very learning of 'and'. Similarly for the other laws of conjunction, and correspondingly for the laws of alternation and other truth functions. Correspondingly, again, for laws of quantification. The law of inference that leads from '$(x)Fx$' to 'Fa' should be traceable back, through the derivation of quantification that I have passed over, until it is found finally to hinge upon the substitution transformation by which we learn to use the relative clause. Thus, in general, the acquisition of our basic logical habits is to be accounted for in our acquisition of grammatical constructions.

Related remarks hold true of inferential habits that exceed pure logic. We learn when to assent to 'dog', and to 'animal', only by becoming disposed to assent to 'animal' in all circumstances where we will assent to 'dog'. Connections more accidental and casual in aspect can also come about through the learning of words; thus a child may have begun to learn the term 'good' in application to chocolate.

I characterized science as a linguistic structure that is keyed to observation here and there. I said also that it is an instrument for predicting observations on the basis of earlier observations. It is keyed to observations, earlier and later, forming a labyrinthine connection between them; and it is through this labyrinth that the prediction takes place. A powerful improvement, this, over simple induction from past observations to future ones; powerful and costly. I have now sketched the nature of the connection between the observations and the labyrinthine interior of scientific theory. I have sketched it in terms of the learning of language. This seemed reasonable, since the scientist himself can make no sense of the language of scientific theory beyond what goes into his learning of it. The paths of language learning, which lead from observation sentences to theoretical sentences, are the only connection there is between observation and theory. This has been a sketch, but a fuller understanding may be sought along the same line: by a more painstaking investigation of how we learn theoretical language.

One important point that already stands forth, regarding the relation of theory to observation, is the vast freedom that the form of the theory must enjoy, relative even to all possible observation. Theory is empirically under-determined. Surely even if we had an observational oracle, capable of assigning a truth value to every standing observational report expressible in our language, still this would not suffice to adjudicate between a host of possible physical theories, each of them completely in accord with the oracle. This seems clear in view of the tenuousness of the connections that we have noted between observation sentences and theoretical ones. At the level of observation sentences, even the general form of the eventual theoretical language remained indeterminate, to say nothing of the ontology. The observation sentences were associated, as wholes, with the stimulatory situations that warranted assent to them; but there was in this no hint of what aspects of the stimulatory situations to single out somehow as objects, if indeed any. The question of ontology simply makes no sense until we get to something recognizable as quantification, or perhaps as a relative clause, with pronouns as potential variables. At the level of observation sentences there was no foreseeing even that the superimposed theoretical language would contain anything recognizable as quantification or relative clauses. The steps by which the child was seen to progress from observational language to relative clauses and categoricals and quantification had the arbitrary character of historical accident and cultural heritage; there was no hint of inevitability. It was a tremendous achievement, on the part of our long-term culture and our latter-day scientists, to develop a theory that leads from observation to predicted observation as successfully as ours. It is a near miracle. If our theory were in full conformity with the observational oracle that we just now imagined, which surely it is not, that would be yet a nearer miracle. But if, even granted that nearer miracle, our theory were not still just one of many equally perfect possible theories to the same observational effect, that would be too miraculous to make sense.

But it must be said that the issue of underdetermination proves slippery when we try to grasp it more firmly. If two theories conform to the same totality of possible observations, in what sense are they two? Perhaps they are both stated in English, and they are alike, word for word, except that one of them calls molecules electrons and electrons molecules. Literally the two theories are in contradiction, saying incompatible things about so-called molecules. But of course we would not want to count this case; we would call it terminological. Or again, following Poincaré, suppose the two theories are alike except that one of them assumes an infinite space while the other has a finite space in which bodies shrink in proportion to their distance from centre. Even here we want to say that the difference is rather terminological than real; and our reason is that we see how to bring the theories into agreement by translation: by reconstruing the English of one of the theories.

At this point it may be protested that after all there can never be two complete theories agreeing on the total output of the observational oracle. It may be protested that since such theories would be empirically equivalent, would have the same empirical meaning, their difference is purely verbal. For surely there is no meaning but empirical meaning, and theories with the same meaning must be seen as translations one of the other. This argument simply rules out, by definition, the doctrine that physical theory is under-determined by all possible observation.

The best reaction at this point is to back away from terminology and sort things out on their merits. Where the significant difference comes is perhaps where we no longer see how to state rules of translation that would bring the two empirically equivalent theories together. Terminology aside, what wants recognizing is that a physical theory of radically different form from ours, with nothing even recognizably similar to our quantification or objective reference, might still be empirically equivalent to ours, in the sense of predicting the same episodes of sensory bombardment on the strength of the same past episodes. Once this is recognized, the scientific achievement of our culture becomes in a way more impressive than ever. For, in the midst of all this formless freedom for variation, our science has developed in such a way as to maintain always a manageably narrow spectrum of visible alternatives among which to choose when need arises to revise a theory. It is this narrowing of sights, or tunnel vision, that has made for the continuity of science, through the vicissitudes of refutation and correction. And it is this also that has fostered the illusion of there being only one solution to the riddle of the universe.

NOTE

1. This paper is meant as a summary statement of my attitude towards our knowledge of nature. Consequently I must warn the more omnivorous of my readers (dear souls) that they are apt to experience a certain indefinable sense of déjà vu. The main traces of novelty come towards the end.

W. V. O. QUINE

Norms and Aims

I am of that large minority or small majority who repudiate the Cartesian dream of a foundation for scientific certainty firmer than scientific method itself. But I remain occupied, we see, with what has been central to traditional epistemology, namely the relation of science to its sensory data. I approach it as an input-output relation within flesh-and-blood denizens of an antecedently acknowledged external world, a relation open to inquiry as a chapter of the science of that world. To emphasize my dissociation from the Cartesian dream, I have written of neural receptors and their stimulation rather than of sense or sensibilia. I call the pursuit naturalized epistemology, but I have no quarrel with traditionalists who protest my retention of the latter word. I agree with them that repudiation of the Cartesian dream is no minor deviation.

But they are wrong in protesting that the normative element, so characteristic of epistemology, goes by the board. Insofar as theoretical epistemology gets naturalized into a chapter of theoretical science, so normative epistemology gets naturalized into a chapter of engineering: the technology of anticipating sensory stimulation.

The most notable norm of naturalized epistemology actually coincides with that of traditional epistemology. It is simply the watchword of empiricism: *nihil in mente quod non prius in sensu.* This is a prime specimen of naturalized epistemology, for it is a finding of natural science itself, however fallible, that our information about the world comes only through impacts on our sensory receptors. And still the point is normative, warning us against telepaths and soothsayers.

Moreover, naturalized epistemology on its normative side is occupied with heuristics generally—with the whole strategy of rational conjecture in the framing of scientific hypotheses. In the present pages I have been treating rather of the testing of a theory after it has been thought up, this being where

the truth conditions and empirical content lie; so I have passed over the thinking up, which is where the normative considerations come in. Ullian and I did go into it somewhat in *The Web of Belief,* listing five virtues to seek in a hypothesis: conservatism, generality, simplicity, refutability, and modesty. Further counsel is available anecdotally in the history of hard science. In a more technical vein, normative naturalized epistemology tangles with margin of error, random deviation, and whatever else goes into the applied mathematics of statistics.

But when I cite predictions as the checkpoints of science, I do not see that as normative. I see it as defining a particular language game, in Wittgenstein's phrase: the game of science, in contrast to other good language games such as fiction and poetry. A sentence's claim to scientific status rests on what it contributes to a theory whose checkpoints are in prediction.

I stressed in §1 that prediction is not the main purpose of the science game. It is what decides the game, like runs and outs in baseball. It is occasionally the purpose, and in primitive times it gave primitive science its survival value. But nowadays the overwhelming purposes of the science game are technology and understanding.

The science game is not committed to the physical, whatever that means. Bodies have long since diffused into swarms of particles, and the Bose-Einstein statistic has challenged the particularity of the particle. Even telepathy and clairvoyance are scientific options, however moribund. It would take some extraordinary evidence to enliven them, but, if that were to happen, then empiricism itself—the crowning norm, we saw, of naturalized epistemology—would go by the board. For remember that that norm, and naturalized epistemology itself, are integral to science, and science is fallible and corrigible.

Science after such a convulsion would still be science, the same old language game, hinging still on checkpoints in sensory prediction. The collapse of empiricism would admit extra input by telepathy or revelation, but the test of the resulting science would still be predicted sensation.

In that extremity it might indeed be well to modify the game itself, and take on as further checkpoints the predicting of telepathic and divine input as well as of sensory input. It is idle to bulwark definitions against implausible contingencies.

JAEGWON KIM

What Is "Naturalized Epistemology"?

1. EPISTEMOLOGY AS A NORMATIVE INQUIRY

Descartes' epistemological inquiry in the *Meditations* begins with this question: What propositions are worthy of belief? In the *First Meditation* Descartes canvasses beliefs of various kinds he had formerly held as true and finds himself forced to conclude that he ought to reject them, that he ought not to accept them as true. We can view Cartesian epistemology as consisting of the following two projects: to identify the criteria by which we ought to regulate acceptance and rejection of beliefs, and to determine what we may be said to know according to those criteria. Descartes' epistemological agenda has been the agenda of Western epistemology to this day. The twin problems of identifying criteria of justified belief and coming to terms with the skeptical challenge to the possibility of knowledge have defined the central tasks of theory of knowledge since Descartes. This was as true of the empiricists, of Locke and Hume and Mill, as of those who more closely followed Descartes in the rationalist path.[1]

It is no wonder then that modern epistemology has been dominated by a single concept, that of *justification,* and two fundamental questions involving it: What conditions must a belief meet if we are justified in accepting it as true? and What beliefs are we in fact justified in accepting? Note that the first question does not ask for an "analysis" or "meaning" of the term "justified belief". And it is generally assumed, even if not always explicitly stated, that not just any statement of a necessary and sufficient condition for a belief to be justified will do. The implicit requirement has been that the stated conditions must constitute "criteria" of justified belief, and for this it is necessary that the conditions be stated *without the use of epistemic terms.* Thus, formulating conditions of justified belief in such terms

as "adequate evidence", "sufficient ground", "good reason", "beyond a reasonable doubt", and so on, would be merely to issue a promissory note redeemable only when these epistemic terms are themselves explained in a way that accords with the requirement.[2]

This requirement, while it points in the right direction, does not go far enough. What is crucial is this: *the criteria of justified belief must be formulated on the basis of descriptive or naturalistic terms alone, without the use of any evaluative or normative ones, whether epistemic or of another kind.*[3] Thus, an analysis of justified belief that makes use of such terms as "intellectual requirement"[4] and "having a right to be sure"[5] would not satisfy this generalized condition; although such an analysis can be informative and enlightening about the inter-relationships of these normative concepts, it will not, on the present conception, count as a statement of *criteria* of justified belief, unless of course these terms are themselves provided with nonnormative criteria. What is problematic, therefore, about the use of epistemic terms in stating criteria of justified belief is not its possible circularity in the usual sense; rather it is the fact that these epistemic terms are themselves essentially normative. We shall later discuss the rationale of this strengthened requirement.

As many philosophers have observed,[6] the two questions we have set forth, one about the criteria of justified belief and the other about what we can be said to know according to those criteria, constrain each other. Although some philosophers have been willing to swallow skepticism just because what we regard as correct criteria of justified belief are seen to lead inexorably to the conclusion that none, or very few, of our beliefs are justified, the usual presumption is that our answer to the first question should leave our epistemic situation largely unchanged. That is to say, it is expected to turn out that according to the criteria of justified belief we come to accept, we know, or are justified in believing, pretty much what we reflectively think we know or are entitled to believe.

Whatever the exact history, it is evident that the concept of justification has come to take center stage in our reflections on the nature of knowledge. And apart from history, there is a simple reason for our preoccupation with justification: it is the only specifically epistemic component in the classic tripartite conception of knowledge. Neither belief nor truth is a specifically epistemic notion: belief is a psychological concept and truth a semantical-metaphysical one. These concepts may have an implicit epistemological dimension, but if they do, it is likely to be through their involvement with essentially normative epistemic notions like justification, evidence, and rationality. Moreover, justification is what makes knowledge itself a normative concept. On surface at least, neither truth nor belief is normative or evaluative (I shall argue below, though, that belief does have an essential normative dimension). But justification manifestly is normative. If a belief is justified for us, then it is *permissible* and *reasonable,* from the epistemic point of view, for us to hold it, and it would be *epistemically irresponsible* to hold beliefs that contradict it. If we consider believing or accepting a proposition to be an "action" in an appropriate sense, belief justification would then be a special case of justification of action, which in its broadest terms is the central concern of normative ethics. Just as it is the business of normative ethics to delineate the conditions under which acts and decisions are justified from the moral point of view, so it is the business of epistemology to identify and analyze the conditions under which beliefs, and perhaps other propositional attitudes, are justified from the epistemological point of view. It probably is only an historical accident that we standardly speak of "normative ethics" but not of "normative epistemology". Epistemology is a normative discipline as much as, and in the same sense as, normative ethics.

We can summarize our discussion thus far in the following points: that justification is a central concept of our epistemological tradition, that justification, as it is understood in this tradition, is a normative concept, and in consequence that epistemology itself is a normative inquiry whose principal aim is a systematic study of the conditions of justified belief. I take it that these points are uncontroversial, although of course there could be disagreement about the details—for example, about what it means to say a concept or theory is "normative" or "evaluative".

2. THE FOUNDATIONALIST STRATEGY

In order to identify the target of the naturalistic critique—in particular, Quine's—it will be useful to take a brief look at the classic response to the epistemological program set forth by Descartes. Descartes' approach to the problem of justification is a familiar story, at least as the textbook tells it: it takes the form of what is now commonly called "foundationalism". The foundationalist strategy is to divide the task of explaining justification into two stages: first, to identify a set of beliefs that are "directly" justified in that they are justified without deriving their justified status from that of any other belief, and then to explain how other beliefs may be "indirectly" or "inferentially" justified by standing in an appropriate relation to those already justified. Directly justified beliefs, or "basic beliefs", are to constitute the foundation upon which the superstructure of "nonbasic" or "derived" beliefs is to rest. What beliefs then are directly justified, according to Descartes? Subtleties aside, he claimed that beliefs about our own present conscious states are among them. In what does their justification consist? What is it about these beliefs that make them directly justified? Somewhat simplistically again, Descartes' answer is that they are justified because they are *indubitable,* that the attentive and reflective mind *cannot but assent* to them. How are nonbasic beliefs justified? By "deduction"—that is, by a series of inferential steps, or "intuitions", each of which is indubitable. If, therefore, we take Cartesian indubitability as a psychological notion, Descartes' epistemological theory can be said to meet the desideratum of providing nonepistemic, naturalistic criteria of justified belief.

Descartes' foundationalist program was inherited, in its essential outlines, by the empiricists. In particular, his "mentalism", that beliefs about one's own current mental state are epistemologically basic, went essentially unchallenged by the empiricists and positivists, until this century. Epistemologists have differed from one another chiefly in regard to two questions: first, what else belonged in our corpus of basic beliefs, and second, how the derivation of the non-basic part of our knowledge was to proceed. Even the Logical Positivists were, by and large, foundationalists, although some of them came to renounce Cartesian mentalism in favor of a "physicalistic basis".[7] In fact, the Positivists were foundationalists twice over: for them "observation", whether phenomenological or physical, served not only as the foundation of knowledge but as the foundation of all "cognitive meaning"—that is, as both an epistemological and a semantic foundation.

3. QUINE'S ARGUMENTS

It has become customary for epistemologists who profess allegiance to a "naturalistic" conception of knowledge to pay homage to Quine as the chief contemporary provenance of their inspiration—especially to his influential paper "Epistemology Naturalized".[8] Quine's principal argument in this paper against traditional epistemology is based on the claim that the Cartesian foundationalist program has failed—that the Cartesian "quest for certainty" is "a lost cause". While this claim about the hopelessness of the Cartesian "quest for certainty" is nothing new, using it to discredit the very conception of normative epistemology is new, something that any serious student of epistemology must contend with.

Quine divides the classic epistemological program into two parts: *conceptual reduction* whereby physical terms, including those of theoretical science, are reduced, via definition, to terms referring to phenomenal features of sensory experience, and *doctrinal reduction* whereby truths about the physical world are appropriately obtained from truths about sensory experience. The "appropriateness" just alluded to refers to the requirement that the favored epistemic status ("certainty" for classic epistemologists, according to Quine) of our basic beliefs be transferred, essentially undiminished, to derived beliefs, a necessary requirement if the derivational process is to yield knowledge from knowledge. What

derivational methods have this property of preserving epistemic status? Perhaps there are none, given our proneness to err in framing derivations as in anything else, not to mention the possibility of lapses of attention and memory in following lengthy proofs. But logical deduction comes as close to being one as any; it can at least be relied on to transmit truth, if not epistemic status. It could perhaps be argued that no method can preserve certainty unless it preserves (or is known to preserve) truth; and if this is so, logical deduction is the only method worth considering. I do not know whether this was the attitude of most classic epistemologists; but Quine assumes that if deduction doesn't fill their bill, nothing will.

Quine sees the project of conceptual reduction as culminating in Carnap's *Der Logische Aufbau der Welt*. As Quine sees it, Carnap "came nearest to executing" the conceptual half of the classic epistemological project. But coming close is not good enough. Because of the holistic manner in which empirical meaning is generated by experience, no reduction of the sort Carnap and others so eagerly sought could in principle be completed. For definitional reduction requires point-to-point meaning relations[9] between physical terms and phenomenal terms, something that Quine's holism tells us cannot be had. The second half of the program, doctrinal reduction, is in no better shape; in fact, it was the one to stumble first, for, according to Quine, its impossibility was decisively demonstrated long before the *Aufbau*, by Hume in his celebrated discussion of induction. The "Humean predicament" shows that theory cannot be logically deduced from observation; there simply is no way of deriving theory from observation that will transmit the latter's epistemic status intact to the former.

I don't think anyone wants to disagree with Quine in these claims. It is not possible to "validate" science on the basis of sensory experience, if "validation" means justification through logical deduction. Quine of course does not deny that our theories depend on observation for evidential support; he has said that sensory evidence is the only evidence there is. To be sure, Quine's argument against the possibility of conceptual reduction has a new twist: the application of his "holism". But his conclusion is no surprise; "translational phenomenalism" has been moribund for many years.[10] And, as Quine himself notes, his argument against the doctrinal reduction, the "quest for certainty" is only a restatement of Hume's "skeptical" conclusions concerning induction: induction after all is not deduction. Most of us are inclined, I think, to view the situation Quine describes with no great alarm, and I rather doubt that these conclusions of Quine's came as news to most epistemologists when "Epistemology Naturalized" was first published. We are tempted to respond: of course we can't define physical concepts in terms of sense-data; of course observation "underdetermines" theory. That is why observation is observation and not theory.

So it is agreed on all hands that the classical epistemological project, conceived as one of deductively validating physical knowledge from indubitable sensory data, cannot succeed. But what is the moral of this failure? What should be its philosophical lesson to us? Having noted the failure of the Cartesian program, Quine goes on:[11]

> The stimulation of his sensory receptors is all the evidence anybody has had to go on, ultimately, in arriving at his picture of the world. Why not just see how this construction really proceeds? Why not settle for psychology? Such a surrender of the epistemological burden to psychology is a move that was disallowed in earlier times as circular reasoning. If the epistemologist's goal is validation of the grounds of empirical science, he defeats his purpose by using psychology or other empirical science in the validation. However, such scruples against circularity have little point once we have stopped dreaming of deducing science from observation. If we are out simply to understand the link between observation and science, we are well advised to use any available information, including that provided by the very science whose link with observation we are seeking to understand.

And Quine has the following to say about the failure of Carnap's reductive program in the *Aufbau*:[12]

> To relax the demand for definition, and settle for a kind of reduction that does not eliminate, is to renounce the last remaining advantage that we supposed rational reconstruction to have over straight psychology; namely, the advantage

of translational reduction. If all we hope for is a reconstruction that links science to experience in explicit ways short of translation, then it would seem more sensible to settle for psychology. Better to discover how science is in fact developed and learned than to fabricate a fictitious structure to a similar effect.

If a task is entirely hopeless, if we know it cannot be executed, no doubt it is rational to abandon it; we would be better off doing something else that has some hope of success. We can agree with Quine that the "validation"—that is, logical deduction—of science on the basis of observation cannot be had; so it is rational to abandon this particular epistemological program, if indeed it ever was a program that anyone seriously undertook. But Quine's recommendations go further. In particular, there are two aspects of Quine's proposals that are of special interest to us: first, he is not only advising us to quit the program of "validating science", but urging us to take up another specific project, an empirical psychological study of our cognitive processes; second, he is also claiming that this new program replaces the old, that both programs are part of something appropriately called "epistemology". Naturalized epistemology is to be a kind of epistemology after all, a "successor subject"[13] to classical epistemology.

How should we react to Quine's urgings? What should be our response? The Cartesian project of validating science starting from the indubitable foundation of first-person psychological reports (perhaps with the help of certain indubitable first principles) is not the whole of classical epistemology—or so it would seem at first blush. In our characterization of classical epistemology, the Cartesian program was seen as one possible response to the problem of epistemic justification, the two-part project of identifying the criteria of epistemic justification and determining what beliefs are in fact justified according to those criteria. In urging "naturalized epistemology" on us, Quine is not suggesting that we give up the Cartesian foundationalist solution and explore others within the same framework[14]—perhaps, to adopt some sort of "coherentist" strategy, or to require of our basic beliefs only some degree of "initial credibility" rather than

Cartesian certainty, or to permit some sort of probabilistic derivation in addition to deductive derivation of non-basic knowledge, or to consider the use of special rules of evidence, like Chisholm's "principles of evidence",[15] or to give up the search for a derivational process that transmits undiminished certainty in favor of one that can transmit diminished but still useful degrees of justification. Quine's proposal is more radical than that. He is asking us to set aside the entire framework of justification-centered epistemology. That is what is new in Quine's proposals. Quine is asking us to put in its place a purely descriptive, causal-nomological science of human cognition.[16]

How should we characterize in general terms the difference between traditional epistemological programs, such as foundationalism and coherence theory, on the one hand and Quine's program of naturalized epistemology on the other? Quine's stress is on the *factual* and *descriptive* character of his program; he says, "Why not see how [the construction of theory from observation] *actually proceeds?* Why not settle for psychology?";[17] again, "Better to *discover how science is in fact developed and learned than.* . . ."[18] We are given to understand that in contrast traditional epistemology is not a descriptive, factual inquiry. Rather, it is an attempt at a "validation" or "rational reconstruction" of science. Validation, according to Quine, proceeds via deduction, and rational reconstruction via definition. However, their *point* is justificatory—that is, to rationalize our sundry knowledge claims. So Quine is asking us to set aside what is "rational" in rational reconstruction.

Thus, it is normativity that Quine is asking us to repudiate. Although Quine does not explicitly characterize traditional epistemology as "normative" or "prescriptive", his meaning is unmistakable. Epistemology is to be "a chapter of psychology", a law-based predictive-explanatory theory, like any other theory within empirical science; its principal job is to see how human cognizers develop theories (their "picture of the world") from observation ("the stimulation of their sensory receptors"). Epistemology is to go out of the business of justification. We earlier characterized traditional epistemology as essentially normative; we see why Quine wants us to reject it. Quine is urging us to replace a normative theory of cognition with a descriptive science.

4. LOSING KNOWLEDGE FROM EPISTEMOLOGY

If justification drops out of epistemology; knowledge itself drops out of epistemology. For our concept of knowledge is inseparably tied to that of justification. As earlier noted, knowledge itself is a normative notion. Quine's nonnormative, naturalized epistemology has no room for our concept of knowledge. It is not surprising that, in describing naturalized epistemology, Quine seldom talks about knowledge; instead, he talks about "science" and "theories" and "representations". Quine would have us investigate how sensory stimulation "leads" to "theories" and "representation" of the world. I take it that within the traditional scheme these "theories" and "representations" correspond to beliefs, or systems of beliefs; thus, what Quine would have us do is to investigate how sensory stimulation leads to the formation of beliefs about the world.

But in what sense of "lead"? I take it that Quine has in mind a causal or nomological sense. He is urging us to develop a theory, an empirical theory, that uncovers lawful regularities governing the processes through which organisms come to develop beliefs about their environment as a causal result of having their sensory receptors stimulated in certain ways. Quine says:[19]

> [Naturalized epistemology] studies a natural phenomenon, viz., a physical human subject. This human subject is accorded experimentally controlled input—certain patterns of irradiation in assorted frequencies, for instance—and in the fullness of time the subject delivers as output a description of the three-dimensional external world and its history. *The relation between the meager input and torrential output* is a relation that we are prompted to study for somewhat the same reasons that always prompted epistemology; namely, in order to see *how evidence relates to theory,* and in what ways one's theory of nature transcends any available evidence.

The relation Quine speaks of between "meager input" and "torrential output" is a causal relation; at least it is qua causal relation that the naturalized epistemologist investigates it. It is none of the naturalized epistemologist's business to assess whether, and to what degree, the input "justifies" the output, how a given irradiation of the subject's retinas makes it "reasonable" or "rational" for the subject to emit certain representational output. His interest is strictly causal and nomological: he wants us to look for patterns of lawlike dependencies characterizing the input-output relations for this particular organism and others of a like physical structure.

If this is right, it makes Quine's attempt to relate his naturalized epistemology to traditional epistemology look at best lame. For in what sense is the study of causal relationships between physical stimulation of sensory receptors and the resulting cognitive output a way of "seeing how evidence relates to theory" in an epistemologically relevant sense? The causal relation between sensory input and cognitive output is a relation between "evidence" and "theory"; however, it is not an *evidential relation*. This can be seen from the following consideration: the nomological patterns that Quine urges us to look for are certain to vary from species to species, depending on the particular way each biological (and possibly non-biological) species processes information, but the evidential relation in its proper normative sense must abstract from such factors and concern itself only with the degree to which evidence supports hypothesis.

In any event, the concept of evidence is inseparable from that of justification. When we talk of "evidence" in an epistemological sense we are talking about justification: one thing is "evidence" for another just in case the first tends to enhance the reasonableness or justification of the second. And such evidential relations hold in part because of the "contents" of the items involved, not merely because of the causal or nomological connections between them. A strictly nonnormative concept of evidence is not our concept of evidence; it is something that we do not understand.[20]

None of us, I think, would want to quarrel with Quine about the interest or importance of the psychological study of how our sensory input causes our epistemic output. This is only to say that the study of human (or other kinds of) cognition is of interest. That isn't our difficulty; our difficulty is whether, and in what sense, pursuing Quine's "epistemology" is a way of doing epistemology—that is, a way of studying "how evidence relates to theory". Perhaps, Quine's recommendation that we discard justification-centered epistemology is worth pondering; and his exhortation to take up the study of psychology perhaps deserves to be heeded also. What is mysterious is why this recommendation has to be coupled with the rejection of normative epistemology (if normative epistemology is not a possible inquiry, why shouldn't the would-be epistemologist turn to, say, hydrodynamics or ornithology rather than psychology?). But of course Quine is saying more; he is saying that an understandable, if misguided, motivation (that is, seeing "how evidence relates to theory") does underlie our proclivities for indulgence in normative epistemology, but that we would be better served by a scientific study of human cognition than normative epistemology.

But it is difficult to see how an "epistemology" that has been purged of normativity, one that lacks an appropriate normative concept of justification or evidence, can have anything to do with the concerns of traditional epistemology. And unless naturalized epistemology and classical epistemology share some of their central concerns, it's difficult to see how one could *replace* the other, or be a way (a better way) of doing the other.[21] To be sure, they both investigate "how evidence relates to theory". But putting the matter this way can be misleading, and has perhaps misled Quine: the two disciplines do not investigate the same relation. As lately noted, normative epistemology is concerned with the evidential relation properly so-called—that is, the relation of justification—and Quine's naturalized epistemology is meant to study the causal-nomological relation. For epistemology to go out of the business of justification is for it to go out of business.

5. BELIEF ATTRIBUTION AND RATIONALITY

Perhaps we have said enough to persuade ourselves that Quine's naturalized epistemology, while it may be a legitimate scientific inquiry, is not a kind of epistemology, and, therefore, that the question whether it is a better kind of epistemology cannot arise. In reply, however, it might be said that there was a sense in which Quine's epistemology and traditional epistemology could be viewed as sharing a common subject matter, namely this: they both concern beliefs or "representations". The only difference is that the former investigates their causal histories and connections whereas the latter is concerned with their evidential or justificatory properties and relations. This difference, if Quine is right, leads to another (so continues the reply): the former is a feasible inquiry, the latter is not.

I now want to take my argument a step further: I shall argue that the concept of belief is itself an essentially normative one, and in consequence that if normativity is wholly excluded from naturalized epistemology it cannot even be thought of as being about beliefs. That is, if naturalized epistemology is to be a science of beliefs properly so called, it must presuppose a normative concept of belief.

Briefly, the argument is this. In order to implement Quine's program of naturalized epistemology, we shall need to identify, and individuate, the input and output of cognizers. The input, for Quine, consists of physical events ("the stimulation of sensory receptors") and the output is said to be a "theory" or "picture of the world"—that is, a set of "representations" of the cognizer's environment. Let us focus on the output. In order to study the sensory input-cognitive output relations for the given cognizer, therefore, we must find out what "representations" he has formed as a result of the particular stimulations that have been applied to his sensory transducers. Setting aside the jargon, what we need to be able to do is to attribute *beliefs,* and other contentful intentional states, to the cognizer. But belief attribution ultimately requires a "radical interpretation" of the cognizer, of his speech and intentional states; that is, we must construct an "interpretive theory" that simultaneously assigns meanings to his utterances and attributes to him beliefs and other propositional attitudes.[22]

Even a cursory consideration indicates that such an interpretation cannot begin—we cannot get a foothold in our subject's realm of meanings and intentional states—unless we assume his total system of beliefs and other propositional attitudes to be largely and essentially rational and coherent. As Davidson has emphasized, a given belief has the content it has in part because of its location in a network of other beliefs and propositional attitudes; and what at bottom grounds this network is the evidential relation, a relation that regulates what is reasonable to believe given other beliefs one holds. That is, unless our cognizer is a "rational being", a being whose cognitive "output" is regulated and constrained by norms of rationality—typically, these norms holistically constrain his propositional attitudes in virtue of their contents—we cannot intelligibly interpret his "output" as consisting of beliefs. Conversely, if we are unable to interpret our subject's meanings and propositional attitudes in a way that satisfies a minimal standard of rationality, there is little reason to regard him as a "cognizer", a being that forms representations and constructs theories. This means that there is a sense of "rational" in which the expression "rational belief" is redundant; every belief must be rational in certain minimal ways. It is not important for the purposes of the present argument what these minimal standards of rationality are; the only point that matters is that unless the output of our cognizer is subject to evaluation in accordance with norms of rationality, that output cannot be considered as consisting of beliefs and hence cannot be the object of an epistemological inquiry, whether plain or naturalized.

We can separate the core of these considerations from controversial issues involving the so-called "principle of charity", minimal rationality, and other matters in the theory of radical interpretation. What is crucial is this: for the interpretation and attribution of beliefs to be possible, not only must we assume the overall rationality of cognizers, but also we must continually evaluate and re-evaluate the putative beliefs of a cognizer in their evidential relationship to one another and other propositional attitudes. It is not merely that belief attribution requires the umbrella assumption about the overall rationality of cognizers. Rather, the point is that *belief attribution requires belief evaluation,* in accordance with normative standards of evidence and justification. If this is correct, rationality in its broad and fundamental sense is not an optional property of beliefs, a virtue that some beliefs may enjoy and others lack; it is a precondition of the attribution and individuation of belief—that is, a property without which the concept of belief would be unintelligible and pointless.

Two objections might be raised to counter these considerations. First, one might argue that at best they show only that the normativity of belief is an epistemological assumption—that we need to assume the rationality and coherence of belief systems when we are trying to *find out* what beliefs to attribute to a cognizer. It does not follow from this epistemological point, the objection continues, that the concept of belief is itself normative.[23] In replying to this objection, we can by-pass the entire issue of whether the rationality assumption concerns only the epistemology of belief attribution. Even if this premise (which I think is incorrect) is granted, the point has already been made. For it is an essential part of the business of naturalized epistemology, as a theory of how beliefs are formed as a result of sensory stimulation, to *find out* what particular beliefs the given cognizers have formed. But this is precisely what cannot be done, if our considerations show anything at all, unless the would-be naturalized epistemologist continually evaluates the putative beliefs of his subjects in regard to their rationality and coherence, subject to the overall constraint of the assumption that the cognizers are largely rational. The naturalized epistemologist cannot dispense with normative concepts or disengage himself from valuational activities.

Second, it might be thought that we could simply avoid these considerations stemming from belief attribution by refusing to think of cognitive output as consisting of "beliefs", namely as states having propositional contents. The "representations" Quine speaks of should be taken as appropriate neural states, and this means that all we need is to be able to discern neural states of organisms. This requires only neurophysiology and the like, not the normative theory of rational belief. My reply takes the form of a dilemma: either the "appropriate" neural states are identified by seeing how they correlate with beliefs,[24] in which case we still need to contend with the problem of radical interpretation, or beliefs are entirely by-passed. In the latter case, belief, along with justification, drops out of Quinean epistemology, and it is unclear in what sense we are left with an inquiry that has anything to do with knowledge.[25]

6. THE "PSYCHOLOGISTIC" APPROACH TO EPISTEMOLOGY

Many philosophers now working in theory of knowledge have stressed the importance of systematic psychology to philosophical epistemology. Reasons proffered for this are various, and so are the conceptions of the proper relationship between psychology and epistemology.[26] But they are virtually unanimous in their rejection of what they take to be the epistemological tradition of Descartes and its modern embodiments in philosophers like Russell, C. I. Lewis, Roderick Chisholm, and A. J. Ayer; and they are united in their endorsement of the naturalistic approach of Quine we have been considering. Traditional epistemology is often condemned as "aprioristic", and as having lost sight of human knowledge as a product of natural causal processes and its function in the survival of the organism and the species. Sometimes, the adherents of the traditional approach are taken to task for their implicit antiscientific bias or indifference to the new developments in psychology and related disciplines. Their own approach in contrast is hailed as "naturalistic" and "scientific", better attuned to significant advances in the relevant scientific fields such as "cognitive science" and "neuroscience", promising philosophical returns far richer than what the aprioristic method of traditional epistemology has been able to deliver. We shall here briefly consider how this new naturalism in epistemology is to be understood in relation to the classic epistemological program and Quine's naturalized epistemology.

Let us see how one articulate proponent of the new approach explains the distinctiveness of his position vis-à-vis that of the traditional epistemologists. According to Philip Kitcher, the approach he rejects is characterized by an "apsychologistic" attitude that takes the difference between knowledge and true belief—that is, justification—to consist in "ways which are independent of the causal antecedents of a subject's states".[27] Kitcher writes:[28]

> . . . we can present the heart of [the apsychologistic approach] by considering the way in which it would tackle the question of whether a person's true belief that *p* counts as knowledge that *p*. The idea would be to

disregard the psychological life of the subject, looking just at the various propositions she believes. If p is 'connected in the right way' to other propositions which are believed, then we count the subject as knowing that p. Of course, apsychologistic epistemology will have to supply a criterion for propositions to be 'connected in the right way' . . . but proponents of this view of knowledge will emphasize that the criterion is to be given in *logical* terms. We are concerned with logical relations among propositions, not with psychological relations among mental states.

On the other hand, the psychologistic approach considers the crucial difference between knowledge and true belief—that is, epistemic justification—to turn on "the factors which produced the belief", focusing on "processes which produce belief, processes which will always contain, at their latter end, psychological events."[29]

It is not entirely clear from this characterization whether a psychologistic theory of justification is to be *prohibited* from making *any* reference to logical relations among belief contents (it is difficult to believe how a theory of justification respecting such a blanket prohibition could succeed); nor is it clear whether, conversely, an apsychologistic theory will be permitted to refer at all to beliefs qua psychological states, or exactly what it is for a theory to do so. But such points of detail are unimportant here; it is clear enough, for example, that Goldman's proposal to explicate justified belief as belief generated by a reliable belief-forming process[30] nicely fits Kitcher's characterization of the psychologistic approach. This account, one form of the so-called "reliability theory" of justification, probably was what Kitcher had in mind when he was formulating his general characterization of epistemological naturalism. However, another influential form of the reliability theory does not qualify under Kitcher's characterization. This is Armstrong's proposal to explain the difference between knowledge and true belief, at least for non-inferential knowledge, in terms of "a *law-like connection* between the state of affairs [of a subject's believing that p] and the state of affairs that makes 'p' true such that, given the state of affairs [of the subject's believing that p], it must be the case that p."[31] There is here no reference to the causal *antecedents*

of beliefs, something that Kitcher requires of apsychologistic theories.

Perhaps, Kitcher's preliminary characterization needs to be broadened and sharpened. However, a salient characteristic of the naturalistic approach has already emerged, which we can put as follows: justification is to be characterized in terms of *causal* or *nomolocal* connections involving beliefs as *psychological states* or *processes,* and not in terms of the *logical* properties or relations pertaining to the *contents* of these beliefs.[32]

If we understand current epistemological naturalism in this way, how closely is it related to Quine's conception of naturalized epistemology? The answer, I think, is obvious: not very closely at all. In fact, it seems a good deal closer to the Cartesian tradition than to Quine. For, as we saw, the difference that matters between Quine's epistemological program and the traditional program is the former's total renouncement of the latter's normativity, its rejection of epistemology as a normative inquiry. The talk of "replacing" epistemology with psychology is irrelevant and at best misleading, though it could give us a momentary relief from a sense of deprivation. When one abandons justification and other valuational concepts, one abandons the entire framework of normative epistemology. What remains is a descriptive empirical theory of human cognition which, if Quine has his way, will be entirely devoid of the notion of justification or any other evaluative concept.

As I take it, this is not what most advocates of epistemological naturalism are aiming at. By and large they are not Quinean eliminativists in regard to justification, and justification in its full-fledged normative sense continues to play a central role in their epistemological reflections. Where they differ from their nonnaturalist adversaries is the specific way in which criteria of justification are to be formulated. Naturalists and nonnaturalists ("apsychologists") can agree that these criteria must be stated in descriptive terms—that is, without the use of epistemic or any other kind of normative terms. According to Kitcher, an apsychologistic theory of justification would state them primarily in terms of *logical* properties and relations holding for propositional contents of beliefs, whereas the psychologistic approach advocates the exclusive use of *causal* properties and relations holding for beliefs as events or states. Many traditional epistemologists may prefer criteria that confer upon a cognizer a position of special privilege and responsibility with regard to the epistemic status of his beliefs, whereas most self-avowed naturalists prefer "objective" or "externalist" criteria with no such special privileges for the cognizer. But these differences are among those that arise within the familiar normative framework, and are consistent with the exclusion of normative terms in the statement of the criteria of justification.

Normative ethics can serve as a useful model here. To claim that basic ethical terms, like "good" and "right", are *definable* on the basis of descriptive or naturalistic terms is one thing; to insist that it is the business of normative ethics to provide *conditions* or *criteria* for "good" and "right" in descriptive or naturalistic terms is another. One may properly reject the former, the so-called "ethical naturalism", as many moral philosophers have done, and hold the latter; there is no obvious inconsistency here. G. E. Moore is a philosopher who did just that. As is well known, he was a powerful critic of ethical naturalism, holding that goodness is a "simple" and "nonnatural" property. At the same time, he held that a thing's being good "follows" from its possessing certain naturalistic properties. He wrote:[33]

> I should never have thought of suggesting that goodness was 'non-natural', unless I had supposed that it was 'derivative' in the sense that, whenever a thing is good (in the sense in question) its goodness . . . 'depends on the presence of certain non-ethical characteristics' possessed by the thing in question: I have always supposed that it did so 'depend', in the sense that, if a thing is good (in my sense), then that it is so *follows* from the fact that it possesses certain natural intrinsic properties. . . .

It makes sense to think of these "natural intrinsic properties" from which a thing's being good is thought to follow as constituting naturalistic criteria of goodness, or at least pointing to the existence of such criteria. One can reject ethical naturalism, the doctrine that ethical concepts are definitionally eliminable in favor of naturalistic terms, and at the same time hold that ethical properties, or the ascription of ethical terms, must be governed by naturalistic criteria. It is clear, then, that we are here using "naturalism" ambiguously in "epistemological naturalism" and "ethical naturalism". In our present usage, epistemological naturalism does not include (nor does it necessarily exclude) the claim that epistemic terms are definitionally reducible to naturalistic terms. (Quine's naturalism is eliminative, though it is not a definitional eliminativism.)

If, therefore, we locate the split between Quine and traditional epistemology at the descriptive vs. normative divide, then currently influential naturalism in epistemology is not likely to fall on Quine's side. On this descriptive vs. normative issue, one can side with Quine in one of two ways: first, one rejects, with Quine, the entire justification-based epistemological program; or second, like ethical naturalists but unlike Quine, one believes that epistemic concepts are naturalistically definable. I doubt that very many epistemological naturalists will embrace either of these alternatives.[34]

7. EPISTEMIC SUPERVENIENCE– OR WHY NORMATIVE EPISTEMOLOGY IS POSSIBLE

But why should we think that there *must be* naturalistic criteria of justified belief and other terms of epistemic appraisal? If we take the discovery and systematization of such criteria to be the central task of normative epistemology, is there any reason to think that this task can be fruitfully pursued, that normative epistemology is a possible field of inquiry? Quine's point is that it is not. We have already noted the limitation of Quine's negative arguments in "Epistemology Naturalized", but is there a positive reason for thinking that normative epistemology is a viable program? One could consider a similar question about the possibility of normative ethics.

I think there is a short and plausible initial answer, although a detailed defense of it would involve complex general issues about norms and values. The short answer is this: we believe in the supervenience of epistemic properties on naturalistic ones, and more generally, in the supervenience of all valuational and normative properties on naturalistic conditions. This comes out in various ways. We think, with R. M. Hare,[35] that if two persons or acts coincide in all descriptive or naturalistic details, they cannot differ in respect of being good or right, or any other valuational aspects. We also think that if something is "good"—a "good car", "good drop shot", "good argument"—then that must be so "in virtue of" its being a "certain way", that is, its having certain "factual properties". Being a good car, say, cannot be a brute and ultimate fact: a car is good *because* it has a certain contextually indicated set of properties having to do with performance, reliability, comfort, styling, economy, etc. The same goes for justified belief: if a belief is justified, that must be so *because* it has certain factual, nonepistemic properties, such as perhaps that it is "indubitable", that it is seen to be entailed by another belief that is independently justified, that it is appropriately caused by perceptual experience, or whatever. That it is a justified belief cannot be a brute fundamental fact unrelated to the kind of belief it is. There must be a *reason* for it, and this reason must be grounded in the factual descriptive properties of that particular belief. Something like this, I think, is what we believe.

Two important themes underlie these convictions: first, values, though perhaps not reducible to facts, must be "consistent" with them in that objects that are indiscernible in regard to fact must be indiscernible in regard to value; second, there must be nonvaluational "reasons" or "grounds" for the attribution of values, and these "reasons" or "grounds" must be *generalizable*—that is, they are covered by *rules* or *norms*. These two ideas correspond to "weak supervenience" and "strong supervenience" that I have discussed elsewhere.[36] Belief in the supervenience of value upon fact, arguably, is fundamental to the very concepts of value and valuation.[37] Any valuational concept, to be significant, must be governed by a set of criteria, and these criteria must ultimately rest on factual characteristics and relationships of objects and events being evaluated. There is something deeply incoherent about the idea of an infinitely descending series of valuational concepts, each depending on the one below it as its criterion of application.[38]

It seems to me, therefore, that epistemological supervenience is what underlies our belief in the possibility of normative epistemology, and that we do not need new inspirations from the sciences to acknowledge the existence of naturalistic criteria for epistemic and other valuational concepts. The case of normative ethics is entirely parallel: belief in the possibility of normative ethics is rooted in the belief that moral properties and relations are supervenient upon non-moral ones. Unless we are prepared to disown normative ethics as a viable philosophical inquiry, we had better recognize normative epistemology as one, too.[39] We should note, too, that epistemology is likely to parallel normative ethics in regard to the degree to which scientific results are relevant or useful to its development.[40] Saying this of course leaves large room for disagreement concerning how relevant and useful, if at all, empirical psychology of human motivation and action can be to the development and confirmation of normative ethical theories.[41] In any event, once the normativity of epistemology is clearly taken note of, it is no surprise that epistemology and normative ethics share the same metaphilosophical fate. Naturalized epistemology makes no more, and no less, sense than naturalized normative ethics.[42]

NOTES

1. In making these remarks I am only repeating the familiar textbook history of philosophy; however, what *our* textbooks say about the history of a philosophical concept has much to do with *our* understanding of that concept.

2. Alvin Goldman explicitly states this requirement as a desideratum of his own analysis of justified belief in "What is Justified Belief?", in George S. Pappas (ed.), *Justification and Knowledge* (Dordrecht: Reidel, 1979), p.1. Roderick M. Chisholm's definition of "being evident" in his *Theory of Knowledge,* 2nd ed. (Englewood Cliffs, N.J.: Prentice-Hall, 1977) does not satisfy this requirement as it rests ultimately on an unanalyzed epistemic concept of one belief being *more reasonable* than another. What does the real "criteriological" work for Chisholm is his "principles of evidence". See especially (A) on p. 73 of *Theory of Knowledge,* which can usefully be regarded as an attempt to provide nonnormative, descriptive conditions for certain types of justified beliefs.

3. The basic idea of this stronger requirement seems implicit in Roderick Firth's notion of "warrant-increasing property" in his "Coherence, Certainty, and Epistemic Priority", *Journal of Philosophy* 61

(1964): 545–57. It seems that William P. Alston has something similar in mind when he says, ". . . like any evaluative property, epistemic justification is a supervenient property, the application of which is based on more fundamental properties" (at this point Alston refers to Firth's paper cited above), in "Two Types of Foundationalism", *Journal of Philosophy* 73 (1976): 165–85 (the quoted remark occurs on p. 170). Although Alston doesn't further explain what he means by "more fundamental properties", the context makes it plausible to suppose that he has in mind nonnormative, descriptive properties. See Section 7 [of this reading] for further discussion.

4. See Chisholm, ibid., p. 14. Here Chisholm refers to a "person's responsibility or duty *qua* intellectual being".

5. This term was used by A. J. Ayer to characterize the difference between lucky guessing and knowing; see *The Problem of Knowledge* (New York & London: Penguin Books, 1956), p. 33.

6. Notably by Chisholm in *Theory of Knowledge,* 1st ed., ch. 4.

7. See Rudolf Carnap, "Testability and Meaning", *Philosophy of Science* 3 (1936), and 4 (1937). We should also note the presence of a strong coherentist streak among some positivists; see, e.g., Carl G. Hempel, "On the Logical Positivists' Theory of Truth", *Analysis* 2 (1935): 49–59, and "Some Remarks on 'Facts' and Propositions", *Analysis* 2 (1935): 93–96.

8. In W. V. Quine, *Ontological Relativity and Other Essays* (New York: Columbia University Press, 1969). Also see his *Word and Object* (Cambridge: MIT Press, 1960); *The Roots of Reference* (La Salle, Ill.: Open Court, 1973); (with Joseph Ullian) *The Web of Belief* (New York: Random House, 1970); and especially "The Nature of Natural Knowledge" in Samuel Guttenplan (ed.), *Mind and Language* (Oxford: Clarendon Press, 1975). See Frederick F. Schmitt's excellent bibliography on naturalistic epistemology in Hilary Kornblith (ed.), *Naturalizing Epistemology* (Cambridge: MIT/Bradford, 1985).

9. Or confirmational relations, given the Positivists' verificationist theory of meaning.

10. I know of no serious defense of it since Ayer's *The Foundations of Empirical Knowledge* (London: Macmillan, 1940).

11. "Epistemology Naturalized", pp. 75–76.

12. Ibid., p. 78.

13. To use an expression of Richard Rorty's in *Philosophy and the Mirror of Nature* (Princeton: Princeton University Press, 1979), p. 11.

14. Elliott Sober makes a similar point: "And on the question of whether the failure of a foundationalist programme shows that questions of justification cannot be answered, it is worth noting that Quine's advice 'Since Carnap's foundationalism failed, why not settle for psychology' carries weight only to the degree that Carnapian epistemology exhausts the possibilities of epistemology", in "Psychologism", *Journal of Theory of Social Behaviour* 8 (1978): 165–91.

15. See Chisholm, *Theory of Knowledge,* 2nd ed., ch. 4.

16. "If we are seeking only the causal mechanism of our knowledge of the external world, and not a justification of that knowledge in terms prior to science . . .", Quine, "Grades of Theoreticity", in L. Foster and J. W. Swanson (eds.), *Experience and Theory* (Amherst: University of Massachusetts Press, 1970), p. 2.

17. Ibid., p. 75. Emphasis added.

18. Ibid., p. 78. Emphasis added.

19. Ibid., p. 83. Emphasis added.

20. But aren't there those who advocate a "causal theory" of evidence or justification? I want to make two brief points about this. First, the nomological or causal input/output relations are not in themselves evidential relations, whether these latter are understood causally or otherwise. Second, a causal theory of evidence attempts to state *criteria* for "e is evidence for h" in causal terms; even if this is successful, it does not necessarily give us a causal "definition" or "reduction" of the concept of evidence. For more details see section 6 below.

21. I am not saying that Quine is under any illusion on this point. My remarks are directed rather at those who endorse Quine without, it seems, a clear appreciation of what is involved.

22. Here I am drawing chiefly on Donald Davidson's writings on radical interpretation. See Essays 9, 10, and 11 in his *Inquiries into Truth and Interpretation* (Oxford: Clarendon Press, 1984). See also David Lewis, "Radical Interpretation", *Synthese* 27 (1974): 331–44.

23. Robert Audi suggested this as a possible objection.

24. For some considerations tending to show that these correlations cannot be lawlike see my "Psychophysical Laws", in Ernest LePore and Brian McLaughlin (eds.), *Actions and Events: Perspectives on the Philosophy of Donald Davidson* (Oxford: Blackwell, 1985).

25. For a more sympathetic account of Quine than mine, see Hilary Kornblith's introductory essay,

"What is Naturalistic Epistemology?", in Kornblith (ed.), *Naturalizing Epistemology*.

26. See for more details Alvin I. Goldman, *Epistemology and Cognition* (Cambridge: Harvard University Press, 1986).

27. *The Nature of Mathematical Knowledge* (New York: Oxford University Press, 1983), p. 14.

28. Ibid.

29. Ibid., p. 13. I should note that Kitcher considers the apsychologistic approach to be an aberration of the twentieth century epistemology, as represented by philosophers like Russell, Moore, C. I. Lewis, and Chisholm, rather than an historical characteristic of the Cartesian tradition. In "The Psychological Turn", *Australasian Journal of Philosophy* 60 (1982): 238–253, Hilary Kornblith gives an analogous characterization of the two approaches to justification; he associates "justification-conferring processes" with the psychologistic approach and "epistemic rules" with the apsychologistic approach.

30. See Goldman, "What is Justified Belief?".

31. David M. Armstrong, *Truth, Belief and Knowledge* (London: Cambridge University Press, 1973), p. 166.

32. The aptness of this characterization of the "apsychologistic" approach for philosophers like Russell, Chisholm, Keith Lehrer, John Pollock, etc. can be debated. Also, there is the issue of "internalism" vs. "externalism" concerning justification, which I believe must be distinguished from the psychologistic vs. apsychologistic division.

33. Moore, "A Reply to My Critics", in P.A. Schilpp (ed.), *The Philosophy of G. E. Moore* (Chicago & Evanston: Open Court, 1942), p. 588.

34. Richard Rorty's claim, which plays a prominent role in his arguments against traditional epistemology in *Philosophy and the Mirror of Nature,* that Locke and other modern epistemologists conflated the normative concept of justification with causal-mechanical concepts is itself based, I believe, on a conflation of just the kind I am describing here. See Rorty, ibid., pp. 139ff. Again, the critical conflation consists in not seeing that the view, which I believe is correct, that epistemic justification, like any other normative concept, must have factual, naturalistic criteria, is entirely consistent with the rejection of the doctrine, which I think is incorrect, that justification itself *is*, or is *reducible* to, a naturalistic-nonnormative concept.

35. *The Language of Morals* (London: Oxford University Press, 1952), p.145.

36. See "Concepts of Supervenience", *Philosophy and Phenomenological Research* 65 (1984): 153–176.

37. Ernest Sosa, too, considers epistemological supervenience as a special case of the supervenience of valuational properties on naturalistic conditions, in "The Foundation of Foundationalism", *Nous* 14 (1980): 547–64; especially p. 551. See also James Van Cleve's instructive discussion in his "Epistemic Supervenience and the Circle of Belief", *The Monist* 68 (1985): 90–104; especially, pp. 97–99.

38. Perhaps one could avoid this kind of criteriological regress by embracing directly apprehended valuational properties (as in ethical intuitionism) on the basis of which criteria for other valuational properties could be formulated. The denial of the supervenience of valuational concepts on factual characteristics, however, would sever the essential connection between value and fact on which, it seems, the whole point of our valuational activities depends. In the absence of such supervenience, the very notion of valuation would lose its significance and relevance. The elaboration of these points, however, would have to wait for another occasion; but see Van Cleve's paper cited in the preceding note for more details.

39. Quine will not disagree with this: he will "naturalize" them both. For his views on values see "The Nature of Moral Values" in Alvin I. Goldman and Jaegwon Kim (eds.), *Values and Morals* (Dordrecht: Reidel, 1978). For a discussion of the relationship between epistemic and ethical concepts see Roderick Firth, "Are Epistemic Concepts Reducible to Ethical Concepts?" in the same volume.

40. For discussions of this and related issues see Goldman, *Epistemology and Cognition*.

41. For a detailed development of a normative ethical theory that exemplifies the view that it is crucially relevant, see Richard B. Brandt, *A Theory of the Good and the Right* (Oxford: The Clarendon Press, 1979).

42. An early version of this paper was read at a meeting of the Korean Society for Analytic Philosophy in 1984 in Seoul. An expanded version was presented at a symposium at the Western Division meetings of the American Philosophical Association in April, 1985, and at the epistemology conference at Brown University in honor of Roderick Chisholm in 1986. I am grateful to Richard Foley and Robert Audi who presented helpful comments at the APA session and the Chisholm Conference respectively. I am also indebted to Terence Horgan and Robert Meyers for helpful comments and suggestions.

ROBERT ALMEDER

On Naturalizing Epistemology

I. INTRODUCTION

There are three distinct forms of naturalized epistemology. The first form asserts that the only legitimate questions about the nature of human knowledge are those we can answer in natural science. So described, naturalized epistemology is a branch of natural science wherein the questions asked about the nature of human knowledge make sense only because they admit of resolution under the methods of such natural sciences as biology and psychology. Characterized in this way, naturalized epistemology consists in empirically describing and scientifically explaining how our various beliefs originate, endure, deteriorate or grow. Unlike traditional epistemology, this form of naturalized epistemology does not seek to determine whether the claims of natural science are more or less justified. For this reason, it is not "normative" in the way traditional epistemology is normative. Not surprisingly, this first form of naturalized epistemology regards traditional "philosophical" questions about human knowledge, questions whose formulation and solution do not emerge solely from the practice of natural science, as pointless. Accordingly, this first form of naturalized epistemology seeks to *replace* traditional epistemology with the thesis that while we certainly have scientific knowledge, and whatever norms are appropriate for the successful conduct of natural science, we have no philosophical theory of knowledge sitting in judgment over the claims of natural science to determine whether they live up to a philosophically congenial analysis of justification or knowledge. As we shall see shortly, the classical defense of this first form of naturalized epistemology appears in Quine's "*Naturalized Epistemology*".[1]

The second form of naturalized epistemology seeks less to *replace* traditional epistemology than it does to *transform* and supplement it by connecting it with the methods and insights of psychology, biology and cognitive science. In *Epistemology and Cognition*, for example, Alvin Goldman has argued for this second form which allows for traditionally normative elements but is "naturalized" for the reason that the practitioners of natural science, especially biology and psychology, will have the last word on whether anybody knows what they claim to know. For Goldman, although defining human knowledge and other epistemic concepts is legitimately philosophical and traditionally normative, whether anybody knows what they claim to know, and just what cognitive processes are involved, is ultimately a matter we must consign to psychologists or cognitive scientists. Unlike the first form of naturalized epistemology, this second form allows traditional epistemology to sit in judgment on the claims of natural science but the judgment must be made by the practitioners of natural science using the methods of natural science.

The third distinct form of naturalized epistemology simply insists that the method of the natural sciences is the only method for acquiring a proper understanding of the nature of the physical universe. On this view, natural science, and all that it implies, is the most epistemically privileged activity for understanding the nature of the physical world. Adopting this last form of naturalized epistemology is, however, quite consistent with rejecting both of the above forms of naturalized epistemology. This third form is quite compatible with traditional epistemology because it does not seek to *replace* traditional epistemology in the way that the Quine thesis does; nor does it seek to *transform* traditional epistemology by turning the question of who knows what over to psychologists and cognitive scientists in the way that the Goldman thesis does.

At any rate, the most currently pervasive and challenging form of naturalized epistemology is the radically anti-traditional, anti-philosophical thesis offered originally by Quine and recently defended by others. So, in the next few pages we shall focus *solely* on the Quinean thesis and five distinct arguments recently offered in defense of it. Along the way, we will discuss various objections to such a naturalized epistemology, objections proponents of the thesis have recently confronted. Unfortunately, because space here is limited, we will not examine the second and distinct form of naturalized epistemology offered by Alvin Goldman. To do so would involve a long discussion of the merits of the reliabilist theory of justification upon which Goldman's type of naturalism squarely rests.[2]

Finally, the modest conclusion of this paper is that there is no sound argument available for the Quinean form of naturalized epistemology. The immodest conclusion is that any argument proposed for the thesis will be incoherent, and that consequently there is no rational justification for anybody taking such a naturalistic turn.

II. QUINE'S ARGUMENT

In "Epistemology Naturalized", Quine began his defense of naturalized epistemology by asserting that traditional epistemology is concerned with the foundations of science, broadly conceived. As such, it is supposed to show how the foundations of knowledge, whether it be the foundations of mathematics or natural science, reduce to certainty. In short, showing how certainty obtains is the core of traditional epistemology, and this implies that the primary purpose of traditional epistemology is to refute the Cartesian skeptic whose philosophical doubts over whether we can attain certainty has set the program for traditional epistemology.

But, for Quine, traditional epistemology has failed to refute the skeptic, and will never succeed in refuting the skeptic. Mathematics reduces only to set theory and not to logic; and even though this reduction enhances clarity it does nothing by way of establishing certainty because the axioms of set theory have less to recommend them by way of certainty than do most of the mathematical theorems we would derive from them. As he says:

> Reduction in the foundations of mathematics remains mathematically and philosophically fascinating, but it does not do what the

epistemologist would like of it: it does not reveal the ground of mathematical knowledge, it does not show how mathematical certainty is possible. (p. 71).

Moreover, mathematics aside, the attempt to reduce natural knowledge to a foundation in the certainty of statements of sense experience has also failed miserably. Common sense about sensory impressions provides no certainty. And, when it come to justifying our knowledge about truths of nature, Hume taught us that general statements and singular statements about the future do not admit of justification by way of allowing us to ascribe certainty to our beliefs associated with such statements. For Quine, the problem of induction is still with us; "The Humean predicament is the human predicament." (p. 72). As Quine sees it, Hume showed us quite clearly that any attempt to refute the skeptic by uncovering some foundation of certainty associated with sense statements, whether about sense impressions or physical objects, is doomed equally to failure. (p. 72)

This last consideration is crucial because as soon as we accept Quine's rejection of the analytic/synthetic distinction in favor of only synthetic propositions, Hume's argument casts a long despairing shadow over our ever being able to answer the skeptic because such propositions could never be certain anyway. The conclusion Quine draws from all this is that traditional epistemology is dead. There is no "first philosophy". There are no strictly philosophical truths validating the methods of the natural sciences. Nor can we validate in any non-circular way the methods of the natural sciences by appeal to psychology or the methods of the natural sciences. As he says, "If the epistemologist's goal is validation of the grounds of empirical science, he defeats his purpose by using psychology or other empirical science in the validation." (pp. 75–76). We may well have justified beliefs based upon induction, but we cannot have any justified belief that we can have justified beliefs based upon induction. Accordingly, if epistemology is to have any content whatever, it will seek to explain, *via* the methods of natural science, the origin and growth of beliefs we take to be human knowledge and natural science. Construed in this way, epistemology continues as a branch of natural science wherein the only meaningful questions are questions answerable in science by scientists using the methods of natural science. This reconstrual of the nature of epistemology consigns the enterprise to a descriptive psychology whose main function is to describe the origin of our beliefs and the conditions under which we take them to be justified. On this view, all questions and all doubts are scientific and can only be answered or resolved in science by the methods of science. Philosophical discussions on the nature and limits of scientific knowledge, questions that do not lend themselves to resolution via the methods of natural science are simply a part of traditional philosophy that cannot succeed. What can we say about all this?

III. RESPONSE TO QUINE'S ARGUMENT

In "The Significance of Naturalized Epistemology," Barry Stroud criticizes Quine's defense of naturalized epistemology.[3] After a brief description of Quine's position, Stroud argues that Quine is inconsistent for arguing *both* that there is no appeal to scientific knowledge that could non-circularly establish the legitimacy of scientific knowledge in the presence of the traditional epistemological skeptic, *and* in *Roots of Reference* that we should take seriously the project of validating our knowledge of the external world.[4] For Stroud, it was in *Roots of Reference* that Quine came to believe in the coherent use of the resources of natural science to validate the deliverances of natural science. But that would be to countenance the basic question of traditional epistemology when in fact the thrust of Quine's thesis on naturalized epistemology is that such a question forms part of 'first philosophy', which is impossible. Apart from such an inconsistency, Stroud also argues that Quine's attempt to validate scientific inference fails. (p. 81) Stroud's thesis here is that Quine attempts to offer a naturalized defense of science in "The Nature of Natural Knowledge,"[5] but the effort fails because, on Quine's reasoning, we can see how others acquire their beliefs but we are denied thereby any evidence of whether such beliefs are correct beliefs about the world. By implication, we have no reason for thinking our own beliefs are any better off. (p. 81) In commenting on Quine's defense, Stroud says:

Therefore, if we follow Quine's instructions and try to see our own position as 'just like' the position we can find another 'positing' or 'projecting' subject to be in, we will have to view ourselves as we view another subject when we can know nothing more than what is happening at his sensory surfaces and what he believes or is disposed to assert. (p. 81)

His point here is that when we examine how another's beliefs originate, we have no way to look beyond his positing to determine whether his beliefs are true or correct. In that position we never can understand how the subject's knowledge or even true belief is possible. Therefore, we never can understand how our own true beliefs are possible either. Stroud says:

The possibility that our own view of the world is a *mere* projection is what had to be shown not to obtain in order to explain how our knowledge is possible. Unless that challenge has been met, or rejected, we will never understand how our knowledge is possible at all. (p. 83)

. . . if Quine's naturalized epistemology is taken as an answer to the philosophical question of our knowledge of the external world, then I think that for the reasons I have given, no satisfactory explanation is either forthcoming or possible. (p. 83)

He goes on to conclude that if naturalized epistemology is *not* taken as answer to the philosophical question of our knowledge of the external world, and if the question is a legitimate question (and Quine has not shown that it is not) then naturalized epistemology cannot answer the question:

I conclude that even if Quine is right in saying that skeptical doubts are scientific doubts, the scientific source of these doubts has no anti-skeptical force in itself. Nor does it establish the relevance and legitimacy of a scientific epistemology as an answer to the traditional epistemological question. If Quine is confident that a naturalized epistemology can answer the traditional question about knowledge, he must have some other reason for that confidence. He believes that skeptical doubts are scientific doubts and he believes that in resolving those doubts we may make free use of all the scientific knowledge we possess. But if, as he allows, it is possible for the skeptic to argue by *reductio* that science is not known, then it cannot be that second of those beliefs (that a naturalized epistemology is all we need) follows from the first.

Until the traditional philosophical question has been exposed as in some way illegitimate or incoherent, there will always appear to be an intelligible question about human knowledge in general which, as I have argued, a naturalized epistemology cannot answer. And Quine himself seems committed at least to the coherence of that traditional question by his very conception of knowledge. (pp. 85–86)

Stroud's closing remark is that the traditional question has not been demonstrated as illegitimate, and Quine's attempt to resolve skeptical doubts as scientific doubts within science has failed. Moreover, for Stroud, apart from the question of whether Quine succeeded, his effort is predicated on the legitimacy of the traditional question of whether science provides us with knowledge of the external world.

Some naturalized epistemologists will probably disagree with Stroud's analysis and urge that Quine's attempt to validate scientific knowledge is misunderstood when construed as an attempt to establish first philosophy. Better by far that we read Quine as asserting that there is simply no way to validate the deliverance of science as more or less warranted. Whether this last response is adequate, we cannot now discuss.

At any rate, Quine has responded to Stroud with the following remarks:

What then does our overall scientific theory really claim regarding the world? Only that it is somehow structured as to assure the sequences of stimulation that our theory gives us to expect . . . .

In what way then do I see the Humean predicament as persisting? Only in the fallibility of prediction: the the fallibility of induction and the hypthetico-deductive method in anticipating experience.

I have depicted a barren scene. The furniture of our world, the people and sticks and stones along with the electrons and molecules, have dwindled to manners of speaking. And other purported objects would serve as well, and may as well be said already to be doing so.

So it would seem. Yet people, sticks, stones, electrons and molecules are real indeed, on my view, and it is these and no dim proxies that science is all about. Now, how is such robust realism to be reconciled with what we have just been through? The answer is naturalism: the recognition that it is within science itself, and not in some prior philosophy, that reality is properly to be identified and described.[6]

In reflecting on this response to Stroud, Ernest Sosa has been quick to note the incoherence involved in accepting science as the "reality-claims court coupled with the denial that it is anything but free and arbitrary creation."[7] Continuing his criticism of Quine, Sosa goes on to say:

The incoherence is not removed, moreover, if one now adds:

(Q1)   What then does our overall scientific theory really claim regarding the world? Only that it is somehow so structured as to assure the sequence of stimulation that our theory gives us to expect.

(Q2)   Yet people, sticks, stones, electrons and molecules are real indeed.

(Q3)   [It] . . . is within science itself and not in some prior philosophy, that reality is properly to be identified and described.

If it is within science that we settle, to the extent possible for us, the contours of reality; and if science really claims regarding the world only that it is so structured as to assure certain sequences of stimulation; then how can we possibly think reality to assume the contours of people, sticks, stones and so on?

We cannot have it all three ways: (Q1), (Q2) and (Q3) form an incoherent triad. If we trust science as the measure of reality, and if we think there really are sticks and stones, then we can't have science accept only a world 'somehow so structured as to assure' certain sequences of stimulations or the like. Our science must also claim that there really are sticks and stones.

What is more, if science really is the measure of reality it cannot undercut itself by saying that it really isn't, that it is only convenient 'manners of speaking' to guide us reliably from stimulation to stimulation. (p. 69)

Sosa's criticism seems quite pointed. Moreover, even if the critique offered by both Stroud and Sosa should turn out to be a misconstrual of Quine's position, there are other plausible objections we might raise to Quine's argument for naturalized epistemology. For one thing, it is obvious that Quine's argument itself for naturalized epistemology is a philosophical argument, which, *ex hypothesi,* should not count by way of providing evidence for the thesis of naturalized epistemology. Further, the thesis of naturalized epistemology is arguably fundamentally incoherent. It argues against there being a "first philosophy" by appealing to two premises both of which are sound only if philosophical arguments about the limits of human knowledge are permissible and sound. The first premise consists in asserting that Hume's skepticism about factual knowledge is indeed established. Hume's thesis is certainly not empirically confirmable. The so-called "problem of induction" is a philosophical problem based upon a certain philosophical view about what is necessary for scientific knowledge. It is certainly not a problem in natural science or naturalized epistemology. The second premise is the denial of analytic/synthetic distinction; and that is a thesis largely resting on a philosophical argument about the nature of meaning. Such premises only make sense within a commitment to the validity of some form of first philosophy and the legitimacy of traditional epistemology. Finally, there is the problematic premise that traditional epistemology has been exclusively concerned to establish the foundations of certainty in order to show that we have knowledge of the world. A close look at traditional epistemology, however, suggests that the primary concern it as much a matter of getting clear on, or (as Sosa has noted) understanding just what it *means* to know, and just what the concept of certainty relative to different senses of "knows" consists in, as it is a matter of validating knowledge claims or seeking the foundations of certainty (pp. 50–51). Indeed, there is good reason to think that the primary concern of traditional epistemology is one of *defining* concepts of knowl-edge, certainty, justification and truth; and only then of determining whether anybody has the sort of certainty associated with the correct definition of knowledge. The history of epistemology is as apt to criticize the program of the Cartesian skeptic (and the definition of knowledge implied therein) as it is to accept it. Certainly, if the concept of knowledge and justification had been defined differently than Hume had defined them, Hume's predicament would never have occurred. Traditional epistemology is probably as concerned with what it means for a belief to be certain, as it is with determining whether scientific knowledge is certain. With these few considerations in mind, and realizing that much more can be said on the issue, it would appear that Quine's defense of naturalized epistemology admits of a number of solid objections. Let us turn to a more recent and quite distinct defense of the Quinean thesis.

IV. THE "PHILOSOPHY IS SCIENCE" ARGUMENT

Among recent arguments for the Quine thesis, the argument offered by William Lycan in *Judgment and Justification* is quite different from Quine's.[8] Unlike the Quinean argument, it does not rest on the alleged failure of the analytic/synthetic distinction and upon the subsequent classification of all propositions as synthetic. Nor does it feed upon Quine's Humean argument that synthetic propositions cannot be justified from the viewpoint of a first philosophy and so, if epistemology is to continue, it can only be in terms of the deliverances of a descriptive psychology. What is the argument?

Lycan begins by characterizing classical philosophy in terms of the deductivist model. He calls it "deductivism" and under this model philosophy gets characterized in a certain way:

Philosophers arrive at conclusions that are guaranteed to be as indisputably true as the original premises once the ingenious deductive arguments have been hit upon. This attitude has pervaded the rationalist tradition and survives among those who are commonly called 'analytic philosophers' in a correctly narrow sense of that expression. Of course the quality of self-evidence that the deductivist premises are supposed to have and to transmit to his conclusion has been variously described (as for example, analyticity, a prioricity, clarity and distinctness, mere obviousness, or just the property of having been agreed upon by all concerned.). . . .

In any case, the deductivist holds that philosophy and science differ in that deductive argument from self-evident premises pervades the former but not the latter. (Some deductivists have held a particularly strong version of this view, identifying the philosophy/science distinction with the a priori/empirical distinction.) Now Quine (1960, 1963, 1970) has a rather special reason for rejecting the dichotomy between philosophy and science, or, to put the point more accurately, between philosophical method and scientific method. He rejects the analytic-synthetic distinction, and thus the proposal that there are two kinds of truths ("conceptual" or "a priori", and "empirical" or scientific), one of which is the province of science and the other the province of science. . . .

I side with Smart and Quine against the deductivist, but for what I think is a more fundamental and compelling reason, one that does not depend on the rejection of the analytic/synthetic distinction. If my argument is sound, then one can countenance that distinction and still be forced to the conclusion that the Smart/Quine methodological view is correct.

Suppose we try to take a strict deductivist stance. Now, as is common knowledge, one cannot be committed (by an argument) to the conclusion of that argument unless one accepts the premises. Upon being presented with a valid argument, I always have the option of denying its conclusion, so long as I am prepared to accept the denial of at least one of the premises.

Thus, every deductive argument can be set up as an inconsistent set. (Let us, for simplicity, consider only arguments whose premises are internally consistent.) Given an argument $P, Q \therefore R$ the cognitive cash value of which is that R follows deductively from the set of P and

Q, we an exhaustively convey its content simply by asserting that the set (P, Q, not-R) is inconsistent, and all the original argument has told us, in fact, is that for purely logical reasons we must deny either P, Q, or not-R. The proponent of the original argument, of course, holds that P and Q are true; therefore, she says, we are committed to the denial of not-R, that is to R. But how does she know that P and Q are true? Perhaps she has constructed deductive arguments with P and Q as conclusions. But, if we are to avoid regress, we must admit that she relies ultimately on putative knowledge gained nondeductively; so let us suppose that she has provided nondeductive arguments for P and Q. On what grounds then does she accept them? The only answer that can be given is that she finds each of P and Q more plausible than not-R, just as Moore found the statement "I had breakfast before I had lunch" more plausible than any of the metaphysical premises on which rested the fashionable arguments against the reality of time.

But these are just the sorts of considerations to which the theoretical scientist appeals. If what I have said here is (more or less) right, then we appear to have vindicated some version of the view that (1) philosophy, except for that relatively trivial part of it that consists in making sure that controversial arguments are formally valid, is just very high level science and that consequently (2) the proper philosophical method for acquiring interesting new knowledge cannot differ from proper scientific method. (pp. 116–118).

In defending this general argument, Lycan then responds to two basic objections which he offers against his own thesis. The first objection is that even if all philosophical arguments rest on plausibility arguments, the above argument has not established what is necessary, namely, that considerations that make for plausibility in science are the same considerations that make for plausibility in philosophy. The second objection is that even if we were to establish as much, it would not thereby obviously follow that philosophy is just very high-level science. Philosophy and science might have the same method but differ by way of subject matter. (pp. 116–118). The core of Lycan's defense of his general argument consists in responding to the first objection. So, let us see whether the response overcomes the objection.

In response to the first objection, Lycan constructs the following argument:

P1. The interesting principals of rational acceptance are not the deductive ones (even in philosophy).

P2. There are, roughly speaking, three kinds of ampliative, non-deductive principles of inference: principles of self-evidence (gnostic access, incorrigibility, a priority, clarity and distinctness, etc.), principles of what might be called 'textbook induction' (enumerative induction, eliminative induction, statistical syllogism, Mill's Methods, etc.), and principles of sophisticated ampliative inference (such as PS principles and the other considerations of theoretical elegance and power mentioned earlier, which are usually construed as filling out the 'best' in 'inference to the best explanation').

P3. Principles of textbook induction are not the interesting principles of rational acceptance in philosophy.

P4. Principles of 'self-evidence,' though popular throughout the history of philosophy and hence considered interesting principles of rational acceptance, cannot be used to settle philosophical disputes.

Therefore: If there are any interesting and decisive principles of rational acceptance in philosophy, they are the elegance principles (p.119).

Lycan adds that the elegance principles are to be extracted mainly from the history of science, and that we can obtain precise and useful statements of such principles only by looking to the history of science, philosophy, and logic in order to see exactly what considerations motivate the replacement of an old theory by a new theory. (pp. 119–120). So, the answer to the question "Why does it follow that the considerations that make for plausibility in philosophy are the same as those that make for plausibility

in science?" is simply "there is nowhere else to turn" (p. 120). For a number of reasons, however, this response to the objection seems problematic.

To begin with, P1 is not true. It is common knowledge that one cannot be rationally justified in accepting the conclusion of an argument unless the argument is valid and consistent in addition to the premises being true. So, we cannot construe P1 to assert that validity and consistency are redundant or eliminable as conditions necessary for the rational acceptability of an argument. Lycan does not mean to argue that point. Rather P1 asserts that even though validity and consistency are necessary conditions for the soundness of an argument, validity and consistency provide no grounds for thinking that the conclusion deduced is plausible. In short, P1 asserts that it is not even a necessary condition for the *plausibility* of a proposed argument that it be both sound and consistent. The reasons offered for P1, however, seem particularly questionable and the reasons for thinking P1 false seem straightforwardly compelling. Let me explain.

Lycan claims that P1 is true because deductive rules are not controversial in their application (p. 119). But how exactly would that establish that such rules of inference are not interesting, meaning thereby not plausibility-conferring on the conclusion? Why not say instead that *because* such rules are noncontroversially applied they are interesting, that is, plausibility conferring? In other words, what does the fact that such rules are non-controversial in their application have to do with their not being plausibility-conferring on the conclusions that follow from them? Is it meant to be obvious that a deductive rule of inference is plausibility-conferring only when its application is controversial? Why should anyone accept such a definition of plausibility, especially because it seems to endorse saying such things as "Your argument is perfectly plausible even though it is both invalid and inconsistent." Why aren't deductive rules interesting (or plausibility-conferring) because they are more likely to guarantee truth from premises that are true? If "interest" is relative to purpose and, if one's purpose is to provide a system of inferential rules that is strongly truth-preserving, then such rules are quite interesting, even if their application is non-controversial. This in itself is sufficient to show P1 is involved in a questionable bit of semantic legislation.

Moreover, Lycan's second reason for $P1$ is that any deductive argument can be made valid in a perfectly trivial way by the addition of some inference-licensing premise (p. 119). But how exactly does it follow from the fact (if it be a fact) that any deductive argument can be made trivially valid that *no* deductive principle (including consistency) is interesting in the sense of conferring plausibility in any degree on what follows from the deductive principle? Here again, is it meant to be obvious that deductive principles are plausibility-conferring only if they function in arguments incapable of being rendered valid and consistent in non-trivial ways? Does not such a claim presuppose a definition of plausibility which, by stipulation, asserts that the plausibility of a deductive conclusion has nothing to do with the fact that the argument is valid and consistent? And is not that precisely what needs to be shown? Indeed, if any deductive argument could be rendered valid and consistent in wholly trivial ways and the conclusion still be plausible, why insist, as we do, on validity and consistency for soundness as a necessary condition for rational acceptance? Why insist on rules that are truth-preserving for soundness if one can get it in trivial ways and it has nothing to do with the plausibility of the conclusion?

Lycan's third reason for $P1$ is that deductive rules are not plausibility conferring because such rules are uninteresting. They are uninteresting precisely because deductive inferences obviously do not accomplish the expansion of our total store of explicit and implicit knowledge, since they succeed only in drawing out information already implicit in the premises (p. 119). Here again, however, even if deductive inference only renders explicit what is implicitly contained in the premises that would only show that deductive inference is not inductive inference, and, unless one *assumes* that the only plausibility considerations that will count are those relevant to expanding our factual knowledge base, rather than showing that one's inferences are the product of truth-preserving rules, why would the fact that deductive inference is not inductive inference be a sufficient reason for thinking that deductive inference is uninteresting as a way of enhancing the plausibility of one's conclusions deductively inferred? The reason Lycan offers here (like the two offered above) strongly implies that the plausibility of a person's beliefs has nothing to do

with whether it is internally consistent, or follows logically from well-confirmed beliefs, or is consistent with a large body of well-confirmed belief or is the product of truth-preserving rules of inference; and this just flies in the face of our epistemic practices.

Lycan's last reason for $P1$ is that any deductive argument can be turned upon its head (p. 120). Once again, what needs proving is assumed. Even if we can turn a valid deductive argument on its head, so to speak, does that mean that there are no valid arguments? If the answer is yes, why say that valid deductive inference is uninteresting rather than impossible? But if we are not arguing that valid deductive inference is impossible, why exactly would such inference be uninteresting if it is truth-preserving, and would guarantee consistency, coherence with well-confirmed beliefs, and the explicit addition of true verifiable sentences not formerly in the corpus of our beliefs? If such considerations do not count as plausibility-conferring, it could only be because "plausibility" is stipulatively defined to rule out such considerations as plausibility-conferring. Such a definition needs defending rather than pleading.

By way of general observation with regard to $P1$, it seems clear that plausibility considerations rest quite squarely on questions of consistency and derivability. One of the traditional tests for theory confirmation (and hence by implication for plausibility) is derivability from above. For example, the fact that Balmer's formula for the emission spectra for gases derives logically from Bohr's theory on the hydrogen atom, counts strongly in favor of Balmer's formula above and beyond the evidence Balmer gave for his formula. What is that to say except that considerations purely deductive in nature function to render theories more or less plausible? What about the rest of Lycan's argument against the first objection to his general argument?

Well, suppose, for the sake of discussion that $P2$ and $P3$ are true. Will $P4$ be true? In other words, will it be true that principles of self-evidence do not count for plausibility unless they can be used to settle some philosophical disputes. Here the argument seems to be suggesting that a common-sense principle will be plausibility-conferring only if it can be used to "settle" (in the sense of everybody agreeing henceforth to the answer) some philosophical dispute. But such a requirement seems arbitrarily too strong. Obviously, a conclusion can be plausible and worthy of rational acceptance even when others will disagree to some degree. Two mutually exclusive conclusions may both be rationally plausible without the principle that renders them plausible "settling" the dispute once and for all. Moreover, are we sure that appeals to common sense principles have failed to resolve or settle philosophical disputes? In a very strong sense of "settle," of course, nothing is settled in philosophy. But that would be to impose an arbitrarily strong sense of "settle" on philosophy, a sense we certainly would not impose on science. In a suitably weak sense, "appeals to obviousness or self-evidence" often, but not always, settles disputes. Indeed, isn't the basic reason that the question of solipsism consistently fails to capture anybody's sustained attention is that it is so implausible by way of appeal to common sense? Who these days really takes the possibility of solipsism seriously? Isn't that a philosophical problem pretty much settled by appeal to common sense or self-evidence? Of course, not all appeals to common sense are so successful, and some are more successful than others as clean "conversation stoppers."

These reasons show that Lycan's reply to the first objection fails. Further, it would have been surprising if the reply had succeeded because it seems clear that in science, but not in philosophy, a necessary condition for any explanation being even remotely plausible is that it be in principle empirically testable. As a mater of fact, if we consult practicing scientists and not philosophers, unless one's scientific explanations are ultimately testable, and we know what empirical evidence would need to occur to falsify the hypothesis, we say that the explanation is not plausible. We may even go so far as to say that it is meaningless because it is not testable. Minimally, in science a hypothesis or a theory will be plausible only if it is empirically testable, and it will be testable only if what the hypothesis virtually predicts is in principle observable under clearly specifiable conditions, and would occur as expected if we were to accept the hypothesis as worthy. On the other hand, if we are not to beg the question against philosophy as distinct from science, and look at philosophical theses, we will find that a philosophical thesis can be more or less plausible quite independently of whether the thesis is empirically

confirmable or testable. As a matter of fact, consider, for example, the dispute between classical scientific realists and classical anti-realists of an instrumental sort. What empirical test might one perform to establish or refute the view that the long-term predictive success of some scientific hypotheses is a function of the truth of claims implied or assumed by the hypotheses? Surely one of these theses must be correct, and yet neither the realist nor the anti-realist position here is testable by appeal to any known experimental or non-experimental test.[9] Does that mean that while one position must be correct *neither* is plausible? Paradox aside, if we say yes, how is that anything more than assuming what needs to be proven, namely that considerations that count for plausibility in science are the same as those that count for plausibility in philosophy?

Surely, however, there are also other philosophical arguments that in fact do depend for their plausibility on the verification and falsification of certain factual claims. For example, Aristotle once argued that humans are quite different from animals because they use tools, whereas animals do not. Aristotle's argument here is implausible because readily falsified by careful observations of the sort Jane Goodall and others continually make. So, in philosophy plausibility may sometimes root in considerations of testability just because one of the premises in the argument asserts that some factual claim about the world is true or false. But, as we just showed in the case of the dispute between the scientific realist and the scientific anti-realist, plausibility may have very little or nothing to do with the empirical testability of the hypothesis. It may simply be a matter of showing the internal inconsistency of a particular argument, or the dire consequences of adopting one position over the other, or the informal (or formal) fallacies attending the argumentation of one position over the other. In short, as practiced, philosophical reasoning often requires both deductive and inductive principles of rational acceptance for plausibility. But it certainly is not a necessary condition for philosophical plausibility that one's philosophical positions be testable or explainable in a way that accommodates empirical testability as a necessary condition for significance. Moreover, it should be apparent by now that to insist that plausibility in philosophy must accommodate the canons of empirical testability or the canons of explanation in the natural sciences is simply a blatant question-begging move against the objection offered against Lycan's main argument. As such, it would be a rationally unmotivated stipulation against philosophy as distinct from natural science.

In sum, Lycan's reply to the first objection to his general argument fails unless one wants to suppose that there is nothing at all plausible about any philosophical argument primarily because philosophical arguments are not straightforwardly verifiable or falsifiable in the way that empirical claims are. Besides, it seems that the dark shadow of Quine's "Epistemology Naturalized" is having an unrealized effect on the main argument Lycan offers. This is because if one excludes philosophical arguments from the realm of the analytic or a priori (as Quine does), it would appear that if there is anything to them at all, they must fall into the realm of the synthetic; and hence it seems only too natural to suppose that synthetic claims are meaningful only if testable and confirmable in some basic way by the method of the natural sciences. But the very argument offered from this view supposes, once again, what needs defending, namely, that philosophical plausibility depends on plausibility considerations that are appropriate only to the methods of the natural sciences. When we look to the actual practice of philosophy that assumption seems quite false or the argument Lycan offers begs the question against the distinctness of philosophy. Let's turn to another recent argument for the Quine thesis.

V. THE "TRADITIONAL EPISTEMOLOGY WILL BECOME IRRELEVANT" ARGUMENT

In his recent book *Explaining Science: A Cognitive Approach,* Ron Giere argues that the justification for the naturalizing of philosophy will not come from explicitly refuting the old paradigm of traditional epistemology, by explicitly refuting on a philosophical basis the philosophical arguments favoring the traditional posture. Rather the argument for naturalizing epistemology will simply be a function of the empirical success of those practitioners in showing how to answer certain questions and, at the same

time, showing the irrelevance of the questions asked under the old paradigm.[10] Comparing the naturalized epistemologist with the proponents of seventeenth century physics, he says:

> Proponents of the new physics of the seventeenth century won out not because they explicitly refuted the arguments of the scholastics but because the empirical success of their science rendered the scholastic's arguments irrelevant (p. 9).

This same sort of argument has been offered by philosophers such as Patricia Churchland and Paul Churchland, who have claimed that traditional epistemology or "first philosophy" will disappear as a consequence of the inevitable elimination of folk psychology in favor of some future successful neuroscientific account of cognitive functioning.[11]

While there are various reasons for thinking that the eliminative materialism implied by the above argument cannot occur,[12] what seems most obvious is that the assertion made by Giere and the Churchlands is simply not an *argument* for naturalized epistemology. Rather, it is a buoyantly optimistic prediction that, purely and simply because of the expected empirical success of the new model, we will naturally come to regard traditional epistemology (normative epistemology) as having led us nowhere. In short, we will come to view the questions of traditional epistemology as sterile and no longer worth asking. In spite of the optimism of this prediction, it is difficult to see what successes to date justify such a prediction. What central traditional epistemological problems or questions have been rendered trivial or meaningless by the advances in natural science or neuroscience? Unless one proves that a basic question in traditional epistemology is "How does the Brain Work?" the noncontroversial advances made in neuroscience will be quite irrelevant to answering the questions of traditional epistemology. While some people seem to have *assumed* as much,[13] it is by no means clear that knowing how ones beliefs originate is in any way relevant to their being justified or otherwise worthy of acceptance.[14] Without being able to point to such successes, the eliminative thesis amounts to an unjustified assertion that traditional philosophy is something of an unwholesome disease for which the doing of natural science or neuroscience is the sure cure. In the absence of such demonstrated success, however, no traditional epistemologist need feel compelled by the prediction to adopt the posture of naturalized epistemology.

As a program committed to understanding the mechanisms of belief-acquisition, naturalized epistemology may very well come to show that our traditional way of understanding human knowledge is in important respects flawed and, as a result, we may indeed need to recast dramatically our understanding of the nature of human knowledge. It would be silly to think that this could not happen. After all, Aristotle's conception of human rationality, and the way in which it was allegedly distinct from animal rationality, was shown to quite wrong when we all saw Jane Goodall's films showing Gorillas making and using tools. Thereafter, Aristotle's philosophical argument that humans think, whereas animals do not, because the former but the not the latter use tools, disappeared from the philosophical landscape. So, it is quite possible that there are certain empirical assumptions about the nature of human knowledge that may well be strongly and empirically falsified in much the same way that Aristotle's position was falsified. But even that sort of progress is still quite consistent with construing epistemology in non-naturalized ways. Traditional epistemology should have no difficulty with accepting the view that some philosophical theses can be conclusively refuted by the occurrence of certain facts. That would be simply to acknowledge that philosophy, and philosophical arguments, are not purely a priori and hence immune from rejection by appeal to the way the world is. So, the traditional epistemologist will need to wait and see just what naturalized epistemology comes up with. Whether it lives up to the expectations of Giere and others who, like the Churchlands, offer the same basic argument is still an open question, at best. As things presently stand, there are good reasons, as we shall see, for thinking that no amount of naturalized epistemology will ever be able in principle to answer certain crucial questions about the nature of justification.

Otherwise Giere's defense of naturalized epistemology consists in responding to others who argue against naturalized epistemology. In responding to these objections, Giere seeks to show that there is certainly no compelling reason why one should not proceed on the new model. He considers the following three arguments.

A. Putnam's Objection

In his "Why Reasons Can't be Naturalized" (*Synthese,* vol. 52, 1982, pp. 3–23) Putnam says:

> A cognitive theory of science would require a definition of rationality of the form: A belief is rational if and only if it is acquired by employing some specified cognitive capacities. But any such formula is either obviously mistaken or vacuous, depending on how one restricts the range of beliefs to which the definition applies. If the definition is meant to cover *all* beliefs, then it is obviously mistaken because people do sometimes acquire irrational beliefs using the same cognitive capacities as everyone else. But restricting the definition to rational beliefs renders the definition vacuous. And so the program of constructing a naturalistic philosophy of science goes nowhere (*Synthese,* vol. 52, 1982, pp. 3–23).

In response to this particular argument, Giere says:

> The obvious reply is that a naturalistic theory of science need not require any such definition. A naturalist in epistemology, however, is free to deny that such a conception can be given any coherent content. For such a naturalist, there is only hypothetical rationality which many naturalists, including me, would prefer to describe simply as 'effective goal-directed action,' thereby dropping the world 'rationality' altogether (p. 9).

In short, for Giere, Putnam is just begging the question by insisting that there must be a coherent concept of categorical rationality. In defense of Putnam's intuition, however, one can argue that Giere missed Putnam's point. Putnam's point is just as easily construed as asserting that if the naturalized epistemologist is not to abandon altogether the concept of rationality, (and thereby abandon any way of sorting justifiable or warranted beliefs from those that are not) the rationality of a belief will be purely and simply a function of the reliability of the mechanisms that cause the beliefs. But because a belief can be produced by a reliable belief-making mechanism and be rationally unjustified, such a definition will not work. Putnam's objection, when construed in this way, is compelling. Unfortunately, Giere's response seems to miss the point Putnam makes. Presumably, Putnam would respond that even if we were to stop talking about rationality, we would still need some way of determining which beliefs are more less justified; and the naturalized epistemologist would need to define such concepts in terms of the mechanisms that produce certain beliefs. And Putnam's point is that that just will not work because unjustified beliefs can emerge just as easily from reliable mechanisms.

B. Siegel's Objection

In his "Justification, Discovery and the Naturalizing of Epistemology,"[15] Harvey Siegel challenges the naturalistic approach by arguing that rationality of means is not enough. There must be a rationality of goals as well because there is no such thing as rational action in pursuit of an irrational goal. In response to this objection, Geire notes:

> This sort of argument gains its plausibility mainly from the way philosophers use the vocabulary of 'rationality.' If one simply drops this vocabulary, the point vanishes. Obviously, there can be effective action in pursuit of any goal whatsoever—as illustrated by the proverbial case of the efficient Nazi. . . .
>
> Nor does the restriction to instrumental rationality prevent the study of science from yielding normative claims about how science should be pursued. Indeed, it may be argued that the naturalistic study of science provides the only legitimate basis for sound science policy (Campbell, 1985). (p. 10)

Along with Giere, we may find it difficult to take Siegel's objection seriously for two reasons. Firstly, it is not at all obvious that naturalized epistemology is committed to rationality of means only and not also to the rationality of goals. It is not even clear what that claim amounts to. Secondly, as Giere also points out, there certainly seems to be cases in which irrational ends can be pursued by rational action. Anyway, as we shall see later, there are much more persuasive objections to naturalized epistemology.

C. The Objection from Vicious Circularity

There is another common objection to eliminating traditional epistemological questions in favor of questions about effective means to desired goals. Giere characterizes it in the following way:

> To show that some methods are effective, one must be able to show that they can result in reaching the goal. And this requires being able to say what it is like to reach the goal. But the goal in science is usually taken to be 'true' or 'correct' theories. And the traditional epistemological problem has always been to justify the claim that one has in fact found a correct theory. Any naturalistic theory of science that appeals only to effective means to the goal of discovering correct theories must beg this question. Thus a naturalistic philosophy of science can be supported only by a circular argument that assumes some means to the goal are in fact effective. (p. 11)

Giere then proceeds to show that this sort of objection (which he does not cite anybody in fact offering) is based on some dubious items of Cartesian epistemology. A more direct response, however, is that this objection is unacceptable because it assumes rather than proves that the goal of scientific theories is to achieve truth rather than empirical adequacy. In other words, a proper response would consist in straightforwardly denying that the goal of science is to discover "true" or "correct" theories rather than ones that are instrumentally reliable as predictive devices. So, for other reasons, we need not take this objection very seriously. In the end, apart from Putnam's objection, these last two objections to naturalized epistemology do not have the necessary bite, and Giere seems quite justified in rejecting them. Later we shall see better objections. For now, however, we need only note that the above argument in favor of naturalized epistemology is not an argument, and that the author's response to the above three objections to naturalized epistemology selects only three and fails to deal effectively with Putnam's objection.

In the end, for Giere, evolutionary theory provides an alternative foundation for the study of science:

It explains why the traditional projects of epistemology, whether in their Cartesian, Humean, or Kantian form, were misguided. And it shows why we should not fear the charge of circularity (p. 12).

But what exactly is it about traditional epistemology that made it misguided? That it sought to refute universal skepticism? Whoever said that that was *the goal* of traditional epistemology? As we noted earlier when we examined Quine's argument, to define the concept of knowledge and then to determine whether, and to what extent, human knowledge exists in the various ways we define it seems equally the major goal of traditional epistemology. And why, exactly, is that a misguided activity? Such an activity seems justified by the plausible goal that if we get very clear on just what we mean by basic epistemological concepts, we might just be in a better position to determine the snake-oil artist from those whose views are worthy of adoption. This goal is based on the noncontroversial point that knowledge just isn't a matter of accepting everything a passerby might say. At the root of most arguments for naturalized epistemology, as we shall see, is this peculiar claim to the effect that traditional epistemology somehow has failed or been misguided in its search for some cosmic skyhook. Certainly we saw as much when we examined Quine's argument. But when the arguments are laid on the table, some philosophers may come to think that what gets characterized as traditional epistemology is quite different from the real thing. Socrates, after all, began his discussion in *Theatetus* with the question "What is knowledge?" and not "Is Human knowledge possible?" or "How does the mind represent reality?" or (as one philosopher recently claimed) "How does the brain work?"[16] That anybody could seriously think that Socrates was really asking for an account of how the brain works is difficult to comprehend. And to say that that is what he *should* have been asking (because nobody has or can answer whatever other question he might have asked) presupposes that one can show that the questions he did ask are misguided or bad questions, and that is yet to be shown in any way that does not beg the question against philosophy. We may now turn to the fourth argument in favor of Quine's thesis.

VI. THE ARGUMENT FROM EVOLUTIONARY THEORY

Evolutionary epistemology is a form of naturalized epistemology which insists that the only valid questions about the nature of human knowledge are those that can be answered in biological science by appeal to evolutionary theory. For the evolutionary epistemologist, the Darwinian revolution underscored the point that human beings, as products of evolutionary development, are natural beings whose capacities for knowledge and belief can be understood by appeal to the basic laws of biology under evolutionary theory. As Michael Bradie has recently noted, evolutionary epistemologists often seem to be claiming that Darwin or, more generally, biological considerations are relevant in deciding in favor of a non-justificational or purely descriptive approach to the theory of knowledge.[17] When we examine the arguments proposed by specific evolutionary epistemologsts, there seems to emerge two distinct arguments. The first argument, allegedly offered by philosophers such as Karl Popper, and reconstructed by Peter Munz is as follows:

*P*1. We do in fact have human knowledge.

*P*2. No justification is possible.

Therefore: *P*3. Human knowledge does not involve justification.

Therefore: *P*4. Every item of knowledge is a provisional proposal or hypothesis subject to revision.[18]

For this reason Popper held that the only problem in epistemology was the problem of the growth of human knowledge, or the biological question of how human knowledge originates and grows. Therefore, epistemology is not normative in the way that traditional epistemology is normative but rather purely descriptive. As Bradie has noted, Popper's argument for *P*2 is based on his acceptance of Hume's critique of induction and the corollary that no empirical universal statements are provable beyond doubt. (p. 10.) The second argument, inspired by Quine's reference to Darwin, is offered by Hilary Kornblith and reconstructed by Bradie as follows:

*P*1. Believing truths has survival value.

Therefore: *P2*. Natural selection guarantees that our innate intellectual endowment gives us a predisposition for believing truths.

Therefore: *P3*. Knowledge is a necessary by-product of natural selection.

In order to get the desired conclusion of a purely descriptive epistemology, Kornblith supplies the following premise

Therefore: *P4*. If nature has so constricted us that our belief-generating processes are inevitably biased in favor of true beliefs, then it must be that the processes by which we arrive at beliefs just are those by which we ought to arrive at them.

warranting the final conclusion:

Therefore: *P5*. The processes by which we arrive at our beliefs are just those by which we ought to arrive at them.[19]

What can we say about these two arguments?

With regard to the first argument, the one Peter Munz ascribes to Popper, the first thing to note is that there is nothing particularly "biological" or "evolutionary" about it at all. It is simply a philosophical argument based on a philosophical acceptance of Hume's philosophical skepticism to the effect that no factual claim about the world could be justified sufficiently for knowledge. So, the argument does not provide a justification deriving from evolutionary theory for taking the naturalistic turn. Secondly, as we saw when we discussed Quine's argument above, accepting a philosophical argument for a purely descriptive epistemology is radically incoherent. A philosophical argument to the effect that there is no first philosophy because Hume was correct in his defense of the problem of induction, is radically incoherent and self-defeating in a way apparently not yet appreciated by naturalized epistemologists.

The second argument has already been well criticized by Michael Bradie who has noted (along with many other, including Stich, Leowontin, and Wilson) that *P2* is quite questionable. The fact that certain beliefs endure and have survival value by no means implies that they are the product of natural

selection. There are many traits that evolve culturally which have no survival value (See Bradie, p. 16.) Moreover, even if it were true that our cognitive capacities have evolved by natural selection, the important point is that that by itself is no reason for thinking that we are naturally disposed to believe truths rather than falsity. On the contrary, the evidence seems pretty strong that, given the history of scientific theorizing, the species is more disposed to accept empirically adequate rather than true hypotheses.

One interesting response to this last line of reasoning come from Nicholas Rescher who has argued in *Methodological Pragmatism* that say what we will, the methods of the natural sciences have indeed been selected out by nature, otherwise they would not have endured as such reliable instruments for prediction and control. Rescher's basic point is that on any given occasion, an instrumentally reliable belief or thesis may well fail to be true. But that is no reason for thinking that nature has not selected out the methods of the natural sciences because in the long run the methods of the natural sciences provide truth.[20] Rescher's point is well taken, but it is certainly not an argument for the thesis that epistemology is purely descriptive. Rescher certainly is not a naturalized epistemologist in that sense. Rather it is an argument for regarding the deliverances of the methods of natural science as epistemically privileged. In offering the argument he does here, Rescher is merely showing how the usual arguments against Pragmatism hold for *thesis* Pragmatism and not for *methodological* Pragmatism. Nor does his argument provide the evidence necessary for making sound Kornblith's reconstructed argument from evolution. This is because Kornblith's proposed argument still falters on *P2*. Rescher's argument by no means shows or supports the view that people by nature are innately disposed to believe only true propositions. If that were so, it would be difficult to see why we would ever need the methods of the natural sciences anyway. Nature selected out the methods of the natural sciences just *because* we are not natively disposed to believe only true propositions.

But, if the above two arguments are the best evolutionary biologists can offer in defense of the first form of naturalized epistemology, it would seem that biology itself, and especially evolutionary biology, is yet to offer a persuasive argument for naturalized epistemology. Along with Bradie, we can only conclude that there does not seem to be any persuasive argument from evolutionary theory in favor of the first form of naturalized epistemology.[21]

VII. THE "IMPOSSIBILITY OF DEFINING JUSTIFICATION" ARGUMENT

The last, and perhaps the most interesting, argument for the first form of naturalized epistemology appears in a forthcoming paper by Richard Ketchum entitled "The Paradox of Epistemology: A Defense of Naturalism." Ketchum's argument is the following: An adequate traditional epistemology will require, among other things, an acceptable definition, or explication of the concept of justification. But there is no non-question begging definition, or explication of the concept of justification. This latter claim rests on the reason that whatever definition one would offer for the concept of justification admits of the question "Are you justified in accepting or believing this definition of justification?" And, of course, if one were to answer yes and then defend the answer by saying it is an instance of the definition (which presumably one would need to say), the questioner would reply that the appeal is question-begging because what is at issue is whether *that* definition itself is justified. Appealing to the analysans of the definition to justify the definition is a patent bit of question-begging. So, no matter what one's definition might be, there would be no non-question-begging way of answering the question of whether one is justified in accepting that definition. Thus, traditional epistemology is dead.[22] What about this argument?

One possible response is that while one may not be justified in believing one's definition of justification, one might certainly have good reasons for accepting one's definition of justification. But the problem with this response is that it arbitrarily prevents one from defining justification in terms of having good reasons. Besides, if having good reasons for accepting a definition of justification is sufficient for accepting it, then why is that not the definition of justification? Can one have sufficient reasons for accepting something and not be justified in accepting it?

Another possible response asserts that the problem with this argument is not in the assumption that we must be justified in believing our definition of justification. Rather it is in the assumption that justification in believing a definition has the same meaning as justification when the term applies to non-definitions. On this view, being justified in believing a definition is simply a matter of whether one has correctly generalized from the conditions of correct usage in natural or scientific discourse (or, if our definitions are stipulative, a matter of whether they lead us to conclusions that satisfy the purpose behind defining things the way we do); whereas being justified in believing a non-definition, or a proposition about the world, is a matter of whether one can give (if necessary) good reasons for thinking that the proposition is a reasonably adequate description of one's mental content or of the non-mental world. Is there anything wrong with this proposed solution?

Yes, and it is this: The original question returns in the form of the question "Are you justified in believing that the concept of justification differs for reportive definitions and non-definitions in the way indicated? Here again, if one answers affirmatively, one could only defend the answer by making it an instance of the concept of justification appropriate for non-definitions, and that is what is at issue. In short, the question returns with a sting even when we try to distinguish various senses of justification.

By implication, suppose one were to say "I am justified in accepting my definition of justification because the definition conforms to the rules we require for generating acceptable definitions.." Once again, the obvious response is "Are you justified in accepting the rules for generating acceptable definitions?"; if the answer is yes (as presumably it would be), then the answer is defensible only if it is an instance of one's definition of justification for non-definitions; but one's definition of justification for non-definitions is justifiable only if it is in an instance of the definition of justification for non-definitions. But the latter is itself what is at issue, and so we come back to the original question and the impossibility of answering it in a non-question-begging way.

Yet another response consists in trying to rule against the meaningfulness of the question on the grounds that if we take it seriously, then it would lead to an infinite regress and that in itself is good evidence for the inappropriateness of the question. On this view, whatever answer one gives, the respondent could still ask "But are you justified in believing that?" Differently stated, to countenance the question in the first instance is to countenance more properly the assumption that one must be justified in all one's beliefs and, as we know from Aristotle's argument in the first book of *Prior Analytics,* that requirement guarantees skepticism, because the need for an infinite amount of justification prevents there ever being any demonstrative knowledge. Is this response acceptable?

It is not acceptable as a way of establishing non-traditional epistemology because the same question cuts equally strongly against the naturalized epistemologist. The naturalized epistemologist like Quine, still says that one's beliefs about the world are more or less justified by appeal to the canons of scientific inference. Accordingly, suppose we grant that traditional epistemology is dead and that one could still be justified in one's beliefs about the world because we need only follow the canons of justification as practiced in science. But if the question "Are you justified in believing that your definition of justification is appropriate or correct?" is a legitimate question to ask of the classical epistemologist, it is also a legitimate question to ask of the naturalized epistemologist who asserts that "In natural science, being justified in one's beliefs is simply a matter of x." And if this is so, the nature of justification in science is as problematic as it would be in traditional epistemology. Why is it that for the naturalized epistemologist the natural scientist (but not the traditional epistemologist) can well ignore the philosopher's question "Are you justified in accepting x as the correct definition of justification in science?" Indeed, it would seem that the question cuts both ways, and is not any more devastating for the traditional epistemologist than it is for the practice of science in general or for the naturalized epistemologist. If the naturalized epistemologist feels justified in ignoring such questions because they are so obviously philosophical, why exactly is that an argument in favor of naturalized epistemology rather than an unargued rejection of philosophy in general? Thus if the question is persuasive, it tends to show the truth of skepticism in general and not simply the failure of traditional epistemology. This is hardly a desirable result for anybody.

By way of confronting this pesky argument for the impossibility of traditional epistemology, another interesting response consists in asserting that we must begin by accepting the fact that we know something, and that just means that we must reject any and all questions about human knowledge that can only be answered with a question-begging response. So, the truth of the matter is that there is no non-question-begging way to answer questions such as "Are you justified in believing your definition of justification?" But if we insist on answering such questions we make global skepticism certain. Presumably, even naturalized epistemologists do not want to go that far. Consequently, such questions are not permissible. What this means is that generalizing from the facts of ordinary usage and scientific practice to determine what we mean by certain epistemic concepts is simply where we start and what we do to get clear about what human knowledge is. To ask that we be justified in the conclusions we draw here is to demand that we begin somewhere else when there is in fact nowhere else to go, and if we do not stop here or somewhere else (which will certainly happen if we allow the skeptic's eternal question "But are you justified in believing that?") there could be no knowledge about anything at all.

Is this a compelling response, or is it merely a grand way of begging the question against global skepticism which, if the original question is permissible, turns out to be forceful? Are we dismissing the question as meaningful because otherwise we would need to accept global skepticism? It is tempting to think not, but the skeptic will doubtless see things differently. It appears that we have no knock-down argument against the skeptic except to say that he begins with a view that we cannot accept, namely, that it is possible that nobody knows anything. But that is not an argument.

In the end, however, the best way to confront the claim that there is no non-question-begging way to justify any definition or analysis of justification consists in arguing as follows: Whoever asks the question "Are you justified in accepting your definition of justification?" can be met with the response "What do you mean when you ask whether I am justified in accepting this definition?" When anyone asks the question "Are you justified in accepting or believing your definition of justification?" he must have in mind just what it means to be justified, otherwise it is not a meaningful question because if he did not have in mind just what it meant, he would not know what would count for a good answer if an answer were possible. So, if the question makes any sense at all, the questioner must be prepared to say just what he means when he asks the question "Are you justified in believing your definition of justification?" In fact, then, it is a necessary condition for this question being meaningful that the questioner be able to say what it would mean for someone to be justified in believing that a particular definition of justification is correct. If the questioner cannot answer the question "What do you mean?" then the question need not be taken seriously. If he can, then his question is easily answered. For example, if the questioner is asking for a good reason for accepting the definition, the response might well be that we have a good reason because the definition is a sound generalization of the facts of ordinary usage (and that's a good reason because evolution selects out this way of determining the meaning of expressions).

In sum, if the question is an honest one, then the questioner is asking for a justification and if he cannot say what would count as an answer to his question (thereby saying what he means by justification) then we need not, and will not, take his question seriously. On the other hand, as soon as he tells us just what he means by "justification" his question seems meaningful and answerable. But now comes the rub: we can still refuse to take his question seriously because *we* can now raise the question of whether his understanding of "justification" is justified, because if it is not, we do not need to answer his question; and if he says our question is meaningless, then so too was his initial question. But now the shoe is on the other foot, as it were. The person who questions the original definition of justification can make sense of his question only if he is willing to say what justification consists in; but if the original question makes sense then it will make equal sense when the question is asked of him—meaning that *he* has no non-question-begging way of answering a question necessary for his meaningfully asking "Are you justified in believing your definition of justification?" Thus it appears that we justified in ignoring the question because the questioner cannot, ex hypothesi, satisfy a condition necessary for the meaningfulness of the proposition. He cannot, ex hypothesi, answer in any non-question-begging way the question we can ask of him, namely, "Are you justified in accepting your definition of justification?"

VIII. CONCLUSION

Given the above considerations, it seems that, in spite of the popularity of the thesis, there is no sound argument presently available supporting the Quinean version of naturalized epistemology. Nor should we be tempted to suppose that because we have never achieved a consensus in traditional epistemology, it looks as though we have good inductive grounds that the program of traditional epistemology will never work. That sort of argument blatantly begs the question in favor of a concept of success that is appropriate to the methods of the natural sciences and so, by implication, begs the question in favor of the naturalized epistemology for which it is supposed to be an argument. The interesting question is whether there is something fundamentally incoherent about arguing philosophically for such a naturalized epistemology. As was suggested above in the discussion on Quine's argument, it certainly seems that offering a philosophical argument in favor of denying that philosophical arguments will count when it comes to answering questions about the nature of epistemology is incoherent when the point of it is to defend a particular view about the nature of human knowledge. But perhaps this is merely a philosophical point.[23]

NOTES

1. In *Ontological Relativity and Other Essays,* (New York: Columbia University Press, 1969).
2. For a full discussion of Goldman's thesis as it occurs in *Epistemology and Cognition* (Cambridge, Mass: Harvard University Press, 1985) see R. Almeder and F. Hogg, "Reliabilism and Goldman's Theory of Justification," *Philosophia* (vol. # 1989) pp.
3. In Hilary Kornblith, ed., *Naturalizing Epistemology* (Cambridge: MIT Press, 1985), pp. 71–85

4. *Roots of Reference* (LaSalle: Open Court, 1975).

5. In S. Guttenplan, ed., *Mind and Language* (Oxford: Clarendon Press, 1975).

6. See "Reply to Stroud" in *Midwest Studies in Philosophy Vol. VI*, P. French, E. Uehling, and H. Wettstein, (eds) (Minneapolis: University of Minnesota Press, 1981), p. 474.

7. See "Nature Unmirrored, Epistemology Naturalized" in *Synthese* vol. 55 (1983), p. 69.

8. See *Judgement and Justification* (Cambridge: Cambridge University Press, 1988).

9. This same point is made by P. Skagestadt in "Hypothetical Realism" in Brewer and Collins (eds.) *Scientific Inquiry and the Social Sciences: A Volume in Honor of Donald T. Campbell* (San Fransico: Jossey-Bass, 1981), p. 92.

10. Ron Giere, *Explaining Science" A Cognitive Approach* (Chicago: University of Chicago Press, 1988).

11. See P. S. Churchland's *Neurophilosophy* (Cambridge: MIT Press, 1986); P. M. Churchland's "Eliminative Materialism and the Propositional Attitudes," *Journal of Philosophy* (1981), vol. 78, pp. 67–90 and "Some Reductive Strategies in Cognitive Neurobiology," *MIND* (1986), vol. 95, pp. 279–309. For a similar argument see S. Stitch's, *From Folk Psychology to Cognitive Science* (Cambridge: MIT Press, 1983).

12. For an interesting argument to the effect that folk psychology is not likely to be eliminated in the way the Churchlands assert that it will, see Robert McCauley's "Epistemology in an Age of Cognitive Science," *Philosophical Psychology*, vol. 1 (1988), pp. 147–149.

13. See, for example P. S. Churchland's "Epistemology in an Age of Neuroscience," *The Journal of Philosophy*, vol. LXXXIV, No. 10 (Oct. 1987), p. 546, where she asserts, without benefit of argument, that the basic question in epistemology is indeed the question "How does the brain work?" Also, as an interesting example of an argument seeking to show that traditional epistemological questions can be eliminated owing to advances in cognitive science (advances that presumably show how we can understand human knowledge on a non-propositional basis), see William Bechtel and Adel Abrahamson, "Beyond the Exclusively Propositional Era," *Synthese*, vol. 82 (1990).

14. This same point is made by Ernest Sosa in "Nature Unmirrored: Epistemology Naturalised," *Synthese*, vol. 55 (1983), p. 70. Naturally, if one were able to defend a form of reliabilism similar to that offered by Alvin Goldman, the question "How does the brain work?" would turn out to be a most crucial question in epistemology; but at that point we would not be defending the sort of naturalized epistemology defended by Quine rather than the form offered and defended by Goldman.

15. See Harvey Siegel, *Philosophy of Science,* vol. 47 (1980), pp. 297–321.

16. See P. S. Churchland, "Epistemology in the Age of Neuroscience," *Journal of Philosophy* (Oct. 1987), p. 546.

17. See Michael Bradie, "Evolutionary Epistemology as Naturalised Epistemology," (forthcoming), p. 3.

18. See Peter Munz, *Our Knowledge of the Growth of Knowledge; Popper or Wittgenstien?* (London: Routledge and Kegan Paul, 1987), p. 371. For a defense of a similar argument, see also Michael Ruse's *Taking Darwin Seriously: A Naturalistic Approach to Philosophy* (Oxford: Blackwell, 1986), and W. W. Bartley III, "Philosophy of Biology versus Philosophy of Physics," in G. Radnitzky and W. W. Bartley, III. (eds.) *Evolutionary Epistemology, Theory of Rationality and the Sociology of Knowledge,* LaSalle: Open Court, 1987), p. 206.

19. See Hillary Kornblith, *Naturalizing Epistemology* (Cambridge: MIT Press, 1985), p. 4.

20. Nicholas Rescher, *Methodological Pragmatism* (Oxford: Basil Blackwell, 1977), Ch. 6.

21. For further reasons why evolutionary epistemology has in fact failed to offer any compelling explanation of how what we take to be knowledge, especially scientific knowledge, has developed, see William Bechtel's "Toward Making Evolutionary Epistemology Into a Truly Naturalized Epistemology" in N. Rescher, *Evolution, Cognition and Realism* (Washington, D. C.: University Press of America, 1990).

22. This is an informal reconstruction of the argument defended by Richard Ketchum in his forthcoming paper in *Philosophical Studies*.

23. I would like to thank the Center for the Philosophy of Science at the University of Pittsburgh for the Senior Fellowship and the stimulating environment that made the writing of this essay possible. For the same reason, I am grateful to the Hambridge Center. Also, Nicholas Rescher, David Blumfeld, Bill Bechtel, Milton Snoeyenbos, Douglas Winblad, and Richard Ketchum all provided valuable comments and criticisms.

ELIZABETH ANDERSON

Feminist Epistemology: An Interpretation and a Defense

Feminist epistemology is about the ways gender influences what we take to be knowledge. Consider impersonal theoretical and scientific knowledge, the kind of knowledge privileged in the academy. Western societies have labeled this kind of knowledge "masculine" and prevented women from acquiring and producing it, often on the pretext that it would divert their vital energies from their "natural" reproductive labor (Hubbard 1990; Schiebinger 1989). Theoretical knowledge is also often tailored to the needs of mostly male managers, bureaucrats, and officials exercising power in their role-given capacities (H. Rose 1987; Smith 1974; Collins 1990). Feminist epistemologists claim that the ways gender categories have been used to understand the character and status of theoretical knowledge, whether men or women have produced and applied this knowledge, and whose interests it has served have often had a detrimental impact on its content. For instance, feminist epistemologists suggest that various kinds of practical know-how and personal knowledge (knowledge that bears the marks of the knower's biography and identity), such as the kinds of untheoretical knowledge that mothers have of children, are undervalued when they are labeled "feminine." Given the androcentric need to represent the "masculine" as independent of the "feminine," this labeling has led to a failure to use untheoretical knowledge effectively in theoretical reasoning (Smith 1974; H. Rose 1987).

Traditional epistemology finds these claims of feminist epistemology to be highly disturbing, if not plainly absurd. Some feminist epistemologists in turn have rejected empiricism (Harding 1986) or even traditional epistemology as a whole (Flax 1983) for its seeming inability to comprehend these claims. I argue, contrary to these views, that a naturalized empiricist epistemology offers excellent prospects for advancing a feminist epistemology of theoretical knowledge.

The project of feminist epistemology with respect to theoretical knowledge has two primary aims (Longino 1993a). First, it endeavors to explain the achievements of feminist criticism of science, which is devoted to revealing sexism and androcentrism in theoretical inquiry. An adequate feminist epistemology must explain what it is for a scientific theory or practice to be sexist and androcentric, how these features are expressed in theoretical inquiry and in the application of theoretical knowledge, and what bearing these features have on evaluating research. Second, the project of feminist epistemology aims to defend feminist scientific practices, which incorporate a commitment to the liberation of women and the social and political equality of all persons. An adequate feminist epistemology must explain how research projects with such moral and political commitments can produce knowledge that meets such epistemic standards as empirical adequacy and fruitfulness. I will argue that these aims can be satisfied by a branch of naturalized, social epistemology that retains commitments to a modest empiricism and to rational inquiry. Feminist naturalized epistemologists therefore demand no radical break from the fundamental internal commitments of empirical science. They may propose changes in our conceptions of what these commitments amount to, or changes in our methods of inquiry. But these can be derived from the core concept of reason, conjoined with perhaps surprising yet empirically supported hypotheses about social or psychological obstacles to achieving them, and the social and material arrangements required for enabling better research to be done. To see how such derivations are possible, modest conceptions of empiricism and reason must be explained before I outline a feminist epistemology that employs these notions.

A MODEST EMPIRICISM

I shall call "empiricism" the view that experience ultimately provides all the evidence we have about the world (Nelson 1990), or more modestly, that observation provides the least defeasible evidence we have about the world (Longino 1993a). No thought process operating independently of empirical evidence can rule out any conceivable hypothesis about the world. I believe that empiricism, so understood, is congenial to the puzzling and seemingly bizarre hypotheses of feminist epistemology because it implies two things. First, for all we know, *anything* can cause *anything,* and *anything* might provide an illuminating fruitful model for *any other phenomenon.* There are no sound a priori restrictions on the concepts or vocabulary we use in describing and explaining the world, so long as these concepts "turn wheels" in theories that have empirical implications. Second, empiricism implies that the discovery of the best theories demands the fullest and freest development of our imaginations. There is no reason to think our presently cramped and stunted imaginations set the actual limits of the world, but they do set the limits of what we now take to be possible. We can never know what further stretch of the imagination might uncover and explain what further expanse of the world. Since feminist epistemology and feminist criticism of science contain many empirical claims about the influence of gender on science that appear at first glance to be unimaginable, it is important to note that nothing in empiricism justifies dismissing such claims out of hand.

Empiricism is commonly taken to mean something else: a doctrine that imposes a priori substantive restrictions on the kinds of entities and concepts that can ultimately figure in science. Various self-described empiricists have tried to eliminate from science reference to unobservables, and use of intentional, modal, and evaluative concepts, or to reduce these to concepts thought to be more "naturalistic." These substantive commitments are simply bets as to how empirical science will actually turn out. Transformed into restrictions on the permissible content of theories, they are attempts to win the bets by rigging the game in advance, preventing the exploration of hypotheses that might show them wrong. This contradicts what I take to be the fundamental commitments of modest empiricism. Since feminist epistemology and feminist criticism of science contain many empirical claims couched in unreduced social, intentional, and evaluative vocabularies, it is important to note that modest empiricism is not committed to eliminating such claims from scientific theories.

I take modest empiricism, then, to be a purely methodological doctrine, which rejects a priori commitments to what the content of our theories and models must be. Empiricism is promiscuous in its permissible ontology and opportunistic in its methods and models. Any hypothesis or method is permitted that advances the goals of discovering and explaining novel phenomena consistent with the constraint that the theories produced seek empirical adequacy.

RATIONALITY AS REFLECTIVE ENDORSABILITY

Reason is the power to change our attitudes, intentions, and practices in response to reflection on the merits of having them or engaging in them. Theoretical reason is the power to acquire, reject, and revise our cognitive attitudes (beliefs and theoretical commitments) and our practices of inquiry through reflection on our reasons for holding them and engaging in them—that is, through reflection on arguments and evidence for our beliefs and about the consequences of our practices. Reflective endorsement is the only test for whether a consideration counts as a reason for having any attitude or engaging in any practice of inquiry: we ask, on reflecting on the ways the consideration could or does influence our attitudes and practices and the implications of its influencing us, whether we can endorse its influencing us in those ways. If we can reflectively endorse its influence, we count the consideration as a reason for our attitudes or practices (Anderson 1993, 91–98).

This conception of reason as reflective self-government rejects the ideal of individualistic self-sufficiency, which some feminists have argued is androcentric, or expressive of specifically male needs (Bordo 1987; Duran 1991). Rational inquiry is a social enterprise (Longino 1990; Nelson 1993).

Anything that counts as evidence for a theory must be publicly accessible, and in experimental contexts, replicable by others. Individuals must use tools, methods, and conceptual frameworks developed by others in order to get their own inquiries under way. They must rely on the testimony of others to get evidence that is too costly or difficult for them to gather on their own, and even to interpret the evidence of their own senses (Coady 1992). Thus it is impossible for individuals to rely only on themselves, for the very reason and interpretations of their experience on which they rely and which seems most to be their own, is a social achievement, not an individual endowment (Nelson 1990; Scheman 1983).

The social character of rational inquiry suggests two things. First, the theories produced by our practices of inquiry may bear the marks of the social relations of the inquirers. To the extent that conceptions of gender inform these social relations, we might expect these conceptions to influence theoretical inquiry. Second, insofar as we reflectively reject certain ways that gender influences the practices and products of inquiry, we need not try to correct these problems by demanding that individual investigators somehow abstract from their gender or gender-related values and commitments. Each individual might be subject to perhaps ineradicable cognitive biases or partiality due to gender or other influences. But if the social relations of inquirers are well arranged, then each person's biases can check and correct the others'. In this way, theoretical rationality and objectivity can be expressed by the whole community of inquirers even when no individual's thought processes are perfectly impartial, objective, or sound (Longino 1990; Nelson 1990; Solomon 1994).

FEMINIST EPISTEMOLOGY AS A BRANCH OF NATURALIZED, SOCIAL EPISTEMOLOGY

Many theorists have proposed that we think of feminist epistemology as a social branch of naturalized epistemology (Nelson 1990; Harding 1986; Potter 1993; Tuana 1992; Antony 1993; Duran 1991). Naturalized epistemologists consider knowledge

production as an activity in which inquirers are subject to the same causal forces that affect their objects of study (Quine 1969). They ask of science that it provide an account of its own activity. This point of view enables us to investigate empirically how knowledge changes as we change factors concerning the inquirers. Social epistemology is the branch of naturalized epistemology that investigates the influence of specifically social factors on knowledge production: who gets to participate in theoretical inquiry, who listens to whom, the relative prestige of different styles and fields of research, the political and economic conditions in which inquirers conduct their investigations, the social settings in which they interact with the subjects of study, their ideological commitments, the availability of models and narrative forms in the culture that can be used to structure scientific observation and explain phenomena, and so forth. Feminist epistemology can be regarded as the branch of social epistemology that investigates the influence of *socially constructed conceptions and norms of gender and gender-specific interests and experiences* on the production of knowledge. It asks how the historical exclusion of women from theoretical inquiry has affected the direction and content of research in fields such as anthropology, philosophy, and psychology; how the use of gender metaphors in biology has made some phenomena more salient than others; how history, economics, and medicine would change if we viewed phenomena from the standpoint of women's rather than men's lives; how the feminist movement has changed our data, our ways of describing the data, and our theories about differences between men and women.

These are all empirical questions. By framing the questions of feminist epistemology as empirical ones, feminist theorists can challenge mainstream theorists, who are largely empiricists, in a way that they cannot responsibly ignore or dismiss. This way of framing feminist epistemology also enables feminists to make arguments for reforming theoretical practice in terms internal to the self-critical commitments of science itself. Feminist criticisms and remedies can be seen as particular, if surprising, instances of general types of criticism and remedy already acknowledged and accommodated by scientific practice. For naturalized epistemology, considered as a tool for improving scientific practices, is already incorporated into the self-critical and self- reforming institutions of science.

How can naturalized epistemology, which studies how knowledge claims are actually produced, support normative views about how we ought to produce knowledge claims? This gap between "is" and "ought" is bridged by the reflective self-endorsement test. Naturalized epistemology considers inquirers in their social relations as systems of belief-formation processes, and theoretical inquiry as a social practice that uses these processes to generate new beliefs. These beliefs in turn are related to one another through various explanatory theories, models, or narratives that aim to produce understanding of the phenomena being studied. This two-level representation of theoretical inquiry suggests two ways naturalized epistemology can get critical leverage on our knowledge practices. First, we can examine our belief-formation processes. Some of these processes are such that, once we reflect on how they work or what they do, we lose confidence in the beliefs to which they give rise, since they do not reliably lead to true beliefs (consider optical illusions). Other processes satisfy the reflective endorsement test: reflecting on how they work or what they do leads us to endorse them and the beliefs to which they give rise (consider deductive inference). A knowledge practice is rational to the extent that it promotes such critical self-reflections and responds to them by checking or canceling out the unreliable belief-formation mechanisms and enabling the reliable ones.

The institution of placebo-controlled, double-blind, multi-center trials as the standard for testing drugs represents an exemplary critical achievement of naturalized epistemology. Each feature of this experimental standard was instituted in response to the discovery of an unreliable belief-formation mechanism that had to be checked. The well-known placebo effect, in which subjects report symptom improvement when they receive *any* intervention they believe may help them, is checked by requiring that the therapeutic effects of drugs be measured against a control group which is administered a placebo, and by requiring that subjects not know whether they belong to the control or the experimental group. Wishful thinking on the part of ex-

perimenters, which leads to exaggerated reports of the therapeutic effectiveness of drugs on trial, is checked by making the tests double-blind, so that even the experimenter does not know which group subjects belong to. Multi-center trials ensure that experimental outcomes are not merely an artifact of the micro-culture of researchers at a single site. These are all reforms scientific institutions have made in the past few decades, in response to scientific studies of its own practice.

The normative implications of much feminist epistemology and feminist criticism of science can be modeled on the case of double-blind testing. If a gendered norm is found to influence the production of knowledge claims in ways that cannot be reflectively endorsed, then we have epistemic reasons to reform our knowledge practices so that this norm is changed or its effects are blocked. Feminist empiricist epistemology thus produces arguments of the same logical type as those already accepted by our knowledge practices.

Feminist empiricist epistemology can generate normative implications for theory in a second way. The model of double-blind testing works only at the level of weeding out false beliefs. But getting an adequate understanding of phenomena is not simply a matter of removing sexist or androcentric bias from factual claims so as to allow scientists to see unvarnished truth. For theoretical inquiry does not aim simply to generate true beliefs. One can add to the stock of true beliefs without the aid of systematic theorizing. Although empirical adequacy poses a fundamental constraint on theorizing, the point of theory is to organize beliefs and generate understanding through models that explain phenomena that people find significant, important, or fundamental, and that abstract from phenomena thought to be unimportant. But whether a phenomenon is considered important or fundamental depends on practical needs and interests, which may be gendered or staked in other socially constructed positions such as class (Tiles 1987). Theories or models offer us only partial maps of the world. Thus different people may find different models satisfactory, depending on which aspects of the world the models highlight (Longino 1993b, 114–16).

This relativity of the value of a model to the socially conditioned interests and experiences of the people to whom it is offered does not imply that theoretical explanations must be false, or that all are equally good, or that there is no common basis for comparing their merits. Empirical adequacy provides the fundamental and common standard for comparing all theories. But a theory can be empirically adequate without being interesting or useful.

Thus, feminist naturalized epistemology uses reason both to constrain and to expand the range of acceptable theories, given what we know about how theories are formed. By raising the standards for evaluating methods of data collection and interpretation in the light of the reflective endorsement test, feminist epistemologists limit the field of credible theories. By legitimizing the explicit introduction of feminist interests to justify the choice of different models, feminist epistemologists use reason in its permissive mode to open up space for alternative theories oriented toward liberatory ends and to contest theories that close off possibilities for social change by representing the subjects of study as if they had no room to maneuver (Longino 1989, 210–13).

Such moves to multiply available explanatory models, like the moves to reform scientific practices on the lines of the double-blind experiment, are internal to the practices of science. These two types of critical activity correspond to the two goals of the feminist epistemology of theoretical knowledge: to legitimate science oriented toward feminist ends and to underwrite feminist criticism of sexist and androcentric science. The fact that these activities can be situated inside science does not mean that the changes feminist epistemology recommends for science must be modest. The sorts of criticisms that generate internal reform of scientific practices today focus on such matters as improving data-gathering instruments and technical features of experimental method. Feminist epistemology and feminist criticism of science focus on changing the background social conditions in which science is practiced. It is therefore an explicitly political enterprise, but one that is justified by epistemic values, such as reason and empirical adequacy, to which science already declares its allegiance.

The variety of claims made by feminist epistemologists and feminist critics of science is bewildering. Without attempting to account for or endorse all the conflicting claims made in the name of feminist epistemology, I shall follow the strategy of reading most of them as contributions to a research program in naturalized social epistemology. I propose that we can sort most of them into four categories, each specifying a particular type of gender influence on theoretical inquiry. Feminist epistemology has generally been better at identifying the ways gender is implicated in our knowledge practices than at explaining how these findings should affect our evaluations of the practices or the theories they produce (Longino 1993a). Naturalized epistemology provides a framework for developing such explanations. So I suggest some questions that probe the normative implications of each category of gender influence on theorizing.

First, studies that investigate *gender structures* focus on the ways gender norms structure the division of labor in society, including the divisions between intellectual and manual and service labor, and within the academy, among different disciplines and subfields, and among primary researchers, teachers, and assistants. These studies consider how the content of theories has been affected by historical discrimination against women entering the sciences, by the difficulties women scientists have getting their work recognized, and by the ways women have changed the orientation of fields of study once they have entered the elite ranks in significant numbers. These studies seek to answer the question, What difference does, or would, an equal representation and status of women researchers make to theoretical inquiry?

Second, some studies consider the uses of *gender symbolism*, which occurs when we represent nonhuman or inanimate phenomena as "masculine" or "feminine" and model them after gender ideals or stereotypes. Feminist epistemologists have found gender symbolism to be pervasive in theoretical inquiry. It is used to represent the relations of scientists to their subjects of study and the relations of different types of knowledge or of different disciplines and subfields to one another, to describe the character of scientific objectivity, and to model nonhuman and inanimate phenomena. These studies seek to answer the question, What difference does it make to our theories and our scientific practices that we conceive of theoretical inquiry itself and its subjects of study as gendered phenomena? How would our theories and practices of inquiry change if we altered our conceptions of the "masculine" and the "feminine," or ceased to employ gender symbolism in understanding our own theorizing or inanimate objects?

Third, some studies focus on *androcentrism* in biology, the social sciences, and cultural and literary studies. Androcentrism occurs when theories take males, men's lives, or "masculinity" to set the norm for humans or animals generally, with female differences either ignored or represented as deviant; when phenomena are viewed from the perspective of men's lives, without regard to how women see them differently; and when male activities or predicaments are represented as the primary causes or sites of important changes, without regard to the roles of females in initiating or facilitating changes or the ways the situation of females has been crucial to determining structural constraints and potentials for change. These studies ask, How would the content of theories be different if we viewed phenomena from the perspective of women's lives, or refused to accept either "masculinity" or "femininity" as setting the norm for humans or animals generally?

Fourth, some studies focus on *sexism* in theory, which can appear either in practices that apply the theory or in the content of the theory itself. Sexism is evident when theories are *applied* in ways that undermine women's interests or that reinforce their subordination to men. The *content* of a theory is sexist when it asserts that women are inferior to men, justly or inevitably subordinated to men, or properly confined to gender-stereotyped roles, or when it judges or describes women according to sexist ideals or double standards, or when it uses such claims as background assumptions to secure an evidential link between observations and theoretical claims. Feminist studies of sexism in theories explore the prospects for alternative scientific theories that meet criteria of empirical adequacy while seeking to serve women's interests and to promote universal equality.

THE GENDERED DIVISION OF THEORETICAL LABOR

Feminist critics of science have carefully documented the history of women's exclusion from theoretical inquiry (Rossiter 1982; Schiebinger 1989). Although formal barriers to women's entry into var-

ious academic disciplines are now illegal in the United States, informal barriers at all levels remain. Girls are socialized by parents and peers to avoid studying or excelling in subjects considered "masculine," such as mathematics and the natural sciences. Teachers and school counselors actively discourage girls from pursuing these subjects (Curran 1980, 30–32). The classroom climate in mixed-gender schools favors boys. Teachers pay more attention and offer more encouragement to white boys than to girls, solicit their participation more, and expect them to achieve more, especially in mathematics courses (Becker 1981; AAUW 1992). Boys marginalize girls in class by interruption and sexual harassment (AAUW 1992). These behaviors in mixed-gender schools have a detrimental impact on girls' academic ambitions and performance. Girls in all-girl schools express a wider diversity of academic interests and perform better academically than girls in mixed-gender schools (Curran 1980, 34). The disadvantage to women's academic performance and interests from attending mixed-gender schools extends to college. The predominantly male faculty in mixed-gender colleges support women students' academic ambitions less than male and female faculty at women's colleges. Women's colleges produce 50 percent more high-achieving women relative to the number of their female graduates than coeducational institutions (Tidball 1980). Graduate schools present women with informal barriers or costs to advancement, including sexual harassment and exclusion from networks of male mentors and colleagues often vital to the advancement of aspiring academics (Reskin 1979; S. Rose 1989).

Women who overcome these obstacles and obtain advanced degrees are not treated as equals once they enter academic positions. Women whose qualifications are comparable to their male colleagues get lower pay, less research support, jobs in less prestigious institutions, lower-ranking positions, and positions that assign more and lower-level teaching (Astin and Beyer 1973; Fox 1981). The prestige of the graduate institution, publications, and having one's work cited aid men's career advancement much more than women's (Rosenfeld 1981). Women in scientific and engineering professions with publication rates equal to those of their male peers have higher unemployment rates, lower starting salaries, and lower academic rank than men. These differences cannot be explained by the greater impact on women of marriage and children (Vetter 1981). The National Science Foundation (1984) found that after adjusting for factors such as women interrupting their careers to take care of children, half the salary differential between male and female scientists could be explained only by sex discrimination.

The gendered division of theoretical labor does not simply prevent women from doing research or getting published. It fits into a broader gendered structure of epistemic authority which assigns greater credibility, respect, and importance to men's than women's claims. Laboratory, field, and natural experiments alike show that the perceived gender of the author influences people's judgments of the quality of research, independent of its content. Psychologists M. A. Paludi and W. D. Bauer (1983) found that a group told that a paper's author was "John T. McKay" assigned it a much higher average ranking than a group told that the same paper's author was "Joan T. McKay." A group told that its author was "J. T. McKay" rated the paper between the other groups' evaluations, reflecting the suspicion that the author was a woman trying to conceal her gender identity. Academics are no less disposed than others to judge the quality of work higher simply because they believe a man has done it. L. S. Fidell (1970) sent vitae identical in all but name to heads of psychology departments that advertised open rank positions. The jobs the psychologists said they would offer to the purportedly male applicant were higher-ranking than those they were willing to offer to the purportedly female applicant. When the Modern Language Association reviewed papers submitted for their meetings with authors' names attached, men's submissions were accepted at significantly higher rates than women's. After the MLA instituted blind reviewing of papers, women's acceptance rates rose to equality with men's (Lefkowitz 1979).

The concerns raised by the influence of sexist norms on the division of theoretical labor and epistemic authority are not simply matters of justice. Feminist epistemology asks what impact these injustices toward women students and researchers have

had on the content, shape, and progress of theoretical knowledge. In some cases, sex discrimination in the academy has demonstrably retarded the growth of knowledge. It took more than three decades for biologists to understand and recognize the revolutionary importance of Barbara McClintock's discovery of genetic transposition. Her attempts to communicate this discovery to the larger scientific community met with incomprehension and disdain. This failure can be partly explained by the fact that no biology department was willing to hire her for a permanent position despite her distinguished record of discoveries and publications. Lacking the opportunities such a position would have provided to recruit graduate students to her research program, McClintock had no one else doing research like hers who could replicate her results or help communicate them to a wider scientific community (Keller 1983).

Cases such as McClintock's demonstrate that the gendered structure of theoretical labor and cognitive authority sometimes slows the progress of knowledge. But does it change the content or shape of knowledge or the direction of knowledge growth? If the gender of the knower is irrelevant to the content of what is investigated, discovered, or invented, then the impact of removing sex discrimination would be to add to the pace of knowledge growth by adding more inquirers and by raising the average level of talent and dedication in the research community. Feminist epistemology would then recommend strictly "gender-blind" changes in the processes by which research jobs get assigned and epistemic authority distributed. The MLA's adoption of blind reviewing of papers to reduce cognitive bias due to sexism in the evaluation of research represents an exemplary application of this side of feminist epistemology. It is logically on a par with the institution of double-blind testing in drug research to reduce cognitive bias due to wishful thinking.

But if the gender of the inquirer makes a difference to the content of what is accepted as knowledge, then the exclusion and undervaluation of women's participation in theoretical inquiry does not merely set up randomly distributed roadblocks to the improvement of understanding. It imparts a systematic bias on what is taken to be knowledge. If the gender of the inquirer makes a difference to what is known, then feminist epistemology would not confine its recommendations to purely gender-blind reforms in our knowledge practices. It could recommend that these knowledge practices actively seek gender diversity and balance among inquirers and actively attend to the gender of the researchers in evaluating their products.

The gender of the researcher is known to make a difference to what is known in certain areas of social science. In survey research, subjects give different answers to questions depending on the perceived gender of the interviewer (Sherif 1987, 47–48). The perceived race of the interviewer also influences subjects' responses. It is a highly significant variable accounting for subjects' responses to questions about race relations (Schuman and Hatchett 1974). In anthropology, informants vary their responses depending on the gender of the anthropologist. In many societies, male anthropologists have less access to women's social worlds than female anthropologists do (Leacock 1982). The race of the researcher affects access to social worlds as well. Native Americans sometimes grant Asian anthropologists access to religious rituals from which they ban whites (Pai 1985).

Where the perceived gender and race of the researcher are variables influencing the phenomena being observed or influencing access to the phenomena, sound research design must pay attention to the gender and racial makeup of the researchers. In survey research, these effects can be analytically excised by ensuring a gender balanced and racially diverse research team and then statistically isolating the variations in responses due to factors other than subjects' responses to the characteristics of the interviewers. In anthropology, the method of reflexive sociology, instead of attempting to analyze away these effects, treats them as a subject of study in their own right. It advises researchers to interpret what informants tell them not as straightforward native observation reports on their own culture, but as reflections of a strategic interaction between informant and researcher and between the informant and other members of the community being studied (Bourdieu 1977). To obtain a complete representation of informants' report strategies with respect to gender, both male and female researchers must interact with both male and female informants and consider why informants varied their responses according to their own and the researcher's gender (see Bell, Caplan, and Karim [1993] for exemplary cases of feminist reflexive anthropology). Similar reasoning applies to factors such as race, class, nationality, and sexual orientation. So reflexive sociology, like survey research, requires a diversity of inquirers to obtain worthwhile results.

The phenomena just discussed concern the *causal* impact of the gender of the researcher on the *object* of knowledge. Many feminist epistemologists claim that the gender of the inquirer influences the *character* of knowledge itself by another route, which travels through the subjectivity of the researcher herself. The gender of the researcher influences what is known not just through her influence on the object of knowledge but by what are claimed to be gender-specific or gender-typical cognitive or affective dispositions, skills, knowledge, interests, or methods that she brings to the study of the object. The variety of claims of this type must be sorted through and investigated with great care. Some are local and modest. No one disputes that personal knowledge of what it is like to be pregnant, undergo childbirth, suffer menstrual cramps, and have other experiences of a female body is specific to women. Gynecology has certainly progressed since women have entered the field and have brought their personal knowledge to bear on misogynist medical practices. The claims get more controversial the more global they are in scope. Some people claim that women have gender-typical "ways of knowing," styles of thinking, methodologies, and ontologies that globally govern or characterize their cognitive activities across all subject matters. For instance, various feminist epistemologists have claimed that women think more intuitively and contextually, concern themselves more with particulars than abstractions, emotionally engage themselves more with individual subjects of study, and frame their thoughts in terms of a relational rather than an atomistic ontology (Belenky, Clinchy, Goldberger and Tarule 1986; Gilligan 1982; H. Rose 1987; Smith 1974; Collins 1990).

There is little persuasive evidence for such global claims (Tavris 1992, chap. 2). I believe the temptation to accept them is based partly on a confusion between gender symbolism—the fact that certain styles of thinking are *labeled* "feminine"—and the actual characteristics of women. It is also partly due to the lack of more complex and nuanced models of how women entering certain fields have changed the course of theorizing for reasons that seem connected to their gender or their feminist commitments. I will propose an alternative model toward the end of this essay, which does not suppose that women theorists bring some shared feminine difference to all subjects of knowledge. Controversies over supposed global differences in the ways men and women think have tended to overshadow other highly interesting work in feminist epistemology that does not depend on claims that men and women think in essentially different ways. The influence of gendered concepts and norms in our knowledge practices extends far beyond the ways male and female individuals are socialized and assigned to different roles in the division of labor. To see this, consider the role of *gender symbolism* in theoretical knowledge.

GENDER SYMBOLISM (I): The Hierarchy of Knowledge

It is a characteristic of human thought that our concepts do not stay put behind the neat logical fences philosophers like to erect for them. Like sly coyotes, they slip past these flimsy barriers to range far and wide, picking up consorts of all varieties, and, in astonishingly fecund acts of miscegenation shocking to conceptual purists, leave offspring who bear a disturbing resemblance to the wayward parent and inherit the impulse to roam the old territory. The philosophical guardians of these offspring, trying to shake off the taint of sexual scandal but feeling guilty about the effort, don't quite know whether to cover up a concept's pedigree or, by means of the discovery/justification distinction, deny that it matters. The latter strategy can work only if, like keepers of a zoo, the philosophers can keep their animals fenced in. Feminist epistemologists track these creatures sneaking past their fences while their keepers dream of tamed animals happy to remain confined.

The most cunning and promiscuous coyotes are our gender concepts. In a manner befitting their own links to sex, they will copulate with *anything*. Feminist epistemologists note that there is hardly any concep-

tual dichotomy that has not been modeled after and in turn used to model the masculine/feminine dichotomy: mind/body, culture/nature, reason/emotion, objective/subjective, tough-minded/soft-hearted, and so forth. These scandalous metaphorical unions generate conceptions of knowledge, science, and rational inquiry, as well as conceptions of the objects of these inquiries, that are shaped in part by sexist views about the proper relations between men and women. Feminist epistemologists investigate how these conceptions are informed and distorted by sexist imagery. They also consider how alternative conceptions are suppressed by the limits imposed by sexism on the imagination, or by the sexist or androcentric interests served by their present symbolic links to gender (Rooney 1991).

Gender symbolism appears on at least two levels of our knowledge practices: in the construction of a hierarchy of prestige and authority among kinds and fields of knowledge and in the content of theoretical inquiry itself. Consider first the ways different kinds and fields of knowledge are gendered. At the most general level, impersonal theoretical knowledge is coded "masculine." Personal knowledge—the kind of knowledge that is inseparable from the knower's identity, biography, and emotional experiences—is coded "feminine." Theoretical knowledge is thought to be masculine in part because it lays claims to objectivity, which is thought to be achieved through the rigorous exclusion from thought of feminine subjectivity—of emotions, particularity, interests, and values. These uses of gender symbolism have *epistemic* import because they structure a hierarchy of prestige and cognitive authority among kinds of knowledge, and hence of knowers, that is homologous with the gender hierarchy. As men in sexist society express contempt for women and enjoy higher prestige than women, so do theoretical knowers express contempt for those with "merely" personal knowledge of the same subject matters, and enjoy higher prestige than they. Echoing the sexist norms that women must obey men but men need not listen to women, the gender-coded hierarchy of knowledge embodies the norm that personal knowledge must submit to the judgments of impersonal theoretical knowledge, while theoretical knowledge has nothing to learn from personal knowledge and may ignore its claims.

These epistemic norms cannot withstand reflective scrutiny. Successful theorizing deeply depends on personal knowledge, particularly embodied skills, and often depends on emotional engagement with the subjects of study (Polanyi 1958; Keller 1983, 1985). Cora Diamond's (1991) insightful discussion of Vicki Hearne's personal knowledge as an animal trainer provides a particularly fine illustration of this point. Hearne's writings (1982) expose the failures of knowledge that occur when theorists ignore the experiences, skills, and language of animal trainers. In her animal training classes, Hearne observed that people's success in training their pets was inversely related to their training in the behavioral sciences. The anthropomorphic and value-laden language of animal trainers enables them to understand what animals are doing in ways not readily accessible to the impersonal, behavioristic language favored by most behavioral scientists. And their skills and personal knowledge of the animals they work with empower trainers to elicit from animals considerably more complex and interesting behaviors than scientists elicit. These powers are not irrelevant to theorizing about animals. Reflecting on Hearne's story about the philosopher Ray Frey, Diamond writes:

> [Frey] attempted to set up a test for his dog's capacity to rank rational desires. When, in order to see how the dog would rank desires, he threw a stick for his dog . . . and at the same time put food before the dog, the dog stood looking at him. Frey could not see that the dog wanted to know what Frey wanted him to do; Frey's conception of the dog as part of an experimental set-up (taken to include two possible desired activities but not taken to include queer behavior by the dog's master), with Frey as the observer, blocked his understanding. Frey's past experience with his dog did not feed an understanding of how the dog saw him; he could not grasp his own failure, as the dog's master, to make coherent sense, so could not see the dog as responding to that failure to make sense. (Diamond 1991, 1014 n. 15)

Diamond diagnoses this epistemic failure as the product of Frey's attachment to a theory of knowledge that distrusts personal experience on the ground that it is distorted by the subject's emotional engagement with the object of knowledge. The theory supposes that we can't achieve objective knowledge of our object through such engagement because all it will offer is a reflection of the subject's own emotions. Subjectivity merely projects qualities onto the object and does not reveal qualities of the object. But the theory is mistaken. Love and respect for another being, animal or person, and trust in the personal experiences of engagement that are informed by such love and respect may be essential both for drawing out and for grasping that being's full potentialities. One of the reasons why behaviorists tend to elicit such boring behavior from animals and humans is that they don't give them the opportunities to exhibit a more impressive repertoire of behaviors that respect for them would require them to offer.

The gender-coded hierarchy of knowledge extends to specific subject matters and methods within theoretical knowledge. The natural sciences are "harder," more like the male body and hence more prestigious, than the social sciences or the "soft" humanities, supposed to be awash in feminine emotionality and subjectivity. Mathematics is coded masculine and is the language of physics, the most prestigious science. Through their closer association with physics, quantitative subfields of biology and the social sciences enjoy higher prestige than subfields of the same discipline or branch of science employing a qualitative, historical, or interpretive methodology. Experimentation asserts more control over subjects of study than observation does. So experimental subfields in biology and psychology are coded masculine and command more cognitive authority than observational subfields of the same disciplines. Values are designated feminine. So normative subfields in philosophy such as ethics and political philosophy enjoy less prestige than supposedly nonnormative fields such as philosophy of language and mind. Social interpretation is thought to be a feminine skill. So interpretive anthropology is designated less masculine, scientific, and rigorous than physical anthropology, which deals with "hard" facts like fossil bones. In each of these cases, the socially enforced norm for relations between fields of knowledge mirrors that of the relations between husband and wife in the ideal patriarchal family: the masculine science is autonomous from and exercises authority over the feminine science, which is supposedly dependent on the former's pronouncements to know what it should think next.

This gendered hierarchy of theoretical subfields produces serious cognitive distortions. Carolyn Sherif (1987) has investigated how the hierarchy of prestige generates cognitive biases in psychology. Forty years ago, experimental psychology dominated developmental and social psychology. The gendered character of this difference in cognitive authority is not difficult to read. Experimental psychologists, by imitating the methods of the "hard" sciences through manipulating quantified variables, claim some of the prestige of the natural sciences. Developmental and social psychologists engage in labor that looks more like the low-status labor conventionally assigned to women. Developmental psychologists work with children; social psychologists deal with human relationships, and forty years ago usually did so in settings not under the control of the researcher. Following the norm that "masculine" sciences need not pay attention to findings in "feminine" sciences, which it is assumed cannot possibly bear on their more "fundamental" research, experimental psychology has a history of constructing experiments that, like Ray Frey's, ignore the ways the social context of the experiment itself and the social relation between experimenter and subject influence outcomes. The result has been a history of findings that lack robustness because they are mere artifacts of the experimental situation. In experimental research on sex differences, this error has taken the form of ascribing observed differences in male and female behavior under experimental conditions to innate difference in male and female psychology rather than to the ways the experiment has socially structured the situation so as to elicit different responses from men and women.

The notorious claim in experimental psychology that women are more suggestible than men offers an instructive illustration of the perils of ignoring social psychology (Sherif 1987, 49–50). The original experiments that confirmed the hypothesis of greater suggestibility involved male researchers trying to persuade men and women to change their beliefs with respect to subject matters

oriented to stereotypical male interests. Unaware of how their own gender-typical interests had imparted a bias in the selection of topics of persuasion, the predominantly male researchers confidently reported as a sex difference in suggestibility what was in fact a difference in suggestibility owing to the degree of interest the subjects had in the topics. Differences in the gender-typed cognitive authority of the researcher also affect subjects' responses. Men are more open to the suggestions of a female researcher when the topic is coded feminine, while women are more open to the suggestions of a male researcher when the topic is coded masculine.

Cognitive distortions due to the gender-coding of types and fields of knowledge are strictly separable from any claims about differences in the ways men and women think. Although it is true that the "feminine" sciences and subfields attract more women researchers than the "masculine" sciences do, the differences in cognitive authority between the various sciences and subfields were modeled on differences in social authority between men and women before women constituted a significant portion of the researchers in any field. Men still predominate even in fields of study that are designated feminine. And scientists' neglect of personal knowledge deprives many men who engage in stereotypically male activities of cognitive authority. For example, animal behaviorists ignore the personal knowledge male policemen have about their police dogs (Diamond 1991). For these reasons, Diamond and Sherif have questioned how gender figures into the cognitive distortions instituted by the hierarchy of knowledge and by scientistic conceptions of objectivity.[1] By shifting our focus from gender structure and supposed gender differences in ways of knowing to gender symbolism, we can see how ideas about gender can distort the relations between forms of knowledge independently of the gender of the knower. In the light of the cognitive distortions caused by the gender-coding of types and domains of knowledge, feminist naturalized epistemologists should recommend that we no longer model the relations between different kinds of knowledge on a sexist view of the authority relations between men and women.

GENDER SYMBOLISM (II): The Content of Theories

Gender symbolism figures in the *content* of theories as well as in their relations of cognitive authority whenever conceptions of human gender relations or gendered characteristics are used to model phenomena that are not gendered. Biology is particularly rich with gender symbolism—in models of gamete fertilization, nucleus-cell interaction, primatology, and evolutionary theory (Biology and Gender Study Group 1988; Haraway 1989; Keller 1985, 1992). Evelyn Fox Keller, a mathematical biologist and feminist philosopher of science, has explored gender symbolism in evolutionary theory most subtly (Keller 1992). Consider the fact that evolutionary theory tends to delineate the unit of natural selection, the entity accorded the status of an "individual," at the point where the theorist is willing to use complex and cooperative rather than competitive models of interaction. Among individuals, antagonistic competition predominates and mutualistic interactions are downplayed. The individual is considered "selfish" in relation to other individuals. Thus, theories that take the gene to be the unit of selection characterize the gene as a ruthless egoist ready to sacrifice the interests of its host organism for the sake of reproducing itself (Dawkins 1976). Where the organism is taken to be the unit of selection, it is represented as selfishly competitive with respect to other individual organisms. But within the individual, cooperation among constitutive parts prevails. Cooperation is modeled after the family, often a patriarchal family. The cells of an individual organism cooperate because of the bonds of kinship: they share the same genes. The constitutive parts of an individual cell cooperate because they are ruled by a wise and benevolent patriarch, the "master molecule" DNA, which autonomously tells all the other parts of the cell what to do, solely on the basis of information it contains within itself. Thus, evolutionary theory models the biological world after a sexist and androcentric conception of liberal society, in which the public sphere is governed by competition among presumably masculine selfish individuals and the private sphere of the family is governed by male heads of households enforcing cooperation among its members (Keller 1992, chap. 8). This model is not rigidly or consistently applied in evolutionary theory, but it does mark theoretical tendencies that can be traced back to the fact that Darwin modeled his theory of natural selection after Malthus's dismal model of capitalist society.

Taken by itself, that evolutionary theory employs a sexist ideology of liberal society to model biological phenomena does not have any straightforward normative implications. Defenders of the theory can appeal to the discovery/justification distinction here: just because a theory had its origins in politically objectionable ideas or social contexts does not mean that it is false or useless. Evolutionary theory is extraordinarily fruitful and empirically well confirmed. The model-theoretic view of theories, widely used by feminist empiricists and feminist postmodernists to analyze the roles of gender in the construction of theoretical knowledge, affirms the epistemic legitimacy of any coherent models, hence of any coherent sexist models, in science (Longino 1993b; Haraway 1986).

In the model-theoretic view, scientific theories propose elaborate metaphors or models of phenomena. Their virtues are empirical adequacy, simplicity, clarity, and fruitfulness. Theories are empirically adequate to the extent that the relations among entities in the model are homologous with the observed relations among entities in the world. Empirically adequate models offer a satisfactory explanation of phenomena to the extent that they model unfamiliar phenomena in ways that are simple, perspicuous and analytically tractable. They are fruitful to the extent that they organize inquirers' conceptions of their subjects in ways that suggest lines of investigation that uncover novel phenomena that can be accommodated by further refinements of the model. Empiricists place no a priori constraints on the things that may constitute useful models for phenomena. Anything might be an illuminating model for anything else. So, empiricists can offer no a priori epistemic objections to modeling nongendered phenomena after gendered ones, even if the models are overtly sexist or patriarchal. Such models may well illuminate and effectively organize important aspects of the objects being studied.

So the trouble with using sexist gender symbolism in theoretical models is not that the models are sexist. The trouble lies rather in the extraordinary political salience and rhetorical power of sexist gender ideology, which generates numerous cognitive distortions. Keller has carefully delineated several such distortions in evolutionary theory, especially with respect to its privileging of models of competitive over cooperative or mutualist interactions among organisms. First, to the extent that political ideology incorporates false conceptual identities and dichotomies, a scientific model borrowing its vocabulary and structure is likely to overlook the alternatives suppressed by that ideology or to elide distinctions between empirically distinct phenomena. The ideology of possessive individualism falsely identifies autonomy with selfishness and falsely contrasts self-interest with cooperation. When used to model phenomena in evolutionary biology, it leads to a false identification of peaceful, passive consumption activity with violent, competitive behavior, and to a neglect of mutualist interactions among organisms. Thus, the mathematical tools of population biology and mathematical ecology are rarely used to model cooperation among organisms although they could do so; in contrast with sociobiology, these mathematical subfields of biology have even neglected the impact of sexual intercourse and parenting behavior on the fitness of organisms (Keller 1992,119–21). Although the technical definition of competition avoids false identities and dichotomies, biologists constantly turn to its colloquial meanings to explain their findings and frame research questions. In this way, "the use of a term with established colloquial meaning in a technical context permits the simultaneous transfer and denial of its colloquial connotations" (Keller 1992,121). When the language used in a model has particularly strong ideological connotations, the cognitive biases it invites are particularly resistant to exposure and criticism.

The symbolic identification of the scientific with a masculine outlook generates further cognitive distortions. The ideology of masculinity, in representing emotion as feminine and as cognitively distorting, falsely assimilates emotion-laden thoughts—and even thoughts about emotions—to sentimentality. In identifying the scientific outlook with that of a man who has outgrown his tutelage, cut his dependence on his mother, and is prepared to meet the competitive demands of the public sphere with a clear eye, the ideology of masculinity tends to confuse seeing the natural world as indifferent in the sense of devoid of teleological laws with seeing the social world as hostile in the sense of full of agents who pursue their interests at others' expense (Keller 1992, 116–18). This confusion tempts biologists into thinking that the selfishness their models ascribe to genes and the ruthless strategic rationality their models ascribe to individual organisms (mere metaphors, however theoretically powerful) are more "real" than the actual care a dog expresses toward her pups. Such thoughts also reflect the rhetoric of unmasking base motivations behind policies that seem to be benevolent, a common if overused tactic in liberal politics and political theory. The power of this rhetoric depends on an appearance/reality distinction that has no place where the stakes are competing social *models* of biological phenomena, whose merits depend on their metaphorical rather than their referential powers. Thus, to the extent that the theoretical preference for competitive models in biology is underwritten by rhetoric borrowed from androcentric political ideologies, the preference reflects a confusion between models and reality as well as an unjustified intrusion of androcentric political loyalties into the scientific enterprise.

These are not concerns that can be relieved by deploying the discovery/justification distinction. To the extent that motivations tied to acquiring a masculine-coded prestige as a theorist induce mathematical ecologists to overlook the epistemic defects of models of natural selection that fail to consider the actual impact of sexual selection, parenting, and cooperative interactions, they distort the context of justification itself. Some of the criteria of justification, such as simplicity, are also distorted in the light of the androcentric distinction between public and private values. For example, simplicity in mathematical biology has been characterized so as to prefer explanations of apparently favorable patterns of group survival in terms of chance to explanations in terms of interspecific feedback loops, if straight forward individualistic mechanisms are not available to explain them (Keller 1992,153). Finally, to the extent that gender ideologies inform the context of discovery by influencing the direction of inquiry and development of mathematical tools, they prevent the growth of alternative models and the tools that could make them tractable, and hence they bias our views of what is "simple" (Keller 1992,160). The discovery/ justification distinction, while useful when considering the epistemic relation of a theory to its confirming or disconfirming evidence, breaks down once we consider the relative merits of alternative theories. In the latter context, any influence that biases the development of the field of alternatives will bias the evaluation of theories. A theoretical approach may appear best justified not because it offers an adequate model of the world but because androcentric ideologies have caused more thought and resources to be invested in it than in alternatives.

So feminist naturalized epistemologists should offer a complex verdict on gender symbolism in the content of theories. They should leave open the possibility that gendered models of ungendered phenomena may be highly illuminating and successful, and hence legitimately used in theoretical inquiry. The impressive explanatory successes of evolutionary theory demonstrate this. At the same time, the ideological power of gender symbolism sometimes gets the better of otherwise careful theorists. It can generate conceptual confusion in ways that are hard to detect, and obscure theoretical possibilities that may be worth pursuing. The most reliable way to tell when the use of gender symbolism is generating such cognitive distortions is to critically investigate the gender ideology it depends on and the role this ideology plays in society. In other words, theorists who use gendered models would do well to consider how feminist theory can help them avoid cognitive distortion. Feminist naturalized epistemologists therefore should recommend that theorists attracted to gendered models of ungendered phenomena proceed with caution, in consultation with feminist theorists. It recommends an important change in the cognitive authority of disciplines, through its demonstration that biologists have something to learn from feminist theory after all.

ANDROCENTRISM

A knowledge practice is androcentric if it reflects an orientation geared to specifically or typically male interests or male lives. Androcentrism can appear in a knowledge practice in at least two ways: in the content of theories or research programs and in the interests that lead inquirers to frame their research in certain terms or around certain problems. Feminists in the natural and social sciences have advanced feminist epistemology most fully and persuasively by exposing androcentrism in the content of social-scientific and biological theories.

The content of theories can be androcentric in several ways. A theory may reflect the view that males, male lives, or "masculinity" set the norm for humans or animals generally. From this point of view, females, their lives, or "feminine" characteristics are represented as problematic, deviations from the norm, and hence in need of a type of explanation not required for their male counterparts. Androcentrism of this sort often appears in the ways theoretical questions are framed. For decades, psychological and biological research about sex differences has been framed by the question, "Why are women different from men?" and the presumed sex difference has cast women in a deviant position. Researchers have been preoccupied with such questions as why girls are more suggestible, less ambitious, less analytically minded, and have lower self-esteem than boys. Let us leave aside the fact that all these questions are based on unfounded beliefs about sex differences (Maccoby and Jacklin 1974). Why haven't researchers asked why boys are less responsive to others, more pushy, less synthetically minded, and more conceited than girls? The framing of the problem to be investigated reflects not just a commitment to asymmetrical explanation of men's and women's characteristics, but to an evaluation of women's differences as dimensions of inferiority (Tavris 1992, chap. 1). It is thus sexist as well as androcentric.

Another way in which the content of theories can be androcentric is in describing or defining phenomena from the perspective of men or typically male lives, without paying attention to how they would be described differently if examined from the point of view of women's lives. Economists and political scientists have traditionally defined class and socioeconomic status from the point of view of men's lives: a man's class or socioeconomic status is defined in terms of his own occupation or earnings, whereas a women's status is defined in terms of her father's or husband's occupation or earnings. Such definitions obscure the differences in power, prestige, and opportunities between male managers and their homemaker wives, and between homemaker wives and female managers (Stiehm 1983). They also prevent an analysis of the distinctive economic roles and status of full-time homemakers and of adult independent unmarried women. The distinction between labor and leisure, central to standard economic analyses of the supply of wage labor, also reflects the perspective of male heads of households (Waring 1990). Classically, the distinction demarcates the public from the private spheres by contrasting their characteristic activities as having negative versus positive utility, or instrumental versus intrinsic value, or as controlled by others versus freely self-directed. From the standpoint of the lives of women with husbands or children, these demarcations make no sense. These women are not at leisure whenever they are not engaged in paid labor. Professional women often find much of their unpaid work to constitute a drudgery from which paid labor represents an escape with positive intrinsic value. Middle-class and working-class women who engage in paid labor and who cannot afford to hire others to perform their household tasks and child care are better represented as engaged in (sometimes involuntary) dual-career or double-shift labor than in trading off labor for leisure. Full-time mothers and homemakers often view what some consider to be their leisure activities as highly important work in its own right, even if it is unpaid.

The androcentrism implicit in the standard economic definition of productive labor has profound implications for national income accounting, the fundamental conceptual framework for defining and measuring what counts as economically relevant data for macroeconomic theory. It effectively excludes women's gender-typical unpaid domestic labor from gross national product (GNP) calculations, making women's work largely invisible in the economy. In the advanced industrialized nations, economists explain this omission by arguing that GNP figures properly measure only the economic value of production for market exchange. In developing nations, where only a modest proportion of productive activity shows up in market exchanges,

economists have long recognized the uselessness of measures of national production that look only at the market; so they impute a market value to various unmarketed domestic production activities associated with subsistence agriculture, home construction, and the like. But which of these household activities do economists choose to count as productive? In practice, they have defined the "production boundary" in such societies by imposing an obsolete Western androcentric conception of the household. They assume that households consist of a productive primary producer, the husband, who supports a wife engaged in "housework," which is assumed to be economically unimportant or unproductive. "Housework" has no clear definition in societies where most production takes place within the household. So economists apply the concept of "housework" to whatever productive activities a society conventionally assigns to women. Thus, women's unmarketed labor in these societies counts as productive only if men usually perform it too, whereas men's unmarketed labor is usually counted in the national income statistics regardless of its relation to women's labor (Waring 1990, 74–87). The result is that in Africa, where women do 70 percent of the hoeing and weeding of subsistence crops, 80 percent of crop transportation and storage, and 90 percent of water and fuel collecting and food processing, these vital activities rarely appear in the national income accounts (Waring 1990, 84). Here, androcentrism is built into the very data for economic theorizing, in such a way that women's gender-typical activities become invisible.

Even when a theory does not go so far as to define the phenomena in a way that excludes female activities, it may still be androcentric in assuming that male activities or predicaments are the sole or primary sources of important changes or events. Until recently, primatologists focused almost exclusively on the behavior of male primates. They assumed that male sexual and dominance behaviors determined the basic structure of primate social order, and that the crucial social relationships among troop-dwelling primates that determined the reproductive fitness of individuals and maintained troop organization were between the dominant male and other males. The assumption followed from a sociobiological argument that claimed to show that females of any species will typically be the "limiting resource" for reproduction: most females will realize an equal and maximum reproductive potential, while males will vary enormously in their reproductive fitness. Natural selection, the driving force of evolutionary change, would therefore operate primarily on male characteristics and behavior (Hrdy 1986).

These assumptions were not seriously challenged until women, some inspired by the feminist movement, started entering the field of primatology in substantial numbers in the mid-1970s. Many studied female-female and female-infant interactions, female dominance and cooperative behavior, and female sexual activity. By turning their focus from male to female behaviors and relationships, they found that infant survival varied enormously, depending on the behavior and social status of the mothers, that troop survival itself sometimes depended on the eldest female (who would teach others the location of distant water holes that had survived droughts), and that female-directed social and sexual behaviors play key roles in maintaining and changing primate social organizations (Hrdy 1981; Haraway 1989). Today the importance of female primates is widely recognized and studied by both male and female primatologists.

What normative implications should be drawn about the epistemic status of androcentric theories? Some feminist epistemologists propose that theory can proceed better by viewing the world through the eyes of female agents. Gynocentric theory can be fun. What could be a more amusing retort to a study that purports to explain why women lack self-esteem than a study that explains why men are conceited? It can also be instructive. Richard Wrangham (1979) has proposed a gynocentric model of primate social organization that has achieved widespread recognition in primatology. The model assumes the centrality of female competition for food resources, and predicts how females will space themselves (singly or in kin-related groups) according to the distribution of the foods they eat. Males then space themselves so as to gain optimum access to females. The model is gynocentric both in defining the core of primate social groups around female kin-relations rather than around relations to a dominant male and in taking the situation of females to constitute the primary variable that accounts for variations in male

and general primate social organization. According to the feminist primatologist Sarah Hrdy (1981,126), Wrangham's model offers the best available explanation of primate social organization.

The three androcentric theoretical constructs mentioned correspond to three different ways in which a theory could be "gender-centric": in taking one sex or gender to set the norm for both, in defining central concepts with respect to the sex- or gender-typical characteristics, behaviors, or perspectives of males or females alone, and in taking the behaviors, situation, or characteristics of one sex or gender to be causally central in determining particular outcomes. These logical differences in gender-centric theorizing have different epistemic implications. As Wrangham's theory shows, gynocentric causal models can sometimes be superior to androcentric models. Whether they are superior in any particular domain of interest is an empirical question. It can only be answered by comparing rival gender-centric models to one another and to models that do not privilege either male- or female-typical activities or situations in their causal accounts, but rather focus on activities and situations common to both males and females. An important contribution of feminist scholarship in the social sciences and biology has been to show that the activities and situations of females have been far more causally important in various domains than androcentric theories have recognized.

The other two types of gender-centrism are much more problematic than this causal type. A theory that takes one gender to set the norm for both must bear an explanatory burden not borne by theories that refuse to represent difference as deviance. It must explain why an asymmetrical explanation is required for male- and female-specific characteristics. Given the dominant background assumption of modern science that the cosmos does not have its own telos, it is hard to justify any claim that one gender naturally sets the norm for both. Claims about norms must be located in human value judgments, which is to say that the only justification for normative gender-centrism would have to lie in a substantive sexist moral or political theory. As we shall see below, empiricism does not rule out the use of value judgments as background assumptions in scientific theories. Nevertheless, this analysis of normative gender-centrism suggests why feminists should not be satisfied with a table-turning, "why men are so conceited" type of gynocentric theorizing. Posing such questions may expose the androcentrism of standard ways of framing research problems in sex-differences research to healthy ridicule. But because feminists are interested in upholding the equality of all persons, not the domination of women over men, they have no interest in claiming that women set the norm for humans generally.

Theories that tailor concepts to the activities or positions specific to or typical of one gender only and then apply them to everyone are straightforwardly empirically inadequate. As the case of androcentric definitions of class showed, they obscure actual empirical differences between men and women and between differently situated women. As the case of the labor/leisure distinction showed, they overgeneralize from the typical situation of one gender to that of both. When conceptually androcentric theories guide public policy, the resulting policies are usually sexist, since theories cannot respond to phenomena they make invisible. Thus, when GNP statistics fail to count women's labor as productive, and public policies aim to increase GNP, they may do so in ways that fail to improve the well-being of women and their families and may even reduce it. In Malawi and Lesotho, where women grow most of the food for domestic consumption, foreign aid projects have provided agricultural training to the men who have no use for it, and offered only home economics education to women (Waring 1990, 232, 234). In the Sahel, a USAID drought-relief project forced women into economic dependency on men by replacing only men's cattle herds, on the androcentric assumption that women did not engage in economically significant labor (Waring 1990,176–77).

Feminist naturalized epistemologists therefore pass different judgments on different kinds of gender-centrism in theoretical inquiry. Conceptual gender-centrism is plainly inadequate in any society with overlapping gender roles, because it leads to overgeneralization and obscures the differences between empirically distinct phenomena. It could work only in societies where men and women inhabit completely and rigidly segregated spheres, and only for concepts that apply exclusively to one or the other gender in such a society. Normative gender-centrism either depends on a problematic cosmic teleology or on sexist values. This does not automatically make it epistemically inadequate, but it does require the assumption of an explanatory burden (why men's and women's traits do not receive symmetrical explanatory treatment) that non-gender-centric theories need not assume. In addition, its dependence on sexist values give theorists who repudiate sexism sufficient reason to conduct inquiry that is not normatively gender-centric. Finally, causal gender-centrism may or may not be empirically justified. Some events do turn asymmetrically on what men or women do, or on how men or women are situated.

The chief trap in causal gender-centrism is the temptation to reify the domain of events that are said to turn asymmetrically on the actions or characteristics of one or the other gender. The selection of a domain of inquiry is always a function of the interests of the inquirer.[2] Failure to recognize this may lead androcentric theorists to construct their domain of study in ways that confine it to just those phenomena that turn asymmetrically on men's activities. They may therefore declare as an objective fact that, say, women have little causal impact on the "economy," when all that is going on is that they have not taken any interest in women's productive activities, and so have not categorized those activities as "economic." Feminist naturalized epistemologists caution against the view that domains of inquiry demarcate natural kinds. Following Quine, they question supposed conceptual barriers between natural and social science, analytic and synthetic knowledge, personal and impersonal knowledge, fact and value (Nelson 1990, chap. 3). Their empiricist commitments enable them to uncover surprising connections among apparently distant points in the web of belief. If naturalized epistemologists use space-age technology to explore the universe of knowledge, feminist naturalized epistemologists could be said to specialize in the discovery of wormholes in that universe. Gender and science are not light-years apart after all; subspace distortions in our cognitive apparatus permit surprisingly rapid transport from one to the other, but feminist navigators are needed to ensure that we know the route we are travelling and have reason to take it.

SEXISM IN SCIENTIFIC THEORIES

One frequently traveled route between gender and science employs normative assumptions about the proper relations between men and women, or about the respective characteristics and interests of men and women, in the content or application of scientific theories. When a theory asserts that women are inferior to men, properly subordinated to men, or properly confined to gender-stereotyped roles, or when it judges or describes women according to sexist or double standards, the content of the theory is sexist. When people employ such assumptions in applying theories, the application of the theory is sexist. Naturalized feminist epistemology considers how our evaluations of theories should change once their sexism is brought to light.

The application of theories can be sexist in direct or indirect ways. Theories may be used to provide direct ideological justification for patriarchal structures. Steven Goldberg (1973) uses his theory of sex differences in aggression to justify a gendered division of labor that deliberately confines women to low-prestige occupations. More usually, the application of theories is indirectly sexist in taking certain sexist values for granted rather than trying to justify them. For example, research on oral contraceptives for men and women uses a double standard for evaluating the acceptability of side effects. Oral contraceptives for men are disqualified if they reduce libido, but oral contraceptives for women are not rejected for reducing women's sexual desire.

In a standard positivist analysis, neither form of sexism in the application of theories has any bearing on the epistemic value of the theories in question. That a theory is used to support unpopular political programs does not show that the theory is false. At most, it reflects a failure of the proponents of the program to respect the logical gap between fact and value. But opponents of the program fail to respect this gap in attacking a theory for the uses to which it is put. According to this view, theories supply facts that all persons must accept, regardless of their political commitments. That a theory is indirectly applied in sexist ways provides even less ground for attacking its content. The question of truth must be strictly separated from the uses to which such truths are put.

Naturalized epistemology does not support such a sanguine analysis of theories that are applied in sexist ways. "Successful" technological applications of theories are currently taken to provide evidence of their epistemic merits. If knowledge is power, then power is a criterion of adequate understanding. The prevailing interpretation of this criterion does not consider whose power is enhanced by the theory and whose interests are served by it. Feminists urge that these considerations be taken explicitly into account when one evaluates whether technological applications of theories supply evidence of an adequate understanding of the phenomena they control (Tiles 1987). It may be true that certain drugs would be effective in controlling the phenomena of women's hormonal cycles that are currently designated as pathologies constitutive of premenstrual syndrome. Such control may come at the expense of women's interests, not just because of undesirable side effects but also because the legitimation of drug treatment reinforces the medicalization of women's complaints, as if these complaints were symptoms to be medicated rather than as claims on others to change their behavior (Zita 1989). Doctors may be satisfied that such a "successful" drug treatment of PMS supplies evidence that the theory it applies provides them with an adequate understanding of women's menstrual cycles. But should women be satisfied with this understanding? Suppose the phenomena associated with PMS could also be eliminated, or revalued, by widespread acceptance of feminist conceptions of women's bodies or by egalitarian changes that would make social arrangements less frustrating to women. (This would be possible if women's symptoms of distress in PMS were partly caused by misogynist social expectations that represent women's menstrual cycles as pathological.) Such a successful "technological" application of feminist theory would provide women with an understanding of their own menstrual cycles that would empower them. Where the sexist medical technology would enable women to adapt their bodies to the demands of a sexist society, the feminist technology would empower women to change society so that their bodies were no longer considered "diseased." Thus, applications of theories may influence the content of theories whenever "success" in application is taken to justify the theory in question. Sexist or feminist values may inform criteria of success in application, which may in turn inform competing criteria of adequate understanding. The epistemic evaluation of theories therefore cannot be sharply separated from the interests their applications serve.

Feminist naturalized epistemology also rejects the positivist view that the epistemic merits of theories can be assessed independently of their direct ideological applications (Longino 1990; Antony 1993; Potter 1993). Although any acceptable ideology must make sure that it does not fly in the face of facts, theories do not merely state facts but organize them into systems that tell us what their significance is. Theories logically go beyond the facts; they are "underdetermined" by all the empirical evidence that is or ever could be adduced in their favor (Quine 1960, 22). The evidential link between an observed fact and a theoretical hypothesis can only be secured by background auxiliary hypotheses. This leaves open the logical possibility that ideological judgments may not be implications of an independently supported theory but figure in the justification of the theory itself, by supplying evidential links between empirical observations and hypotheses.

A particularly transparent example of this phenomenon may be found in theories about sex differences in intelligence. Girls scored significantly higher than boys on the first Stanford-Binet IQ tests developed by Lewis Terman. To correct for this "embarrassment," Terman eliminated portions of the test where girls scored higher than boys and inserted questions on which boys scored higher than girls. The substitution was considered necessary to ensure the validity of the test against school grades, the only available independent measures of children's intelligence, which did not differ by gender. But Terman did not adjust his test to eliminate sex differences on subtests of the IQ, such as those about quantitative reasoning. These differences seemed unproblematic because they conformed to prevailing ideological assumptions about appropriate gender roles (Mensh and Mensh 1991, 68–69). Today, that IQ scores are good predictors of a child's school grades is still taken to provide key evidence for the claim that differences in IQ scores measure differences in children's innate intelligence.

But the evidential link tying school grades to this theoretical claim depends on the background value judgment that schools provide fair educational opportunities to all children with respect to all fields of study. Those schools that discourage girls from pursuing math and science assume that girls have inferior quantitative reasoning ability; they do not recognize that lack of encouragement can cause relatively lower performance on math tests.

From a positivist point of view, this reasoning is defective on two counts. First, it is circular to claim that IQ tests demonstrate innate sex differences in quantitative reasoning ability when the assumption of innate sex differences is built into the background hypotheses needed to validate the tests. Second, no reasoning is scientifically sound that incorprates value judgments into the background assumptions that link observations to theory. The salience of positivist views of science as well as their usefulness to feminists in criticizing research about sex differences has tempted some feminists to use the positivist requirement that science be value-free to discredit all scientific projects that incorporate sexist values in the explicit or implicit content of their theories. But this appropriation of positivism puts at odds the two aims of femmist epistemology—to criticize sexist science and to promote feminist science. If incorporating sexist values into scientific theories is illegitimate on positivist grounds, then so is incorporating feminist values into scientific theories (Longino 1993a, 259).

Feminist naturalized epistemologists offer a more nuanced response to the presence of value judgments in scientific inference. Even "good science" can incorporate such value judgments. The logical gap between theory and observation ensures that one cannot in principle rule out the possibility that value judgments are implicit in the background assumptions used to argue that a given observation constitutes evidence for a given hypothesis (Longino 1990). From the perspective of an individual scientist, it is not unreasonable to use any of one's firm beliefs, including beliefs about values, to reason from an observation to a theory. Nor does the prospect of circularity threaten the scientific validity of one's reasoning, as long as the circle of reasoning is big enough. In a coherent web of belief, every belief offers some support for every other belief, and no belief is perfectly self-supporting. Theories that incorporate value judgments can be scientifically sound as long as they are empirically adequate.

This reasoning underwrites the legitimacy of feminist scientific research, a which incorporates feminist values into its theories. Such values may be detected in the commitment of feminist researchers to regard women as intelligent agents, capable of reflecting on and changing the conditions that presently constrain their actions. This commitment tends to support a theoretical preference for causal models of female behavior that highlight feedback loops between their intentional states and their social and physical environments, and that resist purely structuralist accounts of female "nature" that leave no room for females to resist their circumstances or maneuver among alternate possibilities (Longino 1989, 210–13; Haraway 1989, chap. 13). In contrast, most behaviorist and some sociobiological theories favor models that highlight linear causal chains from fixed physiological or physical conditions to determinate behaviors, and that emphasize the structural constraints on action. The epistemic values of simplicity, prediction, and control might seem to support linear, structural causal models. But we have seen that control at least is a contested value; the kinds of control taken to warrant claims of adequate understanding depend on substantive value judgments about the importance of particular human interests. Is adequate understanding achieved when a theory empowers scientists to control women's lives, or when it empowers women to control their own lives? Rival interpretations of the other epistemic values also depend on contested nonepistemic values. The kind of simplicity one favors depends on one's aesthetic values. In any event, other epistemic values, such as fruitfulness, appear to favor complex, non-linear causal models of human behavior. Such models support experiments that generate novel behaviors disruptive of presumed structural constraints on action.

Naturalized feminist epistemology thus permits scientific projects that incorporate feminist values into the content and application of theories. It does not provide methodological arguments against the pursuit of sexist theories. It does claim, however, that it is irrational for theorists to pursue sexist re-

search programs if they do not endorse sexist values. Moral and political arguments about the rationality of particular values may therefore have a bearing on the rationality of pursuing particular research programs. In addition, the objectivity of science demands that the background assumptions of research programs be exposed to criticism. A scientific community composed of inquirers who share the same background assumptions is unlikely to be aware of the roles these assumptions play in licensing inferences from observations to hypotheses, and even less likely to examine these assumptions critically. Naturalized epistemology therefore recommends that the scientific community include a diversity of inquirers who accept different background assumptions. A community of inquirers who largely accept sexist values and incorporate them into their background assumptions could enhance the objectivity of the community's practice by expanding its membership to include researchers with feminist commitments (Longino 1993a, 267–269).

THE LOCAL CHARACTER OF NATURALIZED FEMINIST EPISTEMOLOGY

In reading the project of feminist epistemology along naturalized, empiricist lines, I have tried to show how its interest and critical power do not depend on the global, transcendental claims that all knowledge is gendered or that rationality as a regulatory epistemic ideal is masculine. Naturalized feminist epistemologists may travel to distant locations in the universe of belief, but they always remain inside that universe and travel from gender to science by way of discrete, empirically discovered paths. They have an interest in constructing new paths to empirically adequate, fruitful, and useful forms of feminist science and in breaking up other paths that lead to cognitively and socially unsatisfactory destinations. All the paths by which naturalized epistemologists find gender to influence theoretical knowledge are local, contingent, and empirically conditioned. All the paths by which they propose to change these influences accept rationality as a key epistemic ideal and empirical adequacy as a fundamental goal of acceptable theories. This ideal and this goal are in principle equally open to pursuit by male and female inquirers, but may be best realized by mixed-gender research communities. Naturalized epistemologists find no persuasive evidence that indicates that all women inquirers bring some shared global feminine difference in ways of thinking to all subjects of study nor that such a feminine difference gives us privileged access to the way the world is.

In rejecting global, transcendental claims about differences in the ways men and women think, naturalized feminist epistemologists do not imply that the entry and advancement of significant numbers of women into scientific communities makes no systematic difference to the knowledge these communities produce. But, following their view of inquiry as a social, not an individual, enterprise, they credit the improvements in knowledge such entry produces to the greater diversity and equality of membership in the scientific community rather than to any purportedly privileged subject position of women as knowers (Tuana 1992; Longino 1993a). Men and women do have *some* gender-specific experiences and personal knowledge due to their different socialization and social status. We have seen that such experiences and forms of knowledge can be fruitfully brought to bear upon theoretical inquiry. So it should not be surprising that women researchers have exposed and criticized androcentrism in theories much more than men have. The diversity and equality of inquirers help ensure that social models do not merely reflect or fit the circumstances of a narrow demographic segment of the population when they are meant to apply to everyone. They correct a cognitive bias commonly found among inquirers belonging to all demographic groups, located in the habit of assuming that the way the world appears to oneself is the way it appears to everyone.

This survey of some findings of naturalized feminist epistemology has also identified improvements in knowledge that have or would come about through the entry of *feminist* theorists into various fields, and through revisions in the systems of cognitive authority among fields that would bring the findings of feminist theorists to bear upon apparently distant subjects.[3] We have seen that the use of gender symbolism to model nonhuman phenomena

is fraught with cognitive traps. So it should not be surprising that feminist researchers, who make it their business to study the contradictions and incoherences in our conceptions of gender, can improve theories by exposing and clearing up the confusions they inherit from the gender ideologies they use as models. By pursuing feminist research in the humanities, social sciences, and biology, feminist researchers also pose challenges to prevailing theories. Here again, the kinds of changes we should expect in theoretical knowledge from the entry of feminist researchers into various fields do not typically consist in the production of specifically feminist ontologies, methodologies, standpoints, paradigms, or doctrines. Feminist contributions to theorizing are more usefully conceived as altering the field of theoretical possibilities (Haraway 1986, 81, 96). Research informed by feminist commitments makes new explanatory models available, reframes old questions, exposes facts that undermine the plausibility of previously dominant theories, improves data-gathering techniques, and shifts the relations of cognitive authority among fields and theories. In these and many other ways, it reconfigures our assessments of the prospects and virtues of various research programs. Without claiming that women, or feminists, have a globally different or privileged way of knowing, naturalized feminist epistemology explains how feminist theory can productively transform the field of theoretical knowledge.

NOTES

I wish to thank Ann Cudd, Sally Haslanger, Don Herzog, David Hills, Peter Railton, Justin Schwartz, Miriam Solomon, and the faculties at the Law Schools of Columbia University, the University of Chicago, and Northwestern University for helpful comments and criticisms.
1. Diamond (1991, 1009) writes that the exclusion of animal trainers' knowledge from the realm of authoritative knowledge "cannot in any very simple way be connected to gender." Pointing out that the terms "hard" and "soft" as applied to forms of knowledge are used by "men trying to put down other men," Sherif argues that for this reason it is "particularly misleading" to infer that these terms

symbolize "masculine" and "feminine" (1987, 46–47). 1 would have thought that her observation supports the gendered reading, since a standard way for men to put down other men is to insinuate that they are feminine.

2. The interests at stake need not be self-interests or even ideological interests of a broader sort. One might just be curious about how rainbows form, without seeking this knowledge for the sake of finding out how to get the proverbial pot of gold at the end. Curiosity is one kind of interest we can express in a phenomenon.

3. The question of the impact of feminist theorists on knowledge is distinct from but related to the question of the impact of women theorists on knowledge. Not all women theorists are feminists, and some feminist theorists are men. At the same time, there could be no genuine feminist theory that was conducted by men alone. Feminist theory is theory committed to the liberation and equality of women. These goals can only be achieved through the exercise of women's own agency, especially in defining and coming to know themselves. Feminist theory is one of the vehicles of women's agency in pursuit of these goals, and therefore cannot realize its aims if it is not conducted by women. So it should not be surprising that most of the transformations of knowledge induced by feminist theory were brought about by women.

REFERENCES

Alcoff, Linda, and Elizabeth Potter, eds. 1993. *Feminist epistemologies.* New York: Routledge.

American Association of University Women. 1992. *The AAUW report: How schools shortchange girls.* Prepared by Wellesley College Center for Research on Women.

Anderson, Elizabeth. 1993. *Value in ethics and economics.* Cambridge: Harvard University Press.

Antony, Louise. 1993. Quine as feminist: The radical import of naturalized epistemology. In *A mind of one's own: Feminist essays on reason and objectivity.* See Antony and Witt 1993.

Antony, Louise, and Charlotte Witt. 1993. *A mind of one's own: Feminist essays on reason and objectivity.* Boulder, CO: Westview.

Astin, Helen S., and Alan E. Beyer. 1973. Sex discrimination in academe. In *Academic women on the move,* ed. Alice S. Rossi and Ann Calderwood. New York: Russell Sage Foundation.

Becker, Joanne Rossi. 1981. Differential treatment of females and males in mathematics classes. *Journal for Research in Mathematics Education* 12(1): 40-53.

Belenky, Mary, Blythe Clinchy, Nancy Goldberger, and Jill Tarule. 1986. *Women's ways of knowing.* New York: Basic Books.

Bell, Diane, Pat Caplan, and Wazir Karim, eds. 1993. *Gendered fields: Women, men, and ethnography.* New York: Routledge.

Biology and Gender Study Group. 1988. The importance of feminist critique for contemporary cell biology. *Hypatia* 3(1): 61-76.

Bordo, Susan. 1987. *The flight to objectivity: Essays on cartesianism and culture.* Albany: State University of New York Press.

Bourdieu, Pierre. 1977. *Outline of a theory of practice.* Cambridge: Cambridge University Press.

Coady, C. A. J. 1992. *Testimony.* Oxford: Clarendon Press.

Collins, Patricia Hill. 1990. *Black feminist thought: Knowledge, consciousness, and the politics of empowerment.* Boston: Unwin Hyman.

Curran, Libby. 1980. Science education: Did she drop out or was she pushed? In *Alice through the microscope,* ed. Brighton Women and Science Group. London: Virago.

Dawkins, Richard. 1976. *The selfish gene.* New York: Oxford University Press.

Diamond, Cora. 1991. Knowing tornadoes and other things. *New Literary History* 22: 1001-15.

Duran, Jane. 1991. *Toward a feminist epistemology.* Totowa, NJ: Rowman and Littlefield.

Fidell, L. S. 1970. Empirical verification of sex discrimination in hiring practices in psychology. *American Psychologist* 25(12): 1094-98.

Flax, Jane. 1983. Political philosophy and the patriarchal unconscious. In *Discovering reality.* See Harding and Hintikka 1983.

Fox, Mary Frank. 1981. Sex segregation and salary structure in academia. *Sociology of Work and Occupations* 8(1): 39-60.

Gilligan, Carol. 1982. *In a different voice.* Cambridge: Harvard University Press.

Goldberg, Steven. 1973. *The inevitability of patriarchy.* New York: Morrow.

Haraway, Donna. 1986. Primatology is politics by other means. In *Feminist approaches to science,* ed. Ruth Bleier. New York: Pergamon.

———.1989. *Primate visions.* New York: Routledge.

Harding, Sandra. 1986. *The science question in feminism.* Ithaca: Cornell University Press.

Harding, Sandra, and Merrill B. Hintikka, eds. 1983. *Discovering Reality*. Dodrecht, Holland: D. Reidel.

Hearne, Vicki. 1982. *Adam's task*. New York: Vintage.

Hrdy, Sarah. 1981. *The woman that never evolved*. Cambridge: Harvard University Press.

———.1986. Empathy, polyandry, and the myth of the coy female. In *Feminist approaches to science,* ed. Ruth Bleier. New York: Pergamon.

Hubbard, Ruth. 1990. *The politics of women's biology*. New Brunswick, NJ: Rutgers University Press.

Keller, Evelyn Fox. 1983. *A feeling for the organism*. New York: Freeman.

———.1985. The force of the pacemaker concept in theories of aggregation in cellular slime mold. In *Reflections on gender and science*. New Haven: Yale University Press.

———.1992. *Secrets of life, secrets of death*. New York: Routledge.

Leacock, Eleanor. 1982. *Myths of male dominance*. New York: Monthly Review Press.

Lefkowitz, M. R. 1979. Education for women in a man's world. *Chronicle of Higher Education,* 6 August, p. 56.

Longino, Helen. 1989. Can there be a feminist science? In *Women, knowledge, and reality,* ed. Ann Carry and Marilyn Pearsall. Boston: Unwin Hyman.

———.1990. *Science as social knowledge*. Princeton, NJ: Princeton University Press.

———.1993a. Essential tensions—Phase two: Feminist, philosophical, and social studies of science. In *A mind of one's own*. See Antony and Witt 1993.

———.1993b. Subjects, power, and knowledge: Description and prescription in feminist philosophies of science. In *Feminist epistemologies*. See Alcoff and Potter 1993.

Maccoby, Eleanor, and Carol Jacklin. 1974. *The psychology of sex differences*. Stanford: Stanford University Press.

Mensh, Elaine, and Harry Mensh. 1991. *The IQ mythology*. Carbondale: Southern Illinois University Press.

National Science Foundation. 1984. *Women and minorities in science and engineering*.

Nelson, Lynn. 1990. *Who knows? From Quine to a feminist empiricism*. Philadelphia: Temple University Press.

———.1993. Epistemological communities. In *Feminist epistemologies*. See Alcoff and Potter 1993.

Pai, Hyong I1.1985. (Anthropologist, University of California, Santa Barbara). Personal communication.

Paludi, Michele Antoinette, and William D. Bauer. 1983. Goldberg revisited: What's in an author's name. *Sex Roles* 9(3). 287-390.

Polanyi, Michael. 1958. *Personal knowledge*. Chicago: University of Chicago Press.

Potter, Elizabeth. 1993. Gender and epistemic negotiation. In *Feminist epistemologies*. See Alcoff and Potter 1993.

Quine, W.V 0.1960. *Word and object*. Cambridge.. MIT Press.

———.1969. Epistemology naturalized. In *Ontological relativity and other essays*. New York: Columbia University Press.

Reskin, Barbara. 1979. Academic sponsorship and scientists' careers. *Sociology of Education* 52(3): 129-46.

Rooney, Phyllis. 1991. Gendered reason: Sex metaphor and conceptions of reason. *Hypatia* 6(2): 77-103.

Rose, Hilary. 1987. Hand, brain, and heart: A feminist epistemology for the natural sciences. In *Sex and scientific inquiry,* ed. Sandra Harding and Jean O'Barr. Chicago: University of Chicago Press.

Rose, Suzanna. 1989. Women biologists and the "old boy" network. *Women's Studies International Forum* 12(3): 349-54.

Rosenfeld, Rachel. 1981. Academic career mobility for psychologists. In *Women in scientific and engineering professions,* ed. Violet Haas and Carolyn Perrucci. Ann Arbor: University of Michigan Press.

Rossiter, Margaret. 1982. *Women scientists in America: Struggles and strategies to 1940*. Baltimore: Johns Hopkins University Press.

Scheman, Naomi. 1983. Individualism and the objects of psychology. In *Discovering reality*. See Harding and Hintikka 1983.

Schiebinger, Londa. 1989. *The mind has no sex?* Cambridge: Harvard University Press.

Schuman, Howard, and Shirley Hatchett. 1974. *Black racial attitudes: Trends and complexities*. Ann Arbor: University of Michigan Press.

Sherif, Carolyn. 1987. Bias in psychology. In *Feminism and methodology,* ed. Sandra Harding. Bloomington: Indiana University Press

Smith, Dorothy. 1974. Women's perspective as a radical critique of sociology. *Sociological inquiry* 44(1): 7-13.

Solomon, Miriam. 1994. Social epistemology. *Nous* 28: 325-343.

Stiehm, Judith. 1983. Our aristotelian hangover. In *Discovering reality*. See Harding and Hintikka 1983.

Tavris, Carol. 1992. *The mismeasure of woman*. New York: Simon and Schuster.

Tidball, M. Elizabeth. 1980. Women's colleges and women achievers revisited. *Signs* 5(3): 504-17.

Tiles, Mary. 1987. A science of Mars or of Venus? *Philosophy* 62(July): 293-306.

Tuana, Nancy. 1992. The radical future of feminist empiricism. *Hypatia* 7(1):100-14.

Vetter, Betty. 1981. Changing patterns of recruitment and employment. In *Women in scientific and engineering professions*, ed. Violet Haas and Carolyn Perrucci. Ann Arbor: University of Michigan Press.

Waring, Marilyn. 1990. *If women counted*. San Francisco: Harper Collins.

Wrangham, Richard. 1979. On the evolution of ape social systems. *Biology and Social Life: Social Sciences Information* 18: 335-68.

Zita, Jacquelyn. 1989. The premenstrual syndrome: "Dis-easing" the female cycle. In *Feminism and science*, ed. Nancy Tuana. Bloomington: Indiana University Press.

FOR FURTHER READING

Almeder, Robert. "On Naturalizing Epistemology." *American Philosophical Quarterly*, 27 (1990), 263–79.

Bloor, David. *Knowledge and Social Imagery*, 2d ed. Chicago: University of Chicago Press,1991.

Dancy, Jonathan and Ernest Sosa, eds. *A Companion to Epistemology*. Oxford: Basil Blackwell, 1992.

French, Peter, et. al., eds. *Midwest Studies in Philosophy*, Vol. XIX. Notre Dame: University of Notre Dame Press, 1994.

Fumerton, Richard. *Metaepistemology and Skepticism*. Lanham, Md.: Rowman & Littlefield, 1995.

Gibson, Roger. *Enlightened Empiricism*. Tampa: University of Florida Press, 1988.

Goldman, Alvin. *Epistemology and Cognition*. Cambridge: Harvard University Press, 1986.

Hahn, L. E. and P. A. Schilpp, eds. *The Philosophy of W. V. O. Quine*. LaSalle, Il.: Open Court, 1986.

Kitcher, Philip. "The Naturalists Return." *Philosophical Review*, 101 (1992), 53–114.

Kornblith, Hilary, ed. *Naturalizing Epistemology*. Cambridge: MIT Press, 1987.

Laudan, Larry. *Science and Values*. Berkeley: University of California Press, 1982.

Lehrer, Keith. *Self-Trust: A Study of Reason, Knowledge, and Autonomy*. Oxford: Oxford University Press, 1997.

Lehrer, Keith. *Theory of Knowledge*. Boulder, Colo.: Westview Press, 1990.

Maffie, James. "Recent Work on Naturalized Epistemology." *American Philosophical Quarterly*, 27 (1990), 281–93.

Moser, Paul. *Empirical Knowledge*, 2d ed. Lanham, Md. Rowman & Littlefield, 1996.

Putnam, Hilary. "Why Reason Can't Be Naturalized." In *Realism and Reason*, 229–47.

Putnam, Hilary. *Realism and Reason: Philosophical Papers*, Vol. 3. Cambridge: Cambridge University Press, 1983.

Quine, W. V. O. "The Nature of Natural Knowledge." *Mind and Language*, ed. Samuel Guttenplan. Oxford: Oxford University Press, 1975, 67–81.

Quine, W. V. O. *Theories and Things*. Cambridge, Mass.: Belknap Press, 1981, 1–23.

Quine, W. V. O. *From a Logical Point of View*, 2d ed. New York, Harper,1961.

Quine, W. V. O. *Roots of Reference*. LaSalle, Ill.: Open Court, 1986.

Quine, W. V. O. *The Pursuit of Truth*. Cambridge: Harvard University Press, 1990.

Rescher, Nicholas, ed. *Evolution, Cognition, and Realism*. Lanham Md.: University Press of America, 1990.

Ruse, M. *Taking Darwin Seriously*. Oxford: Basil Blackwell, 1986.

Schmitt, Frederick. *Knowledge and Belief*. London: Routledge, 1990.

Sosa, Ernest. *Knowledge in Perspective*. Cambridge: Cambridge University Press, 1991.

Stein, Edward. *Without Good Reason: The Rationality Debate in Philosophy and Cognitive Science*. Oxford: Claredon Press, 1997.

Stich, Stephen. "Could Man Be an Irrational Animal?" Reprinted in *Naturalizing Epistemology*. Ed. Hilary Kornblith, 257–58.

Stich, Stephen. *The Fragmentation of Reason*. Cambridge: MIT Press, 1990.

Tomberlin, James, ed. *Philosophical Perspectives*, 2, *Epistemology*. Atascadero, Calif.: Ridgeview Press, 1988.

Wagner, Richard, and Steven Warner, eds. *Naturalism: A Critical Appraisal*. Notre Dame: University of Notre Dame Press, 1993.

STUDY QUESTIONS

1. Explain Quine's distinction between the conceptual and doctrinal aspects of epistemology. Quine writes in "Epistemology Naturalized" that "The Humean predicament is the human predicament." What does he mean by this?

2. What is rational reconstruction? Why does Quine think that this project cannot succeed? Quine claims that naturalized epistemology

continues in a new setting and a clarified status; what does he have in mind here?

3. Quine claims that naturalized epistemology can resolve the problem of epistemological priority. What is this problem, and how is it resolved, according to Quine?

4. In "The Nature of Natural Knowledge," why does Quine think that we are free to use science in responding to the skeptic? What do you think of Quine's response?

5. What is an observation sentence, according to Quine? What is the role of such sentences? How are observation sentences important for our understanding the connection between evidence and theory?

6. Why does Quine think naturalized epistemology is normative?

7. According to Kim, what constraints must be placed on the criteria for justified belief? In what way does Kim agree with Quine about the "classical epistemological project"? Why does Kim disagree with Quine's version of naturalized epistemology?

8. Why does Kim think that the concept of belief is normative? Why is this important for epistemology? What is the notion of supervenience, and why is it important in Kim's view?

9. What are the three forms of naturalized epistemology that Almeder describes?

10. Why does Almeder object to Quine's dismissal of "first philosophy"? What is Almeder's ob-

jection to Giere's claim that traditional epistemology will disappear as a result of eliminative materialism?

11. State the argument from evolutionary theory offered by Kornblith. Why is this argument important? What are Almeder's criticisms of this argument?

12. What, in Anderson's view, are the two primary aims of feminist epistemology? According to her, what are the two implications of empiricism? How does her view of empiricism differ from what she refers to as a common view of empiricism? Why does Anderson think that rational inquiry is essentially social?

13. In what sense is feminist epistemology a branch of social epistemology? Why does Anderson consider naturalized epistemology to be normative?

14. Anderson identifies four categories by which we may recognize the normative implications of feminist epistemology. Briefly explain these categories. In Anderson's view, should a model be rejected just because it relies on a particular type of gender symbolism? What are the real difficulties of such models? How might feminist naturalized epistemology revise our notions of the success of theories? Does Anderson think that an epistemically acceptable theory must be value free? Explain.

PART IV

Sources of Knowledge

9

A Priori Knowledge

We are very familiar with the idea that we acquire knowledge from the operations of our senses. We hear a car pull into the driveway or see the keys on the desk. We see that a certain man has brown hair or blue eyes. Or we learn from a friend that the man is a bachelor. But once we learn that he is bachelor, we know something else without further investigation or inquiry. We know that since he is a bachelor, he is an unmarried male. This bit of knowledge seems perfectly general: All bachelors are unmarried males. We acquire this bit of knowledge in a manner unlike that by which we typically acquire our knowledge of the world around us.

For example, if we want to know whether all eucalyptus trees grow in temperate climates or all swans are white, we conduct an investigation or inquiry. But we do not similarly survey all the bachelors in the world to find out if each one is an unmarried male. If we know that all bachelors are unmarried males, we know this independently of our senses. Moreover, we can find a great number of propositions that we know independently of our senses. Simple mathematical truths, for example that a triangle has three sides, seem to be instances of knowledge that do not derive from our senses. More interesting examples might be that nothing is red and green all over or that everything that happens has a cause. We acquire knowledge of this sort in a different way than we acquire a posteriori knowledge, knowledge that derives from the senses.

Theories of a priori knowledge, knowledge that does not depend on our senses, attempt to explain not only the types of propositions that can be known a priori, but also how we can have a priori knowledge. A venerable answer to the question of how we acquire a priori knowledge is by means of reason alone. The appropriate exercise of our reasoning abilities enables us to know that all bachelors are unmarried males, that all triangles have three sides, or even that all events have a cause.

That reason alone can lead to at least some knowledge is characteristic of *rationalism*. Rationalists, such as Descartes and Leibniz, hold that we know certain interesting truths about the world by means of reason. Descartes, for example, claims that there are two distinct substances in the world: minds and bodies. Leibniz claims that simple substances, the ultimate constituents of all things, cannot be destroyed. But contemporary discussion of a priori knowledge begins with Immanuel Kant, an eighteenth-century philosopher.

Three distinctions drawn by Kant frame most current debate. The first, of course, is the epistemological distinction between a priori knowledge and a posteriori knowledge. But Kant draws two other distinctions, one metaphysical and the other semantic. Kant claims that propositions known a priori are necessarily true; they cannot be false. On the other hand, propositions known a posteriori are contingent propositions. If we know a priori that all triangles have three sides, then the proposition that all triangles have three sides cannot be false. But the a posteriori proposition ("a posteriori proposition" abbreviates the more precise "proposition known a posteriori") that this glass is green is contingent. The glass might have been some other color; hence that proposition might have been false.

There is an intuitive argument for thinking that a priori propositions are necessary, while a posteriori propositions are contingent. A posteriori propositions are known as a result of information we receive from our senses. Our senses tell us what is going on in the world. Thus, a posteriori information depends on certain facts about the world. Of course, the world might have been different. My parents might never have met and, much to my dismay, I would not now be sitting and typing. Facts about the world are contingent facts because they might have been different. A priori knowledge, however, does not depend on such facts, for it is knowledge that does not depend on the senses. Thus, an a priori proposition appears to be true independently of any facts about the world. Imagine, for example, that societies developed in such a way that at the very moment of birth, each male baby was instantly wed. In such a world, there would be no bachelors. Seemingly, however, it remains true that if someone is a bachelor, then he is an unmarried male. No societal custom could change that; indeed nothing we ever perceived could change that. Consequently, it appears as though there is no way that the proposition that all bachelors are unmarried males could turn out to be false. This is what it means to say that the proposition is necessary.

The last distinction is that between types of propositions. Intuitively *analytic* propositions are those that do not provide us with any new information about the subjects of the proposition, whereas *synthetic* propositions provide us with new information. If you are told that a man is both a bachelor and an unmarried male, you do not have two pieces of information; you have one. If you are told that this bachelor is a Republican, you learn something new in addition to the simple fact of his bachelorhood.

Kant claims that all analytic propositions are knowable a priori. If there is no new information about the subject, then there would appear to be no need to rely on the senses for knowing an analytic proposition. Once you grasp or understand the subject of the proposition, you already grasp or understand the information contained in the predicate of the proposition. Equally obvious is the thought that many synthetic propositions are known a posteriori. You learn that the television is off by looking at it, that the President is in Africa by listening to the radio, or that the roast is burning by a distinctive odor. Kant's distinctive and controversial claim is that there are synthetic propositions known a priori. Reason alone can lead us to know certain synthetic propositions. Of course, they are not the simple sort like Sara is walking the dog. Rather, synthetic a priori propositions are of a more general nature, such as all events have a cause. More recently, some have suggested that propositions such as nothing can be red and green all over are also synthetic a priori propositions.

Kant's account of how it is that we know such propositions is one of the more celebrated and controversial views in epistemology. He holds that our experience of the world is governed by certain concepts or categories. It is by virtue of these categories that our experience, our perception of the world, has the structure that it does. We can learn by reflection what these categories are. Once we know what these categories are we thereby know essential features of any particular experience.

Theories of a priori knowledge should provide us with the answers to certain questions. First, they should answer the question of the type of propositions knowable a priori. Second, we should expect them to tell us how we acquire such knowledge. It is one thing to say that reason alone enables us to know such things; it is quite another to say how reason does this.

The readings begin with excerpts from the *Critique of Pure Reason,* where Kant elaborates the distinctions between synthetic and analytic propositions and his claim that there are synthetic propositions knowable a priori. The linguistic view of the a priori, articulated in A. J. Ayer's selection, "The A Priori," holds that we do have a priori knowledge, but only of analytical propositions. The necessity and a priori character of analytic propositions are due, Ayer claims, to the "rules of language." Linguistic conventions or rules tell us that certain propositions are true; or as it is often expressed, analytic propositions are true solely in virtue of the meanings of the terms. The selection from Roderick Chisholm, "Reason and the A priori," presents a defense of the traditional or historic view of a priori knowledge, of which Kant is a representative. Chisholm also attacks the linguistic view on the grounds that the truth of a proposition is not determined by meaning alone. Consequently, you cannot know whether a proposition is true simply by knowing the meaning of the constituent concepts.

Ayer explicitly claims that a motivation of the linguistic theory is the undermining of rationalism. Ayer wants to resist the rationalist claim that there are synthetic propositions known a priori. But the empiricist cannot simply deny the existence of a priori knowledge. Ayer thinks, for example, that mathematical and logical propositions are not synthetic; they are analytic. Consequently, if they are knowable, they are knowable a priori, in Ayer's view. The linguistic view is thus partly an attempt to explain how we could have knowledge a priori of analytic propositions but not of synthetic propositions.

In the last half of this century, the traditional framework for understanding a priori knowledge has been challenged. In his essay, "Two Dogmas of Empiricism," W. V. Quine challenges the distinction between analytic and synthetic propositions. Quine claims that any attempt to explain the notion of analytic propositions leads inevitably back to the very concept with which we began. Consequently, there is no clear line separating analytic from synthetic propositions. The rejection of the analytic-synthetic distinction has a significant consequence, according to Quine. Empiricists like Ayer had hoped to separate our knowledge into two aspects, the content that is given by the world and the content we bring to the world. Certain aspects of our knowledge are

but a reflection of the way we think, and this is embodied in the linguistic conventions that govern our language. Consequent upon the rejection of analytic-synthetic distinction, Quine claims that we can no longer hope to know what is given to us by the world and what is given by us.

Philip Kitcher's essay, "A Priori Knowledge," outlines a reliabilist account of a priori knowledge. Kitcher argues that the reliabilist view retains the essential features of more traditional views. To this end, he describes the kinds of cognitive processes that result in beliefs for which there is an a priori justification. Kitcher suggests that a consequence of his view is that there are contingent propositions that can be known a priori.

IMMANUEL KANT

from Critique of Pure Reason

B1 I. THE DISTINCTION BETWEEN PURE AND EMPIRICAL KNOWLEDGE

There can be no doubt that all our knowledge begins with experience. For how should our faculty of knowledge be awakened into action did not objects affecting our senses partly of themselves produce representations, partly arouse the activity of our understanding to compare these representations, and, by combining or separating them, work up the raw material of the sensible impressions into that knowledge of objects which is entitled experience? In the order of time, therefore, we have no knowledge antecedent to experience, and with experience all our knowledge begins.

But though all our knowledge begins with experience, it does not follow that it all arises out of experience. For it may well be that even our empirical knowledge is made up of what we receive through impressions and of what our own faculty of knowledge (sensible impressions serving merely as the occasion) supplies from itself. If our faculty of knowledge makes any such addition, it may be that B2 we are not in a position to distinguish it from the raw material, until with long practice of attention we have become skilled in separating it.

This, then, is a question which at least calls for closer examination, and does not allow of any off-hand answer: —whether there is any knowledge that is thus independent of experience and even of all impressions of the senses. Such knowledge is entitled *a priori*, and distinguished from the *empir-ical*, which has its sources a *posteriori*, that is, in experience.

The expression '*a priori*' does not, however, indicate with sufficient precision the full meaning of our question. For it has been customary to say, even of much knowledge that is derived from empirical sources, that we have it or are capable of having it *a priori*, meaning thereby that we do not derive it immediately from experience, but from a universal rule—a rule which is itself, however, borrowed by us from experience. Thus we would say of a man who undermined the foundations of his house, that he might have known *a priori* that it would fall, that is, that he need not have waited for the experience of its actual falling. But still he could not know this completely *a priori*. For he had first to learn through experience that bodies are heavy, and therefore fall when their supports are withdrawn.

In what follows, therefore, we shall understand by *a priori* knowledge, not knowledge independent of this or that experience, but knowledge absolutely independent of all experience. Opposed to it is empirical knowledge, which is knowledge possible only *a posteriori*, that is, through experience. *A priori* modes of knowledge are entitled pure when there is no admixture of anything empirical. Thus, for instance, the proposition, 'every alteration has its cause', while an *a priori* proposition, is not a pure proposition, because alteration is a concept which can be derived only from experience.

I. THE IDEA OF TRANSCENDENTAL PHILOSOPHY
A1

Experience is, beyond all doubt, the first product to which our understanding gives rise, in working up the raw material of sensible impressions. Experience is therefore our first instruction, and in its progress

The first edition of the *Critique of Pure Reason* was published in 1781. In response to various comments, Kant published a second edition in 1787, in which there were various additions, changes, and some of the first edition was left unchanged. "A1" or "B1", for example, refer to pages in the first and second editions, respectively. Where the two editions are the same, both editions numbers appear in the margin.

is so inexhaustible in new information, that in the interconnected lives of all future generations there will never be any lack of new knowledge that can be thus ingathered. Nevertheless, it is by no means the sole field to which our understanding is confined. Experience tells us, indeed, what is, but not that it must necessarily be so, and not otherwise. It therefore gives us no true universality; and reason, which is so insistent upon this kind of knowledge, is therefore more stimulated by it than satisfied. Such universal modes of knowledge, which at the same time possess the character of inner necessity, must in themselves, independently of experience, be clear and certain. They are therefore entitled knowledge *a priori*; whereas, on the other hand, that which is borrowed solely from experience is, as we say, known only *a posteriori*, or empirically.

Now we find, what is especially noteworthy, that even into our experiences there enter modes of knowledge which must have their origin *a priori*, and which perhaps serve only to give coherence to our sense-representations. For if we eliminate from our experiences everything which belongs to the senses, there still remain certain original concepts and certain judgments derived from them, which must have arisen completely *a priori*, independently of experience, inasmuch as they enable us to say, or at least lead us to believe that we can say, in regard to the objects which appear to the senses, more than mere experience would teach—giving to assertions true universality and strict necessity, such as mere empirical knowledge cannot supply.

II. WE ARE IN POSSESSION OF CERTAIN MODES OF *A PRIORI* KNOWLEDGE, AND EVEN THE COMMON UNDERSTANDING IS NEVER WITHOUT THEM

What we here require is a criterion by which to distinguish with certainty between pure and empirical knowledge. Experience teaches us that a thing is so and so, but not that it cannot be otherwise. First, then, if we have a proposition which in being thought is thought as *necessary*, it is an *a priori* judgment; and if, besides, it is not derived from any proposition except one which also has the validity of

a necessary judgment, it is an absolutely *a priori* judgment. Secondly, experience never confers on its judgments true or strict, but only assumed and comparative *universality*, through induction. We can properly only say, therefore, that, so far as we have hitherto observed, there is no exception to this or that rule. If, then, a judgment is thought with strict universality, that is, in such manner that no exception is allowed as possible, it is not derived from experience, but is valid absolutely *a priori*. Empirical universality is only an arbitrary extension of a validity holding in most cases to one which holds in all, for instance, in the proposition, 'all bodies are heavy'. When, on the other hand, strict universality is essential to a judgment, this indicates a special source of knowledge, namely, a faculty of *a priori* knowledge. Necessity and strict universality are thus sure criteria of *a priori* knowledge, and are inseparable from one another. But since in the employment of these criteria the contingency of judgments is sometimes more easily shown than their empirical limitation, or, as sometimes also happens, their unlimited universality can be more convincingly proved than their necessity, it is advisable to use the two criteria separately, each by itself being infallible.

Now it is easy to show that there actually are in human knowledge judgments which are necessary and in the strictest sense universal, and which are therefore pure *a priori* judgments. If an example from the sciences be desired, we have only to look to any of the propositions of mathematics; if we seek an example from the understanding in its quite ordinary employment, the proposition, 'every alteration must have a cause', will serve our purpose. In the latter case, indeed, the very concept of a cause so manifestly contains the concept of a necessity of connection with an effect and of the strict universality of the rule, that the concept would be altogether lost if we attempted to derive it, as Hume has done, from a repeated association of that which happens with that which precedes, and from a custom of connecting representations, a custom originating in this repeated association, and constituting therefore a merely subjective necessity. Even without appealing to such examples, it is possible to show that pure *a priori* principles are indispensable for the possibility of experience, and so to prove their existence *a priori*. For whence could experience derive its certainty, if all the rules, according to which it proceeds, were always themselves empirical, and therefore contingent? Such rules could hardly be regarded as first principles. At present, however, we may be content to have established the fact that our faculty of knowledge does have a pure employment, and to have shown what are the criteria of such an employment.

Such *a priori* origin is manifest in certain concepts, no less than in judgments. If we remove from our empirical concept of a body, one by one, every feature in it which is [merely] empirical, the colour, the hardness or softness, the weight, even the impenetrability, there still remains the space which the body (now entirely vanished) occupied, and this cannot be removed. Again, if we remove from our empirical concept of any object, corporeal or incorporeal, all properties which experience has taught us, we yet cannot take away that property through which the object is thought as substance or as inhering in a substance (although this concept of substance is more determinate than that of an object in general). Owing, therefore, to the necessity with which this concept of substance forces itself upon us, we have no option save to admit that it has its seat in our faculty of *a priori* knowledge. . . .

IV. THE DISTINCTION BETWEEN ANALYTIC AND SYNTHETIC JUDGMENTS

In all judgments in which the relation of a subject to the predicate is thought (I take into consideration affirmative judgments only, the subsequent application to negative judgments being easily made), this relation is possible in two different ways. Either the predicate B belongs to the subject A, as something which is (covertly) contained in this concept A; or B lies outside the concept A, although it does indeed stand in connection with it. In the one case I entitle A7 the judgment analytic, in the other synthetic. Analytic judgments (affirmative) are therefore those in which the connection of·the predicate with the subject is thought through identity; those in which this connection is thought without identity should B11 be entitled synthetic. The former, as adding nothing through the predicate to the concept of the subject,

but merely breaking it up into those constituent concepts that have all along been thought in it, although confusedly, can also be entitled explicative. The latter, on the other hand, add to the concept of the subject a predicate which has not been in any wise thought in it, and which no analysis could possibly extract from it; and they may therefore be entitled ampliative. If I say, for instance, 'All bodies are extended', this is an analytic judgment. For I do not require to go beyond the concept which I connect with 'body' in order to find extension as bound up with it. To meet with this predicate, I have merely to analyse the concept, that is, to become conscious to myself of the manifold which I always think in that concept. The judgment is therefore analytic. But when I say, 'All bodies are heavy', the predicate is something quite different from anything that I think in the mere concept of body in general; and the addition of such a predicate therefore yields a synthetic judgment.

*Judgments of experience, as such, are one and all synthetic. For it would be absurd to found an analytic judgment on experience. Since, in framing the judgment, I must not go outside my concept, there is no need to appeal to the testimony of experience in its support. That a body is extended is a proposition that holds *a priori* and is not empirical. For, before appealing to experience, I have already in the B12 concept of body all the conditions required for my judgment. I have only to extract from it, in accordance with the principle of contradiction, the required predicate, and in so doing can at the same time become conscious of the necessity of the judgment—and that is what experience could never have taught me. On the other hand, though I do not include in the concept of a body in general the predicate 'weight', none the less this concept indicates an object of experience through one of its parts, and I can add to that part other parts of this same experience, as in this way belonging together with the concept. From the start I can apprehend the concept of body analytically through the characters of extension, impenetrability, figure, etc., all of which are thought in the concept. Now, however, looking back on the experience from which I have derived this concept of body, and finding weight to be invariably connected with the above characters, I attach it as a predicate to the concept; and in doing so I attach it synthetically, and am therefore extending my knowledge. The possibility of the synthesis of the predicate 'weight' with the concept of 'body' thus rests upon experience. While the one concept is not contained in the other, they yet belong to one another, though only contingently, as parts of a whole, namely, of an experience which is itself a synthetic combination of intuitions.

A9   But in *a priori* synthetic judgments this help is
B13 entirely lacking: [I do not here have the advantage of looking around in the field of experience.] Upon what, then, am I to rely, when I seek to go beyond the concept A, and to know that another concept B is connected with it? Through what is the synthesis made possible? Let us take the proposition, 'Everything which happens has its cause'. In the concept of 'something which happens', I do indeed think an existence which is preceded by a time, etc., and from this concept analytic judgments may be obtained. But the concept of a 'cause' lies entirely outside the other concept, and signifies something different from 'that which happens', and is not therefore in any way contained in this latter representation. How come I then to predicate of that which happens something quite different, and to apprehend that the concept of cause, though not contained in it, yet belongs, and indeed necessarily belongs, to it? What is here the unknown=X which gives support to the understanding when it believes that it can discover outside the concept A a predicate B foreign to this concept, which it yet at the same time considers to be connected with it? It cannot be experience, because the suggested principle has connected the second representation with the first, not only with greater universality, but also with the character of necessity, and therefore completely *a priori* and on the basis of mere concepts. Upon such synthetic, that is, ampliative prin-

ciples, all our *a priori* speculative knowledge must ultimately rest; analytic judgments are very important, and indeed necessary, but only for obtaining that clearness in the concepts which is requisite for such a sure and wide synthesis as will lead to a genuinely new addition to all previous knowledge.

NOTE

* ["Judgments of experience" to end of paragraph substituted in B in place of the following:]

Thus it is evident: 1. that through analytic judgments our knowledge is not in any way extended, and that the concept which I already have is merely set forth and made intelligible to me; 2. that in synthetic judgments I must have besides the concept of the subject something else (X), upon which the understanding may rely, if it is to know that a predicate, not contained in this concept, nevertheless belongs to it.

In the case of empirical judgments, judgments of experience, there is no difficulty whatsoever in meeting this demand. This X is the complete experience of the object which I think through the concept A—a concept which forms only one part of this experience. For though I do not include in the concept of a body in general the predicate 'weight', the concept none the less indicates the complete experience through one of its parts; and to this part, as belonging to it, I can therefore add other parts of the same experience. By prior analysis I can apprehend the concept of body through the characters of extension, impenetrability, figure, etc., all of which are thought in this concept. To extend my knowledge, I then look back to the experience from which I have derived this concept of body, and find that weight is always connected with the above characters. Experience is thus the X which lies outside the concept A, and on which rests the possibility of the synthesis of the predicate 'weight' (B) with the concept (A).

A. J. AYER

The *A Priori*

The view of philosophy which we have adopted may, I think, fairly be described as a form of empiricism. For it is characteristic of an empiricist to eschew metaphysics, on the ground that every factual proposition must refer to sense-experience. And even if the conception of philosophizing as an activity of analysis is not to be discovered in the traditional theories of empiricists, we have seen that it is implicit in their practice. At the same time, it must be made clear that, in calling ourselves empiricists, we are not avowing a belief in any of the psychological doctrines which are commonly associated with empiricism. For, even if these doctrines were valid, their validity would be independent of the validity of any philosophical thesis. It could be established only by observation, and not by the purely logical considerations upon which our empiricism rests.

Having admitted that we are empiricists, we must now deal with the objection that is commonly brought against all forms of empiricism; the objection, namely, that it is impossible on empiricist principles to account for our knowledge of necessary truths. For, as Hume conclusively showed, no general proposition whose validity is subject to the test of actual experience can ever be logically certain. No matter how often it is verified in practice, there still remains the possibility that it will be confuted on some future occasion. The fact that a law has been substantiated in $n - 1$ cases affords no logical guarantee that it will be substantiated in the nth case also, no matter how large we take n to be. And this means that no general proposition referring to a matter of fact can ever be shown to be necessarily and universally true. It can at best be a probable hypothesis. And this, we shall find, applies not only to general propositions, but to all propositions which have a factual content. They can none of them ever become logically certain. This conclusion, which we shall elaborate later on, is one which must be accepted by every consistent empiricist. It is often

thought to involve him in complete scepticism; but this is not the case. For the fact that the validity of a proposition cannot be logically guaranteed in no way entails that it is irrational for us to believe it. On the contrary, what is irrational is to look for a guarantee where none can be forthcoming; to demand certainty where probability is all that is obtainable. We have already remarked upon this, in referring to the work of Hume. And we shall make the point clearer when we come to treat of probability, in explaining the use which we make of empirical propositions. We shall discover that there is nothing perverse or paradoxical about the view that all the "truths" of science and common sense are hypotheses; and consequently that the fact that it involves this view constitutes no objection to the empiricist thesis.

Where the empiricist does encounter difficulty is in connection with the truths of formal logic and mathematics. For whereas a scientific generalisation is readily admitted to be fallible, the truths of mathematics and logic appear to everyone to be necessary and certain. But if empiricism is correct no proposition which has a factual content can be necessary or certain. Accordingly the empiricist must deal with the truths of logic and mathematics in one of the two following ways: he must say either that they are not necessary truths, in which case he must account for the universal conviction that they are; or he must say that they have no factual content, and then he must explain how a proposition which is empty of all factual content can be true and useful and surprising.

If neither of these courses proves satisfactory, we shall be obliged to give way to rationalism. We shall be obliged to admit that there are some truths about the world which we can know independently of experience; that there are some properties which we can ascribe to all objects, even though we cannot conceivably observe that all objects have them. And we shall have to accept it as a mysterious inexplicable fact that our thought has this power to reveal to us authoritatively the nature of objects which we have never observed. Or else we must accept the Kantian explanation which, apart from the epistemological difficulties which we have already touched on, only pushes the mystery a stage further back.

It is clear that any such concession to rationalism would upset the main argument of this book. For the admission that there were some facts about the world which could be known independently of experience would be incompatible with our fundamental contention that a sentence says nothing unless it is empirically verifiable. And thus the whole force of our attack on metaphysics would be destroyed. It is vital, therefore, for us to be able to show that one or other of the empiricist accounts of the propositions of logic and mathematics is correct. If we are successful in this, we shall have destroyed the foundations of rationalism. For the fundamental tenet of rationalism is that thought is an independent source of knowledge, and is moreover a more trustworthy source of knowledge than experience; indeed some rationalists have gone so far as to say that thought is the only source of knowledge. And the ground for this view is simply that the only necessary truths about the world which are known to us are known through thought and not through experience. So that if we can show either that the truths in question are not necessary or that they are not "truths about the world," we shall be taking away the support on which rationalism rests. We shall be making good the empiricist contention that there are no "truths of reason" which refer to matters of fact.

The course of maintaining that the truths of logic and mathematics are not necessary or certain was adopted by Mill. He maintained that these propositions were inductive generalizations based on an extremely large number of instances. The fact that the number of supporting instances was so very large accounted, in his view, for our believing these generalizations to be necessarily and universally true. The evidence in their favour was so strong that it seemed incredible to us that a contrary instance should ever arise. Nevertheless it was in principle possible for such generalizations to be confuted. They were highly probable, but, being inductive generalizations, they were not certain. The difference between them and the hypotheses of natural science was a difference in degree and not in kind. Experience gave us very good reason to suppose that a "truth" of mathematics or logic was true universally; but we were not possessed of a guarantee. For these "truths" were only empirical hypotheses which had worked particularly well in the past; and, like all empirical hypotheses, they were theoretically fallible.

I do not think that this solution of the empiricist's difficulty with regard to the propositions of logic and mathematics is acceptable. In discussing it, it is necessary to make a distinction which is perhaps already enshrined in Kant's famous dictum that, although there can be no doubt that all our knowledge begins with experience, it does not follow that it all arises out of experience.[4] When we say that the truths of logic are known independently of experience, we are not of course saying that they are innate, in the sense that we are born knowing them. It is obvious that mathematics and logic have to be learned in the same way as chemistry and history have to be learned. Nor are we denying that the first person to discover a given logical or mathematical truth was led to it by an inductive procedure. It is very probable, for example, that the principle of the syllogism was formulated not before but after the validity of syllogistic reasoning had been observed in a number of particular cases. What we are discussing, however, when we say that logical and mathematical truths are known independently of experience, is not a historical question concerning the way in which these truths were originally discovered, nor a psychological question concerning the way in which each of us comes to learn them, but an epistemological question. The contention of Mill's which we reject is that the propositions of logic and mathematics have the same status as empirical hypotheses; that their validity is determined in the same way. We maintain that they are independent of experience in the sense that they do not owe their validity to empirical verification. We may come to discover them through an inductive process; but once we have apprehended them we see that they are necessarily true, that they hold good for every conceivable instance. And this serves to distinguish them from empirical generalizations. For we know that a proposition whose validity depends upon experience cannot be seen to be necessarily and universally true.

In rejecting Mill's theory, we are obliged to be somewhat dogmatic. We can do no more than state the issue clearly and then trust that his contention will be seen to be discrepant with the relevant logical facts. The following considerations may serve to show that of the two ways of dealing with logic and mathematics which are open to the empiricist, the one which Mill adopted is not the one which is correct.

The best way to substantiate our assertion that the truths of formal logic and pure mathematics are necessarily true is to examine cases in which they might seem to be confuted. It might easily happen, for example, that when I came to count what I had taken to be five pairs of objects, I found that they amounted only to nine. And if I wished to mislead people I might say that on this occasion twice five was not ten. But in that case I should not be using the complex sign "$2 \times 5 = 10$" in the way in which it is ordinarily used. I should be taking it not as the expression of a purely mathematical proposition, but as the expression of an empirical generalization, to the effect that whenever I counted what appeared to me to be five pairs of objects I discovered that they were ten in number. This generalization may very well be false. But if it proved false in a given case, one would not say that the mathematical proposition "$2 \times 5 = 10$" had been confuted. One would say that I was wrong in supposing that there were five pairs of objects to start with, or that one of the objects had been taken away while I was counting, or that two of them had coalesced, or that I had counted wrongly. One would adopt as an explanation whatever empirical hypothesis fitted in best with the accredited facts. The one explanation which would in no circumstances be adopted is that ten is not always the product of two and five.

To take another example: if what appears to be a Euclidean triangle is found by measurement not to have angles totalling 180 degrees, we do not say that we have met with an instance which invalidates the mathematical proposition that the sum of the three angles of a Euclidean triangle is 180 degrees. We say that we have measured wrongly, or, more probably, that the triangle we have been measuring is not Euclidean. And this is our procedure in every case

in which a mathematical truth might appear to be confuted. We always preserve its validity by adopting some other explanation of the occurrence.

The same thing applies to the principles of formal logic. We may take an example relating to the so-called law of excluded middle, which states that a proposition must be either true or false, or, in other words, that it is impossible that a proposition and its contradictory should neither of them be true. One might suppose that a proposition of the form "x has stopped doing y" would in certain cases constitute an exception to this law. For instance, if my friend has never yet written to me, it seems fair to say that it is neither true nor false that he has stopped writing to me. But in fact one would refuse to accept such an instance as an invalidation of the law of excluded middle. One would point out that the proposition "My friend has stopped writing to me" is not a simple proposition, but the conjunction of the two propositions "My friend wrote to me in the past" and "My friend does not write to me now": and, furthermore, that the proposition "My friend has not stopped writing to me" is not, as it appears to be, contradictory to "My friend has stopped writing to me," but only contrary to it. For it means "My friend wrote to me in the past, and he still writes to me." When, therefore, we say that such a proposition as "My friend has stopped writing to me" is sometimes neither true nor false, we are speaking inaccurately. For we seem to be saying that neither it nor its contradictory is true. Whereas what we mean, or anyhow should mean, is that neither it nor its apparent contradictory is true. And its apparent contradictory is really only its contrary. Thus we preserve the law of excluded middle by showing that the negating of a sentence does not always yield the contradictory of the proposition originally expressed.

There is no need to give further examples. Whatever instance we care to take, we shall always find that the situations in which a logical or mathematical principle might appear to be confuted are accounted for in such a way as to leave the principle unassailed. And this indicates that Mill was wrong in supposing that a situation could arise which would overthrow a mathematical truth. The principles of logic and mathematics are true universally simply because we never allow them to be anything else.

And the reason for this is that we cannot abandon them without contradicting ourselves, without sinning against the rules which govern the use of language, and so making our utterances self-stultifying. In other words, the truths of logic and mathematics are analytic propositions or tautologies. In saying this we are making what will be held to be an extremely controversial statement, and we must now proceed to make its implications clear.

The most familiar definition of an analytic proposition, or judgement, as he called it, is that given by Kant.[5] He said that an analytic judgement was one in which the predicate B belonged to the subject A as something which was covertly contained in the concept of A. He contrasted analytic with synthetic judgements, in which the predicate B lay outside the subject A, although it did stand in connection with it. Analytic judgements, he explains, "add nothing through the predicate to the concept of the subject, but merely break it up into those constituent concepts that have all along been thought in it, although confusedly." Synthetic judgements, on the other hand, "add to the concept of the subject a predicate which has not been in any wise thought in it, and which no analysis could possibly extract from it." Kant gives "all bodies are extended" as an example of an analytic judgement, on the ground that the required predicate can be extracted from the concept of "body," "in accordance with the principle of contradiction"; as an example of a synthetic judgement, he gives "all bodies are heavy." He refers also to "7 + 5 = 12" as a synthetic judgement, on the ground that the concept of twelve is by no means already thought in merely thinking the union of seven and five. And he appears to regard this as tantamount to saying that the judgement does not rest on the principle of contradiction alone. He holds, also, that through analytic judgements our knowledge is not extended as it is through synthetic judgements. For in analytic judgements "the concept which I already have is merely set forth and made intelligible to me."

I think that this is a fair summary of Kant's account of the distinction between analytic and synthetic propositions, but I do not think that it succeeds in making the distinction clear. For even if we pass over the difficulties which arise out of the use of the vague term concept," and the unwarranted assumption that every judgement, as well as every German or English sentence, can be said to have a subject and a predicate, there remains still this crucial defect. Kant does not give one straightforward criterion for distinguishing between analytic and synthetic propositions; he gives two distinct criteria, which are by no means equivalent. Thus his ground for holding that the proposition "7 + 5 = 12" is synthetic is, as we have seen, that the subjective intension of "7 + 5" does not comprise the subjective intension of "12"; whereas his ground for holding that "all bodies are extended" is an analytic proposition is that it rests on the principle of contradiction alone. That is, he employs a psychological criterion in the first of these examples, and a logical criterion in the second, and takes their equivalence for granted. But, in fact, a proposition which is synthetic according to the former criterion may very well be analytic according to the latter. For, as we have already pointed out, it is possible for symbols to be synonymous without having the same intensional meaning for anyone: and accordingly from the fact that one can think of the sum of seven and five without necessarily thinking of twelve, it by no means follows that the proposition "7 + 5 = 12" can be denied without self-contradiction. From the rest of his argument, it is clear that it is this logical proposition, and not any psychological proposition, that Kant is really anxious to establish. His use of the psychological criterion leads him to think that he has established it, when he has not.

I think that we can preserve the logical import of Kant's distinction between analytic and synthetic propositions, while avoiding the confusions which mar his actual account of it, if we say that a proposition is analytic when its validity depends solely on the definitions of the symbols it contains, and synthetic when its validity is determined by the facts of experience. Thus, the proposition "There are ants which have established a system of slavery" is a synthetic proposition. For we cannot tell whether it is true or false merely by considering the definitions of the symbols which constitute it. We have to resort to actual observation of the behaviour of ants. On the other hand, the proposition "Either some ants are parasitic or none are" is an analytic proposition. For one need not resort to observation to discover that there either are or are not ants which are parasitic.

If one knows what is the function of the words "either," "or," and "not," then one can see that any proposition of the form "Either *p* is true or *p* is not true" is valid, independently of experience. Accordingly, all such propositions are analytic.

It is to be noticed that the proposition "Either some ants are parasitic or none are" provides no information whatsoever about the behaviour of ants, or, indeed, about any matter of fact. And this applies to all analytic propositions. They none of them provide any information about any matter of fact. In other words, they are entirely devoid of factual content. And it is for this reason that no experience can confute them.

When we say that analytic propositions are devoid of factual content, and consequently that they say nothing, we are not suggesting that they are senseless in the way that metaphysical utterances are senseless. For, although they give us no information about any empirical situation, they do enlighten us by illustrating the way in which we use certain symbols. Thus if I say, "Nothing can be coloured in different ways at the same time with respect to the same part of itself," I am not saying anything about the properties of any actual thing; but I am not talking nonsense. I am expressing an analytic proposition, which records our determination to call a colour expanse which differs in quality from a neighbouring colour expanse a different part of a given thing. In other words, I am simply calling attention to the implications of a certain linguistic usage. Similarly, in saying that if all Bretons are Frenchmen, and all Frenchmen Europeans, then all Bretons are Europeans, I am not describing any matter of fact. But I am showing that in the statement that all Bretons are Frenchmen, and all Frenchmen Europeans, the further statement that all Bretons are Europeans is implicitly contained. And I am thereby indicating the convention which governs our usage of the words "if" and "all."

We see, then, that there is a sense in which analytic propositions do give us new knowledge. They call attention to linguistic usages, of which we might otherwise not be conscious, and they reveal unsuspected implications in our assertions and beliefs. But we can see also that there is a sense in which they may be said to add nothing to our knowledge. For they tell us only what we may be said to know

already. Thus, if I know that the existence of May Queens is a relic of tree-worship, and I discover that May Queens still exist in England, I can employ the tautology "If *p* implies *q*, and *p* is true, *q* is true" to show that there still exists a relic of tree-worship in England. But in saying that there are still May Queens in England, and that the existence of May Queens is a relic of tree-worship, I have already asserted the existence in England of a relic of tree-worship. The use of the tautology does, indeed, enable me to make this concealed assertion explicit. But it does not provide me with any new knowledge, in the sense in which empirical evidence that the election of May Queens had been forbidden by law would provide me with new knowledge. If one had to set forth all the information one possessed, with regard to matters of fact, one would not write down any analytic propositions. But one would make use of analytic propositions in compiling one's encyclopedia, and would thus come to include propositions which one would otherwise have overlooked. And, besides enabling one to make one's list of information complete, the formulation of analytic propositions would enable one to make sure that the synthetic propositions of which the list was composed formed a self-consistent system. By showing which ways of combining propositions resulted in contradictions, they would prevent one from including incompatible propositions and so making the list self-stultifying. But in so far as we had actually used such words as "all" and "or" and "not" without falling into self-contradiction, we might be said already to know what was revealed in the formulation of analytic propositions illustrating the rules which govern our usage of these logical particles. So that here again we are justified in saying that analytic propositions do not increase our knowledge.

The analytic character of the truths of formal logic was obscured in the traditional logic through its being insufficiently formalized. For in speaking always of judgements, instead of propositions, and introducing irrelevant psychological questions, the traditional logic gave the impression of being concerned in some specially intimate way with the workings of thought. What it was actually concerned with was the formal relationship of classes, as is shown by the fact that all its principles of inference are subsumed in the Boolean class-calculus, which is subsumed in its turn in the propositional calculus of Russell and Whitehead.[6] Their system, expounded in *Principia Mathematica,* makes it clear that formal logic is not concerned with the properties of men's minds, much less with the properties of material objects, but simply with the possibility of combining propositions by means of logical particles into analytic propositions, and with studying the formal relationship of these analytic propositions, in virtue of which one is deducible from another. Their procedure is to exhibit the propositions of formal logic as a deductive system, based on five primitive propositions, subsequently reduced in number to one. Hereby the distinction between logical truths and principles of inference, which was maintained in the Aristotelian logic, very properly disappears. Every principle of inference is put forward as a logical truth and every logical truth can serve as a principle of inference. The three Aristotelian "laws of thought," the law of identity, the law of excluded middle, and the law of non-contradiction, are incorporated in the system, but they are not considered more important than the other analytic propositions. They are not reckoned among the premises of the system. And the system of Russell and Whitehead itself is probably only one among many possible logics, each of which is composed of tautologies as interesting to the logician as the arbitrarily selected Aristotelian "laws of thought."[7]

A point which is not sufficiently brought out by Russell, if indeed it is recognised by him at all, is that every logical proposition is valid in its own right. Its validity does not depend on its being incorporated in a system, and deduced from certain propositions which are taken as self-evident. The construction of systems of logic is useful as a means of discovering and certifying analytic propositions, but it is not in principle essential even for this purpose. For it is possible to conceive of a symbolism in which every analytic proposition could be seen to be analytic in virtue of its form alone.

The fact that the validity of an analytic proposition in no way depends on its being deducible from other analytic propositions is our justification for disregarding the question whether the propositions of mathematics are reducible to propositions of formal logic, in the way that Russell supposed.[8] For even if it is the case that the definition of a cardinal number as a class of classes similar to a given class is circular, and it is not possible to reduce mathematical notions to purely logical notions, it will still remain true that the propositions of mathematics are analytic propositions. They will form a special class of analytic propositions, containing special terms, but they will be none the less analytic for that. For the criterion of an analytic proposition is that its validity should follow simply from the definition of the terms contained in it, and this condition is fulfilled by the propositions of pure mathematics.

The mathematical propositions which one might most pardonably suppose to be synthetic are the propositions of geometry. For it is natural for us to think, as Kant thought, that geometry is the study of the properties of physical space, and consequently that its propositions have factual content. And if we believe this, and also recognise that the truths of geometry are necessary and certain, then we may be inclined to accept Kant's hypothesis that space is the form of intuition of our outer sense, a form imposed by us on the matter of sensation, as the only possible explanation of our *a priori* knowledge of these synthetic propositions. But while the view that pure geometry is concerned with physical space was plausible enough in Kant's day, when the geometry of Euclid was the only geometry known, the subsequent invention of nonEuclidean geometries has shown it to be mistaken. We see now that the axioms of a geometry are simply definitions, and that the theorems of a geometry are simply the logical consequences of these definitions.[9] A geometry is not in itself about physical space; in itself it cannot be said to be "about" anything. But we can use a geometry to reason about physical space. That is to say, once we have given the axioms a physical interpretation, we can proceed to apply the theorems to the objects which satisfy the axioms. Whether a geometry can be applied to the actual physical world or not, is an empirical question which falls outside the scope of the geometry itself. There is no sense, therefore, in asking which of the various geometries known to us are false and which are true. In so far as they are all free from contradiction, they are all true. What one can ask is which of them is the most useful on any given occasion, which of them can be applied most easily and most fruitfully to an actual empirical situation. But the proposition which states that a certain application of a geometry is possible is not itself a proposition of that geometry. All that the geometry itself tells us is that if anything can be brought under the definitions, it will also satisfy the theorems. It is therefore a purely logical system, and its propositions are purely analytic propositions.

It might be objected that the use made of diagrams in geometrical treatises shows that geometrical reasoning is not purely abstract and logical, but depends on our intuition of the properties of figures. In fact, however, the use of diagrams is not essential to completely rigorous geometry. The diagrams are introduced as an aid to our reason. They provide us with a particular application of the geometry, and so assist us to perceive the more general truth that the axioms of the geometry involve certain consequences. But the fact that most of us need the help of an example to make us aware of those consequences does not show that the relation between them and the axioms is not a purely logical relation. It shows merely that our intellects are unequal to the task of carrying out very abstract processes of reasoning without the assistance of intuition. In other words, it has no bearing on the nature of geometrical propositions, but is simply an empirical fact about ourselves. Moreover, the appeal to intuition, though generally of psychological value, is also a source of danger to the geometer. He is tempted to make assumptions which are accidentally true of the particular figure he is taking as an illustration, but do not follow from his axioms. It has, indeed, been shown that Euclid himself was guilty of this, and consequently that the presence of the figure is essential to some of his proofs.[10] This shows that his system is not, as he presents it, completely rigorous, although of course it can be made so. It does not show that the presence of the figure is essential to a truly rigorous geometrical proof. To suppose that it did would be to take as a necessary feature of all geometries what is really only an incidental defect in one particular geometrical system.

We conclude, then, that the propositions of pure geometry are analytic. And this leads us to reject Kant's hypothesis that geometry deals with the form of intuition of our outer sense. For the ground for this hypothesis was that it alone explained how the propositions of geometry could be both true *a priori* and synthetic: and we have seen that they are not

synthetic. Similarly our view that the propositions of arithmetic are not synthetic but analytic leads us to reject the Kantian hypothesis[11] that arithmetic is concerned with our pure intuition of time, the form of our inner sense. And thus we are able to dismiss Kant's transcendental aesthetic without having to bring forward the epistemological difficulties which it is commonly said to involve. For the only argument which can be brought in favour of Kant's theory is that it alone explains certain "facts." And now we have found that the "facts" which it purports to explain are not facts at all. For while it is true that we have *a priori* knowledge of necessary propositions, it is not true, as Kant supposed, that any of these necessary propositions are synthetic. They are without exception analytic propositions, or, in other words, tautologies.

We have already explained how it is that these analytic propositions are necessary and certain. We saw that the reason why they cannot be confuted in experience is that they do not make any assertion about the empirical world. They simply record our determination to use words in a certain fashion. We cannot deny them without infringing the conventions which are presupposed by our very denial, and so falling into self-contradiction. And this is the sole ground of their necessity. As Wittgenstein puts it, our justification for holding that the world could not conceivably disobey the laws of logic is simply that we could not say of an unlogical world how it would look.[12] And just as the validity of an analytic proposition is independent of the nature of the external world; so is it independent of the nature of our minds. It is perfectly conceivable that we should have employed different linguistic conventions from those which we actually do employ. But whatever these conventions might be, the tautologies in which we recorded them would always be necessary. For any denial of them would be self-stultifying.

We see, then, that there is nothing mysterious about the apodeictic certainty of logic and mathematics. Our knowledge that no observation can ever confute the proposition "7 + 5 = 12" depends simply on the fact that the symbolic expression "7 + 5" is synonymous with "12," just as our knowledge that every oculist is an eye-doctor depends on the fact that the symbol "eye-doctor" is synonymous with "oculist." And the same explanation holds good for every other *a priori* truth.

What is mysterious at first sight is that these tautologies should on occasion be so surprising, that there should be in mathematics and logic the possibility of invention and discovery. As Poincaré says: "If all the assertions which mathematics puts forward can be derived from one another by formal logic, mathematics cannot amount to anything more than an immense tautology. Logical inference can teach us nothing essentially new, and if everything is to proceed from the principle of identity, everything must be reducible to it. But can we really allow that these theorems which fill so many books serve no other purpose than to say in a roundabout fashion 'A = A'?"[13] Poincaré finds this incredible. His own theory is that the sense of invention and discovery in mathematics belongs to it in virtue of mathematical induction, the principle that what is true for the number 1, and true for $n + 1$ when it is true for n,[14] is true for all numbers. And he claims that this is a synthetic *a priori* principle. It is, in fact, *a priori*, but it is not synthetic. It is a defining principle of the natural numbers, serving to distinguish them from such numbers as the infinite cardinal numbers, to which it cannot be applied.[15] Moreover, we must remember that discoveries can be made, not only in arithmetic, but also in geometry and formal logic, where no use is made of mathematical induction. So that even if Poincaré were right about mathematical induction, he would not have provided a satisfactory explanation of the paradox that a mere body of tautologies can be so interesting and so surprising.

The true explanation is very simple. The power of logic and mathematics to surprise us depends, like their usefulness, on the limitations of our reason. A being whose intellect was infinitely powerful would take no interest in logic and mathematics.[16] For he would be able to see at a glance everything that his definitions implied, and, accordingly, could never learn anything from logical inference which he was not fully conscious of already. But our intellects are not of this order. It is only a minute proportion of the consequences of our definitions that we are able to detect at a glance. Even so simple a tautology as "$91 \times 79 = 7189$" is beyond the scope of our immediate apprehension. To assure ourselves that "7189" is synonymous with "91×79" we have to resort to calculation, which is simply a process of tautological transformation—that is, a process by which we change the form of expressions without altering their significance. The multiplication tables are rules for carrying out this process in arithmetic, just as the laws of logic are rules for the tautological transformation of sentences expressed in logical symbolism or in ordinary language. As the process of calculation is carried out more or less mechanically, it is easy for us to make a slip and so unwittingly contradict ourselves. And this accounts for the existence of logical and mathematical "falsehoods," which otherwise might appear paradoxical. Clearly the risk of error in logical reasoning is proportionate to the length and the complexity of the process of calculation. And in the same way, the more complex an analytic proposition is, the more chance it has of interesting and surprising us.

It is easy to see that the danger of error in logical reasoning can be minimized by the introduction of symbolic devices, which enable us to express highly complex tautologies in a conveniently simple form. And this gives us an opportunity for the exercise of invention in the pursuit of logical enquiries. For a well-chosen definition will call our attention to analytic truths, which would otherwise have escaped us. And the framing of definitions which are useful and fruitful may well be regarded as a creative act.

Having thus shown that there is no inexplicable paradox involved in the view that the truths of logic and mathematics are all of them analytic, we may safely adopt it as the only satisfactory explanation of their *a priori* necessity. And in adopting it we vindicate the empiricist claim that there can be no *a priori* knowledge of reality. For we show that the truths of pure reason, the propositions which we know to be valid independently of all experience, are so only in virtue of their lack of factual content. To say that a proposition is true *a priori* is to say that it is a tautology. And tautologies, though they may serve to guide us in our empirical search for knowledge, do not in themselves contain any information about any matter of fact.

NOTES

1. Introduction to L. Wittgenstein's *Tractatus Logico-Philosophicus,* p. 23.
2. Concerning logical paradoxes, see Russell and Whitehead, *Principia Mathematica,* Introduction,

Chapter ii; F. P. Ramsey, *Foundations of Mathematics,* pp. 1–63; and Lewis and Langford, *Symbolic Logic,* Chapter xiii.

3. Vide *Logische Syntax der Sprache,* Parts I and II.

4. *Critique of Pure Reason,* 2nd ed., Introduction, section i.

5. *Critique of Pure Reason,* 2nd ed., Introduction, sections iv and v.

6. Vide Karl Menger, "Die Neue Logik," *Krise und Neuaufbau in den Exakten Wissenschaften,* pp. 94–6; and Lewis and Langford, *Symbolic Logic;* Chapter v.

7. Vide Lewis and Langford, *Symbolic Logic,* Chapter vii, for an elaboration of this point.

8. Vide *Introduction to Mathematical Philosophy,* Chapter iii.

9. cf. H. Poincaré, *La Science et l'Hypothèse,* Part II, Chapter iii.

10. cf. M. Black, *The Nature of Mathematics,* p. 154.

11. This hypothesis is not mentioned in the *Critique of Pure Reason,* but was maintained by Kant at an earlier date.

12. *Tractatus Logico-Philiosophicus,* 3.031.

13. *La Science et l'Hypothèse,* Part I, Chapter i.

14. This was wrongly stated in previous editions as "true for n when it is true for $n + 1$."

15. cf. B. Russell's *Introduction to Mathematical Philosophy,* Chapter iii, p. 27.

16. cf. Hans Hahn, "Logik, Mathematik und Naturerkennen," *Einheitswissenschaft,* Heft II, p. 18. "Ein allwissendes Wesen braucht keine Logik und keine Mathematik."

RODERICK CHISHOLM

Reason and the *A Priori*

*The identity of each essence with itself and differ-
ence from every other essence suffices to distinguish
and define them all in eternity, where they form the
Realm of Essence. True and false assertions may be
made about any one of them, such, for instance, as
that it does not exist; or that it includes or excludes
some other essence, or is included or excluded by it.
[George Santayana,* The Realms of Being.*]*

*Pure reason is unable to produce any real knowl-
edge, its only business is the arrangement of symbols
which are used for the expression of knowledge.
[Moritz Schlick, "A New Philosophy of
Experience."]*

Our apprehension of such truths as the following is
traditionally ascribed to "reason": being a square includes being rectangular, and excludes being circular; being a man includes being an animal, and
excludes being an angel. Or, what may come to the
same thing, it is *necessarily true* that if anything is a
square then it is a rectangle and not a circle, and that
if anything is a man then it is an animal and not an
angel. Or it is true, not only in this world but in *all
possible worlds,* that all squares are rectangles and no
squares are circles, and that all men are animals and
no men are angels. But being a square neither includes nor excludes being red, and being a man neither includes nor excludes being a Greek. Again:
some men being Greek includes some Greeks being
men and excludes no Greeks being men; it is necessarily true, or true in all possible worlds, that if some
men are Greek then some Greeks are men; but some
men being Greek neither includes nor excludes
some men being Roman.

The period of American philosophy with which
we are here concerned has been dominated by an attitude of skepticism toward such truths and faculties. The keynote of this attitude was struck by

Moritz Schlick in his second public lecture at the
College of the Pacific: "Empiricism now has the
right and power to claim the whole field of knowledge. We know nothing except by experience, and
experience is the only criterion of the truth or falsity
of any real proposition."[1] Subsequent debate has indicated, I think, that Schlick's confidence was not
justified.

To understand the debate and the issues it involved, we must consider the following topics: (1)
the Kantian distinction between analytic and synthetic judgments, its reinterpretation by recent
philosophers as a distinction between types of *statement,* and the relation of "analytic statements" to
statements that are sometimes said to be "logically
true"; (2) the Kantian distinction between a priori
and a posteriori knowledge; (3) the attempt to construe the a priori knowledge, which is expressed in
analytic statements, as a type of knowledge that is
intimately connected with language; and (4) the
question whether there is any a priori knowledge
that is not expressible in statements that are either
analytic or logically true.

1

An analytic judgment, according to Kant, is a judgment in which "the predicate adds nothing to the
concept of the subject." If I judge that all squares are
rectangles, then, in Kant's terminology, the concept
of the subject of my judgment is the property of being square, and the concept of the predicate is the
property of being rectangular. The concept of the
predicate—and this is the reason for using the term
"analytic"—helps us to "break up the concept of the
subject into those constituent concepts that have all
along been thought in it."[2] Kant would have said
that the "constituent concepts" of being square are
being equilateral and being rectangular; perhaps it

would be clearer to say that being a square is a conjunctive property" the components of which are being equilateral and being rectangular. In either case, the predicate of the judgment that all squares are rectangles may be said to "analyze out" what is already contained in the subject.

Synthetic judgments, on the other hand, are those in which the concept of the predicate is *not* thus "contained in" that of the subject. The judgment that all men are mortal is a synthetic judgment since the concept of being mortal is not included in that of being a man; hence, in the terminology of Leibniz, the judgment though true of this world is not true of "all possible worlds."

Anything that exemplifies the concept of the subject of an analytic judgment will, ipso facto, exemplify that of the predicate; anything that is a square is, ipso facto, a rectangle. To *deny* an analytic judgment—to judge that some squares are *not* rectangles—would be to contradict oneself, for it would be to judge that there are things that both do and do not have a certain property. Kant made this point by saying that "the common principle of all analytic judgments is the law of contradiction."[3]

All analytic judgments are true, but synthetic judgments may be either true or false. The synthetic judgment that all men are mortal is true; the synthetic judgment that all men are Greeks is false. If we deny the former judgment, holding that some men are not mortal, we go wrong but we do not contradict ourselves.

In recent philosophy, the terms "analytic" and "synthetic" are applied not to judgments but to statements or sentences. The linguistic concept of a *statement* is in some respects clearer than the psychological concept of a judgment; but the emphasis on statements, particularly in recent American philosophy, has led some philosophers to confuse certain fundamental questions of epistemology with certain quite different questions of the philosophy of language.

One of the best contemporary accounts of the distinction between analytic and synthetic statements is that given in C. I. Lewis's Carus Lectures, *An Analysis of Knowledge and Valuation* (Open Court, 1946). His account is substantially the following:

The word "square" has as its meaning the property of being square; it denotes, or applies to, anything that happens to have that property. The word "rectangle," similarly, has for its meaning the property of being rectangular, and it denotes, or applies, to anything that happens to have that property. The property of being rectangular, we have noted, is included in that of being square—i.e., it is a component of the conjunctive property of being both equilateral and rectangular; hence the meaning of "rectangular" is included in that of "square." We may say, then, that an affirmative subject-predicate statement, such as "All squares are rectangles," is *analytic* if the meaning of the predicate is included in that of the subject, and a negative subject-predicate statement, such as "No spinster is married," is analytic if the meaning of the negation of the predicate (in this case, the meaning of "nonmarried") is included in the meaning of the subject. A subject-predicate statement may be called *synthetic* if it is not analytic. "All men are mortal" is therefore synthetic, since the meaning of "mortal" is not included in that of "man"—even though, as it happens, the predicate applies to all those things that the subject applies to.[4]

The statement "Socrates is mortal or it is false that Socrates is mortal" is not analytic, as "analytic" has just been defined, for it is a compound statement and not a simple subject-predicate statement; but it is similar, in important respects, to those statements that are analytic. It is necessarily true, or true for all possible worlds, since Socrates being mortal excludes Socrates not being mortal. Kant would have said that it "has its principle in the law of contradiction" and we may express the same point by saying that it is a logical truth. W. V. Quine proposed a useful definition of "logically true," as a phrase that may be predicated of statements or sentences. After we have formulated his definition, we will be in a position to understand some of the philosophical questions that these concepts involve.

Quine first enumerates a list of words to be called "logical words"; the list includes "or," "not," "if," "then," "and," "all," "every," some." A sentence or statement is then said to be logically true if it is one in which only the logical words *occur essentially*. In "Socrates is mortal or it is false that Socrates is mortal," which is logically true, the expressions "or" and "it is false that" occur essentially, but the nonlogical words, "Socrates," "is," and "mortal," do not. What this means, put somewhat loosely, is that the truth of the statement is independent of the particular nonlogical words that happen to occur in it. Put somewhat more exactly: a logically true statement is one such that, if, for any nonlogical word in the sentence, we replace each of its occurrences by any other "grammatically admissible" word (making sure that all occurrences of the old word are replaced by occurrences of the same new word), then the new statement we derive will also be true. If the word "Socrates," in "Socrates is mortal or it is false that Socrates is mortal," is replaced by "these stones," if "is" is replaced by "are," and "mortal" by "blue," then the result—"These stones are blue or it is false that these stones are blue"—will be true. On the other hand, if we replace the logical words by other grammatically admissible words, the result may be false—as it would be if, in our example, we replaced "or" by "and." A logical truth on this interpretation, then, is "a statement that is true and remains true under all reinterpretations of its components other than logical particles."[5] (But if, in the logical truth "All elderly thieves are thieves," the nonlogical term "elderly" is replaced by such a term as "suspected," possible," or "potential," the result will be a false statement. Certain qualifications must be added to "grammatic admissibility" to preclude this type of result. Moreover, as Quine recognized, such a definition of "logical truth" has this limitation: the question of *which* statements thus remain true under all reinterpretations of their nonlogical words remains problematic. The following are often said to be logical truths: "If it is true that either I am now in Providence or I am not now in Providence, then either it is true that I am now in Providence or it is not true that I am now in Providence," and "If it is true that either Zeno is in Athens or Zeno is in Sparta, and if it is also true that Zeno is walking either one mile an hour or Zeno is walking two miles an hour, then it is true that either Zeno is in Athens and walking one mile an hour, or Zeno is in Athens and walking two miles an hour, or Zeno is in Sparta and walking one mile an hour, or Zeno is in Sparta and walking two miles an hour." But if we change the tense of the first of these statements from present to future, then, according to some philosophers, we must reject the result on the ground that it conflicts with certain doctrines about freedom and human agency.[6] And if the second statement is revised, so as to refer to the position and velocity, not of Zeno, but of certain subatomic particles, then, according to some philosophers, we must reject the result on the ground that it conflicts with certain doctrines of contemporary quantum physics.[7] These issues involve epistemological questions similar to those discussed in the first section. For the present discussion, we may assume that we have a general characterization of logical truth, even though we have no definite way of fixing the boundary between logical and nonlogical truth.)

The analytic statements "All squares are rectangles" and "No spinsters are married" are not themselves logical truths on the above account. If in the former we replace the nonlogical word "squares" by "circles,"' the resulting statement will be false; and if in the latter we replace the nonlogical word "married" by "happy," the result will be false. But we may paraphrase any analytic statement—we may reexpress what it expresses—by means of statements that *are* logically true. The term "squares" has among its synonyms (i.e., those terms having the same meaning that it has) a term—viz., "equilateral rectangles"—that includes the predicate term of "All squares are rectangles"; if we replace "square" by this synonym, then the result—"All equilateral rectangles are rectangles"—will be a logical truth. The term "spinster" has among its synonyms a term—viz., "adult lady who is nonmarried"—that includes the negation of the predicate of "No spinster is married"; replacement will thus yield the logical truth "No adult lady who is nonmarried is married." And similarly for other analytic statements; e.g., "All ornithologists are students of birds" and "All quadrupeds have feet." In each case by providing the proper synonyms and then substituting, we can turn the analytic statement into a logical truth. And we can recognize a logical truth, informally, by noting that it is a statement that is explicitly redundant—e.g., "All professional students of birds are students of birds," "No adult ladies who are nonmarried are married," and "All things that have four feet have feet." It will be convenient to describe both analytic statements and logical truths as redundancies—the former being sometimes implicit, and the latter always explicit.

In opposition to the view, mentioned at the beginning of this chapter, that these truths are concerned with relations among essences or properties, and relations among situations or possible states of affairs, and that they are apprehended by a kind of "rational insight," it has been maintained in recent years that they are expressions of our linguistic "rules" or "conventions" and strictly speaking, not truths at all. It has also been held that the distinction between analytic and synthetic is untenable. These views exhibit that "insurgence against reason," which, according to Morris Cohen, "has its roots deep in the dominant temper of our age." What Cohen said about the limitations of "psychologism," "historicism," and "empiricism," may also be said, if I am not mistaken, about these more recent doctrines.

2

"In the realm of logic and pure mathematics," Cohen wrote in *Reason and Nature* (Harcourt, 1931), "we have absolute and a priori truth." Even if "the more objective classical philosophies have overreached themselves in their abuse of the tests of self-evidence and self-contradiction, and in their sanctioning of false and meaningless propositions as a priori, it still remains true that in the Platonic ideas they have recognized the objectivity of the logical and mathematical forms of nature" (pp. 144–45). We can understand the concept of the a priori if we return to our Socratic questions about justification. What if such questions were raised in connection with that knowledge that is expressed in statements that are analytic or logically true? (The reader is referred again to the type of dilemma discussed in the first section. If there is doubt whether anyone *can* be said to know that all squares are rectangles, or that if some men are Greeks then some Greeks are men, it may well be that such doubt is incapable of being resolved. But we may still discuss the consequences of supposing that people *do* have such knowledge. And it will be well to note, so far as *this* question is concerned, that skepticism with respect to what is thought to be such knowledge is not to the point.) "What justification do you have for believing you know that all squares are rectangles, or for believing you know that if some men are Greeks then some Greeks are men?"

If a man *does* know, as most of us think we do, that all squares are rectangles, or that if some men

are Greeks then some Greeks are men, then there are only two ways he could answer our Socratic question. (1) He could say, simply: "I *see* that all squares are rectangles—that whatever is a square must be a rectangle—that being a rectangle is part of what it is to be a square. And I *see* that if some men are Greeks then some Greeks are men, that some men being Greeks and some Greeks being men are one and the same thing." Here we have a stopping place again for our Socratic questioning—but a stopping place that differs in a significant way from those considered in the previous section. (2) He might justify his claim to know these statements, not by saying that he sees that they are true, but rather by showing how to deduce them logically from *other* statements that are analytic or that are logically true. If we ask him what his justification is for believing he knows these other statements to be true, and if we continue our questioning, then sooner or later, he will stop with some such statements and say that he simply sees that they are true.

Let us now contrast the two statements "I see that Mr. Jones is in his garden" and "I see that all squares are rectangles." Both have subordinate statements as the objects of their principal verbs, and both are such that, if they are justified, then their subordinate statements are also justified. I may justify my claim to know that Mr. Jones is in his garden by saying "I see that he is" and I may justify my claim to know that all squares are rectangles by saying "I see that they are." And, as we have seen, if I am asked "What justification do you have for believing you *see* that Mr. Jones is in his garden?" then, if I do see that he is there, I can state my justification for believing that I see that he is there—and what I say will not merely reiterate the claim to see that he is there. But if I am asked "What justification do you have for claiming to see that all squares are rectangles?" and if my justification does not consist in the fact that I can deduce it logically from other analytic statements or from statements that are logically true, then I can *not* provide any further answer; in this case, unlike the case of Mr. Jones being in his garden, I can only reiterate that I *do* see it.

It is traditional to say, following Kant, that most, if not all, of the analytic statements and logical truths that express what we know are statements that express what we know a priori, and to say that what is known, but not known a priori, is known a posteriori. The point of using "a priori" and "a posteriori" may be suggested by this fact: we can know that all squares are rectangles *before* we have examined any particular square; but we cannot know that all men are mortal until *after* some particular men have been examined. One might speak of contemplating certain members of the realm of essence before examining any of their particular exemplifications in the realm of matter; this is the way that Santayana and Cohen expressed themselves. But we need not speak in this way, for one may also "contemplate" essence, or properties, in their particular exemplifications. As Aristotle said, "I may come to see that man is a rational animal—that the property of being rational and animal includes that of being rational—by considering some particular man, Callias; but what I thus learn will not be restricted to this particular fact, nor will it depend for its justification upon this particular fact."[8] And I may, by reflecting on some particular situation (say, on the fact that this apple is not, in the same part at the same time, both red and not red), come to know some more general fact that holds of all possible situations (say, that, for any possible object, being red excludes not being red). According to R. M. Eaton, this is the way we come to know some of the truths of logic.[9]

The statements we know a priori to be true differ in a number of respects from the "self-justifying" statements described in the previous chapter. For one thing, the "self-justifying" statements—e.g., "I believe that Socrates is mortal" and "That appears white"—are restricted to a psychological or subjective subject matter, but a priori statements are not so restricted. (The program of "psychologism," referred to in the first section, might be described as an attempt to reduce the a priori to the self-justifying, by transforming the statements of logic and mathematics into statements about the way in which people think.) For another thing, as Kant pointed out, the statements that we know a priori are statements that are *necessarily* true. All squares are rectangles—in this world and in all possible worlds. But "I cannot help believing that if a thing is a square it is a rectangle" is contingent and not necessary. (Consequently, the program of "psychologism" was not successful.) Finally, if what I suggested in the previous chapter is accurate, a person's statement may be said to be

"self-justifying" for her provided that her justification for thinking she knows it to be true is simply the fact that it *is* true; the point may be put alternatively by saying that such statements are "neither justified nor unjustified" but may constitute one's justification for other statements. Whether we may speak similarly of a priori statements remains problematic.[10]

What it is that we thus know a priori may seem meager and not worthy of being called "knowledge" at all. Schlick said, in his California lectures, that the statements of logic are "empty" and even Santayana, who wrote about "the realm of essence," said that there can be no *knowledge* of essences, that "there are no necessary truths," and that truth "never enters the field of mathematics at all."[11] But Schlick was saying only that the statements of logic *are* statements of logic and are not synthetic, and so, too, apparently was Santayana. (When Santayana wrote about the "realm of truth," he restricted the adjective "true" to what can be truly said only about the "realm of matter," about *this* possible world, and he did not apply the adjective as he did the quotation at the beginning of this chapter—to what can be truly said about the "realm of essence." But he did truly say, of essences, and this is what matters, that "every essence involves its parts, considered as the elements which integrate it," and, "excludes everything not itself."[12] The interesting question is not whether analytic statements and the statements of logic are "empty truths," but whether they are truths at all.

3

Schlick had contended, and many still agree, that once we have exposed the relations between logic and language, we will be able to account for our "so-called 'rational knowledge.'" But just what relation between logic and language would account for such knowledge remained obscure.

Schlick said three quite different things in his California lecture: (1) that the so-called propositions of logic and mathematics are "nothing but certain rules which determine the use of language, i.e., of expression by combination of signs"; (2) that their "absolute truth" cannot be denied; and (3) that "they do not deal with any facts, but only with the symbols by means of which the facts are expressed."[13]

Herbert Feigl and Albert Blumberg, reporting to America in 1931 on the speculations of the Vienna Circle (of which Schlick was one of the leading members), said substantially the same three things: (1) logic is "the system of conventions which determines the syntactical order required if we are to have a consistent language"; (2) the propositions of logic are "tautologically true"; and (3) "all formal sciences are engaged, then, in elaborating symbol-patterns and assert nothing about experience"[14] What, then, is the relation between logic and language that provides the key to our so-called rational knowledge? If we say, as in (1), that logical statements are *rules*, or *conventions*, then it may seem strange to go on to say, as in (2), that they are *true*; for we do not ordinarily think of rules, or of conventions, as being true, or as being false. Statements *about* rules, however, are either true or false; and what (3) suggests is, not that logical statements are themselves the rules or conventions of our language, but rather that they are statements *about* the rules of conventions of our language, statements telling us *what* these rules or conventions happen to be. Statements *about* the rules or conventions of language, however, need not be "tautologically true" (consider, e.g., "In French, adjectives of color are customarily placed after the noun they modify")— and the statements of logic with which we are concerned (e.g., "Either Socrates is mortal or it is false that Socrates is mortal") *are* tautologically true, and are *not*, in any clear sense, statements *about* the rules or conventions of our language.

What is usually maintained, in the face of such objections, is that the sentiments of logic are true *because* of the rules or conventions of our language. Thus, Feigl and Blumberg said: "For example, '*p* or not-*p* is tautologically true because of the very definitions of 'or' and 'not'" (p.284). Others have said that analytic statements are true *because* of the way in which we use the words that make them up. What does this mean?

The doctrine of "truth by convention" will seem most plausible in the case of analytic statements. It may be recalled that the concept of the meaning of the words that make up a statement is essential to the definition of "analytic statement." The statement "All squares are rectangles," as it is understood in ordinary English, is analytic, inasmuch as the meaning of the predicate term is included in that of the subject term. But, as Plato had argued in the *Cratylus*, it is "by custom" and "convention," and not "by nature," that our worlds have the meanings they happen to have. Had the English language developed in a different way, as it quite conceivably could have, then those statements that happen now to be analytic might not be analytic and might even be false. If the word "square" were used to denote, not the geometrical objects that it does happen to denote, but, say, those things we now call "horses," then the English statement "All squares are rectangles" would be synthetic and false. Therefore, one may say that the English statement "All squares are rectangles" is analytic—and thus true—because we happen to use words the way we do. Similarly for the class of logical truths: if the word "some," for example, were used in the way in which, as it happens, we now use "all," then the statement "If some men are Greeks then some Greeks are men" would not be logically true.

May we infer from all of this that statements that are analytic or logically true are "true only by convention" and that the so-called rational contemplation of essence is merely knowledge or belief about our language? If such reasoning were valid, then we could infer, not only that analytic and logical statements are "true only by convention," but also that all of those *synthetic* statements that are true are "true only by convention." For, as Quine was to point out, "even so factual a sentence as 'Brutus killed Caesar' owes its truth, in part, to our using the component words the way we do."[15] Had "killed," for example, been given the use which the phrase "was survived by" came to have, then "Brutus killed Caesar" would be false—unless, of course, Brutus were called "Caesar" and Caesar "Brutus."

What if it is said that an analytic statement—e.g., "All squares are rectangles"—owes its truth *solely* to the fact that we use the component words the way we do, or, as the matter is sometimes put, that it is true "solely in virtue of the rules of our language"? We may suppose that the following is a "rule of English":

a) When the word "square" is used in English to designate something, the thing it designates should be square.

The rule seems more significant, of course, when it is formulated in a language other than English, e.g., as "Wenn das Wort 'square' auf Englisch angewendet wird, um etwas zu bedeuten, muss das, was es bedeutet, quadratisch sein." The following, then, would also be a "rule of English":

> b) When the word "rectangular" is used in English to designate something, the thing it designates should be rectangular.

("'Rectangular' darf nur das bedeuten, was rechtwinkelig ist.") According to the thesis in question, the analytic statement "All squares are rectangles" owes its truth to the fact—and only to the fact—that the following is also a "rule of English":

> c) When the word "square" is used in English to designate something, the thing it designates should be rectangular.

But (c) is a rule of quite a different sort from either (a) or (b). This may be seen as follows. If we were to teach English to an educated man, say to a native German, and taught him that (a) and (c) are rules of English, he would not be able to find out on his own that (b) is also a rule of English; or if we were to teach him that (b) and (c) are rules of English, he would not be able to find out on his own that (a) is a rule of English. But if we were to teach him that (a) and (b) are rules of English, he *would* then be able to find out on his own, to see by himself, that (c) is, or ought to be, an additional rule of English. How is it, then, that his knowledge of (a) and (b) enables him to know that (c) is also a rule? The only answer that seems reasonable to me is that, since he knows that all squares are rectangles, he knows that if (a) and (b) are rules, then (c) ought to be a rule as well. And, *ex hypothesi*, his knowledge that all squares are rectangles is now knowledge about the rules of English. I would say, therefore, that "All squares are rectangles" does not "owe its truth" solely to the fact that we use the component words the way we do; it owes it also to the fact that the conjunctive property of being both equilateral and rectangular has the property of being rectangular as one of its components.

Lewis wrote, in *An Analysis of Knowledge and Valuation*: "The *mode of expression* of any analytic truth is . . . dependent on linguistic conventions; as is also the manner in which any empirical fact is to be formulated and *conveyed*. But the meanings that are conveyed by symbols, on account of a stipulated or a customary usage of them, and the relation of meanings conveyed by an order of symbols, on account of syntactic stipulations or customary syntactic usage, are matters antecedent to and independent of any conventions affecting the linguistic manner in which they are to be conveyed" (p. 148).[16] What this passage makes clear to us is the need of keeping the following two questions distinct:

> 1) How does one find out whether the English statement "All squares are rectangles" is analytic?
>
> 2) How does one find out whether all squares are rectangles?

We can answer the first question only by making a linguistic investigation of English speaking people; but the answer to the second refers to what is a priori and depends only upon the "contemplation of essences," or however else we wish to describe that consideration of properties which is the source of our a priori knowledge. The linguistic study that is essential to the answer of (1) is not essential to the answer of (2); to realize this, we have only to consider that many people do not know English, and do not, therefore, know the answer to (1), but do know the answer to (2)—do know that all squares are rectangles. We need not answer (1), then to answer (2), but—and this is still another point—we *do* need to answer (2) to answer (1). For when we answer (1) we study the "linguistic behavior" of English speaking people and find out, as best we can, what properties constitute, for most such people, the meanings of the words "square" and "rectangle"; then, having found one property that we suppose to be the meaning of "square" and another that we suppose to be the meaning of "rectangle," we "look to see" whether the latter is included in the former—and this is something we can know a priori.[17]

To be sure, when I formulate question (2)— "How does one find out whether all squares are rectangles?"—I assume that the reader will understand what I have written; I assume, indeed, that I have used the words "squares" and "rectangles," as well as most of the other words that appear, in the way in which they are ordinarily used in English. But if the reader is tempted to infer from these facts that, when I write that all squares are rectangles, I am saying something *about* the English language, then he may be referred back to the possible confusion between "use" and "mention" noted at the end of the previous section.

In *Mind and the World-Order* (1929) and earlier, C. I. Lewis had defended a "pragmatic conception of the a priori," a view that was easily misread as being a kind of conventionalism. But this "pragmatic conception" was a view, not about the nature of a priori truth or our knowledge of it, but about our ways of classifying things. Whether, for example, it is better to use the word "fish" in such a way that it will apply to whales, or in such a way that it will not apply to anything that is a mammal—such questions as these are to be decided wholly on the basis of practical utility. "I *may* categorize experience as I will; but what categorical distinction will best serve my interests . . . ?" (p. 265). I *may* let properties A, B, and C be the properties that constitute the meaning of "fish," as I use the word, or I may choose properties B, C, and D instead; the choice is a matter of convenience. In the first use, but not the second, "All fish are A" will be analytic, and in the second, but not the first, "All fish are D" will be analytic. But (as Lewis recognized) the choice of these two classifications has no effect on the two a priori truths—that the properties A, B, and C include the property A, and that the properties B, C, and D include the property D—truths that do not at all depend on anyone's convenience. Thus Lewis said that "the pragmatic element in knowledge concerns the choice in application of conceptual modes of interpretation," but does not touch that "abstract a priori truth" which is "absolute and eternal" (pp. 272–73).

I think it is fair to say that, for any clear interpretation that has been found for the phrase "true only by convention," the phrase cannot be said to refer to any merely *linguistic* characteristic that is peculiar to analytic statements and the truths of logic. There remains, however, the possibility that the statements *are* linguistic conventions—not that they are *true* "by convention" but that they are themselves conventions, rules, or stipulations and are thus not true (or false) at all. This possibility, as we saw, was suggested by Schlicks's California lecture and by Feigl and Blumberg's report; it was defended by Ernest Nagel, writing on "Logic without Ontology." Logical principles, he said, are "regulative principles," which are

"*prescriptive* for the use of language"; the choice between alternative systems of such principles may be grounded "on the relatively greater adequacy of one of them as an instrument for achieving a certain systematization of knowledge."[18] But even if it be conceded that some logical statements are no more than rules or conventions, there is a difficulty of principle in saying that *all* such statements are rules or conventions. "Briefly the objection is that whatever rules one may have initially stipulated, and however arbitrary such stipulations may be, one will thereafter have to *find out* what these rules entail, and the statement that such and such is entailed by the rules could hardly be characterized as itself a rule."[19] What we find out, when we discover with respect to two statements in our language that our rules allow us to derive one from the other, includes a logical truth—something that we can know a priori.

I think that Schlick and his followers were mistaken, then, in saying that there are certain facts about language that will enable us to set aside our "so-called rational knowledge." Other attacks on the traditional conception of the a priori have proceeded from a skeptical position—a skepticism about our knowledge of properties and states of affairs. According to Lewis, as we have noted, if the word "square" is used to mean the property of being square and if the word "rectangular" is used to mean the property of being rectangular, then the statement "All squares are rectangular" is analytic; for, as he said, one can *see* by a kind of experiment in the imagination, that the property of being rectangular is included in that of being square (i.e., in that of being equilateral and rectangular). Morton White was skeptical about this kind of seeing or understanding: "One either sees or doesn't see the relationship and that is the end of the matter. It is very difficult to argue one's difficulties with such a position and I shall only say dogmatically that I do not find this early retreat to intuition satisfactory."[20] On the basis of a similar skepticism, Quine concluded that acceptance of the traditional distinction between analytic and synthetic is "an unempirical dogma of empiricists, a metaphysical article of faith."[21]

Here again I take the liberty of referring the reader to the discussion of skepticism in the first section.

4

There remains the question of the synthetic a priori. Is anything that is known a priori to be true expressible only in statements that are synthetic, i.e., in statements that are neither analytic nor logically true? Or, as we may say for short, do we have any synthetic a priori knowledge? According to the tradition of British empiricism, which has dominated much of the philosophical thought of the period with which we are concerned, all of our a priori knowledge is "empty" and "nonfactual"—that is to say, all of our a priori knowledge is expressible in statements that are analytic or logically true. But some American philosophers have argued, with some plausibility, that some of our a priori knowledge can be expressed only in statements that are synthetic.

The concept of the synthetic a priori, however, has been taken in two quite different ways, with the result that our question—"Do we have any synthetic a priori knowledge?"—has a certain ambiguity that is often overlooked. The technical term "a priori" is sometimes taken in a positive sense, as it has been here, and "a posteriori" is then defined as what is not a priori. If, for the moment, we take "rational knowledge" as a synonym for this positive sense of "a priori," then we may say that our a posteriori knowledge is any knowledge that is not rational knowledge. But sometimes "a posteriori" is taken as the positive term and the "a priori" is then defined as what is not a posteriori. When "a posteriori" is taken in this positive sense it then becomes a synonym for "empirical knowledge." (Our empirical knowledge may be thought of roughly, as comprising: first, what we know by means of the "external senses"; second, those facts about our own psychological states and about appearing that were discussed in the previous section; third, those facts of the first two types that we *remember*; and, last, whatever is inductively supported by any of the foregoing. The concepts of *empirical knowledge* and *rational knowledge* are thus exclusive but not necessarily exhaustive. If Burch's views about revelation, referred to in the first section, are correct, then there is a religious knowledge that is neither empirical nor rational.) Hence our question "Do we have any synthetic a priori knowledge?" may be taken in these two ways:

A) Is there any rational knowledge that is expressible only in synthetic statements?

B) Is there any knowledge that is not empirical and is expressible only in synthetic statements?

An affirmative answer to (A) would imply an affirmative answer to (B). An affirmative answer to (B), however, need not imply an affirmative answer to (A); for if there is knowledge that is neither empirical nor rational, and if that knowledge is the only nonempirical knowledge that must be expressed in synthetic statements, then (A) would be answered in the negative and (B) in the affirmative. In the present chapter, we are concerned with (A).

Our problem may be discussed by reference to the following six statements, each of which has been taken, by some American philosopher, to indicate an area of synthetic a priori knowledge:

1) Anything that is red is colored.

2) Nothing is both red and green.

3) If anything is orange, then it has a color that is intermediate between red and yellow.

4) Anything that is colored is extended.

5) Anything that is a cube has twelve edges.

6) Seven and five are twelve.

If we wish to show that there is no synthetic a priori knowledge, then we must show, with respect to each of these statements, either that it is analytic, or that it expresses what is known but not known a priori, or that it does not express what is known at all. The statements may thus be thought of as presenting us with six puzzles or riddles. The way in which we deal with these puzzles or riddles will obviously have important implications concerning the nature of our knowledge.

C. H. Langford has defended the thesis of the synthetic a priori with respect to statements (1), (2), (3), and (5); Hector Neri Castañeda, following Kant, has defended it with respect to (6); and various philosophers have defended it with respect to (4).[22]

Statement (1)—"Anything that is red is colored"—is very much like our earlier statement, "Anything that is square is rectangular." I think we may assume that, if the latter can be known a priori, then so, too can the former; in each case, knowledge of a single instance of the generalization is enough, if not more than enough, to enable us to see that the generalization itself is true. To show that "Anything that is square is rectangular" is analytic, we may "analyze the predicate out of the subject" in such a way that we turn the statement into an explicit redundancy; that is to say, we replace the subject term "square" with a synonymous expression, "equilateral and rectangular," containing the original predicate, and the result—"Anything that is equilateral and rectangular is rectangular"—is a statement that is logically true. Can we similarly "analyze the predicate out of the subject" in the case of statement (1)? Can we find some term, which along with "colored" can be used to make up a synonym for "red," and which will then enable us to turn "Anything that is red is colored" into an explicit redundancy? I believe that no one has been able to find a term that will do.

Suppose, however, that we had a list of all the colors, and suppose (for simplicity) that the list comprised just the colors red, yellow, green, and blue. Could we then say that "colored" is synonymous with "either red, yellow, green, or blue?" If we could, then by replacing the *predicate* instead of the subject we could turn "Anything that is red is colored" into the following logical truth: "Anything that is red is either red, yellow, green, or blue." But if our list of colors is not complete, then, of course, we cannot say that "colored" is synonymous with "either red, yellow, green, or blue," for the color that our list omits will be a color and neither red, yellow, green, nor blue. And even if our list of colors should happen to be complete, we may, at least, speculate on the possibility that it is not: "Were we all in the position of those people we now call 'color-blind,' we would have been mistaken about the completeness of any list we might have made. Might it not be that we are also mistaken about this present list? Perhaps there is some color that none of us is acquainted with, and that therefore is not on our list, but is such that if we were to become acquainted with it we would see that it is a further color to be added to our list." This speculation may be false, but, as Langford said (concerning a slightly different example), "it is logically and conceptually possible, which is all that is required for our purposes."[23] If it is logically and conceptually possible that a thing be colored and neither red, yellow, blue, nor green, then "colored" cannot mean "either red, yel-

low, blue, or green"; for there is *no* possibility that a thing could be either red, yellow, blue, or green, but neither red, yellow, blue nor green. And so runs the principal objection to this method of showing that statement (1) is analytic.

But if the objection is unfounded and if we can say that the list "red, yellow, blue, and green" (possibly with some additions), constitutes a complete list of colors, then we may also be able to say that statement (2)—"Nothing is both red and green"—is analytic. We might say, for example, that "green" means the same as "colored, but neither red, yellow, nor blue," and statement (2) could then be transformed into the logical truth "Nothing is both red and colored but neither red, yellow, nor blue." But if the objection we have just considered is valid, then we will have to deny that "green" means the same as "colored, but neither red, yellow, nor blue," and this method of transforming (2) into a logical truth will have to be rejected.

More technical devices have been proposed: we might try to [form] our color vocabulary in such a way that, in our revised vocabulary, we can say everything we need to say about colors but cannot formulate the troublesome statement (2). If we can do this—and the technique that has been applied with considerable success elsewhere in philosophy and in logic—then perhaps we can say that our difficulties with (2) can be traced, not to the fact that (2) is synthetic a priori, but to the fact that our ordinary color vocabulary is defective. In applying this method, however, we must be on guard lest, when we use our new vocabulary, our difficulties reappear in connection with some other sentence. The following is a simple example of this method.

Think of two objects, A and B, which are red and green, respectively; define "is red" as "has the same color as A and does not have the same color as B," and define "is green" as "has the same color as B and does not have the same color as A"; then "Nothing is both red and green" may be replaced by "There is nothing that has the same color as A and does not have the same color as B and has the same color as B and does not have the same color as A," which latter statement is a logical truth. But, if I am not mistaken, we will have only transferred the problem of the synthetic a priori—transferred the problem from "Nothing is both red and green" to

"If one object is red and another object is green, then the two objects do not have the same color." A method somewhat similar to this, though with added technical detail and refinement, was proposed by Hilary Putnam.[24] Arthur Pap subsequently suggested that the troublesome statements with which such an analysis leaves us—e.g., "Red and green are different colors"—*are* synthetic a priori, but that they are *also* statements that have "a linguistic origin" and therefore "may even be purely *verbal* and not 'about the world' at all! . . . What capital could a rationalist make of such synthetic a priori knowledge?"[25] We have noted, however, that serious difficulties are involved in saying, of statements that do not mention language, that they are "purely verbal" or that they have their "origin in language." I think it is more plausible to say of statement (2)—"Nothing is both red and green"—that it has its "origin" in the relation of *exclusion*, which obtains between the properties of being red and being green, and to which Santayana referred in the quotation at the beginning of this section.

Statement (3) on our list—"If anything is orange, then it has a color that is intermediate between red and yellow"—raises no new questions of principle. Of (3), Langford wrote: "We may suppose a person who has never seen anything that was either red or yellow, but has seen all his life things that were orange in color. Such a person will easily be able to understand the antecedent of this proposition; but he will not be able to understand its consequent, and that will not be due merely to a defect in vocabulary."[26] And this Langford took to be evidence for saying that (3) is synthetic a priori.

Perhaps we may deal with statement (4)—"Anything that is colored is extended"—in a simpler way. Instead of trying to prove that it is analytic, we might suggest, on the ground that it is not known at all, that it is now known a priori. For how are we to tell, of things that are not extended, whether or not they are colored?

What of statement (5), "Anything that is a cube has twelve edges"? Langford proposed the following argument to show that this statement, which seems clearly a priori, is not analytic. There are many people, he said, who know *what* a cube is, who can recognize dice and other such objects as being cubes, and who do *not* realize that being a cube requires having twelve edges. From this he deduced that "the notion of having twelve edges can be no part of the notion of being a cube" and hence that the statement "Anything that is a cube has twelve edges" is not analytic.[27] The conclusion follows, however, only if we assume that a man cannot recognize an object as exemplifying a certain complex of properties unless he also recognizes it as exemplifying each of the components of that complex. But it is at least problematic, I think, whether this assumption is true; the theories of the Gestalt psychologists suggest that it may be false.[28]

Our statement (6)—"Seven and five are twelve"—involves technical questions of logic and mathematics that fall outside the scope of the present survey. According to Kant and Castañeda, such mathematical statements are synthetic a priori; according to John Stuart Mill, they are synthetic but not a priori; and according to the "logistic thesis," defended in Russell and Whitehead's *Principia Mathematica* and elsewhere, such statements may be translated into the statements of logic and are therefore not synthetic. The status of (6) in contemporary controversy turns upon the question whether the "logistic thesis" is true. If the thesis is true, then the translations of (6) and the other statements of pure mathematics would turn out to be very long; Professor Quine told a Brazilian audience in 1942 that, if the binomial theorem were written out in the vocabulary of logic and in type the size of this, it would "extend from the North Pole to the South Pole.[29] But the objection to the "logistic thesis" is not, of course, to the length of the translations in question; the controversy concerns, first, whether these lengthy translations *would* be translations of such statements as (6), as the statements are ordinarily understood, and, second, whether all of the statements needed for the logistic translation or paraphrase of (6) are statements that are logically true. But these are not questions of epistemology.

Other statements sometimes thought to be synthetic a priori involve questions of ethics and of metaphysics; examples are "To the extent that an act is charitable it is good, whatever its consequences" and "If there are complexes, then there are simples."[30] The philosophical significance of the particular examples we have considered lies partly in this fact: if some of them must be acknowledged as exemplifying the synthetic a priori, then, in order to defend skepticism with respect to the statements of ethics and of metaphysics, it will not be sufficient merely to point out that some such statements, if they are known to be true, are synthetic a priori.

NOTES

1. Moritz Schlick, "A New Philosophy of Experience, in P. A. Schilpp, ed., *Lectures . . . .*, (Publications in Philosophy, The College of the Pacific, 1932); reprinted in Schlick's *Gesammelte Aufsätze* (Vienna, 1938).
2. *Critique of Pure reason,* A 7.
3. *Prolegomena to Any Further Metaphysics*, sec. 2.
4. For refinement of detail, see Lewis, *An Analysis,* book 1, and Rudolf Carnap, *Meaning and Necessity* (U. of Chicago, 1974), chap. 1.
5. W.V. Quine, *From a Logical Point of View.* Quine first sets forth this view in "Truth by Convection," in Otis Lee, ed., *Philosophical Essays for Alfred North Whitehead* (Longmans, 1936).
6. Cf. Paul Weiss, *Nature and Man* (Holt, 1947), pp. 13, 203; Charles Hartshorne, *Man's Vision of God and the Logic Theism* (Willet, 1941); Richard Taylor, "The Problem of Future Contingencies," *Philosophical Review*, 66 (1957), 1-28, and "Fatalism," *Philosophical Review*, 71 (1962), 55-66; Donald C. Williams, "The Sea Fight Tomorrow," in Paul Henle, Horace M. Kallen, and Susanne K. Langer, eds., *Structure, Method, and Meaning: Essays in Honor of Henry M. Sheffer* (liberal Arts, 1951).
7. Cf. Garrett Birkhoff and John von Neumann, "The Logic of Quantum Mechanics," *Annals of Mathematics*, 37 (1936); Hilary Putnam, "Three Valued Logic," *Philosophical Studies*, 8 (1957).
8. *Posterior Analytics*, 100a-100b.
9. R. M. Eaton, *General Logic* (Scribner, 1931), pp. 495-501. Cf. W. P. Montague, *The Ways of Knowing* (Macmillan, 1925), chap. 11; Charles A. Baylis, "Universals, Communicable Knowledge and Metaphysics," *Journal of Philosophy*, 48 (1951), 634-44; Donald Williams, 'The Nature and Variety of the *A Priori*," *Analysis*, 5 (1938), 85-94.
10. "What we require is a picture of the employment of mathematical propositions and of sentences beginning 'I believe that . . . .' where a mathematical proposition is the object of belief," (Ludwig Wittgenstein, *Remarks on the Foundations of Mathematics* [Blackwell, 1956], p. 33e.)
11. George Santayana, *The Realms of Being* (Scribner, 1942), pp.407, 421.
12. *Ibid.*, pp. 401, 82, 88.
13. *Gesammelte Aufsätze*, pp. 146-47.
14. Albert E. Blumberg and Herbert Feigl, "Logical Positivism," *Journal of Philosophy*, 28 (1931), 281-96. It was in this article that the name "logical positivism" was introduced.
15. W. V. Quine, "Carnap e la verità logica," *Revista di filosofia*, 48 (1957), 4.
16. Cf. Gustav Bergmann, *The Metaphysics of Logical Positivism* (Longmans, 1954), p. 45 ff.
17. On the problem of finding a definition or a criterion of s*ameness of meaning* that does *not* refer to relations between properties, see: Nelson Goodman, "On Likeness of Meaning," in Leonard Linsky, ed. *Semantics and the Philosophy of Language*, pp 67-74: Morton White, "The Analytic and the Synthetic: An Untenable Dualism," in the same book, pp. 272-86; W. V. Quine, *Word and Object*, chap. 2, and Paul Ziff, *Semantic Analysis* (Cornell, 1960).
18. Ernest Nagel, "*Logic without Ontology,*" in Y. H. Krikorian, ed., *Naturalism and the Human Spirit* (Columbia, 1944): reprinted in Herbet Feigl and W.S. Sellars, eds., *Readings in Philosophical Analysis*.
19. Arthur Pap, *Semantics and Necessary Truth* (Yale, 1958), p. 184. Compare Quine's "Carnap e la verita logica," p. 11. The latter paper is an excellent statement of the entire problem. Quine's critique of conventionalism goes back to his "Truth by Convention" (1936), and "Is Logic a Matter of Words?" (1937), read at the Princeton meeting of the American Philosophical Association and abstracted in the *Journal of Philosophy*, 34 (1937), 674.
20. Morton White, "The Analytical and the Synthetic: An Untenable Dualism" p. 280. White also noted that attempts to define "analytic statement" *without* reference to meaning and to relations between properties were inadequate; he took these facts to indicate that the traditional distinction between analytical and synthetic is "untenable." For a criticism of this reasoning, see Richard Taylor, "Disputes about Synonymy," *Philosophical Review*, 63 (1954), 517-29.
21. *From a Logical Point of View,* p. 37. He also said, what is obviously true, that is the traditional distinction between a priori and a posteriori were replaced by a "behavioristic" contrast "between more or less firmly accepted statements," then the distinction might well turn out to be merely a matter of degree.

22. C.H. Langford, "Moore's Notion of Analysis," in Schilpp, ed., *The Philosophy of G.E. Moore*, and "A Proof That Synthetic A Priori Propositions Exist," *Journal of Philosophy*, (1949), 20-24; Hector Neri Castañeda, "'7 + 15 =12' as a Synthetic Proposition," *Philosophy and Phenomenological Research*, 21 (1960), 141-58. For a useful general discussion, see Oliver A. Johnson, "Denial of the Synthetic *A Priori*," *Philosophy*, 35 (1960), 1-10.

23. "A Proof That Synthetic A Priori Propositions Exist," p. 24.

24. Hilary Putnam, "Reds, Green, and Logical Analysis." *Philosophical Review*, 45 (1956), 206-17.

25. Arthur Pap, "Once more: Colors and Synthetic A Priori," *Philosophical Review*, 66 (1957), 94-99. Pap's discussion of these questions in his *Semantics and Necessary Truth* is more in the spirit of what I have tried to say here than in that of the passage just quoted. His book is a useful account of the issues that the concept of the a priori has involved in recent philosophy.

26. "A Proof That Synthetic A Priori Propositions Exist," p. 24.

27. *Ibid.*, p. 21

28. Langford introduced this example in connection with what he called the "paradox of analysis"; viz., if the philosphical analysis of a concept is such that "the verbal expression representing the analysan-dum has the same meaning as the verbal expression representing the analysans, the analysis states a bare identity and is trivial; but if the two verbal expressions do not have the same meaning, the analysis is incorrect" ("The Notion of Analysis in Moore's Philosophy," p. 323). For further discussion of this "paradox," see: Moore's reply to Langford, *The Philosophy of G. E. Moore*, pp. 660-67; Morton G. White, "A Note on the 'Paradox of Anaysis,'" *Mind*, 54 (1945); Max Black, "The 'Paradox of Analysis' Again: A Reply," *ibid.*, pp. 272-73; Morton G. White, "Analysis and Identity; A Rejoinder," *ibid.*, pp. 357-61; Max Black, "How Can Analysis Be Informative?" *Philosophy and Phenomenological Research*, 6 (1946), 628-31; a review of White's and Black's papers by Alonzo Church, *Journal of Symbolic Logic*, 11 (132-33; and Arthur Pap, *Semantics and Necessary Truth*, pp. 275-82.

29. W. V. Quine, "Os estados unidos e o ressurgimento da logical," in *Vida intelectual nos estados unidos*, vol. 2 (Uniao Cultural Brasil-Estados Unidos, Sao Paulo, 1946); the quotation is from p. 277. Quine's Truth by Convention" is a clear discussion of some of the issues that the "logistic thesis" involves.

30. On statements of the latter sort, see Henry Veatch, "Matrix, Matter, and Method in Metaphysics," *Review of Metaphysics*, 14 (1961), 581-600.

W. V. O. Quine

Two Dogmas of Empiricism

Modern empiricism has been conditioned in large part by two dogmas. One is a belief in some fundamental cleavage between truths which are *analytic,* or grounded in meanings independently of matters of fact, and truths which are *synthetic,* or grounded in fact. The other dogma is *reductionism:* the belief that each meaningful statement is equivalent to some logical construct upon terms which refer to immediate experience. Both dogmas, I shall argue, are ill-founded. One effect of abandoning them is, as we shall see, a blurring of the supposed boundary between speculative metaphysics and natural science. Another effect is a shift toward pragmatism.

1. BACKGROUND FOR ANALYTICITY

Kant's cleavage between analytic and synthetic truths was foreshadowed in Hume's distinction between relations of ideas and matters of fact, and in Leibniz's distinction between truths of reason and truths of fact. Leibniz spoke of the truths of reason as true in all possible worlds. Picturesqueness aside, this is to say that the truths of reason are those which could not possibly be false. In the same vein we hear analytic statements defined as statements whose denials are self-contradictory. But this definition has small explanatory value; for the notion of self-contradictoriness, in the quite broad sense needed for this definition of analyticity, stands in exactly the same need of clarification as does the notion of analyticity itself. The two notions are the two sides of a single dubious coin.

Kant conceived of an analytic statement as one that attributes to its subject no more than is already conceptually contained in the subject. This formulation has two shortcomings: it limits itself to statements of subject-predicate form, and it appeals to a notion of containment which is left at a metaphorical level. But Kant's intent, evident more from the use he makes of the notion of analyticity than from his definition of it, can be restated thus: a statement is analytic when it is true by virtue of meanings and independently of fact. Pursuing this line, let us examine the concept of *meaning* which is presupposed.

Meaning, let us remember, is not to be identified with naming. Frege's example of "Evening Star" and "Morning Star," and Russell's of "Scott" and "the author of *Waverley,*" illustrate that terms can name the same thing but differ in meaning. The distinction between meaning and naming is no less important at the level of abstract terms. The terms "9" and "the number of the planets" name one and the same abstract entity but presumably must be regarded as unlike in meaning; for astronomical observation was needed, and not mere reflection on meanings, to determine the sameness of the entity in question.

The above examples consist of singular terms, concrete and abstract. With general terms, or predicates, the situation is somewhat different but parallel. Whereas a singular term purports to name an entity, abstract or concrete, a general term does not; but a general term is *true of* an entity, or of each of many, or of none. The class of all entities of which a general term is true is called the *extension* of the term. Now paralleling the contrast between the meaning of a singular term and the entity named, we must distinguish equally between the meaning of a general term and its extension. The general terms "creature with a heart" and "creature with kidneys," for example, are perhaps alike in extension but unlike in meaning.

Confusion of meaning with extension, in the case of general terms, is less common than confusion of meaning with naming in the case of singular terms. It is indeed commonplace in philosophy to oppose intension (or meaning) to extension, or, in a variant vocabulary, connotation to denotation.

The Aristotelian notion of essence was the forerunner, no doubt, of the modern notion of intension or meaning. For Aristotle it was essential in men to be rational, accidental to be two-legged. But there is an important difference between this attitude and the doctrine of meaning. From the latter point of view it may indeed be conceded (if only for the sake of argument) that rationality is involved in the meaning of the word "man" while two-leggedness is not; but two-leggedness may at the same time be viewed as involved in the meaning of "biped" while rationality is not. Thus from the point of view of the doctrine of meaning it makes no sense to say of the actual individual, who is at once a man and a biped, that his rationality is essential and his two-leggedness accidental or vice versa. Things had essences, for Aristotle, but only linguistic forms have meanings. Meaning is what essence becomes when it is divorced from the object of reference and wedded to the word.

For the theory of meaning a conspicuous question is the nature of its objects: what sort of things are meanings? A felt need for meant entities may derive from an earlier failure to appreciate that meaning and reference are distinct. Once the theory of meaning is sharply separated from the theory of reference, it is a short step to recognizing as the primary business of the theory of meaning simply the synonymy of linguistic forms and the analyticity of statements; meanings themselves, as obscure intermediary entities, may well be abandoned.

The problem of analyticity then confronts us anew. Statements which are analytic by general philosophical acclaim are not, indeed, far to seek. They fall into two classes. Those of the first class, which may be called *logically true*, are typified by:

(1) No unmarried man is married.

The relevant feature of this example is that it not merely is true as it stands, but remains true under any and all reinterpretations of "man" and "married." If we suppose a prior inventory of *logical* particles, comprising "no," "un-," "not," "if," "then," "and," etc., then in general a logical truth is a statement which is true and remains true under all reinterpretations of its components other than the logical particles.

But there is also a second class of analytic statements, typified by:

(2) No bachelor is married.

The characteristic of such a statement is that it can be turned into a logical truth by putting synonyms for synonyms; thus (2) can be turned into (1) by putting "unmarried man" for its synonym "bachelor." We still lack a proper characterization of this second class of analytic statements, and therewith of analyticity generally, inasmuch as we have had in the above description to lean on a notion of 'synonomy' which is no less in need of clarification than analyticity itself.

In recent years Carnap has tended to explain analyticity by appeal to what he calls state-descriptions.[1] A state-description is any exhaustive assignment of truth values to the atomic, or noncompound, statements of the language. All other statements of the language are, Carnap assumes, built up of their component clauses by means of the familiar logical devices, in such a way that the truth value of any complex statement is fixed for each state-description by specifiable logical laws. A statement is then explained as analytic when it comes out true under every state description. This account is an adaptation of Leibniz's "true in all possible worlds." But note that this version of analyticity serves its purpose only if the atomic statements of the language are, unlike "John is a bachelor" and "John is married," mutually indpendent. Otherwise there would be a state-description which assigned truth to "John is a bachelor" and "John is married," and consequently "No bachelors are married" would turn out synthetic rather than analytic under the proposed criterion. Thus the criterion of analyticity in terms of state-descriptions serves only for languages devoid of extralogical synonym-pairs, such as "bachelor" and "unmarried man"—synonym-pairs of the type which give rise to the 'second class' of analytic statements. The criterion in terms of state-descriptions is a reconstruction at best of logical truth, not of analyticity.

I do not mean to suggest that Carnap is under any illusions on this point. His simplified model language with its state-descriptions is aimed primarily not at the general problem of analyticity but at another purpose, the clarification of probability and induction. Our problem, however, is analyticity; and here the major difficulty lies not in the first class of analytic statements, the logical truths, but rather in the second class, which depends on the notion of synonymy.

2. DEFINITION

There are those who find it soothing to say that the analytic statements of the second class reduce to those of the first class, the logical truths, by *definition;* "bachelor," for example, is *defined* as "unmarried man." But how do we find that "bachelor" is defined as "unmarried man"? Who defined it thus, and when? Are we to appeal to the nearest dictionary, and accept the lexicographer's formulation as law? Clearly this would be to put the cart before the horse. The lexicographer is an empirical scientist, whose business is the recording of antecedent facts; and if he glosses "bachelor" as "unmarried man" it is because of his belief that there is a relation of synonymy between those forms, implicit in general or preferred usage prior to his own work. The notion of synonymy presupposed here has still to be clarified, presumably in terms relating to linguistic behavior. Certainly the 'definition' which is the lexicographer's report of an observed synonymy cannot be taken as the ground of the synonymy.

Definition is not, indeed, an activity exclusively of philologists. Philosophers and scientists frequently have occasion to 'define' a recondite term by paraphrasing it into terms of a more familiar vocabulary. But ordinarily such a definition, like the philologist's, is pure lexicography, affirming a relation of synonymy antecedent to the exposition in hand.

Just what it means to affirm synonymy, just what the interconnections may be which are necessary and sufficient in order that two linguistic forms be properly describable as synonymous, is far from clear; but, whatever these interconnections may be, ordinarily they are grounded in usage. Definitions reporting selected instances of synonymy come then as reports upon usage.

There is also, however, a variant type of definitional activity which does not limit itself to the reporting of pre-existing synonymies. I have in mind what Carnap calls *explication*—an activity to which philosophers are given, and scientists also in their more philosophical moments. In explication the purpose is not merely to paraphrase the definiendum into an outright synonym, but actually to improve upon the definiendum by refining or supplementing its meaning. But even explication, though not merely reporting a pre-existing synonymy between definiendum and definiens, does rest nevertheless on *other* pre-existing synonymies. The matter may be viewed as follows. Any word worth explicating has some contexts which, as wholes, are clear and precise enough to be useful; and the purpose of explication is to preserve the usage of these favored contexts while sharpening the usage of other contexts. In order that a given definition be suitable for purposes of explication, therefore, what is required is not that the definiendum in its antecedent usage be synonymous with the definiens, but just that each of these favored contexts of the definiendum, taken as a whole in its antecedent usage, be synonymous with the corresponding context of the definiens.

Two alternative definientia may be equally appropriate for the purposes of a given task of explication and yet not be synonymous with each other; for they may serve interchangeably within the favored contexts but diverge elsewhere. By cleaving to one of these definientia rather than the other, a definition of explicative kind generates, by fiat, a relation of synonymy between definiendum and definiens which did not hold before. But such a definition still owes its explicative function, as seen, to pre-existing synonymies.

There does, however, remain still an extreme sort of definition which does not hark back to prior synonymies at all: namely, the explicitly conventional introduction of novel notations for purposes of sheer abbreviation. Here the definiendum becomes synonymous with the definiens simply because it has been created expressly for the purpose of being synonymous with the definiens. Here we have a really transparent case of synonymy created by definition; would that all species of synonymy were as intelligible. For the rest, definition rests on synonymy rather than explaining it.

The word "definition" has come to have a dangerously reassuring sound, owing no doubt to its frequent occurrence in logical and mathematical writings. We shall do well to digress now into a brief appraisal of the role of definition in formal work.

In logical and mathematical systems either of two mutually antagonistic types of economy may be striven for, and each has its peculiar practical utility.

On the one hand we may seek economy of practical expression—ease and brevity in the statement of multifarious relations. This sort of economy calls usually for distinctive concise notations for a wealth of concepts. Second, however, and oppositely, we may seek economy in grammar and vocabulary; we may try to find a minimum of basic concepts such that, once a distinctive notation has been appropriated to each of them, it becomes possible to express any desired further concept by mere combination and iteration of our basic notations. This second sort of economy is impractical in one way, since a poverty in basic idioms tends to a necessary lengthening of discourse. But it is practical in another way: it greatly simplifies theoretical discourse *about* the language, through minimizing the terms and the forms of construction wherein the language consists.

Both sorts of economy, though prima facie incompatible, are valuable in their separate ways. The custom has consequently arisen of combining both sorts of economy by forging in effect two languages, the one a part of the other. The inclusive language, though redundant in grammar and vocabulary, is economical in message lengths, while the part, called primitive notation, is economical in grammar and vocabulary. Whole and part are correlated by rules of translation whereby each idiom not in primitive notation is equated to some complex built up of primitive notation. These rules of translation are the so-called *definitions* which appear in formalized systems. They are best viewed not as adjuncts to one language but as correlations between two languages, the one a part of the other.

But these correlations are not arbitrary. They are supposed to show how the primitive notations can accomplish all purposes, save brevity and convenience, of the redundant language. Hence the definiendum and its definiens may be expected, in each case, to be related in one or another of the three ways lately noted. The definiens may be a faithful paraphrase of the definiendum into the narrower notation, preserving a direct synonymy[2] as of antecedent usage; or the definiens may, in the spirit of explication, improve upon the antecedent usage of the definiendum; or finally, the definiendum may be a newly created notation, newly endowed with meaning here and now.

In formal and informal work alike, thus, we find that definition—except in the extreme case of the explicitly conventional introduction of new notations—hinges on prior relations of synonymy. Recognizing then that the notion of definition does not hold the key to synonymy and analyticity, let us look further into synonymy and say no more of definition.

3. INTERCHANGEABILITY

A natural suggestion, deserving close examination, is that the synonymy of two linguistic forms consists simply in their interchangeability in all contexts without change of truth value—interchangeability, in Leibniz's phrase, *salva veritate*.[3] Note that synonyms so conceived need not even be free from vagueness, as long as the vaguenesses match.

But it is not quite true that the synonyms "bachelor" and "unmarried man" are everywhere interchangeable *salva veritate*. Truths which become false under substitution of "unmarried man" for "bachelor" are easily constructed with the help of "bachelor of arts" or "bachelor's buttons"; also with the help of quotation, thus:

"Bachelor" has less than ten letters.

Such counterinstances can, however, perhaps be set aside by treating the phrases "bachelor of arts" and "bachelor's buttons" and the quotation "bachelor" each as a single indivisible word, and then stipulating that the interchangeability *salva veritate*, which is to be the touchstone of synonymy, is not supposed to apply to fragmentary occurrences inside of a word. This account of synonymy, supposing it acceptable on other counts, has indeed the drawback of appealing to a prior conception of 'word' which can be counted on to present difficulties of formulation in its turn. Nevertheless, some progress might be claimed in having reduced the problem of synonymy to a problem of wordhood. Let us pursue this line a bit, taking 'word' for granted.

The question remains whether interchangeability *salva veritate* (apart from occurrences within words) is a strong enough condition for synonymy, or whether, on the contrary, some heteronymous expressions might be thus interchangeable. Now let us be clear that we are not concerned here with synonymy in the sense of complete identity in psychological associations or poetic quality; indeed no two expressions are synonymous in such a sense. We are concerned only with what may be called *cognitive* synonymy. Just what this is cannot be said without successfully finishing the present study, but we know something about it from the need which arose for it in connection with analyticity in §1. The sort of synonymy needed there was merely such that any analytic statement could be turned into a logical truth by putting synonyms for synonyms. Turning the tables and assuming analyticity, indeed, we could explain cognitive synonymy of terms as follows (keeping to the familiar example): To say that "bachelor" and "unmarried man" are cognitively synonymous is to say no more nor less than that the statement:

(3) All and only bachelors are unmarried men

is analytic.[4]

What we need is an account of cognitive synonymy not presupposing analyticity—if we are to explain analyticity conversely with help of cognitive synonymy as undertaken in §1. And indeed such an independent account of cognitive synonymy is at present up for consideration, namely, interchangeability *salva veritate* everywhere except within words. The question before us, to resume the thread at last, is whether such interchangeability is a sufficient condition for cognitive synonymy. We can quickly assure ourselves that it is, by examples of the following sort. The statement:

(4) Necessarily all and only bachelors are bachelors

is evidently true, even supposing "necessarily" so narrowly construed as to be truly applicable only to analytic statements. Then, if "bachelor" and "unmarried man" are interchangeable *salva veritate,* the result:

(5) Necessarily all and only bachelors are unmarried men

of putting "unmarried man" for an occurrence of "bachelor" in (4) must, like (4), be true. But to say that (5) is true is to say that (3) is analytic, and hence that "bachelor" and "unmarried man" are cognitively synonymous.

Let us see what there is about the above argument that gives it its air of hocus-pocus. The condition of interchangeability *salva veritate* varies in its force with variations in the richness of the language at hand. The above argument supposes we are working with a language rich enough to contain the adverb "necessarily," this adverb being so construed as to yield truth when and only when applied to an analytic statement. But can we condone a language which contains such an adverb? Does the adverb really make sense? To suppose that it does is to suppose that we have already made satisfactory sense of "analytic." Then what are we so hard at work on right now?

Our argument is not flatly circular, but something like it. It has the form, figuratively speaking, of a closed curve in space.

Interchangeability *salva veritate* is meaningless until relativized to a language whose extent is specified in relevant respects. Suppose now we consider a language containing just the following materials. There is an indefinitely large stock of one-place predicates (for example, "F" where "Fx" means that x is a man) and many-place predicates (for example, "G" where "Gxy" means that x loves y), mostly having to do with extralogical subject matter. The rest of the language is logical. The atomic sentences consist each of a predicate followed by one or more variables "x," "y," etc.; and the complex sentences are built up of the atomic ones by truth functions ("not," "and," "or," etc.) and quantification. In effect such a language enjoys the benefits also of descriptions and indeed singular terms generally, these being contextually definable in known ways. Even abstract singular terms naming classes, classes of classes, etc., are contextually definable in case the assumed stock of predicates includes the two-place predicate of class membership. Such a language can be adequate to classical mathematics and indeed to scientific discourse generally, except in so far as the latter involves debatable devices such as contrary-to-fact conditionals or modal adverbs like "necessarily".[5] Now a language of this type is extensional, in this sense: Any two predicates which agree extensionally (that is, are true of the same objects) are interchangeable *salva veritate.*[6]

In an extensional language, therefore, interchangeability *salva veritate* is no assurance of cognitive synonymy of the desired type. That "bachelor" and "unmarried man" are interchangeable *salva veritate* in an extensional language assures us of no more than that (3) is true. There is no assurance here that the extensional agreement of "bachelor" and "unmarried man" rests on meaning rather than merely on accidental matters of fact, as does the extensional agreement of "creature with a heart" and "creature with kidneys."

For most purposes extensional agreement is the nearest approximation to synonymy we need care about. But the fact remains that extensional agreement falls far short of cognitive synonymy of the type required for explaining analyticity in the manner of §1. The type of cognitive synonymy required there is such as to equate the synonymy of "bachelor" and "unmarried man" with the analyticity of (3), not merely with the truth of (3).

So we must recognize that interchangeability *salva veritate*, if construed in relation to an extensional language, is not a sufficient condition of cognitive synonymy in the sense needed for deriving analyticity in the manner of §1. If a language contains an intensional adverb "necessarily" in the sense lately noted, or other particles to the same effect, then interchangeability *salva veritate* in such a language does afford a sufficient condition of cognitive synonymy; but such a language is intelligible only in so far as the notion of analyticity is already understood in advance.

The effort to explain cognitive synonymy first, for the sake of deriving analyticity from it afterward as in §1, is perhaps the wrong approach. Instead we might try explaining analyticity somehow without appeal to cognitive synonymy. Afterward we could doubtless derive cognitive synonymy from analyticity satisfactorily enough if desired. We have seen that cognitive synonymy of "bachelor" and "unmarried man" can be explained as analyticity of (3). The same explanation works for any pair of one-place predicates, of course, and it can be extended in obvious fashion to many-place predicates. Other syntactical categories can also be accommodated in fairly parallel fashion. Singular terms may be said to be cognitively synonymous when the statement of identity formed by putting "=" between them is analytic. Statements may be said simply to be cognitively synonymous when their biconditional (the result of joining them by "if and only if") is analytic.[7] If we care to lump all categories into a single formulation, at the expense of assuming again the notion of 'word' which was appealed to early in this section, we can describe any two linguistic forms as cognitively synonymous when the two forms are interchangeable (apart from occurrences within 'words') *salva* (no longer *veritate* but) *analyticitate*. Certain technical questions arise, indeed, over cases of ambiguity or homonymy; let us not pause for them, however, for we are already digressing. Let us rather turn our backs on the problem of synonymy and address ourselves anew to that of analyticity.

4. SEMANTICAL RULES

Analyticity at first seemed most naturally definable by appeal to a realm of meanings. On refinement, the appeal to meanings gave way to an appeal to synonymy or definition. But definition turned out to be a will-o'-the-wisp, and synonymy turned out to be best understood only by dint of a prior appeal to analyticity itself. So we are back at the problem of analyticity.

I do not know whether the statement "Everything green is extended" is analytic. Now does my indecision over this example really betray an incomplete understanding, an incomplete grasp of the 'meanings', of "green" and "extended?" I think not. The trouble is not with "green" or "extended," but with "analytic."

It is often hinted that the difficulty in separating analytic statements from synthetic ones in ordinary language is due to the vagueness of ordinary language and that the distinction is clear when we have a precise artificial language with explicit 'semantical rules'. This, however, as I shall now attempt to show, is a confusion.

The notion of analyticity about which we are worrying is a purported relation between statements and languages: A statement S is said to be *analytic for* a language L, and the problem is to make sense of this relation generally, that is, for variable "S" and "L". The gravity of ths problem is not perceptibly less for artificial languages than for natural ones. The problem of making sense of the idiom "S is analytic for L," with variable "S" and "L," retains its stubbornness even if we limit the range of the variable "L" to artificial languages. Let me now try to make this point evident.

For artificial languages and semantical rules we look naturally to the writings of Carnap. His semantical rules take various forms, and to make my point I shall have to distinguish certain of the forms. Let us suppose, to begin with, an artificial language L_0 whose semantical rules have the form explicitly of a specification, by recursion or otherwise, of all the analytic statements of L_0. The rules tell us that such and such statements, and only those, are the analytic statements of L_0. Now here the difficulty is simply that the rules contain the word "analytic," which we do not understand! We understand what expressions the rules attribute analyticity to, but we do not understand what the rules attribute to those expressions. In short, before we can understand a rule which begins "A statement S is analytic for language L_0 if and only if . . . .," we must understand the general relative term "analytic for"; we must understand "S" is analytic for "L" where "S" and "L" are variables.

Alternatively we may, indeed, view the so-called rule as a conventional definition of a new simple symbol "analytic-for-L_0" which might better be written untendentiously as "K" so as not to seem to throw light on the interesting word "analytic." Obviously any number of classes K, M, N, etc. of statements of L_0 can be specified for various purposes or for no purpose; what does it mean to say that K, as against M, N, etc., is the class of the 'analytic' statement of L_0?

By saying what statements are analytic for L_0 we explain "analytic-for-L_0" but not "analytic," not "analytic for." We do not begin to explain the idiom "S is analytic for L" with variable "S" and "L," even if we are content to limit the range of "L" to the realm of artificial languages.

Actually we do know enough about the intended significance of "analytic" to know that analytic statements are supposed to be true. Let us then turn to a second form of semantical rule, which says not that such and such statements are analytic but simply that such and such statements are included among the truths. Such a rule is not subject to the criticism of containing the un-understood word "analytic"; and we may grant for the sake of argument that there is no difficulty over the broader term "true." A semantical rule of this second type, a rule of truth, is not supposed to specify all the truths of the language; it merely stipulates, recursively or otherwise, a certain multitude of statements which, along with others unspecified, are to count as true. Such a rule

may be conceded to be quite clear. Derivatively, afterward, analyticity can be demarcated thus: a statement is analytic if it is (not merely true but) true according to the semantical rule.

Still there is really no progress. Instead of appealing to an unexplained word "analytic," we are now appealing to an unexplained phrase "semantical rule." Not every true statement which says that the statements of some class are true can count as a semantical rule—otherwise *all* truths would be 'analytic' in the sense of being true according to semantical rules. Semantical rules are distinguishable, apparently, only by the fact of appearing on a page under the heading "Semantical Rules"; and this heading is itself then meaningless.

We can say indeed that a statement is *analytic-for-L_0* if and only if it is true according to such and such specifically appended 'semantical rules,' but then we find ourselves back at essentially the same case which was originally discussed: "S is analytic-for-L_0 if and only if . . . ." Once we seek to explain "S is analytic for L" generally for variable "L" (even allowing limitation of "L" to artificial languages), the explanation "true according to the semantical rules of L" is unavailing; for the relative term "semantical rule of" is as much in need of clarification, at least, as "analytic for."

It may be instructive to compare the notion of semantical rule with that of postulate. Relative to a given set of postulates, it is easy to say what a postulate is: it is a member of the set. Relative to a given set of semantical rules, it is equally easy to say what a semantical rule is. But given simply a notation, mathematical or otherwise, and indeed as thoroughly understood a notation as you please in point of the translations or truth conditions of its statements, who can say which of its true statements rank as postulates? Obviously the question is meaningless—as meaningless as asking which points in Ohio are starting points. Any finite (or effectively specifiable infinite) selection of statements (preferably true ones, perhaps) is as much *a* set of postulates as any other. The word "postulate" is significant only relative to an act of inquiry; we apply the word to a set of statements just in so far as we happen, for the year or the moment, to be thinking of those statements in relation to the statements which can be reached from them by some set of transformations to which we have seen fit to direct our attention. Now the notion of semantical rule is as sensible and meaningful as that of postulate, if conceived in a similarly relative spirit—relative, this time, to one or another particular enterprise of schooling unconversant persons in sufficient conditions for truth of statements of some natural or artificial language L. But from this point of view no one signalization of a subclass of the truths of L is intrinsically more a semantical rule than another; and, if "analytic" means "true by semantical rules," no one truth of L is analytic to the exclusion of another.[8]

It might conceivably be protested that an artificial language L (unlike a natural one) is a language in the ordinary sense *plus* a set of explicit semantical rules—the whole constituting, let us say, an ordered pair; and that the semantical rules of L then are specifiable simply as the second component of the pair L. But, by the same token and more simply, we might construe an artificial language L outright as an ordered pair whose second component is the class of its analytic statements; and then the analytic statements of L become specifiable simply as the statements in the second component of L. Or better still, we might just stop tugging at our bootstraps altogether.

Not all the explanations of analyticity known to Carnap and his readers have been covered explicitly in the above considerations, but the extension to other forms is not hard to see. Just one additional factor should be mentioned which sometimes enters: sometimes the semantical rules are in effect rules of translation into ordinary language, in which case the analytic statements of the artificial language are in effect recognized as such from the analyticity of their specified translations in ordinary language. Here certainly there can be no thought of an illumination of the problem of analyticity from the side of the artificial language.

From the point of view of the problem of analyticity the notion of an artificial language with semantical rules is a *feu follet par excellence*. Semantical rules determining the analytic statements of an artificial language are of interest only in so far as we already understand the notion of analyticity; they are of no help in gaining this understanding.

Appeal to hypothetical languages of an artificially simple kind could conceivably be useful in clarifying analyticity, if the mental or behavioral or cultural factors relevant to analyticity—whatever they may be—were somehow sketched into the simplified model. But a model which takes analyticity merely as an irreducible character is unlikely to throw light on the problem of explicating analyticity.

It is obvious that truth in general depends on both language and extralinguistic fact. The statement "Brutus killed Caesar" would be false if the world had been different in certain ways, but it would also be false if the word "killed" happened rather to have the sense of "begat." Thus one is tempted to suppose in general that the truth of a statement is somehow analyzable into a linguistic component and a factual component. Given this supposition, it next seems reasonable that in some statements the factual component should be null; and these are the analytic statements. But, for all its a priori reasonableness, a boundary between analytic and synthetic statements simply has not been drawn. That there is such a distinction to be drawn at all is an unempirical dogma of empiricists, a metaphysical article of faith.

5. THE VERIFICATION THEORY AND REDUCTIONISM

In the course of these somber reflections we have taken a dim view first of the notion of meaning, then of the notion of cognitive synonymy, and finally of the notion of analyticity. But what, it may be asked, of the verification theory of meaning? This phrase has established itself so firmly as a catchword of empiricism that we should be very unscientific indeed not to look beneath it for a possible key to the problem of meaning and the associated problems.

The verification theory of meaning, which has been conspicuous in the literature from Peirce onward, is that the meaning of a statement is the method of empirically confirming or infirming it. An analytic statement is that limiting case which is confirmed no matter what.

As urged in §1, we can as well pass over the question of meanings as entities and move straight to sameness of meaning, or synonymy. Then what the verification theory says is that statements are synonymous if and only if they are alike in point of method of empirical confirmation or infirmation.

This is an account of cognitive synonymy not of linguistic forms generally, but of statements.[9] However, from the concept of synonymy of statements we could derive the concept of synonymy for other linguistic forms, by considerations somewhat similar to those at the end of §3. Assuming the notion of 'word' indeed, we could explain any two forms as synonymous when the putting of the one form for an occurrence of the other in any statement (apart from occurrences within 'words') yields a synonymous statement. Finally, given the concept of synonymy thus for linguistic forms generally, we could define analyticity in terms of synonymy and logical truth as in §1. For that matter, we could define analyticity more simply in terms of just synonymy of statements together with logical truth; it is not necessary to appeal to synonymy of linguistic forms other than statements. For a statement may be described as analytic simply when it is synonymous with a logically true statement.

So, if the verification theory can be accepted as an adequate account of statement synonymy, the notion of analyticity is saved after all. However, let us reflect. Statement synonymy is said to be likeness of method of empirical confirmation or infirmation. Just what are these methods which are to be compared for likeness? What, in other words, is the nature of the relation between a statement and the experiences which contribute to or detract from its confirmation?

The most naïve view of the relation is that it is one of direct report. This is *radical reductionism*. Every meaningful statement is held to be translatable into a statement (true or false) about immediate experience. Radical reductionism, in one form or another, well antedates the verification theory of meaning explicitly so called. Thus Locke and Hume held that every idea must either originate directly in sense experience or else be compounded of ideas thus originating; and taking a hint from Tooke we might rephrase this doctrine in semantical jargon by saying that a term, to be significant at all, must be either a name of a sense datum or a compound of such names or an abbreviation of such a compound. So stated, the doctrine remains ambiguous as between sense data as sensory events and sense data as sensory qualities, and it remains vague as to the admissible ways of compounding. Moreover, the doc-

trine is unnecessarily and intolerably restrictive in the term-by-term critique which it imposes. More reasonably, and without yet exceeding the limits of what I have called radical reductionism, we may take full statements as our significant units—thus demanding that our statements as wholes be translatable into sense-datum language, but not that they be translatable term by term.

This emendation would unquestionably have been welcome to Locke and Hume and Tooke, but historically it had to await an important reorientation in semantics—the reorientation whereby the primary vehicle of meaning came to be seen no longer in the term but in the statement. This reorientation, explicit in Frege ([1], §60), underlies Russell's concept of incomplete symbols defined in use; also it is implicit in the verification theory of meaning, since the objects of verification are statements.

Radical reductionism, conceived now with statements as units, set itself the task of specifying a sense-datum language and showing how to translate the rest of significant discourse, statement by statement, into it. Carnap embarked on this project in the *Aufbau*.

The language which Carnap adopted as his starting point was not a sense-datum language in the narrowest conceivable sense, for it included also the notations of logic, up through higher set theory. In effect it included the whole language of pure mathematics. The ontology implicit in it (that is, the range of values of its variables) embraced not only sensory events but classes, classes of classes, and so on. Empiricists there are who would boggle at such prodigality. Carnap's starting point is very parsimonious, however, in its extralogical or sensory part. In a series of constructions in which he exploits the resources of modern logic with much ingenuity, Carnap succeeds in defining a wide array of important additional sensory concepts which, but for his constructions, one would not have dreamed were definable on so slender a basis. He was the first empiricist who, not content with asserting the reducibility of science to terms of immediate experience, took serious steps toward carrying out the reduction.

If Carnap's starting point is satisfactory, still his constructions were, as he himself stressed, only a fragment of the full program. The construction of even the simplest statements about the physical world was left in a sketchy state. Carnap's suggestions on this subject were, despite their sketchiness, very suggestive. He explained spatio-temporal point-instants as quadruples of real numbers and envisaged assignment of sense qualities to point-instants according to certain canons. Roughly summarized, the plan was that qualities should be assigned to point-instants in such a way as to achieve the laziest world compatible with our experience. The principle of least action was to be our guide in constructing a world from experience.

Carnap did not seem to recognize, however, that his treatment of physical objects fell short of reduction not merely through sketchiness, but in principle. Statements of the form "Quality q is at point-instant $x; y; z; t$" were, according to his canons, to be apportioned truth values in such a way as to maximize and minimize certain overall features, and with growth of experience the truth values were to be progressively revised in the same spirit. I think this is a good schematization (deliberately oversimplified, to be sure) of what science really does; but it provides no indication, not even the sketchiest, of how a statement of the form "Quality q is at $x; y; z; t$" could ever be translated into Carnap's initial language of sense data and logic. The connective "is at" remains an added undefined connective; the canons counsel us in its use but not in its elimination.

Carnap seems to have appreciated this point afterward; for in his later writings he abandoned all notion of the translatability of statements about immediate experience. Reductionism in its radical form has long since ceased to figure in Carnap's philosophy.

But the dogma of reductionism has, in a subtler and more tenuous form, continued to influence the thought of empiricists. The notion lingers that to each statement, or each synthetic statement, there is associated a unique range of possible sensory events such that the occurrence of any of them would add to the likelihood of truth of the statement, and that there is associated also another unique range of possible sensory events whose occurrence would detract from that likelihood. This notion is of course implicit in the verification theory of meaning.

The dogma of reductionism survives in the supposition that each statement, taken in isolation from its fellows, can admit of confirmation or infirmation at all. My countersuggestion, issuing essentially from Carnap's doctrine of the physical world in the *Aufbau*, is that our statements about the external world face the tribunal of sense experience not individually but only as a corporate body.[10]

The dogma of reductionism, even in its attenuated form, is intimately connected with the other dogma—that there is a cleavage between the analytic and the synthetic. We have found ourselves led, indeed, from the latter problem to the former through the verification theory of meaning. More directly, the one dogma clearly supports the other in this way: as long as it is taken to be significant in general to speak of the confirmation and infirmation of a statement, it seems significant to speak also of a limiting kind of statement which is vacuously confirmed, *ipso facto*, come what may; and such a statement is analytic.

The two dogmas are, indeed, at root identical. We lately reflected that in general the truth of statements does obviously depend both upon language and upon extralinguistic fact; and we noted that this obvious circumstance carries in its train, not logically but all too naturally, a feeling that the truth of a statement is somehow analyzable into a linguistic component and a factual component. The factual component must, if we are empiricists, boil down to a range of confirmatory experiences. In the extreme case where the linguistic component is all that matters, a true statement is analytic. But I hope we are now impressed with how stubbornly the distinction between analytic and synthetic has resisted any straightforward drawing. I am impressed also, apart from prefabricated examples of black and white balls in an urn, with how baffling the problem has always been of arriving at any explicit theory of the empirical confirmation of a synthetic statement. My present suggestion is that it is nonsense, and the root of much nonsense, to speak of a linguistic component and a factual component in the truth of any individual statement. Taken collectively, science has its double dependence upon language and experience; but this duality is not significantly traceable into the statements of science taken one by one.

The idea of defining a symbol in use was, as remarked, an advance over the impossible term-by-term empiricism of Locke and Hume. The statement, rather than the term, came with Frege to be recognized as the unit accountable to an empiricist critique. But what I am now urging is that even in taking the statement as unit we have drawn our grid too finely. The unit of empirical significance is the whole of science.

6. EMPIRICISM WITHOUT THE DOGMAS

The totality of our so-called knowledge or beliefs, from the most casual matters of geography and history to the profoundest laws of atomic physics or even of pure mathematics and logic, is a man-made fabric which impinges on experience only along the edges. Or, to change the figure, total science is like a field of force whose boundary conditions are experience. A conflict with experience at the periphery occasions readjustments in the interior for the field. Truth values have to be redistributed over some of our statements. Reevaluation of some statements entails reevaluation of others, because of their logical interconnections—the logical laws being in turn simply certain further statements of the system, certain further elements of the field. Having reevaluated one statement we must reevaluate some others, which may be statements logically connected with the first or may be the statements of logical connections themselves. But the total field is so underdetermined by its boundary conditions, experience, that there is much latitude of choice as to what statements to reevaluate in the light of any single contrary experience. No particular experiences are linked with any particular statements in the interior of the field, except indirectly through considerations of equilibrium affecting the field as a whole.

If this view is right, it is misleading to speak of the empirical content of an individual statement—especially if it is a statement at all remote from the experiential periphery of the field. Furthermore it becomes folly to seek a boundary between synthetic statements, which hold contingently on experience, and analytic statements, which hold come what may. Any statement can be held true come what may, if we make drastic enough adjustments elsewhere in the system. Even a statement very close to the periphery can be held true in the face of recal-

citrant experience by pleading hallucination or by amending certain statements of the kind called logical laws. Conversely, by the same token, no statement is immune to revision. Revision even of the logical law of the excluded middle has been proposed as a means of simplifying quantum mechanics; and what difference is there in principle between such a shift and the shift whereby Kepler superseded Ptolemy, or Einstein Newton, or Darwin Aristotle?

For vividness I have been speaking in terms of varying distances from a sensory periphery. Let me try now to clarify this notion without metaphor. Certain statements, though *about* physical objects and not sense experience, seem peculiarly germane to sense experience—and in a selective way: some statements to some experiences, others to others. Such statements, especially germane to particular experiences, I picture as near the periphery. But in this relation of 'germaneness' I envisage nothing more than a loose association reflecting the relative likelihood, in practice, of our choosing one statement rather than another for revision in the event of recalcitrant experience. For example, we can imagine recalcitrant experiences to which we would surely be inclined to accommodate our system by reevaluating just the statement that there are brick houses on Elm Street, together with related statements on the same topic. We can imagine other recalcitrant experiences to which we would be inclined to accommodate our system by reevaluating just the statement that there are no centaurs, along with kindred statements. A recalcitrant experience can, I have urged, be accommodated by any of various alternative reevaluations in various alternative quarters of the total system; but, in the cases which we are now imagining, our natural tendency to disturb the total system as little as possible would lead us to focus our revisions upon these specific statements concerning brick houses or centaurs. These statements are felt, therefore, to have a sharper empirical reference than highly theoretical statements of physics or logic or ontology. The latter statements may be thought of as relatively centrally located within the total network, meaning merely that little preferential connection with any particular sense data obtrudes itself.

As an empiricist I continue to think of the conceptual scheme of science as a tool, ultimately, for predicting future experience in the light of past experience. Physical objects are conceptually imported into the situation as convenient intermediaries—not by definition in terms of experience, but simply as irreducible posits comparable, epistemologically, to the gods of Homer. For my part I do, qua lay physicist, believe in physical objects and not in Homer's gods; and I consider it a scientific error to believe otherwise. But in point of epistemological footing the physical objects and the gods differ only in degree and not in kind. Both sorts of entities enter our conception only as cultural posits. The myth of physical objects is epistemologically superior to most in that is has proved more efficacious than other myths as a device for working a manageable structure into the flux of experience.

Positing does not stop with macroscopic physical objects. Objects at the atomic level are posited to make the laws of macroscopic objects, and ultimately the laws of experience, simpler and more manageable; and we need not expect or demand full definition of atomic and subatomic entities in terms of macroscopic ones, any more than definition of macroscopic things in terms of sense data. Science is a continuation of common sense, and it continues the common-sense expedient of swelling ontology to simplify theory.

Physical objects, small and large, are not the only posits. Forces are another example; and indeed we are told nowadays that the boundary between energy and matter is obsolete. Moreover, the abstract entities which are the substance of mathematics—ultimately classes and classes of classes and so on up—are another posit in the same spirit. Epistemologically these are myths on the same footing with physical objects and gods, neither better nor worse except for differences in the degree to which they expedite our dealings with sense experiences.

The overall algebra of rational and irrational numbers is underdetermined by the algebra of rational numbers, but is smoother and more convenient; and it includes the algebra of rational numbers as a jagged or gerrymandered part. Total science, mathematical and natural and human, is similarly but more extremely underdetermined by experience. The edge of the system must be kept squared with experience; the rest, with all its elaborate myths or fictions, has as its objective the simplicity of laws.

Ontological questions, under this view, are on a par with questions of natural science.[11] Consider the question whether to countenance classes as entities. This, as I have argued elsewhere, is the question whether to quantify with respect to variables which take classes as values. Now Carnap [3] has maintained that this is a question not of matters of fact but of choosing a convenient language form, a convenient conceptual scheme or framework for science. With this I agree, but only on the proviso that the same be conceded regarding scientific hypotheses generally. Carnap ([3], p. 32n) has recognized that he is able to preserve a double standard for ontological questions and scientific hypotheses only by assuming an absolute distinction between the analytic and the synthetic; and I need not say again that this is a distinction which I reject.[12]

The issue over there being classes seems more a question of convenient conceptual scheme; the issue over there being centaurs, or brick houses on Elm Street, seems more a question of fact. But I have been urging that this difference is only one of degree, and that it turns upon our vaguely pragmatic inclination to adjust one strand of the fabric of science rather than another in accommodating some particular recalcitrant experience. Conservatism figures in such choices, and so does the quest for simplicity.

Carnap, Lewis, and others take a pragmatic stand on the question of choosing between language forms, scientific frameworks; but their pragmatism leaves off at the imagined boundary between the analytic and the synthetic. In repudiating such a boundary I espouse a more thorough pragmatism. Each man is given a scientific heritage plus a continuing barrage of sensory stimulation; and the considerations which guide him in warping his scientific heritage to fit his continuing sensory promptings are, where rational, pragmatic.

NOTES

1. Carnap [1], pp. 9ff; [2], pp. 70ff.
2. According to an important variant sense of "definition," the relation preserved may be the weaker relation of mere agreement in reference. But definition in this sense is better ignored in

the present connection, being irrelevant to the question of synonymy.

3. Cf. Lewis [1], p. 373.

4. This is cognitive synonymy in a primary, broad sense. Carnap ([1], pp. 56ff) and Lewis ([2], pp. 83ff) have suggested how, once this notion is at hand, a narrower sense of cognitive synonymy which is preferable for some purposes can in turn be derived. But this special ramification of concept-building lies aside from the present purposes and must not be confused with the broad sort of cognitive synonymy here concerned.

5. On such devices see also Quine [1].

6. This is the substance of Quine [2], ⋆121.

7. The 'if and only if' itself is intended in the truth functional sense. See Carnap [1], p. 14.

8. The foregoing paragraph was not part of the present essay as originally published. It was prompted by Martin.

9. The doctrine can indeed be formulated with terms rather than statements as the units. Thus Lewis describes the meaning of a term as "*a criterion in mind,* by reference to which one is able to apply or refuse to apply the expression in question in the case of presented, or imagined, things or situations" ([2], p. 133).—For an instructive account of the vicissitudes of the verification theory of meaning, centered however on the question of meaning*fulness* rather than synonymy and analyticity, see Hempel.

10. This doctrine was well argued by Duhem, pp. 303–328. Or see Lowinger, pp. 132–140.

11. "L'ontologie fait corps avec la science elle-même et ne peut en être separée." Meyerson, p. 439.

12. For an effective expression of further misgivings over this distinction, see White.

REFERENCES

Carnap, R. [1]. *Meaning and Necessity.* (Chicago: University of Chicago Press, 1947.)

————[2]. *Logical Foundations of Probability.* (Chicago: University of Chicago Press, 1950.)

————[3]. "Empiricism, semantics, and ontology," *Revue Internationale de Philosophie,* vol. IV (1950), pp. 20–40.

Duhem, P. *La Théorie physique: son objet et sa structure.* (Paris: 1906.)

Frege, Gottlob. *Foundations of Arithmetic.* (New York: Philosophical Library, 1950.)

Hempel, C. G. "Problems and Changes in the Empiricist Criterion of Meaning." *Revue International de Philosophie,* vol. IV (1950), pp. 41–63.

Lewis, C. I. [1]. *A Survey of Symbolic Logic.* (Berkeley: 1918.)

————[2]. *An Analysis of Knowledge and Valuation.* (LaSalle, Ill.: Open Court Publishing co., 1946).

Lowinger, A. *The Methodology of Pierre Duhem.* (New York: Columbia University Press, 1941.)

Martin, R. M., "On 'Analytic'." *Philosophical Studies,* vol. III (1952), pp. 42–47.

Meyerson, Émile. *Identité et realité.* (Paris: 1908; 4th ed., 1932.)

Quine, W. V. [1]. *From a Logical Point of View.* (New York: Harper & Row, 1961.)

————[2]. *Mathematical Logic.* (New York: W. W. Norton & Company, Inc., 1940; Cambridge: Harvard University Press, 1947; rev. ed., 1951.)

White, Morton. "The Analytic and the Synthetic: An Untenable Dualism." In Sidney Hook, ed., *John Dewey: Philosopher of Science and Freedom.* (New York: The Dial Press, Inc., 1950.) pp. 3160–30.

PHILIP KITCHER

A Priori Knowledge

I

"A priori" has been a popular term with philosophers at least since Kant distinguished between a priori and a posteriori knowledge. Yet, despite the frequency with which it has been used in twentieth century philosophy, there has been little discussion of the concept of apriority. Some writers seem to take it for granted that there are propositions, such as the truths of logic and mathematics, which are a priori; others deny that there are any a priori propositions. In the absence of a clear characterization of the a priori/a posteriori distinction, it is by no means obvious what is being asserted or what is being denied.

"A priori" is an epistemological predicate. What is *primarily* a priori is an item of knowledge. Of course, we can introduce a derivative use of "a priori" as a predicate of propositions: a priori propositions are those which we could know a priori. Somebody might protest that current practice is to define the notion of an a priori proposition outright, by taking the class of a priori propositions to consist of the truths of logic and mathematics (for example). But when philosophers allege that truths of logic and mathematics are a priori, they do not intend merely to recapitulate the definition of a priori propositions. Their aim is to advance a thesis about the epistemological status of logic and mathematics.

To understand the nature of such epistemological claims, we should return to Kant, who provided the most explicit characterization of a priori knowledge: "we shall understand by a priori knowledge, not knowledge which is independent of this or that experience, but knowledge absolutely independent of all experience." While acknowledging that Kant's formulation sums up the classical notion of apriority, several recent writers who have discussed the topic have despaired of making sense of it. I shall try to show that Kant's definition can be clarified,

and that the concept of a priori knowledge can be embedded in a naturalistic epistemology.

II

Two questions naturally arise. What are we to understand by "experience"? And what is to be made of the idea of independence from experience? Apparently, there are easy answers. Count as a person's experience the stream of her sensory encounters with the world, where this includes both "outer experience," that is, sensory states caused by stimuli external to the body, and "inner experience," that is, those sensory states brought about by internal stimuli. Now we might propose that someone's knowledge is independent of her experience just in case she could have had that knowledge whatever experience she had had. To this obvious suggestion there is an equally obvious objection. The apriorist is not ipso facto a believer in innate knowledge: indeed, Kant emphasized the difference between the two types of knowledge. So we cannot accept an analysis which implies that a priori knowledge could have been obtained given minimal experiences.

Many philosophers (Kant included) contend both that analytic truths can be known a priori and that some analytic truths involve concepts which could only be acquired if we were to have particular kinds of experience. If we are to defend their doctrines from immediate rejection, we must allow a minimal role to experience, even in a priori knowledge. Experience may be needed to provide some concepts. So we might modify our proposal: knowledge is independent of experience if any experience which would enable us to acquire the concepts involved would enable us to have the knowledge.

It is worth noting explicitly that we are concerned here with the *total* experience of the knower. Suppose that you acquire some knowledge empirically. Later

567

you deduce some consequences of this empirical knowledge. We should reject the suggestion that your knowledge of those consequences is independent of experience because, at the time you perform the deduction, you are engaging in a process of reasoning which is independent of the sensations you are then having. As Kant recognized, your knowledge, in cases like this, is dependent on your total experience: different total sequences of sensations would not have given you the premises for your deductions.

Let us put together the points which have been made so far. A person's experience at a particular time will be identified with his sensory state at the time. (Such states are best regarded physicalistically in terms of stimulation of sensory receptors, but we should recognize that there are both "outer" and "inner" receptors.) The total sequence of experiences X has had up to time t is *X's life at t*. A life will be said to be *sufficient for X for p* just in case X could have had that life and gained sufficient understanding to believe that p. (I postpone, for the moment, questions about the nature of the modality involved here.) Our discussion above suggests the use of these notions in the analysis of a priori knowledge: X knows a priori that p if and only if X knows that p and, given any life sufficient for X for p, X could have had that life and still have known that p. Making temporal references explicit: at time t X knows a priori that p just in case, at time t, X knows that p and, given any life sufficient for X for p, X could have had that life at t and still have known, at t, that p. In subsequent discussions I shall usually leave the temporal references implicit.

Unfortunately, the proposed analysis will not do. A clear-headed apriorist should admit that people can have empirical knowledge of propositions which can be known a priori. However, on the account I have given, if somebody knows that p and if it is possible for her to know a priori that p, then, apparently, given any sufficiently rich life she could know that p, so that she would meet the conditions for a priori knowledge that p. (This presupposes that modalities "collapse," but I don't think the problem can be solved simply by denying the presupposition.) Hence it seems that my account will not allow for empirical knowledge of propositions that can be known a priori.

We need to amend the analysis. We must differentiate situations in which a person knows something empirically which could have been known a priori from situations of actual a priori knowledge. The remedy is obvious. What sets apart corresponding situations of the two types is a difference in the ways in which what is known is known. An analysis of a priori knowledge must probe the notion of knowledge more deeply than we have done so far.

III

We do not need a general analysis of knowledge, but we do need the *form* of such an analysis. I shall adopt an approach which extracts what is common to much recent work on knowledge, an approach which may appropriately be called "the psychologistic account of knowledge." The root idea is that the question of whether a person's true belief counts as knowledge depends on whether the presence of that true belief can be explained in an appropriate fashion. The difference between an item of knowledge and mere true belief turns on the factors which produced the belief; thus the issue revolves around the way in which a particular mental state was generated. It is important to emphasize that, at different times, a person may have states of belief with the same content, and these states may be produced by different processes. The claim that a process produces a belief is to be understood as the assertion that the presence of the current state of belief is to be explained through a description of that process. Hence the account is not committed to supposing that the original formation of a belief is relevant to the epistemological status of later states of belief in the same proposition.

The question of what conditions must be met if a belief is to be explained in an appropriate fashion is central to epistemology, but it need not concern us here. My thesis is that the distinction between knowledge and true belief depends on the characteristics of the process which generates the belief, and this thesis is independent of specific proposals about what characteristics are crucial. Introducing a useful term, let us say that some processes *warrant* the beliefs they produce, and that these processes are *warrants* for such beliefs. The general view of knowledge I have adopted can be recast as the thesis that X knows that p just in case X correctly believes that p and X's belief was produced by a process which is a warrant for it. Leaving the task of specifying the conditions on warrants to general epistemology, my aim is to distinguish a priori knowledge from a posteriori knowledge. We discovered above that the distinction requires us to consider the ways in which what is known is known. Hence I propose to reformulate the problem: let us say that X knows a priori that p just in case X has a true belief that p and that belief was produced by a process which is an *a priori warrant* for it. Now the crucial notion is that of an a priori warrant, and our task becomes that of specifying the conditions which distinguish a priori warrants from other warrants.

At this stage, some examples may help us to see how to draw the distinction. Perception is an obvious type of process which philosophers have supposed *not* to engender a priori knowledge. Putative a priori warrants are more controversial. I shall use Kant's notion of pure intuition as an example. This is not to endorse the claim that processes of pure intuition are a priori warrants, but only to see what features of such processes have prompted Kant (and others) to differentiate them from perceptual processes.

On Kant's theory, processes of pure intuition are supposed to yield a priori mathematical knowledge. Let us focus on a simple geometrical example. We are supposed to gain a priori knowledge of the elementary properties of triangles by using our grasp on the concept of triangle to construct a mental picture of a triangle and by inspecting this picture with the mind's eye. What are the characteristics of this kind of process which make Kant want to say that it produces knowledge which is independent of experience? I believe that Kant's account implies that three conditions should be met. The same type of process must be *available* independently of experience. It must produce *warranted* belief independently of experience. And it must produce *true* belief independently of experience. Let us consider these conditions in turn.

According to the Kantian story, if our life were to enable us to acquire the appropriate concepts (the concept of a triangle and the other geometrical concepts involved) then the appropriate kind of pure intuition would be available to us. We could represent a triangle to ourselves, inspect it, and so reach the same beliefs. But, if the process is to generate *knowledge* independently of experience, Kant must require more of it. Given any sufficiently rich life, if we were to undergo the same type of process and gain the same beliefs, then those beliefs would be warranted by the process. Let us dramatize the point by imagining that experience is unkind. Suppose that we are presented with experiments which are cunningly contrived so as to make it appear that some of our basic geometrical beliefs are false. Kant's theory of geometrical knowledge presupposes that if, in the circumstances envisaged, a process of pure intuition were to produce geometrical belief then it would produce warranted belief, despite the background of misleading experience.

So far I have considered how a Kantian process of pure intuition might produce warranted belief independently of experience. But to generate *knowledge* independently of experience, a priori warrants must produce warranted *true* belief in counterfactual situations where experiences are different. This point does not emerge clearly in the Kantian case because the propositions which are alleged to be known a priori are taken to be necessary, so that the question of whether it would be possible to have an a priori warrant for a false belief does not arise. Plainly, we could ensure that a priori warrants produce warranted *true* belief independently of experience by declaring that a priori warrants only warrant necessary truths. But this proposal is unnecessarily strong. Our goal is to construe a priori knowledge as knowledge which is independent of experience, and this can be achieved, without closing the case against the contingent a priori, by supposing that, in a counterfactual situation in which an a priori warrant produces belief that p then p. On this account, a priori warrants are ultra-reliable; they never lead us astray.

Summarizing the conditions that have been uncovered, I propose the following analysis of a priori knowledge.

(1) X knows a priori that p if and only if X knows that p and X's belief that p was produced by a process which is an a priori warrant for it.

(2) α is an a priori warrant for X's belief that p if and only if α is a process such that, given any life e, sufficient for X for p, then

    (a) some process of the same type could produce in X a belief that p

    (b) if a process of the same type were to produce in X a belief that p then it would warrant X in believing that p

    (c) if a process of the same type were to produce in X a belief that p then p.

It should be clear that this analysis yields the desired result that, if a person knows a priori that p then she could know that p whatever (sufficiently rich) experience she had had. But it goes beyond the proposal of §II in spelling out the idea that the knowledge be obtainable in the same way. Hence we can distinguish cases of empirical knowledge of propositions which could he known a priori from cases of actual a priori knowledge.

IV

In this section, I want to be more explicit about the notion of "types of processes" which I have employed, and about the modal and conditional notions which figure in my analysis. To specify a process which produces a belief is to pick out some terminal segment of the causal ancestry of the belief. I think that, without loss of generality, we can restrict our attention to those segments which consist solely of states and events internal to the believer. Tracing the causal ancestry of a belief beyond the believer would identify processes which would not be available independently of experience, so that they would violate our conditions on a priori warrants.

Given that we need only consider psychological processes, the next question which arises is how we divide processes into types. It may seem that the problem can be sidestepped: can't we simply propose that to defend the apriority of an item of knowledge is to claim that that knowledge was produced by a psychological process and that *that very process* would he available and would produce warranted true belief in counterfactual situations where experience is different? I think it is easy to see how to use this proposal to rewrite (2) in a way which avoids reference to "types of processes." I have not

adopted this approach because I think that it shortcuts important questions about what makes a process the same in different counterfactual situations.

Our talk of processes which produce belief was originally introduced to articulate the idea that some items of knowledge are obtained in the same way while others are obtained in different ways. To return to our example, knowing a theorem on the basis of hearing a lecture and knowing the same theorem by following a proof count, intuitively, as different ways of knowing the theorem. Our intuitions about this example, and others, involve a number of different principles of classification, with different principles appearing in different cases. We seem to divide belief-forming processes into types by considering content of beliefs, inferential connections, causal connections, use of perceptual mechanisms and so forth. I suggest that these principles of classification probably do not give rise to one definite taxonomy, but that, by using them singly, or in combination, we obtain a number of different taxonomies which we can and do employ. Moreover, within each taxonomy, we can specify types of processes more or less narrowly. Faced with such variety, what characterization should we pick?

There is probably no privileged way of dividing processes into types. This is not to say that our standard principles of classification will allow *anything* to count as a type. Somebody who proposed that the process of listening to a lecture (or the terminal segment of it which consists of psychological states and events) belongs to a type which consists of itself and instances of following a proof, would flout *all* our principles for dividing processes into types. Hence, while we may have many admissible notions of types of belief-forming processes, corresponding to different principles of classification, some collections of processes contravene all such principles, and these cannot be admitted as genuine types.

My analysis can be read as issuing a challenge to the apriorist. If someone wishes to claim that a particular belief is an item of a priori knowledge then he must specify a segment of the causal ancestry of the belief, consisting of states and events internal to the believer, and type-identity conditions which conform to some principle (or set of principles) of classification which are standardly employed in our divisions of belief-forming processes (of which the principles I have indicated above furnish the most obvious examples). If he succeeds in doing this so that the requirements in (2) are met, his claim is sustained; if he cannot, then his claim is defeated.

The final issue which requires discussion in this section is that of explaining the modal and conditional notions I have used. There are all kinds of possibility, and claims about what is possible bear an implicit relativization to a set of facts which are held constant. When we say, in (2), that, given any sufficiently rich life, X could have had a belief which was the product of a particular type of process, should we conceive of this as merely logical possibility or are there some features of the actual world which are tacitly regarded as fixed? I suggest that we are not just envisaging any logically possible world. We imagine a world in which X has similar mental powers to those he has in the actual world. By hypothesis, X's experience is different. Yet the capacities for thinking, reasoning, and acquiring knowledge which X possesses as a member of *homo sapiens* are to remain unaffected: we want to say that X, *with the kinds of cognitive capacities distinctive of humans*, could have undergone processes of the appropriate type, even if his experiences had been different.

Humans might have had more faculties for acquiring knowledge than they actually have. For example, we might have had some strange ability to "see" what happens on the other side of the Earth. When we consider the status of a particular type of process as an a priori warrant, the existence of worlds in which such extra faculties come into play is entirely irrelevant. Our investigation focuses on the question of whether a particular type of process would be available to a person with the kinds of faculties people actually have, not on whether such processes would be available to creatures whose capacities for acquiring knowledge are augmented or diminished. Conditions (2(b)) and (2(c)) are to be read in similar fashion. Rewriting (2(b)) to make the form of the conditional explicit, we obtain: for any life e sufficient for X for p and for any world in which X has e, in which he believes that p, in which his belief is the product of a process of the appropriate kind, and *in which X has the cognitive capacities distinctive of humans*, X is warranted in believing that p. Similarly, (2(c)) becomes: for any life e sufficient for X for p and for any world in which X has e, in which he believes that p, in which his belief is the product of a process of the appropriate kind, *and in*

which X has the cognitive capacities distinctive of humans, p. Finally, the notion of a life's being sufficient for X for p also bears an implicit reference to X's native powers. To say that a particular life enables X to form certain concepts is to maintain that, given the genetic programming with which X is endowed, that life allows for the formation of the concepts.

The account I have offered can be presented more graphically in the following way. Consider a human as a cognitive device, endowed initially with a particular kind of structure. Sensory experience is fed into the device and, as a result, the device forms certain concepts. For any proposition p, the class of experiences which are sufficiently rich for p consists of those experiences which would enable the device, with the kind of structure it actually has, to acquire the concepts to believe that p. To decide whether or not a particular item of knowledge that p is an item of a priori knowledge we consider whether the type of process which produced the belief that p is a process which would have been available to the device, with the kind of structure it actually has, if different sufficiently rich experiences had been fed into it, whether, under such circumstances, processes of the type would warrant belief that p, and would produce true belief that p.

Seen in this way, claims about apriority are implicitly indexical, in that they inherit the indexical features of "actual." If this is not recognized, use of "a priori" in modal contexts can engender confusion. The truth value of "Possibly, X knows a priori that p" can be determined in one of two ways: we may consider the proposition expressed by the sentence at our world, and inquire whether there is a world at which that proposition is true; or we may ask whether there is a world at which the sentence expresses a true proposition. Because of the covert indexicality of "a priori," these lines of investigation may yield different answers. I suspect that failure to appreciate this point has caused trouble in assessing theses about the limits of the a priori. However, I shall not pursue the point here.

V

At this point, I want to address worries that my analysis is too liberal, because it allows some of our knowledge of ourselves and our states to count as a priori. Given its Kantian psychologistic underpinnings, the theory appears to favor claims that some of our self-knowledge is a priori. However, two points should be kept in mind. Firstly, the analysis I have proposed can only be applied to cases in which we know enough about the ways in which our beliefs are warranted to decide whether or not the conditions of (2) are met. In some cases, our lack of a detailed account of how our beliefs are generated may mean that no firm decision about the apriority of an item of knowledge can be reached. Secondly, there may be cases, including cases of self-knowledge, in which we have no clear pre-analytic intuitions about whether a piece of knowledge is a priori.

Nevertheless, there are some clear cases. Obviously, any theory which implied that I can know a priori that I am seeing red (when, in fact, I am) would be suspect. But, when we apply my analysis, the unwanted conclusion does not follow. For, if the process which leads me to believe that I am seeing red (when I am) can be triggered in the absence of red, then (2(c)) would be violated. If the process cannot be triggered in the absence of red, then, given some sufficiently rich experiences, the process will not be available, so that (2(a)) will be violated. In general, knowledge of any involuntary mental state—such as pains, itches or hallucinations—will work in the same way. Either the process which leads from the occurrence of pain to the belief that I am in pain can be triggered in the absence of pain, or not: if it can, (2(c)) would be violated, if it cannot, then (2(a)) would be violated.

This line of argument can be sidestepped when we turn to cases in which we have the power, independently of experience, to put ourselves into the appropriate states. For, in such cases, one can propose that the processes which give us knowledge of the states cannot be triggered in the absence of the states themselves *and* that the processes are always available because we can always put ourselves into the states. On this basis, we might try to conclude that we have a priori knowledge that we are imagining red (when we are) or thinking of Ann Arbor (when we are). However, the fact that such cases do not fall victim to the argument of the last paragraph does not mean that we are compelled to view them as cases of a priori knowledge. In the first place, the thesis that the processes through which we come to know our imaginative feats and our voluntary thoughts cannot be triggered in the absence of the

states themselves requires evaluation—and, lacking detailed knowledge of those processes, we cannot arrive at a firm judgment here. Secondly, the processes in question will be required to meet (2(b)) if they are to be certified as a priori warrants. This means that, whatever experience hurls at us, beliefs produced by such processes will be warranted. We can cast doubt on this idea by imagining that our experience consists of a lengthy, and apparently reliable, training in neurophysiology, concluding with a presentation to ourselves of our own neurophysiological organization which appears to show that our detection of our imaginative states (say) is slightly defective, that we always make mistakes about the contents of our imaginings. If this type of story can be developed, then (2(b)) will be violated, and the knowledge in question will not count as a priori. But, even if it cannot be coherently extended, and even if my analysis does judge our knowledge of states of imagination (and other "voluntary" states) to be a priori, it is not clear to me that this consequence is counterintuitive.

In fact, I think that one can make a powerful case for supposing that *some* self-knowledge is a priori. At most, if not all, of our waking moments, each of us knows of herself that she exists. Although traditional ideas to the effect that self-knowledge is produced by some "non-optical inner look" are clearly inadequate, I think it is plausible to maintain that there are processes which do warrant us in believing that we exist—processes of reflective thought, for example—and which belong to a general type whose members would be available to us independently of experience. Trivially, when any such process produces in a person a belief that she exists that belief is true. All that remains, therefore, is to ask if the processes of the type in question inevitably warrant belief in our own existence, or whether they would fail to do so, given a suitably exotic background experience. It is difficult to settle this issue conclusively without a thorough survey of the ways in which reflective belief in one's existence can be challenged by experience, but perhaps there are Cartesian grounds for holding that, so long as the belief is the product of reflective thought, the believer is warranted, no matter how wild his experience may have been. If this is correct, then at least some of our self-knowledge will be a priori. However, in cases like this, attributions of apriority seem even less vulnerable to the criticism that they are obviously incorrect.

At this point we must consider a doctrinaire objection. If the conclusion of the last paragraph is upheld then we can know some contingent propositions a priori. Frequently, however, it is maintained that only necessary truths can be known a priori. Behind this contention stands a popular argument. Assume that a person knows a priori that p. His knowledge is independent of his experience. Hence he can know that p without any information about the kind of world he inhabits. So, necessarily p.

This hazy line of reasoning rests on an intuition which is captured in the analysis given above. The intuition is that a priori warrants must be ultra-reliable: if a person is entitled to ignore empirical information about the type of world she inhabits then that must be because she has at her disposal a method of arriving at belief which guarantees *true* belief. (This intuition can be defended by pointing out that if a method which could produce false belief were allowed to override experience, then we might be blocked from obtaining knowledge which we might otherwise have gained.) In my analysis, the intuition appears as (2(c)).

However, when we try to clarify the popular argument we see that it contains an invalid step. Presenting it as a *reductio*, we obtain the following line of reasoning. Assume that a person knows a priori that p but that it is not necessary that p. Because p is contingent there are worlds at which p is false. Suppose that the person had inhabited such a world and behaved as she does at the actual world. Then she would have had an a priori warrant for a false belief. This is debarred by (2(c)). So we must conclude that the initial supposition is erroneous: if someone really does know a priori that p then p is necessary.

Spelled out in this way, the argument fails. We are not entitled to conclude from the premise that there are worlds at which p is false the thesis that there are worlds at which p is false *and* at which the person behaves as she does at the actual world. There are a number of propositions which, although they could be false, could not both be false and also believed by us. More generally, there are propositions which could not both be false and also believed by us in particular, definite ways. Obvious examples are

propositions about ourselves and their logical consequences: such propositions as those expressed by tokens of the sentences "I exist," "I have some beliefs," "There are thoughts," and so forth. Hence the attempted *reductio* breaks down and allows for the possibility of a priori knowledge of some contingent propositions.

I conclude that my analysis is innocent of the charge of being too liberal in ascribing to us a priori knowledge of propositions about ourselves. Although it is plausible to hold that my account construes some of our self-knowledge as a priori, none of the self-knowledge it takes to be a priori is clearly empirical. Moreover, it shows how a popular argument against the contingent a priori is flawed, and how certain types of contingent propositions—most notably propositions about ourselves—escape that argument. Thus I suggest that the analysis illuminates an area of traditional dispute.

VI

I now want to consider two different objections to my analysis. My replies to these objections will show how the approach I have developed can be further refined and extended.

The first objection, like those considered above, charges that the analysis is too liberal. My account apparently allows for the possibility that a priori knowledge could be gained through perception. We can imagine that some propositions are true at any world of which we can have experience, and that, given sufficient experience to entertain those propositions, we could always come to know them on the basis of perception. Promising examples are the proposition that there are objects, the proposition that some objects have shapes, and other, similar propositions. In these cases, one can argue that we cannot experience worlds at which they are false and that any (sufficiently rich) experience would provide perceptual warrant for belief in the propositions, regardless of the specific content of our perceptions. If these points are correct (and I shall concede them both, for the sake of argument) then perceptual processes would qualify as a priori warrants. Given any sufficiently rich experience, some perceptual process would be available to us, would produce warranted belief and, *ex hypothesi*, would produce warranted *true* belief.

Let us call cases of the type envisaged cases of *universally empirical* knowledge. The objection to my account is that it incorrectly classifies universally empirical knowledge as a priori knowledge. My response is that the classical notion of apriority is too vague to decide such cases: rather, this type of knowledge only becomes apparent when the classical notion is articulated. One could defend the classification of universally empirical knowledge as a priori by pointing out that such knowledge requires no particular type of experience (beyond that needed to obtain the concepts, of course). One could oppose that classification by pointing out that, even though the content of the experience is immaterial, the knowledge is still gained by perceiving, so that it should count as a posteriori.

If the second response should seem attractive, it can easily be accommodated by recognizing a stronger and a weaker notion of apriority. The weaker notion is captured in (1) and (2). The stronger adds an extra requirement: no process which involves the operation of a perceptual mechanism is to count as an a priori warrant.

At this point, it is natural to protest that the new condition makes the prior analysis irrelevant. Why not define a priori knowledge outright as knowledge which is produced by processes which do not involve perceptual mechanisms? The answer is that the prior conditions are not redundant: knowledge which is produced by a process which does not involve perceptual mechanisms need not be independent of experience. For the process may fail to generate warranted belief against a backdrop of misleading experience. (Nor may it generate true belief in all relevant counterfactual situations.) So, for example, certain kinds of thought-experiments may generate items of knowledge given a particular type of experience, but may not be able to sustain that knowledge against misleading experiences. Hence, if we choose to exclude universally empirical knowledge from the realm of the a priori in the way suggested, we are building on the analysis given in (1) and (2), rather than replacing it.

A different kind of criticism of my analysis is to accuse it of revealing the emptiness of the classical notion of apriority. Someone may suggest that, in exposing the constraints on a priori knowledge, I have shown that there could be very little a priori knowledge. Although I believe that this suggestion is incorrect, it is worth pointing out that, even if it is granted, my approach allows for the development of weaker notions which may prove epistemologically useful.

Let me first note that we can introduce approximations to a priori knowledge. Suppose that A is any type of process all of whose instances culminate in belief that p. Define the *supporting class* of A to be that class of lives, e, such that, (a) given e, some process in A could occur (and so produce belief that p), (b) given e, any process in A which occurred would produce warranted true belief that p. (Intuitively, the supporting class consists of those lives which enable processes of the type in question to produce knowledge.) The *defeating class* of A is the complement of the supporting class of A within the class of lives which are sufficient for p. A priori warrants are those processes which belong to a type whose defeating class is null. But we can be more liberal, and allow approximations to a priori knowledge by considering the size and/or nature of the defeating class. We might, for example, permit the defeating class to contain those radically disruptive experiences beloved of skeptics. Or we can define a notion of *contextual* apriority by allowing the defeating class to include experiences which undermine "framework principles." Or we may employ a concept of *comparative* apriority by ordering defeating classes according to inclusion relations. Each of these notions can serve a useful function in delineating the structure of our knowledge.

VII

Finally, I want to address a systematic objection to my analysis. The approach I have taken is blatantly psychologistic. Some philosophers may regard these psychological complications as objectionable intrusions into epistemology. So I shall consider the possibility of rival apsychologistic approaches.

Is there an acceptable view of a priori knowledge which rivals the Kantian conception? The logical positivists hoped to understand a priori knowledge without dabbling in psychology. The simplest of their proposals was the suggestion that X knows a priori that p if and only if X believes that p and p is analytically true.

Gilbert Harman has argued cogently that, in cases of factual belief, the nature of the reasons for which a person believes is relevant to the question of whether he has knowledge. Similar considerations arise with respect to propositions which the positivists took to be a priori. Analytic propositions, like synthetic propositions, can be believed for bad reasons, or for no reasons at all, and, when this occurs, we should deny that the believer knows the propositions in question. Assume, as the positivists did, that mathematics is analytic, and imagine a mathematician who comes to believe that some unobvious theorem is true. This belief is exhibited in her continued efforts to prove the theorem. Finally, she succeeds. We naturally describe her progress by saying that she has come to know something she only believed before. The positivistic proposal forces us to attribute knowledge from the beginning. Worse still, we can imagine that the mathematician has many colleagues who believe the theorem because of dreams, trances, fits of Pythagorean ecstasy, and so forth. Not only does the positivistic approach fail to separate the mathematician after she has found the proof from her younger self, but it also gives her the same status as her colleagues.

A natural modification suggests itself: distinguish among the class of analytic truths those which are elementary (basic laws of logic, immediate consequences of definitions, and, perhaps, a few others), and propose that elementary analytic truths can be known merely by being believed, while the rest are known, when they are known a priori, by inference from such truths. Even this restricted version of the original claim is vulnerable. If you believe the basic laws of logic because you have learned them from an eminent mathematician who has deluded himself into believing that the system of *Grundgesetze* is consistent and true, then you do not have a priori knowledge of those laws. Your belief in the laws of logic is undermined by evidence which you do not currently possess, namely the evidence which would expose your teacher as a misguided fanatic. The moral is obvious: apsychologistic approaches to a priori knowledge fail because, for a priori knowledge as for factual knowledge, the reasons for which a person believes are relevant to the question of whether he knows.

Although horror of psychologizing prevented the positivists from offering a defensible account of a priori knowledge, I think that my analysis can be used to articulate most of the doctrines that they wished to defend. Indeed, I believe that many classical theses, arguments and debates can be illuminated by applying the analysis presented here. My aim has been to prepare the way for investigations of traditional claims and disputes by developing in some detail Kant's conception of a priori knowledge. "A priori" has too often been a label which philosophers could attach to propositions they favored, without any clear criterion for doing so. I hope to have shown how a more systematic practice is possible.

FOR FURTHER READING

Audi, Robert. *Belief, Justification, and Knowledge.* Belmont, Calif.: Wadsworth, 1988.

Ayer, A. J. *Language, Truth, and Logic*, 2d ed. New York: Dover, 1952.

BonJour, Laurence. *The Structure of Empirical Knowledge.* Cambridge: Harvard University Press, 1985.

Casullo, Albert. "A priori/A posteriori." In *A Companion to Epistemology*, ed. Jonathan Dancy and Ernest Sosa, 1–3.

Casullo, Albert. "A priori Knowledge." In *A Companion to Epistemology*, ed. Jonathan Dancy and Ernest Sosa, 3–8.

Casullo, Albert. "Kripke on the A Priori and the Necessary." In *A Priori Knowledge*, ed. Paul Moser.

Chisholm, Roderick. *The Foundations of Knowing.* Minneapolis: University of Minnesota Press, 1982.

Chisholm, Roderick. *Theory of Knowledge*, 2d ed. Dover, Del.: Prentice Hall, 1977.

Dancy, Jonathan, and Ernest Sosa, eds. *A Companion to Epistemology.* Oxford: Basil Blackwell, 1992.

Frankfurt, Harry G., ed. *Leibniz: A Collection of Critical Essays.* Garden City, N.Y.: Anchor, 1972.

Gibson, Roger. *Enlightened Empiricism.* Tampa: University of Florida Press, 1988.

Grice, H. P., and P. F. Strawson. "In Defense of a Dogma." In *Analyticity*, ed. James F. Harris and Richard H. Severens, 56–74.

Hamlyn, D. W. *The Theory of Knowledge.* London: Macmillan Press, 1970.

Harris, James F., and Richard H. Severens, eds. *Analyticity.* Chicago: Quadrangle Books, 1970.

Kant, Immanuel. *Critique of Pure Reason.* Trans. Norman Kemp Smith. New York: St. Martin's Press, 1965.

Kitcher, Philip. "A Priori Knowledge." In *Naturalizing Epistemology*, ed. Hilary Kornblith, 129–45.

Kripke, Saul. *Naming and Necessity*. Cambridge: Harvard University Press, 1980.

Lewis, Clarence I. *Mind and the World Order*. London: George Allen and Unwin, 1929.

Linsky, Leonard. *Names and Descriptions*. Chicago: University of Chicago Press, 1977.

Moser, Paul, ed. *A Priori Knowledge*. Oxford: Oxford University Press, 1987.

Penelhum, Terence, and J. J. MacIntosh, eds. *The First Critique: Reflections on Kant's Critique of Pure Reason*. Belmont, Calif.: Wadsworth Publishing, 1969.

Quine, W. V. O. "Two Dogmas of Empiricism." In W. V. O. Quine, *From a Logical Point of View*, 20–46.

Quine, W. V. O. *From a Logical Point of View*, 2d ed. New York: Harper, 1961

Russell, Bertrand. *The Problems of Philosophy*. 1912. Reprint, London: Oxford University Press, 1959.

Stroll, Avrum. "What Water Is: Or Back to Thales." In *Midwest Studies in Philosophy*, ed. Peter A. French, et. al. Notre Dame: University of Notre Dame Press, 1989, 258–74.

STUDY QUESTIONS

1. How does Kant distinguish between a priori and a posteriori judgments? In Kant's view what are the criteria of a priori judgments? How does Kant distinguish between analytic and synthetic judgments? Why does Kant think that there are synthetic a priori judgments?

2. Why does Ayer think that mathematical and logical propositions are important for the dispute between rationalism and empiricism? Why does Ayer disagree with Mill's view that logical and mathematical truths have the same status as empirical hypotheses?

3. Explain Ayer's view of the a priori status of mathematical and logical propositions. Why, in Ayer's view, are such propositions necessary?

4. What is the traditional view of a priori knowledge, according to Chisholm? What is the connection between logical truths and analytic propositions? What is Chisholm's response to the claim that some propositions are true in virtue of linguistic conventions?

5. Why does Chisholm think that "Nothing is both red and green" is synthetic a priori?

6. According to Quine, what are the two dogmas of empiricism?

7. Quine considers three ways by which we might try to explain the concept of an analytic proposition. Briefly explain each of these three ways and why Quine rejects them.

8. What is the doctrine of reductionism, according to Quine? What consequence does the rejection of the analytic/synthetic distinction have for this doctrine? What does Quine mean by the claim that "Any statement can be held true come what may, if we make drastic enough adjustments elsewhere in the system"?

9. Kitcher develops a traditional definition of a priori; why does he object to this account? What is Kitcher's definition of a proposition that is known a priori? Why does Kitcher think that his view is psychologistic?

10. Why does Kitcher think that some of our self-knowledge is a priori? Why does he think that an apyschologistic account of a priori knowledge is unacceptable?

10

Perception

WYSIWYG—what you see is what you get—is a familiar acronym to the technologically inclined. It also seems appropriate as a description of our commonsense view of perception. If Sara sees a red rose, it is because the rose is red; and if she smells the sweet fragrance of the the same rose or feels the softness of its petals, it is because the rose is fragant and the petals soft. As our most pervasive and fundamental contact with the world, perception conveys information to us about objects and their properties. Perceptual information reflects the way things really are. Independently of what we think or believe, the world contains objects that have certain kinds of properties. These objects, along with their properties, exist even if they are never perceived. It is the business of our perceptual capacities to tell us about the objects and their various characteristics. Of courses, somtimes things go wrong. From a distance Sam may think he sees a friend, only to find out otherwise when he runs up to a total stranger. Under abnormal lighting, a wall might appear green rather than its actual color. From one angle a round penny may appear elliptical. We are nonetheless confident that most of the time, perception tells us about genuine features of the world. This view of perception is sometimes described as commonsense or naïve realism.

In the view of some, however, commonsense realism cannot explain certain aspects of perception. For example, we do not perceive objects directly; moreover, some of the properties we attribute to objects are not really properties of those objects. Arguments from illusion are thought to undermine our commonsense view.

In the eighteenth century, George Berkeley observed that if we place one hand in hot water and the other in cold water, and then place both hands in lukewarm water, we will experience quite different sensations. The water will feel cold to the hand previously in hot water, and it will feel hot to the hand previously in cold water. Nothing can have contrary properties; the water cannot be both cold and hot at the same time. Berkeley thus draws what he thinks is the appropriate conclusion: the sensible properties of objects are not in the objects themselves. In the early part of the twentieth century, Bertrand Russell made a similar observation about the color of a table. Russell notes that depending on the angle and the observer, a brown table could appear different colors. There is, he concludes, no color that can be said to be *the* color of the table. Instead, Russell claims, the color of the table is not a feature of the table itself, but depends on the table, the perceiver, and the conditions under which the table is perceived.

These types of argument purport to show that we directly experience only our own sensations, and these sensations are not properties of objects, but properties of the perceiver. At this point there seem to be two options for understanding perception. The first option is indirect, or representative, realism, and the second is phenomenalism.

In the representative realist's view, our sensations are representations of objects and are what we directly experience. But the representative realist, as a realist, holds that our sensations represent mind-independent objects. You need not be a skeptic about perception to be somewhat puzzled by the representative realist's view. If all we ever experience are our own sensations, how can we ever find out if those sensations actually represent mind-independent objects? How can we ever perform an independent check to find out if our sensations are genuinely representative? We know in general what it is to perform an independent check. For example, if you have doubts about a newspaper report, you can check the accuracy of the story in any number of ways. You can read another paper, turn to a cable news station, or turn on the radio. Lamentably, in representative realism, we do not seem to have access to such an independent check. We have no access to objects other

than sensation; we can only check our sensations, by other sensations and this is hardly an independent check.

The representative realist does have a response, a type of causal explanation: our sensations are caused by objects, and some of our sensations cue us to actual properties of sensations. John Locke, a seventeenth-century philosopher, distinguishes between primary and secondary qualities. Our idea of the former, Locke claims, resembles the actual properties of the object. Motion, figure, number, and solidity are among the types of primary qualities. Colors, scents, and tastes are typical of secondary qualities. These do not actually resemble any features of the objects. There are, according to Locke, features of the object that indeed cause us to have the ideas of color or taste, but there is no redness in the rose or sweetness in the grape. Initially this seems a bit strange to us, yet science tells us that the rose is actually composed of colorless molecules. This provides us with the clue we need to understand the representative realist.

Molecules are not visible to the unaided eye, but long before the advent of electron microscopes, scientists inferred the existence of molecules and even much smaller particles. They thought that certain kinds of phenomena could be explained if we appealed to the notion of molecules. If molecules had certain properties, then our observations would have an explanation. Moreover, invoking the notion of molecules allowed us to predict that we would subsequently observe various other phenomena. If we observed the predicted phenomena, then this would be further evidence of the existence of molecules. This is a simple picture of a complicated scientific process, but it does help us understand the representative realist.

We experience sensations of various kinds. One way to explain the existence of these sensations is that they are caused by mind-independent objects that have particular properties. As our picture of this mind-independent world becomes more articulate and elaborate, we are able to predict the kinds of sensations we will have under various circumstances. The more these predictions are borne out, the more confident we are in them.

The phenomenalist, on the other hand, rejects the inference to mind-independent physical objects.

The phenomenalist agrees that we only directly experience our own sensations, but denies the existence of mind-independent physical objects. Despite the apparent conflict with common sense, the phenomenalist steadfastly maintains that phenomenalism is in greater accord with common sense than is representative realism. Consider, for example, our notion of a simple physical object, an apple. What properties does this apple have? It is red on the outside, white on the inside with small flecks of brown; it is also rather spherical, sweet, juicy, and crunchy. Each of these properties is a sensible property, the phenomenalist notes. That is, each of these properties requires a perceiver. Now, one by one, remove these properties. What is left of the apple? According to phenomenalism, not much; indeed it looks a lot like nothing. Our idea of an object is exhausted by its sensible properties. But sensible properties require perceivers, and hence it makes no sense to talk of mind-independent objects.

A recent theory of perception, adverbial theory, attempts to rehabilitate the directness of commonsense realism. The adverbial theorist claims that we should not view sensations as special mental objects that represent physical objects. We perceive objects directly, according to the adverbial theorist. Our sensations are merely indicative of the way or manner in which we sense. For example, suppose that Sam sees that the book is blue. Sam does not have a blue, rectangular sensation, although he does have a particular kind of visual experience. Rather Sam senses in a blue, rectangular manner. The blue and rectangular features of the book cause certain modifications in Sam's sensory capacities that are described by adverbial theorists as Sam sensing bluely and rectangularly. An analogy sometimes used is that of a smile. The smile is not an object distinct from the face. It is a modification or property of the face, a smiling face.

Adverbial theorists seem to be more in line with the commonsense view. They hold that there are mind-independent objects that we perceive directly. Moreover, they suggest that the appropriate way of handling arguments from illusion is to recognize that modifications of our senses are sometimes caused in nonstandard ways.

Rather than opting for representative realism, phenomenalism or adverbialism, some have attempted to retain direct, or commonsense, realism. Because arguments from illusion are thought to undermine the commonsense view, attention turns to whether such arguments are compelling. Arguments from illusion often trade on the assumption that if something seems to have a property, then something must indeed have the property. It is not obvious, however, that we must accept this assumption. There are any number of occasions where an object looks to have a property, but does not, and we do not suppose that there must be something that does have the property. If, from a distance, it looks as though Sam has a lot of hair, but in fact does not, we do not suppose that there must be some object that has the property of having a lot of hair. There is, of course, a cause for Sam's hairy appearance, but this cause need not have the property "hairy." A commonsense view will need to give up the claim that objects have every property that we perceive them to have. This, however, does not require the commonsense realist to give up the claim that, in general, we directly perceive mind independent objects and their properties.

In the first selection, from his classic work, *Perception*, H. H. Price considers the significance of arguments from illusion for naïve realism. Price develops two versions of the argument from illusion, one of which he thinks is stonger than the other. Although Price contends that naïve realism cannot be maintained, consideration of the argument leads to a better understanding of what the naïve realist might be claiming.

The next selections, from John Locke and George Berkeley, provide accounts of representative realism and phenomenalism, respectively. Both accept the view that the mind can be aware of only its own ideas, but each develops this view in a different direction. It is worth noting that Berkeley does consider some of the standard objections to phenomenalism, such as how we are to understand the idea of objects existing when there is no one there to perceive them. In Berkeley's theistic phenomenalism, God is always there to perceive objects, but he also provides some suggestion as to how the nontheistic phenomenalist might deal with such objections.

The selection from W. T. Stace attempts to tie phenomenalism to our scientific understanding of the world. Stace contends that the laws of science and its theoretical entities are merely instruments for predicting the sequences of sensations we can expect to have. Fred Dretske argues there is a noncognitive, nonepistemic element in perception and it is this element that we often characterize as sensation or perceptual experience. In the last selection, John Heil critiques the idea of a noncognitve perceptual experience. Once we abandon this type of view, Heil thinks we are led back to a more direct realism, where our experience is of objects and their properties.

H. H. PRICE

from Perception

CHAPTER I. SENSE DATA "THE GIVEN"

. . .We may sum up this discussion as follows. When I am in the situation which is described as seeing something, touching something, hearing something, etc., it is certain in each case that a colour-patch, or a pressure, or a noise exists at that moment and that I am acquainted with this colour-patch, pressure or noise. Such entities are called sense-data, and the acquaintance with them is conveniently called sensing; but it differs from other instances of acquaintance only in its object, not in its nature, and it has no species. The usual arguments against the reality and against the knowability of sense-data break down on examination. They only prove at most that there is no sense-datum which is not the object of other sorts of consciousness besides sensing, and that the causes of most sense-data are more complicated than might have been expected: and in these conclusions there is nothing to disturb us.

In conclusion we may point out that the admission that there are sense-data is not a very large one; it commits us to very little. It may be worth while to mention explicitly a number of things which we are *not* committed to.

1. We are not committed to the view that sense-data *persist* through the intervals when they are not being sensed. We have only to admit that they *exist* at the times when they are being sensed.

2. We are not committed to the view that several minds can be acquainted with the *same* sense-datum. We have only to admit that every mind is acquainted with *some* sense-data from time to time.

3. We are not committed to any view about what is called 'the status' of sense-data in the Universe, either as regards the *category* they fall under, or as regards their relations with other types of existent entities. They may be events, or substances, or states of substances. They may be physical; i.e. they may be parts of, or events, in material objects such as chairs and tables or (in another theory) brains. They may be mental, as Berkeley and many others have held. They may be neither mental nor physical.

4. We are not committed to any view about their *origin*. They may originate as a result of processes in material objects, or of mental processes, or of both. Or again, it may be that the boot is on the other leg: it may be that they are the ultimate constituents of the Universe, and material things (perhaps minds as well) may be just collections of them; in which case they 'just are', and have no origin and no explanation, since everything else is explained by reference to them.

Thus the term sense-datum is meant to be a *neutral* term. The use of it does not imply the acceptance of any particular theory. The term is meant to stand for something whose existence is indubitable (however fleeting), something from which all theories of perception ought to start, however much they may diverge later.

And I think that all past theories have in fact started with sense-data. The Ancients and the Schoolmen called them *sensible species*. Locke and Berkeley called them *ideas of sensation*, Hume *impressions*, Kant *Vorstellungen*. In the nineteenth century they were usually known as *sensations*, and people spoke of visual and auditory sensations when they meant colour-patches and noises; while many contemporary writers, following Dr. C. D. Broad, have preferred to call them *sensa*.

All these terms have the defect of begging questions. If we speak of *sensible species* we assume that sense-data are physical, a sort of effluences flying off the external objects into our sense-organs. If we use terms like *idea, impression,* and *sensation* we commit ourselves to the view that sense-data are mental events. *Sensum* is very much the best. But it is generally used to mean a 'third kind' of entity, neither mental nor physical. And although we are not at present in a position to assert that sense-data are physical or that they are mental, neither are we in a position to deny either of these alternatives. (Thus 'sense-data are sensa' is not a tautology, but a synthetic proposition.)

An incidental virtue of the term *sense-datum* is that it enables us to give a brief and intelligible account of the traditional theories concerning perception and the external world, and so to make us use the work of our predecessors without wasting time in tedious historico-lexicographical investigations.

CHAPTER II. NAÏVE REALISM AND THE ARGUMENT FROM ILLUSION

It is now clear that all our beliefs about the material world are based directly or indirectly upon the sensing of visual and tactual sense-data, meaning by 'based' that if we were not from time to time acquainted with visual and tactual sense-data, these beliefs could neither exist nor be justified. But is this their whole basis? Plainly it is not. To see that it is not, we have only to consider any such belief, and ask what exactly it is that the belief is about. For instance, I believe that this tomato is red, smooth, soft, and sweet-tasting. It is obvious that this is not a belief about a sense-datum. For no single sense-datum has all these qualities. Further, I believe that the tomato is ripe and vitaminous: and these characteristics do not seem to characterize any sense-datum at all. It follows that though sensing is *necessary* for the holding of such beliefs, it is certainly not *sufficient*. There must be some further process or act, by which the subjects of such beliefs are brought before the mind.

It is true that according to Berkeley and many other philosophers material things are wholly composed of sense-data. But even so, sensing would not be sufficient. For even on this view, a material thing is not *a* sense-datum, but a complicated *group* of sense-data. And it is plain that even if all the members of the group are sensed, yet the group itself is not given in sense. In order to bring the group before the mind, we should have to 'collect' the sense-

data (to use a term of Mr. Russell's)—or perhaps this would *be* the bringing of it before the mind. And the collecting would have to include at least two processes distinct from sensing. The sense-data are sensed successively, so that memory will be required. And even when (with the help of memory) a number of sense-data past and present are assembled before the mind, we have still to recognize that they stand in such and such relations to each other, say of similarity or spatial collocation or what not; otherwise, though aware of the members, we are not aware of the group. Nor would that be all. For it would probably be admitted, first, that such a group would have no finite number of members; and secondly, that sense-data are private, i.e. that no one mind can sense sense-data sensed by any other mind, while the group is not restricted to any one mind's sense-data. It would follow that no one mind *could* sense all the sense-data which (on this view) compose an object. And even if these admissions were not made, still it is certain that hardly any one who entertains beliefs about a particular material object has in fact sensed more than a very few of the data which are alleged to compose it; it is quite possible that he has only sensed one of them, i.e. has 'just glanced at' the thing as we say, or 'just felt it'. Thus the so-called collecting will have to include the *supplementation* of the given members of the group by not-given ones; i.e. the knowing or believing that in addition to the colour-patches, pressures, smells etc., actually given to me as I observe the object, there is a vastly—perhaps infinitely—greater multitude of colour-patches, pressures, smells, etc., related to them in the appropriate object-composing manner, but not actually given to me at all. The most we could say would be that, in the case of beliefs based directly on observation, at least one member of the group must have been actually sensed by the holder of the belief, and each of the members *could* be sensed by some observer, human or animal.

Thus even if a material object is wholly composed of sense-data, sensing is not a sufficient (though it is a necessary) condition of holding beliefs about it. Some further mental process or attitude is needed. And *a fortiori* this will be true on other theories concerning the nature of material objects. Since the time of Thomas Reid, this further mental process has often been called 'perceiving':

thus it would often be said that we *sense* colour-patches, noises, pressures, etc., but we *perceive* tables, mountains and tomatoes. This usage of 'perceive' is very convenient and has been adopted by the majority of philosophers and psychologists. But unfortunately there is an ambiguity in it. Let us consider any illusion of sense, e.g. seeing double, and let us suppose that the observer is actually deceived by it. Everybody agrees that he senses two sense-data. Are we to say that he perceives two candles or not? I think the majority of philosophers would say that he does. If so, it is possible to perceive what does not exist (though of course what we *sense* always exists when we sense it) and it would be necessary to distinguish between true and false perceiving.

But in another sense of 'perceive', and one that comes closer to ordinary speech, it is not possible to perceive what does not exist, and the distinction between true and false does not apply to perceiving at all. In this sense 'I perceive a candle' means: (1) I sense a sense-datum; (2) this sense-datum is related to a candle in a peculiar and intimate manner; (3) there is no other thing to which this sense-datum is related in that manner. In this sense, perceiving is not a specific form of consciousness, like acquaintance or believing or wondering; it does indeed involve a specific form of consciousness, namely sensing (acquaintance with sense-data), but that which it involves in addition is not a form of consciousness at all—it is a merely *de facto* relation. (Hence certain philosophers, believing that acquaintance too is a relation, have described perceiving as a *relative product* like 'being a nephew of'.) It follows that if a material thing is in this sense perceived, then that thing necessarily exists. But this by no means implies that all perceiving is true (or 'veridical'). It cannot indeed be called false, but that is only because it cannot be called true either; just as, if Smith has a brother and I have met Smith, there is a complex involving me, Smith, and Smith's brother, but this complex is not the sort of thing to which the distinction between true and false applies. It follows too that just as I can meet Smith without knowing or even guessing that he has a brother, so too I can perceive a material object and yet not know or even guess that that object exists: either because I believe that it does *not* exist (or is somewhere else), as when Jones whom I believe to be dead or in Greenland en-

ters the room, and I do not recognize him but take him for some one else—yet it is certainly Jones himself that I have 'perceived';—or again because I just have no conscious attitude towards it at all, whether of knowledge or of belief, true or false, or even of wondering. Yet still I should be 'perceiving' that object of whose very existence I was utterly ignorant, provided I was sensing a sense-datum which was in fact related to it in the required manner.

Both these senses of the term 'perceive'—both that in which it stands for a specific mental process capable of truth and falsity, and that in which it stands merely for a complex situation—are of great importance. Which of the two usages are we to adopt? Common sense, or rather common language, points on the whole to the second, though not without vacillation. (Of course it does not very often use the word 'perceive' at all, but prefers to speak of 'seeing', 'touching', 'smelling', etc.) Usually when we speak of seeing a lion or smelling a rose, we do mean to convey that the lion or the rose exist. Also we say when looking for some distant object in the dusk, 'I am not sure whether I see anything or not'; whereas if 'seeing' meant a specific act of consciousness (as 'believing' or 'apprehending' does) we could hardly fail to know whether we were seeing anything or not. On the other hand, we do sometimes say that a delirious person 'sees things that aren't there' or 'hears' non-existent voices; but when we do, we are apt to correct ourselves and say 'of course he didn't really see them, for there was nothing there to be seen, only he was in such a state that he thought he did'. (The state presumably was one of sensing certain sense-data, and this was due to his abnormal physical and mental condition.)

In this situation, the only safe course is to avoid the word 'perceive' altogether. It might indeed seem allowable to adopt the *first* sense of the word and use it as a name for that other mode of consciousness, additional to sensing, which is presupposed by the holding of beliefs about material objects; for we must have some name for this. We should then be following the majority of the philosophers and psychologists of recent times. Since the term is in any case mainly a technical one, does it matter much whether we follow the usage of ordinary language or not? But unfortunately there are several philosophers, including Professor G. E. Moore, who have adopted the *second* sense. And although we can perhaps afford to neglect ordinary language, we cannot neglect these philosophers. But neither can we follow them, for the first sense of the word is equally familiar, and if we adopted the second, many readers would certainly be misled. And as both senses are extremely important for our inquiry, we shall have to invent substitutes for both.

First, we must find some name for the non-sensuous mode of consciousness of which we have spoken. For the present we shall simply call it *perceptual consciousness*. Later on, when we come to discuss it more fully, we shall suggest a more definite term. But for the present it seems desirable to use a vague one which commits us to as little as possible.

Secondly, we need some name for the situation where a sense-datum is sensed which is related in a peculiar manner (to be discussed later) to one material thing and one only. We shall describe this as *having a material thing present to one's senses*. There is now no excuse for mixing this up with *being perceptually conscious of a material thing*. It is clear that an object can be 'present to my senses' when I am mistaken about its nature, or even when I am unaware of its very existence: thus the straight stick is present to the senses of the man who takes it to be bent; and the house which I pass every day, without ever noticing it, is repeatedly present to my senses, but I am never aware of its existence.

Also, thirdly, we need a name for the relation subsisting between the sense-datum and the material thing when the material thing is present to the senses of the being who is sensing that sense-datum. For the present we shall follow Professor Moore in calling it the relation of *belonging to*.

It is plain from this discussion that there are two main questions which confront us.

1. What is perceptual consciousness and how is it related to sensing?
2. What is the relation between a sense-datum and a material thing when the thing is present to the senses of the being who senses the sense-datum? i.e. what is the relation of belonging to?

These two questions are different, but they are not entirely separable. Any answer to one greatly narrows the range of possible answers to the other,

so that to a large extent they can be discussed together. Also we shall find that in discussing question (2) we cannot avoid saying something about the nature of material things themselves. For instance, if it be suggested that the relation of belonging to is that of member to group, we must perforce discuss the view that a material thing is a group of sense-data.

It is convenient to begin by discussing certain plausible but erroneous answers to our questions. And it is natural to consider first the view called *Naïve Realism*. The name is not a very suitable one (for the view is hardly a faithful analysis of the unreflective assumptions of the plain or naïve man), but it is well known and serves as a convenient label.

Naïve Realism offers answers to both our questions. First, it holds that my consciousness of an object is the *knowing that* there exists an object to which the sense-datum now sensed by me belongs. Perceptual consciousness would not be acquaintance or intuitive apprehension of a particular, as sensing is. It would be knowledge about, or apprehension of a fact. But it would be like sensing in that it would be knowledge, and not mere belief or mere taking for granted.

Secondly, Naïve Realism holds that in the case of a visual or tactual sense-datum, belonging to means the same as *being a part of the surface of*: in that literal sense in which the surface of one side of this page is part of the whole surface of this page. Thus if we ask a Naïve Realist what sort of thing it is whose existence he knows of in an act of perceptual consciousness, he answers: It is that which visual and tactual sense-data are parts of the surface of. And having a surface, it must be a three-dimensional entity located in space. No doubt he would add that it persists through time and has various causal properties, and that it makes no difference to these spatial and temporal characteristics and these causal properties whether we sense the sense-data belonging to it or not; for this is universally admitted to be part of the meaning of the term 'material thing'.

It is commonly held that the *Argument from Illusion* (as it is called) is sufficient to refute Naïve Realism. And this seems substantially true. But what exactly the argument proves is not very clear. The fact seems to be that there are really two distinct arguments: for want of better names we will call them respectively the Phenomenological Argument and the Causal Argument. Contrary to common opinion, the first is by far the more important. It seeks to show directly that there are visual and tactual sense-data which cannot be identical with parts of the surfaces of material objects. The second seeks to show that visual and tactual sense-data only exist while certain processes, other than sensing but contemporary with it, are going on in the nervous system and perhaps in the mind of the being who senses them. And it is inferred from this that they cannot be identical with parts of the surfaces of objects; for such an object (and therefore the surfaces of it) *ex hypothesi* continues to exist at times when we are not sensing, and it is now contended that at those times the sense-data do not exist.

It is not at all easy to state either of these arguments clearly, and in a form which will survive obvious criticisms. The first thing to do is to say what the term 'illusion' means. We must be careful not to define it in causal terms, for this, as we shall see, would lead to a vicious circle. I suggest the following provisional definition: An illusory sense-datum of sight or touch is a sense-datum which is such that we tend to take it to be part of the surface of a material object, but if we take it so we are wrong. It is not necessary that we should *actually* so take it. Thus if I were to see a mirage knowing it to be a mirage, I should not be deceived. But the sense-datum would be none the less illusory: since I do *tend* to take it for part of the surface of a pool of water, and if I actually did I should be wrong. Nor have we begged the question against Naïve Realism in saying this. For we have only been saying what the term 'illusory' *means*: whether there are really any instances of it, remains to be seen.

Does the notion of illusoriness apply to data of the other senses? Could there be an illusory sound or smell? It seems clear that there could. But here for 'being part of the surface of' we must substitute something like 'emanating from'. By *s* emanates from O we should mean roughly (1) *s* is caused by O, (2) *s* is more intense in the neighborhood of O than elsewhere.

Now there is no doubt that there are illusory visual and tactual sense-data in the sense defined. Let us begin with visual ones. First, *Perspective* provides plenty of instances. We all know that stereoscopic vision is possible only within a relatively narrow range. Outside this range there is what is called Collapse of Planes, and objects undergo various sorts of 'distortion'. Thus a distant hillside which is full of protuberances, and slopes upwards at quite a gentle angle, will appear flat and vertical, like a scene painted on cardboard. This means that the sense-datum, the colour-expanse which we sense, actually *is* flat and vertical. And if so, it cannot be part of the surface of something protuberant and gently sloping.

Again in *Reflection* the sense-datum is dislocated from the object and reversed as to right and left. Often too it is 'distorted', i.e. its shape differs from the shape of the object, as with the reflection of a tree in water ruffled by a breeze, or that of a lamp in the polished surface of a shoe. In *Refraction* there is distortion and commonly dislocation too, as with things seen through uneven glass. The like occurs with *physiological* disorders: as for instance in seeing double, where there are two sense-data which cannot both be parts of the surface of the object, for at least one is in the wrong place, and moreover both are flattened. (It is worth remembering that in binocular vision things not in focus are always seen double; and that in the visual experience of an insect every piece of matter is probably multiplied fifty or a hundred fold.) The phenomena of giddiness provide an analogous instance, particularly that giddiness which precedes a fainting fit, where the walls of the room not only 'turn round' but 'move in and out'. *After-images,* which are sense-data completely cut off as it were from the thing, changing and moving independently of its changes and motions, and even capable of existing after its destruction, are the transitional cases between these distorted and dislocated sense-data, and completely 'wild' ones which are characteristic of *Hallucination*. In hallucination the sense-datum fails to belong to any object in any way at all, though of course the sentient still *takes* it to belong to one. Total hallucination in which the entire field of view consists of 'wild' data is probably confined to lunatics and delirious patients. But partial hallucination, where part of the field of view is wild and part is not, is far from uncommon; for emotion and habitual expectations often cause one to see what one expects to see, for instance (to take some cases from the writer's own experience) they cause one to see 3 instead of 8 when one is waiting for No. 3 bus, or to see a log of wood with protruding branches as a recumbent black and white cow, or a cyclist carrying a milk-can in one hand as a pedestrian leading a goat. In such cases the sense-datum is 'cooked' and supplemented by the mind. And such 'cookery' may be negative as well as positive: some part of what is physically before our eyes has at a certain moment no visual sense-datum belonging to it though other parts have (Negative Hallucination). The failure to see misprints, and sometimes entire words, will illustrate this. When we see the right word instead of the misprint—the most common case—there is a combination of negative and positive hallucination.

Nor must we forget that there are illusions of touch as well as of sight, though they are much less frequent. It will not do to say, with some philosophers, that at least all tactual sense-data are parts of the surfaces of material objects, even if many visual ones are not. Thus a man whose leg has been amputated feels pressure upon his now non-existent foot: i.e. he has a tactual sense-datum similar to those which he used to have before; but there is now no foot with part of whose surface it could be identical. Again, a case has been described in which the patient's brain was operated upon while he remained conscious: when the appropriate region of it was stimulated with a mild electric current, he reported that he felt as if some one was stroking his finger, though nobody was. Thus he sensed a certain tactual sense-datum in the absence of the material thing to which such a datum would ordinarily belong. It is less often realized that there is something corresponding to perspective in touch. Thus a sixpence feels bigger if laid on the tongue than if laid on the back of the hand; and a pair of fixed compass-points drawn across the face appear to diverge as they pass the lips. And it has been pointed out that there are occasional after-images of touch. Thus when my hat is taken off my head, I still continue to feel it there for a time: and the same is true if some small object such as a match-box is placed on one's head for a minute or two and then removed.

The Phenomenological form of the Argument from illusion simply points to such facts as these and contends that they directly refute Naïve Realism. And it certainly does seem clear that there are a great many visual and tactual sense-data which cannot possibly be parts of the surface of material objects in any natural sense of the words 'surface' and 'part'. It follows that perceptual consciousness cannot always be a form of knowing, as the Naïve Realists say it is, for it is certainly sometimes erroneous. The Causal Argument uses the same facts in another way. According to it, they show that sense-data vary with variations in the medium between the observer and the object, with variations in the observer's sense-organs, and with variations in his nervous system. And we never find a sense-datum in the absence of a sense-organ and a nervous system, and in sight, hearing and smell we always find a medium as well. Such constant conjunction and concomitant variation, it is urged, are obviously signs of causal dependence. Moreover, this causal dependence is in all cases a dependence on the *brain*. For the states of the intervening medium and of the sense-organs and afferent nerves only make a difference to the sense-datum in so far as they make a difference to processes in that: otherwise they are irrelevant. And the state of the external object itself is only relevant in so far as it indirectly affects the brain, while in hallucination the external object is dispensed with altogether. Further, this dependence of sense-data upon the brain is a *complete* dependence. There is no quality possessed by sense-data which is not subject to this concomitant variation. Thus sense-data are not merely affected by brain-processes, but entirely produced by them. It even begins to seem conceivable that they are themselves cerebral events qualified in a certain way.

If all this is so, no sense-datum can continue to exist in the absence of the cerebral processes which generate it, and therefore no sense-datum can be part of the surface of an external (i.e. extra-cerebral) object, e.g. of a table. If the sense-datum is a cerebral event, this is obvious. If it is produced by cerebral events without being one, the conclusion still follows. For when we cease from sensing, the table *ex hypothesi* remains unchanged. But it now appears that when we cease from sensing, the sense-datum itself ceases to exist: it is not merely that the colour-patch or pressure ceases to be a datum, i.e. ceases to be sensed by a mind; it is altogether abolished. (Not that it depends for its existence upon being sensed—that is absurd, since sensing is a form of knowing—but upon another process which only occurs when sensing does.) But if no change occurs in the object when I cease from sensing, then the abolition of the sense-datum cannot be a change in the object, and therefore the sense-datum cannot have been a part of its surface; and we may add, cannot have been a constituent of the object in any other way either.

It might be thought that both arguments could be met by drawing a distinction between *normal* and *abnormal* sense-data. We should then say that normal sense-data of sight and touch *are* parts of the surfaces of material things and are *not* dependent on processes in the observer's brain: while abnormal ones are dependent on processes in the brain and are not part of the surfaces of material things, but are related to the things in some more complicated way. The material thing would still be the remote though not the immediate cause of them, and they might still resemble parts of its surface though they would not *be* such parts. This is a considerable modification in the original theory, but quite a plausible one. We should also have to modify the original account of perceptual consciousness. When I sense an abnormal sense-datum, we must say I merely *believe* that there exists a material thing part of whose surface it is: only when I sense a normal one do I *know* that there exists such a material thing.

But this will not do. The difficulty is that there is no qualitative difference between normal sense-data as such and abnormal sense-data as such. Indeed the whole trouble about abnormal sense-data is precisely that they simulate normal ones. Otherwise it would not even be possible for us to be deceived by them; they would be strange, but they would not be illusory. We shall give two examples. The abnormal crooked sense-datum of a straight stick standing in water is qualitatively indistinguishable from a normal sense-datum of a crooked stick. Again a mirror-image of a right-hand glove 'looks exactly like' a real left-hand glove; i.e. the two sense-data are indistinguishable, though one is abnormal, the other normal. Is it not incredible that two entities so similar in all these qualities should really be so utterly different: that the one should be a real constituent of a material object, wholly independent of the observer's mind and organism, while the other is merely the fleeting product of his cerebral processes?

We may also appeal to considerations of continuity. When a cricket ball, for instance, is seen from twenty yards off, the sense-datum is flat and therefore abnormal. From a short distance, say two yards, which is within the range of stereoscopic vision, the sense-datum is no longer flat but bulgy and accordingly normal. (We will suppose that there are no complications arising from bad light or drugs or ocular disorders.) But what about intermediate distances? I start from two yards off, and walk slowly backwards, keeping my eye on the ball. At a certain point in my walk, the sense-datum just begins to be flattened; and this must mean that the normal sense-datum is replaced by an abnormal one. There is all the difference in the world between these two sense-data, if the theory is correct. The first is a physical entity, which continues to exist whether my body is present or not, the second is a mere cerebral product. We should expect at least a jerk or a flicker as the one is replaced by the other. But in point of fact we find nothing of the sort. There is a sensibly continuous transition from the bright bulgy patch sensed from two yards off to the faint, small, flat one sensed from twenty yards off, without any break at all. Moreover, if the last normal member of the series to be taken (and according to the theory there must be a last one), then it will be possible to find an abnormal member which differs from it as little as you please, in size, colour, and bulginess. Now it seems most extraordinary that there should be a total difference of nature where there is only an infinitesimal difference of quality. It also seems most extraordinary that so radical a replacement should be brought about by an infinitesimal backward movement of the observer's body.

Nor is the other part of the theory more plausible. There is no discernible difference in our consciousness when we pass from sensing a normal sense-datum to sensing an abnormal one, or vice versa. In both cases there is acquaintance with something, and in both cases there is also 'perceptual consciousness'. What the nature of this 'perceptual consciousness' may be we are to consider later, but certainly it is the same in both cases. It is impossible to hold that it is knowledge in the one and mere belief in the other.

It might indeed be thought that we could avoid this particular difficulty by making the knowledge less determinate. Might there not be a different sorts of 'belonging to'? Normal sense-data might then belong to the thing in one way and abnormal in some other way. And this would enable us to admit that the consciousness is of the same nature in both cases. In each case, it might then be maintained, it is knowledge; and what we know is that there exists some material thing or other to which this sense-datum belongs in some way or other; in which way, and therefore also what particular sort of material thing, would remain to be determined later. But apart from the difficulty of understanding how this determining is to be done, the existence of hallucinations is a fatal objection to the theory. In hallucination, for instance in the visions of delirium, the sense-datum is completely wild; it does not belong to any material thing in any way at all. The pink sense-datum, to take the usual case, not only does not belong to a pink rat, as the sentient himself assumes: it does not *belong to* anything, and indeed owns no allegiance of any sort except to the disordered nervous system which generates it.

Thus if these two arguments are correct, Naïve Realism is certainly false. If they are correct, it cannot be held that all visual and tactual sense-data are parts of the surfaces of material objects, and considerations of continuity suggest strongly that none are. Nor can it be held that all instances of perceptual consciousness are instances of knowing: and it is strongly suggested that none are. The positive conclusion is that all sense-data are produced by processes in the brains of the beings who sense them.

Both arguments seem very strong ones. But unfortunately both are open to objection. We shall find on examination that the Phenomenological Argument survives with but slight alteration. But the Causal Argument has to be radically restated, and when this has been done, its conclusions turn out to be much less important than they seemed, and to admit of two entirely different interpretations.

The objection against both arguments is in essence this: that both of them tacitly assume in their premises the truth of the very theory which they profess to disprove.

The Phenomenological Argument relies entirely upon the citation of negative instances. With regard to each instance it argues as follows: 'Here is a par-

ticular sense-datum *s* and here is a particular material thing M. According to Naïve Realism *s* ought to be part of the surface of M. But it is obvious on inspection that *s* is not part of the surface of M because M is in another place or because it has another shape or size.' Now unless we know such facts about M, the argument obviously breaks down. How can we know that the flat sense-datum is not part of the surface of the cricket-ball, unless we know that there really is a cricket-ball and that it really does have a surface which is spherical? Or how do we know that the reflection of the glove is dislocated as to position and reversed as to right and left, unless we know where the glove itself is and how its parts are arranged? And even with 'wild' sense-data there is the same difficulty. The man with the amputated leg is aware of a tactual sense-datum, which he takes to be located on the surface of his foot. Here it is said there is not really any material object at all for the sense-datum to belong to. But how can we be sure that there is not? Clearly only by knowing that where the foot purports to be there is in fact some *other* piece of matter, e.g. a chair-leg or a volume of air. In the same way we profess to know a number of facts about mirrors, physical media, lenses, eyes, and so forth.

But where do we get this knowledge about material objects which the argument demands? Clearly from observation (how else?)—that is, from sensing sense-data. Must we not assume that *these* sense data at least are, and are known to be, parts of the surfaces of objects, in order to show that others are not? Thus with regard to these sense-data, and with regard to these acts of perceptual consciousness, Naïve Realism would have to be true. And we should be refuting Naïve Realism at one point only by assuming its truth at another.

Now I suppose that every one feels that there is something wrong with this objection, and that it does not really save Naïve Realism. Indeed the Phenomenological Argument is in the opposite case from those sceptical arguments which Hume mentions. It admits of an answer, and yet it does not cease to produce conviction. The truth is, I think, that the objection does hold against many people who have used the argument, but that by stating our case more carefully we can avoid it: and that in two ways.

First, we might admit that we do have knowledge of the existence and nature of the cricket-ball, the glove, the chair leg; that this knowledge is essential to the argument; and that we do get it from sensing sense-data. But, we might say, there is no reason to assume that we get it in the way Naïve Realism alleges. It might be necessary not just to sense one sense-datum, but to compare a large number of sense-data and find that they stand in certain relations to each other. There might really be a relation of 'belonging to'—as indeed there obviously is—and we might be capable of knowing that particular sense-data belong to particular material things: and yet this relation might be different from what Naïve Realism thinks it is, e.g. it might be much more complex or less direct, or it might be many-one instead of one-one.

But secondly, we are not obliged to admit as much as this. All that the argument strictly requires is that we possess the conception of *material thing-hood* or know what the term 'material thing' *means*. Knowledge about particular material things is not needed. We might have this conception without knowing whether it had any instances or not. (Not perhaps without *believing* that it had some, but the belief need never have been true.) Now there are in the conception of material thinghood two important elements. On the one hand, by 'a material thing' is meant something which can be present to the senses from many different places and in many different manners. It must be *multiply accessible*. Thus if there is anything which is a material thing, it must be possible for a multitude of different sense-data to belong to it. But also by 'a material thing' is meant something which is a single three-dimensional whole, having one closed surface, one shape, one size, and one position in relation to other material things. It must be *spatially unitary*.

But if Naïve Realism were right it would be impossible for anything to possess both multiple accessibility and spatial unity at the same time. For among the multitude of visual and tactual sense-data which the Naïve Realist and every one else regard as belonging to one single material thing M, the greater part will not fit together into one single three-dimensional whole. They differ from each other in size, in shape, in respect of flatness and solidity, in respect of amount of detail (thus of two sense-data alleged to belong to the same toothed wheel one is circular and the other serrated). And some are spatially dissociated from the rest as in double vision, or as reflections and mirages are dissociated from normal views. Thus they cannot all be parts of the surface of one unitary three-dimensional entity. And we know that they cannot, merely by inspecting the data themselves. We do not have to know that there is in fact such a spatially unitary entity, or that all these sense-data in fact belong to it. For we are only asserting that *if* there is such an entity to which they all belong, then they cannot all be parts of its surface.

The Causal version of the Argument from Illusion is not nearly so easy to defend. It is constantly talking of physical media, of mirrors, lenses and prisms, of drugs and physical diseases, and especially of sense-organs, nerves and brains. Thus it presupposes a vast amount of detailed knowledge concerning a variety of material objects. And this knowledge is certainly not *a priori*. It is got from observation: it presupposes both sensing and what we have called perceptual consciousness. Or, if it is not knowledge but only a body of beliefs, then the argument is proportionally weakened; and even so the beliefs are still based on sensing and on perceptual consciousness. Thus whatever the argument proves, it certainly cannot have the slightest tendency to prove that there are not material objects to which sense-data belong, or that if there are, they are not accessible to our minds; otherwise it would be contradicting its own premises. Yet it is frequently thought to prove these things. It even begins to seem doubtful whether it can refute Naïve Realism, which is a particular theory *about* this relation of belonging to, and about the accessibility of material objects to our minds. At any rate, we can be fairly certain that many people have used it who were themselves naïve realists with regard to the observation of mirrors, lenses, brains, nervous systems, and scientific apparatus. Such people, it has been said, are 'naïve realists in the laboratory and subjective idealists outside it'. Or perhaps they are naïve realists with regard to the observations of common men. There is many a thinker who assumes without question that his own sense-data were parts of the surfaces of the eyes or nerves or brains which he has examined, while he assures us that the sense-data sensed by his patients or his readers are mere products of their nervous systems, having but a dubious correspondence with Reality. I pass over the even more extraordinary *naïveté* of those philosophers who argue that all sense-data are dependent upon the brain, and conclude that they depend upon the mind—and then, having done this, gravely urge that the whole material world is but a mental construction or a set of vicious abstractions, so that there are really no brains at all.

Despite these gross confusions in the statement of it, the Argument from Illusion obviously does prove something, even in its Causal form: and we must now try to see what. Obviously we shall never clear the matter up so long as we remain at the standpoint of Physiology. Let us be quite plain about this. An inquiry about 'belonging to' and about perceptual consciousness is concerned (among other things) with the foundations of Physiology itself: for all the empirical sciences are based on observation. No proposition in Physiology can possibly be *more* probable than such observational propositions as 'This that I now see is a human head', 'This is a lens', 'That is a microscope': it can hardly fail to be *less* probable. No doubt some observational propositions are false (else there would be no illusion). But unless a great many of them have at least a considerable probability, no proposition in Physiology has any probability at all. And as a matter of fact some observational propositions are so obviously true (whatever the correct analysis of them may be) that no argument purporting to prove them false can possibly have any weight in comparison.

It is necessary, then, to give up the 'external' standpoint of Physiology, and to take up instead what is called the 'immanent' standpoint, that of the individual experiment himself. We must try to return to what is indubitable, putting all prepossessions (including scientific prepossessions) out of our minds. This requires a peculiar mental effort, somewhat like that required when we look at a picture or a view in an aesthetic way, discarding the practical attitude of everyday life. We have to go back to the sense-data themselves: for they are what we are quite certain of. This argument which we are examining, if it has anything in it, must be based upon facts about sense-data, and these ought to be discoverable.

Now what we are acquainted with at any one time is not one single sense-datum but a number of generically different sense-data. Indeed at most moments of our waking life we are acquainted with tactual, auditory and organic sense-data, and usually with visual ones also, if we are not blind. Let us call this group of simultaneously given data the *Totum Datum*.

The Casual form of the Argument from Illusion does not so much prove anything, as draw our attention to two very important facts about the organization of this Totum Datum.

1. It points out that at any moment the Totum Datum consists of two parts. The one part consists of what we may call *somatic* sense-data: the other of what we may call *environmental* sense-data. When I call the first set of data 'somatic' I do not mean to imply that they belong to a particular material object called my own body, though I think that as a matter of fact this is nearly always true. And likewise when I call the second set 'environmental' I do not mean to imply that they belong to material objects other than my own body. By 'somatic' sense-data I only mean those which I ordinarily *take* to belong to my own body, and by 'environmental' ones, those which I ordinarily take to belong to other objects. That I do habitually take some to belong to the one, and others to the others, is perfectly certain, whether I am right or wrong in my takings.

2. The second thing pointed out is that somatic and environmental data *vary concomitantly* in certain respects, and this concomitant variation never ceases so long as there is a Totum Datum at all. For instance, visual data vary in size, shape, position, and intensity with variations in kinaesthetic data.

(Of course there are many other sets of parts into which a particular Totum Datum may be divided besides this: e.g. into vivid data and faint ones, into extended and non-extended ones, into those taken to belong to solids, liquids and gases respectively. And there are many other types of concomitant variation which it may display. But *every* Totum Datum can be divided into a somatic and an environmental part, and in every Totum Datum there is concomitant variation of these two.)

We may sum up the thesis as follows: Somatic and environmental sense-data are always co-present and co-variant. We shall express this by saying that *the Totum Datum is always somato-centric*. This is what those who use the Causal form of the Argument from Illusion are really trying to show—little as they may be aware of it.

But this established, what follows? It is not at all easy to say. But certainly it does not follow that all sense-data are products of the brain (though of course there may be other reasons for thinking that they are).

For in the somato-centric *totum* there is no reason to give priority to the somatic side rather than to the environmental. What we always find is both sides together, and a *concomitant* variation between them. Of course it is also true that a variation on the somatic side sometimes *precedes* a particular variation on the other side. Thus the staggering of the whole field of view when one is about to faint is preceded by a marked change in the whole quality of the somatic datum. But equally it is sometimes the other way about. Thus I am aware of the succession of visual data purporting to belong to an approaching cricket-ball before I feel the blow on my hand or head.

Thus if somato-centricity is a sign of causal dependence, it is no one-way dependence of the environmental on the somatic. But is it a sign of dependence at all? It can indeed be taken *connectively,* as a sign of dependence. But it can also be taken *selectively.* Let us consider these two alternatives a little.

On the *connective* interpretation, the most we could maintain would be this: that as somatic and environmental data are never in fact found apart, therefore they cannot exist apart. Of course a particular environmental datum could exist without a particular somatic datum, e.g. a distant view of a tree without the feeling of sitting, but not without *some* somatic datum. Equally a particular somatic datum, say a twinge of toothache, could exist without a particular environmental datum, say a square blue patch: but not in the absence of *all* environmental data. We are never wholly destitute of tactual data; and very rarely (if at all) of auditory ones, for what we call 'silence' can be heard. Thus the contention would be that environmental data in general cannot exist without somatic data in general, nor somatic without environmental. The somato-centric *totum* would be a kind of *organic whole*.

Now it is true that on this interpretation the argument does refute Naïve Realism. But it is by no means true that it refutes *all* forms of Realism, as is sometimes thought, i.e. all forms of the theory that there are material objects to which sense-data 'belong', and which exist at times when we are not sensing. For *if* the argument tended to show that in the absence of my body other material objects cease to exist (as what we may call Physiological Idealism maintains), it would equally tend to show that in the absence of other objects my body ceases to exist: for I have no experience of my body existing in isolation. The plausible view for a sceptic to take is rather that nothing exists except this that and the other Totum Datum, each of which is both somatic and environmental at once. On such a theory the environment does not exist without the nervous system, nor the nervous system without the environment (so far as we can speak of such things at all); they are correlatives, and really there is only the whole consisting of both in mutual correlation. This twofold whole would constitute the knowable world, and it would be a series of short-lived somato-centric complexes punctuated by gaps (periods of unconsciousness) containing just nothing at all. And if you will, there is a single unknown something which produces both correlatives alike. I do not say that this theory is true—far from it. But at least it is not stupid, as Physiological Idealism is.

Now let us turn to the *selective* interpretation. According to this, the somatic data are merely *instrumental.* They enable us to be conscious of environmental data. When I have one sort of somatic datum, one sort of environmental datum is revealed to me; when I have another, another. But between environmental and somatic there is no relation of dependence, either mutual or one-sided. What is connected with the somatic datum is the act of sensing, and that only. We may illustrate by an analogy. If I am to select a bun from the counter my hand must be there to pick it up. If I move my hand to the left I pick up bun No. 1, if to the right, bun No. 2. But the bun which I do pick up is in no way dependent upon my hand for its existence, nor my hand upon the bun. Hand plus bun do not form an organic whole, and either could exist without the other. Still less can we say that the hand creates the bun. Physiological Idealism, which says that the somatic datum creates the environmental, is no less absurd than such a 'Manual Idealism' would be. And it is plain that on *this* interpretation of it, somato-centricity is not in the least incompatible even with Naïve Realism. But of course Naïve Realism would still be refuted by the Phenomenological Argument.

We may notice an alternative way of stating this selective theory, according to which the function of the somatic sense-data is obsuration rather than revelation. In the absence of all somatic data, it might be said, we should be conscious of everything that exists. But as this would be very confusing, the somatic data (for good biological reasons) are so arranged as to cut off most things from our view, and leave only a few at any one moment, so that we may be able to act.

We may now consider the further implications of the Selective Theory. The most important is that there is no reason left for believing that colour-patches cease to exist when our eyes are shut, sounds when our ears are removed, prement patches in the absence of our skin, and so on. Of course there was never any reason for thinking that these entities depended in any manner upon the sensing of them, for sensing is a form of knowing. But there did seem to be reason for thinking that they were dependent upon *other* processes contemporary with sensing, namely processes in the brain: the Causal form of the Argument from Illusion seemed to have shown this. However, our criticism of it has revealed that it is thoroughly confused. And it is now open to us to interpret these cerebral processes selectively (or 'instrumentally') like those somatic data which are their overt manifestations. If so, we have no reason for thinking that sense-data do not persist before and after we are acquainted with them, as other *cognita* do. Or, if it sounds odd to speak of unsensed sense-data, we may call them *sensibilia* with Mr. Bertrand Russell, the difference between a sensibile and sense-datum being solely that we are acquainted with the latter and not with the former. (Of course this does not mean that every sensibile exists for ever or in all circumstances. It only means that the not being included in a somato-centric complex does not stop it from existing. And a sensibile could become a sense-datum without any change in its qualities, and vice vera.)

This suggests, though it does not strictly necessitate, a new view of the nature of objects, and of the relation of belonging to. Let us consider the visual and tactual sense-data belonging to the table. It is obvious that there will be no finite number of them, if only because there is no finite number of points of view from which the table can be present to our senses. Thus there will be an infinite multitude of sensibilia belonging to the table. And as all these in any case exist unsensed, why not say that the whole collection of them *is* the table? Would not the collection of them have all the causal and other characteristics which we expect a table to have? (Of course these 'physical' characteristics would be manifested by the collection as a whole, not by the individual sensibilia.) It would follow from this that the relation of 'belonging to' is the same as the relation of member to group. And as for the hallucinatory or wild sense-data which gave so much trouble to Naïve Realism, these we should say exist unsensed like any others. Only, such a sense-datum would either belong to no group at all, and this would constitute its 'wildness': or not to the sort of group which has physical characteristics—in which case it would belong to an object of some sort, but not to an object 'in this world'.

Such a theory is of course different from Naïve Realism. Yet I think we may maintain that it gives the Naïve Realist all that he really wanted, and indeed more than he dared to ask. For what he really wanted was a theory in which visual and tactual sense-data were somehow *constituents* of the material object itself, not mere effects or representatives of it. He wanted to interpret the statement. '*this* is a table' as literally as possible. Since 'this' is the sense-datum with which I am now acquainted, it obviously cannot literally *be* a table. No one could suppose that a patch of colour or a pressure is the object that you can sit on or have your dinner off. But if it is in some way a constituent of the table, that is the next best thing. And when asked what sort of constituent it is, the Naïve Realist merely jumped to the most obvious answer. Moreover, the Selective Theory gives him more than he hoped for, because it allows him to say that not merely visual and tactual data, but also sounds, smells and tastes, are constituents of the object.

It is evident that the Selective Theory is extremely attractive; the more so because it makes the 'secondary' qualities no less part of Nature than spatial, temporal, and causal characteristics. Thus it heals the breach between the Nature of the poets and the Nature of the physicists, and perhaps no one but a poet could do full justice to it. In spite of these attractions, the theory has been rejected by almost all philosophers. The usual arguments against it do not however appear very strong.

It is sometimes thought to be just obvious that there cannot be unsensed sensibilia, e.g. colour-patches or sounds with which no one is acquainted, in which case the Selective Theory would not even be worth discussion. Now of course it may in fact be true that there are none, but I cannot see that it is obvious. Of course if by 'sensing', one means *sense-datum-genesis,* it is plausible to say that what is sensed cannot exist apart from sensing; this would be just a way of saying that colour-patches, sounds, etc., are events. But if that what one means by 'sensing,' then one has got to face the possibility that 'sensing' can go on in the absence of minds. That the coming-into-being of a sound or colour-patch is a pyschical (or a physiological) process must be proved, not merely assumed. Or if its psychical nature is a matter of *definition,* so that sensing just means the coming into being a psychical event which is coloured, or noisy, or hot, then the question has been begged against the Selective Theory in the definition. It must be proved, and not merely assumed, that there is any real process answering to the definition. For the whole point of the Selective Theory is to maintain that there is no process which is both the genesis of a colour-patch or sound, and psychical in character, i.e. that there is in *this* sense of the word 'sensing' no sensing at all.

But it is surely plain that sensing does not ordinarily means anything of the sort. If it means what it ordinarily means, viz. acquaintance or intuitive awareness, then it is obvious that sense-data are not dependent on sensing, even if they are dependent upon some other process which accompanies it (which, as we have seen, has not yet been shown). Even if they are psychical events, they are still not in any way dependent upon the sensing of them. For to say that anything, even so humble an entity as a sense-datum, is dependent for its existence or for any of its qualities upon our being aware of it, is to deny that there is any such thing as awareness; and thereby to contradict oneself.

Secondly, the Selectivist is asked whether he really thinks that roses are red in the dark and that bells are noisy in a vacuum. This is a silly objection. The Selective Theory does not say that red sensibilia continue to exist in *all* conditions, but only that they continue to exist outside the somato-centric complexes. It can perfectly well hold that in the absence of a source of light nothing is coloured, and that when the light is altered, red sensibilia are replaced, say, by grey ones. (Of course prement sensibilia would be unaffected.) And there might be coloured sensibilia which are not accessible to human senses at all, and which still exist in what we call darkness. Thus to living creatures otherwise constituted, X-rays might reveal sensibilia with which no human being can be acquainted.

Thirdly, with regard to the so-called Secondary Qualities, the Selectivist is asked to say *which* colour belongs to the rose when nobody is looking at it. For when it is being looked at, it appears to have one colour to A, another to B, another to C and so on *ad indefinitum.* The answer is obvious. It has them all. Or rather all these sensibilia, each with its colour-quality, are constituents of the rose. We need to have a more catholic conception of the rose's nature. A sees only one of the colours. But he must not suppose that if this colour belongs to the rose when his eyes are shut, then no other colour belongs to it. What B sees or C or D (to say nothing of non-human sentients) belong to it just as much. There is no colour which is *the* colour of the rose at a given moment, as there is a colour which is *the* colour of this patch which I am now sensing. Or if you insist on speaking of 'the colour' of the rose you must mean by this a certain class or series of colours.

A similar reply may be made to a similar objection about *intensity.* How loud is the sound of a waterfall in the unvisited wilds of Labrador? The reply is that what the objector calls 'the sound' of the waterfall is really an infinitely numerous group of sounds each having its own degree of loudness; and these degrees would range from a certain maximum, characteristic of that particular waterfall at that particular moment, all the way down to zero.

These two objections and the replies to them suggest another, which is perhaps the one most commonly urged. Does not the Selective Theory make the world exceedingly complicated? Things appear to grow larger and brighter as we walk towards them, and to alter in their shapes as we move about. The Selective Theory says that all these shapes, sizes and brightnesses persist in our absence, and that the observer's motion merely reveals now one now another of them. This is odd enough. But when we consider the more striking forms of illusion, the result is even odder. The sense-data sensed in the various types of reflection and refraction, in double vision, in after-sensation, and in all kinds of physiological and psychological disorders—all these are real constituents of the external world and quite independent of the minds and bodies of those who sense them. The abnormal state or situation of the observer's organism merely serves to reveal to him what is hidden from other people. For instance, if a drunkard sees double, both of the sense-data which he senses are independent of him and of his organism, and exist when his eyes are shut; but a man is not able to sense the second one unless he first gets his eyes into an unusual state by dosing himself with alcohol or in some other way. Nor must we forget the sense-data of other animals. When the table is present to my senses, I generally see a single brown patch; but the fly probably sees a hundred. Yet the fly's data are just as real as mine, and they persist in its absence, just as mine persist in my absence.

In short, all the sense-data that any one senses from any place at any time in any surroundings, be he healthy or diseased, mad or sane, drunk or sober, insect or man—all these exist in his absence and are real constituents of the material world. Every observer counts for one and nobody for more than one. Thus even the simplest-seeming object will really be an infinitely multitudinous and infinitely complicated swarm of miscellaneous sensibilia. Surely such a multiplication of entities is monstrous and incredible? Can the world really be so complicated and so chaotic?

This objection sounds formidable, but there is not really much force in it. First, mere oddness can hardly be a difficulty. The material world is an odd place on any theory, and it certainly was not made for the convenience of philosophers. And as for the multiplication of entities, we must remember that it is Nature and not the Selective theory which is responsible for it. The only multiplication which is objectionable is a multiplication of *assumed* entities.

But these 'odd' and 'abnormal' sense-data are there in any case: they are not assumed, but found. They certainly exist, for they are certainly sensed. Their existence is beyond all comparison more certain than any theory can be. You do not get rid of them by calling them 'abnormal' or 'merely subjective'. And one cannot excuse oneself from finding some place for them in one's metaphysical scheme. All the Selectivist does is to say that they exist not only when sensed but also at other times, and to argue by analogy that others like them exist which do not happen to be sensed at all.

Thirdly, with regard to complexity, we must remember that there are at least two distinct ways in which a world, or a conception of the world, can be called simple or complicated: (1) in respect of the number of *entities* in it, (2) in respect of the number of *kinds* of entities in it. In the first respect the world as the Selective Theory conceives it is undoubtedly complicated. But we have just seen that this complexity is innocuous. But in the second respect it is not complicated at all; and in so far, the Selective Theory is the simplest of all theories. For whereas other theories postulate at least two distinct kinds of entities, namely, sense-data and material objects, it postulates only sense-data and says that material objects are composed of them. (Likewise it does not have to postulate a new *relation* of 'belonging to'. It says that 'belonging to' is simply a special case of the old and familiar relation of member to group.)

Fourthly, there is nothing chaotic about these groups. Each group contains an infinitely numerous multitude of members, but this does not means that the members are not *ordered*. For instance, the infinitely numerous 'perspectified' colour-patches falling within some one object are united in a continuous series. Between this elliptical patch and that circular one there are infinitely numerous gradations. And the like applies to colour, premency, and other secondary qualities. So too with the dissociated and distorted sense-data of reflection, refraction and so on. They are united with the ordinary perspectified ones by a like gradual transition. And the sense-data characteristic of physiological and psychological disorder can be dealt with in the same way. An observer who had the same disorder in a slightly smaller degree would 'select' a sensibile slightly more like the ordinary perspectified one, until as the disorder is reduced he selects one which is only just distinguishable from that. It is true that there are some few hallucinatory sense-data, which are entirely 'wild'. But even they stand in *some* relation with these ordered groups. We can at least say that *if* this colour-patch were a member of an ordinary object, then that object would have such and such a position in space: e.g. it would be between the table-leg and the door.

Thus it is misleading to say (as is commonly done) 'that the theory abolishes the distinction between reality and illusion'. True, in one important respect it makes no distinction between the illusory sense-datum and the ordinary one. It holds that both alike persist outside the somato-centric complex, as unsensed sensibilia. But there may still be extremely important differences within the world of sensibilia. Some are related in one way to their fellow-sensibilia, others in other ways. Some have one status within their object-group, some have another: some are merely perspectified, others are dislocated or distorted; some are members of no object-group at all. And in certain cases a sensibile is such that on sensing it we tend to misconceive the specific character of the object of which it is a member: e.g. we think it is the sort of group commonly called a bent stick whereas in fact it is the sort commonly called a straight stick. In some few cases the sensibile, though still perfectly independent of us, is completely 'wild', i.e. belongs to no object-group at all; but we naturally take it to belong to one (for it really is similar in quality to others that do), and this is hallucination. And here the Selective Theory is surely right, in principle at any rate. Whatever the distinction between normal and abnormal sense-data may turn out to be, there is no *special* connexion between abnormality and mind-dependence, or for that matter between normality and mind-independence: so far as dependence or independence on the mind (and the nervous system) are concerned, all sense-data must stand or fall together. The difference between normal and abnormal lies in another dimension altogether: it concerns the relation between this sense-datum and other sense-data. Whether these sense-data do or do not exist as unsensed sensibilia also, is irrelevant.

We must conclude, then, that the objections commonly urged against the Selective Theory can be answered. But it is very difficult to believe seriously that the theory is true, however attractive it appears in the study. And it seems to me that there are two other objections against it which have more force.

One of these is that the theory really proves too much: that by refusing to interpret somato-centricity in a connective way, it in effect denies causal connexion everywhere. The theory admits that in certain respects there is a constant concomitant variation of somatic and environmental data, and that we never find the one sort without the other. And it can hardly deny that the connective interpretation of this is the natural and obvious one. Both the Method of Agreement and Method of Concomitant Variations concur in suggesting that interpretation. None the less the theory holds that constant compresence and concomitant variation is *not* here a sign of causal connexion direct or indirect. But if so, we must ask, why should it be a sign of causation in other cases either? Why should we not hold that other alleged instances of causal connexion are really only instances of selection? The higher the temperature, the more the metal expands, and we commonly think that the increase of temperature causes the expansion. But why should we not say that the several elongated states *really* coexist with the original state, but the increase of temperature reveals now one and now another to our consciousness? Nor could we save causation by appealing to the Method of Difference. In the absence of the spark, we commonly argue, the powder magazine does not blow up: when the spark is introduced, all other conditions remaining constant, it does; therefore the spark is at least a part-cause of the explosion. But why should we not take a selective view of this too, and say that really both states of the magazine, the exploded and unexploded, coexist all along: and that all the spark does is to reveal the exploded state to our consciousness, and to make the unexploded state (not non-existent but) unobservable by us? In short, whenever A is said to cause B, it could always be suggested that B existed all along, and A merely revealed it. And in any case we chose to take, all evidence for causal connexion, however strong, could in this way be discredited.

And we could not stop short of a further extension of the selective principle; we should have to hold that there is no *temporal order* except the order of our successive apprehendings. The ordinary view is that every event has what we call 'its place' in an objective temporal order. It is thought that Tuesday's events can only *exist* if Monday's events have existed first. But ought we not to say that Tuesday's events can only be *observed* if Monday's events have first been *observed*—that really they are all contemporary? Thus what we are accustomed to regard as successive events would be in all cases coexistent, and the only successiveness would be that of successive apprehending. And having got so far, we could not avoid a vicious infinite regress. For how could we avoid saying that our seemingly successive apprehendings are themselves really coexistent, and that the real succession is in our apprehendings of these apprehendings? But then there would be the same difficulty about the successiveness of these new apprehendings, and so on *ad inf.* Thus a theory which professes to be the most 'realistic' of all theories ends by making Time itself an illusion.

Now obviously in an argument of this kind everything depends on the first step. If the Selective Theory could show that there is some difference of principle between the somato-centric sort of co-presence and co-variation and all other sorts, it might still be saved. But can it? Of course in so far as my state of *sensing* may be said to be constantly co-present and co-variant with what is sensed—being variously 'directed', now upon this and now upon the other—that is no sign of causal connexion. For sensing (as we are using the term) is a form of apprehension or knowing, and all forms of apprehension are selective. If I apprehend first A and then B, this by itself determines nothing whatever as to the temporal order of A and B themselves. They might even both of them be timeless, as when A is one geometrical theorem and B another. And they are both sense-data, it still remains possible so far that they really coexist though successively apprehended. For the relation between the apprehended and the mind apprehending is an 'external' relation. But then it is not this relation that we are talking of. What concerns us is a relation *within* the apprehended itself, i.e. within the Totum Datum; and if the first relation is external, it does not follow that the second is. And it is suggested that in fact, we have the strongest evidence we could hope for to show that it is *not* external.

It is true that *if* we could see that from their very nature somatic and environmental data could not be mutually dependent, this evidence would go for nothing. Thus if I apprehend an isosceles triangle of a certain height, I can see that the equality of the angles at the base is from its very nature independent of the height, and the height independent of it: and this would still be so, and could be known to be so, even if all other isosceles triangles I ever met with were of that height, while all triangles of other heights had other shapes, and conversely. Such a concomitant variation of height and shape would be held to be 'accidental', however often repeated. But then there is nothing in the nature of, say, colour-patches and kinaesthetic feelings to show that *their* concomitant variation (as we walk about or read just our eyes) is thus accidental. The conclusion, then, is that if there is *ever* any empirical reason for believing that two entities are connected, then somato-centricity must be interpreted connectively and not selectively: so that the Selective Theory must be false. And since the connexion must extend to all the qualities of all the sense-data within the Totum Datum (for none are exempt from this co-presence and co-variancy) we must also conclude that neither part of it, neither the somatic data nor the environmental, could exist at all apart from the other; we cannot compromise and say that they continue to exist as sensibilia, but with a change of quality; i.e. that they are modified but not abolished by leaving the somato-centric complex, and again modified but not created by entering it. Thus the somato-centric *totum* is not only an organic whole, but an organic whole of a very intimate kind.

The other objection concerns the teleological or instrumental character of sense-data. The Selective Theory says that the sense-organs and nervous processes are instrumental, regarding the sensing of sense-data as their 'end': but the truth is that the sense-data themselves are 'means' to something else, namely, to perceptual consciousness, which would be impossible without them. It seems likely that the *meaningfulness* of the sense-datum, the fact that it is pre-adapted to be taken as belonging to a particular material object, is part of its essential nature and not a mere accident of it. It is plain, too, that a man's sense-data even adapt themselves in certain cases to his prejudices and prepossessions concerning particular material objects (right or wrong), and that this is a large part of the explanation of hallucinations. This strongly suggests that sense-data, though independent of the mind in respect of *sensing,* are dependent upon it in respect of its *perceptual dispositions.*

Thus the Selective Theory seems to be false. But we must hasten to add that its falsity does nothing to strengthen any form of solipsism or scepticism. So far as the second objection goes, this is obvious: for it is wholly founded upon the fact that we are conscious of matter as well as of sense-data. But it is also true with regard to the first. Though the somato-centric complex is an organic whole, this does not in the least prevent the sense-data in it from belonging to material things, which persist and have their being before and after these sense-data come into existence. And it does not in the least prevent the sense-data from revealing those things to us. It does indeed show that the things cannot be wholly composed of sense-data: but it does not show that sense-data do not stand in an extremely intimate relation to them. It does show that they cannot be permanent constituents of material things. But it does show that they cannot be temporary and occasional elements in the thing's total being, along with others more permanent; the fact that they exist only when and so long as certain complicated conditions are fulfilled is no obstacle to this. And it might accordingly be possible to say that the 'total object' has from time to time such secondary qualities as red or hard or hot, though its persistent and physically operative part does not.

We can go farther. The argument against the Selective Theory is not only *compatible* with the existence of material objects accessible to our consciousness, but would have no force whatever without it. For the notions of substance and of causal connexion seem to be closely bound up that we may almost call them two aspects of one single notion—that of the causative-continuant or continuing-causant. It does not matter here whether this is regarded as a complex continuum of successive events, or as a persisting substrate in which diverse events inhere: the point is only that in some sense or other it retains its identity through time. Unless sense-data belong to and somehow reveal to us such persistent yet changing objects—the environmental ones revealing one sort, the somatic another—the

compresence and co-variation of sense-data, however often repeated, is nothing but a rather curious phenomenon, a fact as it were of a merely geographical kind, and gives no evidence of causal connexion at all. Thus the very argument which shows the Totum Datum is an organic whole, show too that this whole has a *parasitic* and not an autonomous character.

Lastly, if we reject the Selective Theory, we should do so with reluctance. For it lays stress on some important facts which we are liable to forget. Odd, abnormal, and illusory sense-data do not really exist outside the somato-centric complex, as unsensed sensibilia. But within it they certainly do exist. And a theory which fails to find a place for them, by determining their relations to other sense-data, to material things, and to our consciousness of such things, is perfectly worthless. Even the 'wild' ones have their corner in the real universe, humble though it may be. Doubtless they are of no interest to Science (though their causes sometimes are) and of no importance to the practical man. But it is well to remember that the Real includes more than the objects of scientific inquiry and of practical manipulation. And the fact that some of these odd sense-data are met with only in certain forms of mental or bodily disease is a poor reason for not investigating them. For the notions of 'disease' and 'abnormality' are very relative ones: a 'diseased' state of mind or body usually mean no more than a state which makes us inefficient in action. But if our state of practical inefficiency enables us to be aware of new sorts of existents, then so far it is not worse but better than our ordinary state. And if these existents are but short-lived and conditional in their existence, they none the less exist. In Philosophy we must discard our standing prejudices in favour of the practical, the persistent and the efficacious. And this the Selective Theory helps us to do, by treating all sense-data alike whether they are odd or ordinary.

Again, though it is a mistake to say that a material object is wholly composed of sense-data, the mistake is an instructive one. For the fact that the object can be present to the senses of various people in various ways, i.e. that there are various sense-data belonging to it and could in assignable circumstances be various others, is an extremely important fact about it: so important, perhaps, that 'material objectness' cannot be defined without mention of it. If so, it becomes important to investigate this set of sense-data and the relations between them, and in doing so to consider not only the actual data but also the fact that various others *would* exist if the thing were present to our senses (or other people's) in other ways. These actual and those obtainable sense-data do form a group of a peculiar sort: and until we understand what sort of group it is we shall not be able to say what a material object is, still less to describe our consciousness of such objects. The investigation of such groups (which we shall later call 'families of sense-data') is a puzzling and a complicated task. And in the course of it we may often be able to help ourselves by asking what the Selective Theory would say about the group which according to it is the object, and about the relations between its members.

On these two grounds we might reasonably maintain that although the Selective Theory is false, a temporary belief in it is the best introduction to the problems of perception.

We may now try to summarize the argument of this chapter. We first saw that there are two main subjects to be considered in this book: 1 the relation of 'belonging to'; 2. the nature of 'perceptual consciousness', sometimes (but ambiguously) called 'perceiving'. *Naïve Realism* puts forward a theory on both these points. It is commonly thought to be re-futed by the *Argument from Illusion*. This really has two distinct forms, the Phenomenological and the Causal, which are commonly confused. Even when distinguished, they are apt to be stated in an incoherent way, in which the alleged conclusions contradict the premises. Still, the Phenomenological form, properly stated, does refute *Naïve Realism,* and the distinction between normal and abnormal sense-data is no answer. The Causal form, however, really proves only somato-centricity; and though on the *connective* interpretation of this the falsity of Naïve Realism would follow, another interpretation is possible, viz. the *selective.* And this with its further developments constitutes the *Selective Theory.* According to it a material object is simply a complex group of sensibilia: and it is thus enabled to put forward a new view of 'belonging to' which it identifies with the relation of member to group. This theory deserves very serious consideration, and the ordinary objections to it can fairly easily be met; but there are two others which seem to refute it. Our conclusions are *negatively* that neither Naïve Realism nor the Selective Theory is tenable; and *positively* that sense-data are somato-centric, and further that they exist only within the somato-centric complex. But we have reached no positive conclusion concerning the relation of 'belonging to', nor concerning perceptual consciousness. In subsequent chapters we shall consider other theories about both.

JOHN LOCKE

from An Essay Concerning Human Understanding

BOOK II.

Chapter I. Of Ideas in General, and Their Original

1. *Idea is the object of thinking.*—Every man being conscious to himself, that he thinks, and that which his mind is applied about, whilst thinking, being the ideas that are there, it is past doubt that men have in their mind several ideas, such as are those expressed by the words, "whiteness, hardness, sweetness, thinking, motion, man, elephant, army, drunkenness," and others: it is in the first place then to be inquired, How he comes by them? I know it is a received doctrine, that men have native ideas and original characters stamped upon their minds in their very first being. This opinion I have at large examined already; and, I suppose, what I have said in the foregoing book will be much more easily admitted, when I have shown whence the understanding may get all the ideas it hath, and by what ways and degrees they may come into the mind; for which I shall appeal to every one's own observation and experience.

2. *All ideas come from sensation or reflection.*—Let us then suppose the mind to be, as we say, white paper, void of all characters, without any ideas; how comes it to be furnished? Whence comes it by that vast store, which the busy and boundless fancy of man hath painted on it with an almost endless variety? Whence hath it all the materials of reason and knowledge? To this I answer, in one word, From experience; in that all our knowledge is founded, and from that it ultimately derives itself. Our observation, employed either about external sensible objects, or about the internal operations of our minds, perceived and reflected on by ourselves, is that which supplies our understandings with all the materials of thinking. These two are the fountains of knowledge, from whence all the ideas we have, or can naturally have, do spring.

3. *The object of sensation one source of ideas.*—First. Our senses, conversant about particular sensible objects, do convey into the mind several distinct perceptions of things, according to those various ways wherein those objects do affect them; and thus we come by those ideas we have of yellow, white, heat, cold, soft, hard, bitter, sweet, and all those which we call sensible qualities; which when I say the senses convey into the mind, I mean, they from external objects convey into the mind what produces there those perceptions. This great source of most of the ideas we have, depending wholly upon our senses, and derived by them to the understanding, I call, "sensation."

4. *The operations of our minds the other source of them.*—Secondly. The other fountain, from which experience furnisheth the understanding with ideas, is the perception of the operations of our own minds within us, as it is employed about the ideas it hath got; which operations when the soul comes to reflect on and consider, do furnish the understanding with another set of ideas which could not be had from things without; and such are perception, thinking, doubting, believing, reasoning, knowing, willing, and all the different actings of our own minds; which we, being conscious of, and observing in ourselves, do from these receive into our understandings as distinct ideas, as we do from bodies affecting our senses. This source of ideas every man hath wholly in himself; and though it be not sense as having nothing to do with external objects, yet it is very like it, and might properly enough be called "internal sense." But as I call the other "sensation," so I call this "reflection," the ideas it affords being such only as the mind gets by reflecting on its own operations within itself. By reflection, then, in the following part of this discourse, I would be understood to mean that notice which the mind takes of its own

operations, and the manner of them, by reason whereof there come to be ideas of these operations in the understanding. These two, I say, viz., external material things as the objects of sensation, and the operations of our own minds within as the objects of reflection, are, to me, the only originals from whence all our ideas take their beginnings. The term "operations" here, I use in a large sense, as comprehending not barely the actions of the mind about its ideas, but some sort of passions arising sometimes from them, such as is the satisfaction or uneasiness arising from any thought.

5. *All our ideas are of the one or the other of these.*— The understanding seems to me not to have the least glimmering of any ideas which it doth not receive from one of these two. External objects furnish the mind with the ideas of sensible qualities, which are all those different perceptions they produce in us; and the mind furnishes the understanding with ideas of its own operations.

These, when we have taken a full survey of them, and their several modes, [combinations, and relations,] we shall find to contain all our whole stock of ideas; and that we have nothing in our minds which did not come in one of these two ways. Let any one examine his own thoughts, and thoroughly search into his understanding, and then let him tell me, whether all the original ideas he hath there, are any other than of the objects of his senses, or of the operations of his mind considered as objects of his reflection; and how great a mass of knowledge he imagines to be lodged there, he will, upon taking a strict view, see that he hath not any idea in his mind but what one of these two have imprinted, though perhaps with infinite variety compounded and enlarged by the understanding, as we shall see hereafter. . . .

Chapter VIII. Some Farther Considerations Concerning Our Simple Ideas of Sensation

1. *Positive ideas from privative causes.*—Concerning the simple ideas of sensation it is to be considered, that whatsoever is so constituted in nature as to be able by affecting our senses to cause any perception in the mind, doth thereby produce in the understanding a simple idea; which, whatever be the external cause of it, when it comes to be taken notice of by our discerning faculty, it is by the mind looked on and considered there to be a real positive idea in the understanding as much as an other whatsoever; though perhaps the cause of it be but a privation in the subject.

2. Thus the ideas of heat and cold, light and darkness, white and black, motion and rest, are equally clear and positive ideas in the mind, though perhaps some of the causes which produce them are barely privations in those subjects from whence our senses derive those ideas. These the understanding, in its view of them, considers all as distinct positive ideas without taking notice of the causes that produce them; which is an inquiry not belonging to the idea as it is in the understanding, but to the nature of the things existing without us. These are two very different things, and carefully to be distinguished; it being one thing to perceive and know the idea of white or black, and quite another to examine what kind of particles they must be, and how ranged in the superficies, to make any object appear white or black.

3. A painter or dyer who never inquired into their causes, hath the ideas of white and black and other colours as clearly, perfectly, and distinctly in his understanding, and perhaps more distinctly than the philosopher who hath busied himself in considering their natures, and thinks he knows how far either of them is in its cause positive or privative; and the idea of black is no less positive in his mind than that of white, however the cause of that colour in the external object may be only a privation.

4. If it were the design of my present undertaking to inquire into the natural causes and manner of perception, I should offer this as a reason why a privative cause might, in some cases at least, produce a positive idea, viz., that all sensation being produced in us only by different degrees and modes of motion in our animal spirits, variously agitated by external objects, the abatement of any former motion must as necessarily produce a new sensation as the variation or increase of it; and so introduce a new idea, which depends only on a different motion of the animal spirits in that organ.

5. But whether this be so or not I will not here determine, but appeal to every one's own experience, whether the shadow of a man, though it consists of

nothing but the absence of light (and the more the absence of light is, the more discernible is the shadow), doth not, when a man looks on it, cause as clear and positive an idea in his mind as a man himself, though covered over with clear sunshine! And the picture of a shadow is a positive thing. Indeed, we have negative names, [which stand not directly for positive ideas, but for their absence, such as *insipid, silence, nihil,* &c., which words denote positive ideas, v.g., *taste, sound, being,* with a signification of their absence.]

6. *Positive ideas from privative causes.*—And thus one may truly be said to see darkness. For, supposing a hole perfectly dark, from whence no light is reflected, it is certain one may see the figure of it, or it may be painted; or whether the ink I write with make any other idea, is a question. The privative causes I have here assigned of positive ideas are according to the common opinion; but, in truth, it will be hard to determine whether there be really any ideas from a privative cause, till it be determined whether rest be any more a privation than motion.

7. *Ideas in the mind, qualities in bodies.*—To discover the nature of our ideas the better, and to discourse of them intelligibly, it will be convenient to distinguish them as they are ideas or perceptions in our minds, and as they are modifications of matter in the bodies that cause such perceptions in us; that so we may not think (as perhaps usually is done) that they are exactly the images and resemblances of something inherent in the subject; most of those of sensation being in the mind no more the likeness of something existing without us than the names that stand for them are the likeness of our ideas, which yet upon hearing they are apt to excite in us.

8. Whatsoever the mind perceives in itself, or is the immediate object of perception, thought, or understanding, that I call "idea;" and the power to produce any idea in our mind I call "quality" of the subject wherein that power is. Thus a snowball having the power to produce in us the ideas of white, cold, and round, the powers to produce those ideas in us as they are in the snowball, I call "qualities;" and as they are sensations or perceptions in our understandings, I call them "ideas;" which ideas, if I speak of them sometimes as in the things themselves, I would be understood to mean those qualities in the objects which produce them in us.

9. *Primary qualities.*—[Qualities thus considered in bodies are, First, such as are utterly inseparable from the body, in what estate soever it be;] and such as, in all the alterations and changes it suffers, all the force can be used upon it, it constantly keeps; and such as sense constantly finds in every particle of matter which hath bulk enough to be perceived, and the mind finds inseparable from every particle of matter, though less than to make itself singly be perceived by our senses: *v.g.,* take a grain of wheat, divide it into two parts, each part hath still solidity, extension, figure, and mobility; divide it again, and it retains still the same qualities: and so divide it on till the parts become insensible, they must retain still each of them all those qualities. For, division (which is all that a mill or pestle or any other body doth upon another, in reducing it to insensible parts) can never take away either solidity, extension, figure, or mobility from any body, but only makes two or more distinct separate masses of matter of that which was but one before; all which distinct masses, reckoned as so many distinct bodies, after division; make a certain number. [These I call *original* or *primary* qualities of body, which I think we may observe to produce simple ideas in us, viz., solidity, extension, figure, motion or rest, and number.

10. *Secondary qualities.*—Secondly. Such qualities, which in truth are nothing in the objects themselves, but powers to produce various sensations in us by their primary qualities, *i.e.,* by the bulk, figure, texture, motion of their insensible parts, as colours, sounds, tastes, &c., these I call *secondary* qualities. To these might be added a third sort, which are allowed to be barely powers, though they are as much real qualities in the subject as those which I, to comply with the common way of speaking, call qualities, but, for distinction, *secondary* qualities. For, the power in fire to produce a new colour or consistency in wax or clay, by its primary qualities, is as much a quality in fire as the power it hath to produce in me a new idea or sensation of warmth or burning, which I felt not before, by the same primary qualities, viz., the bulk, texture, and motion of its insensible parts.]

11. [*How primary qualities produce their ideas.*—The next thing to be considered is, how bodies produce ideas in us; and that is manifestly by impulse, the only way which we can conceive bodies to operate in.]

12. If, then, external objects be not united to our minds when they produce ideas therein, and yet we perceive these original qualities in such of them as singly fall under our senses, it is evident that some motion must be thence continued by our nerves, or animal spirits, by some parts of our bodies, to the brains or the seat of sensation, there to produce in our minds the particular ideas we have of them. And since the extension, figure, number, and motion of bodies of an observable bigness, may be perceived at a distance by the sight, it is evident some singly imperceptible bodies must come from them to the eyes, and thereby convey to the brain some motion which produces these ideas which we have of them in us.

13. *How secondary.*—After the same manner that the ideas of these original qualities are produced in us, we may conceive that the ideas of secondary qualities are also produced, viz., by the operation of insensible particles on our senses. For it being manifest that there are bodies, and good store of bodies, each whereof are so small that we cannot by any of our senses discover either their bulk, figure, or motion (as is evident in the particles of the air and water, and other extremely smaller than those, perhaps as much smaller than the particles of air or water as the particles of or water are smaller than peas or hailstones): let us suppose at present that the different motions and figures, bulk and number, of such particles, effecting the several organs of our senses, produce in us those different sensations which we have from the colours and smells of bodies, *v.g.,* that a violet, by the impulse of such insensible particles of matter of peculiar figures and bulks, and in different degrees and modifications of their motions, causes the ideas of the blue colour and sweet scent of that flower to be produced in our minds; it being no more impossible to conceive that God should annex such ideas to such motions, with which they have no similitude, than that he should annex the idea of pain to the motion of a piece of steel dividing our flesh, with which the idea hath no resemblance.

14. What I have said concerning colours and smells may be understood also of tastes and sounds, and other the like sensible qualities; which, whatever reality we by mistake attribute to them, are in truth nothing in the objects themselves, but powers to produce various sensations in us, and depend on those primary qualities, viz., bulk, figure, texture, and motion of parts [as I have said.]

15. *Ideas of primary qualities are resemblances; of secondary, not.*—From whence I think it is easy to draw this observation, that the ideas of primary qualities of bodies are resemblances of them, and their patterns do really exist in the bodies themselves; but the ideas produced in us by these secondary qualities have no resemblance of them at all. There is nothing like our ideas existing in the bodies themselves. They are, in the bodies we denominate from them, only a power to produce those sensations in us; and what is sweet, blue, or warm in idea, is but the certain bulk, figure, and motion of the insensible parts in the bodies themselves, which we call so.

16. Flame is denominated *hot* and *light;* snow, *white* and *cold;* and manna, *white* and *sweet,* from the ideas they produce in us, which qualities are commonly thought to be the same in those bodies that those ideas are in us, the one the perfect resemblance of the, other, as they are in a mirror; and it would by most men be judged very extravagant, if one should say otherwise. And yet he that will consider that the same fire that at one distance produces in us the sensation of warmth, doth at a nearer approach produce in us the far different sensation of pain, ought to bethink himself what reason he hath to say, that this idea of warmth which was produced in him by the fire, is actually in the fire, and his idea of pain which the same fire produced in him the same way is not in the fire. Why is whiteness and coldness in snow and pain not, when it produces the one and the other idea in us, and can do neither but by the bulk, figure, number, and motion of its solid parts?

17. The particular bulk, number, figure, and motion of the parts of fire or snow are really in them, whether any one's senses perceive them or no; and therefore they may be called *real* qualities, because they really exist in those bodies. But light, heat, whiteness, or coldness are no more really in them than sickness or pain is in manna. Take away the sensation of them; let not the eyes see light or colours, nor the ears hear sounds; let the palate not taste, nor the nose smell; and all colours, tastes, odours, and sounds, as they are such particular ideas, vanish and cease, and are reduced to their causes, *i. e.,* bulk, figure, and motion of parts.

18. A piece of manna of a sensible bulk is able to produce in us the idea of a round or square figure; and, by being removed from one place to another, the idea of motion. This idea of motion represents it as it really is in the manna moving; a circle or square are the same, whether in idea or existence, in the mind or in the manna; and this both motion and figure are really in the manna, whether we take notice of them or no: this every body is ready to agree to. Besides, manna, by the bulk, figure, texture, and motion of its parts, hath a power to produce the sensations of sickness, and sometimes of acute pains or grippings, in us. That these ideas of sickness and pain are not in the manna, but effects of its operations on us, and are nowhere when we feel them not; this also every one readily agrees to. And yet men are hardly to be brought to think that sweetness and whiteness are not really in manna, which are but the effects of the operations of manna by the motion, size, and figure of its particles on the eyes and palate; as the pain and sickness caused by manna, are confessedly nothing but the effects of its operations on the stomach and guts by the size, motion, and figure of its insensible parts (for by nothing else can a body operate, as hath been proved): as if it could not operate on the eyes and palate, and thereby produce in the mind particular distinct ideas which in itself it hath not, as well as we allow it can operate on the guts and stomach, and thereby produce distinct ideas which in itself it hath not. These ideas being all effects of the operations of manna on several parts of our bodies, by the size, figure, number, and motion of its parts, why those produced by the eyes and palate should rather be thought to be really in the manna than those produced by the stomach and guts: or why the pain and sickness, ideas that are the effects of manna, should be thought to be nowhere when they are not felt: and yet the sweetness and whiteness, effects of the same manna on other parts of the body, by ways equally as unknown, should be thought to exist in the manna, when they are not seen nor tasted would need some reason to explain.

19. *Ideas of primary qualities are resemblances; of secondary, not.*—Let us consider the red and white colours in porphyry; hinder light but from striking on it, and its colours vanish; it no longer produces any such ideas in us. Upon the return of light, it produces these appearances on us again. Can any one think any real alterations are made in the porphyry by the presence or absence of light, and that those ideas of whiteness and redness are really in porphyry in the light, when it is plain it hath no colour in the dark? It hath indeed such a configuration of particles, both night and day, as are apt, by the rays of light rebounding from some parts of that hard stone, to produce in us the idea of redness, and from others the idea of whiteness. But whiteness or redness are not in it at any time, but such a texture that hath the power to produce such a sensation in us.

20. Pound an almond, and the clear white colour will be altered into a dirty one, and the sweet taste into an oily one. What real alteration can the beating of the pestle make in any body, but an alteration of the texture of it?

21. Ideas being thus distinguished and understood, we may be able to give an account how the same water, at the same time, may produce the idea of cold by one hand, and of heat by the other; whereas it is impossible that the same water, if those ideas were really in it, should at the same time be both hot and cold. For if we imagine warmth as it is in our hands, to be nothing but a certain sort and degree of motion in the minute particles of our nerves or animal spirits, we may understand how it is possible that the same water may at the same time produce the sensation of heat in one hand, and cold in the other; which yet figure never doth, that never producing the idea of a square by one hand which hath produced the idea of a globe by another. But if the sensation of heat and cold be nothing but the increase or diminution of the motion of the minute parts of our bodies, caused by the corpuscles of any other body, it is easy to be understood that if that motion be greater in one hand than in the other, if a body be applied to the two hands, which hath in its minute particles a greater motion than in those of one of the hands, and a less than in those of the other, it will increase the motion of the one hand, and lessen it in the other, and so cause the different sensations of heat and cold that depend thereon.

22. I have, in what just goes before, been engaged in physical inquiries a little farther than perhaps I intended. But it being necessary to make the nature of sensation a little understood, and to make the difference between the qualities in bodies, and the ideas produced by them in the mind, to be distinctly conceived, without which it were impossible to discourse

intelligibly of them, I hope I shall be pardoned this little excursion into natural philosophy, it being necessary in our present inquiry to distinguish the primary and real qualities of bodies, which are always in them, (viz., solidity, extension, figure, number, and motion or rest and are sometimes perceived by us, viz., when the bodies they are in are big enough singly to be discerned,) from those secondary and imputed qualities, which are but the powers of several combinations of those primary ones, when they operate without being distinctly discerned; whereby we also may come to know what ideas are, and what are not, resemblances of something really existing in the bodies we denominate from them. . . .

BOOK IV

Chapter I. Of Knowledge in General

1. *Our knowledge conversant about our ideas.*—Since the mind, in all its thoughts and reasonings, hath no other immediate object but its own ideas, which it alone doth or can contemplate, it is evident that our knowledge is only conversant about them.

2. *Knowledge is the perception of the agreement or disagreement of two ideas.*—Knowledge then seems to me to be nothing but the perception of the connection of and agreement, or disagreement and repugnancy, of any of our ideas. In this alone it consists. Where this perception is, there is knowledge; and where it is not, there, though we may fancy, guess, or believe, yet we always come short of knowledge. For, when we know that white is not black, what do we else but perceive that these two ideas do not agree? When we possess ourselves with the utmost security of the demonstration that the three angles of a triangle are equal to two right ones, what do we more but perceive, that equality to two right ones doth necessarily agree to, and is inseparable from, the three angles of a triangle? . . .

Chapter III. Of the Extent of Human Knowledge

1. KNOWLEDGE, as hath been said, lying in the perception of the agreement or disagreement of any of our ideas, it follows from hence that,

First, No farther than we have ideas.—First, We can have knowledge no farther than we have ideas.

2. *Secondly, No farther than we can perceive their agreement or disagreement.*—Secondly, That we can have no knowledge farther than we can have perception of that agreement or disagreement: which perception being, (1.) Either by intuition, or the immediate comparing any two ideas; or, (2.) By reason, examining the agreement or disagreement of two ideas by the intervention of some others; or, (3.) By sensation, perceiving the existence of particular things; hence it also follows,

3. *Thirdly, Intuitive knowledge extends itself not to all the relations of all our ideas.*—Thirdly, that we cannot have an intuitive knowledge that shall extend itself to all our ideas, and all that we would know about them; because we cannot examine and perceive all the relations they have one to another by juxtaposition, or an immediate comparison one with another. Thus having the ideas of an obtuse and an acute-angled triangle, both drawn from equal bases, and between parallels, I can by intuitive knowledge perceive the one not to be the other; but cannot that way know whether they be equal or no: because their agreement or disagreement in equality can never be perceived by an immediate comparing them; the difference of figure makes their parts incapable of an exact immediate application; and therefore there is need of some intervening qualities to measure them by, which is demonstration or rational knowledge.

4. *Fourthly, Nor demonstrative knowledge.*—Fourthly, It follows also, from what is above observed, that our rational knowledge cannot reach to the whole extent of our ideas: because between two different ideas we would examine, we cannot always find such mediums as we can connect one to another with an intuitive knowledge, in all the parts of the deduction; and wherever that fails, we come short of knowledge and demonstration. . . .

Chapter XI. Of Our Knowledge of the Existence of Other Things

1. *It is to be had only by sensation*—The knowledge of our own being we have by intuition. The existence of a God reason clearly makes known to us, as hath been shown.

The knowledge of the existence of any other thing, we can have only by sensation: for, there being no necessary connexion of real existence with any idea a man hath in his memory, nor of any other existence but that of God with the existence of any particular man, no particular man can know the existence of any other being, but only when by actual operating upon him it makes itself perceived by him. For, the having the idea of any thing in our mind no more proves the existence of that thing than the picture of a man evidences his being in the world, or the visions of a dream make thereby a true history.

2. *Instance whiteness of this paper.*—It is therefore the actual receiving of ideas from without that gives us notice of the existence of other things, and makes us know that something doth exist at that time without us which causes that idea in us, though perhaps we neither know nor consider how it doth it: for it takes not from the certainty of our senses, and the ideas we receive by them, that we know not the manner wherein they are produced; *v.g.,* whilst I write this, I have, by the paper affecting my eyes, that idea produced in my mind which whatever object causes, I call "white;" by which I know that that quality or accident (*i.e.,* whose appearance before my eyes always causes that idea) doth really exist and hath a being without me. And of this the greatest assurance I can possibly have, and to which my faculties can attain, is the testimony of my eyes, which are the proper and sole judges of this thing; whose testimony I have reason to rely on as so certain that I can no more doubt, whilst I write this, that I see white and black, and that something really exists that causes that sensation in me, than that I write or move my hand; which is a certainty as great as human nature is capable of concerning the existence of any thing but a man's self alone and of God.

3. *This, though not so certain as demonstration, yet may be called "knowledge," and proves the existence of things without us.*—The notice we have by our senses of the existing of things without us, though it be not altogether so certain as our intuitive knowledge, or the deductions of our reason employed about the clear abstract ideas of our own minds; yet it is an assurance that deserves the name of knowledge. If we persuade ourselves that our faculties act and inform us right concerning the existence of those objects that affect them, it cannot pass for an ill-grounded confidence: for I think nobody can, in earnest, be so skeptical as to be uncertain of the existence of those things which he sees and feels. At least, he that can

doubt so far, (whatever he may have with his own thoughts,) will never have any controversy with me: since he can never be sure I say any thing contrary to his own opinion. As to myself, I think God hath given me assurance enough of the existence of things without me; since; by their different application, I can produce in myself both pleasure and pain, which is one great concernment of my present state. This is certain, the confidence that our faculties do not herein deceive us is the greatest assurance we are capable of concerning the existence of material beings. For we cannot act any thing but by our faculties, nor talk of knowledge itself but by the help of those faculties which are fitted to apprehend even what knowledge is. But, besides the assurance we have from our senses themselves, that they do not err in the information they give us of the existence of things without us, when they are affected by them, we are farther confirmed in this assurance by other concurrent reasons.

4. *First, Because we cannot have them but by the inlet of the senses.*—First, It is plain those perceptions are produced in us by exterior causes affecting our senses, because those that want the organs of any sense never can have the ideas belonging to that sense produced in their minds. This is too evident to be doubted: and therefore we cannot but be assured that they come in by the organs of that sense, and no other way. The organs themselves, it is plain, do not produce them; for then the eyes of a man in the dark would produce colours, and his nose smell roses in the winter: but we see nobody gets the relish of a pineapple till he goes to the Indies where it is, and tastes it.

5. *Secondly, Because an idea from actual sensation and another from memory are very distinct perceptions.*—Secondly, Because sometimes I find that I cannot avoid the having those ideas produced in my mind: for though when my eyes are shut, or windows fast, I can at pleasure recall to my mind the ideas of light or the sun, which former sensations had lodged in my memory; so I can at pleasure lay by that idea, and take into my view that of the smell of a rose, or taste of sugar. But if I turn my eyes at noon towards the sun, I cannot avoid the ideas which the light or sun then produces in me. So that there is a manifest difference between the ideas laid up in my memory (over which, if they were there only, I should have constantly the same power to

dispose of them, and lay them by at pleasure), and those which force themselves upon me and I cannot avoid having. And therefore it must needs be some exterior cause, and the brisk acting of some objects without me, whose efficacy I cannot resist, that produces those ideas in my mind, whether I will or no. Besides, there is nobody who doth not perceive the difference in himself between contemplating the sun as he hath the idea of it in his memory, and actually looking upon it: of which two his perception is so distinct, that few of his ideas are more distinguishable one from another: and therefore he hath certain knowledge that they are not both memory, or the actions of his mind and fancies only within him; but that actual seeing hath a cause without.

6. *Thirdly, Pleasure or pain, which accompanies actual sensation, accompanies not the returning of those ideas without the external objects.*—Thirdly, Add to this, that many of those ideas are produced in us with pain, which afterwards we remember without the least offence. Thus the pain of heat or cold, when the idea of it is revived in our minds, gives us no disturbance; which, when felt, was very troublesome, and is again when actually repeated: which is occasioned by the disorder the external object causes in our bodies when applied to them. And we remember the pain of hunger, thirst, or the headache, without any pain at all; which would either never disturb us, or else constantly do it as often as we thought of it, were there nothing more but ideas floating in our minds, and appearances entertaining our fancies, without the real existence of things affecting us from abroad. The same may be said of pleasure accompanying several actual sensations ; and, though mathematical demonstration depends not upon sense, yet the examining them by diagrams gives great credit to the evidence of our sight, and seems to give it a certainty approaching to that of demonstration itself. For it would be very strange that a man should allow it for an undeniable truth, that two angles of a figure which he measures by lines and angles of a diagram, should be bigger one than the other, and yet doubt of the existence of those lines and angles which, by looking on, he makes use of to measure that by.

7. *Fourthly, Our senses assist one another's testimony of the existence of outward things.*—Fourthly, Our senses, in many cases, bear witness to the truth of each other's report concerning the existence of sensible things without us. He that sees a fire may, if he doubt whether it be any thing more than a bare fancy, feel it too, and be convinced by putting his hand in it; which certainly could never be put into such exquisite pain by a bare idea or phantom, unless that the pain be a fancy too: which yet he cannot, when the burn is well, by raising the idea of it, bring upon himself again.

Thus I see, whilst I write this, I can change the appearance of the paper; and, by designing the letters, tell beforehand what new idea it shall exhibit the very next moment, by barely drawing my pen over it; which will neither appear (let me fancy as much as I will) if my hand stand still, or though I move my pen, if my eyes be shut; nor, when those characters are once made on the paper, can I choose afterwards but see them as they are; that is, have the ideas of such letters as I have made. Whence it is manifest that they are not barely the sport and play of my own imagination, when I find that the characters that were made at the pleasure of my own thoughts do not obey them; nor yet cease to be, whenever I shall fancy it, but continue to affect my senses constantly and regularly, according to the figures I made them. To which if we will add, that the sight of those shall, from another man, draw such sounds as I beforehand design they shall stand for, there will be little reason left to doubt that those words I write do really exist without me, when they cause a long series of regular sounds to affect my ears, which could not be the effect of my imagination, nor could my memory retain them in that order.

8. *This certainty is as great as our condition needs.*—But yet, if after all this any one will be so skeptical as to distrust his senses, and to affirm that all we see and hear, feel and taste, think and do, during our whole being, is but the series and deluding appearances of a long dream whereof there is no reality, and therefore will question the existence of all things or our knowledge of any thing; I must desire him to consider, that if all be a dream, then he doth but dream that he makes the question; and so it is not much matter that a waking man should answer him. But yet, if he pleases, he may dream that I make him this answer, that the certainty of things existing in *rerum natura*, when we have the testimony of our senses for it, is not only as great as our frame can attain to, but as our condition needs. For, our faculties being

suited not to the full extent of being, nor to a perfect, clear, comprehensive knowledge of things free from all doubt and scruple, but to the preservation of us, in whom they are, and accommodated to the use of life, they serve to our purpose well enough, if they will but give us certain notice of those things which are convenient or inconvenient to us. For he that sees a candle burning, and hath experimented the force of its flame by putting his finger in it, will little doubt that this is something existing without him, which doth him harm and puts him to great pain; which is assurance enough, when no man requires greater certainty to govern his actions by than what is as certain as his actions themselves. And if our dreamer pleases to try whether the glowing heat of a glass furnace be barely a wandering imagination in a drowsy man's fancy, by putting his hand into it, he may, perhaps, be awakened into a certainty, greater than he could wish, that it is something more than bare imagination. So that this evidence is as great as we can desire, being as certain to us as our pleasure or pain, *i.e.*, happiness or misery; beyond which we have no concern either of knowing or being. Such an assurance of the existence of things without us, is sufficient to direct us in the attaining the good and avoiding the evil which is caused by them, which is the important concern we have of being made acquainted with them.

9. *But reaches no farther than actual sensation.*—In fine, then, when our senses do actually convey into our understandings any idea, we cannot but be satisfied that there doth something at that time really exist without us which doth affect our senses, and by them give notice of itself to our apprehensive faculties, and actually produce that idea which we then perceive: and we cannot so far distrust their testimony as to doubt that such collections of simple ideas as we have observed by our senses to be united together, do really exist together. But this knowledge extends as far as the present testimony of our senses, employed about particular objects that do then affect them, and no farther. For if I saw such a collection of simple ideas as is wont to be called "man" existing together one minute since, and am now alone; I cannot be certain that the same man exists now, since there is no necessary connexion of his existence a minute since with his existence now: by a thousand ways he may cease to be, since I had the testimony of my senses for his existence. And if I cannot be certain that the man I saw last to-day is now in being, I can less be certain that he is so who hath been longer removed from my senses, and I have not seen since yesterday, or since the last year; and much less can I be certain of the existence of men that I never saw. And therefore, though it be highly probable that millions of men do now exist, yet, whilst I am alone writing this, I have not that certainty of it which we strictly call "knowledge;" though the great likelihood of it puts me past doubt, and it be reasonable for me to do several things upon the confidence that there are men (and men also of my acquaintance, with whom I have to do) now in the world: but this is but probability, not knowledge.

from Of the Principles of Human Knowledge

PART I

It is evident to anyone who takes a survey of the *objects* of human knowledge that they are either ideas actually imprinted on the senses, (or else such as are perceived by attending to the passions and operations of the mind,) or lastly, ideas formed by help of memory and imagination—either compounding, dividing, or barely representing those originally perceived in the aforesaid ways. By sight I have the ideas of light and colors, with their several degrees and variations. By touch I perceive, for example, hard and soft, heat and cold, motion and resistance, and of all these more and less either as to quantity or degree. Smelling furnishes me with odors, the palate with tastes, and hearing conveys sounds to the mind in all their variety of tone and composition. And as several of these are observed to accompany each other, they come to marked by one name, and so to be reputed as one thing. Thus, for example, a certain color, taste, smell, figure, and consistence having been observed to go together, are accounted one distinct thing signified by the name "apple"; other collections of ideas constitute a stone, a tree, a book, and the like sensible things—which as they are pleasing or disagreeable excite the passions of love, hatred, joy, grief, and so forth.

2. But, besides all that endless variety of ideas or objects of knowledge, there is likewise something which knows or perceives them and exercises divers operations, as willing, imagining, remembering, about them. This perceiving, active being is what I call "mind," "spirit," "soul," or "myself." By which words I do not denote any one of my ideas, but a thing entirely distinct from them, wherein they exist or, which is the same thing, whereby they are perceived—for the existence of an idea consists in being perceived.

3. That neither our thoughts, nor passions, nor ideas formed by the imagination exist without the mind is what everybody will allow. And it seems no less evident that the various sensations or ideas imprinted on the sense, however blended or combined together (that is, whatever objects they compose), cannot exist otherwise than in a mind perceiving them.—I think an intuitive knowledge may be obtained of this by anyone that shall attend to what is meant by the term "exist" when applied to sensible things. The table I write on I say exists, that is, I see and feel it; and if I were out of my study I should say it existed—meaning thereby that I was in my study I might perceive it, or that some other spirit actually does perceive it. There was an odor, that is, it was smelled, there was a sound, that is to say, it was heard; a color or figure, and it was perceived by sight or touch. This is all that I can understand by these and the like expressions. For as to what is said of the absolute existence of unthinking things without any relation to their being perceived, that seems perfectly uninelligible. Their *esse* is *percipi*, nor is it possible they should have any existence out of the minds or thinking things which perceive them.

4. It is indeed an opinion strangely prevailing amongst men that houses, mountains, rivers, and, in a word, all sensible objects have an existence, natural or real, distinct from their being perceived by the understanding. But with how great an assurance and acquiescence soever this principle may be entertained in the world, yet whoever shall find in his heart to call it in question may, if I mistake not, perceive it to involve a manifest contradiction. For what are the forementioned objects but the things we perceive by sense? And what do we perceive besides our own ideas or sensations? And is it not plainly repugnant that any one of these, or any combination of them, should exist unperceived?

5. If we thoroughly examine this tenet it will, perhaps, be found at bottom to depend on the doctrine of *abstract ideas.* For can there be a nicer strain of abstraction than to distinguish the existence of sensible

objects from their being perceived, so as to conceive them existing unperceived? Light and colors, heat and cold, extension and figures—in a word, the things we see and feel—what are they but so many sensations, notions, ideas, or impressions on the sense? And is it possible to separate, even in thought, any of these from perception? For my part, I might as easily divide a thing from itself. I may, indeed, divide in my thoughts, or conceive apart from each other, those things which, perhaps, I never perceived by sense so divided. Thus I imagine the trunk of a human body without limbs, or conceive the smell of a rose without thinking on the rose itself. So far, I will not deny, I can abstract—if that may properly be called "abstraction" which extends only to the conceiving separately such objects as it is possible may really exist or be actually perceived asunder. But my conceiving or imagining power does not extend beyond the possibility of real existence or perception. Hence, as it is impossible for me to see or feel anything without an actual sensation of that thing, so it is impossible for me to conceive in my thoughts any sensible thing or object distinct from the sensation or perception of it.

6. Some truths there are so near and obvious to the mind that a man need only open his eyes to see them. Such I take this important one to be, to wit, that all the choirs of heaven and furniture of the earth, in a word, all those bodies which compose the mighty frame of the world, have not any subsistence without a mind—that their *being* is to be perceived or known, that, consequently, so long as they are not actually perceived by me or do not exist in my mind or that of any other created spirit, they must either have no existence at all or else subsist in the mind of some eternal spirit—it being perfectly unintelligible, and involving all the absurdity of abstraction, to attribute to any single part of them an existence independent of a spirit. To be convinced of which, the reader need only reflect, and try to separate in his own thoughts, the *being* of a sensible thing from its *being perceived.*

7. From what has been said it follows there is not any other substance than *spirit,* or that which perceives. But, for the fuller proof of this point, let it be considered the sensible qualities are color, figure, motion, smell, taste, and such like —that is, the ideas perceived by sense. Now, for an idea to exist in an unperceiving thing is a manifest contradiction, for to have an idea is all one as to perceive; that, therefore, wherein color, figure, and the like qualities exist must perceive them; hence it is clear there can be no unthinking substance or *substratum* of those ideas.

8. But, say you, though the ideas themselves do not exist without the mind, yet there may be things like them, whereof they are copies or resemblances, which things exist without the mind in an unthinking substance. I answer, an idea can be like nothing but an idea; a color or figure can be like nothing but another color or figure. If we look but ever so little into our thoughts, we shall find it impossible for us to conceive a likeness except only between our ideas. Again, I ask whether those supposed originals or external things, of which our ideas are the pictures or representations, be themselves perceivable or no? If they are, then they are ideas and we have gained our point; but if you say they are not, I appeal to anyone whether it be sense to assert a color is like something which is invisible; hard or soft, like something which is intangible; and so of the rest.

9. Some there are who make a distinction betwixt *primary* and *secondary* qualities. By the former they mean extension, figure, motion, rest, solidity or impenetrability, and number; by the latter they denote all other sensible qualities, as colors, sounds, tastes, and so forth. The ideas we have of these they acknowledge not to be the resemblances of anything existing without the mind, or unperceived, but they will have our ideas of the primary qualities to be patterns of images of things which exist without the mind, in an unthinking substance which they call "matter." By "matter," therefore, we are to understand an inert, senseless substance, in which extension, figure, and motion do actually subsist. But it is evident from what we have already shown that extension, figure, and motion are only ideas existing in the mind, and that an idea can be like nothing but another idea, and that consequently neither they nor their archetypes can exist in an unperceiving substance. Hence it is plain that the very notion of what is called "matter" or "corporeal substance" involves a contradiction in it.

10. They who assert that figure, motion, and the rest of the primary or original qualities do exist without the mind in unthinking substances do at the

same acknowledge that colors, sounds, heat, cold, and suchlike secondary qualities do not—which they tell us are sensations existing in the mind alone, that depend on and are occasioned by the different size, texture, and motion of the minute particles of matter. This they take for an undoubted truth which they can demonstrate beyond all exception. Now, if it be certain that those original qualities are inseparably united with the other sensible qualities, and not, even in thought, capable of being abstracted from them, it plainly follows that they exist only in the mind. But I desire anyone to reflect and try whether he can, by any abstraction of thought, conceive the extension and motion of a body without all other sensible qualities. For my own part, I see evidently that it is not in my power to frame an idea of a body extended and moved, but I must withal give some color or other sensible quality which is acknowledged to exist only in the mind. In short, extension, figure, and motion, abstracted from all other qualities are, there must these be also, to wit, in the mind and nowhere else.

11. Again, *great* and *small, swift* and *slow* are allowed to exist nowhere without the mind, being entirely relative, and changing as the frame or position of the organs of sense varies. The extension, therefore, which exists without the mind is neither great nor small, the motion neither swift nor slow; that is, they are nothing at all. But, say you, they are extension in general, and motion in general: thus we see how much the tenet of extended movable substances existing without the mind depends on that strange doctrine of *abstract ideas*. And here I cannot but remark how nearly the vague and indeterminate description of matter or corporeal substance, which the modern philosophers are run into by their own principles, resembles that antiquated and so much ridiculed notion of *materia prima*, to be met with in Aristotle and his followers. Without extension, solidity cannot be conceived; since, therefore, it has been shown that extension exists not in an unthinking substance, the same must also be true of solidity.

12. That number is entirely the creature of the mind, even though the other qualities be allowed to exist without, will be evident to whoever considers that the same thing bears a different denomination of number as the mind views it with different respects. Thus the same extension is one, or three, or thirty-six, according as the mind considers it with reference to a yard, a foot, or an inch. Number is so visibly relative and dependent on men's understanding that it is strange to think how anyone should give it an absolute existence without the mind. We say one book, one page, one line; all these are equally units, though some contain several of the others. And in each instance it is plain the unit relates to some particular combination of ideas arbitrarily put together by the mind.

13. Unity I know some will have to be a simple or uncompounded idea accompanying all other ideas into the mind. That I have any such idea answering the word "unity" I do not find; and if I had, methinks I could not miss finding it; on the contrary, it should be the most familiar to my understanding since it is said to accompany all other ideas and to be perceived by all the ways of sensation and reflection. To say no more, it is an *abstract idea*.

14. I shall further add that, after the same manner as modern philosophers prove certain sensible qualities to have no existence in matter, or without the mind, the same thing may be likewise proved of all other sensible qualities whatsoever. Thus, for instance, it is said that heat and cold are affections only of the mind, and not all patterns of real being existing in the corporeal substances which excite them. For that the same body which appears cold to one hand seems warm to another. Now, why may we not as well argue that figure and extension are not patterns or resemblances of qualities existing in matter, because to the same eye at different stations, or eyes of a different texture at the same station, they appear various and cannot, therefore, be the images of anything settled and determinate without the mind? Again, it is proved that sweetness is not really in the sapid thing, because, the thing remaining unaltered, the sweetness is changed into bitter, as in case of a fever or otherwise vitiated palate. Is it not as reasonable to say that motion is not without the mind, since if the succession of ideas in the mind become swifter, the motion, it is acknowledged, shall appear slower without any alteration in any external object?

15. In short, let anyone consider those arguments which are thought manifestly to prove that colors and tastes exist only in the mind, and he shall find they may with equal force be brought to prove the

same thing of extension, figures, and motion. Though it must be confessed this method of arguing does not so much prove that there is no extension or color in an outward object as that we do not know by sense which is the true extension or color of the object. But the arguments foregoing plainly show it to be impossible that any color or extension at all, or other sensible quality whatsoever, should exist in an unthinking subject without the mind, or, in truth, that there should be any such thing as an outward object.

16. But let us examine a little the received opinion.—It is said extension is a mode or accident of matter, and that matter is the *substratum* that supports it. Now I desire that you would explain what is meant by matter's "supporting" extension. Say you, I have no idea of matter and, therefore, cannot explain it. I answer, though you have no positive, yet, if you have any meaning at all, you must at least have a relative idea of matter; though you know not what it is, yet you must be supposed to know what relation it bears to accidents, and what is meant by its supporting them. It is evident "support" cannot here be taken in its usual or literal sense—as when we say that pillars support a building; in what sense therefore must it be taken?

17. If we inquire into what the most accurate philosophers declare themselves to mean by "material substance," we shall find them acknowledge they have no other meaning annexed to those sounds but the idea of being in general together with the relative notion of its supporting accidents. The general idea of being appears to me the most abstract and incomprehensible of all other; and as for its supporting accidents, this, as we have just now observed, cannot be understood in the common sense of those words; it must, therefore, be taken in some other sense, but what that is they do not explain. So that when I consider the two parts or branches which make the signification of the words "material substance," I am convinced there is no distinct meaning annexed to them. But why should we trouble ourselves any further in discussing this material *substratum* or support of figure and motion and other sensible qualities? Does it not suppose they have an existence without the mind? And is not this a direct repugnancy and altogether inconceivable?

18. But, though it were possible that solid, figured, movable substances may exist without the mind, corresponding to the ideas we have of bodies, yet how is it possible for us to know this? Either we must know it by sense or by reason. As for our senses, by them we have the knowledge only of our sensations, ideas, or those things that are immediately perceived by sense, call them what you will; but they do not inform us that things exist without the mind, or unperceived, like to those which are perceived. This the materialists themselves acknowledge. It remains therefore that if we have any knowledge at all of external things, it must be by reason, inferring their existence from what is immediately perceived by sense. But what reason can induce us to believe the existence of bodies without the minds, from what we perceive, since the very patrons of matter themselves do not pretend there is any necessary connection betwixt them and our ideas? I say it is granted on all hands (and what happens in dreams, frenzies, and the like, puts it beyond dispute) that it is possible we might be affected with all the ideas we have now, though no bodies existed without resembling them. Hence it is evident the supposition of external bodies is not necessary for producing our ideas; since it is granted they are produced sometimes, and might possibly be produced always in the same order we see them in at present, without their concurrence.

19. But though we might possibly have all our sensations without them, yet perhaps it may be thought easier to conceive and explain the manner of their production by supposing external bodies in their likeness rather than otherwise; and so it might be at least probable there are such things as bodies that excite their ideas in our minds. But neither can this be said, for, though we give the materialists their external bodies, they by their own confession are never the nearer to knowing how our ideas are produced, since they own themselves unable to comprehend in what manner body can act upon spirit, or how it is possible it should imprint any idea in the mind. Hence it is evident the production of ideas or sensations in our minds can be no reason why we should suppose matter or corporeal substances, since that is acknowledged to remain equally inexplicable with our without this supposition. If therefore it were possible for bodies to exist without the

mind, yet to hold they do so must needs be a very precarious opinion, since it is to suppose, without any reason at all, that God has created innumerable beings that are entirely useless and serve to no manner of purpose.

20. In short, if there were external bodies, it is impossible we should ever come to know it; and if there were not, we might have the very same reasons to think there were that we have now. Suppose—what no one can deny possible—an intelligence without the help of external bodies, to be affected with the same train of sensations or ideas that you are, imprinted in the same order and with like vividness in his mind. I ask whether that intelligence has not all the reason to believe the existence of corporeal substances, represented by his ideas and exciting them in his mind, that you can possibly have for believing the same thing? Of this there can be no question—which one consideration is enough to make any reasonable person suspect the strength of whatever arguments he may think himself to have for the existence of bodies without the mind.

21. Were it necessary to add any further proof against the existence of matter after what has been said, I could instance several of those errors and difficulties (not to mention impieties) which have sprung from that tenet. It has occasioned numberless controversies and disputes in philosophy, and not a few of far greater moment in religion. But I shall not enter into the detail of them in this place as well because I think arguments a posteriori are unnecessary for confirming what has been, if I mistake not, sufficiently demonstrated a priori, as because I shall hereafter find occasion to speak somewhat of them.

22. I am afraid I have given cause to think me needlessly prolix in handling this subject. For to what purpose is it to dilate on that which may be demonstrated with the utmost evidence in a line or two to anyone that is capable of the least reflection? It is but looking into your own thoughts, and so trying whether you can conceive it possible for a sound, or figure, or motion, or color to exist without the mind or unperceived. This easy trial may make you see that what you contend for is a downright contradiction. Insomuch that I am content to put the whole upon this issue: if you can but conceive it possible for one extended movable substance, or, in

general, for any one idea, or anything like an idea, to exist otherwise than in a mind perceiving it, I shall readily give up the cause. And, as for all that compages of external bodies which you contend for, I shall grant you its existence, though you cannot either give me any reason why you believe it exists, or assign any use to it when it is supposed to exist. I say the bare possibility of your opinion's being true shall pass for an argument that it is so.

23. But, say you, surely there is nothing easier than to imagine trees, for instance, in a park, or books existing in a closet, and nobody by to perceive them. I answer you may so, there is no difficulty in it; but what is all this, I beseech you, more than framing in your mind certain ideas which you call books and trees, and at the same time omitting to frame the idea of anyone that may perceive them? But do not you yourself perceive or think of them all the while? This therefore is nothing to the purpose; it only shows you have the power of imagining or forming ideas in your mind; but it does not show that you can conceive it possible the objects of your thought may exist without the mind. To make out this, it is necessary that you conceive them existing unconceived or unthought of, which is a manifest repugnancy. When we do our utmost to conceive the existence of external bodies, we are all the while only contemplating our own ideas. But the mind, taking no notice of itself, is deluded to think it can and does conceive bodies existing unthought of or without the mind, though at the same time they are apprehended by or exist in itself. A little attention will discover to anyone the truth and evidence of what is here said, and make it unnecessary to insist on any other proofs against the existence of *material substance*.

24. It is very obvious, upon the least inquiry into our own thoughts, to know whether it be possible for us to understand what is meant by "the absolute existence of sensible objects in themselves, or without the mind." To me it is evident those words mark out either a direct contradiction or else nothing at all. And to convince others of this, I know no readier or fairer way than to entreat they would calmly attend to their own thoughts; and if by this attention the emptiness or repugnancy of those expressions does appear, surely nothing more is requisite for their conviction. It is on this, therefore, that I insist, to wit, that "the absolute existence of unthinking

things" are words without a meaning, or which include a contradiction. This is what I repeat and inculcate, and earnestly recommend to the attentive thoughts of the reader.

25. All our ideas, sensations, or the things which we perceive, by whatsoever names they may be distinguished, are visibly inactive—thee is nothing of power or agency included in them. So that one idea or object of thought cannot produce or make any alteration in another. To be satisfied or the truth of this, there is nothing else requisite but a bare observation of our ideas. For since they and every part of them exist only in the mind, it follows that there is nothing in them but what is perceived; but whoever shall attend to his ideas, whether of sense or reflection, will not perceive in them any power or activity; there is, therefore, no such thing contained in them. A little attention will discover to us that the very being of an idea implies passiveness and inertness in it, insomuch that it is impossible for an idea to do anything or, strictly speaking, to be the cause of anything; neither can it be the resemblance or pattern of any active being, as is evident from sec. 8. Whence it plainly follows that extension, figure, and motion cannot be the cause of our sensations. To say, therefore, that these are the effects of powers resulting from the configuration, number, motion and size of corpuscles must certainly be false.

26. We perceive a continual succession of ideas, some are anew excited, others are changed or totally disappear. There is, therefore, some cause of these ideas, whereon they depend and which produces and changes them. That this cause cannot be any quality or idea or combination of ideas is clear from the preceding section. It must therefore be a substance; but it has been shown that there is no corporeal or material substance: it remains, therefore, that the cause of ideas is an incorporeal, active substance or spirit.

27. A spirit is one simple, undivided, active being—as it perceives ideas it is called "the understanding," and as it produces or otherwise operates about them it is called "the will." Hence there can be no *idea* formed of a soul or spirit; for all ideas whatever, being passive and inert (*vide* sec. 25), they cannot represent unto us, by way of image or likeness, that which acts. A little attention will make it plain to anyone that to have an idea which shall be like that active principle of motion and change of ideas is absolutely impossible. Such is the nature of *spirit*, or that which acts, that it cannot be of itself perceived, but only by the effects which it produces. If any man shall doubt of the truth of what is here delivered, let him but reflect and try if he can frame the idea of any power or active being, and whether he has ideas of two principal powers marked by the names "will" and "understanding," distinct from each other as well as from a third idea of substance or being in general, with a relative notion of its supporting or being the subject of the aforesaid powers-which is signified by the name "soul" or "spirit." This is what some hold; but, so far as I can see, the words "will," "soul," "spirit" do not stand for different ideas or, in truth, for any idea at all, but for something which is very different from ideas, and which, being an agent, cannot be like unto, or represented by, any idea whatsoever. Though it must be owned at the same time that we have some notion of soul, spirit, and the operations of the mind, such as willing, loving, hating—in as much as we know or understand the meaning of those words.

28. I find I can excite ideas in my mind at pleasure, and vary and shift the scene as oft as I think fit. It is no more than willing, and straightway this or that idea arises in my fancy; and by the same power it is obliterated and makes way for another. This making and unmaking of ideas does very properly denominate the mind active. Thus much is certain and grounded on experience; but when we talk of unthinking agents or of exciting ideas exclusive of volition, we only amuse ourselves with words.

29. But, whatever power I may have over my own thoughts, I find the ideas actually perceived by sense have not a like dependence on my will. When in broad daylight I open my eyes, it is not in my power to choose whether I shall see or no, or to determine what particular objects shall present themselves to my view, and so likewise as to the hearing and other senses; the ideas imprinted on them are not creatures of my will. There is therefore some *other* will or spirit that produces them.

30. The ideas of sense are more strong, lively, and distinct than those of the imagination; they have likewise a steadiness, order, and coherence, and are not excited at random, as those which are the effects of human wills often are, but in a regular train or series,

the admirable connection whereof sufficiently testifies the wisdom and benevolence of its Author. Now the set rules or established methods wherein the mind we depend on excites in us the ideas of sense are called "the laws of nature"; and these we learn by experience, which teaches us that such and such ideas are attended with such and such other ideas in the ordinary course of things.

31. This gives us a sort of foresight which enables us to regulate our actions for the benefit of life. And without this we should be eternally at a loss; we could not know how to act anything that might procure us the least pleasure or remove the least pain of sense. That food nourishes, sleep refreshes, and fire warms us; that to sow in the seedtime is the way to reap in the harvest; and in general that to obtain such or such ends, such or such means are conducive—all this we know, not by discovering any necessary connection between our ideas, but only by the observation of the settled laws of nature, without which we should be all in uncertainty and confusion, and a grown man no more know how to manage himself in the affairs of life than an infant just born.

32. And yet this consistent, uniform working which so evidently displays the goodness and wisdom of that Governing Spirit whose Will constitutes the laws of nature, is so far from leading our thoughts to Him that it rather sends them awandering after second causes. For when we perceive certain ideas of sense constantly followed by other ideas, and we know this is not of our own doing, we forthwith attribute power and agency to the ideas themselves and make one the cause of another, than which nothing can be more absurd and unintelligible. Thus, for example, having observed that when we perceive by sight a certain round, luminous figure, we at the same time perceive by touch the idea or sensation called "heat," we do from thence conclude the sun to be the cause of heat. And in like manner perceiving the motion and collision of bodies to be attended with sound, we are inclined to thing the latter an effect of the former.

33. The ideas imprinted on the senses by the Author of Nature are called "real things"; and those excited in the imagination, being less regular, vivid, and constant, are more properly termed "ideas" or "images of things" which they copy and represent.

But then our sensations, be they never so vivid and distinct, are nevertheless ideas, that is, they exist in the mind, or are perceived by it, as truly as the ideas of its own framing. The ideas of sense are allowed to have more reality in them, that is, to be more strong, orderly, and coherent than the creatures of the mind; but this is no argument that they exist without the mind. They are also less dependent on the spirit, or thinking substance which perceives them, in that they are excited by the will of another, and more powerful spirit; yet still they are *ideas*; and certainly no idea, whether faint or strong, can exist otherwise than in a mind perceiving it.

34. Before we proceed any further it is necessary to spend some time in answering objections which may probably be made against the principles hitherto laid down. In doing of which, if I seem too prolix to those of quick apprehensions, I hope it may be pardoned, since all men do not equally apprehend things of this nature, and I am willing to be understood by everyone.

First, then, it will be objected that by the foregoing principles all that is real and substantial in nature is banished out of the world, and instead thereof a chimerical scheme of *ideas* takes place. All things that exist, exist only in the mind, that is, they are purely notional. What therefore becomes of the sun, moon, and stars? What must we think of houses, rivers, mountains, trees, stones, nay, even of our own bodies? Are all of these but so many chimeras and illusions on the fancy? To all which, and whatever else of the same sort may be objected, I answer that by the principles premised we are not deprived of any one thing in nature. Whatever we see, feel, hear, or anywise conceive or understand remains as secure as ever, and is as real as ever. There is a *rerum natura*, and the distinction between realities and chimeras retains its full force. This is evident from secs. 29, 30, and 33, where we have shown what is meant by "real things" in opposition to "chimeras" or ideas of our own framing; but then they both equally exist in the mind, and in that sense they are alike *ideas*.

35. I do not argue against the existence of any one thing that we can apprehend either by sense or reflection. That the things I see with my eyes and touch with my hands do exist, really exist, I make not the least question. The only thing whose existence

we deny is that which philosophers call matter or corporeal substance. And in doing of this there is no damage done to the rest of mankind, who, I dare say, will never miss it. The atheist indeed will want the color of an empty name to support his impiety; and the philosophers may possibly find they have lost a great handle for trifling and disputation.

36. If any man thinks this detracts from the existence or reality of things, he is very far from understanding what has been premised in the plainest terms I could think of. Take here an abstract of what has been said: there are spiritual substances, minds, or human souls, which will or excite these ideas in themselves at pleasure, but these are faint, weak, and unsteady in respect of others they perceive by sense—which, being impressed upon them according to certain rules or laws of nature, speak themselves the effects of a mind more powerful and wise than human spirits. These latter are said to have more *reality* in them than the former—by which is meant that they are more affecting, orderly, and distinct, and that they are not fictions of the mind perceiving them. And in this sense the sun that I see by day is the real sun, and that which I imagine by night is the idea of the former. In the sense here given of "reality" it is evident that every vegetable, star, mineral, and in general each part of the mundane system, is as much a *real being* by our principles as by any other. Whether others mean anything by the term "reality" different from what I do, I entreat them to look into their own thoughts and see.

37. It will be urged that this much at least is true, to wit, that we take away all corporeal substances. To this my answer is that if the word "substance" be taken in the vulgar sense—for a combination of sensible qualities, such as extension, solidity, weight, and the like—this we cannot be accused of taking away; but if it be taken in a philosophic sense— for the support of accidents or qualities without the mind—then indeed I acknowledge that we take it away, if one may be said to take away that which never had existence, not even in the imagination.

38. But, say you, it sounds very harsh to say we eat and drink ideas, and are clothed with ideas. I acknowledge it does so—the word "idea" not being used in common discourse to signify the several combinations of sensible qualities which are called 'things"; and it is certain that any expression which varies from the familiar use of language will seem harsh and ridiculous. But this does not concern the truth of the proposition which, in other words, is no more than to say we are fed and clothed with those things which we perceive immediately by our senses. The hardness or softness, the color, taste, warmth, figure, and suchlike qualities, which combined together constitute the several sorts of victuals and apparel, have been shown to exist only in the mind that perceives them; and this is all that is meant by calling them "ideas," which word if it was as ordinarily used as "thing," would sound no harsher nor more ridiculous than it. I am not for disputing about the propriety, but the truth of the expression. If therefore you agree with me that we eat and drink and are clad with the immediate objects of sense, which cannot exist unperceived or without the mind, I shall readily grant it is more proper or conformable to custom that they should be called "things" rather than "ideas."

39. If it be demanded why I make use of the word "idea," and do not rather in compliance with custom call them "things," I answer I do it for two reasons; first, because the term "thing" in contradistinction to "idea" is generally supposed to denote somewhat existing without the mind; secondly, because "thing" has a more comprehensive signification than "idea," including spirits or thinking things as well as ideas. Since therefore the objects of sense exist only in the mind and are withal thoughtless and inactive, I chose to mark them by the word "idea," which implies those properties.

40. But, say what we can, someone perhaps may be apt to reply he will still believe his senses, and never suffer any arguments, how plausible soever, to prevail over the certainty of them. Be it so; assert the evidence of sense as high as you please, we are willing to do the same. That what I see, hear, and feel does exist—that is to say; is perceived by me—I no more doubt than I do of my own being. But I do not see how the testimony of sense can be alleged as a proof for the existence of anything which is not perceived by sense. We are not for having any man turn skeptic and disbelieve his senses; on the contrary, we give them all the stress and assurance imaginable; nor are there any principles more opposite to skepticism than those we have laid down, as shall be hereafter clearly shown.

41. *Secondly*, it will be objected that there is a great difference betwixt real fire, for instance, and the idea of fire, betwixt dreaming or imagining oneself burned, and actually being so. This and the like may be urged in opposition to our tenets. To all which the answer is evident from what has been already said; and I shall only add in this place that if real fire be very different from the idea of fire, so also is the real pain that it occasions very different from the idea of the same pain, and yet nobody will pretend the real pain either is, or can possibly be, in an unperceiving thing, or without the mind, any more than its idea. . . .

45. *Fourthly*, it will be objected that from the foregoing principles it follows things are every moment annihilated and created anew. The objects of sense exist only when they are perceived; the trees, therefore, are in the garden, or the chairs in the parlor, no longer than while there is somebody by to perceive them. Upon shutting my eyes all the furniture in the room is reduced to nothing, and barely upon opening them it is again created. In answer to all which I refer the reader to what has been said in secs. 3, 4, etc., and desire he will consider whether he means anything by the actual existence of an idea distinct from its being perceived. For my part, after the nicest inquiry I could make, I am not able to discover that anything else is meant by those words; and I once more entreat the reader to sound his own thoughts and not suffer himself to be imposed on by words. If he can conceive it possible either for his ideas or their archetypes to exist without being perceived, then I give up the cause; but if he can stand up in defense of he knows not what and pretend to charge on me as an absurdity the not assenting to those propositions which at bottom have no meaning in them. . . .

54. In the *eighth* place, the universal concurrent assent of mankind may be thought by some an invincible argument in behalf of matter, or the existence of external things. Must we suppose the whole world to be mistaken? And if so, what cause can be assigned of so widespread and predominant an error? I answer, first, that, upon a narrow inquiry, it will not perhaps be found so many as is imagined do really believe the existence of matter or things without the mind. Strictly speaking, to believe that which involves a contradiction, or has no meaning in it, is impossible; and whether the foregoing expressions are not of that sort, I refer it to the impartial examination of the reader. In one sense, indeed, men may be said to believe that matter exists, that is, they act as if the immediate cause of their sensations, which affects them every moment and is so nearly present to them, were some senseless unthinking being. But that they should clearly apprehend any meaning marked by those words, and form thereof a settled speculative opinion, is what I am not able to conceive. This is not the only instance wherein men impose upon themselves, by imagining they believe those propositions they have often heard, though at bottom they have no meaning in them.

55. But secondly, though we should grant a notion to be ever so universally and steadfastly adhered to, yet this is but a weak argument of its truth to whoever considers what a vast number of prejudices and false opinions are everywhere embraced with the utmost tenaciousness by the unreflecting (which are the far greater) part of mankind. There was a time when the antipodes and motion of the earth were looked upon as monstrous absurdities even by men of learning; and if it be considered what a small proportion they bear to the rest of mankind, we shall find that at this day those notions have gained but a very inconsiderable footing in the world.

56. But it is demanded that we assign a cause of this prejudice and account for its obtaining in the world. To this I answer that men, knowing they perceived several ideas whereof they themselves were not the authors—as not being excited from within nor depending on the operation of their wills—this made them maintain those ideas, or objects of perception, had an existence independent of and without the mind, without ever dreaming that a contradiction was involved in those words. But philosophers having plainly seen that the immediate objects of perception do not exist without the mind, they in some degree corrected the mistake of the vulgar, but at the same time run into another which seems no less absurd, to wit, that there are certain objects really existing without the mind or having a subsistence distinct from being perceived, of which our ideas are only images or resemblances, imprinted by those objects on the mind. And this notion of the philosophers owes its origin to the same

cause with the former, namely, their being conscious that they were not the authors of their own sensations, which they evidently knew were imprinted from without, and which therefore must have some cause distinct from the minds on which they are imprinted.

57. But why they should suppose the ideas of sense to be excited in us by things in their likeness, and not rather have recourse to *spirit* which alone can act, may be accounted for, first because they were not aware of the repugnancy there is, as well in supposing things like unto our ideas existing without, as in attributing to them power or activity. Secondly, because the supreme spirit which excites those ideas in our minds is not marked out and limited to our view by any particular finite collection of sensible ideas, as human agents are by their size, complexion, limbs and motions. And thirdly, because His operations are regular and uniform. Whenever the course of nature is interrupted by a miracle, men are ready to own the presence of a superior agent. But when we see things on in the ordinary course, they do not excite in us any reflection; their order and concatenation, though it be an argument of the greatest wisdom, power, and goodness in their Creator, is yet so constant and familiar to us that we do not think them the immediate effects of a *free spirit*, especially since inconstancy and mutability in acting, though it be an imperfection, is looked on as a mark of *freedom*.

58. *Tenthly*, it will objected that the notions we advance are inconsistent with several sound truths in philosophy and mathematics. For example, the motion of the earth is now universally admitted by astronomers as a truth grounded on the clearest and most convincing reasons. But on the foregoing principles there can be no such thing. For, motion being only an idea, it follows that if it be not perceived it exists not; but the motion of the earth is not perceived by sense I answer, that tenet, if rightly understood, will be found to agree with the principles we have premised, for the question whether the earth moves or no amounts in reality to more than this, to wit, whether we have reason to conclude, from what has been observed by astronomers, that if we were placed in such and such circumstances, and such or such a position and distance both from the earth and sun, we should perceive the former to move among the choir of the planets, and appearing in all respects like one of them; and this, by the established rules of nature which we have no reason to mistrust, is reasonably collected from the phenomena.

59. We may, from the experience we have had of the train and succession of ideas in our minds, often make, I will not say uncertain conjectures, but sure and well-grounded predictions concerning the ideas we shall be affected with pursuant to a great train of actions, and be enabled to pass a right judgment of what would have appeared to us in case we were placed in circumstances very different from those we are in present. Herein consists the knowledge of nature, which may preserve its use and certainty very consistently with what has been said. It will be easy to apply this to whatever objections of the like sort may be drawn from the magnitude of the stars or any other discoveries in astronomy or nature.

W. T. STACE

Science and the Physical World

So far as I know scientists still talk about electrons, protons, neutrons, and so on. We never directly perceive these, hence if we ask how we know of their existence the only possible answer seems to be that they are an inference from what we do directly perceive. What sort of an inference? Apparently a causal inference. The atomic entities in some way impinge upon the sense of the animal organism and cause that organism to perceive the familiar world of tables, chairs, and the rest.

But is it not clear that such a concept of causation, however interpreted, is invalid? The only reason we have for believing in the law of causation is that we *observe* certain regularities or sequences. We observe that, in certain conditions, *A* is always followed by *B*. We call *A* the cause, *B* the effect. And the sequence *A-B* becomes a causal law. It follows that all *observed* causal sequences are between sensed objects in the familiar world of perception, and that all known causal laws apply solely to the world of sense and not to anything beyond or behind it. And this in turn means that we have not got, and never could have, one jot of evidence for believing that the law of causation can be applied *outside* the realm of perception, or that that realm can have any causes (such as the supposed physical objects) which are not themselves perceived.

Put the same thing in another way. Suppose there is an observed sequence *A-B-C*, represented by the vertical lines in the diagram below.

The observer X sees, and can see, nothing except things in the familiar world of perception. What *right* has he, and what *reason* has he, to assert causes of A, B, and C, such as *a′, b′, c′*, which he can never observe, behind the perceived world? He has no *right,* because the law of causation on which he is relying has never been observed to operate outside the series of perceptions, and he can have, therefore, no evidence that it does so. And he has no *reason* because the phenomenon C is *sufficiently* accounted for by the cause B, B by A, and so on. It is unnecessary and superfluous to introduce a *second* cause *b′* for B, *c′* for C, and so forth. To give two causes for each phenomenon, one in one world and one in another, is unnecessary, and perhaps even self-contradictory.

Is it denied, then, it will be asked, that the star causes light waves, that the waves cause retinal changes, that these cause changes in the optic nerve, which in turn causes movements in the brain cells, and so on? No, it is not denied. But the observed causes and effects are all in the world of perception. And no sequences of sense-data can possibly justify going outside that world. If you admit that we never observe anything except sensed objects and their relations, regularities, and sequences, then it is obvious that we are completely shut in by our sensations and can never get outside them. Not only causal relations, but all other observed relations, upon which *any* kind of inferences might be founded, will lead only to further sensible objects and their relations. No inference, therefore, can pass from what is sensible to what is not sensible.

The fact is that atoms are *not* inferences from sensations. No one denies, of course, that a vast amount of perfectly valid inferential reasoning takes place in the physical theory of the atom. But it will not be found to be in any strict logical sense inference *from sense-data to atoms.* An *hypothesis* is set up, and the inferential processes are concerned with the

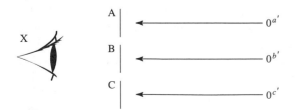

A | ⟵――――――――――― $0^{a'}$

X

B | ⟵――――――――――― $0^{b'}$

C | ⟵――――――――――― $0^{c'}$

application of the hypothesis, that is, with the prediction by its aid of further possible sensations and with its own internal consistency.

That atoms are not inferences from sensations means, of course, that from existence of sensations we cannot validly infer the existence of atoms. And this means that we cannot have any reason at all to believe that they exist. And that is why I propose to argue that they do not exist—or at any rate that no one could know it if they did, and that we have absolutely no evidence of their existence.

What status have they, then? Is it meant that they are false and worthless, merely untrue? Certainly not. No one supposes that the entries in the nautical almanac "exist" anywhere except on the pages of that book and in the brains of its compilers and readers. Yet they are "true," inasmuch as they enable us to predict certain sensations, namely, the positions and times of certain perceived objects which we call the stars. And so the formulae of the atomic theory are true in the same sense, and perform a similar function.

I suggest that they are nothing but shorthand formulae, ingeniously worked out by the human mind, to enable it to predict its experience, i.e. to predict what sensations will be given to it. By "predict" here I do not mean to refer solely to the future. To calculate that there was an eclipse of the sun visible in Asia Minor in the year 585 S.C. is, in the sense in which I am using the term, to predict.

In order to see more clearly what is meant, let us apply the same idea to another case, that of gravitation. Newton formulated a law of gravitation in terms of "forces." It was supposed that this law—which was nothing but a mathematical formula—governed the operation of these existent forces. Nowadays it is no longer believed that these forces exist at all. And yet the law can be applied just as well without them to the prediction of astronomical phenomena. It is a matter of no importance to the scientific man whether the forces exist or not. That may be said to be a purely philosophical question. And I think the philosopher should pronounce them fictions. But that would not make the law useless or untrue. If it could still be used to predict phenomena, it would be just as true as it was.

It is true that fault is now found with Newton's law, and that another law, that of Einstein, has been substituted for it. And it is sometimes supposed that the reason for this is that forces are no longer believed in. But this is not the case. Whether forces exist or not simply does not matter. What matters is the discovery that Newton's law does *not* enable us accurately to predict certain astronomical facts such as the exact position of the planet Mercury. Therefore another formula, that of Einstein, has been substituted for it which permits correct predictions. This new law, as it happens, is a formula in terms of geometry. It is pure mathematics and nothing else. It does not contain anything about forces. In its pure form it does not even contain, so I am informed, anything about "humps and hills in space-time." And it does not matter whether any such humps and hills exist. It is truer than Newton's law, not because it substitutes humps and hills for forces, but solely because it is a more accurate formula of prediction.

Not only may it be said that forces do not exist. It may with equal truth be said that "gravitation" does not exist. Gravitation is not a "thing," but a mathematical formula, which exists only in the heads of mathematicians. And as a mathematical formula cannot cause a body to fall, so gravitation cannot cause a body to fall. Ordinary language misleads us here. We speak of the law "of" gravitation, and suppose that this law "applies to" the heavenly bodies. We are thereby misled into supposing that there are *two* things, namely, the gravitation and the heavenly bodies, and that one of these things, the gravitation, causes changes in the other. In reality nothing exists except the moving bodies. And neither Newton's law nor Einstein's law is, strictly speaking, a law of gravitation. They are both laws of moving bodies, that is to say, formulae which tell us how these bodies will move.

Now, just as in the past "forces" were foisted into Newton's law (by himself, be it said), so now certain popularizers of relativity foisted "humps and hills in space-time" into Einstein's law. We hear that the reason why the planets move in curved courses is that they cannot go through these humps and hills, but have to go round them! The planets just get "shoved about," not by forces, but by the humps and hills! But these humps and hills are pure metaphors. And anyone who takes them for "existences" gets asked awkward questions as to what "curved space" is curved "in."

It is not irrelevant to our topic to consider *why* human beings invent these metaphysical monsters of forces and bumps in space-time. The reason is that they have never emancipated themselves from the absurd idea that science "explains" things. They were not content to have laws which merely told them *that* the planets will, as a matter of fact, move in such and such ways. They wanted to know "why" the planets move in those ways. So Newton replied, "Forces." "Oh," said humanity, "that explains it. We understand forces. We feel them every time someone pushes or pulls us." Thus the movements were supposed to be "explained" by entities familiar because analogous to the muscular sensations which human beings feel. The humps and hills were introduced for exactly the same reason. They seem so familiar. If there is a bump in the billiard table, the rolling billiard ball is diverted from a straight to a curved course. Just the same with the planets. "Oh, I see!" says humanity, "that's quite simple. That *explains* everything."

But scientific laws, properly formulated, never "explain" anything. They simply state, in an abbreviated and generalized form, *what happens*. No scientist, and in my opinion no philosopher, knows *why* anything happens, or can "explain" anything. Scientific laws do nothing except state the brute fact that "when *A* happens, *B* always happens too." And laws of this kind obviously enable us to predict. If certain scientists substituted humps and hills for forces, then they have just substituted one superstition for another. For my part I do not believe that *science* has done this, though some *scientists* may have. For scientists, after all, are human beings with the same craving for "explanations" as other people.

I think that atoms are in exactly the same position as forces and the humps and hills of space-time. In reality the mathematical formulae which are the scientific ways of stating the atomic theory are simply formulae for calculating what sensations will appear in given conditions. But just as the weakness of the human mind demanded that there should correspond to the formula of gravitation a real "thing" which could be called "gravitation itself" or "force," so the same weakness demands that there should be a real thing corresponding to the atomic formulae, and this real thing is called the atom. In reality the atoms no more cause sensations than gravitation causes apples to fall. The only causes of sensations are other sensations. And the relation of atoms to sensations to be felt is not the relation of cause to effect, but the relation of a mathematical formula to the facts and happenings which it enables the mathematician to calculate.

Some writers have said that the physical world has no color, no sound, no taste, no smell. It has no spatiality. Probably it has not even number. We must not suppose that it is in any way like our world, or that we can understand it by attributing to it the characters of our world. Why not carry this progress to its logical conclusion? Why not give up the idea that it has even the character of "existence" which our familiar world has? We have given up smell, color, taste. We have given up even space and shape. We have given up number. Surely, after all that, mere existence is but a little thing to give up. No? Then is it that the idea of existence conveys "a sort of halo"? I suspect so. The "existence" of atoms is but the expiring ghost of the pellet and billiard-ball atoms of our forefathers. They, of course, had size, shape, weight, hardness. These have gone. But thinkers still cling to their existence, just as their fathers clung to the existence of forces, and for the same reason. Their reason is not in the slightest that science has any use for the existent atom. But the *imagination* has. It seems somehow to explain things, to make them homely and familiar.

It will not be out of place to give one more example to show how common fictitious existences are in science, and how little it matters whether they really exist or not. This example has no strange and annoying talk of "bent spaces" about it. One of the foundations of physics is, or used to be, the law of the conservation of energy. I do not know how far, if at all, this has been affected by the theory that matter sometimes turns into energy. But that does not affect the lesson it has for us. The law states, or used to state, that the amount of energy in the universe is always constant, that energy is never either created or destroyed. This was highly convenient, but it seemed to have obvious exceptions. If you throw a stone up into the air, you are told that it exerts in its fall the same amount of energy which it took to throw it up. But suppose it does not fall. Suppose it lodges on the roof of your house and stays there. What has happened to the energy which you can nowhere perceive as being exerted? It seems to have disappeared out of the universe. No, says the scientist, it still exists as *potential* energy. Now what does this blessed word "potential"—which is thus brought in to save the situation—mean as applied to energy? It means, of course, that the energy does not exist in any of its regular "forms," heat, light, electricity, etc. But this is merely negative. What positive meaning has the term? Strictly speaking, none whatever. Either the energy exists or it does not exist. There is no realm of the "potential" half-way between existence and non-existence. And the existence of energy can only consist in its being exerted. If the energy is not being exerted, then it is not energy and does not exist. Energy can no more exist without energizing than heat can exist without being hot. The "potential" existence of the energy is, then, a fiction. The actual empirically verifiable facts are that if a certain quantity of energy *e* exists in the universe and then disappears out the universe (as happens when the stone lodges on the roof) the same amount of energy *e* will always reappear, begin to exist again, in certain known conditions. That is the fact which the law of

the conservation of energy actually expresses. And the fiction of potential energy is introduced simply because it is convenient and makes the equations easier to work. They could be worked quite well without it, but would be slightly more complicated. In either case the function of the law is the same. Its object is to apprise us that if in certain conditions we have certain perceptions (throwing up the stone), then in certain other conditions we shall get certain other perceptions (heat, light, stone hitting skull, or other such). But there will always be a temptation to hypostatize the potential energy as an "existence," and to believe that it is a "cause" which "explains" the phenomena.

If the views which I have been expressing are followed out, they will lead to the conclusion that, strictly speaking, *nothing exists except sensations* (and the minds which perceive them). The rest is mental construction or fiction. But this does not mean that the conception of a star or the conception of an electron are worthless or untrue. Their truth and value consist in their capacity for helping us to organize our experience and predict our sensations.

FRED DRETSKE

from "Sensation and Perception"

THE OBJECTS OF PERCEPTION

It has been argued that perception is a process (or, if you will, the result of a process) in which sensory information is coded in analog form in preparation for cognitive utilization. The sense modality (seeing, hearing, etc.) is determined, not by *what information* is encoded, but by the particular *way* it is encoded. I can *see* that it is 12:00 p.m. (by looking at a clock), but I can also get this information by auditory means (hearing the noon whistle). What makes one an instance of seeing and the other an instance of hearing is not the information carried by the two sensory representations (in this case the information is the same), but the differences in the vehicle by means of which this information is delivered—a difference in the representations (in contrast to what is represented).

I have argued, furthermore, that to pass from a perceptual to a cognitive state, to go from *seeing* Herman to *recognizing* Herman, from *hearing* the noon whistle to *knowing* that it is noon, from *smelling* or *tasting* a Moselle wine to *identifying* it as a Moselle wine (by the way it tastes or smells) is a process that involves a conversion in the way such information is encoded—a conversion from analog to digital. Cognitive states always, either explicitly or implicitly, have a specific propositional content. We know (or believe, or judge, or think) *that s is F* (identify, classify, or categorize *s* as *F*). We have a variety of ways to describe our cognitive states. Herman *realizes* that the wine has gone bad, *sees that* he needs a new typewriter ribbon, and can hear that there has been a change of key. Frequently the propositional content is not explicitly displayed in the nominal expression following the verb. We may say, for example, that Herman detects a *difference* between the two tastes, recognizes *his uncle*, or identifies *the object*. In each of these cases the propositional content is left unspecified, but there must always be some specific content if the attitudes in question are to qualify as cognitive. If Herman detects a difference between the two tastes, if he can distinguish between them, then he must know *that* the two tastes differ in some respect. Perhaps he only knows that they differ. If he recognizes his uncle, he must know that the man is such and such for some value of "such and such" (his uncle, the man who brings him candy, the stranger who kisses Mommy). And if he identifies the object, he must identify it as something—take it to be (and hence believe that it is) so and so for *some* value of "so and so."

Our perceptual states are different. We perceive (see, hear, smell, taste, and feel) *objects* and *events*. We see the man, smell the burning toast, taste the wine, feel the fabric, and hear the tree fall. What determines what we perceive (what object or event) is not what we believe (if anything) about what we perceive. For, as we have argued, one can see (say) a pentagon and think it is a square, taste a burgundy and take it to be a chianti, and hear a bell and believe one is hallucinating. Or one may have no relevant beliefs at all about the thing perceived. What is it, then, that determines the perceptual object? What makes it *Herman* I see when I mistake him for my Uncle Emil or see him under circumstances in which I fail to even notice him?

Suppose you are sitting on a train and someone tells you that it is moving. You cannot feel it move, see it move, or hear it move. You learn that it is moving by being told that it is moving. The information that the train is moving is acquired auditorily. Yet, we do not say that you could hear the train moving. The train, or the movement of the train, is not the object of your perceptual state. We can say that you *heard that* the train was moving, indicating by this choice of words that the information was received by auditory means, but what you actually heard was your friend say, "The train is moving," or words to that effect. *That* the train is moving is the propositional object of your cognitive state, but the train's movement is not the object your *perceptual* state.

A similar pattern is exhibited by all the sense modalities. When you read about an accident in the newspapers, you may come to know that a particular event occurred. Information is received by visual means, and we typically express this by the verb "to see" —you could see (by the newspapers) that there had been a tragic accident. Yet, you did not see the accident. To be told that K learned that s was F by seeing, hearing, smelling, or tasting is not to be told what K saw, heard, smelled, or tasted.

What, then, determines what it is that we see, hear, taste, smell, and feel? What determines the perceptual object, the object our sensory experience is an experience *of*?

There is a familiar, if not very adequate, reply to this question. The causal theory of perception tells us that we see and hear those objects (or events) which are causally responsible for our perceptual experience. I see the man (not the book he is holding behind him) because the man (not the book) is directly involved in a causal sequence of events (involving the reflection of light rays) which generates in me a visual experience of the appropriate kind. Since the book is not involved in this causal sequence, we do not see the book. And if I mistake Herman for my Uncle Emil, what makes it *Herman* I see (and not my Uncle Emil) is the fact that *Herman* is causally responsible for my sensory experience.

The difficulties with this analysis are well known. *How* must X be "causally involved" in the sequence of events that culminates in the sensory experience in order to qualify as the object of that experience? Suppose Herman hears the doorbell ring and goes to the door to see who is there. For the sake of the illustration we may suppose that Herman knows (at least believes) that someone is at the door. We have the following sequence of events: (1) Someone presses the door button, thereby closing an electric circuit; (2) current flows through the electromagnets of the doorbell; (3) a clapper is pulled against a bell (simultaneously breaking the electric circuit); (4) the resulting vibration of the clapper against the bell sets up an acoustic wave that strikes Herman's eardrums; (5) the pattern of pressure on Herman's eardrums causes a series of electrical pulses to be transmitted to Herman's brain; and finally (6) Herman undergoes an experience that we ordinarily describe by saying that he hears the bell ring.

We say he hears *the bell*, or *the bell ringing*. Why does he not hear the button being depressed? Why does he not hear the membrane vibrating in his ear? Each of these events is causally involved in the process that results in Herman's auditory experience, and each of these events is what H. H. Price calls a *differential condition*. What makes the bell so special that we designate *it* as the thing heard? It is certainly true that if the bell had not rung, Herman would not have had the auditory experience he had, but just as certainly if the button had not been depressed (if the membrane in his ear had not vibrated), he would not have had that experience. It will not do to say that in such situations the depression of the button is not *audible*. This is doubtless true if we trust our ordinary intuitions about *what can be heard*. But the question we now face is how the audibility and inaudibility of these events can be explained on purely causal grounds.

I do not think that a causal analysis can give a satisfactory account of the objects of our sensory experience. It provides no way of discriminating among the variety of eligible candidates. What is missing, I suggest, is an appreciation of the way the informational relationships operate to determine what it is that we perceive. There are two key facts about the difference between a causal and an informational relationship that are fundamental to a proper understanding of this matter. The first is that (as we saw in Chapter 1) C can cause E without E carrying any significant information about C. Second, E can carry information about some of its causal antecedents in virtue of carrying information about others. These facts, taken together, single out some causal antecedents as unique, and it is these objects (and events), I submit, that constitute the objects of our perceptual states.

Let us first consider, in a highly schematic way, some relevant features of certain (but not all) information-transmission systems. Consider the situation diagrammed in [Figure 1]. A certain state of affairs exists at the source, c's being B, and this causes d to be E. This second event, in turn, produces the state (structure, signal) I have labeled S. The solid lines indicate the route of the causal chain. Sometimes, however, c's being B causes d to be F instead of E. This

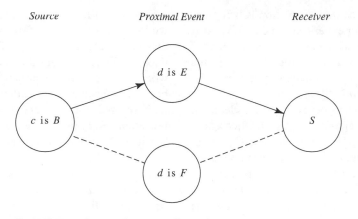

Source   Proximal Event   Receiver

FIGURE 1. Source Proximal Event Receiver

alternative route has no effect on S; the same state of affairs is produced at the receiver whether or not d is E or F. The broken line indicates an alternative causal sequence, a sequence that is occasionally (say 40 percent of the time) the one that actually occurs.

What is interesting about this diagram (for our purposes) is that it illustrates a pattern of information delivery in which a situation (S) carries information about a distant causal antecedent (c's being B) *without* carrying information about the more proximal members of the causal chain (viz., d's being E) *through which* this information (about c) is communicated. S, as it were, skips over (or "sees through") the intermediate links in the causal chain in order to represent (carry information about) its more distant causal antecedents. This is so because the features of S that carry the information that c is B (from which one could learn that something was B) *do not* carry the information that d is E (one could not learn from them that d was E). Since d is E only 60 percent of the time that S occurs (carrying the information that something is B), S "says" that c is B without "saying" that d is E.

In such situations the state of affairs designated as S carries information about the property B (the information that something—in fact c—is B) without carrying information about the property (viz., E) whose instantiation (by d) is the causal intermediary through which the information about c is transmitted.

This is the first important point of contrast between a causal and an informational relationship. If

we confine ourselves to a causal analysis, there is no non-arbitrary way of singling out one of the causal antecedents of S as more special than the others. They are all equally *involved* in the production of the final state (S). Some of these causal antecedents are more remote than others, but this is obviously a matter of degree. Why should some of these (more remote) antecedents be singled out as the object of our sensory states to the exclusion of others. From the point of view of information theory we can begin to see why this should be so. There may be no difference between the way events occurring in our head depend, *causally*, on a number of different antecedent events, but there may be a significant difference in the information these sensory states carry about these causal antecedents.

There is, however, a second fact about information transmission that is relevant to understanding the nature of the perceptual object. Recall our example of the doorbell. It was said that the listener's auditory experience carried information about the bell—information to the effect that it was ringing. But since the ringing bell carries information to the effect that the door button is being depressed (this is why we can know someone is at the door when we hear the bell ring), the auditory experience also carries the information that the door button is depressed. This, it should be noted, is a specific piece of information about a causal antecedent. Yet, as we have seen, the button's being depressed is not the object of our sensory state. We do not hear the button's being depressed. We hear the *bell ringing* (and come to know, thereby, that the button is being depressed—*hear that* someone is at the door). What is the information-theoretical basis for this distinction? Why is one the object and not the other when the auditory experience (by hypothesis) carries specific information about *both*?

The situation may become somewhat clearer if we embellish [Figure 1] as in [Figure 2]. Once again, S does not carry the information that *d* is *E* (though this is a proximal cause of *S*). Nonetheless, it carries the information that *c* (the doorbell) is *B* (ringing) *and* the information that *f* (the doorbutton) is *G* (being depressed). Why is *c* (the bell) and not *f* (the button) the perceptual object?

The distinction between *c* and *f* is simply that *S* gives what I shall call *primary representation* to the properties of *c* but not to the properties of *f*. *S* carries information about *c* (that it is *B*) and about *f* (that it is *G*) but it represents *f*'s properties *by means of* representing *c*'s properties. That is, *S*'s representation of *f*'s being *G* depends on the informational link between *f* and *c* while its representation of *c*'s properties does not depend on it.

> *S* gives *primary representation* to property *B* (relative to property *G*) = *S*'s representation of something's being *G* depends on the informational relationship between *B* and *G* but not *vice versa*.

Our auditory experience represents the bell ringing and it represents the button's being depressed. But only the former is given a primary representation because the information the experience carries about the depression of the button depends on the informational link between the button and the bell while its representation of the bell's ringing does not depend on this relationship. If we short-circuit the doorbell wires (causing the bell to ring periodically when no one is at the door), the informational tie between the bell and the button is broken. When this tie is severed, the auditory experience continues to represent (carry information about) the ringing bell, but it no longer carries information about the depression of the button.

If, contrary to hypothesis, the auditory experience *continued* to represent the button's being depressed (continued to carry the information that the button was depressed) even when its informational link with the ringing bell was broken, *then* we could speak about the button's being depressed as itself receiving primary representation (relative to the bell at least) in the auditory experience of the subject. Its representation would no longer depend on its connection with the ringing bell. But in precisely this situation we would speak of our ability to *hear* the button's being depressed (as well, perhaps, as the bell's ringing). If the button was very rusty, for example, and squeaked loudly whenever it was depressed, we might be able to hear the button being depressed whether or not it was connected to the bell. The explanation for this fact is that, in these altered circumstances, the button's being depressed is no longer being given a *secondary representation* in terms of the bell's ringing.

The signals arriving over a communication system always have their *proper qualities*—the magnitudes to which they give primary representation. Voltmeters, pressure gauges, and speedometers have

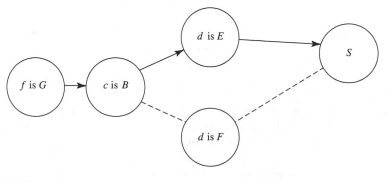

FIGURE 2

their proper qualities. By this I mean that whatever information such systems deliver, some properties or magnitudes are, given the nature of the devices, always given primary representation. The voltmeter can tell us about the voltage difference between points A and B (in an external circuit), but it does so by means of registering the current flow (through the instrument itself) that such external voltages generate (when the instrument is properly connected). The flow of electric current constitutes the instrument's proper magnitude. An altimeter can tell us how high we are, but this information about altitude is delivered in terms of pressure. Pressure is the instrument's proper quantity. And (certain) tachometers can tell us how fast our engine is running, but they do so by means of representing the frequency with which the ignition coil is firing. The instrument is sensitive to the *frequency* of these pulses, and it is capable of delivering any information that happens to be embedded in this, its proper, magnitude. If information is to be relayed, transmitted, or carried by such devices, the information must first be transformed into the appropriate magnitude so that the instrument can process it. Voltmeters are used to carry information about a great many things besides voltage differences (temperature, weight, resistance, depth, etc.—anything, in fact, that can be converted into electrical form by a proper transducer), but it can do so only when the information is first translated into the instrument's language, only when it is converted into a *proper* dimension.

Our sensory systems are similar. They have their proper objects, the qualities and quantities to which they give primary representation. If information about temperature is to be coded visually, if we are to be allowed to *see that* the temperature is increasing, the information must be transformed or coded in a way suitable for visual pick-up and processing. Thermometers, of course, effect such a transformation. If the information that it is lunchtime is to be represented auditorily, it must be given an acoustic embodiment. The bell (tone, chimes, buzz, or whatever) does precisely that. Litmus paper is a way of encoding information about acidity into visually processible form, and speech is our main instrument for converting *any* piece of information into auditory form.

Assuming, then, that our sensory experience *does* carry information about our surroundings (assuming, that is, that we can *learn* something about our surroundings by having these experiences), the object of the experience in question (what it is we see, hear, smell and taste) is that object (or set of objects) whose properties the experience represents in a primary way. An experience *need not* (and obviously does not) carry information about *all* the properties of the perceptual object. Nevertheless, of all those properties the experience does carry information about, some comprise the sense modality's proper qualities. The *perceptual object* is the thing that has *these* qualities. The reason we hear the bell, not the button, is because, although our auditory experience carries information about the properties of both the bell (that it is ringing) and the button (that it is depressed), the ringing (of the bell) is represented in a primary way while the depression (of the button) is not.

The distinction between primary and secondary representation serves to explain why we hear the doorbell ringing and not the door button being depressed. But it does *not* help explain why we hear the doorbell ringing and not, say, the vibration of the membranes in our ear. Isn't the ringing of the bell given secondary representation relative to the behavior of the membranes in our ear? Don't we get information about what the bell is doing *in virtue of* (or *by means of*) getting information about what is happening in our ears? If so, we don't (on this account) hear the bell. We hear the (vibration of the) membranes in our ear or, perhaps, the firing of neurons in our brain.

Generally speaking, an organism's way of coding sensory information puts the perceptual object *outside* the perceiving organism. The reason for this should be apparent from [Figure 1] and the operation of what are called *constancy mechanisms*. Our visual experience, for example, carries highly specific information about the properties of objects (their color, shape, size, movement) without carrying the same kind of specific information about the more proximal events (on the retina, say) on which the delivery of this information depends (causally). Size, shape and color constancy testify to the fact that it is the *properties of objects*, and not (say) the properties of the retinal stimulation (or the firing of neural cells), that is represented by our visual experience under normal viewing conditions. The visual experience that constitutes our sensory encoding of information about ordinary physical objects can, and generally *does*, remain unchanged in response to *quite different proximal stimulation*, and such a pattern of information delivery exemplifies that which is diagrammed in [Figure 1]. Our sensory experience is sensitive to (hence, carries information about), *not* the behavior of our receptors or neural pathways, but the behavior of more distant elements in the causal chain. Since the proximal (peripheral, neural) antecedents of an experience are not (generally speaking) represented in the experience at all, they are not given *primary* representation. They do not, therefore, qualify as the object of that experience.

For example, an object (a piece of paper, say) that looks white in daylight continues to look white under drastically diminished illumination even though the intensity of light it reflects is (in near darkness) less than that which a black object reflects in normal daylight. Hence, the experience of whiteness carries information about the reflectance of the paper and not about the intensity of the (local) retinal stimulation reflected *by the paper*. Similarly, objects do not appear to change size and shape as we (or they) move about and change their orientation even though the retinal projection (and, hence, the pattern of neural firings) is constantly changing. The visual representation of a round object (its *looking* round) carries information about the shape *of the object* without carrying information about the shape *of the image* projected on the retina (this can be round or variously elliptical). We experience movement of objects *whether or not* there is any motion of the object's retinal projection. Stationary objects do not appear to move when we change the direction of our gaze (movement of the retinal image), but we experience motion when we "track" a moving object (when there is *no* movement of the retinal image). To experience movement, then, is to receive information, not about what is happening on the retina (there may or may not be movement occurring here) but about what the more distal source is doing.

Woodworth puts the point nicely:

The retinal image continually changes without much changing the appearance of objects. The apparent size of a person does not change as he moves away from you. A ring turned at various angles to the line of sight, and therefore projected as a varying ellipse on the retina, continues to appear circular. Part of a wall, standing in shadow, is seen as the same in color as the well-lighted portion. Still more radical are the changes in the retinal image that occur when we move about a room and examine its contents from various angles. In spite of the visual flux the objects seem to remain in the same place.[1]

The sensory experience carries information about, and therefore represents, not the proximal events on which it causally depends, but the more distal ancestors in this causal chain. And since the proximal events aren't represented, they are not, a fortiori, represented in any primary way. This, indeed, is why we do not see or hear them. We see (and hear) *through* them.

One plausible explanation of the constancy phenomena is that our sensory systems are sensitive, not to localized stimuli (e.g., the light reflected from object X), but to more global characteristics of the entire stimulus pattern (e.g., the differences between the light reflected from X and the light reflected from X's surroundings). One way of describing this is to say that our perceptual systems are sensitive to "higher order" variables in the stimulus array. The neural circuits in the visual cortex are sensitive, not to local stimulus x (light reaching the retina from X) and local stimulus y (light reaching the retina from Y), but to various *ratios*, *gradients*, and *rates of change* in or among the local (proximal) counterparts of the distal stimuli. So, for example, what accounts for brightness constancy is not (just) the intensity of light coming from X (this can change radically without any apparent change in brightness), but the *ratio* of intensities coming from X and its surroundings (nearby objects). What accounts for size constancy is (among other things) the relative amount of textural details (in the background) occluded by the object. Since there is a gradient in the textural field, the amount of texture occluded will remain constant as the object moves away. Aside from these higher order variables, it also seems clear that our sensory experience is determined, in part at least, by information from other sense modalities. That is, the perceptual system "takes account" of information about the body's tilt (relative to gravity), the position and movement of the eyes, head and trunk, and so on.

Such explanations are plausible enough, and I do not wish to dispute them. These are matters that should be left to the scientific specialists. The only point that concerns me here is that whatever the correct explanation of constancy phenomena may be, they certainly exist. And it is on the existence of such phenomena (not their correct explanation) that the *externality* of the perceptual object depends. It is the *fact* of constancy not the psychological or neurological basis for it, that accounts for the fact that our sensory experience gives primary representation to the properties of distal objects and not to the properties of those more proximal events on which it (causally) depends. It is this fact that explains why we see physical objects and not the effects that these objects have on our perceptual systems.

Whether or not we see ordinary physical objects is (on this account of things) an empirical question—something that must be decided by looking at the kind of information embodied in our sensory experience. There is, as I have tried to indicate, an impressive amount of experimental evidence to support the view that our visual experience (and, to a lesser extent, the other sense modalities) carries highly specific information about the properties of ordinary objects without carrying the same kind of specific information about the intermediate events responsible for the delivery of this information. There is, therefore, an impressive body of evidence to support the commonsense view that we see trees, cats, people and houses and not the neurological events (peripheral or central) that are equally "involved" (causally) in the production of our experience.

This should not be taken to imply that our mode of processing sensory information cannot be changed so as to generate different perceptual objects. The psychologist J. J. Gibson has suggested a distinction between the *visual world* and the *visual field*. According to Gibson the visual world consists of our everyday world of chairs, trees, buildings and people. These are the things we see under normal perceptual conditions. We can, however, get ourselves into a different frame of mind—what is sometimes called a phenomenological frame of mind—or put ourselves under abnormal perceptual conditions (in so-called "perceptual reduction" where much of

the information is removed from the stimulus) in which we (according to Gibson) perceive a different constellation of objects. In these altered states we no longer see a stable world of objects but an ensemble of continuously varying entities—things that are continuously changing their brightness and color (as the illumination changes), their size and shape (as we and they move about), their position and orientation. Under such altered (or reduced) perceptual conditions, it is no longer true to say that the subject sees physical objects. One's visual experience still carries information about physical objects, but the properties of these objects is no longer given *primary* representation in the sensory experience. Under such conditions the physical object comes to occupy the status of the depressed button in our doorbell example.

The possibility of confronting a visual field instead of a visual world raises the question of what human infants and animals perceive. They look out on the same world we do, and they doubtless receive much of the same information we do, but how do they perceptually code this information? It *may* be that as we mature we evolve a different way of coding sensory information so that (referring to [Figure 1]) we begin by representing the properties of *d* (e.g., that it is *E*) and only later, after sustained interaction with such information bearing signals, begin to give more distal properties (e.g., *B*) primary representation. That is, our perceptual experience may develop by moving the perceptual object *outward,* away from the perceiving organism. Infants may literally see a different world from adult members of the species.

Paradoxical as this may sound, we can witness something comparable in our auditory processing of information. Listening to an unfamiliar language we hear (as we often express it) *sounds* but not *words*. It will not do to say that since the sounds we hear *are* words, to hear the sounds is to hear the words. Sounds have a certain pitch and loudness; the *word* "bear" has neither of these properties. And the question of whether we hear the *sound* "bear" or the *word* "bear" is a question of whether our auditory experience gives primary representation to the properties of the sound or the properties of the word. Studies suggest that the way we encode information when listening to a familiar language is different from the way we do it when listening to an unfamiliar language. With a familiar language we hear breaks between words even when the *sound* is continuous (no drop in acoustic energy). We hear subtleties associated with the grammatical structure and meaning of the utterance that are totally absent from the pattern of acoustic vibrations reaching the auditory receptors. To learn a language is, to some extent at least, to start hearing properties associated with the words and sentences and to stop hearing acoustic properties.

I do not know whether anything comparable to this occurs when an infant "learns" to see the world. Most of our learning consists of our greater *cognitive* utilization of information already made perceptually available in some determinate sensory representation (e.g., the transition from seeing a daffodil to seeing *that it is* a daffodil). In such learning there is no significant *perceptual* change, no change in what we see. Only a change in what we *know* about what we see. But the possibility exists that normal maturation involves a change, not only in our cognitive resources, but a change in the manner in which things are perceptually represented. Whether this occurs, and, if so, to what extent, is a scientific, not a philosophical, issue.

One point, however, should be stressed before leaving this discussion of the perceptual object. The fact that an animal successfully avoids obstacles and predators, the fact that it efficiently locates food and mates, is a fact that is no certain guide to what it sees, hears, smells and tastes. Success in these practical activities tells us something about the animal's *cognitive* capabilities, but it provides no infallible criterion for determining the way it perceptually represents the elements around it. A rabbit, for example, need not give *primary* visual representation to the fox, need not see the fox, in order to get accurate and detailed information concerning the whereabouts, movements, and identity of the fox by visual means. The fact that I answer the door every time someone depresses the door button, the fact that I am so extraordinarily sensitive to the position of the door button, does not mean that I can hear (or somehow *sense*) the button being depressed. All it shows is that something I *do* hear carries accurate information about the state of the button. To say that I *know* that the button is being depressed (to specify the object of my *cognitive* state), and that I know this by *auditory* means, is not to say what I hear. As we all know, what I actually hear is the bell. It is this which "tells me" that someone is at the door pressing the button. Practical success in responding to someone's presence on my front porch, even when this success is to be explained in auditory terms, does not imply that I can hear people on my front porch. And, for the same reason, the rabbit's success in evading the fox should not be taken to imply that the rabbit can see, hear or smell the fox. It *may*, of course, but it will take more than facts about the rabbit's cognitive abilities to establish this conclusion.

NOTE

1. R. Woodworth, *Experimental Psychology*, (London: Methuen, 1938), p. 595.

JOHN HEIL

Perceptual Experience

PERCEPTS WITHOUT CONCEPTS

Philosophers cut their teeth on talk about perceptual experiences. Seeing, hearing, tasting, smelling, and touching things is, we are taught, a matter of our having *experiences* of those things. Experiences differ from one another *qualitatively*. *Seeing* a bell toll and *hearing* it are not at all the same. Experiences are *nondoxastic*. An experience may *give rise* to belief, but experience is not *reducible* to belief. More generally, experiences are noncognitive, nonpropositional. An experience may be propositionally *characterized,* perhaps, but the content of an experience is not itself a proposition. Experiences are of objects and events, particulars and particular goings-on, not facts. And experiences are, or often are, in some degree, *conscious*.

That we have perceptual experiences with these characteristics is widely assumed, hence rarely defended. The attitude is one inherited from Locke:

> What [perceptual experience] is every one will know better by reflecting on what he does himself when he sees, hears, feels, etc. . . . than by any discourse of mine. Whoever reflects on what passes in his own mind cannot miss it: and if he does not reflect, all the words in the world cannot make him have any notion of it. (Locke [1690] 1979, book II, chapter 9, section 2, p. 143)

Indeed in considering the matter, one may feel a certain sense of foreboding. Like time, perceptual experience is something we have a grip on so long as we postpone thinking about it. It is only after we trouble to reflect on the topic that it loses its obviousness. We regard perceptual experience in the way we might regard income from a distant but disreputable source: we make sure of it gladly, while preferring not to reflect on its origins.

The epistemological role of experiences is controversial. Philosophers disagree, for instance, on whether experiences play a part in warranting or undermining the warrant of beliefs, whether they are *epistemic,* or whether only doxastic states—beliefs based on experiences, perhaps—are relevant epistemologically. Suppose, for instance, that beliefs I now hold support the proposition *p,* but that my experiences are inapposite. I have sufficient evidence—where having evidence is a matter of having beliefs—that there is a cat on the mat, no evidence to the contrary. I have an experience of Tabby being nudged aside and displaced by Spot, a large Dalmatian. I do not, however, form the belief that Tabby has been displaced. I do not change any of my beliefs at all about the mat's occupant. Is my belief that there is a cat on the mat (still) warranted?

The example may seem in some way impossible. So long as we uphold a distinction between the having of experiences and the forming of beliefs, however, this is unlikely. Given the distinction, then, what is to be said about the case? On the one hand, it seems patent that I should *not* be justified in believing that there is a cat on the mat given the content of my experiences. On the other hand, my having no beliefs at all about Tabby's giving way to Spot makes it difficult to see how my experience *could* be thought to undermine the warrant I have for the proposition that there is a cat on the mat, any more than would my idly forming an image of Spot's routing Tabby. Perhaps our ambivalence about the case stems from our appreciation of a powerful albeit contingent psychological fact about human beings: on the whole, beliefs are tailored to experiences. The move from the one to the other is a move we are conditioned to make spontaneously and unselfconsciously in childhood.

Although philosophers help themselves to features of perceptual experiences in various ways, it is

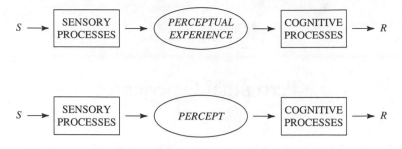

FIGURE 1a The Psychological Place of Perceptual Experience.
FIGURE 1b Perception as an Information-Processing Stage.

rare that anyone takes the trouble to scrutinize the role they might be thought to play in our mental lives. Fred Dretske is a notable exception. Indeed, Dretske's defense of "nonepistemic" or "simple" perceiving is perhaps best appreciated as an account of the category of perceptual experience.[1] The idea is admirably straightforward. In perceiving, we register our surroundings in a certain way. The process can be broken down into distinct components. It begins with sub-perceptual sensory events elicited by a stimulus, passes into perception, and culminates in judgment (and, often enough, an appropriate response; see [Figure 1a]).

Consider visual perception. As I gaze about the world, photons bombard my retina. When conditions are right, when there are *enough* photons, sensations are produced. Sensations, the constituents of perceptual experience, incorporate information about distal objects and events, those objects and events, namely, structuring the light reaching my retina, hence, indirectly, the pattern of responses occurring there. My visual system, in this way, captures incoming information about my surroundings.

The mere capturing or registering of information by sensory organs, however, cannot, according to Dretske, be counted perception. Information thus picked up must be available to the system as a whole, to the *perceiver*. Incoming light might carry information about the chemical composition of the surface reflecting it, for instance, and this information might be registered somehow by retinal cells. Unless the larger system is equipped to extract it, however, unless that information can be *passed along* up the informational chain of command, it is perceptually irrelevant. We may think of a perceptual

episode as culminating in a *percept,* a perceptual state incorporating information registered by the senses and made available to the perceiver's cognitive centers. Typically, a percept will contain far more information than we can hope to extract cognitively. A percept is worth a thousand beliefs.

Dretske worries that psychologists and philosophers have tended to conflate perceiving with cognizing. If one supposes that perception involves an *appreciation* of what is perceived, he suggests, one is confusing a judgmental operation following on the heels of perception with perception itself. The mistake is easily made. We may decide what an agent perceives by asking him or by observing his nonverbal behavior. Descriptions supplied, however, and deeds, are a function not merely of what is perceived, but also of beliefs formed on the basis of what is perceived. The point is implicit in [Figure 1b]. Dretske concedes that psychologists and philosophers nowadays use the expression "visual perception" to refer to cognitive—belief-like—states that succeed perceiving proper. The practice is encouraged by a tendency to regard perceiving in a functional light. In going to bat for simple perceiving, his aim is to persuade us that this is a mistake, that there is a useful and important distinction to be made between perceiving and cognizing.

SEEING *TOUT COURT*

In one respect the psychological account of perceptual processes as depicted in [Figure 1b] is uncontroversial. One who accepts a causal theory of perception, for instance, might assign a functional role to a Dretske-style percept, while insisting that *perceiving* occurs only at some later stage of the process. Showing that this is wrong requires showing that perceiving and conceiving (or cognizing) are *conceptually* distinct. Ordinarily a demonstration of this point might proceed by invoking either a bottom-up or a top-down strategy, that is, either by providing clear-cut instances of simple perceiving or by generating an explanatorily satisfying theory that independently motivated appeals to some such notion. In this case, however, the latter route is blocked. One could accept the psychological picture Dretske sketches without conceding the notion that perceiving, in some ordinary, pretheoretical sense, is what he says it is. This would be so if, as in the cases above, one thought that Dretske had characterized in an interesting way an intelligent perceptual system but misidentified the *place* in that system occupied by perception.[2]

We are, then, obliged to consider *instances* of perceiving that might be thought to have the properties required by Dretske's view. As we noted at the outset, the instances in question are most naturally appreciated as corresponding to what philosophers have learned to call *experiences*. To focus discussion, let us follow Dretske and concentrate on visual experiences, Dretske's *simple seeing*, what I shall call seeing *tout court*. Such seeing is to be distinguished from seeing *that* something is so or seeing a thing *as* a such and such. Dretske's contention is that seeing (*tout court*—the qualification will be presumed in what follows) is to be identified with the having of distinctive nonconceptualized, nonepistemic experiences. My seeing the cat on the mat is a matter of my being in a certain state, one the character of which in no way depends upon my conceptual resources. Dretske does not deny that we often, even typically, form beliefs about what

we see. Simple, nonepistemic seeing is not something that occurs only in isolation from judgment or belief, but something that in no way *depends* on judgment or belief. Seeing a thing is like stepping on it. In stepping on Tabby, I may form many beliefs including, perhaps, the belief that it is Tabby I am stepping on. But my *stepping* on Tabby is conceptually independent of these beliefs. I might have stepped on Tabby without recognizing that I had done so, without having any beliefs at all about my circumstances.

Simple seeing, then, is not an eccentric or primitive form of seeing, not something that we grow out of or that occurs only in infants and creatures lacking our conceptual sophistication, not something we might induce by putting ourselves in a special frame of mind. If there is seeing at all, visual perceiving, there is simple seeing: seeing *is* simple seeing. More generally, perceiving is the having of unconceptualized, nonepistemic perceptual experiences. Judgment, belief, and the rest commonly *accompany* perception, at least in noninfant human beings, but remain conceptually distinct from it.

How is seeing, on Dretske's view, related to *conscious awareness*? Are percepts *conscious* states? In addressing this question caution must be exercised. It is, in the first place, a notable feature of the flow chart set out in [Figure 1b] that there is no obvious need for conscious awareness at the perceptual stage. Is it, then, merely a contingent fact that seeing, in the case of human beings, involves consciousness? The very same question might be raised about the philosopher's category of experience. Experiences are invariably described as conscious states, but it is by no means obvious that their being conscious is required for them to play the role they are most often thought to play.

Second, care must be taken not to confuse simple seeing with *noticing* or *attending*. On Dretske's

FIGURE 2 Ambiguous Figures.

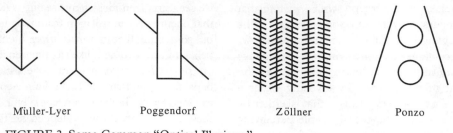

Müller-Lyer   Poggendorf   Zöllner   Ponzo

FIGURE 3 Some Common "Optical Illusions."

view, what we see, for the most part, far outstrips what we attend to or notice. Noticing requires a focusing of attention. In so doing, the visual field comes to be organized into figure and ground. When our attention is attracted by something, its surroundings recede. When we shift attention, the relationship is altered, even reversed. The phenomenon is most easily appreciated in the case of ambiguous figures (see [Figure 2]). I may fail to notice the likeness of a rabbit or a white cross on a black ground. Nevertheless, these seem to be included in my visual experience of the figures. (How could they *fail* to be included given their boundaries are congruent?) Dretske might say that they are *seen* by me, despite my failing to appreciate or recognize their presence.[3]

I may, then, see much that I never notice, much that I fail to appreciate. It is on this feature of seeing *tout court* that Dretske has most wanted to focus. I gaze at a flag and *see* 50 stars, though I have no clue as to how many there are. You *see* Garbo ducking into a taxi, though you are entirely ignorant that it is Garbo you see.[4] In each case, according to Dretske, what each of us *sees*, what we visually experience, exceeds our *grasp* of what we see, the beliefs we may chance to form on the basis of our respective visual experiences. And this will be so even for what we *notice*. I notice the stars on the flag, yet fail to *appreciate* their number; you notice Garbo, yet fail to *recognize* her.

Dretske finds further confirmation for his view in the experimental work of Sperling and others (see, e.g., Sperling 1960; Neisser 1967, chapter 2). Typical experiments involve the tachistoscopic presentation of arrays of elements (nine letters of the alphabet, for instance, arranged in three rows) to subjects for brief durations (50 milliseconds). The duration is such that subjects are unable to identify more than three or four of the letters after exposure to the stimulus. *Which* letters subjects identify, however, can be manipulated by visual prompts occurring *after* the removal of the stimulus. Experiments of this sort have encouraged the postulation of visual *icons,* fleeting, after-image-like replicas of stimuli. During the momentary persistence of an icon, subjects seem capable of adjusting their attention in the way they might were the stimulus still available. What is preserved in the icon, though only for an instant, might be thought of as something close to the original visual experience in all its fullness.

The character and even existence of icons is a matter of some controversy (see, e.g., Neisser 1976, pp. 46ff). Nevertheless, we may agree with Dretske that it is possible to regard the underlying phenomenon in a way that fits nicely with his notion of seeing *tout court.* Iconic memory seems to capture something at least close to what is simply seen, a visual experience *naked,* prior to any cognitive manipulation.

Another sort of case, a sort that Dretske does not discuss, but one that might be thought to support his position is provided by familiar perceptual illusions (see [Figure 3]). These call attention to a familiar distinction between the way things *look* or *appear* to us and our beliefs about them. A visual experience that we should describe as an object's looking a certain way is possible even when there is no such object. An oar may *look* bent to me, I may have the visual *experience* of a bent oar, without coming to believe that there *is* a bent oar. If I am a naive perceiver, an infant say, I may know nothing whatever of oars. If I am sophisticated, I may know that ordinary oars immersed in water will *look* bent without *being* bent.

This will be true as well for ordinary optical illusions.[5] One line may continue to *look* longer than another even after I assure myself that this is not so.

These facts, long recognized, seem to support the notion that seeing is fundamentally a matter of having visual experiences, of coming to be in perceptual states that are themselves unaffected by judgments we may make about what is seen. Cases in which lines *look* unequal, oars *look* bent, are to be explained by reference to features of my experiences. The apparent inequality and bentness are features of my visual experience, properties of *me*, not properties of the objects outside me.

Although Dretske holds that his conception of seeing *tout court* accommodates what we have in mind in speaking of the look of things, there is no reason to think that he would be sympathetic to such arguments. There are at least two reasons for this, one quite general, one attaching to Dretske's information-theoretic perspective on perception. The general point is a familiar one. It seems unpromising to explain how it is that X can appear to have some property, P, by reference to a second, posited item, Y, distinct from X, that actually possesses P. Applied to the case of lines looking of unequal length, for instance, we should have to posit something—an image, perhaps—containing lines that *really are* unequal. The move offends a number of sensibilities.

Consider a case in which you examine the Müller-Lyer lines in [Figure 3] and take them to be of different lengths. A companion tells you that this is not so. Skeptical, you measure them against one another by marking off their end points on a scrap of paper. You gaze at the lines and at the scrap of paper. Can what you encounter in so doing coherently be described in terms of the continued presence of an item (an image, sense datum, percept, or whatever) that includes lines of unequal length? However we elect to explain the possibility of things appearing to have properties they lack, it is surely wrong to do so by conjuring up *other* things actually possessing those properties.

A second reason Dretske would be reluctant to appeal in this way to illusory figures to bolster the case for seeing *tout court* is related to the information-theoretic character of the doctrine he advances. Perceptual states contain information that is accessible to various higher cognitive centers. When I look at the Müller-Lyer figure, however, the resulting perceptual state could not contain the information

that its lines are of unequal length for the simplest of reasons: the lines are *not* unequal in length.[6] What might occur, instead, is the formation of a percept that would, normally perhaps, carry information that the lines differ in length but which, on this occasion, does not.

These points pose no special difficulties for Dretske. Even if a satisfactory explanation of such cases turned out to be a problem for his view, it remains a problem, as well, for competing views. For the moment I want merely to put aside a line of argument that has traditionally been used to defend accounts of perception that identify perceiving with the having of experiences.

EVIDENCE FOR SEEING *TOUT COURT*

I have likened Dretske's conception of simple perceiving, perceiving *tout court*, to the philosophical notion of perceptual experience. Although philosophers, on the whole, regard the latter as uncontroversial, not everyone has been persuaded by Dretske's arguments. This might be due to Dretske's simply getting it wrong; perhaps there is some better, more winning account of perceptual experience available. Or it might be that what Dretske has in mind when he speaks of percepts and simple perception has nothing at all to do with what everyone else has in mind in speaking of perceptual experiences. Both possibilities seem to me unlikely. The concept of perceptual experience—as commonly deployed by philosophers—appears innocent only so long as it is not scrutinized. When we set out to make the notion explicit, when we inspect it more closely, it loses much of its initial charm. In this section, and in the next, I shall advance reasons for doubting that perceiving *is* simple perceiving and for doubting, as well, the innocence of the philosophical category of perceptual experience. Dretske has done more than anyone else, perhaps, to capture and motivate that category, and we can learn much from uncovering respects in which his conception goes awry. There is, as well, a larger moral to be drawn, one pertaining to the legitimacy of philosophical appeals to experiences.

Do the sorts of case Dretske regards as relevant for the establishment of the concept of simple seeing require what he contends they require? Let us first consider those cases, then examine a possibility that seems at odds with Dretske's account.

I look at a flag featuring 50 stars, see *all* the stars, yet fail to realize that there are 50 of them. It is not merely that my seeing something, *X*, that possesses a certain property, *P*, does not require that I in any sense *recognize* or *take X* to be *P*. That is altogether unremarkable. Objects have countless properties, and we may come to know a great deal about an object without coming to know about all of these. I may recognize that a flag has *stars,* for instance, without recognizing that it has 50 stars, just as I may recognize you without recognizing that you are *n* centimeters tall. Dretske, however, advances a conception of seeing according to which *X* can be seen without being taken to possess any properties whatever.[7] On this conception, my recognizing *X* to be *P* is based on *X*'s possessing *P* being seen by me. It is not enough in such cases merely that *X* be seen. Dretske's thesis is that *X's being P* is part of what is seen and entirely distinct from my seeing *that X is P*, my *taking X* to be *P*, and the like.

It is difficult to know what to say about the possibility of episodes of this sort. On the one hand, it is easy to imagine cases in which, for any given property, *P*, possessed by *X*, *S* sees *X* without *taking X* to have *P*. And we might describe such cases as ones in which *S* fails to see *X* under a certain aspect. On the other hand, the plausibility of these cases may well rest at least in part on the tacit assumption that *X*, if not seen under *this* aspect, is seen under some *other* aspect, if not taken to have *P*, then taken to have some other property, *P'*. Dretske's notion of seeing *tout court* requires that there be cases in which *S* encounters *X* perceptually, but does not take X in any way at all. It is far from clear, however, that there are any such cases, or that, even if there are, they are in any way illuminating.[8]

When I see the flag, according to Dretske, I see its 50 stars, *each* of them, though I do not (thereby) form the belief that there are 50 stars, much less 50 distinct beliefs, one for each star. If I see each of the 50 stars, however, and *this* star is one of the 50, then I see *this* star without forming any beliefs about it at all, without taking it to have any property whatever. But how apt is this description of the case? I scan a televised image of a football crowd taken from a blimp. You are somewhere in that crowd. Do I see you? Do I *see* you, the man in the red hat seated next to you, the hotdog vendor with a tattoo on his left forearm standing in the aisle? This seems wrong just as it seems wrong to say that I see individual hairs on your head, when I see you walk beneath my window. When I set foot on the beach, I step on 20,000 grains of sand. Do I step on *each* grain? Putting it thus is bound to mislead.

Such considerations do not, I think, establish that Dretske is wrong about visual perception. Indeed, they may, if anything, incline one to suppose that the dispute between Dretske and those who regard perceiving as essentially cognitive or belief-like is merely terminological, one that boils down to a dispute over what labels belong in which boxes in [Figure 1b]. Do I see you in the football crowd; each of the 50 stars on the flag? Well, someone might say *yes and no*; it depends on what you mean by seeing in each case.

There are, however, reasons to doubt the appropriateness of Dretske's terminology. I shall suggest below a way of accounting for the locutions favored by Dretske for describing these cases, one that does not require that we embrace his conception of simple seeing. Then, in a concluding section, I shall offer what appear to be counterexamples to that conception. My argument, then, will be that we *need* not regard perception as Dretske would have us regard it, and that we *ought* not to so regard it.

SEEING WITHOUT BELIEVING

It is true, certainly, that we have occasion to say that someone sees things that fall outside his ken. You see Garbo ducking into a taxi without an inkling that it is *Garbo* you see; indeed you may never have *heard* of Garbo. This may be less a feature of your sensory state, however, than a feature of our ordinary ways of *describing* such states. I may describe your perception either by reference to its *content* or by reference to its *object*. You notice an elderly woman hailing a taxi. This, it might be said, constitutes the *content* of your perception. The elderly woman in question is, as it happens, Garbo. The *object* of your perception, then, the elderly woman, is Garbo. When reporting what you saw, I may mention either the content or the object of this state. Reference to the former is called for in circumstances in which the focus is on *you*, on what you are likely to do or say, for instance. Mention of the latter is appropriate in circumstances in which attention is focused, not on you, but on the object. In these circumstances, the way *you* take what you see, the properties *you* recognize it to have, are mostly irrelevant. My describing the object of your perception in this way, however, *seems* to require your having a perception with a particular content. That is, my aptly characterizing your seeing by reference to the object seen, might be thought to depend on my taking you to have come to be in a perceptual state with a particular content.

The plausibility of the cases Dretske describes, then, seems to rest on our accepting the uncontroversial notion that the object of one's perception can have properties one does not take it to have, not on our accepting the less obvious notion that one might perceive *this* object despite one's not taking it to be anything at all. One cannot, at any rate, conclude from the fact that, for any property, P, possessed by X, it is possible to perceive X without taking X to possess P, that it is possible to perceive X without taking X to possess any property whatsoever.[9]

The point need not be thought to depend on a theory of mental content according to which reference is fixed internally—by one's beliefs, for instance (see Dretske 1979, p. 8). My beliefs about a given perceptual object, X, may be largely false, or they may hold for some other object, Y. *What* I perceive, what counts as a perceptual object for me, could turn out to be fixed *causally*. I now see Polly, not her twin Holly, because I am causally interacting in a certain way with Polly, not Holly, even though some of my beliefs about what I am seeing may be true of Holly, not Polly.

Even if we suppose that the content of perceptual states is fixed at least in part causally, however, we need not image that seeing has the character Dretske takes it to have. More particularly, it is possible to accept the notion that perceptual *objects* are not (or not *exclusively*) determined by belief-*contents*, without conceding that perceptual states are belief-independent or nonepistemic. A theory that identified perceiving with the having of certain sorts of belief, for instance, might well incorporate a causal component (theories of this sort are discussed in Armstrong 1973, and in Heil 1983). That the content of a given

mental state is, or might be, at least in part, externally fixed, then, is perfectly consistent with that state's being essentially cognitive and epistemic.

WHAT *ARE* PERCEPTUAL EXPERIENCES?

We must conclude, I think, that Dretske has offered no compelling reasons for supposing that seeing is essentially noncognitive, nonepistemic. Even so, we may continue to feel that there is something importantly right about the conception he defends. It certainly seems, for instance, that in gazing about our surroundings, we are, in some sense, *aware* of far more than we recognize or bother to identify. And it seems, as well, that the *constituents* of this awareness are not, or need not be, cognized, brought under concepts, judged to be this or that. The constituents of an infant's visual awareness might be identical to those of an adult, though the adult, owing to a degree of conceptual sophistication, is able to extract more from those constituents than the infant.

This *seems* right. But what are we to make of it? A standard philosophical move is to launch into a discussion of perceptual experiences. In this way, entities and properties that naive perceivers take to be external, public features of the world are moved inside, made into features of perceivers. My visual field is thus populated not by tables, trees, and clouds, but by *images* of these, *sensations*, sensory *qualia*. These elements are part of *me*, constituents of a particular sort of mental state, the having of which is an experience. The occurrence of experiences in me is a fundamental aspect of perceiving.

Dretske's view is usefully seen as falling squarely into this tradition, or so I have contended. His notion of simple perceiving is readily identifiable as an updated version of the classical empiricist notion of bare experience, what Locke and Hume, respectively, identified as the having of *ideas* and *impressions*. So long as we focus solely on functional aspects of such views, the point is apt to be missed. We have noted already that the notion that perceivers might be regarded as incorporating functional states with the properties Dretske attributes to percepts is something that any causal theorist could accept. The rub comes in Dretske's making these, in a certain way, central: seeing just *is* the having of such states. To convince us of this, Dretske is obliged to move beyond a purely functional or theory-driven perspective on perceiving to a consideration of instances. The implicit aim in this is to encourage the identification of certain functional states with the having of perceptual experiences, and, in turn, an identification of the having of perceptual experiences with perceiving *tout court*.

If we are to abandon such a view, then, we shall want to show either that perceiving is more than (or perhaps distinct from) the having of nonepistemic, unconceptualized experiences, or show that there is something objectionable about the notion of experiences thus conceived. We have seen already that the examples Dretske provides do not establish his point. This way of putting it suggests that he bears the burden of proof: the notion that perceiving is simple, nonepistemic is presumed false until proven true. Perhaps this is unfair. What reasons might there be for thinking Dretske *wrong*? Let us consider the matter in this light, and examine evidence suggesting both that it is a mistake to identify perceiving with the having of noncognitive states and that the identification of perceptual states with experiences is misguided.

First, let us pretend that the notion of visual experience is entirely unproblematic. A visual experience is an internal episode phenomenologically and informationally characterizable. If this is unclear, the reader is directed to the passage from Locke quoted at the outset. Experiences are, we may suppose, produced causally, the products of agents' interactions with their surroundings. The properties of experiences, and indeed experiences themselves, depend not merely on external causes that give rise to them but also, and crucially, on properties of agents in whom they occur. An agent lacking a certain piece of equipment, photosensitive receptors in the retina, for instance, will lack the capacity for certain sorts of experience, what we should call *visual* experience. A perceiver with damaged or maladjusted equipment may enjoy experiences that differ qualitatively from those had by normal perceivers. If certain cells in my retina are deficient, I will experience colors differently than you do, or perhaps altogether lack the capacity to experience colors visually.

Now imagine that we are visited by creatures from a remote galaxy, creatures, in most respects, exactly like us. Eventually we learn to communicate with these visitors, and we set out to investigate their psychology. We discover that they exhibit a range of perceptual abilities comparable to our own. That is, they can describe the colors and shapes of things at a distance providing the illumination is adequate. In the dark they lose this ability. They are sometimes fooled, just as we are, by trick mirrors, and by objects placed under conditions of nonstandard illumination. Thus, so long as we disguise the conditions, they judge white objects under red light to be red. The alien creatures turn out to be comparable to human beings, as well, along the whole range of perceptual aptitudes. Researchers capture this aspect of their psychology be means of the chart in [Figure 1b].

One day an accident befalls one of the visitors, and it dies. Seizing the opportunity, anatomists open it up and explore its biology. A wonderful discovery is made: the aliens lack a capacity for perceptual experiences. Their neural hardware is functionally identical to ours, but the biological components responsible for the having of experiences are entirely lacking. The creatures have mechanisms for processing and storing information. Like human beings, they take in far more information than they could possibly use—a fact already established in the course of ordinary psychological testing and now confirmed. But they evidently lack anything plausibly describable as perceptual experiences. Although they nicely fit the characterization afforded by [Figure 1b], they fail to fit that set out in [Figure 1a].

What are we to conclude about such creatures? Must we say that our original assessment was in error, that their lacking appropriate experiences shows that they cannot (or cannot, *strictly speaking*) perceive? I doubt that anyone without a philosophical axe to grind would be tempted to say this. But if that is so, it seems to follow that, on our ordinary conception, perceiving does not require the having of particular sorts of experience—where *experience* is understood in the philosophical sense set out above. Compare the case with that of another tribe of alien creatures, a tribe psychologically very different from us. The creatures seem intelligent, but they altogether fail at standard visual tasks. We conclude that these aliens cannot see. If one of creatures dies and, on examination, we discover that it has, after all, almost certainly had experiential visual states identical to ours, it is far from clear that we should be tempted to revise our original assessment.[10]

One might balk at these examples on the grounds that they are, in some way, incoherent. If we suppose, however, that perceptual experiences are states of perceivers of certain particular sorts, then a charge of incoherence is difficult to support. Of course, there may well be something fishy about this notion of perceptual experience. If that were so, however, then there would be something fishy, as well, about the model of perceiving we have been considering.

There may, in fact, be cases in which it seems natural to regard certain unfortunate human beings as resembling alien creatures of the first sort discussed above. I have in mind instances of what is called *blind-sight* (see Heil 1983, chapter 4 for a discussion and further references). Lesions in a particular region of the brain produce apparent blindness in certain regions of the visual field. We might wish to describe these cases as ones in which agents, thus afflicted, *experience* nothing in those regions. Tests however, reveal that, despite this deficit, blind-sighters are adept at regulating their behavior in ways that suggest that they are picking up information available in the blind field. Such agents might be described as *seeing* what is in the blind field despite lacking appropriate visual experiences. [11]

The blind-sight phenomenon may turn out to be otherwise explicable. The point of mentioning it here is only to show that it is not at all obvious that there is a conceptual connection between perceiving and the having of experiential states. To the extent that Dretske's account of perceiving denies this, then, we must be suspicious of it.

WHITHER PERCEPTUAL EXPERIENCES?

For the sake of the discussion, we have conformed to the traditional practice of taking these to be uncontroversial sensory givens. If a Dretske-style account of perceiving is objectionable in the ways I have suggested, however, the whole notion that perceiving involves essentially the having of perceptual experiences seems much less compelling. What then might be said about the sort of unconceptualized awareness we all seem to have of our surroundings?

One possibility is that the naive view of perceiving is right: items constituting the content of that awareness are simply objects and events outside us in the world. If asked to describe elements of our visual field, for instance, and then to say where we imagine these elements to reside, most of us will take ourselves to be describing features of the world, not features of ourselves. Only someone in the grip of a philosophical theory is likely to differ. The notion that external objects could not possibly have the properties we perceive them to have—hence that the properties in question must be properties of experiences or sensory episodes, not properties of external objects—is a manifestly philosophical notion, one resting on arguments that ought to arouse suspicion. It is sometimes imagined that the move from what we take to be facts about perceiving to the postulation of specialized mental episodes is motivated by purely empirical considerations. This is a mistake. It is only when we see those empirical considerations in a certain light, only when they are illuminated by a certain philosophical doctrine, that we are tempted to construe them as evidence for impressions or experiences (in the nonordinary, philosophical senses of these things).

Many of the features philosophers commonly ascribe to phenomenal perceptual states are in fact perfectly objective features of the world. Evidence suggests, for instance, that the visual icon discussed earlier is, if it is anything, a retinal occurrence (see e.g., Neisser 1976). Many of the differences cited to distinguish the *looks* of things from the things themselves (and thus to the postulation of distinct internal objects or episodes to which these looks can be ascribed) are explicable by reference to the optical properties of ambient illumination (see, e.g., Gibson 1979; Heil 1983). In cases where such explanations are more difficult to find—the optical illusions, for instance—it is not obvious how appeals to mediating sensory objects in any way advance our understanding.

My suggestion is that we should be better off dropping talk about perceptual experiences altogether. Dretske is right: there *is* an important sense in which we enjoy a primitive, noncognitive sort of awareness that far outstrips our capacity to conceptualize or make judgments. But the field of this awareness is not some internal state or process. It comprises, rather, ordinary objects and goings-on in the world outside us. These objects and goings on, of course, do not depend on judgments we make. Mostly they persist independently of our thoughts about them. They are the same for me as for an infant. And they are, often enough, objects of perception. But perceiving such

things must be more than their simply being there—
as they indisputably are when we open our eyes and
gaze about. Perceiving them involves *taking* them in
various ways, forming beliefs about them, judging
them to be one way rather than another.

Our doing this, perhaps, requires much in the way
of sensory machinery. And that machinery may well,
as Dretske plausibly contends, supply us with far
more information than we should ever want or need.
But this fact, if it is a fact, pertains to the mechanisms
underlying our capacity to perceive. It does not settle
the question of what it is to perceive.

NOTES

Work on this paper was supported by a National
Endowment for the Humanities fellowship (FB–
24078–86). I am indebted to Fred Dretske, Alfred
Mele, and Paul Snowdon for their comments on
earlier drafts.

1. See, e.g., Dretske 1969, chapter 2; 1978; 1979; and
   1981 chapters 6 and 7. The account of simple seeing, seeing *tout court*, offered here is a hybrid constructed from all of these sources.
2. Putting it this way suggests that the issue between
   Dretske and those who take perceiving to be essentially cognitive is, at bottom *verbal*. Even if that
   were so, however, there might be reasons for preferring one system of labels to another. And *one*
   way to motivate a Dretske-style taxonomy would
   be to show that it nicely accommodates a full-
   blooded notion of perceptual experience. The aim
   here is to raise doubts about the philosophical category of perceptual experience and thus, by extension, doubts about Dretske's preference for a
   non-cognitive account of perceiving.
3. Dretske (1978 p. 110) says that in "the shifting perception of ambiguous figures . . . there is a change in
   the percept without a change in the corresponding
   stimulus. . . ." This comes perilously close to identifying percepts—simple, unadulterated seeing, seeing
   tout court—with *seeing as*, however, an identity
   Dretske is bound to deny. My seeing the figure as a
   duck, your seeing it as a rabbit, and an infant's seeing it (but *as* nothing at all) are all cases presumably
   of seeing the *same* figure. The percepts might differ,
   but not, I gather, simply because each of us sees the
   figure *as* something different.
4. Such examples are discussed in Dretske 1978,
   1979. See, also, Heil 1982; and 1983, chapter 4.

5. Evidence suggests that the illusions depicted in
   [Figure 3] are not uniquely visual. In each case,
   tactual analogues are possible. See Heil 1987 for
   discussion and references.
6. Notice that these cases differ from those, for instance, in which a white thing, under a red light,
   looks red to me. Here we may say that light reaching my retina contains information that, in certain
   crucial respects, is identical to that contained in
   light reflected from a genuinely red thing. The case
   of an apparently bent oar may be similar. In each
   instance, however, there is a perfectly objective feature of the world—light radiation of particular
   structured sort—to which one might appeal in explaining the looks of the things in question.
7. Which is, of course, not the same as taking it to
   have no properties whatever.
8. Here is a possibility suggested to me by C. B. Martin.
   S, blind from birth, undergoes an operation that re-
   vives his sight. When the bandages are removed and
   S opens his newly restored eyes for the first time, he
   is sitting in a chair that faces a pale blue wall. S sees
   the blueness of the wall, yet is so awestruck by the experience that he makes nothing whatever of it. If
   Dretske is right, then all seeing is like this.
9. In the case of infants, it is significant that we begin
   to speak of their *seeing* this or that only once they
   begin to manifest signs of *recognition*. It would be,
   at any rate, misleading to say of a newborn baby
   gazing aimlessly about that it *sees its mother* solely
   on the grounds that its eyes are open and functioning properly, and its mother falls somewhere
   within its visual field.
10. Dretske would perhaps agree on this point. He in-
    sists that perceptual states, although themselves
    noncognitive, must be available to a perceiver's
    cognitive centers. For him a perceptual state is a
    functional state with certain additional, nonfunc-
    tional properties. We might then wonder about a
    case in which aliens, psychologically resembling
    the first group, were discovered to have the appro-
    priate experiential states, but it turned out that
    these were functionally inert: information for per-
    ceptual judgments came from mechanisms entirely
    unrelated to these states.
11. Paul Snowdon has reminded me that blind-
    sighters typically manifest surprise that their
    "guesses" are correct. Does this show that such
    people lack the corresponding perceptual beliefs?
    Not at all. Unless one imagines that beliefs are in-
    evitably conscious, it shows, a best, only that blind-
    sighters do not *believe* that they have such beliefs.

Indeed, it is altogether natural to ascribe to them first-order perceptual beliefs, on the basis of which they issue "guesses" about their surroundings, together with second-order beliefs, on the basis of which they report that they are merely guessing. See Marcel 1983.

REFERENCES

Armstrong, D. M. 1973: *Belief, Truth and Knowledge.* Cambridge: Cambridge University Press

Dretske, F. I. 1969: *Seeing and Knowing.* London: Routledge and Kegan Paul

———1978. The Role of the Percept in Visual Cognition. In *Perception and Cognition: Issues in the Foundations of Psychology* (Minnesota studies in the philosophy of science, vol. 9), ed. W. Savage, Minneapolis: University of Minnesota Press.

———1979. Simple Seeing. In *Body, Mind, and Method*, ed. D. F. Gustafson and B. L. Tapscott, Cambridge: MIT Press/Bradford Books.

Gibson, J. J. 1979: *The Ecological Approach to Visual Perception.* Boston: Houghton Mifflin.

Heil, J. 1982: Seeing is Believing. *American Philosophical Quarterly*, 19, pp. 229–39.

———1983: *Perception and Cognition.* Berkeley: University of California Press.

———1987: The Molyneux Question. *Journal for the Theory of Social Behavior*, 17, pp. 227–41.

Locke, J. [1690] 1979: *An Essay Concerning Human Understanding*, ed. P. H. Nidditch, Oxford: Oxford University Press.

Marcel, A. J. 1983: Conscious and Unconscious Perception: An approach to the relations between phenomenal experiences and perceptual processes. *Cognitive Psychology*, 15, 238–300.

Neisser, U. 1967: *Cognitive Psychology.* New York: Appleton-Century-Crofts.

—1976: *Cognition and Reality.* San Francisco: W. H. Freeman.

Sperling, G. A. 1960: The Information Available in Brief Perceptual presentation. *Psychological Monographs*, 74, no. 498.

FOR FURTHER READING

Armstrong, D. M. *Belief, Truth and Knowledge,* London: Cambridge University Press, 1973.

Audi, Robert. *Belief, Justification, and Knowledge.* Belmont, Calif.: Wadsworth, 1988.

Ayer, A. J. *The Problem of Knowledge.* Harmondsworth, England: Penguin Books, 1956.

Berckeley, George. *A Treatise Concerning the Principles of Human Knowledge.* Indianapolis: Bobbs-Merrill, 1965.

Chisholm, Roderick. *Perceiving: A Philosophical Study.* Ithaca, N.Y.: Cornell University Press, 1957.

Cornman, James. *Perception, Common Sense, Science.* New Haven: Yale University Press, 1975.

Dancy, Jonathan, and Ernest Sosa, eds. *A Companion to Epistemology.* Oxford: Basil Blackwell, 1992.

Dancy, Jonathan, ed. *Perceptual Knowledge.* Oxford: Oxford University Press, 1988.

Dicker, Georges. *Perceptual Knowledge.* Dordrecht, Netherlands: Kluwer Academic Publishing, 1980.

Dretske, Fred. *Knowledge and the Flow of Infomation.* Cambridge: MIT Press, 1981.

Dretske, Fred. *Seeing and Knowing.* London: Routledge & Kegan Paul, 1969.

Fales, Evan. *A Defense of the Given.* Lanham, Md.: Rowman & Littlefield, 1996.

Fumerton, Richard. *Metaphysical and Epistemological Problems of Perception.* Lincoln: University of Nebraska Press, 1985.

Heil, John. *Perception and Cognition.* Berkeley: University of California Press, 1983.

Goldman, Alan. *Empirical Knowledge.* Berkeley: University of California Press, 1988.

Goldman, Alvin. "Discrimination and Perceptual Knowledge." *Journal of Philosophy* 73 (1976), 771–79.

Hamlyn, D.W. *The Theory of Knowledge.* London: Macmillan Press, 1970.

Hardin, C. L. *Color for Philosophers.* Indianapolis: Hackett, 1986.

Jackson, Frank. *Perception.* Cambridge: Cambridge University Press, 1977.

Maclahlan, D.L.C. *The Philosopy of Perception.* Englewood Cliffs, N.J.: Prentice Hall, 1989.

McLaughlin, Brian, ed. *Dretske and His Critics.* Oxford: Basil Blackwell, 1991.

Nelkin, Norton. "How Sensations Get Their Names." *Philosophical Studies* 51 (1987) 325–39.

Price, H. H. *Perception.* London: Methuen, 1932.

Pollock, John. *Contemporary Theories of Knowledge.* Totowa, N.J.: Rowman & Littlefield, 1986.

Robinson, Howard. *Perception.* London: Routledge, 1994.

Russell, Bertrand. *The Problems of Philosophy.* 1912. Reprint, London: Oxford University Press, 1959.

Weiskrantz, Larry. *Blindsight.* Oxford: Oxford University Press, 1986.

STUDY QUESTIONS

1. According to Price, what are the two claims characteristic of naïve realism? Describe the phenomenological and causal forms of the argument from illusion. What is the central objection to each of these forms of the argument? Does Price think that either form of the argument can meet the objection? Explain.

2. What is the Selective Theory? Why does Price think that it helps the naïve realist? Why does Price think that naïve realisim should be rejected?

3. What does Locke mean by "idea"? What, according to Locke, are the sources of all our ideas? What is the difference between primary and secondary qualities? How do we obtain ideas of primary qualities?

4. Explain Locke's argument that our ideas of secondary qualities do not resemble objects.

5. What is knowledge, according to Locke? Why does Locke think we have knowledge of objects?

6. What are the objects of knowledge, according to Berkeley? In his view, what does it mean to say that the table exists? In general, what is Berkeley's view of the essence of objects?

7. What do you think Berkeley means when he refers to external objects or bodies? How does Berkeley respond to the objection that in his view we can no longer distinguish between the real and chimeras? How does he respond to the claim that his view eliminates the sun, moon, stars, and the other familiar objects of our world? How do you think that Berkeley might explain the existence of dinosaurs?

8. Does Stace think we can justify our claims about the existence of theoretical entities? What is the purpose, in Stace's view, of such entities? What is the purpose of scientific laws? Would you classify Stace as a phenomenalist or a representative realist? Explain.

9. Why does Dretske object to the causal theory of perception? Briefly describe Dretske's information theory of perception. What, in this view, is the object of perception?

10. How does Heil distingush between simple seeing and seeing *tout court*? Why does Heil reject this distinction? What is Heil's attitude toward perceptual experiences? Why does he hold this view, and why is it important for his own view of the nature of perception?

Credits

LINDA ALCOFF, from *Real Knowing: New Versions of the Coherence Theory,* Cornell University Press, 1996. Used by permission of Cornell University Press.

ROBERT ALMEDER, "On Naturalizing Epistemology," *American Philosophical Quarterly,* Vol. 27, 1990. Used with permission of the publisher.

WILLIAM P. ALSTON, "Concepts of Epistemic Justification," *Monist,* Vol. 68, 1985, 57–83. Reprinted with permission; "Two Types of Foundationalism," Journal of Philosophy, LXXIII, 7, April 8, 1976, 165–185. Reprinted with permission from the publisher and the author.

ELIZABETH ANDERSON, "Feminist Epistemology: An Interpretation and Defense," *Hypatia,* Vol. 10, 1995. Reprinted with permission from the author, Associate Professor, Philosophy & Women's Studies, University of Michigan.

ROBERT AUDI, "The Foundationalism-Coherentism Controversy" from *The Structure of Justification,* Cambridge University Press, 1993, pp. 117–164. Reprinted with permission of Cambridge University Press; "Justification, Truth and Reliability," *Philosophy and Phenomenological Research,* Vol. 49, 1988, 1–29. Reprinted with permission.

A. J. AYER, "Skepticism and Certainty," *The Problem of Knowledge,* Penguin Books Ltd., 1976, 41–44, 52–57, 61–68, 75–81. Copyright © 1956 A. J. Ayer. Reprinted with permission from the publisher; "The *A Priori,*" *Language, Truth and Logic,* Second Edition, Dover Publications, 1952, pp 71–87. Reprinted with permission from the publisher.

LAURENCE BONJOUR, "The Concept of Epistemic Justification," "Elements of Coherence," "Coherence and Truth." Reprinted by permission of the publisher from *The Structure of Empirical Knowledge* by Laurence BonJour, Cambridge, Mass.: Harvard University Press. Copyright © 1985 by the President and Fellows of Harvard College; "Externalist Theories of Empirical Knowledge," Midwest Studies in Philosophy, Vol. V, 1980, 53–71, Peter French et al., editors. Reprinted with permission from University of Minnesota Press and the author.

RODERICK CHISHOLM, "Reason and the *A Priori,*" *Philosophy,* edited by R. Chisholm, H. Feigl, W. K. Frankera, J. Passmore, M. Thompson, Prentice-Hall, 1964, 287–311. Reprinted with permission of the publisher.

RENÉ DESCARTES, "Meditations I," "Meditations II," "Meditations III" from *The Philosophical Works of Descartes,* Vol. 1, 1967, pp. 144–171, translated by Elizabeth S. Haldane and G. R. T. Ross. Reprinted with permission from Cambridge University Press.

FRED DRETSKE, "Sensation and Perception" from *Knowledge and the Flow of Information,* The MIT Press, 1981, 153–168. Reprinted with permission from the publisher.

PAUL EDWARDS, "Russell's Doubts about Induction," *Mind,* Vol. 68(1949), pp. 141–163. Reprinted by permission of Oxford University Press.

RICHARD FELDMAN, "Epistemic Obligations," *Philosphical Perspectives, 2, Epistemology,* 1988 edited by James E. Tomberlin. Copyright ©1988 by Ridgeview Publishing Co., Atascadero, CA. Reprinted by permission of Ridgeview Publishing Company.

RICHARD FOLEY, "What Am I to Believe?" *Naturalism: A Critical Appraisal,* edited by Steven J. Wagner and Richard Warner, University of Notre Dame Press, 1993, 147–161. Copyright ©1993 by University of Notre Dame Press. Used by permission of the publisher.

RICHARD FUMERTON, "The Internalism/Externalism Controversy," *Philosophical Perspectives, 2, Epistemology,* 1988 edited by James E. Tomberlin. Copyright ©1988 by Ridgeview Publishing Co., Atascadero, CA. Reprinted by permission of Ridgeview Publishing Company.

EDMUND L. GETTIER, "Is Justified True Belief Knowledge?" *Analysis,* Vol. 23, 1963, 121–123. Reprinted with permission.

ALVIN I. GOLDMAN, "A Causal Theory of Knowing," *Journal of Philosophy,* LXIV, 12, June 22, 1967, pp 357–372. Used with permission of the author and the publisher; "What Is Justified Belief?" *Justification and Knowledge,* G. Pappas, editor, 1979, pp. 1–23. With kind permission from Kluwer Academic Publishers; "Strong and Weak Justification," *Philosophical Perspectives, 2, Epistemology,* 1988 edited by James E. Tomberlin. Copyright ©1988 by Ridgeview Publishing Company, Atascadero, CA. Reprinted by permission of Ridgeview Publishing Company.

NELSON GOODMAN, "The New Riddle of Induction." Reprinted by permission of the publisher from *Fact, Fiction, and Forecast,* 4th Edition by Nelson

BRIAN SKYRMS, "The Pragmatic Justification of Induction," *Choice and Chance,* 1966, pp. 37–42. Reprinted with permission from Wadsworth Publishing Company.

ERNEST SOSA, "Knowledge and Intellectual Virtue," *The Monist,* 1985. Copyright ©1985 *The Monist,* La Salle, IL 61301. Reprinted by permission.

WILLIAM STACE, "Science and the Physical World" from *Man Against Darkness* by W. T. Stace. Copyright ©1967 by University of Pittsburgh Press. Reprinted by permission of the University of Pittsburgh Press.

P. F. STRAWSON, "Hume, Wittgenstein and Induction," from *Skepticism and Naturalism* by P. F. Strawson. Copyright ©1985 Columbia University Press. Reprinted with the permission of the publisher.

BARRY STROUD, "Understanding Human Knowledge in General," *Knowledge and Skepticism,* edited by Marjorie Clay and Keith Lehrer, Westview Press, 1989, 31–49. Reprinted with permission.